Keighley Campus Leeds City College
Tel: 01535 685010
Please return by the date stamped below. To renew by telephone please give your student number and the barcode number of the item to be renewed

Sociology

Sixth Edition

Anthony Giddens

Revised and updated with

Philip W. Sutton

polity

The right of Anthony Giddens to be identified as Author of this Work has been asserted in accordance with the UK Copyright, Designs and Patents Act 1988.

First published in 2009 by Polity Press
Reprinted 2011
Polity Press
65 Bridge Street
Cambridge CB2 1UR, UK

Polity Press
350 Main Street
Malden, MA 02148, USA

ISBN-13: 978-0-7456-4357-1
ISBN-13: 978-0-7456-4358-8(pb)

A catalogue record for this book is available from the British Library.

Book Design by Peter Ducker MISTD

Typeset in 9.5 on 12.5pt Utopia
by Servis Filmsetting Ltd, Stockport, Cheshire
Printed in Italy by Rotolito Lombarda

The publisher has used its best endeavours to ensure that the URLs for external websites referred to in this book are correct and active at the time of going to press. However, the publisher has no responsibility for the websites and can make no guarantee that a site will remain live or that the content is or will remain appropriate.

Every effort has been made to trace all copyright holders, but if any have been inadvertently overlooked the publishers will be pleased to include any necessary credits in any subsequent reprint or edition.

For further information on Polity, visit our website: www.politybooks.com

Contents

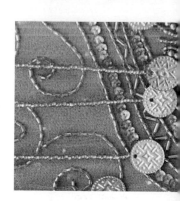

Detailed contents

Preface to the sixth edition

It is now 20 years since the first edition of *Sociology* was published. In 1989, when the book first came out, some readers of the current edition weren't even born. That year was a time of dramatic social change, with the end of the Cold War and the opening up of former Soviet bloc countries. Events such as the Tiananmen Square massacre in China made headlines worldwide. Throughout the 1980s, more and more people in the developed world had acquired luxury goods such as microwaves and video recorders. Yet at that time the current pervasiveness of the Internet, email and other digital media in everyday life was unimaginable. I dictated much of the first edition onto tape, and it was then typed up on a word processor, a kind of electronic typewriter.

Over the years, consecutive editions have mapped out the myriad changes we have experienced in the social world, as well as sociologists' attempts to understand them. This sixth edition has been carefully revised to make sure it takes account of recent global developments and new ideas in sociology. You'll see that there is now a chapter dedicated to war and terrorism, as well as substantive new material in the chapters on the media, education, theoretical thinking, politics and government. Other revisions have been made throughout.

I have all the previous editions of *Sociology* on my shelves at home, as well as copies in the multiple languages into which the book has been translated. What all previous editions of this book have in common is their attempt to help readers see the value of thinking sociologically. I hope this sixth edition will again serve that purpose.

Students sometimes find sociological ideas and evidence difficult to understand. In part, I think that's because sociology demands a concerted attempt to set aside personal beliefs and opinions when analysing research findings and theories. In this sense, thinking sociologically involves a profound intellectual challenge. Most people who study sociology are changed by the experience. The reason is that sociology offers a different perspective on the world from that which most people have when they start out in the subject. Sociology helps us look beyond the immediate contexts of our lives and so helps us understand the causes of our own actions better. Sociology can also help us change the world for the better. I hope you enjoy the book.

Acknowledgements

I would like to thank everyone who has helped in the preparation of this book in all six of its editions. This sixth edition has benefited enormously from the involvement of Philip W. Sutton, a sociologist with 17 years' experience of teaching at university level. Philip's contribution to this edition has helped to ensure that the book is fully up to date with the ways in which sociology is currently being taught. His longstanding experience of designing and delivering introductory sociology courses has given this edition a fresh, interactive dimension. This revision also owes much to the research skills of Ann P. Love, who worked tirelessly to collect contemporary materials across the varied sociological subjects. I am greatly indebted to her. I should like to thank all those who read draft chapters and made constructive suggestions for improvement. Thanks are also owed to the worldwide readers of the fifth edition who wrote to tell me about their experiences of using the book.

At Polity, I thank the following in particular: John Thompson, David Held, Gill Motley, Neil de Cort and Breffni O'Connor. Emma Longstaff and Jonathan Skerrett have managed the project from start to finish and have been marvellous to work with. The book owes much to Emma's clear vision and constructive advice, even – perhaps especially – in occasional periods of adversity. Finally, as always, I should like to thank Alena Ledeneva for her constant help and encouragement.

AG

About this book

One of the things that's so exciting about sociology is its constant engagement with the ever-changing social world. Events we find hard to make sense of, or that frighten us – such as climate change or terrorism – are all of interest to sociologists. My aim in this sixth edition, as in the previous five, has been to capture the sense of excitement that pervades the very best of sociology, and to inspire a new generation of sociologists. The book was written in the firm belief that sociology has a key role to play in modern intellectual culture and a central place in the social sciences. It does not try to introduce overly sophisticated notions nor does it make a virtue of sociological jargon. Nevertheless, findings drawn from the cutting edge of the discipline are incorporated throughout, along with contemporary issues and data. My own work is, of course, included across the book and I have referred to it in the first person so that readers are clear when I am writing about my own contributions to the field. I have also included the views of my critics where necessary. I hope it is not a partisan treatment; as usual I endeavoured to cover the major perspectives in sociology and the major findings of contemporary research in an even-handed, though not indiscriminate, way.

Major themes

The book is constructed around a number of basic themes, each of which helps to give the work a distinctive character. One central theme is that of *social change*. Sociology was born of the transformations that wrenched the industrializing social order of the West away from the ways of life characteristic of preceding societies. The world created by these changes is the primary concern of sociological analysis. The pace of social change has continued to accelerate, and it is possible that we stand on the threshold of transitions as significant as those that occurred in the late eighteenth and nineteenth centuries. Sociology has prime responsibility for charting the transformations that have taken place in the past and for grasping the major lines of development taking place today.

A second, connected, theme of the book is the *globalizing of social life*. For too long, sociology has been dominated by the view that societies can be studied as independent entities. But even in the past, societies never really existed in isolation. In the contemporary world, we can see a clear acceleration in processes of global integration. The emphasis on globalization also connects closely with the weight given to the *interdependence* of the industrialized and developing worlds today. The book's first edition, published in 1989, broke new ground in discussing the impact of globalization, an examination of which was only just beginning, even in the more technical areas of the discipline. Since then the debate about globalization has intensified, while globalization itself has advanced much further, as have some of the changes in information technology associated with it.

Third, the book adopts a strongly *comparative* stance. Sociology cannot be taught solely by understanding the institutions of one particular society and the discussions contain a rich variety of materials drawn from across the world. The book continues to cover developing countries as well as the industrialized ones and in this way, it contributes to the globalization of sociology. Given the close connections that now mesh societies across the world with one another, and the virtual disappearance of traditional social systems, sociology and anthropology are becoming increasingly indistinguishable.

A fourth theme is the necessity of taking an *historical approach* to sociology. This involves more than just filling in the historical context within which events occur. One of the most important developments in sociology over the past few years has been an increasing emphasis on historical analysis. This should be understood not solely as applying a sociological outlook to the past, but as a way of contributing to our understanding of institutions in the present. Recent work in historical sociology is discussed throughout and provides a framework for the interpretations offered within most of the chapters.

Fifth, particular attention is given throughout the text to *issues of gender*. The study of gender is ordinarily regarded as a specific field within sociology as a whole – and this volume contains one chapter that specifically explores thinking and research on the subject. However, questions about gender relations are so fundamental to sociological analysis today that they cannot simply be considered a subdivision. Thus, many chapters contain sections concerned with issues of gender.

A sixth theme is the *micro and macro link*. In many places in the book, I show that interaction in micro-level contexts affects larger social processes and that such macro-level processes influence our day-to-day lives. Social situations can be better understood by analysing them at both the micro and macro levels.

A final theme is the relation between the *social* and the *personal*. Sociological thinking is a vital help to self-understanding, which in turn can be focused back on an improved understanding of the social world. Studying sociology should be a liberating experience that enlarges our sympathies and imagination, opens up new perspectives on the sources of our own behaviour and creates an awareness of cultural settings different from our own. In so far as sociological ideas challenge dogma, teach the appreciation of cultural variety and provide insights into the working of social institutions, the *practice* of sociology enhances the possibilities of human freedom.

New features

The sixth edition incorporates a range of new features, all designed to help make the book more engaging, support students' learning, and to stretch their sociological imaginations. First, throughout the book you'll now find *Classic Studies* boxes. These are intended to introduce students to some of sociology's most influential research. I have tried to pick examples which have had a big impact in the field, and which will engage or provoke readers. The selections are not definitive, exhaustive or comprehensive, but are illustrative of key problems or concerns. The Classic Studies may date from the early days of sociology or be relatively recent, as sheer age does not define them. Instead, the studies are chosen for the deep-seated influence they've had on subsequent research, be it methodologically, theoretically, empirically, or a mixture of these. Above all, I have tried to choose examples that will inspire students, and help them to appreciate the many possibilities opened up by thinking sociologically.

Second, the interactivity of the text has been increased to reflect the growing focus in education on student-centred learning. In all the chapters you'll find a series of new boxes labeled *Thinking Critically*. These can be seen as 'stopping off' points where the reader is encouraged to reflect on what they've been reading, before coming back to pick up the thread. The notion of 'critical' thinking may seem irrelevant to those who see sociology as an inherently critical discipline. However, the questions posed often require the reader to be critical not only of political dogma or social practices, but also of sociology and sociological debates themselves. In this sense, 'thinking critically' serves as a useful reminder that a *constantly* critical approach extends to all ideas – including my own and the so-called 'classics' I discussed earlier! I strongly recommend that readers work through these boxes as part and parcel of getting the most from the book.

Third, many more boxed sections have been included. Numerous lecturers and students have found these very helpful in previous editions and have requested more. To this end, in addition to the *Classic Studies* already mentioned, the book now features two more styles of box. *Global Society* boxes reflect the increasingly global frame of reference within which sociologists work, and will hopefully encourage students to orientate themselves globally when thinking of even the most apparently local or domestic issues. Boxes labelled *Using your Sociological Imagination* often contain quirky or arresting material, designed to illustrate or expand themes found in the main body of the text. They finish with a series of questions on the material featured, providing another opportunity to stimulate students' critical thinking.

In addition, the number of terms in the *glossary* has been expanded. Terms included in the glossary are highlighted in a different colour in the text. *Further readings* are annotated for the first time in this edition, so readers can make a more informed choice about what they choose to read. At the end of each chapter *Summary points* bring readers back to the main points of each chapter – a way of checking understanding, and to reinforce the key messages of each chapter. *Internet links* have been included again, but this time with explicit guidance on why each site is being recommended.

In addition to the *Internet links*, the book is also designed to be used in conjunction with the extensive material on its own website: www.polity.co.uk/giddens. Both lecturers and students will find a wealth of resources to aid further research into the themes explored throughout the book, and to support students' learning.

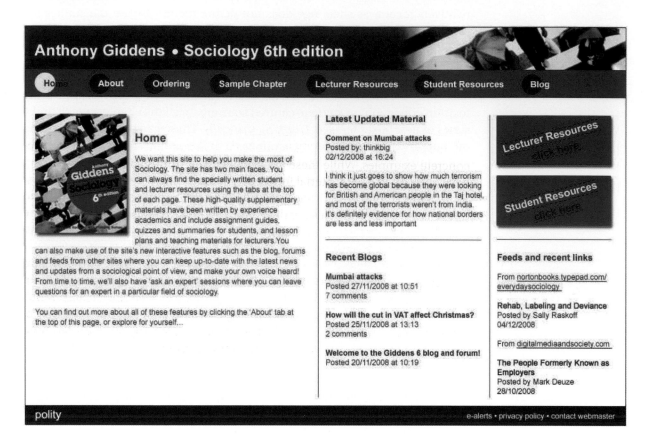

Visit the interactive website that accompanies this book at

www.politybooks.com/giddens6

where you'll find specially written materials for students and lecturers, including assignment guides, quizzes and useful links, lesson plans and teaching resources.

The site also features regularly updated content and blogs, so don't miss out on the opportunity to put across your questions in the 'ask an expert' sessions and to make your voice heard.

Organization of the book

There is not much abstract discussion of sociological concepts in the book. Instead, I have sought to illustrate ideas, concepts and theories by means of concrete examples. While these are usually taken from sociological research, I have quite often used material from other sources (such as newspaper reports) for illustrative purposes. I have tried to keep the writing style as simple and direct as possible, whilst also endeavouring to make the book a good read. The overall aim is to create a fairly seamless narrative throughout each chapter and indeed the book as a whole.

The chapters follow a sequence designed to help achieve a progressive mastery of the different fields of sociology, but I have taken care to ensure that the book can be used flexibly and is easy to adapt to the needs of teachers, which are necessarily diverse. Chapters can be ignored or studied in a different order without much loss as each one has been written as a fairly autonomous unit, with substantial cross-referencing to relevant chapters.

Figures

Tables

Boxes

Classic Studies

USING YOUR SOCIOLOGICAL IMAGINATION

1
What is Sociology?

CHAPTER 1

· ·

What is Sociology?

We live today – in the first decade of the twenty-first century – in a world that is intensely worrying, yet full of the most extraordinary promise for the future. It is a world marked by rapid changes, deep conflicts, tensions and social divisions, as well as by increasing concerns about the destructive impact of human societies on the natural environment. Yet we also have new opportunities for controlling our destiny and shaping our lives for the better that would have been unimaginable to earlier generations.

How did this world come about? Why are our conditions of life so different from those of our parents and grandparents? What directions will societies take in the future? If you have ever asked yourself such questions, then consider yourself a novice sociologist. These questions are the prime concern of sociology, a field of study that consequently has a fundamental role to play in modern intellectual life.

Sociology is the scientific study of human life, social groups, whole societies and the human world as such. It is a dazzling and compelling enterprise, as its subject-matter is our own behaviour as social beings. The scope of sociology is extremely wide, ranging from the analysis of passing encounters between individuals on the street to the investigation of international relations and global forms of terrorism.

Most of us see the world in terms of the familiar features of our own lives – family, friendships and work. But sociology demonstrates the need to take a much broader view of our own lives in order to explain why we act as we do. It teaches us that what we regard as natural, inevitable, good or true may not be so, and that things we take for granted are strongly influenced by historical events and social processes. Understanding the subtle yet complex and profound ways in which our individual lives reflect the contexts of our social experience is basic to the sociological outlook.

The sociological imagination

Learning to think sociologically – looking, in other words, at the broader view – means cultivating our imagination. Studying sociology is not just a routine process of acquiring knowledge. A sociologist is someone who is able to break free from the immediacy of personal circumstances and put things into a wider context. Doing sociological work depends on what the American author C. Wright Mills, in a famous phrase, called the **sociological imagination** (Mills 1970).

The sociological imagination requires us, above all, to 'think ourselves away' from the familiar routines of our daily lives in order to look at them anew. Consider the simple act of drinking a cup of coffee. What could we find to say, from a sociological point of view, about such an apparently

Getting together with friends for coffee is part of a social ritual.

Coffee is more than a pleasant drink for these workers, whose livelihoods depend on the coffee plant.

uninteresting piece of behaviour? An enormous amount.

We could point out, first of all, that coffee is not just a refreshment. It has symbolic value as part of our day-to-day social activities. Often the ritual associated with coffee-drinking is much more important than the simple act of consuming the drink. For many Westerners, the morning cup of coffee stands at the centre of a personal routine. It is an essential first step to starting the day. Morning coffee is often followed later in the day by coffee with others – the basis of a social, not just individual, ritual. Two people who arrange to meet for coffee are probably more interested in getting together and chatting than in what they actually drink. In all societies, drinking and eating provide occasions for social interaction and the enactment of rituals – and these offer a rich subject matter for sociological study.

Second, coffee is a drug that contains caffeine, which has a stimulating effect on the brain. Many people drink coffee for the 'extra lift' it provides. Long days at the office or late nights studying are made more tolerable by regular coffee breaks. Coffee is a habit-forming substance, but coffee addicts are not normally regarded by most people in Western cultures as 'drug-users'. Like alcohol, coffee is a socially acceptable drug, whereas marijuana, for instance, is not. Yet there are societies that tolerate the consumption of marijuana or even cocaine, but frown on both coffee and alcohol. Sociologists are interested in why these differences exist and how they came about.

Third, an individual who drinks a cup of coffee is caught up in a complicated set of social and economic relationships stretching right across the world. Coffee is a product that links people in some of the wealthiest and most impoverished parts of the planet: it is consumed in great quantities in wealthy countries, but is grown primarily in poor ones. Next to oil, coffee is the most valuable commodity in international trade; it provides many

Eighteenth-century coffee houses were centres of gossip and political intrigue for British social elites.

countries with their largest source of foreign exchange. The production, transportation and distribution of coffee require continuous transactions between people thousands of miles away from the coffee drinker. Studying such global transactions is an important task of sociology, since many aspects of our lives are now affected by worldwide social influences and communications.

Fourth, the act of sipping a coffee presumes a long process of social and economic development. Along with other familiar items of Western diets – like tea, bananas, potatoes and white sugar – coffee became widely consumed only from the late 1800s, though it was fashionable amongst the elite before then. Although the drink originated in the Middle East, its mass consumption dates from the period of Western expansion some two centuries ago. Virtually all the coffee we drink today comes from areas such as South America and Africa that were colonized by Europeans; it is in no sense a 'natural' part of the Western diet. The colonial legacy has had an enormous impact on the development of the global coffee trade.

Fifth, coffee is a product that lies at the heart of contemporary debates about globalization, international fair trade, human rights and environmental destruction. As coffee has grown in popularity, it has become 'branded' and politicized; the decisions that consumers make about what kind of coffee to drink and where to purchase it have become lifestyle choices. People may choose to drink only organic coffee, decaffeinated coffee or coffee that has been 'fairly traded' through schemes that pay the full market price to small producers in developing countries. They may opt to patronize 'independent' coffee houses, rather than 'corporate' coffee chains such as Starbucks. Coffee-drinkers might decide to boycott coffee from countries with poor human rights and environmental records. Sociologists are interested to understand how globalization heightens people's awareness of issues occurring in distant corners of the planet and prompts them to act on new knowledge in their own lives. For sociologists, the apparently trivial act of drinking coffee could hardly be more interesting.

Studying people and society

Adopting a sociological imagination allows us to see that many events which appear to concern only the individual actually reflect larger issues. Divorce, for instance, may be a very difficult process for someone who goes through it – what Mills calls a 'personal trouble'. But divorce is also a significant 'public issue' in many societies across the world. In Britain, over a third of all marriages end in divorce within ten years. Unemployment, to take another example, may be a personal tragedy for anyone who loses their job and is unable to find another. Yet it goes far beyond a matter of private despair when millions of people in a society are in the same situation: it is a public issue expressing large social trends.

Try to apply a sociological imagination to your own life. It is not necessary to think only of troubling events. Consider, for instance, why you are turning the pages of this book at all – why did you decide to study sociology? You could be a reluctant sociology student, taking the course only to fulfil the degree requirement for a future career. Or you might just be enthusiastic to find out more about your society and the subject of sociology. Whatever your motivation, you are likely to have a good deal in common, without necessarily knowing it, with others who also study sociology. Your private decision reflects your position within the wider society.

Do the following characteristics apply to you? Are you young? White? From a professional or white-collar background? Have you done, or do you still do, some part-time work to boost your income? Do you want to find a good job when you finish your education, but are not especially dedicated to studying? Do you not really know what sociology is, but think it has something to do with how people behave in groups? More than three-quarters of you will answer 'yes' to all these questions. University students are not typical of the population as a whole, but tend to be drawn from more privileged social backgrounds. And their attitudes usually reflect those held by friends and acquaintances. The social backgrounds from which we come have a great deal to do with what kinds of decision we think appropriate.

Did some or none of the characteristics above apply to you? You might come from a minority-group background or from one of poverty. You may be someone in mid-life or older. All the same, further conclusions probably follow. You are likely to have had to struggle to get where you are; you might have had to overcome hostile reactions from friends and others when you told them you were intending to go to college; or you might be combining higher education with full-time parenthood.

Although we are all influenced by the social contexts in which we find ourselves, none of us is completely determined in our behaviour by those contexts. We possess, and create, our own individuality. It is the business of sociology to investigate the connections between what society makes of us and what we make of ourselves and society. Our activities both structure – give shape to – the social world around us and, at the same time, are structured by that social world. The concept of **social structure** is an important one in sociology. It refers to the fact that the social contexts of our lives do not consist of random assortments of events or actions; they are structured, or patterned, in distinct ways. There are regularities in the ways we behave and in the relationships we have with one another.

But social structure is not like a physical structure, such as a building, which exists independently of human actions. Human societies are always in the process of **structuration**. They are reconstructed at every moment by the very 'building blocks' that compose it – human beings like you and me. Consider again the case of coffee. A cup of coffee does not automatically arrive in your hands. You choose to go to a particular coffee shop and you choose whether to drink a latte or an espresso. As you make these decisions, along with millions of other people, you shape the market for coffee and affect the lives of coffee producers living perhaps thousands of miles away on the other side of the world.

The development of sociological thinking

When they first start studying sociology, many students are puzzled by the diversity of approaches they encounter. Sociology has never been a discipline in which there is a body of ideas that everyone accepts as valid, though there have been times when some theories have been more widely accepted than others. Sociologists often quarrel amongst themselves about how to study human behaviour and how research results should best be interpreted. Why should this be so? Why can sociologists not agree with one another more consistently, as natural scientists seem able to do? The answer is bound up with the very nature of our subject-matter. Sociology is about our own lives and our own behaviour and studying ourselves is the most complex and difficult endeavour we can undertake.

Theories and theoretical perspectives

Trying to understand something as complex as the impact of industrialization on societies, for example, raises the importance of theory to sociology. Factual research shows how things occur; but sociology does not just consist of collecting facts, however important and interesting they may be. For example, it is a fact that I bought a cup of coffee this morning, that it cost a certain amount of money and that the coffee beans used to make it were grown in Central America. But in sociology we also want to know

In this painting by Brueghel, there are a large number of people engaged in a range of often bizarre activities. The painting at first seems to make little sense. However, its title, Netherlandish Proverbs, helps explain its meaning: this picture shows more than 100 proverbs that were common when it was painted in the sixteenth century. In the same way, sociologists need theory as a context to help make sense of their observations.

why things happen, and in order to do so we have to learn to construct explanatory theories. For instance, we know that industrialization has had a major influence on the emergence of modern societies, but what are the origins of and preconditions for industrialization? Why do we find differences between societies in their industrialization processes? Why is industrialization associated with changes in forms of criminal punishment or in family structures and marriage systems? To answer such questions, we have to develop theoretical thinking.

Theories involve constructing abstract interpretations that can be used to explain a wide variety of empirical or 'factual' situations. A **theory** about industrialization, for example, would be concerned with identifying the main features that processes of industrial development share in common and would try to show which of these are of importance in explaining industrial development. Of course, factual research and theories can never be completely separated. We can only develop valid theoretical explanations if we are able to test them by means of factual research.

We need theories to help us make sense of the many facts that we find. Contrary to popular assertion, facts do *not* speak for themselves. Many sociologists do work primarily on factual research, but unless they are guided by some knowledge of theory, their work is unlikely to be able to *explain* the complexity of societies. This is true even of research carried out with strictly practical objectives in mind.

Many 'practical people' tend to be suspicious of theorists and may like to see themselves as too 'down to earth' to have to pay any attention to more abstract ideas. Yet all practical decisions have some theoretical assumptions lying behind them. The manager of a business, for example, might have scant regard for 'theory'. Nonetheless, every approach to business activity involves theoretical assumptions, even if these remain unstated. Thus, the manager might

assume that employees are motivated to work hard mainly by money – the level of wages they receive. This is an underlying theoretical interpretation of human behaviour, though it is also a mistaken one, as research in industrial sociology tends to demonstrate.

Without a theoretical approach, we would not know what to look for when beginning a study or when interpreting our results at the end of the research. However, the illumination of factual evidence is not the only reason for the prime position of theory in sociology. Theoretical thinking must respond to general problems posed by the study of human social life, including issues that are philosophical in nature. Deciding the extent to which sociology should be modelled on the natural sciences and how we should best conceptualize human consciousness, action and institutions are problems that do not have easy solutions. They have been handled in different ways in the various theoretical approaches that have developed within the discipline. This chapter will introduce sociology's founders and describe the way they theorized about modern societies; chapter 3, 'Theories and Perspectives in Sociology', provides a more up-to-date overview of the development of sociological theorizing over the course of the twentieth and into the twenty-first century.

Founders of sociology

We human beings have always been curious about the sources of our own behaviour, but for thousands of years our attempts to understand ourselves relied on ways of thinking passed down from generation to generation, often expressed in religious terms. For example, before the rise of modern science, many people believed that gods or spirits were the cause of natural events such as earthquakes and other natural disasters. Although writers from earlier periods provided insights into human behaviour, the systematic study of society is

Auguste Comte (1798–1857).

a relatively recent development, whose beginnings date back to the late 1700s and early 1800s. The background to the origins of sociology lies in the series of sweeping changes ushered in by the French Revolution and the mid-eighteenth-century **Industrial Revolution** in Europe. The shattering of traditional ways of life wrought by these changes resulted in the attempts of thinkers to understand and explain how they had come about and what their consequences were likely to be. To do this, scholars were led to develop new understandings of both the social and the natural worlds.

One key development was the use of science instead of religion to understand the world. The type of questions that nineteenth-century thinkers sought to answer – What is human nature? Why is society structured the way it is? How and why do societies change? – are much the same as those that sociologists try to answer today. However, our modern world is radically different from that of the past and it is sociology's task to help us understand this world and what the future is likely to hold.

Auguste Comte

No single individual can found a whole field of study and there were many contributors to early sociological thinking. However, particular prominence is usually given to the French author Auguste Comte (1798–1857), if only because he actually invented the word 'sociology'. Comte had originally used the term 'social physics' to describe the new field, but some of his intellectual rivals at the time were also using that term. Comte wanted to distinguish his own ideas from theirs, so he coined the term 'sociology' to describe the subject he wished to establish.

Comte's thinking reflected the turbulent events of his age. The French Revolution of 1789 had significantly changed French society, while the spread of industrialization was altering the traditional lives of the population. Comte sought to create a science of society that could explain the laws of the social world just as natural science explained the functioning of the physical world. Although Comte recognized that each scientific discipline has its own subject-matter, he argued that studying the latter could be done using the same common logic and scientific method aimed at revealing universal laws. Just as the discovery of laws in the natural world allows us to control and predict events around us, so uncovering the laws that govern human society could help us shape our destiny and improve the welfare of humanity. Comte argued that society conforms to invariable laws in much the same way that the physical world does.

Comte's vision for sociology was for it to become a 'positive science'. He wanted sociology to apply the same rigorous scientific methods to the study of society that physicists and chemists use to study the physical world. Positivism holds that science should be concerned only with observable entities that are known directly to experience. On the basis of careful observations, one can infer laws that explain the relationship between the observed phenomena. By understanding the causal relationships between events, scientists can then predict how future events will occur. A positivist approach to sociology aims for the production of knowledge about society based on empirical evidence drawn from observation, comparison and experimentation.

Comte's *law of three stages* claims that human efforts to understand the world have passed through theological, metaphysical and positive stages. In the theological stage, thinking was guided by religious ideas and the belief that society was an expression of God's will. In the metaphysical stage, which came to the forefront around the time of the Renaissance, society came to be seen in natural, not supernatural, terms. The positive stage, ushered in by the discoveries and achievements of Copernicus, Galileo and Newton, encouraged the application of scientific techniques to the social world. In keeping with this view, Comte regarded sociology as the last science to develop – following on from physics, chemistry and biology – but also as the most significant and complex of all the sciences.

In the latter part of his career, Comte drew up ambitious plans for the reconstruction of French society in particular and for human societies in general, based on his sociological viewpoint. He urged the establishment of a 'religion of humanity' that would abandon faith and dogma in favour of a scientific grounding. Sociology would be at the heart of the new religion. Comte was keenly aware of the state of the society in which he lived; he was concerned with the inequalities being produced by industrialization and the threat they posed to social cohesion. The long-term solution, in his view, was the production of a new moral consensus that would help to regulate, or hold together, society, despite the new patterns of inequality. Although Comte's vision for the reconstruction of society was never realized, his contribution to systematizing and unifying the science of society was important to the later professionalization of sociology as an academic discipline.

Emile Durkheim

The writings of another French sociologist, Emile Durkheim (1858–1917), have had a more lasting impact on modern sociology than those of Comte. Although Durkheim drew on aspects of Comte's work, he thought that many of his predecessor's ideas were too speculative and vague and that Comte had not successfully carried out his programme – to establish sociology on a

Emile Durkheim (1858–1917).

scientific basis. Durkheim saw sociology as a new science that could be used to elucidate traditional philosophical questions by examining them in an empirical manner. Like Comte before him, Durkheim argued that we must study social life with the same objectivity as scientists study the natural world. His famous first principle of sociology was 'Study social facts as things!' By this, he meant that social life could be analysed as rigorously as objects or events in nature.

Durkheim's writings spanned a broad spectrum of topics. Three of the main themes he addressed were the importance of sociology as an empirical science, the rise of the individual and the formation of a new social order, and the sources and character of moral authority in society. We will encounter Durkheim's ideas again in our discussions of sociological theories, religion, deviance and crime, and work and economic life.

For Durkheim, the main intellectual concern of sociology is the study of **social facts**. Rather than applying sociological methods to the study of individuals, sociologists should instead examine social facts – aspects of social life that shape our actions as individuals, such as the state of the economy or the influence of religion. Durkheim argued that societies have a reality of their own – that there is more to society than simply the actions and interests of its individual members. According to Durkheim, social facts are ways of acting, thinking or feeling that are external to individuals and have their own reality outside the lives and perceptions of individual people. Another attribute of social facts is that they exercise a coercive power over individuals. The constraining nature of social facts is often not recognized by people as coercive. This is because people generally comply with social facts freely, believing they are acting out of choice. In fact, Durkheim argues, people often simply follow patterns that are general to their society. Social facts can constrain human action in a variety of ways, ranging from outright punishment (in the case of a crime, for example) to social rejection (in the case of unacceptable behaviour) to simple misunderstanding (in the case of the misuse of language).

Durkheim conceded that social facts are difficult to study. Because they are invisible and intangible, social facts cannot be observed directly. Instead, their properties must be revealed indirectly by analysing their effects or by considering attempts that have been made at their expression, such as laws, religious texts or written rules of conduct. In studying social facts, Durkheim stressed the importance of abandoning prejudices and ideology. A scientific attitude demands a mind which is open to the evidence of the senses and free of preconceived ideas which come from outside. Durkheim held that scientific concepts could only be generated through scientific practice. He challenged sociologists to study things as they really are and to construct new concepts that reflect the true nature of social things.

Like the other founders of sociology, Durkheim was preoccupied with the changes transforming society in his own lifetime. He was particularly interested in social and moral solidarity – in other words, what holds society together and keeps it from descending into chaos. Solidarity is maintained when individuals are successfully integrated into social groups and are regulated by a set of shared values and customs. In his first major work, *The Division of Labour in Society*, Durkheim presented an analysis of social change that argued that the advent of the industrial era meant the emergence of a new type of solidarity (Durkheim 1984 [1893]). In making this argument, Durkheim contrasted two types of solidarity, mechanical and organic, and related them to the **division of labour** – the growth of distinctions between different occupations.

According to Durkheim, traditional cultures with a low division of labour are characterized by mechanical solidarity. Because most members of the society are

Karl Marx (1818–83).

their recognition of the importance of others' contributions. As the division of labour expands, people become increasingly dependent upon one another, because each person needs goods and services that those in other occupations supply. Relationships of economic reciprocity and mutual dependency come to replace shared beliefs in creating social consensus.

Yet, processes of change in the modern world are so rapid and intense that they give rise to major social difficulties. They can have disruptive effects on traditional lifestyles, morals, religious beliefs and everyday patterns without providing clear new values. Durkheim linked these unsettling conditions to **anomie**: feelings of aimlessness, dread and despair provoked by modern social life. Traditional moral controls and standards, which used to be supplied by religion, are largely broken down by modern social development, and this leaves many individuals in modern societies feeling that their daily lives lack meaning.

One of Durkheim's most famous studies was concerned with the analysis of suicide (see Classic Studies 1.1 below). Suicide seems to be a purely personal act, the outcome of extreme personal unhappiness. Durkheim showed, however, that social factors exert a fundamental influence on suicidal behaviour, anomie being one of these influences. Suicide rates show regular patterns from year to year and these patterns must be explained sociologically.

Karl Marx

The ideas of Karl Marx (1818–83) contrast sharply with those of both Comte and Durkheim, but, like them, he sought to explain the changes that were taking place in society during the time of the Industrial Revolution. As a young man, Marx's political activities brought him into conflict with the German authorities; after a brief stay in France, he settled permanently in exile in Britain. Marx witnessed the growth of factories and industrial production, as well as the

involved in similar occupations, they are bound together by common experience and shared beliefs. The strength of these shared beliefs is repressive – the community swiftly punishes anyone who challenges conventional ways of life. In this way, there is little room for individual dissent. Mechanical solidarity, therefore, is grounded in consensus and similarity of belief. The forces of industrialization and urbanization, however, led to a growing division of labour that contributed to the breakdown of this form of solidarity. Durkheim argued that the specialization of tasks and the increasing social differentiation in advanced societies would lead to a new order featuring organic solidarity. Societies characterized by organic solidarity are held together by people's economic interdependence and

Classic Studies 1.1 **Durkheim's study of suicide rates**

The research problem

One of the most unsettling aspects of our lives is the phenomenon of suicide, which often leaves those left behind with more questions than answers. Why do some people decide to take their own lives? Where do the pressures they experience actually come from? One of the early sociological classics which explores the relationship between the individual and society is Emile Durkheim's analysis of suicide rates, *Suicide: A Study in Sociology* (Durkheim 1952 [1897]). Even though people see themselves as individuals exercising free will and choice, their behaviours are often socially patterned and shaped and Durkheim's study showed that even a highly personal act like suicide is influenced by what happens in the social world.

Research had been conducted on suicide prior to Durkheim's study, but he was the first to insist on a sociological explanation. Previous writers had acknowledged the influence of some social factors on suicide, but generally resorted to race, climate or mental disorder to explain an individual's likelihood of committing suicide.

According to Durkheim, though, suicide was a social fact that could only be explained by other social facts. The suicide rate was more than simply the aggregate of individual suicides – it was a phenomenon with patterned properties. Suicide rates, for example, vary widely across the world's societies (see figure 1.1).

In examining official suicide statistics in France, Durkheim found that certain categories of people were more likely to commit suicide than others. He discovered, for example, that there were more suicides amongst men than amongst women, more Protestants than Catholics, more wealthy than poor, and more single people than married people. Durkheim also noted that suicide rates tended to be lower during times of war and higher during times of economic change or instability. Why should this be so?

Durkheim's explanation

These findings led Durkheim to conclude that there are social forces *external to the individual*

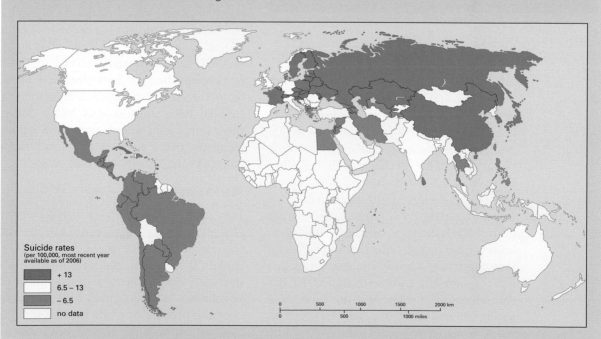

Figure 1.1 Global suicide rates, 2002

Source: World Health Organization 2002

which affect suicide rates. He related his explanation to the idea of social solidarity and to two types of bonds within society – social integration and social regulation. Durkheim argued that people who were strongly integrated into social groups, and whose desires and aspirations were regulated by social norms, were less likely to commit suicide. He identified four types of suicide, in accordance with the relative presence or absence of integration and regulation.

1. *Egoistic suicides* are marked by low integration in society and occur when an individual is isolated, or when his or her ties to a group are weakened or broken. For example, the low rates of suicide amongst Catholics could be explained by their strong social community, while the personal and moral freedom of Protestants mean that they 'stand alone' before God. Marriage protects against suicide by integrating the individual into a stable social relationship, while single people remain more isolated within society. The lower suicide rate during wartime, according to Durkheim, can be seen as a sign of heightened social integration in the face of an external enemy.
2. *Anomic suicide* is caused by a lack of social regulation. By this, Durkheim was referring to the social conditions of anomie when people are rendered 'normless' as a result of rapid change or instability in society. The loss of a fixed point of reference for norms and desires – such as in times of economic upheaval or in personal struggles like divorce – can upset the balance between people's circumstances and their desires.
3. *Altruistic suicide* occurs when an individual is 'over-integrated' – social bonds are too strong – and values society more than him- or herself. In such a case, suicide becomes a sacrifice for the 'greater good'. Japanese kamikaze pilots or Islamic 'suicide bombers' are examples of altruistic suicides. Durkheim saw these as characteristic of traditional societies where mechanical solidarity prevails.

4. The final type of suicide is *fatalistic suicide*. Although Durkheim saw this as of little contemporary relevance, he believed that it results when an individual is over-regulated by society. The oppression of the individual results in a feeling of powerlessness before fate or society.

Suicide rates vary between societies but show regular patterns *within* societies over time. Durkheim took this as evidence that there are consistent social forces that influence suicide rates. An examination of suicide rates reveals how general social patterns can be detected within individual actions.

Critical points

Since the publication of *Suicide*, many objections have been raised to Durkheim's study, particularly in relation to his uncritical use of official statistics, his dismissal of non-social influences on suicide and his insistence in classifying all types of suicide together. Some critics have also shown that it is vitally important to understand the social process involved in collecting data on suicides, as coroners' definitions and criteria influence the number of deaths actually recorded as 'suicides'. Because of this, suicide statistics may be highly variable across societies, not necessarily because of differences in suicidal behaviour, but because of different practices used by coroners in recording unexplained deaths.

Contemporary significance

Nonetheless, despite such legitimate criticisms, Durkheim's study remains a classic. It helped to establish sociology as a discipline with its own subject – the study of social facts – and his fundamental argument in his book on suicide retains its force: that to grasp fully even the apparently most personal act of suicide demands a sociological explanation rather than simply one rooted in the exploration of personal motivation.

resulting inequalities. His interest in the European labour movement and socialist ideas were reflected in his writings, which covered a diversity of topics. Most of his work concentrated on economic issues, but since he was always concerned to connect economic problems to social institutions, his work was, and remains, rich in sociological insights. Even his sternest critics regard his work as important in the development of sociology.

Capitalism and class struggle

Though he wrote about various phases of history, Marx concentrated primarily on change in modern times. For him, the most important changes were bound up with the development of capitalism. Capitalism is a system of production that contrasts radically with all previous economic systems, involving as it does the production of goods and services sold to a wide range of consumers. Marx identified two main elements within capitalist enterprises. The first is capital – any asset, including money, machines or even factories, that can be used or invested to make future assets. The accumulation of capital goes hand in hand with the second element, wage-labour. Wage-labour refers to the pool of workers who do not own the means of their livelihood but who must find employment provided by the owners of capital. Marx argued that those who own capital – capitalists – form a ruling class, while the mass of the population make up a class of waged workers – a working class. As industrialization spread, large numbers of peasants who used to support themselves by working the land moved to the expanding cities and helped to form an urban-based industrial working class. This working class is also referred to as the proletariat.

According to Marx, capitalism is inherently a class system in which class relations are characterized by conflict. Although owners of capital and workers are each dependent on the other – the capitalists need labour and the workers need wages –

the dependency is highly unbalanced. The relationship between classes is an exploitative one, since workers have little or no control over their labour and employers are able to generate profit by appropriating the product of workers' labour. Marx saw that class conflict over economic resources would become more acute with the passing of time.

Social change: the materialist conception of history

Marx's viewpoint was grounded in what he called the materialist conception of history. According to this view, it is not the ideas or values which human beings hold that are the main sources of social change; rather, social change is prompted primarily by economic influences. Conflicts between classes provide the motivation for historical development – they are the 'motor of history'. As Marx wrote at the beginning of *The Communist Manifesto*, 'The history of all hitherto existing society is the history of class struggles' (Marx and Engels 2001 [1848]). Although Marx focused most of his attention on capitalism and modern society, he also examined how societies had developed over the course of history. According to him, social systems make a transition from one mode of production to another – sometimes gradually, sometimes through revolution – as a result of contradictions in their economies. He outlined a progression of historical stages that began with primitive communist societies of hunters and gatherers and passed through ancient slave-owning systems and feudal systems based on the division between landowners and serfs. The emergence of merchants and craftspeople marked the beginning of a commercial or capitalist class that came to displace the landed nobility. In accordance with this view of history, Marx argued that, just as the capitalists had united to overthrow the feudal order, so too would the capitalists be supplanted and a new order installed: communism.

Marx theorized the inevitability of a workers' revolution which would overthrow the capitalist system and usher in a new society in which there would be no classes – no large-scale divisions between rich and poor. He did not mean that all inequalities between individuals would disappear. Rather, society would no longer be split into a small class that monopolizes economic and political power and the large mass of people who benefit little from the wealth their work creates. The economic system would come under communal ownership, and a more humane society than we know at present would be established. Marx argued that, in the society of the future, production would be more advanced and efficient than production under capitalism.

Marx's work had a far-reaching effect on the twentieth-century world. Until only a generation ago, more than a third of the earth's population lived in societies, such as the Soviet Union and the countries of Eastern Europe, whose governments claimed to derive their inspiration from Marx's ideas.

Max Weber

Like Marx, Max Weber (pronounced 'veybur') (1864–1920) cannot simply be labelled a sociologist; his interests and concerns ranged across many areas. Born in Germany, where he spent most of his academic career, Weber was an individual of wide learning. His writings covered the fields of economics, law, philosophy and comparative history, as well as sociology. Much of his work was also concerned with the development of modern capitalism and the ways in which modern society was different from earlier forms of social organization. Through a series of empirical studies, Weber set forth some of the basic characteristics of modern industrial societies and identified key sociological debates that remain central for sociologists today.

In common with other thinkers of his time, Weber sought to understand the nature and causes of social change. He was influenced by Marx but was also strongly critical of some of Marx's major views. He rejected the materialist conception of history and saw class conflict as less significant than did Marx. In Weber's view, economic factors are important, but ideas and values have just as much impact on social change. Weber's celebrated and much discussed work, *The Protestant Ethic and the Spirit of Capitalism* (1992 [1904–5]), proposes that religious values – especially those associated with Puritanism – were of fundamental importance in creating a capitalistic outlook. Unlike other early sociological thinkers, Weber argued that sociology should focus on social action, not social structures. He argued that human

Max Weber (1864–1920).

motivation and ideas were the forces behind change – ideas, values and beliefs had the power to bring about transformations. According to Weber, individuals have the ability to act freely and to shape the future. He did not see, as did Durkheim and Marx, that structures existed external to or independent of individuals. Rather, structures in society were formed by a complex interplay of actions. It was the job of sociology to understand the meanings behind those actions.

Some of Weber's most influential writings reflected this concern with social action in analysing the distinctiveness of Western society as compared with other major civilizations. He studied the religions of China, India and the Near East, and in the course of these researches made major contributions to the sociology of religion. Comparing the leading religious systems in China and India with those of the West, Weber concluded that certain aspects of Christian beliefs strongly influenced the rise of capitalism. He argued that the capitalist outlook of Western societies did not emerge, as Marx supposed, only from economic changes. In Weber's view, cultural ideas and values help shape society and our individual actions.

An important element in Weber's sociological perspective was the idea of the **ideal type**. Ideal types are conceptual or analytical models that can be used to understand the world. In the real world, ideal types rarely, if ever, exist – often only some of their attributes will be present. These hypothetical constructions can be very useful, however, as any situation in the real world can be understood by comparing it to an ideal type. In this way, ideal types serve as a fixed point of reference. It is important to point out that by 'ideal' type Weber did not mean that the conception was a perfect or desirable goal. Instead, he meant that it was a 'pure' form of a certain phenomenon. Weber utilized ideal types in his writings on forms of bureaucracy and economic markets.

Rationalization

In Weber's view, the emergence of modern society was accompanied by important shifts in patterns of social action. He saw that people were moving away from traditional beliefs grounded in superstition, religion, custom and long-standing habit. Instead, individuals were increasingly engaging in rational, instrumental calculations that took into account efficiency and the future consequences of their actions. In industrial society, there was little room for sentiment and for doing things simply because they had been done that way for generations. The development of science, modern technology and **bureaucracy** was described by Weber collectively as **rationalization** – the organization of social and economic life according to the principles of efficiency and on the basis of technical knowledge. If, in traditional societies, religion and long-standing customs largely defined people's attitudes and values, modern society was marked by the rationalization of more and more areas of life, from politics to religion to economic activity.

In Weber's view, the Industrial Revolution and the rise of capitalism were evidence of the larger trend towards rationalization. Capitalism is not dominated by class conflict, as Marx argued, but by the rise of science and bureaucracy: large-scale organizations. Weber saw the scientific character of the West as one of its most distinctive features. Bureaucracy, the only way of organizing large numbers of people effectively, expands with economic and political growth. Weber used the term 'disenchantment' to describe the way in which scientific thinking in the modern world had swept away the forces of sentimentality from the past.

Weber was not entirely optimistic about the outcome of rationalization, however. He was fearful that the spread of modern bureaucracy to all areas of life would imprison us in a 'steel-hard cage' from which there would be little chance of

1.1   Neglected founders of sociology?

Although Comte, Durkheim, Marx and Weber are, without doubt, foundational figures in sociology, there were some in the same period and others from earlier times whose contributions should also be taken into account. Sociology, like many academic fields, has not always lived up to its ideal of acknowledging the importance of every thinker whose work has intrinsic merit. Very few women or members of racial minorities were given the opportunity to become professional sociologists during the 'classical' period of the late nineteenth and early twentieth centuries. In addition, the few who were given the opportunity to do sociological research of lasting importance have frequently been neglected. Important scholars like Harriet Martineau and the Muslim scholar Ibn Khaldun have attracted the attention of sociologists in recent years.

Harriet Martineau (1802–76)

Harriet Martineau (1802–76).

Harriet Martineau has been called the 'first woman sociologist', but, like Marx and Weber, cannot be thought of simply as a sociologist. She was born and educated in England and was the author of more than 50 books, as well as numerous essays. Martineau is now credited with introducing sociology to Britain through her translation of Comte's founding treatise of the field, *Positive Philosophy* (see Rossi 1973). In addition, Martineau conducted a first-hand, systematic study of American society during her extensive travels throughout the United States in the 1830s, which is the subject of her book *Society in America* (Martineau 1962 [1837]). Martineau is significant to sociologists today for several reasons.

First, she argued that when one studies a society, one must focus on all its aspects, including key political, religious and social institutions. Second, she insisted that an analysis of a society must include an understanding of women's lives. Third, she was the first to turn a sociological eye on previously ignored issues, including marriage, children, domestic and religious life, and race relations. As she once wrote: 'The nursery, the boudoir, and the kitchen are all excellent schools in which to learn the morals and manners of a people' (1962 [1837]). Finally, she argued that sociologists should do more than just observe; they should also act in ways to benefit a society. As a result, Martineau was an active proponent of both women's rights and the emancipation of slaves.

Ibn Khaldun (1332–1406)

The Muslim scholar Ibn Khaldun was born in what is today Tunisia and is famous for his historical, sociological and political economic studies. Ibn Khaldun wrote many books, the most widely known of which is a six-volume work, the *Muqaddimah* ('Introduction'), completed in 1378. This is viewed by some scholars today as essentially an early foundational work of sociology (see Alatas 2006). The *Muqaddimah* criticized existing historical approaches and methods as dealing only with description, claiming instead the discovery of a new 'science of social organization' or 'science of society', capable of getting at the underlying meaning of events.

Ibn Khaldun devised a theory of social conflict based on understanding the central characteristics of the 'nomadic' and 'sedentary' societies of his time. Central to this theory was the concept of 'group feeling' or solidarity (*asabiyyah*). Groups and societies with a strong group feeling were able to dominate and control those with weaker forms of internal solidarity. Ibn Khaldun developed these ideas in an attempt to explain the rise and decline of Maghribian and Arab states, and in this sense he may be seen as studying the process of state-formation – itself a main concern of modern, Western historical sociology. Nomadic Bedouin tribes tended towards a very strong group feeling, which enabled them to overrun and dominate the weaker sedentary town-dwellers and establish new dynasties. However, the Bedouin then became settled into more urbanized lifestyles and their previously strong group feeling and military force diminished, thus leaving them open to attack from external enemies once again. This completed a long cycle in the rise and decline of states. Although Western historians and sociologists of the late nineteenth and early twentieth centuries referred to Ibn Khaldun's work, only in very recent years have they again come to be seen as potentially significant.

Ibn Khaldun (1332–1406).

escape. Bureaucratic domination, although based on rational principles, could crush the human spirit by attempting to regulate all spheres of social life. He was particularly troubled by the potentially suffocating and dehumanizing effects of bureaucracy and its implications for the fate of democracy. The seemingly progressive agenda of the eighteenth-century Age of Enlightenment, of scientific progress, increasing wealth and happiness produced by rejecting traditional customs and superstitions, also had a dark side with new dangers.

Modern theoretical approaches

The early sociologists were united in their desire to make sense of the changing soci-

> **THINKING CRITICALLY**
>
> What factors might account for the neglect of Harriet Martineau's sociological work on marriage, children and the domestic life of women in the nineteenth century? Why do you think Ibn Khaldun's fourteenth-century ideas are finding a new audience at the start of the twenty-first century?

eties in which they lived. They wanted to do more than simply depict and interpret the momentous events of their time, however. They all looked to develop ways of studying the social world that could explain how societies functioned and what were the causes of social change. Yet, as we have seen, Durkheim, Marx and Weber employed very different approaches in their studies. For example, where Durkheim and Marx focused on the strength of forces external to the individual, Weber took as his point of departure the ability of individuals to act creatively on the outside world. Where Marx pointed to the predominance of economic issues, Weber considered a much wider range of factors to be significant. Such differences in approach have persisted throughout the history of sociology. Even when sociologists agree on the subject of analysis, they often undertake that analysis from different theoretical positions.

The three recent theoretical approaches examined below – functionalism, the conflict approach and symbolic interactionism – have connections with Durkheim, Marx and Weber respectively. Throughout this book, you will encounter arguments and ideas that draw upon and illustrate these theoretical approaches.

> In chapter 3, 'Theories and Perspectives in Sociology', we return to the major theoretical approaches in more detail and examine the development of sociological theory during the twentieth century.

Functionalism

Functionalism holds that society is a complex system whose various parts work together to produce stability and solidarity. According to this approach, the discipline of sociology should investigate the relationship of parts of society to each other and to society as a whole. We can analyse the religious beliefs and customs of a society, for example, by showing how they relate to other institutions within it, for the different parts of a society develop in close relation to one another.

To study the function of a social practice or institution is to analyse the contribution which that practice, or institution, makes to the continuation of society. Functionalists, including Comte and Durkheim, have often used an organic analogy to compare the operation of society to that of a living organism. They argue that the parts of society work together, just as the various parts of the human body do, for the benefit of society as a whole. To study a bodily organ like the heart, we need to show how it relates to other parts of the body. By pumping blood around the body, the heart plays a vital role in the continuation of the life of the organism. Similarly, analysing the function of a social item means showing the part it plays in the continued existence and health of a society.

Functionalism emphasizes the importance of moral consensus, in maintaining order and stability in society. Moral consensus exists when most people in a society share the same values. Functionalists regard order and balance as the normal state of society – this social equilibrium is grounded in the existence of a moral consensus among the members of society. For instance, Durkheim argued that religion reaffirms people's adherence to core social values, thereby contributing to the maintenance of social cohesion.

Until the 1960s, functionalist thought was probably the leading theoretical tradition in sociology, particularly in the United States. Talcott Parsons (1902–79) and Robert K. Merton (1910–2003), who each drew extensively on Durkheim, were two of its most prominent adherents. Merton's version of functionalism has been particularly influential. Merton distinguished between manifest and latent functions. Manifest functions are those known to, and intended by, the participants in a specific type of social activity. Latent functions are consequences of that activity of which participants are unaware. To illustrate this distinction, Merton used the example of a rain dance performed by the Hopi Tribe of Arizona and New Mexico. The Hopi believe that the ceremony will bring the rain they need for their crops (manifest function). This is why they organize and participate in it. But the rain dance,

Merton argued, using Durkheim's theory of religion, also has the effect of promoting the cohesion of the Hopi society (latent function). A major part of sociological explanation, according to Merton, consists in uncovering the latent functions of social activities and institutions.

Merton also distinguished between functions and **dysfunctions**. To look for the dysfunctional aspects of social behaviour means focusing on features of social life that challenge the existing order of things. For example, it is mistaken to suppose that religion is always functional – that it contributes only to social cohesion. When two groups support different religions or even different versions of the same religion, the result can be major social conflicts, causing widespread social disruption. Thus, wars have often been fought between religious communities – as can be seen in the struggles between Protestants and Catholics in European history.

In recent years, the popularity of functionalism has begun to wane, as its limitations have become apparent. While this was not true of Merton, many functionalist thinkers (Talcott Parsons is an example) unduly stressed factors leading to social cohesion at the expense of those producing division and conflict. The focus on stability and order means that divisions or inequalities in society – based on factors such as class, race and gender – are minimized. There is also less emphasis on the role of creative social action within society. Many critics have argued that functional analysis attributes to societies social qualities that they do not have. Functionalists often wrote as though societies have 'needs' and 'purposes', even though these concepts make sense only when applied to individual human beings.

Conflict perspectives

Like functionalists, sociologists employing **conflict theories** emphasize the importance of structures within society. They also advance a comprehensive 'model' to explain how society works. However, conflict theorists reject functionalism's emphasis on consensus. Instead, they highlight the importance of divisions in society. In doing so, they concentrate on issues of power, inequality and struggle. They tend to see society as composed of distinct groups pursuing their own interests. The existence of separate interests means that the potential for conflict is always present and that certain groups will benefit more than others. Conflict theorists examine the tensions between dominant and disadvantaged groups within society and seek to understand how relationships of control are established and perpetuated.

An influential approach within conflict theory is Marxism, named after Karl Marx, whose work emphasized class conflict. Numerous interpretations of Marx's major ideas are possible, and there are today schools of Marxist thought that take very different theoretical positions. In all of its versions, Marxism differs from most other traditions of sociology in that its authors see it as a combination of sociological analysis and political reform. Marxism is supposed to generate a programme of radical political change.

However, not all conflict theories take a Marxist approach. Some conflict theorists have also been influenced by Weber. A good example is the contemporary German sociologist Ralf Dahrendorf (1929–). In his now classic work, *Class and Class Conflict in Industrial Society* (1959), Dahrendorf argues that functionalist thinkers only consider one side of society – those aspects of social life where there is harmony and agreement. Just as important, or more so, are areas marked by conflict and division. Conflict, Dahrendorf says, comes mainly from different interests that individuals and groups have. Marx saw differences of interest mainly in terms of classes, but Dahrendorf relates them more broadly to authority and power. In all societies there is a division between those who hold authority and those who are largely excluded from it – between rulers and ruled.

Symbolic interactionism

The work of the American social philosopher G. H. Mead (1863–1931) had an important influence on sociological thought, in particular through a perspective called **symbolic interactionism**. Symbolic interactionism springs from a concern with language and meaning. Mead claims that language allows us to become self-conscious beings – aware of our own individuality and able to see ourselves from the outside as others see us. The key element in this process is the symbol. A symbol is something that stands for something else. For example, words that we use to refer to certain objects are in fact symbols which represent what we mean. The word 'spoon' is the symbol we use to describe the utensil that we use to eat soup. Non-verbal gestures or forms of communication are also symbols. Waving at someone or making a rude gesture has symbolic value. Mead argued that humans rely on shared symbols and understandings in their interactions with one another. Because human beings live in a richly symbolic universe, virtually all interactions between human individuals involve an exchange of symbols.

Symbolic interactionism directs our attention to the detail of interpersonal interaction and how that detail is used to make sense of what others say and do. Sociologists influenced by symbolic interactionism often focus on face-to-face interaction in the contexts of everyday life. They stress the role of such interaction in creating society and its institutions. Max Weber was an important indirect influence on this theoretical approach because, although he acknowledged the existence of social structures – such as classes, parties, status groups and others – he held that these structures were created through the social actions of individuals.

While the symbolic interactionist perspective can yield many insights into the nature of our actions in the course of day-to-day social life, it has been criticized for ignoring the larger issues of power and structure within society and how they serve to constrain individual action.

One classic example of symbolic interactionism that does take into account the issues of power and structure in our society is Arlie Hochschild's *The Managed Heart: Commercialization of Human Feeling* (1983). Hochschild, a sociology professor at the University of California, observed training sessions and carried out interviews at Delta Airlines' Stewardess Training Center in Atlanta in the USA. She watched flight attendants being trained to manage their feelings as well as learning other skills. Hochschild recalled the comments of one instructor, a pilot, at the training sessions: 'Now girls, I want you to go out there and really smile', the pilot instructed. 'Your smile is your biggest asset. I want you to go out there and use it. Smile. Really smile. Really lay it on.'

Through her observations and interviews, Hochschild found that as Western economies have become increasingly based on the delivery of services, the emotional style of the work we do needs to be understood. Her study of 'customer service' training amongst flight attendants might feel familiar to anyone who has worked in the service industry before, perhaps in a shop, restaurant or bar. Hochschild calls this training in 'emotional labour' – labour that requires that one manages one's feelings in order to create a publicly observable (and acceptable) facial and body display. According to Hochschild, the companies you work for lay claim not only to your physical movements, but also to your emotions. They own your smile when you are working.

Hochschild's research opened a window on an aspect of life that most people think they understand, but which needed to be understood at a deeper level. She found that service workers – like physical labourers – often feel a sense of distance from the particular aspect of themselves that is given up in work. The physical labourer's arm, for

In many service industries, people's management of the public display of their emotions has become a key part of their skills training.

example, might come to feel like a piece of machinery, and only incidentally a part of the person moving it. Likewise, service workers often told Hochschild that their smiles were *on* them but not *of* them. In other words, these workers felt a sense of distance from their own emotions. This is interesting when we consider the fact that emotions are usually thought of as a deep and personal part of ourselves.

Hochschild's book is an influential application of symbolic interactionism and many other scholars have built on her ideas. Although she conducted her research within one of the world's most developed 'service economies' – the United States – Hochschild's findings are applicable to many societies in the present age. Service jobs are expanding rapidly in countries around the world, demanding that more and more people engage in 'emotional labour' at the workplace. In some cultures, such as amongst the Inuit of Greenland, where there is not the same tradition of public smiling as there is in Western Europe and North America, training in emotional labour has proved to be a somewhat difficult task. In these countries, employees in service jobs are sometimes required to take part in special 'smiling training sessions' not so different from the ones attended by Delta Airlines stewardesses.

Theoretical thinking in sociology

So far in this chapter we have been concerned with theoretical *approaches*, which refer to broad, overall orientations to the subject-matter of sociology. However, we can draw a distinction between the theoretical approaches discussed above and actual theories. Theories are more narrowly focused and represent attempts to explain particular social conditions or types of event. They are usually formed as part of the process of research and in turn suggest problems to which research investigations should be devoted. An example would be Durkheim's theory of suicide, referred to earlier in this chapter.

Many theories have been developed in the many different areas of research in which sociologists work. Sometimes theories are very precisely set out and are even occasionally expressed in mathematical form – although this is more common in other social sciences (especially economics) than in sociology.

Some theories are also much more encompassing than others. Opinions vary about whether it is desirable or useful for sociologists to concern themselves with very wide-ranging theoretical endeavours. Robert K. Merton (1957), for example, argued forcefully that sociologists should concentrate their attention on what he calls 'theories of the middle range'. Rather than attempting to create grand theoretical schemes (in the manner of Marx, for instance), we should be concerned with developing theories that are more modest.

Middle-range theories are specific enough to be directly tested by empirical research, yet sufficiently general to cover a range of different phenomena. A case in point is the theory of relative deprivation. This theory holds that the way people evaluate their circumstances depends on whom they compare themselves to. Thus, feelings of deprivation do not conform directly to the level of material poverty that people experience. A family living in a small home in a poor area, where everyone is in more or less similar circumstances, is likely to feel less deprived than a family living in a similar house in a neighbourhood where the majority of the other homes are much larger and the other people more affluent.

It is indeed true that the more wide-ranging and ambitious a theory is, the more difficult it is to test empirically. Yet there seems no obvious reason why theoretical thinking in sociology should be confined to the 'middle range'.

Assessing theories, and especially theoretical approaches, in sociology is a challenging and formidable task. Theoretical debates are, by definition, more abstract than controversies of a more empirical kind. The fact that sociology is not dominated by a single theoretical approach might seem to be a sign of weakness in the subject, but this is not the case. The jostling of rival theoretical approaches and theories is an expression of the vitality of the sociological enterprise. In studying human beings – ourselves – theoretical variety rescues us from dogma and stagnation. Human behaviour is complicated and many-sided, and it is very unlikely that a single theoretical perspective could cover all of its aspects. Diversity in theoretical thinking provides a rich source of ideas that can be drawn on in research and which stimulate the imaginative capacities so essential to progress in sociological work.

Levels of analysis: microsociology and macrosociology

One important distinction between the different theoretical perspectives we have discussed in this chapter involves the level of analysis at which each is directed. The study of everyday behaviour in situations of face-to-face interaction is usually called microsociology. Macrosociology is the analysis of large-scale social systems, like the political system or the economic order. It also includes the analysis of long-term processes of change, such as the development of industrialism. At first glance, it might seem that microanalysis and macroanalysis are distinct from one another. In fact, the two are closely connected (Knorr-Cetina and Cicourel 1981; Giddens 1984).

Macroanalysis is essential if we are to understand the institutional background of daily life. The ways in which people live their everyday lives are greatly affected by the broader institutional framework, as is obvious when the daily cycle of activities of a culture like that of the medieval period is compared with life in an industrialized urban environment. In modern societies, we are constantly in contact with strangers. This contact may be indirect and impersonal. However, no matter how many indirect or electronic relations we enter into today, even in the most complex societies, the presence of other people remains crucial. While we may choose just to send an acquaintance an email message, we can also choose to fly thousands of miles to spend the weekend with a friend.

Micro-studies are in turn necessary for illuminating broad institutional patterns. Face-to-face interaction is clearly the main basis of all forms of social organization, no matter how large scale. Suppose we are studying a business corporation. We could understand much about its activities simply by looking at face-to-face behaviour. We could analyse, for example, the interaction of directors in the boardroom, people working in the various offices, or the workers on the factory floor. We would not build up a picture of the whole corporation in this way, since some of its business is transacted through printed materials, letters, the telephone and computers. Yet we could certainly contribute significantly to understanding how the organization works.

Of course, people do not live their lives as isolated individuals, nor are their lives completely determined by national states. Sociology tells us that our everyday life is lived in families, social groups, communities and neighbourhoods. At this level – the meso (or 'middle') level of society – it is possible to see the influences and effects of both micro- and macro-level phenomena. Many sociological studies of specific local communities deal with the macrosociological impact of huge social changes, such as industrialization and economic globalization. But they also explore the way that individuals, groups and social movements cope with such changes and attempt to turn them to their advantage. For example, when the UK government decided to reduce the role of coal in its energy policy in the 1980s, the impact was disastrous for many traditional mining communities, as people's livelihoods were threatened by large-scale unemployment (Waddington et al. 2001). Mining communities initially organized to protest against the policy, but, when this eventually failed, many individual miners retrained to find work in other industries. Such studies of the community-level of social life can provide a window through which to observe and understand the interaction of micro- and macro-levels of society and much applied work in sociology takes place at this *meso* level of social reality.

In later chapters, we will see further examples of how interaction in micro-contexts affects larger social processes, and how macro-systems in turn influence more confined settings of social life.

Why study sociology?

Sociology has several practical implications for our lives, as C. Wright Mills emphasized when developing his idea of the sociological imagination. First, sociology gives us an awareness of cultural differences that allows us to see the social world from many perspectives. Quite often, if we properly understand how others live, we also acquire a better understanding of what their problems are. Practical policies that are not based on an informed awareness of the ways of life of people they affect have little chance of success. For example, a white social worker operating in a predominantly Latin American community in South London will not gain the confidence of its members without developing a sensitivity to the differences in social experience between members of different groups in the UK.

Second, sociological research provides practical help in assessing the results of policy initiatives. A programme of practical reform may simply fail to achieve what its designers sought or may produce unintended consequences of an unfortunate kind. For instance, in the years following the Second World War, large public housing blocks were built in city centres in many countries. These were planned to provide high standards of accommodation for low-income groups from slum areas and offered shopping amenities and other civic services nearby. However, research later showed that many people who had moved from their previous dwellings to large apartment blocks felt isolated and unhappy. High-rise apartment blocks and shopping centres in poorer areas often became dilapidated and provided breeding grounds for muggings and other violent crimes.

Third, and in some ways this is the most important, sociology can provide us with self-enlightenment – increased self-understanding. The more we know about why we act as we do and about the overall workings of our society, the more likely we are to be able to influence our own futures. We should not see sociology as assisting only policy-makers – that is, powerful groups – in making informed decisions. Those in power cannot be assumed always to consider the interests of the less powerful or underprivileged in the policies they pursue. Self-enlightened groups can often benefit from sociological research by using the information gleaned to respond in an effective way to government policies or form policy initiatives of their own. Self-help groups like Alcoholics Anonymous and social movements like the environmental movement are examples of social groups that have directly sought to bring about practical reforms, with some degree of success.

Finally, it should be mentioned that many sociologists concern themselves directly with practical matters as professionals. People trained in sociology are to be found as industrial consultants, researchers, urban planners, social workers and personnel managers, as well as in many other jobs. An understanding of society can also help

for future careers in law, journalism, business and health professions.

There is often a connection between studying sociology and the prompting of social conscience. Should sociologists themselves actively advocate and agitate for programmes of reform or social change? Some argue that sociology can preserve its intellectual independence only if sociologists are studiously neutral in moral and political controversies. Yet are those scholars who remain aloof from current debates necessarily more impartial in their assessment of sociological issues than others? No sociologically sophisticated person can be unaware of the inequalities that exist in the world today. It would be strange if sociologists did not take sides on political issues, and it would be illogical to try to ban them from drawing on their expertise in so doing.

In this chapter, we have seen that sociology is a discipline in which we often set aside our personal view of the world in order to look more carefully at the influences that shape our lives and those of others. Sociology emerged as a distinct intellectual endeavour with the development of modern societies, and the study of such societies remains a central concern. However, in an increasingly interconnected global world, sociologists must increasingly take a similarly global view of their subject matter if they are properly to understand and explain it. Of course, sociologists remain preoccupied with a broad range of issues about the nature of social interaction and human societies in general.

As we will see in chapter 3, *Theories and Perspectives in Sociology*, the central problems that exercise sociologists change along with the societies they aim to explore and understand. During the period of the discipline's classical founders, the central problems included social class conflict, wealth distribution, the alleviation of absolute as well as relative poverty, the secularization of religious belief and the question of where the process of modernization was headed. In the contemporary period, though most of these issues remain, it can forcefully be argued that sociology's central problems are shifting. Today, societies are grappling with the problems created by rapid globalization, environmental degradation and its impact on human health and well-being, the awareness of risks with potentially high consequences, how to create successful models of multiculturalism and the achievement of a genuine gender equality: to name just a few. This means that sociologists will need to question whether the theories designed to grasp the different problems of an earlier period have any purchase on the problems facing today's societies. If not, then they will need to design new theories that *can* grasp what Karl Mannheim once called 'the secret of these new times'.

Readers can expect the ongoing debate about the status and continuing relevance of the classical sociological theories and attempts to construct new theories to occur throughout this book.

Sociology is not just an abstract intellectual field, but has major practical implications for people's lives. Learning to become a sociologist should not be a dull or tedious endeavour. The best way to make sure it does not become so is to approach the subject in an imaginative way and to relate sociological ideas and findings to situations in your own life. In that way, you should learn important things about yourself, about your society and about the wider human world.

Summary points

1. Sociology is the systematic study of human societies, giving special, but not exclusive emphasis, to modern industrialized societies.

2. The practice of sociology involves the ability to think imaginatively and to detach oneself from preconceived ideas about social life.

3. Sociology came into being as an attempt to understand the far-reaching changes that have occurred in human societies over the past two or three centuries. The changes involved are not just large-scale ones; they also involve shifts in the most intimate and personal aspects of people's lives.

4. Among the classical founders of sociology, four figures are particularly important: Auguste Comte, Karl Marx, Emile Durkheim and Max Weber. Comte and Marx, working in the mid-nineteenth century, established some of the basic issues of sociology, later elaborated on by Durkheim and Weber. These issues concern the nature of sociology and the impact of modernization on the social world.

5. A diversity of theoretical approaches is found in sociology. Theoretical disputes are difficult to resolve even in the natural sciences, but in sociology we face special difficulties because of the complex problems involved in subjecting our own behaviour to study.

6. The main theoretical approaches in sociology are functionalism, conflict perspectives and symbolic interactionism. There are some basic differences between each of these approaches, which have strongly influenced the development of the subject in the post-war period.

7. One way of thinking about sociology's approaches is in terms of their level of analysis. Microsociology is the study of everyday behaviour in face-to-face encounters. Macrosociology analyses large-scale social systems and whole societies. Micro- and macro-levels are closely connected, however, and this can be seen in research studies of communities and neighbourhoods – the meso (or middle) level of social life.

8. Sociology is a subject with important practical implications. It can contribute to social criticism and practical social reform in several ways. The improved understanding of social circumstances gives us all a better chance of controlling them. At the same time, sociology provides the means of increasing

our cultural sensitivities, allowing policies to be based on an awareness of divergent cultural values. In practical terms, we can investigate the consequences of the adoption of particular policy programmes. Finally, and perhaps most important, sociology provides self-enlightenment, offering groups and individuals an increased opportunity to understand and alter the conditions of their own lives.

Further reading

For anyone new to sociology, Steve Bruce's *Sociology: A Very Short Introduction* (Oxford: Oxford University Press, 2000) is a good place to start your reading. This is a brief but stimulating guide. Following this, Zygmunt Bauman and Tim May's *Thinking Sociologically* (Oxford: Blackwell, 2001) is a more involved introduction to developing and using your sociological imagination and the book contains many everyday examples. If these motivate you to take on something a little more advanced, then Richard Jenkins's *Foundations of Sociology: Towards a Better Understanding of the Human World* (Basingstoke: Palgrave Macmillan, 2002) contains a central argument about the role of sociology and sociologists in an age of globalization. This is not an easy read but it is worthwhile.

One other useful resource for all newcomers to the discipline is a good sociology dictionary and there are several possibilities. Among them, both John Scott and Gordon Marshall's *Oxford Dictionary of Sociology* (Oxford: Oxford University Press, 2005) and Nicholas Abercrombie, Stephen Hill and Bryan Turner's *The Penguin Dictionary of Sociology* (London: Penguin Books, 2006) are reliable and comprehensive.

Internet links

Additional information and support for this book at Polity:
www.polity.co.uk/giddens

The International Sociological Association:
www.isa-sociology.org/

The European Sociological Association:
www.valt.helsinki.fi/esa/

The British Sociological Association:
www.britsoc.co.uk/

Intute – a social science information gateway with lots of sociology resources:
www.intute.ac.uk/socialsciences/sociology/

SocioSite – the Social Science Information System, based at the University of Amsterdam:
www.sociosite.net/index.php

2

Asking and Answering Sociological Questions

CHAPTER 2

Asking and Answering Sociological Questions

(opposite) Why hang out in public toilets?

Towards the end of a working day, the public toilets of a particular park in St Louis, Missouri, in the United States, are suddenly busier than one might expect. One man walks in dressed in a grey suit; another has on a baseball cap, trainers, shorts and a T-shirt; a third is wearing the mechanic's uniform from the garage where he has repaired cars all day. What are these men doing here? Surely other toilets are more conveniently located. Is there some common interest besides the toilets themselves that brings them to this place?

None of these men is visiting the toilets to use them for the purposes for which they were officially built: they are there for 'instant sex'. Many

In contrast to Humphrey's covert research, increasingly the subjects of research are themselves involved in the research process and may help to formulate questions or comment on the researcher's interpretation of their views.

men – married and unmarried, those with straight identities and those who see themselves as gay – seek sex with people they do not know. They are hoping to experience sexual excitement, but they want to avoid involvement. They do not want any commitments that extend beyond the particular encounters they will have in this public convenience.

This kind of search for anonymous, instant sex between men happens all over the world, yet until the late 1960s the phenomenon persisted as a widespread but rarely studied form of human interaction. In the USA, the gay community called the toilets where these activities occur 'tearooms' (in the UK the activity is known as 'cottaging'). Laud Humphreys, a sociologist, visited these public lavatories to conduct research on the participants. He wrote about them in his book *Tearoom Trade* (Humphreys 1970). Unsurprisingly,

the book caused widespread controversy when it was published, and for some people the issue is still a difficult one to deal with today. For example, Humphreys' research methodology was heavily criticized for being unethical because his fieldwork had to be covert; it did not involve seeking the informed consent of the men he studied. However, his research in the 'tearooms' was able to cast new light on the struggles of men who were forced to keep their sexual proclivities secret. He showed that many men who otherwise live 'normal' lives – the people next door – find ways to engage in embarrassing behaviours that will not harm their careers or family lives. Humphreys' research was conducted at a time when there was much more stigma associated with gay and lesbian identities and when police were vigilant in enforcing laws against such behaviour. Many lives were ruined in the process of harsh law enforcement.

Humphreys spent an extended period of time researching public toilets because one excellent way to understand social processes is to participate in and observe them. He also conducted survey interviews that enabled him to gather more information than he would have obtained by simply observing the toilets. Humphreys' research opened a window on an aspect of life that many people were shocked to know existed at all and that certainly needed to be understood at a deeper level. His work was based on systematic research, but it also carried a note of passion; it was conducted with a certain scientific detachment, but at the same time Humphreys was involved in the search for solutions to social problems.

Humphreys argued that persecution of gay lifestyles leads men to live anguished existences in which they must resort to extreme secrecy and often dangerous activities. His study was conducted before the onset of AIDS; such activity would be much more dangerous today. He argued that tolerance for a gay subculture would put gays in a position where they could provide one another with self-esteem, mutual support and relief from torment.

Human subjects and ethical problems

All research concerned with human beings can pose ethical dilemmas. A key question that sociologists agree must be asked is whether the research 'poses risks to the subjects that are greater than the risks they face in their everyday lives'. Ethical issues have become much more prominent today than in the past. In particular, researchers are no longer seen as *the* knowledgeable experts or participants as mere *subjects* of research. Increasingly, the subjects of research are themselves involved in the research process and may help to formulate questions, comment on the researcher's interpretation of their views and in some cases expect to receive a copy of the final research report.

Clearly, as is the case in other areas of social life (such as doctors and their patients or university professors and their students), 'lay people' no longer automatically defer to 'experts' in the way they might have done a few decades ago. This broad social change is also transforming research practice. Indeed, all research funding bodies now routinely ask research teams what ethical issues they expect to confront and how they will deal with these, whether deception will be used, what measures will be put in place to protect their participants from risk and how their findings will be fed back to participants at the end of the study.

In writing *Tearoom Trade*, Humphreys said he was less than truthful to those whose behaviour he was studying. He said he did not reveal his identity as a sociologist when observing the tearoom. People who came into the tearoom assumed he was there for the same reasons they were and that his presence could be accepted at face value. Although he did not tell any direct lies during his observations, neither did he reveal the real reason for his presence in the tearoom. Was this particular aspect of his behaviour ethical? The answer is that, on balance, this particular aspect of his study did not put any of his subjects at risk. On the basis of what he observed in the tearoom, Humphreys did not collect information about the participants that would have identified them. What he knew about them was similar to what all the other people in the tearoom knew. In this way, his presence did not subject them to any more risk than they already encountered in their everyday lives. At the same time, had Humphreys been completely frank at every stage, the research might not have progressed as far as it did. Indeed, some of the most valuable data that have been collected by sociologists could never have been gathered if the researcher had first explained the project to each person encountered in the research process.

If this were the only dilemma posed by Humphreys' research project, it would not stand out as a notable problem in the ethics of social research. What raised more eyebrows was that Humphreys wrote down the car number-plates of the people who came into the 'tearooms', obtained their home addresses from a friend who worked at the Department of Motor Vehicles and then visited their homes in the guise of conducting a neutral survey. Even though Humphreys did not reveal to the men's families anything about their activities in the tearooms, and even though he took great pains to keep the data confidential, the knowledge he gained could have been damaging. Since the activity he was documenting was illegal, police officers might have demanded that he release information about the identities of the subjects. It is also possible that a less skilled investigator could have slipped up when interviewing the subjects' families, or that Humphreys could have lost his notes, which might then have been found by someone else.

Considering the number of things that could go wrong in the research process, researchers today do not consider projects of this kind to be legitimate. Around the world, government funding bodies for sociological research, such as the European Science Foundation or the UK's Economic and Social Research Council (ESRC), as well as the professional organizations to which sociologists belong, such as the International Sociological Association (ISA), now have much stricter ethical guidelines for researchers engaging in sociological research of whatever kind.

Humphreys was one of the first sociologists to study the lives of gay men. His account was a humane treatment that went well beyond the existing stock of knowledge on sexual communities. Although none of his research subjects actually suffered as a result of his book, Humphreys himself later agreed with his critics on the key ethical controversy. He said that were he to do the study again, he would not trace number-plates or go to people's homes. Instead, after gathering his data in the public 'tearooms', he might try to get to know a subset of the people well enough to inform them of his goals for the study and then ask them to talk about the significance of these activities in their lives.

Sociological questions

The toilets under study in *Tearoom Trade* are a perfect example of a phenomenon that is the subject of many of the kinds of question that sociologists ask. For example, in looking at the surprising activities that occur in public toilets, Humphreys was asking how society works in ways that are different from the official versions of how it should work. He also found that what we take to be natural – a public toilet – is actually *socially constructed*, depending on how it is used. **Social constructionism** is a perspective which begins from the premise that social reality is – to varying degrees – the product of interactions between individuals and groups, not something that is

obvious to all (see chapter 7, 'Social Interaction and Everyday Life' and chapter 5, 'The Environment'). In this case, what most people believed to be simply a public building with an immediately obvious function was, for a particular social group, *primarily* a venue for the pursuit of sexual satisfaction.

It is also interesting to note that elements of modern theoretical approaches can help us understand the issues addressed by Humphreys' study. An *interactionist* might ask: how does this behaviour take place through processes of interaction? What *kinds* of interaction take place? Humphreys found that people who went into the tearooms learnt from others to be silent. This was a response to the demand for privacy without involvement. Another finding was that men who went into the toilet and who did not respond to initial sexual advances were not approached any further. Each party must collaborate to make a sexual situation occur. A *functionalist* approach might ask: what contribution does the tearoom make to the continuation of society as a whole? The answer is that it provides an outlet for sexual activity that, when carried out in secret, enables the participants and other members of society to carry on as 'normal' people in their everyday lives without challenging the accepted order of things. A *Marxist* approach might ask: is thinking about economic class relations apparent in the tearooms? Humphreys found that the impersonal sex of the tearooms had a democratic quality. Men of all social classes and races would come together in these places for sexual contact. Finally, a *feminist* approach might ask: how can women's lives be considered in this study of an all-male group? This approach was not dominant at the time Humphreys conducted his study, but a feminist today might ask how women's lives – perhaps wives and partners who know nothing about the activity of their male partners – are affected and put at risk by the secret behaviour in the

Law enforcement exists in all countries, but comparative empirical studies of police forces are needed to reveal their similarities and differences.

tearooms. We explore some of these theoretical approaches in chapter 3.

It is almost 40 years since *Tearoom Trade* was first published and in the interim society has become more tolerant of gay identities and gay sex. After the publication of his book, Humphreys became part of the political movement – the gay rights movement – that made this change possible. He used his findings to convince courts and police to ease up on prosecuting men for engaging in gay sex so as to alleviate the damaging side effects of covert sexual activity.

It is the business of sociological research in general to go beyond surface-level understandings of ordinary life, as Humphreys clearly did. Good research should help us understand our social lives better, sometimes in a new way. It could take us by surprise, both in the questions that it asks

and in the findings it comes up with. The issues that concern sociologists, in both their theorizing and their research, are often similar to those that worry other people. But the results of such research frequently run counter to our common-sense beliefs.

What are the circumstances in which racial or sexual minorities live? How can mass starvation exist in a world that is far wealthier than it has ever been before? What effects will the increasing use of the Internet have on our lives? Is the family beginning to disintegrate as an institution? Sociologists try to provide answers to these and many other questions. Their findings are by no means conclusive. Nevertheless, it is always the aim of sociological theorizing and research to break away from the speculative manner in which the ordinary person usually considers such questions. Good sociological work tries to make the questions as precise as possible and seeks to gather factual evidence before coming to conclusions. To achieve these aims, we must know the most useful **research methods** to apply in a given study and how best to analyse the results.

In their research studies, sociologists will often ask empirical or **factual questions**. For example, many aspects of sexual behaviour, such as those Humphreys studied, need direct and systematic sociological investigation. Thus, we might ask: what kinds of occupation and domestic arrangement are most common among people who go to the tearooms? What proportion of tearoom participants do the police catch? Factual questions of this kind are often difficult to answer. Official statistics on tearooms do not exist. Even official statistics on crime are of dubious value in revealing the real level of criminal activity. Researchers who have studied crime levels have found that only about half of all serious crimes are reported to the police.

Factual information about one society, of course, will not always tell us whether we are dealing with an unusual case or a general set of influences. Sociologists often want to ask **comparative questions**, relating one social context within a society to another or contrasting examples drawn from different societies. There are signifi-cant differences, for example, between the social and legal systems of the USA, Italy and South Africa. A typical comparative question might be: how much do patterns of criminal behaviour and law enforcement vary between the two countries?

In sociology, we need not only to look at existing societies in relation to one another but also to compare their present and past. The questions sociologists ask in this case are historical or **developmental questions**. How did we get from there to here? To understand the nature of the modern world, we have to look at previous forms of society and also study the main direction that processes of change have taken. Thus we can investigate, for example, how the first prisons originated and what they are like today.

Factual investigations – or, as sociologists usually prefer to call them, **empirical investigations** – concern *how* things occur. Yet sociology does not consist of just collecting facts, however important and interesting they may be. We always need to interpret what facts mean, and to do so we must learn to pose theoretical questions – concerned with *why* things occur. Many sociologists work primarily on empirical questions, but unless they are guided in research by some knowledge of theory, their work is unlikely to be illuminating (see table 2.1).

Table 2.1 The sociologist's line of questioning

Factual question	What happened?	Since the 1980s, girls have been attaining better educational results in school than boys.
Comparative question	Did this happen everywhere?	Was this a global phenomenon, or did it occur just in Britain, or only in a certain region of Britain?
Developmental question	Has this happened over time?	What have been the patterns of girls' educational attainment over time?
Theoretical question	What underlies this phenomenon?	Why are girls now performing better in school? What factors would we look at to explain this change?

At the same time, sociologists strive not to attain theoretical knowledge for its own sake. A standard view is that while the sociologist's values should not be permitted to bias their conclusions, social research should be relevant to real-world concerns. In this chapter, we look further into such issues by asking whether it is possible to produce 'objective' knowledge. We begin by stressing the scientific nature of sociology, before examining the stages involved in sociological research. Some of the most widely used research methods are then compared, as we consider some actual investigations. As we shall see, there are often significant differences between the way research should ideally be carried out and real-world studies. Sociological research, like other scientific research, is the art of the possible.

Is sociology scientific?

As discussed in chapter 1, Auguste Comte saw sociology as an emerging science, which should adopt the successful (positivist) methods of the natural sciences such as physics and chemistry. Durkheim, Marx and the other founders of sociology also thought of sociology as a scientific subject; but can we really study human social life in a scientific way? Are Laud Humphreys' observations on the tearooms really scientific? Before we can answer, we must first understand what this word means; what exactly is science?

Science is the use of *systematic methods* of empirical investigation, the *analysis of data, theoretical thinking* and the *logical assessment* of arguments to develop a *body of knowledge* about a particular subject-matter. Sociology *is* a scientific endeavour, according to this definition, because it involves systematic methods of empirical investigation, the analysis of data and the assessment of theories in the light of evidence and logical argument.

Studying human beings, however, is different from observing events in the phys-

"*I'm a social scientist, Michael. That means I can't explain electricity or anything like that, but if you ever want to know about people I'm the man.*"

ical world, so sociology and the natural sciences cannot be identical. Unlike objects in nature, humans are self-aware beings who confer meaning and purpose on what they do. We cannot even describe social life accurately unless we first grasp the concepts that people apply in their own behaviour. For instance, to describe a death as a 'suicide' means knowing what the person in question was intending when he died. Suicide can only occur when an individual actively has self-destruction in mind. If he accidentally steps in front of a car and is killed, he cannot be said to have committed suicide.

The fact that we cannot study human beings in exactly the same way as objects in nature is in some ways an advantage to sociology. Sociological researchers profit from being able to ask questions directly of those they study – other human beings – and get responses that they understand. This opportunity to converse with the participants of research studies and confirm the researcher's interpretations means that sociological findings are, at least potentially, even more *reliable* (different researchers would arrive at the same results) and *valid* (the research actually measures what it is supposed to) than those from the natural sciences. However, in other respects, sociology creates difficulties that are not encountered by natural scientists. People who are aware that their activities are being scrutinized may not behave in the same way that they normally do. They may consciously or unconsciously portray themselves in a way that differs from their usual attitudes. They may even try to 'assist' the researcher by giving the responses they believe he or she wants. Researchers studying the behaviour of, say, chemicals or frogs do not have this problem.

THINKING CRITICALLY

Reflecting on the discussion so far, in what ways does sociology differ from the natural sciences, such as physics and chemistry? Were Laud Humphreys' *research methods* 'scientific', for example? If we were allowed to use the same methods to carry out a similar study today, would we be likely to get the same or different results? Thinking more generally and sociologically now, how might recent social changes affect such a study and its potential findings?

The research process

Let us first look at the stages normally involved in research work. The research process takes in a number of distinct steps, leading from when the investigation is begun to the time its findings are published or made available in written form (see figure 2.1).

Defining the research problem

All research starts from a research problem. This is sometimes an area of factual ignorance: we may simply wish to improve our

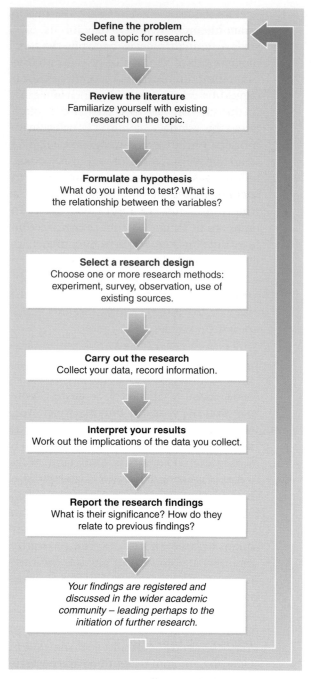

Figure 2.1 Steps in the research process

knowledge about certain institutions, social processes or cultures. A researcher might set out to answer questions like 'What proportion of the population holds strong religious beliefs?' 'Are people today really disaffected with "big government"?' 'How far does the economic position of women lag behind that of men?'.

The best sociological research, however, begins with problems that are also puzzles. A puzzle is not just a lack of information, but a *gap in our understanding*. Much of the skill in producing worthwhile sociological research consists in correctly identifying puzzles. Rather than simply answering the question 'What is going on here?', puzzle-solving research tries to contribute to our understanding of why events happen as they do. Thus we might ask: why are patterns of religious belief changing? What accounts for the decline in the proportions of the population voting in elections in recent years? Why are women poorly represented in high-status jobs?

No piece of research stands alone. Research problems come up as part of ongoing work; one research project may easily lead to another because it raises issues the researcher had not previously considered. A sociologist may discover puzzles by reading the work of other researchers in books and professional journals or by being aware of specific trends in society. For example, over recent years, there have been an increasing number of programmes that seek to treat the mentally ill within the community, rather than confining them in asylums. Sociologists might be prompted to ask: what has given rise to this shift in attitude towards the mentally ill? What are the likely consequences both for the patients themselves and for the rest of the community?

Reviewing the evidence

Once the problem is identified, the next step taken in the research process is usually to review the available evidence in the field; it might be that previous research has already satisfactorily clarified the problem. If not, the sociologist will need to sift through whatever related research does exist, to see how useful it is for his or her purpose. Have previous researchers spotted the same puzzle? How have they tried to resolve it?

What aspects of the problem has their research left unanalysed? Drawing upon others' ideas helps the sociologist to clarify the issues that might be raised and the methods that might be used in the research.

Making the problem precise

A third stage involves working out a clear formulation of the research problem. If relevant literature already exists, the researcher might return from the library with a good notion of how the problem should be approached. Hunches about the nature of the problem can sometimes be turned into a definite hypothesis. Although rooted in an educated guess about what is going on, a hypothesis clearly states this in exact language so that it can be tested. If the research is to be effective, hypotheses must be formulated in such a way that the factual material gathered will provide evidence that either supports or disproves them.

Working out a design

The researcher must then decide just how the research materials are to be collected. A range of different research methods exists, and which one is chosen depends on the overall objectives of the study, as well as the aspects of behaviour to be analysed. For some purposes, a survey (in which questionnaires are normally used) might be suitable. In other circumstances, interviews or an observational study, such as that carried out by Laud Humphreys, might be more appropriate. We shall learn more about various research methods later in this chapter.

Carrying out the research

At the point of actually proceeding with the research, unforeseen practical difficulties can easily crop up. It might prove impossible to contact some of those to whom questionnaires are to be sent or those people the researcher wishes to interview. A business firm or government agency may be unwilling to let the researcher carry out the work planned. Difficulties such as these could

Table 2.2 Number of motor vehicles per 1,000 inhabitants: selected countries

	1990	1991	1992	1993	1994	1995	1996	1997	1998	1999	2000	2001	2002
Austria	462	463	503	515	528	543	495	509	529	544	555	565	537
Belgium	432	442	441	454	464	487	494	482	490	500	511	517	520
Canada	600	619	627	595	569	565	565	564	580	566	569	572	581
Germany	527	527	427	478	523	540	547	551	556	564	570	582	589
Greece	248	246	257	271	283	298	313	328	351	378	406	428	450
Portugal	310	370	407	439	438	501	533	569	610	654	698	711	756
Turkey	57	47	53	61	64	68	97	105	111	116	124	148	148
UK	443	433	453	441	439	428	448	458	474	486	493	516	533
United States	842	718	779	725	719	771	783	784	792	798	810	816	807

Source: OECD Factbook 2005

USING YOUR SOCIOLOGICAL IMAGINATION

2.1 Reading and interpreting tables

You will often come across tables when reading sociological literature. They sometimes look complex, but are easy to decipher if you follow a few basic steps, listed below; with practice, these will become automatic. Do not succumb to the temptation to skip over tables; they contain information in concentrated form, which can be read more quickly than would be possible if the same material were expressed in words. By becoming skilled in the interpretation of tables, you will also be able to check how far the conclusions drawn by a writer actually seem justified.

1. Read the title in full. Tables frequently have longish titles, which represent an attempt by the researcher to state accurately the nature of the information conveyed. The title of table 2.2 gives first the subject of the data, second the fact that the table provides material for comparison, and third the fact that data are given only for a limited number of countries.
2. Look for explanatory comments, or notes, about the data. Notes may say how the material was collected, or why it is displayed in a particular way. Many of the tables used throughout this book contain explanatory notes. If the data have not been gathered by the researcher but are based

on findings originally reported elsewhere, a *source* will be included. The source sometimes gives you some insight into how reliable the information is likely to be, as well as showing where to find the original data. In table 2.2, the source note makes clear that the data have been taken from a publication by the OECD.

3. Read the headings along the top and left-hand side of the table. (Sometimes tables are arranged with 'headings' at the foot rather than the top.) These tell you what type of information is contained in each row and column. In reading the table, keep in mind each set of headings as you scan the figures. In our example, the headings on the left give the countries involved, while those at the top refer to the levels of car ownership and the years for which they are given.
4. Identify the units used; the figures in the body of the table may represent cases, percentages, averages or other measures. Sometimes it may be helpful to convert the figures to a form more useful to you: if percentages are not provided, for example, it may be worth calculating them.
5. Consider the conclusions that might be reached from the information in the table. Most tables are discussed by the author, and what he or she has to say should of course be borne in mind. But you should also ask what further issues or questions could be suggested by the data.

Several interesting trends can be seen in the figures in our table. First, the level of car ownership varies considerably between different countries. The number of cars per 1,000 people was more than five times greater in the United States than in Turkey in 2002. Second, there is a clear connection between car ownership and the level of affluence of a country. In fact, we could probably use car ownership ratios as a rough indicator of differential prosperity. Third, in nearly all countries represented, the level of car ownership increased between 1990 and 2002, but in some the rate of increase has been higher than in others – probably indicating differences in the degree to which countries have successfully generated economic growth or are catching up.

DOONESBURY   by Garry Trudeau

potentially bias the result of the study and give a false interpretation. For example, if the researcher is studying how business corporations have complied with equal opportunities programmes for women, then companies that have not complied may not want to be studied. Clearly, this could result in a systematic bias in the results.

Bias can enter the research process in many ways. For example, if a piece of research is based on surveys of participants' views, it may be easy for the researcher to push the discussion in a particular way, such as asking leading questions that follow their own particular prejudices (as the Doonesbury cartoon shows). Alternatively, interviewees may evade a question that for various reasons they do not want to answer. The use of questionnaires with fixed wording can help to reduce interview bias, but it will not eliminate it. Another source of bias comes when *potential* participants in a survey, such as a voluntary questionnaire, decide that they do not want to take part. This is known as *non-response bias*, and as a

general rule the higher the proportion of non-responses in the sample, the more likely it is that the survey of those who do take part will be biased. Even if every attempt is made to reduce bias in the survey, the observations that sociologists make in carrying out a piece of research are

> **THINKING CRITICALLY**
>
> Familiarize yourself again with table 2.2 and reflect on what questions might follow from this. For example, did you find anything surprising here? How could we find out *why* vehicle ownership in Canada and the USA has fallen from its highpoint in the early 1990s, while in the UK and other European countries ownership continues to rise? Next, track down the same data from 2003–9 yourself: what has happened to vehicle ownership since this table was produced? What place is there, if any, for qualitative methods in helping us to address such questions?

likely to reflect their own cultural assumptions. This *observer bias* can be difficult, or perhaps even impossible, to eliminate. Later in this chapter we look at some of the other pitfalls and difficulties of sociological research, and discuss how some of these can be avoided.

Interpreting the results

Once the material has been gathered together for analysis, the researcher's troubles are not over – they may be only just beginning! Working out the implications of the data collected and relating these back to the research problem are rarely easy. While it may be possible to reach a clear answer to the initial questions, many investigations are, in the end, less than fully conclusive.

Reporting the findings

The research report, usually published as a journal article or book, provides an account of the nature of the research and seeks to justify whatever conclusions are drawn. In Humphreys' case, this report was the book *Tearoom Trade*. This is a final stage only in terms of the individual research project. Most reports indicate questions that remain unanswered and suggest further research that might profitably be done in the future. All individual research investigations are part of the continuing process of research taking place within the sociological community. Other scholars have built on Humphreys' research findings.

Reality intrudes!

The preceding sequence of steps is a simplified version of what happens in actual research projects (see figure 2.1). In real sociological research, these stages rarely succeed each other so neatly, and there is almost always a certain amount of 'muddling through'. The difference is a bit like that between the recipes outlined in a cookbook and the actual process of preparing a meal. People who are experienced cooks often do not work from recipes at all,

yet their food may be better than that cooked by those who do. Following fixed schemes can be unduly restricting and many outstanding pieces of sociological research have not fitted rigidly into this sequence, although most of the steps would be there somewhere.

Understanding cause and effect

One of the main problems to be tackled in research methodology is the analysis of cause and effect. A **causal relationship** between two events or situations is an association in which one event or situation produces another. If the handbrake is released in a car that is pointing downhill, the car will roll down the incline, gathering speed progressively as it does so. Taking the brake off caused this to happen; the reasons for this can readily be understood by reference to the physical principles involved. Like natural science, sociology depends on the assumption that all events have causes. Social life is *not* a random array of occurrences, happening without rhyme or reason. One of the main tasks of sociological research – in combination with theoretical thinking – is to identify causes and effects.

Causation and correlation

Causation cannot be directly inferred from **correlation**. Correlation means the existence of a regular relationship between two sets of occurrences or variables. A **variable** is any dimension along which individuals or groups vary. Age, differences in income, crime rates and social-class differences are among the many variables that sociologists study. It might seem as though, when two variables are found to be closely correlated, one must be the cause of the other. However, this is very often not the case. There are, in fact, many correlations without any causal relationship between variables. For example, over the period since the

Second World War, a strong correlation can be found between the decline in pipe-smoking and the decrease in the number of people who regularly go to the cinema. Clearly one change does not cause the other, and we would find it difficult to discover even a remote causal connection between them.

There are many instances, however, in which it is not so obvious that an observed correlation does not imply a causal relationship. Such correlations are traps for the unwary and easily lead to questionable or false conclusions. In his classical work of 1897, *Suicide* (discussed in chapter 1), Emile Durkheim found a correlation between rates of suicide and the seasons of the year. In the societies that Durkheim studied, levels of suicide increased progressively from January to around June or July. From that time onward they declined over the remainder of the year. It might be supposed that this demonstrates that temperature or climatic change are *causally related* to the propensity of individuals to kill themselves. We might perhaps surmise that as temperatures increase, people become more impulsive and hot-headed, leading to higher suicide rates. However, the causal relationship here has nothing *directly* to do with temperature or climate at all. In spring and summer, most people engage in a more intensive social life than they do in the winter months. Individuals who are isolated or unhappy tend to experience an intensification of these feelings as the activity level of other people rises. Hence they are likely to experience acute suicidal tendencies more in spring and summer than they do in autumn and winter, when the pace of social activity slackens. We always have to be on our guard both in assessing whether correlation involves causation and deciding in which direction causal relations run.

Causal mechanisms

Working out the causal connections involved in correlations is often a difficult process. There is a strong correlation, for

Sociologists might be interested in the reasons why some young children, but not others, smoke. However, it can be difficult to establish a causal relationship between the different factors involved.

instance, between level of educational achievement and occupational success in modern societies. The better the grades an individual gets in school, the better-paid the job he is likely to get. What explains this correlation? Research tends to show that it is not mainly school experience itself; levels of school attainment are influenced much more by the type of home from which the person comes. Children from better-off homes, whose parents take a strong interest in their learning skills and where books are abundant, are more likely to do well than those coming from homes where these

qualities are lacking. The causal mechanisms here are the attitudes of parents towards their children, together with the facilities for learning that a home provides.

Causal connections in sociology should not be understood in too mechanical a way. The attitudes people have and their subjective reasons for acting as they do are causal factors in relationships between variables in social life.

 A discussion of some recent 'critical realist' approaches to environmental sociology can be found in chapter 5, 'The Environment'.

Controls

In assessing the cause or causes that explain a correlation, we need to distinguish **independent variables** from **dependent variables**. An independent variable is one that produces an effect on another variable. The variable affected is the dependent one. In the example just mentioned above, academic achievement is the independent variable and occupational income the dependent variable. The distinction refers to the direction of the causal relation we are investigating. The same factor may be an independent variable in one study and a dependent variable in another. It all depends on what causal processes are being analysed. If we were looking at the effects of differences in occupational income on lifestyles, occupational income would then be the independent variable rather than the dependent one.

To find out whether a correlation between variables is a causal connection, we use **controls**, which means we hold some variables constant in order to look at the effects of others. By doing this, we are able to judge between explanations of observed correlations, separating causal from non-causal relationships. For example, researchers studying child development have claimed that there is a causal connection between maternal deprivation in infancy and serious personality problems in adulthood. ('Maternal deprivation' means that an infant is separated from its mother for a long period – several months or more – during the early years of its life.) How might we test whether there really is a causal relationship between maternal deprivation and later personality disorders? We would do so by trying to control, or 'screen out', other possible influences that might explain the correlation.

One source of maternal deprivation is the admission of a child to a hospital for a lengthy period, during which it is separated from its parents. Is it attachment to the mother, however, that really matters? Perhaps if a child receives love and attention from *other* people during infancy, she might subsequently be a stable person. To investigate these possible causal connections, we would have to compare cases where children were deprived of regular care from anyone with other instances in which children were separated from their mothers but received love and care from *someone* else. If the first group developed severe personality difficulties but the second group did not, we would suspect that regular care from someone in infancy is what matters, regardless of whether or not it is the mother. In fact, children do seem to prosper normally as long as they have a loving, stable relationship with someone looking after them; this person does not have to be the mother herself.

Identifying causes

There are a large number of possible causes that could be invoked to explain any given correlation. How can we ever be sure that we have covered them all? The answer is that we cannot be sure. We would never be able to carry out and interpret the results of a piece of sociological research satisfactorily if we were compelled to test for the possible influence of every causal factor we could imagine as potentially relevant. Identifying causal relationships is normally guided by previous research into the area in question. If we do not have some reasonable idea beforehand of the causal mechanisms involved in a correlation, we would probably find it very difficult to discover what the real causal connections are. We would not know what to test *for*.

A good example of how difficult it is to be sure of the causal relations involved in a correlation is given by the long history of studies of smoking and lung cancer. Research has consistently demonstrated a strong correlation between the two. Smokers are more likely to contract lung cancer than non-smokers, and very heavy smokers are more likely to do so than light smokers. The correlation can also be expressed the other way around. A high proportion of those who have lung cancer are smokers or have smoked for long periods in their past. There have been so many studies confirming these correlations that it is generally accepted that a causal link is involved, but the exact causal mechanisms are thus far largely unknown.

However much correlational work is done on any issue, there always remains some doubt about possible causal relationships.

Other interpretations of the correlation are possible. It has been proposed, for instance, that people who are predisposed to get lung cancer are also predisposed to smoke. In this view, it is not smoking that causes lung cancer, but rather some built-in biological disposition to smoking and cancer.

Research methods

A common distinction is often made in sociology between **quantitative** and **qualitative** research methods and traditions; the former is associated with functionalism and positivism, the latter with interactionism and the search for meanings and understanding. As the term suggests, quantitative methods try to *measure* social phenomena and will use mathematical models and, often, statistical analysis to explain them. Qualitative methods, on the other hand, attempt to gather detailed, rich data allowing for an in-depth understanding of individual action in the context of social life. As a rough-and-ready guide to a diverse range of sociological research methods, this distinction is a starting point and many sociologists will tend to specialize in, or even favour, one tradition rather than another. However, there is a danger that the two traditions will be seen as opposing 'camps' with entirely different approaches to research. This would not be very productive.

In fact, many research projects today make use of **mixed methods** – both quantitative and qualitative – in order to gain a more comprehensive understanding and explanation of the subject being studied. The findings from separate quantitative and qualitative studies can also be combined. For example, some feminist sociologists favour qualitative methods, which, they argue, allow the authentic voices of women to be heard in ways that quantitative studies do not. But without quantitative studies it would not have been possible to measure the extent of gender inequalities in society

Table 2.3 **Four of the main methods used in sociological research**

Research method	Strengths	Limitations
Fieldwork	Usually generates richer and more in-depth information than other methods.	Can only be used to study relatively small groups or or communities.
	Ethnography can provide a broader understanding of social processes.	Findings might only apply to the groups or communities studied; it is not easy to generalize on the basis of a single fieldwork study.
Surveys	Make possible the efficient collection of data on large numbers of individuals.	The material gathered may be superficial; where a questionnaire is highly standardized, important differences between respondents' viewpoints may be glossed over.
	Allow for precise comparisons to be made between the answers of respondents.	Responses may be what people profess to believe rather than what they actually believe.
Experiments	The influence of specific variables can be controlled by the investigator.	Many aspects of social life cannot be brought into the laboratory.
	Are usually easier for subsequent researchers to repeat.	The responses of those studied may be affected by their experimental situation.
Documentary research	Can provide source of in-depth materials as well as data on large numbers, depending on the type of documents studied.	The researcher is dependent on the sources that exist, which may be partial.
	Is often essential when a study is either wholly historical or has a defined historical dimension.	The sources may be difficult to interpret in terms of how far they represent real tendencies, as in the case of some official statistics.

or set those individual women's voices into their wider societal context. Sociologists have to be prepared to use the most appropriate methods for the questions they want to answer.

Next, we look at the various research methods sociologists commonly employ in their work (see table 2.3).

Ethnography

Laud Humphreys used **ethnography**, a type of fieldwork, or first-hand study of people, using **participant observation** and/or interviews as his main research methods. Here, the investigator hangs out, works or lives with a group, organization or community and perhaps takes a direct part in their activities. Where it is successful, ethnography provides information on the behaviour of people in groups, organizations and communities, and also on how those people understand their own behaviour. Once we see how things look from inside a given group, we are likely to develop a better understanding not only of that group, but of social processes that transcend the situation under study. Ethnography is one

of a number of **qualitative research methods** used in sociology that aims to gain an in-depth knowledge and understanding of relatively small-scale social phenomena.

In recent years, sociologists have made use of **focus groups**, which have previously been widely used in marketing and surveys of political attitudes, as a qualitative research method. Focus groups are essentially 'group interviews' in which a particular group of people – usually between four and ten individuals – are gathered together to discuss a subject and exchange views. The researcher acts as a moderator but also asks specific questions relating to the research study, to direct the discussion. Focus groups can increase the size of a sample quite easily and because of their interactive nature, any possible misunderstandings can be clarified, thereby increasing the validity of a study's findings. However, critics point out that the

researcher in a focus group is more participant than detached observer and may well influence the responses of the group. There is therefore a danger that participants will perform according to their perception of the researcher's expectations.

In the traditional works of ethnography, accounts were presented without very much information about the researchers themselves. This was because it was believed that an ethnographer could present objective pictures of the societies they studied. More recently, ethnographers have increasingly tended to talk about themselves and the nature of their connection to the people under study. Sometimes, for example, it might be a matter of trying to consider how one's race, class or gender affected the work, or how the power differences between observer and observed distorted the dialogue between them.

For a long while, it was usual for research based on participant observation to exclude any account of the hazards or problems that had to be overcome, but more recently the published reminiscences and diaries of fieldworkers have been more open about them. Frequently, feelings of loneliness must be coped with – it is not easy to fit into a social context or community where you do not really belong. The researcher may be constantly frustrated because the members of the group refuse to talk frankly about themselves; direct queries may be welcomed in some contexts but met with a chilly silence in others. Some types of fieldwork may even be physically dangerous; for instance, a researcher studying a delinquent gang might be seen as a police informer or might become unwittingly embroiled in conflicts with rival gangs.

Ethnographic studies also have other major limitations. Only fairly small groups or communities can be studied and much depends on the skill of the researcher in gaining the confidence of the individuals involved. Without this skill, the research is unlikely to get off the ground at all. The reverse is also possible. A researcher could

In fieldwork, sociologists have to become close to the communities they are studying, but not so close that they lose their outsider's eye.

begin to identify so closely with the group that he or she becomes too much of an 'insider' and loses the perspective of an outside observer.

Surveys

Interpreting field studies usually involves problems of generalization. Since only a small number of people are under study, we cannot be sure that what is found in one context will apply in other situations as well, or even that two different researchers would come to the same conclusions when studying the same group. This is usually less of a problem in survey research. In a **survey**, questionnaires are either sent out or administered directly in interviews to a selected group of people – sometimes as many as several thousand. Sociologists refer to this group of people, whatever its size, as a **population**. Whilst ethnographic work is well suited to in-depth studies of small slices of social life, survey research tends to produce information that is less detailed but which can usually be applied over a broader area. Surveys are the most widely used type of **quantitative research method**, allowing social phenomena to be measured and then analysed using mathematical models and statistical techniques.

Many government bodies and private polling agencies also make extensive use of surveys to gain knowledge of people's attitudes and voting intentions. These may be conducted through face-to-face interviews, telephone calls, postal questionnaires and, increasingly, online, via the Internet and email. Whichever method is adopted, the great advantage of surveys is that they allow researchers to collect large amounts of comparable data, which can be manipulated, usually using computer software, to find out whether there are any significant correlations between variables.

Standardized, open-ended, semi-structured questionnaires

Three types of questionnaire are used in surveys. Some contain a standardized, or fixed-choice, set of questions, to which only a fixed range of responses is possible – for instance, '*Yes / No / Don't know*' or '*Very likely / Likely / Unlikely / Very unlikely*'. Such surveys have the advantage that responses are easy to count and compare, since only a small number of categories are involved. On the other hand, because they do not allow for subtleties of opinion or verbal expression, the information they yield is likely to be restricted in scope and sometimes misleading.

Other questionnaires are open-ended: respondents have more opportunity to express their views in their own words and are not limited to making fixed-choice responses. Open-ended questionnaires typically provide more detailed information than standardized ones. The researcher can follow up answers to probe more deeply into what the respondent thinks. On the other hand, the lack of standardization means that responses may be more difficult to compare statistically.

A very popular and widely used compromise between these two is the semi-structured interview questionnaire, which presents some standardized questions – the data from which may be analysed statistically later – but also includes interview prompts for more in-depth answers and sometimes allows interviewees to stray from the schedule when necessary. Semi-structured interview schedules tend to pursue relevant research themes rather than highly specific, researcher-defined questions.

Questionnaire items are normally listed so that a team of interviewers can ask the questions and record responses in the same predetermined order. All the items must be readily understandable to interviewers and interviewees alike. In the large national surveys undertaken regularly by government agencies and research organizations, interviews are carried out more or less simultaneously across the whole country. Those who conduct the interviews and those who analyse the results could not do their work effectively if they constantly had to check with each other about ambiguities in the questions or answers.

Questionnaires should also take into consideration the characteristics of respondents. Will they see the point the researcher has in mind in asking a particular question? Have they enough information to answer usefully? Will they answer at all? The terms of a questionnaire might be unfamiliar to the respondents. For instance, the question

'What is your marital status?' might baffle some people. It would be more appropriate to ask, 'Are you single, married, separated, or divorced?' Most surveys are preceded by **pilot studies** in order to pick up problems not anticipated by the investigator. A pilot study is a trial run in which just a few people complete a questionnaire. Any difficulties can then be ironed out before the main survey is done.

Sampling

Often sociologists are interested in the characteristics of large numbers of individuals – for example, the political attitudes of the British population as a whole. It would be impossible to study all these people directly, so in such situations researchers engage in sampling – they concentrate on a sample, or small proportion, of the overall group. One can usually be confident that results from a population sample, as long as it was properly chosen, can be generalized to the total population. Studies of only two to three thousand voters, for instance, can give a very accurate indication of the attitudes and voting intentions of the entire population. But to achieve such accuracy, a sample must be **representative**: the group of individuals studied must be typical of the population as a whole. Representative sampling is more complex than it might seem, and statisticians have developed rules for working out the correct size and nature of samples.

A particularly important procedure used to ensure that a sample is representative is **random sampling**, in which a sample is chosen so that every member of the population has the same probability of being included. The most sophisticated way of obtaining a random sample is to give each member of the population a number and then use a computer to generate a random list, from which the sample is derived – for instance, by picking every tenth number.

One famous early example of survey research was called, 'The People's Choice?', a study carried out by Paul Lazarsfeld and colleagues more than 60 years ago

(Lazarsfeld et al. 1948). This study, which investigated the voting intentions of residents of Erie County, Ohio, during the 1940 campaign for the US presidency, pioneered several of the main techniques of survey research in use to this day. In order to probe a little more deeply than a single questionnaire could do, the team interviewed each member of a sample of voters on seven separate occasions. The aim was to trace and understand the reasons for changes in voting attitudes.

The research had a number of hypotheses to test. One was that relationships and events close to voters in a community can influence voting intentions more than distant world affairs, and the findings on the whole confirmed this. The researchers developed sophisticated measurement techniques for analysing political attitudes; yet their work also made significant contributions to theoretical thinking. The study showed that some individuals – opinion leaders – tend to shape the political opinions of those around them. People's views are not formed in a direct fashion, but in a two-step process. In the first step, opinion leaders react to political events; in the second step, those leaders influence people around them – relatives, friends and colleagues. The views expressed by opinion leaders, filtered through personal relationships, then influence the responses of other individuals towards political issues of the day. This study shows that good survey research does more than simply describe social phenomena, it can also aid our theoretical understanding.

There are other types of sampling that are used by sociologists. In some types of research, it may be necessary to use **convenience sampling**. This means taking your sample from wherever you can! Because convenience sampling is less systematic and rigorous than other types, the results it generates have to be treated with caution. Nonetheless, in applied research or studies of hard-to-reach social groups who may be reluctant to come forward (substance misusers or people who self-harm, for example), it may be the only practical way of gathering an adequate sample. Similarly, snowball sampling, in which existing participants are used to recruit other participants (usually via their own network of contacts and friends) is a tried and tested method of gaining access to a larger sample than would otherwise be the case.

Advantages and disadvantages of surveys

Surveys are widely used in sociological research, for several reasons. Responses to questionnaires can be more easily quantified and analysed than material generated by most other research methods; large numbers of people can be studied; and, given sufficient funds, researchers can employ an agency specializing in survey work to collect the responses. The scientific method is the model for this kind of research, as surveys give researchers a statistical measure of what they are studying.

Many sociologists today, however, are critical of the survey method. They argue that an *appearance* of precision can be given to findings whose accuracy may be dubious, given the relatively shallow nature of most survey responses. Levels of non-response are sometimes high, especially when questionnaires are sent and returned through the mail. It is not uncommon for studies to be published, based on results derived from little over half of those in a sample, although normally an effort is made to re-contact non-respondents or to substitute other people. Little is known about those who choose not to respond to surveys or refuse to be interviewed, but survey research is often experienced as intrusive and time-consuming.

Experiments

An **experiment** can be defined as an attempt to test a hypothesis under highly controlled conditions established by an

2.2 Statistical terminology

Research in sociology often makes use of statistical techniques in the analysis of findings. Some are highly sophisticated and complex, but those most often used are easy to understand. The most common are **measures of central tendency** (ways of calculating averages) and **correlation coefficients** (measures of the degree to which one variable relates consistently to another).

There are three methods of calculating averages, each of which has certain advantages and shortcomings. Take as an example the amount of personal wealth (including all assets such as houses, cars, bank accounts and investments) owned by 13 individuals. Suppose they own the following amounts:

1. £000 (zero)
2. £5,000
3. £10,000
4. £20,000
5. £40,000
6. £40,000
7. £40,000
8. £80,000
9. £100,000
10. £150,000
11. £200,000
12. £400,000
13. £10,000,000

The mean corresponds to the average, arrived at by adding together the personal wealth of all 13 people and dividing the result by 13. The total is £11,085,000; dividing this by 13, we reach a mean of £852,692.31. This mean is often a useful calculation because it is based on the whole range of data provided. However, it can be misleading where one or a small number of cases are very different from the majority. In the above example, the mean is not in fact an appropriate measure of central tendency, because the presence of one very large figure, £10,000,000, skews the picture. One might get the impression when using the mean to summarize this data that most of the people own far more than they actually do.

In such instances, one of two other measures may be used. The **mode** is the figure that occurs most frequently in a given set of data. In our example, it is £40,000. The problem with the mode is that it does not take into account the overall distribution of the data – i.e., the range of figures covered. The most frequently occurring case in a set of figures is not necessarily representative of their distribution as a whole and thus may not be a useful average. In this case, £40,000 is too close to the lower end of the figures.

The third measure is the **median**, which is the middle of any set of figures; here, this would be the seventh figure, again £40,000. Our example gives an odd number of figures: 13. If there had been an even number – for instance, 12 – the median would be calculated by taking the mean of the two middle cases, figures 6 and 7. Like the mode, the median gives no idea of the actual range of the data measured.

Sometimes a researcher will use more than one measure of central tendency to avoid giving a deceptive picture of the average. More often, he will calculate the **standard deviation** for the data in question. This is a way of calculating the **degree of dispersal**, or the range, of a set of figures – which in this case goes from zero to £10,000,000.

Correlation coefficients offer a useful way of expressing how closely connected two (or more) variables are. Where two variables correlate completely, we can speak of a perfect positive correlation, expressed as 1.0. Where no relation is found between two variables – they have no consistent connection at all – the coefficient is zero. A perfect negative correlation, expressed as -1.0, exists when two variables are in a completely inverse relation to one another. Perfect correlations are never found in the social sciences. Correlations of the order of 0.6 or more, whether positive or negative, are usually regarded as indicating a strong degree of connection between whatever variables are being analysed. Positive correlations on this level might be found between, say, social class background and voting behaviour.

Classic Studies 2.1 | **The social psychology of prison life**

The research problem

Most people have not experienced life in prison and find it hard to imagine how they would cope 'inside'. How would you fare? Could you work as a prison officer? What kind of a prison officer would you be? A disciplinarian maybe? Or perhaps you would adopt a more humanitarian approach to your prisoners? In 1971, a research team led by Philip Zimbardo decided to try and find out what impact prison would have on 'ordinary people'.

In a study funded by the US Navy, Zimbardo set out to test the 'dispositional hypothesis', which dominated within the armed forces. This hypothesis suggested that constant conflicts between prisoners and guards were due to the individual characters of the guards and inmates – their personal dispositions. Zimbardo thought this may be wrong and set up an experimental prison to find out.

Zimbardo's explanation

Zimbardo's research team set up a fake jail at Stanford University, advertised for male volunteers to participate in a study of prison life and selected 24 mainly middle-class students who did not know each other prior to the experiment. Each participant was then randomly assigned as guard or prisoner. Following a standard induction process which involved being stripped naked, de-loused and photographed, also naked, prisoners stayed in jail 24 hours a day, but guards worked shifts and went home in between times. Standardized uniforms were used for both roles. The aim was to see how playing these different roles would lead to changes in attitude and behaviour. The results shocked the investigators.

Students who played at being guards quickly assumed an authoritarian manner; they displayed real hostility towards the prisoners, ordering them around and verbally abusing and bullying them. The prisoners, by contrast, showed a mixture of apathy and rebelliousness – a response often noted among inmates in real prisons. These effects were so marked and the level of tension so high that the 14-day experiment had to be called off after just 6 days

Reaction to the mock prison regime during the Stanford prison experiment led to one inmate staging a hunger strike to be let out.

because of the distress of the participants. Even before this, five 'prisoners' were released because of extreme anxiety and emotional problems. Many 'guards', though, were unhappy that the study had ended prematurely.

On the basis of the findings, Zimbardo concluded that the dispositional hypothesis could not account for the participants' reactions. Instead, he proposed an alternative 'situational' explanation – behaviour in prisons is influenced by the prison situation itself, not by the individual characteristics of those involved. In particular, the expectations attached to the roles being played tended to shape behaviour. Some of the guards' behaviour had deteriorated – they treated prisoners badly, regularly handing out punishments and appearing to take pleasure in the distress of the prisoners. Zimbardo suggests that this is due to the power relationships the jail had established. Their control over prisoners' lives very quickly became a source of enjoyment for the guards. On the other hand, following a short period of rebelliousness, prisoners very rapidly exhibited a 'learned helplessness' and dependency. As researchers, the study tells us something important about why social relationships very often deteriorate within prisons and, by implication, other 'total institutions' (Goffman 1968 [1961]). This has little to do with individual personalities and much more to do with the prison environment and the social roles within it.

Critical points

Critics argue that there were real ethical problems with the study. Participants were not given full information about the purpose of the research and it is therefore questionable whether they could really have given 'informed consent'. Should the study even have been allowed to go ahead? The sample selected was clearly not representative of the population as a whole; all were students and male. Generalizing about the effects of 'prison life' would therefore be very difficult with such a small and unrepresentative sample. A final criticism is that the constructed situation may invalidate the findings. For example, participants knew their imprisonment would only last 14 days and they were paid $15 a day for their participation. Established problems of prisons such as racism and involuntary homosexuality were also absent. Critics say that the experiment is therefore not a meaningful comparison with real prison life.

Contemporary significance

In spite of the somewhat artificial situation – it was an experiment, after all – Zimbardo's findings have been widely referred to since the 1970s. For example, Zygmunt Bauman's (1989) *Modernity and the Holocaust* draws on this study to help explain the behaviour of inmates and guards in Nazi-run concentration camps in the Second World War. Just as importantly, the general thesis emerging from the research – that institutional settings can shape social relations and behaviour – continues to inform contemporary sociological studies, such as those investigating care homes for older people, residential homes for disabled people and many more.

investigator. Experiments are often used in the natural sciences, as they offer major advantages over other research procedures. In an experimental situation the researcher directly controls the circumstances being studied. Psychologists studying individual behaviour also use laboratory-based experimentation extensively. However, compared with these disciplines, the scope for experimentation in sociology is quite restricted. Most sociological studies, even those of individual actions, look to investigate the relationship between micro- and macrosocial phenomena. To remove individuals from their social context for the purposes of experimentation effectively prevents this.

Sometimes, sociologists may want to explore group dynamics – the way individuals behave when in groups – and experiments may then be possible. However, only small groups of individuals can be brought into a laboratory setting, and in such experiments people know that they are being studied and may not behave normally. Such

---

THINKING CRITICALLY

What is your first response to the Zimbardo study – can such an experimental situation really reproduce the authentic experience of a prison? Which aspects of the prison experience could an experiment *never* replicate? Thinking more critically now, should social scientists be allowed to 'experiment' on human beings at all? If not, does that mean there are things we will just never know about? If they should, what limits should there be on such experiments?

changes in subject behaviour are referred to as the 'Hawthorne effect'. In the 1930s, researchers conducting a work-productivity study at the Western Electric Company's Hawthorne plant near Chicago found to their surprise that worker productivity continued to rise regardless of which experimental conditions were imposed (levels of lighting, break patterns, work team size and so forth). The workers were conscious of being under scrutiny and accelerated their natural work pace. Nevertheless, as 'Classic Studies 2.1' shows, we can still learn things about social life from small-scale experiments.

Biographical research

In contrast to experiments, **biographical research** belongs purely to sociology and the other social sciences; it has no place in natural science. Biographical research has become much more popular and widely used in sociology in recent decades and includes oral histories, narratives, autobiographies, biographies and life histories (Bryman 2008). These methods are used to explore how individuals experience social life and periods of social change, and how they interpret their relationships with others in the context of a changing world. In this way, biographical methods allow new voices to enter sociological research; life histories are an example of such research methods.

Life histories consist of biographical material assembled about particular individuals – usually as recalled by the individuals themselves. Life histories have been successfully employed in studies of major importance. One celebrated early study was *The Polish Peasant in Europe and America*, by W. I. Thomas and Florian Znaniecki, the five volumes of which were first published between 1918 and 1920 (Thomas and Znaniecki 1966). Thomas and Znaniecki were able to provide a more sensitive and subtle account of the experience of migration than would have been possible without the interviews, letters and newspaper articles they collected.

Other procedures of research do not usually yield as much information as the life-history method does about the development of beliefs and attitudes over time. Life-historical studies rarely rely wholly on people's memories, however. Normally, sources such as letters, contemporary reports and newspaper descriptions are used to expand on and check the validity of the information that individuals provide.

Sociologists' views differ on the value of biographical methods. Some feel they are too unreliable to provide useful information, but others believe they offer sources of insight that few other research methods can match. Indeed, some sociologists have begun to offer reflections on their own lives within their research studies, as a way of offering insights into the origins and development of their theoretical assumptions (see Mouzelis 1995).

Comparative research

The research methods described so far are generally applied in a comparative context. **Comparative research** is of central importance in sociology, because making comparisons allows us to clarify what is going on in a particular area of research. Let us take the rate of divorce in many developed societies- – i.e. the number of divorces granted each year – as an example. In the early 1960s there were fewer than 30,000 divorces per year in the UK; by the early 1980s this figure had risen to around 160,000 or more. Do these changes reflect specific features of British society? We can find out by comparing divorce rates in the UK with those of other countries. Such a comparison reveals that compared to most other Western societies the overall trends are similar. A majority of Western countries have experienced steadily climbing divorce rates over the past half century.

Historical analysis

As discussed in chapter 1, a historical perspective is often essential in sociological research. For we frequently need a *time perspective* to make sense of the material we collect about a particular problem.

Sociologists commonly want to investigate past events directly. Some periods of history can be studied in a direct way while there are still survivors around – such as in the case of the Holocaust in Europe during the Second World War. Research in oral history means interviewing people about events they witnessed at some point earlier in their lives. This kind of research work, obviously, can only stretch at the most some 60 or 70 years back in time.

For historical research on an earlier period, sociologists use **documentary research** from written records, often contained in the special collections of libraries or archives. The range of useful documents is extensive, taking in personal sources such as diaries; official sources such as policy documents, records of births and deaths and tax records; documents from private bodies like businesses and voluntary organizations; as well as magazines and newspapers. Depending on the research question, historical documents such as these can all constitute **primary sources**, just as much as the data recorded in interviews with war survivors. However, historical sociologists also make much use of **secondary sources**: accounts of historical events written by people afterwards. Most documentary studies make use of both types. However, sociologists face the same issues as historians when they make use of such sources. How authentic are the documents? Is the information within them reliable? Do they represent only a partial viewpoint? Documentary research requires a patient, systematic approach to sources and their interpretation.

An interesting example of the use of historical documents is sociologist Anthony Ashworth's study of trench warfare during the First World War (Ashworth 1980). Ashworth was concerned with analysing what life was like for men who had to endure being under constant fire, crammed in close proximity for weeks on end. He drew on a diversity of documentary sources: official histories of the war, including those written about different military divisions and battalions; official publications of the time; the notes and records kept informally by individual soldiers; and personal accounts of war experiences. By drawing on such a variety of sources, Ashworth was able to develop a rich and detailed description of life in the trenches. He discovered that most soldiers formed their own ideas about how often they intended to engage in combat with the enemy and often effectively ignored the commands of their officers. For example, on Christmas Day, German and Allied soldiers suspended hostilities, and in one place the two sides even staged an informal soccer match.

Comparative-historical research

Ashworth's research concentrated on a relatively short time period, but there have been many studies that have investigated social change over much longer periods and applied comparative research in that historical context. One of the more recent modern classics of comparative historical sociology is Theda Skocpol's (1979) analysis of social revolutions, discussed in 'Classic Studies 2.2'.

Sociological research in the real world

All research methods, as was stressed earlier, have their advantages and limitations. Hence, it is common to combine several methods in a single piece of research, using each to supplement and check on the others, in a process known as **triangulation**. We can see the value of combining methods – and, more generally,

Classic Studies 2.2 **Theda Skocpol's comparison of social revolutions**

The research problem

As all students of sociology and history are taught, the French Revolution of 1789 transformed France forever. But why did it happen then and not at some other time? Was it an historical accident or was it inevitable? The early twentieth-century revolutions in China and Russia not only turned those countries into communist societies, but significantly shaped the direction of the modern world itself. Again, why did they happen then? What caused them? The American sociologist Theda Skocpol (1947–), set out to address these questions and to uncover the similarities and differences between them. Skocpol set herself an ambitious task: to produce a theory of the origins and nature of revolution grounded in detailed empirical study. The result was a book, published as *States and Social Revolutions* (1979), that is now one of the classic studies of long-term social transformation.

Skocpol's explanation

Skocpol looked at the processes of revolution in three different historical contexts: the 1789 French Revolution (1786–1800); the 1917 revolutions in Russia (1917–21) and the revolutionary period in China (1911–49). Given the essentially historical questions she asked, her main method was the use and careful interpretation of a range of primary and secondary documentary sources. Although there are many differences between the three cases of revolution, Skocpol argues that their underlying structural causes are in fact similar. She rejects the Marxist idea that revolutions are the product of mass (class-based) movements with deep grievances. Instead, she agrees with the thesis that, 'revolutions are not made, they come'. That is, social revolutions are largely the result of the unintended consequences of intentional human action. Before the Russian Revolution, for instance, various political groups

Social unrest does not necessarily lead to revolution. It is unclear what the outcome of protests in Tibet against Chinese rule will be.

were trying to overthrow the pre-existing regime, but none of these – including the Bolsheviks, who eventually came to power – anticipated the revolution that occurred. A series of clashes and confrontations gave rise to a process of social transformation much deeper and more radical than anyone had foreseen.

Skocpol's explanation is that all three revolutions occurred in predominantly agrarian societies and were made possible only when the existing state structures (administrative and military) were breaking down as they came under intense competitive pressure from other states. In this context, it was peasant revolts and mass mobilizations that brought about social revolutions in France, China and Russia. Thus Skocpol argued against the widespread notion that peasants were *not* a 'revolutionary class'. Some similarities with other revolutions in Vietnam, Cuba, Mexico and Yugoslavia can also be seen. Skocpol's causal explanation focuses on state structures; as these began to break down, a power vacuum was created and states lost their legitimacy, enabling revolutionary forces to take power.

Skocpol's research makes use of the 'logic of scientific experiment' for comparative studies, outlined by John Stuart Mill in the mid-nineteenth century. Skocpol adopts Mill's 'method of similarity', taking three similar events (revolutions) in very different national contexts. This allows her to look for possible key similarities across the three cases which can be identified as *independent variables* and thus, help to explain the causes of political revolutions.

Critical points

Some of Skocpol's critics have raised questions about her thesis's structural argument. This, they say, leaves little room for active agency on the part of people. How did peasant groups revolt? Did leaders not play a part in the revolutions?

Could things have turned out differently if individual actors and groups had chosen alternative courses of action? Are individuals so powerless to influence change in the face of structural pressures? A further criticism is of Skocpol's notion of 'cause' in this context. Some have argued that what her argument amounts to is really a set of sophisticated generalizations in relation to the cases she studied. And although such generalizations work quite well for these specific cases, this is not the same thing as a general causal theory of social revolutions. So, critics say, despite setting out to discover the underlying causes and nature of social revolutions, in the end, Skocpol's study showed that each revolution has to be studied in its own right.

Contemporary significance

Skocpol's study has become a modern classic for two reasons. First, it developed a powerful causal explanation of revolutionary change, which emphasized the underlying social structural conditions of revolution. Such a strong central thesis was, nevertheless, underpinned by very detailed analysis of primary and secondary documentary sources. Hence, Skocpol successfully demonstrated that comparative-historical sociology could combine the study of large-scale, long-term social change with the empirical investigation of historical events 'on the ground'. In essence, she brought together the macro- and microsociological aspects into one theoretical framework. Second, Skocpol made a very significant contribution to our understanding of revolutions. She showed that there are enough similarities across different revolutions to warrant pursuing general theories of social change. In this way, her thesis helped to bridge the gap between mainstream historical studies and the sociology of revolutions.

the problems and pitfalls of real sociological research – by looking once again at Laud Humphreys' *Tearoom Trade*.

One of the questions that Humphreys wanted to answer was: 'What kind of men came to the tearooms?' But it was very hard

for him to find this out, because all he could really do in the toilets was observe. The norm of silence in the toilets made it difficult to ask any questions, or even to talk. In addition, it would have been very odd if he had begun to ask personal questions of people who basically wanted to be anonymous.

Humphreys' solution was to try to find out more about the men in the 'tearooms' using survey methods. Standing by the door of the toilets, he would write down the car number-plates of people who pulled up to the car park and went into the toilets for sex. He then gave the numbers to a friend who worked at the Department of Motor Vehicles, securing the addresses of the men.

Months later, Washington University in St Louis, in the United States, where Laud was working, was conducting a door-to-door survey of sexual habits. Humphreys asked the principal investigators in that survey if he could add the names and addresses of his sample of tearoom participants. Humphreys then disguised himself as one of the investigators and went to interview these men at their homes, supposedly just to ask only the survey questions but actually also to learn more about their social backgrounds and lives. He found that most of these men were married and otherwise led very conventional lives. He often interviewed wives and other family members as well.

THINKING CRITICALLY

Do you think Zimbardo's project would be allowed today? On reflection, *should* such projects be allowed in sociology at all? Considering Laud Humphreys' study of tearooms *and* Zimbardo's prison experiment, can the knowledge benefits of a research study ever justify compromising a researcher's own ethical position?

Restating the obvious?

Because sociologists often study things that we have some personal experience of, one can sometimes wonder if sociology is merely 'a painful elaboration of the obvious' (Wright 2000). Is sociology merely a restatement, in abstract jargon, of things we already know? Is it simply the tedious definition of social phenomena with which we are already familiar? Sociology at its worst can be all of these things, but it is never appropriate to judge any discipline by what its worst practitioners do. In fact, good sociology sharpens our understanding of the obvious (Berger 1963) or it completely transforms our common sense. In either event, good sociology is neither tedious nor a restatement of the obvious. Discussions of a new topic in this text sometimes begin with definitions of things that you may already understand. It is necessary for any academic discipline to define its terms. However, when we define a family, for example, as a unit of people who are related to one another, we do so not as an endpoint but instead as a beginning. Without defining our terms, we often cannot move forward to sharper levels of understanding later on – good sociology never defines terms as an end in itself.

The influence of sociology

Sociological research is rarely of interest only to the intellectual community of sociologists. For a start, much sociological research funding comes from government sources and is directly linked to social issues and problems. Many studies of crime and deviance, for example, target specific offences or types of offender with a view to gaining a better knowledge so that the social problems associated with crime can be tackled more effectively. Sociologists also work with voluntary agencies, public bodies and businesses, bringing their research skills to bear on matters of interest not just to the sociologist. A fair amount of this work is **applied social research**, which does not simply aim to produce better knowledge, but also seeks to inform interventions aimed at improving social life. A study of the effects on children of parental alcohol use, for example, may be interested in whether a particular treatment programme has any effect on reducing alcoholism. Sociology's impact is not restricted to policy-oriented research, however.

The results of sociological research are often disseminated throughout society. Sociology, it must be emphasized, is not just the *study* of societies; it is a significant element *in the continuing life* of those societies. Take the transformations taking place in relation to marriage, sexuality and the family (discussed in chapters 9 and 14). Few people do not have some knowledge of these changes, as a result of the filtering down of sociological research. Our thinking and behaviour are affected by sociological knowledge in complex and often subtle ways, thus reshaping the very field of socio-logical investigation. A way of describing this phenomenon, using the technical concepts of sociology, is to say that sociology stands in a 'reflexive relation' to the human beings whose behaviour is studied. **Reflexivity**, as we shall see in chapter 3, describes the interchange between sociological research and human behaviour. We should not be surprised that sociological findings often correlate closely with common sense. The reason is not simply that sociology comes up with findings we knew already; it is, rather, that sociological research continually influences what our common-sense knowledge of society actually is.

Summary points

1. Sociologists investigate social life by posing distinct questions and trying to find the answers to these by systematic research. These questions may be factual, comparative, developmental or theoretical.

2. All research begins from a research problem, which interests or puzzles the investigator. Gaps in the existing literature, theoretical debates, or practical issues in the social world may suggest research problems. There are a number of clear steps in the development of research strategies – although these are rarely followed exactly in actual research.

3. A causal relationship between two events or situations is one in which one event or situation brings about the other. This is more problematic than it seems at first. Causation must be distinguished from correlation, which refers to the existence of a regular relationship between two variables. A variable can be differences in age, income, crime rates, etc. We need to also distinguish independent variables from dependent variables. An independent variable is a variable that produces an effect on another. Sociologists often use controls to ascertain a causal relationship.

4. In fieldwork or participant observation, the researcher spends lengthy periods of time with a group or community being studied. Survey research involves sending or administering questionnaires to samples of a larger population. Documentary research uses printed materials, from archives or other resources, as a source for information. Other research methods include experiments, biographical methods, historical analysis and comparative research.

5. Each of these various methods of research has its limitations. For this reason, researchers will often combine two or more methods in their work, each being used to check or supplement the material obtained from the others. This process is called triangulation.

6. Sociological research often poses ethical dilemmas. These may arise either where deception is practised against those who are the subjects of the research, or where the publication of research findings might adversely affect the feelings or lives of those studied. There is no entirely satisfactory way to deal with these issues, but all researchers have to be sensitive to the dilemmas they pose.

Further reading

Books on research methods are very numerous, especially those pitched at introductory level students. This selection is therefore merely the tip of a large iceberg of literature.

Novice researchers need a text that is both informative and practical, so something like Judith Bell's *Doing Your Research Project: A Guide for First-time Researchers in Education, Health and Social Science*, 4th edn (Buckingham: Open University Press, 2007) is a very good place to begin thinking about and planning a research project. Similarly, Keith F. Punch's *Introduction to Social Research: Quantitative and Qualitative Approaches*, 2nd edn (London: Sage Publications, 2005) does exactly what it says and covers a lot of issues and debates. Gary D. Bouma and Rod Ling's *The Research Process, Fifth Edition* (Melbourne: Oxford University Press, 2005) is also an excellent introduction to research methods.

For something more sophisticated and comprehensive, you could then try Alan Bryman's *Social Research Methods*, 3rd edn (Oxford: Oxford University Press, 2008), which has become very widely adopted by lecturers for their research methods courses. Tim May's *Social Research: Issues, Methods and Process*, 3rd edn (Buckingham: Open University Press, 2003) is a similarly much-used and reliable guide.

One other book worth looking at is Darrell Huff's *How to Lie with Statistics* (London: Penguin Books Ltd, 1991), which is apparently the best-selling statistics book ever written (see J. M. Steele, 'Darrell Huff and fifty years of how to lie with statistics', *Statistical Science*, 20/3 (2005): 205–9). This is probably because its irreverent tone makes it attractive to students. It is, however, an excellent guide to the misuse of statistical information in society, which carries a serious message.

Finally, a good dictionary is usually a good investment, so Victor Jupp's *The SAGE Dictionary of Social Research Methods* (London: Sage Publications, 2006) is well worth consulting.

Internet links

Ipsos MORI – a merged company (Ipsos UK and MORI) focusing on market research and social research:
www.ipsos-mori.com/

Intute – social science web resources for education and research:
www.intute.ac.uk/socialsciences/

UK National Statistics Online, which includes lots of survey research, but other types as well:
www.statistics.gov.uk/default.asp

The UK Data Archive – a centre of expertise in relation to the collection and storage of data on a variety of subjects:
www.data-archive.ac.uk/

CESSDA – Council of European Social Science Data Archives – houses many social science data archives from across Europe covering many types of research:
www.nsd.uib.no/cessda/home.html

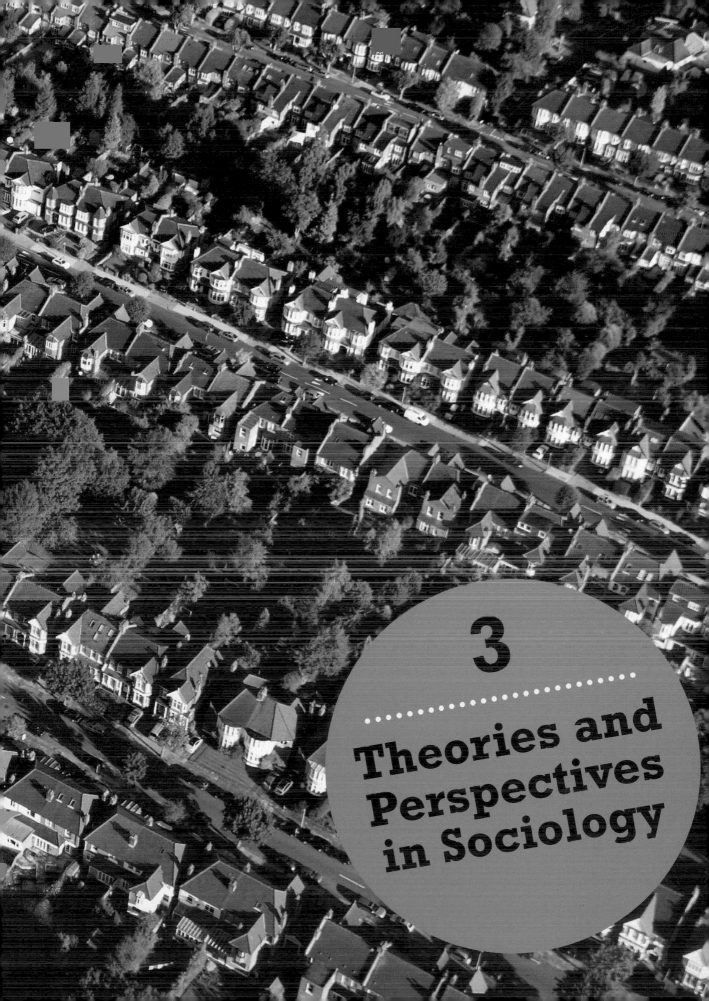

3

Theories and Perspectives in Sociology

CHAPTER 3

Theories and Perspectives in Sociology

(opposite) Does the environmental issue of global climate change demand new forms of sociological theorizing?

In chapter 1 we saw that, like other scientific disciplines, sociologists need to devise abstract interpretations – theories – to explain the variety of facts and evidence they collect in their research studies. They also need to adopt a theoretical approach at the outset of their empirical studies if they are to formulate adequate research questions and narrow down the search for evidence. But sociological theorizing does not take place in a vacuum outside the wider society. This is clear from the questions posed by the discipline's founders, which were closely tied to some of the major social issues of the day. For example, Marx sought to explain the dynamics of the capitalist economy and the causes of poverty and social inequality. Durkheim's studies investigated the character of industrial society and the process of secularization. Weber tried to explain the emergence of capitalism and the consequences of modern bureaucratic forms of organization. And all three were concerned to understand what was unique about modern societies and where they were heading. Some sociologists continue to be motivated today by these 'big questions'.

However, the central problems within societies seem to be changing, as are the sociological theories that aim to understand and explain them. What are the social and political consequences of globalization? How and why are gender relations being transformed? What is the future for multicultural societies? Indeed, what is the future for human populations across the world in the light of dire scientific forecasts of global warming and other environmental problems? In order to address these new issues, sociologists have been forced to re-evaluate the utility of the classical perspectives and, where these are found wanting, to develop novel theories of their own. We will look at some of the latter in this chapter. Before that, we have to establish why a chapter dedicated to theory is needed and what you should expect from it.

So what is left to do? This chapter rounds off an interlinked block of three at the start of the book. Taken together, the block provides a basic introduction to the discipline of sociology. In chapter 1 we explored what sociology – the study of human societies – adds to the sum total of scientific knowledge. Chapter 2 then presented some of the main research methods and techniques which sociologists use in their research – their 'tools of the trade', as it were. And in this chapter, we provide a relatively brief account of the history and development of sociological theorizing, along with some of the central problems that have exercised generations of sociologists since the nineteenth century. For all newcomers to sociology, such an historical perspective is vital. Not only will it help readers to understand better how the discipline emerged and changed into its current state, but it should prevent us

all from trying too hard to reinvent the (theoretical) wheel, when there is no need to do so. Critics of sociological theorizing – more than a few from within the discipline itself – complain that too many 'new' theories are really 'old' theories dressed up in new language. But an awareness of the development of sociological theory can help us to avoid falling into this particular trap.

Coming to terms with the array of theories and perspectives in sociology is challenging for those new to the discipline. It would be much easier if sociology had a central theory around which all sociologists could work, and for a time in the 1950s and '60s, the structural functionalist approach of Talcott Parsons did come close to being that central theory. However, as we saw in chapter 1, this is just not the case today, as the present period of sociological theorizing is characterized by a diversity of theoretical approaches and perspectives. And of course, with such diversity comes more competition and disagreement. All this makes the task of evaluating competing theories more difficult than it once was, but you should not be put off. Sociological theories are necessary because without theory our understanding of social life would be very weak. Good theories help us to arrive at a deeper understanding of societies and to explain the social changes that affect us all.

Robert K. Merton (1957) argued strongly for 'middle-range' theories that try to explain a specific aspect of social life, rather than grand theories aiming to explain large-scale social structures or the historical development of modern societies (see chapter 1). One reason why we might well agree with Merton is that it is very difficult to test **grand theories** by empirical research. But sociology can easily accommodate *both* types. Indeed, the insights we can garner from grand theories often makes the difficulties associated with empirical testing well worth the effort. Over the last decade or two, we have seen something of a return to grand theorizing as social scientists try to understand the momentous social, political

1750	European Enlightenment philosophers (1750–1800)
1800	Auguste Comte (1798–1857) **Harriet Martineau (1802–76)**
1850	**Karl Marx (1818–83)** Herbert Spencer (1820–1903)
1900	Emile Durkheim (1858–1917)
	Max Weber (1864–1920)
	Georg Simmel (1858–1918) Edmund Husserl (1859–1938)
1930	George H. Mead (1863–1931) Alfred Schutz (1899–1959)
	Chicago School (1920s) Antonio Gramsci (1891–1937)
1940	Talcott Parsons (1902–79)
	Frankfurt School (1930)
	Simone de Beauvoir (1908–86)
1950	Robert Merton (1910–2003)
1960	Erving Goffman (1922–82)
	Betty Friedan (1921–2006)
	Howard Becker (1928–)
	Harold Garfinkel (1917–) Norbert Elias (1897–1990)
1970	Jürgen Habermas (1929–)
	Michel Foucault (1926–84)
1980	Pierre Bourdieu (1930–2002) Immanuel Wallerstein (1930–)
	Jean Baudrillard (1929–2007)
1990	Anthony Giddens (1938–) Ulrich Beck (1944–) Judith Butler (1956–)
	Vandana Shiva (1952–) Zygmunt Bauman (1925–)
2000	Manuel Castells (1942–)

Key:
Selected theorists associated with or inspired by the different sociological perspectives are identified thus:

▪ Philosophical thinkers
▪ Functionalism
▪ Marxism
▪ Interactionism
▪ Feminism
▪ Postmodernism/poststructuralism
▪ Theoretical syntheses

Figure 3.1 Chronology of major sociological theorists and schools, 1750–2000

and technological transformations of recent times (Skinner 1990). Such an enterprise has been part of the sociological tradition from the start, and it appears ever more necessary for it to continue in the rapidly globalizing world we live in today.

Next, we trace the emergence of sociological theory and the establishment of the discipline of sociology through the work of the 'classical founders' and the traditions of enquiry they began. We then explore some key theoretical issues around which debates in sociological theory have focused, before ending the chapter with a look at the way in which the rapid and wide-ranging social changes since the 1970s have forced sociologists to devise new approaches to their theorizing. Figure 3.1 provides a simple chronological chart, which illustrates the emergence and development of sociological theories and perspectives through certain influential theorists and schools. The place of individuals in the time-sequence is determined roughly by the date of their major publication(s) and the place of schools by their date of formation. This is of course merely a selection and is not intended to be exhaustive. The chart aims to provide some key theoretical signposts, which can be referred to throughout the chapter and, indeed, the book as a whole.

> ### THINKING CRITICALLY
>
> Read carefully and reflect on the simplified chronology of theorists and schools in figure 3.1. Why do you think there seem to be more attempts to produce theoretical syntheses, mixing elements from the different perspectives, at the present time than there were in the past?

Towards sociology

As we saw in chapter 1, a sociological perspective was made possible by two revolutionary transformations. The Industrial Revolution of the late eighteenth and nineteenth centuries radically transformed the material conditions of life and the ways of making livings forever, bringing with it, initially at least, many new social problems such as urban overcrowding, poor sanitation and accompanying disease and industrial pollution on an unprecedented scale. Social reformers looked for ways to mitigate and solve such problems, which led them to carry out research and gather evidence on the extent and nature of the problems to reinforce their case for change.

The French Revolution of 1789 marked the symbolic endpoint of the older European agrarian regimes and absolute monarchies as republican ideals of freedom, liberty and citizenship rights came to the fore. This revolution is often seen as, in part, the outcome of mid-eighteenth-century European Enlightenment ideas that challenged religious and traditional authorities and promoted philosophical and scientific notions of reason, rationality and critical thinking as the keys to progress in human affairs.

Enlightenment philosophers saw the advancement of reliable knowledge in the natural sciences, particularly in astronomy, physics and chemistry, as showing the way forward for the study of social life. The English physicist, Sir Isaac Newton (1643–1727), was singled out as an exemplary scientist whose notions of Natural Law and scientific method appealed to Enlightenment scholars, who argued that such laws could be found (and should be sought using similar methods) in social and political life as well.

Positivism and social evolution

Auguste Comte saw the science of society (which he termed 'sociology') as essentially similar to natural science. His **positivist** approach was based on the principle of direct observation, which could be explained by theoretical statements based on establishing causal, law-like generalizations. The task of sociology, according to Comte, was to gain reliable knowledge of the social world in order to make predictions about it, and, on the basis of those predictions, to intervene and shape social life in progressive ways. Comte's positivist philosophy was clearly inspired by what he saw as the fabulous predictive power of the natural sciences. Anyone who has watched (probably on television) NASA's space shuttles taking off and spending days orbiting the Earth before landing in the manner of an aeroplane has witnessed this predictive power in action. Thinking about the different types of accurate knowledge that are required to achieve such a feat of science and engineering shows why the natural sciences are held in high regard.

But could such reliable, predictive knowledge ever be achieved in relation to human beings? Most sociologists today think not and even fewer would use the term 'positivist' to describe their own work. Probably the main reason why so many sociologists reject Comtean positivism is because they see the idea of shaping and controlling people and societies as impossible, potentially dangerous or both. Critics say that self-conscious human beings cannot be studied in the same way as, say, frogs, because they are capable of acting in ways that confound our predictions about them. But even if Comte was right and humans *could* be scientifically studied, their behaviour forecast and interventions made to direct it in positive directions, who would decide what constitutes a 'positive direction'? Scientists themselves? Politicians? Religious authorities? The twentieth century saw many attempts to control human populations, including those of hard-line communist regimes based on 'scientific Marxism' and fascist governments drawing on theories of 'scientific racism' to justify mass murder. Social scientists today cannot un-know the appalling human consequences of such uses of scientific theories and there has been increasing scepticism about Comte's notion of sociology as a predictive science.

Nevertheless, although Comte is not held in particularly high regard by most sociologists today, it is important to remember his formative role in establishing the case for a science of society.

> See chapter 1, 'What is Sociology?', for a wider discussion of Comte's ideas.

Comte's ideas were extremely influential and his theory of the development of the sciences was an inspiration to other thinkers working with theories of evolutionary social development. Comte saw each science as passing through three stages: the theological (or religious), the metaphysical (or philosophical) and finally the positive (or scientific), with each stage representing a form of human mental development. He argued that the history of the sciences demonstrated this pattern of movement, with social life being the last area to move into the positive stage and sociology the final discipline.

English philosopher and sociologist Herbert Spencer (1820–1903) drew on Comte's ideas and was among the first to argue that, just as the world of nature was subject to biological evolution, so societies were subject to **social evolution**. This took the form of *structural differentiation* – through which simple societies develop over time into more and more complex forms with an increasingly diverse array of separate social institutions; and *functional adaptation* – the way that societies accommodate themselves to their environment. Spencer argued that it was through structural differentiation that societies became functionally better adapted, and the industrial societies of the nineteenth century were essentially demonstrating a form of social evolution, emerging out of the more static and hierarchical societies that preceded them. Spencer also thought that the principle of 'survival of the fittest' applied in social as well as biological evolution, and he was not in favour of state intervention to support the vulnerable or disadvantaged (Taylor 1992).

Although Spencer's theory of social evolution was widely known and his books were well received in his lifetime, like many other evolutionary theories in sociology, in the twentieth century his work fell into decline within the discipline and few sociology courses now make more than passing reference to him. His fate stands in stark contrast to another of the grand theorists of the nineteenth century, Karl Marx, whose influence, not only on sociology, but also on world history itself, it is hard to overestimate.

Karl Marx: the capitalist revolution

In chapter 1, Marx's basic ideas on class conflict and social change were introduced and at this point you may want to refresh your knowledge of these. Marx and his collaborator, Friedrich Engels, never considered themselves professional sociologists. They did seek a scientific understanding of society, however, and, from this, an explanation of long-term social change. Marx viewed the emergence of his social scientific work as marking a break with philosophy and philosophical forms of thought. He argued that 'the philosophers have only interpreted the world in various ways, the point however is to change it'. His interest in and commitment to the European industrial working class was closely linked to his studies of capitalism and its workings.

Marx's theoretical approach: historical materialism

Marx's work is important for sociology in a number of ways and references to it will occur regularly throughout this book, but we will concentrate on just one aspect in this chapter: his analysis of capitalism, which is part of his broader theory of class conflicts as being the driving force of history. This 'grand theory' has formed the basis of many later research studies and theoretical developments in sociology and the social sciences. Recognizably 'Marxist' ideas also formed the basis of many political movements and governments in the twentieth century, including the communist regimes of the former Soviet Union, Eastern Europe, Cuba, Vietnam and China.

Marx's theoretical perspective is sometimes referred to as historical materialism; more accurately perhaps, it is a **materialist conception of history**. This means that Marx is opposed to idealism, a philosophical doctrine which says that the historical development of societies is driven by abstract ideas or ideals, like freedom and democracy. Instead, Marx argues that the dominant ideas and ideals of an age are reflections of the dominant way of life, specifically of a society's **mode of production**. For example, in an age when absolute monarchs reigned, it is not surprising that the dominant ideas suggested that kings and queens had a 'divine right [from God] to rule'; in our own age of free-market capitalism, it is again unsurprising that the dominant ideas are those of sovereign individuals who 'make free choices'. As Marx argues, the dominant ideas of an age are those of the ruling groups. Marx's 'historical materialism' is, therefore, primarily concerned with how people work collectively to produce a life together. How do they produce food, shelter and other material goods and what kind of division of labour exists which enables them to do so?

> **THINKING CRITICALLY**
>
> What is your own assumption about social change? Can ideas change history? Marx suggests not, but can you think of any examples where theories and ideas *have* had the effect of changing society? How might Marxists respond? How would an historical materialist explanation differ from the idealist one?

Successive modes of production: a successful grand theory?

Marx's historical studies led him to argue that there had been a very long, but structured, historical development of human societies. In the ancient past, small-scale human groups existed with no developed system of property ownership. Instead, all the resources acquired were communally owned and no class divisions were present. Marx called this a form of *primitive communism*. As the production of these groups increased, this mode of production was effectively outgrown and a new mode emerged, this time with some private prop-

Marx argued that as workers were brought together in large numbers, class-consciousness would develop.

erty ownership (including slavery), such as in ancient Greece and Rome. From here, societies developed based on settled agriculture and feudal property relations. The European system of *feudalism* was based on a class division between landowners and landless peasants and tenant farmers, who were forced to work for the landowners in order to survive.

But the feudal mode of production also reached its productive limitations and the system gave way to the *capitalist society* with which we are now familiar. The first capitalists began to invest in workshops and manufacturing in the sixteenth century; by the time of the French Revolution in 1789, they had grown numerous and powerful enough to become a revolutionary force in history.

Under capitalism, class antagonisms were greatly simplified, with society 'splitting into two great camps' – the property owners (capitalists or the *bourgeoisie*) and the workers (or *proletariat*). The capitalist revolution broke the bounds of traditional feudal production systems, demanding a new discipline and long hours from workers so that capitalists could extract a profit from using their labour power. Marx produces a glowing account of capitalism. In its first 100 years it had 'created more massive and more colossal productive forces than have all preceding generations together' (Marx and Engels 2001[1848]). Capitalism has been a genuinely revolutionary mode of production. But such achievements have been based on terrible exploitation of workers and, consequently, inevitable and endemic

Neo-Marxism: the Frankfurt School of critical theory

The apparent 'failure' of the European working classes to overthrow capitalism and install communist regimes, the rise of fascism and Nazism in the 1930s and the 'corruption' of communism within the Soviet Union and its allies all presented later Marxists with a dilemma. Is Marx's theory still adequate for understanding the development of capitalism or not? If it is, then an orthodox form of Marxism remains valuable. But if not, then new forms of Marxist theory (neo-Marxism) will be needed, which may have to break with some of Marx's original ideas.

Marxist thought, in fact, developed in several directions over the twentieth century, particularly amongst 'Western Marxists', who rejected the Soviet version of communism (Kolakowski 2005). One group of Marxists within Western Marxism has been especially influential – namely the Frankfurt School of critical theory. Originally based at the Institute for Social Research in Frankfurt under the directorship of Max Horkheimer, many critical theorists were forced out of Germany when the National Socialists expelled around one-third of the University's staff, resulting in their relocation to Europe and America. The Nazis systematically undermined universities and removed or forced out many Jewish intellectuals.

Drawing on the ideas of Marx, Freud and the philosophy of Immanuel Kant, the Frankfurt School produced a series of important studies of capitalism, fascism, mass culture and the emerging consumer society in the USA. For example, Theodore Adorno (1976 [1950]) and his colleagues analysed the emergence and popularity of fascism as, in part, a consequence of the rise of an authoritarian personality-type, susceptible to the attractions of a strong leader. Herbert Marcuse's *One-Dimensional Man* (1964)

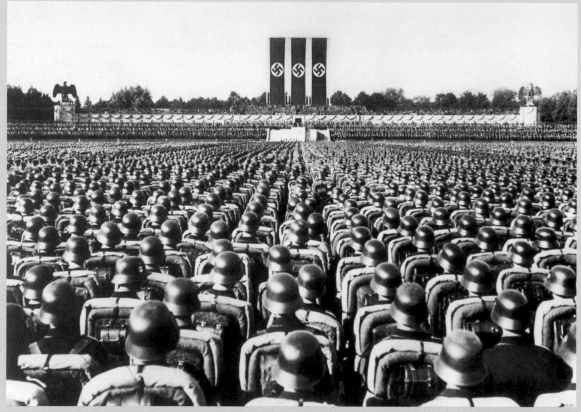

The rise of facism in Europe forced Western Marxists to rethink Marx's ideas.

distinguished between 'real' human needs and the many 'false' needs produced by the consumer form of industrial capitalism with its seductive advertising, which suppressed people's ability to think critically, instead producing a one-dimensional and uncritical form of thinking.

In studies such as these, we can see the Frankfurt thinkers attempting to come to terms with a very different form of capitalism from that which Marx had investigated. At the same time, the optimistic Marxist vision of a working-class revolution began to fade, as the obstacles to revolution seemed to mount up in the consumer-centred capitalist societies.

The latest critical theorist to exert an influence in sociology is the German social philosopher Jürgen Habermas. Amongst other things, Habermas devised a theory of 'communicative action' based on the deceptively simple notion that when people make statements to each other (he calls these 'speech acts'), they expect to be understood. But much of the time, he argues, asymmetrical power relations in society work systematically to distort such communication, giving rise to fundamental misunderstandings and a lack of genuine debate and communication. The solution is not to abandon modern ways of rational thinking, as some postmodern thinkers would have it, but to deepen our modernity by defending and extending democracy and eliminating the huge inequalities of power and status that prevent proper human communication. Habermas continues to this day to work in the tradition of neo-Marxist critical theory.

Since the collapse of the communist bloc countries of Eastern Europe following the fall of the Berlin Wall in 1989, and the ending of the Soviet Union's communist regime in 1991, Marx's ideas, and Marxist theories generally, have lost ground in sociology. Some have even talked of a crisis in Marxist thought as a result of the demise of actually existing socialism and communism (Gamble 1999). However, a broadly Marxist analysis of capitalist economies continues to play a part in debates about the direction of contemporary social change.

alienation amongst the industrial work-force.

Just like feudalism, Marx expected capitalism itself to give way to another mode of production, communism, brought about by disaffected workers who develop class-consciousness (an awareness of their exploited position) in which private property is abolished and communal social relations are established. Unlike primitive communism though, modern communism would have all the benefits of the highly productive capitalist system at its disposal. This would be an advanced, humane and sophisticated form of communism, which was able to deliver on the communist principle 'from each, according to his [sic] ability, to each, according to his need' (Marx 1978[1875]).

Evaluation

Marx's theory of capitalism has been important for sociology. It challenged the early assumption that the problems brought about by industrialization could be resolved within the system itself. For Marx, a theory of industrialism per se makes no sense. Industrial development required industrialists, and these were capitalist entrepreneurs. To understand the industrial system as debated and discussed by Comte and Spencer also means being able to grasp the new structural social relationships: capitalistic social relationships, favouring a few and disadvantaging the majority. Marx's

> ### THINKING CRITICALLY
>
> What is your own answer to why the communist revolution, forecast by Marx, has not materialized? List all the factors that may have prevented the working class from revolting against capitalism. How serious is the absence of Marxist-style revolution for Marxist theory? Can we now say that the theory has been definitively falsified?

perspective also provides a useful reminder that factories, workshops and offices, along with computers, robots and the Internet, do not simply materialize from thin air. They are the products of social relations, which can be riven with conflict rather than agreement.

Marx also shows that grand theorizing can be helpful. The concept of a mode of production is a useful one, insofar as it allows us to place the welter of historical evidence into a common framework, which is then easier to understand. Many social scientists have worked with this framework, expanding, refining or criticizing it since Marx's death. Many continue to do so even today. Though Marx's theory may be flawed, most sociologists would agree that discovering those flaws has been immensely fruitful for sociology as a whole.

However, Marx's work also illustrates the main problem with grand theories – namely the difficulty of subjecting them to empirical testing. How could this thesis be tested against the available evidence? What would we have to find in order conclusively to prove it to be wrong or to falsify it? Does the fact that a communist revolution has not – so far – happened in the highly industrialized countries show that the theory's central prediction was misguided? If so, does that also mean that other aspects of it are similarly wrong-headed? What about the historical materialist approach in general – is it, too, badly flawed? How long should we wait for the revolution to occur, before discarding the theory? Later Marxists have sought to explain exactly why a global communist revolution has not occurred and in doing so have been forced to modify Marx's ideas. 'Classic Studies 3.1' looks at one especially influential group, whose theories have influenced the development of conflict sociology.

Establishing sociology

Comte, Spencer, Marx and other early theorists laid some of the foundations for sociology's development. But in the period they lived through, there was no formal discipline of sociology, nor did the subject have any institutional presence within universities. If sociology was to become part of Comte's 'hierarchy of the sciences', then it needed to carve out a place alongside the natural sciences in the academy, where a sociological training could be offered to students. In short, sociology needed to become respectable, and Emile Durkheim's work in France went a long way towards achieving this aim. However, it took much longer for sociology to become a firmly established subject within universities.

Emile Durkheim: the social level of reality

Durkheim is a pivotal figure in the development of academic sociology. Following a conventional philosophical training, he moved decisively away from philosophy – which he saw as too far removed from the big issues of the day – and towards social science, which he perceived to be closer to making clear what were the main moral questions facing French society. Durkheim's first academic position was at the University of Bordeaux, where he taught sociology and education, or 'pedagogy'. While he was in Bordeaux, he published widely and was the first French scholar to be promoted to Professor of Social Science. In 1902 Durkheim's reputation took him to the prestigious Sorbonne, The University of Paris, and in 1906 he became Professor of the Science of Education. Seven years later, Durkheim became the first ever Professor of the Science of Education and Sociology (Coser 1977). Sociology finally had a foothold within the academic establishment.

The second aspect of Durkheim's influence on modern sociology was in relation to the nature of the discipline itself. Durkheim saw that the study of specifically *social* phenomena was needed whenever research into people's actions went beyond their individual interactions. Social institutions and social forms – such as social movements or the family – outlive the particular individuals who inhabit them and they therefore must have a reality of their own. This reality cannot adequately be understood by an individualistic psychology or abstract philosophical speculation, but demands a genuinely sociological explanation. In Durkheim's terms, what we call 'the social' is a level of reality *in its own right* that cannot be reduced to mere action, nor is it a simple aggregate of individual consciousnesses.

This explains why Durkheim focused on group phenomena and **social facts** such as comparative suicide rates (see chapter 1), social solidarity and religion. In his view, the psychology of individuals was not the proper subject for sociologists to study. Just one example of this perspective can be seen in *The Division of Labour in Society* (1893), where Durkheim outlined his now famous distinction between the *mechanical* forms of solidarity found in less complex societies and the *organic* solidarity that characterizes large-scale, modern, industrial societies. Mechanical solidarity exists when individualism is minimized and the individual is subsumed within the collectivity. By contrast, *organic solidarity* is generated by the extensive division of labour within industrial societies, which tends to produce differences rather than similarities.

Durkheim therefore rejected the idea – common at the time and since – that modern industrialism inevitably destroys social solidarity and threatens the social fabric of society. In fact, said Durkheim, *stronger* bonds of mutual interdependence are created under organic forms of solidarity, which hold out the potential for a better balance between individual differences and collective purpose. Here we can see how Durkheim's scientific sociological analysis is closely tied to the moral and social problems of the day – how can industrial societies hold together in an age of increasing individualism?

Evaluation

As we saw in chapter 1, Durkheim's approach to sociology is known as functionalism; the study of society and the way its institutions connect together and change. And though functionalism has been very influential in sociology in the past, today it is in retreat. There are several reasons why.

First, many critics have argued that functionalism is good at explaining consensus – why societies hold together and share a common morality – but it is much less able to explain conflict and radical social change. Others argue that Durkheimian functionalism seems to prioritize societies' constraints over people and does not allow enough room for the creative actions of individuals. Finally, functional analysis tends to impute purposes and needs to society itself. For example, we might say that the function of the education system is to train young people for the *needs* of a modern society. This functionalist argument seems to suggest that societies can have 'needs' in the same way the people do. But is this really an adequate form of explanation? Modern economies may well require certain skills from people, but is the present education system the only or even the best way to provide for them? What we really want to know is how, exactly, the modern education system came into being. How did it develop over time into its present form, and could things have been different? Functionalism does not prioritize such questions.

THINKING CRITICALLY

Reflecting on Durkheim's ideas, what did he mean by 'social facts' and in what ways are they 'thing-like'? Durkheim rejected the idea that sociologists should study individual psychology. Do you agree with him or are there good reasons why sociologists should be interested in the psyche of the human individual? What reasons can you suggest?

Twentieth-century structural functionalism

In the 1940s, '50's and '60s, a version of functionalist theory, **structural functionalism**, became the central paradigm of sociology. Although the perspective was never totally dominant, it is hard for students today, who may be used to the idea that sociology as a discipline is *inevitably* pluralistic, argumentative and theoretically diverse, to appreciate just how different *doing* sociology was at that time. Sociology and structural functionalism were often seen as one and the same thing (Davis 1949). Two American sociologists particularly stand out during this period: Robert Merton and his mentor Talcott Parsons.

Parsons combined the ideas of Durkheim, Weber and Vilfredo Pareto into his own brand of structural functionalism, which began from the so-called, 'problem of social order' (Lee and Newby 1983). This problem asks how society can hold together when all the individuals within it are self-interested and pursue their own wants and needs, often at the expense of others.

Philosophers like Thomas Hobbes (1588–1679) answered this by saying that the emergence of the modern state, with all of its policing and military powers, was the crucial factor. The state protected all individuals from one another and from external enemies but, in return, citizens were required to accept the state's legitimate right to exercise its powers. An informal contract existed between state and each individual.

Parsons rejected this solution. He saw that people's conformity to social rules was not simply produced through the *negative* fear of punishment; instead, people conformed in *positive* ways, teaching others society's moral rules and norms of behaviour. Such positive commitment to an orderly society showed, says Parsons, that social rules are not merely an external force acting on individuals, but have become internalized via the continual process of socialization. Society does not simply exist 'out there' but exists 'in here' as well.

Having established the primacy of a sociological understanding of social order,

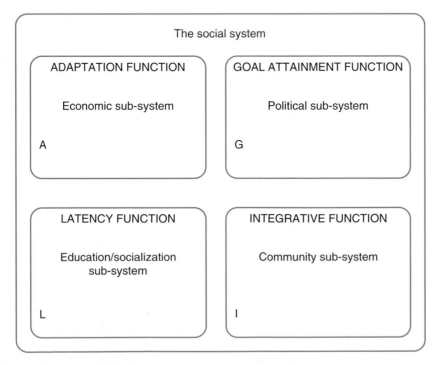

Figure 3.2 Parsons's AGIL scheme

What is the main social function of ceremonies and rituals such as rain dances? Can you think of any ceremonies which perform similar functions in modern societies?

Parsons turned his attention to the functioning of the social system itself. To do this, he devised a model based on identifying the needs of the system, known as the AGIL paradigm (Parsons and Smelser 1956). Parsons argued that if a social system is to continue, then there are four basic functions it must perform. First, it must be capable of adapting to its environment and gather enough resources to do so. Second, it must set out and put in place goals to be attained and the mechanisms for their achievement. Third, the system must be integrated and the various sub-systems must be coordinated effectively. Finally, the social system must have ways of preserving and transmitting its values and culture to new generations.

In less abstract terms, Parsons saw the economic sub-system as performing an adaptive function, the political sub-system as setting society's goals and means of attaining them, the community sub-system ('societal community') as doing integrative work and the educational sub-system (along with other socializing agencies) as transmitting culture and values – the latency function (see figure 3.2). Clearly, Parsons's structural functionalism was a form of systems theory, which tended to give priority to the overall system and its 'needs'. But it was always vulnerable to the charge that it over-emphasized consensus and agreement, while paying less attention to fundamental conflicts of interest and small-scale interactional processes, through which social order and disorder are produced and reproduced. The task of solving these problems passed to Robert Merton, who pursued a version of Parsons's functionalism, but did so in a much more critical way.

As we have already noted above, Merton saw that while many sociological studies focused on either the macro-level of society as a whole or the micro-level of social interactions, this polarization had failed to 'fill in the gaps' between macro- and micro-levels. To rectify this, Merton argued for middle-range theories in particular areas or on specific subjects. An excellent example from his own work is his study of working-class criminality and deviance. He set out to explain why there was so much acquisitive crime amongst the working classes. His explanation was that in an American society which promotes the cultural goal of material success, but offers very few legitimate opportunities for lower social-class groups, working-class criminality represented an adaptation to the social circumstances that many young people found themselves in. But the fact that they aimed to achieve the kind of material success the system promoted also meant that these people were not evil or incapable of being reformed. Rather, it was the structure of social life that was in need of reform.

This thesis shows that Merton did not simply follow Parsons's version of functionalism, but actually tried to develop it into new directions. In doing so, his perspective moved closer to conflict theory. He distinguished between **manifest** and **latent functions**: the former are observable consequences of action, the latter are those aspects that remain unspoken. In studying latent functions, Merton argued, we can learn much more about the way that societies work. For example, we might observe a rain dance amongst tribal people, the manifest function of which appears to be to bring about rain. But if we look deeper, we may find that the rain dance often fails and yet continues to be practised, because its latent function is to build and sustain group solidarity.

Similarly, where Parsons had focused on the functional aspects of society's institu-

tions and legitimate forms of behaviour, Merton argued that these also contained certain **dysfunctional** elements. The existence of dysfunctions allowed Merton to discuss the potential for conflicts within society in ways that Parsons did not.

 See chapter 21, 'Crime and Deviance', for a more detailed discussion and critique of Merton's ideas.

What became of structural functionalism? Following the death of Parsons in 1979, Jeffrey Alexander (1985) sought to revisit and revive the approach, aiming to tackle its theoretical flaws to make it more useful to modern sociology. But by 1997, even Alexander was forced to concede that the internal contradictions of neofunctionalism meant that it was finished. Instead, he argued for a new reconstruction of sociological theory going beyond functionalism (Alexander 1997). Parsonian structural functionalism is, to all intents and purposes, for the time being at least, defunct within mainstream sociology.

> **THINKING CRITICALLY**
>
> What conclusions do you draw from the rise and fall of structural functionalism? What are the main problems with Parsons's systems theory, and are such theories appropriate for studying human societies?

Nonetheless, some reference to the functions of social institutions continues to inform sociological research, and the concept of 'function' in social analysis does have a place. More importantly, Durkheim's notion that sociology should take society's central problems and apply a sociological perspective to our understanding of them is a valuable one. It is typical of all of the early sociological theorists and of many contemporary sociologists too. For example, Parsons's ideas became so influential partly because they spoke to the developed societies about their post-1945 situation, which was one of gradually increasing affluence and political consensus. But they lost ground in the late 1960s and '70s as internal and external social conflicts began to mount, with new peace and anti-nuclear movements, protests against the American war in Vietnam and radical student movements emerging across Europe and North America. At that point, conflict theories came to be perceived as more capable of understanding and accounting for the situation.

As we will see later in the chapter, one important reason why contemporary theorists are seeking out new theoretical directions is precisely because the central problems of our societies have changed. While the early sociologists tried to understand industrialism, urbanization and capitalism, a new series of issues faces sociologists today. Globalization, multiculturalism and environmental degradation are amongst the new central problems of societies today and, arguably, these demand different theories and perspectives that take us away from the classical traditions.

Max Weber: capitalism and religion

In a major work, *The Protestant Ethic and the Spirit of Capitalism* (1992 [1904–5]), Weber set out to tackle a fundamental problem: why did capitalism develop in the West and nowhere else? For some 13 centuries after the fall of ancient Rome, other civilizations were much more prominent than the West in world history. Europe, in fact, was a rather insignificant area of the globe, while China, India and the Ottoman Empire in the Near East were all major powers. The Chinese, in particular, were a long way ahead of the West in terms of their level of technological and economic development. What happened to bring about a surge in economic progress in Europe from the seventeenth century onwards?

To answer this question, Weber reasoned, we must show what it is that separates modern industry from earlier types of economic activity. We find the desire to accumulate wealth in many different civilizations, and this is not difficult to explain: people have valued wealth for the comforts, security, power and enjoyment it can bring. They wish to be free of want, and, having accumulated wealth, they use it to make themselves comfortable.

Religion in the heart of capitalism?

If we look at the economic development of the West, Weber argued, we find something quite different: an attitude towards the accumulation of wealth found nowhere else in history. This attitude is what Weber called the 'spirit of capitalism' – a set of beliefs and values held by the first capitalist merchants and industrialists. These people had a strong drive to accumulate personal wealth. Yet, quite unlike the wealthy elsewhere, they did not seek to use their accumulated riches to follow a luxurious lifestyle. Their way of life was in fact self-denying and frugal; they lived soberly and quietly, shunning the ordinary manifestations of affluence. This very unusual combination of characteristics, Weber tried to show, was vital to early Western economic development. For unlike the wealthy in previous ages and in other cultures, these groups did not dissipate their wealth: instead, they reinvested it to promote the further expansion of the enterprises they headed.

The core of Weber's theory is that the attitudes involved in the spirit of capitalism derived from religion. Christianity in general played a part in fostering such an outlook, but the essential motivating force was provided by the impact of Protestantism and one variety of Protestantism in particular: Puritanism. The early capitalists were mostly Puritans, and many subscribed to Calvinist views. Weber argued that certain Calvinistic doctrines were the direct source of the spirit of capitalism. One was the idea that human beings are God's instruments on earth, required by the Almighty to work in a vocation – an occupation for the greater glory of God.

A second important aspect of Calvinism was the notion of predestination, according to which only certain predestined individuals are to be among the 'elect' – to enter heaven in the afterlife. In Calvin's original doctrine, nothing a person does on this earth can alter whether he or she happens to be one of the elect; this is pre-determined by God. However, this belief caused such anxiety among his followers that it was modified to allow believers to recognize certain signs of election.

Success in working in a vocation, indicated by material prosperity, became the main sign that a person was truly one of the elect. A tremendous impetus towards economic success was created among groups influenced by these ideas. Yet this was accompanied by the believer's need to live a sober and frugal life. The Puritans believed luxury to be an evil, so the drive to accumulate wealth became joined to a severe and unadorned lifestyle.

The early entrepreneurs had little awareness that they were helping to produce momentous changes in society; they were impelled above all by religious motives. The ascetic – that is, self-denying – lifestyle of the Puritans has subsequently become an intrinsic part of modern civilization. As Weber wrote:

> The Puritan wanted to work in a calling; we are forced to do so. For when asceticism was carried out of the monastic cells into everyday life, and began to dominate worldly morality, it did its part in building the tremendous cosmos of the modern economic order. . . . Since asceticism undertook to remodel the world and to work out its ideals in the world, material goods have gained an increasingly and finally an inexorable power over the lives of men as at no previous period in history. . . . The idea of duty in one's calling prowls about in our lives like the ghost of dead religious beliefs. (1992: 182)

Evaluation

Weber's theory has been criticized from many angles. Some have argued, for example, that the outlook he called 'the spirit of capitalism' can be discerned in the early Italian merchant cities in the twelfth century, long before Calvinism was ever heard of. Others have claimed that the key notion of 'working in a vocation', which Weber associated with Protestantism, already existed in Catholic beliefs. Yet the essentials of Weber's account are still accepted by many and the thesis he advanced remains as bold and illuminating as it did when first formulated. If Weber's thesis is valid, then modern economic and social development has been decisively influenced by something that seems at first sight utterly distant from it – a set of religious ideals. This is something that Marx did not see within capitalist economic relations.

Weber's theory meets several important criteria in theoretical thinking in sociology. First, it is counterintuitive – it suggests an interpretation that breaks with what common sense would suggest. The theory thus develops a fresh perspective on the issues it covers. Most authors before Weber gave little thought to the possibility that religious ideas could have played a fundamental role in the origins of capitalism. Second, the theory makes sense of something that is otherwise puzzling: why individuals would want to live frugally while making great efforts to accumulate wealth. Third, the theory is capable of illuminating circumstances beyond those it was originally developed to understand. Weber emphasized that he was trying to understand only the early origins of modern capitalism. Nonetheless, it seems reasonable to suppose that parallel values to those instilled by Puritanism might be involved in other situations of successful capitalist development. Finally, a good theory is not just one that happens to be valid. It is also one that is fruitful in terms of how far it generates new ideas and stimulates further research.

Weber's theory, like Marx's analysis of capitalism, has certainly been highly successful in these respects, providing the springboard for a vast amount of subsequent research and theoretical analysis. Weber's approach to sociology also forms the basis for the tradition known as interactionism.

> ### THINKING CRITICALLY
>
> Weber's theory of the origins of capitalism goes way beyond Merton's concept of a 'middle range theory'. But could the available evidence ever effectively test it? List all the elements of capitalism described by Weber. What, if anything, does this theory add to our understanding of the nature, character and likely future development of modern capitalism?

Symbolic interactionism, phenomenology and ethnomethodology

Along with Max Weber, the American social behaviourist George Herbert Mead is credited as laying the foundations for a general approach to sociology called *interactionism*. This is a general label covering all those approaches that investigate the social interactions amongst individuals, rather than starting from society or its constituent social structures. Interactionists often reject the very idea that social structures exist objectively or they just do not focus on them at all. Herbert Blumer (who coined the term 'symbolic interactionism') argued that all talk of social structures or social systems is unjustified, as only individuals and their interactions can be said really to exist at all.

Symbolic interactionism focuses on micro-level interaction and the way in which meanings are constructed and transmitted across the members of society. G. H. Mead (1934) argued that the individual's self is a **social self**, produced in the process of interaction rather than being biologically

given. Mead's theory traces the emergence and development of the self through a series of stages in childhood and his ideas on the social self underpins much interactionist research (see chapter 1 for a detailed discussion of Mead's ideas). The home of this perspective for some 30 years until 1950 was the University of Chicago's Department of Sociology (known as The Chicago School), though by no means all Chicago sociologists were symbolic interactionists. The department was also home to the 'ecological' approach of Louis Wirth, Robert E. Park and Ernest Burgess (see chapter 6, 'Cities and Urban Life', for a discussion of this approach). Nonetheless, the institutional base for key interactionists, including Mead, was an important factor in extending this approach.

Arguably, the most successful symbolic interactionist is Erving Goffman. Goffman's studies of mental 'asylums', processes of stigmatization and the ways in which people present their selves in social encounters have all become sociological classics, as much for their methodological and observational style as for their findings. In developing his 'dramaturgical analysis', which works with the metaphor of the theatre, Goffman's ideas have had a very wide influence on students across the world.

 See chapter 7, 'Social Interaction and Everyday Life', for a wider discussion of Goffman's perspective.

Phenomenology is a second interactionist perspective, which deals with the ways in which social life is actually experienced. Literally, it is the systematic study of phenomena; things as they appear in our experience. Its roots lie in the philosophical work of the German philosopher Edmund Husserl, though in sociological research, the Austrian-born philosopher and sociologist Alfred Schutz has been the more important figure. Schutz concentrated attention on people's experiences of everyday life and the ways in which they come to be

Children who struggle at school may be labelled as failures, which in turn can be a powerful force in shaping their concept of self.

taken-for-granted. Schutz calls this adopting a 'natural attitude'. For Schutz, the task of phenomenological sociology is to understand better how this happens and what its consequences are.

Schutz was particularly interested in *typifications* – the way that experienced phenomena are classified according to previous experience. Typification is commonplace. When we meet someone we will perhaps think, 'Oh she's *that* kind of person' or 'He seems an honest type'. Typification helps to order our world and make it more predictable. But if it becomes stereotypification, it can also be dangerous – the illegitimate generalization about people based simply on their membership of a certain social group. Examples include racism, sexism and negative attitudes towards all disabled people.

People also tend to make the assumption that everyone thinks in much the same way as they do, and they can therefore safely forget about possible problems of interpersonal communication. Once these kinds of assumption become internalized, they fade from view and become sedimented below the surface of conscious existence to form the basis of the natural attitude. In this way, people come to experience important aspects of the social world, such as language and culture, as objective and external to themselves. Phenomenology has not had the same impact on sociology as some of the other perspectives, though it did give rise to ethnomethodology.

Ethnomethodology – the systematic study of the methods used by 'natives' (members of a particular society) to construct their social worlds – is the third interactionist perspective. It traces its roots back to phenomenological philosophy, but only rose to prominence in the 1960s with the research studies of Harold Garfinkel and Aaron Cicourel. Ethnomethodologists were highly critical of mainstream sociology, particularly Parsonian structural function-alism, which Garfinkel saw as treating people as if they were 'cultural dopes' – passive recipients of society's socializing agents, rather than creative actors in their own right. Garfinkel took issue with Durkheim's famous statement that sociologists should 'treat social facts as things'. For Garfinkel, this should only be the starting point for ethnomethodological enquiry, not assumed in advance of it. This means that ethnomethodology seeks instead to uncover just how Durkheim's social facts are created by society's members.

> Ethnomethodology is discussed more widely in chapter 7, 'Social Interaction and Everyday Life'.

In contrast to many symbolic interactionist, phenomenological and ethnomethodological studies, the work of Max Weber appears to sit much more closely to the mainstream of sociology. Although he certainly was interested in social interactions and the micro level of social life, Weber's work on world religions, economic sociology and legal systems was also historically informed, strongly comparative in orientation and concerned with the overall development and direction of the modern world. This is in contrast to the interactionist tradition as it developed after Weber's death, which has become rather more exclusively focused on the micro level during the twentieth century.

Theoretical dilemmas

Controversies sparked by the work of the classical theorists, as well as by the later theoretical ideas and perspectives discussed above, continue today. But since the time of the classical sociologists, it has become commonplace to argue that their work, and that of sociology in general, has set up a series of theoretical dilemmas. There are several basic theoretical dilem-mas – matters of continuing or recurring controversy or dispute – which these clashes of viewpoint bring to our attention, some of which concern very general matters to do with how we should interpret human activities and social institutions. In short, these are questions about how we *can* or *should* 'do' sociology. We shall outline four such dilemmas here.

1   One dilemma concerns human action and social structure. The issue is the following: how far are we creative human actors, actively controlling the conditions of our own lives? Or is most of what we do the result of general social forces outside our control? This issue has always divided, and continues to divide, sociologists. Weber and the symbolic interactionists, for example, stress the active, creative components of human behaviour. Other approaches, such as that of Durkheim and functionalism, emphasize the constraining nature of social influences on our free actions.

2   A second theoretical controversy concerns consensus and conflict in society. Some standpoints in sociology, as we have seen – including functionalism – emphasize the inherent order and harmony of human societies. Those taking this view regard continuity and consensus as the most evident characteristics of societies, however much they may change over time. Other sociologists, such as Marxists, accentuate the pervasiveness of social conflict. They see societies as plagued with divisions, tensions and struggles. To them, it is illusory to claim that people tend to live amicably with one another most of the time; even when there are no open confrontations, they say, there remain deep divisions of interest, which at some point are liable to break out into active conflicts.

3   There is a third basic theoretical dilemma which hardly figures at all in the orthodox traditions of sociology, but

which cannot be ignored. This is the problem of how we are to incorporate a satisfactory understanding of gender within sociological analysis. The founding figures of sociology were all men, as we saw in chapter 1, and they paid virtually no attention to the fact that human beings are gendered. Even those women who were involved in sociology were, until recently, largely neglected. In the works of the early male sociologists, human individuals appear as if they were 'neuter' – they are abstract 'actors', rather than differentiated women and men. Since we have very little to build on in relating issues of gender to the more established forms of theoretical thinking in sociology, this is perhaps, at the current time, the most acutely difficult problem to grapple with.

One of the main theoretical dilemmas associated with gender is the following: should we build 'gender' as a general category into our sociological thinking? Or, alternatively, do we need to analyse gender issues by breaking them down into more specific influences affecting the behaviour of women and men in different contexts? We can put this in another way: are there characteristics that separate men and women, in terms of their identities and social behaviour, in all cultures? Or are gender differences always to be explained mainly in terms of other differences which divide societies (such as class divisions)?

4   A fourth problem concerns not so much the general characteristics of human behaviour or of societies as a whole, but rather features of modern social development. It is to do with the determining influences affecting the origins and nature of modern societies, and derives from the differences between non-Marxist and Marxist approaches. The dilemma centres on the following issue: how far has the modern world been shaped by the economic factors which Marx singled out – in particular, the mechanisms of capitalist economic enterprise? How far, on the other hand, have other influences – such as social, political or cultural factors – shaped social development in the modern era? These controversies are so fundamental for sociological theory that we shall consider the different ideas developed about them in some detail.

Social structure and human action

A major theme pursued by Durkheim, and many other sociologists since, is that the societies of which we are members exert social constraint over our actions. Durkheim argued that society has primacy over the individual person. Society is far more than the sum of individual acts; it has a 'firmness' or 'solidity' comparable to structures in the material environment. Think of a person standing in a room with several doors. The structure of the room constrains the range of her or his possible activities. The siting of the walls and the doors, for example, defines the routes of exit and entry. Social structure, according to Durkheim, constrains our activities in a parallel way, setting limits to what we can do as individuals. It is 'external' to us, just as the walls of the room are.

This point of view is expressed by Durkheim in a famous statement:

> When I perform my duties as a brother, a husband or a citizen and carry out the commitments I have entered into, I fulfil obligations which are defined in law and custom and which are external to myself and my actions. . . . Similarly, the believer has discovered from birth, ready fashioned, the beliefs and practices of his religious life; if they existed before he did, it follows that they exist outside him. The systems of signs that I employ to express my thoughts, the monetary system I use to pay my debts, the credit instruments I utilize in my commercial relationships, the practices I follow in my profession, etc. – all function independently of the use I make of them. (1982 [1895])

Although the type of view Durkheim expresses has many adherents, it has also met with sharp criticism. What is 'society', the critics ask, if it is not the composite of many individual actions? If we study a group, we do not see a collective entity, only individuals interacting with one another in various ways. What we call 'society' is only an aggregate of many individuals behaving in regular ways in relation to each other. According to the critics, including most sociologists influenced by symbolic interactionism, as human beings we have reasons for what we do, and we inhabit a social world permeated by cultural meanings. Social phenomena, according to them, are precisely *not* like 'things', but depend on the symbolic meanings with which we invest what we do. We are not the creatures of society, but its creators.

It is unlikely that this controversy will ever be fully resolved, since it has existed since modern thinkers first started systematically to try to explain human behaviour. Moreover, it is a debate which is not just confined to sociology, but preoccupies scholars in all fields of the social sciences. You must decide, in the light of your reading of this book, which position you think more nearly correct.

Yet the differences between the two views can be exaggerated. While both cannot be wholly right, we can fairly easily see connections between them. Durkheim's view is clearly in some respects valid. Social institutions do precede the existence of any given individual; it is also evident that they exert constraint over us. Thus, for example, I did not invent the monetary system which exists in Britain. Nor do I have a choice about whether I want to use it or not if I wish to have the goods and services that money can buy. The system of money, like all other established institutions, exists independently of every individual member of society, and it constrains the activities of each individual.

On the other hand, it is obviously mistaken to suppose that society is 'external' to us in the same way that the physical world is. For the physical world would go on existing whether or not any human beings were alive, whereas it would plainly be nonsensical to say this of society. While society is external to each individual taken singly, by definition it cannot be external to all individuals taken together.

Moreover, although what Durkheim calls 'social facts' might constrain what we do, they do not *determine* what we do. I could choose to live without using money, should I be firmly resolved to do so, even if it were to prove very difficult to eke out an existence from day to day. As human beings, we do make choices, and we do not simply respond passively to events around us. The way forward in bridging the gap between 'structure' and 'action' approaches is to recognize that we actively make and remake social structure during the course of our everyday activities. For example, the fact that I use the monetary system contributes in a minor, yet necessary, way to the very existence of that system. If everyone, or even the majority of people, at some point decided to avoid using money, the monetary system would dissolve.

As mentioned in chapter 1, a useful term for analysing this process of the active making and remaking of social structure is structuration. This is a concept which I (Anthony Giddens) have introduced into sociology in recent years. 'Structure' and 'action' are necessarily related to one another. Societies, communities or groups only have 'structure' insofar as people behave in regular and fairly predictable ways. On the other hand, 'action' is only possible because each of us, as an individual, possesses an enormous amount of socially structured knowledge.

The best way to explain this is through the example of language. To exist at all, language must be socially structured – there are properties of language use which every speaker must observe. What someone says in any given context, for instance, would not make sense unless it followed certain grammatical rules. Yet the structural qualities of language only exist insofar as individual language users actually follow those rules in practice. Language is constantly in the process of structuration.

Erving Goffman and other writers on social interaction (discussed in chapter 7) are quite right to suggest that all human agents are highly knowledgeable. We are what we are as human beings largely because we follow a complex set of conventions – for example, the rituals that strangers observe when passing by on the street. On the other hand, as we apply that knowledge ability to our actions, we give force and content to the very rules and conventions we draw on. Structuration always presumes what the author calls 'the duality of structure'. This means that all social action presumes the existence of structure. But at the same time, structure presumes action, because 'structure' depends on regularities of human behaviour.

THINKING CRITICALLY

How satisfactory do you think the concept of structuration is in resolving the structure-action problem? Does it mean that the interactionists are wrong – that there are social structures after all? If so, can structuration theory explain their emergence?

Consensus or conflict?

It is also useful to begin with Durkheim when contrasting the consensus and conflict viewpoints. Durkheim sees society as a set of interdependent parts. For most functionalist thinkers, in fact, society is treated as an integrated whole, composed of structures which mesh closely with one another. This is very much in accord with Durkheim's emphasis on the constraining, 'external' character of 'social facts'. However, the analogy here is not with the walls of a building, but with the physiology of the body.

A body consists of various specialized parts (such as the brain, heart, lungs, liver

and so forth), each of which contributes to sustaining the continuing life of the organism. These necessarily work in harmony with one another; if they do not, the life of the organism is under threat. So it is, according to Durkheim, with society. For a society to have a continuing existence over time, its specialized institutions (such as the political system, religion, the family and the educational system) must work in harmony with one another. The continuation of a society thus depends on cooperation, which in turn presumes a general consensus, or agreement, among its members over basic values.

Those who focus mainly on conflict have a very different outlook. Their guiding assumptions can easily be outlined using Marx's account of class conflict as an example. According to Marx, societies are divided into classes with unequal resources. Since such marked inequalities exist, there are divisions of interest, which are 'built into' the social system. These conflicts of interest at some point break out into active change. Not all of those influenced by this viewpoint concentrate on classes to the degree to which Marx did; other divisions are regarded as important in promoting conflict – for example, divisions between racial groups or political factions. Society is seen as essentially full of tension regardless of which conflict groups are stronger than others; even the most stable social system represents an uneasy balance of antagonistic groupings.

As with the case of structure and action, it is not likely that this theoretical debate can be completely brought to a close. Yet, once more, the difference between the consensus and conflict standpoints seems wider than it is. The two positions are by no means wholly incompatible. All societies probably involve some kind of general agreement over values, and all certainly involve conflict.

Moreover, as a general rule of sociological analysis we always have to examine the connections between consensus and conflict within social systems. The values held by different groups and the goals that their members pursue often reflect a mixture of common and opposed interests. For instance, even in Marx's portrayal of class conflict, different classes share some common interests as well as being pitted against one another. Thus capitalists depend on a labour force to work in their enterprises, just as workers depend on capitalists to provide their wages. Open conflict is not continuous in such circumstances; rather, sometimes what both sides have in common tends to override their differences, while in other situations the reverse is the case.

A useful concept which helps analyse the interrelations of conflict and consensus is that of ideology – values and beliefs which help secure the position of more powerful groups at the expense of less powerful ones. Power, ideology and conflict are always closely connected. Many conflicts are about power, because of the rewards it can bring. Those who hold most power may depend mainly on the influence of ideology to retain their dominance, but are usually also able to use force if necessary. For instance, in feudal times aristocratic rule was supported by the idea that a minority of people were 'born to govern', but aristocratic rulers often resorted to the use of violence against those who dared to oppose their power.

The neglected issue of gender

Issues of gender scarcely feature in the writings of the major figures who established the framework of modern sociology. The few passages in which they did touch on gender questions, however, allow us at least to specify the outlines of a basic theoretical dilemma – even if there is little in their works to help us try to resolve it. We can best describe this dilemma by contrasting a theme which occasionally occurs in Durkheim's writings with one that appears in those of Marx. Durkheim (1952 [1897]) notes at one point, in the course of his discussion of suicide, that man is 'almost entirely the product of society', while woman is 'to a far greater extent the product of nature'. Expanding on these observations, he says of man: 'his tastes, aspirations and humour have in large part a collective origin, while his companion's are more directly influenced by her organism. His needs, therefore, are quite different from hers.' In other words, women and men have different identities, tastes and inclinations because women are less socialized and are 'closer to nature' than men.

No one today would accept a view stated in quite this manner. Female identity is as much shaped by socialization as that of males. Yet, when modified somewhat, Durkheim's claim does represent one possible view of the formation and nature of gender. This is that gender differences rest fundamentally on biologically given distinctions between men and women. Such a view does not necessarily mean believing that gender differences are mostly inborn. Rather, it presumes that women's social position and identity are mainly shaped by their involvement in reproduction and childrearing. If this view is correct, differences of gender are deeply embedded in all societies. The discrepancies in power between women and men reflect the fact that women bear children and are their primary caretakers, whereas men are active in the 'public' spheres of politics, work and war.

Marx's view is substantially at odds with this. For Marx, gender differences in power and status between men and women mainly reflect other divisions, especially, in his eyes, class divisions. According to him, in the earliest forms of human society neither gender nor class divisions were present. The power of men over women only came about as class divisions appeared. Women came to be a form of 'private property' owned by men, through the institution of marriage. Women will be freed from their situation of bondage when class divisions are overcome. Again, few if any would accept this analysis today, but we can make it more plausible by further generalizing it. Class is not the only factor shaping social divisions which affects the behaviour of men and women. Other factors include ethnicity and cultural background. For instance, it might be argued that women in a minority group (say, black people in the United States) have more in common with men in that minority group than they do with women in the majority (that is, with white women). Or it may be the case that women from a particular culture (like a small hunting and gathering culture) share more common characteristics with the males of that culture than they do with women in an industrial society.

The issues involved in this third dilemma are highly important, and bear directly on the challenge that feminist authors have thrown down to sociology. No one can seriously dispute that a great deal of sociological analysis in the past has either ignored women or has operated with interpretations of female identity and behaviour that are drastically inadequate. In spite of all the new research on women carried out in sociology over the past 20 years, there are still many areas in which the distinctive activities and concerns of women have been insufficiently studied. But 'bringing the study of women into sociology' is not in and of itself the same as coping with problems of gender, because gender concerns the relations between the identities and behaviour of women and men. For the moment, it has to be left as an open question how far gender differences can be illuminated by means of other sociological concepts (class, ethnicity, cultural background and so forth), or how far, on the contrary, other social divisions need to be explained in terms of gender. Certainly some of the major explanatory tasks of sociology in the future will depend on tackling this dilemma effectively.

The direction of social change

The Marxist perspective

As we saw earlier in the chapter, Marx's writings threw down a powerful challenge to sociological analysis, which has not been ignored. From his own time to the present day, many sociological debates have centred on Marx's ideas about the development of modern societies. Marx sees modern societies as capitalistic and the driving impulse behind social change in the modern era is the pressure towards constant economic transformation, which is an integral part of capitalist production. Capitalism is a vastly more dynamic economic system than any preceding one. Capitalists compete with one another to sell their goods to consumers, and, in order to survive in a competitive market, firms have to produce their wares as cheaply and efficiently as possible. This leads to constant technological innovation, because increasing the effectiveness of the technology used in a particular production process is one way in which companies can secure an edge over their rivals.

There are also strong incentives to seek out new markets in which to sell goods, acquire cheap raw materials and make use of cheap labour power. Capitalism, therefore, according to Marx, is a restlessly expanding system, pushing outwards across the world. This is how Marx explains the spread of Western industry globally.

Marx's interpretation of the influence of capitalism has found many supporters, and subsequent authors have considerably refined Marx's own portrayal. On the other hand, numerous critics have set out to rebut his view, offering alternative analyses of the influences shaping the modern world. Virtually everyone accepts that capitalism has played a major part in creating the world in which we live. But other sociologists have argued both that Marx exaggerated the impact of purely economic factors in producing change, and that capitalism is less central to modern social development

---

Marx and Weber on the shaping of the modern world

Broadly Weberian ideas

1. The main dynamic of modern development is the expansion of capitalistic economic mechanisms.
2. Modern societies are riven with class inequalities, which are basic to their very nature.
3. Major divisions of power, like those affecting the differential position of men and women, derive ultimately from economic inequalities.
4. Modern societies (capitalist societies) are a transitional type – we may expect them to become radically reorganized in the future. Socialism will eventually replace capitalism.
5. The spread of Western influence across the world is mainly a result of the expansionist tendencies of capitalist enterprise.

Broadly Marxist ideas

1. The main dynamic of modern development is the rationalization of production.
2. Class is one type of inequality among many – such as inequalities between men and women – in modern societies.
3. Power in the economic system is separable from other sources. For instance, male–female inequalities cannot be explained in economic terms.
4. Rationalization is bound to progress further in the future, in all spheres of social life. All modern societies are dependent on the same basic modes of social and economic organization.
5. The global impact of the West comes from its command over industrial resources, together with superior military power.

---

than he claimed. Most of these writers have also been sceptical of Marx's belief that a socialist system would eventually replace capitalism.

Weber's alternative view

One of Marx's earliest and most acute critics was Max Weber, whose writings have sometimes been described as involving a lifelong struggle with 'the ghost of Marx' – that is, with the intellectual legacy that Marx left behind. The alternative position, which Weber worked out, remains important today. According to him, *non-economic* factors have played a key role in modern social development. This argument, in fact, is one of the main points of his book, *The Protestant Ethic and the Spirit of Capitalism*. Religious values – especially those associated with Puritanism – were of fundamental importance in creating a capitalistic outlook. This outlook did not emerge, as Marx supposed, from economic changes as such.

Weber's understanding of the nature of modern societies and the reasons for the spread of Western ways of life across the world, contrasts substantially with that of Marx. According to Weber, capitalism – a distinct way of organizing economic enterprise – is one among other major factors shaping social development in the modern period. Underlying capitalistic economic mechanisms, and in some ways more fundamental than them, is the impact of science and bureaucracy. Science has shaped modern technology – and will presumably continue to do so in any future socialist society. Bureaucracy is the only way of organizing large numbers of people effectively, and therefore inevitably expands with economic and political growth. Weber refers to the development of science, modern technology and bureaucracy collectively as 'rationalization'. Rationalization means the organization of social and economic life according to principles of efficiency, on the basis of technical knowledge.

Marx or Weber?

Which type of interpretation of modern societies, that deriving from Marx or that coming from Weber, is correct? Again, scholars are divided on the issue. And it must be remembered that within each camp there are variations, so not every theorist on each side will agree with the others. The contrasts between Marxist and Weberian standpoints inform many areas of sociology. They influence not only how we analyse the nature of the industrialized societies, but our view of less developed societies also.

In addition, the two perspectives are linked to differing political positions, with authors on the left on the whole adopting views on the first side, liberals and conservatives those on the second side. Yet the factors with which this particular dilemma is concerned are of a more directly empirical nature than those involved in the other dilemmas. Factual studies of the paths of evolution of modern societies and less developed countries help us assess how far patterns of change conform to one side or the other.

The transformation of societies – and sociology

The dilemma of how the modern world was shaped is still important, but more recent theorists have tried to go beyond both Marx and Weber. Yet other sociologists, including postmodernists (some of whom were originally Marxists), now discount Marx altogether. They believe that his attempt to find general patterns of history was inevitably doomed to failure. For such postmodern thinkers, sociologists should simply give up on the sorts of theory that both Marx and Weber sought to develop – overall interpretations of social change or what we have here called 'grand theory'. Many sociologists now view contemporary societies as developing in ways that the classical theorists could not have foreseen. This is why they have come to the conclusion that it may be time to develop alternative ways of thinking about and theorizing the globalizing social world in which, increasingly, we all live.

Judith Butler's ideas on the performance of gender have been influential in undermining essentialist notions of gender identity.

Gender equality and feminist theory

The rise of the women's movement led to some radical changes within sociology and other disciplines. Feminism has led to a broad-based assault on the perceived male bias both in sociological theory and methodology, and in the very subject matter of sociology. Look back at figure 3.1 (page 71) and count the number of women in the chart to see just how male-dominated sociology has been. Not only has this male domination of sociology been challenged, but there have also been calls for a comprehensive reconstruction of the discipline itself – both the questions that form its core and the presentation of discussions surrounding them.

Feminist perspectives in sociology emphasize the centrality of gender in analysing the social world. While the diversity of feminist viewpoints makes it difficult to speak in generalities, we can safely say that most feminists agree that knowledge is integrally related to questions of sex and gender. Because men and women have different experiences and view the world from different perspectives, they do not construct their understandings of the world in identical ways. Feminists often charge that traditional sociological theory has denied or ignored the 'gendered' nature of knowledge and has instead projected conceptions of the social world, which are male-dominated. Males have traditionally occupied positions of power and authority in society and have an investment in maintaining their privileged roles, according to feminists. Under such conditions, gendered knowledge becomes a vital force in perpetuating established social arrangements and legitimating male domination.

 Feminism approaches in sociology are discussed further in chapter 14, 'Sexuality and Gender'.

Some feminist writers have argued that it is a mistake to suppose that either 'men' or 'women' are groups with their own interests or characteristics. Several of these writers, such as Donna Haraway (1989, 1991), Hélène Cixous (1976) and Judith Butler (1990, 1997, 2004), have been influenced by poststructuralist and postmodern thinking, which is discussed further below. According to Butler, gender is not a fixed category, an essence, but a fluid one, exhibited in what people *do* rather than what they *are*. If, as Butler (1990) argues, gender is something

that is 'done' or performed, then it is also something that we should fight to 'undo' when it is used by one group to exert power over another (see chapter 7, 'Social Interaction and Everyday Life').

Susan Faludi has also pursued the theme of gender identity. In *Stiffed: The Betrayal of Modern Man* (2000), a book on masculinity, Faludi shows that the idea that men dominate in all spheres is a myth. On the contrary, there is something of a crisis of masculinity today in the world that men supposedly own and run. Some groups of men are still confident and feel in control; many others find themselves marginalized and lacking in self-respect. The success that at least some women have achieved is part of the reason, but so too are changes in the nature of work. The impact of information technology, for example, has made many less-skilled men redundant to society's needs, while the shift towards the service sector has led to a 'feminization of the workplace', which many men seem reluctant to enter.

 See chapter 20, 'Work and Economic Life', for a discussion of service employment.

Feminist theory has changed and developed markedly since the 1980s and the themes it pursues are very different from those that emerged from within 1960s feminist movements. Whilst the latter saw feminism as a movement primarily concerned with equalizing the life chances of men and women, today feminist and queer theory question what exactly men and women are. Is there, in fact, any essential gendered being at all? The main issue for contemporary feminist theory may well be whether such questions are able to connect with the lives of women in both the developed and developing societies (see Shiva 1993).

Feminist movements are discussed further in chapter 22, 'Politics, Government and Social Movements'.

THINKING CRITICALLY

From your own experience, has substantial gender equality now been achieved in the developed world? Is there still a place for feminist movements and theory in an age of broad gender equality? Thinking more critically, what issues should feminists concentrate on today if they are to tap into the concerns of younger women ?

Poststructuralism and postmodernity

Michel Foucault and poststructuralism

Michel Foucault (1926–84), Jacques Derrida (1976, 1978) and Julia Kristeva (1974, 1977) are the most influential figures in an intellectual movement known as **poststructuralism**. However, it is the work of Foucault that has had by far the most influence on sociology and the social sciences. In his work, he attempted to illustrate shifts of understanding which separate thinking in our modern world from that of earlier ages. In his writings on crime, the body, madness and sexuality, Foucault analysed the emergence of modern institutions such as prisons, hospitals and schools that have played an increasing role in controlling and monitoring the social population. He wanted to show that there was 'another side' to Enlightenment ideas about individual liberty – one concerned with discipline and surveillance. Foucault advanced important ideas about the relationship between power, ideology and discourse in relation to modern organizational systems.

The study of power – how individuals and groups achieve their ends against those of others – is of fundamental importance in sociology. Marx and Weber, among the classical founders, laid particular emphasis on power; Foucault continued some of the lines of thought they pioneered. The role of

discourse is central to his thinking about power and control in society. He used the term to refer to ways of talking or thinking about particular subjects that are united by common assumptions. Foucault demonstrated, for example, the dramatic way in which discourses of madness changed from medieval times through to the present day. In the Middle Ages, for example, the insane were generally regarded as harmless; some believed that they may even have possessed a special 'gift' of perception. In modern societies, however, 'madness' has been shaped by a medicalized discourse, which emphasizes illness and treatment. This medicalized discourse is supported and perpetuated by a highly developed and influential network of doctors, medical experts, hospitals, professional associations and medical journals.

 Foucault's work is discussed in more detail in chapter 10, 'Health, Illness and Disability'.

According to Foucault, power works through discourse to shape popular attitudes towards phenomena such as crime, madness or sexuality. Expert discourses established by those with power or authority can often be countered only by competing expert discourses. In such a way, discourses can be used as a powerful tool to restrict alternative ways of thinking or speaking. Knowledge becomes a force of control. A prominent theme throughout Foucault's writings is the way power and knowledge are linked to technologies of surveillance, enforcement and discipline.

Foucault's radical new approach to social theory stands in opposition to the general consensus about the nature of scientific knowledge. This approach, which characterized many of his early works, has become known as Foucault's 'archaeology' of knowledge. Unlike other social scientists, who aim to make sense of the unfamiliar by drawing analogies with that which is familiar, Foucault set about the opposite task: to make sense of the familiar by digging into the past.

He energetically attacked the present – the taken-for-granted concepts, beliefs and structures which are largely invisible precisely because they are familiar. For example, he explored how the notion of 'sexuality' has not always existed, but has been created through processes of social development. Similar comments can be made about our modern-day conceptions of normal and deviant activity, of sanity and madness, and so forth. Foucault attempted to reveal the assumptions behind our current beliefs and practices and to make the present 'visible' by accessing it from the past. However, we cannot have general theories about society, social development or modernity; we can only understand fragments of them.

The postmodern turn in social theory

Since the mid-1980s, advocates of postmodernism claim that the classic social thinkers took their inspiration from the idea that history has a shape – it 'goes somewhere' and leads to progress. But this notion has now collapsed. There are no longer any 'grand narratives' or 'metanarratives' – overall conceptions of history or society – that make any sense (Lyotard 1985). Not only is there no general notion of progress that can be defended, there is also no such thing as history. The postmodern world is not destined, as Marx hoped, to be a socialist one. Instead, it is one dominated by the new media, which 'take us out' – disembed us – from our past.

Postmodern society is highly pluralistic and diverse. In countless films, videos, TV programmes and websites, images circulate around the world. We come into contact with many ideas and values, but these have little connection with the history of the areas in which we live, or indeed with our own personal histories. Everything seems constantly in flux. As one group of authors expressed things:

> Our world is being remade. Mass production, the mass consumer, the big city, big-brother state, the sprawling housing estate, and the nation-state are in decline: flexibility, diversity, differentiation, and mobility, communication, decentralisation and internationalisation are in the ascendant. In the process our own identities, our sense of self, our own subjectivities are being transformed. We are in transition to a new era. (Hall and Jacques 1988)

One important theorist of postmodernity is the French author Jean Baudrillard (whose work is discussed in more detail in chapter 17, 'The Media'). Baudrillard believes that the electronic media have destroyed our relationship to the past and created a chaotic, empty world. He was strongly influenced by Marxism in his early years. However, he argues that the spread of electronic communication and the mass media has reversed the Marxist theorem that economic forces shape society. Instead, social life is influenced, above all, by signs and images.

In a media-dominated age, Baudrillard says, meaning is created by the flow of images, as in TV programmes. Much of our world has become a sort of make-believe universe in which we are responding to media images rather than to real persons or places. Thus when Diana, Princess of Wales, died in 1997, there was an enormous outpouring of grief, not only in Britain but all over the world. Yet were people mourning a real person? Baudrillard would say not. Princess Diana existed for most people only through the media. Her death was more like an event in a soap opera than a real event in the way in which people experienced it; Baudrillard speaks of 'the dissolution of life into TV'.

Polish sociologist Zygmunt Bauman (1992) offers a helpful distinction, offering two ways of thinking about postmodern ideas. On the one hand, we could argue that the social world has rapidly moved in a postmodern direction. The enormous growth and spread of the mass media, new information technologies, more fluid movement of people across the world and the development of multicultural societies: all of these

Postmodern theory is exemplified by Baudrillard's ideas on the domination of social life by the mass media, particularly television.

ment to rationally shape society no longer makes sense, at least not in the way thought possible by Comte, Marx or other classical theorists. However, since the turn of the century he has moved away from the term 'postmodern' – which he says has become corrupted through too diverse usage – and now describes our world as one of 'Liquid Modernity', reflecting the fact that it is in constant flux and uncertainty *in spite of* all attempts to impose (a modern) order and stability onto it (Bauman 2000, 2007).

One staunch critic of postmodern theory is Jürgen Habermas (1983), who argued that now is not the time to give up on the 'project' of modernity. He sees modernity as 'an incomplete project' and instead of resigning it to the dustbin of history, we should be extending it: pushing for more democracy, more freedom and more rational policies. Postmodernists were essentially pessimists and defeatists. It does seem that postmodern analyses are now losing ground to the theory of globalization, which has become the dominant theoretical framework for understanding the direction of social change in the twenty-first century.

> ### THINKING CRITICALLY
>
> Postmodern theory suggests that the 'project of modernity', with its ideas of reason, rationality and progress, is dead. List all the social changes which could support such a view. Does this list amount to the kind of fundamental social transformation identified by Baudrillard and others?

Globalization, risk and the 'revenge' of nature

mean that we no longer live in a modern world, but in a postmodern one. Modernity is dead and we are entering a period of post-modernity. The question then is, can a modern sociology adequately analyse a postmodern world? Is a *sociology of post-modernity* possible? The second view is that the postmodern changes above cannot be analysed using old sociological theories and concepts and we need to devise new ones. In short, we need a *postmodern sociology* for a postmodern world.

Bauman accepts that the modern project that originated in the European Enlighten-

The theory of globalization will be discussed extensively in chapter 4 and we will not anticipate that discussion here. Instead, we will look at three significant contemporary theories, which assume that globalization is rapidly changing human societies. These theories are chosen as representative of sociologists who reject the radical postmodern idea of the death of modernity, but seek new ways of theorizing the changes globalization brings. You will have to decide whether such theories give us any more purchase on the direction of contemporary social change than the classical traditions built on the work of Marx, Durkheim and Weber.

Manuel Castells: the network economy

Manuel Castells began his academic career as a Marxist. As an expert on urban affairs, he sought to apply Marx's ideas to the study of cities. In recent years, however, Castells has moved away from Marxism. Like Baudrillard, he has become concerned with the impact of media and communications technologies. The information society, Castells argues, is marked by the rise of networks and a network economy. The new economy, which depends on the connections made possible by global communications, is certainly capitalist. However, the capitalist economy and society of today are quite different from those of the past. The expansion of capitalism is no longer based primarily, as Marx thought it would be, either on the working class or the manufacture of material goods. Instead, telecommunications and computers are the basis of production.

> Castells' ideas on the 'network society' are discussed more fully in chapter 18, 'Organizations and Networks'.

Castells does not reveal much about how these changes are affecting gender relations. However, he does say a good deal about their effects on personal identity and everyday life. In the network society, personal identity becomes a much more open matter. We do not any longer take our identities from the past; we have actively to create them in interacting with others. This directly affects the sphere of the family and also more generally the structuring of male and female identities. Men and women no longer get their identities from traditional roles. Thus women's 'place' was once in the home, whereas that of men was to be 'out at work'. That division has now broken down.

Castells calls the new global economy the 'automaton' – he thinks that we no longer fully control the world we have created. His statements here echo those made a century earlier by Weber, who thought that the increase in bureaucracy would imprison us all in an 'iron cage'. As Castells puts it: 'Humankind's nightmare of seeing our machines taking control of our world seems on the edge of becoming reality – not in the form of robots that eliminate jobs or government computers that police our lives, but as an electronically based system of financial transactions' (2000: 56).

Yet Castells has not forgotten his Marxist roots altogether. He thinks that it may be possible to regain more effective control of the global marketplace. This will not come through any sort of revolution, but through the collective efforts of international organizations and countries which have a common interest in regulating international capitalism. Information technology, Castells concludes, can often be a means of local empowerment and community renewal. He quotes as an example the case of Finland. Finland is the most developed information society in the world. All schools in the country have Internet access and most of the population is computer literate. At the same time, Finland has a well-established and effective welfare state, which has been adapted to meet the needs of the new economy.

Anthony Giddens on social reflexivity

In my own writings, I also develop a theoretical perspective on the changes happening in the present-day world. We live today in what I call a 'runaway world', a world marked by new risks and uncertainties of the sort diagnosed by Beck (1999). But we should place the notion of trust alongside that of risk. Trust refers to the confidence we have either in individuals or in institutions.

In a world of rapid transformation, traditional forms of trust tend to become dissolved. Trust in other people used to be based in the local community. Living in a more globalized society, however, our lives are influenced by people we never see or meet, who may be living on the far side of the world from us. Trust means having confidence in 'abstract systems' – for example, we have to have confidence in agencies for food regulation, the purification of water or the effectiveness of banking systems. Trust and risk are closely bound up with one another. We need to have confidence in such authorities if we are to confront the risks which surround us, and react to them in an effective way.

Living in an information age, in my view, means an increase in social reflexivity. Social reflexivity refers to the fact that we have constantly to think about, or reflect upon, the circumstances in which we live our lives. When societies were more geared to custom and tradition, people could follow established ways of doing things in a more unreflective fashion. For us, many aspects of life that for earlier generations were simply taken for granted become matters of open decision-making. For example, for hundreds of years people had no effective ways of limiting the size of their families. With modern forms of contraception, and other forms of technological involvement in reproduction, parents can not only choose how many children they have, but can even decide what sex their children will be. These new possibilities, of course, are fraught with new ethical dilemmas.

We have not *inevitably* lost control of our own future. In a global age, nations certainly lose some of the power they used to have. For instance, countries have less influence over economic policy than they once had. However, governments retain a good deal of power. Acting collaboratively, nations can get together to reassert their influence over

the runaway world. The groups to which Beck points – agencies and movements working outside the formal framework of politics – can have an important role. But they will not supplant orthodox democratic politics. Democracy is still crucial, because groups in the area of 'sub-politics' make divergent claims and have different interests. Such groups may include, for example, those who are actively campaigning in favour of more tolerance of abortion, and those who believe entirely the opposite. Democratic government must assess and react to these varying claims and concerns.

There is a potential 'democracy of the emotions' emerging in everyday life. A democracy of the emotions refers to the emergence of forms of family life in which men and women participate in an equal fashion. Virtually all forms of traditional family were based on the dominance of men over women, something that was usually sanctioned in law. The increasing equality between the sexes cannot be limited only to the right to vote; it must also involve the personal and intimate sphere. The democratizing of personal life advances to the degree to which relationships are founded on mutual respect, communication and tolerance.

Ulrich Beck and ecological politics in an age of risk

Another German sociologist, Ulrich Beck, also rejects postmodernism. Rather than living in a world 'beyond the modern', we are moving into a phase of what he calls 'the second modernity'. The second modernity refers to the fact that modern institutions are becoming global, while everyday life is breaking free from the hold of tradition and custom. The old industrial society is disappearing and is being replaced by a 'risk society'. What the postmodernists see as chaos, or lack of pattern, Beck sees as risk or uncertainty. The management of risk is the prime feature of the global order.

Beck is not arguing that the contemporary world is more risky than that of previous ages. Rather, it is the nature of the risks we must face that is changing. Risk now derives less from natural dangers or hazards than from uncertainties created by our own social development and by the development of science and technology. For example, global warming – or climate change – represents possibly the most serious environmental issue today. But the scientific consensus is that this is not a simple natural disaster, but the product of excessive greenhouse gases from industrial pollution and modern transportation emissions over the past 250 years. Popular science writers have dubbed such reactions, the 'revenges of nature'.

The advance of science and technology creates new risk situations that are very different from those of previous ages. Science and technology obviously provide many benefits for us. Yet they create risks that are hard to measure. Thus no one quite knows, for example, what the risks involved in the development of new technologies, such as genetic modification or nanotechnology, might be. Supporters of genetically modified crops, for example, claim that at best they give us the possibility of ending malnutrition in the world's poorest countries and providing cheap food for everyone. Sceptics claim that they could have dangerous, unintended health consequences.

> Beck's ideas on risk are discussed in more detail in chapter 5, 'The Environment'.

According to Beck, an important aspect of the risk society is that its hazards are not restricted spatially, temporally or socially. Today's risks affect all countries and all social classes; they have global, not merely personal, consequences. Many forms of manufactured risk, such as those to do with terrorism or pollution for example, cross national boundaries. The explosion at the Chernobyl nuclear power plant in Ukraine in 1986 provides a clear illustration of this point. Everyone living in the immediate vicinity of Chernobyl – regardless of age, class, gender or status – was exposed to dangerous levels of radiation. At the same time, the effects of the accident stretched far beyond Chernobyl itself; throughout Europe and beyond, abnormally high levels of radiation were detected long after the explosion.

Many decisions taken at the level of everyday life also become infused with risk. Risk and gender relations are actually closely linked, for example, as many new uncertainties have entered the relationships between the sexes (see chapter 9, 'Families and Intimate Relationships'). One example concerns the areas of love and marriage. A generation ago, in the developed societies, marriage was a fairly straightforward process of life transition – people moved from being unmarried to being married, and this was assumed to be a fairly permanent situation. Today, many people live together without getting married and divorce rates are high. Anyone contemplating a relationship with another person must take these facts into account, and is therefore involved in risk calculations. The individual must judge his or her likelihood of gaining happiness and security against this uncertain backdrop.

The threat of terrorism provides another example of how risk affects our society. The self-defined 'Islamic' terrorist attacks on New York and Washington in 2001, Bali in 2002, Casablanca and Madrid in 2004, London in 2005 and many more all changed the extent to which people thought of their communities as being at risk from violence. The fear of terrorism created inertia in economies around the world, particularly in the months after September 2001, as businesses became reluctant to risk large-scale investment. The terrorist attacks also changed the assessment that states made over the balance between the freedom of its citizens and their security.

In recent years, Beck's thinking has followed that of others (Vertovec and Cohen 2002; Benhabib 2006), developing into a

Shaira Khatoon lost both her eyes in an industrial disaster at a pesticide plant in Bhopal, India, in 1984. More than 15,000 people lost their lives in the month following the toxic explosion and some 500,000 were left permanently injured.

theory of **cosmopolitanism** (Beck 2006; Beck and Grande 2007). Beck's version of cosmopolitanism begins from a critique of 'nation-state-based' thinking; that is, theories within the social sciences which take national societies as the main unit of analysis. In *The Cosmopolitan Vision* (2006: 18) Beck argues that this 'national outlook', now 'fails to grasp that political, economic and cultural action and their (intended and unintended) consequences know no borders'. In our age of globalization, where national borders are becoming more permeable and individual states are less powerful, social reality is being transformed in a thoroughly cosmopolitan direction. This process of 'cosmopolitanization' is occurring even behind the backs of sociologists who continue to think in terms of national societies and their international relationships. If allowed to develop without direction, cosmopolitanization presents as many threats as opportunities, particularly for those who are exploited by multinational corporations traversing the globe seeking cheaper labour and maximal profits.

Beck argues that the nation-state is no longer able to cope in a world of global risks. Instead, there must be transnational cooperation between states. The narrow viewpoint of the nation-state becomes an impediment when it comes to dealing with new risks, such as global warming. When it comes to fighting against international terrorism, we must ask what we are fighting *for*. His ideal is a cosmopolitan system based on the acknowledgement and acceptance of cultural diversity. Cosmopolitan states do not fight only against terrorism, but also against the *causes* of terrorism in the world. To Beck, they provide the most positive way to deal with global problems, which appear insoluble at the level of the individual state, but manageable through cooperation.

The social changes of recent decades do not spell the end of attempts at social and political reform. Beck argues to the contrary: new forms of activism are appearing. We see the emergence of a new field of what Beck calls 'sub-politics'. This refers to the activities of groups and agencies operating outside the formal mechanisms of democratic politics, such as ecological, consumer or human rights groups. Responsibility for risk management cannot be left to politicians or scientists alone: other groups of citizens need to be brought in. Groups and movements that develop in the arena of sub-politics, however, can have a big influence on orthodox political mechanisms. For instance, responsibility for the environment, which was previously the province of ecological activists, has now been accepted as part of the conventional political framework.

Beck concedes that thinking in universal or cosmopolitan terms is not really new. Previously, the idea of citizenship beyond the nation-state was the preserve of well travelled and well-connected social elites who *voluntarily* chose to see themselves as 'Europeans', for example, or as 'citizens of the world'. But this form of cosmopolitanism now has much stronger roots in reality and is therefore potentially more effective. Beck argues that it is not enough for sociologists simply to analyse the emerging cosmopolitan world society; they should also be involved in shaping it in positive directions if the problems associated with globalization are to be tackled.

Conclusion: out with the old, in with the new?

Perhaps today we are at the beginning of a major new phase in the development of sociological theorizing. The ideas of the classic thinkers – Marx, Durkheim and Weber – were formed during times of great social, political and economic change, which their theories sought to understand. We are now living through a period of global transformation that is probably just as profound and yet is much more widely felt across larger areas of the world. We seem to need new theories to help us understand and explain the new developments that are transforming our societies today.

But this conclusion does not necessarily mean we should abandon the older theoretical perspectives altogether. Sociological theory cannot be successful if it only develops through internal debate. It has to give us insights into the key issues of the day and must be empirically adequate as well as internally coherent. What is likely to be more productive is to bring the older perspectives into contact with the new, in order to test and compare their effectiveness in helping us understand and explain the dramatic changes we are living through.

THINKING CRITICALLY

Beck argues that we are moving into a global risk society. What are the implications of the environmental risks discussed above for the world's developing countries? Why might environmental risks be more evenly distributed globally than, say, poverty and malnutrition?

Summary points

1. A diversity of theoretical approaches is found in sociology. The reason for this is not particularly puzzling: theoretical disputes are difficult to resolve even in the natural sciences, and in sociology we face special difficulties because of the complex problems involved in subjecting our own behaviour to study. However, the dominance of Parsonian functionalism in the 1950 and '60s shows us that things have not always been this way and may change again in the future. Sociological theorizing needs to remain close to the central problems of the day in order to stay relevant.

2. Clashes of viewpoint in sociology bring to our attention several basic theoretical dilemmas. An important one concerns how we should relate human action to social structure. Are we the creators of society, or created by it? The choice between these alternatives is not as stark as it may initially appear, and the real problem is how to relate the two aspects of social life to one another.

3. A second dilemma concerns whether societies should be pictured as harmonious and orderly, or whether they should be seen as marked by persistent conflict. Again, the two views are not completely opposed, and we need to show how consensus and conflict interrelate.

4. A third basic dilemma concerns gender, and in particular whether we should build it as a general category into our sociological thinking. Feminist theorists have brought changes both in what sociologists think about, and in the way they think it.

5. A fourth dilemma is to do with the analysis of modern social development. Are processes of change in the modern world mainly shaped by capitalist economic development or by other factors, including non-economic ones? Positions taken in this debate are influenced to some extent by the political beliefs and attitudes held by different sociologists.

6. In tackling the issues of social development, recent theorists have tried to go beyond both Marx and Weber. Postmodern thinkers deny that we can develop any general theories of history or society at all, but these are now losing ground to theories of globalization.

7. Other theorists are critical of postmodernism, arguing that we can still develop overall theories of the social world, and in a way that will enable us to intervene to shape it for the better. Castells, Beck and Giddens are amongst this more recent strand of theorizing, which attempts to develop new ways of theorizing for a global age.

Further reading

Books on social and sociological theory are amongst the most numerous of any subject in sociology, so there should something to suit everyone's taste. For a well-written introduction to the theories discussed in this chapter, try Pip Jones, *Introducing Social Theory* (Cambridge: Polity, 2003). An alternative is Shaun Best's *A Beginner's Guide to Social Theory* (London: Sage, 2002). A different approach is taken by Steven Miles in *Social Theory in the Real World* (London: Sage, 2001), which shows how theory can help us to understand the world we live in.

From here, a somewhat more challenging text is Derek Layder's *Understanding Social Theory*, 2nd edn (London: Sage, 2005), which is very good on critical commentary. George Ritzer's *Sociological Theory*, 7th edn (Maidenhead: McGraw-Hill, 2007) is a similarly excellent book by a renowned expert in sociological theory.

For the more contemporary theorists, Austin Harrington's (ed.) *Modern Social Theory: An Introduction* (Buckingham: Open University Press, 2004) is a useful collection, and for the classical theorists, Kenneth Morrison's *Marx, Durkheim, Weber: Formations of Modern Social Thought* (London: Sage, 2006) is deservedly into its second edition.

Of course, at some point it will be necessary to consult the ideas of the theorists in this chapter in their original texts. Ultimately this is the only way to form your own assessment of their relative merits and for that reason is strongly recommended.

Internet links

The Dead Sociologists' Society – sadly, exactly what it says. Very good resources on the classical theorists:
http://media.pfeiffer.edu/lridener/DSS/DEADSOC.HTML.

Feminist theories and perspectives:
www.cddc.vt.edu/feminism/enin.html

The Frankfurt School of Critical Theory:
www.marxists.org/subject/frankfurt-school/index.htm

Phenomenologists and ethnomethodologists:
www.phenomenologyonline.com/scholars/scholars.html

A series of webpages below devoted to the work of some individual theorists:
Jean Baudrillard – http://englishscholar.com/baudrillard.htm
Judith Butler – www.theory.org.uk/ctr-butl.htm
Ulrich Beck – www.lse.ac.uk/collections/sociology/whoswho/beck.htm
Manuel Castells – http://sociology.berkeley.edu/faculty/castells/
Michel Foucault – www.foucault.info/documents/
Anthony Giddens – http://old.lse.ac.uk/collections/meetthedirector.20031001/
Erving Goffman – www.mdx.ac.uk/WWW/STUDY/xgof.htm

4

Globalization and the Changing World

CHAPTER 4

• •

Globalization and the Changing World

(opposite) A view of the Pyramids at Giza through a Pizza Hut window, juxtaposing one of the earliest civilizations with twenty-first-century life.

• •

Planet Earth, geologists tell us, is a barely imaginable four and a half *billion* years old. Human beings have existed on earth for less than half a million years or so. Agriculture, the necessary basis of fixed settlements, is much more recent, being just 12,000 years old. Large-scale human civilizations date back no more than 6,000 years. If we can think of the entire span of human existence thus far as a 24-hour day, agriculture would have come into existence at 11.56 p.m. – four minutes to midnight – and civilizations at 11.57 p.m. Over this very long timescale of human history, human beings gradually spread into most parts of the planet as relationships between human groups became more regular and often riven with conflicts (Mennell 1990). This global development of humanity has occupied most of human history.

The development of modern societies would get under way only at 11.59 and 30 seconds. Yet the last 30 seconds of this human day have arguably produced more rapid social and environmental change than in all the time leading up to it. The period sociologists call **modernity** has witnessed a much more *rapid* globalization of social life, connecting large-scale societies together in a whole variety of ways, from long-range economic exchanges and international political agreements to global tourism, electronic communications technology and more fluid migration patterns. In all these ways, people across the world have become more interconnected and interdependent than in previous times.

The sheer pace of change in the modern era is evident if we look at rates of population growth and technological development. Italian demographer, Massimo Livi-Bacci (1992), has studied the global human population and its long-term growth. From an estimated 6 *million* people in 10,000 BCE, the global population rose to almost 6 *billion* by 1990 (see table 4.1) and in 2007 stood at 6.6 billion. In itself, such a recent increase is staggering enough. However, Livi-Bacci's study shows that the pace of population growth has been very uneven, speeding up from around 1750, the start of the industrial era. Perhaps the most striking demographic aspect here is the 'doubling time' of the global population. Even in 1750, the time it took for the population to double in size was quite slow, taking more than 1,000 years; but by 1950 this was down to 118 years and in 1990 a mere 38 years. If such predictions are borne out in the future, there will be more than 10 billion people on planet Earth by 2025, all trying to eke out a living. Whether they will be able to do so is, in part, dependent on the carrying capacity of the natural environment and this is strongly influenced by the creativity of human technological development.

 Chapter 5, 'The Environment', looks more closely at the impact of such rapid human expansion on the natural environment and other species.

What Livi-Bacci's work shows us is the change of pace in the process of globalization introduced with the modern era, leading to a much more effective form of global society since the 1950s. In this chapter, we will look at previous types of society and some key turning points in the long-term, overall history of human affairs, before moving on to look at evidence and current debates on the rapid globalization process that, arguably, has occurred only over the last 60 years or so. Many social scientists see this contemporary form of globalization as *the* most significant development that will shape all of our futures.

First though, we look at the main types of society that existed in the past and which can still be found in parts of the world. Today we are accustomed to societies that contain tens of millions of people, many of them living together in crowded urban areas. But this situation is historically unusual. For most of human history, populations were much less densely populated than now and it is only over the past 100 years or so that any societies have existed in which the *majority* of the population are urban dwellers. To understand the forms of society that existed prior to modern industrialism, we have to call on the historical dimension of the sociological imagination.

Types of society

A disappearing world: the fate of pre-modern societies

The explorers, traders and missionaries sent out during Europe's great age of discovery met with many different peoples. As the anthropologist Marvin Harris has written, in his work, *Cannibals and Kings* (1978):

Table 4.1 Population, total births, and years lived (10,000 BCE – 1990)

Demographic index	10,000 BCE*	0	1750	1950	1990
Population (millions)	6	252	771	2530	5292
Annual growth (%)	0.008	0.037	0.064	0.596	1.845
Doubling time (years)	8369	1854	1083	116	38
Births (billions)	9.29	33.6	22.64	10.42	4.79
Life expectancy	20	22	27	35	55

NB: For births and life expectancy, the data refer to interval between the date at the head of the column and that of the preceding column (for the first column the interval runs from the hypothetical origin of the human species to 10,000 BCE).
*Many historians now use BCE (Before the Common Era) and CE (Common Era) rather than BC and AD.

Source: Adapted from Livi-Bacci 1992: 31

In some regions – Australia, the Arctic, the southern tips of South America and Africa – they found groups still living much like Europe's own long-forgotten stone age ancestors: bands of twenty or thirty people, sprinkled across vast territories, constantly on the move, living entirely by hunting animals and collecting wild plants. These hunter-collectors appeared to be members of a rare and endangered species. In other regions – the forests of eastern North America, the jungles of South America, and East Asia – they found denser populations, inhabiting more or less permanent villages, based on farming and consisting of perhaps one or two large communal structures, but here too the weapons and tools were relics of prehistory. . . . Elsewhere of course, the explorers encountered fully developed states and empires, headed by despots and ruling classes, and defended by standing armies. It was these great empires, with their cities, monuments, palaces, temples and treasures that had lured all the Marco Polos and Columbuses across the oceans and deserts in the first place. There was China – the greatest empire in the world, a vast, sophisticated realm whose leaders scorned the 'red-faced barbarians', suppliants from puny kingdoms beyond the pale of the civilised world. And there was India – a land where cows were venerated and the unequal burdens of life were apportioned according to what each soul had merited in its previous incarnation. And then there were the native American states and empires, worlds unto themselves, each

with its distinctive arts and religions: the Incas, with their great stone fortresses, suspension bridges, over-worked granaries, and state-controlled economy; and the Aztecs, with their bloodthirsty gods fed from human hearts and their incessant search for fresh sacrifices.

This seemingly unlimited variety of pre-modern societies can actually be grouped into three main categories, each of which is referred to in Harris's description: *hunters and gatherers* (Harris calls these, 'hunter-collectors' in his description above); larger *agrarian* or *pastoral societies* (involving agriculture or the tending of domesticated animals); and *non-industrial civilizations* or *traditional states*. As table 4.2 shows, with the emergence of each successive societal type came larger societies and an increase in the size of the global human population.

The earliest societies: hunters and gatherers

For all but a tiny part of their existence on this planet, human beings have lived in **hunting and gathering societies**. Hunters and gatherers gain their livelihood from hunting, fishing and gathering edible plants growing in the wild. These cultures continue to exist in some parts of the world, such as in a few arid parts of Africa and the jungles of Brazil and New Guinea. Most hunting and gathering cultures, however, have been destroyed or absorbed by the spread of

Table 4.2 **Types of pre-modern human society**

Type	Period of Existence	Characteristics
Hunting and gathering societies	50,000 BCE to the present. Now on the verge of complete disappearance.	Consist of small numbers of people gaining their livelihood from hunting, fishing and the gathering of edible plants. Few inequalities. Differences of rank limited by age and gender.
Agrarian societies	12,000 BCE to the present. Most are now part of larger political entities and are losing their distinct identity.	Based on small rural communities, without towns or cities. Livelihood gained through agriculture, often supplemented by hunting and gathering. Stronger inequalities than among hunters and gatherers. Ruled by chiefs.
Pastoral societies	12,000 BCE to the present. Today mostly part of larger states; their traditional ways of life are being undermined.	Size ranges from a few hundred people to many thousands. Dependent on the tending of domesticated animals for their subsistence. Marked by distinct inequalities. Ruled by chiefs, or warrior kings.
Traditional societies or civilizations	6000 BCE to the nineteenth century. All traditional states have disappeared.	Very large in size, some numbering millions of people (though small compared with larger industrialized societies). Some cities exist, in which trade and manufacture are concentrated. Based largely on agriculture. Major inequalities exist among different classes. Distinct apparatus of government headed by a king or emperor.

Western culture (the culture of Europe, the United States, Australasia) and those that remain are unlikely to stay intact for much longer. Currently, fewer than a quarter of a million people in the world support themselves through hunting and gathering – only 0.001 per cent of the world's population (see figure 4.1).

Compared with larger societies – particularly those in the developed world – little inequality is found in most hunting and gathering groups. Hunters and gatherers do not accumulate material wealth beyond what is needed to cater for their basic wants. Their main preoccupations are normally with religious values and with ceremonial and ritual activities. The material goods they need are limited to weapons for hunting, tools for digging and building, traps and cooking utensils. Thus there is little difference among members of the society in the number or kinds of material possessions – there are no divisions of rich and poor. Differences of position or rank tend to be

Pre-historic cave paintings show us something of the lives of the earliest hunter-gatherers.

limited to age and sex; men are almost always the hunters, while women gather wild crops, cook, and bring up the children. This division of labour between men and women, however, is very important: men tend to dominate public and ceremonial positions.

Hunters and gatherers are not merely 'primitive' peoples whose ways of life no longer hold any interest for us. Studying their cultures allows us to see more clearly that modern institutions are far from being 'natural' features of all human life. Of course, we should not idealize the circumstances in which hunters and gatherers have lived, but, nonetheless, the absence of war, the lack of major inequalities of wealth and power and the emphasis on cooperation rather than competition are all instructive reminders that the world created by modern industrial civilization is not necessarily to be equated in any obvious way with 'progress'.

Pastoral and agrarian societies

About 20,000 years ago, some hunting and gathering groups turned to the raising of domesticated animals and the cultivation of fixed plots of land as their means of livelihood. Pastoral societies are those that rely mainly on domesticated livestock, while agrarian societies are those that grow crops (practise agriculture). Many societies have had mixed pastoral and agrarian economies.

Depending on the environment in which they live, pastoralists rear and herd animals such as cattle, sheep, goats, camels and horses. Many pastoral societies still exist in the modern world, concentrated especially in areas of Africa, the Middle East and Central Asia. These societies are usually found in regions where there are dense grasslands, or in deserts or mountains. Such regions are not amenable to fruitful agriculture, but may support various kinds of livestock. Pastoral societies usually migrate

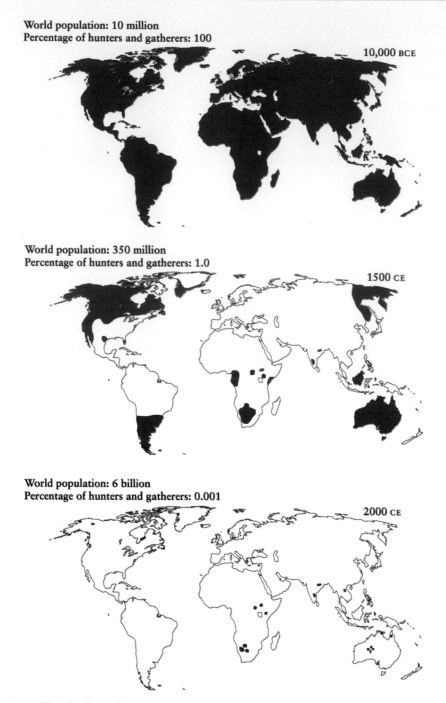

World population: 10 million
Percentage of hunters and gatherers: 100

10,000 BCE

World population: 350 million
Percentage of hunters and gatherers: 1.0

1500 CE

World population: 6 billion
Percentage of hunters and gatherers: 0.001

2000 CE

Figure 4.1 The decline of hunting and gathering societies

Source: Lee and De Vore (1968)

between different areas according to seasonal changes. Given their nomadic habits, people in pastoral societies do not normally accumulate many material possessions, although their way of life is more complex in material terms than that of hunters and gatherers.

At some point, hunting and gathering

groups began to sow their own crops rather than simply collect those growing in the wild. This practice first developed as what is usually called 'horticulture', in which small gardens were cultivated with the use of simple hoes or digging instruments. Like pastoralism, horticulture provided for a more assured supply of food than was possible by hunting and gathering and could therefore support larger communities. Since they were not on the move, people gaining a livelihood from horticulture could develop larger stocks of material possessions than either hunting and gathering or pastoral communities. Some people in the world still rely primarily on agriculture for their livelihood (see table 4.3).

Non-industrial or traditional civilizations

From about 6000 BCE onwards, we find evidence of larger societies than ever existed before, which contrast in distinct ways with earlier types (see figure 4.2). These societies were based on the development of cities, showed very pronounced inequalities of wealth and power and were associated with the rule of kings or emperors. Because they involved the use of writing, and science and art flourished, they are often called *civilizations*.

The earliest civilizations developed in the Middle East, usually in fertile river areas. The Chinese Empire originated in about 2000 BCE, when powerful states were also founded in what are now India and Pakistan. A number of large civilizations existed in Mexico and Latin America, such as the Aztecs of Mexico, the Mayas of the Yucatan Peninsula and the Incas of Peru.

Most traditional civilizations were also *empires*; they achieved the size they did through the conquest and incorporation of other peoples (Kautsky 1982). This was true, for instance, of traditional China and Rome. At its height, in the first century CE, the Roman Empire stretched from Britain in north-west Europe to beyond the Middle

These Masai warriors from Tanzania are among some of the few remaining pastoralists in the world today.

East. The Chinese empire, which lasted for more than 2,000 years, up to the threshold of the twentieth century, covered most of the massive region of eastern Asia now occupied by modern China. The emergence of these large-scale civilizations and empires shows that the long-term process of globalization has involved invasion, wars and violent conquest every bit as much as cooperation and mutual exchange between societies. Nevertheless, by the dawn of the modern era, human settlement had already taken place right across the globe.

Table 4.3 Some agrarian societies remain

Country	Percentage of workers in agriculture
Rwanda	90
Uganda	82
Ethiopia	80
Nepal	76
Bangladesh	63
How the industrialized societies differ	
Japan	4.6
Australia	3.6
Germany	2.8
Canada	2.0
United Kingdom	1.4
United States	0.7

Source: CIA World Factbook 2007

The modern world: the industrialized societies

What has happened to destroy the forms of society which dominated the whole of history up to two centuries ago? The answer, in a word, is **industrialization** – a term we introduced in chapter 1. Industrialization refers to the emergence of machine production, based on the use of inanimate power resources (like steam or electricity). The **industrial societies** (sometimes also called 'modern' or 'developed' societies) are utterly different from any previous type of social order and their development has had consequences stretching far beyond their European origins.

In even the most advanced of traditional civilizations, most people were engaged in working on the land. The relatively low level of technological development did not permit more than a small minority to be freed from the chores of agricultural production. Modern technology has certainly transformed the ways of life enjoyed by a large proportion of the human population. As the economic historian David Landes (1969) has observed:

Modern technology produces not only more, faster; it turns out objects that could not have been produced under any circumstances by the craft methods of yesterday. The best Indian hand-spinner could not turn out yarn so fine and regular as that of the [spinning] mule; all the forges in eighteenth-century Christendom could not have produced steel sheets so large, smooth and homogeneous as those of a modern strip mill. Most important, modern technology has created things that could scarcely have been conceived in the pre-industrial era: the camera, the motor car, the airplane, the whole array of electronic devices from the radio to the high-speed computer, the nuclear power plant, and so on almost ad infinitum.

Even so, the continuing existence of gross global inequalities means that such technological development is still not equally shared. The modes of life and social institutions characteristic of the modern world are radically different from those of even the recent past. During a period of only two or three centuries – a minute sliver of time in the context of human history – human social life has been wrenched away from the types of social order in which people lived for thousands of years.

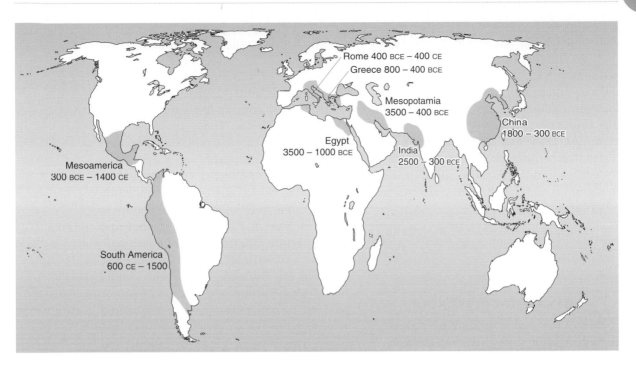

Figure 4.2 Civilizations in the ancient world

A central feature of industrial societies today is that a large majority of the employed population work in factories, offices or shops rather than in agriculture (as we saw in table 4.2). And over 90 per cent of people live in towns and cities, where most jobs are to be found and new job opportunities are created. The largest cities are vastly greater in size than the urban settlements found in traditional civilizations. In the cities, social life becomes more impersonal and anonymous than before and many of our day-to-day encounters are with strangers rather than with individuals known to us. Large-scale organizations, such as business corporations or government agencies, come to influence the lives of virtually everyone.

> The role of cities in the new global order is discussed in chapter 6, 'Cities and Urban Life'.

A further feature of modern societies concerns their political systems, which are more developed and intensive than forms of government in traditional states. In traditional civilizations, the political authorities (monarchs and emperors) had little direct influence on the customs and habits of most of their subjects, who lived in fairly self-contained local villages. With industrialization, transportation and communication became much more rapid, making for a more integrated 'national' community.

The industrial societies were the first nation-states to come into existence. Nation-states are political communities, divided from each other by clearly delimited borders rather than the vague frontier areas that used to separate traditional states. National governments have extensive powers over many aspects of citizens' lives, framing laws that apply to all those living within their borders. Virtually all societies in the world today are nation-states.

The application of industrial technology has by no means been limited to peaceful processes of economic development. From the earliest phases of industrialization, modern production processes have been put to military use and this has radically altered ways of waging war, creating weaponry and modes of military organization much more advanced than those of non-industrial cultures. Together, superior economic strength, political cohesion and military superiority account for the seemingly irresistible spread of Western ways of life across the world over the past two centuries. Once again, as we noted in our discussion of older types of society, we have to acknowledge that the globalization process has very often been characterized by violence and conquest.

> Issues of war and violence are taken up in chapter 23, 'Nations, War and Terrorism'.

THINKING CRITICALLY

Take a few moments to reflect on just how different industrialized, modern societies are from previous types. What *three features* would you pick out as being the most significant ones that mark them out as very different types, and why? Marx once forecast that the industrialized countries showed to the non-industrialized ones a picture of their own future. In what ways has he been proved right, and how might it be argued that in important respects, he was wrong?

Global development

From the seventeenth to the early twentieth century, the Western countries established colonies in numerous areas that were previously occupied by traditional societies, using their superior military strength where necessary. Although virtually all of these colonies have now attained their independence, the policy of **colonialism** was central to shaping the social map of the globe as we know it today (colonialism was discussed in chapter 1 in relation to the coffee trade). In some regions, such as North America, Australia and New Zealand, which were only thinly populated by hunting and gathering communities, Europeans became the majority population. In other areas, including much of Asia, Africa and South America, local populations remained in the majority.

Societies of the first of these types, including the United States, have become industrialized and are often referred to as *developed* societies. Those in the second category are mostly at a much lower level of industrial development and are often referred to as *developing* societies, or the developing world. Such societies include China, India, most of the African countries (such as Nigeria, Ghana and Algeria) and those in South America (for example, Brazil, Peru and Venezuela). Since many of these societies are situated south of the United States and Europe, they are sometimes referred to collectively as the South and contrasted to the wealthier, industrialized North. This is a generalization, though, and as countries of the global south become industrialized, this simple division of the world becomes less and less accurate.

You may often hear developing countries referred to as part of the **Third World**. The term Third World was originally part of a contrast drawn between three main types of society found in the early twentieth century. **First World** countries were (and are) the industrialized states of Europe, the United States, Canada, Greenland, Australasia (Australia and New Zealand), South Africa and Japan. Nearly all First World societies have multiparty, parliamentary systems of government. **Second World** societies meant the communist countries of what was then the Soviet Union (USSR) and Eastern Europe, including, for example, Czechoslovakia, Poland, East Germany and Hungary. Second World societies had centrally planned economies, which allowed little room for private property or competitive economic enterprise. They were also one-party states: the Communist Party dominated both the political and economic systems. For some 75 years, world history was affected by a global rivalry known as the Cold War, between the Soviet Union and Eastern European countries on the one

Life in Russia has changed dramatically after the fall of communism. Older people have sometimes found it difficult to adapt, which has led to nostalgia for former communist leaders such as Stalin and Lenin.

hand and the capitalistic societies of the West and Japan on the other. Today that rivalry is over. With the ending of the **Cold War** and the disintegration of communism in the former USSR and Eastern Europe, the Second World has effectively disappeared.

Even though the Three Worlds model is still sometimes used in sociology textbooks, today it has outlived whatever usefulness it might once have had as a way of describing the countries of the world. For one thing, the Second World of socialist and communist countries no longer exists and even exceptions such as China are rapidly adopting capitalist economies. It can also be argued that the ranking of First, Second and Third Worlds always reflected a value judgement,

in which 'first' means 'best' and 'third' means 'worst'. It is therefore best avoided.

The developing world

Many developing societies are in areas that underwent colonial rule in Asia, Africa and South America. A few colonized areas gained independence early, like Haiti, which became the first autonomous black republic in January 1804. The Spanish colonies in South America acquired their freedom in 1810, while Brazil broke away from Portuguese rule in 1822. However, most nations in the developing world have become independent states only since the Second World War, often following bloody anti-colonial struggles. Examples include

India, a range of other Asian countries (like Burma, Malaysia and Singapore) and countries in Africa (including, for example, Kenya, Nigeria, Zaire, Tanzania and Algeria).

While they may include peoples living in traditional fashion, developing countries are very different from earlier forms of traditional societies. Their political systems are modelled on systems that were first established in the societies of the West – that is to say, they are nation-states. While most of the population still live in rural areas, many of these societies are experiencing a rapid process of urban development.

>> The growth of cities in the developing world is discussed in chapter 6, 'Cities and Urban Life'.

Although agriculture remains the main economic activity, crops are now often produced for sale in world markets rather than for local consumption. Developing countries are not merely societies that have 'lagged behind' the more industrialized areas. They have been in large part created by contact with Western industrialism, which has undermined earlier, more traditional systems. Conditions in some of the most impoverished of these societies have deteriorated rather than improved over more recent years. There are still around one billion people living on the equivalent of less than one US dollar a day.

>> Global poverty is discussed briefly in chapter 12, 'Poverty, Social Exclusion and Welfare', and in more detail in chapter 13, 'Global Inequality'.

The world's poor are concentrated particularly in South and East Asia and in Africa and Latin America, although there are some important differences between these regions. For example, poverty levels in East Asia and the Pacific have declined over the past decade, while they have risen in the nations of sub-Saharan Africa. During the 1990s, the number of people living on less than one dollar per day in this region has grown from 241 million to 315 million

(World Bank 2004). There have also been significant increases in poverty in parts of South Asia, Latin America and the Caribbean. Many of the world's poorest countries also suffer from a serious debt crisis. Payments of interest on loans from foreign lenders can often amount to more than governments' investments in health, welfare and education.

Newly industrializing countries

While the majority of developing countries are not as economically developed as the societies of the West, some have successfully embarked on a process of industrialization. These countries are sometimes referred to as *newly industrializing countries* (NICs), including Brazil and Mexico in Latin America and Hong Kong, South Korea, Singapore and Taiwan in East Asia. The rates of economic growth of the most successful NICs, such as those in East Asia, are several times those of the Western industrial economies. No developing country figured among the top 30 exporters in the world in 1968, but 25 years later South Korea was in the top 15.

The East Asian NICs have shown the most sustained levels of economic prosperity. They are investing abroad as well as promoting growth at home. South Korea's production of steel has doubled in the last decade and its shipbuilding and electronics industries are among the world's leaders. Singapore is becoming the major financial and commercial centre of Southeast Asia. Taiwan is an important presence in the manufacturing and electronics industries. All these changes in the NICs have directly affected countries such as the United States, whose share of global steel production, for example, has dropped significantly over the past 30 years. Types of society in the modern world are summarized in table 4.4.

Social change

We saw at the start of this chapter how the modern world is characterized by modes of

Table 4.4 Societies in the modern world

Type	First World societies	Second World societies	Developing societies ('Third World societies')	Newly industrializing societies (NICs)
Period of existence	Eighteenth century to the present.	Early twentieth century (Russian Revolution of 1917 to early 1990s).	Eighteenth century (mostly as colonized areas) to the present.	1970s to the present.
Characteristics	Based on industrial production and generally free enterprise. Majority of people live in towns and cities; a few work in rural agricultural pursuits. Major class inequalities, though less pronounced than in traditional states. Distinct political communities or nation-states, including the nations of West, Japan, Australia and New Zealand.	Based on industry, but the economic system is centrally planned. Small proportion of the population work in agriculture; most live in towns and cities. Major class inequalities persist. Distinct political communities or nation-states. Until 1989, composed of the Soviet Union and Eastern Europe, but social and political changes began to transform them into free enterprise economic systems, according to the model of First World societies.	Majority of the population work in agriculture, using traditional methods of production. Some agricultural produce sold on world markets. Some have free enterprise systems, while others are centrally planned. Distinct political communities or nation-states, including China, India and most African and South American nations.	Former developing societies now based on industrial production and generally free enterprise. Majority of people live in towns and cities, a few work in agricultural pursuits. Major class inequalities, more pronounced than First World societies. Average per capita income considerably less than First World societies. Include Hong Kong, South Korea, Singapore, Taiwan, Brazil and Mexico.

life and social institutions that are radically different from those of even the recent past. Social change is difficult to define, because there is a sense in which everything changes, all of the time. Every day is a new day; every moment is a new instant in time. The Greek philosopher Heraclitus pointed out that a person cannot step into the same river twice. On the second occasion, the river is different, since water has flowed along it and the person has changed in subtle ways too. While this observation is in a sense correct, we do of course normally want to say that it is the same river and the same person stepping into it on the two occasions. There is sufficient continuity in the shape or form of the river and in the physique and personality of the person with wet feet to say that each remains 'the same' through the changes that occur. Given this problem, how do sociologists account for the processes of change that have transformed the way humans lived?

Identifying significant change involves showing how far there are alterations in the *underlying structure* of an object or situation over a period of time. In the case of human societies, to decide how far and in what ways a system is in a process of change we have to show to what degree there is any modification of *basic institutions* during a specific period. All accounts of social change also involve showing what remains stable, as a baseline against which to measure alterations. The nineteenth-century sociologist, Auguste Comte, once described this as the study of social *dynamics* (change) and social *statics* (stability). Even in the rapidly moving world of today there are still continuities with the distant past. Major religious systems, for example, such as Christianity or Islam, retain their ties with ideas and practices initiated some 2,000 years ago. Yet most institutions in modern societies clearly change much more rapidly than did institutions of the traditional world.

Influences on social change

Over the past 200 years, sociologists and other social theorists have tried to develop a grand theory that explains the nature of social change. But no single factor theory could account for the diversity of human social development, from hunting and gathering and pastoral societies to traditional civilizations, and finally to the highly complex social systems of today. We can, however, identify the main factors that have consistently influenced patterns of social change: *cultural* factors, the *physical environment* and *political* organization.

Cultural factors

The first main influence on social change consists of cultural factors, which include the effects of religion, communication systems and leadership. Religion may be either a conservative or an innovative force in social life (see chapter 16, 'Religion'). Some forms of religious belief and practice have acted as a brake on change, emphasizing above all the need to adhere to traditional values and rituals. Yet, as Max Weber

emphasized, religious convictions frequently play a mobilizing role in pressures for social change.

A particularly important cultural influence that affects the character and pace of change is the nature of communication systems. The invention of writing, for instance, allowed for the keeping of records, making possible increased control of material resources and the development of large-scale organizations. In addition, writing altered people's perception of the relation between past, present and future. Societies that write keep a record of past events and know themselves to have a history. Understanding history can develop a sense of the overall movement or line of development a society is following and people can then actively seek to promote it further. With the advent of the Internet, communication has become much faster and distance is less of an obstacle. It has also generated a more effective sense of global society than previously, which is one important aspect of globalization.

Under the general heading of cultural factors, we should also place leadership. Individual leaders have had an enormous influence in world history. We have only to think of great religious figures (like Jesus), political and military leaders (like Julius Caesar) or innovators in science and philosophy (like Isaac Newton) to see that this is the case. A leader capable of pursuing dynamic policies and generating a mass following or radically altering pre-existing modes of thought can overturn a previously established order. The classical sociologist Max Weber examined the role of charismatic leadership in social change.

 Weber's conception of leadership is discussed in chapter 16, 'Religion'.

However, individuals can only reach positions of leadership and become effective if favourable social conditions exist. Adolf Hitler rose to power in Germany in the 1930s, for instance, partly as a result of the tensions and crises that beset the country at that time, which prompted people to look

Gandhi – shown here on an Indian banknote – fits Weber's concept of a charismatic leader. He helped bring about independence for India from British rule.

for simple solutions. If those circumstances had not existed, he would probably have remained an obscure figure within a minor political faction. The same was true at a later date of Mahatma Gandhi, the famous pacifist leader in India during the period after the Second World War. Gandhi was able to be effective in securing his country's independence from Britain because the war and other events had unsettled the existing colonial institutions in India.

The physical environment

The physical environment has an effect on the development of human social organization. This is clearest in more extreme environmental conditions, where people must organize their ways of life in relation to weather conditions. Inhabitants of polar regions necessarily develop habits and practices different from those living in subtropical areas. People who live in Alaska, where the winters are long and cold, tend to follow different patterns of social life from people who live in the much warmer Mediterranean countries. Alaskans spend more of their lives indoors and, except for the short summer period, plan outdoor activities very carefully, given the inhospitable environment in which they live.

Less extreme physical conditions can also affect society. The native population of Australia has never stopped being hunters and gatherers, since the continent contained hardly any indigenous plants suitable for regular cultivation, or animals that could be domesticated to develop pastoral production. The world's early civilizations mostly originated in areas that contained rich agricultural land – for instance, in river deltas. The ease of communications across land and the availability of sea routes are also important: societies cut off from others by mountain ranges, impassable jungles or deserts

Global Society 4.1 | Humans and the domestication of fire

Over the course of human history, human beings gradually learned how to exert more control over the natural environment and were able to pass on this useful knowledge to geographically distant groups and to their own younger generations. In *Fire and Civilization* (1992), Dutch sociologist Johan Goudsblom (1932–) argues that an especially significant development in early human development was the discovery of fire and the invention of techniques for making, managing and keeping it under control.

Human groups that learned how to make and use fire gained dominance over those that did not. Eventually all human societies were able to make and use fire. The domestication of fire also enabled human beings to dominate over other animal species. Goudsblom's developmental history of fire shows something of the way that human societies try to manipulate and manage the natural environment to their own advantage. In the process, though, there is also new pressure on societies to change their own social organization.

From small domestic fires used for keeping warm and cooking food, all the way to modern central heating systems and large power plants, the gradual expansion of fire-making has necessitated more complex forms of social organization. When early humans learned how to make and manage small fires, they had to organize themselves to keep fires going, to monitor them and, at the same time, to stay safe. Much later, with the introduction of domesticated forms of fire into private homes, societies needed specialists in fire control, fire brigades and fire-prevention advisers. With the advent of large power-generating stations, it has become important to protect these, militarily if necessary, from potential attacks. Today, more people are more dependent on the easy availability and control of fire than ever before.

Goudsblom notes one further consequence of the domestication of fire: the changing psychology of individuals. To be able to use fire, people had to overcome their previous fears of it, perhaps borne of seeing naturally occurring bush fires, lightning strikes or volcanoes. This was not an easy task. It meant controlling their fears and emotions long enough to be able to take advantage of the possible benefits of fire use. Such emotional control slowly came to be experienced as 'natural', so that people today hardly ever think about how long it has taken for humans to arrive at such high levels of emotional control over their feelings and deep-seated fears.

However, even today, fires still cause harm; destroying homes, families and businesses. Fire is always threatening to escape the control of human societies, however firmly established that control might seem. The sociological lesson we can take from this study is that the relationship between human societies and the natural environment is an unavoidable two-way process: human societies try to exert control over the natural environment, but, as they do so, the natural environment also imposes certain constraints and requirements on them.

---

often remain relatively unchanged over long periods of time.

Although the natural environment is a physical constraint on social change, many human groups thrive and generate wealth even within the most inhospitable areas. This is true, for example, of Alaskans, who have been able to develop oil and mineral resources in spite of the harsh nature of their environment. Conversely, hunting and gathering cultures have frequently lived in highly fertile regions without becoming involved in pastoral or agricultural production.

Political organization

A third factor that strongly influences social change is the type of political organization. In hunting and gathering societies, this influence is at a minimum, since there are no political authorities capable of mobilizing the community. In all other types of society, however, the existence of distinct political agencies – chiefs, lords, kings and governments – strongly affects the course of development a society takes. Political systems are not, as Marx argued, direct expressions of underlying economic organization; quite different types of political order may exist in societies that have similar production systems. For instance, some societies based on industrial capitalism have had authoritarian political systems (examples are Nazi Germany and South Africa under apartheid), while others are much more democratic (for example, the United States, Britain or Sweden).

Military power played a fundamental part in the establishment of most traditional states; it influenced their subsequent survival or expansion in an equally basic way. But the connections between the level of production and military strength are again indirect. A ruler may choose to channel resources into building up the military, for example, even when this impoverishes most of the rest of the population – as has happened in North Korea under the rule of Kim Il Sung and his son, Kim Jong Il.

Change in the modern period

Why has the period of modernity seen such a tremendous acceleration of social change in the direction of globalization? This is a complex issue, but the key factors can be categorized along lines similar to those that have influenced social change throughout history, except that the impact of the physical environment can be subsumed within the overall importance of *economic* factors.

Cultural influences

Among the cultural factors affecting processes of social change in modern times, both the development of science and the secularization of thought have contributed to the critical and innovative character of the modern outlook. We no longer assume that customs or habits are acceptable merely because they have the age-old authority of tradition. On the contrary, our ways of life increasingly require a 'rational'

basis. For instance, a design for a hospital would not be based mainly on traditional tastes, but would consider its capability for serving the purpose of a hospital – effectively caring for the sick.

In addition to *how* we think, the *content* of ideas has also changed. Ideals of self-betterment, freedom, equality and democratic participation are largely creations of the past two or three centuries. Such ideals have served to mobilize processes of social and political change, including revolutions. These ideas cannot be tied to tradition, but rather suggest the constant revision of ways of life in the pursuit of human betterment. Although they were initially developed in the West, such ideals have become genuinely universal in their application, promoting change in most regions of the world.

Economic influences

Of economic influences, the most far-reaching is the impact of capitalism. Capitalism differs in a fundamental way from pre-existing production systems, because it involves the constant expansion of production and the ever-increasing accumulation of wealth. In traditional production systems, levels of production were fairly static, as they were geared to habitual, customary needs. Capitalism promotes the constant revision of the technology of production, a process into which science is increasingly drawn. The rate of technological innovation fostered in modern industry is vastly greater than in any previous type of economic order.

Consider the current development of information technology. In recent decades, the power of computers has increased many thousands of times over. A large computer in the 1960s was constructed using thousands of handmade connectors; an equivalent device today is not only much smaller, but requires just a handful of elements in an integrated circuit.

The impact of science and technology on how we live may largely be driven by economic factors, but it also stretches beyond the economic sphere. Science and technology both influence and are influenced by political and cultural factors. Scientific and technological development, for example, helped create modern forms of communication such as radio and television. As we have seen, such electronic forms of communication have produced changes in politics in recent years. Radio, television and the other electronic media have also come to shape how we think and feel about the world.

Political influences

The third major type of influence on change in the modern period consists of political developments. The struggle between nations to expand their power, develop their wealth and triumph militarily over their competitors has been an energizing source of change over the past two or three centuries. Political change in traditional civilizations was normally confined to elites. One aristocratic family, for example, would replace another as rulers, while for the majority of the population life would go on relatively unchanged. This is not true of modern political systems, in which the activities of political leaders and government officials constantly affect the lives of the mass of the population. Both externally and internally, political decision-making promotes and directs social change far more than in previous times.

Political development in the past two or three centuries has certainly influenced economic change as much as economic change has influenced politics. Governments now play a major role in stimulating (and sometimes retarding) rates of economic growth and in all industrial societies there is a high level of state intervention in production, the government being far and away the largest employer.

Military power and war have also been of far-reaching importance. The military strength of the Western nations from the seventeenth century onwards allowed them to influence all quarters of the world – and provided an essential backing to the global spread of Western lifestyles. In the twentieth century, the effects of the two world wars have been profound: the devastation of many countries led to processes of rebuilding that brought about major institutional changes, for example in Germany and Japan after the Second World War. Even those states that were the victors – like the UK – experienced major internal changes as a result of the impact of the war on the economy.

Globalization

The concept of globalization has become widely used in debates in politics, business and the media over recent years. Thirty years ago, the term globalization was relatively unknown, but today it seems to be on the tip of everyone's tongue. **Globalization** refers to the fact that we all increasingly live in one world, so that individuals, groups and nations become ever more *interdependent*. As we saw in the chapter introduction, globalization in this sense has been occurring over a very long period of human history and is certainly not restricted to the contemporary world. Nevertheless, current debates are much more focused on the sheer pace and intensity of globalization over the past 30 years or so. It is this central idea of an intensification of the globalization process which marks this short period out as rather different, and it is this sense of the concept that will concern us here.

The process of globalization is often portrayed solely as an economic phenomenon. Much is made of the role of transnational corporations whose massive operations now stretch across national borders, influencing global production processes and the international distribution of labour. Others point to the electronic integration of global financial markets and the enormous volume of global capital flows. Still others focus on the unprecedented scope of world trade, involving a much broader range of goods and services than ever before.

| **Global Society 4.2** | **Sociology and globalization in the sixth edition** |

The concept of globalization has had an enormous impact on the social sciences, including sociology. Indeed, there is hardly a sociological topic that has *not* been influenced by the emerging global frame of reference. For this reason, it is not possible to cover the impact of globalization on sociology in this single chapter. What we *can* offer here is a quick reference guide to the presence of global issues and globalization throughout the various chapters that make up the book.

Chapter 1 – Introduction to globalization in sociology and illustrative example of coffee.
Chapter 5 – The global risk society; global environmental issues (including global warming).
Chapter 6 – Global cities and their governance.
Chapter 8 – Global life expectancy and issues of ageing societies across the world.
Chapter 9 – Families in a global context.
Chapter 10 – Globalization and disability; HIV/AIDS in global context.
Chapter 11 – Impact of globalization on stratification systems.
Chapter 13 – Globalization, inequalities and unequal life chances across the world.
Chapter 14 – Globalization and the gender order; the global sex industry.
Chapter 15 – The 'age of migration' and globalization.
Chapter 16 – Religious belief and responses to globalization.
Chapter 17 – Global mass media; the role of new technologies in processes of globalization.
Chapter 18 – International organizations and global social networks.
Chapter 19 – Education in global context; globalization and e-universities.
Chapter 20 – Globalization, the workplace and employment trends.
Chapter 21 – Globalization, organized crime and cybercrime.
Chapter 22 – Global spread of democracy; globalization and social movements.
Chapter 23 – Terrorism and globalization; old and new wars

Although economic forces are an integral part of globalization, it would be wrong to suggest that they *alone* produce it. The coming together of political, social, cultural and economic factors creates contemporary globalization.

Factors contributing to globalization

Intensified globalization has been driven forward above all by the development of information and communication technologies that have intensified the speed and scope of interaction between people all over the world. As a simple example, think of the last football World Cup. Because of global television links, some matches are now watched by *billions* of people across the world.

The rise of information and communications technology

The explosion in global communications has been facilitated by a number of important advances in technology and the world's telecommunications infrastructure. In the post-Second World War era, there has been a profound transformation in the scope and intensity of telecommunications flows. Traditional telephonic communication, which depended on analogue signals sent through wires and cables with the help of mechanical crossbar switching, has been replaced by integrated systems in which vast amounts of information are compressed and transferred digitally. Cable technology has become more efficient and less expensive; the development of fibre-optic cables has dramatically expanded the number of channels that can be carried. The earliest transatlantic cables laid in the 1950s were capable of carrying fewer than

Classic Studies 4.1 **Immanuel Wallerstein on the modern world-system**

The research problem

Many students come to sociology to find answers to the big questions of social life. For example, why are some countries rich and others desperately poor? How have some previously poor countries managed to develop to become relatively wealthy, while others have not? Such questions concerning global inequalities and economic development underpin the work of the American historical sociologist, Immanuel Wallerstein (1930–). In addressing these issues, Wallerstein also sought to take forward Marxist theories of social change in a global age. In 1976 he helped to found the Fernand Braudel Center for the Study of Economies, Historical Systems and Civilizations at Binghamton University, New York, which has become a focus for his world-system research.

Wallerstein's explanation

Before the 1970s, social scientists had tended to discuss the world's societies in terms of those within the First, Second and Third worlds, based on their levels of capitalist enterprise, industrialization and urbanization (see table 4.4 above). The solution to Third World 'underdevelopment' was therefore thought to be more capitalism, industry or urbanization. Wallerstein rejected this dominant way of

categorizing societies, arguing instead that there is only one world and that all societies are connected together within it via capitalist economic relationships. He described this complex intertwining of economies as the 'modern world-system', which was a pioneer of globalization theories. His main arguments about how this world-system emerged were outlined in a three-volume work, *The Modern World-System* (1974; 1980; 1989), which sets out his macrosociological perspective.

The origins of the modern world-system lie in sixteenth- and seventeenth-century Europe, where colonialism enabled countries like Britain, Holland and France to exploit the resources of the countries they colonized. This allowed them to accumulate capital, which was ploughed back into the economy, thus driving forward production even further. This global division of labour created a group of rich countries, but also impoverished many others, thus preventing their development. Wallerstein argues that the process produced a world-system made up of a *core*, a *semi-periphery* and a *periphery* (see figure 4.3). And although it is clearly possible for individual countries to move 'up' into the core – as have some newly industrialized societies – or to drop 'down' into the semi-periphery and periphery, the structure of the modern world-system remains constant.

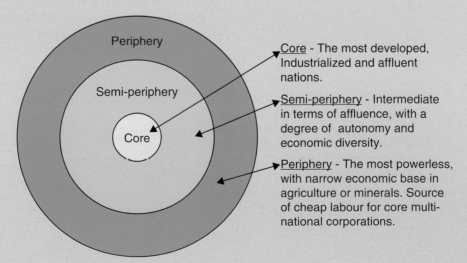

Figure 4.3   The modern world-system

Wallerstein's theory tries to explain why developing countries have found it so difficult to improve their position, but it also extends Marx's class-based conflict theory to the global level. In global terms, the world's periphery becomes the working class, while the core forms the exploitative capitalist class. In Marxist theory, this means any future socialist revolution is now more likely to occur in the developing countries, rather than the wealthy core as forecast by Marx. This is one reason why Wallerstein's ideas have been well received by political activists in the anti-capitalist and anti-globalization movements (the latter are discussed in chapter 22, 'Politics, Government and Social Movements').

Critical points

With its origins in the work of Karl Marx and Marxism, world-systems theory has faced some similar criticisms. First, world-systems theory tends to emphasize the economic dimension of social life and underplays the role of culture in explanations of social change. It has been argued, for example, that one reason why Australia and New Zealand were able to move out of the economic periphery more easily than others was due to their close ties with British industrialization, which enabled an industrial culture to take root more quickly. Second, the theory underplays the role of ethnicity, which is seen as merely a defensive reaction against the globalizing forces of the world-system. Therefore, major differences of religion and language are not seen as particularly important. Finally, it has been argued that Wallerstein uses his world-systems perspective to explain current events but is never prepared to consider that such events may falsify the theory or that alternative theories may provide a better explanation.

Contemporary significance

Wallerstein's work has been important in alerting sociologists to the interconnected character of the modern capitalist world economy and its globalizing effects. He therefore has to be given credit for early recognition of the significance of globalization, even though his emphasis on economic activity is widely seen as somewhat limited. Wallerstein's approach has attracted many scholars, and with an institutional base in the Fernand Braudel Center and an academic journal devoted to its extension – *The Journal of World-Systems Research* (since 1995) – world-systems analysis now seems to be an established research tradition.

100 voice paths, but by 1997 a single transoceanic cable could carry some 600,000 voice paths (Held et al. 1999). The spread of communications satellites, beginning in the 1960s, has also been significant in expanding international communications. Today, a network of more than 200 satellites is in place to facilitate the transfer of information around the globe.

The impact of these communications systems has been staggering. In countries with highly developed telecommunications infrastructures, homes and offices now have multiple links to the outside world, including telephones (both landlines and mobile phones), digital, satellite and cable television, electronic mail and the Internet. The Internet has emerged as the fastest-growing communication tool ever developed – some 140 million people worldwide were using the Internet in mid-1998. More than a billion people were estimated to be using the Internet by 2007 (table 4.5).

These forms of technology facilitate the compression of time and space (Harvey 1989): two individuals located on opposite sides of the planet – in Tokyo and London, for example – can not only hold a conversation in real time, but can also send documents and images to one another with the help of satellite technology. Widespread use of the Internet and mobile phones is deepening and accelerating processes of globalization; more and more people are becoming interconnected through the use of these technologies and are doing so in places that have previously been isolated or poorly served by

Internet access has become more freely available in more public settings, enabling online access to those without a personal computer at home.

traditional communications. Although the telecommunications infrastructure is not evenly developed around the world, a growing number of countries can now access international communications networks in a way that was previously impossible; over the past decade or so, Internet usage has been growing fastest in those areas that previously lagged behind – Africa and the Middle East for example (see table 4.5).

Information Flows

If, as we have seen, the spread of information technology has expanded the possibilities for contact among people around the globe, it has also facilitated the flow of information about people and events in distant places. Every day, the global media bring news, images and information into people's homes, linking them directly and continuously to the outside world. Some of the most gripping events of the past two or three decades – such as the fall of the Berlin Wall, the violent crackdown on democratic protesters in China's Tiananmen Square and the terrorist attacks of 11 September 2001 – have unfolded through the media before a truly global audience. Such events, along with thousands of less dramatic ones, have resulted in a reorientation in people's thinking from the level of the nation-state to the global stage. Individuals are now more aware of their interconnectedness with others and more likely to identify with global issues and processes than was the case in times past.

This shift to a global outlook has two significant dimensions. First, as members of

Table 4.5 **The global spread of Internet usage**

World Regions	Population (2007 est.)	Population % of world	Internet usage, latest data	% Population (penetration)	Usage % of world	% Usage growth 2000–7
Africa	933,448,292	14.2	33,334,800	3.6	3.0	638.4
Asia	3,712,527,624	56.5	398,709,065	10.7	35.8	248.8
Europe	809,624,686	12.3	314,792,225	38.9	28.3	199.5
Middle East	193,452,727	2.9	19,424,700	10.0	1.7	491.4
North America	334,538,018	5.1	233,188,086	69.7	20.9	115.7
Latin America/ Caribbean	556,606,627	8.5	96,386,009	17.3	8.7	433.4
Oceania / Australia	34,468,443	0.5	18,439,541	53.5	1.7	142.0
WORLD TOTAL	6,574,666,417	100.0	1,114,274,426	16.9	100.0	208.7

Source: www.internetworldstats.com, 2007

a global community, people increasingly perceive that social responsibility does not stop at national borders but instead extends beyond them. Disasters and injustices facing people on the other side of the globe are not simply misfortunes that must be endured but are legitimate grounds for action and intervention. There is a growing assumption that the international community has an obligation to act in crisis situations to protect the physical well-being or human rights of people whose lives are under threat. In the case of natural disasters, such interventions take the form of humanitarian relief and technical assistance. In recent years, earthquakes in Turkey and China, the Indian Ocean tsunami, famine in Africa and hurricanes in Central America have all been rallying points for global assistance.

There have also been stronger calls in recent years for interventions in the case of war, ethnic conflict and the violation of human rights, although such mobilizations are more problematic than in the case of natural disasters. Yet in the case of the first Gulf War in 1991 and the violent conflicts in the former Yugoslavia (Bosnia and Kosovo), military intervention was seen as justified by many people who argued that human

rights and national sovereignty had to be defended.

Second, a global outlook means that people are increasingly looking to sources other than the nation-state in formulating their own sense of identity. This is a phenomenon that is both produced by and further accelerates processes of globalization. Local cultural identities in various parts of the world are experiencing powerful revivals at a time when the traditional hold of the nation-state is undergoing profound transformation. In Europe, for example, inhabitants of Scotland and the Basque region of Spain might be more likely to identify themselves as Scottish or Basque – or simply as Europeans – rather than as British or Spanish. The nation-state as a source of identity is waning in many areas, as political shifts at the regional and global levels loosen people's orientations towards the states in which they live.

Economic factors

Globalization is also being driven forward by the continuing integration of the world economy. In contrast to previous eras, the global economy is no longer primarily agricultural or industrial in its basis. Rather, it is increasingly dominated by activity that is

Coca-Cola is a transglobal enterprise, selling its products all over the world. This picture shows Diet Coke on sale in Jordan, in the Middle East.

weightless and intangible (Quah 1999). This *weightless economy* is one in which products have their base in information, as is the case with computer software, media and entertainment products and Internet-based services. This new economic context has been described using a variety of terms, which we will discuss in more detail in chapter 20, including 'post-industrial society', 'the information age' and 'the new economy'. The emergence of the knowledge society has been linked to the development of a broad base of consumers who are technologically literate and eagerly integrate new advances in computing, entertainment and telecommunications into their everyday lives.

The very operation of the global economy reflects the changes that have occurred in the information age. Many aspects of the economy now work through networks that cross national boundaries, rather than stopping at them (Castells 1996). In order to be competitive in globalizing conditions, businesses and corporations have restructured themselves to be more flexible and less hierarchical in nature. Production practices and organizational patterns have become more flexible, partnering arrangements with other firms have become commonplace and participation in worldwide distribution networks has become essential for doing business in a rapidly changing global market.

Transnational corporations

Among the many economic factors that are driving globalization, the role of transnational corporations is particularly important. Transnational corporations are companies that produce goods or market services in more than one country. These

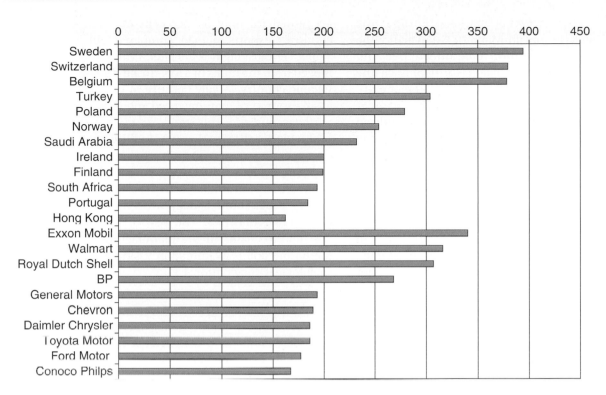

Figure 4.4 Revenue of world's biggest companies compared with GDP of selected countries, 2005–6

Source: Compiled from *Fortune* magazine's 'Global 500', 4 July 2006, and *The Economist*, 2005

may be relatively small firms with one or two factories outside the country in which they are based, or gigantic international ventures whose operations criss-cross the globe. Some of the biggest transnational corporations are companies known all around the world: Coca-Cola, General Motors, Colgate-Palmolive, Kodak, Mitsubishi and many others. Even when transnational corporations have a clear national base, they are oriented towards global markets and global profits.

Transnational corporations are at the heart of economic globalization. They account for two-thirds of all world trade, they are instrumental in the diffusion of new technology around the globe and they are major actors in international financial markets. As one observer has noted, they are 'the lynchpins of the contemporary world economy' (Held et al. 1999). Some 500 transnational corporations had annual sales of more than $10 billion in 2001, while only 75 *countries* could boast gross domestic products of at least that amount. In other words, the world's leading transnational corporations are larger economically than most of the world's countries (see figure 4.4). In fact, the combined sales of the world's largest 500 transnational corporations totalled $14.1 trillion – nearly half of the value of goods and services produced by the entire world.

Transnational corporations became a global phenomenon in the years following the Second World War. Expansion in the initial post-war years came from firms based in the United States, but by the 1970s, European and Japanese firms increasingly began to invest abroad. In the late 1980s and 1990s, transnational corporations expanded dramatically with the establishment of three powerful regional markets: Europe (the Single European Market), Asia-Pacific (the Osaka Declaration guaranteed free and open trade by 2010) and North America (the North American Free Trade Agreement). Since the early 1990s, countries in other areas of the world have also liberalized restrictions on foreign investment. By the turn of the twenty-first century, there were few economies in the world that stood beyond the reach of transnational corporations. Over the past decade, transnational corporations based in industrialized economies have been particularly active in expanding their operations in developing countries and in the societies of the former Soviet Union and Eastern Europe.

THINKING CRITICALLY

Reflecting on your knowledge of transnational corporations to date, are they really more powerful than national governments? How could national governments increase the possibility of influencing their own nation's development? Which of the sociological theories we introduced in chapter 1 would best explain the rise and increasing power of transnational corporations?

The argument that manufacturing is becoming increasingly globalized is often expressed in terms of **global commodity chains**, the worldwide networks of labour and production processes yielding a finished product. These networks consist of all pivotal production activities that form a tightly interlocked 'chain' that extends from the raw materials needed to create the product to its final consumer (Gereffi 1995; Hopkins and Wallerstein 1996; Appelbaum and Christerson 1997).

Manufactures accounted for approximately three-quarters of the world's total economic growth during the period 1990–8. The sharpest growth has been among middle-income countries: manufactures

accounted for only 54 per cent of these countries' exports in 1990, compared with 71 per cent just eight years later. China has moved from the ranks of a low- to a middle-income country, largely because of its role as an exporter of manufactured goods, and partly accounts for this trend. Yet the most profitable activities in the commodity chain – engineering, design and advertising – are likely to be found in the core countries, while the least profitable activities, such as factory production, usually are found in peripheral countries. The use of global commodity chains in the manufacture of the Barbie doll is examined in 'Using your sociological imagination 4.1'.

THINKING CRITICALLY

Which social groups, organizations and societies stand to benefit from the operation of global commodity chains? What are the negative consequences of such global economic activity and who stands to lose out? Does the globalizing of economic life primarily help or hinder the progress of the world's developing countries?

The electronic economy

The 'electronic economy' now underpins economic globalization. Banks, corporations, fund managers and individual investors are able to shift funds internationally with the click of a mouse. This new ability to move 'electronic money' instantaneously carries with it great risks, however. Transfers of vast amounts of capital can destabilize economies, triggering international financial crises such as the ones that spread from the Asian 'tiger economies' to Russia and beyond in 1998. As the global economy becomes increasingly integrated, a financial collapse in one part of the world can have an enormous effect on distant economies.

The political, economic, social and technological factors described above are joining together to produce a phenomenon that

4.1 'Barbie' and the development of global commodity chains

One illustration of the global commodity chain can be found in the manufacture of the Barbie doll, the most profitable toy in history. The 40-something teenage doll sells at a rate of two per second, bringing the Mattel Corporation, based in Los Angeles, USA, well over a billion dollars in annual revenues. Although the doll sells mainly in the United States, Europe and Japan, Barbie can also be found in 140 countries around the world. Barbie is a truly global citizen (Tempest 1996). Barbie is global not only in sales, but in terms of her birthplace as well. Barbie was never made in the United States. The first doll was made in Japan in 1959, when that country was still recovering from the Second World War and wages were low. As wages rose in Japan, Barbie moved to other low-wage countries in Asia. Her multiple origins today tell us a great deal about the operation of global commodity chains.

Barbie is designed in the United States, where her marketing and advertising strategies are devised and where most of the profits are made. But the only physical aspect of Barbie that is 'made in the USA' is her cardboard packaging, along with some of the paints and oils that are used to decorate the doll.

Barbie's body and wardrobe span the globe in their origins:

USA (manufacture plastic moulding machinery)

JAPAN (hair)

CHINA, INDONESIA, MALAYSIA (body moulding)

TAIWAN (plastic production)

CHINA (cotton for clothing, and clothing manufacturer)

SAUDI ARABIA (oil)

HONG KONG (import of raw materials)

'Global Barbie'

1   Barbie begins her life in Saudi Arabia, where oil is extracted and then refined into the ethylene that is used to create her plastic body.
2   Taiwan's state-owned oil importer, the Chinese Petroleum Corporation, buys the ethylene and sells it to Taiwan's Formosa Plastic Corporation, the world's largest producer of polyvinyl chloride (PVC) plastics, which are used in toys. Formosa Plastics converts the ethylene into the PVC pellets that will be shaped to make Barbie's body.
3   The pellets are then shipped to one of the four Asian factories that make Barbie – two in southern China, one in Indonesia and one in Malaysia. The plastic mould injection machines that shape her body, which are the most expensive part of

Barbie's manufacture, are made in the United States and shipped to the factories.
4   Once Barbie's body is moulded, she gets her nylon hair from Japan. Her cotton dresses are made in China, with Chinese cotton – the only raw material in Barbie that actually comes from the country where most Barbies are made.
5   Hong Kong plays a key role in the manufacturing process of the Chinese Barbies. Nearly all the material used in her manufacture is shipped into Hong Kong – one of the world's largest ports – and then trucked to the factories in China. The finished Barbies leave by the same route. Some 23,000 trucks make the daily trip between Hong Kong and southern China's toy factories.

So where is Barbie actually from? The cardboard and cellophane box containing the 'My First Tea Party' Barbie is labelled 'Made in China', but, as we have seen, almost none of the materials that go into making her actually originate in that country. Out of her $9.99 retail price in the USA (about £5), China gets only about 35 cents, mainly in wages paid to the 11,000 peasant women who assemble her in the two factories. Back in the United States, on the other hand, Mattel makes about $1 in profits.

What about the rest of the money that is made when Barbie is sold for $9.99? Only 65 cents is needed to cover the plastics, cloth, nylon and other materials used in her manufacture. Most of the money goes to pay for machinery and equipment, transoceanic shipping and domestic trucking, advertising and merchandising, retail floor space – and, of course, the profits of Toys 'Я' Us and other retailers. What Barbie production and consumption shows us is the effectiveness of globalization processes in connecting together the world's economies. However, it also demonstrates the unevenness of globalization's impact, which enables some countries to benefit at the expense of others. This means that we cannot assume that global commodity chains will inevitably promote development right across the chain of societies involved.

lacks any earlier parallel in terms of its intensity and scope. The consequences of globalization are many and far-reaching, as we shall see later in this chapter. But first we will turn our attention to the main views about globalization that have been expressed in recent years.

Political changes

Contemporary globalization is also related to political change. There are several aspects to this. First, the collapse of Soviet-style communism that occurred in a series of dramatic revolutions in Eastern Europe in 1989 and culminated in the dissolution of the Soviet Union itself in 1991. Since the fall of communism, countries in the former Soviet bloc – including Russia, Ukraine, Poland, Hungary, the Czech Republic, the Baltic states, the states of the Caucasus and Central Asia and many others – have been moving towards Western-style political and economic systems. They are no longer isolated from the global community, but are becoming integrated within it. This development has meant the end to the system that existed during the Cold War, when countries of the First World stood apart from those of the Second World. The collapse of communism has hastened processes of globalization, but should also be seen as a result of globalization itself. The centrally planned communist economies and the ideological and cultural control of communist political authority were ultimately unable to survive in an era of global media and an electronically integrated world economy.

A second important political factor leading to intensifying globalization is the growth of international and regional mechanisms of government. The United Nations and the European Union are the two most prominent examples of international organizations that bring together nation-states into a common political forum. While the UN does this as an association of individual nation-states, the EU is a more pioneering form of transnational governance in which a certain degree of national sovereignty is relinquished by its member states. The governments of individual EU states are bound by directives, regulations and court judgements from common EU bodies, but they also reap economic, social and political benefits from their participation in the regional union.

Finally, globalization is being driven by international governmental organizations (IGOs) and international non-governmental organizations (INGOs). An IGO is a body that is established by participating governments and given responsibility for regulating or overseeing a particular domain of activity that is transnational in scope. The first such body, the International Telegraph Union, was founded in 1865. Since that time, a great number of similar bodies have been created to regulate issues ranging from civil aviation to broadcasting to the disposal of hazardous waste. In 1909, there were 37 IGOs in existence to regulate transnational affairs; by 1996, there were 260 (Held et al. 1999).

As the name suggests, international non-governmental organizations differ from IGOs in that they are not affiliated with government institutions. Rather, they are independent organizations that work alongside governmental bodies in making policy

Table 4.6	Conceptualizing globalization: three tendencies		
	Hyperglobalizers (Ohmae 1990, 1995; Albrow 1997)	Sceptics (Boyer & Drache 1996; Hirst 1997; Hirst & Thompson 1999)	Transformationalists (Sassen 1991; Rosenau 1997)
What's new?	A global age	Trading blocs, weaker geo-governance than in earlier periods	Historically unprecedented levels of global inter-connectedness
Dominant features?	Global capitalism, global governance, global civil society	World less interdependent than in 1890s	'Thick' (intensive and extensive) globalization
Power of national governments?	Declining or eroding	Reinforced or enhanced	Reconstituted, restructured
Driving forces of globalization?	Capitalism and technology	Governments and markets	Combined forces of modernity
Pattern of stratification?	Erosion of old hierarchies	Increased marginalization of South	New architecture of world order
Dominant motif?	McDonald's, Madonna, etc.	National interest	Transformation of political community
Conceptualization of globalization?	A reordering of the framework of human action	Internationalization and regionalization	Reordering of inter-regional relations and action at a distance
Historical trajectory?	Global civilization	Regional blocs / clash of civilizations.	Indeterminate: global integration and fragmentation.
Summary argument	The end of the nation-state	Internationalization depends on government acquiescence and support	Globalization transforming government power and world politics

Source: Adapted from Held et al. 1999: 10

decisions and addressing international issues. Some of the best-known INGOs – such as Greenpeace, Médecins Sans Frontières (Doctors Without Borders), the Red Cross and Amnesty International – are involved in environmental protection and humanitarian efforts. But the activities of thousands of lesser-known groups also link together countries and communities.

Contesting globalization

In recent years, globalization has become a hotly debated topic. Most people accept that there are important transformations occurring around us, but the extent to which it is valid to explain these as 'globalization' is contested. This is not entirely surprising. As an unpredictable and turbulent process, globalization is seen and understood very differently by observers.

David Held and colleagues (Held et al. 1999) have surveyed the controversy and divided its participants into three schools of thought: sceptics, hyperglobalizers and transformationalists. These three tendencies within the globalization debate are summarized in table 4.6. Note that the authors cited under each school are selected because their work contains some of the key arguments that define that particular school's approach.

The sceptics

Some analysts argue that the idea of globalization is overstated and that most theories of globalization amount to a lot of talk about something that is not really new. The sceptics in the globalization controversy argue that present levels of economic interdependence are not unprecedented. Pointing to nineteenth-century statistics on world trade and investment, they contend that modern globalization differs from the past only in the intensity of interaction between nations.

The sceptics agree that there may now be more contact between countries than in previous eras, but in their eyes the current world economy is not sufficiently integrated to constitute a truly globalized economy. This is because the bulk of trade occurs within three regional groups – Europe, Asia-Pacific and North America – rather than a genuinely globalized context. The countries of the European Union, for example, trade predominantly amongst themselves. The same is true of the other regional groups, thereby invalidating the notion of a single global economy (Hirst 1997).

Many sceptics focus on processes of *regionalization* within the world economy – such as the emergence of major financial and trading blocs. To sceptics, the growth of regionalization is evidence that the world economy has become *less* integrated rather than more so (Boyer and Drache 1996; Hirst and Thompson 1999). Compared with the patterns of trade that prevailed a century ago, it is argued that the world economy is actually less global in its geographical scope and more concentrated on intense pockets of activity.

Sceptics also reject the view that globalization is fundamentally undermining the role of national governments and producing a world order in which they are less central. According to the sceptics, national governments continue to be key players because of their involvement in regulating and coordinating economic activity. Governments, for example, are the driving force behind many trade agreements and policies of economic liberalization.

The hyperglobalizers

Hyperglobalizers take an opposing position to that of the sceptics. They argue that globalization is a very real phenomenon whose consequences can be felt everywhere. Globalization is seen as a process that is indifferent to national borders, producing a new global order, swept along by powerful flows of cross-border trade and production. One of the best-known hyperglobalizers, the Japanese writer Kenichi Ohmae (1990, 1995), sees globalization as leading to a 'borderless world' – a world in which market forces are more powerful than national governments.

Much of the analysis of globalization offered by hyperglobalizers focuses on the changing role of the nation-state. It is argued that individual countries no longer control their economies because of the vast growth in world trade. National governments and the politicians within them are increasingly unable to exercise control over the issues that cross their borders – such as volatile financial markets and environmental threats. Citizens recognize that politicians are limited in their ability to address these problems and, as a result, lose faith in existing systems of governance. Some hyperglobalizers suggest that the power of national governments is also being challenged from above – by new regional and international institutions, such as the European Union, the World Trade Organization and others.

Taken together, these shifts signal to the hyperglobalizers the dawning of a global age in which national governments decline in importance and influence (Albrow 1997).

The transformationalists

Transformationalists take a position somewhere between sceptics and hyperglobalizers. They see globalization as the central force behind a broad spectrum of changes that are currently shaping modern societies, but though the global order *is* being transformed, many of the old patterns remain. National governments, for instance, still retain a good deal of power in spite of the advance of global interdependence. These transformations are not restricted to economics alone, but are equally prominent within the realms of politics, culture and personal life. Transformationalists contend that the current level of globalization is breaking down established boundaries between the internal and external, the international and domestic. In trying to adjust to this new order, societies, institutions and individuals are being forced to navigate contexts where previous structures have been shaken up.

Unlike hyperglobalizers, transformationalists see globalization as a dynamic and open process that is subject to influence and change. It is developing in a contradictory fashion, encompassing tendencies that frequently operate in opposition to one another. Globalization is, therefore, not a one-way process but a two-way flow of images, information and influences. Global migration, mass media and telecommunications are contributing to the diffusion of cultural influences. The world's vibrant 'global cities' such as London, New York and Tokyo are thoroughly multicultural, with ethnic groups and cultures intersecting and living side by side (Sassen 1991). According to transformationalists, globalization is a decentred and reflexive process characterized by links and cultural flows that work in a multidirectional way. Because globalization is the product of numerous intertwined global networks, it cannot be seen as being driven from one particular part of the world.

Rather than losing sovereignty, as the hyperglobalizers argue, nation-states are restructuring in response to new forms of economic and social organization that are non-territorial in basis, including corporations, social movements and international bodies. Transformationalists argue that we are no longer living in a state-centric world; governments are being forced to adopt a more active and outward-looking stance towards governance under the complex conditions of globalization (Rosenau 1997).

Evaluation

Which view is best supported by the evidence? At this point, probably that of the transformationalists, which suggests that global processes are having a great impact on many aspects of life across the world, but that this impact is not completely transforming the world's societies. However, we cannot be certain how globalization will progress in the future, as this partly depends on the actions and reactions of those groups, organizations and governments caught up in it, which are difficult to forecast.

Sceptics tend to underestimate just how much the world is changing; world finance markets, for example, are organized on a global level much more than they ever were before. It is also the case that the increasing movement of people around the world, alongside more immediately effective forms of communication, are transforming people's everyday experience of the world and their view of it. The sceptical viewpoint tends to underplay this experiential aspect of the process.

Hyperglobalizers, on the other hand, focus on *economic* globalization and tend to see this as a linear, or one-way process with a clearly defined endpoint: a global economy and, hence, a global society. In reality, the globalization process is more complex than this picture implies and the endpoint cannot be determined from present trends as these may well change. For example, the idea of a 'borderless world' may be an accurate description of the forces at work in economic globalization, but whether or not it becomes reality will depend on political decisions taken at national government level. Indeed, many countries around the world are seeking to tighten their border controls precisely to prevent that borderless world ever being created in the first place.

Held et al's (1999) threefold scheme is useful, in so far as it alerts us to some of the main points at issue, but it is not the only way of thinking about globalization. For example, in this debate, all three positions focus primarily on the *modern* process of rapid globalization and its consequences for the future. However, it may be better to set contemporary globalization processes into a longer timeframe. In this chapter we made an early distinction between the global spread of human societies over the very long term and the intensified globalization process of recent times. In this way it is possible to see the extended development of human societies as leading *towards* more global patterns of interdependent relations, while also acknowledging that this was not and is not inevitable. An example will make this point clear.

As we noted earlier, historically, globalization has been as much the product of conflicts, wars and invasion as of cooperation and agreement between social groups and societies. Since 1945, the world has lived with the immense destructive potential of nuclear weapons and the prospect of conflict between nuclear powers resulting in mutually assured destruction (MAD) for the combatants (and others). Such a conflict would surely halt the current process of rapid globalization and eliminate most of those interdependent relations that some see as inevitably leading to a global society. With nuclear proliferation still a very significant international issue and nuclear power increasingly seen by governments as a solution to global warming (see chapter 5, 'The Environment'), this scenario cannot be completely ruled out even today. Human conflicts *have* made a major contribution to globalization, but they also have the potential to send it into reverse.

>> Chapter 23, 'Nations, War and Terrorism', contains an extended discussion of war and conflict.

The impact of globalization

In chapter 1, we found that the chief focus of sociology has historically been the study of the industrialized societies. However, as sociologists we must also pay attention to the developing world, rather than leaving this to anthropologists. The industrialized and the developing societies have developed in interconnection with one another and are today more closely related than ever before. Those of us living in the industrialized societies depend on many raw materials and manufactured products from developing countries to sustain our lives. Conversely, the economies of most developing states depend on trading networks that bind them to the industrialized countries. We can only fully understand the industrialized order against the backdrop of societies in the developing world – in which by far the greater proportion of the world's population lives – sometimes described as the 'majority world'.

Take a close look at the array of products on display the next time you walk into a local shop or supermarket. The diversity of goods we in the West have come to take for granted as available for anyone with the money to buy them depends on amazingly complex economic connections stretching across the world. The store products have been made in, or use ingredients or parts from, a hundred different countries. These parts must be regularly transported across the globe, and constant flows of information are necessary to coordinate the millions of daily transactions.

As the world rapidly moves towards a single, unified economy, businesses and people move about the globe in increasing numbers in search of new markets and economic opportunities. As a result, the cultural map of the world changes: networks of peoples span national borders and even continents, providing cultural connections between their birthplaces and their adoptive countries (Appadurai 1986). Although there are between 5,000 and 6,000 languages spoken on the planet, around 98

Classic Studies 4.2 | **Anthony Giddens: riding the juggernaut of modernity**

The research problem

What impact is globalization likely to have on people's everyday lives? How will globalization change the modern world that we all increasingly inhabit? Can anyone just ignore or escape the forces of globalization? In a series of books, articles and lectures since the early 1990s, I have tried to explore the characteristics of the emerging global form of modernity and its consequences for everyday life (1991a, 1991b, 1993, 2001). In particular, I have been interested in the decline of traditions, our increasing risk awareness and the changing nature of trust within our relationships.

Giddens's explanation

In *The Consequences of Modernity*, I outlined my view that the global spread of modernity tends to produce a 'runaway world', in which, it appears, no one and no government is in overall control. While Marx used the image of a monster to describe modernity, I liken it to riding onboard a huge truck or 'juggernaut':

> I suggest we should substitute that of the juggernaut – a runaway engine of enormous power, which, collectively as human beings, we can drive to some extent but which also threatens to rush out of our control and which could rend itself asunder. The juggernaut crushes those who resist it, and while it sometimes seems to have a steady path, there are times when it veers away erratically in directions we cannot foresee. The ride is by no means unpleasant or unrewarding; it can often be exhilarating and charged with hopeful anticipation. But, as long as the institutions of modernity endure, we shall never be able to control completely either the path or the pace of the journey. In turn, we shall never be able to feel entirely secure, because the terrain across which it runs is fraught with risks of high consequence. Feelings of ontological security and existential anxiety will co-exist in ambivalence. (1991b: 139)

The globalizing form of modernity is marked by new uncertainties, new risks and changes to people's trust in other individuals and social institutions. In a world of rapid change, traditional forms of trust are dissolved. Our trust in other people used to be based in local communities, but in more globalized societies, our lives are influenced by people we never meet or know, who may live on the far side of the world from us. Such impersonal relationships means we are pushed to 'trust' or have confidence in 'abstract systems', such as food production and environmental regulation agencies or international banking systems. In this way, trust and risk are closely bound together. Trust in authorities is necessary if we are to confront the risks around us and react to them in an effective way. But *this* type of trust is not habitually given, but the subject of reflection and revision.

When societies were more reliant on knowledge gained from custom and tradition, people could follow established ways of doing things without too much reflection. For modern people, aspects of life that earlier generations were able to take for granted become matters of open decision-making, producing what I call 'reflexivity' – the continuous reflection on our everyday actions and reformation of these in the light of new knowledge. For example, whether to marry (or divorce) is a very personal decision, which may take account of family and friends' advice. But official statistics and sociological research on marriage and divorce also filter into social life, becoming widely known and shared, thus becoming part of an individual's decision-making.

For me, these characteristic features of modernity point to the conclusion that global modernity is a form of social life that is discontinuous with previous forms. In many ways, the globalization of modernity marks not the ending of modern societies or a movement beyond them (as in *post*modernism – see chapter 3), but a new stage of 'late' or 'high' modernity which takes the tendencies embedded within modern life into a more far-reaching global phase.

Critical points

My critics argue that perhaps I exaggerate the discontinuity between modernity and previous societies and that tradition and habit continues to structure people's everyday activities. The modern period is not so unique, they say, and modern people are not so different from those that went before. Others think that my account of globalizing modernity underplays the central sociological question of power; in particular the power of transnational corporations to influence governments and promote a form of globalization that privileges the needs of business at the expense of the world's poor. The concept of 'modernity' essentially masks the power of capitalist corporations. Finally, some have argued that I see reflexivity as a wholly positive development, reflecting the opening up of social life to more choice. However, such reflexivity could also be leading to heightened levels of 'anomie', as described by Durkheim, and in that sense, reflexivity may be more of a problem to be solved than a welcome element to be promoted.

Contemporary significance

Because theories of globalization are relatively recent and I continue to develop my theories of modern life, it is very much a 'work in progress'. The ideas I have developed have been taken in fruitful directions by other sociologists and, in that sense, it is satisfying to have provided a theoretical framework and some conceptual tools for younger generations to take forward and develop. As is evident from the contribution of the critics of my work on modernity, reflexivity and trust relationships, this has provoked much sociological debate. I hope that it will continue to do so in the future and readers will, no doubt, come to their own assessment of it.

per cent of these are used by just 10 per cent of the global population. Just a dozen languages have come to dominate the global language system, with more than 100 million speakers each: Arabic, Chinese, English, French, German, Hindi, Japanese, Malay, Portuguese, Russian, Spanish and Swahili. And just one language – English – has become 'hypercentral', as first choice for most second-language speakers. It is these 'bilinguals' who bind together the whole global language system (de Swaan 2001).

It is increasingly impossible for discrete cultures to exist as islands. There are few, if any, places on earth so remote as to escape radio, television, air travel – and the throngs of tourists they bring – or the computer. A generation ago, there were still tribes whose way of life was completely untouched by the rest of the world. Today, these peoples use machetes and other tools made in the United States or Japan, wear T-shirts and shorts manufactured in garment factories in the Dominican Republic or Guatemala, and take medicine manufactured in Germany or Switzerland to combat diseases contracted through contact with outsiders. These people also have their stories broadcast to people around the world through satellite television and the Internet. Within a generation or two at the most, all the world's once-isolated cultures will be touched and transformed by global culture, despite their persistent efforts to preserve their age-old ways of life.

The forces that produce a global culture will be discussed throughout this book. They include:

1 Television, which brings British and American culture (through networks and programmes such as the BBC, MTV or *Friends*) into homes throughout the world daily, while adapting cultural products from the Netherlands (such as *Big Brother*) or Sweden (such as *Expedition: Robinson*, which became *Survivor*) for British and American audiences.
2 The emergence of a unified global economy, with business whose factories, management structures and markets often span continents and countries.
3 'Global citizens', such as managers of large corporations, who may spend as much time criss-crossing the globe as

Global Society 4.3 | Globalization and reggae music

When those knowledgeable about popular music listen to a song, they can often pick out the stylistic influences that helped shape it. Each musical style, after all, represents a unique way of combining rhythm, melody, harmony and lyrics. And while it does not take a genius to notice the differences between rock, R&B or folk, for example, musicians often combine a number of styles in composing songs. Identifying the components of these combinations can be difficult. But for sociologists, the effort is often rewarding. Different musical styles tend to emerge from different social groups, and studying how styles combine and fuse is a good way to chart the cultural contacts between groups.

Some sociologists have turned their attention to reggae music because it exemplifies the process whereby contacts between social groups result in the creation of new musical forms. Reggae's roots can be traced to West Africa. In the seventeenth century, large numbers of West Africans were enslaved by British colonists and brought by ship to work in the sugar-cane fields of the West Indies. Although the British attempted to prevent slaves from playing traditional African music for fear it would serve as a rallying cry to revolt, the slaves managed to keep alive the tradition of African drumming, sometimes by integrating it with the European musical styles imposed by the slave-owners. In Jamaica, the drumming of one group of slaves, the Burru, was openly tolerated by slave holders because it helped meter the pace of work. Slavery was finally abolished in Jamaica in 1834, but the tradition of Burru drumming continued, even as many Burru men migrated from rural areas to the slums of Kingston.

It was in these slums that a new religious cult began to emerge – one that would prove crucial to the development of reggae. In 1930 a man named Haile Selassie was crowned emperor of the African country of Ethiopia. While opponents of European colonialism throughout the world cheered Selassie's ascension to the throne, a number of people in the West Indies came to believe that he was a god, sent to earth to lead the oppressed of Africa to freedom. One of Selassie's names was 'Prince Ras Tafari', and the West Indians who worshipped him called themselves 'Rastafarians'. The Rastafarian cult soon merged with the Burru, and Rastafarian music came to combine Burru styles of drumming with biblical themes of oppression and liberation. In the 1950s, West Indian musicians began mixing Rastafarian rhythms and lyrics with elements of American jazz and black rhythm and blues. These combinations eventually developed into 'ska' music, and then, in the late 1960s, into reggae, with its relatively slow beat, its emphasis on bass, and its stories of urban deprivation and of the power of collective social consciousness. Many reggae artists, such as Bob Marley, became commercial successes, and by the 1970s people the world over were listening to reggae music. In the 1980s and 1990s, reggae was fused with hip-hop (or rap) to produce new sounds (Hebdige 1997), heard in the work of the groups like The Wu-Tang Clan, Shaggy or Sean Paul.

The history of reggae is thus the history of contact between different social groups, and of the meanings – political, spiritual and personal – that those groups expressed through their music. Globalization has increased the intensity of these contacts. It is now possible for a young musician in Scandinavia, for example, to grow up listening to music produced by men and women in the basements of Notting Hill in London, and to be deeply influenced as well by, say, a mariachi performance broadcast live via satellite from Mexico City. If the number of contacts between groups is an important determinant of the pace of musical evolution, it can be predicted that there will be a veritable profusion of new styles in the coming years as the process of globalization continues to unfold.

---

they do at home, identifying with a global, cosmopolitan culture rather than with that of their own nation.

4 A host of international organizations, including United Nations agencies, regional trade and mutual defence asso-ciations, multinational banks and other global financial institutions, interna-tional labour and health organizations, and global tariff and trade agreements, that are creating a global political, legal and military framework.

Even societies which we might consider as 'untouched' by globalization are not out of the reach of global culture. Many of the goods they use and consume are imported from all over the world.

5   Electronic communications (telephone, fax, electronic mail, the Internet and the World Wide Web), which makes instantaneous communication with almost any part of the planet an integral part of daily life in the business world.

Does the Internet promote a global culture?

Many have argued that the rapid growth of the Internet around the world will hasten the spread of a global culture – one resembling the cultures of Europe and North America, currently home to more than half the world's Internet users (see table 4.7). Belief in such values as equality between men and women, the right to speak freely, democratic participation in government and the pursuit of pleasure through consumption are readily diffused throughout the world over the Internet. Moreover, Internet technology itself would seem to foster such values: global communication, seemingly unlimited (and uncensored) information, and instant gratification are all characteristics of the new technology.

Yet it may be premature to conclude that the Internet will sweep aside traditional cultures, replacing them with radically new cultural values. As the Internet spreads around the world, there is evidence that it is in many ways compatible with traditional cultural values as well, perhaps even a means of strengthening them. To capture this balancing of the consequences of globalization, British sociologist Roland Robertson (1992) coined the term glocalization – a mixture of globalization and localization. This means that local communities are often very active rather than passive in modifying and shaping global processes to fit their own cultures, or that global businesses have to tailor their products and services to take account of local conditions. In the light of such cases, we may find that globalization does not lead inevitably to a uniform, global culture, but instead leads to diversity and multidirectional flows of cultural products across the world's societies.

Consider, for example, the Middle Eastern country of Kuwait, a traditional Islamic culture that has recently experienced strong American and European influences. Kuwait, an oil-rich country on the Persian Gulf, has one of the highest average per person incomes in the world. The government provides free public education through the university level, resulting in high rates of literacy and education for both men and women. Kuwaiti television frequently carries American football from the USA for example, although broadcasts are regularly

Table 4.7	Global Internet connectivity in 2005: PCs, hosts and Internet users					
	PCs		Internet			
	Total (1,000s)	Per 100 people	Hosts total	Hosts per 10,000 people	Users (1,000s)	Users per 100 people
Africa	17,726	2.22	424,968	4.92	33,132.8	3.72
Americas	308,078	35.35	205,502,481	2,339.05	304,834.8	34.23
Asia	230,317	6.44	27,986,795	73.95	368,621.8	9.64
Europe	239,833	30.69	29,058,680	363.24	259,224.3	32.4
Oceania	16,130	50.46	4,572,838	1,404.68	17,383.7	53.21
World	812,084	13.4	267,545,762	420.69	983,197.4	15.27

PCs: numbers of personal computers
A host is a computer directly linked to the global Internet network
Users refers to estimates of people accessing the Internet

Source: International Telecommunications Union 2005

interrupted for the traditional Muslim calls to prayer. Half of Kuwait's approximately 2 million people are under the age of 25, and, like their counterparts in Europe and North America, many surf the Internet for new ideas, information and consumer products.

Although Kuwait is in many respects a modern country, cultural norms that treat men and women differently are very strong. Women are generally expected to wear traditional clothing that leaves only the face and hands visible and are forbidden to leave home at night or be seen in public at any time with a man who is not a spouse or relative.

Deborah Wheeler (1998) spent a year studying the impact of the Internet on Kuwaiti culture. The Internet is increasingly popular in Kuwait; half of all Internet users in Middle Eastern Arab countries live in this tiny country. Kuwaiti newspapers frequently carry stories about the Internet and the Web, and Kuwait University was the first university in the Arab world to hook its students up to the Internet.

Wheeler reports that Kuwaiti teenagers are flocking to Internet cafés, where they spend most of their time in chat rooms or visiting pornographic sites – two activities strongly frowned upon by traditional Islamic culture. According to Wheeler (1998): 'Many young people told me of encounters they were having with the opposite sex in cyberspace. There are even keyboard symbols for kisses (*), kisses on the lips (:*), and embarrassed giggles (LOL) – all those interactions and reactions that make courtship exciting and, in this case, safe.' The new communications technologies are clearly enabling men and women to talk with one another in a society where such communications outside marriage are extremely limited. Wheeler also notes that, ironically, men and women are segregated in the Internet cafés. Furthermore, she finds that Kuwaitis are extremely reluctant to voice strong opinions or political views online. With the exception of discussing conservative Islamic religious beliefs, which are freely disseminated over the Internet, Kuwaitis are remarkably inhibited online. Wheeler (1998) attributes this to the cultural belief that giving out too much information about oneself is dangerous:

In Kuwait, information is more of a potential threat than a means for individual empowerment. It is a weapon to use against your enemies, a tool for keeping conformity, or a reinforcement of regulations of daily life. . . . Kuwait's transition to the information age is influenced by these attitudes and the desire to keep one's reputation protected. This keeps the Internet from registering significant political and social impacts, except for the rise in Kuwaiti Islamist discourses on the Internet. . . . In Kuwait, there is an ethos that states that having and/or pronouncing a political opinion publicly is bad. No one wants to talk on the record or to be quoted. The idea makes people scared or nervous. Only those who are elite feel they can speak freely and openly.

Wheeler concludes that Kuwaiti culture, which is hundreds of years old, is not likely to be easily transformed by simple exposure to different beliefs and values on the Internet. The fact that a few young people are participating in global chat rooms does not mean that Kuwaiti culture is adopting the sexual attitudes of the United States or even the form of everyday relations found between men and women in the West. The culture that eventually emerges as a result of the new technologies will not be the same as American culture; it will be uniquely Kuwaiti.

The rise of individualism

Although globalization is often associated with changes within big systems – such as the world financial markets, production and trade, and telecommunications – the effects of globalization are felt equally strongly in the private realm. Globalization is not

> **THINKING CRITICALLY**
>
> What is your initial reaction? Is globalization leading to a homogenous global culture? Now think of some examples where Western products, brands or culture have changed non-Western cultures. Next, list some examples where Western influence has been significantly altered at the local level. Does such localization really mean that indigenous cultures can defend themselves against the forces of globalization?

something that is simply out there, operating on a distant plane and not intersecting with individual affairs. Globalization is an 'in here' phenomenon that is affecting our intimate and personal lives in many diverse ways. Inevitably, our personal lives have been altered as globalizing forces enter into our local contexts, our homes and our communities through impersonal sources – such as the media, the Internet and popular culture – as well as through personal contact with individuals from other countries and cultures.

Globalization is fundamentally changing the nature of our everyday experiences. As the societies in which we live undergo profound transformations, the established institutions that used to underpin them have become out of place. This is forcing a redefinition of intimate and personal aspects of our lives, such as the family, gender roles, sexuality, personal identity, our interactions with others and our relationships to work. The way we think of ourselves and our connections with other people is being profoundly altered through globalization.

In our current age, individuals have much more opportunity to shape their own lives than once was the case. At one time, tradition and custom exercised a very strong influence on the path of people's lives. Factors such as social class, gender, ethnicity and even religious affiliation could close off certain avenues for individuals, or open up others. Being born the eldest son of a tailor, for example, would probably ensure that a young man would learn his father's craft and carry on practising that craft throughout his lifetime. Tradition held that a woman's natural sphere was in the home; her life and identity were largely defined by those of her husband or father. In times past, individuals' personal identities were formed in the context of the community into which they were born. The values, lifestyles and ethics prevailing in that community provided relatively fixed guidelines according to which people lived their lives.

Under conditions of globalization, however, we are faced with a move towards a new *individualism*, in which people have actively to construct their own identities. The weight of tradition and established values is retreating, as local communities interact with a new global order. The social codes that formerly guided people's choices and activities have significantly loosened. Today, for example, the eldest son of a tailor could choose any number of paths in constructing his future, women are no longer restricted to the domestic realm and many of the other signposts that shaped people's lives have disappeared. Traditional frameworks of identity are dissolving and new patterns of identity are emerging. Globalization is forcing people to live in a more open, reflexive way. This means that we are constantly responding and adjusting to the changing environment around us; as individuals, we evolve with and within the larger context in which we live. Even the small choices we make in our daily lives – what we wear, how we spend our leisure time and how we take care of our health and our bodies – are part of an ongoing process of creating and re-creating our self-identities.

Conclusion: the need for global governance

As globalization progresses, existing political structures and models appear unequipped to manage a world full of the challenges that transcend national borders. It is not within the capacity of individual governments to control the spread of AIDS, to counter the effects of global warming or to regulate volatile financial markets. Many of the processes affecting societies around the world elude the grasp of current governing mechanisms. In the light of this governing deficit, some have called for new forms of global governance that could address global issues in a global way. As a growing number of challenges operate above the level of individual countries, it is argued that responses to them must also be transnational in scope.

Although it may seem unrealistic to speak of governance above the level of the nation-state, some steps have already been taken towards the creation of a global democratic structure, such as the formation of the United Nations and the European Union. The EU in particular can be seen as an innovative response to globalization and could well become a model for similar organizations in other parts of the world where regional ties are strong. New forms of global governance could help to promote a cosmopolitan world order in which transparent rules and standards for international behaviour, such as the defence of human rights, are established and observed.

The decade that has passed since the end of the Cold War has been marked by violence, internal conflict and chaotic transformations in many areas of the world. While some have taken a pessimistic view, seeing globalization as accelerating crisis and chaos, others see vital opportunities to harness globalizing forces in the pursuit of greater equality, democracy and prosperity. The move towards global governance and more effective regulatory institutions is certainly not misplaced at a time when global interdependence and the rapid pace of change link all of us together more than ever before. It is not beyond our abilities to reassert our will on the social world. Indeed, such a task appears to be both the greatest necessity and the greatest challenge facing human societies in the twenty-first century.

 We learn more about global governance in chapter 22, 'Politics, Government and Social Movements'.

Summary points

1. Several types of pre-modern society can be distinguished. In hunting and gathering societies, people gain their livelihood from gathering plants and hunting animals. Pastoral societies are those that raise domesticated animals as their major source of subsistence. Agrarian societies depend on the cultivation of fixed plots of land. Larger, more developed, urban societies form traditional states or civilizations.

2. The development of industralized societies and the expansion of the West led to the conquest of many parts of the world through the process of colonialization, which radically changed long-established societies and cultures.

3. In industrialized societies, industrial production is the main basis of the economy. Industrialized countries include the nations of the West and Japan, Australia and New Zealand. The developing world, in which a majority of the world's population live, are almost all formerly colonized areas. The majority of the population works in agricultural production, some of which is geared to world markets.

4. Social change may be defined as the transformation, over time, of the institutions and culture of a society. The modern period, although occupying only a small fraction of human history, has seen rapid and major changes and the pace of change is accelerating.

5. The development of social organization and institutions, from hunting and gathering to agrarian to modern industrial societies, is far too diverse to be accounted for by any single-factor theory of social change. At least three broad categories of influences can be identified. The *physical environment* includes such factors as climate or the availability of communication routes (rivers, mountain passes); these are important to consider, especially as they affect early economic development. *Political* organization (especially military power) affects all societies, traditional and modern, with the possible exception of hunting and gathering societies. *Cultural* factors include religion (which can act as a brake on change), communication systems (such as the invention of writing) and individual leadership.

6. The most important *economic* influence on modern social change is industrial capitalism, which depends on and promotes constant innovation in productive technology. Science and technology also affect and are affected by political factors, the most important of which is the emergence of the modern state. Cultural influences include another effect of science and technology: the critical and innovative character of modern thinking, which constantly challenges tradition and cultural habits.

7. Globalization is often portrayed as an economic phenomenon, but this is too simple. Globalization involves political, economic, cultural and social factors. It is driven forward by advances in information and communication technologies that have intensified the speed and scope of interaction between people around the world.

8. Globalization has become a hotly debated topic. Sceptics think it is overrated and that current levels of interconnectedness are not unprecedented. Some sceptics focus instead on processes of regionalization that are intensifying activity within major financial and trade groups. Hyperglobalizers take an opposing position, arguing that globalization is a real and powerful phenomenon that threatens to erode the role of national governments altogether. A third group, the transformationalists, argue that globalization is transforming many aspects of the current global order, but that old patterns still remain. According to this view, globalization is a contradictory process, involving a multidirectional flow of influences that sometimes work in opposition to each other.

9. Globalization is producing challenges that cross national borders and elude the reach of existing political structures. Because individual governments are not equipped to handle these transnational issues, there is a need for new forms of global governance that can address global problems in a global way. Reasserting our will on the rapidly changing social world may be the greatest challenge of the twenty-first century.

Further reading

The subject-matter of this chapter is so wide-ranging that a single book will not cover it. In general terms, however, there are two types of book you should find useful. First are those that cover the global human history and development of the human species. A good place to begin is with Noel Cowan's *Global History: A Short Overview* (Cambridge: Polity, 2001). This is a well-written, concise, yet comprehensive account which assumes no specialist knowledge. This can be followed with Bruce Mazlish's *The New Global History* (London: Routledge, 2006), which traces global history and globalization processes over the very long term and successfully links both historical and sociological approaches.

Second are those books that deal with current theories and debates on globalization. As you might expect, there are now many of these. Picking out two short introductions, you could try Malcolm Waters's *Globalization*, 2nd edition (London: Routledge, 2001), which is quite brief, divides globalization into economic, political and cultural forms, and moves at a brisk pace. Jan Aart Scholte's *Globalization: A Critical*

Introduction (Basingstoke: Palgrave Macmillan, 2005) is another possibility. This book is exactly what it says it is: a critical approach to globalization, but also one that is accessible and engaging. Jürgen Osterhammel and Niels P. Petersson's *Globalization: A Short History* (Princeton, NJ: Princeton University Press, 2005) traces the history of globalization over the past eight centuries, giving a longer-term view of the process.

After at least one of these, you would then be in a position to move on to more comprehensive and detailed accounts of globalization, such as David Held and Anthony McGrew's (eds) *The Global Transformations Reader*, 2nd edition (Cambridge: Polity, 2003) or Joseph Stiglitz's *Globalization and its Discontents* (London: Allen Lane, 2003).

In addition, a good dictionary of world history is always a useful resource for key dates and events, so something suitably large and reliable like Bruce Lenman and Hilary Marsden's (eds) *Chambers Dictionary of World History, New Edition* (London: Harrap, 2005) would fit the bill, as would *A Dictionary of World History* (Oxford: Oxford Paperbacks, 2000).

Internet links

BBC World Service on globalization:
www.bbc.co.uk/worldservice/programmes/
globalisation/

The Global Site – social science thinking on globalization:
www.theglobalsite.ac.uk/globalization/

1999 Reith Lectures – Anthony Giddens on 'The runaway world':
http://news.bbc.co.uk/hi/english/static/
events/reith_99/

International Forum – an alliance of activists, scholars and researchers looking to better understand globalization processes:
www.ifg.org/

Tradewatch – US-based activist site against globalization:
www.citizen.org/trade/

Centre for Research on Globalization – Canadian-based 'think-site' with lots of comment by researchers and academics:
www.globalresearch.ca/

World Bank globalization pages:
www1.worldbank.org/economicpolicy/
globalization/

Global Policy Forum – monitors policy-making at the United Nations:
www.globalpolicy.org/globaliz/index.ht

5

The
Environment

CHAPTER 5

The Environment

(opposite) The 2004 Indian Ocean earthquake was the third largest ever recorded and caused massive loss of human life.

Just before one o'clock a.m. UTC (Coordinated Universal Time) on 26 December 2004, the largest earthquake in 40 years occurred beneath the Indian Ocean. The earthquake shifted the seabed and displaced hundreds of cubic kilometres of water. A large wave known as a tsunami, caused by the tremor, began moving across the Indian Ocean away from the quake's epicentre at a speed of around 500 miles per hour. As it neared the coast, the tsunami slowed dramatically to just 30 miles per hour and began to increase in height. The tsunami reached the nearest landmass, Aceh in northern Indonesia, just 15 minutes after the initial quake, in many places destroying everything in its path and sweeping debris hundreds of metres inland. Thailand was hit after 90 minutes, Sri Lanka after two hours, the Maldives after three and a half hours; finally, the wave reached the African coast, thousands of miles from the epicentre of the quake, some seven hours after the earthquake that caused it.

The scale of the tragedy was not immediately apparent. By the end of the day on 26 December it was reported that 12,000 people had been killed. A few weeks later the United Nations estimated that more than 175,000 people had died. Most deaths were in Indonesia, where it is thought that around 160,000 people lost their lives. Figures for the total number of people killed around the Indian Ocean vary hugely, but the British Red Cross has estimated a death toll closer to the region of a staggering 1 million. In Sri Lanka more than 30,000 people were killed, more than a 1,000 of whom drowned when an 80-tonne train was lifted off its tracks and submerged under water. In India, just fewer than 10,000 people are thought to have died. Travelling west, the wave caused devastation as far away as Africa, killing around 140 people along the continent's east coast. Many millions of people around the Indian Ocean were left homeless.

Although much sociological research tends to focus on how human institutions and citizens respond to ecological hazards, the 2004 tsunami reminds us that natural processes can be complex and unpredictable. The natural environment is not simply an inert, passive backdrop to the dramas of social life, but is an active force, which often plays a large part in the shaping of societies. The Asian tsunami also shows that in a globalized world, events thousands of miles away have a great impact on everyone's lives.

Although the vast majority of people killed in the tsunami were locals, several thousands were tourists from around the world, many of whom had been enjoying an idyllic Christmas break in the region. For instance, the tsunami claimed the lives of 149 people who were British citizens or had close links with the UK: the greatest loss of British lives in any one incident since the Second World War and far greater than the number of Britons who died in the terrorist attacks in New York and Washington in 2001. The high loss of life amongst Westerners reflects the processes of globalization. Thailand, where most holiday-makers were killed, has only become a destination for mass tourism in the past two decades or so, as people from the rich world are increasingly prepared to travel further afield for their holidays. The relief effort was also global in scope, as the world's news stations beamed pictures and reports of the suffering around the planet. In rich countries, millions of dollars were donated by the general public and governments, troops and expertise were sent to the region and it was agreed that debt repayments from the worst hit countries should be suspended. In early January 2005, millions of people across Europe stopped what they were doing to take part in a three-minute silence in memory of those killed.

Why should sociologists be interested in events such as the Asian tsunami? Surely this was a 'natural disaster', an example of the massive power of nature? If so, then isn't it the proper subject for environmental scientists and geologists rather than sociologists? After all, what institutional training do sociologists receive on understanding earthquakes or plate tectonics? For most of the twentieth century, this apparently common-sense division of academic labour was taken for granted. Natural scientists investigated the non-human world, while social scientists concentrated on people and their societies. However, by the 1980s and '90s things were changing, as knowledge of global environmental problems emerged and it became much clearer that the fate of the 'natural' and 'social' worlds were inevitably intertwined.

In this chapter we look at ideas of nature and environment and what constitutes an environmental issue, before outlining sociological approaches to the study of such issues. From here we discuss some important environmental issues, including pollution, resource depletion, genetic modification and global warming before looking at sociological theories of consumerism and the risk society and proposals aimed at dealing with environmental dilemmas such as sustainable development and ecological modernization. The chapter ends with an evaluation of their prospects for success, looking ahead to the future of society–environment relations.

Nature, the environment and sociology

Defining nature and the environment

The environmental issues noted above all seem to involve nature. But 'nature' is not a simple word with a single meaning. In fact, dictionary definitions usually describe some twelve distinct meanings of the word. Raymond Williams (1987) says that **nature** is one of the most complex and difficult words in the English language because its dominant meaning has changed over time along with the development of societies.

'Nature' can mean something that is *essential* to a person or a thing. Why do some birds build their nests at the same time every year, for instance? We may be told that this is instinctive behaviour and an essential part of the 'nature' of birds. In fourteenth-century Europe, however, a new dominant meaning began to emerge. Nature came to be seen instead as a *series of forces* that directed the world and ultimately explained why things happen. For example, even today many people consult astrological charts looking for their birth date-based 'star sign' and what guidance it can offer on their life decisions. When they do this, they implicitly draw on the same idea of 'natural forces' – in this case the movement of stars and planets – directing human affairs. By the nineteenth century, the dominant

meaning of 'nature' had changed again. This time it was seen as the whole *material world of things* rather than as a series of forces. The natural world was a world full of *natural things* – animals, fields, mountains and much more. For instance, there was a trend towards looking at 'scenery' as landscapes and pictorials, with nature literally framed for our appreciation and enjoyment.

Two major and related causes of this latest change in meaning were **industrialization**, which shifted people away from working the land in agricultural settings, and **urbanization**, which led to larger human settlements that generated new living environments largely divorced from natural things (Thomas 1984). Nature was seen as an obstacle that society had to tame and overcome in order to make progress, as the popular ideas of nature 'in the raw' or nature 'red in tooth and claw' suggest.

For a minority of people, nature and society were seen as distinct, but nature was not seen as in need of taming. Instead, it was modern industrial society that was the problem, polluting and wasting nature to feed new urban lifestyles. Wild nature needed protection not domestication. Nevertheless, for both the tamers and the protectors, society and nature were seen as *separate things*. Nature was that which society was not, and vice versa. This meaning remains the dominant one today, though more people would probably now agree with the nature-protectors than did so in earlier periods.

Since the 1950s, use of the word, 'nature' has started to give way to another term: the **environment**. Dictionary definitions of 'environment' suggest that it is the external conditions or surroundings of people, especially those in which they live or work. David Harvey (1993) notes that this definition can apply to a number of situations. For example, we have a working environment, a business environment and an urban environment. However, none of these environments is what most of us think of when the term is used today. Indeed, this chapter's

From the seventeenth century onwards, wealthy social groups began to take pleasure in, and appreciate, landscape scenes such as this one, which also became the focus of the 'tourist gaze' (Urry 1990).

title, *The Environment*, does not refer to any of these 'environments'. Most people today would probably expect this chapter to discuss pollution, climate change, animal welfare and so on, indicating that *the* environment has taken on a widespread and special meaning. *The* environment is assumed to mean all of those non-human, natural surroundings within which human beings exist – sometimes called the 'natural environment' – and in its widest sense this is simply planet Earth as a whole. We will use this as our working definition throughout this chapter.

Sociology and the environment

In our age of global environmental problems and international environmental movements, sociologists can and must take a direct interest in our relationship to the environment within which we live. But just how can sociology help us to understand environmental issues?

> **THINKING CRITICALLY**
>
> How satisfactory is our working definition of 'the environment' above? What things would it include and what would it exclude? Should human beings be considered part of nature? If so, explain why many people see human creations such as cities and urban environments as somehow artificial.

First, sociology can help us to understand how environmental problems are distributed. Although the tsunami in Asia killed people from all over the globe, most of those who died were native to the coastal regions around the Indian Ocean. If it had occurred in the richer countries of the Pacific Ocean, the Pacific Tsunami Warning System, based in the American state of Hawaii, would quickly have alerted the emergency authorities in the endangered countries where the infrastructure should be in place to move people away from the coast before a wave strikes. In 2005, the United Nations began to plan for an early warning system for the Indian Ocean, with money from Western donors. The distribution of risks from the environment varies with other types of environmental issue too. For example, although global warming – the increase in average temperature across the globe – will affect everyone on the planet, it will do so in different ways. Flooding kills many more people in low-lying, poor countries, such as Bangladesh, where housing and emergency infrastructures are less able to cope with severe weather than in Europe, for instance. In richer countries, such as the USA, the issues raised by global warming for policymakers are likely to concern indirect effects, such as rising levels of immigration as people try to enter the country from areas more directly affected.

Second, sociologists can provide an account of how patterns of human behaviour create pressure on the natural environment (Cylke 1993). Although the 2004 tsunami was not a direct result of human action, many of the environmental challenges discussed in this chapter are. For example, the levels of pollution produced by industrialized countries would cause catastrophe if repeated in the world's poorer, non-industrial nations. If the impoverished regions of the world are to catch up with the richer ones, then citizens of the rich world are going to have to revise their expectations about constant

Modern consumerism generates huge amounts of waste, much of which has conventionally been simply dumped in landfill sites.

economic growth. Sociological theories of capitalist expansion, globalization or rationalization can all help us to understand how human societies are transforming the environment.

Third, sociology can help us to evaluate policies and proposals aimed at providing solutions to environmental problems. For example, some environmental activists and 'green' writers argue that people in the rich countries must turn away from consumerism and return to simpler ways of life living close to the land if global ecological disaster is to be avoided (Devall 1990; Schumacher 1977; Stead and Stead 1996). They argue that rescuing the global environment will thus mean radical social as well as technological change. However, given the enormous global inequalities that currently exist, there is little chance that the poor countries of the developing world will sacrifice their own economic growth because of environmental problems created largely by the rich countries. For instance, some governments in developing countries have argued that in relation to global warming there is no parallel between the 'luxury emissions' produced by the developed world and their own 'survival emissions'. In this way, sociological accounts of international relations and global inequality can clarify some of the underlying causes of the environmental problems we face today.

Sociology's founders – Marx, Durkheim and Weber – paid little attention to what we now call 'environmental issues'. Marx analysed capitalism and its exploitative class relationships (see chapter 1, 'What is Sociology?' and chapter 11, 'Stratification and Social Class'), Durkheim sought to understand the sources of social solidarity and to establish sociology within academic institutions (see chapter 1, 'What is Sociology?' and chapter 3, 'Theories and Perspectives in Sociology'), while Weber investigated the connections between religion, rationality and modern capitalism. The relationship between human societies and the natural environment was not seen as

especially problematic by a majority of people in the societies of the time; nor, therefore, was it a central problem for social scientists. Instead, the important social issues occupying scholars were social inequality, poverty and its alleviation, transforming unhealthy urban living conditions and assessing the future direction of industrial development. The natural environment was very much taken for granted, simply as the backdrop to the much more pressing and urgent social problems generated by industrial capitalism.

Although there are ideas within the work of the classical founders of sociology that have been pursued in an environmental direction by later sociologists, the environment was not a central problem of classical sociology. This situation became increasingly difficult once sociologists began to explore the problems identified by environmental campaigners. Could the classical theories provide any insights into human–environment relations? Do we need to abandon them altogether to understand how environmental problems have come about and how they might be solved? Some sociologists *have* returned to classical sociology, reinterpreting the classics in the light of environmental issues (Dickens 2004; Dunlap et al. 2002; Murphy 1997). However, most have not. Rather, sociological studies of the environment have been characterized by a dispute amongst social constructionist and critical realist approaches over just *how* environmental issues should be studied sociologically.

Social constructionism and critical realism

Social constructionism is an approach to studying social problems, including environmental problems. Social constructionists have investigated how some environmental issues come to be seen as significant while others are seen as less important or are largely ignored (Braun and Castree 1998; Hannigan 2006). Are the environmental problems that are thought to be most important today really the ones which are

For more on social constructionism, see chapter 3, 'Theories and Perspectives in Sociology', and chapter 7, 'Social Interaction and Everyday Life'.

the most serious and in need of urgent action?

Constructionists ask a series of important questions about environmental problems. What is the *history of the problem* and how has it developed? *Who* is making the claim that it is a problem; do they have any vested interest and stand to benefit from doing so? *What do they say* about it and does the evidence support this? *How* do they say it? Do they use scientific, emotional, political or moral arguments and why do they do so? Who *opposes* the claim and on what grounds? Do opponents stand to lose if the claim is successful and could that, rather than the evidence, explain their opposition? Such questions give sociologists a clearly defined role in the study of environmental issues, which no other discipline performs. They also add something new to our understanding of environmental issues and problems.

Social constructionists remind us that all environmental problems are, in part, socially created or 'constructed' by groups of people. Nature never does 'speak for itself', but people do speak on its behalf. This process of construction can be examined, understood and explained. And in doing so, the public should be in a better position to assess whether an environmental problem really is as serious as the claims-makers say it is.

For some sociologists though, constructionism is problematic, particularly when studying environmental issues. Social constructionism tends to be 'agnostic' about the central problem at issue (Irwin 2001). For example, a constructionist study of the depletion of the ozone layer would tell us a lot about how this problem came to be seen as important, what arguments were made about it and who opposed the claim. But on the central question – is the ozone layer really becoming dangerously depleted? – social constructionism remains agnostic. For environmental activists and those committed to solving environmental problems, this is just not helpful. In short, constructionism tells us a lot about people and social interactions, but nothing about society–environment relations.

An alternative approach, known as 'environmental realism' (Bell 2004) or **critical realism**, attempts to approach environmental issues in a scientific way, which brings together evidence from across the social and natural sciences in order to understand better why environmental problems occur. Critical realism aims to get beneath the surface of the visible evidence to uncover the underlying causes of events and problems (Benton 1994; Dickens 1996, 2004; Martell 1994). In contrast to the agnosticism of social constructionism towards the reality of environmental problems, critical realists are prepared to accept and debate knowledge and evidence from the natural and environmental sciences in its explanations. 'Using your sociological imagination 5.1', on BSE in the UK, illustrates some key points of this approach.

Realist approaches such as that described above require the findings from a range of academic disciplines: biology, zoology, history, sociology, political science and more. Only in this way can we properly explain how and why BSE and vCJD posed such a problem in the 1980s and '90s. Like social constructionists, realists would agree that cows are social as well as natural creatures. Arguing a constructionist case, Alan Irwin says: 'The modern cow is the product of generations of human-controlled cattle-breeding, feeding and housing' (2001: 80). But unlike constructionists, realists search for *causal explanations* and are prepared to explore and debate the natural science of environmental issues in ways that social constructionists do not. Critical realism takes into account the *objective reality* of natural objects and environments, and this means rethinking our sociological theories and concepts with this in mind.

5.1 'Mad cow disease' in the UK

In 1996, British government ministers admitted the possibility that at least 10 recent human deaths had been caused by a new variant of Creutzfeldt-Jakob Disease (vCJD) in humans, which may have developed as a result of people eating beef infected with Bovine Spongiform Encephalopathy (BSE) during the 1980s. This was a huge shock. Millions of people had eaten beef in this period and, at least theoretically, could develop the disease. How had this happened?

BSE is a fatal neurodegenerative disease of cattle, whose symptoms are similar to those of Creutzfeldt-Jakob Disease (CJD) in human beings. These symptoms include the loss of coordination, nervousness, loss of memory, and aggression (hence 'mad' cows). From the experience of sheep farming, it was thought that BSE could not cross the species barrier into the human population. CJD is a recognized but very rare disease in human beings, but is unrelated to BSE. The UK BSE Inquiry (1998–2000) identified the cause of BSE in cattle as a gene mutation in a single cow (named Cow 133). But the most widely accepted explanation for the *spread* of BSE is that cattle were being fed BSE-infected offal (Macnaghten and Urry 1998: 253–65). The Inquiry Report said that the problem was 'the recycling of animal protein in ruminant feed'.

The Report also noted that the link between BSE and the human vCJD, 'was now clearly established'. As of 7 January 2008, the National Creutzfeldt-Jakob Disease Surveillance Unit in Edinburgh reports that 163 people have died from vCJD. Meat-rendering practices were changed and new rules brought in to prevent a recurrence, but public confidence in science, politics, regulatory bodies and the meat industry was thoroughly shaken by the episode.

On the face of it, this seems like an episode of a naturally occurring disease in animals, unrelated to social processes. However, the transmission and spread of BSE was the product of decisions taken within the animal feed production system. The previous scientific assumption that BSE would not cross the species barrier was shown to be wrong. BSE-infected beef *did* lead to vCJD in humans. Treating cattle as commercial products and denying their herbivorous nature by feeding them dead cattle produced an unexpected outcome that no one had forecast. A critical realist approach would suggest that to understand this event properly (and therefore to put in place the right measures to prevent it from happening again), we need to know what kind of creatures cows are: what are their natural capacities? We also need to understand human beings to know why the disease had such devastating effects on people. What happens when infected foodstuff finds its way into the human body? We also need to know how the food production system operates and what political and economic decisions were made that allowed dead animals to be fed to others. And we need culturally specific knowledge – just why do so many people eat so much beef in the UK?

From this brief sketch of these two approaches, we can say that social constructionism leads in the direction of a *sociology of the environment* that explores environmental issues from a conventional sociological position, using concepts and theories from within the discipline. By contrast, critical realism leads towards an *environmental sociology*, which demands the revision of existing sociological approaches to take account of the complex intertwining of society and environment (Sutton 2007). However, as we will see during the chapter, many research studies in this field tend to veer between these two polarized alternatives.

> **THINKING CRITICALLY**
>
> What advantages are there in sociologists taking an 'agnostic' stance to environmental problems? Why might this not be such a good idea? How would social constructionists investigate the BSE epidemic and its consequences, as outlined above?

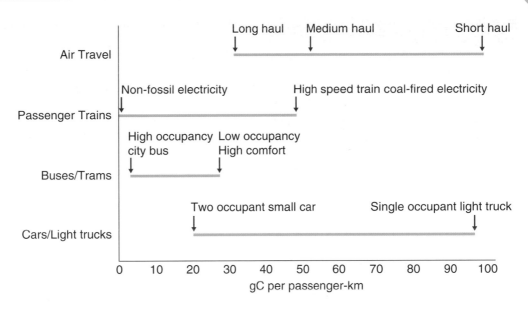

Figure 5.1 European carbon emissions (grams of carbon per kilometre) by mode of transport, 2007

Source: ATAG http://atag.org/files/PR%20LON-170002A.pdf (Slide 6, accessed 18 January 2008)

What are environmental issues?

As we have seen, there are many different environmental issues confronting the contemporary world. Some are local or regional in character, while others have an impact on the global human population. However, what they all share and what makes them specifically environmental issues is that they involve both social relationships and interactions and non-human, natural phenomena. In this sense, they are *hybrid* issues of society and the environment (Irwin 2001: 26). Keep this point in mind when you read the rest of this section, which covers a range of environmental issues.

Pollution and waste

Air pollution

Air pollution, caused by toxic emissions into the atmosphere, is thought to claim more than 2.7 million lives per year. It is possible to make a distinction between two types of air pollution: 'outdoor pollution', produced mainly by industrial pollutants and automobile emissions, and 'indoor pollution', which is caused by burning fuels in the home for heating and cooking. Traditionally, air pollution has been seen as a problem that afflicts industrialized countries, with their greater numbers of factories and motorized vehicles. In recent years, however, attention has been drawn to the dangers of 'indoor pollution' in the developing world. It is suggested that more than 90 per cent of deaths linked to air pollution occur in the developing world. This is because many of the fuels that are burned by people in developing countries, such as wood and dung, are not as clean as modern fuels such as kerosene and propane.

Until the middle of the twentieth century, air pollution in many countries was caused primarily by the widespread burning of coal – a fossil fuel – which emits sulphur dioxide and thick black smoke into the atmosphere. In many Eastern European countries and the developing world, the practice remains widespread. Coal was used extensively to heat homes and as power in factories. In 1956, in an attempt to reduce smog, a Clean Air Act was passed in Britain to regulate emissions from chimneys. Smokeless types of fuels, such as kerosene, propane and natural gas, were promoted and are now widely used in the industrialized countries.

Since the 1960s the main source of air pollution has been the growth in the use of motorized vehicles. Vehicle emissions are particularly harmful because they enter the atmosphere at a much lower level than emissions from chimneys. As figure 5.1 shows, the range of emissions that are produced by different types of vehicle is quite large. Cars, which account for some 80 per cent of travel in Europe, have a particularly harmful impact on the environment. A single occupancy car journey can cause the same weight of carbon emissions per kilometre travelled as a long-haul flight. For this reason, attempts to reduce air pollution in many industrialized countries have focused on the use of low-emission travel alternatives such as passenger trains, high occupancy buses and the sharing of car journeys.

Air pollution has been linked to a number of health problems among humans, including respiratory difficulties, cancers and lung disease. Although outdoor pollution has long been associated with industrialized countries, it is growing rapidly in the developing world. As countries undergo rapid processes of industrialization, factory emissions increase and the number of vehicles on the roads also grows. In many developing countries, leaded petrol is still in use, although it has been phased out in much of the developed world. Levels of air pollution were particularly high in many areas of Eastern Europe and the (former) Soviet Union, though economic restructuring and the collapse of industrial manufacturing in these areas has reduced this somewhat since the 1990s.

Air pollution does not only affect the health of human and animal populations; it also has a damaging impact on other elements of the ecosystem. One harmful consequence of air pollution is acid rain, a phenomenon which occurs when sulphur and nitrogen oxide emissions in one country drift across borders and produce acidic rainfalls in another. Acid rain is harmful to forests, crops and animal life, and leads to the acidification of lakes. Canada, Poland and the Nordic countries have been particularly hard hit by acid rain. In Sweden, for example, 20,000 lakes out of a total of 90,000 have been acidified.

Like many environmental issues, acid rain is difficult to counteract because it is transnational in its origins and consequences. Much of the acid rain in eastern Canada, for example, has been shown as linked to industrial production in the state of New York, across the US–Canadian border. Other countries suffering from acid rain have similarly found that it is not within their control to tackle the problem, since its origins lie across national borders. In some instances, bilateral or regional agreements have been concluded in an attempt to reduce the severity of acid rain. Yet emissions remain high in some areas and are growing quickly in the developing world.

Water pollution

Throughout history, people have depended on water to fulfil a host of important needs – drinking, cooking, washing, irrigating crops, fishing and many other pursuits. Although water is one of the most valuable and essential natural resources, it has also suffered enormous abuse at the hands of human beings. For many years, waste products – both human and manufactured – were dumped directly into rivers and oceans with barely a second thought. Only in the past half century or so have concerted efforts been made in many countries to protect the quality of water, to preserve the fish and wildlife that depend on it, and ensure access to clean water for the human population. Regardless of these efforts, water pollution remains a serious problem in many parts of the world.

Even in lush rainforest where water is abundant, urban settlements, factories and intensive farming practices can make getting access to clean water a difficult task.

One of the 'Millennium Development Goals' set by the United Nations in 2000 is to 'reduce by half the proportion of people without access to safe drinking water' by 2015. Water pollution can be understood broadly to refer to the contamination of the water supply by elements such as toxic chemicals and minerals, pesticides or untreated sewage. It poses the greatest threat to people in the developing world. Currently, more than one billion people around the world lack access to safe drinking water and more than two billion lack sanitation. Sanitation systems remain underdeveloped in many of the world's poorest countries and human waste products are often emptied directly into streams, rivers and lakes. The high levels of bacteria that result from untreated sewage lead to a variety of water-borne diseases, such as diarrhoea, dysentery and hepatitis. Some

two billion cases of diarrhoea are caused annually by contaminated water; five million people die each year from diarrhoeal diseases.

Some progress is being made to improve access to the world's resources of water. During the 1990s, nearly one billion people gained access to safe water and the same number to sanitation, though ensuring safe water supplies remains a problem, particularly in some parts of Africa (UNDP 2002; see also figure 5.2). The problem may actually be worsening as water supplies in developing countries are privatised, raising the cost for customers, whilst the effects of global warming produce more regular droughts (see 'Global Society 5.1').

In industrialized countries, cases of water pollution are often caused by the overuse of fertilizers in agricultural areas. Over a period of years, nitrates from chemical pesticides

Global Society 5.1 | The privatization of water

Western companies have the know-how – and the financial incentive – to supply water to poor nations. But, as Richard Wachman reports, their involvement is already provoking unrest ...

Water becomes the new oil as world runs dry

The midday sun beats down on a phalanx of riot police facing thousands of jeering demonstrators, angry at proposals to put up their water bills by more than a third. Moments later a uniformed officer astride a horse shouts an order and the police charge down the street to embark on a club-wielding melée that leaves dozens of bloodied protesters with broken limbs.

A film clip from the latest offering from Hollywood? Unfortunately not. It's a description of a real-life event in Cochabamba, Bolivia's third largest city, where a subsidiary of Bechtel, the US engineering giant, took over the municipal water utility and increased bills to a level that the poorest could not afford.

Welcome to a new world, where war and civil strife loom in the wake of chronic water shortages caused by rising population, drought (exacerbated by global warming) and increased demand from the newly affluent middle classes in the emerging economies of Asia and Latin America. At a City briefing by an international bank last week, a senior executive said: 'Today everyone is talking about global warming, but my prediction is that in two years water will move to the top of the geopolitical agenda.'

The question for countries as far apart as China and Argentina is whether to unleash market forces by allowing access to private European and American multinationals that have the technological know-how to help bring water to the masses – but at a price that many may be unable, or unwilling, to pay.

As Cochabamba illustrates, water is an explosive issue in developing countries, where people have traditionally received supplies for free from local wells and rivers. But in the past 15 years rapid industrialisation, especially in places such as China, has led to widespread pollution and degradation of the local environment.

A report out today from accountancy giant Deloitte & Touche says humans seem to have a peculiar talent for making previously abundant resources scarce: 'This is especially the case with water', it observes. According to the firm's findings, more than one billion people will lack access to clean water by next year. Paul Lee, research director at Deloitte, and one of the authors of the report, says: 'Demand for water is expected to be driven by economic growth and population increases. India's demand for water is expected to exceed supply by 2020.'

The World Wildlife Fund has forecast that in the Himalayas, the retreat of glaciers could reduce summer water flows by up to two-thirds. In the Ganges area, this would cause a water shortage for 500 million people. Lee says: 'The lack of the most important form of liquid in the world is therefore a fundamental issue and one that the technology sector can play a major role in addressing.'

But the crux of the problem remains: according to a report from Credit Suisse, annual world water use has risen sixfold during the past century, more than double the rate of population growth. By 2025, almost two-thirds of the global population will live in countries where water will be a scarce commodity. And that could lead to conflict, as United Nations secretary-general Ban Ki-moon warned last week.

Asia looks vulnerable, with China planning to syphon off Tibet's water supply to make up for shortages in the parched north. Elsewhere, the Israel-Palestine conflict is at least partly about securing supplies from the River Jordan; similarly, water is a major feature of the strife in Sudan that has left Darfur devastated. When it comes to this most basic of commodities, the stakes could hardly be higher.

Source: Richard Wachman, *Observer*, 9 December 2007

seep into the groundwater supply; nearly 25 per cent of groundwater in Europe shows levels of contamination higher than that deemed permissible by the European Union (UNDP 1998). Some of the most polluted water can be found near former industrial areas, where traces of mercury, lead and other metals have lodged in the sediments and continue slowly to emit pollutants into the water supply over a period of years.

The quality of rivers in most Western industrialized countries has been improving in recent years. In Eastern Europe and the former Soviet Union, however, river pollution remains a very real concern. Four-fifths of the water samples taken from 200 rivers in the former Soviet Union revealed levels of contamination that were dangerously high.

Solid waste

Next time you visit a supermarket, toy store or fast-food restaurant, pay attention to the amount of packaging that accompanies the products you see there. There are few things you can buy without packaging in our present age. Although there are clear benefits to packaging in terms of displaying goods attractively and guaranteeing the safety of products, there are enormous drawbacks as well. One of the clearest indicators of increasing consumption is the growing amount of domestic waste – what goes into our rubbish bins – being produced worldwide. Where the developing countries generated 100–330 kilograms of domestic solid waste per capita in the early 1990s, the figure was 414 kilograms for the European Union and 720 for North America (UNDP 1998). As figure 5.3 illustrates, waste generation is closely tied to the relative prosperity of countries as consumption of goods increases; Poland, the Czech Republic and the Slovak Republic, countries that have only recently started to emulate the model of Western consumerism, generate less than half the waste per capita of the USA, Denmark and Australia. There have been increases in both the absolute amount of waste produced, and the amount produced per person, in a majority of countries around the world.

The industrialized societies have been called 'throw-away societies' because the

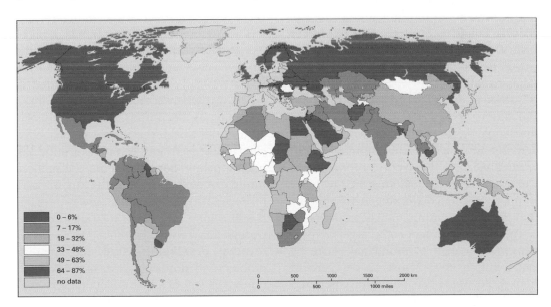

Figure 5.2 Percentage of population with lack of access to safe water, by country, 2004

Source: www.theglobaleducationproject.org/earth/human-conditions.php (accessed 17 January 2008)

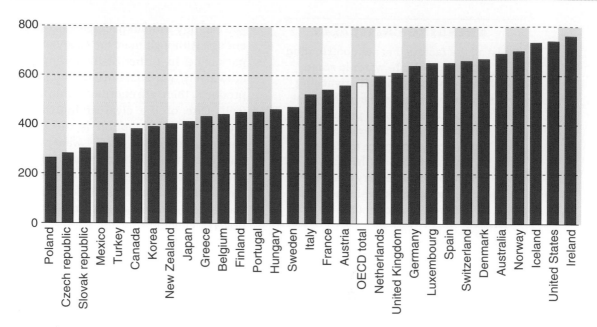

Figure 5.3 Municipal waste generation in kilogram per capita, OECD countries, 2003 (or latest year available)

Source: OECD 2007

volume of items discarded as a matter of course is so large. In most countries of the industrialized world, waste collection services are almost universal, but it is becoming increasingly difficult to dispose of the enormous amounts of refuse. Landfill sites are quickly filling up, and many urban areas have run out of disposal room for domestic waste. In Scotland for example, around 90 per cent of household waste goes into landfill sites and the Scottish Environment Protection Agency reported that in 2006 household waste was still growing at 2 per cent per annum. The international trade in waste has led to the export of recycling to China where waste is often sorted by hand in poorly regulated working environments that produce environmental degradation.

The UK government set a target of recycling 40 per cent of municipal waste by 2005. But in 2001–2 just 12 per cent of household waste was recycled, compared with 7 per cent in 1996–7. During the same period, the amount of waste produced by each household in England increased by 17

per cent (HMSO 2004). Table 5.1 shows how waste is managed in England. Although this amount of recycling may seem low compared to the overall amount of domestic waste that is produced, a large proportion of what is thrown away cannot be easily reprocessed or reused. Many kinds of plastics widely employed in food packaging simply become unusable waste; there is no way of recycling it, and it has to be buried in refuse tips where it remains for centuries. Recycling is becoming a huge industry around the world; the formal global recycling industry currently employs around 1.5 million people handling some 500 million tonnes of waste, generating an annual turnover of US$200 billion. However, there is still a long way to go to transform the world's 'throw-away societies'.

In the developing world, the greatest problem with domestic waste at the present time is the *lack* of refuse collection services. It has been estimated that 20–50 per cent of domestic waste in the developing world goes uncollected. Poorly managed waste

Table 5.1 Management of municipal waste, England: by method

	1996/7	1998/9	2000/1	2001/2
Landfill	20,631	21,534	22,039	22,317
Incineration with energy from waste	1,446	2,117	2,391	2,459
Recycled/composted[a]	1,750	2,525	3,446	3,907
Other[b]	761	160	182	140
Total	24,588	26,337	28,057	28,823

[a] Includes household and non-household sources collected for recycling or for centralized composting; home composting estimates are not included in this total

[b] Includes incineration without energy from waste and refuse derived fuel manufacture. Excludes any processing prior to landfilling and materials sent to materials reclamation facilities (MRFs)

Source: HMSO (2004)

systems mean that refuse piles up in the streets, contributing to the spread of disease. With the passing of time, it is very likely that the developing world will face problems with waste disposal that are even more acute than the current situation in the industrialized countries. As societies become richer, there is a gradual shift from organic waste, such as food remains, to plastic and synthetic materials, like packaging, that take much longer to decompose.

Resource depletion

Human societies depend on very many resources from the natural world – for example, water, wood, fish, animals and plant life. These elements are often termed 'renewable resources', because in a healthy ecosystem they replace themselves automatically with the passing of time. Yet if the consumption of renewable resources gets out of balance or is too extreme, there is a danger that they will be depleted altogether. Some evidence suggests that such a process may be occurring. The deterioration of renewable resources is of great concern to many environmentalists.

Water

You may not think of water as a depletable resource – after all, it constantly replenishes itself through rainfall. If you live in Europe or North America, you probably do not give much thought to your water supply at all, except occasionally when restrictions are put on its use in the summer months. Yet for people in many parts of the world, access to a constant water supply is a more chronic and severe problem. In some densely populated regions, the high demand for water cannot be met by available water resources. In the arid climates of North Africa and the Middle East, for example, the pressure on water supply is acute and shortages have become commonplace. This trend is almost sure to intensify in the years to come.

There are several reasons why this is so. The first is that much of the projected world population growth over the next quarter-century is likely to be concentrated in areas that are already experiencing problems with water shortages. Furthermore, much of this growth will occur in urban areas, where the infrastructure will struggle to accommodate the water and sanitation needs of this expanded population.

Climate change also has a potential impact on the depletion of the water supply. As temperatures rise, more water will be needed for drinking and irrigation. Yet it is also likely that groundwater may not replenish itself as rapidly as before and that rates of evaporation may also increase.

Recycling has become a huge industry worldwide; many people have built the recycling of domestic waste into their everyday routines.

Finally, changes in climate patterns which may accompany global warming will be likely to affect existing patterns of precipitation, altering access to water supplies in ways that are quite unpredictable.

Soil degradation and desertification

According to the 1998 UN Human Development Report, a third of the world's population lives more or less directly from the land – on the food they can grow or gather, and the game they can catch. Because they are largely dependent on the earth, they are particularly vulnerable to changes affecting their ability to live off the land. In many areas of Asia and Africa that are experiencing rapid population growth, the problem of soil degradation threatens to impoverish millions of people. Soil degradation is the process by which the quality of the earth is worsened and its valuable natural elements are stripped away through over-use, drought or inadequate fertilization.

The long-term effects of soil degradation are extremely severe and difficult to reverse. In areas where the soil has been degraded, agricultural productivity declines and there is less arable land available per head. It becomes difficult or impossible to keep cattle or other livestock because of a lack of fodder. In many instances, people are forced to migrate in search of more fertile land. Desertification refers to instances of intense land

Global Society 5.2 | Soil degradation and economic development in Africa

Soil crisis is holding back African recovery

The fertility of Africa's soil is being depleted at a rate that threatens to undermine the continent's attempts at eradicating hunger with sustainable agricultural development.

A study has found three-quarters of Africa's farmland is plagued by severe soil degradation caused by wind and soil erosion and the loss of vital mineral nutrients.

This degradation can partly explain why agricultural productivity in Africa has remained largely stagnant for 40 years while Asia's productivity has increased threefold, the authors claim. Julio Henao and Carlos Baanante of the non-profit International Centre for Soil Fertility and Agricultural Development in Muscle Shoals, Alabama, found bad farming practices have damaged soil health on the continent between 1980 and 2004.

Farmers in Africa have traditionally relied on clearing land to grow crops then leaving it fallow to regain some of its fertility. 'But population pressure now forces farmers to grow crop after crop, ''mining'' or depleting the soil of nutrients while giving nothing back', the report says.

'With little access to fertilisers, the farmers are forced to bring less fertile soils on marginal land into production, at the expense of Africa's wildlife and forests.' Mr Henao and Mr Baanante found that during 2002 to 2004 about 85 per cent of African farmland was haemorrhaging mineral nutrients at an annual rate greater than 30 kg per hectare, and 40 per cent of farmland was losing nutrients at the higher rate of 60 kg per hectare a year.

'The very resources on which African farmers and their families depend for welfare and survival are being undermined by soil degradation caused by nutrient mining and associated factors, such as deforestation, use of marginal lands and poor agricultural practices', the report says.

The worst-affected countries in terms of soil depletion are Guinea Bissau, the Democratic Republic of Congo, Angola, Rwanda, Burundi and Uganda. With a population growth of 3 per cent per year, the number of malnourished people in sub-Saharan Africa has grown from about 88 million in 1970 to more than 200 million by the end of the last century, the report says.

Source: Steve Connor, *Independent*, 31 March 2006

---

degradation which result in desert-like conditions over large areas. This phenomenon has already affected territory adding up to the size of Russia and Indonesia combined, putting more than 110 countries at risk.

Deforestation

Forests are an essential element of the ecosystem: they help to regulate water supplies, release oxygen into the atmosphere and prevent soil erosion. They also contribute to many people's livelihoods as sources of fuel, food, wood, oils, dyes, herbs and medicines. Yet despite their crucial importance, more than a third of the earth's original forests have now disappeared. Deforestation describes the destruction of forested land, usually through commercial logging. Deforestation claimed 15 million hectares of land in the 1980s, with the largest amounts occurring in Latin America

and the Caribbean (losing 7.4 million hectares) and sub-Saharan Africa (losing 4.1 million hectares).

Although many types of forest are involved in the process of deforestation, the fate of tropical rainforests has attracted the greatest attention. Tropical rainforests, which cover some 7 per cent of the earth's surface, are home to a great number of plant and animal species that contribute to the earth's biodiversity – the diversity of species of life forms. They are also home to many of the plants and oils from which medicines are developed. Tropical rainforests are currently shrinking at a rate of approximately 1 per cent a year, and may well disappear altogether by the end of this century if current trends are not halted. In many areas of South America where tropical rainforests are most extensive, rainforests have been burned to make room for more land to graze

Deforestation threatens significantly to reduce the diversity of life forms on the planet.

cattle. In other areas of the world, such as West Africa and the South Pacific, the international demand for exotic hardwoods has fuelled the destruction of rainforests. Trends in increasing consumption therefore encourage developing countries to export their natural commodities – a process which results in both environmental destruction and a loss of biodiversity.

Deforestation has both human and environmental costs. In terms of human costs, some poor communities which were previously able to sustain or supplement their livelihoods through forests are no longer able to do so. Deforestation can further impoverish marginalized populations, which rarely share in the enormous revenues generated from the granting of logging rights and the sale of timber. The environmental costs of deforestation include soil erosion and floods: when they are intact, mountainous forests perform the important function of absorbing and recycling much of the water from rainfall. Once

the forests are missing, rain cascades off the slopes, causing floods and then droughts.

Genetic modification of food

As we will see in chapter 13, 'Global Inequality', some 830 million people around the globe go hungry each day and, as we saw above, increasing soil degradation threatens to undermine economic development in Africa. The process of global warming may also contribute to increased desertification and poor harvests, all of which has led to fears that food shortages may become even more widespread. In some of the world's most densely populated areas, people are highly dependent on staple food crops – such as rice – whose stocks are dwindling. Many worry that present farming techniques will not be able to produce rice yields sufficient to support the growing population. As with many environmental challenges, the threat of famine is not evenly distributed. The industrialized countries have extensive surpluses of grain. It is the poorer countries, where the population growth is projected to be greatest, that grain shortfalls are likely to be a chronic problem.

Some scientists and politicians argue that the key to averting a potential food crisis may lie in recent advances in science and biotechnology. By manipulating the genetic composition of basic crops, such as rice, it is now possible to boost a plant's rate of photosynthesis and to produce bigger crop yields. This process is known as genetic modification; plants that are produced in such a way are called **genetically modified organisms** (GMOs). Genetic modification can be carried out for a variety of purposes – not only to enhance the crop yield. Scientists have produced GMOs with higher than normal vitamin content, for example; other genetically modified crops are resistant to commonly used agricultural herbicides that are used to kill the weeds round them, as well as insects and fungal and viral pests. Food products that are made from, or contain traces of, GMOs are known as GM foods.

GM crops are different from anything that has existed before, because they involve transplanting genes between different organisms. This is a much more radical intervention into nature than the older methods of cross-breeding that have been used for many years. GMOs are produced by techniques of gene splicing that can be used to transplant genes between animals as well as plants. For instance, in recent experiments human genes have been introduced into farm animals, such as pigs, with a view to eventually providing replacement parts for human transplants. Human genes have even been spliced into plants, although the GM crops that have been marketed so far do not involve this kind of radical bioengineering.

Scientists claim that a GM strain of 'super-rice' could boost rice yields by as much as 35 per cent. Another strain called 'golden rice' – which contains added amounts of vitamin A – could reduce vitamin A deficiency in more than 120 million children worldwide. You might think that such advances in biotechnology would be welcomed enthusiastically by people around the world. But in fact, the issue of genetic modification has become one of the most controversial issues of our age. For many people, it highlights the fine line that exists between the benefits of technology and scientific innovation, on the one hand, and the risks of environmental destruction, on the other.

Controversy over GM foods

The saga of GM foods began only a few years ago when some of the world's leading chemical and agricultural firms decided that new knowledge about the workings of genes could transform the world's food supply. These companies had been making pesticides and herbicides, but wanted to move into what they saw as a major market for the future. The American firm Monsanto was the leader in developing much of the new technology. Monsanto bought up seed companies, sold off its chemical division and devoted much of its energies to bringing the new crops to the market. Led by its then Chief Executive Robert Shapiro, Monsanto launched a gigantic advertising campaign promoting the benefits of its GM crops to farmers and to consumers. The early responses were just as the company had confidently anticipated. By early 1999, 55 per cent of the soya beans and 35 per cent of the maize produced in the United States contained genetic alterations. GM crops at that point were already growing on 35 million hectares of land across the world – an area one and a half times the size of Britain. In addition to North America, GM crops were also being widely grown in China.

Monsanto's sales campaign stressed a number of positive virtues of GM foods. The company claimed that GM crops could help feed the world's poor and reduce the use of chemical pollutants, especially the chemicals used in pesticides and herbicides. It is claimed, for example, that GM potatoes

Greenpeace has led some of the anti-GM protests in recent years, such as this attack on a field of genetically modified corn in Norfolk.

need 40 per cent less chemical insecticide than would be required using traditional farming techniques. Biotechnology, according to Monsanto, will allow us to grow better-quality crops with higher yields, while at the same time sustaining and protecting the environment.

Since GM crops are essentially quite new, no one can be certain about what their effects will be once they are introduced into the environment. Many ecological and consumer groups became concerned about the potential risks involved with the adoption of this largely untested technology. Concern about GM foods was especially widespread in Europe (Toke 2004). In Britain, hostility to the commercial growing of GM crops was stimulated by the findings of Dr Arpad Pusztai, an internationally renowned geneticist working in a government laboratory in Scotland. In his research, Dr Pusztai had tested potatoes which had a gene for a particular natural insecticide

inserted – a protein known as lectin, extracted from a certain type of flower. The results indicated that rats which ate the GM potatoes experienced significant damage to their immune systems and reduced organ growth. Dr Pusztai's findings were criticized by other leading scientists and he was dismissed from his post at the government laboratory after speaking on television about his worries concerning GM foods.

By this time, GM foods had become a front-page story in the news almost every day. Numerous TV and radio debates, chat shows and phone-ins were organized to discuss the issue. Many members of the British public registered their antagonism to GM crops; some even engaged in 'direct action', pulling GM crops out of the ground at official trial sites across the country. Similar responses occurred in a range of other European countries. These eventually spread back to the USA, where there had previously been little debate. In the UK,

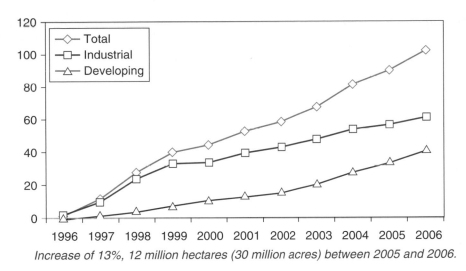

Increase of 13%, 12 million hectares (30 million acres) between 2005 and 2006.

Figure 5.4   Global area of genetically modified crops, 2006

Source: ISAAA Brief 35, 2006

seven out of the eight major supermarket chains changed their policy on GM foods. Five of them imposed a complete ban on GM ingredients in their own-brand products, which is still in place, and all of them insisted on better labelling in their stores. Two large companies, Unilever and Nestlé, announced that they would withdraw their acceptance of genetically modified foodstuffs. Some farmers in the USA who had been engaged in the large scale cultivation of GM crops changed back to conventional crop production. One survey in 2003 showed that 59 per cent of the UK population strongly agreed that genetically modified foods should be banned (HMSO 2005).

The protests of environmentalists and consumer groups had a major impact on the fate of Monsanto, and caused a serious decline in its share value. Robert Shapiro appeared on television to admit that his company had made major mistakes: 'We have probably irritated and antagonized more people than we have persuaded', he said. 'Our confidence in this technology and our enthusiasm for it has, I think, been widely seen – and understandably so – as condescension or indeed arrogance.' It was an extraordinary turnaround from the world-beating confidence with which he had spoken only a few months before. Monsanto was forced to drop altogether one of its most controversial plans – the idea of using a gene called 'the terminator'. This gene would have ensured that seeds which Monsanto sold to farmers would be sterile after one generation. The farmers would have had to order seeds each year from the company. Critics of Monsanto claimed that the company was trying to lure farmers into a form of 'bioslavery', and the issue highlights again the inequalities of power between those companies looking to take advantage of globalization processes and those at their sharp end.

GM food continues to generate controversy in Europe and large parts of Africa. The European Union refused patents of new GM crops between 1998 and 2004. The complete moratorium was raised in 2004 when imports of a further GM maize crop were approved, and a scheme was introduced to label foods containing GM products. However, the EU's actions were too slow for the big GM producers, particularly in the United States, who filed a complaint with the World Trade Organization (WTO) in 2003 against the EU's failure to authorize the commercialization of GM crops, claiming that the European position had no scientific basis and broke free trade laws. In 2006 the WTO ruled that a series of European countries, including Austria, Germany, Greece, France and Luxembourg, *had* broken international trade rules by imposing bans on the marketing and growing of GM foods. However, it is hard to imagine that European consumers, who have consistently refused to buy GM foods, will suddenly drop their opposition based purely on such a ruling.

In Africa, GM food aid has also run into trouble. In 2002, Zambia refused to accept American food-aid donations of corn and soya because much of it was genetically modified and reduced the genetic diversity which was essential for long-term sustainable agriculture. Zambia's president, Levy Mwanawasa, called the imports 'poison'. By 2004 Zambia had been joined by Zimbabwe, Malawi, Mozambique, Lesotho and Angola in refusing genetically modified food aid.

Evaluating the risks of GM foods

The issue of GM crops highlights the point we noted at the start of the chapter, namely that environmental issues always involve complex combinations of the natural and the social and it is not realistic to expect them to be easily separated. Despite the assertions of the GM producers, no one can say with certainty that genetically modified crops are risk-free. The genetic code is highly complicated – adding new genes into plants or organisms could produce as yet unpredicted diseases or other harmful consequences. Because the technology is so unknown, new findings and discoveries are being uncovered with startling frequency. In May 2000, the British government admitted that thousands of acres of conventional oilseed rape that had been planted by farmers had in fact been 'contaminated' as GM crops pollinated those nearby. German research published just weeks later claimed that a gene commonly used to modify oilseed rape had jumped the species barrier

into the guts of bees. In the short period between these two startling revelations, Monsanto itself acknowledged that its modified soybeans – the GMO that has been cultivated most extensively for commercial purposes – contain unexpected gene fragments that had previously gone undetected.

Such findings reinforce what many environmental activists have been warning for some time. Although genetic modification may have enormous potential benefits, the risks involved are unpredictable and difficult to calculate. Once released into the environment, GMOs may set off a string of knock-on effects that will be difficult to monitor and control. In the face of this dilemma, many environmentalists favour what is often termed the **precautionary principle**. This principle proposes that where there is sufficient doubt about the possible risks of new departures, it is better to stick to existing practices than to change them.

Despite the concerns of environmentalists, the amount of land given over to growing GM crops has continued to increase, particularly in the developing world, where the environmental movement is not as strongly established and laws restricting the growth of GM crops are generally less strict (see figure 5.5).

Assessing the debate about GM foods, Matsuura (2004) argues that in the early days the biotechnology industry made two mistakes: first it tried to ignore public concerns and then it attempted to address

---

THINKING CRITICALLY

In what ways can the GM crops/food issue be seen as a specifically *environmental* issue? What makes it so? How realistic is the 'precautionary principle' – that we should always err on the side of caution and not go ahead with any new technologies that have not been exhaustively tested? What real-world examples of unproven technologies are there which may call this idea into question?

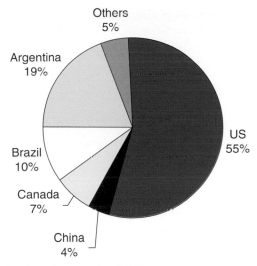

Figure 5.5 GM crop plantings by country, 2005

Source: Brookes and Barfoot 2005

them through purely rational arguments. Later in this chapter, we will look at a broader approach to the concept of risk, taken by the German sociologist Ulrich Beck.

Global warming

Based on average global temperature, 1998 and 2005 were the two warmest years on record since reliable measurements began in the late nineteenth century. Many scientists have argued that this is a good example of how global warming is now affecting the Earth's climate. The effects of very hot weather can be catastrophic. The Earth Policy Institute, an environmental think-tank, has estimated that a heat wave in 2003 killed more than 35,000 people in Europe, with France suffering the worst losses. It was estimated that 14,802 people died from causes attributable to the high temperatures – with older people being particularly affected (*New Scientist*, 10 October 2003).

Scientists have recently estimated that global warming kills about 160,000 people every year, with children in developing countries being most at risk. It has also been estimated that the numbers dying from the 'side-effects' of climate change, such as malaria and malnutrition, could almost double by 2020 (*New Scientist*, 1 October 2003).

The environmental issue of global warming – a form of climate change – is the clearest example of a genuinely *global* environmental problem. Its effects will have an impact on every society on the planet, albeit to varying degrees. To understand it we have to see 'the environment' in its widest sense – planet Earth as a whole – as the atmosphere shrouds the entire planet rather than one region. The problem of global warming cannot be understood without modern science; sociologists need to engage with debates on the science of climate change if they want to say anything useful about the social causes and consequences of global warming. Our own experience of the environment will change as the climate itself becomes a political issue, as happened after New Orleans in the USA was flooded in 2005, when journalists and commentators blamed the US government for not doing enough to tackle climate change.

Global warming also makes us aware of a type of 'pollution' (excessive CO_2) that few of us ever knew existed. One consequence of this knowledge is that it has speeded up the

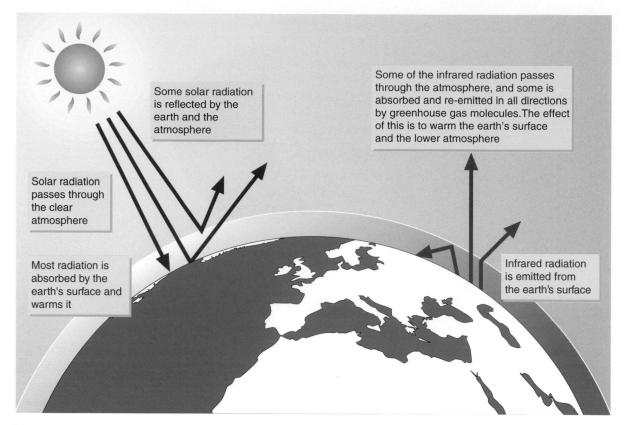

Figure 5.6 The greenhouse effect

Source: USA Environmental Protection Agency,
www.epa.gov/climatechange/science/index.html (accessed 18 January 2008)

globalization of environmental politics, helping to define 'nature' in planetary terms. Finally, tackling global warming is the foundation for any sustainable future for the human species and it is widely recognized as the most significant long-term environmental problem. There is an increasingly strong argument which suggests that this issue has to be tackled as an urgent priority if other sustainability projects are to have any chance. Clearly, we need to understand what global warming is and why it is happening.

What is global warming?

Global warming is regarded by many people to be the most serious environmental challenge of our time. If scientific forecasts are correct, then it has the potential to alter irreversibly the functioning of the earth's climate and to produce a series of devastating environmental consequences which will be felt worldwide. Global warming refers to the gradual rise in the earth's average temperature due to changes in the chemical composition of the atmosphere. The current scientific consensus is that this is caused in large part by humans, because the gases that have built up and altered the earth's atmosphere are ones that are produced in great quantities by human activities.

The process of global warming is closely related to the idea of the greenhouse effect – the build-up of heat-trapping greenhouse gases within the earth's atmosphere. The principle is a simple one. Energy from the sun passes through the atmosphere and

Global Society 5.3 What are greenhouse gases?

Some greenhouse gases such as carbon dioxide occur naturally and are emitted to the atmosphere through natural processes and human activities. Other greenhouse gases (e.g., fluorinated gases) are created and emitted solely through human activities. The principal greenhouse gases that enter the atmosphere because of human activities are:

- *Carbon dioxide (CO₂)*: Carbon dioxide enters the atmosphere through the burning of fossil fuels (oil, natural gas, and coal), solid waste, trees and wood products, and also as a result of other chemical reactions (e.g., manufacture of cement). Carbon dioxide is also removed from the atmosphere (or 'sequestered') when it is absorbed by plants as part of the biological carbon cycle.
- *Methane (CH₄)* : Methane is emitted during the production and transport of coal, natural gas, and oil. Methane emissions also result from livestock and other agricultural practices and by

the decay of organic waste in municipal solid waste landfills.
- *Nitrous oxide (N₂O)*: Nitrous oxide is emitted during agricultural and industrial activities, as well as during combustion of fossil fuels and solid waste.
- *Fluorinated gases*: Hydrofluorocarbons, perfluorocarbons and sulfur hexafluoride are synthetic, powerful greenhouse gases that are emitted from a variety of industrial processes. Fluorinated gases are sometimes used as substitutes for ozone-depleting substances (i.e., CFCs, HCFCs and halons). These gases are typically emitted in smaller quantities, but because they are potent greenhouse gases, they are sometimes referred to as High Global Warming Potential gases ('High GWP gases').

Source. Environmental Protection Agency (EPA): www.epa.gov/climatechange/emissions/index.html #ggo

heats the earth's surface. Although most of the solar radiation is absorbed directly by the Earth, some of it is reflected back. The greenhouse gases act as a barrier to this outgoing energy, trapping heat within the Earth's atmosphere much like the glass panels of a greenhouse (see figure 5.6). This natural greenhouse effect is what keeps the Earth at a reasonably comfortable surface temperature – at about 15.5 degrees Celsius. If it were not for the role of greenhouse gases in retaining heat, the Earth would be a much colder place, with an average temperature of −17 degrees Celsius.

When concentrations of atmospheric greenhouse gases rise, the greenhouse effect is intensified and much warmer temperatures are produced. Since the start of industrialization, the concentration of greenhouse gases has risen significantly. Concentrations of carbon dioxide – the main greenhouse gas – have increased by around 30 per cent since 1880, continuing

to rise steeply from the 1980s. Methane concentrations have also doubled, nitrous oxide concentrations are up by about 15 per cent and other greenhouse gases that do not occur naturally have been generated by industrial development (see 'Global Society 5.3'). Most scientists now agree that the large increase in carbon dioxide in the atmosphere can be attributed to the burning of fossil fuels and other human activities, such as industrial production, large-scale agriculture, deforestation, mining, landfills and vehicle emissions. The Inter-governmental Panel on Climate Change (IPCC 2007) reports that on the basis of analysis comparing actual observations with a model forecast based only on natural climate changes and second model based on natural changes *plus* anthropogenic (human-created) climate changes, it is *very likely* that the increase in observed temperatures during the twentieth century is due to increasing anthropogenic green-

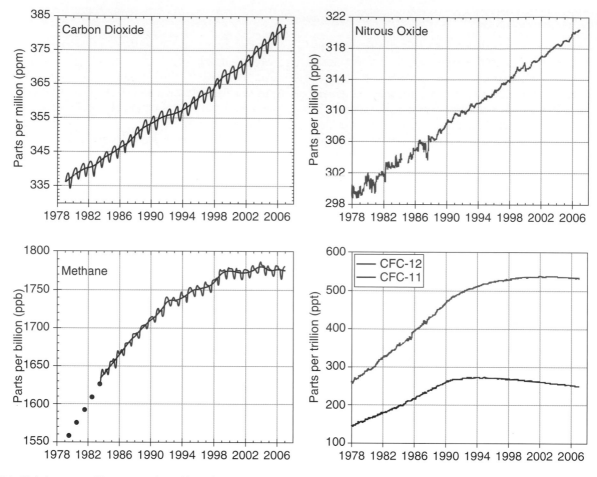

Note: Global averages of the concentrations of the major, well-mixed, long-lived greenhouse gases – carbon dioxide, methane, nitrous oxide, CFC-12 and CFC-11 from the NOAA global flask sampling network since 1978. These gases account for about 97 per cent of the direct radiative forcing by long-lived greenhouse gases since 1750. The remaining 3 per cent is contributed by an assortment of 10 minor halogen gases (see text). Methane data prior to 1983 are annual averages from Etheridge et al. (1998), adjusted to the NOAA calibration scale (Dlugokencky et al. 2005).

Figure 5.7 Global trends in major greenhouse gases, 1978–2006
Source: Hofman 2007

house gas emissions (see figure 5.7). This is a stronger conclusion than that arrived at just six years earlier.

Figure 5.8 shows the upward trend in surface temperatures since the late nineteenth century, charting them against the average temperature in the period 1961–90 in central England and globally. The IPCC notes that 11 of the 12 years 1995–2006 are among the 12 warmest years on record since 1850.

> **THINKING CRITICALLY**
>
> How convincing are the arguments for and evidence of an anthropogenic cause of global warming? Given the enormity of this environmental problem, what might be the social psychological responses of individuals faced with knowledge of it? How has knowledge of global warming affected you personally?

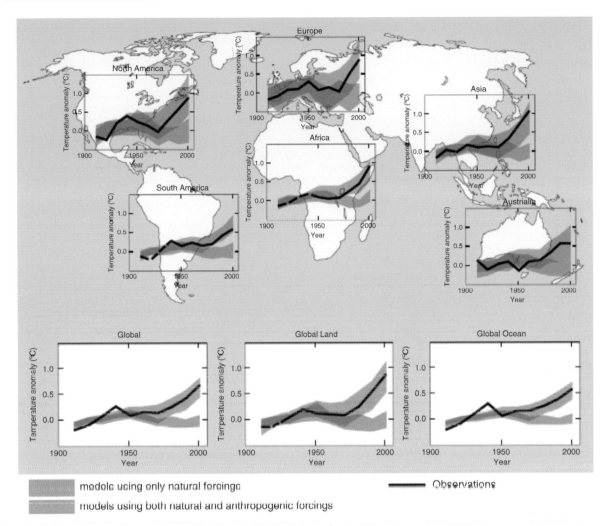

Figure 5.8 Global and continental temperature change, comparison of natural forcing with natural plus anthropogenic forcing

Source: Figure SPM.4 from the Summary for Policymakers of the Climate Change 2007: Synthesis Report. Contribution of Working Groups I, II and III to the Fourth Assessment Report of the Intergovernmental Panel on Climate Change, p. 6 © 2007 IPCC.

The potential consequences of global warming

The consequences of global warming are likely to be devastating, with some of the potentially harmful effects worldwide including:

1 *Rising sea levels.* Global warming may cause the polar ice caps to melt and the oceans to warm and expand. As glaciers and other forms of land ice melt, sea levels will rise. Cities that are near the coasts or in low-lying areas will be flooded and become uninhabitable. If sea levels were to rise by one metre, Bangladesh would lose 17 per cent of its total land area, Egypt would lose 12 per cent and the Netherlands would lose 6 per cent (UNDP 1998). The Indian Ocean tsunami, which we discussed at the beginning of this chapter, would have caused considerably more devastation if sea levels had already been higher.

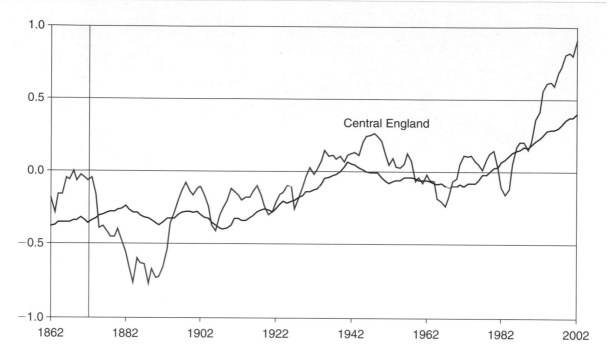

Figure 5.9 Difference in average surface temperature 1861–2002: comparison with 1961–90 average, global and central England (degrees centigrade)

Source: www.statistics.gov.uk/STATBASE/ssdataset.asp?vlnk=7279

2 *Desertification.* Global warming may contribute to large tracts of fertile land becoming desert. Sub-Saharan Africa, the Middle East and South Asia will be further affected by desertification and intense soil erosion.

3 *The spread of disease.* Global warming may extend the geographical range and the seasonality for organisms, such as mosquitoes, which spread diseases like malaria and yellow fever. If temperatures were to rise by 3–5 degrees Celsius, the number of malaria cases could increase by 50–80 million per year.

4 *Poor harvests.* Agricultural yields may fall in many of the poorest areas of the world if global warming progresses. Populations in Southeast Asia, Africa and Latin America would be likely to be most affected.

5 *Changing climate patterns.* Climate patterns that have been relatively stable for thousands of years may undergo rapid disruptions because of global warming. Forty-six million people currently live in areas that could be destroyed by sea storms, while many others may suffer from floods and hurricanes.

6 *Geopolitical instability.* A report published for the US Department of Defense warned that, at their most abrupt, the effects of climate change

Low-lying areas are ever more susceptible to flooding as a result of global climate change, though the effects on the lives of people in these regions will vary tremendously. The picture on the left shows emergency supplies of food and medicines being delivered to a community in Bangladesh. The picture on the right shows RSPCA officers in England rescuing stranded pets.

discussed above could lead to disputes or even wars between nations as they attempt to protect their increasingly limited agricultural, fresh water and energy resources. The report cautions that mass migration could occur as people attempt to move to those regions which posseses the resources to adapt to climate change (Schwartz and Randall 2003).

Some trends associated with global warming seem to be moving much faster than scientists originally predicted. In December 1999, for example, a study by satellite showed that the Arctic ice cap is shrinking much more rapidly than scientists previously thought – a process that could have dramatic effects on the world climate in coming years. Similarly, in early 2002 two huge ice shelves – Larsen B and Thwaites glacier tongue – collapsed in Antarctica, shattering into thousands of icebergs within days. It is possible that the reduction in ice is the result of natural changes, but whatever its origins, the ice seems to be melting at an extraordinary pace. Measurements show that the North Pole sea ice has thinned by 40 per cent in recent decades in the summer and autumn, and has decreased by 10–15 per cent since the 1950s in the spring and summer. Global snow cover has shrunk by 10 per cent since the 1960s, and mountain glaciers have sharply retreated.

Responses to the risks of global warming

For a long time the thesis and scientific evidence of global warming was disputed.

Some scientists doubted whether the claimed effects were real, while others held that changes in the world's climate could be the result of natural trends, rather than the outcome of human intervention. However, there is now a strong consensus behind the view that global warming is indeed occurring and that anthropogenic factors are the main contributor. A 2007 IPCC report states that the average surface temperature of the Earth rose by some 0.74 degrees Celsius between 1906 and 2005. But the report also warns that the warming trend between 1955 and 2005 (0.13 degrees Celsius per decade) is almost double that for the 100 years between 1906 and 2005 (IPCC 2007). Global warming, it seems, is gathering pace. But where should our efforts be concentrated and which countries need to take the lead in reducing their emissions?

As figure 5.10 shows, emissions of carbon dioxide in five of the six largest CO_2 emitting countries continued to increase between 1990 and 2003, in spite of all of the debates and political promises made by governments. However, when we take population size into account and look at emissions per capita, the picture looks rather different. China and India currently produce much less CO_2 per capita than the USA, Europe, the Russian Federation and Japan (see figure 5.11), which shows why some developing countries see their own 'survival' emissions as far less damaging than the 'luxury' emissions of the already rich countries. Clearly, a coordinated global approach to cutting greenhouse gas emissions is made more difficult in the context of such uneven economic development at the national level, which produces as much disagreement as agreement on how to tackle the problem.

The industrial countries currently produce far more greenhouse gases than the developing world, with the United States emitting more carbon dioxide than any other single country, both absolutely and per capita. However, emissions from the developing world are increasing rapidly, particularly in countries that are undergoing rapid industrialization, and are expected to be roughly equal to those of industrialized countries some time around 2035.

The United Nations Framework Convention on Climate Change was created in 1997 in Kyoto, Japan, where agreement was reached to cut greenhouse gas emissions significantly by 2010 in order to stabilize the situation at levels that do not pose a threat to the global climate. This is a very ambitious aim, which some critics have argued is not realistic.

Under the terms of the protocol, industrialized nations committed themselves to a range of targets to reduce emissions to below 1990 levels – the base year – by 2010. World targets range from an average 8 per cent cut for most of Europe to a maximum 10 per cent increase for Iceland and an 8 per cent increase for Australia. (The USA originally committed itself to a 7 per cent cut, but has never ratified the protocol.) Many scientists claim that this target was too modest, and argue that emissions must be cut by as much as 70 or 80 per cent if serious climatic consequences are to be avoided. Whatever governments do to cut emissions, it will be some time before the effects of global warming are altered as it takes more than a century for carbon dioxide to be removed from the atmosphere through natural processes.

In 2001, the US President, George W. Bush, refused to ratify the Kyoto Protocol, arguing that it would damage the US economy. After some debate, most other nations agreed to go ahead without the United States, in spite of it being the world's largest producer of greenhouse gases. Later the same year, talks in Bonn, Germany and Marrakech, Morocco finally agreed the increasingly complicated fine print of the protocol and signatory nations were urged to ratify the deal in their national legislatures by the end of 2002. In recent years, several of the largest producers of greenhouse gases have successfully cut emissions, including the UK, Germany, China and Russia – although Russia's cuts can largely be explained by the decline in its economy.

At the beginning of 2008, 174 countries

In 2003, 22 per cent of total world emissions originated in the United States, followed by China, with 16 per cent. Despite the substantial drop during the 1990s, the Russian Federation is the fourth largest emitter, followed closely by India and Japan.

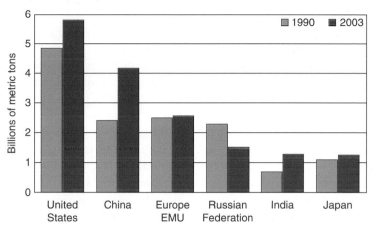

Figure 5.10   The six largest emitters of carbon dioxide, 1990 and 2003

Source: World Bank, *The Little Green Data Book*, 2007. © 2007 by World Bank. Reprinted with permission of World Bank in the format Textbook via Copyright Clearance Center.

Global representation for the top six carbon dioxide emitters is very different once population is taken into account.

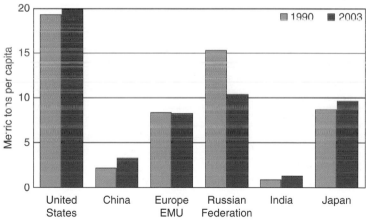

Note: Emissions shown in the figures are from cement manufacturing and fossil fuel combustion. The EMU aggregate in the figures includes the members states of the Economic and Monetary Union of the European Union that have adopted the euro as their currency: Austria, Belgium, Finland, France, Germany, Greece, Ireland, Italy, Luxembourg, Netherlands, Portugal, Slovenia, and Spain.

Figure 5.11   The six largest emitters of carbon dioxide per capita, 1990 and 2003

Source: World Bank, *The Little Green Data Book*, 2007. © 2007 by World Bank. Reprinted with permission of World Bank in the format Textbook via Copyright Clearance Center.

had ratified the Kyoto Protocol: 37 developed countries and 137 developing countries. Australia, which had previously refused to take part, finally did so in December 2007 under the newly elected Labour Federal government. However, it is clear that tackling global warming will be very difficult if the country with the highest national emissions levels – the USA – continues to opt out of international attempts to cap greenhouse gas emissions.

The Kyoto Protocol was and is controversial and one important issue has been the decision to push for emissions cutbacks in the developed countries, while developing countries are only asked to monitor and report their emissions. This is an acknowledgement that the latter have some 'catching up' to do in terms of economic development, which would be severely hampered by an emissions cap or reduction. In the longer term, though, all countries will have to control and reduce their greenhouse gas emissions.

The Kyoto Protocol took 1990 greenhouse emission levels as its starting point. But this was seen by many in the developing world as favouring the industrialized countries, as it fails to take into account their 'historical responsibility' for the problem of global warming and, hence, avoids attributing blame. It is also unclear exactly when developing countries will be asked to reduce their emissions, or by how much. Will it allow for their inevitably higher emission levels as economic development catches up with the industrialized world? If it does not, then it may be seen as unfair and unworkable (Najam et al. 2003). At the time of writing, a successor to Kyoto has been formally approved by the G8+5 countries (the G8 countries plus China, India, Brazil, Mexico and South Africa) in the so-called, 'Washington Declaration' of 2007. This will see the introduction of a global 'cap and trade' system (involving all countries) in which emissions caps will be introduced alongside an emissions trading system (focused on carbon trading) that forces polluters to pay.

The system works by rewarding those countries that reduce emissions (and sell credits) and penalizing those which do not (and are forced to pay for carbon credits). However, the overall effect of the cap and trade system is to push all countries towards lowering their emissions.

As with many new forms of manufactured risk, no one can be sure what the effects of global warming will be. Its causes are so diffuse and its precise consequences are difficult to calculate. Would a 'high' emissions scenario truly result in widespread natural disasters? Will stabilizing the level of carbon dioxide emissions protect most people in the world from the negative effects of climate changes? Is it possible that current processes of global warming have already triggered a series of further climatic disturbances? We cannot answer these questions with any certainty. The Earth's climate is extremely complex and a variety of factors will interact to produce different consequences in individual countries at varying points across the earth.

> **THINKING CRITICALLY**
>
> 'The industrialized countries are responsible for producing global warming and their populations should be prepared to accept a lower material standard of living in order drastically to reduce greenhouse gas emissions.' What arguments could be advanced to persuade people in the industrialized world to accept a lower material standard of living? Would they be likely to accept such a solution?

Sociological theories and ecological sustainability

Natural scientists have been at the forefront of debates on environmental issues. As the examples of pollution, resource depletion, genetic modification and global warming above show, environmental issues are different from many other sociological subjects, because they usually involve getting to grips with *natural scientific* research and evidence. However, the hybrid character of environmental issues means that natural scientists can never have a monopoly on them. Our brief introduction to the problem of global warming is the most striking example of this. The IPCC scientists acknowledge that twentieth-century global warming has largely been the product of human activities – industrialization, urbanization and globalization processes for example – and the experts in these areas are sociologists and other *social* scientists. If environmental problems are to be successfully understood, then social and natural scientists will have to try to understand each other rather better than they have done so far. This must surely be a positive challenge for the whole academic community.

The rest of this section will explore some of the main sociological theories linking social development with environmental damage, along with some of the major approaches to solving global environmental problems.

Consumerism and environmental damage

One important issue surrounding the environment and economic development is that of consumption patterns. Consumption refers to the goods, services, energy and resources that are used up by people, institutions and societies. It is a phenomenon with both positive and negative dimensions. On the one hand, rising levels of consumption around the world mean that people are living under better conditions than in times past. Consumption is linked to economic development – as living standards rise, people are able to afford more food, clothing, personal items, leisure time, holidays, cars and so forth. On the other hand, consumption can have negative impacts as well. Consumption patterns can

damage the environmental resource base and exacerbate patterns of inequality.

The trends in world consumption over the course of the twentieth century are startling to observe. In 1900, world consumption levels were just over 1.5 trillion dollars (UNDP 1998); by the end of the century, private and public consumption expenditures amounted to around 24 trillion dollars – twice the level of 1975 and six times that of 1950. Consumption rates have been growing extremely rapidly over the past 30 years or so. In industrialized countries, consumption per head has been growing at a rate of 2.3 per cent annually; in East Asia growth has been even faster – 6.1 per cent annually. By contrast, the average African household consumes 20 per cent less today than it did 30 years ago. There is widespread concern that the consumption explosion has passed by the poorest fifth of the world's population.

The inequalities in consumption between the world's rich and poor are significant. North America and Western Europe contain only around 12 per cent of the world's population, but their private consumption – the amount spent on goods and services at the household level – is over 60 per cent of the world's total. In contrast, the world's poorest region – sub-Saharan Africa, which contains around 11 per cent of the total global population – has just a 1.2 per cent share of the world's total private consumption.

It has been argued that industrial capitalism sets societies on a 'treadmill of production' leading to environmental damage, using up natural resources at a rapid rate and generating high levels of pollution and waste (Schnaiberg 1980). However, in the twentieth century it was modern consumerism which kept that treadmill running faster in this direction (Bell 2004). Consumption is something that human beings have to engage in to survive, but modern forms of consumption are very different from earlier forms.

Mass production must also be accompanied by large-scale consumption. The products of industry have to be bought and consumed, though producing and consuming may well be acted out in geographically distant locations. Products are made wherever it is cheapest to do so and consumed wherever the best price can be gained. In the past 60 years or so, this has led to industrial production moving to developing countries. The rapid transformation of the newly industrializing countries (NICs) such as Hong Kong, South Korea, Singapore and Taiwan in the 1970s and recent industrial development in India, China and Malaysia testify to this, which is part of the globalization process.

Sociologists of consumerism have argued that it is also a way of thinking, a mentality or even an ideology (Corrigan 1997). We can understand this aspect if we ask, 'Why do people continually consume and want to consume?' Perhaps it is simply because consumer goods have 'use-value' for people; they help to save them time and effort. But luxury items fit this explanation less well. They show another side to modern consumerism; its role in the social status competition within society (see chapter 7, 'Social Interaction and Everyday Life'). Differentiated mass consumption allows for complex, fine-grained distinctions to be made according to the styles and fashions of the day. People may be prepared to pay a premium for the latest fashions because these products allow them to say something about themselves, to communicate their status or their aspirations in highly visible ways to others. Even products with a clear use-value, such as clothes, are also fashionable items that are discarded and replaced before their 'use-value' has expired. Large amounts of such fashion-fuelled waste increases pressure on the environment.

Over time, consumer products become embedded in the routines of everyday life and are taken for granted. When this happens, it becomes difficult to perceive alternatives to their use. A good example of this is the modern motor vehicle, particularly the car. Many households have one, two or more cars, and people use them even

for a short trip to the shops or to visit friends and relatives who may live quite close by. But large-scale car-ownership and use generates large amounts of pollution and waste in both the production and consumption of cars. Why has it proved so difficult to reduce our use of the car?

A survey of attitudes to car-ownership found a range of types of consumer amongst visitors to National Trust properties in north-west England (Anable 2005).

1   *Malcontented Motorists* form the largest group. These drivers are unhappy with many aspects of their car use, but feel that public transport has too many constraints to be viable as a genuine alternative, and so they do not switch.
2   *Complacent Car Addicts* accept that there are alternatives to using the car, but do not feel any pressing moral imperative to changing their pattern of use.
3   *Aspiring Environmentalists* have already reduced their car usage, but feel the car has advantages that force them not to give it up altogether.
4   *Die-hard Drivers* feel they have a right to drive, enjoy driving and tend to have negative feelings towards other modes of transportation, such as buses and trains.
5   *Car-less Crusaders* have given up their cars for environmental reasons and see alternative modes of travel positively as a result.
6   *Reluctant Riders* do use public transport but would prefer to use the car; however, for a variety of reasons, such as health problems, they cannot do this, but will accept lifts from others.

The study shows that blanket appeals to people's emerging environmental awareness are likely to fail. Instead, 'the segmentation approach illustrates that policy interventions need to be responsive to the different motivations and constraints of the sub-groups' (Anable 2005: 77).

THINKING CRITICALLY

THINKING CRITICALLY

Looking at the typology of transport users above, which category best describes you? Think of an appropriate environmental policy aimed at each consumer type that stands the best chance of generating pro-environmental behaviour in that specific group. Are there any universal environmental policies that might have the desired effect on all the groups?

Another element of modern consumerism is its pleasurable aspect. But *why* is it pleasurable? Some sociologists have argued that the pleasure of consumerism does not lie in the *use* of products but in the *anticipation* of purchasing them. Colin Campbell (1992) argues that this is *the most* pleasurable part of the process; the wanting, the longing after, the seeking out and desiring of products, not the use of them. It is a 'romantic ethic' of consumption based on desire and longing. Marketing of products and services draws on this anticipatory consumerism in seductive ways to create and intensify people's desires. That is why we keep going back for more and are never truly satisfied. From an environmental perspective, the 'romantic ethic' of consumerism is disastrous. We constantly demand new products and more of them. That means more production, so the cycle of mass production and mass consumption continues to churn out pollution and wastes natural resources. At the input side of production, natural resources are used up in enormous quantities, and at the output end in consumption, people throw away useful things not because they are *use-less*, but because they are no longer in fashion or fail to represent their status aspirations.

The sociology of consumption shows us that the combination of industrialization, capitalism and consumerism has transformed society–environment relations. Many environmentalists and more than a few social and natural scientists have concluded that this continual expansion of economies and the continuing promotion of economic growth cannot carry on indefinitely. The resulting pollution might have been ecologically insignificant if it had been restricted to a small part of the global human population. But when industrialization spreads across the planet, when a majority of people live in huge cities, and when capitalist companies become multinational and consumerism seduces people in all countries, then the natural environment's capacity for recovery and resilience becomes severely weakened.

Environmentalists argue that current consumption patterns are not only highly unequal, but they are also having a severe impact on the environment and, in the long term, are not sustainable. For example, the consumption of fresh water has doubled since 1960; the burning of fossil fuels, which is the main contributor to global warming discussed below, has almost quintupled in the past 50 years; and the consumption of wood is up by 40 per cent from 25 years ago. Fish stocks are declining, wild species are becoming extinct, water supplies are diminishing and wooded areas are shrinking in size. Patterns of production and consumption are not only depleting existing natural elements, but are also contributing to their degradation through waste products and harmful emissions (UNDP 1998).

Finally, although the rich are the world's main consumers, the environmental damage that is caused by growing consumption has the heaviest impact on the poor. As we saw in our discussion of global warming, the wealthy are in a better position to enjoy the many benefits of consumption without having to deal with its negative effects. On a local level, affluent groups can usually afford to move away from problem areas, leaving the poor to bear most of the costs. Chemical plants, power stations, major roads, railways and airports are often sited close to low-income areas. On a global level, we can see a similar process at work: soil degradation, deforestation, water shortages, lead emissions and air pollution are all concentrated within the developing world. Poverty also intensifies these environmental problems. People with few resources have little choice but to maximize the resources that are available to them. As a result, more and more pressures are put on a shrinking resource base as the human population increases.

Limits to growth and sustainable development

A central motivating idea for environmental campaigners has been that of 'sustainability' – ensuring that human activity does not compromise the ecology of planet Earth. In *The Ecologist*, the UK campaigning magazine, Edward Goldsmith and his colleagues set out the charge against industrial expansion in their 'Blueprint for Survival' (1972: 15): 'The principal defect of the industrial way of life with its ethos of expansion is that it is not sustainable . . . we can be certain . . . that sooner or later it will end.' Such doom-laden forecasts used to be described as 'catastrophist' and were restricted to the wilder fringes of the environmental movement. However, the idea now has a wider currency amongst the general public and policy-makers, for which the scientific predictions of global warming are largely responsible. Anyone who recycles their plastic, paper and glass, conserves water or tries to use their car less is probably aware that they too are trying to put into practice the idea of sustainability.

One important influence on the rise of environmental movements and public concern about environmental problems can be traced back to a famous report first published in the early 1970s, which set out the case that economic growth could not continue indefinitely. The report and its findings are discussed in 'Classic Studies 5.1'.

Classic Studies 5.1 | **Modelling the limits to economic growth**

The research problem
Global human population has grown enormously since industrialization took hold and the resulting pressure on the environment has led to soil degradation, deforestation and pollution. Are there any limits to this pattern of development? Will food supplies keep up with increasing demand or will the world see mass famine? How many people can the planet support without ruining the environment? These hugely significant questions were asked of a group of scientists by a global think-tank, the Club of Rome, almost 40 years ago. The resulting book was published as *The Limits to Growth* (Meadows et al. 1972).

Meadows and colleagues' explanation
The *Limits* study used modern computer-modelling techniques to make forecasts about the consequences of continued economic growth, population growth, pollution and the depletion of natural resources. Their computer model – *World3* – showed what would happen if the trends that were established between 1900 and 1970 were to continue to the year 2100. The computer projections were then altered to generate a variety of possible consequences, depending on different rates of growth of the factors considered. The researchers found that each time they altered one variable, there would eventually be an environmental crisis. If the world's societies failed to change, then growth would end anyway through the depletion of resources, food shortages or industrial collapse, sometime before 2100.

The research team used computer modelling to explore five global trends (Meadows et al. 1974: 21):

- accelerating industrialization across the world
- rapid population growth
- widespread malnutrition in some regions
- depletion of non-renewable resources
- a deteriorating natural environment

The program was then run to test 12 alternative scenarios, each one manipulated to resolve some of the identified problems. This allowed the researchers to ask questions about which combinations of population levels, industrial output and natural resources would be sustainable. The conclusion they drew in 1972 was that there *was* still time to put off the emerging environmental crisis. But if nothing was done, and even if the amount of available resources in the model were doubled, pollution were reduced to pre-1970s levels and new technologies were introduced, economic growth would still grind to a halt before 2100. Some campaigners saw this as vindicating the radical environmental argument that industrial societies were just not sustainable over the long term.

Critical points

Many economists, politicians and industrialists roundly condemned the report, arguing that it was unbalanced, irresponsible and, when its predictions failed to materialize, just plain wrong. The modelling was largely devoid of political and social variables and was therefore just a partial account of reality. The researchers later accepted that some of the criticisms were justified. The method used focused on *physical* limits and assumed existing rates of economic growth and technological innovation, but this did not take account of the capacity of human beings to respond to environmental challenges. For example, market forces could be made to work to limit the over-exploitation of resources. If a mineral like magnesium starts to become scarce, its price will rise. As its price rises it will be used less, and producers might even find

alternatives should costs rise too steeply. *Limits* was seen by many as yet another overly pessimistic, catastrophist tract that engaged in unreliable 'futurology' – predicting the future from current trends.

Contemporary significance

Whatever its limitations, the original report made a significant impact on public debate and environmental activism. It made many more people aware of the damaging consequences of industrial development and technology, as well as warning about the perils of allowing pollution to increase. The report was an important catalyst for the modern environmental movement (for a wider discussion, see chapter 22, 'Politics, Government and Social Movements'). Twenty years later, the team published *Beyond the Limits* (1992) an even more pessimistic report, castigating the world's politicians for wasting the time, identified as crucial in the first report, arguing that ecological 'overshoot' was *already* occurring. Then in 2004, their *30 Year Update* was released, arguing that although some progress had been made in environmental awareness and technological development, the evidence of global warming, declining fish stocks and much more, showed a world 'overshooting' its natural limits. This conclusion was also that of the UN's Millennium Ecosystem Assessment of 2005, which is tellingly titled, *Living Beyond Our Means*. The basic conclusion from the original *Limits* report and its updates continues to resonate in our globalizing world.

Sustainable development

Rather than calling for economic growth to be reined in, more recent developments turn on the concept of **sustainable development**. This term was first introduced in a 1987 report commissioned by the United Nations, *Our Common Future*. This is also known as the *Brundtland Report*, after the chair of the organizing committee, Gro Harlem Brundtland, then Prime Minister of Norway. The report's authors argued that use of the Earth's resources by the present generation was unsustainable:

Over the course of the twentieth century the relationship between the human world and the planet that sustains it has undergone a profound change . . . major, unintended changes are occurring in the atmosphere, in soils, in waters, among plants and animals, and in the relationships among all of these. . . . To keep options open for future generations, the present generation must begin now, and begin together, nationally and internationally. (Brundtland 1987)

The Brundtland Commission regarded sustainable development as, 'development which meets the needs of the present generation, without compromising the ability of future generations to meet their own needs' (ibid.) – a short definition, but one which carries enormous significance. Sustainable development means that economic growth should be carried on in such a way as to recycle physical resources rather than deplete them, and to keep levels of pollution to a minimum.

Following the publication of *Our Common Future*, the phrase 'sustainable development' came to be widely used by both environmentalists and governments. It was employed at the UN Earth Summit in Rio de Janeiro in 1992 and has subsequently appeared in other ecological summit meetings organized by the UN, such as the World Summit on Sustainable Development in Johannesburg in 2002. Sustainable development is also one of the Millennium Development Goals (MDGs), which have been agreed by 191 states around the world as they aim to reduce many forms of poverty in the coming decades. The relevant MDGs include the integration of the principles of sustainable development into country policies and programmes, the reversal of the loss of environmental resources, the reduction by half of the proportion of people without sustainable access to safe drinking water and achieving a significant improvement in the lives of at least 100 million slum-dwellers – all by 2020.

> For more on the Millennium Development Goals, see chapter 13, 'Global Inequality'.

The Brundtland Report attracted much criticism, just as the report of the Club of Rome had done some quarter of a century earlier. Critics see the notion of sustainable development as too vague and as neglecting the specific needs of poorer countries. According to the critics, the idea of sustainable development tends to focus attention only on the needs of richer countries; it does not consider the ways in which the high levels of consumption in the more affluent countries are satisfied at the expense of other people. For instance, demands on Indonesia to conserve its rainforests could be seen as unfair, because Indonesia has a greater need than the industrialized countries for the revenue it must forgo by accepting conservation.

It can also be argued that linking the concept of ecological sustainability to that of economic development is contradictory. This is a particularly pertinent point where sustainability and development clash, for example when considering new roads or retail sites it is often the case that the prospect of many new jobs and economic prosperity means sustainability takes second place. This is even more pronounced for governments in developing countries, which are badly in need of more economic activity. In recent years, ideas of environmental justice and ecological citizenship have come to the fore (as we see below), partly as a result of the severe problems associated with the concept and practice of sustainable development.

It is easy to be sceptical about the future prospects for sustainable development. Its aim of finding ways of balancing human activity with sustaining natural ecosystems may appear impossible. Nonetheless, sustainable development looks to create common ground amongst nation-states and connects the world development movement with the environmental movement in a way that no other project has yet managed

---

THINKING CRITICALLY

Sustainable development is 'development which meets the needs of the present generation, without compromising the ability of future generations to meet their own needs'. What are the *needs* of the present generation? How might we find out what the *needs* of future generations will be? Can sustainable development policies be devised from this definition?

to do. It gives radical environmentalists the opportunity to push for full implementation of its widest goals, but, at the same time, moderate campaigners can be involved locally and have an impact. This inclusivity can be seen as a weakness, but also a potential strength of the sustainable development project.

Living in the global 'risk society'

Humans have always had to face risks of one kind or another, but today's risks are qualitatively different from those that came in earlier times. Until quite recently, human societies were threatened by **external risk** – dangers such as drought, earthquakes, famines and storms that spring from the natural world and are unrelated to the actions of humans. Today, however, we are increasingly confronted with various types of **manufactured risk** – risks that are created by the impact of our own knowledge and technology on the natural world. As we shall see, many environmental and health risks facing contemporary societies are instances of manufactured risk: they are the outcomes of our own interventions into nature.

Global Society 5.4 **Manufactured risks and the survival of humanity**

In 2003, Martin Rees, the British Astronomer Royal, published a book provocatively called *Our Final Century*, subtitled with the question: 'Will the human race survive the twenty-first century?' Rees argues that the explosive advances in science and technology, seen for example in bio-, cyber- and nanotechnology and in the exploration of space, do not just offer exhilarating prospects for the future, but also contain what he calls a dark side.

Scientific advancement can have unintended consequences, as we have seen, and Rees's book examines the likelihood of catastrophic scenarios where human civilization dies out. He describes some of the apocalyptic risks that could occur with the new science of the twenty-first century: these include nuclear holocaust, caused by terrorists or nations and terrorist use of biological weapons or laboratory errors that create new diseases.

Rees's conclusions are sobering. He separates the long term from the short term. In the short term, which he defines as the next 20 years, he is prepared to bet on a major catastrophe killing more than a million people (though he fervently hopes that he will be wrong in his assessment). Returning to the subtitle of his book, Rees argues, over the next 100 years – which he calls the long term – he gives humanity a 50/50 chance of surviving the twenty-first century.

The prognosis may seem desperately pessimistic, but Rees argues that he hopes his book will stimulate discussion on how to guard as far as possible against the worst risks, while deploying new knowledge optimally for human benefit.

Debates on genetically modified foods, global warming and other manufactured risks have presented individuals with new choices and challenges in their everyday lives. Because there is no road map to these new dangers, individuals, countries and transnational organizations must negotiate risks as they make choices about how lives are to be lived. And because there are no definitive answers as to the outcomes of such risks, each individual is forced to make decisions about which risks he or she is prepared to take. This can be a bewildering endeavour. Should we use food and raw materials if their production or consumption might have a negative impact on our own health and on the natural environment? Even seemingly simple decisions about what to eat are now made in the context of conflicting information and opinions about the product's relative merits and drawbacks.

Ulrich Beck (1992) has written extensively about risk and globalization. As technological change progresses more and more rapidly, producing new forms of risk, we must constantly respond and adjust to the changes. Risks today involve a series of interrelated changes in contemporary social life: shifting employment patterns, heightened job insecurity, the declining influence of tradition and custom on self-identity, the erosion of traditional family patterns and the democratization of personal relationships. Because personal futures are much less fixed than they were in traditional societies, decisions of all kinds present risks for individuals. Getting married, for example, is a more risky endeavour today than it was at a time when marriage was a lifelong institution. Decisions about educational qualifications and career paths can also feel risky: it is difficult to predict what skills will be valuable in an economy that is changing as rapidly as ours. 'Classic Studies 5.2' explores Beck's arguments, specifically in relation to environmental risks.

Classic Studies 5.2 | **Ulrich Beck and the global risk society**

The research problem

This chapter has explored some of the environmental consequences of industrial production and high levels of consumption. Taking a long-term view, we can see that the spread of industrialization produces more widespread and potentially serious side-effects in the form of environmental risks. But is modern life really more risky, or are we just more 'risk aware'? Are we worrying unnecessarily about environmental problems? The German sociologist, Ulrich Beck (1944–), has been the foremost sociological theorist of risk, which he sees as much more significant than sociologists previously thought.

Beck's explanation

Throughout the nineteenth and twentieth centuries, the politics of modern societies was dominated by a major conflict of interest between workers and employers – in Marx's terms, between the non-owning working class and the property-owning capitalist class. The conflict centred on issues of wealth distribution as trades unions and labour parties sought a more equal distribution of the socially produced wealth. Such struggles still continue of course. But Ulrich Beck (1992, 1999, 2002) argues that this distributional conflict is losing its significance as environmental risks rise to prominence. He says that more people are beginning to realize that their fight for a share of the 'wealth cake' is futile if the cake itself is be poisoned (Beck 2002: 128) as a result of pollution and environmental damage. Beck argues that:

the knowledge is spreading that the sources of wealth are 'polluted' by growing 'hazardous side effects'. This is not at all new, but it has remained unnoticed for a long time in the efforts to overcome poverty. . . . To put it differently, in the risk society the unknown and unintended consequences come to be a dominant force in history and society. (1992: 20–1)

Industrial societies are slowly dissolving as environmental problems build up; this is an unintended consequence of the rush for economic growth and material prosperity. Beck (1999) argues that we are, in effect, moving into a 'world risk society' – a new type of society in which risk consciousness and risk avoidance are becoming the central features – because environmental pollution does not respect national boundaries. No matter where industrial production or consumption takes place, its consequences can be felt in very distant locations. The relatively rich countries are not immune from industrial pollution and global environmental damage. We will remain dependent on science and high technology though, because it is only through these that industrial processes can be safely and effectively managed.

Beck wants to show us that the environmental issue is moving from the margins of political concern towards the centre. Most of the risks we face are the products of human activity; they are not like the purely natural disasters of film and television. This means that the environment becomes an issue for political debate and decision-making and we can see the creation of environmental organizations and Green political parties in the 1970s as the first step towards inclusion of environmental issues into mainstream politics.

Critical points

One of the main criticisms of Beck's overall thesis is that there is not (yet) enough evidence to support his theory of the transition to a 'risk society', even though there is today more awareness of environmental risks (Hajer 1996; Sutton 2004). Similarly, the idea that older forms of class-based politics are losing out to a new politics of risk seems premature. In most countries, Green political parties have not broken through the conventional party system, and globally the issue of wealth creation and distribution still tends to dominate over environmental protection whenever these objectives clash. Finally, it has been argued that the risk thesis fails to take account of cultural variability in definitions of risk (Douglas 1994; Scott 2000). What some societies define as 'risk',

others may not, in the same way that what is defined as pollution in wealthy industrial societies is often seen as a sign of healthy economic development in poorer developing countries.

Contemporary significance

The concept of risk holds a special place in current sociological debates on environmental issues and the direction of social change. Beck's risk thesis is useful, because it provides part of an explanation for why environmental movement concerns have found such a receptive audience. Once people become sensitized to risks, the arguments of environmentalists begin to make more sense. Beck's *Risk Society* has taken sociological thinking on modernity and its possible futures in a new and highly original direction, making us re-think the sociological tradition, and for this reason it has rightly become a modern classic of social theory.

> ### THINKING CRITICALLY
>
> How aware are you of risk in your everyday life? What actions do you routinely take to minimize personal risk? Do you engage in any 'risk-taking activities' and if so, why do you do it? Is risk always a negative part of modern life or can you think of any positive aspects?

Ecological modernization

For environmentalists, both capitalist and communist forms of modernization have signally failed. They have delivered wealth and material success, but at the price of massive environmental damage. In recent years, groups of academic social scientists have tried to develop a theoretical perspective called **ecological modernization**, which accepts that 'business as usual' is no longer possible, but rejects radical environmentalist solutions involving de-industrialization. Instead they focus on technological

innovation and the use of market mechanisms to bring about positive outcomes, transforming production methods and reducing pollution at its source.

Ecological modernizers see huge potential in leading European industries to reduce the usage of natural resources *without* this affecting economic growth. This is an unusual position, but it does have a certain logic. Rather than simply rejecting more economic growth, they argue that an *ecological form* of growth is theoretically possible. An example is the introduction of catalytic converters and emission controls on motor vehicles, which has been delivered within a short period of time and shows that advanced technologies can make a big difference to greenhouse gas emissions. If environmental protection really can be achieved like this, then we can continue to enjoy our high technology lifestyles.

Ecological modernizers also argue that if consumers demand environmentally sound production methods and products, then market mechanisms will be forced to try and deliver them. The example of opposition to GM food in Europe (discussed above) is a good example of this idea in practice. Supermarkets have not stocked or pushed the supply of GM foods, because large numbers of consumers have made it clear that they will stay on the shelves.

The theory of ecological modernization sees that five social and institutional structures need to be ecologically transformed:

1 *Science and technology*: to work towards the invention and delivery of sustainable technologies.
2 *Markets and economic agents*: to introduce incentives for environmentally benign outcomes.
3 *Nation-states*: to shape market conditions which allow this to happen.
4 *Social movements*: to put pressure on business and the state to continue moving in an ecological direction.
5 *Ecological ideologies*: to assist in persuading more people to get involved in the ecological modernization of society. (Mol and Sonnenfeld 2000)

Science and technology have a particularly crucial role in developing preventative solutions, building in ecological considerations at the design stage. This will transform currently polluting production systems.

Since the mid-1990s, three new areas of debate had entered the ecological modernization perspective. Firstly, research began to expand to the developing countries of the South, significantly challenging the Eurocentrism of the original perspective. Second, once ecological modernizers started to think beyond the West, the theory of globalization became more relevant and current research seeks to link globalization with ecological modernization (Mol 2001). Third, ecological modernization has started to take account of the sociology of consumption and theories of consumer societies. This has led to some interesting studies exploring the ecological moderniza-

tion of domestic consumption as well as of production. These studies look at how consumers can play a part in the ecological modernization of society and on how domestic technologies can be improved to reduce energy consumption, save scarce resources (such as water) and contribute to waste reduction through recycling.

The possibilities offered by ecological modernization can be illustrated by reference to the waste disposal industry – the industry that gets rid of the tonnes of waste products that industries and consumers generate every day. Until recently, most of this waste was simply processed and buried in landfill sites. Today, the whole industry is being transformed. Technological developments make it much cheaper to produce newsprint from recycled paper than from wood pulp. Hence there are good economic reasons, as well as environmental ones, to use and reuse paper instead of endlessly cutting down trees. Not just individual companies, but whole industries are actively pursuing the goal of 'zero waste' – the complete recycling of all waste products for future industrial use. Toyota and Honda have already reached a level of 85 per cent recyclability for the car parts they use. In this context, waste is no longer just the harmful dumping of materials, but a resource for industry and, to some extent, a means of driving further technological innovation.

Significantly, some of the major contributions to recycling, and therefore to sustainable development, have come from areas with a heavy concentration of information technology industries, such as California's Silicon Valley. Information technology, unlike many older forms of industrial production, is environmentally clean. The more it plays a part in industrial production, the greater the likelihood that harmful environmental effects will be reduced. This consideration could have some bearing on the future development of the world's poorer societies. In some areas of production, at least, it might be possible for them to achieve rapid economic development without the pollution produced by the older industrial economies, because information technology will play a much greater role.

Unlike other perspectives, ecological modernization is less concerned with global inequality and more interested in how businesses, individuals and non-state actors can all play a part in transforming society. This makes it different from sustainable development, which begins from the premise that reducing global inequality is a prerequisite for environmental protection. Ecological modernizers also argue that if the capitalist economic system can be made to work for environmental protection then it will continue; if not, then something different will have to emerge because the ecological modernization of global society is already well under way.

Critics have seen ecological modernization as overly reliant on technological fixes and relatively ignorant of cultural, social and political conflicts. It is probably correct to say that ecological modernization is imbued with technological optimism rather than having a fully worked out theory of how to get from here to a future sustainable society. But the myriad real-world examples they produce, of practical technologies and suggestions for change, could collectively make a big difference, especially if ways can be found to make them financially viable in developing countries. However, these will also need to be introduced alongside the

kind of international agreements that characterized the Kyoto Protocol, which could then ensure the spread of best practice and knowledge of what works.

Environmental justice and ecological citizenship

Environmental justice

If ecological modernization perhaps leans too heavily on technological fixes, one way of balancing this is by promoting the active involvement of people from all social groups and classes in the project of achieving sustainable development.

Environmental justice is a term that originated in the USA with the formation of grassroots networks of activists in working-class communities (Szasz 1994; Bell 2004: ch. 1; Visgilio and Whitelaw 2003). One touchstone campaign was that of Lois Gibbs in Niagara Falls, New York in 1978, seeking to relocate the Love Canal community, which she discovered had been built on a 20,000-ton toxic chemical dump. The community campaign was ultimately successful when 900 working-class families were relocated away from the leaking dump in 1980 (Gibbs 2002). Environmental justice groups have focused on campaigns against the siting of toxic waste sites and incinerators in urban areas with high working-class and ethnic minority populations. Linking environmental quality to social class inequalities shows that environmentalism is not just a middle-class concern but can be linked to working-class interests, and takes account of social inequalities and real-world 'risk positions'. In the USA, toxic waste sites have tended to be situated in black and Hispanic communities where citizens' action groups are relatively less powerful, but Gibbs's campaign showed that they are not powerless.

Environmental justice groups can be very significant. Their emergence has the potential to broaden the support base of environmental politics to currently under-represented groups within the wider

THINKING CRITICALLY

Look again at the five social and institutional structures that constitute an ecologically modernist approach to environmental problems. List them in order of current progress – which structure has been transformed the most and which the least? How would you explain this? What obstacles are harder to overcome in transforming the structures of modern societies in environmentally sensitive directions?

environmental movement. For instance, Friends of the Earth International (amongst others) has expanded its agenda, recognizing the need to tackle social problems if pressures on the natural environment are to be relieved (Rootes 2005). Environmental justice takes us into the urban and inner city areas where most of the waste products of modern life end up, and this opens up environmental politics to people who may not have thought about their problems as being at all 'environmental'.

Perhaps the most significant consequence of environmental justice groups is that they offer the possibility of linking environmental politics in the rich countries with that practised in the relatively poorer ones. One important example was the protest against the multinational oil company, Shell's, impact on the environment of the indigenous Ogoni people in Nigeria. The campaign of the *Movement for the Survival of the Ogoni People* (formed in 1990) and the international support it garnered is just one example of the potentially unifying concept of environmental justice. Attempts by the Nigerian government to put down the resistance movement involved torture, ransacking of villages and, in 1995, the eventual execution of nine members of the movement's leadership, including the writer Ken Saro-Wiwa, in the face of international protest (Watts 1997). Such events reinforce the argument that the relatively powerless are made to bear the brunt of environmental pollution. Environmental justice campaigns demonstrate the potential for linking social inequalities and poverty to environmental issues, promising to make environmentalism more than just a nature-defence movement.

Ecological citizenship

One final development worthy of note is the emergence of a type of citizenship linked to the defence of the natural environment. In recent years, some sociologists and political scientists have argued that a new form of citizenship is emerging, something Mark J. Smith (1998) has called **ecological citizenship** and Dobson and Bell (2006) refer to as environmental citizenship.

As discussed in chapter 12, 'Poverty, Social Exclusion and Welfare', the concept of citizenship is not new and can be divided into different types. *Civil citizenship* emerged with modern property-ownership, which imposed certain mutual obligations on people to respect each other's rights to property. *Political citizenship* emerged later, during which voting rights expanded, working-class groups and women were brought into the suffrage and rights of association (as in trades unions) and free speech developed. The third stage, *social citizenship*, saw rights to welfare and responsibilities for collective provision of social benefits. What Smith and others see is that a fourth stage is developing, in which ecological citizenship rights and responsibilities form the centrepiece.

Ecological citizenship involves new obligations: to non-human animals, to future generations of human beings and to maintaining the integrity of the natural environment (Sandilands 1999). Obligations to animals means reconsidering human uses of animals that infringe their rights to leading a natural life and expressing their natures. Hence, vivisection, hunting, farming methods, breeding and pet-keeping would all need to be reassessed. Ecological citizenship's new obligation to future generations of people means working towards sustainability over a long time period. If economic development plans threaten the ability of future generations to provide for their own needs, then other forms will need to be designed and planned. Political and economic planning must become future-oriented and take a long-term view rather than adopting a short-term, free market or laissez-faire approach. Finally, all human activity should be considered with reference to its effects on the natural environment and a *precautionary principle* should be adopted that puts the onus on developers to justify their actions in ecological terms. In essence, then, ecological citizenship introduces a new demand for people to take account of the human 'ecological footprint' – the impact of human activity on the natural environment and natural processes.

Clearly ecological citizenship would demand some fundamental changes to modern societies. Perhaps the most radical change would be to people themselves, as ecological citizenship requires a transformed human experience of nature and the self as tightly bound together. In the same way that people had to start to perceive themselves as citizens with rights in order for political citizenship to take hold, so ecological citizenship is unlikely to develop fully unless people's identities also include the experience of having ecological selves.

Conclusion

At the end of the first decade of a new century, we cannot foresee whether the next 100 years will be marked by peaceful social and economic development or by a multiplication of global problems – perhaps beyond the ability of humanity to solve. Unlike the nineteenth-century sociologists, we see more clearly the dark side of modern industry, technology and science. We know they are by no means wholly beneficial in their consequences. Scientific and technological development have created a world that contains high consequence risks that make possible huge gains and losses. Especially in the developed world, the population is wealthier than ever before, yet the world as a whole is closer to ecological disaster.

Should we resign ourselves to an attitude of despair? Sociology offers us a profound consciousness of the human authorship or social creation of social institutions. We see the possibility of controlling our destiny and shaping our lives for the better, to an extent unimaginable to previous generations.

The ideas of sustainable development, ecological modernization and environmental justice and citizenship are helping to promote some important changes in human–environment relations and the production of ecologically sensitive technologies. Even as late as the 1980s, when the Brundtland Report appeared, it was widely assumed that industrial development and ecological protection were incompatible. However, the central idea of all of these approaches is that this assumption is false. The use of eco-efficient technologies can produce forms of economic development that combine economic growth with positive policies for the environment, while an emerging environmental responsibility could ensure an expanding demand for such developments.

Even the strongest advocates of ecological modernization accept that rescuing the global environment will require changes in the levels of inequality that now exist in the world. As we have seen, industrial countries currently account for only about one-fifth of the world's population, yet they are responsible for over 75 per cent of the emissions that serve to pollute the atmosphere and hasten global warming. The average person in the developed world consumes natural resources at ten times the rate of the average individual in less developed countries. Poverty is itself a prime contributor to practices that lead to environmental damage in poor countries and people living in conditions of economic hardship have no choice but to make maximum use of the local resources available to them. What will be needed, then, are 'just sustainabilities' (Agyeman et al. 2003; Smith and Pangsapa 2008). Achieving ecological sustainability demands that concerted international efforts are made to tackle global inequalities as a necessary condition for environmental protection.

Summary points

1. The environment means all of the non-human, natural surroundings within which human beings exist – sometimes called the 'natural environment' – and in its widest sense this is simply planet Earth as a whole.

2. The classical sociologists paid little direct attention to the environment, though others have tried to rectify that omission. Current environmental debates have been divided between social constructionists and critical realists. The former leads to a sociology of the environment and adopts an agnostic approach to the subject. The latter leads to an environmental sociology that looks for the underlying causes of environmental problems.

3. Environmental issues are hybrids of environment and society, which marks them out as different from many other sociological issues and social problems. This necessitates interdisciplinary understanding and, potentially, collaboration. All societies are now faced by increasingly global environmental problems and international cooperation is needed in order to find workable solutions.

4. Most environmental issues involve manufactured risks, as they have been generated by human activity. Increasingly, issues of pollution and resource depletion are global in scale and developing countries have been particularly badly affected by soil degradation and deforestation.

5. More recent environmental issues, such as genetic modification of crops and global warming, have been subjects of much controversy. GM foods are widely accepted in the USA and are grown in China, Brazil and elsewhere, but European consumers have refused to buy them. Global warming is the most serious environmental issue yet identified and could have severe consequences for human societies, including flooding, the spread of disease, extreme weather and rising sea levels. Scientists generally agree that it has been caused by human activities since the Industrial Revolution which have rapidly increased the concentrations of greenhouse gases in the

atmosphere. The 1997 Kyoto Protocol, which aimed at cutting back on greenhouse gas emissions, has now been ratified by 174 countries, excluding the USA – the world's largest contributor to greenhouse gases.

6. Rising worldwide consumption patterns are linked to industrial production in a 'treadmill of production and consumption', but they also intensify environmental damage and tend to exacerbate global inequality. Energy consumption and the consumption of raw materials are vastly higher in Western countries than in other areas of the world. Yet the environmental damage caused by growing consumption has the most severe impact on the poor.

7. Sustainable development is the dominant framework for environmental policy development. It is defined as 'development which meets the needs of the present generation, without compromising the ability of future generations to meet their own needs'. Sustainable development links economic development to environmental protection and is concerned to equalize global inequalities to help achieve this.

8. Ulrich Beck's theory of an emerging risk society has been very influential in shaping debates on global environmental issues. His argument is that the industrial age is coming to an end as the side-effects of industrialization build up, forcing societies into a new phase which will see the control and management of risk as its central feature. Critics suggest the thesis currently lacks solid supportive empirical evidence.

9. Ecological modernization is a theory of evolutionary social change, which sees an ecological version of modernization emerging in the present period, which marries continuing technological and economic development with environmental solutions. In social science research, ecological modernization represents a body of work that devises small-scale, practical solutions to environmental problems with a view to rolling out solutions that work. Ecological modernization is also interested in modernizing domestic consumption and transforming the practices of everyday life in an ecologically sensitive direction.

10. Taking a long-term view of environmental change suggests that reducing global inequalities will be a necessary step if developing countries are to be fully involved in achieving global sustainable development. There is some evidence of this in recent environmental justice campaigns, though the spread of ecological citizenship may take rather longer.

Further reading

A good place to start your additional reading is with Philip W. Sutton's *The Environment: A Sociological Introduction* (Cambridge: Polity, 2007), which is a genuinely introductory-level text covering all the issues discussed in this chapter and more. Michael M. Bell's *An Invitation to Environmental Sociology, Second Edition* (Thousand Oaks, CA: Pine Forge Press, 2004) is also very well written and uses lots of helpful examples to illustrate key environmental dilemmas.

For something more theoretical, you could try John Hannigan's excellent *Environmental Sociology: A Social Constructionist Perspective* (London: Routledge, 2006), which includes some very effective constructionist case studies. Peter Dickens's *Social Theory and the Environment: Changing Nature, Changing Ourselves* (Cambridge: Polity, 2004) approaches environmental issues from a critical realist position and explains this with great clarity. Riley E. Dunlap, Frederick H. Buttel, Peter Dickens and August Gijswijt's. *Sociological Theory and the Environment: Classical Foundations, Contemporary Insights*

(Oxford: Rowman & Littlefield, 2002) is also a fine edited collection of essays, which covers the classics as well as more recent theories.

On sustainable development, Susan Baker's *Sustainable Development* (London: Routledge, 2005) is a good introduction. On the risk society, Ulrich Beck's own, *World Risk Society* (Cambridge: Polity, 1999) is quite accessible in the original. And for ecological modernization, Arthur P. J. Mol's *Globalization and Environmental Reform: The Ecological Modernization of the Global Economy* (Cambridge, MA: The MIT Press, 2003) is a nicely balanced summary and evaluation of the perspective and its achievements to date.

For environmental justice and ecological citizenship, you could try Mark J. Smith and Piya Pangsapa's *Environment and Citizenship: Integrating Justice, Responsibility and Civic Engagement* (London: Zed Books, 2008) and Andrew Dobson and Derek Bell's edited collection, *Environmental Citizenship* (Cambridge, MA: The MIT Press, 2006), which contains some thought-provoking essays.

Internet links

UK Department for Environment, Food and Rural Affairs:
www.defra.gov.uk/Environment/index.htm

Environment and Society Blog, University of Leeds, UK – lots of interesting stories and weblinks here:
https://elgg.leeds.ac.uk/socenv/weblog/

Environmental Organization Web Directory – USA-based repository with lots of useful resources:
www.webdirectory.com/

European Environment Agency – good resource base with some interesting surveys and other research:
www.eea.europa.eu/

Friends of the Earth International – campaigning environmental organization:
www.foei.org/

Greenpeace International – campaigning environmental organization:
www.greenpeace.org/international/

OECD – Environment site with lots of data from OECD countries:
www.oecd.org/topic/0,3373,en_2649_37465_1_1_1_1_37465,00.html

United Nations Development Programme – link to Human Development Reports and the UN Millennium Goals:
www.undp.org/

World Bank, Environment & Development Series – lots of resources, particularly on environment and developing countries:
http://web.worldbank.org/WBSITE/EXTERNAL/TOPICS/ENVIRONMENT/0,,menuPK:176751~pagePK:149018~piPK:149093~theSitePK:244381,00.html

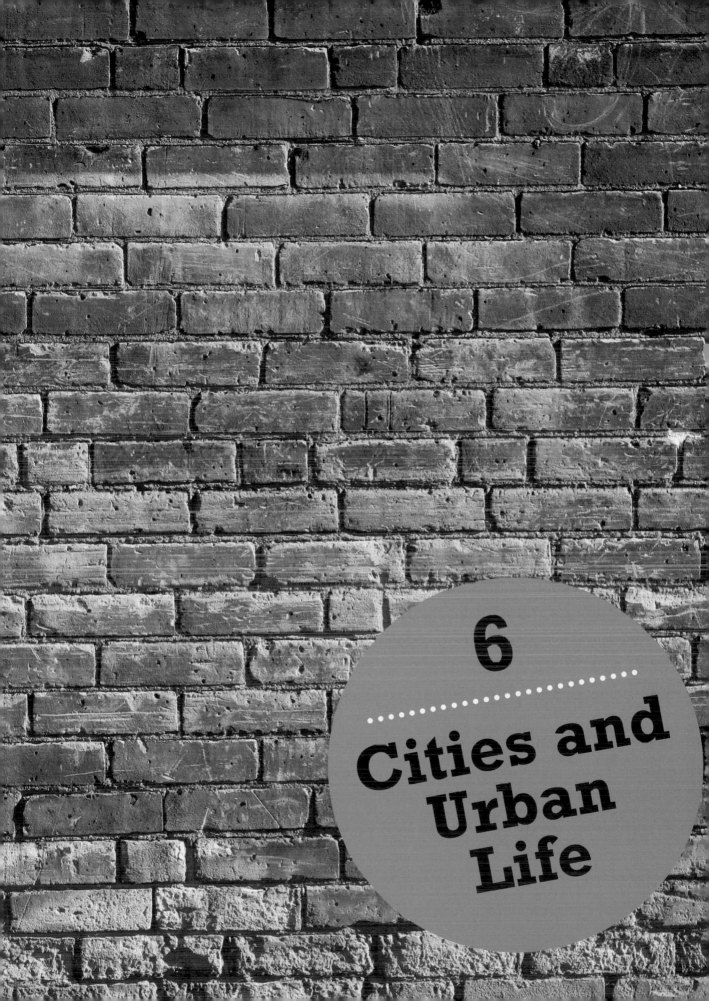

6

Cities and
Urban
Life

CHAPTER 6

Cities and Urban Life

(opposite) Cities make enormous demands on our mental life. Are these people adopting a blasé attitude and exhibiting 'urban reserve'?

London, New York and Tokyo are three of the world's 'global cities', seen as command centres for the world's economy, with influence extending far beyond their own national borders (Sassen 2001). These global cities are the headquarters for large, transnational corporations, as well as a profusion of financial, technological and consulting services.

London has a population of more than 7 million people with more than 300 languages between them and a resident workforce of some 3.4 million. It also has an unrivalled cultural and artistic heritage, helping to confirm its place as a vibrant and dynamic capital – almost 30 million tourists come to stay for a night or more each year. High migration levels have resulted in a young population

(20–24 year-olds) as young people move to London for work, education, culture and perhaps to escape the conformity and provincialism of rural life.

New York houses Wall Street, which, since 1945 has been one of the world's primary economic centres. New York is also a major hub for international diplomacy, being home to the United Nations headquarters. The city has more than 8 million inhabitants and is the most densely populated city in the USA. New York has been influential in the development of some major popular musical trends such as jazz in the 1940s and punk rock in the 1970s. The Bronx area was also the birthplace of new musical genres such as rap music and hip-hop in the 1970s and ' '80s. The city is also extremely culturally diverse with more than one-third of the population born outside the USA.

Tokyo city has a population of around 8 million and the Tokyo urban area is the most populous in the world with around 35 million people. The city also has the highest gross domestic product (GDP) of all the world's cities, as well as the second largest stock exchange (behind New York). Like London and New York, Tokyo is a major cultural centre with many museums, art galleries and festivals, and in recent years it has become a familiar cityscape as the backdrop for numerous globally distributed films – including *Kill Bill* (2003/4) and *Lost in Translation* (2003).

Yet, despite all the rich opportunities that big cities such as these have to offer, many people actually find them lonely or unfriendly places. Why? One distinctive characteristic of modern urban life is the frequency of interactions between strangers. Even within the same neighbourhood or block of flats, it is unlikely that people will know most of their neighbours. If you live in a town or city, think about the number of times that you interact everyday with people you do not know. The list might include the bus driver, people working in shops, students and even people you exchange 'pleasantries' with in the street.

Perhaps this fact alone makes living in cities today a very different proposition from what is on offer elsewhere or during earlier times in history. Indeed, Marshall Berman (1983) sees the experience of modern urban life as definitive of the period sociologists call 'modernity' itself (see chapter 1).

 Social interaction is discussed in detail in chapter 7, 'Social Interaction and Everyday Life'.

In this chapter, we shall first consider some of the main theories of urbanism that have been developed to understand cities and urban life. From there, we will study the origins of cities and the enormous growth in city populations over the twentieth century and some of the important contemporary trends in urbanization around the world. Not surprisingly, rapid globalization is having an enormous impact on city-living and we shall consider this process in the final part of the chapter.

Theorizing urbanism

What is a city? A simple working definition is:

> an inhabited central place differentiated from a town or village by its greater size, and by the range of activities practised within its boundaries, usually religious, military-political, economic, educational and cultural. Collectively, these activities involve the exercise of power over the surrounding countryside. (Jary and Jary 1999: 74)

We can say, then, that cities are relatively large forms of human settlement, within which a wide range of activities are performed, which enable cities to become centres of power in relation to outlying areas and smaller settlements. Thinking back to our introductory example, this definition fits London, New York and Tokyo pretty well.

Many early sociologists were fascinated by the city and by urban life; Max Weber even wrote a book called *The City* (published posthumously in 1921), in which he traced the conditions that made modern capitalism possible back to the medieval, Western city. Other early sociologists were more concerned with the way in which the development of cities changed the social as well as the physical environment. The work of Ferdinand Tönnies and Georg Simmel provided two of the most important early contributions to urban sociology.

German sociologist Ferdinand Tönnies (1855–1936) was particularly concerned about the effects of city life on social bonds and solidarity. He argued that the process of urbanization, which occurred with the Industrial Revolution, irredeemably changed social life. He charted with some sadness the gradual loss of what he called *Gemeinschaft* or community bonds, which he characterized as based on traditional, close-knit ties, personal and steady relationships between neighbours and friends, and a clear understanding of one's social position (Tönnies 2001 [1887]). However, *Gesellschaft*, or 'associational' bonds, were rapidly replacing this type of social bond. These were relatively short-lived, transitory and instrumental in character. And though all societies contain social bonds of both types, with industrialization and urbanization the balance of social bonds was shifting decisively away from *Gemeinschaft* in favour of a more individualistic society. In this society, relationships tend to be specific to a particular setting and purpose, and only take into account a part of the whole person. For example, if we take a bus in the city, our interaction with the driver is likely to be limited to a brief exchange at the door of the bus as we pay, and our use for him will be limited to his ability to get us to our destination – it is an instrumental exchange. For Tönnies, the modern city, unlike older traditional settlements, is a place full of strangers, for good or ill.

The early theorists of the city deeply influenced the work of later urban sociologists. Robert Park, for example, a key member of the Chicago School of Sociology, studied under Simmel in Germany at the turn of the twentieth century, and it is to this that we now turn.

The Chicago School

A number of sociologists associated with the University of Chicago from the 1920s to the 1940s, especially Robert Park, Ernest Burgess and Louis Wirth, developed ideas which were for many years the chief basis of theory and research in urban sociology. Two concepts developed by the Chicago School are worthy of special attention. One is the so-called ecological approach in urban analysis; the other is the characterization of urbanism as a way of life, developed by Wirth (Wirth 1938; Park 1952).

Urban ecology

Ecology is a term taken from a physical science: the study of the adaptation of plant and animal organisms to their environment. This is the sense in which 'ecology' is used in the context of problems of the natural environment (see chapter 5, 'The Environment', for more on ecology and environment). In the natural world, organisms tend to be distributed in systematic ways over the terrain, such that a balance or equilibrium between different species is achieved. The Chicago School argued that the siting of major urban settlements and the distribution of different types of neighbourhood within them could be understood in terms of similar principles. Cities do not grow up at random, but in response to advantageous features of the environment. For example, large urban areas in modern

---

THINKING CRITICALLY

What are your *positive* experiences of city life? What freedoms, opportunities and experiences do city inhabitants enjoy that are not routinely available to those living in small towns and villages? Do these positive aspects outweigh the possible negative ones outlined by Simmel and Tönnies? Was Simmel right, or have cities radically changed since his time?

Classic Studies 6.1 | **Georg Simmel on the mental life of city-dwellers**

The research problem

Many people saw that large-scale urbanization fundamentally changed societies, but what effects would such a shift have on individuals? How would it alter their attitudes and behaviour? And what exactly is it about city-living that produces such dramatic effects? One of Tönnies's German contemporaries, Georg Simmel (1858–1918), provided just such a theoretical account of how the city shapes its inhabitants' 'mental life'; his 'The Metropolis and Mental Life' (1950 [1903]), Tönnies remarked, had managed to capture 'the flavour of the metropolis'.

Simmel's explanation

Simmel's study would today be described as an early piece of **interpretative sociology**, seeking to understand and convey something about how city life is actually *experienced* by people. City life, says Simmel, bombards the mind with images and impressions, sensations and activity. This is 'a deep contrast with the slower, more habitual, more smoothly flowing rhythm' of the small town or village. In this context, it is not possible for individuals to respond to every stimulus or activity they come across, so how do they deal with such a bombardment?

Simmel argues that city-dwellers protect themselves from 'the unexpectedness of violent stimuli' and the assault of 'changing images' by becoming quite blasé and disinterested, adopting a 'seen-it-all-before' attitude. They 'tune out' much of the urban buzz that surrounds them, focusing on whatever they need to, just in order to get by. The result of this blasé attitude, thought Simmel, is that although city-dwellers are part of the 'metropolitan crush', they distance themselves from one another emotionally. Typically, the myriad fleeting contacts with people they do not know result in an 'urban reserve' in interactions with others, which can be perceived as emotionless and rather cold, leading to widespread feelings of impersonality and even isolation. Simmel points out, though, that city people are not by nature indifferent to others and uncaring. Rather, they are forced to adopt such modes of behaviour in order to preserve their social distance and individual selves in the face of pressures from the densely populated urban environment.

Simmel notes that the sheer pace of urban life partly explains the typical urban personality. But he also argues that the fact that the city is 'the seat of the money economy' must be taken into account. Many cities are large capitalistic financial centres, which demand punctuality, rational exchange and an instrumental approach to business. This encourages 'relentless' matter-of-fact dealings between people, with little room for emotional connection, resulting in 'calculating minds' capable of weighing the benefits and costs of involvement in relationships. Like Tönnies, then, Simmel's study points up some of the emerging problems of living in the modern, urbanized world.

Critical points

Critics of Simmel's study have raised a number of objections. His arguments seem to be based on personal observation and insight rather than on any formal or replicable research methods, thus the findings can be seen as somewhat speculative and not rooted in empirical studies. Also, despite Simmel's insistence that he set out merely to understand urban life and not to damn it, many critics have suggested that the overall tone of the study is negative, revealing a value bias against the capitalist city. It is certainly true that his work seems to focus on the ways in which individuals can resist being 'levelled down and worn out by a socio-technological mechanism' (Simmel 1950: 409). In this sense, critics say, Simmel plays down the liberating experience of many people who move to cities to experience greater freedoms and room for individual expression. Finally, the study may be guilty of over-generalizing from a specific type of large city to cities in general. After all, only a minority of cities are financial centres and those that are not may well have less alienating and isolating effects on people than Simmel allows for. Can we really say that *all* urbanites have the same experiences?

Contemporary significance

Simmel's account of life in the modern metropolis provides a sociological explanation of some key characteristics of contemporary urbanism. His theoretical study shows how the quality of social interactions can be shaped by pressures arising from the wider social environment of the city, an important consequence of which is Simmel's view that the city, 'is not a spatial entity with social consequences, but a sociological entity that is formed spatially'. This has proved a very productive starting point for later urban studies. Simmel's influence can also be felt in modern social theory. He argued: '[T]he deepest problems of modern life derive from the claim of the individual to preserve the autonomy and individuality of his existence in the face of overwhelming social forces.' There is more than an echo of this perspective in the more recent work of Ulrich Beck, Zygmunt Bauman and other contemporary theorists of modern individualism.

societies tend to develop along the shores of rivers, on fertile plains or at the intersection of trading routes or railways.

'Once set up,' in Park's words, 'a city is, it seems, a great sorting mechanism which . . . infallibly selects out of the population as a whole the individuals best suited to live in a particular region or a particular milieu' (1952: 79). Cities become ordered into 'natural areas', through processes of competition, invasion and succession – all of which occur in biological ecology. If we look at the ecology of a lake in the natural environment, we find that competition between various species of fish, insects and other organisms operates to reach a fairly stable distribution between them. This balance is disturbed if new species 'invade' – try to make the lake their home. Some of the organisms, which used to proliferate in the central area of the lake, are driven out to suffer a more precarious existence around its fringes. The invading species are their successors in the central sections.

Patterns of location, movement and relocation in cities, according to the ecological view, take a similar form. Different neighbourhoods develop through the adjustments made by inhabitants as they struggle to gain their livelihoods. A city can be pictured as a map of areas with distinct and contrasting social characteristics. In the initial stages of the growth of modern cities, industries congregate at sites suitable for the raw materials they need, close to supply lines. Populations cluster around these workplaces, which come to be increasingly diversified as the number of the city's inhabitants grows. The amenities thus developed become correspondingly more attractive, and greater competition develops for their acquisition. Land values and property taxes rise, making it difficult for families to carry on living in the central neighbourhood, except in cramped conditions or in decaying housing where rents are still low. The centre becomes dominated by businesses and entertainment, with the more affluent private residents moving out to newly forming suburbs around the perimeter. This process follows transport routes, since these minimize the time taken in travelling to work; the areas between these routes develop more slowly.

Cities can be seen as formed in concentric rings, broken up into segments. In the centre are the inner-city areas, a mixture of big business prosperity and decaying private houses. Beyond these are longer established neighbourhoods, housing workers employed in stable manual occupations. Further out still are the suburbs in which higher-income groups tend to live. Processes of invasion and succession occur within the segments of the concentric rings. Thus, as property decays in a central or near-central area, ethnic minority groups might start to move into it. As they do so, more of the pre-existing population start to leave, precipitating a wholesale flight to neighbourhoods elsewhere in the city or out to the suburbs.

Although for a period the **urban ecology** approach fell into disrepute, it was later revived and elaborated in the writings of a number of authors, particularly Amos Hawley (1950, 1968). Rather than concentrating on competition for scarce resources, as his predecessors had done, Hawley emphasized the *interdependence* of different city areas. *Differentiation* – the specialization of groups and occupational roles – is the main way in which human beings adapt to their environment. Groups on which many others depend will have a dominant role, often reflected in their central geographical position. Business groups, for example, like large banks or insurance companies, provide key services for many in a community, and hence are usually to be found in the central areas of settlements. But the zones which develop in urban areas, Hawley points out, arise from relationships not just of space, but also of time. Business dominance, for example, is expressed not only in patterns of land-use, but also in the rhythm of activities in daily life – an illustration being the rush hour. The ordering in time of people's daily lives reflects the hierarchy of neighbourhoods in the city.

The ecological approach has been as important for the empirical research it has helped to promote as for its value as a theoretical perspective. Many studies, both of cities and of particular neighbourhoods, have been prompted by ecological thinking, concerned, for example, with the processes of 'invasion' and 'succession' mentioned above. However, various criticisms can justifiably be made. The ecological perspective tends to underemphasize the importance of conscious design and planning in city organization, regarding urban development as a 'natural' process. The models of spatial organization developed by Park, Burgess and their colleagues were drawn from American experience, and fit only some types of city in the USA, let alone cities in Europe, Japan or the developing world.

Claude Fischer (1984) has put forward an interpretation of why large-scale urbanism tends actually to promote diverse subcultures, rather than swamp everyone within an anonymous mass. Those who live in cities, he points out, are able to collaborate with others of similar backgrounds or interests to develop local connections; and they can join distinctive religious, ethnic, political and other subcultural groups. A small town or village does not allow the development of such subcultural diversity. Those who form ethnic communities within cities, for instance, might have little or no knowledge of one another in their land of origin. When they arrive, they gravitate to areas where others from a similar linguistic and cultural background are living, and new sub-community structures are formed. An artist might find few others to associate with in a village or small town, but in a large city he or she might become part of a significant artistic and intellectual subculture.

A large city is a 'world of strangers', yet it supports and creates personal relationships. This is not paradoxical. We have to separate urban experience between the public sphere of encounters with strangers and the more private world of family, friends and work colleagues. It may be difficult to 'meet people' when one first moves to a large city. But anyone moving to a small, established rural community may find the friendliness of the inhabitants largely a matter of public politeness – it may take years to become 'accepted'. This is not so in the city. As Edward Krupat has commented:

> Yet the overwhelming evidence is that because of the diversity of strangers – each one is a potential friend – and the wide range of lifestyles and interests in the city, people do move from the outside in. And once they are on the inside of one group or network, the possibilities for expanding their connections multiply greatly. As a result, the evidence indicates that the positive opportunities in the city often seem to outweigh the constraining forces, allowing people to develop and maintain satisfying relationships. (1985: 36)

Modern cities do frequently involve impersonal, anonymous social relationships, but they are also sources of diversity – and, sometimes, intimacy.

Urbanism and the created environment

More recent theories of urbanism have stressed that it is not an autonomous process, but has to be analysed in relation to major patterns of political and economic change. The two leading writers in urban analysis, David Harvey (1982, 1985, 2006) and Manuel Castells (1983, 1991, 1997), have both been strongly influenced by Karl Marx.

The restructuring of space

Drawing on broadly Marxist ideas, David Harvey has argued that urbanism is one aspect of the created environment brought about by the spread of industrial capitalism. In traditional societies, city and countryside were clearly differentiated. In the modern world, industry blurs the division between city and countryside. Agriculture becomes mechanized and is run simply according to considerations of price and profit, just like industrial work, and this process lessens the differences in modes of social life between urban and rural people.

In modern urbanism, Harvey points out, space is continually *restructured*. The process is determined by where large firms choose to place their factories, research and development centres and so forth, by the controls asserted by governments over both land and industrial production and by the activities of private investors, buying and selling houses and land. Business firms, for example, are constantly weighing up the relative advantages of new locations against existing ones. As production becomes cheaper in one area than in another, or as the firm moves from one product to another, offices and factories will be closed down in one place and opened up elsewhere. Thus at one period, when there are considerable profits to be made, there may be a spate of office block building in the

The Lozells area of Birmingham in the UK saw an eruption of violence in 2005 between the ethnic communities who make up the majority of its population. Was this the result of ethnic groups leading lives in increasingly segregated communities?

The research problem

We know from Simmel that the urban environment tends to create particular personality types and that there is a certain pattern to the development of cities. But are such personality types limited to the cities? How do cities relate to and interact with the rest of society? Does urbanism exert any influence outside the city boundary? Louis Wirth (1897–1952) explored the idea that urbanism was, in fact, a whole way of life, not an experience limited to just some areas of society.

Wirth's explanation

While other members of the Chicago School focused on understanding the shape of the city – how they came to be internally divided – Wirth was more concerned with **urbanism** as a distinct way of life. Urbanism, he argued, could not be reduced to or understood simply by measuring the size of urban populations. Instead, it has to be grasped as a form of social existence. Wirth observed that:

> The influences which cities exert on the social life of man are greater than the ratio of the urban population would indicate; for the city is not only increasingly the dwelling-place and the workshop of modern man, but it is the initiating and controlling centre of economic, political and cultural life that has drawn the most remote communities of the world into its orbit and woven diverse areas, peoples and activities into a cosmos. (1938: 342)

In cities, large numbers of people live in close proximity to one another, without knowing most of those others personally. This is in fundamental contrast to small, traditional villages and towns. Many contacts between city-dwellers are, as Tönnies suggested, fleeting and partial, they are means to other ends, rather than being satisfying relationships in themselves. Wirth calls these 'secondary contacts', compared to the 'primary contacts' of familial and strong community relationships. For example, interactions with salespeople in shops, cashiers in banks or ticket collectors on trains are passing encounters, entered into not for their own sake, as in communal relations, but merely as means to other aims.

Since those who live in urban areas tend to be highly mobile, moving around to find work and to enjoy leisure and travel, there are relatively weak bonds between them. People are involved in many different activities and situations each day and the 'pace of life' in cities is much faster than in rural areas. Competition tends to prevail over cooperation, and social relationships can appear as flimsy and brittle. Of course, the Chicago School's ecological approach found that the density of social life in cities leads to the formation of neighbourhoods having distinct characteristics, some of which may preserve some of the characteristics of small communities. In immigrant areas, for example, traditional types of connections between families are found, with most people knowing most others on a personal basis. Similarly, Young and Wilmott's (1957) *Family and Kinship in East London*, found strong connections amongst working class families in the city.

However, although Wirth accepted this, he argued that the more these areas became

"*We love the view. It helps to remind us that we're part of a larger community.*"

absorbed into the wider patterns of city life, the less such community characteristics would survive. The urban way of life weakens bonds of kinship, thus eroding families, communities are dissolved and the traditional bases of social solidarity are rendered ineffective. Wirth was not blind to the benefits of urbanism. He saw that modern cities were centres of freedom, toleration and progress, but he also saw that urbanism spread beyond city boundaries, as the process of suburbanization, with all of its necessary transport systems and infrastructure, shows. And in that sense, modern societies themselves are necessarily shaped by the forces of urbanism.

Critical points

Critics have pointed out the limitations of Wirth's ideas on urbanism. Like the ecological perspective, with which it has much in common, Wirth's thesis is rooted in the experience of American cities, and cannot be seen as a general theory of city life. Urbanism is not the same at all times and all places. Ancient cities were quite different from modern ones, for example and cities in developing countries today are often very different from those in the developed ones. Critics argue that Wirth also exaggerates the extent of impersonality in modern cities. Communities involving close

friendship or kinship links are more persistent than he thought. Everett Hughes, a colleague of Wirth, said that, 'Louis used to say all those things about how the city is impersonal – while living with a whole clan of kin and friends on a very personal basis' (cited in Kasarda and Janowitz 1974: 338). Similarly, Herbert Gans (1962) argued that 'urban villagers' – such as Italian-Americans living in inner-city Boston – were quite commonly to be found. These critics question Wirth's picture of modern cities by showing that city life can lead to the *building* of communities rather than *always* destroying them.

Contemporary significance

Wirth's ideas have deservedly enjoyed wide currency. The impersonality of many day-to-day contacts in modern cities is undeniable and, to some degree, this is true of social life more generally. His theory is also important for its recognition that urbanism is not just one part of society, but actually expresses and influences the character of the wider social system. Given the expanding process of urbanization in many developing countries and the fact that a majority of people in the developed world already live in urban areas, Wirth's ideas will continue to be a reference point for sociologists looking to understand urbanism as a way of life.

centre of large cities. Once the offices have been built, and the central area 'redeveloped', investors look for potential for further speculative building elsewhere. Often what is profitable in one period will not be so in another, when the financial climate changes.

The activities of private home-buyers are strongly influenced by how far, and where, business interests buy up land, as well as by rates of loans and taxes fixed by local and central government. After the Second World War, for instance, there was a vast expansion of suburban development in major cities in the United States. This was partly due to ethnic discrimination and the tendency of whites to move away from inner-city areas.

However, it was only made possible, Harvey argues, because of government decisions to provide tax concessions to home-buyers and construction firms, and by the setting up of special credit arrangements by financial organizations. These provided the basis for the building and buying of new homes on the peripheries of cities, and at the same time promoted demand for industrial products such as the motorcar. In recent years, Harvey (2006) has applied his theory of uneven spatial development to global inequalities between the relatively rich countries of the northern hemisphere and the relatively poor developing countries in the south. The turn towards neoliberal ideas, as for example in the USA and UK in the 1970s and '80s, has, he argues, laid bare the 'myth' that developing countries just need to 'catch up with the West'. Such a neoliberal political agenda shows that gross inequalities are built into the global capitalist economy.

Urbanism and social movements

Like Harvey, Castells stresses that the spatial form of a society is closely linked to the overall mechanisms of its development. To understand cities, we have to grasp the processes whereby spatial forms are created and transformed. The layout and architectural features of cities and neighbourhoods express struggles and conflicts between different groups in society. In other words, urban environments represent symbolic and spatial manifestations of broader social forces (Tonkiss 2006). For example, skyscrapers may be built because they are expected to provide profit, but the giant buildings also 'symbolise the power of money over the city through technology and self-confidence and are the cathedrals of the period of rising corporate capitalism' (Castells 1983: 103).

In contrast to the Chicago sociologists, Castells sees the city not only as a distinct location – the urban area – but also as an integral part of processes of **collective consumption**, which in turn are an inherent aspect of industrial capitalism. Schools, transport services and leisure amenities are ways in which people collectively 'consume' the products of modern industry. The taxation system influences who is able to buy or rent where, and who builds where. Large corporations, banks and insurance companies, which provide capital for building projects, have a great deal of power over these processes. But government agencies also directly affect many aspects of city life, by building roads and public housing, planning green belts, on which new development cannot encroach, and so forth. The physical shape of cities is thus a product of both market forces and the power of government.

But the nature of the created environment is not just the result of the activities of wealthy and powerful people. Castells stresses the importance of the struggles of underprivileged groups to alter their living conditions. Urban problems stimulate a range of social movements, concerned with improving housing conditions, protesting against air pollution, defending parks and green belts and combating building development that changes the nature of an area. For example, Castells studied the gay movement in San Francisco, which succeeded in restructuring neighbourhoods around its own cultural values – allowing many gay organizations, clubs and bars to flourish – and gaining a prominent position in local politics.

Cities, Harvey and Castells both emphasize, are almost wholly 'artificial' environments, constructed by people. Even most rural areas do not escape the influence of human intervention and modern technology, for human activity has reshaped and reordered the world of nature. Food is not produced for local inhabitants, but for national and international markets; and in mechanized farming, land is rigorously subdivided and specialized in its use, ordered into physical patterns, which have little relationship to natural features of the environment. Those who live on farms and in isolated rural areas are economically, politically and culturally tied to the larger society, however different some of their modes of behaviour may be from those of city-dwellers.

Evaluation

The views of Harvey and Castells have been widely debated, and their work has been important in redirecting urban analysis. In contrast to the ecologists' approach, it puts emphasis not on 'natural' spatial processes, but on how land and the created environment reflect social and economic systems of power. This marks a significant shift of emphasis. Yet the ideas of Harvey and

Castells are often stated in a highly abstract way, and have not stimulated such a large variety of research studies compared with the work of the Chicago School.

In some ways, the views set out by Harvey and Castells and those of the Chicago School usefully complement each other, and can be combined to give a comprehensive picture of urban processes. The contrasts between city areas described in urban ecology do exist, as does the overall impersonality of city life. But these are more variable than the members of the Chicago School thought, and are primarily governed by the social and economic influences analysed by Harvey and Castells. John Logan and Harvey Molotch (1987) suggested an approach that directly connects the perspectives of authors like Harvey and Castells with some features of the ecological standpoint. They agree with Harvey and Castells that broad features of economic development, stretching nationally and internationally, affect urban life in quite a direct way. But these wide-ranging economic factors, they argue, are focused through local organizations, including neighbourhood businesses, banks and government agencies, together with the activities of individual house-buyers.

Places – land and buildings – are bought and sold, according to Logan and Molotch, just like other goods in modern societies, but the markets which structure city environments are influenced by how different groups of people want to use the property they buy and sell. Many tensions and conflicts arise as a result of this process – and these are the key factors structuring city neighbourhoods. For instance, in modern cities, Logan and Molotch point out, large financial and business firms continually try to intensify land-use in specific areas. The more they can do so, the more there are opportunities for land speculation and for the profitable construction of new buildings. These companies have little concern with the social and physical effects of their activities on a given neighbourhood – with whether or not, for example, attractive older residences are destroyed to make room for large new office blocks. The growth processes fostered by big firms involved in property development often go against the interests of local businesses or residents, who may attempt actively to resist them. People come together in neighbourhood groups in order to defend their interests as residents. Such local associations may campaign for the extension of zoning restrictions, block new building encroaching on parks, or press for more favourable rent regulations.

The development of the city

Although there were great cities in the ancient world, like Athens and Rome in Europe, city life, as we now know it, is very different from that experienced in previous ages. As early sociologists like Simmel and Tönnies showed, the development of the modern city changed the way in which humans felt and thought about the world and the ways in which they interacted with one another. In this section we look at the development of the city from its beginnings in traditional societies to the most recent trends in urban development across the world.

Cities in traditional societies

The world's first cities appeared around 3500 BCE, in the river valleys of the Nile in Egypt, the Tigris and Euphrates in what is now Iraq, and the Indus in what is today Pakistan. Cities in traditional societies were very small by modern standards. Babylon, for example, one of the largest ancient Near Eastern cities, extended over an area of only 3.2 square miles and at its height, around 2000 BCE, probably numbered no more that 15,000–20,000 people. Rome under Emperor Augustus in the first century BCE was easily the largest pre-modern city outside China,

Cityscape of the modern megalopolis. How does it feel to you – a desolate concrete jungle or the very pinnacle of human achivement?

with some 300,000 inhabitants – the size of a 'small' modern city today.

Most cities of the ancient world shared certain common features. High walls, that served as a military defence and emphasized the separation of the urban community from the countryside, usually surrounded them. The central area was usually occupied by a religious temple, a royal palace, government and commercial buildings and a public square. This ceremonial, commercial and political centre was sometimes enclosed within a second, inner wall and was usually too small to hold more than a minority of the citizens. Although it usually contained a market, the centre was different from the business districts found at the core of modern cities, because the main buildings were nearly always religious and political (Sjoberg 1960, 1963; Fox 1964; Wheatley 1971).

The dwellings of the ruling class or elite tended to be concentrated near the centre. The less privileged groups lived towards the perimeter of the city or outside the walls, moving inside if the city came under attack. Different ethnic and religious communities were often allocated to separate neighbourhoods, where their members both lived and worked. Sometimes these neighbourhoods were also surrounded by walls. Communications among city-dwellers were erratic. Lacking any form of printing press, public officials had to shout at the tops of their voices to deliver pronouncements. 'Streets' were usually strips of land on which no one had yet built. A few traditional civilizations boasted sophisticated road systems linking various cities, but these existed mainly for military purposes, and transportation for the most part was slow and limited. Merchants and soldiers were the only people who regularly travelled over long distances.

While cities were the main centres for science, the arts and cosmopolitan culture, their influence over the rest of the country was always weak. No more than a tiny proportion of the population lived in the cities, and the division between cities and countryside was pronounced. By far the majority of people lived in small rural communities and rarely encountered more than the occasional state official or merchant from the towns.

Industrialization and urbanization

The contrast between the largest modern cities and those of pre-modern civilizations is extraordinary. The most populous cities in the industrialized countries number almost 20 million inhabitants. A conurbation – a cluster of cities and towns forming a continuous network – may include even larger numbers of people. The peak of urban life today is represented by what is called the megalopolis, the 'city of cities'. The term was originally coined in ancient Greece to refer to a city-state that was planned to be the envy of all civilizations, but in current usage it bears little relation to that utopia. The term was first applied in relation to the north-eastern seaboard of the United States, a conurbation covering some 450 miles from north of Boston to below Washington, DC. In this region, about 40 million people live at a density of more than 700 persons per square mile.

Britain was the first society to undergo industrialization, a process that began in the mid-eighteenth century. The process of industrialization generated increasing urbanization – the movement of the population into towns and cities, and away from the land. In 1800, fewer than 20 per cent of the British population lived in towns or cities of more than 10,000 inhabitants. By 1900, this proportion had risen to 74 per cent. The capital city, London, was home to

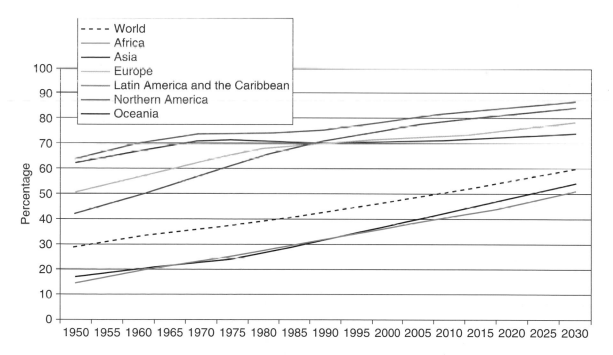

Figure 6.1   Percentage of the world's population living in urban areas, 1950–2030 (projected)

Source: United Nations Urbanization prospects, 2005. Reprinted by permission of the United Nations Population Division.

about 1.1 million people in 1800; by the beginning of the twentieth century, it had increased in size to a population of more than 7 million. London was then by far the largest city ever seen in the world. It was a vast manufacturing, commercial and financial centre at the heart of a still-expanding British Empire.

The urbanization of most other European countries and the United States took place somewhat later – but in some cases, once under way, accelerated even faster. In 1800, the United States was a more rural society than the leading European countries. Less than 10 per cent of the population lived in communities with populations of more than 2,500 people. Today, well over three-quarters of Americans do so. Between 1800 and 1900, the population of New York leapt from 60,000 people to 4.8 million.

Urbanization is now a global process, into which developing countries are increasingly being drawn. In 1950, only 30 per cent of the world's population were urban-dwellers; by 2000, this had reached 47 per cent – 2.9 billion people – and by 2030 it is forecast to reach 60 per cent – some 5 billion people. In 2007, the number of people living in urban areas overtook the number of people in rural areas. Most urbanization is now taking place in the developing world. The urban population of the less developed regions is expected to rise by more than 2 billion people between 2000 and 2030 from around 2 to 4 billion. As figure 6.1 shows, urbanization in Africa, Asia, Latin America and the Caribbean has increased particularly rapidly over the last 60 years, whilst the rate of urban population growth within developed regions such as Europe and Oceania has slowed over the same period (United Nations 2005).

The development of the modern city

Only at the turn of the twentieth century did statisticians and social observers begin to distinguish between the town and the city. Cities with large populations were recognized to be usually more cosmopolitan than smaller centres, with their influence extending beyond the national society of which they were a part.

The expansion of cities came about because of population increase, plus the migration of outsiders from farms, villages and small towns. This migration was often international, with people moving from peasant backgrounds directly into cities in the other countries. The immigration of very large numbers of Europeans from poor farming backgrounds to the United States is the most obvious example.

Cross-national immigration into cities was also widespread between countries in Europe itself. Peasants and villagers migrated to the towns (as they are doing on a massive scale in developing countries today) because of lack of opportunities in the rural areas, coupled with the apparent advantages and attractions of cities, where it was rumoured that the streets were 'paved with gold' (jobs, wealth, a wide range of goods and services). Cities, moreover, became concentrated centres of financial and industrial power, entrepreneurs sometimes creating new urban areas almost from scratch.

The development of modern cities has had an enormous impact, not only on habits and modes of behaviour, but on patterns of thought and feeling. From the time when large urban agglomerations first formed, in the eighteenth century, views about the effects of cities on social life have been polarized. For many people, cities represent 'civilized virtue' and are the fount of dynamism and cultural creativity; cities maximize opportunities for economic and cultural development, and provide the means of living a comfortable and satisfying existence. For others, the city is a smoking inferno thronged with aggressive and mutually distrustful crowds, riddled with crime, violence, corruption and poverty. In the late twentieth century, environmentalists such as Murray Bookchin (1986) have come to see cities as huge sprawling, environmentally damaging monsters that devour energy and generate waste at an unsustainable rate.

> See chapter 5 'The Environment', for a discussion of environmental issues.

As cities mushroomed in size, many people were horrified to see that inequalities and urban poverty seemed to intensify correspondingly. The extent of urban poverty and the vast differences between city neighbourhoods were among the main factors that prompted early sociological analyses of urban life. Unsurprisingly, the first major sociological studies of, and theories about, modern urban conditions originated in Chicago, a US city marked by a phenomenal rate of development – it grew from a virtually uninhabited area in the 1830s to a population of well over 2 million by 1900 – and by very pronounced inequalities.

Urban trends in the developed world

In this section, we consider some of the main patterns in Western urban development in the post-war era, using Britain and the United States as examples. Attention will focus on the rise of suburban areas, the decline of inner-city areas and strategies aimed at urban renewal.

Suburbanization

In the USA, the process of **suburbanization** reached its peak in the 1950s and 1960s. The centres of cities during those decades had a 10 per cent growth rate, while that of the suburban areas was 48 per cent. Most of the early movement to the suburbs involved white families. The enforcement of racial mixing in schools can be seen as a major factor in the decision of many whites to decamp from inner city areas. Moving to the suburbs was an attractive option for families who wished to put their children in all-white schools. Even today, American suburbs remain mostly white.

Many Victorians saw the newly industrializing cities such as Manchester and Leeds as sewers of degeneration and vice.

However, the white domination of suburbia in the United States is being eroded as more and more members of ethnic minorities move there. An analysis of data from the US 2000 Census showed that racial and ethnic minorities make up 27 per cent of suburban populations, up from 19 per cent in 1990. Like the people who began the exodus to suburbia in the 1950s, members of minority ethnic groups who move to the suburbs are mostly middle-class professionals. They move in search of better housing, schools and amenities. According to the chairman of the Chicago Housing Authority, 'suburbanization isn't about race now; it's about class. Nobody wants to be around poor people because of all the problems that go along with poor people: poor schools, unsafe streets, gangs' (De Witt 1994).

In the UK, many of the suburbs around London grew up between the two world wars, and clustered round new roads and links by underground trains that could bring commuters into the centre. Some converts to the big city life have looked with disdain on the large expanses of suburbia, with their semi-detached villas and well-tended gardens blanketing the fringes of English cities. Others, like the poet John Betjeman (1906–84), celebrated the modest eccentricity of the architecture of the suburbs, and the impulse to combine the employment opportunities of the city with a mode of life connected in practical terms with owner-occupation and car-ownership, and in terms of values with traditional family life.

In Britain, the migration of the residential population from central city areas to outlying suburbs and dormitory towns (towns outside the city boundaries lived in mainly by people who work in the city) or villages in the 1970s and early 1980s meant that the population of Greater London dropped by about half a million over the period. In the industrial towns of the North, the rapid loss of manufacturing industry during this period also reduced the population of inner-city areas. At the same time, many

USING YOUR SOCIOLOGICAL IMAGINATION

6.1 'Engendering' the city

Writing from a feminist perspective, several authors have examined how the city reflects the unequal gender relations in society, and have looked at ways to overcome this. Jo Beall (1998) has noted that if social relations, in this case between men and women, are underpinned by power, then cities demonstrate the correlation between power and space in terms of what gets built, where it is built, how and for whom. Beall writes: 'Cities are literally concrete manifestations of ideas on how society was, is and how it should be'.

The growth of the city in the nineteenth century is associated with gender separation. Public life and space was dominated by men, who were free to travel through the city as they wanted. Women were not expected to be seen in most public places, and those who were, were likely to be regarded as prostitutes or 'street walkers'. As the process of suburbanization began, the gender separation grew even more obvious. While the male head of the family commuted into the city on a daily basis, the women (wives) were expected to remain at home to care for the family. Transport links were built for travel between the suburbs and the city centre, but little thought was given by male designers to transportation within the suburbs, as a result of which it was more difficult for women to leave home (Greed 1994).

Elizabeth Wilson (2002) has argued that the development of the city was not all bad for women. She suggests that some feminist arguments reduce the role of women in the city to that of passive victims. In fact, the development of the city provided opportunities that non-urban forms of life could not provide. With the emergence of female white-collar work in the city and later the expansion of service industries, women increasingly entered the workforce. Thus the city offered women an escape from unpaid labour at home that did not exist elsewhere.

smaller cities and towns grew quickly – for example, Cambridge, Ipswich, Norwich, Oxford and Leicester. The 'flight to the suburbs' has had dramatic implications for the health and vitality of both British and American urban centres, as we shall see. Suburbanization has also affected men and women differently, as 'Using your sociological imagination 6.1' suggests.

> **THINKING CRITICALLY**
>
> What examples of the 'built environment' of cities can you think of that make getting around more difficult, particularly for women? Are these simply the result of male dominance in the architectural professions or the product of separate roles for men and women? Is Wilson right – have cities become more 'female-friendly' over time?

Inner-city decay

In the USA, the severe inner-city decay, which has marked all large cities over the past few decades, is a direct consequence of the growth of the suburbs. The movement of high-income groups away from the city centres has meant a loss of their local tax revenues. Since those that remain, or replace them, include many who are living in poverty, there is little scope for replacing that lost income. If rates are raised in the central city, wealthier groups and businesses tend to move further out.

This situation is worsened by the fact that the building stock in city centres becomes more run-down than in the suburbs, crime rates rise and there is higher unemployment. More must therefore be spent on welfare services, schools, the upkeep of buildings and police and fire services. A cycle of deterioration develops in which the more that suburbia expands, the greater become the problems of the city centres. In many American urban areas the effect has

been dramatic, particularly in the older cities, such as New York, Boston and Washington, DC. In some neighbourhoods in these cities, the deterioration of property is probably worse than in large urban areas anywhere else in the industrialized world. Decaying tenement blocks and boarded-up and burnt-out buildings alternate with empty areas of land covered in rubble.

In Britain, inner-city decay has been less marked than in the United States. Yet some inner-city areas are as dilapidated as many neighbourhoods in American cities. An important Church of England report, *Faith in the City*, described the inner-city areas in bleak terms:

> Grey walls, littered streets, boarded-up windows, graffiti, demolition and debris are the drearily standard features of the districts and parishes with which we are concerned . . . the dwellings in the inner cities are older than elsewhere. Roughly one-quarter of England's houses were built before 1919, but the proportion in the inner areas ranged from 40 to 60 per cent. (1985: 18)

One reason for the decay in Britain's inner cities is the financial crises that have affected many of these areas. From the late 1970s onwards, central government put strong pressure on local authorities to limit their budgets and to cut local services, even in inner-city areas most subject to decay. This led to intense conflicts between government and many of the councils that ran distressed inner-city areas, when they could not meet their set budgets. A number of the city councils found themselves with less revenue than before and were compelled to cut back on what were largely regarded as essential services.

Inner-city decay in the UK is also related to changes in the global economy. More recently industrialized countries, such as Singapore, Taiwan or Mexico, often have much cheaper labour costs than places like the UK, which can make them an attractive location for manufacturing industry. In

Global economic restructuring led to the deterioration of many inner-city areas in the 1970s and '80s.

response to this, over the past few decades, some already industrialized nations – for example, Japan and (West) Germany – shifted their economies to the kinds of activity that require a high level of capital investment and a highly skilled, well-educated workforce.

In an important study, *Inside the Inner-City*, Paul Harrison (1983) examined the impact of these global changes on Hackney, still one of London's poorest boroughs. The 1970s saw a dramatic decline in Hackney's manufacturing sector, paralleling a national decline. The number of manufacturing jobs in the borough dropped from 45,500 in 1973 to 27,400 in 1981 – a fall of 40 per cent. Until the mid-1970s, Hackney's male unemployment rate was roughly level with the national average; by 1981 it had risen to 17.1 per cent (50 per cent above the average). As the number of people out of work increased, so too did the number of people living in poverty. Harrison summarizes the effects

of such a concentration of disadvantaged people:

> [L]ocal government poor in resources and sometimes in the quality of staffing; a poor health service, since doctors cannot find a decent accommodation or much in the way of private practice; a low level of educational attainment due primarily to poor home backgrounds and the low average ability in schools; and, finally, high levels of crime, vandalism and family breakdown, and, wherever communities of divergent cultures live together, conflicts based on religion or race. (1983: 23–4)

Sometimes these multiple disadvantages overlap to such an extent that they burst forth openly in the form of urban conflict and riots.

For more on the problems arising from inner-city decay, see chapter 11, 'Stratification and Social Class', and chapter 12, 'Poverty, Social Exclusion and Welfare'.

Riots and urban unrest

In an era of globalization, population movement and rapid change, large cities have become concentrated and intensified expressions of the social problems that afflict society as a whole. All too often, the 'invisible' fault-lines within cities, generally created by unemployment and racial tension, undergo the equivalent of social earthquakes. Simmering tensions flare to the surface, sometimes violently in the form of riots, looting and widespread destruction.

This occurred in the USA in the spring of 1992, when riots engulfed parts of Los Angeles. Similarly, in 2005, some 5,000 people in Sydney, Australia were involved in disturbances (known as the Cronulla Riots) following reports of intimidatory behaviour by 'outsiders', said to be Middle Eastern youths, and the involvement of right-wing groups within the crowds that assembled to protest. While riots are generally relatively disorganized protests involving violence, urban unrest can take other forms, often turning into political protests, and they are certainly not limited to the developed countries. For example, Tiananmen Square in Beijing, China was the scene of protests by students in 1989 calling for political reform, and other activists campaigning against corruption. Between 1,000 and 3,000 people were killed in the military crackdown during and following the ending of the protest.

Many cities across the world have witnessed urban unrest in the late twentieth and early twenty-first centuries. In an age of globalization, cities have become key sites for symbolic protests, demonstrations and unrest associated with ethnic tensions, which are seen across the world via television and the Internet. Such protests have occurred within a number of European societies. For example, ethnic tensions fuelled by decaying infrastructure and housing led to rioting in many French cities in late 2005, reigniting debates across Europe on immigration and relations between ethnic groups. In Britain, neighbourhood riots have taken place in Brixton, South London, in 1981, 1985 and 1995; in Ely, Cardiff in 1991; in Oldham, Burnley and Lidget Green in Bradford in 2001 and in Birmingham in 2005. The 2001 riots in Bradford involved clashes between members of different cultural and ethnic backgrounds, attacks upon the police and the destruction of property.

Following the UK riots in 2001, the government set up a Community Cohesion Review Team, chaired by Ted Cantle, to produce a report into the causes of the riots. The report found a deep polarization between different ethnic communities in Britain's urban areas. It argued that many aspects of people's everyday lives compounded this split; for example, having separate educational arrangements, voluntary bodies, employment patterns, places of worship and language. A Muslim of Pakistani origin, interviewed for the report, summed this up, saying: 'When I leave this meeting with you I will go home and not see another white face until I come back here next week.' The report argued:

> In such a climate, there has been little attempt to develop clear values which focus on what it means to be a citizen of a modern multi-racial Britain and many still look backwards to some supposedly halcyon days of a mono-cultural society, or alternatively look to their country of origin for some form of identity.

The report suggested that greater community cohesion is needed, based upon knowledge of, contact between and respect for the various cultures that make up the UK. To do this, it 'is also essential to establish a greater sense of citizenship, based on (a few) common principles which are shared and observed by all sections of the community. This concept of citizenship would also place a higher value on cultural differences.' To achieve these aims, the report called for a well-resourced national debate, heavily influenced by younger people, and expressed the hope that this debate would lead to a new conception of citizenship, creating a more coherent approach to issues like education, housing, regeneration and employment (Cantle 2001). What we can gather from this report is that what are commonly seen as random acts of violence and destruction can arise from serious underlying social and economic causes that just need the trigger of a local event to spark protests. Attempts to tackle these underlying causes have led to programmes of urban renewal.

> See chapter 15, 'Race, Ethnicity and Migration', for a more detailed discussion of multiculturalism and ethnic relations.

Urban renewal

What kind of approach should local, regional and national governments take in addressing the complex problems crippling inner cities? How can the rapid expansion of outlying suburban areas be checked to prevent the erosion of green areas and countryside? A successful urban renewal policy is particularly challenging because it demands simultaneous action on multiple fronts.

In many developed countries, a range of national schemes – involving, for example, grants for the rehabilitation of houses by their owners or tax incentives to attract business – have been introduced to try to revive the fortunes of the inner cities. Over the last few decades a range of government programmes has been launched that pursue different methods of urban regeneration. The UK Conservative government's 'Action for Cities' programme of 1988, for example, looked more to private investment and free market forces to generate improvement than to state intervention. However, the response from business was much weaker than anticipated. Because of the seeming intractability of many of the problems facing the inner cities, there has been a tendency for programmes to be frequently dropped or replaced when results are not quick to arrive.

Studies indicate that, apart from the odd showpiece project, providing incentives and expecting private enterprise to do the job is ineffective as a way of tackling the fundamental social problems generated by the central cities. So many oppressive circumstances come together in the inner city that reversing processes of decay once they have got under way is in any case exceedingly difficult. Investigations into inner-city decay, such as the Scarman Report on the 1981 Brixton riots, have noted the lack of a coordinated approach to inner-city problems (Scarman 1982). Without major public expenditure – which is unlikely to be forthcoming from government – the prospects for radical improvement are slender indeed (Macgregor and Pimlott 1991).

The 1997 Labour government launched two main regeneration funds: the new deal for communities and the neighbourhood renewal fund. Other sources of funding focused on specific activities are also important in aiding urban renewal, including money from the National Lottery, funding for action zones in health, employment and education, and Housing Corporation cash for new social housing, 60 per cent of which has to support regeneration schemes. An important difference between current programmes and earlier schemes is that the earlier projects tended to focus on physical aspects of regeneration, particularly housing, whereas later programmes have tried to stimulate both social and economic regeneration.

The new deal for communities is the Labour government's flagship regeneration scheme. Launched in 1998, there are currently some 39 communities with projects across the UK. The main goal of the programme is to reduce disadvantages in the poorest areas by focusing on five specific issues: poor job prospects, high levels of crime, educational under-achievement, poor health and problems with housing and the physical environment. The Neighbourhood Renewal Fund, which began in 2001, targets the most deprived urban areas, aiming to narrow the gap between deprived areas and the rest of England (Neighbourhood Renewal Unit 2004).

A number of questions remain about the effectiveness of such regeneration schemes. How can top-down government programmes gain the backing and involvement of local people that is usually crucial to their success? Can public cash really stimulate local economies and create jobs? How can regeneration schemes prevent displacing problems from one area to another (Weaver 2001)?

Gentrification and 'urban recycling'

Urban recycling – the refurbishing or replacement of old buildings and new uses for previously developed land – has become common in large cities. Occasionally this has been attempted as part of planning programmes, but more often it is the result of gentrification – the renovation of buildings in dilapidated city neighbourhoods for

use by those in higher income groups, plus the provision of amenities like shops and restaurants to serve them. The gentrification of inner-city areas has occurred in many cities in Britain, the USA and other developed nations, and seems set to continue in years to come.

In the USA, the sociologist Elijah Anderson analysed the impact of gentrification in his book *Streetwise: Race, Class, and Change in an Urban Community* (1990). While the renovation of a neighbourhood generally increases its value, it rarely improves the living standards of its current low-income residents, who are usually forced to move out. In the Philadelphia neighbourhood that Anderson studied, many black residences were condemned, forcing more than 1,000 people to leave. Although they were told that their property would be used to build low-cost housing that they would be given the first opportunity to buy, instead large businesses and a high school now stand there.

The poor residents who continued to live in the neighbourhood received some benefits in the form of improved schools and police protection, but the resulting increase in taxes and rents finally forced them to leave for a more affordable neighbourhood, most often into areas of greater social exclusion. Black residents interviewed by Anderson expressed resentment at the influx of 'yuppies', whom they held responsible for the changes that drove the poorer people away.

The white newcomers had come to the city in search of cheap 'antique' housing, closer access to their city-based jobs, and a trendy urban lifestyle. They professed to be 'open-minded' about racial and ethnic differences; in reality, however, little fraternizing took place between the new and old residents unless they were of the same social class. Since the black residents were mostly poor and the white residents were middle class, class differences were compounded by ethnic ones. While some middle-class blacks lived in the area, most who could afford to do so chose a more suburban lifestyle, fearing that they would otherwise receive from whites the same treatment that was reserved for the black underclass. Over time, the neighbourhood was gradually transformed into a white middle-class enclave.

One reason behind gentrification is demographic. Young professional people are choosing to marry and start families later in life; as a result, more housing is needed for individuals and couples, rather than for families. In the UK, the government predicts that an additional 3.8 million households will have formed between 1996 and 2021 (Urban Task Force 1999). Because young people are having families later and their careers often demand long hours in inner-city office buildings, life in suburbia becomes more of an inconvenience than an asset. Affluent childless couples are able to afford expensive housing in refurbished inner-city areas and may even prefer to build lifestyles around the high-quality cultural, culinary and entertainment options available in city centres. Older couples whose children have left home may also be tempted back into inner-city areas for similar reasons.

It is important to note that the process of gentrification parallels another trend discussed earlier: the transformation of the urban economy from a manufacturing to a service-industries base. Addressing the concerns of the victims of these economic changes is critical for the survival of the cities.

In London, Docklands has been a notable example of 'urban recycling'. The Docklands area in East London occupies some eight and a half square miles of territory adjoining the Thames – deprived of its economic function by dock closures and industrial decline. Docklands is close to the financial district of the City of London, but also adjoins poor, working-class areas on the other side. From the 1960s onwards there were intense battles – which continue today – about what should happen to the area. Many living in or close to Docklands favoured redevelopment by means of community development projects, which would protect the interests of poorer residents. In the event, with the setting up of the Docklands Development Corporation in 1981, the region became a central part of the Conservative government's strategy of encouraging private enterprise to play the prime part in urban regeneration. The constraints of planning requirements and regulations were deliberately relaxed. The area today is covered in modern buildings, often adventurous in design. Warehouses have been converted into luxury flats, and new blocks have been constructed alongside them. A very large office development, visible from many other parts of London, has been constructed at Canary Wharf. Yet amid the glitter there are still dilapidated buildings and empty stretches of wasteland. Office space quite often lies empty, as do some of the new dwellings which have proved unsaleable at the prices they were originally projected to fetch. The boroughs of the Docklands have some of the poorest housing in the country, but many people living in such housing argue that they have benefited little from the construction that has gone on around them.

In the USA, developers are buying up abandoned industrial warehouses in cities from Milwaukee to Philadelphia and converting them into expensive residential loft and studio apartments. The creation of vibrant public spaces within the blighted urban centres of Baltimore and Pittsburgh has been heralded as a triumph of urban renewal. Yet, it is difficult to conceal the deprivation that remains in neighbourhoods just blocks away from these revitalized city centres.

Arguing against developments such as Docklands in his book about the history of the city, *The Conscience of the Eye* (1993), Richard Sennett argued that attempts should be made by urban planners to preserve, or to return to, what he calls 'the humane city'. The large, impersonal buildings in many cities turn people inwards,

Table 6.1 Cities with more than 10 million inhabitants, 1975, 2005 and 2015 (projected)

Rank	Agglomeration	Country	Population (thousands) 1975	Agglomeration	Country	Population (thousands) 2005	Agglomeration	Country	Population (thousands) 2015
1	Tokyo	Japan	26 615	Tokyo	Japan	35 197	Tokyo	Japan	35 494
2	New York	United States of America	15 880	Ciudad de México (Mexico City)	Mexico	19 411	Mumbai (Bombay)	India	21 869
3	Ciudad de México (Mexico City)	Mexico	10 690	New York	United States of America	18 718	Ciudad de México (Mexico City)	Mexico	21 568
4				São Paulo	Brazil	18 399	São Paulo	Brazil	20 596
5				Mumbai (Bombay)	India	18 196	New York	United States of America	19 876
6	Delhi	India	15 048	Delhi	India	18 604			
7	Shanghai	China	14 503	Shanghai	China	17 225			
8	Kolkata (Calcutta)	India	14 277	Kolkata (Calcutta)	India	16 980			
9	Jakarta	Indonesia	13 215	Dhaka	Bangladesh	16 842			
10	Buenos Aires	Argentina	12 550	Jakarta	Indonesia	16 822			
11	Dhaka	Bangladesh	12 430	Lagos	Nigeria	16 141			
12	Los Angeles	United States of America	12 298	Karachi	Pakistan	15 155			
13	Karachi	Pakistan	11 608	Buenos Aires	Argentina	13 396			
14	Rio de Janeiro	Brazil	11 469	Al-Qahirah (Cairo)	Egypt	13 138			
15	Osaka-Kobe	Japan	11 268	Los Angeles	United States of America	13 095			
16	Al-Qahirah (Cairo)	Egypt	11 128	Manila	Philippines	12 917			
17	Lagos	Nigeria	10 886	Beijing	China	12 850			
18	Beijing	China	10 717	Rio de Janeiro	Brazil	12 770			
19	Manila	Philippines	10 686	Osaka-Kobe	Japan	11 309			
20	Moskva (Moscow)	Russian Federation	10 654	Istanbul	Turkey	11 211			
21				Moskva (Moscow)	Russian Federation	11 022			
22				Guangzhou, Guangdong	China	10 420			

Source: United Nations World Urbanization Prospects 2005. Reprinted by permission of the United Nations Population Division.

away from one another. But cities can turn people outwards, putting them into contact with a variety of cultures and ways of life. We should seek to create city streets that are not only unthreatening but also 'full of life', in a way that 'traffic arteries, for all their rushing vehicular motion, are not'. The suburban shopping mall with its standardized walkways and shops is just as remote from 'the humane city' as is the traffic highway. Sennett argues that we should instead draw our inspiration from older city areas, like those found in many Italian city centres, which are on a human scale and mix diversity with elegance of design.

Urbanization in the developing world

The world's urban population could reach almost 5 billion people by 2030 and the United Nations estimates that almost 4 billion of these urban dwellers will be residents of cities in the developing world. As table 6.1 shows, most of the twenty-two cities projected to have more than 10 million residents by 2015 are located in the developing world.

Manuel Castells (1996) refers to **megacities** as one of the main features of third millennium urbanization. They are not defined by their size alone – although they are vast agglomerations of people – but also by their role as connection points between enormous human populations and the global economy. Megacities are intensely concentrated pockets of activity through which politics, media, communications, finances and production flow. According to Castells, megacities function as magnets for the countries or regions in which they are located. People are drawn towards large urban areas for various reasons; within megacities are those who succeed in tapping into the global system and those who do not. Besides serving as nodes in the global economy, megacities also become 'depositories of all these segments of the population who fight to survive'. For ex-

ample, Mumbai in India is a burgeoning employment and financial centre and home to the extraordinarily popular Bollywood film industry. It is a thriving and expanding city with exactly the kind of magnetic attraction that Castells talks of (see 'Global Society 6.1').

THINKING CRITICALLY

How does Mumbai compare with the megacities of the industrialized world? Are there similarities between Mumbai and, say, Los Angeles (see 'Global Society 6.3' below), London, Tokyo or New York? What seem to be the main differences? Does India's current position within the global capitalist economy effectively prevent Mumbai from 'closing the wealth gap'?

One of the largest urban settlements in history is currently being formed in Asia in an area of 50,000 square kilometres reaching from Hong Kong to mainland China, the Pearl River Delta and Macao. Although the region has no formal name or administrative structure, by 1995 it had already encompassed a population of 50 million people. According to Manuel Castells, it is poised to become one of the most significant industrial, business and cultural centres of the century.

Castells points to several interrelated factors that help to explain the emergence of this enormous conurbation. First, China is undergoing an economic transformation, and Hong Kong is one of the most important 'nodal points' linking China into the global economy. Next, Hong Kong's role as a global business and financial centre has been growing as its economic base shifts away from manufacturing towards services. Finally, between the mid-1980s and the mid-1990s, Hong Kong industrialists initiated a dramatic process of industrialization within the Pearl River Delta. More than 6 million people are employed in 20,000 factories and 10,000 firms. The result of

Global Society 6.1 | Mumbai – a megacity in the developing world

India gained independence from British colonial rule in 1947, at a time when the country was relatively poor and underdeveloped. Since independence, the country has changed quite dramatically and nowhere is this change seen more than in Mumbai, a megacity of some 12 million people in an urban area with more than 21 million inhabitants. Like other such cities across the world, Mumbai is a place of often stark contrasts between rich and poor. The article below, written for the 60th anniversary of independence in 2007, explores Mumbai's present and future.

Can India close the wealth gap?

Sixty years after India was freed from British colonial rule, the country's economy is booming. But will the wealth be shared more equally in the future?

Not enough

In Mumbai, India's financial capital, symbols of India's economic success are all around   from

flashy billboards advertising the latest perfumes to trendy young women dressed in the latest Tommy jeans. The India of today is vibrant, confident and ambitious – and not afraid to show it.

Take Rishi Rajani for example. The 30-something garment tycoon based in Mumbai and Denmark is a self-confessed workaholic who also loves the good life. His latest acquisition is a black Porsche sports car, which he drives through the streets of Mumbai. In the money capital of India, flaunting your wealth is now fashionable. Mr Rajani has always dreamed of owning the mean machine, and now his dream is a reality thanks to the success of the economy and his business.

'I work hard, you know, for my money', he says. 'And I need a reward. This is my reward.

'But it's not enough. My next goal? A yacht. That's when I'll know I've really made it. I'm already working towards it.'

Extremes of wealth and poverty exist side-by-side in many cities of the developing world.

Fast city

This is the stuff dreams are made of. Fast life, fast city – money in Mumbai cannot be spent or made quickly enough. And it is this dream that leads millions of migrants to the city every single day. They come here in packs, having heard legendary tales of Mumbai's streets being paved with gold. Travelling thousands of miles by train, they leave behind their families, their friends and their desperate lives. Many end up in the one of the city's numerous slums and struggling to survive by doing odd jobs on the street. The city they came to conquer, ends up engulfing them.

Demolition job

Saunji Kesarwadi is a potter by profession who lives in a 10 x 10-foot flat in Dharavi, Asia's biggest slum. In this box, he works and supports a family of six who live in the attic. Barely eking out an existence, he fears being thrown out of his home to make way for development.

'We hear the builders are coming', Mr Kesarwadi says as his two little girls look on. 'But no one has told us anything. They say they'll give us a flat if we sell them this land – but how can all of us leave? This is where my work, my life is. It may not be much but it's all I have.' But while life in the big city often falls short of expectations, thanks to the growth in the country's economy there are new opportunities in some villages.

Rural choice

Some 300 kilometres away from India's technology capital, Bangalore, lies Bellary – an industrial town born out of a sleepy village. When you first arrive, all you can see is dusty farmland for miles around. But behind the quiet exterior, there is a dramatic change afoot.

Bellary is home to one of India's first rural outsourcing centres, run by Indian steel maker JSW Steel Limited. The organisation has started two small operations on its Bellary campus, hiring young women from nearby villages to work in their rural processing centres. Here the girls spend their shifts punching in details of American patients' dental records, typing in a language many of them have only recently learned, using a machine many had never seen or heard of before.

Twenty-year-old Savithri Amma has a basic high school diploma. She earns about $80 (£40) a month doing this work – the same as one of her peers might earn working as a house-help in Mumbai. For that money she has to turn up to work every weekday by 7 a.m. – picked up from her village by a JSW bus at 5 a.m. and taken home when her shift ends at 3 p.m. 'At first, when I started this job, my parents were sceptical', she says shyly. 'Girls here used never to go out – but now we can because our position in life has improved financially and socially thanks to our work here. My father makes a little more than I do every month. I'm proud to contribute to the family finances.'

Growth promise

In Ms Amma's village, she is looked upon as a role model for many of her peers. The daily evening prayers at the village temple are a time for her to reflect on her day's work, and give thanks to the ancient Hindu gods for her good fortune. She has much to be thankful for. Ms Amma is one of the lucky ones, she is someone who did not have to leave home to battle the millions in urban India to survive. Growth in India's economy has to make its way off the streets of Mumbai and Delhi and into all of India's villages. Only when it does will it truly be here to stay - and the promise of independence will be met.

Source: Karishma Vaswani, *BBC News Online*, 14 August 2007 © bbc.co.uk/news

these overlapping processes has been an 'unprecedented urban explosion' (Castells 1996).

Why is the rate of urban growth in the world's lesser-developed regions so much higher than elsewhere? Two factors in particular must be taken into account. First, rates of population growth are higher in developing countries than they are in industrialized nations. Urban growth is fuelled by high fertility rates among people already living in cities.

Second, there is widespread internal migration from rural areas to urban ones – as in the case of the developing Hong Kong–Guangdong megacity. People are drawn to cities in the developing world either because their traditional systems of rural production have disintegrated, or because the urban areas offer superior job opportunities. Rural poverty prompts many people to try their hand at city life. They may intend to migrate to the city only for a relatively short time, aiming to return to their villages once they have earned enough money. Some actually do return, but most find themselves forced to stay, having for one reason or another lost their position in their previous communities.

>> See chapter 5, 'The Environment', for a discussion of the consequences of global population growth.

Challenges of urbanization in the developing world

Economic implications

As a growing number of unskilled and agricultural workers migrate to urban centres, the formal economy often struggles to absorb the influx into the workforce. In most cities in the developing world, it is the informal economy that allows those who cannot find formal work to make ends meet. From casual work in manufacturing and construction to small-scale trading activities, the unregulated informal sector offers earning opportunities to poor or unskilled workers.

Informal economic opportunities are important in helping thousands of families to survive in urban conditions, but they have problematic aspects as well. The informal economy is untaxed and unregulated. It is also less productive than the formal economy. Countries where economic activity is concentrated in this sector fail to collect much-needed revenue through taxation. The low level of productivity also hurts the general economy – the proportion of the GDP generated by informal economic activity is much lower than the percentage of the population involved in the sector.

The OECD (Organization of Economic Cooperation and Development) estimates that a billion new jobs will be needed by 2025 to sustain the expected population growth in cities in the developing world. It is unlikely that all of these jobs will be created within the formal economy. Some development analysts argue that attention should be paid to formalizing or regulating the large informal economy, where much of the 'excess' workforce is likely to cluster in the years to come.

Environmental challenges

The rapidly expanding urban areas in developing countries differ dramatically from cities in the industrialized world. Although cities everywhere are faced with environmental problems, those in developing countries are confronted by particularly severe risks. Pollution, housing shortages, inadequate sanitation and unsafe water supplies are chronic problems for cities in less developed countries.

Housing is one of the most acute problems in many urban areas. Cities such as Calcutta and São Paulo are massively congested; the rate of internal migration is much too high for the provision of permanent housing. Migrants crowd into squatters' zones, which mushroom around the edges of cities. In urban areas in the West, newcomers are most likely to settle close to the central parts of the city, but the reverse tends to happen in developing countries, where migrants populate what has been called the 'septic fringe' of the urban areas. Shanty dwellings made of sacking or cardboard are set up around the edges of the city wherever there is a little space.

In São Paulo, it is estimated that there was a 5.4 million shortfall in habitable homes in 1996. Some scholars estimate that the shortage is as high as 20 million, if the definition of 'habitable housing' is interpreted more strictly. Since the 1980s, the chronic deficit of housing in São Paulo has produced a wave of unofficial 'occupations' of empty buildings. Groups of unhoused families initiate 'mass squats' in abandoned hotels, offices and government buildings. Many families believe that it is better to share limited kitchen and toilet facilities with hundreds of others than to live on the streets or in *favelas* – the makeshift shanty-towns on the edges of the city.

City and regional governments in less developed countries are hard-pressed to keep up with the spiralling demand for housing. In cities such as São Paulo there are disagreements among housing authorities and local governments about how to address the housing problem. Some argue that the most feasible route is to improve conditions within the *favelas* – to provide electricity and running water, pave the streets and assign postal addresses. Others fear that makeshift shantytowns are fundamentally uninhabitable and should be demolished to make way for proper housing for poor families.

Congestion and over-development in city centres lead to serious environmental problems in many urban areas. Mexico City is a prime example. There, 94 per cent of the city consists of built-up areas, with only 6 per cent of land being open space. The area of 'green spaces' – parks and open stretches of green land – is far below that found in even the most densely populated North American or European cities. Pollution is a major problem, coming mostly from the cars, buses and trucks which pack the inadequate roads of the city, the rest deriving from industrial pollutants. It has been estimated that living in Mexico City is equivalent to smoking 40 cigarettes a day. In March 1992, pollution reached one of its highest levels ever. Whereas an ozone level of just under 100 points was deemed 'satisfactory' for health, in that month the level climbed to 398 points. The government had to order factories to close down for a period, schools were shut and 40 per cent of cars were banned from the streets on any one day.

 The concept and practices of sustainable development are discussed in more detail in chapter 5, 'The Environment'.

Social effects

Many urban areas in the developing world are overcrowded and under-resourced. Poverty is widespread and existing social services cannot meet the demands for healthcare, family planning advice, education and training. The unbalanced age distribution in developing countries adds to their social and economic difficulties. Compared to industrialized countries, a much larger proportion of the population in the developing world is under the age of fifteen. A youthful population needs support and education, but many developing countries lack the resources to provide universal education. When their families are poor, many children must work full time, and others have to scratch a living as street children, begging for whatever they can. When the street children mature, most become unemployed, homeless or both.

The future of urbanization in the developing world

In considering the scope of the challenges facing urban areas in developing countries, it can be difficult to see prospects for change and development. Conditions of life in many of the world's largest cities seem likely to decline even further in the years to come. But the picture is not entirely negative.

First, although birth rates remain high in many countries, they are likely to drop in the years to come as urbanization proceeds. This in turn will feed into a gradual decrease in the rate of urbanization itself. In West Africa, for example, the rate of urbanization should drop to 4.2 per cent per year by 2020,

 Population growth is discussed chapter 4, 'Globalization and the Changing World', chapter 13, 'Global Inequality', and chapter 5, 'The Environment'.

down from an annual rate of 6.3 per cent growth over the previous three decades.

Second, globalization is presenting important opportunities for urban areas in developing countries. With economic integration, cities around the world are able to enter international markets, to promote themselves as locations for investment and development, and to create economic links across the borders of nation-states. Globalization presents one of the most dynamic openings for growing urban centres to become major forces in economic development and innovation. Indeed, many cities in the developing world are already joining the ranks of the world's 'global cities', as we shall see shortly.

Cities and globalization

Before modern times, cities were self-contained entities that stood apart from the predominantly rural areas in which they were located. Road systems sometimes linked major urban areas, but travel was a specialized affair for merchants, soldiers and others who needed to cross distances with any regularity. Communication between cities was limited. The picture in the first decade of the twenty-first century could hardly be more different. Globalization has had a profound effect on cities by making them more interdependent and encouraging the proliferation of horizontal links between cities across national borders. Physical and virtual ties between cities now abound, and global networks of cities are emerging.

Some people have predicted that globalization and new communications technology might lead to the demise of cities as we know them – the Helsinki virtual village profiled in 'Global Society 6.2' provides one possibility. This is because many of the traditional functions of cities can now be carried out in cyberspace rather than in dense and congested urban areas. For example, financial markets have gone elec-

tronic, e-commerce reduces the need for both producers and consumers to rely on city centres and 'e-commuting' permits a growing number of employees to work from home rather than in an office building.

Yet, thus far, such predictions have not been borne out. Rather than undermining cities, globalization is transforming them into vital hubs within the global economy. Urban centres have become critical in co-ordinating information flows, managing business activities and innovating new services and technologies. There has been a simultaneous dispersion and concentration of activity and power within a set of cities around the globe (Castells 1996).

Global cities

The role of cities in the new global order has been attracting a great deal of attention from sociologists (Marcuse and van Kempen 2000; Massey 2007). Globalization is often thought of in terms of a duality between the national level and the global, yet it is the largest cities of the world that comprise the main circuits through which globalization occurs (Sassen 1998). The functioning of the new global economy is dependent on a set of central locations with developed informational infrastructures and a 'hyperconcentration' of facilities. It is in such points that the 'work' of globalization is performed and directed. As business, production, advertising and marketing assume a global scale, there is an enormous amount of organizational activity that must be done in order to maintain and develop these global networks.

Saskia Sassen has been one of the leading contributors to the debate on cities and globalization. She uses the term global city to refer to urban centres that are home to the headquarters of large, transnational corporations and a superabundance of financial, technological and consulting services. In *The Global City* (1991), Sassen based her work on the study of the three cities we introduced at the start of this chapter: New York, London and Tokyo. The contemporary development of the world economy, she argued, has created a novel strategic role for major cities. Most such cities have long been centres of international trade, but they now have four new traits:

1 They have developed into 'command posts' – centres of direction and policy-making – for the global economy.
2 Such cities are the key locations for financial and specialized service firms, which have become more important in influencing economic development than in manufacturing.
3 They are the sites of production and innovation in these newly expanded industries.
4 These cities are markets on which the 'products' of financial and service industries are bought, sold or otherwise disposed of.

New York, London and Tokyo have very different histories, yet we can trace comparable changes in their nature over the past two or three decades. Within the highly dispersed world economy of today, cities like these provide for central control of crucial operations. Global cities are much more than simply places of coordination, however; they are also contexts of production. What is important here is not the production of material goods, but the production of the specialized services required by business organizations for administering offices and factories scattered across the world, and the production of financial innovations and markets. Services and financial goods are the 'things' made by the global city.

The downtown areas of global cities provide concentrated sites within which whole clusters of 'producers' can work in close interaction, often including personal contact, with one another. In the global city, local firms mingle with national and multinational organizations, including a multi-

plicity of foreign companies. Thus 350 foreign banks have offices in New York City, plus 2,500 other foreign financial corporations; one out of every four bank employees in the city works for a foreign bank. Global cities compete with one another, but they also constitute an interdependent system, partly separate from the nations in which they are located.

Other authors have built on Sassen's work, noting that as globalization progresses, more and more cities are joining New York, London and Tokyo in the ranks of the 'global city'. Castells has described the creation of a tiered hierarchy of world cities – with places such as Hong Kong, Singapore, Chicago, Frankfurt, Los Angeles, Milan, Zurich and Osaka serving as major global centres for business and financial services. Beneath these, a new set of 'regional centres' is developing as key nodes within the global economy. Cities such as Madrid, São Paulo, Moscow, Seoul, Jakarta and Buenos Aires are becoming important hubs for activity within the so-called 'emerging markets'.

> **THINKING CRITICALLY**
>
> The Helsinki virtual village is described as a 'technological utopia'. List the effects – positive and negative – that mobile phones have already had on our society. Based on the your list, what might be some of the unintended consequences of such extensive mobile phone connectivity? Could such technology help to re-create the kind of *Gemeinschaft* or 'community' bonds that Tönnies (2001 [1887]) bemoaned the loss of? Or is it more likely that this technology will make people more isolated? How would that be brought about?

Inequality in the global city

The new global economy is highly problematic in many ways. Nowhere can this be seen more clearly than in the new dynamics of

Global Society 6.2 The Helsinki 'virtual village'

Jari Mielonen and his colleagues have a motto: 'Sanoista tekoihin', which loosely translates to 'Don't talk – make it happen'. Mielonen is chief technology officer of Sonera, Finland's leading telecommunications company and one of Europe's most aggressive players in the wireless market. 'Everyone's been talking about possibilities', he says. 'Nobody's been saying, "This is it. Touch and feel. Try it."'

That's why he and a group of businesspeople, academics and city planners are collaborating to turn a new development on the tussocky shore of the Gulf of Finland into the world's first wireless community. It's a simple but intriguing idea: give the workers and residents of a new Helsinki suburb a state-of-the-art wireless infrastructure and the very latest wireless services; to log on, locals won't even need a computer – just a mobile phone. Then stand back and watch how the info-age town of the future actually functions.

The site, known as Arabianranta (Arabia shore), is a flat, windswept, mostly barren expanse named for the pottery works that once stood there. Even before Mielonen and his colleagues started hatching plans to turn the area into a wireless wonderland, it had been earmarked by the city of Helsinki for development as a tech hub. If all goes as planned, by 2010 the location will be home to about 12,000 residents and 700 IT companies with some 8,000 employees, along with 4,000 students enrolled at local universities. It will also be home to a real-world experiment in community networking that will untangle some of the most pressing questions about the social effects of pervasive connectivity. Will the constant availability of wireless connection make communities more cohesive, or more isolated? How will people balance privacy concerns with the obvious advantages of extended wireless reach? And how much connectivity – once it becomes the status quo – will people really want?

Construction has already begun on the first wave of new office buildings and homes. Alongside the concrete and steel pilings, another, less visible, framework is being built here by Sonera and its partners – IBM, local software producer Digia, and the European-based Symbian Alliance, a joint effort involving Ericsson, Motorola, Nokia, Matsushita and Psion. They are creating what they call the Helsinki virtual village, a wireless interactive community for the entire suburb of Arabianranta. HVV will include a local area network and a wide range of services available through broadband fibre-optic cable and wireless links, which will be accessible anytime, anywhere. Users will be able to participate in HVV via any wireless handset, as well as by PC and digital TV.

For instance, residents could consult their personal calendar wherever they happen to be – in front of a computer at the office, watching TV at home or using a mobile phone on the go. The envisioned menu of offerings will let them create their own social organizations, office networks or mobile commerce opportunities, and a profiling system will let them control and update their personal data minute by minute.

Now HVV is throwing mobility into the mix, making communication casual and unobtrusive. IBM Nordic's Kurt Lönnqvist, who has watched his children grow up in a mobile-tech world, believes Finnish society has changed forever. Young people can be spontaneous about making social plans, he says. On the streets, they're continually sending a stream of messages back and forth to their friends: 'Where R U?' 'Let's meet.' 'C U at the bar.' Lönnqvist believes his children have become freer about the way they lead their lives than his generation is. 'They live with mobility every day. It's a way of life.'

At the Helsinki University of Technology, sociologist Timo Kopomaa has tried to track these changes in Finnish society. 'Spontaneity is something that is going to stay', he says. 'It's a new generation that has grown up with these devices, and their lives are bound up with them.' He studied groups of young phone-users and noted several differences in lifestyle. 'Today's society may be more casual, but that doesn't mean social ties are disappearing. In fact, he found that phones are drawing people together in new ways. Young 'telesurfers' often have larger social circles than non-phone-users. Close friends or relatives are in almost constant contact with each other, tending to share experiences as they happen. For friends, this has brought a new sense of tele-intimacy; for parents, reassurance.

Kopomaa believes the new wireless intimacy affects the workplace as well. 'The mobile phone softens the structure of the working day', he says. 'Workers don't have to plan so rigidly anymore – each day can unfold as meetings are set up when needed.'

Source: © Shaw 2001

inequality visible within the global city. The juxtaposition between the central business district and impoverished inner-city areas of many global cities should be seen as inter-related phenomena, as Sassen and others remind us. The 'growth sectors' of the new economy – financial services, marketing, high technology – are reaping profits far greater than any found within traditional economic sectors. As the salaries and bonuses of the very affluent continue to climb, the wages of those employed to clean and guard their offices are dropping. This process echoes the analysis of sociologists such as Manuel Castells and geographers like David Harvey, both of whom have argued that the city is not just a place or loca-tion for social relations, but is itself the prod-uct of struggles and conflicts amongst social groups. Sassen (2001) argues that we are wit-nessing the 'valorization' of work located at the forefront of the new global economy, and the 'devalorization' of work, which occurs behind the scenes.

> Deprivation and social exclusion are discussed in chapter 12, 'Poverty, Social Exclusion and Welfare', and inequalities in chapter 13, 'Global Inequality'.

Disparities in profit-making capabilities are expected in market economies, but the magnitude of the disparities in the new global economy is having a negative effect on many aspects of the social world, from housing to the labour market. Those who work in finance and global services receive high salaries, and the areas where they live become gentrified. At the same time, ortho-dox manufacturing jobs are lost, and the very process of gentrification creates a vast supply of low-wage jobs – in restaurants, hotels and boutiques. Affordable housing is scarce in gentrified areas, forcing an expan-sion of low-income neighbourhoods. While central business districts are the recipients of massive influxes of investment in real estate, development and telecommunica-tions, marginalized areas are left with few resources.

THINKING CRITICALLY
Does Davis's vision of Los Angeles show us the future for all major cities (see Global Society 6.3)? Which aspects of his thesis are familiar from cities that you know? How widespread is the separation of rich neighbourhoods from poorer communities? If poor people are being excluded from large parts of cities, where are they likely to live in the future? What could governments do to tackle these forms of urban social exclusion?

Governing cities in a global age

Like globalization, urbanization is double-edged and contradictory. It has both creative and destructive effects on cities. On the one hand, it allows for the concentration of people, goods, services and opportuni-ties. But at the same time, it fragments and weakens the coherence of places, traditions and existing networks. Alongside the new potentials created by centralization and economic growth are the dangerous effects of marginalization. Not only in developing countries, but in industrialized ones as well, many city-dwellers operate on the peri-phery, outside the realm of formal employ-ment, the rule of law and civic culture.

Although globalization is aggravating many of the challenges facing cities around the world, it is also making room for cities and local governments to play a revitalized political role. Cities have become more important than ever before as nation-states are increasingly unable to manage global trends. Issues such as ecological risk and volatile financial markets are operating at levels far above that of the nation-state; individual countries – even the most power-ful – are too 'small' to counter such forces. Yet nation-states also remain too 'large' to address adequately the rich diversity of needs found within cosmopolitan urban areas. Where the nation-state is unable to act effectively, local and city governments

Global Society 6.3 | Social inequalities in 'cities of quartz'

Within modern global cities, a geography of 'centrality and marginality' is taking shape. Alongside resplendent affluence, there is acute poverty. Yet although these two worlds coexist side by side, the actual contact between them can be surprisingly minimal. As Mike Davis (1990/2006) has noted in his study of Los Angeles, there has been a 'conscious hardening' of the city's surface against the poor – hence the metaphor of rock-hard 'quartz'. Accessible public spaces have been replaced by walled compounds, neighbourhoods are guarded by electronic surveillance, rich residents hire private police to keep street gangs at bay and 'corporate citadels' have been created. In Davis's words:

> To reduce contact with untouchables, urban redevelopment has converted once vital pedestrian streets into traffic sewers and transformed public parks into temporary receptacles for the homeless and wretched. The American city . . . is being systematically turned inside out – or, rather, outside in. The valorized spaces of the new megastructures and super-

malls are concentrated in the center, street frontage is denuded, public activity is sorted into strictly functional compartments, and circulation is internalized in corridors under the gaze of private police. (1990: 232)

According to Davis, life is made as 'unliveable' as possible for the poorest and most marginalized residents of Los Angeles. Benches at bus stops are barrel-shaped to prevent people from sleeping on them, the number of public toilets is fewer than in any other North American city, and sprinkler systems have been installed in many parks to deter the homeless from living in them. Police and city-planners have attempted to contain the homeless population within certain regions of the city, but in periodically sweeping through and confiscating makeshift shelters, they have effectively created a population of 'urban bedouins'.

 See chapter 21, 'Crime and Deviance', for a discussion of situational crime prevention and other recent crime-prevention techniques.

---

may be more 'agile forms for managing the global' (Borja and Castells 1997).

 For more on social movements, see chapter 22, 'Politics, Government and Social Movements'.

Jordi Borja and Manuel Castells (1997) argue that there are three main realms in which local authorities can act effectively to manage global forces. First, cities can contribute to economic productivity and competitiveness by managing the local 'habitat' – the conditions and facilities that form the social base for economic productivity. Economic competitiveness in the new economy depends on a productive qualified workforce; to be productive, that workforce needs a strong educational system for its children, good public transport, adequate and affordable housing, capable law enforcement, effective emergency services and vibrant cultural resources.

Second, cities play an important role in ensuring socio-cultural integration within

diverse multiethnic populations. Global cities bring together individuals from dozens of countries, varying religious and linguistic backgrounds, and different socio-economic levels. If the intense pluralism found within cosmopolitan cities is not countered by forces of integration, then fragmentation and intolerance can result. Especially in cases where the effectiveness of the nation-states for promoting social cohesion is compromised for historic, linguistic or other reasons, individual cities can be positive forces for social integration.

Third, cities are important venues for political representation and management. Local authorities have two inherent advantages over the nation-state in managing global issues: they enjoy greater legitimacy with those they represent, and they have more flexibility and room for manoeuvre than national structures. As explored in chapter 22, 'Politics, Government and Social Movements', many citizens feel that national political systems do not adequately

Shanghai is one of the ten largest cities in the world and China's financial and economic hub. This risks damaging the social coherence of place and tradition. However, innovative use of city space can reduce this effect. For example, here women are practising tai chi in the heart of the city.

represent their interests and concerns. In cases where the nation-state is too distant to represent specific cultural or regional interests, city and local authorities are more accessible forums for political activity.

Cities as political, economic and social agents

A great many organizations, institutions and groups cross paths within cities. Domestic and international businesses, potential investors, government bodies, civic associations, professional groups, trade unions and others meet and form links in urban areas. These links can lead to collective and joint actions in which cities act as social agents in political, economic, cultural and media spheres.

Examples of cities as economic actors have been increasing in recent years. In Europe, beginning with the recession of the 1970s, cities have banded together to promote investment and generate new forms of employment. The Eurocities movement, which now encompasses Europe's 50 largest cities, was formed in 1989. Asian cities such as Seoul, Singapore and Bangkok have been particularly effective as economic actors, acknowledging the importance of speed of information about international markets and the need for flexible productive and commercial structures.

Some cities construct medium- and long-term strategic plans to address the complex challenges before them. Under such plans, local government authorities, civic groups and private economic agents can work together to refurbish the urban infrastructure, organize a world-class event or shift the employment base away from industrial enterprises to knowledge-based ones. Birmingham, Amsterdam, Lyons, Lisbon, Glasgow and Barcelona are examples of

6.2 Global sport as urban renewal?

USING YOUR SOCIOLOGICAL IMAGINATION

Jowell to tell how Olympics funds will be repaid: Proceeds from land sales to replenish lottery. Agreement aims to dispel fears of arts bodies.
By Andrew Culf

Members of the International Olympic Committee (IOC) were impressed by the importance placed on urban regeneration in London's successful bid for the 2012 Olympic Games. The plan for 2012 focuses on the regeneration of some 500 acres of land in the Stratford area of East London, one of the most deprived areas in the UK. However, although advocates hope that this global sporting event will be a catalyst for urban regeneration, critics are concerned about the financing of the games and its long-term consequences, discussed in the article below, written in June 2007.

The 2012 London Olympics

The government will outline today [27 June 2007] how the national lottery will be repaid the £675m that is to be siphoned off to pay for the rising costs of the 2012 Olympics.

A memorandum of understanding between Tessa Jowell, the Olympics minister, and Ken Livingstone, the mayor of London, will explain how the money is to be clawed back from land

sales from the Olympic Park at Stratford, east London. The deal, which has taken three months, is an attempt by the government to show that lottery good causes will not lose out as a result of the larger than anticipated £9.3bn bill for the games.

Arts, heritage, sports and charity campaigners had expressed dismay that the public sector funding package for London 2012 included an additional £675m diversion from the lottery from 2009. The lottery was originally expected to contribute £1.5bn, but that figure rose to £2.2bn to deal with a black hole in the government's original calculations.

They warned the cuts could have a devastating affect on the cultural sector and also jeopardise the aim of increasing grassroots participation in sport.

Under the terms of the memorandum – which will be deposited in the library of the House of Commons – Ms Jowell and Mr Livingstone explain that the £675m will start to be repaid after 2012 once the London Development Agency has recovered the £650m it has spent on acquiring the Olympic Park site.

The LDA plans to sell 68 hectares for development and is confident that rising land prices will make such a sell-off lucrative. Continuing land sales will fund the staged payback to the lottery. The memorandum says the first phase after the LDA has recovered its costs will be a

An artist's impression of the London 2012 Olympic Stadium in Stratford, a deprived area of London's East End. Is this an example of long-term regeneration or just a short-term political fix?

repayment of £506m to lottery good causes and £125m to the LDA.

Once those sums have been achieved, in the second phase, the lottery will receive the remaining £169m, while the LDA will get £375m. This means that the bulk of the lottery cash will be repaid faster than previously anticipated. The memorandum replaces the deal between Ms Jowell and Mr Livingstone in 2003 when agreement was reached on how the cost would be shared between London's council tax payers and the lottery.

Opposition parties, which have criticized the government over the budget for the games, are expected to react sceptically to the memorandum. They described the old agreement as a 'back of an envelope calculation' cooked up before London really thought it could win the bid.

Last night a Whitehall source said: 'What Tessa Jowell promised in March has been agreed with the mayor of London. It is only fair that lottery good causes, having contributed a further £625m to the costs of the Olympics, should benefit and see their money coming back and they will.'

Source: Guardian newspaper, 27 June 2007

European cities that have carried out successful urban renewal projects with the help of strategic plans.

The case of Barcelona is particularly noteworthy. Launched in 1988, the Barcelona 2000 Economic and Social Strategic Plan brought together public and private organizations under a shared vision and action plan for transforming the city. The Barcelona municipal government and 10 additional bodies (including the chamber of commerce, the university, the city port authority and trade unions) have been overseeing the implementation of the plan's three main objectives: to connect Barcelona with a network of European cities by improving the communication and transport infrastructure, to improve the quality of life of Barcelona's inhabitants and to make the industrial and service sector more competitive, while promoting promising new economic sectors.

One of the cornerstones of the Barcelona 2000 plan took place in 1992, when the city hosted the Olympic Games. Staging the Olympics allowed Barcelona to 'internationalize' itself; the city's assets and vision were on display for the whole world to see. In the case of Barcelona, organizing a world-class event was crucial on two fronts: it enhanced the profile of the city in the eyes of the world and it generated additional enthusiasm within the city for completing the urban transformation (Borja and Castells 1997). Sport, it seems, can now play an important part in urban regeneration (Taylor et al. 1996).

> ## THINKING CRITICALLY
>
> Can sporting events really lead to lasting urban regeneration? Who will benefit from the 2012 London Olympics? Developers? Government or opposition politicians? The deprived communities of East London? What kinds of beneficial infrastructural developments may be left behind for residents to make use of when the games have finished?

The role of city mayors

As cities assume a new importance in the global system, the role of city mayors is also changing. Major world cities are becoming relatively independent actors in the global system and elected mayors of large cities are able to provide a type of personalized leadership that can be crucial in promoting urban agendas and raising a city's international profile. The London-based organization, City Mayors, works to raise the profile of mayors internationally and, since 2004, has awarded the title of 'World Mayor' based on the outcome of an online poll. In 2006, the title was won by John So, mayor of Melbourne, Australia with city mayors from Makati City in the Philippines, Dubrovnik in Croatia and Antananarivo in Madagascar in the top 10 places, showing the global spread of the mayor role.

In several prominent cases in which cities have successfully transformed their image, the role of the city mayor has been decisive. The mayors of Lisbon and Barcelona, for example, were driving forces behind efforts to elevate their cities to the ranks of the world's major urban centres. Likewise, mayors in smaller cities can play a crucial role in making the city known internationally and in attracting new economic investment. In the UK, London's affairs were devolved to an elected mayor, Ken Livingstone, in 2000. He set about pursuing a distinctive set of policies, including investing in public transport, introducing a congestion charge in the city centre and increasing the stock of affordable housing for 'key workers' such as teachers and nurses. Livingstone also strongly supported London's successful bid to host the 2012 Olympic Games. However, in 2008 Livingstone lost the mayoral election to Boris Johnson, who opposed plans to extend congestion charging further into the London suburbs. Many commentators saw this as a major reason for Johnson's success.

In the United States, city mayors have become a powerful economic and political force in recent decades. As gun-related violence has soared in American cities, more than 20 city mayors have abandoned reliance on federal attempts to pass gun control legislation and have filed lawsuits against the gun manufacturers on behalf of their cities. Former New York mayor Rudolph Giuliani generated a firestorm of controversy – but grudging respect from many – by implementing tough 'law-and-order' policies aimed at lowering crime rates. New York's violent crime rate dropped dramatically during the 1990s; strict 'quality of life' policies aimed at the homeless popu-lation transformed the face of New York's busy streets. After the terrorist attacks on 11 September 2001, Giuliani's determined leadership set the tone for the world's media, and he was named *Time* magazine's Person of the Year for 2001.

In many cities around the world, mayors are enjoying increased influence as spokes-people for their cities and regions. City mayors are often able to shape the policy agenda for areas that lie outside the city limits by entering into agreements with communities in the general metropolitan area. These types of partnerships can be drawn on in attracting foreign investment, for example, or in bidding to play host to a world-class event.

Conclusion: cities and global governance

Cooperation between cities is not restricted to the regional level. There is a growing acknowledgement that cities can and should play a significant role in addressing international political, economic and social issues. Informal and formal networks of cities are emerging as globalizing forces draw disparate parts of the world more closely together. The problems facing the world's largest cities are not isolated ones; they are embedded in the larger context of a global economy, international migration, new trade patterns and the power of information technology.

We have noted elsewhere that the complexities of our changing world are demanding new forms of democratic inter-national governance. Networks of cities should figure prominently among these new mechanisms. One such structure already exists – a World Assembly of Cities and Local Authorities is convened in paral-lel to the UN's Habitat Conference. Bodies such as the World Assembly promise to allow the gradual integration of city organi-zations into structures presently composed of national governments.

The heightened involvement of cities has the potential to democratize international relations; it may also make them more efficient. As the world's urban population continues to grow, more and more policies and reforms will need to be targeted at populations living in urban areas. City governments will be necessary and vital partners in these processes.

Summary points

1. Early approaches to urban sociology were dominated by the work of the Chicago School, whose members saw urban processes in terms of ecological models derived from biology. Louis Wirth developed the concept of urbanism as a way of life, arguing that city life breeds impersonality and social distance. These approaches have been challenged, without being discarded altogether.

2. The more recent work of David Harvey and Manuel Castells connects patterns of urbanism to the wider society, rather than treating urban processes as self-contained. The modes of life people develop in cities, as well as the physical lay-out of different neighbourhoods, express broad features of the development of industrial capitalism.

3. In traditional societies, only a small minority of the population lived in urban areas. In the industrialized countries today, between 60 and 90 per cent do so. Urbanism is developing very rapidly in the developing world as well.

4. The expansion of suburbs and dormitory towns has contributed to inner-city decay. Wealthier groups tend to move out of the centre of the city to live in low-rise housing and more homogeneous neighbourhoods. A cycle of deterioration is set under way, so that the more suburbia expands, the greater are the problems faced by those living in the inner cities. Urban recycling – including the refurbishing of old buildings to put them to new uses – has become common in many large cities.

5. Massive processes of urban development are occurring in developing countries. Cities in these societies differ in major respects from those of the West and are often dominated by makeshift illegal housing, where conditions of life are extremely impoverished. The informal economy is pronounced in many cities in the developing world. Governments often cannot meet the growing demands of the population for education, healthcare and family planning.

6. Cities are being strongly influenced by globalization. Global cities are urban centres, such as New York, London and Tokyo, that are home to the headquarters of large corporations and a superabundance of financial, technological and consulting services. A set of regional cities, such as Seoul, Moscow and São Paulo, are also developing as key nodes of the global economy.

7. As cities become more important within the global economy, their relationship with outlying regions is altered. Cities become disconnected from the region and nation in which they are located and horizontal links with other global cities take on greater significance. Global cities are characterized by high levels of inequality. Great affluence and abject poverty coexist side by side, but contact between the two worlds can be minimal.

8. The role of cities as political and economic agents is increasing. City governments are positioned to manage the effects of some global issues better than national governments. Cities can contribute to economic productivity and competitiveness, promote social and cultural integration, and serve as accessible venues for political activity. Some cities construct strategic plans to promote the city's profile by hosting a world-class event or carrying out urban renewal and economic development programmes. City mayors are becoming important political forces for advancing urban agendas.

9. As globalization progresses, the role of cities in addressing international issues is likely to grow. Regional and international networks of cities are emerging and may become more actively involved in forms of global governance currently composed of nation-states.

Further reading

To get an overview of urban sociology, David Byrne's *Understanding the Urban* (Basingstoke: Palgrave Macmillan, 2001) is a good place to begin and Mike Savage, Allan Warde and Kevin Ward's *Urban Sociology, Capitalism and Modernity* (Basingstoke: Palgrave Macmillan, 2002) gives a comprehensive account of this field.

On cities, Doreen Massey's *World City* (Cambridge: Polity, 2007) takes London as a case study of a global city, while the UN-Habitat's *The State of the World's Cities: The Millennium Development Goals and Urban Sustainability* (London: Earthscan Publications, 2006) gives much comparative information on cities across the world.

It may be a little old now, but Marshall Berman's *All That is Solid Melts into Air: The Experience of Modernity* (London: Verso, 1983) remains an inspiring book dealing especially with the *experience* of urban modernity, and is well worth the effort.

Debates on cities and the restructuring of space are well handled in Peter Marcuse and Ronald van Kempen's (eds) *Globalizing Cities: A New Spatial Order?* (Oxford: Blackwell Publications, 2000). Fran Tonkiss's *Space, the City and Social Theory: Social Relations and Urban Forms* (Cambridge: Polity, 2005) is not an easy read, but it does offer an account of social theories of the city.

Finally, Jan Lin's *The Urban Sociology Reader* (London and New York: Routledge, 2005) is an edited collection of urban sociology 'classics' and, as such, is a very helpful resource.

Internet links

A USA site on sustainable architecture, building and culture:
www.sustainableabc.com/

Centre for Urban History, based at the University of Leicester, UK:
www.le.ac.uk/urbanhist/

UK Government's Neighbourhood Renewal Unit:
www.neighbourhood.gov.uk/

City Mayors – a useful resource on the role of mayors across the world:
www.citymayors.com/

H-Urban – A discussion forum for urban history and urban studies:
www.h-net.org/~urban/*Home page
http://h-net.msu.edu/cgi-bin/logbrowse.pl?trx=lm&list=H-Urban*Discussion logs

Radical Urban Theory – 'writings on the modern urban condition':
www.radicalurbantheory.com/

Virtual Cities Resource Centre – online cities:
www.casa.ucl.ac.uk/planning/virtualcities.html

7

Social Interaction and Everyday Life

CHAPTER 7

• •

Social Interaction and Everyday Life

People in close proximity to each other – such as at this gym – engage routinely in 'civil inattention'.

Shaun is a fitness instructor at an expensive city health club, where he has worked for many years. Over time, he has come to know hundreds of people who exercise at the gym. He worked with some of them when they first joined, explaining to them how to use the equipment. He met many others in his role as an instructor of 'spinning' classes (a group session on exercise bikes). Others he has come to know through casual contact, since many of the same people work out at the same time every week.

The personal space is limited within the gym, due to the proximity of the exercise equipment. For example, in the weight-training circuit, one section contains a number of machines that are very near to each other. Members

'Leave me alone!' On public transport, people try to protect their personal space.

must work in close proximity to others working out, and they constantly cross one another's paths as they move from machine to machine.

It is almost impossible for Shaun to walk anywhere in this physical space without making eye contact with someone else he has at least met. He will greet many of these patrons the first time he sees them in the day, but afterwards it is usually understood that they will go about their own business without acknowledging one another in the way they did earlier.

When passers-by quickly glance at one another and then look away again, they demonstrate what Erving Goffman (1967, 1971) calls the **civil inattention** we require of one another in many situations. Civil inattention is not the same as ignoring another person. Each individual indicates recognition of the other person's presence, but avoids any gesture that might be taken as too intrusive. Civil inattention to others is something we engage in more or less unconsciously, but it is of fundamental importance to the existence of social life, which must proceed efficiently and, sometimes amongst total strangers, without fear. When civil inattention occurs among passing strangers, an individual implies to another person that she has no reason to suspect his intentions, be hostile to him or in any other way specifically avoid him.

The best way to see the importance of this

is by thinking of examples where it does not apply. When a person stares fixedly at another, allowing her face openly to express a particular emotion, it is normally with a lover, family member or close friend. Strangers or chance acquaintances, whether encountered on the street, at work or at a party, virtually never hold the gaze of another in this way. To do so may be taken as an indication of hostile intent; for example, racists have been known to give a 'hate stare' to passers-by from other ethnic groups.

Even friends in close conversation need to be careful about how they look at one another. Each individual demonstrates attention and involvement in the conversation by regularly looking at the eyes of the other, but not staring into them. To look too intently might be taken as a sign of mistrust about, or at least failure to understand, what the other is saying. Yet if neither party engages the eyes of the other at all, each is likely to be thought evasive, shifty, or otherwise odd.

Why study daily life?

Why should we concern ourselves with such seemingly trivial aspects of social behaviour? Passing someone on the street or exchanging a few words with a friend seem minor and uninteresting activities, things we do countless times a day without giving them any thought. In fact, the study of such apparently insignificant forms of social interaction is of major importance in sociology – and, far from being uninteresting, is one of the most absorbing of all areas of sociological investigation. There are three reasons for this.

First, our day-to-day routines, with their almost constant interactions with others, give structure and form to what we do; we can learn a great deal about ourselves as social beings, and about social life itself, from studying them. Our lives are organized around the repetition of similar patterns of behaviour from day to day, week to week,

month to month, and year to year. Think of what you did yesterday, for example, and the day before that. If they were both weekdays, in all probability you got up at about the same time each day (an important routine in itself). If you are a student, you may have gone off to a class fairly early in the morning, perhaps making the journey from home to campus that you make virtually every weekday. You perhaps met some friends for lunch, returning to classes or private study in the afternoon. Later, you retraced your steps back home, possibly going out in the evening with other friends.

Of course, the routines we follow from day to day are not identical, and our patterns of activity at weekends usually contrast with those on weekdays. And if we make a major change in our life, like leaving college to take up a job, alterations in our daily routines are usually necessary; but then we establish a new and fairly regular set of habits again.

Second, the study of everyday life reveals to us how humans can act creatively to shape reality. Although social behaviour is guided to some extent by forces such as roles, norms and shared expectations, individuals perceive reality differently according to their backgrounds, interests and motivations. Because individuals are capable of creative action, they continuously shape reality through the decisions and actions they take. In other words, reality is not fixed or static; it is created through human interactions. This notion of the 'social construction of reality' lies at the heart of the symbolic interactionist perspective and was introduced in chapter 1.

Third, studying social interaction in everyday life sheds light on larger social systems and institutions. All large-scale social systems, in fact, depend on the patterns of social interaction that we engage in daily. This is easy to demonstrate. Consider again the case of two strangers passing in the street. Such an event may seem to have little direct relevance to large-scale, more permanent forms of social organization. But when we take into account many such interactions, this is no longer so. In modern societies, most people live in towns and cities and constantly interact with others whom they do not know personally. Civil inattention is one among other mechanisms that give city life, with its bustling crowds and fleeting, impersonal contacts, the character it has.

In this chapter, we shall discuss non-verbal communication such as facial expressions and bodily gestures, and explore how our identities are 'embodied'. We will then move on to analyse everyday speech – how we use language to communicate to others the meanings we wish to get across. Finally, we will focus on the ways in which our lives are structured by daily routines, paying particular attention to how we coordinate our actions across space and time. In this chapter we also find that the study of small, everyday practices that sociologists of social interaction investigate are not separate from any of the large-scale issues examined in the later chapters of this book, such as gender or class; instead, we find that they are intimately linked. We look at two specific examples of the link between micro- and macrosociology in the two 'Using your sociological imagination' boxes in this chapter.

>> Recent theories on the impact of larger social structures on the everyday 'lifeworld' can be found in chapter 3, 'Theories and Perspectives in Sociology'.

Non-verbal communication

Social interaction requires numerous forms of non-verbal communication – the exchange of information and meaning through facial expressions, gestures and movements of the body. Non-verbal communication is sometimes referred to as 'body language', but this is misleading, because we characteristically use such non-verbal cues to eliminate or expand on what is said with words.

The human face, gestures and emotions

One major aspect of non-verbal communication is the facial expression of emotion.

When we compare the human face with that of other species, it does seem remarkably flexible and capable of manipulation. The German sociologist Norbert Elias (1897–1990) argued that studying the face shows how human beings, like all other species, have naturally evolved over a long period of time, but also that this biological basis has been overlain with cultural features in the process of social development. Compare the human face with that of our closest evolutionary relatives, the apes. The ape face is furry and quite rigid in structure, permitting a limited amount of movement. The human face, in contrast, is naked and very flexible, able to contort into a wide variety of postures. In some parts of the world, 'gurning' competitions are even held to see who can pull the strangest facial expressions – some of these are, indeed, *very* strange. Without this evolved physiological malleability, human communication, as we know it, would be impossible. Therefore, Elias (1987) sees the development of the human face as closely linked to the evolutionary 'survival value' of effective communication systems. Whilst apes do make extensive use of 'whole body' communication, humans can communicate a varied range of emotions on just the 'signalling board' of the face. For Elias, such facial communication of emotions demonstrates that in human beings, the natural and the social are always inextricably intertwined.

Paul Ekman and his colleagues developed what they call the Facial Action Coding System (FACS) for describing movements of the facial muscles that give rise to particular expressions (Ekman and Friesen 1978). By this means, they have tried to inject some precision into an area notoriously open to inconsistent or contradictory interpretations – for there is little agreement about how emotions are to be identified and classified. Charles Darwin, the originator of evolutionary theory, claimed that basic modes of emotional expression are the same in all human beings. Although some have disputed the claim, Ekman's research among people from widely different cultural backgrounds seems to confirm this. Ekman and Friesen carried out a study of an isolated community in New Guinea, whose members had previously had virtually no contact with outsiders. When they were shown pictures of facial expressions expressing six emotions (happiness, sadness, anger, disgust, fear, surprise), the New Guineans were able to identify these emotions.

According to Ekman, the results of his own and similar studies of different peoples support the view that the facial expression of emotion and its interpretation are innate in human beings. He acknowledges that his evidence does not conclusively demonstrate this, and it may be that widely shared cultural learning experiences are involved; however, other types of research support his conclusions. Eibl-Eibesfeldt (1973) studied six children born deaf and blind to see how far their facial expressions were the same as those of sighted, hearing individuals in particular emotional situations. He found that the children smiled when engaged in obviously pleasurable activities, raised their eyebrows in surprise when sniffing at an object with an unaccustomed smell and frowned when repeatedly offered a disliked object. Since they could not have seen other people behaving in these ways, it seems that these responses must have been innately determined. Using the FACS, Ekman and Friesen identified a number of the discrete facial muscle actions in newborn infants that are also found in adult expressions of emotion. Infants seem, for example, to produce facial expressions similar to the adult expression of disgust (pursing the lips and frowning) in response to sour tastes.

But although the facial expression of emotion seems to be partly innate, individual and cultural factors influence what exact form facial movements take and the contexts in which they are deemed appropriate. How people smile, for example, the precise movement of the lips and other facial muscles, and how fleeting the smile is all vary between cultures.

There are no gestures or bodily postures that have been shown to characterize all, or even most, cultures. In some societies, for instance, people nod when they mean no, the opposite of Anglo-American practice.

Paul Ekman's photographs of the facial expressions of a tribesman from a remote community in New Guinea helped to test the idea that basic modes of emotional expression are the same amongst all people. Look carefully at each facial expression. Which of the six emotions used by Ekman above do you think is being conveyed in each one? Check to see if you were right by looking at the 'Thinking Critically' box overleaf.

Gestures that Europeans and Americans tend to use a great deal, such as pointing, seem not to exist among certain peoples (Bull 1983). Similarly, a straightened forefinger placed at the centre of the cheek and rotated is used in parts of Italy as a gesture of praise, but appears to be unknown elsewhere. Like facial expressions, gestures and bodily posture are continually used to fill out utterances, as well as conveying meanings when nothing is actually said. All three can be used to joke, or show irony or scepticism.

The non-verbal impressions that we convey often inadvertently indicate that what we say is not quite what we mean. Blushing is perhaps the most obvious example of how physical indicators can contradict our stated meanings. But there are many more subtle signs that can be picked up by other people. As an example, a trained eye can often detect deceit by studying non-verbal cues. Sweating, fidgeting, staring or shifting eyes, and facial expressions held for a long time (genuine facial expressions tend to evaporate after four or five seconds) could indicate that a person is being deceptive. Thus, we use facial expressions and bodily gestures of other people to add to what they communicate verbally and to check how far they are sincere in what they say and whether we can trust them.

Gender and the body

Is there a gender dimension to everyday social interaction? There are reasons to believe that there is. Because interactions are shaped by the larger social context, it is not surprising that both verbal and non-verbal communication may be perceived and expressed differently by men and women. Understandings of gender and gender roles are greatly influenced by social factors and are related broadly to issues of power and status in society.

For example, the political philosopher Iris Marion Young (1949–2006) explored gendered bodily experience in a famous arti-

> ### THINKING CRITICALLY
>
> From left to right, Ekman's instructions were to show how your face would look if:
>
> 1 Your friend had come and you were *happy*.
> 2 Your child had died and you were *sad*.
> 3 You were *angry* and about to fight.
> 4 You saw a dead pig that had been lying there a long time: *disgust*.
>
> How many did you get right? Look at the faces again – is it easier to see the different emotions being expressed when you know the context? Have you ever misunderstood how someone is feeling, and if so, why did their facial expression not give away their emotional state? Are there *different ways* of facially expressing happiness, sadness and so on?

cle, 'Throwing Like a Girl' (1980, 2005). Young argued that the distinctive 'half-hearted' movements – such as throwing a ball or stone – made by women are not biologically determined, but are the product of discourses and practices which encourage girls and young women to experience their bodies as 'objects for others' from an early age. Such bodily training, she suggested, embodies an 'inhibited intentionality', reflecting feminine norms of restricted bodily comportment and movement. In short, male-dominated societies produce a majority of women who are 'physically handicapped'. In contrast, men learn to experience their bodies as active and forceful 'objects for themselves', which is reflected in their more aggressive bodily movements, particularly noticeable in sports, for example. For young boys, therefore, to be accused of 'throwing like a girl' is a dreadful insult and an attack on their identity as a male.

These dynamics are evident even in standard interactions in daily life. Take as an example one of the most common non-verbal expressions: eye contact. Individuals use eye contact in a wide variety of ways, often to catch someone's attention or to begin a social interaction. In societies where men on the whole dominate women in both public and private life, men may feel freer than women to make eye contact with strangers.

A particular form of eye contact – staring – illustrates the contrasts in meaning between men and women of identical forms of non-verbal communication. A man who stares at a woman can be seen as acting in a 'natural' or 'innocent' way; if the woman is uncomfortable, she can evade the gaze by looking away or choosing not to sustain the interaction. On the other hand, a woman who stares at a man is often regarded as behaving in a suggestive or sexually leading manner. Taken individually, such cases may seem inconsequential; when viewed collectively, they help reinforce patterns of gender inequality (Burgoon et al. 1996).

There are other gender differences in non-verbal communication as well. Men tend to sit in more relaxed ways than women. Men tend to lean back with their legs open, whereas women tend to have a more closed body position, sitting upright, with their hands in their lap and their legs crossed. Women tend to stand closer to the person they are talking to than men; and men make physical contact with women during conversation far more often than the other way around (women are generally expected to view this as normal). Studies have also shown that women tend to show their emotions more obviously (through facial expressions), and that they seek and break eye contact more often than men. Sociologists have argued that these seemingly small-scale micro-level interactions reinforce the wider macro-level inequality in our society. Men control more space when standing and sitting than women because they tend to stand further away from the person they are talking to and because they tend to sprawl when sitting, and they demonstrate control through more

frequent physical contact. Women, it has been argued, seek approval through eye contact and facial expression; when men make eye contact, a woman is more likely to look away than another man. Thus, it is argued, micro-level studies of non-verbal forms of communication provide subtle cues, which demonstrate men's power over women in wider society (Young 1990).

In *Gender Trouble* (1990), Judith Butler argued that these expressions of gendered identities illustrate that gender is 'performative'. What does she mean by this? Butler says that many feminists rejected the idea that gender is biologically or naturally fixed. But, in doing so, they separated gender (culture) from sex (biology), arguing that gendered norms of behaviour were built upon biologically determined male and female bodies. Butler rejects this position, arguing that there are *no* biologically determined identities lying beneath the cultural expressions of gender. Instead, gender identities are established precisely *through* their continuous performance. There is simply no essential, natural or biological basis to gender even though the belief that there is such a basis is very widespread within many societies and such beliefs shape people's behaviour. Butler's position is that gender identity is not a question of *who you are*, but of *what you do*, and it therefore follows that gender identity is much more fluid and unstable than was previously thought. If Butler is right, then there may be much more scope for people to choose how they perform gender and thus to resist the dominant or hegemonic forms of gendered identity.

 See chapter 14, 'Sexuality and Gender', for R. W. Connell's wider theory of hegemony in relation to gender and identity.

Embodiment and identities

The gendering of bodily experience and movement described above complements theories of gender identity, which are

7.1 Women and men in public

As we saw in chapter 1, microsociology, the study of everyday behaviour in situations of face-to-face interaction and macrosociology, the study of the broader features of society like class or gender hierarchies, are inextricably connected (Knorr-Cetina and Cicourel 1981; Giddens 1984). Here, we look at an example of how an event that may seem to be a prime example of microsociology – a woman walking down the street is verbally harassed by a group of men – is in fact also linked to the bigger issues that make up macrosociology.

In her study *Passing By: Gender and Public Harassment* (1995), Carol Brooks Gardner found that in various settings – most famously, the edge of construction sites – these types of unwanted interaction occur as something women frequently experience as abusive.

Although the harassment of a single woman might be analysed in microsociological terms by looking at a single interaction, it is not fruitful to view it so simply. Such harassment is typical of street talk involving men and women who are strangers (Gardner 1995). And these kinds of interaction cannot simply be understood without also looking at the larger background of gender hierarchy in society. In this way, we can see how micro- and macroanalysis are connected. For example, Gardner linked the harassment of women by men to the larger system of gender inequality,

"So far, so good. Now let's hear your wolf-whistling."

represented by male privilege in public spaces, women's physical vulnerability and the omnipresent threat of rape.

Without making this link between micro- and macrosociology, we can only have a limited understanding of these interactions. It might seem as though these types of interaction are isolated instances or that they could be eliminated by teaching people good manners. Understanding the link between micro and macro helps us see that in order to attack the problem at its root cause, one would need to focus on eliminating the forms of gender inequality that give rise to such interactions.

discussed in detail in chapter 8, 'The Life-Course'. As that chapter shows, both Sigmund Freud and Nancy Chodorow argued – in different ways – that people *learn* gender roles and gendered behaviour in interaction with significant other people, such as key family members, from a very early age. What we can add to this from the sociological work on bodily experience and non-verbal communication above, is that a person's gender identity is also expressed through experience of their own and other people's bodies and bodily movements.

Gender identity is both socially created and 'embodied'. In fact the general concept of **identity** has become central to many areas of sociology over recent years. But what is an identity?

Richard Jenkins (1996) says that identity is, 'our understanding of who we are and of who other people are', and of course this also includes *their* understanding of themselves and of us too. It follows then, that all human identities must be 'social identities', because they are formed in the continuing processes of interaction in social life. Identities are made, not given. Nevertheless, we can see three central parts to identities; they are partly individual or personal; they are partly collective or social; and they are always 'embodied'. As Jenkins puts it:

> Selves without bodies don't make much sense in human terms. Even ghosts or spirits, if we recognise them as human, once had bodies; even the disembodied world of cyberspace depends, in the not-so-final-resort, on bodies in front of computer screens. We reach out with our selves and others reach out to us. (1996: 47)

A good example of the close linkage between social identity and embodiment is in Goffman's study of 'stigma' (discussed in chapter 10). He shows how disabled people, for example, can be stigmatized on the basis of readily observable physical impairments (discredited stigma), which then make individual identities more difficult to 'manage' than some non-physical impairments, which can be more easily hidden (discrediting stigma).

Identities are also multilayered, consisting of several sources. A simple distinction can be made between *primary* and *secondary* identities, which are connected to the processes of primary and secondary socialization respectively. Primary identities are those that are formed in early life and include gender, race/ethnicity and perhaps also disability/impairment. Secondary identities build on these and would include those associated with **social roles** and **achieved statuses** such as occupational roles and social status positions. Clearly, social identities are quite complex and fluid, changing as people gain new roles or leave behind old ones.

An important consequence of the discussion so far is that identities mark out *similarities* and *differences* in social interactions. Individual or personal identity feels quite unique and different from other people, especially in the individualized modern societies, and is perceived by others as such. Our personal names are one illustration of this individual difference. In many societies today, parents increasingly seek out unique names for their offspring to mark them out as unique and different from the crowd, rather than choosing names that are commonly used. In contrast, collective identities display similarity with others. To identify yourself (and be identified) as working class, an environmentalist or a professional sociologist can be sources of group solidarity, pride or perhaps even individual shame at being part of a particular group. Whatever the perception we may have of our own social identities, the example demonstrates that individual and social identities are tightly bound together within the embodied self (Burkitt 1999).

The social rules of interaction

Although we routinely use non-verbal cues in our own behaviour and in making sense of the behaviour of others, much of our interaction is done through talk – casual verbal exchange – carried on in informal conversations with others. It has always been accepted by sociologists that language is fundamental to social life. Recently, however, an approach has been developed that is specifically concerned with how people use language in the ordinary contexts of everyday life.

Ethnomethodology is the study of the 'ethnomethods' – the folk, or lay, methods – people use to *make sense* of what others do, and particularly of what they say. Harold Garfinkel, whose work is discussed below, coined the term 'ethnomethodology'. We all apply these methods, normally without having to give any conscious attention to them. Often we can only make sense of what is said in conversation if we know the social context, which does not appear in the words themselves. Take the following conversation (Heritage 1985):

A: I have a 14-year-old son.
B: Well, that's all right.
A: I also have a dog.
B: Oh, I'm sorry.

What do you think is happening here? What is the relation between the speakers? What if you were told that this is a conversation between a prospective tenant and a landlord? The conversation then becomes sensible: some landlords accept children but do not permit their tenants to keep pets. Yet if we do not know the social context, the responses of individual B seem to bear no relation to the statements of A. *Part* of the sense is in the words, and *part* is in the way in which the meaning emerges from the social context.

Shared understandings

The most inconsequential forms of daily talk assume complicated, shared knowledge brought into play by those speaking. In fact, our small talk is so complex that it has so far proved impossible to program even the most sophisticated computers to converse convincingly with human beings for very long. The words used in ordinary talk do not always have precise meanings, and we 'fix' what we want to say through the unstated assumptions that back it up. If Maria asks Tom: 'What did you do yesterday?' there is no obvious answer suggested by the words in the question themselves. A day is a long time, and it would be logical for Tom to answer: 'Well, at 7.16, I woke up. At 7.18, I got out of bed, went to the bathroom and started to brush my teeth. At 7.19, I turned on the shower. . . .' We understand the type of response the question calls for by knowing Maria, what sort of activities she and Tom consider relevant, and what Tom usually does on a particular day of the week, among other things.

'Interactional vandalism'

We have already seen that conversations are one of the main ways in which our daily lives are maintained in a stable and coherent manner. We feel most comfortable when the tacit conventions of small talk are adhered to; when they are breached, we can feel threatened, confused and insecure. In most everyday talk, conversants are carefully attuned to the cues being given by others – such as changes in intonation, slight pauses or gestures – in order to facilitate conversation smoothly. By being mutually aware, conversants 'cooperate' in opening and closing interactions, and in taking turns to speak. Interactions in which one party is conversationally 'uncooperative', however, can give rise to tensions.

Garfinkel's students created tense situations by intentionally undermining conversational rules as part of a sociological experiment. But what about situations in the real world in which people 'make trouble' through their conversational practices? One US study investigated verbal interchanges between pedestrians and street people in New York City to understand why such interactions are often seen as problematic by passers-by. The researchers used a technique called **conversation analysis** to compare a selection of street interchanges with samples of everyday talk. Conversation analysis is a methodology that examines all facets of a conversation for meaning – from the smallest filler words (such as 'um' and 'ah') to the precise timing of interchanges (including pauses, interruptions and overlaps).

The study looked at interactions between black men – many of whom were homeless, alcoholic or drug-addicted – and white women who passed by them on the street. The men would often try to initiate conversations with passing women by calling out to them, paying them compliments or asking them questions. But something 'goes wrong' in these conversations, because the women rarely respond as they would in a normal interaction. Even though the men's comments are seldom hostile in tone, the women tend to quicken their step and stare fixedly ahead. The following shows attempts by Mudrick, a black man in his late 50s, to engage women in conversation (Duneier and Molotch 1999):

[Mudrick] begins this interaction as a white woman, who looks about 25, approaches at a steady pace:
1 MUDRICK: I love you baby.
   She crosses her arms and quickens her walk, ignoring the comment.
2 MUDRICK: Marry me.
   Next, it is two white women, also probably in their mid-twenties:
3 MUDRICK: Hi girls, you all look very nice today. You have some money? Buy some books.

They ignore him. Next, it is a young black woman:
4 MUDRICK: Hey pretty. Hey pretty.
   She keeps walking without acknowledging him.
5 MUDRICK: 'Scuse me. 'Scuse me. I know you hear me.
   Then he addresses a white woman in her thirties:
6 MUDRICK: I'm watching you. You look nice, you know.
   She ignores him.

Negotiating smooth 'openings' and 'closings' to conversations is a fundamental requirement for urban civility. These crucial aspects of conversation were highly problematic between the men and women. When the women resisted the men's attempts at opening a conversation, the men ignored the women's resistance and persisted. Similarly, if the men succeeded in opening a conversation, they often refused to respond to cues from the women to close the conversation once it had got under way:

1 MUDRICK: Hey pretty.
2 WOMAN: Hi how you doin'.
3 MUDRICK: You alright?
4 MUDRICK: You look very nice you know. I like how you have your hair pinned.
5 MUDRICK: You married?
6 WOMAN: Yeah.
7 MUDRICK: Huh?
8 WOMAN: Yeah.
9 MUDRICK: Where the rings at?
10 WOMAN: I have it home.
11 MUDRICK: Y'have it home?
12 WOMAN: Yeah.
13 MUDRICK: Can I get your name?
14 MUDRICK: My name is Mudrick, what's yours?
   She does not answer and walks on.
(Duneier and Molotch 1999)

In this instance, Mudrick made 9 out of the 14 utterances that comprised the interaction to initiate the conversation and to elicit further responses from the woman. From the

Classic Studies 7.1 | **Harold Garfinkel's ethnomethodological experiments**

The research problem

Misunderstandings are commonplace in social life. Sometimes they go unresolved but at others, they can provoke irritation and frustration. Anyone who has been told, 'listen when I'm talking to you', or, 'you just don't get it, do you?', will be aware of just how quickly apparently trivial misunderstandings can escalate into anger and aggression. But why do people get so upset when the minor conventions of talk are not followed? The founder of ethnomethodology, Harold Garfinkel, investigated this issue with some of his students.

Garfinkel's explanation

For a smooth-running everyday existence, people must be able to take for granted certain aspects of their lives. These 'background expectancies' include the organization of ordinary conversations, such as knowing when to speak and when not to, what we can assume without formally stating it – and so on. Garfinkel (1963) explored such unspoken assumptions with student volunteers who set out to 'breach' the conventions of daily life. The students were asked to engage a friend or relative in conversation and to insist that casual remarks or general comments be actively pursued to make their meaning more precise. So, if someone said, 'Have a nice day', the student was to respond, 'Nice in what sense, exactly?' 'Which part of the day do you mean?' and so on. One of these exchanges ran as follows (E is the student volunteer, S is their friend):

> S: How are you?
> E: How am I in regard to what? My health, my finance, my school work, my peace of mind, my … ?
> S: [*red in the face and suddenly out of control*]: Look! I was just trying to be polite. Frankly, I don't give a damn how you are.

Why would a friend get so upset so quickly?

Garfinkel's answer is that the stability and meaningfulness of our daily social lives depend on the sharing of unstated cultural assumptions about what is said and why. If we were not able to

take these for granted, meaningful communication would be impossible. Any question or contribution to a conversation would have to be followed by a massive 'search procedure' of the sort Garfinkel's subjects were told to initiate, and interaction would simply break down. What seem at first sight to be unimportant conventions of talk, therefore, turn out to be fundamental to the very fabric of social life, which is why their breach is so serious.

In everyday life, people sometimes deliberately feign ignorance of unstated knowledge. This may be done to rebuff the others, poke fun at them, cause embarrassment or call attention to a double meaning in what was said. Consider, for example, this all too typical exchange between parent (P) and teenager (T):

> P: Where are you going?
> T: Out.
> P: What are you going to do?
> T: Nothing.

The responses of the teenager are effectively the opposite of those of the student volunteers above. Rather than pursuing enquiries where this is not normally done, the teenager provides no appropriate answers at all – essentially saying, 'Mind your own business!'

The first question might elicit a different response from another person in another context:

> A: Where are you going?
> B: I'm going quietly round the bend.

B deliberately misreads A's question in order ironically to convey worry or frustration. Comedy and joking thrive on such deliberate misunderstandings of the unstated assumptions involved in talk. There is nothing threatening about this so long as the parties concerned recognize that the intent is to provoke laughter.

By delving into the everyday world which we all inhabit, Garfinkel shows us that the normal, smooth-running social order that some sociologists simply take for granted is in fact a social process of interaction, which has to be continually reproduced over the course of every day. Social order is hard work! However, in his 'breaching experiments', Garfinkel was also able amply to demonstrate just how robust is the fabric of daily life. The students were able to explain and apologize to their friends and families once the experiment was over, but what might have happened had they carried on behaving in such pedantic and uncooperative ways? Would they have been shunned and thrown out of the family home or referred to a doctor or psychiatrist as suffering from a mental illness? Social reality may be socially constructed, but this is still a very hard construction that is impossible to ignore.

Critical points

Given that ethnomethodology set out to criticize much mainstream sociology and is usually seen as an alternative to, rather than a school of thought within, sociology, it has been the subject of much criticism. However, we need only note the most important ones. First, ethnomethodology seeks to understand the world from the viewpoint of 'ordinary actors'. While this may bring about some useful insights, critics argue that it leaves the conclusions from ethnomethodological research open to a charge of subjectivism – that they only apply to the particular subjects being studied – and therefore it is not legitimate to generalize from them. Second, many sociologists argue that the focus on micro level order and disorder leaves

ethnomethodology remarkably detached from the key structural determinants affecting people's life chances, such as gender, race/ethnicity and social class. Ethnomethodology's aversion to social structural analysis and general theories of society seem to leave its studies cast adrift from crucial questions about the operation of power in the structuring of social life. Finally, ethnomethodology does not look for the causes of social phenomena, but only to describe how they are experienced and made sense of by people 'on the ground'. Again, many sociologists see this lack of causal explanation to be a major problem, which essentially rules out the idea that the study of social life could be 'scientific'.

Contemporary significance

Ethnomethodology is an important approach to the study of everyday life and social interaction, which is usually seen alongside other microsociologies such as phenomenology and symbolic interactionism. Sociologists who are interested in large-scale social structures, power relations within the international system of nation-states and long-term socio-historical change will always find ethnomethodology disappointing. But taken on its own terms, this theoretical approach has produced much insightful work on the operation of daily life and how it is experienced and made sense of by the people who constitute and reproduce it. It therefore remains an influential perspective amongst scholars and students of everyday life.

transcript alone, it is quite evident that the woman is not interested in talking, but when conversation analysis is applied to the tape recording, her reluctance becomes even clearer. The woman delays all her responses – even when she does give them, while Mudrick replies immediately, his comments sometimes overlapping hers. Timing in conversations is a very precise indicator; delaying a response by even a fraction of a second is adequate in most everyday interactions to signal the desire to change the course of a conversation. By betraying these

tacit rules of sociability, Mudrick was practising conversation in a way that was 'technically rude'. The woman, in return, was also 'technically rude' in ignoring Mudrick's repeated attempts to engage her in talk. It is the 'technically rude' nature of these street interchanges that make them problematic for passers-by to handle. When standard cues for opening and closing conversations are not adhered to, individuals feel a sense of profound and inexplicable insecurity.

The term **interactional vandalism** describes cases like these, in which a subordinate person breaks the tacit rules of everyday interaction that are of value to the more powerful. The men on the street often conform to everyday forms of speech in their interactions with one another, local shopkeepers, the police, relatives and acquaintances. But when they choose to, they subvert the tacit conventions for everyday talk in a way that leaves passers-by disoriented. Even more than physical assaults or vulgar verbal abuse, interactional vandalism leaves victims unable to articulate what has happened.

This study of interactional vandalism provides another example of the two-way links between micro-level interactions and forces that operate on the macro-level. To the men on the street, the white women who ignore their attempts at conversation appear distant, cold and bereft of sympathy – legitimate 'targets' for such interactions. The women, meanwhile, may often take the men's behaviour as proof that they are indeed dangerous and best avoided. Interactional vandalism is closely tied up with over-arching class, gender and racial structures. The fear and anxiety generated in such mundane interactions help to constitute the outside statuses and forces that, in turn, influence the interactions themselves. Interactional vandalism is part of a self-reinforcing system of mutual suspicion and incivility.

Response cries

Some kinds of utterance are not talk but consist of muttered exclamations, or what Goffman (1981) has called **response cries**. Consider Lucy, who exclaims, 'Oops!' after knocking over a glass of water. 'Oops!' seems to be merely an uninteresting reflex response to a mishap, rather like blinking your eye when a person moves a hand sharply towards your face. It is not a reflex, however, as shown by the fact that people do not usually make the exclamation when alone. 'Oops!' is normally directed towards others present. The exclamation demonstrates to witnesses that the lapse is only

Being approached by a stranger who breaks the tacit rules of 'standard' social interaction can leave people feeling threatened or uncomfortable.

minor and momentary, not something that should cast doubt on Lucy's command of her actions.

'Oops!' is used only in situations of minor failure, rather than in major accidents or calamities – which also demonstrates that the exclamation is part of our controlled management of the details of social life. Moreover, the word may be used by someone observing Lucy, rather than by Lucy herself, or it may be used to sound a warning to another. 'Oops!' is normally a curt sound, but the 'oo' may be prolonged in some situations. Thus, someone might extend the sound to cover a critical moment in performing a task. For instance, a parent may utter an extended 'Oops!' or 'Oopsadaisy!' when playfully tossing a child in the air. The sound covers the brief phase when the child may feel a loss of control, reassuring him and probably at the same time developing his understanding of response cries.

This may all sound very contrived and exaggerated. Why should we bother to analyse such an inconsequential utterance in this detail? Surely we do not pay as much attention to what we say as this example suggests? Of course not – on a conscious level. The crucial point, however, is that we take for granted an immensely complicated, continuous control of our appearance and actions. In situations of interaction, we are never expected just to be present on the scene. Others expect, as we expect of them, that we will display what Goffman calls 'controlled alertness'. A fundamental part of being human is continually demonstrating to others our competence in the routines of daily life.

Face, body and speech in interaction

Let us summarize at this point what we have learned so far. Everyday interaction depends on subtle relationships between what we convey with our faces and bodies and what we express in words. We use the facial expressions and bodily gestures of other people to fill in what they communicate verbally and to check if they are sincere in what they say. Mostly without realizing it, each of us keeps a tight and continuous control over facial expression, bodily posture and movement in the course of our daily interaction with others.

Face, bodily management and speech, then, are used to convey certain meanings and to hide others. We also organize our activities in the contexts of social life to achieve the same ends, as we shall now see.

Encounters

In many social situations, we engage in what Goffman calls **unfocused interaction** with others. Unfocused interaction takes place whenever individuals exhibit mutual awareness of one another's presence. This is usually the case anywhere that large numbers of people are assembled together, as on a busy street, in a theatre crowd or at a party. When people are in the presence of others, even if they do not directly talk to them, they continually communicate non-verbally through their posture and facial and physical gestures.

Focused interaction occurs when individuals directly attend to what others say or do. Social interaction will often involve both focused and unfocused exchanges. Goffman calls an instance of focused interaction an **encounter**, and much of our day-to-day life consists of encounters with other people – family, friends, colleagues – frequently occurring against the background of unfocused interaction with others present on the scene. Small talk, seminar discussions, games and routine face-to-face contacts (with ticket attendants, waiters, shop assistants and so forth) are all examples of encounters.

Encounters always need 'openings', which indicate that civil inattention is being discarded. When strangers meet and begin to talk at a party, the moment of ceasing civil inattention is always risky, since misunderstandings can easily occur about the nature of the encounter being established (Goffman 1971). Hence, the making of eye contact may first be ambiguous and tentative. The person who is looking to make eye contact can then act as though he had made no direct move if the overture is not accepted. In focused interaction, each person communicates as much by facial expression and gesture as by the words actually exchanged. Goffman distinguishes between the expressions individuals 'give' and those they 'give off'. The first are the words and facial expressions people use to produce certain impressions on others. The second are the clues that others may spot to check their sincerity or truthfulness. For instance, a restaurant-owner listens with a polite smile to the statements that customers give about how much they enjoyed their meals. At the same time, she is noting the signals the customers give off – how pleased they seemed to be while eating the food, whether a lot was left over, and the tone of voice they use to express their satisfaction, for example.

Waiters and other workers in the service industries are, of course, told to smile and be polite in their social interaction with customers. In a famous study of the airline industry, Arlie Hochschild describes this 'emotional labour' (see chapter 1).

> ## THINKING CRITICALLY
>
> In some societies today, surveys show that women and older people believe it to be unsafe for them to walk out after dark. In recent years, young people in the UK who wear 'hoodies' (a type of jacket with large hood) have been seen as 'threatening' by many older groups of people. How might Anderson's study help us to understand such interactions and what do they tell us about the macrosociological relationships between younger and older generations?

Impression management

Goffman and other writers on social interaction often use notions from the theatre in their analyses. The concept of **social role**, for example, originated in a theatrical setting. Roles are socially defined expectations that a person in a given **status**, or **social position**, follows. To be a teacher is to hold a specific position; the teacher's role consists of acting in specified ways towards her pupils. Goffman sees social life as though played out by actors on a stage – or on many stages, because how we act depends on the roles we are playing at a particular time. People are sensitive to how they are seen by others and use many forms of **impression management** to compel others to react to them in the ways they

"Hmmm... what shall I wear today...?"

wish. Although we may sometimes do this in a calculated way, usually it is among the things we do without conscious attention. When Philip attends a business meeting, he wears a suit and tie and is on his best behaviour; that evening, when relaxing with friends at a football game, he wears jeans and a sweatshirt and tells a lot of jokes. This is impression management.

As we noted above, the social roles that we adopt are highly dependent on our social status. A person's social status can be different depending on the social context. For instance, as a 'student', you have a certain status and are expected to act in a certain way when you are around your professors. As a 'son or daughter', you have a different status from a student, and society (especially your parents) has different expectations for you. Likewise, as a 'friend', you have an entirely different position in the social order, and the roles you adopt would change accordingly. Obviously, a person has many statuses at the same time. Sociologists refer to the group of statuses that you occupy as a **status set**.

Sociologists also like to distinguish between ascribed status and achieved status. An **ascribed status** is one that you

USING YOUR SOCIOLOGICAL IMAGINATION

7.2   Street encounters

Have you ever crossed to the other side of the street when you felt threatened by someone behind you or someone coming towards you? One sociologist who tried to understand simple interactions of this kind is Elijah Anderson. Anderson began by describing social interaction on the streets of two adjacent urban neighbourhoods in the United States. His book, *Streetwise: Race, Class, and Change in an Urban Community* (1990), found that studying everyday life sheds light on how social order is created by the individual building blocks of infinite micro-level interactions. He was particularly interested in understanding interactions when at least one party was viewed as threatening. Anderson showed that the ways many blacks and whites interact on the streets had a great deal to do with the structure of racial stereotypes, which is itself linked to the economic structure of society. In this way, he showed the link between micro-interactions and the larger macro-structures of society.

Anderson began by recalling Erving Goffman's description of how social roles and statuses come into existence in particular contexts or locations. Goffman (1959) wrote:

> When an individual enters the presence of others, they commonly seek to acquire information about him or bring into play information already possessed. ... Information about the individual helps to define the situation, enabling others to know in advance what he will expect of them and they may expect of him.

Following Goffman's lead, Anderson (1990) asked what types of behavioural cues and signs make up the vocabulary of public interaction? He concluded that:

> Skin colour, gender, age, companions, clothing, jewellery, and the objects people carry help identify them, so that assumptions are formed and communication can occur. Movements (quick or slow, false or sincere, comprehensible or incomprehensible) further refine this public communication. Factors like time of day or an activity that 'explains' a person's presence can also

affect in what way and how quickly the image of 'stranger' is neutralized. If a stranger cannot pass inspection and be assessed as 'safe', the image of predator may arise, and fellow pedestrians may try to maintain a distance consistent with that image.

Anderson showed that the people most likely to pass inspection are those who do not fall into commonly accepted stereotypes of dangerous persons: 'Children readily pass inspection, while women and white men do so more slowly, black women, black men, and black male teenagers most slowly of all.' In showing that interactional tensions derive from outside statuses such as race, class and gender, Anderson shows that we cannot develop a full understanding of the situation by looking at the micro-interactions themselves. This is how he makes the link between micro-interactions and macro-processes.

Anderson argues that people are 'streetwise' when they develop skills such as 'the art of avoidance' to deal with their felt vulnerability towards violence and crime. According to Anderson, whites who are not streetwise do not recognize the difference between different kinds of black men (such as between middle-class youths and gang members). They may also not know how to alter the number of paces to walk behind a 'suspicious' person or how to bypass 'bad blocks' at various times of day.

Studies such as this one demonstrate how microsociology is useful in illuminating the broad institutional patterns that are the content of macrosociology. Face-to-face interaction is clearly the main basis of all forms of social organization, no matter how large scale. We could not build up a full account of gender and race in our society from these studies alone, yet we could certainly contribute significantly to understanding these issues better.

are 'assigned' based on biological factors such as race, sex or age. Thus, your ascribed statuses could be 'white', 'female' and 'teenager'. An **achieved status** is one that is earned through an individual's own effort. Your achieved statuses could be 'graduate', 'athlete' or 'employee'. While we may like to believe that it is our achieved statuses that are most important, society may not agree. In any society, some statuses have priority over all other statuses and generally determine a person's overall position in society. Sociologists refer to this as a **master status** (Hughes 1945; Becker 1963). The most common master statuses are those based on gender and race. Sociologists have shown that in an encounter, one of the first things that people notice about one another is gender and race (Omi and Winant 1994). As we shall see shortly, both race and gender strongly shape our social interactions.

Adopting roles: intimate examinations

For an example of collaboration in impression management that also borrows from

the theatre, let us look at one particular study in some detail. James Henslin and Mae Biggs studied a specific, highly delicate type of encounter: a woman's visit to a gynaecologist (1971, 1997). At the time of the study, most pelvic examinations were carried out by male doctors and the experience was therefore (and sometimes still is) fraught with potential ambiguities and embarrassment for both parties. Men and women in the West are socialized to think of the genitals as the most private part of the body, and seeing, and particularly touching, the genitals of another person is ordinarily associated with intimate sexual encounters. Some women feel so worried by the prospect of a pelvic examination that they refuse to visit the doctor, male or female, even when they suspect there is a strong medical reason to do so.

Henslin and Biggs analysed material collected by Biggs, a trained nurse, from a large number of gynaecological examinations. They interpreted what they found as having several typical stages. Adopting a dramaturgical metaphor, they suggested that each phase could be treated as a distinct scene, in which the parts played by the actors alter as the episode unfolds. In the prologue, the woman enters the waiting room preparing to assume the role of patient and temporarily discarding her outside identity. Called into the consulting room, she adopts the 'patient' role, and the first scene opens. The doctor assumes a business-like, professional manner and treats the patient as a proper and competent person, maintaining eye contact and listening politely to what she has to say. If he decides an examination is called for, he tells her so and leaves the room; scene one is over.

As he leaves, the nurse comes in. She is an important stagehand in the main scene shortly to begin. She soothes any worries that the patient might have, acting as both a confidante – knowing some of the 'things women have to put up with' – and a collaborator in what is to follow. Crucially, the nurse helps alter the patient from a person to a 'non person' for the vital scene – which features a body, part of which is to be scrutinized, rather than a complete human being. In Henslin and Biggs's study, the nurse not only supervises the patient's undressing, but also takes over aspects that normally the patient would control. Thus, she takes the patient's clothes and folds them. Most women wish their underwear to be out of sight when the doctor returns, and the nurse makes sure that this is so. She guides the patient to the examining table and covers most of her body with a sheet before the physician returns.

The central scene now opens, with the nurse as well as the doctor taking part. The presence of the nurse helps ensure that the interaction between the doctor and the patient is free of sexual overtones and also provides a legal witness should the physician be charged with unprofessional conduct. The examination proceeds as though the personality of the patient were absent; the sheet across her separates the genital area from the rest of her body, and

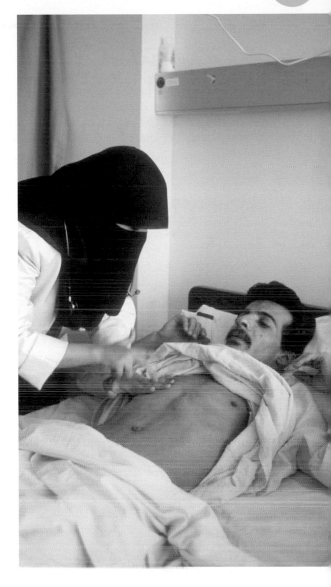

In normal social life in Saudi Arabia, interaction between men and women is highly regulated and intimate contact in public is forbidden. However, in a medical setting, other social rules take precedence, although these are still carefully managed.

her position does not allow her to watch the examination itself. Apart from any specific medical queries, the doctor ignores her, sitting on a low stool, out of her line of vision. The patient collaborates in becoming a temporary non-person, not initiating

Classic Studies 7.2 **Erving Goffman on the drama of everyday life**

The research problem

Very often we watch people in public situations who seem to be 'performing' or 'playing to the crowd'. If we are honest, we would probably admit that we also treat the world a little like a stage at times, putting on a show for the benefit of other people. But why do we do this? And when we do it, is it really *us* – our 'real selves' – doing the performing? If 'all the world's a stage', what happens *behind the scenes* of public life? And what is the relationship between the front and backstage regions? Erving Goffman (1922–82) studied this issue in several publications and research studies, producing the most detailed accounts of people's 'performances' and backstage behaviour.

Goffman's explanation

Much of social life, Goffman suggests, can be divided into front regions and back regions. **Front regions** are social occasions or encounters in which individuals act out formal roles; they are essentially, 'on-stage performances'. *Teamwork* is often involved in creating front-region performances. Two prominent politicians in the same party may put on an elaborate show of unity and friendship before the television cameras, even though each privately detests the other. A wife and husband may take care to conceal their quarrels from their children, preserving a front of harmony, only to fight bitterly once the children are safely tucked up in bed.

The **back regions** are where people assemble the props and prepare themselves for interaction in the more formal settings. Back regions resemble the backstage of a theatre or the off-camera activities of filmmaking. When they are safely behind the scenes, people can relax and give vent to feelings and styles of behaviour they keep in check when on stage. Back regions permit 'profanity, open sexual remarks, elaborate griping … rough informal dress, "sloppy" sitting and standing posture, use of dialect or substandard speech, mumbling and shouting, playful aggressiveness and "kidding," inconsiderateness for the other in minor but potentially symbolic acts, minor self-involvement such as humming, whistling, chewing, nibbling, belching and flatulence' (Goffman 1959). Thus, a

waitress may be the soul of quiet courtesy when serving a customer, but become loud and aggressive once behind the swing doors of the kitchen. Probably few people would continue to patronize restaurants if they could see all that goes on in the kitchens.

American sociologist, Spencer Cahill, led a research team studying social interaction in the public toilets (or 'bathrooms') of shopping centres, college campuses, bars and restaurants (Cahill et al. 1985). Using Goffman's idea of front and back regions, Cahill found that what Goffman (1959) called 'performance teams' would sometimes retreat into public toilets to conceal embarrassment when a collective performance goes wrong. Cahill recounts a conversation between three young women in the bathroom of a student centre on a college campus:

A: That was sooo embarrassing! I can't believe that just happened. [*general laughter*]

B: He must think we are the biggest bunch of losers.

A: I can't believe I just screamed loud enough for everyone to hear.

C: It really wasn't all that loud. I'm sure he didn't hear you.

B: ——, we didn't see him right away, and I did try to tell you but you were so busy talking that I …

A: I can't believe that just happened. I feel like such an asshole.

B: Don't worry 'bout it. At least he knows who you are now. Are you ready?

A: I'm so embarrassed. What if he's still out there?

B: You're going to have to see him at some point.

Such defensive strategies buy individuals and teams the time to gather themselves before going out to face the 'audience' again.

Goffman (1959) argued that performance teams routinely use backstage regions for such purposes. They also discuss and rehearse the performance before it actually takes place. At times, backstage discussions will be concerned with morale of particular individuals or of the whole team.

The division between front and backstage of social life is vividly depicted here by two doctors relaxing together after a busy day in the hospital.

Goffman's approach is usually described as 'dramaturgical'; that is, it is an approach based on an analogy with the theatre, with its front and backstage regions. However, we have to bear in mind that this is an analogy. Goffman is *not* suggesting that the social world really *is* a stage, but that, using the dramaturgical analogy, we can study certain aspects of it and learn more about why people behave in the ways they do.

Critical points

Critics of Goffman's approach make some similar points to those levelled at other microsociologies. Perhaps he does not give enough recognition to the role that power plays in shaping social relations, tending to understand interactions from the participants' point of view. The dramaturgical analogy can also be questioned. This may be a good model for studies of organizations and 'total institutions', but may not be so useful outside elsewhere. Similarly, Goffman's theatrical analogy works best in modern Western societies which have developed a division between the public and the private realms of life (front and back stages). But

in other societies, this division is either less pronounced or just does not exist in the same form (see discussion of the !Kung on page 272); Goffman's perspective may not have quite the same purchase on life within these societies.

Contemporary significance

Goffman's work has had a profound influence not only on sociology as a discipline, but on numerous scholars, who have been inspired to become professional sociologists after reading his works. He is widely acknowledged to have made some of the most thoughtful and stimulating contributions to the discipline. Many sociologists today continue to refer to his original works for examples of how to carry out microsociological work and the concepts he developed (stigma, master status, front and back stage, and so on), have become part of the very fabric of sociology in a variety of fields. For example, his work is discussed in many places in this book, including chapter 10, 'Health, Illness and Disability', chapter 21, 'Crime and Deviance' and chapter 8, 'The Life-Course'.

conversation and keeping any movements to a minimum.

In the interval between this and the final scene, the nurse again plays the role of stagehand, helping the patient to become a full person once more. After the doctor has left the room, the two may again engage in conversation, the patient expressing relief that the examination is over. Having dressed and re-groomed herself, the patient is ready to face the concluding scene. The doctor re-enters the room and, in discussing the results of the examination, again treats the patient as a complete and responsible person. Resuming his polite, professional manner, he conveys that his reactions to her are in no way altered by the intimate contact with her body. The epilogue is played out when she leaves the doctor's surgery, taking up again her identity in the outside world. The patient and the doctor have thus collaborated in such a way as to manage the interaction and the impression each participant forms of the other.

Personal space

There are cultural differences in the definition of personal space. In Western culture, people usually maintain a distance of at least three feet when engaged in focused interaction with others; when standing side by side, they may stand more closely together. In the Middle East, people often stand closer to one another than is thought acceptable in the West. Westerners visiting that part of the world are likely to find themselves disconcerted by this unexpected physical proximity.

Edward T. Hall, who has worked extensively on non-verbal communication, distinguishes four zones of personal space. *Intimate distance*, of up to one and a half feet, is reserved for very few social contacts. Only those involved in relationships in which regular bodily touching is permitted, such as lovers or parents and children, operate within this zone of private space.

Personal distance, from one and a half to four feet, is the normal spacing for encounters with friends and close acquaintances. Some intimacy of contact is permitted, but this tends to be strictly limited. *Social distance*, from four to twelve feet, is the zone usually maintained in formal settings such as interviews. The fourth zone is that of *public distance*, beyond twelve feet, preserved by those who are performing to an audience.

In ordinary interaction, the most fraught zones are those of intimate and personal distance. If these zones are invaded, people try to recapture their space. We may stare at the intruder as if to say, 'Move away!' or elbow him aside. When people are forced into proximity closer than they deem desirable, they might create a kind of physical boundary; a reader at a crowded library desk might physically demarcate a private space by stacking books around its edges (Hall 1969, 1973).

Here, gender issues also play a role, in much the same way as in other forms of non-verbal communication. Men have traditionally enjoyed greater freedom than women in the use of space, including movement into the personal space of women who may not necessarily be intimates or even close acquaintances. A man who guides a woman by the arm when they walk together, or who places a hand on her lower back when showing her through a door, may be doing so as a gesture of friendly care or politeness. The reverse phenomenon, however – a woman entering a man's personal space – is often construed as flirtation or a sexual advance. New laws and standards regarding sexual harassment in many Western countries seek to protect people's personal space – both men and women – from unwanted touching or contact by others.

Interaction in time and space

Understanding how activities are distributed in time and space is fundamental to analysing encounters, and also to understanding social life in general. All interaction is situated – it occurs in a particular place and has a specific duration in time. Our actions over the course of a day tend to be 'zoned' in time as well as in space. Thus, for example, most people spend a zone – say, from 9.00 a.m. to 5.00 p.m. – of their daily time working. Their weekly time is also zoned: they are likely to work on weekdays and spend weekends at home, altering the pattern of their activities on the weekend days. As we move through the temporal zones of the day, we are also often moving across space as well: to get to work, we may take a bus from one area of a city to another, or perhaps commute in from the suburbs. When we analyse the contexts of social interaction, therefore, it is often useful to look at people's movements across time-space.

The concept of regionalization will help us understand how social life is zoned in time-space. Take the example of a private house. A modern house is regionalized into rooms, hallways and floors if there is more than one storey. These spaces are not just physically separate areas, but are zoned in time as well. The living rooms and kitchen are used most in the daylight hours, the bedrooms at night. The interaction that occurs in these regions is bound by both spatial and temporal divisions. Some areas of the house form back regions, with 'performances' taking place in the others. At times, the whole house can become a back region. Once again, this idea is beautifully captured by Goffman:

> Of a Sunday morning, a whole household can use the wall around its domestic establishment to conceal a relaxing slovenliness in dress and civil endeavour, extending to all rooms the informality that is usually restricted to kitchen and bedrooms. So, too, in American middle-class neighbourhoods, on afternoons the line between children's playground and home may be defined as backstage by mothers, who pass along it wearing jeans, loafers, and a minimum of make-up. … And, of course, a region that is thoroughly established as a front region for the regular performance of a particular routine often functions as a back region before and after each performance, for at these times the permanent fixtures may undergo repairs, restoration, and rearrangement, or the performers may hold dress rehearsals. To see this we need only glance into a restaurant, or store, or home, a few minutes before these establishments are opened to us for the day. (1959: 128)

Clock time

In modern societies, the zoning of our activities is strongly influenced by clock time. Without clocks and the precise timing of activities, and thereby their coordination across space, industrialized societies could not exist (Mumford 1973). The measuring of time by clocks is today standardized across the globe, making possible the complex international transport systems and communications we now depend on. World standard time was first introduced in 1884 at a conference of nations held in Washington. The globe was then partitioned into 24 time zones, each one hour apart, and an exact beginning of the universal day was fixed.

Fourteenth-century monasteries were the first organizations to try to schedule the activities of their inmates precisely across the day and week. Today, there is virtually no group or organization that does not do so – the greater the number of people and resources involved, the more precise the scheduling must be. Eviatar Zerubavel (1979, 1982) demonstrated this in his study of the temporal structure of a large modern hospital. A hospital must operate on a 24-hour basis, and coordinating the staff and resources is a highly complex matter. For instance, the nurses work for one time period in ward A, another time period in ward B, and so on, and are also called on to alternate between day- and night-shift work. Nurses, doctors and other staff, plus the resources they need, must be integrated together both in time and in space.

The ordering of space and time

The Internet is another example of how closely forms of social life are bound up with our control of space and time. The Internet makes it possible for us to interact with people we never see or meet, in any corner of the world. Such technological change 'rearranges' space – we can interact with anyone without moving from our chair. It also alters our experience of time, because communication on the electronic highway is almost immediate. Until about 50 years ago, most communication across space required a duration of time. If you sent a letter to someone abroad, there was a time gap while the letter was carried by ship, train, truck or plane to the person to whom it was written.

People still write letters by hand today, of course, but instantaneous communication has become basic to our social world. Our lives would be almost unimaginable without it. We are so used to being able to switch on the TV and watch the news or make a phone call or send an email to a friend in another part of the world that it is hard for us to imagine what life would be like otherwise.

Everyday life in cultural and historical perspective

Some of the mechanisms of social interaction analysed by Goffman, Garfinkel and others seem to be universal. But much of Goffman's discussion of civil inattention and other kinds of interaction primarily concerns societies in which contact with strangers is commonplace. What about small-scale traditional societies, where there are no strangers and few settings in which more than a handful of people are together at any one time?

To see some of the contrasts between social interaction in modern and traditional societies, let's take as an example one of the least developed cultures in terms of technology remaining in the world: the !Kung (sometimes known as the Bushmen), who live in the Kalahari Desert area of Botswana and Namibia, in southern Africa (Lee 1968, 1969; the exclamation mark refers to a click sound one makes before pronouncing the name). Although their way of life is changing because of outside influences, their traditional patterns of social life are still evident.

The !Kung live in groups of some 30 or 40 people, in temporary settlements near water-holes. Food is scarce in their environment, and they must walk far and wide to find it. Such roaming takes up most of the average day. Women and children often stay back in the camp, but equally often the whole group spends the day walking. Members of the community will sometimes fan out over an area of up to a 100 square miles in the course of a day, returning to the camp at night to eat and sleep. The men may be alone or in groups of two or three for much of the day. There is one period of the year, however, when the routines of their daily activities change: the winter rainy season, when water is abundant and food much easier to come by. The everyday life of the !Kung during this period is centred on ritual and ceremonial activities, the preparation for and enactment of which is very time-consuming.

The members of most !Kung groups never see anyone they do not know reasonably well. Until contacts with the outside became more common in recent years, they had no word for 'stranger'. While the !Kung, particularly the males, may spend long periods of the day out of contact with others, in the community itself there is little opportunity for privacy. Families sleep in flimsy, open dwellings, with virtually all activities open to public view. No one has studied the !Kung with Goffman's observations on everyday life in mind, but it is easy to see that some aspects of his work have limited application to !Kung social life. There are few opportunities, for example, to create front and back regions. The closing off of different gatherings and encounters by the walls of rooms, separate buildings and the various neighbourhoods of cities common in modern societies are remote from the activities of the !Kung.

The form of social interaction of the !Kung is very different from the interaction that takes place in the modern city. City life forces us to interact almost constantly with strangers.

THINKING CRITICALLY

Think about your recent holidays and note the reasons why you chose those locations. Did you ever consider the impact your visit would have on:

- the *society* and *people* you were visiting - what *resources* are needed? what kind of *jobs* are required to service the tourist's needs?
- the *natural environment* – in terms of *travel*, *infrastructure* needed, damage to *ecosystems*.

Do the benefits of global tourism outweigh the damage it causes? What are those benefits?

A famous account of urban social interaction is that of Georg Simmel, whose work is discussed in chapter 6, 'Cities and Urban Life'.

The social construction of reality: the sociological debate

Within sociology, many different theoretical frameworks are used to explain social reality. These theories differ in their explanations of social phenomena, yet they share the assumption that social reality exists independently of people's talking about it or living in it. This assumption has been challenged by a broad body of sociological thought known as **social constructionism**.

Social constructivists believe that what individuals and society perceive and understand as reality is itself a construction, a creation of the social interaction of individuals and groups. Trying to 'explain' social reality is to overlook and to reify (regard as a given truth) the processes through which such reality is constructed. Therefore, social constructivists argue that sociologists need to document and analyse these processes and not simply be concerned with the concept of social reality they give rise to. Social constructionism has been seen as an important influence on the postmodern school of thought in sociology (see chapter 1, 'What is Sociology?').

In their 1966 classic study, *The Social Construction of Reality*, sociologists Peter Berger and Thomas Luckmann examined common-sense knowledge – those things that individuals take for granted as real. They emphasized that these 'obvious' facts of social reality may differ among people from different cultures, and even among different people within the same culture. The task becomes an analysis of the processes by which individuals come to perceive what is 'real' to them as real.

Social constructivists apply the ideas of Berger and Luckmann to the investigation of social phenomena, to illuminate the ways in which members of society come to know and simultaneously create what is real. While social constructivists have examined such diverse topics as medicine and medical treatment, gender relations and emotions, much of their work has focused on social problems, such as the crime 'problem'.

The work of Aaron Cicourel (1968) provides an example of social constructionist research in the area of youth crime. Sometimes, data regarding rates and cases of youth crime are taken as given (that is, as real), and theories are created to explain the patterns observed in the data. For example, at first glance arrest and court data would seem to indicate that young people from

Global Society 7.1 | International tourist interactions

Have you ever had a face-to-face conversation with someone from another country? Or connected to an overseas website? Have you ever travelled to another part of the world? If you answered 'yes' to any of these questions, you have witnessed the effects of globalization on social interaction. Globalization – a relatively recent phenomenon – has changed both the frequency and the nature of interactions between people of different nations. The historical sociologist Charles Tilly, in fact, defines globalization in terms of these changes. According to Tilly, 'globalization means an increase in the geographic range of locally consequential social interactions' (Tilly 1995: 1–2). In other words, with globalization, a greater proportion of our interactions come to involve, directly or indirectly, people from other countries.

What are the characteristics of social interactions that take place between individuals of different nations? Important contributions to the study of this problem have been made by those working in the area of the sociology of tourism. Sociologists of tourism note that globalization has greatly expanded the possibilities for international travel, both by encouraging an interest in other countries and by facilitating the movement of tourists across international borders. Between 1982 and 2002, the number of visits to the UK made by overseas residents doubled, and spending on these visits more than tripled. These visitors now pump almost £12 billion a year into the UK economy. Britons are also travelling the world in record numbers (ONS 2004b).

High levels of international tourism, of course, translate into an increase in the number of face-to-face interactions between people of different countries. The sociologist John Urry (1990) argues that the 'tourist gaze' – the expectation on the part of the tourist that he or she will have 'exotic' experiences while travelling abroad – shapes many of these interactions. Urry compares the tourist gaze to Foucault's conception of the medical gaze (see chapter 10, 'Health, Illness and Disability'). Urry argues that the tourist gaze is just as socially organized by professional experts, systematic in its application and as detached as the medical gaze, but this time it is organized in its search for 'exotic' experiences. These are experiences that violate our everyday expectations about how social interaction and interaction with

the physical environment are supposed to proceed.

Britons travelling in the United States, for example, may delight in the fact that the Americans drive on the right-hand side of the road. At the same time, such behaviour is disconcerting to drivers from the UK. Our rules of the road are so ingrained that we experience systematic violations of those rules as strange, weird and exotic. Yet, as tourists, we take pleasure in this strangeness. In a sense, it is what we have paid money to see when we go abroad – along with the Empire State Building or the Eiffel Tower. Imagine how disappointed you would be if you were to travel to a different country only to find that it was almost exactly the same as the city or town in which you grew up.

Yet most tourists do not want their experiences to be too exotic. A popular destination for young, particularly US, travellers in Paris, for example, is a McDonald's restaurant. Some go to see if there is any truth to the line from Quentin Tarantino's movie *Pulp Fiction* that, because the French use the metric system, McDonald's 'quarter pounder with cheese' hamburgers are called 'Royales with cheese' (it is true, by the way). Britons travelling abroad often cannot resist eating and drinking in British- and Irish-style pubs. Sometimes such diversions are the result of curiosity, but often people enjoy the comfort of eating familiar food in a familiar setting. The contradictory demands for the exotic and the familiar are at the heart of the tourist gaze.

The tourist gaze may put strains on face-to-face interactions between tourists and locals. Locals who are part of the tourist industry may appreciate overseas travellers for the economic benefits they bring to the places they visit. Other locals may resent tourists for their demanding attitudes or for the overdevelopment that often occurs in popular tourist destinations. Tourists may interrogate locals about aspects of their everyday lives, such as their food, work and recreational habits; they may do this either to enhance their understanding of other cultures or to judge negatively those who are different from themselves.

As tourism increases with the march of globalization, sociologists will have to watch carefully to see what dominant patterns of interaction emerge between tourists and locals, and to determine, among other things, whether these interactions tend to be friendly or antagonistic.

single-parent families are more likely to commit delinquent acts than those from two-parent homes. Some sociologists have therefore developed explanations for this observed relationship: perhaps children from single-parent homes have less supervision, or perhaps they lack appropriate role models.

By contrast, Cicourel observed the *processes* involved in the arrest and classification of youths suspected of committing crimes; that is, he observed the creation of the 'official' crime data. He discovered that police procedures in the handling of young offenders rely on common-sense understandings of what young offenders are 'really like'.

For example, when youths from lower-class families were arrested, police were more likely to view their offences as results of poor supervision or a lack of proper role models, and would retain the young people in custody. Offenders from upper-class homes, however, were more likely to be released to their parents' care, where police and parents believed the young person could receive proper discipline. Thus, the practices of police serve formally to assign the label of 'young offender' more often to those from lower-class homes than to those from upper-class homes – even when the youths have committed similar offences. This assignment produces the very data, which in turn confirm the relationships held by the common-sense views; for example, that young people from poor families are more likely to engage in crime. Cicourel's study shows that, through interacting with other people in society, we transform our common-sense notions of reality into independent, 'objective' proof of their own validity.

Social constructionism is not without its critics. Sociologists Steve Woolgar and Dorothy Pawluch (1985) argue that social constructivists aim to show the subjective creation of social reality, yet in doing so selectively view certain features as objective and others as constructed. For example, in analyses examining which young people become labelled as delinquent, social constructivists often argue that the initial behaviours reported for the young people are identical; therefore, any differences between those labelled as criminals and those avoiding such a label must be due to the construction of the label itself. Critics argue that social constructionism inconsistently presents the initial behaviours as objective, while arguing that the labelling process is subjective (ibid.).

Other sociologists have criticized social constructionism for its unwillingness to accept broader social forces as powerful influences on observable social outcomes. For example, some critics have argued that while reality may be a constructed perpetuation of common-sense beliefs, these beliefs themselves may be caused by existing social factors such as capitalism or patriarchy.

Ultimately, social constructionism offers a theoretical approach to understanding social reality that radically differs from most other sociological approaches. Rather than assuming that social reality objectively exists, social constructivists work to document and analyse the processes through which social reality is constructed, such that the construction then serves to confirm its own status as social reality.

Social interaction in cyberspace

In modern societies, in complete contrast to the !Kung, we constantly interact with others whom we may never see or meet. Almost all of our everyday transactions, such as buying groceries or making a bank deposit, bring us into contact – but *indirect* contact – with people who may live thousands of miles away.

Now that email, instant messaging, online communities and chat rooms have become facts of life for many people in industrialized countries, what is the nature of these interactions, and what new complexities are emerging from them?

Sceptics argue that indirect communication through email and the Internet contains a wealth of problems not found in face-to-face social interaction. As Katz et al. put it: 'To type is not to be human, to be in cyberspace is not to be real; all is pretence and alienation, a poor substitute for the real thing' (2001: 407). In particular, supporters of this view argue that computer-mediated communication technology is too limited to prevent users hiding behind false identities. This also allows trickery, lechery, manipulation, emotional swindles and so on:

> The problem lies in the nature of human communication. We think of it as a product of the mind, but it's done by bodies: faces move, voices intone, bodies sway, hands gesture. ... On the Internet, the mind is present but the body is gone. Recipients get few clues to the personality and mood of the person, can only guess why messages are sent, what they mean, what responses to make. Trust is virtually out the window. It's a risky business.
> (Locke and Pascoe 2000)

Yet defenders of new technology argue that there are ways in which good or bad reputations can be built and trust can be established, thereby reducing the risks of online communication.

Furthermore, Internet enthusiasts argue that online communication has many inherent advantages that cannot be claimed by more traditional forms of interaction such as the telephone and face-to-face meetings. The human voice, for example, may be far superior in terms of expressing emotion and subtleties of meaning, but it can also convey information about the speaker's age, gender, ethnicity or social position – information that could be used to the speaker's disadvantage. Electronic communication, it is noted, masks all these identifying markers and ensures that attention focuses strictly on the content of the message. This can be a great advantage for women or other traditionally disadvantaged groups whose opinions are sometimes devalued in other settings (Locke and Pascoe 2000). Electronic interaction is often presented as liberating and empowering, since people can create their own online identities and speak more freely than they would elsewhere.

Internet sceptics have also argued that indirect, online communication encourages isolation and prevents real friendships from forming, but this does not seem to reflect the reality. A survey of Internet users carried out between 1995 and 2000 showed that, far from increasing social isolation, Internet usage is associated with significant and increased online and offline social interactions. The survey found that Internet users tend to communicate with others through other media – especially by the telephone – more than non-users do, meet face-to-face with friends more than non-users and interact with others more in general (Katz et al. 2001).

THINKING CRITICALLY

From your own experience, can the online environment ever match the trust established by relationships in face-to-face relationships? Could the wider use of personal webcams increase the trust we have in Internet communications? What can we learn about online trust from the eBay system and experience described in 'Global Society 7.2'?

Conclusion: the compulsion of proximity?

Despite the rise in indirect communication, however, it seems that humans still value direct contact. People in business, for instance, continue to attend meetings, sometimes flying halfway around the world to do so, when it would seem much cheaper and more efficient to transact business through a conference call or video link. Family members could arrange 'virtual' reunions or holiday gatherings using electronic real-time communications, but we all recognize that they would lack the warmth and intimacy of face-to-face celebrations.

Global Society 7.2 | Building trust in cyberspace?

Public debate on Internet security has tended to focus on issues of online banking fraud, the use of false identities and the problems associated with children using chatrooms that may be monitored by predatory paedophiles. Such worries make many people wary and erode trust in the online environment. Sociologists have been interested in the auction website, eBay, which has become a global phenomenon; some 165,000 Americans alone are estimated to be making a living purely from selling via eBay (Epley et al. 2006). Below is a short extract which discusses how eBay has sought to increase levels of trust for buyers and sellers in its services.

The 'eBay' feedback system

Currently the largest, and one of the oldest person-to-person Internet auction houses is eBay. Launched in 1995, eBay soon attracted more than 100 million people around the world who buy and sell products on the eBay websites. Remarkably, eBay offers no warranties or guarantees for any of the goods that are auctioned off – buyers and sellers assume all risks for the transaction, with eBay serving as a listing agency. It would seem to be a market ripe with the possibility of large-scale fraud and deceit, and yet the default rate for trades conducted through eBay is remarkably small. Both eBay and the participants in its market credit an institutionalized reputation system at the site known as the Feedback Forum – for the very high rate of successful trades.

After every seller's or bidder's name is a number in parenthesis. In the case of a seller, the information is displayed as follows:

Seller name (265)

The number is a summary measure of a person's reputation in the eBay market. Registered users are allowed to post positive, negative or neutral comments about users with whom they have traded. Each positive comment is given a score of +1, each negative comment is given a score of −1, with neutral comments not affecting one's score in either direction. At certain levels, market participants are also awarded a colour star which marks the number of net positive comments they have received. . . .

One is able to contact the person via email by clicking on the name; clicking on the number following someone's name leads to their full feedback profile. There one finds the full list of comments, with email links and ratings numbers for every evaluator as well (thus, one can explore the reputation of the evaluators just as one can for the evaluated). A typical positive comment might be 'Well packaged, fast delivery. Highly recommended. A1'. . . .

A high feedback rating is an extremely valuable asset. Many participants report that they are more willing to trade with someone with a high rating, or even that they will only trade with individuals with high ratings. In that sense, some traders are able to create a brand identity that increases their volume of sales or even the price at which they are able to sell items. . . . Even a few negative ratings can seriously damage a reputation, and so frequent traders are very careful about nurturing their rating by providing swift execution of honest trades. The potential damage of a negative comment is a subject of great concern among frequent participants. . . . One can choose to make one's entire feedback profile private, but this is a huge disadvantage in a market which relies on these reputations.

Source: Adapted from Kollock (1999)

An explanation for this phenomenon comes from Deirdre Boden and Harvey Molotch (1994), who have studied what they call the **compulsion of proximity**: the need of individuals to meet with one another in situations of co-presence, or face-to-face interaction. People put themselves out to attend meetings, Boden and Molotch suggest, because situations of co-presence, for reasons documented by Goffman in his studies of interaction, supply much richer information about how other people think and feel, and about their sincerity, than any form of electronic communication. Only by actually being in the presence of people who make decisions affecting us in important ways do we feel able to learn what is going on and feel confident that we can impress them with our own views and our own sincerity. 'Co-presence', Boden and Molotch (1994) say, 'affects access to the body part that "never lies", the eyes – the "windows on the soul". Eye contact itself signals a degree of intimacy and trust; co-present interactants continuously monitor the subtle movements of this most subtle body part.'

Summary points

1. Many apparently trivial aspects of our day-to-day behaviour turn out on close examination to be both complex and important aspects of social interaction. An example is the gaze – looking at other people. In most interactions, eye contact is fairly fleeting. To stare at another person could be taken as a sign of hostility – or on some occasions, of love. The study of social interaction is a fundamental area in sociology, illuminating many aspects of social life.

2. Many different expressions are conveyed by the human face. It is widely held that basic aspects of the facial expressions of emotion are innate. Cross-cultural studies demonstrate quite close similarities between members of different cultures both in facial expression and in the interpretation of emotions registered on the human face.

3. The study of ordinary talk and conversation has come to be called 'ethnomethodology', a term first coined by Harold Garfinkel. Ethnomethodology is the analysis of the ways in which we actively – although usually in a taken-for-granted way – make sense of what others mean by what they say and do.

4. We can learn a great deal about the nature of talk by studying response cries (exclamations).

5. Unfocused interaction is the mutual awareness individuals have of one another in large gatherings when not directly in conversation together. Focused interaction, which can be divided up into distinct encounters, or episodes of interaction, is when two or more individuals are directly attending to what the other or others are saying and doing.

6. Social interaction can often be illuminatingly studied by applying the dramaturgical model – studying social interaction as if those involved were actors on a stage, having a set and props. As in the theatre, in the various contexts of social life there tend to be clear distinctions between front regions (the stage itself) and back regions, where the actors prepare themselves for the performance and relax afterwards.

7. All social interaction is situated in time and space. We can analyse how our daily lives are 'zoned' in both time and space combined by looking at how activities occur during definite durations and at the same time involve spatial movement.

8. Some mechanisms of social interaction may be universal, but many are not. The !Kung of southern Africa, for example, live in small mobile bands, where there is little privacy and thus little opportunity to create front and back regions.

9. Modern societies are characterized largely by indirect interpersonal transactions (such as making bank deposits), which lack any co-presence. This leads to what has been called the compulsion of proximity, the tendency to want to meet in person whenever possible, perhaps because this makes it easier to gather information about how others think and feel, and to accomplish impression management.

Further reading

There is no single introductory text covering all of the issues in this chapter, but the main themes can be approached in some of the following.

A good place to start is with the idea of 'everyday life', so Tony Bennett and Diane Watson's edited *Understanding Everyday Life* (Oxford: Blackwell, 2002) contains some worthwhile chapters. Brian Roberts's *Micro Social Theory* (Basingstoke: Palgrave Macmillan, 2006) is a well-written introduction to the development of the microsociological tradition.

Following on from the chapter's introduction to social identities, Richard Jenkins's *Social Identity*, 2nd edn (London: Routledge, 2004) is very readable and contains many everyday examples. Issues of identity and social inequality can then be taken further in Kath Woodward's *Questioning Identity: Gender, Class and Ethnicity* (London: Routledge, 2004).

For something more specific on the work of Garfinkel and others, you could try David Francis and Stephen Hester's *An Invitation to Ethnomethodology: Language, Society and Interaction* (London: Sage, 2004).

Or, if Goffman's ideas are more to your taste, there is no one better to introduce it then Goffman himself, so see his *The Presentation of Self in Everyday Life* (Harmondsworth: Penguin, 1990 [1969]), which is a brilliant example of what he has to offer sociology. Then, should you want to place Goffman's work into wider context, Phil Manning's *Erving Goffman and Modern Sociology* (Cambridge: Polity. 1992) or Greg Smith's *Erving Goffman* (London: Routledge, 2006) are well worth the effort.

Internet links

ComResources Online – Online resources for non-verbal communications:
www.natcom.org/ctronline/nonverb.htm

An introduction to symbolic interactionism based at Grinnell College, USA:
http://web.grinnell.edu/courses/soc/s00/soc11 1-01/IntroTheories/Symbolic.html

Ethno/CA News – online resource for ethnomethodology and conversation analysis:
www2.fmg.uva.nl/emca/

Website with information on the life and work of Erving Goffman:
http://people.brandeis.edu/~teuber/ goffmanbio.html

8

The Life-Course

CHAPTER 8

The Life-course

At the start of J. K. Rowling's first Harry Potter adventure, *Harry Potter and the Philosopher's Stone*, the shrewd wizard Albus Dumbledore leaves Harry, a newly orphaned infant, at the doorstep of his non-magician (or 'Muggle') uncle and aunt's house. Harry has already shown himself to have unique powers, but Dumbledore is concerned that if left in the wizard world, Harry will not mature healthily. 'It would be enough to turn any boy's head', he says. 'Famous before he can walk and talk! Famous for something he won't even remember. Can't you see how much better off he'll be, growing up away from all that until he's ready to take it?' (Rowling 1998).

The Harry Potter novels, each of which follows Harry through a single school year, are based on the principle that there is no adventure greater than that of growing up. Hogwarts School of Witchcraft and Wizardry may be unusual, but it is still a school, which helps young people to develop a set of values for life. We all pass through important life stages, such as the passage from childhood into adolescence and then on to adulthood, and the Harry Potter books also trace these transitions. For example, as the series progresses, Harry feels the onset of sexual urges, to which he responds with an entirely common awkwardness. Sport is an important activity during which children learn about camaraderie and ambition, and Harry plays the wizard sport 'Quidditch'. The function of many classic children's stories is to make the process of growing up understandable, whether they're set in a fairy-tale universe, our own world or – as in the Harry Potter series – both.

For sociologists, **socialization** is the process whereby the helpless human infant gradually becomes a self-aware, knowledgeable person, skilled in the ways of the culture into which he or she was born. Socialization of the young allows for the more general phenomenon of social reproduction – the process whereby societies have structural continuity over time. During the course of socialization, especially in the early years of life, children learn the ways of their elders, thereby perpetuating their values, norms and social practices. All societies have characteristics that endure over long stretches of time, even though their existing members die and new ones are born. Societies have many distinctive social and cultural aspects that have persisted for generations – not least the different languages spoken by their members.

As we will see in this chapter, socialization connects the different generations to one another. The birth of a child alters the lives of those who are responsible for its upbringing – who themselves therefore undergo new learning experiences. Parenting usually ties the activities of adults to children for the remainder of their lives. Older people still remain parents when they become grandparents, of course, thus forging another set of relationships connecting the different generations with each other. Although the process of cultural learning is much more intense in infancy and early childhood than later, learning and adjustment go on throughout a person's life.

The sections that follow deal with the theme of 'nature versus nurture', a common debate in sociology. We shall first examine the main theoretical interpretations put forward by different writers on how and why children develop as they do, including theories that explain how we develop gender identities. Then we move on to discuss the main groups and social contexts that influence socialization during the course of individuals' lives, from childhood to later life. Finally, we explore some of the most important sociological issues surrounding ageing.

Culture, society and child socialization

Theories of child development

One of the most distinctive features of human beings, compared to other animals, is that humans are *self-aware*. How should we understand the emergence of a sense of self – the awareness that the individual has a distinct identity separate from others? During the first months of his life, the infant possesses little or no understanding of differences between human beings and material objects in his environment, and has no awareness of self. Children do not begin to use concepts like 'I', 'me' and 'you' until the age of 2 or later. Only gradually do they then come to understand that others have distinct identities, consciousness and needs separate from their own.

Classic Studies 8.1 **George Herbert Mead on the social self**

The research problem

It has often been said that human beings are the only creatures who know that they exist and that they will die. Sociologically, this means that human individuals are *self-aware*. With a moment's reflection, we may all accept that this is so. But just how do humans gain that self-awareness? Is it innate or learned? Surely this is a research problem for psychology though? Why would sociologists be interested in the individual self? The American sociologist and philosopher, George Herbert Mead, investigated how children learn to use the concepts of 'I' and 'me' to describe themselves. But unusually at the time, Mead insisted that a sociological perspective was necessary if we are to understand how the self emerges and develops.

Mead's explanation

Since Mead's ideas formed the main basis of a general tradition of theoretical thinking – **symbolic interactionism** – they have had a very broad impact in sociology. Symbolic interactionism emphasizes that interaction between human beings takes place through symbols and the interpretation of meanings (see chapter 1). But in addition, Mead's work provides an account of the main phases of child development, giving particular attention to the emergence of a sense of self.

According to Mead, infants and young children first of all develop as *social* beings by imitating the actions of those around them. Play is one way in which this takes place, and in their play small children often imitate what adults do. A small child will make mud pies, having seen an adult cooking, or dig with a spoon, having observed someone gardening. Children's play evolves from simple imitation to more complicated games in which a child of 4 or 5 years old will act out an adult role. Mead called this 'taking the role of the other' – learning what it is like to be in the shoes of another person. It is only at this stage that children acquire a developed sense of self. Children achieve an understanding of themselves as separate agents

Children's play has a serious side, enabling them to start to develop a social self.

– as a 'me' – by seeing themselves through the eyes of others.

We achieve self awareness, according to Mead, when we learn to distinguish the 'me' from the 'I'. The 'I' is the unsocialized infant, a bundle of spontaneous wants and desires. The 'me', as Mead used the term, is the **social self**. Individuals develop **self-consciousness**, Mead argued, by coming to see themselves as others see them, which allows for an 'internal conversation' between the individual 'I' and the social 'me'. According to Mead's theory, this conversation is what we call 'thinking'.

A further stage of child development, according to Mead, occurs when the child is about 8 or 9 years old. This is the age at which children tend to take part in organized games, rather than unsystematic play. It is at this period that they begin to understand the overall **values** and *morality* according to which social life is conducted. To learn organized games, children must understand the rules of play and notions of fairness and equal participation. Children at this stage learn to grasp what Mead termed the **generalized other** – the general values and moral rules of the culture in which they are developing.

Critical points

Mead's theory of the social self has been criticized on several grounds. First, some argue that it effectively eliminates all biological influences on the development of the self, when it is clear from biology and neuroscience that there is a biological basis to the human self. However, this criticism appears not to recognize that Mead's notion of the 'I' represents the 'unsocialized infant'. Second, Mead's theory seems to rely on the 'I' and the 'me' working cooperatively to ensure the smooth functioning of the self. But critics argue that this downplays the internal tensions and conflicts that people experience deeply, and which Freud and Chodorow's theories seem better able to explain (see pages 292–5 for details of Freud and Chodorow's theories). Mead also has little to say about the effects of unbalanced power relationships on the socialization of children. Finally, and again unlike Freud, Mead's

explanation has no room for the unconscious mind as a motive force in human behaviour and consequently lacks the concept of 'repression', which has proved essential to psychoanalytic practice.

Contemporary significance

Mead's work was very important for the development of sociology. His was the first genuinely sociological theory of self formation and development, which insisted that if we are properly to understand ourselves, then we must start with the social process of human interaction. In this way he showed that the self is not an innate part of our biology, nor does it emerge simply with the developing human brain. What Mead demonstrated is that the study of the individual's self cannot be divorced from the study of society – and that requires a sociological perspective.

Although Freud's approach to the human psyche has perhaps overshadowed Mead's during the twentieth century, at least in relation to psychological practice and the treatment of mental disorders, symbolic interactionism continues to produce insightful findings from a perspective rooted in Mead's sociological theories. And in this sense, Mead's ideas still have much to offer new generations of sociological researchers.

The problem of the emergence of self is a much-debated one and is viewed rather differently in contrasting theoretical perspectives. To some extent, this is because the most prominent theories about child development emphasize different aspects of socialization.

Jean Piaget and the stages of cognitive development

The Swiss student of child behaviour, Jean Piaget, worked on many aspects of child development, but his most well-known writings concern cognition – the ways in which children learn to think about them-

selves and their environment. Piaget placed great emphasis on the child's active capability to make sense of the world. Children do not passively soak up information, but instead select and interpret what they see, hear and feel in the world around them. Piaget described several distinct stages of cognitive development during which children learn to think about themselves and their environment. Each stage involves the acquisition of new skills and depends on the successful completion of the preceding one.

Piaget called the first stage, which lasts from birth up to about the age of 2, the **sensorimotor stage**, because infants learn mainly by touching objects, manipulating them and physically exploring their environment. Until the age of about four months or so, infants cannot differentiate themselves from their environment. For example, a child will not realize that her own movements cause the sides of her crib to rattle. Objects are not differentiated from persons, and the infant is unaware that anything exists outside her range of vision. Infants gradually learn to distinguish people from objects, coming to see that both have an existence independent of their immediate perceptions. The main accomplishment of this stage is that, by its close, children understand their environment to have distinct and stable properties.

The next phase, called the **pre-operational stage**, is the one to which Piaget devoted the bulk of his research. This stage lasts from the ages of 2 to 7. During the course of it, children acquire a mastery of language and become able to use words to represent objects and images in a symbolic fashion. A 4-year-old might use a sweeping hand, for example, to represent the concept 'aeroplane'. Piaget termed the stage 'pre-operational' because children are not yet able to use their developing mental capabilities systematically. Children in this stage are egocentric. As Piaget used it, this concept does not refer to selfishness, but to the tendency of the child to interpret the world exclusively in terms of his own position. A child during this period does not understand, for instance, that others see objects from a different perspective from his own. Holding a book upright, the child may ask about a picture in it, not realizing that the other person sitting opposite can only see the back of the book.

Children at the pre-operational stage are not able to hold connected conversations with another. In egocentric speech, what each child says is more or less unrelated to what the other speaker said. Children talk together, but not to one another in the same sense as adults. During this phase of development, children have no general understanding of categories of thought that adults tend to take for granted: concepts such as causality, speed, weight or number. Even if the child sees water poured from a tall, thin container into a shorter, wider one, she will not understand that the volume of water remains the same – and concludes rather that there is less water because the water level is lower.

A third period, the **concrete operational stage**, lasts from the ages of 7 to 11. During this phase, children master abstract, logical notions. They are able to handle ideas such as causality without much difficulty. A child at this stage of development will recognize the false reasoning involved in the idea that the wide container holds less water than the thin, narrow one, even though the water levels are different. She becomes capable of carrying out the mathematical operations of multiplying, dividing and subtracting. Children by this stage are much less egocentric. In the pre-operational stage, if a girl is asked, 'How many sisters do you have?' she may correctly answer 'one'. But if asked, 'How many sisters does your sister have?' she will probably answer 'none', because she cannot see herself from the point of view of her sister. The concrete operational child is able to answer such a question with ease.

The years from 11 to 15 cover what Piaget called the **formal operational stage**. During adolescence, the developing child becomes able to grasp highly abstract and hypothetical ideas. When faced with a problem, children at this stage are able to review all the possible ways of solving it and go through them theoretically in order to reach a solution. The young person at the formal operational stage is able to understand why some questions are trick ones. To the question, 'What creatures are both poodles and dogs?' the individual might not be able to give the correct reply but will understand why the answer 'poodles' is right and appreciate the humour in it.

According to Piaget, the first three stages of development are universal; but not all adults reach the third, formal operational stage. The development of formal operational thought depends in part on processes of schooling. Adults of limited educational attainment tend to continue to think in more concrete terms and retain large traces of egocentrism.

The Russian psychologist, Lev Vygotsky (1986 [1934]) provided a useful critique of Piaget's influential ideas. He argued that the processes of learning which Piaget describes are dependent on social structures and interactions. Vygotsky saw that the opportunities for learning available to children from various social groups differed considerably, and this strongly influenced children's ability to learn from their engagements with the world outside their self. In short, learning and cognitive development are not immune from the social structures within which they are embedded. Just as these structures constrain some groups and enable others to become wealthy, so they also constrain and enable their cognitive development.

> **THINKING CRITICALLY**
>
> Reflecting on the processes of socialization, how do these differ from common-sense ideas of 'brainwashing' or 'indoctrination'? What impact might a *lack* of early socialization have on the formation of the human infant's self-awareness? Explain your answer with reference to the theories above.

Agencies of socialization

Sociologists often speak of socialization as occurring in two broad phases, involving a number of different agencies of socialization. **Agencies of socialization** are groups or social contexts in which significant processes of socialization occur. Primary socialization occurs in infancy and childhood and is the most intense period of cultural learning. It is the time when children learn language and basic behavioural patterns that form the foundation for later learning. The family is the main agent of socialization during this phase. Secondary socialization takes place later in childhood

and into maturity. In this phase, other agents of socialization take over some of the responsibility from the family. Schools, peer groups, organizations, the media and, eventually, the workplace become socializing forces for individuals. Social interactions in these contexts help people learn the values, norms and beliefs that make up the patterns of their culture.

The family

Since family systems vary widely, the range of family contacts that the infant experiences is by no means standard across cultures. The mother everywhere is normally the most important individual in the child's early life, but the nature of the relationships established between mothers and their children is influenced by the form and regularity of their contact. This is, in turn, conditioned by the character of family institutions and their relation to other groups in society.

In modern societies, most early socialization occurs within a small-scale family context and children spend their early years within a domestic unit containing mother, father and perhaps one or two other children. In many other cultures, by contrast, aunts, uncles and grandparents are often part of a single household and serve as caretakers even for very young infants. Yet even within modern societies there are many variations in the nature of family contexts. Some children are brought up in single-parent households, some are cared for by two mothering and fathering agents (divorced parents and step-parents). A high proportion of women with families are now employed outside the home and return to their paid work relatively soon after the births of their children. In spite of these variations, the family normally remains the major agency of socialization from infancy to adolescence and beyond –

 We look at issues concerning families in more detail in chapter 9, 'Families and Intimate Relationships'.

in a sequence of development connecting the generations.

Families have varying 'locations' within the overall institutions of a society. In most traditional societies, the family into which a person was born largely determined the individual's social position for the rest of his or her life. In modern societies, social position is not inherited at birth in this way, yet the region and social class of the family into which an individual is born affects patterns of socialization quite distinctly. Children pick up ways of behaviour characteristic of their parents or others in their neighbourhood or community.

 We look at issues of class in more depth in chapter 11, 'Stratification and Social Class'.

Varying patterns of childrearing and discipline, together with contrasting values and expectations, are found in different sectors of large-scale societies. It is easy to understand the influence of different types of family background if we think of what life is like, say, for a child growing up in a poor ethnic-minority family living in a run-down area of a city compared to one born into an affluent white family in the suburbs (Kohn 1977).

Of course, few if any children simply take over unquestioningly the outlook of their parents. This is especially true in the modern world, in which change is so pervasive. Moreover, the very existence of a range of socializing agencies in modern societies leads to many divergences between the outlooks of children, adolescents and the parental generation.

Schools

Another important socializing agency is the school. Schooling is a formal process: students pursue a definite curriculum of subjects. Yet schools are agencies of socialization in more subtle respects. Children are expected to be quiet in class, be punctual at lessons and observe rules of school discipline. They are required to accept and respond to the authority of the teaching

staff. Reactions of teachers also affect the expectations children have of themselves. These expectations in turn become linked to their job experience when they leave school. Peer groups are often formed at school, and the system of keeping children in classes according to age reinforces their impact.

We discuss socialization within education systems in chapter 19, 'Education'.

Peer relationships

Another socializing agency is the **peer group**. Peer groups consist of children of a similar age. In some cultures, particularly small traditional societies, peer groups are formalized as age-grades (normally confined to males). There are often specific ceremonies or rites that mark the transition of men from one age-grade to another. Those within a particular age grade generally maintain close and friendly connections throughout their lives. A typical set of age-grades consists of childhood, junior warriorhood, senior warriorhood, junior elderhood and senior elderhood. Men move through these grades not as individuals, but as whole groups.

The family's importance in socialization is obvious, since the experience of the infant and young child is shaped more or less exclusively within it. It is less apparent, especially to those of us living in Western societies, how significant peer groups are. Yet even without formal age-grades, children over the age of 4 or 5 usually spend a great deal of time in the company of friends the same age. With both partners now working, peer relationships amongst young children who play together in day-care centres are likely to become even more important today than they were before (Corsaro 1997; Harris 1998).

Peer relations are likely to have a significant impact beyond childhood and adolescence. Informal groups of people of similar ages, at work and in other situations, are usually of enduring importance in shaping individuals' attitudes and behaviour.

8.1 Socialization in the school playground

In her book *Gender Play* (1993), the sociologist Barrie Thorne looked at socialization by observing how children interact in the playground. As others had before her, she wanted to understand how children come to know what it means to be male and female. Rather than seeing children as passively learning the meaning of gender from their parents and teachers, she looked at the way in which children actively create and recreate the *meaning* of gender in their interactions with each other. The social activities that schoolchildren do together can be as important as other agents for their socialization.

In school playgrounds, girls tend to play only with other girls and boys with other boys. Why should this be so?

Thorne spent two years observing fourth and fifth graders at two schools in Michigan and California, sitting in the classroom with them and observing their activities outside the classroom. She watched games such as 'chase and kiss' – known by names such as 'kiss-catch' in the UK – so as to learn how children construct and experience gender meanings in the classroom and on the playground. Thorne found that peer groups have a great influence on gender socialization, particularly as children talk about their changing bodies, a subject of great fascination. The social context created by these children determined whether a child's bodily change was experienced with embarrassment or worn with pride. As Thorne (1993) observed:

If the most popular women started menstruating or wearing bras (even if they didn't need to), then other girls wanted these changes too. But if the popular didn't wear bras and hadn't … gotten their periods, then these developments were viewed as less desirable.

Thorne's research is a powerful reminder that children are social actors who help create their social world and influence their own socialization. Still, the impact of societal and cultural influences is tremendous, since the activities that children pursue and the values they hold are determined by influences such as their families and the media.

The mass media

Newspapers, periodicals and journals flourished in the West from the early 1800s onward, but they were confined to a fairly small readership. It was not until a century later that such printed materials became part of people's daily experience. The spread of **mass media** involving printed documents was soon accompanied by electronic communication – radio, television, records and videos, bringing with them concerns about undue influence on opinions, attitudes and behaviour. The media plays a large role in shaping our understanding of the world and therefore in socialization.

Much early research on the influence of the media, especially television, on childhood development has tended to see children as passive and undiscriminating in their reactions to what they see. But Hodge and Tripp (1986) emphasized that children's responses to TV involve interpreting, or 'reading', what they see, not just registering the content of programmes. Since then, researchers have arrived at a more balanced understanding of the influence of the mass media in socialization processes and now see television, for example, as one important agency of socialization alongside several others.

Gender socialization

Agencies of socialization play an important role in how children learn **gender roles**. Let us now turn to the study of **gender socialization**, the learning of gender roles through social factors such as the family and the media.

Reactions of parents and adults

Many studies have been carried out on the degree to which gender differences are the result of social influences. Studies of mother–infant interaction show differences in the treatment of boys and girls even when parents believe their reactions to both are the same. Adults asked to assess the personality of a baby give different answers according to whether or not they believe the child to be a girl or a boy. In one experiment, five young mothers were observed in interaction with a six-month-old called Beth. They tended to smile at her often and offer her dolls to play with. She was seen as 'sweet', having a 'soft cry'. The reaction of a second group of mothers to a child the same age, named Adam, was noticeably different. The baby was likely to be offered a train or other 'male toys' to play with. Beth and Adam were actually the same child, dressed in different clothes (Will et al. 1976).

Gender learning

Gender learning by infants is almost certainly unconscious. Before children can accurately label themselves as either a boy or a girl, they receive a range of pre-verbal cues. For instance, male and female adults usually handle infants differently. The cosmetics used by women contain scents different from those the baby might learn to associate with males. Systematic differences in dress, hairstyle and so on provide visual cues for the infant in the learning process. By the age of 2, children have a partial understanding of what gender is. They know whether they are a boy or a girl, and they can usually categorize others accurately. Not until the age of 5 or 6, however, does a child know that a person's gender does not change, that everyone has gender and that sex differences between girls and boys are anatomically based.

The toys, picture books and television programmes with which young children come into contact all tend to emphasize differences between male and female attributes. Toy stores and mail-order catalogues usually categorize their products by gender. Even some toys that seem neutral in terms of gender are not so in practice. For example, toy kittens and rabbits are recommended for girls, while lions and tigers are seen as more appropriate for boys.

Vanda Lucia Zammuner (1986) studied the toy preferences of children aged between 7 and 10 in Italy and Holland. Children's attitudes towards a variety of toys were analysed; stereotypically masculine and feminine toys, as well as toys presumed not to be gender-typed, were included. Both the children and their parents were asked to assess which toys were suitable for boys and which for girls. There was close agreement between the adults and the children. On average, the Italian children chose gender-differentiated toys to play with more often than the Dutch children – a finding that conformed to expectations, since Italian culture tends to hold a more traditional view of gender divisions than does Dutch society. As in other studies, girls

8.2 Children's stories, TV and film

More than 30 years ago, Lenore Weitzman and her colleagues (1972) carried out an analysis of gender roles in some of the most widely used pre-school children's books and found several clear differences in gender roles. Males played a much larger part in the stories and pictures than females did, outnumbering females by a ratio of 11 to 1. When animals with gender identities were included, the ratio was 95 to 1. The activities of males and females also differed. The males engaged in adventurous pursuits and outdoor activities that demanded independence and strength. Where girls did appear, they were portrayed as passive and were confined mostly to indoor activities. Girls cooked and cleaned for the males or awaited their return. Much the same was true of the adult men and women represented in the storybooks. Women who were not wives and mothers were imaginary creatures like witches or fairy godmothers. There was not a single woman in all the books analysed who held an occupation outside the home. By contrast, the men were depicted as fighters, policemen, judges, kings and so forth.

More recent research suggests that things have changed somewhat but that the large bulk of children's literature nevertheless remains much the same (Davies 1991). Fairy-tales, for example, embody traditional attitudes towards gender and towards the sorts of aims and ambitions that girls and boys are expected to have. 'Some day my prince will come': in versions of fairy-tales from several centuries ago, this usually implied that a girl from a poor family might dream of wealth and fortune. Today, its meaning has become more closely tied to the ideals of romantic love. Some feminists have tried to rewrite some of the most celebrated fairy-tales, reversing their usual emphases: 'I really didn't notice that he had a funny nose. And he certainly looked better all dressed up in fancy clothes. He's not nearly as attractive as he seemed the other night. So I think I'll just pretend that this glass slipper feels too tight' (Viorst 1986). Like this version of Cinderella, however, these rewrites are found mainly in books directed at adult audiences, and have hardly affected the tales told in innumerable children's books.

Analyses of television programmes and films designed for children show that most still conform to the findings about children's books. Studies of the most frequently watched cartoons show that most of the leading figures are male and that males dominate the active pursuits. Similar images are found in the commercials that appear throughout the programmes.

However, there are some exceptions to this repetitively gendered pattern. The 2001 film Shrek (and its sequels) told a fairly conventional fairy-tale story of princes, princesses and ogres, whilst also subverting conventional fairy-tale gender and character roles. The film's marketing tagline was: 'The greatest fairytale never told' – 'The Prince isn't charming. The Princess isn't sleeping. The sidekick isn't helping. The ogre is the hero. Fairy-tales will never be the same again.' Shrek (the ugly ogre) is actually the hero of the film, while Fiona (the beautiful princess) is an independent woman with martial arts skills who turns into an ogress at night. The 'happy ending' arrives when Shrek kisses Fiona, she turns permanently into an ogress and they get married, thus reversing the traditional story of the ogre turning into a handsome young prince, reflecting Western ideals of beauty and bodily perfection. Such representations remain a small minority of total output at present, however.

from both societies chose gender-neutral or boys' toys to play with far more than boys chose girls' toys. Clearly, gender socialization is very powerful, and challenges to it can be upsetting. Once a gender is 'assigned', society expects individuals to act like 'females' and 'males'. It is in the practices of everyday life that these expectations are fulfilled and reproduced (Bourdieu 1990; Lorber 1994).

The sociological debate

Sigmund Freud's theory

Perhaps the most influential – and controversial – theory of the emergence of gender identity is that of Sigmund Freud (1856–1939). According to Freud, the learning of gender differences in infants and young children is centred on the possession or absence of the penis. 'I have a penis' is equivalent to 'I am a boy', while 'I am a girl' is equivalent to 'I lack a penis'. Freud is careful to say that it is not just the anatomical distinctions that matter here; the possession or absence of the penis are symbolic of masculinity and femininity.

At around the age of 4 or 5, the theory goes, a boy feels threatened by the discipline and autonomy his father demands of him, fantasizing that the father wishes to remove his penis. Partly consciously, but mostly on an unconscious level, the boy recognizes the father as a rival for the affections of his mother. In repressing erotic feelings towards the mother and accepting the father as a superior being, the boy identifies with the father and becomes aware of his male identity. The boy gives up his love for his mother out of an unconscious fear of castration by his father. Girls, on the other hand, supposedly suffer from 'penis envy' because they do not possess the visible organ that distinguishes boys. The mother becomes devalued in the little girl's eyes, because she is also seen to lack a penis and to be unable to provide one. When the girl identifies with the mother, she takes over the submissive attitude involved in the recognition of being 'second best'.

Once this phase is over, the child has learned to repress his erotic feelings. The period from about the age of 5 to puberty, according to Freud, is one of latency – sexual activities tend to be suspended until the biological changes involved in puberty reactivate erotic desires in a direct way. The latency period, covering the early and middle years of school, is the time at which same-gender peer groups are most important in the child's life.

Major objections have been raised to Freud's views, particularly by feminists, but also by many other authors (Mitchell 1975; Coward 1984). First, Freud seems to identify gender identity too closely with genital awareness; other more subtle factors are surely involved. Second, the theory seems to depend on the notion that the penis is superior to the vagina, which is thought of as just a lack of the male organ. Yet why should the female genitals not be considered superior to those of the male? Third, Freud treats the father as the primary disciplining agent, whereas in many cultures the mother plays the more significant part in the imposition of discipline. Fourth, Freud argues that gender learning is concentrated at the age of 4 or 5. Most later authors have emphasized the importance of earlier learning, beginning in infancy.

Carol Gilligan's theory

Carol Gilligan (1982) has further developed Chodorow's analysis (see 'Classic Studies 8.2'). Her work concentrates on the images that adult women and men have of themselves and their attainments. Women, she agrees with Chodorow, define themselves in terms of personal relationships and judge their achievements by reference to the ability to care for others. Women's place in the lives of men is traditionally that of caretaker and helpmate. But the qualities developed in these tasks are frequently devalued by men, who see their own emphasis on individual achievement as the only form of 'success'. Concern with relationships on the part of women appears to them as a weakness rather than as the strength that in fact it is.

Gilligan carried out intensive interviews with about 200 American women and men of varying ages and social backgrounds. She

Classic Studies 8.2 Nancy Chodorow on attachment and separation

The research problem

You may think or have been told that men find it difficult to express their emotions and, instead, tend to 'bottle it up' or 'keep a stiff upper lip'. Conversely, women are apparently more likely to express how they are feeling. But why should this be so? Are women really just naturally better than men at forming close emotional relationships? Such common-sense assumptions formed the basis of Nancy Chodorow's (1978) work on gender identity. Like many others, Chodorow made use of Freud's approach in studying gender development, but modified it in major respects to account for important gender differences.

Chodorow's explanation

Chodorow (1978, 1988) argues that learning to feel male or female derives from the infant's attachment to his parents from an early age. She places much more emphasis than Freud does on the importance of the mother rather than the father. Children tend to become emotionally involved with the mother, since she is easily the most dominant influence in their early lives. This attachment has at some point to be broken in order for the child to achieve a separate sense of self – the child is required to become less closely dependent.

Chodorow argues that the breaking process occurs in a different way for boys and girls. Girls remain closer to the mother - able, for example, to go on hugging and kissing her and imitating what she does. Because there is no sharp break from the mother, the girl, and later the adult woman, develops a sense of self that is more continuous with other people. Her identity is more likely to be merged with or dependent on another's: first her mother, later a man. In Chodorow's view, this tends to produce characteristics of sensitivity and emotional compassion in women.

Boys gain a sense of self via a more radical rejection of their original closeness to the mother, forging their understanding of masculinity from what is not feminine. They learn not to be 'sissies' or 'mummy's boys'. As a result, boys are relatively unskilled in relating closely to others; they develop more analytical ways of looking at the world. They take a more active view of their lives, emphasizing achievement, but they have repressed their ability to understand their own feelings and those of others.

To some extent, Chodorow reverses Freud's emphasis. Masculinity, rather than femininity, is defined by a loss, the forfeiting of continued close attachment to the mother. Male identity is formed through separation; thus, men later in life unconsciously feel that their identity is endangered if they become involved in close emotional relationships with others. Women, on the other hand, feel that the absence of a close relation to another person threatens their self-esteem. These patterns are passed on from generation to generation, because of the primary role women play in the early socialization of children. Women express and define themselves mainly in terms of relationships. Men have repressed these needs and adopt a more manipulative stance towards the world.

Critical points

Chodorow's work has met with various criticisms. Janet Sayers (1986), for example, has suggested that Chodorow does not explain the struggle of women, particularly in current times, to become autonomous, independent beings. Women (and men), she points out, are more contradictory in their psychological make-up than Chodorow's theory suggests. Femininity may conceal feelings of aggressiveness or assertiveness, which are revealed only obliquely or in certain contexts (Brennan 1988). Chodorow has also been criticized for her narrow conception of the family, one based on a white, middle-class model. What happens, for example, in one-parent households or, as in many Chicano communities, families where children are cared for by more than one adult (Segura and Pierce 1993)?

Contemporary significance

These legitimate criticisms do not undermine Chodorow's central ideas, which remain important in the study of gender socialization. They teach us a good deal about the nature of femininity and masculinity, and they help us to understand the origins of what has been called 'male inexpressiveness' - the difficulty men have in revealing their feelings to others (Bourdieu 2001).

asked all the interviewees a range of questions concerning their moral outlook and conceptions of self. Consistent differences emerged between the views of the women and the men. For instance, the interviewees were asked: 'What does it mean to say something is morally right or wrong?' Whereas the men tended to respond to this question by mentioning abstract ideals of duty, justice and individual freedom, the women persistently raised the theme of helping others. Thus a female college student answered the question in the following way: 'It [morality] has to do with responsibilities and obligations and values, mainly values. … In my life situation I relate morality with interpersonal relationships that have to do with respect for the other person and myself.' The interviewer then asked: 'Why respect other people?' and received the answer: 'Because they have a consciousness or feelings that can be hurt, an awareness that can be hurt' (Gilligan 1982).

The women were more tentative in their moral judgements than the men, seeing possible contradictions between following a strict moral code and avoiding harming others. Gilligan suggests that this outlook reflects the traditional situation of women, anchored in caring relationships, more than it does the 'outward-looking' attitudes of men. Women have in the past deferred to the judgements of men, while being aware that they have qualities that most men lack. Their views of themselves are based on successfully fulfilling the needs of others, rather than on pride in individual achievement (Gilligan 1982).

The life-course

The various transitions through which individuals pass during their lives seem at first to be biologically fixed. This common-sense view of the human **life-cycle** is widely accepted in society and strongly suggests that there exists a universal and uniform set of stages through which all people pass. For example, everyone who lives to old age has been an infant, a child, a youth and an adult, and everyone dies eventually. However, historically and sociologically, this is not correct. These apparently natural biological stages are part of the human **life-course**, which is social as well as biological (Vincent 2003). The concept of the life-course rather than life-cycle reflects the acknowledgement by sociologists that there is considerable variation in different societies and over time and therefore variation also across the life-course. Stages of the life-course are influenced by cultural differences and also by the material circumstances of people's lives in given types of society.

For example, in modern Western societies, death is usually thought of in relation to elderly people, because most people live to be over 70. In the traditional societies of the past, however, more people died at a younger age than survived to old age, and death therefore carried a different meaning and set of expectations.

Other social factors, such as social class, gender and ethnicity, also influence the way that the life-course is experienced. For example, in nineteenth-century Britain and elsewhere, children of the upper classes routinely attended boarding schools and continued their education over an extended period. However, for children from working-class families, the expectation was of labour not education, and it was not unusual for 13-year-old boys to work in coal-mining and other industries, while many girls of the same age went into domestic service. Clearly, the notion of a set of *universal* and age-related stages making up the life-course is not borne out by the evidence.

The individual life-course is not only structured by the major social divisions of social class, gender and ethnicity, but is also historically situated. One way of thinking about this aspect is to consider the concepts of birth cohorts and generations. **Cohorts** are simply groups of people with something in common and birth cohorts are therefore groups of people who are born in the same year. Why should this be important? Sociologists argue that such groups tend to be influenced by the same major events and, though they may well respond differently to these, they nonetheless share a common experience. In large measure, their life-course experiences have common cultural and political reference points, such as specific governments, conflicts, musical trends and so on. Recent examples would be the terror attacks in New York, Madrid, London and elsewhere, as well as the invasion of Iraq and its aftermath. Although people do have divergent different views about these events, they still share a common currency of experiences which gives shape to the life-course.

Finally, the Hungarian-born sociologist Karl Mannheim (1893–1947), made a strong claim regarding the influence of particular **generations** on life-course experience. Generations can be thought of as groups of people who are born in either the same year or series of years. Mannheim (1972 [1928]:105) said: 'Individuals who belong to the same generation . . . are endowed . . . with a common location in the historical dimension of the social process.' Mannheim's claim is that generational location can be as influential in shaping people's attitudes and beliefs as their social-class position. Generations tend to experience

the world, and their place in it, rather differently. Hence we can speak of a 'generation gap', a 'lost generation [of youth]' or 'generation X' to describe the historical location of different generations. The assumption behind all such descriptions is that the generation of people in question is very different from that which came before.

For example, sociologists and historians have identified the different attitudes and experiences of the 'baby-boom' generation (Gillon 2004) and the 'Beat generation' (Charters 2001), to name but two. The baby-boomers are said to be those born after the Second World War, roughly between 1946 and 1964, when many countries experienced large increases in their birth rates, arguably in large measure as a result of post-war economic growth and prosperity. Baby-boomers had many new experiences; television in the home which consolidated a specific generational experience and identity, a new youth culture, rising income levels and more liberal attitudes to sex and morality. The experiences of baby-boomers were significantly different from those of their parents, and, with the creation of 'youth' as a stage of life, so too was their experience of the life-course. Indeed, Mannheim's argument suggests that this generation actually changed society itself. This dual aspect of giving shape to the life-course and for producing social change is one reason why Mannheim sees generations as akin to social classes in their potential impact on individual identities and social life.

Childhood

To people living in modern societies, **childhood** is a clear and distinct stage of life. Children are distinct from babies or toddlers; childhood intervenes between infancy and the teen years. Yet the concept of childhood, like so many other aspects of social life today, has only come into being over the past two or three centuries.

Until recently, sociologists tended to discuss children and childhood in the

The hippy youth culture of the 1960s and '70s was an important generational influence on social identities in the USA and other developed societies.

context of primary socialization within the family (see chapter 9). This often gave the impression that childhood is merely a transitory stage leading towards the more sociologically significant period of adulthood when *individuals* become involved in work, reproduction and building relationships. However, this conception is based on the notion of a stable *adulthood*, which is increasingly being challenged as permanent 'jobs for life' diminish along with permanent, lifelong relationships in the more fluid or 'liquid modernity' that characterizes the contemporary world (Lee 2001; Bauman 2000).

The idea of childhood as mere transition also ignores the *social structural* position of children within different societies. That is, children should be conceptualized as a distinct social group, in the same way as, for example, social classes and ethnic groups

are. As a distinct social group, children tend to experience life through their own culture, with its unique symbols and rituals, and they also have a similar status to some other minority groups, which has often led to them being exploited as a cheap source of labour (James et al. 1998). Childhood has also been shown to be socially constructed; the experience of childhood and its meaning for society are diverse, both in different historical periods and across geographical regions in the same time period (Jenks 2005).

In many earlier societies, young people moved directly from a lengthy infancy into working roles within the community. The French historian Philippe Ariès (1965) argued that 'childhood', conceived of as a separate phase of development, did not exist in medieval times. In the paintings of medieval Europe, children are portrayed as little adults, with mature faces and the same style of dress as their elders. Children took part in the same work and play activities as adults, rather than in the childhood games we now take for granted.

Into the early twentieth century, in most Western countries, children were put to work at what now seems a very early age. There are countries in the world today, in which young children are engaged in full-time work, sometimes in physically demanding circumstances (such as coal-mines and agriculture). The idea that children have distinctive rights and that the use of child labour is 'obviously' morally repugnant are really quite recent developments and are not universally accepted. The United Nations Convention on the Rights of the Child (UNCRC) came into force in 1990, setting out the basic rights of all children across the world, which all UN member states have ratified (except the USA and Somalia). The UNCRC defines a child as anyone under the age of 18, unless nation-states already have an earlier definition.

The attempt to universalize the rights of children and definitions of childhood in very different social and economic contexts is a bold one that raises some important issues. Is the UN definition culturally sensitive to different societies, or does it impose Western ideas of children and childhood onto the rest of the world? Can the governments of the developing world really put in place the same safeguards for protecting children's rights that already largely exist in the developed societies? And if they do, will it restrict economic development and effectively restrict the income-generating capacity of the poorest families? For example, in many developing countries, 'street children' earn money for poor families by selling goods, and if states penalize such practices as 'deviant', then how will such families survive? These are very difficult questions which are currently being worked out in policy and practice across the world.

The issue of child labour is discussed in chapter 13, 'Global Inequality'.

Because of the long period of childhood that we recognize today, societies are now in some respects more child-centred than traditional ones. But a child-centred society, it must be emphasized, is not one in which all children experience love and care from parents or other adults. The physical and sexual abuse of children is a commonplace feature of family life in present-day society, although the full extent of such abuse has only recently come to light. Child abuse has clear connections with what seems to us today like the frequent mistreatment of children in pre-modern Europe.

It seems possible that as a result of changes currently occurring in modern societies, the separate character of childhood is diminishing once more, bringing adult-child relations towards crisis point (Prout 2004). The uncertainties associated with globalization processes and the kind of rapid social changes we explored in chapter 4 are leading to new social constructions of childhood. Prout (2004: 7) suggests: 'These new representations construct children as more active, knowledgeable and socially participative than older discourses allowed. They are more difficult to manage, less biddable and hence are more troublesome and troubling.' It seems that relationships between adults and children are in a period of flux and major disturbance.

Other observers have suggested that children now grow up so fast that the previously solid boundary between adults and children is rapidly diminishing, leading to the 'disappearance' of childhood in the developed societies (Postman 1995; Buckingham 2000). They point out that even small children may watch the same television programmes as adults, thereby becoming much more familiar early on with the adult world than did preceding generations. Children are becoming consumers at an earlier age and are consuming adult products such as TV programmes, mobile phones and advertising. All of this may mean that the protected period of childhood which characterized the developed countries for most of the twentieth century, may be being eroded today.

The teenager and youth culture

The idea of the 'teenager', so familiar to us today, also did not exist until recently. The biological changes involved in puberty (the point at which a person becomes capable of adult sexual activity and reproduction) are universal. Yet in many cultures these do not produce the degree of turmoil and uncertainty often found among young people in modern societies. In cultures that foster age-grades, for example, with distinct ceremonials that signal a person's transition to adulthood, the process of psychosexual development generally seems easier to negotiate. Adolescents in such societies have less to 'unlearn', since the pace of change is slower. There is a time when children in Western societies are required to be children no longer: to put away their toys and break with childish pursuits. In traditional cultures, where children are already working alongside adults, this process of unlearning is normally much less jarring.

In Western societies, teenagers are betwixt and between: they often try to follow adult ways, but they are treated in law as children. They may wish to go to work, but they are constrained to stay in school. Teenagers in the West live in between childhood and adulthood, growing up in a society subject to continuous change.

Linked to the idea of the teenager is that of **youth culture**, a general way of life associated with young people, especially in the developed countries. In many other societies, past and present, the concept of youth culture in this sense does not exist and children move towards adulthood much earlier without the intermediate stage of 'youth'.

Sociologists first reported on youth culture in the 1950s and '60s, when older teenagers moving into employment began to benefit from post-war affluence, using their earnings to buy fashionable clothes, pop records and other products in the

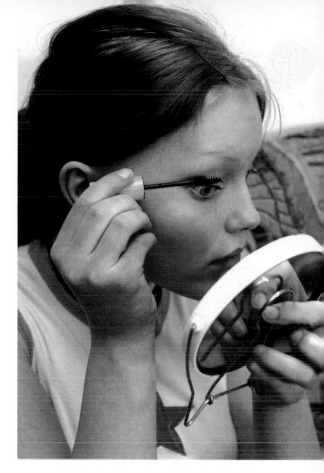

In modern Western societies young teenagers hover between childhood and adulthood.
··

emerging consumer markets (Savage 2007). A 'culture of youth' began to coalesce, which looked different from the mainstream, and which constructed new meaningful worlds out of which sprang the spectacular youth subcultures of teddy boys, mods, rockers and skinheads and, later, hippies, punks, rastas, goths and many more. With hindsight, it seems that sociologists gave disproportionate attention to the small but highly visible subcultures – which tended to be male-dominated – and not enough time to understanding the majority of young people and the ways in which they make sense of their own lives. For instance, Angela McRobbie and Jenny Garber (1975) identified a widespread and more concealed 'culture of the bedroom' amongst girls, which enabled groups of friends to participate in the culture of youth, but which had been largely ignored in the rush to analyse 'deviant' (male) subcultures in the public sphere.

Steven Miles (2000) suggests that the concepts of youth culture and youth subcultures have misled us into seeing all young people as essentially similar, involved in counter-cultural and deviant activity or experiencing unique social disadvantage. Indeed, historian Geoffrey Pearson (1983) did find deviant youth subcultures back in nineteenth-century Britain, including the original 'hooligans', identified by their aggressive attitudes, peaked caps, neck-scarves, bell-bottom trousers and close-cropped hairstyle with a fringe over the fore-head. However, he argued that, like all subsequent deviant subcultures, such as mods and rockers, hooligans were in part socially created, as more traditional social groups sought out scapegoats to blame for their own 'respectable fears' around social problems. Clearly, the mainstream of young people did not – and still do not – fit such deviant descriptions.

> Deviant youth subcultures are discussed in chapter 21, 'Crime and Deviance'.

Instead, Miles proposes the concept of *youth lifestyles*, which suggests a diversity of experience within mainstream youth and focuses on the question, 'How … do young people interact with and negotiate the social worlds in which they construct their everyday lives?' (Miles 2000: 2). Such a perspective reminds us of both the common, shared experiences of youth in a rapidly changing world and the different responses young people adopt towards it.

Young adulthood

Sociologists have started to theorize a relatively new phase within the life-course in developed societies, which we can call **young adulthood** (Goldscheider and Waite 1991), though the systematic study of this stage is not yet as fully developed as that of childhood or later life. Young adulthood seems increasingly to be a specific stage in personal and sexual development in modern societies, which has been described in various ways: as post-adolescence, late adolescence and so on. It is said to characterize those people in their 20s and perhaps early 30s who live relatively independent lives, but have not yet married or had children and as a consequence, are still experimenting with their relationships and lifestyles.

However, this stage is not seen as being experienced in the same way by all social classes and ethnic groups. It is particularly amongst more affluent groups that people in their early 20s are taking the time to travel, and explore sexual, political and religious affiliations (Heath and Cleaver 2003). Indeed, the importance of this post-ponement of the responsibilities of full adulthood is likely to grow, given the extended period of education many people now undergo in the developed world. This stage of life is also likely to become much less gendered, as more young women go on to university and forge careers instead of settling into traditional family life at an early age. We can expect scholars studying the life-course to carry out more research on this stage over the next few years.

Mature adulthood

As we noted above, the sociological study of childhood is a latecomer to the discipline, mainly because childhood itself was seen as simply a transitional period leading to adulthood. Conversely though, the study of adulthood preoccupied sociologists during the twentieth century and most sociological research in many varied fields has simply taken adulthood as an unquestioned assumption underpinning their work. For example, the study of doctor–patient relationships simply assumed mature adult doctors and patients alike, with little or no regard for the different experiences of children or young adults.

Hence, much of this book is concerned primarily with the experiences and lives of mature adults and we can only make some very general comments about this here.

Most young adults in the modern world today can look forward to a life stretching right through to old age. But in pre-modern times, few could anticipate such a future with much confidence – and nor do young adults in the poorer parts of the developing world today. Death through sickness or injury was much more frequent among all age groups than it is today, and women in particular were at great risk because of the high rate of mortality in childbirth.

On the other hand, some of the strains that people experience now were less pronounced in previous times. People usually maintained a closer connection with their parents and other kin than in today's more mobile populations, and the routines of work they followed were much the same as those of their forebears. In current times, major uncertainties must be resolved in marriage, family life and other social contexts. People increasingly have to 'make' their own lives, more so than in the past. Amongst many social groups, the creation of sexual and marital ties now mainly depends on individual initiative and selection rather than being fixed by parents, though this is not, of course, the case in all cultures. Such individual choice can be experienced as a freedom, but the responsibility to *have to* choose can also impose its own pressures.

Keeping a forward-looking outlook in middle age has taken on a particular importance in modern societies. Most people do not expect to be doing the same thing all their lives, as was the case for the majority in traditional cultures. Individuals who have spent their lives in one career may find the level they have reached in middle age unsatisfying and further opportunities blocked. Women who have spent their early adulthood raising a family and whose children have left home may feel themselves to be without any social value. The phenomenon of a 'mid-life crisis' is very real for many middle-aged people. A person may feel she has thrown away the opportunities that life had to offer, or she will never attain goals cherished since childhood. Yet growing older need not lead to resignation or bleak despair; a release from childhood dreams can be liberating.

Later life

In traditional societies, older people were often accorded a great deal of respect. Among cultures that included age-grades, the elders usually had a major – often the final – say over matters of importance to the community. Within families, the authority of both men and women mostly increased with age. In industrialized societies, by contrast, older people tend to lack authority within both the family and the wider social community. Having retired from the labour force, they may be poorer than ever before in their lives. At the same time, there has been a great increase in the proportion of the population over the age of 65, as we see in the next section.

Transition to the age-grade of elder in a traditional culture often marked the pinnacle of the status an individual could achieve. In modern societies, retirement may bring the opposite consequences. No longer living with their children and often having retired from paid work, older people may find it difficult to make the final period of their life rewarding. It used to be thought that those who successfully cope with later life do so by turning to their inner resources, becoming less interested in the material rewards that social life has to offer. While this may often be true, it seems likely that in a society in which many are physically healthy in later life, an outward-looking view will become more and more prevalent. Those in retirement might find renewal in what has been called the 'third age', in which a new phase of education begins (see also the discussion in chapter 19, 'Education').

In the section that follows, we look at the sociological issues surrounding ageing in more detail than the earlier life-course stages. This is for two reasons. First, the study of later life and ageing (gerontology) is very well established, with a significant body of evidence, which is reflected here. Second, major concerns over the consequences of an ageing world population have been at the centre of important social, political and economic debate since the mid-1970s and these claims will also be considered.

Fauja Singh was still running marathons in his 90s.

Ageing

Fauja Singh ran his first London marathon in 2000, at the age of 89. It took him 6 hours and 54 minutes. He had last run seriously 53 years earlier. When he recorded a near-identical marathon time in 2001, he found he had knocked almost an hour off the world record for the over-90s. In 2002 he trimmed his time down to 6 hours and 45 minutes. That year, 407 runners took longer than Singh to complete the London marathon; many were in their 30s. When Singh was that age, he was running cross-country races in his native India. By the time India gained independence in 1947, new priorities had led Singh to hang up his running shoes at the age of 36. A lifetime later – widowed and living in Ilford, East London – with four children, thirteen grandchildren and five great-grandchildren scattered across three continents, he began looking for new challenges. He started to punctuate his daily walks with bursts of jogging. His legs soon regained their lost strength. Then Singh saw a television programme about the marathon and was inspired. He began to run marathons all over the world and raised thousands of pounds for charity (Askwith 2003), even running a 2007 half-marathon in Jalandhar at the age of 94.

People, especially in the richer countries, are leading longer, healthier and more productive lives than ever before. When she became monarch in 1952, Queen Elizabeth II sent 273 birthday telegrams to congratulate British centenarians on their 100th birthdays. By the end of the twentieth century, that figure had risen to more than 3,000 per year (Cayton 2002), and in 2007 there were around 9,000 British people over 100 years of age, 90 times more than in 1911. Growing old can be a fulfilling and rewarding experience; or it can be filled with physical distress and social isolation. For most older people, the experience of ageing lies somewhere in between.

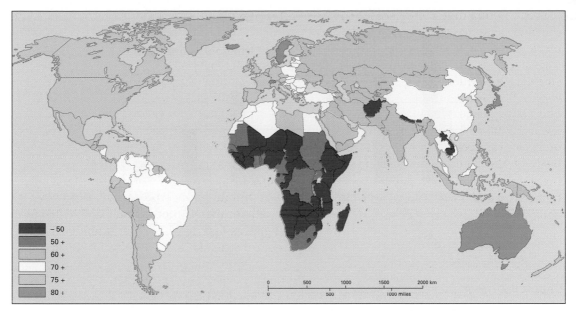

Figure 8.1 Global life expectancy (average life expectancy at birth)

Source: Created from CIA Factbook 2007

The greying of human societies

Throughout the world, societies are ageing, but they are not doing so evenly. One example is the startling national differences in average life expectancy (see figure 8.1). Taking the two extremes, in 2006, average life expectancy at birth for women in Swaziland was 32.62 years and for men just 31.84 years; but in Andorra it was 86.62 for women and 80.62 years for men. Such grossly unequal life chances illustrates in a stark way the very different ageing experiences of people across the world and the various meanings attached to the idea of a 'life-course' in different parts of the world. In the developed world, being 32 years of age does not mean that one is approaching the end of a life but merely indicates the period of young adulthood. As we will see later in this chapter, such wide disparities in average life expectancy also shape the experiences of death, dying and bereavement.

So, although most of this section will focus on debates and evidence from the relatively wealthy developed countries, we have to bear in mind that the situation in the developing world is very different and the 'ageing experience' differs accordingly.

A 1998 report by the United Nations Population Fund (UNFPA 1998) notes that the population of those aged 65 and older worldwide grew by about 9 million in 1998. By 2010, this population will grow by 14.5 million and by 2050 it will grow by 21 million. The most rapid growth of the 65 and older group will take place in the industrialized nations of the world, where families have fewer children and people live longer than in poorer countries. In the industrialized countries, the percentage of the older population grew from 8 per cent in 1950 to 14 per cent in 1998, and it is projected to reach 25 per cent by 2050. After the middle of the century, the developing nations will follow suit, as they experience their own elder explosion.

The populations of most of the world's societies are ageing as the result of a decline in both birth and death rates, although the populations of the developing countries continue to have shorter life spans because of poverty, malnutrition and disease (see chapter 13, 'Global Inequality'). The world's average life expectancy grew from 46 in 1950

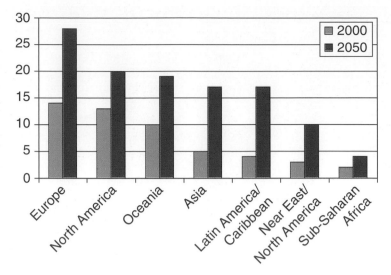

Figure 8.2 Proportion of population over the age of 65 by region, 2000 and 2050 (projected)
Source: UNFPA 2004

to 50 in 1985 and will reach 71 by 2025 (UNFPA 1998). By that time, some 800 million people will be over the age of 65, nearly a threefold increase in numbers from 1990 (see figure 8.2). Among the very old (those over 86), whose medical and service needs are the greatest, the number will increase by half in North America, while it will double in China and grow nearly one and a half times in West Africa (Sokolovsky 1990). This growth will place increasing demands on the resources of many countries that are already too poor to support their populations adequately.

This explosion has enormous implications for social policy. More than 150 nations currently provide public assistance for people who are elderly or disabled, or for their survivors when they die. Older people are especially likely to require costly healthcare services. Their rapid growth in numbers threatens to strain the medical systems in many industrial nations, where the cost of providing healthcare to older people is likely to overwhelm government budgets.

Looking at the changing demographic statistics, some sociologists and gerontologists now refer to the greying of the population (Peterson 1999). 'Greying' is the result of two long-term trends in industrial societies: the tendency of families to have fewer children (discussed in chapter 9, 'Families and Intimate Relationships'), and the fact that people are living longer. As figure 8.3 shows, a long-term shift in the age structure of developed societies is under way, which means, for example, that around one-third of Europe's population will be over the age of 65 by the year 2050.

Over the twentieth century, average life expectancy also increased, and infant mortality decreased. In Britain, for example, average life expectancy at birth will have increased from 45 years for men born in 1900 to 77 years for men born between 2005 and 2010. For a British woman, life expectancy will have risen from 48 to 81 over the same period. Most of these gains occurred in the first half of the twentieth century and were largely due to the improved chances for survival among the young. In 1921 in the UK, 84 infants in 1,000 live births died before the age of one, but by 2002 the rate was just 4.8 deaths for every 1,000 live births (HMSO 2004). An upward trend in life expectancy is shared across most industrialized and developing societies.

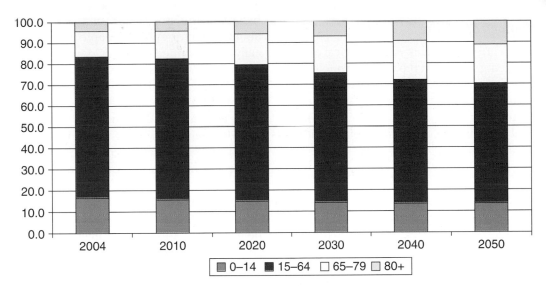

Figure 8.3 Changes in the age structure of European Union population, 2005

Source: European Union 2005

However, in the countries of sub-Saharan Africa, life expectancy has actually reduced since the mid-1980s, mainly because of the enormous and continuing impact of HIV/AIDS. Russia also experienced a lowering of average life expectancy after the mid-1990s, which some analysts ascribe to the effects of increasing poverty and, in particular, widespread alcohol abuse.

How do people age?

In examining the nature of ageing we will draw on studies of **social gerontology**, a discipline concerned with the study of the social aspects of ageing. Studying ageing is a bit like examining a moving target. As people grow older, society itself changes at the same time, and so does the very meaning of being 'old' (Riley et al. 1988). For people born into the developed societies in the first quarter of the twentieth century, a secondary education was regarded as more than sufficient for most of the available jobs, and the majority of people did not expect to live much past their 50s – and then only at the cost of suffering a variety of disabilities. Today, those very same people find them-

selves in their 70s and 80s; many are relatively healthy, unwilling to disengage from work and social life, and in need of more schooling than they ever dreamed would be necessary.

What does it mean to age? **Ageing** can be sociologically defined as the combination of biological, psychological and social processes that affect people as they grow older (Abeles and Riley 1987; Atchley 2000). These processes suggest the metaphor of three different, although interrelated, developmental 'clocks': first, a biological one, which refers to the physical body; second, a psychological one, which refers to the mind and mental capabilities; and, third, a social one, which refers to cultural norms, values and role expectations having to do with age. There is an enormous range of variation in all three of these processes, as will be shown below. Our notions about the meaning of age are rapidly changing, both because recent research is dispelling many myths about ageing, and because advances in nutrition and health have enabled many people to live longer, healthier lives than ever before.

Biological ageing

There are well-established biological effects of ageing, although the exact chronological point at which they occur varies greatly from individual to individual, depending on genetics and lifestyle. In general, for men and women alike, biological ageing typically means:

- declining vision, as the eye lens loses its elasticity (small type is the bane of most people over 50);
- hearing loss, first of higher-pitched tones, then of lower-pitched ones;
- wrinkles, as the skin's underlying structure becomes more and more brittle (millions of pounds invested in skin lotion and increasingly common surgical face-lifts only delay the inevitable);
- a decline of muscle mass and an accompanying accumulation of fat, especially around the middle (eating habits that were offset by exercise when you were 25 come back to haunt you when you are 50); and
- a drop in cardiovascular efficiency, as less oxygen can be inhaled and utilized during exercise (lifelong runners who ran a six-minute mile at the age of 30 are happy to break an eight-minute mile once they turn 60).

The normal processes of ageing cannot be avoided, but they can be partly compensated for and offset by good health, proper diet and nutrition, and a reasonable amount of exercise (John 1988). Lifestyle can make a significant health difference for people of all ages. For many people, the physical changes of ageing do not significantly prevent them from leading active, independent lives well into their 80s. Some scientists have even argued that with a proper lifestyle and advances in medical technology, more and more people will be able to live relatively illness-free lives until they reach their biological maximum, experiencing only a brief period of sickness just before death (Fries 1980). There is a debate about when, or even if, people are genetically programmed to die (Kirkwood 2001). About 90–100 years seems to be the upper end of the genetically determined age distribution for most human beings, although some have argued that it may be as high as 120 (Rusting 1992; Treas 1995). When the world's oldest officially recorded person, the Frenchwoman Jeanne Calment, died in 1997, she was 122, rode a bicycle until the age of 100 and had met Vincent van Gogh as a child. Other people have claimed to be even older, though their ages cannot be verified.

Even though the majority of older people in the developed societies suffer no significant physical impairment and remain physically active, unfortunate stereotypes about the 'weak and frail elderly' continue to exist (Heise 1987). These stereotypes have more to do with the social than the biological meaning of ageing in Western culture, which is increasingly preoccupied with youthfulness and fears of growing old and dying. Traditionally, older people in the West were seen as knowledgeable, wise and a source of good advice and in some cultures they are still seen this way: as active and valuable members of society.

Psychological ageing

The psychological effects of ageing are much less well established than the physical effects, although research into the psychology of ageing is continuing at an expanding pace (Diehl and Dark-Freudeman 2006). Even though such things as memory, learning, intelligence, skills and motivation to learn are widely assumed to decline with age, research into the psychology of ageing suggests a much more complicated process (Birren and Schaie 2001).

Memory and learning ability, for example, do not decline significantly until very late in life for most people, although the speed with which one recalls or analyses information may slow down somewhat, giving the false impression of mental impairment. For most older people whose lives are stimulating and rich, such mental abilities as motivation to learn, clarity of thought and problem-solving capacity do not appear to decline significantly until very late in life (Baltes and Schaie 1977; Schaie 1979; Atchley 2000).

Current research has focused on the extent to which memory loss relates to other variables, such as health, personality and social structures. Scientists and psychologists argue that intellectual decline is not necessarily irreversible, and they are working on ways to identify older people at risk so that medical intervention may be taken which will allow longer maintenance of higher levels of intellectual function (Schaie 1990).

Even Alzheimer's disease, the progressive deterioration of brain cells which is the primary cause of dementia in later life, is relatively rare in non-institutionalized persons under 75, although it may afflict as many as half of all people over 85. Recent research, particularly in the controversial area of stem cells, has created the hope that the treatment of Alzheimer's disease may one day be possible.

Social ageing

Social age consists of the norms, values and roles that are culturally associated with a particular chronological age. Ideas about social age differ from one society to another and, at least in modern industrial societies, change over time as well. Societies such as Japan and China have traditionally revered older people, regarding them as a source of historical memory and wisdom. Societies such as the UK and the USA are more likely to dismiss them as non-productive, dependent people who are out of step with the times – both because they are less likely to have the high-tech skills so valued by young people and because of their culture's obsession with youthfulness. Huge amounts are now being spent on prescription drugs, plastic surgery and home remedies that promise eternal youth. These

"We rarely watch television. Most of our free time is devoted to sex."

include such things as tummy-tucks and face-lifts, anti-baldness pills and lotions, and pills that claim to increase memory and concentration. In the USA, three weeks after it hit the market in 1998, the anti-impotence drug Viagra accounted for a staggering 94 per cent of all prescription drug sales (Hotz 1999).

Role expectations are extremely important sources of one's personal identity. Some of the roles associated with ageing are generally positive: lord and lady, senior advisor, doting grandparent, religious elder, wise spiritual teacher. Other roles may be damaging, leading to lowered self-esteem and isolation. Highly stigmatizing stereotypical roles for older people exist: think of phrases like 'grumpy old', 'silly old', 'boring old' and 'dirty old' man or woman (Kirkwood 2001). In fact, like all people, older people do not simply passively play out assigned social roles; they actively shape and redefine them (Riley et al. 1988). We discuss discrimination against older people below (pp. 317–20).

THINKING CRITICALLY

Are you concerned about ageing? List which elements of the ageing process are particularly worrying. Would you describe these elements as biological, psychological or social aspects of ageing? Sociologically, how would you explain the fact that many people in modern societies try so hard to delay the inevitable *biological* ageing process?

Growing old: competing sociological explanations

Social gerontologists have offered a number of theories regarding the nature of ageing. Some of the earliest theories emphasized individual adaptation to changing social roles as a person grows older. Later theories focused on how social structures shape the lives of older people and on the concept of the life-course. The most recent theories have been more multifaceted, focusing on the ways in which older people actively create their lives within specific institutional contexts.

First generation of theories: functionalism

The earliest theories of ageing reflected the functionalist approach that was dominant in sociology during the 1950s and '60s. They emphasized how individuals adjusted to changing social roles as they aged and how those roles were useful to society. The earliest theories often assumed that ageing brings with it physical and psychological decline and that changing social roles have to take this decline into account (Hendricks 1992).

The American sociologist Talcott Parsons, one of the most influential functionalist theorists of the 1950s, argued that society needs to find roles for older people consistent with advanced age. He expressed concern that the USA, in particular, with its emphasis on youth and its avoidance of the subject of death, had failed to provide roles that adequately drew on the potential wisdom and maturity of its older citizens. Moreover, given the greying of society that was evident even at that time, Parsons argued that this failure could well lead to older people becoming discouraged and alienated from society. In order to achieve a 'healthy maturity', Parsons (1960) argued, older people need to adjust psychologically to their changed circumstances, while society needs to redefine the social roles of older people. Traditional roles (such as work) have to be abandoned, and new forms of productive activity (such as volunteer service) need to be identified.

Parsons's ideas anticipated those of **disengagement theory**, the notion that it is functional for society to remove people from their traditional roles when they grow older, thereby freeing up space for others (Cumming and Henry 1961; Estes et al. 1992). According to this perspective, given the increasing frailty, illness and dependency of older people, it becomes all the more dysfunctional for them to occupy traditional social roles they are no longer capable of adequately fulfilling. Older people should therefore retire from their jobs, pull back from civic life and eventually withdraw from other activities as well. Disengagement is assumed to be functional for the larger society because it opens up roles that were formerly filled by older people to younger ones, who will presumably carry them out with fresh energy and new skills. Disengagement is also assumed to be functional for older people because it enables them to take on less taxing roles consistent with their advancing age and declining health. A number of studies of older adults do indeed report that the large majority feel good about retiring, which they claim has improved their morale and increased their happiness (Palmore 1985; Howard 1986).

While there is obviously some truth to disengagement theory, the idea that older people should completely disengage from the larger society takes for granted the prevailing stereotype that later life necessarily involves frailty and dependence. Critics of functionalist theories of ageing argue that they emphasize the need for older people to adapt to existing conditions, but they do not question whether or not the circumstances faced by older people are just. In reaction, another group of theorists arose – those growing out of the social conflict tradition (Hendricks 1992).

Second generation of theories: age stratification theory and life-course theory

From the mid-1970s, a new range of theories was introduced into gerontology (Estes et al. 2003). Two of the most important contributions were *age stratification theory* and the *life-course model*. Age stratification theory looks at the role and influence of social structures, such as retirement policy, on the process of individual ageing and on the wider stratification of older people in society. One important aspect of age stratification theory is the concept of *structural lag* (Riley et al. 1994). This provides an account of how structures do not keep pace with changes in the population and in individuals' lives. For example, in many European countries, when the retirement age was set at 65 soon after the Second World War, life expectancy and quality of life for older people was considerably lower than it is today.

Like the age stratification approach, the life-course perspective also moved beyond looking at ageing in terms of individual adjustment. This perspective views ageing as one phase of a lifetime shaped by the historical, social, economic and environmental factors that occurred at earlier ages in the life-course. Thus the life-course model views ageing as a process that continues from birth to death. In this, it contrasts with earlier theories that focus solely on the elderly as a distinctive group. The theory bridges micro- and macrosociology in examining the relationships between psychological states, social structures and social processes (Elder 1974).

Third generation of theories: political economy theory

One of the most important strands in the study of ageing in recent years has been the *political economy perspective* pioneered by Carroll Estes. Political economy theory provides an account of the role of the state and capitalism as contributing to systems of domination and marginalization of older people.

Political economy theory focuses on the role of economic and political systems in shaping and reproducing the prevailing power arrangements and inequalities in society. Social policy – in income, health or social security, for example – is understood as the result of social struggles, conflicts and the dominant power relations of the time. Policy affecting older people reflects the stratification of society by gender, race and class. As such, the phenomena of ageing and old age are directly related to the larger society in which they are situated and cannot be considered in isolation from the other social forces (Estes and Minkler 1991; Estes et al. 2003).

Aspects of ageing

Although ageing is a process which presents new possibilities, it is also accompanied by a set of unfamiliar challenges. As people age, they face a combination of physical, emotional and material problems that can be difficult to negotiate. One challenge that marks a significant transition is retirement. For most people, work does not just pay the bills; it also contributes to their sense of personal identity. In this case, retirement does not only lead to a loss of income; it can also lead to a loss of status to which many people find it difficult to adjust. Another significant transition that many older people face is the loss of a spouse. Widowhood can represent the loss of a partner of

40 or 50 years, and someone who has been the main source of companionship and support.

The older population reflects the diversity within societies. Older people are rich, poor and in between; they belong to all ethnic groups; they live alone and in families of various sorts; they vary in their political values and preferences; and they are gay and lesbian as well as heterosexual. Furthermore, like other people, they are diverse with respect to health. These differences can influence the ability of older people to maintain their autonomy and overall well-being.

As well as the diversity of the older population noted above, 'later life' now covers a wide and increasing age span. A distinction is often drawn between the third and fourth ages of life in modern societies. The third age covers the years from 50 to 74, when people are able to lead active independent

lives, increasingly free from day-to-day parenting responsibilities and the labour market. Many in this group have the time and money to fund an expanding consumer market and culture. The success of Saga in the UK, a company that aimed its tours and other products solely at the over-50s market, is evidence of the increasing power of the 'grey pound'. In contrast, the fourth age refers to the years of life when people's independence and ability to care fully for themselves is more seriously challenged.

In this section, we look at the effects of inequality, gender and ethnicity on the experience of ageing.

Inequality and older people

Overall, older people in developed societies tend to be more materially disadvantaged than other segments of the population (figure 8.4). However, older people's

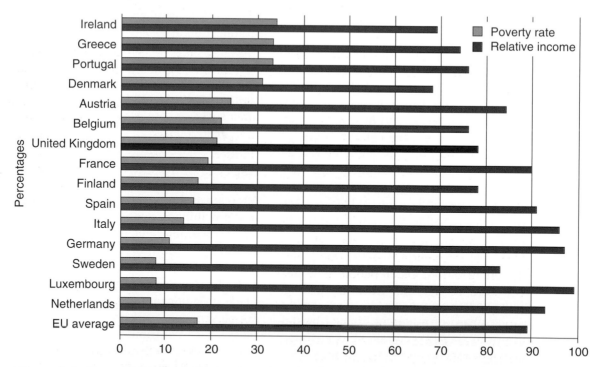

Figure 8.4 Poverty rate[a] and relative income[b] of people aged 65+: EU comparison, 1998
[a] *Percentage with income below 60 per cent of the median equivalized income of the national population*
[b] *Median equivalized income of those aged 65 and over as a percentage of the population aged 0 to 64*
Source: HMSO Social Trends 34 (2004), p. 7

For some, old age is a time of acute poverty, ill health, depression and loneliness.

subjective feelings about their standard of living are not solely based on material factors, but draw on other reference groups to which they compare themselves. Comparisons are possible with their memories of earlier life. In this, they are likely to compare themselves positively with the past in material terms (although not necessarily in moral or social ones). However, they are also likely to compare themselves with the standard of living that they enjoyed before retirement, which is likely to be materially better than their current position. Older people may also compare themselves with the average living conditions of society as a whole or of other retirees. Thus there is no common subjective experience of inequality amongst older people (Vincent 1999).

The inequalities of class, race and gender are often exacerbated when a person stops paid work, so the added inequality of later life means that older women, minorities and manual workers are poorer than peer equivalents in middle age. Retirement can result in a loss of income that may cause a significant drop in an older person's standard of living. The ability to build up a private occupational or personal pension during working life is one of the key determinants of income inequality between pensioners. Consequently, it is older men who were previously employed as professionals or managers who tend to have the highest gross weekly income in later life.

 We look at poverty amongst older people in more detail in chapter 12, 'Poverty, Social Exclusion and Welfare'.

The feminization of later life

Across all the world's societies, women tend to live longer than men.

 A more detailed exploration of such inequalities can be found in chapter 13, 'Global Inequality'.

Because of this, widowhood is the norm for older women. In the UK for example, almost half of women over the age of 65, and four-fifths of women aged 85 and over, are widowed. By contrast, more than three-quarters of men aged between 65 and 69 are married, falling to 60 per cent by their early 80s (HMSO 2004). This numerical predominance of women has been described as the 'feminization of later life' in European countries (see figure 8.5).

Although there were a disproportionate number of women in the older age group in Europe throughout the latter half of the twentieth century, the proportion of women to men has fluctuated and is now declining somewhat. In many European countries, there are currently more than three times as many women as men over the age of 85, but this figure is predicted to fall to just twice as many by 2021. One reason for the change in the proportion of women to men is because so many young men died during the First World War in 1914–18. The women of this generation began to reach retirement age in 1961, which began a sharp rise in the sex ratio imbalance amongst older people. A second reason for the declining imbalance between older men and women is the more rapid fall in male, rather than female, mortality over the age of 65 during the second half of the twentieth century. Figure 8.6 shows how the sex ratio among older people in the UK has fluctuated from 1951 to the predicted ratio in 2031.

'Feminization' is not without its problems, however. Older women are more likely than their male contemporaries to be poor.

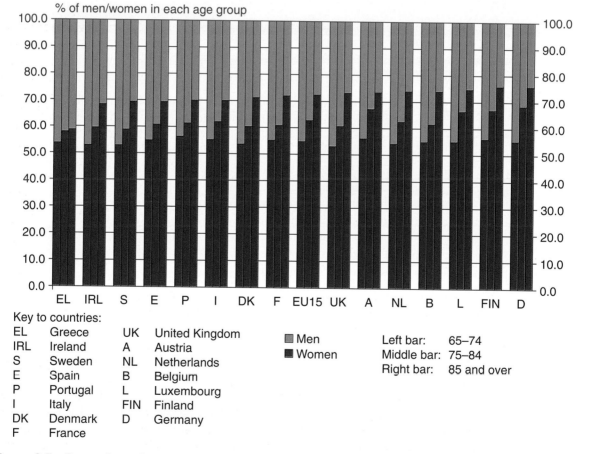

Figure 8.5 Proportions of men and women aged 65+ by age group, 2000

Source: Winqvist, K. (2002) *Women and Men Beyond Retirement*, Statistics in focus: population and social conditions, No 21 (Luxemburg: Eurostat)

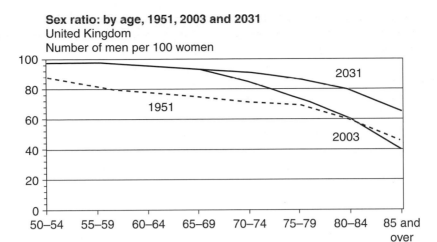

Sex ratio: by age, 1951, 2003 and 2031
United Kingdom
Number of men per 100 women

Figure 8.6   Sex ratios amongst older people

Source: Office for National Statistics, 2005

The ability to build private pension entitlements is one of the main causes of inequalities in wealth between older people. In most countries, women are far less likely to have the same pension entitlements as men because of the gender gap in pay and also the loss of lifetime earnings associated with having children. In 2004, only 43 per cent of older women in the UK had any income from private pensions (including widows' pensions based on their late husbands' private pensions), compared to 71 per cent of men (HMSO 2004).

Studies reveal that, as well as having lower personal incomes than men, older women also suffer inequalities in other resources, such as car-ownership. Only 42 per cent of UK women aged between the ages of 75 and 84 have a car, compared to 66 per cent of men. The discrepancy in car-ownership may not seem a major concern, but it can significantly restrict women's overall mobility and their access to healthcare, shopping and contact with others.

Finally, with increasing age, women suffer more than men from disability. This means that they require more assistance and support simply to carry out everyday tasks and personal care routines, such as bathing

and getting in and out of bed. But the living situations of older men and women also have a gender dimension. As one study of a selection of European countries by Delbès et al. (2006) found, it seems that women grow old alone, but men grow old with a partner (see figure 8.7). Older women were also twice as likely as men to live in an institution, and the authors suggest that perhaps men find it more difficult to deal with their partners' health problems than do women. There are also some differences between Northern and Southern Europe. For instance, 56 per cent of Finnish women and 59 per cent of German women live alone after the age of 75, compared to just 30 per cent of Portuguese women.

There are some cultural and policy differences that may explain such findings. South European countries tend to see 'multigenerational co-residence' as the preferred option for keeping older relatives at home, whereas North European states tend to have better-developed welfare services, which perform some of the same functions, but can lead to individuals being able to live alone. It is clear, then, that there are specific gendered patterns of care amongst the older population.

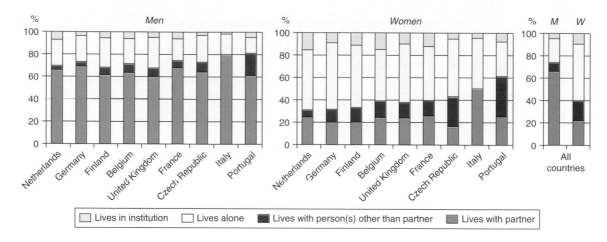

Figure 8.7 Living arrangements of people aged 75+ in nine European countries, 2000, by gender

Source: Delbès, C., Gaymu, J. and Springer, S. (2006) 'Women Grow Old Alone, but Men Grow Old with a Partner. A European Overview', Population & Societies, 419 (January).

Age and ethnicity

The income of older people from ethnic minorities also tends to be lower than that of their white counterparts, and reliance on means-tested benefits is greater (Berthoud 1998). Older people from ethnic minorities groups are also disadvantaged in other measures of wealth, such as car-ownership and housing tenure (although certain groups, such as Indian and Chinese groups, have rates of home-ownership comparable to that of white populations). For example, in general, Pakistanis and Bangladeshis in the UK have high rates of poverty compared to other groups, and this pattern is continued into later life.

Ginn and Arber (2000) examined ethnic and gender differences in the income of individuals amongst the older population in the UK. They found that older Asian women tend to be particularly disadvantaged. Retired ethnic minorities are often unable to supplement their state pension with an occupational or private one. Table 8.1 illustrates this issue: almost three-quarters of the white population are in receipt of an occupational pension compared to fewer than half of the Asian/

Asian British and black/black British populations. The lack of a private pension reflects shorter employment records in Britain for the largely migrant older ethnic population, discrimination in the labour market, the limited availability and type of jobs found in the areas where minorities have settled and sometimes a lack of fluency in English. For older women in some specific minority groups, economic disadvantage may also result from cultural norms acting as a barrier to employment earlier in life. Such patterns of structured disadvantage can be found amongst many other ethnic minority populations in Europe and internationally.

The politics of ageing

'The global ageing crisis'?

As we saw earlier in the chapter, the proportion of the European population over the age of 65 is almost 20 per cent, and will continue to grow. This significant shift in age distribution within the population presents specific challenges for all industrialized countries. One way of understanding why, is by thinking about the **dependency ratio** – the rela-

Table 8.1 **Components of mean gross income of UK pensioner units and the proportion in receipt of income, by ethnic minority group, 2003–6**

Ethnic Minority groups	All	White	Asian/Asian British	Black/Black British
Gross income *of which*	343	346	256	261
Benefit income	154	154	140	149
State Pension	113	114	78	96
Income related benefits	19	19	39	34
Disability benefits	13	13	11	10
Occupational pension	88	89	42	43
Personal pension income	10	10	7	5
Investment income	31	32	21	8
Earnings	56	57	43	53
Other income	3	3	3	3
Proportion of pensioners in receipt of:				
Benefit income	99%	99%	97%	98%
State Pension	97%	97%	80%	92%
Income related benefits	31%	31%	46%	46%
Disability benefits	23%	23%	21%	19%
Occupational pension	72%	73%	45%	42%
Personal pension income	60%	61%	31%	44%
Investment income	11%	12%	4%	5%
Earnings	14%	15%	10%	18%

Notes:
(1) Data based on the average of three years of results from 2003/4, 2005/6 FRS data and uprated to 2005/6 prices

Source: UK Department for Work and Pensions 2007

tionship between the number of *children* and *retired people* (considered 'dependent') on the one hand, and the number of *people of working age* on the other (see figure 8.8 for the UK). Such trends have several causes. Modern agriculture, improved sanitation systems, better epidemic control and medicines have all contributed to a decline in mortality throughout the world. In most societies today, especially in the developed world, fewer children die in infancy and more adults survive to later life. As the proportion of older people continues to grow, the demands on social services and health systems will increase as well. The growth in life expectancy means that pensions will need to be paid for more years than they are at present.

However, the working population funds the programmes that support the older population. As the old-age dependency ratio grows, some argue that increasing strain will be placed on available resources. In the light of demographic projections, governments, interest groups and policy-makers are being forced to look ahead and to develop proposals for meeting the needs of a changing population. Some pension associations are now warning that the current pension payment scheme is not sustainable indefinitely. They have called for an increase in the minimum pension age for both women (now

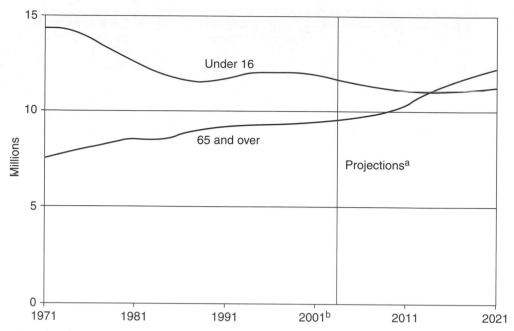

a *2001-based projections.*
b *Population estimates for 2001 and 2002 include provisional results from the Manchester matching exercise.*

Figure 8.8   Dependent population by age, UK, 1971–2021

Source: HMSO Social Trends 34 (2004), p.17

60, rising to 65) and men (now 65) to 70, in order to compensate for increased longevity.

Some critics argue that all this 'dependency talk' is unnecessarily alarmist and is just not an accurate depiction of the implications of contemporary demographic change. It also risks constructing negative interpretations of older people that stigmatize and stereotype them. In a study of the American pension system, *Social Security: The Phony Crisis* (1999), Dean Baker and Mark Weisbrot showed that even on highly conservative assumptions about economic growth, the forecast insolvency of the social security system in the USA within 30 years is highly unlikely to happen. They argue that much of the pressure to privatize the system has come from Wall Street. This is because, if a state-paid system of social security were to be replaced with individual private pensions, America's financial-services

industry would stand to gain 130 million new investment accounts.

In *The Imaginary Time Bomb* (2002), British sociologist Phil Mullan has argued that those who believe the ageing population is a ticking time bomb about to bring about a series of devastating social problems are falling for a series of myths that he seeks to defuse. For example, on healthcare, Mullan argues that it is a myth that an ageing population will mean an exponential rise in ill health and dependency. He responds that ageing is not an illness, and most elderly people are neither ill nor disabled. One of the reasons that people are living longer is the improvement in living conditions over the past century, and he argues that, if this improvement continues, elderly people will be fitter and healthier than their predecessors. Categorizing older people as a 'dependent population' alongside children constructs this social group as a problem for society at large. However, it can be argued that a new affluence has spread across society and across the life-course and although not all older people are uniformly fit and financially secure, later life has changed very much for the better for many people looking forward to retirement (Gilleard and Higgs 2005).

Many of the concepts that have conventionally been applied to the position of people in later life – for example, that they are socially disengaged or dependent upon the state – nowadays seem insufficient. For example, the generation of adults now reaching retirement age grew up in the post-war years of the 1950s and 1960s, when youth culture became dominated by 'conspicuous consumption' of fashion, music and so on. As older people, maintaining the habits they picked up as younger people, they continue to be important consumers, and enjoy an independent lifestyle.

Arber and Ginn (2004) argue that the idea of dependency itself now needs reconsidering. First, the age ranges used to define dependency (under 16 and over 64) no longer reflect the actual patterns of employment in this country. Fewer young people now enter the labour market full time at the age of 16, tending instead to stay in formal education for longer, and most workers leave the labour market some years before the age of 65. At the same time, more women than ever before are in paid employment, off-setting the shorter duration of employment amongst men.

Second, activity that benefits the economy is not confined to active participation in the labour market. Evidence from the UK shows that, rather than being a burden, older people make many productive economic and social contributions. Older people are often involved in providing unpaid and informal care to less able partners, drastically reducing the cost to the state of provision of health and personal care. They are also a major source of care provision for grandchildren, allowing daughters and

"Hello, we're new age pensioners"

daughters-in-law to enter the labour market. Older people are also active in voluntary organizations. Arber and Ginn suggest that older people may also be an important source of financial support for their grown-up children – for example, providing them with loans, educational fees, gifts and help for housing. Many studies have also found that older parents continue to provide emotional support for their adult children, particularly during times of difficulty, such as divorce.

THINKING CRITICALLY

List some of the financial implications brought about by the 'greying' of the world's population. How could national governments and international bodies deal with these implications and the pressure on pension provision, social welfare and health services? Should older people be required to work longer and retire later?

Ageism

Activist groups have started to fight against ageism – discrimination against people on the basis of their age – seeking to encourage

Global Society 8.1 **China's ageing population**

Every day at 8 a.m., home help Wei Qing arrives at pensioner Ge Qigong's one-roomed apartment and sets about cleaning the cramped but tidy space. Mr Ge is not wealthy. Wei Qing's first job is to unlock the bathroom, which is shared by nine families.

'We're just like friends', she said. 'I've been looking after him for a year, when I'm done with my chores we sit down and have a chat.'

Her wages are paid by the Shanghai government. Mr Ge said he would not be able to afford to pay on his own.

'I didn't get any pension from the pen company I used to work for', he said. 'I have to rely on the government, they give us RMB 460 (£30) a month and they take care of our medical bills.'

This level of care – his rent is also paid – is not uncommon in Shanghai. Although China is still a developing country, the city is proud of the way it looks after its many pensioners.

But future generations of pensioners may not be so lucky. Around 7.5 per cent of the Chinese population is over 65, but in the next quarter century that number will increase to 30 per cent. It will be one of the greatest demographic changes in history.

'The pressure on the working age population will be much bigger than before', said Professor Peng Xizhe, a population expert, at Shanghai's Fudan University.

'Ageing is mainly caused by China's population control programmes in the past. At the beginning stage of the one-child policy . . . no one really realized that ageing would be such a serious population or social problem', he added.

The drop in fertility caused by the so-called one-child policy is beginning to feed through into the working population. This generation of Chinese pensioners are supported by at least six workers paying taxes. In 30 years' time there will only be three workers for every Chinese pensioner.

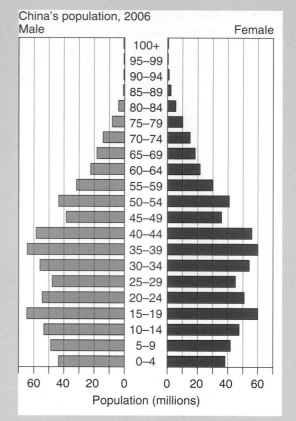

Figure 8.9 China's population, 2006

Source: US Census Bureau

And, as China develops, people are living longer. The average life expectancy for a woman born in Shanghai is now 82 years old, equivalent to many developed countries.

With a population that is living longer and a workforce that is getting smaller, the pressure is on China to get rich before it gets old.

Source: Adapted from BBC News, 16 October 2006

a positive view of later life and older people. Ageism is an ideology just as sexism and racism are. There are as many false stereotypes of older people as there are in other areas. For instance, it is often believed that older workers are less competent than younger ones, that most people over 65 are in hospitals or homes for the elderly, and that a high proportion are senile. All these beliefs are erroneous. The productivity and attendance records of workers over 60 are superior on average to those of younger age groups; 95 per cent of people over 65 live in private dwellings; and only about 7 per cent of those between 65 and 80 show pronounced symptoms of senile decay. In the UK, the government has put forward proposals to ban age discrimination, which could cover recruitment, training (including entry to higher education), promotion, pay, job-retention and – importantly – retirement.

In one study (Levin 1988), college students were shown a photograph of the same man at ages 25, 52 and 73, and were asked to rate him in terms of a variety of personality characteristics. The ratings were significantly more negative for the man depicted at the age of 73. When he looked old in his photograph, the students were more likely to perceive him negatively, even though they knew absolutely nothing about him. The mere fact that he was older was sufficient to trigger a negative cultural stereotype. Widely shared cultural stereotypes of 'grumpy old men' can lead to private opinions that are hurtful to older people.

The sociologist Bill Bytheway has provided a theoretical account of ageism that draws on social constructionism (an approach introduced in chapter 7, 'Social Interaction and Everyday Life'). Bytheway (1995) begins by questioning the reality of the terms 'old age' and 'elderly'. He argues that we presume that these terms have some kind of universal reality that they do not in fact have. He demonstrates by asking what we mean by the term 'old age': 'Is it a condition, a period of life, a state of mind, or what?' Is there any scientific evidence that something exists that can be called old age? If it exists, how do people enter it and become elderly? To Bytheway, the categories we use to describe ageing – such as 'the elderly' and 'the old' – are themselves ageist. They are socially constructed in order to legitimize the separation and management of people on the basis of their chronological age by dominant groups with something to gain from the inequalities associated with ageism.

Countries vary widely in what they are doing to cope with their growing numbers

Older people often provide much-needed help to their communities, for example by looking after grandchildren.
....

of older people. As we have seen already, the UK relies primarily on the state pension and the National Health Service to provide a safety net to serve the financial and health needs of older people. Other industrial nations provide a much broader array of services. In Japan, for example, men and women remain active well into later life because the Japanese culture encourages this activity and because business policies often support post-retirement work with the same company the person worked for before retirement. A number of national laws in Japan support the employment and training of older workers, and private businesses also support retraining.

The combination of greying and globalization will shape the lives of older people throughout the world well into this century. Traditional patterns of family care will be challenged, as family-based economies continue to give way to labour on the farms and in the offices and factories of global businesses (family patterns are already changing in the West, as we see in the discussion of 'the beanpole family' in chapter 9). Like the industrial nations early in the twentieth century, all societies will be challenged to find roles for their ageing citizens. This challenge will include identifying new means of economic support, often financed by government programmes. It will also entail identifying ways to incorporate rather than isolate older people, by drawing on their considerable reserves of experience and talents.

Death, dying and bereavement

The sociology of death and dying

Sociologists have only recently become interested in the universal human experiences of dying, death and bereavement. One reason why the study of death and dying has not been more central to sociology, is that death marks the *end* of an individual's participation in the social world and therefore seems to lie outside sociology's main concerns. Societies continue to develop even though individuals die, and social development, rather than individual deaths, has been the focus of sociology. Another reason is that within modern societies themselves, death and dying have long been 'taboo subjects', not a topic for polite conversation. One early research study was Glaser and Strauss's *Awareness of Dying* (1965), which looked at the experience of death and dying in a US hospital's cancer ward, but this was an exception rather than the norm.

Since the 1990s, the neglect of death and dying has been rectified by the devel-opment of a new research field – the sociology of death, dying and bereavement (Clark 1993). One of the founders of this field is British sociologist Tony Walter, whose work has focused on the ways in which societies organize death, dying and mourning (1994, 1999). How do societies care for the hundreds of thousands of dying people? Practically, how do they deal with this number of dead bodies? What support is provided for the many more bereaved relatives? What beliefs are held about the prospects for the dead when their earthly lives are over? The answer to such questions turns out to be quite varied. Anthropologists have long studied cultural differences in death rituals in small-scale societies and within developing countries, but the modern sociology of death has been primarily focused on the developed world. Even here there are cultural differences in the social organization of death. Nonetheless, sociologists have been struck by some key, *shared* features of modern industrial societies in relation to their handling of death.

Theorizing death in modern societies

One main feature of modern societies is that, until quite recently, death has tended to be hidden 'behind the scenes' of social life. In previous times and in many non-industrialized societies today, a majority of people experience the final process of dying while at home, with family and friends in close attendance. But in most modern societies today, death typically occurs in hospitals and nursing homes – relatively impersonal settings that are distanced from the mainstream of social life. On death, bodies are then moved to different parts of the buildings, thereby maintaining a physical distance between living patients, their families and the dead (Ariès 1965).

In *The Loneliness of the Dying* (1985), Norbert Elias connects this modern hiding away of death and dying to the increasing life expectancy we looked at earlier in this chapter. He argues:

> The attitude to dying and the image of death in our societies cannot be completely understood without reference to this relative security and predictability of individual life and the correspondingly increased life expectancy. Life grows longer, death is further postponed. The sight of dying and dead people is no longer commonplace. It is easier in the normal course of life to forget death. (1985: 8)

However, Elias sees that the modern way of death and dying presents emotional problems for people reaching this stage of their lives. Although hospitals provide the best available nursing care and scientific medicine and use new medical technologies, the patient's contact with family members and friends is usually seen as inconveniencing treatment and care regimes, and is therefore restricted to short, specific times of the day. But this rational management of the patient's treatment may well deny people the essential emotional comfort of being close to their loved ones, which they actually need most in the final period of life. In modern societies, dying can be a very lonely process indeed.

Zygmunt Bauman (1992) offers another perspective on the distancing of modern people from death and dying. He argues that modern societies deny and defer death long into the future, by turning the ultimate and inevitable ending of life into a multitude of smaller, 'non-ultimate' and potentially resolvable 'health hazards' and illnesses. Mortality is therefore effectively 'deconstructed', which brings the endless defensive battles against ageing and death right into the centre of daily life. People become used to treating, curing and managing their chronic illnesses, for example. In particular, modern societies place a high value on youthfulness, and the quest to remain 'young' – both physically and emotionally (staying 'young at heart') – takes up a large part of many people's lives. As we noted above, there are now huge markets for anti-ageing treatments, vitamin supplements, cosmetic surgery and fitness equipment, as the demand for youthfulness increases. Bauman describes such actions as part of a 'life strategy', though of course, people may not always acknowledge that their attempts to stay young and fit are ultimately futile defensive actions to avoid acknowledging their own mortality.

THINKING CRITICALLY

Are you concerned about ageing? List which elements of the ageing process are particularly worrying? Would you describe these elements as biological, psychological or social aspects of ageing? Sociologically, how would you explain the fact that many people in modern societies try so hard to delay the inevitable *biological* ageing process?

Recent developments

Since the mid-1990s, sociologists have noted some significant changes in the way that death, dying and bereavement are dealt with in modern societies. First, the hospice movement, which started in the 1960s, aims to offer an alternative to the impersonality of hospitals for terminally ill people. The first modern hospice was founded in London in 1967 by Dame Cicely Saunders and many hospices in the UK and USA have a Christian basis. The UK has some 231 hospice (29 for children), which are based on the principle that death and dying are a natural part of life and that the quality of life for dying people should be as positive as possible. Hospices encourage family and friends to continue to play a part in the patient's life, even in the final stages. Saunders actually believed that the pain

8.3 An ageless future?

In *Stories of Ageing* (2000), Mike Hepworth uses literature to encourage his readers to 'explore fiction as an imaginative resource for understanding variations in the meaning of the experience of ageing in society'. In the section below, Hepworth discusses how science and technology could radically alter how we understand ageing:

For centuries in Western culture ageing has been imagined as a condition of existence from which human beings can only be rescued by supernatural forces. True, there has always been the quest to prolong active life, but until very recently the search has been a dream rather than a reality. And when people have experienced eternal life it has more often than not been a curse rather than a blessing, as in the legend of *The Wandering Jew* and *The Flying Dutchman*. [In literature, sometimes] supernatural forces do intervene in the apparently natural order of things to arrest the normal processes of physical ageing, as happens in the case of Faust (Fielder 1946), who makes a pact with the Devil and sells his own soul, and in Oscar Wilde's novel about moral corruption *The Picture of Dorian Gray*. Dorian Gray is an aesthete with wondrous good looks whose face and body remain mysteriously unmarked by his excessive indulgence in immoral practices; all external signs of his debauchery (in this story a form of premature ageing) are mysteriously transferred to his portrait. When he finally attacks the painting with a knife in an attempt to destroy the evidence of his past he succeeds only in destroying himself, so close has the affinity between the portrait and himself become. On his death the portrait reverts back to the original image of youth – 'all the wonder of his exquisite youth and beauty' (Wilde 1960: 167) – leaving the dead body unrecognisably that of an old man, 'withered, wrinkled, and loathsome of visage' (ibid.).

Outside the realms of legend and the romantic imagination there was until very recently only one future of ageing in Western culture if one was lucky to live long enough to grow old: the Christian vision of the inevitable

In 2007, South African paralympian, Oscar Pistorius, was allowed to run against able-bodied athletes while sporting authorities debated whether his carbon-fibre prosthetics gave him an unfair advantage. In January 2008, it was decided that they did and he was not allowed to take part in the 2008 Beijing Olympic Games. The idea of the 'cyborg' – part human, part technology – may not be as fanciful as it sounds.

decline of the human body, death and an afterlife of either Heaven or Hell. The dualistic separation of the body from the soul in Christian thought regards the ageing of the body in the temporal world as a brief testing ground for eternal spiritual life beyond the veil. The corruption of the flesh frees the soul or essential self for an other-worldly existence out of time. Heaven is the compensation for graceful or virtuous ageing and not looking for pacts with the Devil to prolong a youthfully active life.

But times are rapidly changing and the emergence of modern scientific medicine and technology has offered an alternative promise to release from the ageing body in this world rather than the next (Katz 1996). One of the interesting features of this development is that contemporary models of an ageless future have become predominantly biological rather than essentially spiritual (Cole 1992). The prevailing belief now is that it is the science of the biological body, and not the religion of the eternal immaterial soul, which will arrest the process of ageing and extend the period of youthful life. The prominent social gerontologist Jabber F. Gubrium (1986) has commented on our reluctance in contemporary society to accept the 'normality' of a biologically limited life span. The widespread faith in the limitless potential of science to solve human problems encourages us to turn expectantly to medical science to transform ageing from the natural termination of the life-course into a disease, which is potentially curable. In this optimistic vision of the future of ageing the biological risks associated with later life will be curable and the human life span extended well beyond the biblical three score years and ten. One of these days ageing will disappear from the human agenda when cures for the illnesses associated with growing older have been found and ailing and malfunctioning body parts can be replaced.

One way of defeating the ageing process is for humans to become cyborgs or to assume the 'post-human' bodies of partly biological and partly technological beings (Featherstone and Renwick 1995). [Unlike Drew Leder's idea of the 'dys-appearing body' (1990), which makes its presence felt as pain, disease and dysfunction], this vision of the future is one where the dys-appearing body literally disappears. Any part of the internal body which causes distress in later life will be removed and replaced with a genetically engineered or transplanted substitute. The story of the ageing body will thus become not a story of how individuals cope or come to terms with its limitations but science fiction come true. The body will be a machine and the meaning of ageing may cease to be a matter of concern.

Source: Hepworth 2000: 124–5

relief regimes within hospices made euthanasia unnecessary. The growth of more personalized forms of care for terminally ill people may make the modern experience of dying much less impersonal than Elias had thought.

Second, there seem to be some emerging ways of dealing with death and bereavement that are much more informal than those in the past. Some sociologists have described these as 'postmodern' developments (see chapter 3 for a discussion of postmodern social theory) in which more individualistic and therefore, diverse approaches to dealing with death, are emerging (Bauman 1992; Walter 1994). For example, it is becoming more common for people to personalize their own or their relatives' funerals: playing pop music, giving their own speeches and insisting on colourful clothing rather than relying on the traditional rituals of the churches. It is also becoming more commonplace for relatives to mark road-accident deaths with flowers at the scene of a crash as an individual way of remembering the dead, rather than, or in addition to, the ritual of attending a cemetery to tend the grave. Since the 1980s, in many of the developed societies, people have embarked on a quest for new rituals in dying and mourning to replace the older, more formal, religious ones (Wouters 2002). This development may represent an attempt by people to find new public rituals which match their own individual and personal needs, and may signal the movement of death and dying out of its previously hidden location within society.

Summary points

1. Socialization is the process whereby the helpless infant gradually becomes a self-aware, knowledgeable human being, skilled in the ways of the given culture and environment.

2. According to G. H. Mead, the child achieves an understanding of being a separate agent by seeing how others behave towards him or her in social contexts. At a later stage, playing organized games and learning the rules of play, the child comes to understand 'the generalized other' – general values and cultural rules.

3. Jean Piaget distinguishes several stages in the development of the child's capability to make sense of the world. Each stage involves the acquisition of new cognitive skills and depends on the successful completion of the preceding one. According to Piaget these stages of cognitive development are universal features of socialization.

4. Agencies of socialization are structured groups or contexts within which significant processes of socialization occur. In all cultures, the family is the principal socializing agency of the child during infancy. Other influences include peer groups, schools and the mass media. Socialization continues throughout the life-cycle.

5. Gender socialization begins virtually as soon as an infant is born. Even parents who believe they treat children equally tend to produce different responses to boys and girls. These differences are reinforced by many other cultural influences.

6. Biological, psychological and social ageing are not the same and may vary considerably within and across cultures. It is important not to confuse a person's social age with their chronological age. Physical ageing is inevitable, but for most people, proper nutrition, diet and exercise can preserve a high level of health well into later life.

7. Because of low mortality and fertility rates, Western societies are rapidly greying or ageing. The older population constitutes a large and rapidly growing category that is extremely diverse economically, socially and politically. However, it is now possible to divide a third and a fourth age representing the 'young-old' and the 'old-old'. The greying of the population has resulted in a greater 'dependency ratio'. This has led to new debates about the funding of services for older people.

8. Functionalist theories of ageing originally argued that the disengagement of older people from society was desirable. Disengagement theory held that older people should pull back from their traditional social roles as younger people move into them. Activity theory, on the other hand, soon came to emphasize the importance of being engaged and busy as a source of vitality. Conflict theorists of ageing have focused on how the routine operation of social institutions produces various forms of inequality among older people. The most recent theories regard older people as capable of taking control over their own lives and playing an active role in politics and the economy.

9. Older people are more likely to be materially disadvantaged than other groups. Older women are also more likely to suffer from poverty than their male counterparts, and older members of ethnic minorities are more likely to suffer poverty than older white people.

10. Death, dying and bereavement have now become part of life-course studies. Many developed societies have hidden death and dying behind the scenes of social life but some now appear to be undergoing an informalization of mourning as people seek new, less rigid, more individualized public rituals and personalized ways of dealing with death and dying.

Further reading

Two very good texts which follow from some of the key issues on ageing in this chapter are, Chris Gilleard and Paul Higgs's *Contexts of Ageing: Class, Cohort and Community* (Cambridge: Polity, 2005), which has a special focus on the 'third age'; and Bill Bytheway's *Ageism* (Buckingham: Open University Press, 1999), which is a very accessible account of discrimination against older people.

From there, you could explore ageing in a European context in John Bond, Sheila M. Peace, Freya Dittmann-Kohli and Gerben Westerhof's edited *Ageing in Society: European Perspectives on Gerontology*, 3rd edn (London: Sage Publications, 2007). Miriam Bernard and Thomas Scharf's edited *Critical Perspectives on Ageing Societies* (Ageing and the Life-course Series) (Bristol: Policy Press, 2007), explores current debates in this field.

Looking to the future, Phil Mullan's *The Imaginary Time Bomb: Why an Ageing Population is Not a Social Problem* (London: A. B. Tauris, 2000) makes a critical argument against the idea that the greying of societies is inevitably problematic. Then John A. Vincent, Chris Phillipson and Murna Downs's edited collection of 21 essays, *The Futures of Old Age* (London: Sage Publications, 2005) takes these issues further by looking ahead to both the possibilities and problems facing ageing societies.

A comprehensive and worthwhile – if very large (770 pages) – book, which can be approached for particular life-course subjects, is Malcolm Johnson's edited *The Cambridge Handbook of Age and Ageing* (Cambridge: Cambridge University Press, 2007).

Finally, anyone interested in reading more about the sociological issues surrounding death, dying and bereavement could try Glennys Howarth's *Death and Dying: A Sociological Introduction* (Cambridge: Polity, 2007) and/or Tony Walter's *The Revival of Death* (London: Routledge, 1994).

Internet links

The World Heath Organization on Ageing and the Life-course:
www.who.int/ageing/en/

HelpAge International – a good source of information on ageing across the world:
www.helpage.org/Home

The Centre for Policy on Ageing (UK):
www.cpa.org.uk/index.html

OECD – research on ageing, mainly in the developed world:
www.oecd.org/topic/0,2686,en_2649_37435_1_1_1_1_37457,00.html

The United Nations Programme on Ageing:
www.un.org/esa/socdev/ageing/

The Centre for Death and Society at the University of Bath, UK:
www.bath.ac.uk/cdas/

9
....

Families and Intimate Relationships

CHAPTER 9

Families and Intimate Relationships

Romantic love has not always been at the centre of intimate relationships.

Have you ever been in love? Almost certainly you have. Most people from their teens onwards know what being in love is like. Love and romance provide, for many of us, some of the most intense feelings we ever experience. But why do people fall in love? The answer at first sight seems obvious. Love expresses a mutual and physical attachment that two individuals feel for one another. These days, we might be sceptical of the idea that love is 'for ever', but falling in love, we tend to think, is an experience arising from universal human emotions. It seems natural for a couple who fall in love also to want personal and sexual fulfilment in their relationship, perhaps by marrying and/or starting a family.

Yet this situation, which may just appear 'natural' to most of us today, is in fact very unusual. Beginning a long-term partnership, or starting a family, with someone with whom you have fallen in love is not an experience that most people across the world have. In early modern Europe, royal and aristocratic marriages were very often arranged primarily on political grounds, or for reasons of enhancing or maintaining family status. And although 'arranged marriages' across the world are now less common than once they were, amongst certain South Asian communities, they remain the norm. In all these cases, falling in love is rarely thought of as having any connection to marriage or starting a family. The idea of basing a long-term partnership on romantic love did not become widespread in European societies until fairly recently, and has never existed at all in many other cultures where more material or pragmatic reasons take precedence.

Only in modern times have love and sexuality come to be seen as closely connected in the Western industrialized societies. John Boswell, a historian of medieval Europe, has remarked on the unusual nature of modern ideas about romantic love. In Europe during the Middle Ages, virtually no one married for love; there was even a medieval saying: 'To love one's wife with one's emotions is adultery.' In those days and for centuries afterwards, men and women married mainly in order to keep property in the hands of the family or to raise children for working on the family farm. Once married, they may have become close companions, but this happened after marriage rather than before. People sometimes had sexual affairs outside marriage, but these inspired few of the emotions we currently associate with love. Romantic love was regarded as at best a weakness and at worst a kind of sickness.

Modern attitudes today are almost completely the opposite. Boswell quite rightly speaks of the 'virtual obsession of modern industrial culture' with romantic love:

> Those immersed in this 'sea of love' tend to take it for granted. . . . Very few premodern or non-industrialized contemporary cultures would agree with the contention – uncontroversial in the West – that 'the purpose of a man is to love a woman, and the purpose of a woman is to love a man.' Most human beings in most times and places would find this a very meagre measure of human value!
> (Boswell 1995: xix)

It was only in the late eighteenth century that the concept of romantic love began to make its presence felt. Romantic love – as distinct from the near universal compulsions of passionate love – involved idealizing its object. The notion of romantic love more or less coincided with the emergence of the novel as a literary form and the spread of romantic novels played a vital part in spreading the idea (Radway 1984). For women in particular, romantic love involved telling stories about how the relationship could lead to personal fulfilment.

Romantic love, therefore, cannot be understood as a natural part of human life; rather, it has been shaped by broad social and historical influences. For most people in the industrialized world today, the couple – married or unmarried – is at the core of what the family is. The couple came to be at the centre of family life as the economic role of the family dwindled and love, or love and sexual attraction, became the basis of forming marriage ties. However, we will also see later in this chapter that the term 'family' should by no means only be understood as involving a heterosexual couple and their children.

Today, most people in the developed countries believe that a good relationship is based on emotional communication or intimacy. The idea of intimacy, like so many other familiar notions we have discussed in this book, is a recent one. Marriage was never in the past based on intimacy and emotional communication, and although this was important to a good marriage, it was not the foundation of it. For the modern couple, it is. Communication is the means of establishing a good relationship in the first place, and it is the chief rationale for its continuation. A good relationship is a relationship of equals, in which both parties have equal rights and obligations. In such a relationship, each person has respect, and wants the best, for the other. Talk, or dialogue, is the basis of making the relationship work. Relationships function best if people do not hide too much from each other: there has to be mutual trust. And trust has to be worked at; it cannot just be taken for granted. Finally, a good relationship is one free from arbitrary power, coercion or violence (Giddens 1993).

The theme of much of this book has been social change. We live in a turbulent, difficult and unfamiliar world today. Whether we like it or not, we all must come to terms with the mixture of opportunity and risk it presents. The discussion of romantic love shows that nowhere is this observation truer than in the domain of personal and emotional life.

How do we begin to understand the nature of these changes and their impact on our lives? It is only possible to understand what is going on with intimate relationships and with the family as a social institution today if we know something about how people lived in the past and how people currently live in societies across the world. So in this chapter, we look at the historical development of marriage and the family. We then examine families and intimate relationships in Europe, using Britain – the first industrializing society (see chapter 4) – as a reference point for our national comparisons. The final section of the chapter looks at some of the theoretical perspectives that attempt to explain the family and intimate relationships, before concluding by turning to the current debate on 'family values'.

Basic concepts

We need first of all to define some basic concepts, particularly those of **family**, kinship and marriage. A family is a group of persons directly linked by kin connections, the adult members of whom assume responsibility for caring for children. **Kinship** ties are connections between individuals, established either through marriage or through the lines of descent that connect blood relatives (mothers, fathers, siblings, offspring, etc.). **Marriage** can be defined as a socially acknowledged and approved sexual union between two adult individuals. When two people marry, they become kin to one another; the marriage bond also, however, connects together a wider range of kinspeople. Parents, brothers, sisters and other blood relatives become relatives of the partner through marriage.

Family relationships are always recognized within wider kinship groups. In virtually all societies we can identify what sociologists and anthropologists call the **nuclear family**, two adults living together with their own or adopted children in a **household**. Households are single individuals or groups of people who share a common housing unit, common living rooms and the essentials for living, such as food. In most traditional societies, the nuclear family was part of a larger kinship network of some type. When close relatives other than a married couple and children live either in the same household or in a close and continuous relationship with one another, we speak of an **extended family**. An extended family may include grandparents, brothers and their wives, sisters and their husbands, aunts and nephews.

In most Western societies, marriage, and therefore the family, are associated with **monogamy**. It is illegal for a man or woman to be married to more than one spouse at any one time. This is not the case everywhere, however. In a famous comparison of several hundred societies in the mid-twentieth century, George Peter Murdock (1949) found that **polygamy**, which allows a husband or wife to have more than one spouse, was permitted in more than 80 per cent of them. There are two types of polygamy: **polygyny**, in which a man may be married to more than one woman at the same time, and **polyandry**, much less common, in which a woman may have two or more husbands simultaneously. In 1998, the Ethnographic Atlas Codebook reported that of 1,231 societies worldwide, 453 had occasional polygyny, 588 had more regular polygyny and just 4 had polyandry – a total of 84 per cent, a similar proportion to that found by Murdock 50 years earlier. The majority of these polygamous societies were in parts of Africa and South Asia. The best-known group to practise polygamy in the West are the Fundamentalist Mormons, based largely in Utah, in the United States, where although the practice is illegal, prosecutions are rare. The practice of having many wives was abandoned by mainstream Mormons a century ago as a condition of Utah becoming part of the United States. It is estimated that 30,000 fundamentalists still practise polygamy in Utah.

Many sociologists believe that we cannot speak about 'the family' as if there is just one model of family life that is more or less universal. There are many different family forms: two-parent families, step-families, lone-parent families and so on. The sociologist Diana Gittins (1993) has argued that it seems more appropriate to speak of 'families' rather than 'the family'. Referring to 'families' emphasizes the diversity of family forms. While as a shorthand term we may often speak of 'the family', it is vital to remember what a variety this covers.

The family in historical context

Sociologists once thought that, prior to the modern period, the predominant form of family in Western Europe was of the extended type. Research has shown this view to be mistaken. The nuclear family, consisting of a father, mother and dependent children, seems long to have been pre-eminent. Pre-modern household size was larger than it is today, but the difference is not especially great. In England, for example, throughout the seventeenth, eighteenth and nineteenth centuries, the average household size was 4.75 persons (though

An unusual family photograph showing Utah polygamist Tom Green with his five wives and some of his 29 children.

this included domestic servants). Today the average household size in the UK is around 2.4 people (HMSO 2004), though this masks some large differences across ethnic groups. For example, white British and black Caribbean households average 2.2 people, while Bangladeshi and Pakistani households average 4.4 and 4.1 persons respectively (HMSO 2007). The UK, Germany, France and the Netherlands lie at the lower end of the European spectrum of household size; Portugal, Spain, Malta and Slovakia are at the higher end, averaging around 3.0 persons per household (Eurostat 2007).

The development of family life

Children in pre-modern Europe were often working – helping their parents on the farm – from the age of 7 or 8. Those who did not remain in the family enterprise frequently left the parental household at an early age to do domestic work in the houses of others or to follow apprenticeships. Children who went away to work in other households would rarely see their parents again.

Other factors made family groups even more impermanent than they are now, in spite of the currently high rates of divorce. Rates of mortality (the number of deaths per 1,000 of the population in any one year) for people of all ages were much higher. A quarter or more of all infants in early modern Europe did not survive beyond the first year of life, in contrast to well under 1 per cent today, and women frequently died in childbirth. The death of children or of one or both spouses often shattered family relations.

The historian John Boswell (mentioned at the start of this chapter) has noted:

> In premodern Europe marriage usually began as a property arrangement, was in its middle mostly about raising children, and ended about love. Few couples in fact married 'for love', but many grew to love each other in time as they jointly managed their household, reared their offspring, and shared life's experiences. Nearly all surviving epitaphs to spouses evince

profound affection. By contrast, in most of the modern West, marriage begins about love, in its middle is still mostly about raising children (if there are children), and ends – often – about property, by which point love is absent or a distant memory. (1995: xxi)

The way we never were? Myths of the traditional family

Many people, generally writing from a conservative point of view, argue that family life is becoming dangerously undermined. They contrast what they see as the decline of the family with more traditional and stable forms of family life. But was the family of the past as peaceful and harmonious as many people recall it, or is this simply an idealized fiction? In *The Way We Never Were* (1992), Stephanie Coontz points out that, as with other visions of a previous golden age, the rosy light shed on the 'traditional family' dissolves when we look back to previous times to see what things really were like.

Many admire the apparent discipline and stability of the nineteenth-century Victorian family. However, because families at this time suffered especially high death rates, the average length of marriages was fewer than 12 years, and more than half of all children saw the death of at least one parent by the time they were 21. The admired discipline of the Victorian family was rooted in the strict authority of parents over their children. The way in which this authority was exercised would be considered exceedingly harsh by today's standards.

If we consider the Victorian family of the 1850s, the ideal family still eludes us. In this period, some middle-class wives were more or less confined to the home. According to Victorian morality, women were meant to be strictly virtuous, while men were sexually licentious: many visited prostitutes and paid regular visits to brothels. In fact, wives and husbands often had little to do with one another, communicating only through their children. Moreover, domesticity was not even an option for poorer social groups of

Classic Studies 9.1 | **Lawrence Stone on the family in Europe**

The research problem

Modern families seem very different from previous families. No one can be unaware that modern family life has undergone much change even within a single generation. But what were families like hundreds of years ago? Did people have the same attitudes to sex and marriage? What functions did families perform in earlier societies? In *The Family, Sex, and Marriage in England, 1500–1800* (1980), historical sociologist, Lawrence Stone, tried to answer these questions, charting some key changes leading from pre-modern to modern forms of family life in Europe. In doing so, he distinguished three phases in the development of the family from the 1500s to the 1800s.

Stone's explanation

In the early 1500s, the main English family form was a type of nuclear family. People lived in fairly small households but maintained relationships that were embedded within the community, including other kin. Families were not so clearly separated from the community as many are today. Stone argues that the family at that time was not a major focus of *emotional* attachment or dependence for its members. For example, people did not experience, or look for, the emotional closeness that we associate with family life today.

Sex within marriage was not regarded as a source of pleasure, but as a necessity to propagate children. Individual freedom of choice in marriage and other matters of family life were subordinated to the interests of parents, other kin or the community. Outside aristocratic circles, where it was sometimes actively encouraged, erotic or romantic love was regarded by moralists and theologians as a sickness. As Stone puts it, the family during this period 'was an open-ended, low-keyed, unemotional, authoritarian institution. . . . It was also very short-lived, being frequently dissolved by the death of the husband or wife or the death or very early departure from the home of the children' (1980: 17).

This type of family was succeeded by a 'transitional form' that lasted from the early seventeenth century to the beginning of the eighteenth. This later type was largely confined to the upper reaches of society, but it was very important because from it spread attitudes that have since become almost universal. The nuclear family became a more separate entity, distinct from ties to other kin and to the local community. There was a growing stress on the importance of marital and parental love, although there was also an increase in the authoritarian power of fathers.

In the third phase, the type of family we are most familiar with in the West today gradually evolved. This family is a group tied by close emotional bonds, enjoying a high degree of domestic privacy, preoccupied with the rearing of children. It is marked by the rise of **affective individualism** – the formation of marriage ties on the basis of personal selection, guided by sexual attraction or romantic love. Sexual aspects of love came to be glorified within marriage instead of in extramarital relationships. The family became geared to consumption rather than production, as a result of the increasing number of workplaces that were separate from the home. Women became associated with domesticity and men with being 'breadwinners'. In recent decades, the idea of a male breadwinner 'heading' the family is being increasingly challenged, as more women enter the workplace and family structures continue to diversify.

Critical points

Stone's three-phase history has been subjected to much critique. First, a series of medieval historians has shown, against his thesis, that love was quite often found in English marriages before the eighteenth century. Second, many have seen Stone's main arguments as rather unoriginal. For instance, describing the demise of extended kin groups and the consequent rise of individualism was a theme in the work of Max Weber and other early social scientists. Third, Stone's linkage of the lack of emotional closeness to harsh material conditions of life ignores many anthropological studies documenting very loving relationships within family groups in very poor communities (by modern standards). Stone's theory of emotional development then appears much weaker.

Contemporary significance

The critical reception of Stone's work has led to some significant revisions to his long story of English family history. However, social science research often develops through empirical criticism of bold theses such as Stone's, which point out where the theory's generalizations claim more than the evidence will support. No single piece of research in historical sociology will ever tell us the whole truth about a period covering as long as three centuries, but the contemporary value of Stone's work is twofold. First, it stimulated others to try and prove him wrong, to refute the thesis in some way and, in so doing, we gained more accurate knowledge of an earlier period of social life; second, Stone was not afraid to adopt a sociological imagination in his study of historical materials, looking for patterns in social development. This is an important aspect of sociological work, which can be traced all the way back to the discipline's founders.

---

this period. In factories and workshops, families worked long hours with little time for a home life. Child labour was also very common in these groups.

Our most recent memory draws us to the 1950s as the time of another possible 'ideal family'. This was a period when many women worked in the home, while men were perceived as responsible for earning the 'family wage'. Yet large numbers of women did not actually want to retreat to a purely domestic role, and felt miserable and trapped in it. Many women had held paid jobs during the Second World War as part of the war effort and they lost these jobs when men returned home. Men were still emotionally removed from their wives and often observed a strong sexual double standard, seeking sexual adventures for themselves but setting a strict code for their spouse.

The American author Betty Friedan (1921–2006) wrote a best-selling book, *The Feminine Mystique* (1963), about women's lives in the 1950s. Friedan struck a chord with many thousands of women within and outside the USA when she spoke of the 'problem with no name'. That is, the oppressive nature of a domestic life bound up with childcare, domestic drudgery and a husband who only occasionally put in an appearance and with whom little emotional communication was possible. Even more severe than an oppressive home life were the alcoholism and violence suffered within many families during a time when society was not fully prepared to confront these issues.

As sociologists, we must be careful not to let people's ideas of how society *ought* to be affect our reporting of the *evidence* of society's reality, however disturbing that might be.

> **THINKING CRITICALLY**
>
> If the traditional family, as described above, is 'a myth', why do so many people still believe in it? What social consequences might follow from people's belief in and commitment to this mythical family form?

Families in global context

There is a diversity of family forms today in different societies across the world. In some areas, such as more remote regions in Asia, Africa and the Pacific Rim, traditional family systems are little altered. In most developing countries, however, widespread changes are occurring. The origins of these changes are complex, but several factors can be picked out as especially important.

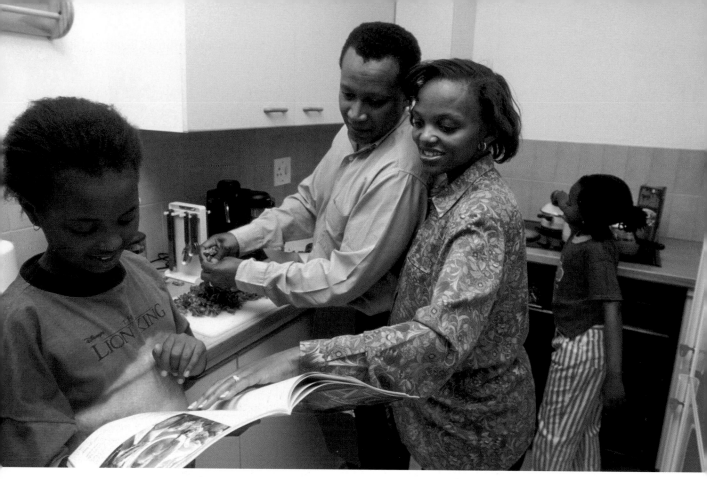

Was the nuclear family ever really the norm?

One is the spread of Western culture. Western ideals of romantic love, for example, have spread to societies in which they were previously unknown. Another factor is the development of centralized government in areas previously composed of autonomous smaller societies. People's lives become influenced by their involvement in a national political system; moreover, governments make active attempts to alter traditional ways of behaviour. Because of the problem of rapidly expanding population growth, for example in China, states frequently introduce programmes that advocate smaller families, the use of contraception, and so forth. A further influence is the large-scale migration from rural to urban areas. Often men go to work in towns or cities, leaving family members in the home village. Alternatively, a nuclear family group will move as a unit to the city. In both cases, traditional family forms and

kinship systems may become weakened. Finally, and perhaps most important, employment opportunities away from the land and in such organizations as government bureaucracies, mines, plantations and – where they exist – industrial firms tend to have disruptive consequences for family systems previously centred on landed production in the local community.

In general, these changes can be seen as creating a worldwide movement towards the breaking down of extended family systems and household kinship groups, though relations between kinspeople continue to be important sources of social bonds. William J. Goode first documented the decline of extended families in his book *World Revolution in Family Patterns* (1963), and though the trends he identified were appropriate given the evidence available at the time, it is now clear that, globally, families are developing in a variety of different directions. A significant criticism of Goode's argument is its reliance on structural functionalist theory, as set out by Talcott Parsons (see chapter 3 for a discussion of Parsons's ideas). For example, Goode argued that as the process of modernization spread across the world, it is likely that the 'conjugal [or nuclear] family' would become the dominant form because of its close 'fit' with the needs of industrialization and industrial culture. Since the 1960s though, the pace of social change and its impact on families has led to some changes that Goode simply could not have foreseen and, as we will see later in this chapter, families today seem to be more notable for their diverse range of forms than for their uniform character.

Recent empirical studies of the family in a global perspective have reinforced this conclusion. One important recent study is Swedish sociologist Göran Therborn's *Between Sex and Power* (2004), an extensive global history of the family over the entire twentieth century and thus beyond Goode's timeframe. Therborn discusses five major family types that have been shaped by particular religious or philosophical worldviews: sub-Saharan African (Animist); European/North American (Christian); East Asian (Confucian); South Asian (Hindu) and West Asia/North Africa (Islamic). Two others – the Southeast Asian and Creole American – are described as 'interstitial systems', combining elements from more than one of the five major types.

The institution of the family, Therborn argues, has been structured by three central elements across all these familial types: patriarchy or male dominance, marriage and non-marriage in the regulation of sexual behaviour, and fertility and birth control measures in the production of demographic trends. Focusing on these three elements allows international comparisons to be made. We can take each element in turn.

Patriarchal power *within* the family has generally declined over the twentieth

century. He identifies two key periods of change. The first was after the First World War, when women were needed to work for the war effort, and the Russian Revolution, which challenged the patriarchal ideology of women's 'natural' domestic role in favour of egalitarian ideals. The second was between the sexual revolution of the late 1960s and the 1975 'International Women's Year', when second-wave feminism reinforced the shifting position of women in society, gaining legislative measures to enable women formally to participate in public life outside of their domestic role. The second period of change, argues Therborn, was more noticeable in Europe and America, with less pronounced changes in the family situations of South Asia, West Asia and North Africa and sub-Saharan Africa. In more recent years, he sees evidence that the economic power of women has been growing in the textile and electronics industries in the developing world, which could reshape patriarchal family relations there too.

Marriage and family patterns have changed across the world in the twentieth century, but Therborn's studies lead to a different conclusion from that reached in Goode's earlier work. The different family types are *not* becoming increasingly similar, conforming to the Western nuclear family model. In most developed countries, intimate relationships have become more open and less bound by tradition, especially since the 1960s. The combination of increasing rates of divorce, high remarriage rates and more people living alone seems to disprove the thesis of a convergence of family structures, even in the West. Therborn also argues that there is no evidence that such change and fluidity in family life is spreading globally. For example, in most of Asia, people remain committed to monogamy within marriage, while in sub-Saharan Africa, polygamous relationships continue to be the norm. The nuclear family, so important in functionalist theory, does not look set to dominate in the twenty-first century.

Finally, Therborn sees possibly the major change of the last century to be a falling global fertility rate, with the significant exception of sub-Saharan Africa. This is the product of more effective birth control methods, rising economic prosperity and the increasing movement of women into the paid workforce, thereby improving their own position within societies. As we discuss in detail in chapter 8, 'The Life-Course', such demographic changes will mean, for most countries, that populations will decline and societies will 'age', with a higher proportion of older people living longer.

If diversity is the most notable feature of families across the world, are there any general patterns emerging? Perhaps the most important general changes we can observe at this point are:

1 Clans and other kin-based groups are declining in influence.
2 There is a widespread trend towards the free selection of a spouse.
3 The rights of women are becoming more widely recognized, in respect to both the initiation of marriage and decision-making within the family.
4 Higher levels of sexual freedom, for men and women, are developing in some societies that were previously very restrictive.
5 There is a general trend towards the extension of children's rights.
6 There is an increased acceptance of same-sex partnerships, though this is unevenly distributed across the world's societies.

It would be a mistake to exaggerate these trends; many of them are still being fought for and are bitterly contested. For example, the suppression of women's rights in Afghanistan under the Taliban from 1996 to 2001 – discussed in chapter 22, 'Politics, Government and Social Movements' – shows that such trends are not uniform. Moreover, there are differences in the speed at which change is occurring, and there are reversals and countertrends that have to be considered too.

Families and intimate relationships

Given the culturally diverse character of modern societies, there are considerable variations in family and marriage too. Some of the most striking include differences between family patterns of white and non-white people, and we need to consider why this is so. We will then move on to examine issues surrounding divorce and remarriage in relation to contemporary patterns of family life. Let us first, however, describe some basic characteristics which nearly all families in Britain, most of Europe and the industrialized world share.

Key features of the family in European and other Western countries, include the following:

1 The family is monogamous, monogamy being established in law. Given the high rate of divorce that now exists in the industrialized countries, however, some observers have suggested that this marriage pattern should be called *serial monogamy*. That is to say, individuals are permitted to have a number of spouses in sequence, although no one may have more than one wife or husband at any one time. It is misleading, though, to muddle legal monogamy with sexual practice. It is obvious that a high proportion of Europeans engage in sexual relations with individuals other than their spouses.
2 European marriage is based on the idea of romantic love. Affective individualism has become the major influence. Couples are expected to develop mutual affection, based on personal attraction and compatibility, as a basis for contracting marriage relationships. Romantic love as part of marriage has become 'naturalized' in the developed

world; it seems to be a normal part of human existence, rather than a distinctive feature of modern culture. Of course, the reality is divergent from the ideology. The emphasis on personal satisfaction in marriage has raised expectations which sometimes cannot be met, and this is one factor involved in the increasing rate of divorce.

3 The modern family is patrilineal and neo-local. **Patrilineal** inheritance involves children taking the surname of the father. In the past it also meant that property would usually pass down the male line, although this is far less common today. (Many societies in the developing world are **matrilineal** – surnames, and often property, pass down the female line.) A **neo-local residence** pattern involves a married couple moving into a dwelling away from both their families. Neo-localism, however, is not an absolutely fixed trait of European family life. Many families, particularly in poorer, working-class or South Asian neighbourhoods, are **matrilocal** – the newly weds settle in an area close to where the bride's parents live (if the couple lives near or with the groom's parents, it is called **patrilocal**).

4 The modern family is often described as nuclear, consisting of one or two parents living in a household with their children, although nuclear family units are by no means completely isolated from other kin ties. However, the dominance of the nuclear family is being eroded in the industrialized world, as we will see below.

Development and diversity in family patterns

In the 1980s, Rapoport et al. argued that, 'families in Britain today are in transition from coping in a society in which there was a single overriding norm of what a family should be like to a society in which a plurality of norms are recognised as legitimate and, indeed, desirable' (1982: 476). Substantiating this argument, they identified five types of diversity: *organizational*, *cultural*, *class*, *life-course* and *cohort*. We could add to this list *sexual* diversity. The diversity of family forms that Rapoport et al. identified is even more obvious across European societies today than when they first wrote about Britain in 1982.

 Socialization and life stages are also discussed in chapter 8, 'The Life-Course'.

Families *organize* their respective individual domestic duties and their links with the wider social environment in a variety of ways. The contrast between 'orthodox' families – the woman as 'housewife', the husband as 'breadwinner' – and dual-career or one-parent families illustrates this diversity. *Culturally*, there is greater diversity of family benefits and values than used to be the case. The presence of ethnic minorities (such as families of South Asian or West Indian origin, which are discussed below) and the influence of movements such as feminism have produced considerable cultural variety in family forms. Persistent *class* divisions between the poor, the skilled working classes and the various groupings within the middle and upper classes sustain major variations in family structure. Variations in family experience during the *life-course* are fairly obvious. For instance, one individual might come into a family in which both parents had stayed together, and go on to marry and then divorce. Another person might be brought up in a single-parent family, be multiply married and have children by each marriage.

The term *cohort* refers to generations within families. Connections between parents and grandparents, for example, have probably now become weaker than they were. On the other hand, more people now live into old age, and three 'ongoing' families might exist in close relation to one another: married grandchildren, their parents and the grandparents. There is also greater *sexual* diversity in family organizations than ever before. As homosexuality becomes increasingly accepted in many Western societies, partnerships and families are formed based on partnerships between homosexual as well as heterosexual couples.

> Gay marriage and civil partnerships are discussed in chapter 14, 'Sexuality and Gender'.

South Asian families

Among the variety of family types in Europe, there is one pattern distinctively different from most others – that associated with South Asian groups. The South Asian population of the UK numbers more than a million people today. Migration began in the 1950s from three main areas of the Indian subcontinent: Punjab, Gujarat and Bengal. In Britain, these migrants formed communities based on religion, area of origin, caste and, most importantly, kinship. Many migrants found their ideas of honour and family loyalty almost entirely absent among the indigenous British population. They tried to maintain family unity, but housing proved a problem. Large old houses were available in run-down areas; moving up-market usually meant moving into smaller houses and breaking up the extended family.

South Asian extended families show strong familial bonds.

South Asian children born in Europe today are often exposed to two very different cultures. At home, their parents expect or demand conformity to the norms of cooperation, respect and family loyalty. At school, they are expected to pursue academic success in a competitive and individualistic social environment. Most choose to organize their domestic and personal lives in terms of the ethnic subculture, as they value the close relationships associated with traditional family life. Yet involvement with Western culture has brought changes. The Western tradition of marrying 'for love' frequently comes into conflict with the practice of arranged marriages within Asian communities. Such unions, arranged by parents and family members, are predicated on the belief that love comes from within marriage. Young people of both sexes are demanding greater consultation in the arrangement of their marriages.

Statistical findings from the UK Policy Study Institute's fourth national survey of ethnic minorities (Modood et al. 1997) indicate that Indians, Pakistanis, Bangladeshis and African-Asians were the ethnic groups most likely to be married. In 2001, among all families with dependent children, 65 per cent of Asian or Asian British one-family households consisted of a married couple, while among whites and African-Caribbeans, the percentages were somewhat lower. Cohabitation was proportionately smaller amongst Asian and Asian British couples with children than it was amongst other ethnic groups (see table 9.1). Although there appear to be some signs of change among South Asian families in Britain – such as young people wanting a greater say in marriages and a slight rise in divorces and lone-parent households – on the whole, South Asian ethnic groups in the UK and across Europe continue to have remarkably strong familial bonds.

Black families

Families of African-Caribbean origin in Europe have a different structure again. In the UK there are far fewer black women aged between 20 and 44 living with a husband than there are white women in the same age group. Rates of divorce and separation are higher among African-Caribbeans than among other ethnic groups in Britain. As a result, lone-parent households are more common among African-Caribbeans than among any other ethnic minority; yet, unlike other groups, single African-Caribbean mothers are more likely to be employed (Modood et al. 1997). The high proportion of lone-parent families (the vast majority of which are headed by the mother) amongst the black or black British population compared to other ethnic groups can be seen in table 9.1.

In the UK, the same factors seem to be at work among black families in the poorer neighbourhoods of London and other European cities. Many discussions of black families concentrate on the low rates of formal marriage, but some observers believe that this emphasis is misplaced. The marriage relationship does not necessarily form the structure of the black family as it does for the family in other groups. Extended kinship networks are important in West Indian groups – much more significant, relative to marital ties, than in most white European communities. A mother heading a lone-parent family is likely to have a close and supportive network of relatives to depend on. Siblings also play an important role in many African-Caribbean families by helping to raise younger children (Chamberlain 1999). This contradicts the idea that black single parents and their children necessarily form unstable families.

Inequality within the family

Balancing work and care

Gender inequalities vary across the world's societies. A 2007 survey by the World Economic Forum found that women had made the most progress towards equal participation in Sweden, with Norway,

Table 9.1 British families with dependent children: by ethnic group,[a] 2001 (%)

	One family households			Other households with dependent children	All
	Married couple families	Cohabiting couple families	Lone-parent families		
White	60	12	22	6	100
Mixed	38	11	39	12	100
Asian or Asian British					
Indian	68	2	10	21	100
Pakistani	61	2	13	24	100
Bangladeshi	63	2	12	23	100
Other Asian	66	3	12	19	100
All Asian or Asian British	65	2	11	22	100
Black or black British					
Black Caribbean	29	11	48	12	100
Black African	38	7	36	19	100
Other Black	24	9	52	15	100
All black or black British	32	9	43	15	100
Chinese	69	3	15	13	100
Other ethnic group	67	3	18	12	100
All ethnic groups	60	11	22	7	100

[a] Of household reference person

Source: HMSO Social Trends 34 (2004): 28

Finland and Iceland making up the top four standings. The UK came ninth. Yemen came in last, with Saudi Arabia, Chad and Pakistan completing the bottom four positions. However, in balancing work and care, one of the major factors affecting women's careers is the male *perception* that for female employees, work comes second to having children.

One study carried out in Britain in the mid-1980s investigated the views of managers interviewing female applicants for positions as technical staff in the health services (Homans 1987). The researchers found that the interviewers always asked the women about whether or not they had, or intended to have, children (in 2004 a European Directive formally prohibited 'discrimination on grounds of pregnancy and maternity'). They virtually never followed this practice with male applicants. When asked why, two themes ran through their answers: women with children may require extra time off for school holidays or if a child falls sick, and responsibility for childcare is a mother's problem rather than a parental one.

Some managers thought their questions indicated an attitude of 'caring' towards female employees. But most saw such a line of questioning as part of their task to assess how far a female applicant would prove a reliable colleague. Thus, one manager remarked:

There is a high proportion of lone parents amongst the UK's African-Caribbean population.

It's a bit of a personal question, I appreciate that, but I think it's something that has to be considered. It's something that cannot happen to a man really, but I suppose in a sense it's unfair – it's not equal opportunity because the man could never find himself having a family as such. (Homans 1987)

While men cannot biologically 'have a family' in the sense of bearing children, they can be fully involved in and responsible for childcare. Such a possibility was not taken into account by any of the managers studied. The same attitudes were held about the promotion of women. Women were seen as likely to interrupt their careers to care for young children, no matter how senior a position they might have reached. The few women in this study who held senior management positions were all without children, and several of those who planned to have children in the future said they

intended to leave their jobs and would perhaps retrain for other positions subsequently. Most managers accepted the principle that women should have the same career opportunities as men, but the bias in their attitudes was closely linked to cultural ideas of who is responsible for parenting.

In addition, as we saw earlier, the average wage of employed women is well below that of men, although the difference has narrowed somewhat over the past 30 years. In the 25 countries of the European Union, the gender pay gap (the difference between average gross hourly pay of men and women) in 2004 stood at 15 per cent, though this has reduced from 17 per cent in 1998 (Eurostat 2007). Even within the same occupational categories, women on average earn lower salaries than men.

In *Working Women Don't Have Wives* (1994), Terri Apter argues that women find themselves struggling with two contradictory forces. They want and need economic independence, but at the same time they want to be mothers to their children. Both goals are reasonable, but while men with wives who take prime responsibility for domestic work can achieve them, women cannot do likewise. Greater flexibility in working life is one partial solution. Much more difficult is getting men to alter their attitudes.

> **THINKING CRITICALLY**
>
> List all of the factors you can think of as to why men tend not to be as involved in domestic tasks as women. What connections are there between these factors and social stereotypes of men and women? How could such gendered stereotypes be changed?

Housework

Although there have been revolutionary changes in women's status in recent decades in Europe, including the entry of women into male-dominated professions, one area of work has lagged far behind: **housework**. Because of the increase in the number of married women in the workforce, and their resulting change in status, it was presumed that men would contribute more to housework. On the whole, this has not been the case. Although men now do more housework than they did three decades ago and women do slightly less (as can be seen from the data in table 9.2), the balance is still unequal and varies widely across Europe. In Greece, Turkey and Malta the female–male difference in time spent on housework remains more than 70 per cent, a disparity that reduces to below 30 per cent in Sweden and Denmark. The European average gender difference sits at 53 per cent, which indicates that in the area of housework, at least, gender equality still has quite a way to go.

This conclusion is borne out in many European studies. Surveys in the UK have found that women still do the majority of housework and childcare, on average

spending 4 hours 3 minutes per day on these activities compared to 2 hours 17 minutes for men (HMSO 2005). Some sociologists have argued that where women are already working in the paid sector, this extra work, in effect, amounts to a 'second shift' (Hochschild 1989; Shelton 1992). In the late 1980s, findings like these led Arlie Hochschild to call the state of relations between women and men a 'stalled revolution'. Why does housework remain women's work? This question has been the focus of a good deal of research in recent years.

One possible explanation for this phenomenon is that it is the result of economic forces: household work is exchanged for economic support. Because women earn, on average, less than men, they are more likely to remain economically dependent on their husbands and thus perform the bulk of the housework. Until the earnings gap is narrowed, women are likely to remain in their dependent position. Hochschild (1989) has suggested that women are thus doubly oppressed by men: once during the 'first shift' and then again during the 'second shift'. But while this dependency model contributes to our understanding of the gendered aspects of housework, it starts to break down when applied to situations where the wife earns more than her husband. For instance, of the husbands studies by Hochschild who earned less than their wives, none of them shared in the housework.

The problem can be approached from a symbolic interactionist perspective, asking how the performance or non-performance of housework is related to the gender roles created by society. For example, through interviews and participant observation, Hochschild found that the assignment of household tasks falls clearly along gendered lines. Wives do most of the daily chores, such as cooking and routine cleaning, while husbands tend to take on more occasional tasks, such as mowing the lawn or doing home repairs. The major difference between these two types of task is the amount of control the individual has over

Table 9.2 People doing daily housework in Europe (%)

Country	Sex respondent		Total	Female–Male difference
	Male	Female		
Finland	64	95	79	31
Sweden	65	90	77	25
Romania	60	93	76	33
Denmark	65	86	74	21
Hungary	46	93	70	47
Slovakia	47	92	70	45
Luxembourg	44	92	69	48
Belgium	44	91	68	47
Estonia	53	84	68	31
Bulgaria	33	95	66	62
Lithuania	44	90	66	46
Netherlands	47	86	66	39
Germany	36	90	64	54
Latvia	43	85	64	42
Portugal	27	96	62	69
France	32	86	61	54
Slovenia	30	96	61	66
Austria	28	89	59	61
Greece	18	94	59	76
UK	36	80	58	44
Italy	26	88	57	62
Turkey	15	91	57	76
Ireland	33	78	56	45
Malta	21	91	54	70
Cyprus	19	80	53	61
European average*	35	88	62	53

* Sample was weighted according to the population size of each country.

Source: Voicu, B., Boicu, M. and Strapcova, K. (2007) Engendered Housework: A Cross European Analysis (IRISS Working Paper, May 2007).

when they do the work. The jobs done by women in the home are those that tend to bind them to a fixed schedule, whereas men's household tasks are done less regularly and are more discretionary.

In *Feeding the Family* (1991), the sociologist Marjorie Devault looked at how the caring activities within a household are socially constructed as women's work. She argues that women perform the bulk of the housework because the family 'incorporates a strong and relatively enduring association of caring activity with the woman's position in the household'. Observing the division of responsibility for cooking, Devault remarks that the gendered relations of feeding and eating 'convey the message that giving service is part of being a woman, and receiving it is fundamentally part of being a man'. Even in households where men contribute, an egalitarian division of household labour between spouses is greatly impeded when the couple have children – children require constant attention, and their care schedules are often unpredictable. Mothers overwhelmingly spend more time on childrearing tasks than do their spouses (Shelton 1992).

Sociologists argue that underlying this inequitable distribution of tasks is the implicit understanding that men and women are responsible for, and should operate in, different spheres. Men are expected to be providers, while women are expected to tend to their families – even if they are breadwinners as well as mothers. Expectations like this reinforce traditional gender roles learned during childhood socialization. By reproducing these roles in everyday life, men and women 'do gender' and reinforce gender as a means for society to differentiate between men and women.

Intimate violence

Since family or kin relations form part of everyone's existence, family life encompasses virtually the whole range of emotional experience. Family relationships – between wife and husband, parents and children, brothers and sisters, or distant relatives – can be warm and fulfilling. But they can equally well contain the most pronounced tensions, driving people to despair or filling them with a deep sense of anxiety and guilt. This side of family life belies the rosy images of harmony that are quite often emphasized in TV commercials and elsewhere in the popular media. Domestic violence and the abuse of children are two of the most disturbing aspects.

Sexual abuse of children

The sexual abuse of children can be defined as the carrying out of sexual acts by adults with children below the age of consent (16 years old in Britain). Incest refers to sexual relations between close kin. Not all incest counts as child sexual abuse. For example, sexual intercourse between brother and sister is incestuous, but does not fit the definition of abuse. In child sexual abuse, an adult is essentially exploiting an infant or child for sexual purposes. Nevertheless, the most common form of incest is one that is also child sexual abuse – incestuous relations between fathers and young daughters.

Incest, and child sexual abuse more generally, are phenomena that have been 'discovered' only in the past few decades. Of course it has long been known that such sexual acts occur, but it was assumed by most social observers that the strong taboos that exist against this behaviour meant that it was extremely uncommon. This is not the case. Child sexual abuse has proved to be disturbingly commonplace. It is probably found more often among poorer families, but exists at all levels of the social hierarchy – as well as in institutions.

Although in its more obvious versions its nature is plain, the full extent of child sexual abuse is difficult, if not impossible, to calculate accurately because of the many forms it can assume. Corrine May-Chahal and Maria Herczog's (2003) 'informed estimate' suggests that 10–20 per cent of children in Europe will be sexually assaulted during

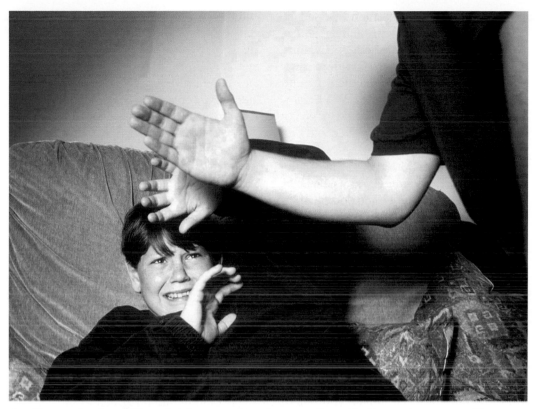

Families can be the setting of violence and tension as well as affection and support, with children later replicating their experiences in adulthood and parenthood.

their childhood. The 1989 UN Convention on the Rights of the Child helped to raise awareness of child sexual abuse and, in a 1999 survey, only 1 per cent of Europeans had never heard of child sexual abuse within the family. In the same survey, 97 per cent thought that child sexual abuse *was* a form of violence (ibid.). However, no fully agreed definitions of either child abuse in general or child sexual abuse in particular have been arrived at, either by researchers or in the courts, and this makes cross-national comparisons highly unreliable.

In the UK, one section of the Children Act 1989 speaks of 'significant harm' being caused by lack of reasonable care – but what is 'significant' is left quite vague. The *National Society for the Prevention of Cruelty to Children* (NSPCC) defines four categories of abuse: 'neglect', 'physical abuse', 'emotional abuse' and 'sexual abuse'. Sexual abuse is defined as 'sexual contact between a child and adult for the purpose of the adult's sexual gratification' (Lyon and de Cruz 1993).

Force or the threat of violence is involved in many cases of incest. In some instances, children are more or less willing participants, but this seems quite rare. Children are sexual beings, of course, and quite often engage in mild sexual play or exploration with one another. But most of the children subjected to sexual contact with adult family members find the experience repugnant, shameful or disturbing. There is now considerable material to indicate that child sexual abuse may have long-term consequences for its sufferers. Studies of prostitutes, juvenile offenders, adolescent runaways and drug-users show that a high proportion have a history of child sexual abuse. Of course, correlation is not causation. Demonstrating that people in these categories have been sexually abused as children does not show that such abuse was a causal influence over their later behaviour. Probably a range of factors is involved, such as family conflicts, parental neglect and physical violence.

Domestic violence

We may define domestic violence as physical abuse directed by one member of the family against another or others. Studies show that the prime targets of physical abuse are children, especially small children. In England, the horrific murder of an 8-year-old girl, Victoria Climbié, in February 2000 brought extreme forms of domestic violence against children to the public's attention. Victoria, who had come to Europe from West Africa, died of hypothermia after months of torture and neglect inflicted by her great-aunt, Marie Therese Kouao, and the woman's boyfriend, Carl Manning. Her abusers were jailed for life in November 2000. During their trial, police and health and social services were all criticized for missing opportunities to save the girl. The government ordered an inquiry, chaired by Lord Laming, which examined the role of the professionals and made recommendations to the government on how to prevent such a tragedy from happening again (Laming 2003).

Violence by men against their female partners is the second most common type of domestic violence. In the UK, two women each week are killed by their partners. At any one time 10 per cent of women are experiencing domestic violence, and it affects between a third and a quarter of women at some point in their lives. Domestic violence is the most common crime against women, who are at greater risk of violence from men in their own families or from close acquaintances than they are from strangers (Rawstorne 2002).

On 27 November 2006, the Council of Europe launched a campaign to combat violence against women, including domestic violence. The campaign stated:

An overview of figures for the prevalence of violence against women suggests that one-fifth to one-quarter of all women have experienced physical violence at least once during their adult lives, and more than one-tenth have suffered sexual violence involving the use of force. Secondary data analysis supports an estimate that about 12% to 15% of all women have been in a relationship of domestic abuse after the age of 16. Many more continue to suffer physical and sexual violence from former partners even after the break-up.

Levels of domestic violence in Eastern Europe were not really known about until after the break-up of the former Soviet Union in 1991, which brought with it a more open exchange of information. Surveys by the Astra Network (Central and Eastern European Women's Network for Sexual and Reproductive Health and Rights) in 1993 found that 29 per cent of women in Romania, 22 per cent in Russia, 21 per cent in Ukraine and more than 42 per cent of married and cohabiting women in Lithuania, said they had been victims of 'physical or sexual violence or threats of violence by their present partner'. In the same year, some 60 per cent of divorced women in Poland reported having been hit at least once by their former husbands (UNICEF 2000b).

Globally, domestic violence is similarly widespread. A study by the *Commonwealth Fund* estimated that almost 4 million women are physically abused each year in the United States, while a 1995 survey by the Beijing Marriage and Family Affairs Research Institute discovered that 23 per cent of husbands admitted to beating their wives. In 1993, some 60 percent of Chilean women involved in a relationship for two years or more were surveyed: 60 per cent said they had been abused by their male partner. The Domestic Violence Research Group in Japan found that 59 percent of the 796 women questioned in 1993 reported having been physically abused by their partner. Finally, in 1992, surveys in Ecuador and

Korea found that 60 percent of low-income women in the former and 38 per cent of women in the latter reported having been beaten by their spouse or partner in the previous year (Marin et al. 1998).

The issue of domestic violence attracted popular and academic attention during the 1970s as a result of the work undertaken by feminist groups with refuge centres for 'battered women'. Before that time, domestic violence, like child abuse, was a phenomenon that was tactfully ignored as a private matter. Feminist studies of patriarchy and domestic violence drew attention to the ways in which such privatization of violence and abuse worked to uphold the dominance of men in patriarchal societies. It was feminist studies which documented the prevalence and severity of violence against women in the home. Most violent episodes between spouses reported to the police involve violence by husbands against their wives. There are far fewer reported cases of women using physical force against their husbands. Feminists have pointed to such statistics to support their claims that domestic violence is a major form of male control over women.

> For theories and evidence of patriarchy, see chapter 14, 'Sexuality and Gender'.

In a backlash against feminist arguments, conservative commentators have claimed that violence in the family is not about patriarchal male power, as feminists contend, but about 'dysfunctional families'. Violence against women is a reflection of the growing crisis of the family and the erosion of standards of morality. They question the finding that violence from wives towards husbands is rare, and suggest that men are less likely to report instances of violence against them from their wives than vice versa (Straus and Gelles 1986).

Such assertions have been strongly criticized by feminists and by other scholars who argue that violence by females is in any case more restrained and episodic than that of men, and much less likely to cause enduring physical harm. They argue that it is not sufficient to look at the 'number' of violent incidents within families. Instead, it is essential to look at the meaning, context and effect of violence. 'Wife battering' – the regular physical brutalizing of wives by husbands – has no real equivalent the other way round. Research found that violence by women against their male partners is often defensive rather than offensive, with women resorting to violence only after suffering repeated attacks over time (Rawstorne 2002). Men who physically abuse children are also much more likely to do so in a consistent way, causing long-standing injuries, than are women.

Why is domestic violence relatively commonplace? Several sets of factors are involved. One is the combination of emotional intensity and personal intimacy characteristic of family life. Family ties are normally charged with strong emotions, often mixing love and hate. Quarrels which break out in the domestic setting can unleash antagonisms that would not be felt in the same way in other social contexts. What seems only a minor incident can precipitate full-scale hostilities between partners or between parents and children. A man tolerant towards eccentricities in the behaviour of other women may become furious if his wife talks too much at a dinner party or reveals intimacies he wishes to keep secret.

A second influence is the fact that a good deal of violence within the family is actually tolerated, and even approved of. Although socially sanctioned family violence is relatively confined in nature, it can easily spill over into more severe forms of assault. Many children in Britain have at some time been slapped or hit, if only in a minor way, by one of their parents. Such actions quite often meet with general approval on the part of others, and they are probably not even thought of as 'violence' – although there is increasing pressure from some groups for the UK to follow many of the other European countries, which have legislation outlawing the physical punishment of children.

Social Class

While no social class is immune to spousal abuse, several studies indicate that it is more common among low-income couples (Cherlin 1999). More than three decades ago, William Goode (1971) suggested that low-income men may be more prone to violence because they have few other means with which to control their wives, such as a higher income or level of education. In addition, the high levels of stress induced by poverty and unemployment may lead to more violence within families. In support of these assertions, Gelles and Cornell (1990) found that unemployed men are nearly twice as likely as employed men to assault their wives.

Divorce and separation

The rise of divorce

For many centuries in the West and other parts of the world, marriage was regarded as virtually indissoluble. A divorce was granted only in very limited cases, such as non-consummation of marriage. Today, however, legal divorce is possible in virtually all of the industrialized and developing societies of the world. Only in Malta and the Philippines is divorce still not legally recognized, though Maltese couples can obtain a 'foreign divorce' from another country if one or both partners are 'habitually resident' there. Seen in a global perspective, these are now isolated examples. Most countries have moved rapidly towards making divorce more easily available.

The so-called adversarial system used to be characteristic of virtually all industrialized countries. For a divorce to be granted, one spouse had to bring charges (for example, cruelty, desertion or adultery) against the other. The first 'no fault' divorce laws were introduced in some countries in the mid-1960s. Since then, many Western states have followed suit, although the details vary. In the UK, the Divorce Reform Act, which made it easier for couples to obtain a divorce and contained 'no fault' provisions, was passed in 1969 and came into effect in 1971. The 'no fault' principle was further consolidated in a new bill passed in 1996.

Between 1960 and 1970 the divorce rate in Britain grew by a steady 9 per cent each year, doubling within that decade. By 1972 it had doubled again, partly as a result of the 1969 Act, which made it easier for many in marriages that had long been 'dead' to get a divorce. Since 1980 the divorce rate has stabilized to some degree, but remains at a very high level compared to any previous period. Around two-fifths of all marriages in the UK now end in divorce. The fall in the number of marriages each year and the rise in the number of divorces are shown in figure 9.1.

Similar trends in marriage and divorce can be seen across the European Community, with some national variations. Marriage rates over the decade 1994–2004 have generally fallen (see figure 9.2), with the notable exception of the Nordic countries: Sweden, Denmark, Norway and Iceland.

Taking a longer view of European divorce rates shows that since the 1960s, rates have risen and remained higher in most national contexts (see figure 9.3), though the exceptions this time are some Eastern European countries such as Romania and Croatia where divorce rates have gone down. The patterns of marriage and divorce in the UK then are far from unique, with British trends actually forming part of much larger Europe-wide social trends.

Divorce rates are obviously not a direct index of marital unhappiness. For one thing, rates of divorce do not include people who are separated but not legally divorced. Moreover, people who are unhappily married may choose to stay together – because they believe in the sanctity of marriage, or worry about the financial or

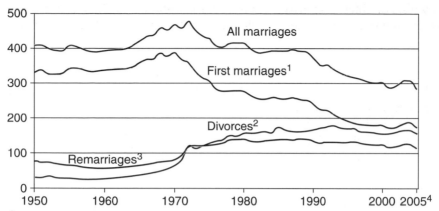

¹ For both partners.
² Includes annulments. Data for 1950 to 1970 for Great Britain only.
   Divorces was permitted in Northern Ireland from 1969.
³ For one or both partners.
⁴ Data for 2005 are provisional. Final figures are likely to be higher.

Figure 9.1   Marriages and divorces in the UK (thousands)

Source: HMSO Social Trends (2007), 18

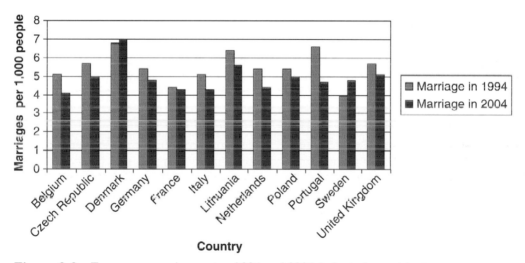

Figure 9.2   European marriage rates, 1994 and 2004 (selected countries)

Source: Adapted from the Eurostat Yearbook 2006–07

emotional consequences of a break-up, or wish to remain with one another to give their children a 'family' home.

Why is divorce becoming more common? Several factors are involved, to do with wider social changes. Except for a very small proportion of wealthy people, marriage today no longer has much connection with the desire to perpetuate property and status from generation to generation. As women become more economically independent, marriage is less of a necessary economic

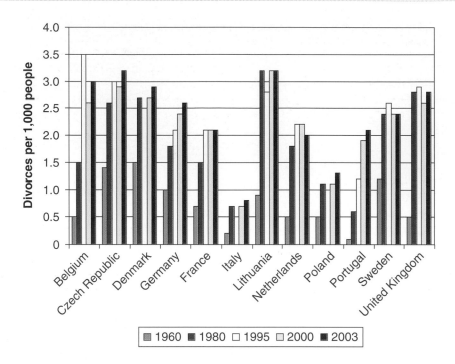

Figure 9.3 Divorce rates in Europe, 1960–2004 (selected countries)

Source: Eurostat Yearbook 2006–07

partnership than it used to be. Greater overall prosperity means that it is easier to establish a separate household, if there is marital disaffection, than used to be the case. The fact that little stigma now attaches to divorce is in some part the result of these developments, but also adds momentum to them. A further important factor is the growing tendency to evaluate marriage in terms of the levels of personal satisfaction it offers. Rising rates of divorce do not seem to indicate a deep dissatisfaction with marriage as such, but an increased determination to make it a rewarding and satisfying relationship.

Lone-parent households

Lone-parent households have become increasingly common in the developed countries over recent decades, though the pattern is quite varied. Lone parents make up a relatively low percentage of households with dependent children in Greece (6.7 per cent), Spain (7.1 per cent) and Portugal (8.4 per cent), with much higher proportions in Belgium (13.7 per cent), Denmark (18.8 per cent) and Sweden (22 per cent). The USA and New Zealand have even higher proportions of lone parents, at 31 and 29 per cent respectively, but Japan has just 8 per cent (Institute for Child and Family Policy 2004).

The UK currently has the highest proportion of lone-parent families in Europe, increasing from 7 per cent in 1971 to 24 per cent in 2006 (HMSO 2007: 16). It is important

---

THINKING CRITICALLY

Reflecting on the experience of your family and friends, what reasons do people give for getting divorced? Do such reasons support the thesis that high rates of divorce do *not* mean that people are rejecting marriage? What sociological evidence is there that marriage remains a highly valued social institution?

9.1   Diane Vaughan on 'uncoupling': the experience of breaking up

It is extremely difficult to draw up a balance sheet of the social advantages and costs of high levels of divorce. More tolerant attitudes mean that couples can terminate an unrewarding relationship without incurring social ostracism. On the other hand, the break-up of a marriage is almost always emotionally stressful for both the couple and their children, and may create financial hardship for one or both parties.

In *Uncoupling: The Turning Points in Intimate Relationships* (1990), Diane Vaughan analysed the relationships between partners during the course of separation or divorce. She carried out a series of interviews with more than 100 recently separated or divorced people (mainly from middle-class backgrounds) to chart the transition from living together to living apart. The notion of uncoupling refers to the break-up of a long-term intimate relationship. She found that in many cases, before the physical parting, there had been a social separation – at least one of the partners developed a new pattern of life, becoming interested in new pursuits and making new friends in contexts in which the other was not present. This usually meant keeping secrets from the other – especially, of course, when a relationship with a lover was involved.

According to Vaughan's research, uncoupling is often unintentional at first. One individual – whom she called the initiator – becomes less satisfied with the relationship than the other, and creates a 'territory' independent of the activities in which the couple engages together. Today, some 90 per cent of initiators are women. For some time before this, the initiator may have been trying unsuccessfully to change the partner, to get him or her to behave in more acceptable ways, foster shared interests and so forth. At some point, the initiator feels that the attempt has failed and that the relationship is fundamentally flawed. From then onwards, he or she becomes preoccupied with the ways in which the relationship or the partner is defective. Vaughan suggests this is the opposite of the process of 'falling in love' at the beginning of a relationship, when an individual focuses on the attractive features of the other, ignoring those that might be less acceptable.

Initiators seriously considering a break notably discuss their relationship extensively with others, 'comparing notes'. In doing so, they weigh the costs and benefits of separation. Can I survive on my own? How will friends and parents react? Will the children suffer? Will I be financially solvent? Having thought about these and other problems, some decide to try again to make the relationship work. For those who proceed with a separation, these discussions and enquiries help make the break less intimidating, building confidence that they are doing the right thing. Most initiators become convinced that a responsibility for their own self-development takes priority over commitment to the other.

Of course, uncoupling is not always entirely led by one individual. The other partner may also have decided that the relationship cannot be saved. In some situations, an abrupt reversal of roles occurs. The person who previously wanted to save the relationship becomes determined to end it, whilst the erstwhile initiator wishes to carry on.

to note that lone parenthood with dependent children is an overwhelmingly female category in the UK (table 9.3) and everywhere else. On average, they are among the poorest groups in contemporary societies. Many lone parents, whether they have ever been married or not, still face social disapproval as well as economic insecurity. Earlier and more judgemental terms such as 'deserted wives', 'fatherless families' and 'broken homes' are tending to disappear, however.

The category of lone-parent household is an internally diverse one. For instance, more than half of widowed mothers are owner-occupiers, but the vast majority of

Table 9.3 **UK households, 1971–2006: by type of household and family (%)**

	1971	1981	1991	2001	2006
One person					
Under state pension age	6	8	11	14	14
Over state pension age	12	14	16	15	14
One-family households					
Couple[1]					
No children	27	26	28	29	28
1–2 dependent children[2]	26	25	20	19	18
3 or more dependent children[2]	9	6	5	4	4
Non-dependent children only	8	8	8	6	7
Lone parent[1]					
Dependent children[2]	3	5	6	7	7
Non-dependent children only	4	4	4	3	3
Two or more unrelated adults	4	5	3	3	3
Multi-family households	1	1	1	1	1
All households (=100%) (=millions)	18.6	20.2	22.4	23.8	24.2

1   Other individuals who were not family members may also be included.
2   May also include non-dependent children.

Source: HMSO Social Trends 37 (2007), 14

never-married lone mothers live in rented accommodation. Lone parenthood tends to be a changing state, and its boundaries are rather blurred: there are multiple paths both entering into and exiting from lone parenthood. In the case of a person whose spouse dies, the break is obviously clear-cut – although even here a person might have been living on his or her own in practical terms if the partner was in hospital for some while before they died. About 60 per cent of lone-parent households today, however, are brought about by separation or divorce.

Amongst the lone-parent families in the UK, the fastest growing category is that of single, never-married mothers. By the late 1990s, they constituted 9 per cent of the total number of families with dependent children. Of these, it is difficult to know how many have deliberately opted to raise children alone. Most people do not wish to

be lone parents. The ongoing *Millennium Cohort Study*, which is currently following the lives of children born in the first few years of this century, has found that younger women are more likely to become solo mothers, and that the more educated the woman, the more likely she is to have a baby within marriage. The research also revealed that for 85 per cent of solo mothers, their pregnancy was unplanned, in contrast to 52 per cent of cohabiting couples and 18 per cent of married women. For the majority of unmarried or never-married mothers, there is also a high correlation between the rate of births outside marriage and indicators of poverty and social deprivation. As we saw earlier, these influences are very important in explaining the high proportion of lone-parent households among families of West Indian background in the UK. However, a growing minority of women are now

Table 9.4 **All families: by type and presence of children, 2004, UK (%)**

	With dependent children	With non-dependent children only	With no children	All
Married	38	13	49	100
Cohabiting couple	38	4	58	100
Lone mother	73	27	–	100
Lone father	50	50	–	100
All families	43	14	42	100

Notes:
Family: a married/cohabiting couple with or without child(ren), or a lone parent with child(ren)
Dependent children: aged under 16, or aged 16–18 in full-time education and never married.
Non-dependent children: never married children aged 16 and over who have no children and are living with their parent(s) (excludes children aged 16–18 in full-time education). There is no age limit.

Source: ONS 2005b

choosing to have a child or children without the support of a spouse or partner. 'Single mothers by choice' is an apt description of some lone parents, normally those who possess sufficient resources to manage satisfactorily as a single parent household.

In *Family Policy, Family Changes*, Patricia Morgan (1999) suggested a direct link between differential levels of welfare support for lone parents and the diverse proportions of lone-parent families across Europe. In particular, she argues that the main reason why Sweden and the UK have the largest proportions of lone-parent families compared with, say, Italy, is because Italian family allowances have been very low and the primary source of support for young people has been the family. Morgan argues that, in states where lone parenting is not subsidized, it is less prevalent.

However, this may be too simplistic. Crow and Hardey (1992) argue that the great diversity of 'pathways' into and out of lone-parent families means that they do not as a whole constitute a uniform or cohesive group. Although lone-parent families may share certain material and social disadvantages in common, they have little collective identity. The plurality of routes means that, for the purposes of social policy, the boundaries of lone parenthood are difficult to define and the needs are difficult to target.

Fathering and the 'absent father'

Recent political debates on the role of fathers have been dominated by the idea of the 'absent father', especially during the period from the late 1930s up to the 1970s. During the Second World War, many fathers, because of war service, only rarely saw their children. In the period following the war, in a high proportion of families women were not in the paid labour force and stayed at home to look after the children. The father was the main breadwinner and, consequently, was out at work all day; he would see his children only in the evenings and at weekends.

With rising divorce rates in more recent years, and the increasing number of lone-parent households, the theme of the **absent father** has come to mean something quite different. It has come to refer to fathers who, as a result of separation or divorce, have only infrequent contact with their children or who lose touch with them altogether. In both Britain and the United States, which have among the highest divorce rates in the world, this situation has provoked intense debate, with some proclaiming the 'death of the dad'.

One outcome of high divorce rates has been the emergence of organizations lobbying for the rights of fathers. In the UK, Netherlands and the USA, the pressure group Fathers 4 Justice (F4J) has gained a high profile as a result of well-publicized stunts, protest marches and direct action carried out by activists. In May 2004, F4J activists threw a condom filled with purple flour at the British Prime Minister in the House of Commons and a few months later one campaigner scaled the walls of Buckingham Palace dressed as the comic-book hero, Batman – 'every father is a superhero to his children'. The group claims that the law, which aims to serve 'the best interests' of the child, is actually biased in favour of the mother when couples split up, by making it difficult for fathers to stay in contact with their children.

Writing from contrasting perspectives, sociologists and commentators have seized on the increasing proportion of fatherless families as the key to a whole diversity of social problems, from rising crime to mushrooming welfare costs for child support. Some have argued that children will never become effective members of a social group unless they are exposed to constant examples of negotiation, cooperation and compromise between adults in their immediate environment (Dennis and Erdos 1992). Boys who grow up without a father will struggle to be successful parents themselves, according to such arguments.

American authors have figured prominently in the debate and have had a great deal of influence over discussions of the issue in Europe, but especially in the UK. In *Fatherless America* (1995), David Blankenhorn argues that societies with high divorce rates are facing not just the loss of fathers but the very erosion of the idea of fatherhood – with lethal social consequences, because many children are growing up now without an authority figure to turn to in times of need. Marriage and fatherhood in all societies up to the present provided a means of channelling men's sexual and aggressive energies. Without them, these energies are likely to be expressed in criminality and violence. As one reviewer of Blankenhorn's book put it: 'better to have a dad who comes home from a nasty job to drink beer in front of the television than no dad at all' (*The Economist* 1995).

Yet, is it? The issue of absent fathers overlaps with that of the more general question of the effects of divorce on children – and there the implications of the available evidence are far from clear. Some scholars have suggested that the key question is not whether the father is present, but how engaged he is in family life and parenting. In other words, the make-up of the household may not be as important as the quality of care, attention and support that children receive from its members. Since the 1980s, issues of good parenting and, in particular, good 'fathering' have become more prominent in political debates and academic research (Hobson 2002).

As women move into paid employment in increasingly larger numbers, men's contribution to domestic tasks and childcare does not seem to be increasing at the same pace. For example, one American study (Yeung et al. 2002) found that on weekdays, neither the earnings of a working mother nor her work hours had any effect on her involvement in childcare; for fathers, on the other hand, both earnings and working hours *did* significantly affect time spent on childcare. This suggests that assumptions of women as primary care-givers remain strong even in dual-earner families. In Europe, two campaigns by the Equal Opportunities Commission have sought ways to promote 'active fatherhood', including increasing paternity-leave entitlement, promoting family-friendly work-

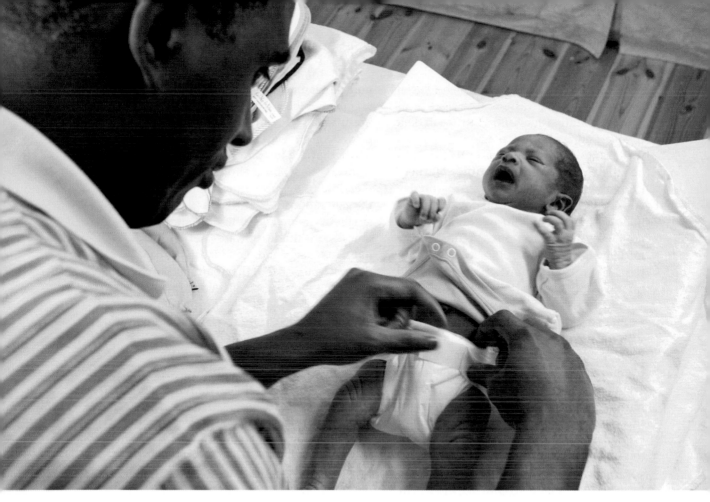

Across European countries, provisions for paternity leave vary greatly.

places and changing the long-hours culture of many European countries, such as the UK and Greece.

European provision for fathers is very diverse. In Sweden, both parents are entitled to 450 days of paid leave at the birth or adoption of a child, 13 months at 80 per cent of salary for most parents and the rest at a lower rate, and employees are entitled to go back to their previous job or a similar one when they do return. However, in Greece, Italy and Spain, fathers do not normally take parental leave. In Spain parental leave is unpaid; in Italy it is not a parent's right to take leave; and in Greece, such leave is not guaranteed in companies with fewer then 50 employees (Flouri 2005). These three countries also have the lowest female labour market participation in the European Union, at around 40 per cent. The USA only

introduced maternity leave in 1993; Australia has no provision for paid maternity or paternity leave and New Zealand introduced paid maternity leave as late as 2002, but still has no provision for paid paternity leave.

Nevertheless, in Sweden, the most generous provider for fathers, it is still mothers who take 85 per cent of all parental leave, an overwhelming majority. Also, many Swedish fathers are reluctant to take their 'papa leave' entitlement for fear of losing out to colleagues for promotion or upsetting employers; in addition, women's wages lag behind those of men and just 2 out of 282 listed companies have female chief executives. We have to be cautious when drawing conclusions about particular national situations, as the introduction of particular policies does not necessarily mean that they will be taken advantage of by the social groups they target.

A comparative analysis of European data (Lamb 2002) showed a wide variety of fathers' involvement in childcare. In Swedish dual-earning families, fathers spent, on average, 10.5 hours per workday and 7.5 hours per non-workday with their infants (more than the mothers in such families), the highest such figure in any European country. Earlier studies found that US fathers spent between 15–20 minutes and 3 hours with infants on workdays, while Israeli fathers spent 2.75 hours. German and Italian fathers spend less time with their infants than do fathers in the UK, Israel or Ireland. What can we conclude from such a diverse body of evidence? It seems that there is a growing interest in fathering, and parenting more generally, in the light of wider concerns about youth crime and the effects of 'bad' parenting or the absence of a 'father figure' in the lives of young men. Such interest and concerns have led to new policies aimed at increasing fathers' engagement in childcare and domestic life. However, even where such policies have been introduced, wider social and economic factors and long-standing gendered assumptions about male and female roles continue to play a strong part in determining the extent to which government policy can shape the dynamics of family life. This means that families and households need to be studied in relation to broader social changes and transformations.

Changing attitudes to family life

There seem to be substantial class differences affecting reactions to the changing character of family life and the existence of high levels of divorce. In *Families on the Fault Line* (1994), Lillian Rubin interviewed the members of 32 working-class families in depth. She concluded that, compared to middle-class families, working-class parents tend to be more traditional. The norms that many middle-class parents have accepted, such as the open expression of pre-marital sex, are more widely disapproved of by working-class people, even where they are not particularly religious. In working-class households, there tends therefore to be more of a conflict between the generations.

The young people in Rubin's study agree that their attitudes towards sexual behaviour, marriage and gender divisions are distinct from those of their parents. But they insist that they are not just concerned with pleasure-seeking. They simply hold to different values from those of the older generation.

Rubin found the young women she interviewed to be much more ambivalent about marriage than were their parents' generation. They were keenly aware of the imperfections of men and spoke of exploring the options available and of living life more fully and openly than was possible for their mothers. The generational shift in men's attitudes was not as great.

Rubin's research was carried out in the United States, but her findings accord closely with those of researchers in European countries. Helen Wilkinson and Geoff Mulgan carried out two large-scale studies of men and women aged between 18 and 34 in the UK (Wilkinson 1994; Wilkinson and Mulgan 1995). They found major changes happening in the outlook of young women in particular; and that the values of this age group contrasted in a general way with those of the older generations in Britain.

Among young women, there is 'a desire for autonomy and self-fulfilment, through work as much as family' and 'the valuing of risk, excitement and change'. In these terms, there is a growing convergence between the traditional values of men and the newer values of women. The values of the younger generation, Wilkinson and Mulgan suggest, have been shaped by their inheritance of freedoms largely unavailable to earlier generations – freedom for women to work and control their own reproduction, freedom of mobility for

USING YOUR SOCIOLOGICAL IMAGINATION

9.2 Carol Smart and Bren Neale's *Family Fragments*?

Between 1994 and 1996, Carol Smart and Bren Neale carried out two rounds of interviews with a group of 60 parents from West Yorkshire who had either separated or divorced after the passage of the 1989 Children Act. This Act altered the situation facing parents and children on divorce by abolishing the old notions of 'custody' and 'access' so that parents would no longer feel that they had to fight over their children. The Act meant that the legal relationship between children and their parents was not changed by divorce; it also encouraged parents to share childrearing and required judges and others to listen more to the views of children. Smart and Neale were interested to know how patterns of parenting were initially formed after divorce and how they changed over time. In their investigation, they compared parents' expectations about post-divorce parenting at the point of separation with the 'reality' of their circumstances one year later.

"Thanks to separations, divorces and remarriages, I've got 20 grandparents."

Smart and Neale found that parenting after divorce involved a process of constant adjustment that many parents had not anticipated and were ill-prepared for. Parenting skills which worked as part of a two-parent team were not necessarily successful in a lone-parent household. Parents were forced to re-evaluate continuously their approaches to parenting, not only in terms of 'big decisions' affecting their children, but also in regard to the everyday aspects of childrearing that were now occurring across two households instead of one. Following a divorce, parents faced two opposing demands – their own needs for separation and distance from their former spouse, and the need to remain connected as part of co-parenting responsibilities.

Smart and Neale found that the lived experience of post-divorce parenting was extremely fluid and changed over time. When interviewed a year after their separation, many parents were able to look back at the initial stages of lone parenting and assess the parenting decisions they had made. They often re-evaluated their behaviour and actions in the light of their changing understandings.

For example, many parents were worried about the harm that their children would suffer as a result of the divorce, but were unsure how to transform their fears and sense of guilt into constructive action. This led some parents to hold on too tightly to their children or to treat them like 'adult' confidants. In other cases it led to alienation, distance and the loss of meaningful connections.

In the media and certain political contexts, according to the authors, there is an implicit – and sometimes explicit – assumption that, after divorce, adults abandon morality and begin to act selfishly and in their own interests. All of a sudden, flexibility, generosity, compromise and sensitivity disappear; the moral framework in which decisions about family and welfare were previously made gets discarded. Smart and Neale's interviews with divorced parents led them to reject this argument. They claim that parents do operate within a moral framework when parenting, but that it is perhaps best understood as a morality of care rather than an unambiguous moral reasoning based on set principles or beliefs. Smart and Neale argue that, as parents care for their children, so decisions emerge about 'the proper thing to do'. These decisions are highly contextual; parents must weigh

[cont'd . . .]

a large number of considerations, including the effects of the decision on the children, whether it is the appropriate time to act and what harmful implications it might have on the co-parenting relationship. Consider the following from a lone mother whose ex-husband requested custody of their children:

> I said, 'Look, if you really, really feel that you can look after these kids on a full-time basis, don't you think you ought to give yourself a weekend with them and then just see how it feels and then maybe after a weekend maybe progress to say you're having them for a full week and see how you cope with them.' He just absolutely hit the roof because he's got this thing in his head that he'd be baby-sitting for me, so he said 'No.' I said, 'Look, in that case I'm not even prepared to discuss it with you because I feel you just don't know how hard it is, you haven't had the children on a full-time basis for three years, I do feel that you're just out of it a little. [I feel you should have them] in a normal everyday routine, bringing them to school, picking them up from school, cooking, cleaning, washing and ironing for them, helping them with their homework, if they're sick, nursing them. And then we will rediscuss, reassess the situation.' (Smart and Neale 1999)

Here the mother was trying to determine the 'right thing to do' while balancing multiple factors. In the context of a difficult relationship with her former spouse and the need to defend the progress she had made in her own self-development, she was still attempting to work constructively with him in the interests of the children.

Smart and Neale conclude that divorce unleashes changes in circumstances which can rarely be 'put straight' once and for all. Successful post-divorce parenting demands constant negotiation and communication. While the 1989 Children's Act has added necessary flexibility to contemporary post-divorce parenting arrangements, its emphasis on the welfare of the child may overlook the crucial role played by the quality of the relationship between divorced parents.

both sexes and freedom to define their own style of life. Such freedoms lead to greater openness, generosity and tolerance; but they can also produce a narrow, selfish individualism and a lack of trust in others. Of those in the sample, 29 per cent of women and 51 per cent of men wanted to 'delay having children as long as possible'. Of women in the 16–24 age group, 75 per cent believed that single parents can bring up children as well as a couple can. The study found that marriage was losing its appeal for both women and men in this age group.

New partnerships, step-families and kin relations

Remarriage

Remarriage can involve various circumstances. Some remarried couples are in their early 20s, neither of them bringing a child to the new relationship. Couples that remarry in their late 20s, their 30s or early 40s might each take one or more children from the first marriage to live with them. Those who remarry at later ages might have adult children who never live in the new homes that the parents establish. There may also be children within the new marriage itself. Either partner of the new couple may previously have been single, divorced or widowed, adding up to eight possible combinations. Generalizations about remarriage therefore have to be made with considerable caution, although some general points are worth making.

In 1900 about nine-tenths of all marriages in the United Kingdom were first marriages. Most remarriages involved at least one widowed person. With the rise in the divorce rate, the level of remarriage also began to climb, and an increasing proportion of remarriages began to involve divorced people. In 1971, 20 per cent of UK marriages were remarriages (for at least one partner); by 2001 that number was more than 40 per cent (as figure 9.1 above shows).

Odd though it might seem, the best way to maximize the chances of getting married, for both sexes, is to have been married before! People who have been married and divorced are more likely to marry again than single people in comparable age groups are to marry for the first time. At all age levels, divorced men are more likely to remarry than divorced women: three in every four divorced women, but five in every six divorced men, remarry. In statistical terms, at least, remarriages are less successful than first marriages. Rates of divorce from second marriages are higher than those from first marriages.

This does not show that second marriages are doomed to fail. People who have been divorced may have higher expectations of marriage than those who have not. Hence they may be more ready to dissolve a new marriage than those only married once. It is possible that the second marriages which endure might be more satisfying, on average, than first marriages.

Step-families

The term 'step-family' refers to a family in which at least one of the adults has children from a previous marriage or relationship. Sociologists often refer to such groups as **reconstituted families**. There are clearly joys and benefits associated with reconstituted families and with the growth of extended families which results. But certain difficulties also tend to arise. In the first place, there is usually a biological parent living elsewhere whose influence over the child or children is likely to remain powerful.

Second, cooperative relations between divorced individuals are often strained when one or both remarries. Take the case of a woman with two children who marries a man who also has two children, and they all live together. If the 'outside' parents insist that children visit them at the same times as before, the major tensions involved in melding such a newly established family together will be exacerbated. For example, it may prove impossible ever to have the new family together at weekends.

Third, reconstituted families merge children from different backgrounds, who may have varying expectations of appropriate behaviour within the family. Since most step-children 'belong' to two households, the likelihood of clashes in habits and outlook is considerable. Here is a step-mother describing her experience, after the problems she faced led to separation:

> There's a lot of guilt. You cannot do what you would normally do with your own child, so you feel guilty, but if you do have a normal reaction and get angry, you feel guilty about that, too. You are always so afraid you will be unfair. Her [step-daughter's] father and I did not agree and he would say I nagged if I disciplined her. The more he did nothing to structure her, the more I seemed to nag. . . . I wanted to provide something for her, to be an element of her life which was missing, but perhaps I am not flexible enough. (Smith 1990)

There are few established norms which define the relationship between step-parent and step-child. Should a child call a new step-parent by name, or is 'Dad' or 'Mum' more appropriate? Should the step-parent discipline the children as a natural parent would? How should a step-parent treat the new spouse of his or her previous partner when collecting the children?

Reconstituted families are developing types of kinship connection, which are quite recent additions to modern Western societies; the difficulties created by remarriage after divorce are also new. Members of these families are developing their own ways of adjusting to the relatively uncharted circumstances in which they find themselves. Some authors today speak of **binuclear families**, meaning that the two households which form after a divorce still comprise one family system where there are children involved.

THINKING CRITICALLY

From your own experience, have step-families become equally acceptable in modern societies? What new problems, issues and opportunities can you think of that might arise for the children growing up within step-families? How might governments tackle the new problems facing step-families?

Kinship relations

As family structures become more fluid and diverse, with high levels of divorce, remarriage and the creation of step-families, sociologists are increasingly interested in understanding what is happening to the relationships between family members. What does it now mean to be a brother or a sister, for example? What ties exist amongst siblings and how do they perceive their obligations towards each other and to parents, grandparents and other family members? Indeed, who counts as kin anyway?

In an early study of kinship in the UK, Raymond Firth (1956) made a distinction between 'effective' and 'non-effective' kin, based on the extent of regular contact between family members. Effective kin are those with whom we have active social relationships; non-effective kin are those with whom we do not have regular contact, but who form part of the extended family group. For example, we may be in contact with sisters and brothers almost every day, but only speak to, or come into contact with, certain cousins or uncles and aunts at annual events such as birthdays. Although it is easy to see the distinction between effective and non-effective kin, it remains the case that all such relationships still fall within conventional family groups assumed to share biological forms of kinship.

USING YOUR SOCIOLOGICAL IMAGINATION

9.3 Bean-pole families

Julia Brannen (2003) argues that the UK has entered an age of the 'bean-pole family'. She suggests that the family household is just one part of a network of kin relations that, increasingly, consists of several generations. This is largely because people are living longer. She notes that at the age of 50, three-fifths of the UK population have at least one parent still alive, and just over a third are grandparents. There is also a rise in the number of four-generation families – families that include great-grandchildren.

As the 'vertical' links between generations of the family are strengthened by increasing life expectancy, so the 'horizontal' links within generations are weakening, as divorce rates rise, fertility rates fall and people have fewer children. Brannen therefore characterizes contemporary families as long and thin 'bean-pole structures' (see figure 9.4).

Brannen found that grandparents are increasingly providing intergenerational services, particularly informal childcare for

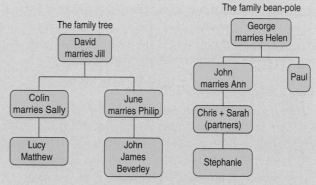

Figure 9.4 The family tree and the family bean-pole

Source: Brannen 2003

their grandchildren. Demand for intergenerational support is particularly high amongst single-parent families, where older generations can also often provide emotional support in times of need, such as during a divorce. In turn, the 'pivot generation', sandwiched between older and younger generations, will often become a carer for their parents (as they become elderly), their children and perhaps even grandchildren.

However, it is not uncommon for people to describe some non-family members in kinship terms. For example, some close friends may come to be described and known as 'uncle' or 'aunt', despite the fact that they have no other link to the family group than friendship. Anthropologists refer to such relationships as 'fictive kin'. An awareness of these different categories of kinship blurs the boundary between family and non-family members, showing that what people perceive to be 'the family' is, in part, socially constructed. As a result, in recent years, kin relations have come to be discussed in terms of the wider concept of 'relatedness', which allows cross-cultural comparisons to be made without imposing the Western idea (and ideal) of what constitutes a 'normal' type of kinship (Carsten 2000). This shifts the focus of research from the sociologist's categorization of kin relations onto people's own sense of what it means to 'be related' to others and the significance they attribute to their relationships. However, such studies tend to exist alongside existing research on family and kinship.

One significant piece of recent research on kin relations is Melanie Mauthner's (2005) study of changing forms of 'sistering' that is, of how women behave as sisters. Mauthner's qualitative study interviewed 37 women from 19 sets of sisters. She identified four 'discourses of sistering' that shaped the women's narratives. 'Best friendship' is a discourse which identifies the sibling relationship as a very intimate one that tends to be closer – both in reality and as an ideal – than other friendships. This comes close to the common-sense idea of the biological closeness of siblings. 'Companionship' is a type of relationship that is less actively engaged than best friendships. 'Close' companionship is less intense but still very close. 'Distant' companionship represents those sibling relations characterized by underlying tensions and problems, leaving sisters' attitudes towards them somewhat ambivalent. Two other discourses – 'posi-tioned' and 'shifting positions' – describe the dynamics of power in sibling relations. Positioned relations are largely shaped by fairly fixed roles defined by families, including older sisters who assume responsibility for younger ones or those who become 'mother substitutes' when required. By contrast, 'shifting positions' applies to the more fluid and egalitarian relations where the exercise of power is negotiated rather than assumed. Mauthner concludes that the practices of sistering are quite varied and are likely to change over the life-course, as the dynamics of power shifts within relationships. Therefore we cannot assume that sibling relations are shaped by fixed biological and familial relations, even though the attitudes and ideals of many women (and men) may be influenced by society-wide discourses suggesting that women are the primary care-givers. In short, sistering implies an active and ongoing attempt to (re)create sibling relations, compared to sisterhood, which can be seen as implying universal role expectations.

In the face of such rich and often confusing familial transformations, perhaps the most appropriate conclusion to be drawn is a simple one: although marriages are broken up by divorce, families on the whole are not. Especially where children are involved, many ties persist despite the reconstructed family connections brought into being through remarriage.

Alternatives to traditional marriage and family life

Cohabitation

Cohabitation – when two people live together in a sexual relationship without being married – has become increasingly widespread in many Western societies. If, previously, marriage was the defining basis of a union between two people, it can no longer be regarded as such. Today it may be more appropriate to speak of coupling and uncoupling, as we do when discussing the

Table 9.5	Marital status of European Union men and women 25–34 years, 2000–1				
Country	Ever-married	Never-partnered	Unmarried currently cohabiting	Unmarried previously cohabited	Number in sample
Sweden	28	13	39	20	891
Denmark	37	14	32	17	957
France	39	15	31	15	1,094
Finland	43	17	30	11	860
Austria	52	13	22	13	1,013
Netherlands	47	23	22	8	954
East Germany	46	17	21	15	718
Great Britain	57	16	18	16	992
Luxembourg	65	11	17	9	512
West Germany	50	19	15	6	905
Ireland	45	32	15	7	913
Belgium	59	20	15	6	964
Spain	44	41	11	4	984
Greece	56	29	10	5	929
Italy	34	55	8	4	964
Portugal	61	32	5	2	753
Total	47	23	19	10	14,730

Source: Kiernan 2004: 37

experience of divorce above. A growing number of couples in committed long-term relationships choose not to marry, but to reside together and raise children together (see table 9.5). It is also the case that many older people choose to cohabit following a divorce rather than or in advance of remarrying.

Across Europe until very recently, cohabitation was generally regarded as somewhat scandalous. In the UK, *The General Household Survey*, the main source of data on British household patterns, included a question on cohabitation for the first time only in 1979. Among young people in Britain and Europe, however, attitudes to cohabitation are changing rapidly. Presented with the statement that 'It is alright for a couple to live together without intending to get married', 88 per cent of British people aged between 18 and 24 now agree, whereas only 40 per cent of respondents aged 65 and over agreed (HMSO 2004). In recent decades, the number of unmarried men and women sharing a household has gone up sharply. Only 4 per cent of UK women born in the 1920s cohabited and 19 per cent of those born in the 1940s did so. But among women born in the 1960s, the percentage is nearly half. By 2001–2, the proportion of cohabiting unmarried women under the age of 60 was 28 per cent; for men the figure was 25 per cent (ibid.). The prevalence of cohabitation was highest for women aged between 25 and 29 and for men aged between 30 and 34. Although cohabitation has become increasingly popular, research suggests that marriage is still more stable. Unmarried couples who live together are three to four times more likely to split up than those who are married.

Cohabitation in many countries seems, for the most part, to be an experimental stage before marriage, although the length of cohabitation prior to marriage is increasing and more and more couples are choosing it as an alternative to marriage. In 2001, for example, 39 per cent of younger adults aged 25–34 in Sweden were unmarried and cohabiting, 32 per cent in Denmark, 31 per cent in France and 30 per cent in Finland (see table 9.5). Young adults often find themselves living together because they drift into it, rather than make calculated plans to do so. Two people who are already having a sexual relationship spend more and more time together, eventually giving up one or other of their individual homes. Young people living together almost always anticipate getting married at some date, but not necessarily to their current partners. Only a minority of such couples pool their finances.

In a 1999 study carried out by researchers at the University of Nottingham, UK, sociologists interviewed a sample of married and cohabiting couples with children aged 11 or under, as well as a sample of their parents who were still married. They were interested in the differences in commitment between older married persons and couples in the younger generation. The researchers found that the younger married and cohabiting couples had more in common with each other than with their parents. While the older generation saw marriage in terms of obligations and duties, the younger generation emphasized freely given commitments. The main difference between the younger respondents was that some of them preferred to have their commitment recognized publicly through marriage (Dyer 1999).

Gay and lesbian partnerships

Many homosexual men and women now live in stable relationships as couples. But because most countries still do not sanction marriage between homosexuals, relationships between gay men and between lesbians have been grounded in personal commitment and mutual trust rather than in law. The term 'families of choice' has sometimes been applied to gay partnerships to reflect the positive and creative forms of everyday life that homosexual couples are increasingly able to pursue together. Many traditional features of heterosexual partnerships – such as mutual support, care and responsibility in illness, the joining of finances, and so forth – are becoming integrated into gay and lesbian families in ways that were not possible earlier.

A very significant recent trend in Western European countries, which has long been campaigned for by lesbian and gay movements, is the introduction of registered or **civil partnerships** for homosexual couples (see figure 9.5).

 Lesbian and gay social movements are discussed in chapter 22, 'Politics, Government and Social Movements'.

Civil partnerships are legally recognized unions between two people of the same sex, though technically they are not 'marriages' in the religious sense. Nonetheless, couples who become 'partnered' generally have the same legal rights as married couples on a range of matters. For example, civil partners can expect equal treatment on financial matters such as inheritance, pensions and child maintenance. They also have rights as 'next of kin', which previously were denied them, and immigration rules take account of civil partnerships in the same way as marriages.

Denmark was first to grant same-sex partners the same rights as married couples in 1989, followed in 1996 by Norway, Sweden and Iceland, and in 2000 by Finland. The Netherlands introduced full civil marriage rights in 2001. Belgium and Spain introduced gay marriage rights in 2003 and 2005 respectively, while in Germany and France, the law gives same-sex couples more limited rights. In Britain, new legislation

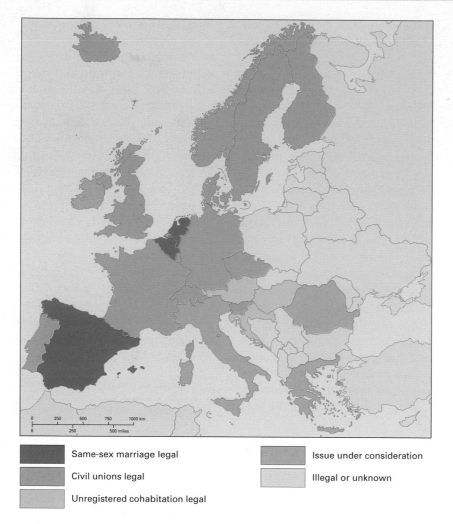

Same-sex marriage legal	Issue under consideration
Civil unions legal	Illegal or unknown
Unregistered cohabitation legal	

Figure 9.5   Status of same-sex partnerships in Europe, 2005

Source: http://en.wikipedia.org/wiki/Image:Same_sex_marriage_map_Europe_detailed.svg

came into force in December 2005, giving same-sex couples in civil partnerships similar rights to married couples. Elsewhere, Argentina (2003), New Zealand (2004) and Canada (2005) have sanctioned same-sex relationships, and in Eastern Europe, both Slovenia and the Czech Republic introduced recognized partnerships in 2006. This trend looks likely to continue and spread, despite opposition from some religious groups, which see legal recognition of same-sex partnerships as legitimizing 'immoral' relationships. Such opposition is particularly strong in many parts of the USA.

Since the 1980s there has been a growing academic interest in gay and lesbian partnerships. Sociologists have seen homosexual relationships as displaying forms of intimacy and equality quite different from those common in heterosexual couples. Because gays and lesbians have been excluded from the institution of marriage, and because traditional gender roles are not easily applicable to same-sex couples, homosexual partnerships must be constructed and negotiated outside the norms and guidelines that govern many heterosexual unions. Some have suggested

Same-sex relationships have been sanctioned across much of the world, but the right of gay parents to adopt and bring up children is a more controversial issue.

that the AIDS epidemic has been an important factor in the development of a distinctive culture of care and commitment among homosexual partners.

Weeks et al. (2004) point to three significant patterns within gay and lesbian partnerships. First, there is more opportunity for equality between partners because they are not guided by the cultural and social assumptions that underpin heterosexual relationships. Gay and lesbian couples may choose to shape their relationships deliberately so as to avoid the types of inequalities and power imbalances that are characteristic of many heterosexual couples. Second, homosexual partners negotiate the parameters and inner workings of their relationships. If heterosexual couples are influenced by socially embedded gender roles, same-sex couples face fewer expectations about

who should do what within the relationship. For example, if women tend to do more of the housework and childcare in heterosexual marriages, there are no such expectations within homosexual partnerships. Everything becomes a matter for negotiation; this may result in a more equal sharing of responsibilities. Third, gay and lesbian partnerships demonstrate a particular form of commitment that lacks an institutional backing. Mutual trust, the willingness to work at difficulties and a shared responsibility for 'emotional labour' seem to be the hallmarks of homosexual partnerships (Weeks et al. 1999). It will be interesting for sociologists to observe how the new civil partnerships and gay marriage rights affect such commitment and mutual trust in the future.

A relaxation of previously intolerant attitudes towards homosexuality has been accompanied by a growing willingness by the courts to allocate custody of children to mothers living in lesbian relationships. Techniques of artificial insemination mean that lesbians may have children and become parents without any heterosexual contacts. While virtually every homosexual family with children in Britain involves two women, for a period in the late 1960s and early 1970s social welfare agencies in several cities in the USA placed homeless gay teenage boys in the custody of gay male couples. The practice was discontinued, largely because of adverse public reaction.

A number of recent legal victories for homosexual couples indicate that their rights are gradually becoming enshrined in law. In Britain, a landmark 1999 ruling declared that a homosexual couple in a stable relationship could be defined as a family. This classification of homosexual partners as 'members of the family' will affect legal categories such as immigration, social security, taxation, inheritance and child support.

> New legal rights of homosexual couples are discussed further in chapter 14, 'Sexuality and Gender'.

In 1999 a US court upheld the paternal rights of a gay male couple to be named jointly on the birth certificate of their children born to a surrogate mother. One of the men who brought the case said: 'We are celebrating a legal victory. The nuclear family as we know it is evolving. The emphasis should not be on it being a father and a mother but on loving, nurturing parents, whether that be a single mother or a gay couple living in a committed relationship' (Hartley-Brewer 1999).

Staying single

Recent trends in European household composition raise the question: are we becoming a community of singles? For instance, the proportion of one-person households in the UK increased from 18 per cent in 1971 to 29 per cent in 2003 (HMSO

Table 9.6 Average age at marriage: England and Wales, 1971–2001

	First marriage	
	Males	Females
1971	24.6	22.6
1981	25.4	23.1
1991	27.5	25.5
2001	30.6	28.4

Source: HMSO Social Trends 34 (2004), 32

2004). Several factors have combined to increase the numbers of people living alone in modern Western societies. One is a trend towards later marriages – in 2001 people in the UK were marrying on average about six years later than was the case in the early 1970s (as table 9.6 shows) and by 2005 was 32 years old for men and 29 for women. Another, as we have seen, is the rising rate of divorce. Yet another is the growing number of older people in the population whose partners have died (discussed in chapter 6). Nearly half of the one-person households in the UK are one-pensioner-only households.

Being single means different things at different periods of the **life-course**. A larger proportion of people in their 20s are unmarried than used to be the case. By their mid-30s, however, only a small minority of men and women have never been married. The majority of single people aged 30–50 are divorced and 'in between' marriages. Most single people over 50 are widowed.

> 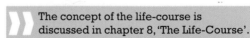 The concept of the life-course is discussed in chapter 8, 'The Life-Course'.

More than ever before, young people are leaving home simply to start an independent life rather than to get married (which had been one of the most common paths out of the home in the past). Hence it seems that the trend of 'staying single' or living on one's own may be part of the societal trend towards valuing independence at the expense of family life. Still, while independence or 'staying single' may be an increasingly common path out of the parental home, most people do eventually marry.

Theoretical perspectives on families and relationships

The study of the family and family life has been taken up by sociologists of contrasting theoretical persuasions. Many of the perspectives adopted even a few decades ago now seem much less convincing in the light of recent research and important changes in the social world. Nevertheless, it is valuable to trace briefly the evolution of sociological thinking before turning to contemporary approaches to the study of the family.

Functionalism

The functionalist perspective sees society as a set of social institutions that perform specific functions to ensure continuity and consensus. According to this perspective, the family performs important tasks that contribute to society's basic needs and helps to perpetuate social order. Sociologists working in the functionalist tradition have regarded the nuclear family as fulfilling certain specialized roles in modern societies. With the advent of industrialization, the family became less important as a unit of economic production and more focused on reproduction, childrearing and socialization.

Feminist approaches

For many people, the family provides a vital source of solace and comfort, love and companionship. Yet as we saw above, it can also be a locus for exploitation, loneliness and profound inequality. Feminism has had a great impact on sociology by challenging the vision of the family as a harmonious and egalitarian realm. During the 1970s and 1980s, feminist perspectives dominated most debates and research on the family. If previously the sociology of the family had focused on family structures, the historical development of the nuclear and extended family and the importance of kinship ties, feminism succeeded in directing attention inside families to examine the experiences of women in the domestic sphere. Many feminist writers have questioned the vision that the family is a cooperative unit based on common interests and mutual support. They have sought to show that the presence of unequal power relationships within the family means that certain family members tend to benefit more than others.

Feminist writings have emphasized a broad spectrum of topics, but three main themes are of particular importance. One of the central concerns – which we will explore in greater depth in chapter 20, 'Work and Economic Life' – is the *domestic division of labour*: the way in which tasks are allocated between members of a household. Among feminists there are differing opinions about the historical emergence of this division. Socialist feminists see it as an outcome of industrial capitalism, while others claim that it is linked to patriarchy, and thus predates the industrialization process. There is reason to believe that a domestic division of labour existed prior to industrialization, but it seems clear that capitalist production brought about a much sharper distinction between the domestic and work realms. This process resulted in the crystallization of 'male spheres' and 'female spheres' and power relationships which are felt to this day. Until recently, the **male breadwinner** model has been widespread in most industrialized societies.

Feminist sociologists have undertaken studies on the way domestic tasks, such as childcare and housework, are shared between men and women. They have investigated the validity of claims such as that of the 'symmetrical family' (Young and Willmott 1973) – the belief that, over time, families are becoming more egalitarian in

Classic Studies 9.2 **Talcott Parsons and the functions of the family**

The research problem

Why is the family such an enduring feature within human societies? Do families do things that other social institutions just cannot do? Is the family really necessary for a well-ordered society? These questions have been part of ongoing debates within sociology from the discipline's earliest days, but the answers are still the subject of heated debate.

Parsons's explanation

According to the American functionalist sociologist Talcott Parsons, the family's two main functions are *primary socialization* and *personality stabilization* (Parsons and Bales 1956). **Primary socialization** is the process by which children learn the cultural norms of the society into which they are born. Because this happens during the early years of childhood, the family is the most important arena for the development of the human personality.

Personality stabilization refers to the role that the family plays in assisting adult family members emotionally. Marriage between adult men and women is the arrangement through which adult personalities are supported and kept healthy. In industrial society, the role of the family in stabilizing adult personalities is said to be critical. This is because the nuclear family is often distanced from its extended kin and is unable to draw on larger kinship ties as families could do before industrialization.

Parsons regarded the nuclear family as the unit best equipped to handle the demands of industrial society. In the 'conventional family', one adult can work outside the home, while the second adult cares for the home and children. In practical terms, this specialization of roles within the nuclear family involved the husband adopting the 'instrumental' role as breadwinner, and the wife assuming the 'affective', emotional role in domestic settings.

Critical points

In our present age, Parsons's view of the family comes across as inadequate and outdated. Functionalist theories of the family have come under heavy criticism for justifying the domestic division of labour between men and women as something natural and unproblematic. We can also criticize functionalist arguments for over-emphasizing the role of the family and neglecting the role that other social institutions, such as government, media and schools, play in socializing children. Parsons also had little to say about variations in family forms that do not correspond to the model of the nuclear family. Families that did not conform to the white, suburban, middle-class 'ideal' could then be seen as deviant.

Finally, the 'dark side' of family life is arguably underplayed in functionalist accounts and therefore not given the significance it deserves.

Contemporary significance

Parsons's functionalist theory of the family is undoubtedly out of favour today, and it is true to say that it must be seen as a partial account of the role of families within societies. Yet it does have historical significance. The immediate post-war years *did* see women returning to their traditional domestic roles and men reassuming positions as sole breadwinners, which was much closer to Parsons's account. Social policy in the UK and USA has also relied on some variant of functionalist theory of the family and its role in tackling social problems. We should also remember that a central tenet of functionalist theory is that, as societies change, social institutions must also change if they are to survive, albeit in new forms. It is possible to see the contemporary diversity of family forms (and marriage) as evidence of this adaptation of a key social institution – the family – to a rapidly changing social life. If so, then it may be too early to dismiss completely Parsons's functionalist analysis just yet.

the distribution of roles and responsibilities. Findings have shown that women continue to bear the main responsibility for domestic tasks and enjoy less leisure time than men, despite the fact that more women are working in paid employment outside the home than ever before (Hochschild 1989; Gershuny 1994; Sullivan 1997). Pursuing a related theme, some sociologists have examined the contrasting realms of paid and unpaid work, focusing on the contribution that women's unpaid domestic labour makes to the overall economy (Oakley 1974). Others have investigated the way in which resources are distributed among family members and the patterns of access to and control over household finances (Pahl 1989).

Second, feminists have drawn attention to the *unequal power relationships* that exist within many families. One topic that has received increased attention as a result of this is the phenomenon of domestic violence. 'Wife battering', marital rape, incest and the sexual abuse of children have all received more public attention as a result of feminists' claims that the violent and abusive sides of family life have long been ignored in both academic contexts and legal and policy circles. Feminist sociologists have sought to understand how the family serves as an arena for gender oppression and even physical abuse.

The study of *caring activities* is a third area where feminists have made important contributions. This is a broad realm which encompasses a variety of processes, from attending to a family member who is ill to looking after an elderly relative over a long period of time. Sometimes caring means simply being attuned to someone else's psychological well-being – several feminist writers have been interested in 'emotion work' within relationships. Not only do women tend to shoulder concrete tasks such as cleaning and childcare, but they also invest large amounts of emotional labour in maintaining personal relationships (Duncombe and Marsden 1993). While caring activities are grounded in love and deep emotion, they are also a form of work which demands an ability to listen, perceive, negotiate and act creatively.

Theorizing the transformation of love and intimacy

Theoretical and empirical studies conducted from a feminist perspective during the last few decades have generated increased interest in the family and intimate relationships in sociology. Terms such as the 'second shift' – referring to women's dual roles at work and at home – have also entered society's everyday vocabulary. But because they often focused on specific issues within the domestic realm, feminist studies of the family did not always reflect larger trends and influences taking place outside the home.

In the past decade, an important body of sociological work on the family has emerged, which draws on feminist perspectives, but is not strictly informed by them. Of primary concern are the larger transformations which are taking place in family forms – the formation and dissolution of families and households, and the evolving expectations within individuals' personal relationships. The rise in divorce and lone parenting, the emergence of 'reconstituted families' and gay families, and the popularity of cohabitation are all subjects of concern. These transformations cannot be understood apart from the larger changes occurring in the contemporary world.

The transformation of intimacy

In my own work, particularly *The Transformation of Intimacy* (1993), I looked at how intimate relationships are changing in modern societies. The introduction to this chapter shows that marriage in pre-modern society was not generally based on sexual attraction or romantic love; instead, it was more often linked to the economic context in which to create a family or to enable the inheritance of property. For the peasantry, a life characterized by unremitting hard labour was unlikely to be conducive to sexual passion – although opportunities for men to engage in extramarital liaisons were numerous.

Romantic love, as distinct from the more or less universal compulsions of passionate love, developed in the late eighteenth century. Despite its promise of an equal relationship based on mutual attraction, romantic love has in practice tended to lead to the dominance of men over women (Evans 2002). For many men, the tensions between the respectability of romantic love and the compulsions of passionate love were dealt with by separating the comfort of the wife and home from the sexuality of the mistress or prostitute. The double standard here was that a woman should remain a virgin until the right man arrives – whereas no such norm applied to the men.

I argue that the most recent phase of modernity has seen another transformation in the nature of intimate relationships in the development of **plastic sexuality**. For people in modern societies there is a much greater choice over when, how often and with whom they have sex than ever before (there is a wider discussion of sexuality in chapter 14, 'Sexuality and Gender'). With plastic sexuality, sex can be untied from reproduction. This is partly due to improved methods of contraception, which have largely freed women from the fear of repetitive pregnancies and childbirths, but the development of a sense of the self that could be actively chosen (a social reflexivity) has also contributed to the emergence of plastic sexuality.

The emergence of plastic sexuality brings with it a change in the nature of love. I argued that the ideals of romantic love are fragmenting and being replaced by **confluent love**. Confluent love is active and contingent. It jars with the forever, one-and-only qualities of romantic love. The emergence of confluent love goes some way towards explaining the rise of separation and divorce discussed earlier in this chapter. Romantic love meant that once people had married they were usually stuck with one another, no matter how the relationship developed. Now people have more choice: whereas divorce was previously difficult or impossible to obtain, married people are now no longer bound to stay together if the relationship does not work.

Rather than basing relationships on romantic passion, people are increasingly pursuing the ideal of the **pure relationship**, in which couples remain because they *choose* to do so. The pure relationship is held together by the acceptance of each partner that, 'until further notice', each gains sufficient benefits from the relationship to make its continuance worthwhile. Love is based upon emotional intimacy that generates trust. Love develops depending on how much each partner is prepared to reveal concerns and needs and to be vulnerable to the other. There is a diversity of forms of pure relationship. Some same-sex relationships, because of their open and negotiated status, come closer to the ideal of pure relationships than do married heterosexual ones.

Some critics have argued that the instability of the pure relationship, which was thought of as a relationship between adults, contrasts with the complexities of family practices which also include children, and neglects the different experiences which men and women tend to have when a (heterosexual) relationship ends. By focusing on relationships between adults, critics have noted, the idea of a pure relationship reflects the marginalization of children and childhood in sociological thought (Smart and Neale 1999). Perhaps the thesis of the pure relationship does not give enough attention to issues of space and time required for its construction. For example, such relationships may still involve home-building and looking after children, both of which can be seen as practical 'joint projects' that also contribute significantly to the maintenance of intimate relationships (Jamieson 1998).

 The sociology of childhood is discussed in chapter 8, 'The Life-Course'.

The 'normal chaos' of love

In *The Normal Chaos of Love* (1995), Ulrich Beck and Elisabeth Beck-Gernsheim exam-

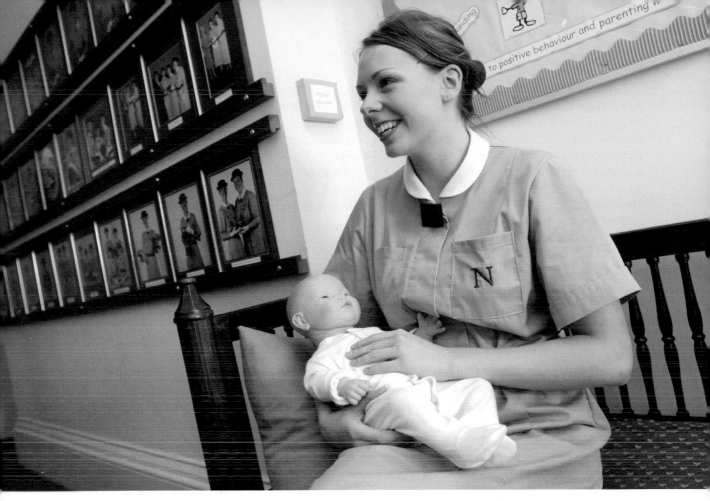

Modern relationships often involve dual-income families where mothers are in full-time work. This has led to the re-emergence of some institutions which might be considered 'old-fashioned', such as schools for professional nannies.

ine the tumultuous nature of personal relationships, marriages and family patterns against the backdrop of a rapidly changing world. The traditions, rules and guidelines which used to govern personal relationships no longer apply, they argue, and individuals are now confronted with an endless series of choices as part of constructing, adjusting, improving or dissolving the unions they form with others. The fact that marriages are now entered into voluntarily, rather than for economic purposes or at the urging of family, brings both freedoms and new strains. In fact, the authors conclude, they demand a great deal of hard work and effort.

Beck and Beck-Gernsheim see our age as one filled with colliding interests between family, work, love and the freedom to pursue individual goals. This collision is felt acutely within personal relationships, particularly when there are two 'labour market biographies' to juggle instead of one, as more women pursue a career. Previous gendered work patterns are less fixed than they once were, both men and women now place emphasis on their professional and personal needs. Relationships in the modern age are not just about relationships; they are also about work, politics, economics, professions and inequality. It is therefore not surprising that antagonisms between men and women are rising. Beck and Beck-Gernsheim claim that the 'battle between the sexes' is the 'central drama of our times', as evidenced in the growth of the marriage-counselling industry, family courts, marital self-help groups and divorce rates. Even though marriage and family life seem to be more 'flimsy' than ever before, they remain very important to people.

Divorce is more common, but rates of remarriage are high. The birth rate may be declining, but there is a huge demand for fertility treatment. Fewer people choose to get married, but the desire to live with someone as part of a couple holds steady. How do we explain such competing tendencies?

Beck and Beck-Gernsheim's answer is: love. They claim that today's 'battle of the sexes' is the clearest possible indication of people's 'hunger for love'. People marry for the sake of love, divorce for the sake of love and engage in an endless cycle of hoping, regretting and trying again. While, on the one hand, the tensions between men and women are high, there remains a deep hope and faith in the possibility of finding true love and fulfilment. This may appear too simple an answer for the complexities of our current age, but Beck and Beck-Gernsheim argue that it is precisely because our world is so overwhelming, impersonal, abstract and rapidly changing that love has become increasingly important. Love is the only place where people can truly find themselves and connect with others:

> Love is a search for oneself, a craving to really get in contact with me and you, sharing bodies, sharing thoughts, encountering one another with nothing held back, making confessions and being forgiven, understanding, confirming and supporting what was and what is, longing for a home and trust to counteract the doubts and anxieties modern life generates. If nothing seems certain or safe, if even breathing is risky in a polluted world, then people chase after the misleading dreams of love until they suddenly turn into nightmares. (1995: 175–6)

Critics have attacked Beck and Beck-Gernsheim's exclusive focus on heterosexuality – the battle between the sexes is the 'central drama of our times' – which, critics say, marginalizes homosexual relationships (Smart and Neale 1999). The thesis can also be criticized for its reliance on the notion of 'individualization', which plays down or fails to acknowledge the importance of social class and community in structuring opportunities and shaping personal relationships – by no means do all women enjoy the kinds of lifetime careers outlined by Beck and Beck-Gernsheim, for instance.

THINKING CRITICALLY

To what extent do you think *love* is capable of holding together the institution of the family? What problems could arise within families when couples place such a high value on love to hold their own relationship together?

Liquid love?

In *Liquid Love* (2003), Zygmunt Bauman argues that, today, relationships are 'the hottest talk of the town and ostensibly the sole game worth playing, despite their notorious risks'. His book is about the 'frailty of human bonds', the feeling of insecurity that this frailty leads to and our responses to it. Bauman writes that the hero of his book is 'the man without bonds' (of, for example, family, class, religion or marriage) or at least the man without fixed, unbreakable ties. Those ties that Bauman's hero does have are loosely knotted, so that they can be released again, with little delay if the circumstances change. To Bauman, the circumstances will change often – he uses the metaphor 'liquid' to describe modern society, which he sees as characterized by constant change and a lack of lasting bonds.

Bauman argues that, in a world of rampant 'individualization', relationships are a mixed blessing; they are filled with conflicting desires, which pull in different ways. On the one hand, there is the desire for freedom, for loose bonds that we can escape from if we so choose and for individualism. On the other, there is the desire for greater security that is gained by tightening the bonds between our partners and ourselves. As it is, Bauman argues, we swing back and forth between the two polarities of security and freedom. Often we run to experts – therapists or columnists, for example – for advice on how we can combine the two. To Bauman, this is attempting 'to have the cake and eat it, to cream off the sweet delights of relationship while omitting its better and tougher bits'. The result is a society of 'semi-detached couples' in 'top pocket relationships'. By the phrase 'top pocket relationships', Bauman means something that can be pulled out when needed, but pushed deep inside the pocket the moment it is not.

One response to the 'frailty of human bonds' is to replace quality in our relationships for quantity. It is not the depth of our relationships, but the number of contacts that we have which becomes important to us. That is partly why, Bauman argues, we are always talking on mobile phones and sending text messages to one another, and even typing them in truncated sentences to increase the speed at which we can send them. It is not the message itself that is important, but the constant circulation of messages, without which we feel excluded. Bauman notes that people now speak more of connections and networks and less of relationships. To be in a relationship means to be mutually engaged; networks suggest moments of being in touch. In a network, connections can be made on demand and broken at will. What really symbolizes the liquid modern relationship for Bauman is computer dating. He cites an interview with a 28-year-old man who notes the one decisive advantage of electronic relations: 'You can always press delete.'

Bauman's ideas are certainly suggestive, but critics see their empirical basis as very weak, leaving them rather speculative, rather than grounded in sociological research. For example, too much is perhaps made of magazines and the short-term impact on social relationships of new technologies such as mobile phones and computers. Like Giddens and Beck and Beck-Gernsheim, Bauman is often accused of being too pessimistic about the contemporary world, especially the transforma-

tion of intimate relationships he identifies. But is his assessment realistic? Carol Smart (2007) thinks not. Indeed, she takes issue with all the theories in the 'Recent perspectives' section above, arguing that they all tend to exaggerate the extent of individualization, family fragmentation and the apparent decline of relationship commitment. Instead, Smart suggests that *personal life* (rather than 'the family' or 'the individual') in modern societies is characterized by strong social and emotional bonds alongside the sharing of memories and experience.

She suggests that the concept of personal life encompasses people's pursuit of a 'life project' (as described in the work of Beck and Giddens, for example), but always relates such individual projects to the wider familial and social context within which they make sense. Smart (2007) argues that Beck's work, for instance, often gives the impression that individuals have been 'cut free' from social structures: a very unrealistic notion. Instead, she argues, 'meaning-constitutive traditions' are important here, as well as such structural factors as social class, ethnicity and gender. Smart attributes particular importance to collective memories, transmitted across generations as well as the way that people are embedded within social structures and 'imagined communities'.

Studying personal life alerts sociologists to something that Smart sees missing in the theories discussed above – namely, *connectedness*. By this, Smart means all the ways in which people maintain their social relationships and associations in different times and contexts, along with the memories, feelings and experiences of being connected to others. She argues that studying connectedness rather than fragmentation allows macrosociological theories to reconnect with the large amount of empirical research on families and relationships and thus get closer to – and understand better – people's real-life experiences.

The relationship networks emerging within 'liquid modernity' can be sustained 'virtually' via electronic forms of communication.

Clearly, these debates and the view we take of recent social change cover some of the big social and political questions of recent times, but what do they mean for the debate about the decline, or otherwise, of family values?

Conclusion: the debate about family values

'The family is collapsing!' cry the advocates of family values, surveying the changes of the past few decades – a more liberal and open attitude towards sexuality, steeply climbing divorce rates and a general seeking for personal happiness at the expense of older conceptions of family duty. We must

recover a moral sense of family life, they argue. We must reinstate the traditional family, which was much more stable and ordered than the tangled web of relationships in which most of us find ourselves now (O'Neill 2002).

These arguments are heard not only in Europe and the United States; changes affecting the personal and emotional spheres go far beyond the borders of any particular country. We find the same issues almost everywhere, differing only in degree and according to the cultural context in which they take place. In China, for example, the state is considering making divorce more difficult to obtain. In the late 1960s, very liberal marriage laws were passed. Marriage is a working contract that can be dissolved 'when husband and wife both desire it'. Even if one partner objects, divorce can be granted when 'mutual affection' has gone from the marriage. Only a two-week wait is required, after which they both pay a few pounds and are henceforth independent. The Chinese divorce rate is still low compared with Western countries, but it is rising rapidly – as is true in the other developing Asian societies. In Chinese cities, not only divorce, but also cohabitation is becoming more frequent. In the vast Chinese countryside, by contrast, everything is different. Marriage and the family are much more traditional – in spite of the official policy of limiting childbirth through a mixture of incentives and punishment. Marriage is an arrangement between two families, fixed by the parents rather than the individuals concerned. A recent study in the province of Gansu, which has only a low level of economic development, found that 60 per cent of marriages are still arranged by parents. As a Chinese saying has it: 'Meet once, nod your head and marry.' There is a twist in the story in modernizing China. Many of those currently divorcing in the urban centres were married in the traditional manner in the country.

In China, there is much talk of protecting the 'traditional' family. In many Western countries, the debate is even more intense and divisive. Defenders of the traditional family argue that the emphasis on relationships comes at the expense of the family as a basic institution of society. Many of these critics now speak of the breakdown of the family. If such a breakdown is occurring, it is extremely significant. The family is the meeting point of a range of trends affecting society as a whole – increasing equality between the sexes, the widespread entry of women into the labour force, changes in sexual behaviour and expectations, the changing relationship between home and work. Among all the changes going on today, none is more important than those happening in our personal lives – in sexuality, emotional life, marriage and the family.

There is a global revolution going on in how we think of ourselves and how we form ties and connections with others. It is a revolution advancing unevenly in different parts of the world, with much resistance.

'Rubbish!' others reply. The family is not collapsing; it is merely diversifying. They argue that we should actively encourage a variety of family forms and sexual life, rather than supposing that everyone has to be compressed into the same mould (Hite 1994).

> ### THINKING CRITICALLY
>
> Using the theories and evidence from this chapter, evaluate the thesis that traditional 'family values' are being eroded. If they are, should we see this as a negative or progressive development for society as a whole? If they are not, then how can we explain why so many people believe they are?

Which side is right? We should probably be critical of both views. A return to the traditional family is not a possibility. This is not only because, as we saw above, the traditional family as it is usually thought of never existed, or because there were too many oppressive facets to families in the past to make them a model for today. It is also because the social changes that have transformed earlier forms of marriage and the family are mostly irreversible. Women will not return in large numbers to a domestic situation from which they have painfully managed to extricate themselves. Sexual partnerships and marriage today, for better or worse, cannot be like they used to be. Emotional communication – more precisely, the active creation and sustaining of relationships – has become central to modern lives in the personal and family domain.

What will be the result? The divorce rate may have levelled off from its previous steep increase, but it is not dropping. All measures of divorce are to some extent estimates, but on the basis of past trends, we can guess that some 60 per cent of all marriages contracted now might end in divorce within ten years.

Divorce, as we have seen, is not always a reflection of unhappiness. People who may in former times have felt constrained to remain in miserable marriages can make a fresh start. But there can be no doubt that the trends affecting sexuality, marriage and the family create deep anxieties for some people at the same time as they generate new possibilities for satisfaction and self-fulfilment for others.

Those who argue that the great diversity in family forms that exists today is to be welcomed, as freeing us from the limitations and sufferings of the past, surely have a certain amount of right on their side. Men and women can remain single if they wish, without having to face the social disapproval that once came from being a bachelor or, even more, a spinster. Couples in live-in relationships no longer face social rejection by their more 'respectable' married friends. Gay couples can set up house together and bring up children without facing the same level of hostility they would have in the past.

These things having been said, it is difficult to resist the conclusion that we stand at a crossroads. Will the future bring about the further decay of long-term marriages or partnerships? Will we more and more inhabit an emotional and sexual landscape scarred by bitterness and violence? None can say for certain. But such a sociological analysis of marriage and the family as we have just concluded strongly suggests that we will not resolve our problems by looking to the past. We must try to reconcile the individual freedoms most of us have come to value in our personal lives with the need to form stable and lasting relations with other people.

Summary points

1. *Kinship*, *family* and *marriage* are closely related terms of key significance for sociology and anthropology. Kinship comprises either genetic ties or ties initiated by marriage. A family is a group of kin having responsibility for the upbringing of children. Marriage is a bond between two people living together in a socially approved sexual relationship.

2. A *nuclear family* is a household in which a married couple (or single parent) live together with their own or adopted children. Where kin other than a married couple and children live in the same household, or are involved in close and continuous relationships, we speak of an *extended family*. During the twentieth century, the predominance of the traditional nuclear family in most industrialized societies has given way to a greater diversity of family forms.

3. In Western societies, marriage – and therefore the family – is associated with *monogamy*. Many other cultures tolerate or encourage *polygamy*, in which an individual may be married to two or more spouses at the same time.

4. There is considerable diversity in family forms among ethnic minority groups. In Britain for example, families of South Asian and African-Caribbean origin differ from the dominant family types.

5. Divorce rates have been rising since 1945 and the number of first marriages has declined. As a result, a growing proportion of the population live in *lone-parent households*.

6. Rates of remarriage are quite high. Remarriage can lead to the formation of a *reconstituted family* – one in which at least one of the adults has children from a previous marriage or relationship.

7. *Cohabitation* (where a couple lives together in a sexual relationship outside marriage) has become more widespread in many industrial countries. Gay men and lesbians are increasingly able to live together as couples, as attitudes to homosexuality become more relaxed. In some instances, homosexual couples have gained the legal right to be defined as a family.

8. Family life is not always happy and harmonious; sexual abuse and domestic violence sometimes occur within it. Most sexual abuse of children and domestic violence is carried out by males, and seems to connect with other types of violent behaviour in which some men are involved.

9. Marriage has ceased to be the condition for regular sexual experience – for either sex – and is no longer the basis of economic activity. However, marriage and the family remain firmly established institutions, while undergoing major stresses and strains.

Further reading

For newcomers to sociology, a good place to begin reading on families and relationships is with Liz Steel and Warren Kidd's *The Family* (Basingstoke: Palgrave Macmillan, 2001), which is a genuinely introductory textbook with lots of guidance. A similar approach is taken by David M. Newman and Liz Grauerholz in their *Sociology of Families*, 2nd edn (London: Sage, 2002), though this is a much larger and more comprehensive book.

From here, it is worth trying something a little more sophisticated, such as Graham Allan and Graham Crow's *Families, Households and Society* (Basingstoke: Palgrave, 2001), which is an excellent account of recent debates in the light of evidence, mainly from the UK. A wider European perspective on changing family forms and policy responses is available in Linda Hantrais's *Family Policy Matters: Responding to Family Change in Europe* (Bristol: Policy Press, 2004).

Sociological theories of the family can be approached via James M. White and David M. Klein's *Family Theories*, 3rd rev. edn (London: Sage, (2007), which also includes perspectives from other disciplines. Then a very comprehensive series of essays covering many of the key issues in this field is Graham Allan's edited collection in *The Sociology of the Family: A Reader* (Oxford: Blackwell, 1999).

Finally, you may want to explore more recent arguments suggesting that changing family forms will need new ways of theorizing. If so, then you could look at Ulrich Beck and Elizabeth Beck-Gernsheim's *Reinventing the Family: In Search of Lifestyles* (Cambridge: Polity, 2002); and Linda McKie and Sarah Cunningham-Burley's edited collection, *Families in Society: Boundaries and Relationships* (Bristol: Policy Press, 2005), which explores families, not as 'things' or 'entities', but rather as 'relationship processes'. Finally, Carol Smart's *Personal Life: New Directions in Sociological Thinking* (Cambridge: Polity, 2007) outlines her thesis of connectedness in people's personal lives.

Internet links

The Centre for Research on Families and Relationships (CRFR) is a research centre founded in 2001, based at the University of Edinburgh, UK, focusing on families:
www.crfr.ac.uk/index.htm

The Centre for Policy Studies (CPS) is a think-tank founded by Margaret Thatcher and Keith Joseph in 1974 to champion a smaller state and foster the family, enterprise and individualism:
www.cps.org.uk/

Civitas – Institute for the Study of Civil Society – was founded in 2000 to promote social cohesion through 'a better division of responsibilities between government and civil society':
www.civitas.org.uk/

Clearinghouse on International Developments in Child, Youth and Family Policies is based at Columbia University, New York; it provides cross-national information on family policies in the industrialized societies:
www.childpolicyintl.org/

The Morgan Centre for the Study of Relationships and Personal Life is a research centre founded in 2005 at the University of Manchester, UK; its research is based on the concept of 'personal life':
www.socialsciences.manchester.ac.uk/morgancentre/

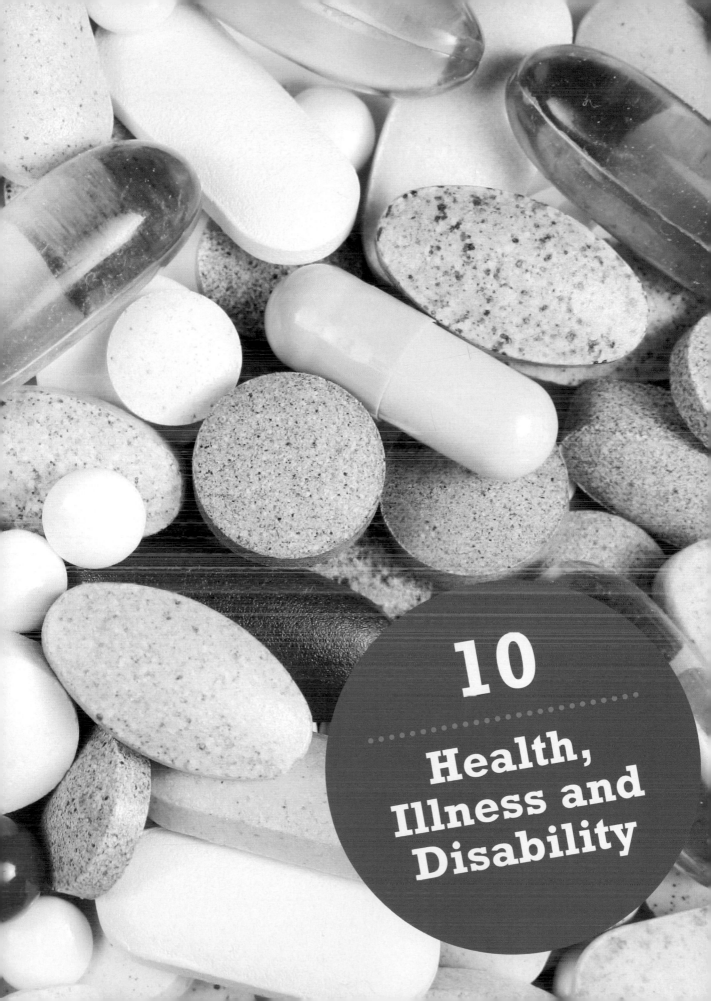

10

Health, Illness and Disability

CHAPTER 10

Health, Illness and Disability

Look at the two photographs above. The images of a sunken face and an emaciated body are almost identical. The young African girl on the left is dying from a simple lack of food. The young woman on the right is a British teenager, dying because, in a society with a superabundance of food, she chose not to eat or to eat so sparingly that her life was endangered.

The social dynamics involved in each case are utterly different. Starvation from lack of food is caused by factors outside people's control and affects only the very poor. The British teenager, living in one of the wealthiest countries in the world, is suffering from anorexia, an illness with no known physical origin. Obsessed with the ideal of achieving a slim body, she has eventually given up eating altogether. Anorexia and other eating disorders are illnesses of the affluent, not of those who have little or no food. They are unknown in the developing countries where food is scarce.

The sociology of the body

Throughout much of human history, a few people – saints or mystics, for example – have deliberately chosen to starve themselves for religious reasons. Anorexia, on the other hand, has no specific connection to religious beliefs, and estimates suggest that some 90 per cent of sufferers are women (Lask and Bryant-Waugh 2000). It is an illness of the body, and thus we might think that we would

This painting by Rubens, completed around 1613, depicts Venus, the goddess of love and beauty

have to look to biological or physical factors to explain it. But health and illness, like other topics we have studied, are also affected by social and cultural influences, such as the pressure to achieve a slim body.

Although it is an illness that expresses itself in physical symptoms, anorexia is closely related to the idea of being on a diet, which in turn is connected with changing views of physical attractiveness, particularly of women, in modern society. In most pre-modern societies, the ideal female shape was a fleshy one. Thinness was not regarded as desirable at all and – partly because it was associated with lack of food and therefore with poverty – the social status of 'thin' was low. Even in Europe in the 1600s and 1700s, the ideal female shape was well proportioned. Anyone who has seen paintings of the period, such as those by Rubens (shown in the photograph), will have noticed how curvaceous (even plump) the women depicted in them are. A contemporary example of the high cultural value traditionally attached to plumpness in some cultures can be seen in the BBC report in 'Global Society 10.1'.

The notion of slimness as the desirable feminine shape originated among some middle-class groups in the late nineteenth century, but it has become generalized as an ideal for most women only recently.

Anorexia thus has its origins in the changing body image of women in the recent history of modern societies. It was first identified as a disorder in France in 1874, but it remained obscure until the past 30 or 40 years (Brown and Jasper 1993). Since then, it has become increasingly common among young women. So has bulimia – bingeing on food, followed by self-induced vomiting. Anorexia and bulimia are often found together in the same individual. Someone may become extremely thin through a starvation diet and then enter a phase of eating enormous amounts and purging in order to maintain a normal weight, followed by a period of again becoming very thin.

Anorexia and other eating disorders are no longer obscure forms of illness confined

Global Society 10.1 Mauritania's 'wife-fattening' farms

Obesity is so revered among Mauritania's white Moor Arab population that the young girls are sometimes force-fed to obtain a weight the government has described as "life-threatening".

A generation ago, over a third of women in the country were force-fed as children – Mauritania is one of the few African countries where, on average, girls receive more food than boys. Now only around one in 10 girls are treated this way. The treatment has its roots in fat being seen as a sign of wealth – if a girl was thin she was considered poor, and would not be respected.

But in rural Mauritania you still see the rotund women that the country is famous for. They walk slowly, dainty hands on the end of dimpled arms, pinching multicoloured swathes of fabric together to keep the biting sand from their faces.

"I make them eat lots of dates, lots and lots of couscous and other fattening food," Fatematou, a voluminous woman in her sixties who runs a kind of "fat farm" in the northern desert town of Atar, told BBC World Service's *The World Today* programme.

Although she had no clients when I met her, she said she was soon expecting to take charge of some seven-year-olds. "I make them eat and eat and eat. And then drink lots and lots of water," she explained. "I make them do this all morning. Then they have a rest. In the afternoon we start again. We do this three times a day – the morning, the afternoon and the evening."

Punishment

She said the girls could end up weighing between 60 to 100 kilograms, "with lots of layers of fat." Fatematou said that it was rare for a girl to refuse to eat, and that if they did, she was helped by the child's parents. "They punish the girls and in the end the girls eat," she said. "If a girl refuses we start nicely, saying 'come on, come on' sweetly, until she agrees to eat."

Fatematou admitted that sometimes the girls cried at the treatment. "Of course they cry – they scream," she said. "We grab them and we force them to eat. If they cry a lot we leave them sometimes for a day or two and then we come back to start again. They get used to it in the end." She argued that in the end the girls were grateful. "When they are small they don't understand, but when they grow up they are fat and beautiful," she said.

"They are proud and show off their good size to make men dribble. Don't you think that's good?"

Change

However, the view that a fat girl is more desirable is now becoming seen as old-fashioned. A study by the Mauritanian ministry of health has found that force-feeding is dying out. Now only 11% of young girls are force fed. "That's not how people think now," Leila – a woman in the ancient desert town of Chinguetti, who herself was fattened as a child – told *The World Today*. "Traditionally a fat wife was a symbol of wealth. Now we've got another vision, another criteria for beauty. Young people in Mauritania today, we're not interested in being fat as a symbol of beauty. Today to be beautiful is to be natural, just to eat normally."

Some men are also much less keen on having a fat wife – a reflection of changes in Mauritanian society. "We're fed up of fat women here," said 19-year-old shop owner Yusuf. "Always fat women! Now we want thin women. In Mauritania if a woman really wants to get married I think she should stay thin. If she gets fat it's not good.

"Some girls have asked me whether they should get fat or stay thin. I tell them if you want to find a man, a European or a Mauritanian, stay thin, it's better for you. But some blokes still like them fat."

Source: Extract from Pascale Harter, BBC World Service, 26 January 2004 © bbc.co.uk/news.

to the wealthiest modern societies. Eating disorders have been increasing in the Middle East, the Far East, South America and Africa (Nasser et al. 2001). A recent review of international research found that, since 1990, problems of eating disorders had been identified in Argentina, Mexico, Brazil, China, Singapore, South Africa, South Korea, Hong Kong, India, Turkey, Iran and the United Arab Emirates (Nasser 2006). In the UK, prevalence rates (the number of cases at any specific time) amongst young adult women have been estimated at around 1–2 per cent for anorexia nervosa and between 1 and 3 per cent for bulimia nervosa. Based on these rates, a best estimate for the total number of British people with a diagnosed or undiagnosed eating disorder is some 1.15 million (Eating Disorders Association 2007).

Nor is obsession with slenderness – and the resulting eating disorders – limited to women in Europe and the United States. As Western images of feminine beauty have spread to the rest of the world, so too have their associated illnesses. Eating disorders were first documented in Japan in the 1960s, a consequence of that county's rapid economic growth and incorporation into the global economy. Anorexia is now found among 1 per cent of young Japanese women, roughly the same percentage as that found in the United States. During the 1980s and 1990s, eating problems surfaced among young, primarily affluent women in Hong Kong and Singapore, as well as in urban areas in Taiwan, China, the Philippines, India and Pakistan (Efron 1997). In a study reported by Medscape's *General Medicine* (Makino et al. 2004), the prevalence of bulimia nervosa in female subjects in Western countries ranged from 0.3 to 7.3 per cent, compared to 0.46 to 3.2 per cent in the non-Western world. Lee (2001) argues that the spread of eating disorders is rooted in the expanding transnational 'culture of modernity'.

Once again, something that may seem to be a purely personal trouble – difficulties with food and despair over one's appearance – turns out to be a public issue. If we include not just life-threatening forms of anorexia but also obsessive concern with dieting and bodily appearance, eating disorders are now part of the lives of millions of people; today they are found in all the industrial countries and are spreading to the developing world too.

> ### THINKING CRITICALLY
> From your knowledge of gender roles and status, why do you think eating disorders seem to affect more women than men? Given that women have achieved more equality with men than in previous generations, is this likely to lead to more eating disorder amongst *young men*? What measures could governments take to stem the increase in eating disorders?

The rapid growth of eating disorders is astonishing, and brings home clearly the influence of social factors on our health and capacity for social interaction. The field known as the **sociology of the body** investigates the ways in which our bodies are affected by these social influences. As human beings, we obviously all possess a body, but this is not something we just have and it is not something physical that exits outside of society. Our bodies are deeply affected by our social experiences, as well as by the norms and values of the groups to which we belong.

One major theme in this chapter is the increasing separation of the body from 'nature' – from our surrounding environment and our biological rhythms. Our bodies are being invaded by the influence of science and **technology**, ranging from machines to diets, and this is creating new dilemmas. The increasing prevalence of forms of plastic surgery, for example, has introduced new options but has also generated intense social controversies. We shall look at one such controversy – plastic surgery for people with facial disfigurements – later in the chapter.

The term 'technology' should not be

In the relatively wealthy countries, a bewildering array of foods from around the world is now available in every supermarket.

....

understood in too narrow a way here. In its most basic sense, it refers to material technologies such as those involved in modern medicine – for example, the scanning machine that allows a doctor to chart a baby's development prior to birth. But we must take account of what Michel Foucault (1988) called 'social technologies' affecting the body. By this phrase, he means that the body is increasingly something we have to 'create' rather than simply accept. A social technology is any kind of regular intervention we make into the functioning of our bodies in order to alter them in specific ways. An example is dieting, so central to anorexia.

In what follows, we will first analyse why eating disorders have become so common. From there, we will study the wider social dimensions of health. Then we turn to the sociology of disability, and look, in particu-

lar, at the social and cultural construction of disablement.

The sociology of health and illness

To understand why eating disorders have become so commonplace in current times, we should think back to the theme of social change analysed elsewhere in the book. Anorexia actually reflects certain kinds of social change, including the impact of globalization.

The rise of eating disorders in Western societies coincides directly with the globalization of food production, which has increased greatly in the past three or four decades. The invention of new modes of refrigeration plus the use of container transportation have allowed food to be stored for long periods and to be delivered from one side of the world to the other. Since the 1950s, supermarkets have stocked foods from all over the world (for those who can afford it – now the majority of the population in Western societies). Most of them are available all the time, not just, as was true previously, when they are in season locally.

Over the past decade or so, many people in developed countries have begun to think more carefully about their diet. This does not mean that everyone is desperately trying to get thin. Rather, when all foods are available more or less all the time, we must decide what to eat – in other words, construct a diet, where 'diet' means the foods we habitually consume. To construct our diet, we have to decide what to eat in relation to the many sorts of new medical information with which science now bombards us – for instance, that cholesterol levels are a factor in causing heart disease. The development of genetically modified (GM) foods presents yet another dilemma for people; in the USA, GM foods are routinely consumed, but in most of Europe, consumers have been anxious about their 'non-natural' (that is, 'man-made') status. Conversely, the recent trend towards organically grown food shows a willingness to 'buy natural' (at least, for those who can afford to do so).

In a society where food is abundant and relatively cheap, we are able for the first time to design our bodies in relation to our lifestyle habits (such as jogging, bicycling, swimming and yoga) and what we eat. Eating disorders have their origins in the opportunities, but also the profound strains and tensions, that this situation produces.

Why do eating disorders affect women in particular and young women most acutely? To begin with, it should be pointed out that not all those suffering from eating disorders are women; globally, around 10 per cent are men (Nasser 2006). But men do not suffer from anorexia or bulimia as often as women, partly because widely held social norms stress the importance of physical attractive-ness more for women than for men and partly because desirable body images of men differ from those of women. Drawing on the diaries of American girls over the last two centuries, Joan Jacobs Brumberg (1997) argues that nowadays, when adolescent girls in the USA ask themselves the questions 'Who am I?' and 'Who do I want to be?', the answer, far more than it was a century ago, is likely to revolve around the body. Brumberg argues that 'commercial interests' increasingly play on the body angst of young girls. She concludes that the body is now so central to American girls' sense of self that it has become their central project.

Anorexia and other eating disorders reflect the current situation in which women play a much larger part in the wider society than they used to but are still judged as much by their appearance as by their attainments. Eating disorders are rooted in feelings of shame about the body. The individual feels herself to be inadequate and imperfect, and her anxieties about how others perceive her become focused through her feelings about her body. Ideals of slimness at that point become obsessive – shedding weight becomes the means of making everything all right in her world. Once she starts to diet and exercise compulsively, she can become locked into a pattern of refusing food altogether or of vomiting up what she has eaten. If the pattern is not broken (and some forms of psychotherapy and medical treatment have proved effective here), the sufferer can actually starve herself to death.

The spread of eating disorders reflects the influence of science and technology on our ways of life today: calorie-counting has only been possible with the advance of technology. But the impact of technology is always conditioned by social factors. We have much more autonomy over the body than ever before, a situation that creates new possibilities of a positive kind as well as new anxieties and problems. What is happening is part of what sociologists call the **socialization of nature**. This phrase refers to the fact that phenomena that used to be 'natural', or given in nature, have now become social – they depend on our own social decisions.

Sociological perspectives on medicine

The rise of the biomedical model of health

Like many of the ideas we explore in this book, 'health' and 'illness' are terms that are culturally and socially defined. Cultures differ in what they consider to be healthy and normal. All cultures have known concepts of physical health and illness, but most of what we now recognize as medicine is a consequence of developments in Western society over the past three centuries. In pre-modern cultures, the family was the main institution coping with sickness or affliction. There have always been individuals who specialized as healers, using a mixture of physical and magical remedies, and many of these traditional systems of treatment survive today in non-Western cultures throughout the world. A large number of them belong to the category of alternative medicines discussed below.

For approximately 200 years now, the dominant Western ideas about medicine have been expressed in the **biomedical model** of health. This understanding of health and illness developed along with the growth of modern societies. In fact, it can be seen as one of the main features of such societies. Its emergence was closely linked to the triumph of science and reason over traditional or religious-based explanations of the world (see the discussion of Max Weber and rationalization in chapter 1). Before looking at the biomedical model in more depth, let us briefly consider the social and historical context in which it arose.

Public health

We mentioned above how members of traditional societies relied largely on folk remedies, treatments and healing techniques which were passed down from generation to generation. Illnesses were frequently regarded in magical or religious terms and were attributed to the presence of evil spirits or 'sin'. For peasants and average town-dwellers, there was no outside authority that was concerned with their health in the way that states and public health systems are today. Health was a private matter, not a public concern.

The rise of both the nation-state and industrialization brought about drastic changes in this situation, however. The emergence of nation-states with defined territories produced a shift in attitudes towards local people, who were no longer simply inhabitants of the land, but were a population falling under the rule of a central authority. The human population was seen as a resource to be monitored and regulated as part of the process of maximizing national wealth and power. The state began to take a heightened interest in the health of its population, as the well-being of its members affected the nation's productivity, level of prosperity, defensive capabilities and rate of growth. The study of **demography** – the size, composition and dynamics of human populations – assumed much greater importance. The Census was introduced in order to record and monitor changes occurring in the population. Statistics of all sorts were collected and calculated: birth rates, mortality rates, average ages of marriage and childbearing, suicide rates, life expectancy, diet, common illnesses, causes of death and so forth.

Michel Foucault (1926–84) made an influential contribution to our understanding of the rise of modern medicine by drawing attention to the regulation and disciplining of bodies by European states (1973). He argued that sexuality and sexual behaviour were of central importance to this process. Sex was both the way in which the population could reproduce and grow, and a potential threat to its health and well-being. Sexuality not linked to reproduction was something to be repressed and controlled. This monitoring of sexuality by the state occurred in part through the collection of data about marriage, sexual behaviour, legitimacy and illegitimacy, the use of contraception and abortions. This surveillance went hand in hand with the promotion of strong public norms about sexual morality and acceptable sexual activity. For example, sexual 'perversions' such as homosexuality, masturbation and sex outside marriage were all labelled and condemned.

> See chapter 14, 'Sexuality and Gender', for a discussion of different forms of sexuality.

The idea of public health took shape in an attempt to eradicate **pathologies** from the population – the 'social body'. The state began to assume responsibility for improving the conditions in which the population lived. Sanitation and water systems were developed to protect against disease. Roads were paved and attention was devoted to housing. Regulations were gradually imposed on slaughterhouses and facilities for food processing. Burial practices were monitored to ensure that they did not pose a health threat to the population. A whole series of institutions, such as prisons, asylums, workhouses, schools and hospitals emerged as part of the move towards monitoring, controlling and reforming the people.

The biomedical model

Medical practices were closely intertwined with the social changes described above. The application of science to medical diagnosis and cure was the major feature of the development of modern healthcare systems. Disease came to be defined objectively, in terms of identifiable objective 'signs' located in the body, as opposed to symptoms experienced by the patient. Formal medical care by trained 'experts' became the accepted way of treating both physical and mental illnesses. Medicine became a tool of reform for behaviours or conditions perceived as 'deviant' – from crime to homosexuality to mental illness.

There are three main assumptions on which the biomedical model of health is predicated. First, disease is viewed as a breakdown within the human body that diverts it from its 'normal' state of being. The germ theory of disease, developed in the late 1800s, holds that there is a specific identifiable agent behind every disease. In order to restore the body to health, the cause of the disease must be isolated and treated.

Second, the mind and body can be treated separately. The patient represents a sick body – a pathology – rather than a whole individual. The emphasis is on curing the disease, rather than on the individual's well-being. The biomedical model holds that the sick body can be manipulated, investigated and treated in isolation, without considering other factors. Medical specialists adopt a 'medical gaze', a detached approach in viewing and treating the sick patient. The treatment is to be carried out in a neutral, value-free manner, with information collected and compiled, in clinical terms, in a patient's official file.

Third, trained medical specialists are considered the only experts in the treatment of disease. The medical profession as a body adheres to a recognized code of ethics and is made up of accredited individuals who have successfully completed long-term training. There is no room for self-taught healers or 'non-scientific' medical practices. The hospital represents the appropriate environment in which to treat serious illnesses; these treatments often rely on some combination of technology, medication or surgery. The main assumptions and critiques of the biomedical model are summarized in table 10.1.

Criticisms of the biomedical model

Over the past few decades, the biomedical model of illness described above has been the object of growing criticism. First, some scholars have claimed that the effectiveness of scientific medicine is 'overrated'. In spite of the prestige that modern medicine

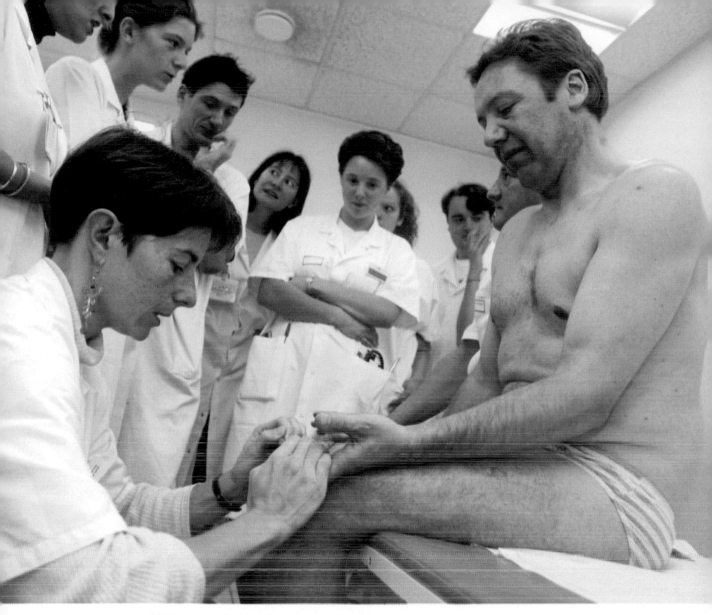

According to the biomedical model of health, to the medical profession patients represent only 'sick bodies'.

has acquired, improvements in overall health can be attributed far more to social and environmental changes than to medical skill. Effective sanitation, better nutrition and improved sewerage and hygiene were more influential, particularly in reducing the infant mortality rates and deaths of young children (McKeown 1979). Drugs, advances in surgery, and antibiotics did not significantly decrease death rates until well into the twentieth century. Antibiotics used to treat bacterial infections first became available in the 1930s and 1940s, while immunizations (against diseases such as polio) were developed later. Ivan Illich (1975) has even suggested that modern medicine has done more harm than good because of iatrogenesis, or 'self-caused' disease. Illich argued that there are three types: clinical, social and cultural iatrogenesis. Clinical iatrogenesis is where medical treatment makes the patient worse or creates new conditions. Social iatrogenesis is where medicine expands into more and more areas, creating an artificial demand for its services. Social iatrogenesis,

Table 10.1 Assumptions and critiques of the biomedical model

Assumptions	Critiques
Disease is a breakdown of the human body caused by a specific biological agent.	Disease is socially constructed, not something that can be revealed through 'scientific truth'.
The patient is a passive being whose 'sick body' can be treated separately from his or her mind.	The patient's opinions and experience of illness is crucial to the treatment. The patient is an active, 'whole' being whose overall well-being – not just physical health – is important.
Medical specialists possess 'expert knowledge' and offer the only valid treatment of disease.	Medical experts are not the only source of knowledge about health and illness. Alternative forms of knowledge are equally valid.
The appropriate arena for treatment is the hospital, where medical technology is concentrated and best employed.	Healing does not need to take place in a hospital. Treatments utilizing technology, medication and surgery are not necessarily superior.

Illich argued, leads to cultural iatrogenesis, where the ability to cope with the challenges of everyday life is progressively reduced by medical explanations and alternatives. To critics like Illich, the scope of modern medicine should be dramatically reduced.

Second, modern medicine has been accused of discounting the opinions and experiences of the patients it seeks to treat. Because medicine is supposedly based on objective, scientific understandings of the causes and cures of specific physical ailments, there is little perceived need to listen to the individual interpretations that patients give to their conditions. Each patient is a 'sick body' to be treated and cured. Critics argue, however, that effective treatment can only take place when the patient is treated as a thinking, capable being with their own valid understandings and interpretations.

Third, critics argue that scientific medicine posits itself as superior to any alternative form of medicine or healing. A belief has been perpetuated that anything that is 'unscientific' is necessarily inferior. As we have already seen, the assertion that modern medicine is somehow a more valid form of knowledge is being undermined by the growing popularity of alternative forms of medicine, such as homeopathy and acupuncture. In many industrialized societies over the last decade, there has been a surge of interest in the potential of **alternative medicine**.

THINKING CRITICALLY

List as many of the health successes of biomedicine as you can think of. Do these provide solid evidence for the belief that scientific medicine is superior to all other types of medicine? What types of health problems has biomedicine not been very effective in tackling? Why do you think this is the case?

THINKING CRITICALLY

Have you ever tried complementary or alternative therapies? What led you to do so? How do the assumptions that underlie the biomedical model of health differ from those found in alternative medicines? Why has there been such a rise in alternative medicines and treatments in recent years?

The number of alternative medical practitioners is expanding, as are the forms of

10.1 Alternative medicine

Earlier in her life Jan Mason enjoyed vibrant health. But when she began experiencing extreme tiredness and depression, she found that her regular doctor was unable to provide her with much relief:

> Before, I was a very fit person. I could swim, play squash, run, and suddenly I just keeled over. I went to the doctor but nobody could tell me what it was. My GP said it was glandular fever and gave me antibiotics which gave me terrible thrush. Then he kept saying that he did not know what it was either. . . . I went through all the tests. I was really very poorly. It went on for six months. I was still ill and they still did not know what it was. (Quoted in Sharma 1992: 37)

Jan's doctor suggested that she try anti-depressants, concluding that she was suffering from the effects of stress. Jan knew that anti-depressants were not the answer for her, even though she acknowledged that her undiagnosed condition had become a great stress in her life. After listening to a radio programme, she suspected that her lethargy might be a result of post-viral fatigue syndrome. On the advice of a friend, she sought out the assistance of a homeopath – an alternative medical practitioner who assesses the state of the whole body and then, using minuscule doses of substances, treats 'like with like', on the assumption that the symptoms of a

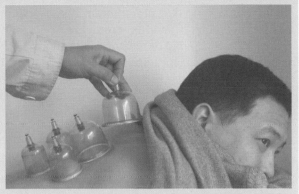

Fire-cupping, a method of applying acupressure in traditional Chinese medicine, is just one of many alternative or complementary therapies, many of which challenge the conventional biomedical model.

disease are part of a body's self-healing process. On finding a homeopath whose approach she was comfortable with, Jan was pleased with the treatment she received (Sharma 1992).

Jan is one of a growing number of people who are incorporating non-orthodox medical practices into their health routines. It has been estimated that as many as one in four Britons have consulted an alternative practitioner. The profile of the typical individual who seeks out alternative forms of healing is female, young to middle-aged, and middle class.

healing that are available. From herbal remedies to acupuncture, from reflexology and chiropractic to light therapy treatments, modern society is witnessing an explosion of healthcare alternatives which lie outside, or overlap with, the 'official' medical system.

Industrialized countries have some of the most well-developed, well-resourced medical facilities in the world. Why, then, are a growing number of people choosing to abandon the healthcare system for 'unscientific' treatments such as aromatherapy and hypnotherapy? First, it is important to stress

that not everyone who uses alternative medicine does so as a substitute for orthodox treatment (although some alternative approaches, such as homeopathy, reject the basis of orthodox medicine entirely). Many people combine elements of both approaches. For this reason, some scholars prefer to call non-orthodox techniques *complementary* medicine rather than alternative medicine (Saks 1992). Some complementary therapies, such as acupuncture, have become part of many mainstream healthcare systems, and are offered alongside biomedical diagnosis and treatment.

There are a number of reasons why individuals might seek the services of a complementary or alternative practitioner. Some people perceive orthodox medicine as deficient, or incapable of relieving chronic, nagging pains or symptoms of stress and anxiety (as in Jan's case in 'Using your sociological imagination 10.1'). Others are dissatisfied with the way modern healthcare systems function – long waiting lists, referrals through chains of specialists, financial restrictions and so forth. Connected to this are concerns about the harmful side-effects of medication and the intrusiveness of surgery – both techniques favoured by modern healthcare systems. The asymmetrical power relationship between doctors and patients is at the heart of some people's choice to avail themselves of alternative medicine. They feel that the role of the 'passive patient' does not grant them enough input into their own treatment and healing. Finally, some individuals profess religious or philosophical objections to orthodox medicine, which tends to treat the mind and body separately. They believe that the spiritual and psychological dimensions of health and illness are often not taken into account in the practice of orthodox medicine.

The growth of alternative medicine presents a number of interesting questions for sociologists to consider. First and foremost, it is a fascinating reflection of the transformations occurring within modern societies. We are living in an age where more and more information is available – from a variety of sources – to draw on in making choices about our lives. Healthcare is no exception in this regard. Individuals are increasingly becoming 'health consumers' – adopting an active stance towards their own health and well-being. Not only are we able to make choices about the type of practitioners to consult, but we are also demanding more involvement in our own care and treatment. In this way, the growth of alternative medicine is linked to the expansion of the self-help movement, which involves support groups, learning circles and self-help books. People are now more likely than ever before to seize control of their lives and actively reshape them, rather than to rely on the instructions or opinions of others.

Another issue of interest to sociologists relates to the changing nature of health and illness in the late modern period. Many of the conditions and illnesses for which individuals seek alternative medical treatment seem to be products of the modern age itself. Insomnia, anxiety, stress, depression, fatigue and chronic pain (caused by arthritis, cancer and other diseases) are all on the rise in industrialized societies. While these conditions have long existed, they appear to be causing greater distress and disruption to people's health than ever before. Recent surveys have revealed that stress has now surpassed the common cold as the biggest cause of absence from work. The World Health Organization (2001) says that depression is the leading cause of disability globally, and by 2020 it is forecast to be the second leading contributor to the global burden of disease. Ironically, it seems that these consequences of living in the modern world are ones which orthodox medicine has great difficulty in addressing. While alternative medicine is unlikely to overtake 'official' healthcare altogether, indications are that its role will continue to grow.

Fourth, some sociologists have argued that the medical profession wields enormous power in defining what does and does not constitute illness. It is able to use its position as the arbiter of 'scientific truth' to bring more and more realms of human life under medical control. Some of the strongest criticisms along these lines have come from women who argue that the processes of pregnancy and childbirth have been appropriated and 'medicalized' by modern medicine. Rather than remaining in the hands of women – with the help of midwives in the home – childbirth now occurs in hospitals under the direction of predominantly male specialists. Pregnancy,

10.2   The medicalization of hyperactivity

In the past 15 years, the number of prescriptions written for the drug Ritalin has grown exponentially. In the United States, some 2 million prescriptions per month are written for ADHD drugs (mainly Ritalin) for children. Between 3 and 5 per cent of America's children live with ADHD. In Britain, 361,832 prescriptions for Ritalin and similar drugs were issued in 2005, most of them for children with diagnosed ADHD (*Guardian*, 11 February 2006). What is Ritalin and why should sociologists be concerned with it?

Ritalin is a drug prescribed to children and adolescents with Attention-Deficit Hyperactive Disorder (ADHD), a psychological disorder which, according to many physicians and psychiatrists, accounts for children's inattentiveness, difficulty in concentrating and inability to learn in school. Ritalin has been described as 'the magic pill'. It helps children to focus, it calms them down and it helps them to learn more effectively. Children who were once disruptive and problematic in the classroom become 'angelic' students, say some teachers, once they begin taking Ritalin.

Critics of Ritalin, however, argue that the drug is far from the harmless 'magic pill' which it is often made out to be. Despite the fact that it has been prescribed in growing quantities in the USA and UK over recent years, no comprehensive research has been carried out on its possible long-term effects on children's brains and bodies. Perhaps more worrying is the claim that Ritalin has become a convenient 'solution' to what is in fact not even a physical problem. Opponents of Ritalin argue that the 'symptoms' of ADHD are in fact reflections of the growing pressure and stress on modern children – an increasingly fast pace of life, the overwhelming effect of information technology, lack of exercise, high-sugar diets and the fraying of family life. Through the use of Ritalin, it is claimed, the medical profession has succeeded in 'medicalizing' child hyperactivity and inattentiveness, rather than drawing attention to the social causes of the observed symptoms.

a common and natural phenomenon, is treated as an 'illness' laden with risks and danger. Feminists argue that women have lost control over this process, as their opinions and knowledge are deemed irrelevant by the 'experts' who now oversee reproductive processes (Oakley 1984). Similar concerns about the medicalization of 'normal' conditions have been raised in relation to hyperactivity in children (see 'Using your sociological imagination 10.2'), unhappiness or mild depression (commonly regulated with the help of medications like Prozac), and tiredness (frequently labelled Chronic Fatigue Syndrome). Many of the assumptions of the biomedical model are being increasingly questioned, as the world in which it developed changes.

Fifth, critics have argued that the assumptions underlying the biomedical model of health have lent themselves to gross political manipulation, in particular through **eugenics**, the attempt to genetically 'improve' the human race through 'good breeding'. Scientific and medical 'experts' in Nazi Germany took these policies to their most extreme, by claiming that they had identified a racially superior, light-skinned 'Aryan' race. Their eugenic programmes led to the genocide of millions of people who belonged to groups the Nazis saw as biologically inferior, such as Jews and gypsies, as well as the systematic murder of more than 250,000 disabled people (Burleigh 1994).

Although Nazi Germany made by far the most murderous use of eugenic policies, it should be remembered that in the twentieth century these techniques – often described as 'population policies' – were also used in several other European countries and the USA against particular sections of the population, notably the disabled. These policies mostly took the form of the compulsory sterilization of 'feeble-minded' women. Racism led to black women being grossly over-represented among the 60,000 people forcibly sterilized in several US states between 1907 and 1960. In Scandinavia, political leaders and geneticists adopted policies for compulsory sterilization because they were concerned that the emerging welfare state would encourage the 'unfit' to reproduce and would therefore reduce the quality of the 'national stock'. In Sweden alone, 63,000 people, 90 per cent of them women, were sterilized between 1934 and 1975. Norway, a much smaller country, sterilized 48,000 people in the same period. British and Dutch medical experts and policy-makers, by contrast, adopted voluntary sterilization, together with the mass institutionalization and segregation of the 'feeble-minded' (Rose 2003).

Today, the rapid development of medical technology is raising new and difficult questions for critics of the biomedical model. A great deal of scientific endeavour is now being devoted to the expansion of genetic engineering, which makes it possible to intervene in the genetic make-up of the foetus so as to influence its subsequent development. The debate about genetic engineering is often polarized between critics, who see it as fatally corrupted by the history of eugenics in the twentieth century discussed above, and supporters who argue it is separate from these events (Kerr and Shakespeare 2002). According to its supporters, genetic engineering will create enormous opportunities. It is possible, for example, to identify the genetic factors that make some people vulnerable to certain diseases. Genetic reprogramming will ensure that these illnesses are no longer passed on from generation to generation. In 2004 a group of people in the UK with a particular form of inherited bowel cancer were granted the right by the government's Human Fertilization and Embryology Authority to select embryos free from genes that might trigger the disease in future generations. The decision means that only those embryos free of the gene that could cause the cancer will be implanted into the mother's womb. Without the screening process, infants would have a 50 per cent chance of inheriting the disease (*The Times*, 1 November 2004). The selection of embryos was previously approved only for childhood or untreatable disorders such as cystic fibrosis and Huntington's disease (*The Times*, 6 November 2004). On the other hand, the ruling by the Human Fertilization and Embryology Authority deepens the controversy over 'designer babies'. It sets a precedent that will allow doctors to 'cherry-pick' embryos for a much wider range of traits than at present. It is now scientifically possible, for example, to 'design' bodies before birth in terms of colour of skin, hair and eyes, weight and so forth.

Several of the criticisms of the biomedical model, discussed above, apply also to the genetic-engineering debate. Many of those with concerns about the biomedical model will question the role of medical experts in exerting their authority over the technology. Will there be unintended consequences of medical intervention? What role will parents-to-be have in making decisions about the selection of embryos? Is this another case of (traditionally male) medical experts giving authoritative medical advice to (obviously female) future mothers? What safeguards should be present to prevent sexism, racism or disablism in embryo selection? And how are these categories defined? Genetic engineering is unlikely to be cheap. Will this mean that those who can afford to pay will be able to programme out from their children any traits they see as socially undesirable? What will happen to the children of more deprived groups, who will continue to be born naturally? Some sociologists have argued that differential access to genetic engineering might lead to the emergence of a 'biological underclass'. Those who do not have the physical advantages genetic engineering can bring might be subject to prejudice and discrimination by those who do enjoy these advantages. They might have difficulty finding employment and life or health insurance (Duster 1990). For sociologists, the rapid pace in which new medical technologies are advancing raises an increasing number of new and difficult questions.

Medicine and health in a changing world

There is a growing realization that it is not only medical experts who possess knowledge and understanding about health and illness. All of us are in a position to interpret and shape our own well-being through our understanding of our bodies, and through choices in our everyday lives about diet, exercise, consumption patterns and general lifestyle. These new directions in popular thinking about health, along with the other criticisms of modern medicine outlined above, are contributing to some profound transformations within healthcare systems in modern societies (see figure 10.1). They also explain the rise in alternative or complementary medicine, discussed above.

Yet other factors are relevant here as well: the nature and the scale of disease itself have both been changing. In earlier times, the major illnesses were infectious diseases such as tuberculosis, cholera, malaria and polio. They often took on epidemic proportions and could threaten a whole population. In industrialized countries today, such acute infectious diseases have become a minor cause of death; some of them have been substantially eradicated. The most common causes of death in industrialized countries are now non-infectious chronic diseases such as cancer, heart disease, diabetes or circulatory diseases. This shift is referred to as the 'health transition'. Whereas in pre-modern societies the highest rates of death were among infants and young children, today death rates rise with increasing age. Because people are living longer and suffering predominantly from chronic degenerative diseases, there is the need for a new approach to health and caring. There is also increased emphasis on 'lifestyle choices' – such as smoking, exercise and diet – which are seen to influence the onset of many chronic illnesses.

HIV and AIDS in global perspective

A powerful reminder that the general shift from acute to chronic conditions is not, however, absolute came in the early 1980s, with the emergence of a deadly new epidemic – AIDS – which rapidly became a pandemic (a global epidemic), killing millions of adults and young people alike. A person is often said to have 'acquired immunodeficiency syndrome' (AIDS) when the number of immune cells in the body falls below a designated minimum required to fight off infections. Once this point is reached, they are likely to be affected by opportunistic infections which their body is then unable to fight off, leading to very serious, life-threatening diseases such as pneumonia, tuberculosis and skin cancers. AIDS is the result of damage caused by previous infection with a virus known as HIV (human immunodeficiency virus). There is still no cure for either HIV infection or AIDS, nor is there a vaccine to prevent infection in the first place.

Transmission of HIV occurs in four main ways:

- from unprotected penetrative sex with an infected person;

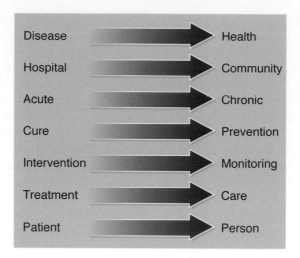

Figure 10.1   Contemporary transformations in health and medicine

Source: Nettleton 2006

- from injection or transfusion of contaminated blood or blood products such as skin grafts or organ transplants from infected people;
- from infected mothers to their babies either during pregnancy, at birth or through breastfeeding;
- sharing unsterilized injection equipment used by an infected person.

The United Nations estimates that some 25 million people died of AIDS-related conditions between 1981 and 2005, making this one of the deadliest pandemics in human history (UNAIDS 2006; see also figure 10.2). The HIV incidence rate is thought to have peaked in the late-1990s, but the number of people living with HIV is rising, partly a result of the effectiveness of anti-retroviral drugs treatments in delaying the onset of AIDS. However, these drugs are expensive and though many people with HIV in the developed world have access to them, this has not been the case in poorer countries, where AIDS has become a major cause of death.

A 2006 UN report estimated that 38.6 million people were living with HIV around the world in 2005, the highest prevalence rates being in Southern Africa, where some epidemics were still expanding (see 'Global society 10.2' for a report on AIDS/HIV in South Africa). There was also some evidence of a resurgent epidemic in the USA, where the disease was first identified in 1981, indicating that there is a long way to go before HIV across the world can be said to be 'under control'.

What then are the sociological lessons to be learned from the emergence of AIDS? First, the links made between particular lifestyles and risk of infection initially led to the stigmatizing of gay men. Erving Goffman (1963) argued that **stigma** is a relationship of devaluation in which one individual is disqualified from full social acceptance. Stigma can take many forms – for example, physical (such as visible impairments), biographical (such as the possession of a criminal record) or contextual (for example, 'hanging out with the wrong crowd'). Stigmas are rarely based on valid understandings. They spring from stereotypes or perceptions, which may be false, or only partially correct. Stigmatization often appears in the medical context. Goffman argued that inherent in the process of stigmatization is social control. Stigmatizing groups is one way in which society controls their behaviour. In some cases, the stigma is never removed and the person is never fully accepted into society.

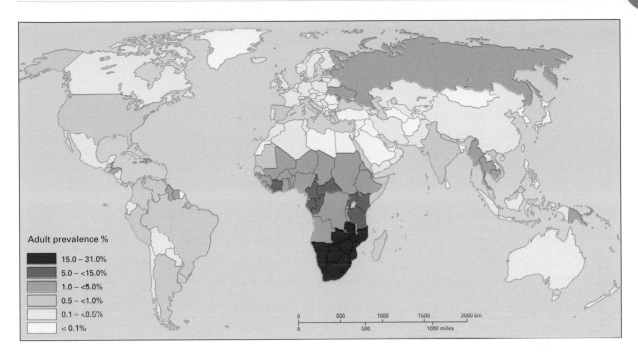

Figure 10.2 A global view of adult HIV infection by prevalence rates, 2005

Source: UNAIDS 2006

This was true of early AIDS patients and continues in some countries.

Sarah Nettleton (2006) notes that because AIDS was first found amongst gay men in the USA, it was originally called GRID – Gay Related Immune Deficiency – and it was suggested that a 'fast lane' gay lifestyle actually *caused* the disease, which was often referred to in the media as a 'gay plague'. Nettleton points out that research findings discredited such beliefs and that it is not being part of a particular social group that is especially risky, but specific *practices*, such as injecting with non-sterilized needles or having unprotected penetrative sex. Nevertheless, epidemiological interpretations of gay men as part of 'high-risk groups' tended to reinforce the division between such groups and the 'heterosexual general public', thus lulling the latter into a false and very dangerous sense of security.

Second, AIDS raises important issues in relation to social inequalities. For example, in many countries, heterosexual norms of masculinity tend to reject the use of condoms, favouring unprotected sex as a way of 'being a man'. The consequences of such widespread social norms could hardly be more serious for heterosexual women. As noted above, the gross global inequalities between the developed and developing worlds are also emphasized by the AIDS pandemic, with HIV-infected people in the relatively rich countries having a much greater chance of survival than those in poorer ones. Attempts to make anti-retroviral drugs more widely available in developing countries have had some success in recent years, though the disparity in healthcare provision remains starkly unequal. Global inequality here literally is a matter of life and death.

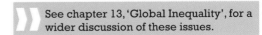

See chapter 13, 'Global Inequality', for a wider discussion of these issues.

Third, the concept of 'risk' has become a central one in social scientific debates on lifestyles, health and medicine since the

Global Society 10.2 HIV/AIDS in South Africa

South Africa is currently experiencing one of the most severe AIDS epidemics in the world. Although it can be hard to collect reliable figures, various data sources suggest that 5.7 million people were living with HIV in South Africa by the end of 2007, and almost 1,000 AIDS deaths were occurring every day. Almost one in five adults are infected and this has serious consequences not only for the infected individual, but also for their family and communities. A recent survey found that South Africans spent more time at funerals than they did having their hair cut, shopping or having barbecues. Less than half as many people had been to a wedding in the past month than had been to a funeral. Mortality rates are so high that in some parts of the country, cemeteries are running out of space for the dead.

Beyond this personal and community level of suffering, the AIDS epidemic has also had a significant effect on the country's general social and economic development. South Africa fell 35 places in the Human Development Index (a worldwide measurement that ranks countries from the most developed down to the least developed) between 1990 and 2003, a period during which the prevalence of HIV saw a dramatic increase. The average life expectancy is 54 years, an estimated 10 years lower than it would otherwise be without the AIDS epidemic. Economically, the crisis is a huge drain on national resources: in 2006 a leading researcher estimated that HIV-positive patients would soon account for 60-70% of medical expenditure in South African hospitals.

The impact on young people is particularly marked. Over half of 15-year-olds are not expected to reach the age of 60. While it is thought that half of all deaths in South Africa are caused by AIDS, this figure is higher amongst young people. Quite apart from many children not being able to attend school because they are ill or need to care for sick relatives, schools have fewer teachers, as an estimated 21% of teachers in South Africa are living with HIV.

Antiretroviral drug treatments have been developed which make it possible for HIV-positive people to remain in good health from day to day and to lead relatively normal lives. However, few people in South Africa have access to this treatment hence the devastation AIDS is causing in South Africa. Such a serious crisis affecting a whole nation is due to a number of different factors such as poverty, social instability and a lack of sufficient government action. People trying to alleviate the problem continue to debate which is the most serious issue in order to most effectively combat the epidemic.

For more information, see the AVERT website (http://www.avert.org/).

---

late twentieth century, and the emergence of AIDS has certainly been instrumental in the creation of a more 'risk-aware' population. As discussed in chapter 5, 'The Environment', Ulrich Beck (1999) has even suggested that we are moving into a 'world risk society'; if this is the case, then one global risk that no one can ignore today is that of HIV infection.

Whether the contemporary transformations in healthcare discussed in this section will result in a new 'health paradigm' to replace the biomedical model, as some scholars have suggested, is unclear. But it is certain that we are witnessing a period of significant and rapid reform in modern medicine and in people's attitudes towards it.

Sociological perspectives on health and illness

One of the main concerns of sociologists is to examine the experience of illness. Sociologists ask how illness, such as anorexia discussed above, is experienced and interpreted by the sick person and by those with whom she comes into contact. If you have ever been ill, even for a short period of time, you will know that patterns in everyday life are temporarily modified and your interactions with others become transformed. This is because the 'normal' functioning of the body is a vital, but often unnoticed, part of our lives. We depend on our bodies to operate as they should; our very sense of self is predicated on the expectation that our bodies will facilitate, not impede, our social interactions and daily activities.

Illness has both personal and public dimensions. When we become ill, not only do we experience pain, discomfort, confusion and other challenges, but others are affected as well. People in close contact with us may extend sympathy, care and support. They may struggle to make sense of the fact of our illness or to find ways to incorporate it into the patterns of their own lives. Others with whom we come into contact may also react to illness; these reactions in turn help to shape our own interpretations and can pose challenges to our sense of self.

Two ways of understanding the experience of illness have been particularly influential in sociological thought. The first, associated with the functionalist school, sets forth the norms of behaviour which individuals are thought to adopt when sick. The second view, favoured by symbolic interactionists, is a broader attempt to reveal the interpretations which are ascribed to illness and how these meanings influence people's actions and behaviour.

> For more on functionalist theory see chapter 1, 'What is Sociology?', and chapter 3, 'Theories and Perspectives in Sociology'.

Functionalist accounts of sick roles and social systems have been influential in shaping sociological studies of health and illness, but we shall now turn to some of the ways that sociologists of the symbolic interactionist school have attempted to understand the *experience* of illness.

Illness as 'lived experience'

Symbolic interactionists are interested in the ways people interpret the social world and the meanings they ascribe to it. Many sociologists have applied this approach to the realm of health and illness in order to understand how people experience being ill or perceive the illness of others. How do people react and adjust to news about a serious illness? How does illness shape individuals' daily lives? How does living with a chronic illness affect an individual's self-identity?

As we saw in the discussion of ageing in chapter 8, people in industrialized societies are now living longer, but suffering later in life from chronic illnesses. Medicine is able to relieve the pain and discomfort associated with some of these conditions, but a growing number of people are faced with the prospect of living with illness over a long period of time. Sociologists are concerned with how illness in such cases becomes incorporated in an individual's personal 'biography'.

One theme that sociologists have explored is how chronically ill individuals learn to cope with the practical and emotional implications of their illness. Certain illnesses demand regular treatments or maintenance which can affect people's daily routines. Dialysis, insulin injections or taking large numbers of pills all demand that individuals adjust their schedules in response to illness. Other illnesses can have unpredictable effects on the body, such as the sudden loss of bowel or bladder control, or violent nausea. Individuals suffering from such conditions are forced to develop strategies for managing their illness in day-to-day life. These include both practical considerations – such as always noting the location of the toilet when in an unfamiliar place – as well as skills for managing interpersonal relations, both intimate and commonplace. Although the symptoms of the illness can be embarrassing and disruptive, people develop coping strategies to live life as normally as possible (Kelly 1992).

At the same time, the experience of illness can pose challenges to and bring about transformations in people's sense of self.

Classic Studies 10.1 | **Talcott Parsons on society's 'sick role'**

The research problem

Have you ever been ill? When you were feeling unwell, how did other people react to you? Were they sympathetic? Did they try to help you get well again? Did you feel they expected you to get better too quickly? The American functionalist theorist, Talcott Parsons (1952), argued that illness has a clear social as well as an individual dimension. People are not only individually sick; they also have to learn what society expects of them when they are sick, and if they fail to conform to the behavioural norms surrounding illness, they may be stigmatized as engaging in deviant behaviour. Why is this?

"We're running a little behind, so I'd like each of you to ask yourself, 'Am I really that sick, or would I just be wasting the doctor's valuable time?'"

Parsons's explanation

Parsons argued that there exists a **sick role** – a concept he used to describe the patterns of behaviour which the sick person adopts in order to minimize the disruptive impact of illness to society. Functionalism holds that society usually operates in a smooth and consensual manner. Illness is therefore potentially dysfunctional as it could disrupt the smooth functioning of society. A sick person, for example, might not be able to perform all of his or her normal responsibilities or might be less reliable and efficient than usual. Because sick people are not able to carry out their normal roles, the lives of people around them are disrupted: work tasks go unfinished causing stress for co-workers, responsibilities at home are not fulfilled, and so on.

According to Parsons, people *learn* the sick role through socialization and enact it – with the cooperation of others – when they fall ill. There are three pillars of the sick role:

1. The sick person is not personally responsible for being sick. Illness is seen as the result of physical causes beyond the individual's control. The onset of illness is unrelated to the individual's behaviour or actions.
2. The sick person is entitled to certain rights and privileges, including a withdrawal from normal responsibilities. Since they bear no responsibility for the illness, they are exempted from certain duties, roles and behaviours which otherwise apply. For example, the sick person might be 'released'

from normal duties around the home. Behaviour that is not as polite or thoughtful as usual might be excused. The sick person gains the right to stay in bed or to take time off from work.
3. The sick person must work to regain health by consulting a medical expert and agreeing to become a 'patient', so the sick role is a temporary and 'conditional' one, which is contingent on the sick person actively trying to get well. In order to occupy the sick role, people must receive the sanction of a medical professional who legitimates the person's claim of illness. Confirmation of illness via expert opinion allows those surrounding the sick person to accept the validity of his or her claims. The patient is expected to cooperate in his or her own recovery by following 'doctor's orders'. But a sick person who refuses to consult a doctor, or who does not heed the advice of a medical authority, puts his or her sick role status in jeopardy.

Parsons's sick role has been refined by later sociologists, who suggest that all illnesses are not 'the same' as far as the sick role is concerned. They argue that the experience of the sick role varies with type of illness, since people's reactions to a sick person are influenced by the severity of the illness and their perception of it. Thus, the added rights and privileges which are part of the sick role may not be uniformly experienced. Freidson (1970) identified three versions of the sick role which correspond with different types and degrees of illness.

The *conditional* sick role applies to people suffering from a temporary condition from which they can recover. The sick person is expected to 'get well' and receives some rights and privileges according to the severity of the illness. For example, someone suffering from bronchitis would reap more benefits than the sufferer of a common cold. The *unconditionally legitimate* sick role refers to individuals who are suffering from incurable illnesses. Because the sick person cannot 'do' anything to get well, he or she is automatically entitled to occupy the sick role long term. The unconditionally legitimate role might apply to individuals suffering from alopecia (total hair loss) or severe acne (in both cases there are no special privileges, but, rather, an acknowledgement that the individual is not responsible for the illness), or from cancer or Parkinson's disease, which result in important privileges and the right to abandon many or most duties.

The final sick role is the *illegitimate role*, which occurs when an individual suffers from a disease or condition that is stigmatized by others. In such cases, there is a sense that the individual might somehow bear responsibility for the illness; additional rights and privileges are not necessarily granted. Alcoholism, smoking-related illness and obesity are possible examples of stigmatized illnesses, which affect a sufferer's right to assume the sick role.

Critical points

Parsons's notion of the sick role has been very influential. It reveals clearly how the sick person is an integral part of a larger social context. But there are a number of important criticisms which can be levelled against it.

Some writers have argued that the sick role 'formula' is unable to capture the *experience* of illness. Others point out that it cannot be applied universally. For example, it does not account for instances when doctors and patients disagree about a diagnosis, or have opposing interests. Furthermore, taking on the sick role is not always a straightforward process. Some individuals suffer for years from chronic pain or from symptoms that are repeatedly

misdiagnosed. They are denied the sick role until a clear diagnosis of their condition is made. In other cases, social factors such as race, class and gender can affect whether, and how readily, the sick role is granted. In sum, the sick role cannot be divorced from the social, cultural and economic influences which surround it and the realities of life and illness are more complex than the sick role suggests.

The increasing emphasis on lifestyle and health in our modern age means that individuals are seen as bearing ever greater responsibility for their own well-being. This contradicts the first premise of the sick role – that individuals are not to blame for their illness. Moreover, in modern societies the shift away from acute infectious disease towards chronic illness has made the sick role less applicable. Whereas the sick role might be useful in understanding acute illness, it is less useful in the case of chronic illness: there is no one formula for chronically ill or disabled people to follow. Living with illness is experienced and interpreted in a multiplicity of ways by sick people – and by those who surround them.

Contemporary significance

Nonetheless, the concept of a 'sick role' remains valuable as it allows us to link individual illness to wider healthcare systems. Bryan S. Turner (1995) argues that most societies *do* develop sick roles – learned norms that promote particular types of behaviour in relation to the control of illness – but that these differ. In many Western societies, for example, an individualized sick role exists, which means that hospital stays for non-life-threatening conditions are generally quite short, visiting hours are limited and the number of visitors strictly controlled. However, in Japan, a more communal sick role is the norm. Patients tend to stay in hospital longer after their medical treatment is completed and the average hospital stay is much longer than in Western societies. Hospital visits are also more informal, with family and friends often eating together and staying for longer periods. Turner suggests that we can still learn much about the social bases of health from such a comparative sociology of sick roles.

Winner of the 'Miss HIV Stigma-Free Beauty Pageant', 2007, held in Botswana, Africa. The competition aims to tackle negative stigmatization of HIV-positive women and put debates about HIV on the public agenda.

These develop both through the actual reactions of others to the illness, and through imagined or perceived reactions. For the chronically ill or disabled, social interactions which are routine for many people become tinged with risk or uncertainty. The shared understandings that underpin standard everyday interactions are not always present when illness or disability is a factor, and interpretations of common situations may differ substantially. An ill person may be in need of assistance but not want to appear dependent, for example. An individual may feel sympathy for someone who has been diagnosed with an illness, but be unsure whether to address the subject directly. The changed context of social interactions can precipitate transformations in self-identity.

Some sociologists have investigated how chronically ill individuals manage their illnesses within the overall context of their lives (Jobling 1988; Williams 1993). Illness can place enormous demands on people's time, energy, strength and emotional reserves. Corbin and Strauss (1985) studied the regimes of health which the chronically ill develop in order to organize their daily lives. They identified three types of 'work' contained in people's everyday strategies. Illness work refers to those activities involved in managing their condition, such as treating pain, doing diagnostic tests or undergoing physical therapy. Everyday work pertains to the management of daily life – maintaining relationships with others, running the household affairs and pursuing professional or personal interests. Biographical work involves those activities that the ill person does as part of building or reconstructing their personal narrative. In other words, it is the process of incorporating the illness into one's life, making sense of it and developing ways of explaining it to others. Such a process can help people restore meaning and order to their lives after coming to terms with the knowledge of chronic illness. From studying how illness affects the individual, we now turn to examine patterns of illness and health within society, and discuss how health outcomes differ between social groups.

The social basis of health

The twentieth century witnessed a significant overall rise in life expectancy for the industrialized countries and a general rise in life expectancy for the world's population to 67 years by 2007 (World Bank 2007a). Of course, such blunt averages hide some major inequalities between the developed and developing countries (see chapter 8, 'The Life-Course'). In the industrialized world, diseases such as polio, scarlet fever and tuberculosis have virtually been eradicated. Compared to other parts of the world, standards of health and well-being are relatively high. Many of these advances in public health have been attributed to the power of modern medicine. There is a commonly held assumption that medical research has been – and will continue to be – successful in uncovering the biological causes of disease and in developing effective treatments to control them. As medical knowledge and expertise grow, the argument runs, we can expect to see sustained and steady improvements in public health.

Although this approach to health and disease has been extremely influential, it is somewhat unsatisfactory for sociologists. This is because it ignores the important role of social and environmental influences on patterns of health and illness. The improvements in overall public health over the past century cannot conceal the fact that health and illness are not distributed evenly throughout the population. Research has shown that certain groups of people tend to enjoy much better health than others. These health inequalities appear to be tied to larger socio-economic patterns.

Sociologists and specialists in social **epidemiology** – scientists who study the distribution and incidence of disease and illness within the population – have attempted to explain the link between health and variables such as social class, gender, race, age and geography. While most scholars acknowledge the correlation between health and social inequalities, there is no agreement about the nature of the connection or about how health inequalities should be addressed. One of the main areas of debate concentrates on the relative importance of individual variables (such as lifestyle, behaviour, diet and cultural patterns) versus environmental or structural factors (such as income distribution and poverty). In this section we will look at variations in health patterns according to social class, gender and ethnicity and review some of the competing explanations for their persistence.

Class and health

Research on health and class has revealed a clear relationship between patterns of mortality and morbidity (illness) and an individual's social class. In fact, Cockerham argues: 'Social class or socioeconomic status (SES) is the strongest predictor of health, disease causation, and longevity in medical sociology' (2007: 75). In the UK, an influential nationwide study – the Black Report (DHSS 1980) – was important in publicizing the extent of class-based health inequalities, which many people found shocking in a wealthy country like Britain. Although there was a trend towards better health in society as a whole, significant disparities existed between classes, affecting health indicators from birth weight to blood pressure to risk of chronic illness. Individuals from higher socio-economic positions are on average healthier, taller and stronger, and live longer

Table 10.2 **Infant deaths per 1,000 live births, by socio-economic classification (based on father's occupation at death registration), England and Wales, 2005**

	Rates[1]				
	Stillbirth	Perinatal	Neonatal	Post-neonatal	Infant
All[2]	5.3	7.8	3.4	1.4	4.8
Inside marriage					
All[3]	5.0	7.4	3.0	1.3	4.3
1.1 Large employers and higher managerial	3.1	4.7	2.0	0.7	2.7
1.2 Higher professional	4.6	6.6	2.7	1.1	3.8
2 Lower managerial and professional	4.3	6.4	2.6	0.8	3.4
3 Intermediate	5.7	8.6	3.5	1.4	5.0
4 Small employers and own-account workers	4.3	6.2	2.6	1.2	3.9
5 Lower supervisory and technical	4.3	6.2	2.3	1.1	3.4
6 Semi-routine	6.3	9.3	4.2	1.9	6.1
7 Routine	6.9	10.1	4.1	1.7	5.8
Other[4]	9.3	13.0	5.1	2.6	7.7
Outside marrage joint registration					
All[3]					
1.1 Large employers and higher managerial	5.7	8.6	3.9	1.6	5.5
1.2 Higher professional	4.2	5.7	2.3	0.8	3.1
2 Lower managerial and professional	4.7	7.1	3.0	0.7	3.6
3 Intermediate	4.4	6.8	3.1	0.8	3.1
4 Small employers and own-account workers	5.1	7.7	3.6	1.8	5.4
5 Lower supervisory and technical	4.1	6.0	2.9	1.4	4.3
6 Semi-routine	4.9	7.4	3.3	1.0	4.3
7 Routine	6.7	10.6	5.0	1.9	6.8
Other[4]	7.4	10.7	4.4	1.8	6.2

[1] Stillbirths and perinatal deaths per 1,000 live births and stillbirths. Neonatal, postneonatal and infant deaths per 1,000 live births.

[2] Inside marriage and outside marriage/joint registration only, including cases where father's occupation was not stated.

[3] Includes cases where father's occupation was not stated.

[4] Students; occupations inadequately described; occupations not classifiable for other reasons; never worked and long-term unemployed.

Source: Adapted from *Health Statistics Quarterly* 32, 2005

than those lower down the social scale. An updated survey in 1990 then confirmed the earlier findings. Differences are greatest in respect to infant mortality (children dying in the first year of life) and child death, but poorer people are at greater risk of dying at all ages than more affluent people.

Some of the main class-based inequalities in health have been summarized by Browne and Bottrill (1999). They include:

1 Unskilled manual workers in the lowest occupational class are twice as likely to die before retirement age than professional white-collar workers in the top occupational class.

2 More than twice as many babies are still-born or die within the first week of life in unskilled families than in higher managerial families. The difference is even more pronounced amongst families of the long-term unemployed (see figure 10.3).

3 An individual born into the highest occupational class (professional white-collar workers) is likely to live on average seven years longer than someone born into the lowest occupational class (unskilled manual workers).

4 Some 90 per cent of the major causes of death are more common in the two lowest occupational classes than the three higher occupational classes (see figure 10.4 for instances).

5 Working-class people visit their doctors more often and for a wider range of ailments than people in professional occupations; long-standing illness is 50 per cent higher among unskilled manual workers than among professionals.

6 Class-based health inequalities are even more pronounced among the long-term unemployed; people in work tend to live longer than those who are without work.

Studies conducted in other industrialized countries have confirmed that there is a clear class gradient to health. Some scholars have found that the relative health inequality between the richest and poorest members of society is widening. Yet despite a growing amount of research aimed at revealing the link between health inequality and social class, scholars have not been entirely successful in locating the actual mechanisms that connect the two. Several competing explanations have been advanced for the causes behind the correlation.

The Black Report concentrated most heavily on *materialist* explanations of health inequality. Materialist or environ-mental explanations see the cause of health inequalities in large social structures, such as poverty, wealth and income distribution, unemployment, housing, pollution and poor working conditions. The patterns in health inequalities between classes are seen as the result of material deprivation. Reducing inequalities in health can only be done by addressing the root causes of social inequalities in general. While not discounting the possible validity of other arguments, the Black Report stressed the need for a comprehensive anti-poverty strategy and for improvements in education to combat health inequalities.

The Conservative government (1979–90) was dismissive of the findings of the Black Report, arguing that it advocated an unrealistic level of public expenditure. The government was more inclined to focus on cultural and behavioural explanations for health inequalities, emphasizing the importance of individual lifestyles on health. It argued that lower social classes tend to engage in certain activities – such as smoking, poor diet and higher consumption of alcohol – which are detrimental to good health. This argument sees individuals as bearing primary responsibility for poor health, as many lifestyle choices are freely made. Some proponents of this approach claim that such behaviours are embedded within the social class context, rather than under the exclusive control of individuals. Nevertheless, they also identify lifestyle and consumption patterns as the main causes of poor health. Subsequent governments have continued to place emphasis on public health campaigns to influence individuals' lifestyle choices. Anti-smoking initiatives and healthy eating and exercise programmes are examples of such efforts to shape public behaviour. Campaigns like these exhort individuals to take responsibility for their own well-being and they pay less attention to the way social position can constrain people's choices and possibilities. For example, fresh fruit and vegetables, which are central to a good diet, are much more expensive than many foods that are

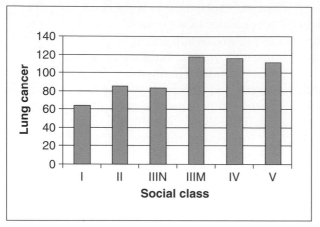

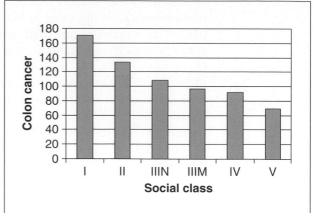

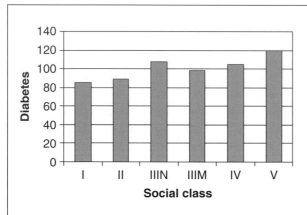

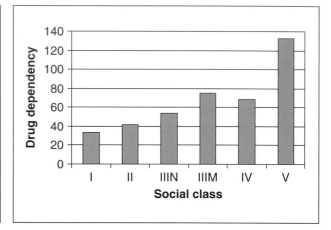

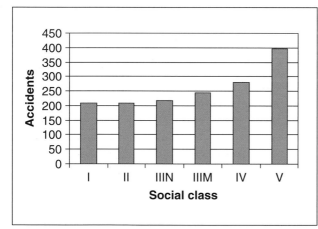

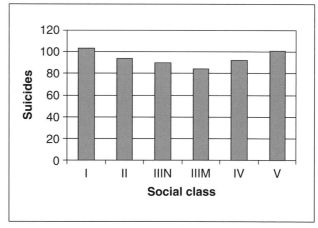

Figure 10.3 UK male mortality by cause of death and social class, selected causes, 1997–2000

Source: White et al. 2003

Poor diet is just one of the factors associated with ill health amongst Britain's most deprived people.

high in fat and cholesterol. The highest consumption of healthy food is, unsurprisingly, among high-income groups.

The 1997 Labour government acknowledged both cultural and material influences on people's health, and commissioned its own report, chaired by Sir Donald Acheson. The Acheson Report (1998) confirmed that for many aspects of health, inequality has generally worsened in the past few decades. Drawing from such evidence, the government's White Paper, *Our Healthier Nation* (1999) emphasized the many diverse influences – social, economic, environmental and cultural – which work together to produce ill health (some of these are illustrated in figure 10.4). It also proposed a set

of initiatives linking health with, for example, unemployment, substandard housing and education, to address not only the symptoms of poor health, but its causes as well. In practice, it remains less expensive, and therefore easier, for governments to concentrate on health promotion and persuasion of individuals than to introduce systematic programmes to tackle major social-structural problems such as unemployment and poor housing.

Gender and health

Disparities in health between men and women have also been noted in many research studies. For example, women

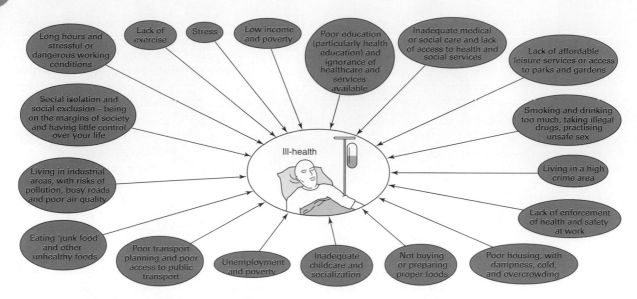

Figure 10.4   Cultural and material influences on health

Source: Browne 2005: 410

generally enjoy a longer life expectancy than men in almost every country in the world (UNDP 2004), while causes of death and patterns of illness show some differences between men and women. In the developed world, although heart disease affects men more than women, it is still the most frequent killer of both men and women under the age of 65. Men, however, suffer from higher rates of death as a result of accidents and violence and are also more prone to drug and alcohol dependency.

Material circumstances appear to influence women's health status, but this has traditionally been a difficult factor to gauge. Many studies have tended to classify women according to the social class of their husbands, thereby producing a distorted picture of women's health (see chapter 11, 'Stratification and Social Class'). We do know, however, that women are more likely to seek medical attention and have higher rates of self-reported illness than men. The gendered pattern is different in South Asian countries like Afghanistan, Bangladesh, India, Nepal and Pakistan, though, where

the life expectancy differential is greatly reduced (Arber and Thomas 2005). Explanatory factors here include conflict and wars, nutritional deficiencies, disadvantages related to lower social status and limited access to medical services for women (Cockerham 2007).

Women in industrialized countries report twice as much anxiety and depression as men. According to some observers, the multiple roles which women tend to perform – domestic work, childcare, professional responsibilities – may increase the stress on women and contribute to higher rates of illness. Lesley Doyal (1995) suggested that patterns of women's health and sickness may best be explained in relation to the main areas of activities which constitute their lives. Women's lives are inherently different from men's in terms of the roles and tasks that are commonly performed – domestic work, sexual reproduction, childbearing and mothering, regulating fertility through birth control, and so forth. (Although it could be argued that this is decreasingly true as more women enter the workplace.) According to Doyal, 'it is the cumulative effects of these various labours that are the major determinants of women's states of health'. Therefore, any analysis of women's health should consider the interaction between social, psychological and biological influences.

Heather Graham has studied the effects of stress on the health of white working-class women. She has highlighted the fact that women at the lower socio-economic end of the spectrum have less access to support networks in times of life crisis than do middle-class women. Working-class women, she notes, tend to encounter life crises (such as job loss, divorce, eviction from housing or the death of a child) more often than other groups, but generally have weaker coping skills and fewer outlets for anxiety. Not only is the resulting stress harmful both physically and psychologically, but some of the coping strategies which are turned to – such as smoking – are also damaging. Graham argues that smoking is a way of reducing tension when personal and material resources are stretched to breaking point. Thus it occupies a paradoxical position in women's lives – increasing the health risk for women and their children, while simultaneously allowing them to cope under difficult circumstances (Graham 1987, 1994).

Ann Oakley and her colleagues (1994) have studied the role of social support in the health of socially disadvantaged women and children in four English cities. She argues that the relationship between stress and health applies both to major life crises and smaller problems, and that it is felt particularly acutely in the lives of working-class people. Oakley notes that social support – such as counselling services, hotlines or home visits – can act as a 'buffer' against the negative health consequences of stress commonly experienced by women. Other studies have shown that social support is an important factor that can help people in adjusting to disease and illness and that women are more likely to form and maintain self-help communities, recently including female communities in cyber-space, such as mothers' forums (Ell 1996; Drentea and Moren-Cross 2005). Conversely, researchers have found that men are not as vigilant about their own health and tend to ignore health problems for longer. Young men also engage in more risk-taking behaviour, such as speeding, drug-taking, early-age sexual activity, getting drunk and so on, than do women (Lupton 1999).

Ethnicity and health

Although health in industrial societies is ethnically patterned, our understanding of the relationship between ethnicity and health is partial at best. An increasing number of sociological studies are being conducted in this area, but the evidence remains inconclusive. In some cases, trends that have been attributed to membership of an ethnic group may have ignored other factors, such as class or gender, which may also be highly significant.

Nevertheless, the incidence of certain illnesses is higher among individuals from African-Caribbean and Asian backgrounds. Mortality from liver cancer, tuberculosis and diabetes are higher among these populations than among whites. African-Caribbeans suffer from higher-than-average rates of hypertension and sickle-cell anaemia (an inherited disorder affecting red blood cells), while people from the Indian subcontinent experience higher mortality from heart disease.

Some scholars have turned to cultural and behavioural accounts to explain ethnic health patterning. In a similar way to cultural explanations of class-based health inequalities, emphasis is placed on individual and group lifestyles which are seen to result in poorer health. These are often seen as linked to religious or cultural beliefs, such as dietary and cooking habits or consanguinity (the practice of intermarriage within families at the level of second cousins). Critics argue that cultural explanations fail to identify the real problems facing ethnic minorities in the industrialized societies: namely, the structural inequalities and the racism and discrimination encountered in healthcare systems.

Social-structural explanations for ethnic patterning in health in many European societies focus on the social context in which African-Caribbeans and Asians live. African-Caribbeans and Asians frequently experience multiple disadvantages which can be harmful to their health. These might include poor or overcrowded housing conditions, high rates of unemployment and over-representation in hazardous, low-paying occupations. Such material factors are then compounded by the effects of racism, either experienced directly in the form of violence, threats or discrimination, or in 'institutionalized' forms. In short: 'Ultimately, what makes race important in a causal sense for health is its close association with class circumstances. Subtract affluence or lack thereof from considerations of race and the causal strength of race in health and disease is severely minimized' (Cockerham 2007: 143).

Nonetheless, **institutional racism** has been noted in the provision of healthcare (Alexander 1999). Ethnic groups may experience unequal or problematic access to health services. Language barriers can present difficulties if information cannot be relayed effectively; culturally specific understandings of illness and treatment are often not considered by professionals within the health service. The National Health Service has been criticized for not requiring more awareness of cultural and religious beliefs among its staff and for paying less attention to diseases that occur predominantly in the non-white population.

> Institutional racism is discussed in detail in chapter 15, 'Race, Ethnicity and Migration'.

There is no consensus on the connection between ethnicity and health inequalities. Indeed, much research still remains to be done. Yet it is clear that the question of ethnicity and health inequalities must be considered in relation to larger social, economic and political factors which affect the experience of ethnic minority groups in the developed societies.

Health and social cohesion

In trying to unravel the causes of health inequalities, a growing number of sociologists are turning their attention to the role of social support and social cohesion in promoting good health. As you may recall from our discussion of Durkheim in chapter 1, 'What is Sociology?', social solidarity is one of the most important concepts in sociology. Durkheim saw the degree and type of solidarity within a culture as one of its most critical features. In his study of suicide, for example, he found that individuals and groups that were well integrated into society were less likely to take their own lives than others.

In several articles, and in his book *Unhealthy Societies: The Afflictions of Inequality* (1996), Richard Wilkinson argues that the healthiest societies in the world are not the richest countries, but those in which income is distributed most evenly and levels of social integration are highest. High levels of national wealth, according to Wilkinson, do not necessarily translate into better health for the population. In surveying empirical data from countries around the world, he notes a clear relationship between mortality rates and patterns of income distribution. Inhabitants of countries such as Japan and Sweden, which are regarded as some of the most egalitarian societies in the world, enjoy better levels of health on average than do citizens of countries where the gap between the rich and the poor is more pronounced, such as the United States.

In Wilkinson's view, the widening gap in income distribution undermines social cohesion and makes it more difficult for people to manage risks and challenges. Heightened social isolation and the failure to cope with stress are reflected in health indicators. Wilkinson argues that social factors – the strength of social contacts, ties within communities, availability of social support, a sense of security – are the main determinants of the relative health of a society.

Wilkinson's thesis has provoked energetic responses. Some claim that his work should become required reading for policy-makers and politicians. They agree that too much emphasis has been placed on market relations and the drive towards prosperity. This approach has failed many members of society, they argue; it is time to consider more humane and socially responsible policies to support those who are disadvantaged. Others criticize Wilkinson's study on methodological grounds and argue that he has failed to show a clear causal relationship between income inequality and poor health (Judge 1995). Illness, critics contend, could be caused by any number of other mediating factors. They argue that the empirical evidence for Wilkinson's claims remains suggestive at best and that the thesis is not confirmed within all developed societies. Recent evidence also shows that the same pattern does not hold within developing countries either. Evidence against the 'Wilkinson thesis' seems to be mounting, and it has been described as, 'a doctrine in search of data' (Eberstadt and Satel 2004) rather than an accurate hypothesis based on the evidence.

THINKING CRITICALLY

Examine figure 10.3 above. Using your sociological imagination, how might the differences in male disease prevalence across social class groups be explained? Would a concerted attempt to tackle poverty help to reduce such inequalities?

Earlier in this chapter we examined some of the assumptions that have historically provided the foundations for the orthodox, biomedical model of health. Many of these assumptions were also found in the way that disability has conventionally been understood in the developed countries. Similarly, the recent trends we discussed above as a reaction to the biomedical model of health – such as scepticism that the medical expert always knows best and the moves to take greater account of the opinions and experiences of patients – have formed part of a more recent rejection of this conventional understanding of disability. It is to a discussion of some of the issues surrounding disability that we now turn.

The sociology of disability

The poet Simon Brisenden neatly summarizes the sense of exclusion that many disabled people feel from orthodox medicine and medical practitioners in his book *Poems for Perfect People*, in which he asked: 'The man who cut your skin / and delved within / has he got any scars?' Brisenden was one of many disabled people whose work has led to a re-evaluation of the conventional understanding of disability in the UK and a number of other countries. Much of this discussion is taking place in the field of disability studies. In this section, we examine the dominant understanding of disability by discussing what has become known as the 'individual model'. We then turn to look at how this model has been challenged, notably by disabled people themselves, through the development of a 'social model' of disability, and offer a brief evaluation of this challenge. Lastly, we look briefly at the level and background of impairments globally. We begin, however, by discussing the language of disability.

Sociologists argue that our awareness and understanding of social issues is, at least partly, shaped by the words we use. In recent decades a critique of the terms which people have historically drawn upon to discuss disability has become increasingly important to those writing in this area. The word 'handicapped', for example, has largely fallen out of use because it was thought to be associated with 'cap in hand' – i.e., charity and begging. Other terms, originally used to describe certain impairments, are rejected because they are now used mainly as insults – terms such as 'spastic' or 'cripple' are examples. Some metaphors, which are still in everyday use, like 'turning a blind eye' or 'a deaf ear', have been criticized because they imply a sense of exclusion. As we shall see, even the way in which we understand the term 'disability' is subject to much debate.

The individual model of disability

Historically, in Western societies, an **individual model of disability** has been dominant. This model contends that individual limitations are the main cause of the problems experienced by disabled people. In the individual model of disability, bodily 'abnormality' is seen as causing some degree of 'disability' or functional limitation – an individual 'suffering' from quadriplegia is incapable of walking, for example. This functional limitation is seen as the basis for a wider classification of an individual as 'an invalid'. Underpinning the individual model is a 'personal tragedy approach' to disability. The disabled individual is regarded as an unfortunate victim of a chance event. Medical specialists play a central role in the individual model because it is their job to offer curative and rehabilitative diagnoses to the 'problems' suffered by the disabled individual. For this reason, the individual model is often described as the 'medical model'. It is the power of the medical expert over disabled people's lives that Simon Brisenden attacked in the poem that started this section. In recent decades, this individual model of disability has been increasingly questioned, as we find below.

The social model of disability

An important early challenge to the individual model of disability was a collection edited by Paul Hunt entitled, *Stigma: The Experience of Disability* (1966). Hunt argued that 'the problem of disability lies not only in the impairment of function and its effects on us individually, but also, more importantly, in the area of our relationship with "normal" people'. Hunt was a leading activist in the early years of the disability movement in Britain and became a founding member of the Union of Physically Impaired Against Segregation (UPIAS). In its manifesto, *Fundamental Principles of Disability* (1976), UPIAS developed a radical alternative to the individual model by arguing that there was a crucial distinction between 'impairment' and 'disability':

- *Impairment*: Lacking part or all of a limb, or having a defective limb, organ or mechanism of the body.
- *Disability*: The disadvantage or restriction of activist caused by a contemporary social organization, which takes no or little account of people who have physical impairments and thus excludes them from participation in the mainstream of social activities.

UPIAS largely accepted the definition of physical 'impairment' as a biomedical property of individuals (although they subsequently extended it to include non-physical, sensory and intellectual forms of impairment). 'Disability', however, was defined in social terms. This challenged conventional understandings of the term. Disability was no longer understood as the problem of an individual, but in terms of the social barriers that people with impairments faced in participating fully in society. Mike Oliver turns the assumptions in the individual model of disability around by rewriting the questions that the UK Office of Population, Censuses and Surveys (OPCS) used to assess 'disability' in the 1980s. Oliver (1983) was the first theorist to make the distinction between the individual and the **social model of disability** explicit (these distinctions are summarized in table 10.3).

Table 10.3 Two models of disability

Individual model	Social model
Personal tragedy model	Social oppression theory
Personal problem	Social problem
Individual treatment	Social action
Medicalization	Self-help
Professional dominance	Individual and collective responsibility
Expertise	Experience
Individual identity	Collective identity
Prejudice	Discrimination
Care	Rights
Control	Choice
Policy	Politics
Individual adjustment	Social change

Source: Adapted from Oliver 1996: 34

The social model of disability was given further academic credibility by the work of Vic Finkelstein (1980, 1981), Colin Barnes (1991) and Oliver himself (1990, 1996).

Social model theorists need to give an explanation of why the social, cultural or historical barriers against disabled people have developed. Some advocates of the social model, influenced by Marx, have argued that a materialist understanding of disability is needed (see chapter 1, 'What is Sociology?' for more on materialism). Oliver (1996), for example, argues that, historically, barriers were erected against disabled people's full participation in society during the Industrial Revolution, when they were excluded from the labour market as the first capitalist factories began to base employment on individual waged labour. As this historical process developed, Oliver argues, 'so many [disabled people] were unable to keep or retain jobs that they became a social problem for the capitalist state whose initial response to all social problems was harsh deterrence and institutionalization'. Even today, disabled people's presence in the workforce is still relatively small.

Evaluation of the social model

The social model has been enormously influential in shaping the way that we think about disability today. Although it originated in the UK, it has gained global influence, and has been described as 'the big idea' of the British disability movement (Hasler 1993). In focusing on the removal of social barriers to full participation, the social model allows disabled people to focus on a political strategy. This has led some to argue that, in accepting this model, disabled people have formed 'a new social movement' (Oliver and Zarb 1989).

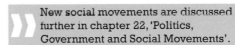

New social movements are discussed further in chapter 22, 'Politics, Government and Social Movements'.

In replacing the individual model, which identifies the 'invalidity' of the individual as the cause of disability, with a model in which disability is the result of oppression, the social model has been seen as 'liberating' by some disabled people (Beresford and Wallcraft 1997).

Since the late 1980s, however, several lines of criticism have been developed

Disabled protesters campaigning for their rights.

against the social model. First, it is argued that it neglects the often painful or uncomfortable experiences of impairment, which are central to many disabled people's lives. Shakespeare and Watson argue: 'We are not just disabled people, we are also people with impairments, and to pretend otherwise is to ignore a major part of our biographies' (2002: 11). Against this accusation, defenders of the social model have claimed that rather than denying everyday experiences of impairment, the social model merely seeks to focus attention on the social barriers to full participation in society that are raised against disabled people.

Second, many people accept that they have impairments, but do not wish to be labelled as 'disabled'. In a recent survey of people claiming government benefits for disability, fewer than half chose to define themselves as disabled. Many people

rejected the term because they saw their health problems related to illness rather than disability or because they did not think that they were ill enough to be so categorized (Department for Work and Pensions 2002). However, Barnes (2003) has pointed out that in a society where disability is too often still associated with abnormality, it is not surprising that some people with impairments chose to reject the label 'disabled'.

Lastly, medical sociologists in particular tend to reject the social model by arguing that the division between impairment and disability, on which it rests, is false. These critics argue that the social model separates impairment, which is defined biomedically, from disability, which is defined socially. Medical sociologists have tended to argue that both disability and impairment are socially structured and are closely interre-

10.3 Applying the social model to assumptions in the OPCS questions

OPCS question	Oliver's question
'Can you tell what is wrong with you?'	'Can you tell me what is wrong with society?'
'What complaint causes you difficulty in holding, gripping or turning things?'	'What defects in the design of everyday equipment like jars, bottles and tins causes you difficulty in holding them?'
'Are your difficulties in understanding mainly due to a hearing problem?'	'Are your difficulties in understanding people mainly due to their inability to communicate with you?'
'Do you have a scar, blemish or deformity which limits your daily activities?'	'Do other people's reactions to any scar, blemish or deformity you may have limit your daily activities?'
'Have you attended a special school because of a long-term health problem or disability?'	'Have you attended a special school because of your education authority's policy of sending people with your health problem/disability to such places?'
'Does your health problem/disability prevent you from going out as often or as far as you would like?'	What is it about the local environment that makes it difficult for you to get about in your neighbourhood?'
'Does your health problem/disability make it difficult for you to travel by bus?'	Are there any transport or financial problems which prevent you from going out as often or as far as you would like?'
'Does your health problem/disability affect your work in any way at present?'	'Do you have problems at work because of the physical environment or the attitudes of others?'
'Does your health problem/disability mean that you need to live with relatives or someone else who can help or look after you?	'Are community services so poor that you need to rely on relatives or someone else to provide you with the right level of personal assistance?'
'Does your present accommodation have any adaptations because of your health problem/disability?'	'Did the poor design of your house mean that you had to have it adapted to suit your needs?'

Source: Oliver 1990

lated. Shakespeare and Watson argue that the division between impairment and disability collapses when one asks, 'Where does impairment end and disability start?' In some cases the division is straightforward – a failure to design suitable wheelchair access in a building clearly creates a socially constructed disabling barrier to wheelchair users. However, there are many more cases where it is impossible to remove all the sources of disability because they are not caused by oppressive conditions in society.

Medical sociologists critical of the social model might argue that to be impaired by constant pain or by significant intellectual limitations, for example, disables the individual from full participation in society in a way that cannot be removed by social change. These critics would argue that a full account of disability must take into account disability caused by impairments and not just those caused by society.

Supporters of the social model have argued that this last claim is based on a

Is this paralympic swimmer disabled?

blurring of the distinction between disability and impairment, which they argue is rooted in the biomedical model of thinking that underlies the individual model of disability. They respond that the social model certainly does not deny that an impairment can be the cause of pain or that there are things that an individual might not be able to do solely because of a particular impairment. Indeed, Carol Thomas (1999, 2002), an advocate of the social model of disability, uses the phrase 'impairment effects' to take into account the ensuing psycho-emotional implications of impairment for disabled people.

Given the contested nature of the term 'disability' and the variety of impairments linked to disability, an account of the numbers of disabled people in the world is difficult. However, it is to these issues that we turn below.

THINKING CRITICALLY

Are people with facial disfigurements 'disabled'? Does Vicky's story ('Using your sociological imagination 10.2') tell us anything about the distinction between impairment and disability, or not? What do Vicky's experiences tell us about the social model of disability and its implications for society as a whole?

Disability, law and public policy

As the social model of disability initially emerged in the UK, we shall begin by outlining the way that British legislation has changed, in part as a result of the campaigning activities of the disabled people's movment

The Disability Discrimination Act (DDA) was passed in 1995, giving disabled people

10.4 'Why I want you to look me in the face'

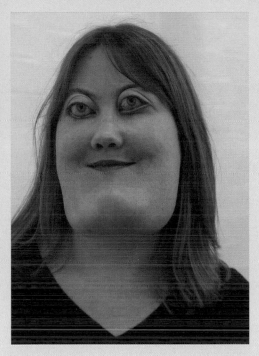

Instead of people looking away, gasping or shuddering, Vicky Lucas wants them to know that her face is integral to who she is. And, as she explains, she likes who she is.

I have a rare genetic disorder called Cherubism, which affects my face. I was diagnosed when I was about 4 years old. I was too young to remember what happened, but visiting hospitals became a regular part of my life.

Although it was only when I was about 6 that my face started to really change shape, I don't remember a time when I didn't look different.

Growing up with a facial disfigurement wasn't easy. When puberty kicked in, it included all the usual developments with a little bit extra – my face became very large and my eyes were more affected too.

Double take

My teenage years were difficult. People would sometimes stare or do a double take. Some people would be downright nasty and call me names.

Even when people said 'Oh you poor thing!' their pity also hurt me and that hurt would stay with me for a long time. I became very withdrawn, afraid of how I might be treated if I went out.

But over time, I gradually started to develop my self-esteem and self-confidence and I started to feel that I shouldn't waste my life just because of other people's attitudes towards me.

At the age of 16 I went to college and studied subjects such as film, media studies and photography. I started to research the representation of disfigured people in the media.

When I looked at how people with facial disfigurements are portrayed in films, well, no wonder people don't know how to react to us! Freddy Krueger in *Nightmare on Elm Street*, the Joker in *Batman*, the various scarred villains in gangster films – the list is endless.

Bad assumption

With stereotypes like that, it's hardly surprising that people assume that if you have a facial difference, there must be something 'different' or 'bad' about you in the inside too.

This was a huge turning point for me because I realized that facial disfigurement was not just a medical issue, but a social issue as well.

I realized that the reason why I was so unhappy was not because of my face, but the way some people would react to it. I decided that it wasn't my face that I wanted to change, but social attitudes. I'm not against plastic surgery. It's just that my personal choice is to not have it.

Now, at the age of 24, I'm used to seeing my face reflected back at me in the mirror and I'm okay with it. Though I could quite happily do without the headaches and double vision. I also dislike being physically unable to wink, but I've overcome this particular disability by doing a nice line in fluttering and blinking.

But my face is integral to who I am. The way people treat me and the way I've had to learn to live my life has created the person I am today.

Lack of imagination

I love the good genuine friends my face has brought me and I appreciate the way it's made me want to be a better person. I also have a boyfriend who thinks I look like a cat. I'm not quite sure if I agree with him, but I'm certainly not complaining!

[cont'd . . .]

Now, whenever a person says I'm ugly, I just pity them for their lack of imagination. For every person who calls me fat chin, I think 'Nah! It's just that you've got a really small weak one. Talk about chin envy!'

For every naturally curious stare I get, I give a friendly smile. And if they don't smile back within my 10-second time limit, I give them a very effective scowl.

Last week, walking in the street with my boyfriend, a man walked towards me and went 'Urghhhhhooooooh!'

Confrontation

It wasn't so much a word as a strange guttural sound, and the kind that only funny-looking people could understand the subtext to. I was so angry that I confronted him.

I won't go into details of what I did but let's just say it's probably the last time he ever gives a strange guttural sound to a funny looking woman in the street ever again.

Two minutes later, as we were walking home, a homeless man came up to me asking for change. He asked me how I was. 'Fine', I said and I told him what had just happened. There was a short pause. Then he smiled and said 'I hope you hurt him!' We all laughed.

It's funny how some strangers can be so cruel and hurtful, and yet others, the ones you'd least expect, the ones you would usually ignore and think nothing of, can be so warm and kind.

That pretty much sums up my life. I go from experiencing the worst in people to the very best, and often within the same five minutes! It makes my life more challenging, but also very interesting. I wouldn't want to change that for the world.

Source: BBC News Magazine, 6 August 2003
© bbc.co.uk/news

certain legal protections from discrimination in several areas, including employment and access to goods and services. Further legislation was introduced in 1999 that led to the creation of the Disability Rights Commission (DRC), set up to work towards 'the elimination of discrimination against disabled people', and a new DDA was introduced in 2005, covering more areas and activities. The 1995 DDA defined a disabled person as 'anyone with a physical or mental impairment, which has a substantial and long-term adverse effect upon their ability to carry out normal day-to-day activities'. This definition of disability includes, for example, people with mental health problems as well as people with facial disfigurements, and it avoids the common misconception that disability mainly concerns mobility impairments or is largely congenital. In fact, around 77 per cent of disabled people became disabled after the age of 16 (Employers' Forum on Disability 2003) and the percentage of the population who are disabled continues to increase with age (see figure 10.5).

Under the DDA definition, in 2003–4 more than 10 million people in the UK (over 10 per cent of the population) were disabled, of whom 6.8 million (one in five of the total working population) were of working age. Of this latter group, only 3.4 million people (50 per cent) were employed, compared with 81 per cent of non-disabled people (Disability Rights Commission 2005) and just 17 per cent of people with learning disabilities were in paid work. The DRC says that around 1 million disabled people without a job want to work. People with impairments linked to disability still belong to one of the most disadvantaged groups in the UK. They are more likely to be out of work than the able-bodied, and those people who have impairments linked to disability who are in employment tend to earn less. In 2005, the DRC reported that the average gross hourly pay of disabled employees was 10 per cent less than that of non-disabled employees – £9.36 per hour compared to £10.39 per hour. Yet disability-related expenditure by governments is high compared to many other areas of spending – the UK government spent more than £19 billion a year on incapacity and disability benefits in 2002 (BBC, 9 April 2002). The wealthiest countries spend at

Per cent

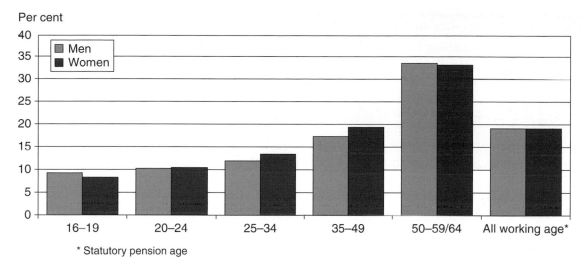

* Statutory pension age

Figure 10.5   Disabled people in the UK 2001, by age (% of age group)

Source: Smith and Twomey 2002: 417

least twice as much on disability-related programmes as they do on unemployment compensation (OECD 2005).

Disability around the world

It is estimated that 10 per cent of the world population, some 650 million people, are disabled, 80 per cent of whom live in developing countries such as India and China (UN Convention on the Rights of Persons with Disabilities 2006). The main cause of disability in developed countries is 'chronic disease and long-term impairments', while in developing countries the main causes are poverty, inadequate sanitation, poor diet and bad housing. Injuries, such as broken bones, will often result in long-term impairment in developing countries, which would not occur if treatment and rehabilitation facilities had been available, as they generally are in the developed world. Iron-deficiency, 'anaemia' and chronic infections of the pelvis (sometimes caused by female circumcision) are major causes of impairment that lead to disability in women in many developing countries. It is estimated that around 250,000 children lose their sight each year because their diet lacks Vitamin A, which is found in green vegetables, and that up to half of the world's impairment could be preventable by improving policies to confront poverty, malnutrition, sanitation, drinking water and employment conditions to reduce accidents (Charlton 1998). War and its aftermath (such as uncleared landmines) comprise another major cause of impairments. Furthermore, in poorer countries disabled children are far less likely to receive the same level of education as other children, which exacerbates their poverty later in life. From the evidence, we can see that poverty in the developing world creates impairments and shapes disability in ways that are very different from the experience in the West.

In 2006, the UN noted that only a minority of countries – 45 – had already introduced legislation aimed at protecting the rights of disabled people. In a majority of countries, therefore, disabled people did not have equal rights with the rest of the population. For example, UNESCO says that around 90 per cent of children with disabilities in developing countries do not attend school and the global literacy rate for adults with disabilities is as low as 3 per cent, and just 1 per cent for women with disabilities (UNDP 1998). In India, a country with anti-discrimination laws, of some 70 million people with disabilities, only about 100,000 have succeeded in obtaining employment in industry and in 2004 just 35 per cent of working-age people with disabilities in the USA were working, compared to 78 per cent of the non-disabled population (UN 2006).

Clearly, anti-discriminatory laws and policies are very patchy and uneven across the world; in many cases disabled people continue to be denied citizenship in their own countries. In an attempt to 'level up' provision for disabled people across the world, the UN launched the first human rights treaty of the twenty-first century: the 2006 UN Convention on the Rights of Persons with Disabilities. The Convention aims to contribute towards a global 'paradigm shift' in attitudes towards disabled people. On the opening day for signatures – 30 March 2007 – some 99 countries signed the new Convention, though the government of the USA said it would not be doing so as it already had extensive provision for disabled people; as we saw above, however, this has not yet guaranteed equal rights in employment. The Convention commits national governments to 'develop and carry out policies, laws and administrative measures for securing the rights recognized in the Convention and to abolish laws, regulations, customs and practices that constitute discrimination'. It also guarantees that disabled people can enjoy a right to life on an equal basis with others, ensures the equal rights and advancement of women and girls with disabilities and protects children with disabilities. In addition, it sets out, for the first time, a global policy agenda to promote equal rights for disabled people.

The very different experiences of impairment and disability encountered by people around the world illustrate a wider idea reflected in this chapter: that our experience of our own bodies and our interactions with others – whether able-bodied or disabled, sick or healthy – are shaped by the changing social contexts in which we find ourselves. In order to develop a sociological perspective on illness, health and disability, we need to examine the social and technological changes that shape our understanding of these aspects of human life.

Summary points

1. Western medicine is based on the biomedical model of health – that disease can be defined in objective terms and that the sick body can be restored to health through scientifically based medical treatment. The biomedical model emerged with modern societies and was linked to the rise of demographics – the study of the size, composition and dynamics of human populations, and a growing state interest in public health. Modern healthcare systems were greatly influenced by the application of science to medical diagnosis and cure.

2. The biomedical model has come under increasing criticism. It has been argued that scientific medicine is not as effective as it is made out to be, that medical professionals do not value the opinions of the patients being treated, and that the medical profession considers itself superior to alternative forms of healing.

3. Sociologists are interested in the *experience* of illness – how being sick, chronically ill or disabled is experienced by the sick person and those nearby. The idea of the *sick role*, developed by Talcott Parsons, suggests that a sick person adopts certain forms of behaviour in order to minimize the disruptive impact of illness. A sick individual is granted certain privileges, such as the right to withdraw from normal responsibilities, but in return must work actively to regain health by agreeing to follow medical advice.

4. Symbolic interactionists have investigated how people cope with disease and chronic illness in their daily lives. The experience of illness can provoke changes in self-identity and daily routines. This sociological dimension of the body is becoming increasingly relevant for many societies;

people are living longer than ever before and tend to suffer more from chronic debilitating conditions than from acute illnesses.

5. The emergence of HIV/AIDS – a deadly pandemic of world-historical significance – showed that modern scientific medicine has not conquered fatal diseases and epidemics once and for all. Many millions of people around the world have died from AIDS-related diseases and there is still no cure or vaccine for HIV or AIDS. The pandemic also contributed to a growing risk-awareness amongst populations and provoked much sociological research into the social inequalities of health and illness across the world.

6. Sociological research reveals close connections between illness and inequality. Within industrial countries, poorer groups have a shorter average life expectancy and are more susceptible to disease than more affluent strata. Richer countries also have higher average life expectancies than poorer ones. Some researchers argue that class-based health inequalities can be explained by cultural and behavioural factors, such as diet and lifestyle. Others place emphasis on structural influences, such as unemployment, sub-standard housing and poor working conditions.

7. Patterns of health and illness have gender and racial dimensions as well. On average, women tend to live longer than men in almost every country of the world, yet they experience a higher incidence of illness than men. Certain illnesses are more common among ethnic minority groups than among the white population. Genetic explanations have been advanced to account for gender and racial differences in health, yet these alone cannot explain the inequalities. While there may be some biological basis to certain health conditions, overall patterns of health and illness must also take into account social factors and differences in material conditions between groups.

8. The individual model of disability holds personal limitations to be the main cause of the problems experienced by disabled people. In the individual model, bodily 'abnormality' is seen as causing some degree of 'disability' or functional limitation. Underpinning the individual model is a 'personal tragedy approach' to disability.

9. The social model of disability locates the causes of disability within society, rather than the individual. It is not the individual's limitations that cause disability, but the barriers that society places in the way of full participation for disabled people.

10. Disabled people make up one of the most socially disadvantaged groups in the developed countries, though the majority of people with impairments actually live in the developing world. The UN Convention on the Rights of Persons with Disabilities (2006) aims to promote equal rights for disabled people globally.

Further reading

The sociology of health and illness is a very large and long-established field, so it is best to start with a shorter introduction. Mike Bury's *Health and Illness* (Cambridge: Polity, 2005) is very good, as is Anne-Marie Barry and Chris Yuill's *Understanding Health: A Sociological Introduction*, 2nd edn (London: Sage, 2007), though there are many more.

From here, you can then try something that covers key debates and evidence in more detail. For example, Sarah Nettleton's *The Sociology of Health and Illness*, 2nd edn (Cambridge: Polity, 2006) or Ellen Annandale's *The Sociology of Health and Medicine: A Critical Introduction* (Cambridge: Polity, 1998) are both engagingly written and well argued.

Critical reviews of sociology's recent engagement with the body can be found in Chris Shilling's *The Body and Social Theory* (London: Sage, 2003) and Alexandra Howson's *The Body in Society: An Introduction* (Cambridge: Polity, 2004). For disability studies in sociology, see Colin Barnes, Geof Mercer and Tom Shakespeare's *Exploring Disability: A Sociological Introduction* (Cambridge: Polity, 1999) and Carol Thomas's *Sociologies of Disability and Illness* (Basingstoke: Palgrave Macmillan, 2007).

If you need a Reference work covering the sociology of health and illness, then Jonathan Gabe, Mike Bury and Mary Ann Elston's *Key Concepts in Medical Sociology* (London: Sage, 2004) should be helpful.

Internet links

European Observatory on Health Systems and Policies:
www.euro.who.int/observatory

Centre for International Public Health Policy:
www.health.ed.ac.uk/CIPHP/

The World Health Organization:
www.who.int/en/

Wellcome Library on the History and Understanding of Medicine, UK:
http://library.wellcome.ac.uk/

The Disability Archive at the University of Leeds, UK:
www.leeds.ac.uk/disability-studies/archiveuk/

The European Disability Forum:
www.edf-feph.org/en/welcome.htm

The Disability Rights Commission, UK:
www.drc-gb.org/

United Nations Convention on the Rights of Persons with Disabilities:
www.un.org/disabilities/convention/

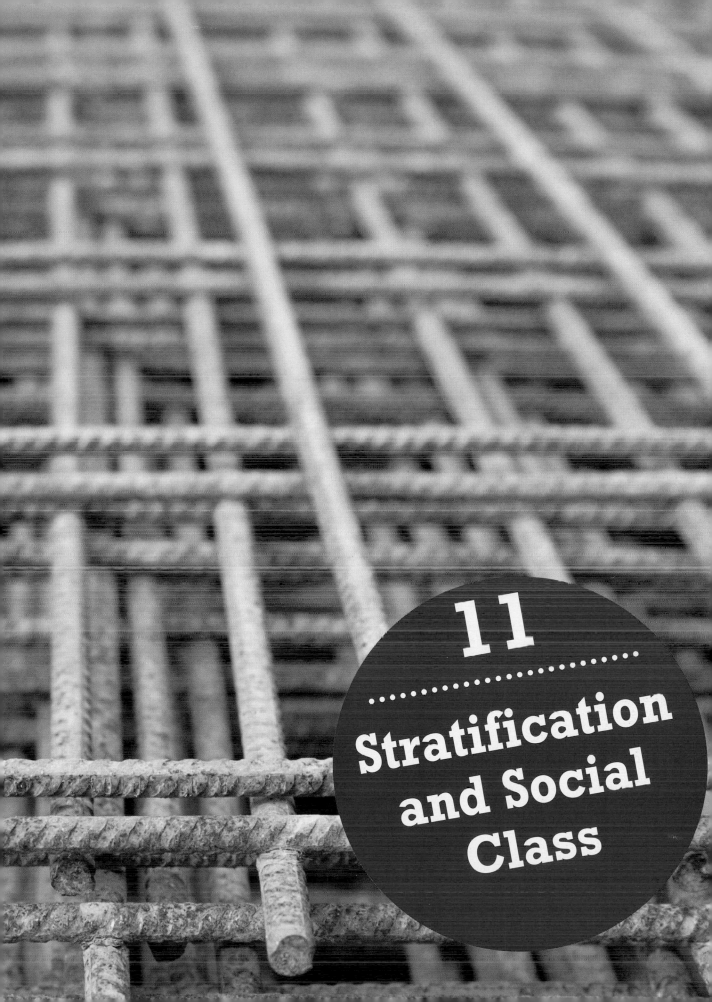

11

·····

Stratification and Social Class

CHAPTER 11

● ●

Stratification and Social Class

(opposite) Prince Charles and Sir Gulam Noon.

Have you ever bought an Indian meal in a supermarket? If you have, there's a strong chance that it was made by Noon Products. The company specializes in supplying Indian food to the big supermarket chains and has an annual turnover of around £90 million. In 2005 it was taken over by Irish food company, Kerry Group. Company founder, Sir Gulam Noon, was estimated to have amassed a fortune of £65 million, according to the 2006 *Sunday Times Rich List*.

Gulam Noon was born in India. His family owned a sweet shop in Bombay: 'Royal Sweets'. They were not particularly well off, but managed to get by until their father's death when Gulam was 7. After that it was a struggle, and, as a young teenager, Gulam would combine school with work in the shop. Having completed school, he joined the family business full time. He soon changed the way the business was marketed, expanded the shop and built a factory. His ambitions, however, were not limited to 'Royal Sweets', and other ventures quickly followed, including printing and construction ventures.

Not satisfied with his successes in India, Gulam looked to England to further his experience. He established 'Royal Sweets' in Southall, London, and brought chefs with him from India to get the business going. Within the year there were nine shops, built around the Asian communities of London and Leicester. Today, the 'Royal Sweets' chain has 40 shops and an annual turnover of £9 million.

Other commercial ventures followed the success of 'Royal Sweets', and in 1989 Noon Products was established. Gulam spotted a niche in the market: 'All the pre-packaged Indian ready meals available from the supermarkets were insipid and frankly unacceptable. I thought I could do better.' The business began with just 11 employees, but soon they were selling authentic Indian foods to the frozen food company Birds Eye, and then to the supermarket chains Waitrose and Sainsbury's.

There are now more than 100 different Noon dishes, produced in three plants, operated by 1,100 employees. Between 250,000 and 300,000 meals are made every day. The produce range has been expanded from Indian food to include Thai and Mexican dishes, amongst others. In 2002 Gulam was knighted for his services to the food industry. Reflecting on what has inspired him during his life, Sir Gulam concludes: 'I'm a self-made man and a quick learner! Nothing comes easily, you've just got to work at it.'

Few of us can expect the kind of wealth that Sir Gulam now possesses. But his rags-to-riches life history raises interesting questions for sociologists. Is it just an isolated incident, or is his story being repeated elsewhere? How much chance does someone from a poor background have of reaching the top of the economic ladder? For every

Gulam Noon in our society, how many people have to work in his businesses, and are they paid their 'fair share' for the success of the company? The issues of wealth and poverty raised by Sir Gulam's life story lead us to broader questions. Why do economic inequalities exist in contemporary societies? What social factors will influence your economic position in society? Are your chances any different if you are a woman? How does the globalization of the economy affect your life chances? These are just a few of the sorts of question that sociologists ask and try to answer, and they are the focus of this chapter.

The study of inequalities in society is one of the most important areas of sociology, because our material resources determine a great deal about our lives. Here, we begin by looking at what sociologists mean when they talk about stratification and class. We then look at some of the most influential theories of class, and attempts to measure it, in sociological thought, after which we take a more detailed look at social class in Western society today. We close with a discussion of social mobility and conclude by briefly considering the continuing importance of social class in helping us to understand the world around us.

Systems of stratification

Sociologists use the concept of **social stratification** to describe inequalities that exist between individuals and groups within human societies. Often we think of stratification in terms of assets or property, but it can also occur because of other attributes, such as gender, age, religious affiliation or military rank.

Individuals and groups enjoy differential (unequal) access to rewards based on their position within the stratification scheme. Thus, stratification can most simply be defined as structured inequalities between different groupings of people. It is useful to think of stratification as rather like the

Access to benefits and rewards in society is affected by factors such as gender and ethnicity, both of which are forms of stratification.

geological layering of rock in the earth's surface. Societies can be seen as consisting of 'strata' in a hierarchy, with the more favoured at the top and the less privileged nearer the bottom.

All socially stratified systems share three basic characteristics:

1 The rankings apply to social categories of people who share a common characteristic without necessarily interacting or identifying with one another. For example, women may be ranked differently from men or wealthy people differently from the poor. This does not mean that individuals from a particular category cannot change their rank; however, it does mean that the category continues to exist even if individuals move out of it and into another category.

2 People's life experiences and opportunities depend heavily on how their social category is ranked. Being male or female, black or white, upper class or working class makes a big difference in terms of your life chances – often as big a difference as personal effort or good fortune (such as winning a lottery).

3 The ranks of different social categories tend to change very slowly over time. In the industrialized societies, for example, only recently have women as a whole begun to achieve equality with men.

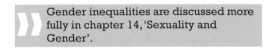

Gender inequalities are discussed more fully in chapter 14, 'Sexuality and Gender'.

As discussed in chapter 4, stratified societies have changed throughout human history. In the earliest human societies, which were based on hunting and gathering, there was very little social stratification – mainly because there was very little by way of wealth or other resources to be divided up. The development of agriculture produced considerably more wealth and, as a result, a great increase in stratification. Social stratification in agricultural societies increasingly came to resemble a pyramid, with a large number of people at the bottom and a successively smaller number of people as you move towards the top. Today, industrial and post-industrial societies are extremely complex; their stratification is more likely to resemble a teardrop, with a large number of people in the middle and lower-middle ranks (the so-called middle class), a slightly smaller number of people at the bottom, and very few people as one moves towards the top.

THINKING CRITICALLY

Should we assume that stratification is 'natural' and therefore inevitable? If not, how might we explain the persistence of stratification in human societies? In what ways could stratification systems be functional for society as a whole?

Historically, four basic systems of stratification can be distinguished: slavery, caste, estates and class. These are sometimes found in conjunction with one another: slavery, for instance, existed alongside classes in ancient Greece and Rome, and in the Southern United States before the Civil War of the 1860s.

Slavery

Slavery is an extreme form of inequality, in which certain people are owned as property by others. The legal conditions of slave-ownership have varied considerably among different societies. Sometimes slaves were deprived of almost all rights by law – as was the case on Southern plantations in the United States – while in other societies, their position was more akin to that of servants. For example, in the ancient Greek city-state of Athens, some slaves occupied positions of great responsibility. They were excluded from political positions and from the military, but were accepted in most other types of occupation. Some were literate and worked as government administrators; many were trained in craft skills. Even so, not all slaves could count on such good luck. For the less fortunate, their days began and ended in hard labour in the mines.

Throughout history, slaves have often fought back against their subjection; the slave rebellions in the American South before the Civil War are one example. Because of such resistance, systems of slave labour have tended to be unstable. High productivity could only be achieved through constant supervision and brutal punishment. Slave-labour systems eventually broke down, partly because of the struggles they provoked and partly because economic or other incentives motivate people to produce more effectively than does direct compulsion. Slavery is simply not economically efficient. Moreover, from about the eighteenth century on, many people in Europe and America came to see slavery as morally wrong. Today, slavery is illegal in every country of the world, but it still exists in some places. Recent research has documented that people are taken by force and held against their will. From enslaved brick-makers in Pakistan to sex slaves in Thailand and domestic slaves in relatively wealthy countries like the UK and France, slavery remains a significant human rights violation in the world today and against many people's assumption, seems to be increasing rather than diminishing (Bales 1999).

Caste

A **caste** system is a social system in which one's social position is given for a lifetime. In caste societies, therefore, all individuals must remain at the social level of their birth

The caste system in India is more than 2,000 years old, but as a form of social organization it has seen significant changes since independence in 1947.

throughout life. Everyone's social status is based on personal characteristics – such as perceived race or ethnicity (often based on such physical characteristics as skin colour), parental religion or parental caste – that are accidents of birth and are therefore believed to be unchangeable. A person is born into a caste and remains there for life. In a sense, caste societies can be seen as a special type of class society, in which class position is ascribed at birth (Sharma 1999). They have typically been found in agricultural societies that have not yet developed industrial capitalist economies, such as rural India or South Africa prior to the end of white rule in 1992.

Prior to modern times, caste systems were found throughout the world. In Europe, for example, Jews were frequently treated as a separate caste, forced to live in restricted neighbourhoods and barred from intermarrying (and in some instances even interacting) with non-Jews. The term 'ghetto' is said to derive from the Venetian word for 'foundry', the site of one of Europe's first official Jewish ghettos, established by the government of Venice in 1516. The term eventually came to refer to those sections of European towns where Jews were legally compelled to live, long before it was used to describe minority neighbourhoods in US cities, with their caste-like qualities of racial and ethnic segregation.

In caste systems, intimate contact with members of other castes is strongly discouraged. Such 'purity' of a caste is often maintained by rules of **endogamy**, marriage within one's social group as required by custom or law.

Caste in India and South Africa

The few remaining caste systems in the world are being seriously challenged by globalization. The Indian caste system, for

Apartheid may be a thing of the past, but the wealth gap between white and black South Africans is still very apparent. These boys live in the rural and impoverished district of Lusikisiki, South Africa.

example, reflects Hindu religious beliefs and is more than 2,000 years old. According to Hindu beliefs, there are four major castes, each roughly associated with broad occupational groupings. The four castes consist of the *Brahmins* (scholars and spiritual leaders) on top, followed by the *Ksyatriyas* (soldiers and rulers), the *Vaisyas* (farmers and merchants) and the *Shudras* (labourers and artisans). Beneath the four castes are those known as the 'untouchables' or *Dalits* ('oppressed people'), who – as their name suggests – are to be avoided at all costs. Untouchables are limited to the worst jobs in society, such as removing human waste, and they often resort to begging and searching in

garbage for their food. In traditional areas of India, some members of higher castes still regard physical contact with untouchables to be so contaminating that a mere touch requires cleansing rituals. India made it illegal to discriminate on the basis of caste in 1949, but aspects of the system remain in full force today, particularly in rural areas.

As India's modern capitalist economy brings people of different castes together, whether it is in the same workplace, aeroplane or restaurant, it is increasingly difficult to maintain the rigid barriers required to sustain the caste system. As more and more of India is influenced by globalization, it seems reasonable to assume that its caste system will weaken still further.

Before its abolition in 1992, the South African caste system, termed **apartheid**, rigidly separated black Africans, Indians, 'coloureds' (people of mixed races) and Asians from whites. In this case, caste was based entirely on race. Whites, who made up only 15 per cent of the total population, controlled virtually all the country's wealth, owned most of the usable land, ran the principal businesses and industries and had a monopoly on political power, since blacks lacked the right to vote. Blacks – who made up three-quarters of the population – were segregated into impoverished *bantustans* ('homelands') and were allowed out only to work for the white minority.

Apartheid, widespread discrimination and oppression created intense conflict between the white minority and the black, mixed-race and Asian majority. Decades of often violent struggle against apartheid finally proved successful in the 1990s. The most powerful black organization, the African National Congress (ANC), mobilized an economically devastating global boycott of South African businesses, forcing South Africa's white leaders to dismantle apartheid, which was abolished by popular vote among South African whites in 1992. In 1994, in the country's first ever multiracial elections, the black majority won control of the government, and Nelson Mandela – the black leader of the ANC, who had spent 27 years imprisoned by the white government – was elected president.

Estates

Estates were part of European feudalism, but also existed in many other traditional civilizations. The feudal estates consisted of strata with differing obligations and rights towards each other, some of these differences being established in law. In Europe, the highest estate was composed of the *aristocracy* and gentry. The *clergy* formed another estate, having lower status but possessing various distinctive privileges. Those in what came to be called the 'third estate' were the *commoners* – serfs, free peasants, merchants and artisans. In contrast to castes, a certain degree of intermarriage and mobility was tolerated between the estates. Commoners might be knighted, for example, in payment for special services given to the monarch; merchants could sometimes purchase titles. A remnant of the system persists in Britain, where hereditary titles are still recognized (though since 1999 peers are no longer automatically entitled to vote in the House of Lords), and business leaders, civil servants and others may be honoured with a knighthood for their services.

Estates have tended to develop in the past wherever there was a traditional aristocracy based on noble birth. In feudal systems, such as in medieval Europe, estates were closely bound up with the manorial community: they formed a local, rather than a national, system of stratification. In more centralized traditional empires, such as China or Japan, they were organized on a more national basis. Sometimes the differences between the estates were justified by religious beliefs, although rarely in as strict a way as in the Hindu caste system.

Class

Class systems differ in many respects from slavery, castes or estates. We can define a class as a large-scale grouping of people who share common economic resources, which strongly influence the type of lifestyle they are able to lead. Ownership of wealth and occupation, are the chief bases of class differences. Classes differ from earlier forms of stratification in four main respects:

1 *Class systems are fluid.* Unlike the other types of strata, classes are not established by legal or religious provisions. The boundaries between classes are never clear-cut. There are no formal restrictions on intermarriage between people from different classes.

2 *Class positions are in some part achieved.* An individual's class is not simply given at birth, as is the case in the other types of stratification systems. Social mobility – movement upward and downward in the class structure – is more common than in the other types.

3 *Class is economically based.* Classes depend on economic differences between groups of individuals – inequalities in the possession of material resources. In the other types of stratification systems, non-economic factors (such as race in the former South African caste system) are generally most important.

4 *Class systems are large-scale and impersonal.* In the other types of stratification systems, inequalities are expressed primarily in personal relationships of duty or obligation – between slave and master or lower- and higher-caste individuals. Class systems, by contrast, operate mainly through large-scale, impersonal associations. For instance, one major basis of class differences is in inequalities of pay and working conditions.

Will caste give way to class?

There is some evidence that globalization may hasten the end of legally sanctioned caste systems throughout the world. Most official caste systems have already given way to class-based ones in industrial capitalist societies; South Africa, mentioned earlier, is the most prominent recent example (Berger 1986). Modern industrial production requires that people move about freely, work at whatever jobs they are suited or able to do, and change jobs frequently according to economic conditions. The rigid restrictions found in caste systems interfere with this necessary freedom. Furthermore, as the world increasingly becomes a single economic unit, caste-like relationships will become increasingly vulnerable to economic pressures. Nonetheless, elements of caste persist even in post-industrial societies. For

example, some Asian immigrants to the West seek to arrange traditional marriages for their children along caste lines.

The next section looks at sociological theories, which seek to explain the persistence of social stratification in human societies. Most sociologists who have addressed this question have been strongly influenced by the social class systems of the modern world and the discussion below reflects this.

THINKING CRITICALLY

What evidence is there from around the world that, in time, social class is likely to become the dominant form of stratification in all the countries of the world? Given what we know about other forms of stratification, on balance, would this be a positive or negative development?

Theories of class and stratification

The theories developed by Karl Marx and Max Weber form the basis of most sociological analyses of class and stratification.

Scholars working in the Marxist tradition have further developed the ideas Marx himself set out and others have tried to elaborate on Weber's concepts. We shall begin by examining the theories set forth by Marx and Weber before analysing the more recent neo-Marxist ideas of American sociologist, Erik Olin Wright.

 Chapter 1, 'What is Sociology?', contains an introduction to Marx and Weber's basic ideas and theoretical perspectives.

Karl Marx's theory of class conflict

Most of Marx's works were concerned with stratification and, above all, with social class, yet surprisingly he failed to provide a systematic analysis of the concept of class. The manuscript Marx was working on at the time of his death (subsequently published as

Classic Studies 11.1 Karl Marx and the theory of class conflict

The research problem

Industrialization in Europe in the nineteenth century transformed societies, arguably, for the better. But it also led to protests and revolutionary movements. Why did workers oppose industrialization? Later, as industrial societies developed in the twentieth century, strikes and militant workers' activity continually occurred. Again, why have workers protested even as societies became more wealthy? Karl Marx (1818–83) spent most of his adult life investigating modern class-based societies in an attempt to understand how they worked, and his crucial argument was that industrial societies were rooted in capitalist economic relations. Marx was not just a detached academic observer though; he was also a key figure in communist political debates and an activist in workers' movements. For Marx, industrial capitalism, for all its progressive elements, was founded in an exploitative system of class relations that led to the oppression of the majority of working people.

Marx's explanation

For Marx, a social class is a group of people who stand in a common relationship to the means of production – the means by which they gain a livelihood. Before the rise of modern industry, the means of production consisted primarily of land and the instruments used to tend crops or pastoral animals. In pre-industrial societies, therefore, the two main classes consisted of those who owned the land (aristocrats, gentry or slave-holders) and those actively engaged in producing from it (serfs, slaves and free peasantry). In modern industrial societies, factories, offices, machinery and the wealth or capital needed to buy them have become more important. The two main classes consist of those who own these new means of production – industrialists or capitalists – and those who earn their living by selling their labour to them – the working class or, in the now somewhat archaic term Marx sometimes favoured, the **proletariat**.

According to Marx, the relationship between classes is an exploitative one. In feudal societies, exploitation often took the form of the direct transfer of produce from the peasantry to the aristocracy. Serfs were compelled to give a certain proportion of their production to their aristocratic master, or had to work for a number of days each month in his fields to produce crops to be consumed by him and his retinue. In modern capitalist societies, the source of exploitation is less obvious, and Marx devoted much attention to trying to clarify its nature. In the course of the working day, Marx reasoned, workers produce more than is actually needed by employers to repay the cost of hiring them. This surplus value is the source of profit, which capitalists are able to put to their own use. A group of workers in a clothing factory, say, might be able to produce 100 suits a day. Selling 75 per cent of the suits provides enough income for the manufacturer to pay the workers' wages and for the cost of plant and equipment. Income from the sale of the remainder of the garments is taken as profit.

Marx was struck by the inequalities created by the capitalist system. Although in earlier times aristocrats lived a life of luxury, completely different from that of the peasantry, agrarian societies were relatively poor. Even if there had been no aristocracy, standards of living would inevitably have been meagre. With the development of modern industry, however, wealth is produced on a scale far beyond anything seen before, but workers have little access to the wealth that their labour creates. They remain relatively poor, while the wealth accumulated by the propertied class grows. Marx used the term **pauperization** to describe the process by which the working class grows increasingly impoverished in relation to the capitalist class. Even if workers become more affluent in absolute terms, the gap separating them from the capitalist class continues to stretch ever wider.

These inequalities between the capitalist and the working class were not strictly economic in nature. Marx noted how the development of modern factories and the mechanization of production means that work frequently becomes dull and oppressive in the extreme. The labour that is the source of our wealth is often both physically wearing and mentally tedious – as in the case of a factory hand whose job consists of routine tasks undertaken day in, day out, in an unchanging environment.

Critical points

Sociological debates on Marx's ideas have been more or less continuous for the past 150 years, and it is quite impossible to do justice to them here. Instead, we can point to several major themes in Marxist criticism. Firstly, Marx's characterization of capitalist society as splitting into 'two main camps' – owners and workers – has been seen as too simple. Even within the working class, there are divisions between skilled and unskilled workers, which work to prevent a clear convergence of class interests. Such divisions have endured and become more complex, with gender and ethnicity also becoming factors leading to internal competition and conflicts. As a result, critics argue, concerted action by the whole of the working class is very unlikely.

Second, Marx's forecast of a communist revolution led by the industrial working class in the advanced societies has not materialized and this calls into question his analysis of the dynamics of capitalism. Some contemporary Marxists continue to see capitalism as a doomed system, which will collapse at some point in the future, but critics (some of them former Marxists) see little evidence of this. Indeed, the majority of the working class have become increasingly affluent property-owners with more of a stake in the capitalist system than ever.

Finally, although Marx saw class-consciousness arising from the increasingly shared experiences of the working class, many critics of Marxism today have found that people identify less rather than more with their social class position. Instead, there are multiple sources of people's social identities, and class identification is not the most important for many people. Without a developing class-consciousness, there can be no concerted class action and, hence, no communist revolution. Again, critics see the long-term social trends moving away from Marx's theoretical predictions.

Contemporary significance

Marx's influence on the world has been enormous, and even though his major predictions have not been proved correct, the analysis of capitalism that he pioneered continues to inform our understanding of globalization processes. Indeed, it can be argued that the widespread acknowledgement of rapid globalization in the social sciences may give fresh impetus to Marxist studies, particularly with the recent emergence of international anti-capitalist and anti-globalization movements.

 See chapter 22, 'Politics, Government and Social Movements', for a discussion of anti-globalization movements.

part of his major work, *Capital*) breaks off just at the point where he posed the question 'What constitutes a class?'. Marx's concept of class has thus to be reconstructed from the body of his writings as a whole. Since the various passages in which he discussed class are not always fully consistent, there have been many disputes between scholars about 'what Marx really meant'. Nevertheless, his main ideas are fairly clear and are discussed in 'Classic Studies 11.1'.

Max Weber: class, status and party

Weber's approach to stratification was built on the analysis developed by Marx, but he modified and elaborated on it. Like Marx, Weber regarded society as characterized by conflicts over power and resources. Yet where Marx saw polarized class relations and economic issues at the heart of all social conflict, Weber developed a more complex, multidimensional view of society. Social stratification is not simply a matter of class, according to Weber, but is shaped by two further aspects: **status** and **party**. These three overlapping elements of stratification produce an enormous number of possible positions within society, rather than the more rigid bipolar model proposed by Marx.

Although Weber accepted Marx's view that class is founded on objectively given economic conditions, he saw a greater variety of economic factors as important in class-formation than were recognized by Marx. According to Weber, class divisions derive not only from control or lack of control of the means of production, but from economic differences that have nothing directly to do with property. Such resources include especially the skills and credentials, or qualifications, which affect the types of work people are able to obtain. Weber argued that an individual's *market position* strongly influences his or her overall life chances. Those in managerial or professional occupations earn more and have more favourable conditions of work, for example, than people in blue-collar jobs. The qualifications they possess, such as degrees, diplomas and the skills they have acquired, make them more 'marketable' than others without such qualifications. At a lower level, among blue-collar workers, skilled craftsmen are able to secure higher wages than the semi- or unskilled.

Status in Weber's theory refers to differences between social groups in the social honour or prestige they are accorded by others. In traditional societies, status was often determined on the basis of the first-hand knowledge of a person gained through multiple interactions in different contexts over a period of years. Yet as societies grew more complex, it became impossible for status always to be accorded in this way. Instead, according to Weber, status came to be expressed through people's *styles of life*. Markers and symbols of status – such as housing, dress, manner of speech and occupation – all help to shape an individual's social standing in the eyes of others. People sharing the same status form a community in which there is a sense of shared identity.

While Marx argued that status distinctions are the result of class divisions in society, Weber argued that status often varies independently of class divisions. Possession of wealth normally tends to confer high status, but there are many exceptions. The term 'genteel poverty' refers to one example. In Britain, for example, individuals from aristocratic families continue to enjoy considerable social esteem even when their fortunes have been lost. Conversely, 'new money' is often looked on with some scorn by the well-established wealthy.

In modern societies, Weber pointed out, party formation is an important aspect of *power*, and can influence stratification independently of class and status. Party defines a group of individuals who work together because they have common backgrounds, aims or interests. Often a party works in an organized fashion towards a specific goal which is in the interest of the party membership. Marx tended to explain both status differences and party organization in terms of class. Neither, in fact, can be reduced to class divisions, Weber argued, even though each is influenced by them; both can in turn influence the economic circumstances of individuals and groups, thereby affecting class. Parties may appeal to concerns cutting across class differences; for example, parties may be based on religious affiliation or nationalist ideals. A Marxist might attempt to explain the conflicts between Catholics and Protestants in Northern Ireland in class terms, since more Catholics than Protestants are in working-class jobs. A follower of Weber would argue that such an explanation is ineffective, because many Protestants are also from working-class backgrounds. The parties to which people are affiliated express religious as well as class differences.

Weber's writings on stratification are important, because they show that other dimensions of stratification besides class strongly influence people's lives. While Marx saw social class as the key social division, Weber drew attention to the complex interplay of class, status and party as separate aspects of social stratification creating a more flexible basis for empirical analyses of stratification.

Erik Olin Wright's theory of class

The American sociologist Erik Olin Wright has developed an influential theory of class which combines aspects of both Marx's and Weber's approaches (Wright 1978, 1985, 1997). According to Wright, there are three dimensions of *control over economic resources* in modern capitalist production, and these allow us to identify the major classes that exist:

- control over investments or money capital;
- control over the physical means of production (land or factories and offices);
- control over labour power.

Those who belong to the capitalist class have control over each of these dimensions in the production system. Members of the working class have control over none of them. In between these two main classes, however, are the groups whose position is more ambiguous – the managers and white-collar workers mentioned above. These people are in what Wright calls *contradictory class locations*, because they are able to influence some aspects of production, but are denied control over others. White-collar and professional employees, for example, have to contract their labour power to employers in order to make a living in the same way as manual workers do. But at the same time they have a greater degree of control over the work setting than most people in blue-collar jobs. Wright terms the class position of such workers 'contradictory', because they are neither capitalists nor manual workers, yet they share certain common features with each.

A large segment of the population – 85 to 90 per cent, according to Wright (1997) – falls into the category of those who are forced to sell their labour because they do not control the means of production. Yet within this population there is a great deal of diversity, ranging from the traditional manual working class to white-collar workers. In order to differentiate class locations within this large population, Wright takes two factors into account: the relationship to authority and the possession of skills or expertise. First, Wright argues that many middle-class workers, such as managers and supervisors, enjoy relationships towards authority that are more privileged than those of the working class. Such individuals are called on by capitalists to assist in controlling the working class – for example, by monitoring an employee's work or by conducting personnel reviews and evaluations – and are rewarded for their 'loyalty' by earning higher wages and receiving regular promotions. Yet, at the same time, these individuals remain under the control of the capitalist owners. In other words, they are both exploiters and exploited.

The second factor which differentiates class locations within the middle classes is the possession of skills and expertise. According to Wright, middle-class employees possessing skills which are in demand in the labour market are able to exercise a specific form of power in the capitalist system. Given that their expertise is in short supply, they are able to earn a higher wage. The lucrative positions available to information technology specialists in the emerging knowledge economy illustrate this point. Moreover, Wright argues, because employees with knowledge and skills are more difficult to monitor and control, employers are obliged to secure their loyalty and cooperation by rewarding them accordingly.

THINKING CRITICALLY

Are Marx and Weber's theories of class at odds with each other or complementary? Explain your answer fully. What does Wright's introduction of the idea of 'contradictory class locations' add to our understanding of class relationships?

Measuring class

Both theoretical and empirical studies have investigated the link between class standing and other dimensions of social life, such as voting patterns, educational attainment and physical health. Yet, as we have seen, the concept of class is far from clear-cut. Both in academic circles and in common usage, the term 'class' is understood and used in a wide variety of ways. How, then, can sociologists and researchers measure such an imprecise concept for the purpose of empirical studies?

When an abstract concept such as class is transformed into a measurable variable in a study, we say that the concept has been *operationalized*. This means that it has been defined clearly and concretely enough to be tested through empirical research. Sociologists have operationalized class through a variety of schemes which attempt to map the class structure of society. Such schemes provide a theoretical framework by which individuals are allocated to social class categories.

A common feature of most class schemes is that they are based on the occupational structure. Sociologists have seen class divisions as corresponding generally with material and social inequalities that are linked to types of employment. The development of capitalism and industrialism has been marked by a growing division of labour and an increasingly complicated occupational structure. Although no longer as true as it once was, occupation is one of the most critical factors in an individual's social standing, life chances and level of material comfort.

Social scientists have used occupation extensively as an indicator of social class because of the finding that individuals in the same occupation tend to experience similar degrees of social advantage or disadvantage, maintain comparable lifestyles, and share similar opportunities in life.

Class schemes based on the occupational structure take a number of different forms. Some schemes are largely descriptive in nature – they reflect the shape of the occupational and class structure in society without addressing the relations between social classes. Such models have been favoured by scholars who see stratification as unproblematic and part of the natural social order, such as those working in the functionalist tradition.

> Functionalism was introduced in chapter 1, 'What is Sociology?', and chapter 3, 'Theories and Perspectives in Sociology'.

Other schemes are more theoretically informed – often drawing on the ideas of Marx or Weber – and concern themselves with explaining the relations between classes in society. 'Relational' class schemes tend to be favoured by sociologists working within conflict paradigms in order to demonstrate the divisions and tensions within society. Erik Olin Wright's theory of class, discussed above, is an example of a relational class scheme, because it seeks to depict the processes of class exploitation from a Marxist perspective. John Goldthorpe's influential work is an example of a relational scheme originally rooted in Weberian ideas of class (see 'Classic Studies 11.2').

Evaluating Goldthorpe's class scheme

As 'Classic Studies 11.2' notes, Goldthorpe's class scheme has been used widely in empirical research. It has been useful in highlighting class-based inequalities, such as those related to health and education, as well as reflecting class-based dimensions in

The research problem

What is the connection between the jobs we do – our occupations – and our social class position? Is class simply the same thing as occupation? Do we then move *between* classes when we move occupations? If we retrain, move into higher education or become unemployed, does our class position change as well? As sociologists, how can we best carry out research into social class?

Some sociologists have been dissatisfied with descriptive class schemes, claiming that they merely reflect social and material inequalities between classes rather than seeking to explain the class processes which give birth to them. With such concerns in mind, British sociologist John Goldthorpe created a scheme for use in empirical research on social mobility. The Goldthorpe class scheme was designed not as a hierarchy, but as a representation of the 'relational' nature of the contemporary class structure.

Goldthorpe's explanation

Goldthorpe's ideas have been highly influential. Although he now underplays any explicit theoretical influence on his scheme (Erikson and Goldthorpe 1993), other sociologists have often pointed to the Goldthorpe classification as an example of a neo-Weberian class scheme. This is because Goldthorpe's original scheme identified class locations on the basis of two main factors: market situation and work situation. An individual's market situation concerns his or her level of pay, job security and prospects for advancement; it emphasizes material rewards and general life chances. The work situation, by contrast, focuses on questions of control, power and authority within the occupation. An individual's work situation is concerned with the degree of autonomy in the workplace and the overall relations of control affecting an employee.

Goldthorpe devised his scheme by evaluating occupations on the basis of their relative market and work situations. In the 1980s and '90s, Goldthorpe's comparative research encompassed a project on social mobility known as the CASMIN project (Comparative Analysis of Social Mobility in Industrial Societies). The results of this project are significant, as the resulting classification was incorporated into the UK Office of National Statistics' own Socio-Economic Classification (ONS-SEC) and is intended to be the basis for a European-wide scheme (Crompton 2008). The Goldthorpe/CASMIN and UK ONS-SEC schemes are shown in table 11.1, alongside the more commonly used sociological terms (on the right-hand side).

Originally encompassing eleven class locations, reduced to eight in the CASMIN research, Goldthorpe's scheme remains more detailed than many others. Yet in common usage, class locations are still compressed into just three main class strata: a 'service' class (classes I and II), an 'intermediate class' (classes III and IV) and a 'working class' (classes V, VI and VII). Goldthorpe also acknowledges the presence of an elite class of property-holders at the very top of the scheme, but argues that it is such a small segment of society that it is not meaningful as a category in empirical studies.

In his more recent writings, Goldthorpe (2000) has emphasized employment relations within his scheme, rather than the notion of 'work situation' described above. By doing this, he draws attention to different types of employment contract. A labour contract supposes an exchange of wages and effort which is specifically defined and delimited, while a service contract has a 'prospective' element, such as the possibility of salary growth or promotion. According to Goldthorpe, the working class is characterized by labour contracts and the service class by service contracts; the intermediate class locations experience intermediate types of employment relations.

Critical points

An extended evaluation of Goldthorpe's work follows, but here we can note two major criticisms. Although his scheme is clearly a useful one for empirical researchers, it is not so clear that it can tell us much about the position of those social groups, such as students, that fall outside social class boundaries. It has also come under fire for underplaying the significance of the gross disparities in wealth within capitalist societies. In a sense, such criticisms are a reflection of the long-standing debate between Marxist and Weberian scholars on social class and its importance.

Contemporary significance

Goldthorpe's work has been at the centre of debates on social class and occupations for some time. In spite of some highly pertinent criticisms, his class scheme has been constantly updated and refined, while remaining within the broadly Weberian tradition of sociology. With the latest version about to become the standard class scheme across the European Union, it would seem that Goldthorpe's ideas are likely to become more rather than less influential in the future.

Table 11.1 Goldthorpe/CASMIN and UK ONS-SEC social class schemes alongside more commonly used sociological categories.

Goldthorpe/CASMIN schema		National Statistics Socio-Economic Classification		Common descriptive term
I	Professional, administrative and managerial employees, higher grade	1	Higher managerial and professional occupations	Salariat (or service class)
II	Professional, administrative and managerial employees, lower grade; technicians, higher grade	2	Lower managerial and professional occupations	
IIIa	Routine non-manual employees, higher grade	3	Intermediate occupations	Intermediate white collar
IV	Small employers and self-employed workers	4	Employers in small organizations, own account workers	Independents (or petty bourgeoisie)
V	Supervisors of manual workers; technicians, lower grade	5	Lower supervisory and lower technical occupations	Intermediate blue-collar
VI	Skilled manual workers	6	Semi-routine occupations	Working class
IIIb	Routine non-manual workers, lower grade	7	Routine occupations	
VII	Semi- and unskilled manual workers			

---

voting patterns, political outlooks and general social attitudes. Yet it is important to note several significant limitations to schemes such as Goldthorpe's, which should caution us against applying them uncritically.

Occupational class schemes are difficult to apply to the *economically inactive*, such as the unemployed, students, pensioners and children. Unemployed and retired individuals are often classified on the basis of their previous work activity, although this

Where do unemployed people and jobseekers fit into a social class scheme?

can be problematic in the case of the long-term unemployed or people with sporadic work histories. Students can sometimes be classified according to their discipline, but this is more likely to be successful in cases where the field of study correlates closely to a specific occupation (such as engineering or medicine).

Class schemes based on occupational distinctions are also unable to reflect the importance of *property-ownership and wealth* to social class. Occupational titles alone are not sufficient indicators of an individual's wealth and overall assets. This is particularly true among the richest members of society, including entrepreneurs, financiers and the 'old rich', whose occupational titles of 'director' or 'executive' place them in the same category as many professionals of much more limited means. In other words, class schemes derived from

occupational categories do not accurately reflect the enormous concentration of wealth among the 'economic elite'. By classifying such individuals alongside other upper-class professionals, the occupational class schemes dilute the relative weight of property relations in social stratification.

John Westergaard is one sociologist who has disputed Goldthorpe's view that because the rich are so few in number they can be excluded from schemes detailing class structure. As Westergaard (1995: 127) argues:

> It is the intense concentration of power and privilege in so few hands that makes these people top. Their socio-structural weight overall, immensely disproportionate to their small numbers, makes the society they top a class society, whatever may be the pattern of divisions beneath them.

11.1   The death of class?

In recent years there has been a vigorous debate within sociology about the usefulness of 'class'. Some sociologists, such as Ray Pahl, have even questioned whether it is still a useful concept in attempting to understand contemporary societies. Australian academics Jan Pakulski and Malcolm Waters have been prominent amongst those who argue that class is no longer the key to understanding contemporary societies. In their book, *The Death of Class* (1996), they argue that contemporary societies have undergone profound social changes and are no longer to be accurately seen as 'class societies'.

A time of social change

Pakulski and Waters argue that industrial societies are now undergoing a period of tremendous social change. We are witnessing a period in which the political, social and economic importance of class are in decline. Industrial societies have changed from being organized class societies to a new stage, which Pakulski and Waters call 'status conventionalism'. They use this term to indicate that inequalities, although they remain, are the result of differences in status (prestige) and in the lifestyle and consumption patterns favoured by such status groups. Class is no longer an important factor in a person's identity, and the class communities exemplified by Young and Willmott's study of Bethnal Green (1973) are a thing of the past. These changes in turn mean that attempts to explain political and social behaviour by reference to class are also out of date. Class, it seems, is well and truly dead.

Property-ownership

One of the reasons for this huge shift is that there have been important changes in property-ownership. Property-ownership, it is claimed, is now less restricted. This means that there is both more competition amongst firms, since there are more of them, and less opportunity for a dominant capitalist or managerial class to reproduce and pass on its own privilege to the next generation of

Is status-based consumption now the main form of stratification in modern societies, rather than social class position?

capitalists. Inequality, however, remains, and, where it does arise, is the result of the failure of groups to achieve a high status, not their class position (their position in a division of labour).

Increase in consumer power

These changes have been accompanied by an increase in consumer power. In ever more competitive and diverse markets, firms have to be much more sensitive in heeding the wishes of consumers. There has thus been a shift in the balance of power in advanced industrial societies. What marks out the underprivileged in contemporary society – what Pakulski and Waters refer to as an 'ascriptively disprivileged underclass' – is their inability to engage in 'status consumption', which is to say, their inability to buy cars, clothes, houses, holidays and other consumer goods.

For Pakulski and Waters, contemporary societies are stratified, but this stratification is achieved through cultural consumption, not class position in the division of labour. It is all a matter of style, taste and status (prestige), not of location in the division of labour.

Processes of globalization

The shift from organized class society to status conventionalism is explained as being the result of processes of globalization, changes in the economy, technology and politics. Pakulski and Waters argue that globalization has led to a new international division of labour, in which the 'first world' is increasingly post-industrial – there are simply fewer of the sort of manual working-class occupations which characterized the previous era of 'organized class society'. At the same time, in a globalized world, nation-states are less self-contained and are less able to govern either their population or market forces than they once were. Stratification and inequality still exist, but they do so more on a global than a national basis; we see more significant inequalities between different nations than we do within a nation-state.

The political and social implications

These changes have had profound political and social implications. As mentioned above, collective class-based communities have collapsed. In the case of the UK this has occurred as old industries, such as coal-mining, have 'down-sized' and populations have shifted to the more affluent urbanized areas in the south. Greater geographical mobility has led to changes in family structure – single-person households are on the increase in the UK. Pakulski and Waters argue that, in the context of greater geographical mobility, the importance of the family as a site of class reproduction (as in Young and Willmott) is now very much in decline.

Nothing but a theory?

John Scott and Lydia Morris argue for a need to make distinctions between the class positions of individuals – their location in a division of labour – and the collective phenomena of social class through which people express a sense of belonging to a group and have a shared sense of identity and values. This last sense of class (a more subjective and collective sense) may or may not exist in a society at a particular time – it will depend on many social, economic and political factors.

It is this last aspect of class that appears to have diminished in recent years. This does not mean that status and the cultural aspects of stratification are now so dominant that the economic aspects of class are of no significance; indeed, mobility studies and inequalities of wealth indicate the opposite. Class is not dead – it is just becoming that bit more complex!

Source: Adapted from Abbott 2001

As we have seen, there are a number of complexities involved in devising class schemes that can reliably 'map' the class structure of society. Even within a relatively 'stable' occupational structure, measuring and mapping social class is fraught with difficulty. Yet the rapid economic transformations occurring in industrial societies have made the measurement of class even more problematic, and have even led some to question the usefulness of class as a concept. New categories of occupations are emerging, there has been a general shift away from industrial production towards service and knowledge work, and an enormous number of women have entered the workforce in recent decades. Occupational class schemes are not necessarily well suited to capturing the dynamic processes of class-formation, mobility and change that are provoked by such social transformations.

THINKING CRITICALLY

Reflecting on your own life experience, to what extent do you feel your identity has been shaped by your family's social class background? What evidence can you point to which suggests that patterns of *consumption* may be becoming more significant in the creation of social divisions?

Contemporary class divisions in the developed world

The question of the upper class

Who is right, Westergaard or Goldthorpe? Is there still a distinctive upper class in the developed societies, founded on ownership of wealth and property? Or should we be talking more of a wider service class, as Goldthorpe suggests? Although Goldthorpe recognizes that a small elite upper class does exist, this is seen as so small that it becomes difficult to build into representative social surveys. On the other hand, for those who argue that an elite upper class is still significant enough to be the focus of research, this is not the same class as the landed aristocracy of estates systems. Instead, it is a capitalist elite whose wealth and power is derived from profit-making in global markets. One way of approaching these issues is to look at how far wealth and income are concentrated in the hands of a few.

Reliable information about the distribution of wealth is difficult to obtain. Some countries keep more accurate statistics than others, but there is always a considerable amount of guesswork involved. The affluent do not usually publicize the full range of their assets; it has often been remarked that we know far more about the poor than we do about the wealthy. What is certain is that wealth is indeed concentrated in the hands of a small minority. In Britain for example, the top 1 per cent own some 21 per cent of

all marketable wealth. The most wealthy 10 per cent of the population has consistently owned 50 per cent or more of the total marketable wealth in the country, while the least wealthy half of the population owns less than 10 per cent of the total wealth (see table 11.2).

Ownership of stocks and bonds is more unequal than holdings of wealth as a whole. The top 1 per cent in the UK own some 75 per cent of privately held corporate shares; the top 5 per cent own over 90 per cent of the total. But there has also been more change in this respect. Around 25 per cent of the population own shares, which compares with 14 per cent in 1986 – many people bought shares for the first time during the privatization programme of the Conservative government that came to power in 1979. The increase is even more dramatic when looked at over a longer period, for in 1979 only 5 per cent of the population held shares. Most of these holdings are small (worth less than £1,000 at 1991 prices), and institutional share-ownership – shares held by companies in other firms – is growing faster than individual share-ownership.

Historically, it has been very difficult to arrive at an overall picture of global wealth distribution because of the problems of data-gathering in some countries. However, a recent study by the Helsinki-based World Institute for Development Economics Research of the United Nations University (UNU-WIDER 2007) covers all the countries of the world and takes in household wealth, shares and other financial assets, as well as land and buildings, making it the most comprehensive global survey of personal wealth ever undertaken. The Helsinki survey found that the richest 2 per cent of the global population own more than half of global household wealth. It also found that while the richest 10 per cent of adults owned 85 per cent of global wealth, the bottom 50 per cent owned just 1 per cent. Clearly, when compared with a single developed country like the UK, the global pattern of wealth distribution is even more unequal,

| Table 11.2 | **UK distribution of wealth, 1976–2003** | | | | | | | |

United Kingdom				Percentages				
Marketable wealth								
Percentage of wealth owned by:								
	1976	1986	1996	1999	2000	2001	2002	2003
Most wealthy 1%	21	18	20	23	23	22	24	21
Most wealthy 5%	38	36	40	43	44	42	45	40
Most wealthy 10%	50	50	52	55	56	54	57	53
Most wealthy 25%	71	73	74	75	75	72	75	72
Most wealthy 50%	92	90	93	94	95	94	94	93
Total marketable wealth (£ billion)	280	955	2,092	2,861	3,131	3,477	3,588	3,783
Marketable wealth less value of dwellings								
Percentage of wealth owned by:								
Most wealthy 1%	29	25	26	34	33	34	37	34
Most wealthy 5%	47	46	49	59	59	58	62	58
Most wealthy 10%	57	58	63	72	73	72	74	71
Most wealthy 25%	73	75	81	87	89	88	87	85
Most wealthy 50%	88	89	94	97	98	98	98	99

Source: National Statistics 2006d

reflecting the gross disparity in wealth and power between the industrialized countries and those in the developing world.

'The rich' do not constitute a homogeneous group. Nor do they form a static category: individuals follow varying trajectories into and out of wealth. Some rich people were born into families of 'old money' – an expression which refers to long-standing wealth that has been passed down through generations. Other affluent individuals are 'self-made', having successfully built up wealth from more humble beginnings. Profiles of the richest members of society vary enormously. Next to members of long-standing affluent families are music and film celebrities, athletes and representatives of the 'new elite' who have made millions through the development and promotion of computers, telecommunications and the Internet. Like poverty, wealth must be regarded in the context of life-cycles. Some individuals become wealthy very quickly, only to lose much or all of it; others may experience a gradual growth or decline in assets over time.

While it is difficult to collect precise information about the assets and lives of the rich, it is possible to trace broad shifts in the composition of the wealthiest segment of society. Some noteworthy trends have arisen in recent years, which we can observe form UK data. First, 'self-made millionaires', like Sir Gulam Noon, whom we discussed at the start of this chapter, appear to be making up a greater proportion of the wealthiest individuals. More than 75 per cent of the 1,000 richest Britons in 2007 made their own wealth rather than inheriting it. Second, a small but growing number of women are entering the ranks of the rich. In 1989, only six women were represented among the wealthiest Britons; by 2007 that number had risen to 92. Third, in recent years many of the wealthiest members of society are quite young – in their 20s or 30s. In 2000, there were 17 Britons under the age of 30 who were worth more than £30 million. Fourth, ethnic minorities, particularly those of Asian origin, have been increasing their presence among the super-rich (*Sunday Times Rich List* 2007). Finally, many of the richest people in Britain – including the richest, Roman Abramovich – were not born in the country, but decided to make it their place of residence for a variety of reasons, including the relatively low rates of tax for the super-rich

Although the composition of the rich is certainly changing, the view that there is no longer a distinguishable upper class is questionable. John Scott (1991) has argued that the upper class today has changed shape but retains its distinctive position. He points to three particular groups that together form a constellation of interests in controlling – and profiting from – big business. Senior executives in large corporations may not own their companies, but they are often able to accumulate shareholdings, and these connect them both to old-style industrial entrepreneurs and to 'finance capitalists'. Finance capitalists, a category that includes the people who run the insurance companies, banks, investment funds and other organizations that are large institutional shareholders, are, in Scott's view, amongst the core of the upper class today. For example, in 2007 one City of London banker took £58.6 million in earnings in less than a year and a half. The Bank of England's deputy governor noted that the situation in private equity and hedge funds was similar to that in English premiership football, where individual pay is set according to a world market, not simply a national one (Crompton 2008: 145).

Policies encouraging entrepreneurship during the 1980s and the information technology boom of the 1990s have led to a new wave of entry into the upper class of people who have made a fortune from business and technological advances. At the same time, the growth of corporate shareholding among middle-class households has broadened the profile of corporate ownership. Yet the concentration of power and wealth in the upper class remains intact. While corporate-ownership patterns may be more diffuse than in earlier times, it is still a small minority who benefit substantially from shareholding.

We can conclude from this that we need a concept both of the upper class and the service class. The upper class consists of a small minority of individuals who have both wealth and power, and who are able to transmit their privileges to their children. This class can be roughly identified as the top 1 per cent of wealth-holders. Below them is the service class, made up, as Goldthorpe says, of professionals, managers and top administrators. They make up some 25 per cent of the population. Those whom Goldthorpe calls the 'intermediate class' are perhaps more simply called the middle class. Let us look in more detail at this class.

The growing middle class

The 'middle class' covers a broad spectrum of people working in many different occupations, from employees in the service industry to school teachers to medical professionals. Some authors prefer to speak of the 'middle classes' so as to draw attention to the diversity of occupations, class and status situations, and life chances that characterize its members. According to most observers, the middle class now encompasses the majority of the population in Britain and most other industrialized countries. This is because the proportion of white-collar jobs has risen markedly relative to blue-collar ones over the course of the century.

See chapter 20, 'Work and Economic Life', for more on the rise of white-collar jobs.

Members of the middle class, by merit of their educational credentials or technical qualifications, occupy positions that provide them with greater material and cultural advantages than those enjoyed by manual workers. Unlike the working class, members of the middle class can sell their mental *and* their physical labour power in order to earn a living. While this distinction is useful in forming a rough division between the middle and working classes, the dynamic nature of the occupational structure and the possibility of upward and downward social mobility make it difficult to define the boundaries of the middle class with great precision.

The middle class is not internally cohesive and is unlikely to become so, given the diversity of its members and their differing interests (Butler and Savage 1995). It is true that the middle class is not as homogeneous as the working class; nor do its members share a common social background or cultural outlook, as is largely the case with the top layers of the upper class. The 'loose' composition of the middle class is not a new phenomenon, however; it has been an abiding feature of the middle class since its emergence in the early nineteenth century.

Professional, managerial and administrative occupations have been among the fastest growing sectors of the middle class. There are several reasons why this is so. The first is related to the importance of large-scale organizations in modern societies.

See chapter 18, 'Organizations and Networks', for more on the nature of organizations.

The spread of bureaucracies has created opportunities and a demand for employees to work within institutional settings. Individuals such as doctors and lawyers, who might have been self-employed in earlier times, now tend to work in institutional environments. Second, the growth of professionals is a reflection of the expanding number of people who work in sectors of the economy where the government plays a major role. The creation of the welfare state led to an enormous growth in many professions involved in carrying out its mandate, such as social workers, teachers and healthcare professionals. Finally, with the deepening of economic and industrial development, there has been an ever-growing demand for the services of experts in the fields of law, finance, accounting, technology and information systems. In this sense, professions can be seen as both a product of the modern era and a central contributor to its evolution and expansion.

Professionals, managers and higher-level administrators gain their position largely from their possession of credentials – degrees, diplomas and other qualifications. As a whole, they enjoy relatively secure and remunerative careers, and their separation from people in more routine non-manual jobs has probably grown more pronounced in recent years. Some authors have seen professionals and other higher white-collar groups as forming a specific class – the 'professional/managerial class' (Ehrenreich and Ehrenreich 1979). The degree of division between them and white-collar workers, however, does not seem either deep or clear-cut enough to make such a position defensible.

Other authors have examined the ways in which white-collar professionals join together to maximize their own interests and to secure high levels of material reward and prestige. The case of the medical profession illustrates this point clearly (Parry and Parry 1976). Some groups within the medical profession, such as doctors, have successfully organized themselves to protect their standing in society and to ensure a high level of material reward. Three main dimensions of *professionalism* have enabled this to happen: entry into the profession is restricted to those who meet a strict set of defined criteria (qualifications); a professional association monitors and disciplines the conduct and performance of its members; and it is generally accepted that only members of the profession are qualified to practise medicine. Through such channels, self-governing professional associations are able to exclude unwanted individuals from the profession and to enhance the market position of their own members.

The changing working class

Marx forecast that the working class – people working in manufacturing as blue-collar labour – would become progressively larger and larger. That was the basis for his view that the working class would create the momentum for a revolutionary transformation of society. In fact, the working class has become smaller and smaller. Only about a quarter of a century ago, some 40 per cent of the working population was in blue-collar work. Now, in the developed countries, this figure stands at only about 18 per cent, and the proportion is still falling. Moreover, the conditions under which working-class people are living, and the styles of life they are following, are changing.

The industrialized countries have significant numbers of poor people. However, the majority of individuals working in blue-collar occupations no longer live in poverty. As was mentioned earlier, the income of manual workers has increased considerably since the turn of the century. This rising standard of living is expressed in the increased availability of consumer goods to all classes. About half of blue-collar workers now own their own homes. Cars, washing machines, televisions and telephones are owned by a very high proportion of households.

 We examine this issue more closely in chapter 12, 'Poverty, Social Exclusion and Welfare.

The phenomenon of working-class affluence suggests yet another possible route towards a more 'middle-class society'.

Perhaps as blue-collar workers grow more prosperous, they become middle class. This idea came to be known as the **embourgeoisement thesis** – simply, the process through which more people become 'bourgeois' or middle class. In the 1950s, when the thesis was first advanced, its supporters argued that many blue-collar workers earning middle-class wages would adopt middle-class values, outlooks and lifestyles as well. There was a seemingly strong argument that progress within industrial society was having a powerful effect on the shape of social stratification.

In the 1960s, John Goldthorpe and his colleagues in the UK carried out what came to be a very well-known study in order to test the embourgeoisement hypothesis. In undertaking the study, they argued that if the thesis was correct, affluent blue-collar employees should be virtually indistinguishable from white-collar employees in terms of their attitudes to work, lifestyle and politics. Based on interviews with workers in the car and chemical industries in Luton, the research was published in three volumes. It is often referred to as the *Affluent Worker* study (Goldthorpe 1968–9). A total of 229 manual workers were studied, together with 54 white-collar workers for purposes of comparison. Many of the blue-collar workers had migrated to the area in search of well-paid jobs; compared to most other manual workers, they were in fact highly paid and earned more than most lower-level white-collar workers.

Goldthorpe and his colleagues focused on three dimensions of working-class attitudes and found very little support for the embourgeoisement thesis. In terms of economic outlooks and attitudes to work, the authors agreed that many workers had acquired a middle-class standard of living on the basis of their income and ownership of consumer goods. Yet this relative affluence was attained through positions characterized by poor benefits, low chances for promotion and little intrinsic job satisfaction. The authors of the study found that affluent workers had an instrumental orientation to their work: they saw it as a means to an end: the end of gaining good wages. Their work was mostly repetitive and uninteresting, and they had little direct commitment to it.

Despite levels of affluence comparable to those of white-collar employees, the workers in the study did not associate with white-collar workers in their leisure time, and did not aspire to rise up the class ladder. Goldthorpe and his colleagues found that most socializing was done at home with immediate family members or kin, or with other working-class neighbours. There was little indication that the workers were moving towards middle-class norms and values. In terms of political outlooks, the authors found that there was a negative correlation between working-class affluence and support for the Conservative Party. Supporters of the embourgeoisement thesis had predicted that growing affluence among the working class would weaken traditional support for the Labour Party.

The results of the study, in the eyes of its authors, were clear-cut: the embourgeoisement thesis was false. These workers were not in the process of becoming more middle class. However, Goldthorpe and his colleagues did concede the possibility of some convergence between the lower-middle class and upper-working class on certain points. Affluent workers shared with their white-collar counterparts similar patterns of economic consumption, a privatized home-centred outlook and support for instrumental collectivism (collective action through unions to improve wages and conditions) at the workplace.

No strictly comparable research has been carried out in the intervening years, and it is not clear how far, if the conclusions reached by Goldthorpe et al. were valid at the time, they remain true now. It is generally agreed that the old, traditional working-class communities have tended to become fragmented, or have broken down altogether, with the decline of manufacturing industry and the impact of consumerism. Just how far such fragmentation has proceeded, however, remains open to dispute.

> **THINKING CRITICALLY**
>
> Look again at the section on the upper class. Does the existence of a very small upper class support Marx's theory of class or Weber's? Explain your answer fully. Explain how it is theoretically possible for the working class to become generally more affluent, when at the same time, social inequality is increasing.

Is there an underclass?

The term 'underclass' is often used to describe the segment of the population located at the very bottom of the class structure. Members of the underclass have living standards that are significantly lower than the majority of people in society. It is a group characterized by multiple disadvantages. Many are among the long-term unemployed, or drift in and out of jobs. Some are homeless, or have no permanent place in which to live. Members of the underclass may spend long periods of time dependent on state welfare benefits. The underclass is frequently described as 'marginalized' or 'excluded' from the way of life that is maintained by the bulk of the population.

The underclass is often associated with underprivileged ethnic minority groups. Much of the debate about the underclass originated in the United States, where the preponderance of poor blacks living in inner-city areas prompted talk of a 'black underclass' (Wilson 1978; Murray 1984, 1990; Lister 1996). This is not simply an American phenomenon, however. In Britain, blacks and Asians are disproportionately represented in the underclass. In some European countries, migrant workers who found jobs in times of greater prosperity 20 or so years ago now make up a large part of this sector. This is true, for instance, of Algerians in France and Turkish immigrants in Germany.

The term 'underclass' is a contested one at the centre of a furious sociological debate. Although the term has now entered everyday speech, many scholars and commentators are wary of using it at all. It is a concept that encompasses a broad spectrum of meanings, some of which are seen as politically charged and negative in connotation. Many researchers in Europe prefer the notion of '**social exclusion**', which is a broader concept than that of underclass, and has the advantage that it emphasizes social processes – mechanisms of exclusion – rather than simply individual positions, though, again, not all agree. Some discussions of social exclusion have tended to underplay the central sociological significance of structural social inequalities and thus risk 'blaming the victims' by focusing on the 'acceptable' and 'unacceptable' behaviour of the unemployed, economic migrants and other socially excluded groups (MacGregor 2003).

> Social exclusion is discussed in detail in chapter 12, 'Poverty, Social Exclusion and Welfare'.

The concept of an underclass has a long history. Marx wrote of a 'lumpenproletariat' composed of individuals located persistently outside the dominant forms of economic production and exchange. In later years, the notion was applied to the 'dangerous classes' of paupers, thieves and vagabonds who refused to work and instead survived on the margins of society as 'social parasites'. In more recent years, the idea of an underclass that is dependent on welfare benefits and bereft of initiative has been similarly influential.

Background to the underclass debate

Recent debates over the underclass have been prompted by several important works published by American sociologists about the position of poor blacks living in inner-city areas. In *The Declining Significance of Race* (1978), drawing on research in Chicago, William Julius Wilson argued that a substantial black middle class – white-collar workers and professionals – had emerged over the previous three or four decades in the United States. Not all African-Americans still live in city ghettos, and those who remain are kept there, Wilson maintained, not so much by active discrimination as by economic factors – in other words, by class rather than by race. The old racist barriers are disappearing; blacks are stuck in the ghetto as a result of economic disadvantages.

Charles Murray agreed about the existence of a black underclass in most big cities. According to him (1984), however, African-Americans find themselves at the bottom of society as a result of the very welfare policies designed to help improve their position. This is a reiteration of the 'culture of poverty' thesis, according to which, it is argued, people become dependent on welfare handouts and then have little incentive to find jobs, build solid communities or make stable marriages.

In response to Murray's claims, in the 1990s Wilson repeated and extended his previous arguments, again using research carried out in Chicago. The movement of many whites from the cities to the suburbs, the decline of urban industries and other urban economic problems, he suggested, led to high rates of joblessness among African-American men. Wilson explained the forms of social disintegration to which Murray pointed, including the high proportion of unmarried black mothers, in terms of the shrinking of the available pool of 'marriageable' (employed) men. In more recent work, Wilson examined the role of such social processes in creating spatially concentrated pockets of urban deprivation populated by a so-called 'ghetto poor'. Members of the ghetto poor – predominantly African-American and Hispanic – experience multiple deprivations, from low educational qualifications and standards of health to high levels of criminal victimization. They

Does the American theory of an underclass make sense in the context of European societies? Consider these Muslims outside a mosque in Whitechapel in East London: is it race, class or something else that keeps them living there?

are also disadvantaged by a weak urban infrastructure – including inadequate public transportation, community facilities and educational institutions – which further reduces their chances of integrating into society socially, politically and economically (Wilson 1999).

This focus on spatial aspects of the underclass debate have been mirrored in the UK with Lydia Morris's (1993, 1995) research into the emergence of long-term unemployment in the wake of the decline of heavy industries in the North-East of England, which once were major sources of employment. Nevertheless, she concluded that, 'there is no direct evidence in my study of a distinctive culture of the "underclass"' (1993: 410). What she did find was that even the long-term unemployed (out of a job for more than a year) were actively seeking work and had not adopted an anti-work culture,

though they lacked the wider social contacts that many employed respondents had. This research again moves away from exploring individual motivations in isolation from the wider social processes that create the circumstances that shape employment opportunities (Crompton 2008). The study was restricted to a region that lacks significant ethnic minority populations however, and its findings cannot easily be generalized to other parts of the country.

Duncan Gallie also argues that there is little basis for the idea of an underclass with a distinct culture. In his analysis of data from the Social Change and Economic Life Initiative, Gallie (1994) argues that there is little difference between working-class individuals and the long-term unemployed in terms of their political outlooks or work histories. For example, he found that people who have been unemployed for long periods of time were more committed to the concept of work than those who were employed.

The underclass, the EU and migration

Much debate on the underclass in the United States centres around its ethnic dimension. Increasingly, this is now the case in Europe as well; the tendencies towards economic division and social exclusion now characteristic of America seem to be hardening both in Britain and other countries in Western Europe. The underclass is closely linked to questions of race, ethnicity and migration. In cities such as London, Manchester, Rotterdam, Frankfurt, Paris and Naples, there are neighbourhoods marked by severe economic deprivation. Hamburg is Europe's richest city, as measured by average personal income, and has the highest proportion of millionaires in Germany; it also has the highest proportion of people on welfare and unemployment – 40 per cent above the national average.

The majority of poor and unemployed people in West European countries are native to their countries, but there are also many first- and second-generation immigrants in poverty and trapped in deteriorating city

---

Global Society 11.1 **The creation of a 'Muslim underclass' in Germany?**

'Berlin integration plan attacked'

Demonstrators from the large Turkish community in Germany have protested in Berlin outside a summit on integration convened by Chancellor Angela Merkel.

Four Turkish groups are boycotting the meeting, saying a new immigration bill treats Turkish-origin people and other immigrants as 'second-class citizens'. The forum will examine ways to improve community relations, including teaching German in nursery schools.

About 15 million people with immigrant backgrounds are living in Germany. The BBC's Tristana Moore in Berlin says the situation of Germany's 3.2 million Muslims, most of whom are of Turkish origin, has generated some anxiety, with fears that a lack of job prospects and the language divide risk creating an embittered Muslim underclass. Ministers have long been concerned that ghettos are springing up in German cities, she reports.

New rules

Chancellor Merkel has invited members of the Muslim community and other immigrant groups to the conference. But several Turkish community groups want the government to change the controversial immigration bill. It stipulates that an immigrant who wants to bring a spouse to

Will tighter rules on immigration in some European countries help to create a new underclass?

Germany has to prove the partner can earn a living and has some knowledge of German.

The new rules do not apply to German nationals who have foreign partners.

The government has ruled out making any changes to the new bill, which has already been approved by both houses of parliament. The Turkish-German groups boycotting the forum have threatened to take the matter to the constitutional court.

Source: BBC News, 12 July 2007, bbc.co.uk/news

neighbourhoods. Sizeable populations of Turks in Germany, Algerians in France and Albanians in Italy, for example, have grown up in each of these countries. Migrants in search of a better standard of living are often relegated to casual jobs that offer low wages and few career prospects (for example, see the article in 'Global Society 11.1'). Furthermore, migrants' earnings are frequently sent home in order to support family members who have remained behind. The standard of living for recent immigrants can be precariously low.

In cases where family members attempt to join a migrant illegally so that the family can be reunited, the potential for exclusion and marginalization is particularly high. Ineligible for state welfare benefits, migrants lacking official status are unable to draw on support from the state in order to maintain a minimum standard of living. Such individuals are extremely vulnerable, trapped in highly constrained conditions with few channels of recourse in the event of crisis or misfortune.

> **THINKING CRITICALLY**
>
> What would be the consequences for the European Union if an underclass consisting of large numbers of immigrants develops within European societies? What are the main differences between the concept of an 'underclass' and that of 'social exclusion' (refer to chapter 12 if necessary)? Which concept best describes the situation of the poorest sections of society?

Evaluation

How can we make sense of these contrasting approaches to the underclass? Does sociological research support the idea of a distinct class of disadvantaged people who are united by similar life chances?

The idea of the underclass was introduced from the United States and continues to make the most sense there. In the USA, extremes of rich and poor are more marked than in Western Europe. Particularly where economic and social deprivation converge with racial divisions, groups of the underprivileged tend to find themselves locked out of the wider society. While the concept of the underclass in these circumstances appears useful, in the European countries its use is more questionable. There is not the same level of separation between those who live in conditions of marked deprivation and the rest of society.

However, even in the USA, recent studies have suggested that, although the urban poor comprise an immobile stratum, accounts of a 'defeated and disconnected underclass' are exaggerated. Thus, more recent studies of fast-food workers and homeless street traders have argued that the separations between the urban poor and the rest of society are not as great as scholars of the underclass think (Duneier 1999; Newman 2000).

Class and lifestyles

In analysing class location, sociologists have traditionally relied on conventional indicators of class location such as market position, relations to the means of production and occupation. Some recent authors, however, argue that we should evaluate individuals' class location not only, or even mainly, in terms of economics and employment, but also in relation to cultural factors such as lifestyle and consumption patterns. According to this approach, our current age is one in which 'symbols' and markers related to consumption are playing an ever greater role in daily life. Individual identities are structured to a greater extent around lifestyle choices – such as how to dress, what to eat, how to care for one's body and where to relax – and less around more traditional class indicators such as employment.

The French sociologist Pierre Bourdieu (1930–2002) supported the view that lifestyle choices are an important indicator of class. He argued that *economic capital* – which consists of material goods such as property, wealth and income – was important, but he argued that it only provided a partial understanding of class. Bourdieu's conception of social class is extremely broad (see Crompton 1993). He identifies four forms of 'capital' that characterize class position, of which economic capital is only one: the others are cultural, social and symbolic (Bourdieu 1986).

> See chapter 19, 'Education', for a discussion of Bourdieu's theoretical scheme.

Bourdieu argues that individuals increasingly distinguish themselves from others, not according to economic factors, but on the basis of *cultural capital* – which includes education, appreciation of the arts, consumption and leisure pursuits. People are aided in the process of accumulating cultural capital by the proliferation of 'need merchants' selling goods and services – either symbolic or actual – for consumption within the capitalist system. Advertisers, marketers, fashion designers, style consult ants, interior designers, personal trainers, therapists, web designers and many others are all involved in influencing cultural tastes and promoting lifestyle choices among an ever-widening community of consumers.

Also important in Bourdieu's analysis of class is *social capital* – one's networks of friends and contacts. Bourdieu defined social capital as the resources that individuals or groups gain 'by virtue of possessing a durable network of more or less institutionalized relationships of mutual acquaintance and recognition' (1992). The concept of social capital has become an important tool in contemporary sociology, and Bourdieu's discussion of the concept marked an important step in the current proliferation of the idea, though social capital forms only one aspect of Bourdieu's broader theoretical scheme.

Last, Bourdieu argues that *symbolic capital* – which includes possession of a good reputation – is a final important indication of social class. The idea of symbolic capital is similar to that of social status.

Each type of capital in Bourdieu's account is related and, to an extent, being in possession of one can help in the pursuit of the others. For example, a businessman who makes a large amount of money (economic capital) might not have particularly fine tastes in the arts, but can pay for his children to attend private schools where these pursuits are encouraged (and so his children gain cultural capital). The businessman's money might lead him to make new contacts with senior people in the business world, and his children will meet the children of other wealthy families, so he, and they, will gain social capital. Similarly someone with a large group of well-connected friends (social capital) might be quickly promoted to a senior position in her company, where she does well, and gains in economic and symbolic capital.

Other scholars have agreed with Bourdieu that class divisions can be linked to distinctive lifestyle and consumption patterns. Thus, speaking of groupings within the middle class, Savage et al. (1992) identify three sectors based on cultural tastes and 'assets'. Professionals in public service, who are high in cultural capital and low in economic capital, tend to pursue healthy, active lifestyles involving exercise, low alcohol consumption and participation in cultural and community activities. Managers and bureaucrats, by contrast, are typified by 'indistinctive' patterns of consumption, which involve average or low levels of exercise, little engagement with cultural activities, and a preference for traditional styles in home furnishings and fashion. The third grouping, the 'postmoderns', pursue a lifestyle that is lacking in any defining principle and may contain elements not traditionally enjoyed alongside each other. Thus, horse-riding and an interest in classical literature may be accompanied by a fascination with extreme sports like rock-climbing and a love of raves and Ecstasy.

More recently, Brigitte LeRoux and colleagues (2007) have argued that although the concept of social exclusion cannot usefully illuminate cultural divisions, since it is based on a pretty blunt distinction between a large mainstream population and a smaller one consisting of marginalized minorities, social class is still central to the organization of cultural tastes and practices. Nonetheless, it is the conception of class used which matters most in attempts to understand cultural practices as structuring forces within society. As LeRoux et al. argue in relation to the UK:

> Our findings suggest that class boundaries are being redrawn through the increasing interplay between economic and cultural capital. Those members of the 'service class' who do not typically possess graduate level credentials, especially those in lower managerial positions, are more similar to the intermediate classes than they are to the other sections of the professional middle class. Boundaries are also being re-drawn within the working class, where lower supervisory and technical occupations have been downgraded so that they have become similar to those in semi-routine and routine positions. (2007: 22)

In general terms, it would be difficult to dispute that stratification within classes, as well as between classes, has come to depend not only on occupational differences but also on differences in consumption and lifestyle. This is borne out by looking at trends in society as a whole. The rapid expansion of the service economy and the entertainment and leisure industry, for example, reflect an increasing emphasis on consumption within industrialized countries. Modern societies have become consumer societies, geared to the acquisition of material goods. In some respects a consumer society is a 'mass society', where class differences are to a degree overridden; thus people from different class backgrounds may all watch similar television programmes or shop for clothing in the same high street shops. Yet class differences

can also become intensified through variations in lifestyle and 'taste' (Bourdieu 1986).

While bearing these shifts in mind, however, it is impossible to ignore the critical role played by economic factors in the reproduction of social inequalities. For the most part, individuals experiencing extreme social and material deprivations are not doing so as part of a lifestyle choice. Rather, their circumstances are constrained by factors relating to the economic and occupational structure (Crompton 2008).

Gender and stratification

For many years, research on stratification was 'gender-blind' – it was written as though women did not exist, or as though, for purposes of analysing divisions of power, wealth and prestige, women were unimportant and uninteresting. Yet gender itself is one of the most profound examples of stratification. There are no societies in which men do not, in some aspects of social life, have more wealth, status and influence than women.

THINKING CRITICALLY

The study described in 'Using your sociological imagination 11.2' concludes that although the women involved saw class as marginally important to them, actually, it fundamentally shaped their lives. Given the obvious gap between the women's own understanding and that of the sociologist, is this a case of sociologists treating 'ordinary people' as 'cultural dopes' (Garfinkel 1963)? How could the sociologist in this study go about validating her research findings?

One of the main problems posed by the study of gender and stratification in modern societies sounds simple, but turns out to be difficult to resolve. This is the question of how far we can understand gender inequalities in modern times mainly in terms of class divisions. Inequalities of gender are

11.2 'Disidentifying' with the working class?

Bourdieu's work on class and status distinctions has been highly influential, and many sociologists have drawn on it in their own studies of social class. One notable example is the British sociologist Beverley Skeggs, who used Bourdieu's account of class and culture to examine the formation of class and gender in her study of women in the north-west of England.

Over a 12-year period, Skeggs (1997) followed the lives of 83 working-class women who had all enrolled, at one point, in a course for carers at a local further education college. Following Bourdieu's terminology, Skeggs found that the women she studied possessed low economic, cultural, social and symbolic capital. They were poorly paid, had limited success in formal education and few relationships that they could draw on with people in powerful positions; they also possessed low status in the eyes of higher social classes. Skeggs claims that the lack of various forms of capital amongst the group of women in her study reflects the wider lack of positive identities for working-class women in the UK. Working-class men, by contrast, do not have the same difficulty gaining a positive identity and Skeggs suggests that this has often been provided through participation in the trade union movement. For women, therefore, to be called 'working class', is to be labelled dirty, valueless and potentially dangerous.

It is this theoretical background, Skeggs argues, that explains why the women in her study were so reluctant to describe themselves as working class. They were well aware of cultural jibes aimed at working-class women about 'white stilettos', 'Sharons' and 'Traceys'. In interviews, Skeggs found that the women tended to 'disidentify' with a perception of themselves as working class. When discussing sexuality for example, the women were keen to avoid the accusation that they were 'tarty' and thus devaluing the limited capital that they did possess as young, marriageable women. It was important amongst the group that they were sexually desirable and that they could 'get a man' if they so wanted. Weddings and marriage offered the chance of respectability and responsibility. The choice to pursue a course in caring emphasized these concerns: training to be a carer taught the women good parenting and offered the possibility of respectable paid work over unemployment after qualification.

Although the group of women tried to disidentify with a view of themselves as working class, and often saw class as of marginal importance in their own lives, Skeggs argues that it is actually fundamental to the way that they lived, and their attempts to distance themselves from a working-class identity made it even more so. Skeggs's account of the lives of a group of women in the north-west of England shows how class is closely interlinked with other forms of identity – in this case, gender.

more deep-rooted historically than class systems; men have superior standing to women even in hunter-gatherer societies, where there are no classes. Yet class divisions are so marked in modern societies that there is no doubt that they 'overlap' substantially with gender inequalities. The material position of most women tends to reflect that of their fathers or husbands; hence, it can be argued that we have to explain gender inequalities mainly in class terms.

Determining women's class position

The view that class inequalities largely govern gender stratification was often an unstated assumption until quite recently. However, feminist critiques and the undeniable changes in women's economic role in many Western societies have broken this issue open for debate.

The 'conventional position' in class analysis was that the paid work of women is relatively insignificant compared to that of men, and that therefore women can be regarded as being in the same class as their husbands (Goldthorpe 1983). According to Goldthorpe, whose own class scheme was originally predicated on this argument, this is not a view based on an ideology of sexism. On the contrary, it recognizes the subordinate position in which most women find themselves in the labour force. Women are more likely to have part-time jobs than men, and tend to have more intermittent experience of paid employment because they may withdraw for lengthy periods to bear and care for children.

> See chapter 20, 'Work and Economic Life', for more about the differences between women and men's working patterns.

Since the majority of women have traditionally been in a position of economic dependence on their husbands, it follows that their class position is most often governed by the husband's class situation.

Goldthorpe's argument has been criticized in several ways. First, in a substantial proportion of households, the income of women is essential to maintaining the family's economic position and mode of life. In these circumstances women's paid employment in some part determines the class position of households. Second, a wife's occupation may sometimes set the standard of the position of the family as a whole. Even where a woman earns less than her husband, her working situation may still be the 'lead' factor in influencing the class of her husband. This could be the case, for instance, if the husband is an unskilled or semi-skilled blue-collar worker and the wife, say, the manager of a shop. Third, where 'cross-class' households exist – in which the work of the husband is in a different category from that of the wife – there may be some purposes for which it is more realistic to treat men and women, even within the same households, as being in different class positions. Fourth, the proportion of households in which women are the sole breadwinners is increasing. The growing numbers of lone mothers and childless working women are testament to this fact. Such women are by definition the determining influence on the class positions of their own households, except in cases where alimony payments put a woman on the same economic level as her ex-husband (Stanworth 1984; Walby 1986).

Goldthorpe and others have defended the conventional position, yet some important changes have also been incorporated into his scheme. For research purposes, the partner of the higher class can be used to classify a household, whether that person be a man or a woman. Rather than classification based on the 'male breadwinner', household classification is now determined by the 'dominant breadwinner'. Furthermore, class III in Goldthorpe's scheme has been divided into two subcategories to reflect the preponderance of women in low-level white-collar work (see page 445). When the scheme is applied to women, class IIIb (non-manual workers in sales and services) is treated as class VII. This is seen as a more accurate representation of the position of unskilled and semi-skilled women in the labour market.

Beyond the household?

Developing the debate over the assignment of class positions, some authors have suggested that the class position of an individual should be determined without reference to the household. Social class, in other words, would be assessed from occupation independently for each individual, without specific reference to that person's domestic circumstances. This approach was taken, for example, in the work of Gordon Marshall and his colleagues in a study of the class system of the UK (Marshall 1988).

Such a perspective, however, also has its difficulties. It leaves on one side those who are not in paid employment, including not only full-time housewives, but also retired people and the unemployed. The latter two groups can be categorized in terms of the last occupations they held, but this can be problematic if they have not worked for some while. Moreover, it seems potentially very misleading to ignore the household altogether. Whether individuals are single or in a domestic partnership can make a large difference in the opportunities open to them.

The impact of women's employment on class divisions

The entry of women into paid employment has had a significant impact on household incomes. But this impact has been experienced unevenly and may be leading to an accentuation of class divisions between households. A growing number of women are moving into professional and managerial positions and earning high salaries. This is contributing to a polarization between high-income 'dual-earner households', on the one hand, and 'single-earner' or 'no-earner' households on the other.

Research has shown that high-earning women tend to have high-earning partners, and that the wives of men in professional and managerial occupations have higher earnings than other employed female partners. Marriage tends to produce partnerships where both individuals are relatively privileged or disadvantaged in terms of occupational attainment (Bonney 1992).

The impact of such dual-earner partnerships is heightened by the fact that the average childbearing age is rising, particularly among professional women. The growing number of dual-earner childless couples is helping to fuel the widening gap between the highest and lowest paid households.

Social mobility

In studying stratification, we have to consider not only the differences between economic positions or occupations, but also what happens to the individuals who occupy them. The term **social mobility** refers to the movement of individuals and groups between different socio-economic positions. **Vertical mobility** means movement up or down the socio-economic scale.

Those who gain in property, income or status are said to be *upwardly mobile* – like Sir Gulam Noon whose life history was summarized at the start of this chapter – while those who move in the opposite direction are *downwardly mobile*. In modern societies there is also a great deal of lateral mobility, which refers to geographical movement between neighbourhoods, towns or regions. Vertical and lateral mobility are often combined. For instance, someone working in a company in one city might be promoted to a higher position in a branch of the firm located in another town, or even in a different country.

There are two ways of studying social mobility. First, we can look at individuals' own careers – how far they move up or down the social scale in the course of their working lives. This is usually called **intragenerational mobility**. Alternatively, we can analyse how far children enter the same type of occupation as their parents or grandparents. Mobility across the generations is called **intergenerational mobility**.

THINKING CRITICALLY

Many people's image of nineteenth-century industrial societies is one of pollution, grimy factories, poor working conditions and mass poverty. In contrast, post-industrial societies are dominated by office-based work, middle-class occupations and information technologies. Explain how it is possible for inequality to be *increasing* in the post-industrial societies, which appear to provide much better working conditions for a majority of their population.

Comparative mobility studies

The amount of vertical mobility in a society is a major index of the degree of its 'openness', indicating how far talented individuals born into lower strata can move up the socio-economic ladder. In this respect,

A high level of social mobility in Britain during the twentieth century means that today's generation can afford luxuries that their grandparents would not have been able to.

social mobility is an important political issue, particularly in states committed to the liberal vision of equality of opportunity for all citizens. How 'open' are the industrialized countries in terms of social mobility?

Studies of social mobility have been carried on over a period of more than 50 years and frequently involve international comparisons. An important early study was conducted by Peter Blau and Otis Dudley Duncan (1967) in America. Their investigation remains the most detailed investigation of social mobility yet carried out in any single country, though like most other studies of mobility, all the subjects were men, which reinforces the point made earlier about the lack of gender balance in this field. Blau and Duncan collected information on a national sample of 20,000 males. They concluded that there was

much vertical mobility in the United States, but that nearly all of this was between occupational positions quite close to one another. 'Long-range' mobility was found to be rare. Although downward movement did occur, both within the careers of individuals and intergenerationally, it was much less common than upward mobility. The reason for this is that white-collar and professional jobs have grown much more rapidly than blue-collar ones, a shift that created openings for sons of blue-collar workers to move into white-collar positions. Blau and Duncan emphasized the importance of education and training on an individual's chances for success. In their view, upward social mobility is generally characteristic of industrial societies as a whole and contributes to social stability and integration.

Perhaps the most celebrated interna-

Global Society 11.2 | Is inequality declining in class-based societies?

There is some evidence that, at least until recently, the class systems in mature capitalist societies became increasingly open to movement between classes, thereby reducing the level of inequality. In 1955, the Nobel Prize-winning economist Simon Kuznets proposed a hypothesis that has since been called the Kuznets Curve: a formula showing that inequality increases during the early stages of capitalist development, then declines, and eventually stabilizes at a relatively low level (Kuznets 1955; see figure 11.1).

Studies of European countries, the United States and Canada suggested that inequality peaked in these places before the Second World War, declined through the 1950s and remained roughly the same through the 1970s (Berger 1986; Nielsen 1994). Lowered post-war inequality was due in part to economic expansion in industrial societies, which created opportunities for people at the bottom to move up, and also to government health insurance, welfare and other programmes which aimed at reducing inequality. However, Kuznets's prediction may well turn out to apply only to industrial societies. The emergence of

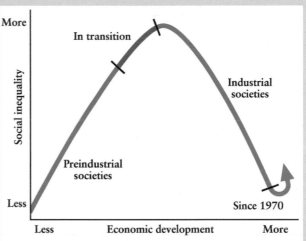

Figure 11.1   The Kuznets Curve

Source: Nielson 1994

post-industrial society has brought with it an increase in inequality in many developed nations since the 1970s (see chapter 12), which calls into question Kuznets's theory.

---

tional study of social mobility was that carried out by Seymour Martin Lipset and Reinhard Bendix (1959). They analysed data from nine industrialized societies – Britain, France, West Germany, Sweden, Switzerland, Japan, Denmark, Italy and the United States, concentrating on mobility of men from blue-collar to white-collar work. Contrary to their expectations, they discovered no evidence that the United States was more open than the European societies. Total vertical mobility across the blue-collar/white-collar line was 30 per cent in the United States, with the other societies varying between 27 and 31 per cent. Lipset and Bendix concluded that all the industrialized countries were experiencing similar changes in respect of the expansion of white-collar jobs. This led to an 'upward surge of mobility' of comparable dimen-

sions in all of them. Others have questioned their findings, arguing that significant differences between countries are found if more attention is given to downward mobility, and if long-range mobility is also brought into consideration (Heath 1981; Grusky and Hauser 1984).

Most studies of social mobility, such as the ones described here, have focused upon 'objective' dimensions of mobility – that is to say, how much mobility exists, in which directions and for what parts of the population. Gordon Marshall and David Firth (1999) took a different approach in their comparative study of social mobility, investigating people's 'subjective' feelings about changing class positions. The authors designed their research in response to what they term 'unsubstantiated speculation' among sociologists about the likely effects of social mobility on individuals' sense of well-being. While some have argued that social mobility produces a sense of disequilibrium and isolation, others have taken a more optimistic view, suggesting that a gradual process of adaptation to a new class inevitably takes place.

Using survey data from ten countries – Bulgaria, the Czech Republic, Slovakia, Estonia, Germany, Poland, Russia, Slovenia, the USA and the UK – Marshall and Firth examined whether class mobility was linked to a heightened sense of satisfaction or dissatisfaction with aspects of everyday life such as family, community, work, income and politics. On the whole, they found little evidence of an association between respondents' class experiences and their overall life satisfaction. This was as true for individuals who had moved from working-class origins to middle-class positions as it was for those who had been downwardly mobile.

Downward mobility

Although downward mobility is less common than upward mobility, it is still a widespread phenomenon. Downward intragenerational mobility is also common. Mobility of this type is quite often associated with psychological problems and anxieties, where individuals become unable to sustain the lifestyles to which they have become accustomed. Redundancy is another of the main sources of downward mobility. Middle-aged people who lose their jobs, for example, either find it hard to gain new employment at all, or can only obtain work at a lower level of income than before.

Thus far, there have been very few studies of downward mobility in the UK. It is probable, however, that downward mobility, in inter- and intragenerational terms, is on the increase in Britain as it is in the United States. In the USA there have been several studies of the phenomenon. Over the 1980s and early 1990s, for the first time since the Second World War, there was a general downturn in the average real earnings

(earnings after adjusting for inflation) of people in middle-level white-collar jobs in the USA. Thus, even if such jobs continue to expand relative to others, they may not support the lifestyle aspirations they once did.

Corporate restructuring and 'downsizing' are the main reasons why these changes are happening. In the face of increasing global competition, many companies have trimmed their workforces. White-collar as well as full-time blue-collar jobs have been lost, to be replaced by poorly paid, part-time occupations. Studies have shown that in the USA downward mobility is particularly common among divorced or separated women with children. Women who enjoyed a moderately comfortable middle-class way of life when they were married often find themselves living 'hand-to-mouth' after a divorce. In many cases, alimony payments are meagre or non-existent; women attempting to juggle work, childcare and domestic responsibilities find it difficult to make ends meet (Schwarz and Volgy 1992).

Social mobility in Britain

Overall levels of mobility have been extensively studied in Britain over the post-war period and there is a wealth of empirical evidence and research studies on the British case. For this reason, we will look at the UK evidence in this section, though, again, until very recently virtually all this research has concentrated on the experience of men.

One important early study was directed by David Glass (1954). Glass's work analysed intergenerational mobility for a longish period up to the 1950s. His findings correspond to those noted above in respect of international data (around 30 per cent mobility from blue-collar to white-collar jobs). Glass's research was in fact widely drawn on by those making international comparisons. On the whole, he concluded that Britain was not a particularly 'open' society. While a good deal of mobility occurred, most of this was short range. Upward mobility was much more common than downward mobility, and was mostly concentrated at the middle levels of the class structure. People right at the bottom tended to stay there; almost 50 per cent of sons of workers in professional and managerial jobs were themselves in similar occupations. Glass also found a high degree of 'self-recruitment' of this sort into elite positions within society.

Another important piece of research, known as the Oxford Mobility Study, was carried out by John Goldthorpe and his colleagues, based on the findings from a 1972 survey (Goldthorpe et al. 1980). They sought to investigate how far patterns of social mobility had altered since the time of Glass's work, and concluded that the overall level of mobility of men was in fact higher than in the previous period, with rather more long-range movement being noted. The main reason for this, however, was once again not that the occupational system had become more egalitarian. Rather, the origin of the changes was the continued acceleration in the growth of higher white-collar jobs relative to blue-collar ones. The researchers found that two-thirds of the sons of unskilled or semi-skilled manual workers were themselves in manual occupations. About 30 per cent of professionals and managers were of working-class origins, while some 4 per cent of men in blue-collar work were from professional or managerial backgrounds.

Despite finding evidence of higher rates of absolute social mobility, the Oxford Mobility Study concluded that the relative chances for mobility among different segments of the population in Britain remained highly unequal, and that inequalities of opportunity remained squarely grounded within the class structure.

The original Oxford Mobility Study was updated on the basis of new material collected about ten years later (Goldthorpe and Payne 1986). The major findings of the earlier work were corroborated, but some

further developments were found. The chances of men from blue-collar backgrounds getting professional or managerial jobs, for example, had increased. Once again, this was traced to changes in the occupational structure, producing a reduction of blue-collar occupations relative to higher white-collar jobs.

Marshall et al. produced results in the 1980s which largely corroborated the findings of Goldthorpe and others. In the Essex Mobility Study, the authors found that about a third of people in higher white-collar or professional jobs were from blue-collar backgrounds. Findings such as these demonstrate a substantial amount of fluidity in British society: for many people, it is indeed possible to move up the social hierarchy, in terms of both intragenerational and intergenerational mobility. Yet the scales are still biased against women whose mobility chances are hampered by their over-representation in routine non-manual jobs. The fluid character of modern society derives mostly from its propensity to upgrade occupations. Marshall (1988: 138) and his co-workers concluded: 'More "room at the top" has not been accompanied by great equality in the opportunities to get there.' However, one should bear in mind a point made earlier: mobility is a long-term process, and if the society is becoming more 'open', the full effects will not be seen for a generation.

However, a study by Jo Blanden et al. (2002) at the London School of Economics found a reversal of this process. They compared intergenerational mobility in Britain between two groups, the first all born in March 1958 and the second in April 1970. Even though these groups are only 12 years different in age, the study documented a sharp fall in intergenerational mobility of economic status between them. It was found that the economic status of the group born in 1970 was much more strongly connected to the economic status of their parents than the group born in 1958. The authors suggested that one of the reasons for the fall in intergenerational mobility from the earlier to the later groups was that the rise in education attainment from the late 1970s onwards benefited children of the wealthy more than children of the less well-off.

In a more recent article, Jackson and Goldthorpe (2007) studied intergenerational social class mobility in the UK by comparing previous and more recent datasets. They found no evidence that intergenerational mobility was falling in an absolute sense, with relative social mobility rates for both men and women remaining fairly constant, but with some indication of a decline in long-range mobility. However, they found a generally less favourable balance between downward and upward mobility emerging for men, which is the product of structural class change. They conclude that there can be no return to the rising rates of upward mobility experienced in the mid-twentieth century.

 See chapter 19, 'Education', for a more detailed discussion of higher education.

An important cohort study funded by the UK's Economic and Social Research Council (ESRC) published as, *Twenty-Something in the 1990s* (Bynner et al. 1997) traced the lives of 9,000 Britons born during the same week in 1970. In 1996, at the age of 26, it was found that for both men and women, family background and class of origin remained powerful influences. The study concluded that the young people who coped best with the transition to adulthood were those who had obtained a better education, postponed children and marriage, and had fathers in professional occupations. Individuals who had come from disadvantaged backgrounds had a greater tendency to remain there.

The study found that, on the whole, women today are experiencing much greater opportunity than their counterparts in the previous generation. Middle-class women have benefited the most from the shifts mentioned above: they were just as likely as their male peers to go to university and to move into well-paid jobs on graduation. This trend towards greater equality was also reflected in women's heightened confidence and sense of self-esteem, compared with a similar cohort of women born just twelve years earlier. As table 11.3 shows, women are now moving into some of the high-status positions in British society, as they are in many other developed countries, though not in particularly large numbers. One way of expressing this change is to suggest that the 'glass ceiling' for women has certainly been cracked, but as yet it has not been completely broken.

Women's chances of entering a good career are improving, but two major obstacles remain. Male managers and employers still discriminate against women applicants. They do so at least partly because of their belief that 'women are not really interested in careers' and they are likely to leave the workforce when they begin a family.

THINKING CRITICALLY

Is social mobility really important in modern societies? If intergenerational social mobility *has* fallen, does it matter? What social consequences are likely to follow from falling levels of social mobility? What can governments do to promote upward social mobility?

Gender and social mobility

Although so much research into social mobility has focused on men, in recent years more attention has begun to be paid to patterns of mobility among women. At a time when girls are 'outperforming' boys in school and females are outnumbering males in higher education, it is tempting to conclude that long-standing gender inequalities in society may be relaxing their hold. Has the occupational structure become more 'open' to women, or are their mobility chances still guided largely by family and social background?

Table 11.3 Percentage of women in Britain's top jobs, 2006

Occupation/role	Female (%)	Occupation / role	Female (%)
MP (House of Commons)	20	High Court judge	7
MSP (Holyrood, Scottish Parliament)	37	FTSE 100 company chief executive officer	1
MEP (Strasbourg, European Parliament)	24	FTSE 100 company director	7
MWA (Cardiff, Welsh Assembly)	50	University professor	14
Local Authority councillor	30	Church of England bishop	0

Source: UK *Economic and Social Research Council Factsheet on social mobility,* accessed 11 January 2008: www.esrcsocietytoday.ac.uk/ESRCInfoCentre/facts/index24.aspx

Having children does indeed still have a very substantial effect on the career chances of women. This is less because they are uninterested in a career than because they are often effectively forced to choose between advancement at work and having children. Men are rarely willing to share full responsibility for domestic work and child-care. Although many more women than before are organizing their domestic lives in order to pursue a career, there are still major barriers in their way.

A meritocratic Britain?

Peter Saunders (1990, 1996) has been one of the most vocal critics of the British tradition of social mobility research encompassing studies such as those done by Glass and Goldthorpe. According to Saunders, Britain is a true meritocracy because rewards go naturally to those who are best able to 'perform' and achieve. In his view, ability and effort are the key factors in occupational success, not class background. Saunders uses empirical data from the National Child Development Study to show that children who are bright and hard-working will succeed regardless of the social advantages or disadvantages they may experience. In his estimation, Britain may be an unequal society, but it is a fair one. Such a conclusion may well be a widely held assumption amongst the populations of industrialized nations.

In response to such claims, Richard Breen and John Goldthorpe (1999) criticize Saunders on both theoretical and method-ological grounds. They accuse Saunders of introducing biases into his analysis of the survey data, such as excluding respondents who were unemployed. Breen and Goldthorpe provide an alternative analysis of the same data used by Saunders and produce radically different findings, which substanti-ate their own argument that class barriers are important to social mobility. They conclude that individual merit is certainly a contribut-ing factor in determining individuals' class positions, but that 'class of origin' remains a powerful influence. According to Breen and Goldthorpe, children from disadvantaged backgrounds must show more merit than those who are advantaged to acquire similar class positions.

A more recent international, compara-tive study of inequality and social mobility by Dan Andrews and Andrew Leigh (2007) also takes issue with Saunders's claims about 'fairness'. Their empirical survey used occupational data on men aged 25–54 in 16 countries around the world (exclud-ing the UK), concentrating on the compar-ative earnings of fathers and their sons. Their main conclusion was: 'Sons who grew up in more unequal countries in the 1970s were less likely to have experienced social mobility by 1999.' In unequal soci-eties around the world, there is less social mobility and the movement from 'rags to riches' becomes much more difficult for those social groups who start from the lower positions. Thus, inequality seems to impede 'fair' outcomes (based on ability and effort) and in order to produce a genuine meritocracy, it will also be necessary to reduce inequalities.

Conclusion: the continuing significance of social class

Although the traditional hold of class is most certainly weakening in some ways, particularly in terms of people's identities, class divisions remain at the heart of core economic inequalities in modern societies. Social class continues to exert a great influence on our lives, and class membership is correlated with a variety of inequalities from life expectancy and overall physical health to access to education and well-paid jobs.

Inequalities between the poor and the more affluent have expanded in Britain over the past three decades. Is growing class inequality a price that has to be paid to secure economic development? Since the 1980s, the pursuit of wealth has been seen as generating economic development because it is a motivating force encouraging innovation and drive. But today many argue that globalization and the deregulation of economic markets are leading to a widening of the gap between rich and poor and a 'hardening' of class inequalities.

Yet it is important to remember that our activities are never completely determined by class divisions: many people do experience social mobility. The entrepreneur Gulam Noon, whose life story we began this chapter with, provides a particularly vivid example of social mobility. The expansion of higher education, the growing accessibility of professional qualifications and the emergence of the Internet and the 'new economy' are all also presenting important new channels for upward mobility. Such developments are further eroding old class and stratification patterns and are contributing to a more fluid social order.

Summary points

1. Social stratification refers to the division of society into layers or strata. When we talk of social stratification, we draw attention to the unequal positions occupied by individuals in society. Analyses of stratification have traditionally been written from a male point of view. This is partly because of the assumption that gender inequalities reflect class differences; this assumption is highly questionable. Gender influences stratification in modern societies to some degree independently of class.

2. Four major types of stratification system can be identified: slavery, caste, estates and class. Whereas the first three depend on legal or religiously sanctioned inequalities, class divisions are not 'officially' recognized, but stem from economic factors affecting the material circumstances of people's lives.

3. The most prominent and influential theories of stratification are those developed by Marx and Weber. Marx placed primary emphasis on class, which he saw as an objectively given characteristic of the economic structure of society. He saw a fundamental split between the owners of capital and the workers who do not own capital. Weber accepted a similar view, but distinguished two other aspects of stratification – status and party. Status refers to the esteem or 'social honour' given to individuals or groups; party refers to the active mobilizing of groups to secure definite ends.

4. Occupation is frequently used as an indicator of social class. Individuals in the same occupation tend to experience similar life chances. Sociologists have traditionally used occupational class schemes to map the class structure of society. Class schemes are valuable for tracing broad class-based

inequalities and patterns, but are limited in other ways. For example, they are difficult to apply to the economically inactive and do not reflect the importance of property-ownership and wealth.

5. Most people in the developed societies are more affluent today than was the case several generations ago, yet wealth remains highly concentrated in a relatively small number of hands. The upper class consists of a small minority of people who have both wealth and power, and the chance of passing on their privileges to the next generation, though the rich are a diverse and changing group with a large number of 'self-made' millionaires.

6. The middle class is composed broadly of those working in white-collar occupations, such as teachers, medical professionals and employees in the service industries. In most industrialized countries, the middle class now encompasses the majority of the population, as professional, managerial and administrative occupations have grown. Members of the middle class generally possess educational credentials or technical qualifications which allow them to sell their mental as well as their physical labour in order to earn a living.

7. The working class is composed of those in blue-collar or manual occupations. The working class shrunk significantly during the twentieth century, with the decline in manufacturing industry, though members of the working class are more affluent than they were 100 years ago.

8. The underclass is said to be a segment of the population that lives in severely disadvantaged conditions at the margins of society. The idea of the underclass was first developed in the United States, and though the notion of the underclass has been applied elsewhere, the concept is perhaps more useful in the US context. Even in the USA, it is a highly controversial concept.

9. Some authors have argued that cultural factors, such as lifestyle and consumption patterns, are important influences on class position, with individual identities now more structured around lifestyle choices than they are around traditional class indicators such as occupation.

10. In the study of social mobility, a distinction is made between intragenerational and intergenerational mobility. The former refers to movement up or down the social scale within an individual's working life. The latter concerns movement across the generations. Social mobility is mostly of limited range. Most people remain close to the level of the families from which they came, although the expansion of white-collar jobs has provided the opportunity for considerable short-range upward mobility. As more women have entered paid employment the glass ceiling has been cracked and women have moved into high status positions, though not in equal numbers to men.

Further reading

A good place to take your studies further is with Wendy Bottero's *Stratification: Social Division and Inequality* (London: Routledge, 2004), which explores social stratification through examples of personal choices and lifestyles. Then, Rosemary Crompton's *Class and Stratification: An Introduction to Current Debates*, 3rd edn (Cambridge: Polity, 2008) is an excellent book written by an expert in the field, which does exactly what it says in the title.

Moving beyond introductions to current debates, Mike Savage's *Class Analysis and Social Transformation* (Buckingham: Open University Press, 2000) brings class debates into contact with recent theories of individualization (in the work of Beck and Giddens), providing a fresh interpretation of the evidence. Similarly innovative is Fiona Devine, Mike Savage, John Scott and Rosemary Crompton's *Rethinking Class: Cultures, Identities and Lifestyles* (Basingstoke: Palgrave Macmillan, 2004), which is an edited collection of chapters focusing on the connections between class analysis and culture.

Christine Zmroczek and Pat Mahony's *Women and Social Class: International Feminist Perspectives* (London: UCL Press, 1999) is a very good edited collection covering the experience of women and class across the world. Finally, Gordon Marshall's *Repositioning Class: Social Inequality in Industrial Societies* (London: Sage Publications, 1997) uses evidence from a range of countries to evaluate theories of the 'death of class'.

Internet links

Social Inequality and Classes – many useful links from Sociosite at the University of Amsterdam:
www.sociosite.net/topics/inequality.php#CLASS

Explorations in Social Inequality – lots of resources, mainly American, based at Trinity University, San Antonio, USA:
www.trinity.edu/mkearl/strat.html

Marxists Internet Archive – exactly what it says; all things Marx and Marxism:
www.marxists.org/

The Progress on Nations 2000 Unicef Report – material on global inequalities:
www.unicef.org/pon00/

ESRC Society Today – Factsheets on inequality and social mobility in the UK:
ww.esrcsocietytoday.ac.uk/ESRCInfoCentre/facts/index24.aspx

12
....
Poverty, Social Exclusion and Welfare

CHAPTER 12

· ·

Poverty, Social Exclusion and Welfare

Lisa is a woman of 24 who works at a telephone call centre, providing information and customer service to people who want to make travel arrangements over the telephone. She works long hours, often late into the evening. The people who work alongside her at the call centre are all women. They sit in a large room in long rows, separated from one another by grey partitions. The women speak into telephone headsets while entering and retrieving information from the computer terminals in front of them.

Like many of her co-workers, Lisa is a lone mother. She supports her two small children on her low wages. Most months she receives a small amount from her ex-husband, but it never seems to be enough to cover everything the children need and sometimes he misses payments. Lisa rarely manages to save money. Three mornings a week she takes on extra work as a cleaner at an office building near her flat. The money she is able to earn from this additional work allows her to pay most of her bills on time, to buy clothes for her children, repay a loan she took out to furnish her flat, and to cover the cost of childcare. Despite working extra hours, Lisa struggles each month to make ends meet. Her prime goal is to save up enough to move herself and her children to a safer, more desirable area.

On the evenings when Lisa works late at the call centre, she rushes from work to fetch her two children from her mother, who cares for them after the nursery closes each afternoon. Lisa is often late because the bus she takes to and from work does not arrive on time. If she is lucky, the children fall back to sleep as soon as she takes them home, but on many nights it is a struggle to get them to bed. By the time the children are asleep, Lisa is too exhausted to do anything but switch on the television. She has little time to shop for food or to cook proper meals, so she and the children eat a lot of frozen foods. She does most of her shopping at the nearest cheap supermarket, but the store is still a bus journey and a difficult walk away with heavy bags, and she is normally exhausted by the time she returns home. She knows that her children would all benefit from a more balanced diet, but there are no shops close by and, in any case, she cannot afford to buy many fresh products.

Lisa worries about spending too much time away from her children, but she does not see any way around her dilemma. After she and her husband divorced, she spent the first 18 months at home with the children, living solely on benefits provided by the government. Although she is struggling to cope with her present situation, she does not want to become dependent on welfare. She hopes that after some years of experience at the call centre, she might be able to rise into a more responsible and better-paid position.

Lisa is British and, as in most industrialized countries, the UK has an established welfare state, which tries to ensure that everyone has enough money to pay for their basic needs, and that no one is forced to live in conditions of absolute poverty. However, as we will see in this chapter, welfare states differ, both in the types of benefits they provide for their citizens and in their underlying philosophies – that is, in what they are trying to achieve. Some look to provide a basic 'safety-net', others aim for a wide range of services that are available 'from the cradle to the grave' and still others (such as the USA) have a minimal welfare state which links benefits to people's commitment to work. This is reflected in state welfare expenditure, which is, for example, relatively high in Denmark, Sweden and France and relatively low in South Korea, the USA and Japan. In the UK, government provides extra money to Lisa and other people in a similar position, to help with costs like housing and childcare, and to supplement their incomes. Many national welfare states today continue to be concerned with the alleviation of poverty, though their methods for doing this are not the same. Similarly, welfare provision in some countries is much more comprehensive than in others. But why do people living in some of the richest societies in the world still live in poverty in the twenty-first century?

Many people who encounter someone like Lisa might make certain assumptions about her life. They might conclude that her poverty and low position in society are a result of her natural abilities or a consequence of her own personal upbringing. Others might blame Lisa for not working hard enough to overcome her difficult situation. How does sociology help us to judge which of these views is most accurate? It is the job of sociology to analyse our assumptions and to develop a broader view of our society that can make sense of the experiences of people like Lisa.

In 1994, Carol Walker analysed research into how people living on income support – a

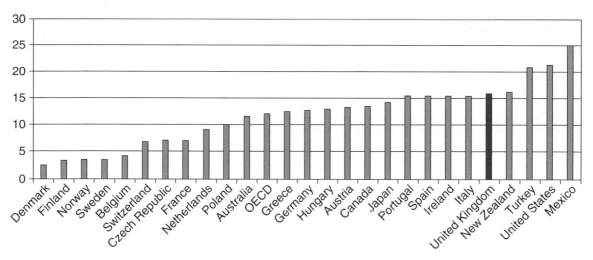

Figure 12.1 Percentage of children living in poverty, OECD countries, 2000

Source: Whiteford and Adema 2007

means-tested benefit for certain groups of people who cannot work full time and do not have enough money to live on – manage to organize their lives. She found a picture very different from that painted by those who argue that living on welfare is an easy option. Of unemployed respondents in one study, 80 per cent had experienced a deterioration in their living standards since living on welfare. For nearly all of them, life became much more of a struggle. Most said they were 'just getting by' or 'getting into difficulties'. In spite of its importance, food is often treated as an item which can be cut back when money is short. For a minority, on the other hand, social assistance can bring improvements in living standards. For instance, when an unemployed person reaches the age of 60, he or she becomes a 'pensioner claimant' (Hernandez et al. 2006) and can claim benefits 30 per cent higher than previously obtained. Walker concludes: 'Despite sensational newspaper headlines, living on social assistance is not an option most people would choose if they were offered a genuine alternative. Most find themselves in that position because of some traumatic event in their lives: loss of a job, loss of a partner or the onset of ill health' (1994: 9).

Lisa and her children are just one example of the many households in the United Kingdom and other developed countries that exist in conditions of poverty. In 2000, the Organization for Economic Cooperation and Development (OECD) reported that, along with Italy, Spain, Portugal and the USA, the UK had one of the worst child poverty records in the developed world. The child poverty rate was above 15 per cent in all of these countries (see figure 12.1). Many people might be shocked to learn that wealthy countries like Britain have such a dubious distinction, as more affluent people often have little accurate knowledge about the extent of the poverty in their midst.

> ### THINKING CRITICALLY
> Before reading any further, take a few moments to reflect on Lisa's story as described above. If a relative or friend were to ask you, 'Why is Lisa poor?', what answer would you give; what *social* and *individual* factors would form part of your explanation?

In this chapter, we examine the concept and experience of poverty more closely. We

Global Society 12.1 **A universal measure of absolute poverty?**

A commonly used measure of absolute or 'extreme' poverty today is the number of people who live on less than US$1 per day. Figure 12.2 shows that, globally, this number has been decreasing since the 1990s in most parts of the world, including East and South Asia. Worldwide, the number of people living in extreme poverty fell from 1.5 billion in 1981 to around 1 billion by 2004. However, in sub-Saharan Africa the reduction has been much lower, and in 2004 more than 40 per cent of people were still trying to live on less than a dollar a day.

The stark contrast in extreme poverty levels between the developed and developing countries is clear from table 12.1, which shows that in the developed countries such as Sweden, Denmark, Britain, the USA, Australia and New Zealand, no one has to try and eke out a living on such a low level of income.

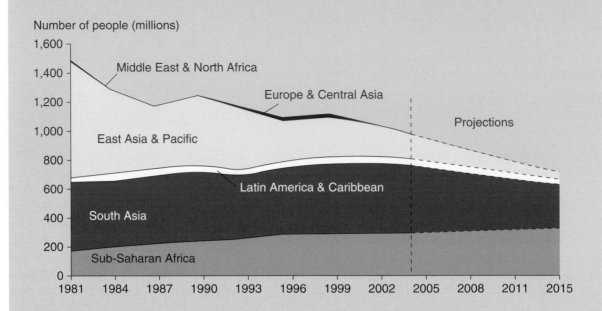

Figure 12.2   Number of people living on less than US$1 per day, 1981–2004, with projections to 2015

Source: Global Monitoring Report 2007 by World Bank. © 2007 by World Bank. Reproduced with permission of World Bank in the format Textbook via Copyright Clearance Center.

also look at the wider concept of social exclusion. In the final section, we look at how the welfare state has grown in response to poverty, and we examine some of the recent attempts to reform it. This chapter focuses primarily on poverty in the UK and other industrialized countries; in the next chapter, 'Global Inequality', we look at issues of poverty and inequality in a global context.

Poverty

What is poverty?

What is poverty and how should it be defined? Sociologists and researchers have favoured two different approaches to poverty: **absolute poverty** and **relative poverty**. The concept of absolute poverty is grounded in the idea of subsistence – the basic conditions that must be met in order to sustain a physically healthy existence. People who lack these fundamental require-

Table 12.1 **Measures of extreme poverty, 2007 (selected countries)**		
Country	Poverty (ratio living on US$1 a day)	Share of revenue to the poorest quintile (%)
Australia	0	5.9
Bangladesh	36	9.1
Brazil	7.5	2.8
China	9.9	4.3
Czech Republic	0	10.3
Denmark	0	8.3
Egypt	3.1	8.6
France	0	7.2
Japan	0	10.6
Kenya	22.8	6
New Zealand	0	7.6
Mozambique	36.2	5.4
Namibia	34.9	1.4
Nigeria	70.8	5.1
Norway	0	9.6
Pakistan	17	9.3
Rwanda	60.3	5.3
Sweden	0	9.1
UK	0	6.1
USA	0	5.4

Source: Global Monitoring Report 2007 by World Bank. © 2007 by World Bank. Reproduced with permission of World Bank in the format Textbook via Copyright Clearance Center.

ments for human existence – such as sufficient food, shelter and clothing – are said to live in poverty. The concept of absolute poverty is seen as universally applicable. It is held that standards for human subsistence are more or less the same for all people of an equivalent age and physique, regardless of where they live. Any individual, anywhere in the world, can be said to live in poverty if he or she falls below this universal standard.

As table 12.1 shows, many developing countries have large sections of their population living in extreme poverty, more than one-third in Bangladesh, Mozambique and Namibia, for example, and over 60 per cent in Rwanda and 70 per cent in Nigeria.

Clearly, material conditions of life in the developed countries are very different from those in developing countries. However, in terms of inequalities *within* individual countries, the share of national revenue which goes to the bottom fifth is often not so starkly different. For example, in Rwanda, some 5.3 per cent of national revenue goes to the poorest fifth of the population, whereas in the USA the figure is 5.4 per cent (table 12.1). As we will see in the next chapter, 'Global Inequalities', this reveals that chronic inequality still exists within the *developed* countries, in spite of their elimination of extreme poverty.

Nevertheless, it remains the case that many people in the developing world today

Who is poor? This child in a refugee camp . . .

still live and die in conditions of absolute or extreme poverty, whilst in the developed world, many people in relative poverty will suffer more illness and die earlier than those in wealthier social groups.

Not everyone accepts that it is possible to identify such a universal standard of absolute poverty however. It is more appropriate, they argue, to use the concept of relative poverty, which relates poverty to the overall standard of living that prevails in a particular society. Advocates of the concept of relative poverty hold that poverty is culturally defined and should not be measured according to some universal standard of deprivation. It is wrong to assume that human needs are everywhere identical – in fact, they differ both within and across societies. Things that are seen as essential in one society might be regarded as luxuries in another. For example, in most industrialized countries, running water,

flush toilets and the regular consumption of fruit and vegetables are regarded as basic necessities for a healthy life; people who live without them could be said to live in poverty. Yet in many developing societies, such items are not standard among the bulk of the population and it would not make sense to measure poverty according to their presence or absence. Critics of the concept of absolute poverty also point out that its definition has changed over time according to the existing knowledge that is available in particular periods (Howard et al. 2001). In short, therefore, even the definition of absolute poverty is relative.

One common technique used in attempts to measure absolute poverty is to determine a **poverty line**, based on the price of the basic goods needed for human survival in a particular society. Individuals or households whose income falls below the poverty line

. . . or these children from a dilapidated housing estate?

are said to live in poverty. Yet using a single criterion of poverty can be problematic, because such definitions fail to take into account variations in human needs within and between societies. It is much more expensive, for example, to live in some areas of a country than others; the cost of basic necessities will differ from region to region. As another example, individuals who are engaged in physical labour outdoors are likely to have greater nutritional needs than, say, office workers who spend their days sitting inside. A single criterion of poverty tends to mean that some individuals are assessed as above the poverty line when in fact their income does not even meet their basic subsistence needs.

The concept of relative poverty presents its own complexities, however. One of the main ones is the fact that, as societies develop, so understandings of relative poverty must also change. As societies become more affluent, standards for relative poverty are gradually adjusted upwards. At one time, for example, refrigerators, central heating and telephones were considered to be luxury goods. Yet in most industrialized societies today, they are seen as necessities for leading a full and active life. Some critics have cautioned that the use of the concept of relative poverty tends to deflect attention away from the fact that even the least affluent members of society are now considerably better off than in earlier times. The question remains of whether 'true' poverty can be said to exist in those relatively wealthy societies, where consumer goods like televisions and washing machines now sit in practically every home. Defenders of relative conceptions of poverty point out that access to consumer goods is valueless if an individual or group is unable to access more basic goods, such as nutritious food and good healthcare.

To illustrate these debates, the next section examines some of the main methods that have been used to measure poverty in the UK.

Measuring poverty

Official measurements of poverty

In contrast to the position in many other countries, UK governments have not recognized or used an 'official poverty line', instead preferring to use a range of separate indicators. This has meant that researchers in the UK have had to rely on other statistical indicators, such as benefit provision, to measure poverty levels. From the mid-1960s onwards researchers followed Abel-Smith and Townsend (1965) in defining anyone with an income at or below the level of supplementary benefit as living 'in poverty'. Supplementary benefit was a means-tested cash benefit paid by the state to people whose income did not reach a level deemed appropriate by Parliament for subsistence. It was replaced in 1998 by income support.

However, since the 1980s there has existed a European Community standard which measures income inequality, whereby poverty is defined as the number of households living on or below 60 per cent (or in earlier measures 50 per cent) of median income – often referred to as 'Households Below Average Income' (HBAI). On this measure, 78 million people in the 25 countries of the EU, some 17 per cent of the population, were at risk of poverty in 2005. Around 14 million of these were 'working poor' – that is, people in work but whose incomes still fell below the EC poverty standard (Eurostat 2007).

The UK government adopted this measure in 1999, with the publication of *Opportunity for All*, setting out measures for tackling poverty and social exclusion. It is important to note that this is a measure of relative poverty – as median income levels change, so does the real income poverty level. Under this measure, the number of people living in poverty increased dramatically throughout the 1980s, peaking in 1991/2, before falling back from the mid-1990s onwards. In 2005–6 the Department for Work and Pensions calculated that 10.4 million people were living in poverty according to this measure (see table 12.2), the same number as in 1994–5.

Other organizations use their own set of indicators. For instance, the New Policy Institute (NPI), with support from the Joseph Rowntree Foundation, produces indicators for poverty and social exclusion for the UK as a whole, but also for Wales, Scotland, England and Northern Ireland separately. This allows for a deeper and more contextually reliable understanding of the extent and spread of poverty in different regions. The tenth NPI Monitoring Poverty and Social Exclusion Report in 2007 found that overall poverty levels in 2005–6 were no improvement on 2002–3 and that the child poverty level was still 500,000 higher than that set for 2004–5.

Poverty and relative deprivation

Some researchers argue that official measures, of the kind discussed above, do not give an accurate picture of poverty. Several important studies have been carried out that define poverty as deprivation. One pioneer of this approach is Peter Townsend, whose work since the late 1950s increased public awareness of poverty in the UK (see 'Classic Studies 12.1').

Building on Townsend's definition of poverty as deprivation, Joanna Mack and Stewart Lansley carried out two highly influential studies of relative poverty in Britain, the first in 1983 and a second in 1990 (published, respectively, in 1985 and 1992). For a television programme in 1983 called *Breadline Britain*, Mack and Lansley conducted an opinion poll to determine what people considered to be 'necessities' for an 'acceptable' standard of living. On the

Table 12.2 Number of individuals living below 60% of median income, 1994/5–2005/6, UK

Number of individuals (millions)

	Before housing costs Below median		All individuals
	50%	60%	
Contemporary income thresholds			
1994/95	5.4	10.4	55.3
1995/96	5.2	9.9	55.5
1996/97	5.9	10.8	55.6
1997/98	6.0	10.9	55.7
1998/99	6.1	11.2	57.5
1999/00	6.1	11.1	57.7
2000/01	6.1	10.7	57.9
2001/02	5.9	10.7	58.1
2002/03	5.9	10.6	58.3
2003/04	5.8	10.4	58.5
2004/05	5.6	10.0	58.8
2005/06	5.9	10.4	59.1
1998/99–2005/06	−0.2	−0.8	1.6
2004/05–2005/06	0.3	0.4	0.4

Source: Office for National Statistics 2007

basis of these responses, they created a list of 22 basic necessities that more than 50 per cent of respondents considered important for a normal life. They then defined poverty as the condition in which three or more items from that list were lacking.

By asking respondents themselves what they thought to be necessities, Mack and Lansley avoided the criticism directed against Townsend's original survey – namely, that his choice of items for the deprivation index was arbitrary. Mack and Lansley also included a question asking whether items which respondents lacked were a matter of personal choice or necessity. If the respondents answered that it was a matter of choice, then they were not classified as being deprived of that item.

The 1983 survey estimated that there were around 7.5 million people in the UK

living in poverty – around 14 per cent of the population. This was a far lower, but still substantial, figure than that arrived at in Townsend's study. Mack and Lansley then repeated the exercise in 1990 and found a significant *growth* in poverty during the 1980s, with the number of people living in poverty (defined in the 1990 study as a lack of three or more of 26 necessities) as high as 11 million. The number living in severe poverty (a lack of seven or more necessities) rose from 2.6 to 3.5 million.

Drawing on Mack and Lansley's earlier research and that of Peter Townsend (who also contributed to this study), David Gordon and his colleagues carried out a similar survey in 2000, the *Millennium Survey of Poverty and Social Exclusion* (known as the PSE survey). Gordon and his team used a questionnaire to determine

| **Classic Studies 12.1** | **Peter Townsend on poverty and deprivation** |

The research problem

Sociologists can understand the extent of poverty in society by collating income statistics, but what is it like to experience poverty? What does poverty feel like and how does it affect people's daily lives? How are low incomes juggled to make ends meet and what do people have to go without to do this? Peter Townsend's studies have concentrated on just this issue of people's subjective experience and understanding of poverty, trying to ascertain exactly what poverty means in terms of deprivation. In his classic study, *Poverty in the United Kingdom* (1979), Townsend examined the responses to more than 2,000 questionnaires filled in by households across the UK during the late 1960s. Respondents provided detailed information about their lifestyles, including their living conditions,

eating habits, leisure and civic activities, as well as their income.

Townsend's explanation

From the information collected, Townsend selected 12 items which he found were relevant across the sample population rather than to particular social groups, and calculated the proportion of the population that were deprived of them (results can be seen in table 12.3). Townsend then gave each household a score on a deprivation index – the higher the score, the more deprived the household was. He then compared the position of households on the index to their total income, making allowances for factors such as the number of people in each household, whether the adults were working, the ages of the children and whether any members of the house were disabled. Townsend

Table 12.3 Townsend's deprivation index (1979)

	Characteristics	% of the population
1	Has not had a holiday away from home in the past 12 months.	53.6
2	Adults only. Has not had a relative or a friend to the home for a meal or snack in the past four weeks.	33.4
3	Adults only. Has not been out in the past four weeks to a relative or friend for a meal or snack.	45.1
4	Children only (under 15). Has not had a friend to play or to tea in the past four weeks.	36.3
5	Children only. Did not have a party on last birthday.	56.6
6	Has not had an afternoon or evening out for entertainment in the past two weeks.	47.0
7	Does not have fresh meat (including meals out) as many as four days a week.	19.3
8	Has gone through one or more days in the past fortnight without a cooked meal.	7.0
9	Has not had a cooked breakfast most days of the week.	67.3
10	Household does not have a refrigerator.	45.1
11	Household does not usually have a Sunday joint (three in four times).	25.9
12	Household does not have sole use of four amenities (flush WC; sink or washbasin and cold water tap; fixed bath or shower and gas / electric cooker).	21.4

Source: "Townsend's Deprivation Index" from Poverty in the United Kingdom, by Peter Townsend (Penguin, 1979).
Copyright © 1979 by Peter Townsend. Reprinted by permission of Penguin Books Ltd.

concluded that his survey had revealed a threshold for levels of income, below which social deprivation rose rapidly. It was these households which Townsend described as suffering from poverty and he calculated that they formed 22.9 per cent of the population, far higher than previous figures had suggested. Based on these findings, he concluded that government rates for means-tested benefits were more than 50 per cent too low, falling well short of the minimum need by a household to participate fully and meaningfully in society. Townsend's study showed that, as household income falls, so families withdraw from taking part in quite ordinary family-type activities: in short, they become 'socially excluded', a concept which is discussed later in the chapter.

Critical points

Although Townsend's approach was highly influential, it was also criticized by some commentators, and one particular criticism stands out. David Piachaud (1987), for example, argued that the items selected by Townsend for his deprivation index have something of an arbitrary quality. He argued: 'It is not clear what they have to do with poverty, nor how they were selected.' Some of the categories seem to have more to do with social or cultural decisions than with poverty and deprivation. If someone chooses not to eat meat or a cooked breakfast, or decides not to socialize regularly or to holiday away from home, it is not immediately obvious that the person is suffering from poverty.

Contemporary significance

The cultural critique is an important one, but over the long term, Townsend's approach to the study of poverty and deprivation has retained its significance. Indeed, it has formed the basis for several significant sociological studies, which have tried to avoid the cultural criticism levelled against Townsend's original study. The attempt to construct a deprivation index based on specific factors remains valuable in our attempts fully to understand how poverty and deprivation are inextricably linked. Townsend's studies have also been instrumental in moving contemporary debates on poverty towards an appreciation of the underlying processes of social exclusion, which deny full citizenship to people in poverty.

what people considered 'necessities' for an acceptable standard of life in modern Britain. Based on the responses, they created a list of 35 items that more than 50 per cent of respondents considered necessary for a normal life (see table 12.4). Of these, 6 items – a TV, a fridge, beds and bedding for everyone, a washing machine, medicines prescribed by a doctor and a deep freezer/fridge freezer – did not add to the reliability or validity of the study and were dropped from the analysis. Gordon and his colleagues then set a threshold for deprivation, based on an enforced lack of *two or more* necessities combined with a low income.

The PSE survey found that 28 per cent of the sample lacked two or more necessities, although this included some 2 per cent whose incomes were high enough to suggest they had now risen out of poverty, leaving 26 per cent of the survey population who could be classified as being in relative poverty (see table 12.5).

Because the PSE survey adopted a similar method to that of Mack and Lansley's two studies, the researchers were able to use their data to compare how the level of poverty in the UK had changed over time. Gordon et al. found that the number of households lacking three or more socially perceived necessities (set as the poverty threshold in Mack and Lansley's studies) increased substantially, from 14 per cent in 1983 to 21 per cent by 1990, rising to 24 per cent by 1999. Thus, although the British population as a whole had become much richer since the early 1980s, by 2000, in terms of a lack of necessities, there had also been a dramatic rise in poverty.

Table 12.4 Perception of adult necessities and how many people lack them (% of adult population)

	Items considered:		Items that respondents:	
	Necessary	Not necessary	Don't have, don't want	Don't have, can't afford
Beds and bedding for everyone	95	4	0.2	1
Heating to warm living areas of the home	94	5	0.4	1
Damp-free home	93	6	3	6
Visiting friends or family in hospital	92	7	8	3
Two meals a day	91	9	3	1
Medicines prescribed by doctor	90	9	5	1
Refrigerator	89	11	1	0.1
Fresh fruit and vegetables daily	86	13	7	4
Warm, waterproof coat	85	14	2	4
Replace or repair broken electrical goods	85	14	6	12
Visits to friends or family	84	15	3	2
Celebrations on special occasions such as Christmas	83	16	2	2
Money to keep home in a decent state of decoration	82	17	2	14
Visits to school, e.g. sports day	81	17	33	2
Attending weddings, funerals	80	19	3	3
Meat, fish or vegetarian equivalent every other day	79	19	4	3
Insurance of contents of dwelling	79	20	5	8
Hobby or leisure activity	78	20	12	7
Washing machine	76	22	3	1
Collect children from school	75	23	36	2
Telephone	71	28	1	1
Appropriate clothes for job interviews	69	28	13	4
Deep freezer/fridge freezer	68	30	3	2
Carpets in living rooms and bedrooms	67	31	2	3
Regular savings (of £10 per month) for rainy days or retirement	66	32	7	25
Two pairs of all-weather shoes	64	34	4	5
Friends or family round for a meal	64	34	10	6
A small amount of money to spend on self weekly, not on family	59	39	3	13
Television	56	43	1	1
Roast joint/vegetarian equivalent once a week	56	41	11	3

Table 12.4 (*continued*)

	Items considered:		Items that respondents:	
	Necessary	Not necessary	Don't have, don't want	Don't have, can't afford
Presents for friends/family once a year	56	42	1	3
A holiday away from home once a year	55	43	14	18
Replace worn-out furniture	54	43	6	12
Dictionary	53	44	6	5
An outfit for social occasions	51	46	4	4

Source: From Poverty and Social Exclusion in Britain by David Gordon et al, published in 2000 by the Joseph Rowntree Foundation. Reproduced by permission of the Joseph Rowntree Foundation.

Table 12.5 **Results of the *Poverty and Social Exclusion Survey* 2000, UK**

Poverty classifications	Percentage (to the nearest whole %)
Poor	26
Vulnerable to poverty	10
Risen out of poverty	2
Not poor	62

Source: Gordon et al. 2000: 18

In a 2006 study commissioned by the Joseph Rowntree Foundation, Guy Palmer and colleagues re-analysed some of the data from Gordon's PSE survey. Combining similar items from the 35 'essential items' scale, they found that the bulk of essential items were directly money-related. That is, the respondents simply did not have enough income to afford to have them (figure 12.3).

Drawing on a Family Resources Survey from 2004–5, the team was then able to compare low-income households with those on average incomes in relation to ten selected essential items (see figure 12.4). Again, significant proportions of low-income households reported that they could not afford these items. Almost 60 per cent could not make savings of £10 or more per month, over 50 per cent could not afford an annual holiday and one-third could not afford to insure their household contents. However, Palmer and his colleagues point out that a significant minority of households on average incomes reported that they could not afford these items either. The report is therefore critical of the use of such subjectively defined measures, which, it argues, are of limited value in providing a reliable and valid measure of 'real' poverty. For example, if almost one-third of people on average incomes cannot afford to make 'savings of £10 per month or more' and one quarter cannot afford 'holidays away from home one week a year', does that mean that they are also living 'in poverty'? What is needed in addition is information about *why* households cannot afford such items, which would enable us to assess the extent to which the lack of each item is an example of 'enforced poverty' (caused by socio-economic circumstances) or the result of personal choice, where other things take priority.

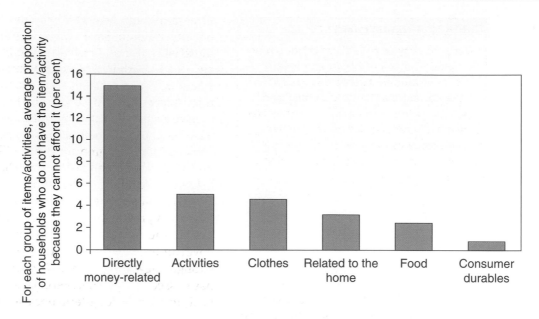

Figure 12.3 Essential items most commonly lacking, by category

Source: Monitoring Poverty and Social Exclusion 2006 by Guy Palmer, Tom MacInnes and Peter Kenway, published in 2006 by the Joseph Rowntree Foundation. Reproduced by permission of the Joseph Rowntree Foundation.

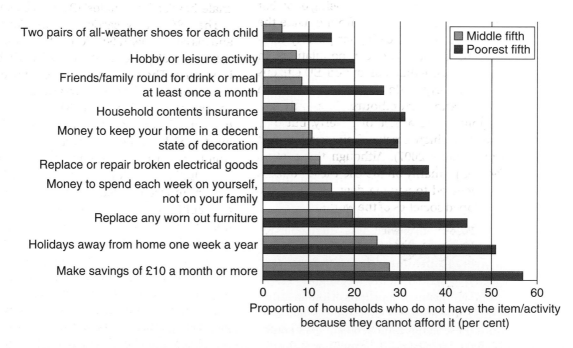

Figure 12.4 Percentage of UK households which cannot afford selected 'essential items', by average and low-income household

Source: Family Resources Survey 2004/05, Department for Work and Pensions, UK.

THINKING CRITICALLY

When society as a whole was becoming wealthier, why did poverty levels increase amongst some groups rather than decrease? Does the concept of 'relative poverty' accurately capture the real-life experiences of people living with disadvantage and deprivation? Can the experience of poverty in the relatively wealthy countries be directly compared with that in the developing world?

Who are the poor?

The face of poverty is diverse and ever changing, so it is difficult to present a profile of 'the poor'. What we do know is that people in some social groups are more likely to be poor than others, including children, older people, women and ethnic minorities. In particular, people who are disadvantaged or discriminated against in other aspects of life have an increased chance of being poor. For example, recent migrants from outside the European Union face higher poverty rates than indigenous European populations. In Belgium, more than half of non-EU citizens live in poverty, as do 45 per cent of those in France and Luxembourg. Not only are migrants more at risk of poverty, but they also face a higher risk of being exploited at work (Lelkes 2007). Although this section focuses primarily on the UK, these patterns are repeated to varying degrees across the developed societies of the world.

Poverty and inequality in the developing societies is discussed in more detail in chapter 13, 'Global Inequality'.

Children

The proportion of children in the UK living in households with an income below 60 per cent of the national average more than doubled between 1979 and 1996/7, from 14 to 34 per cent, but after 1998 this figure fell to stand at around 27 per cent in 2004/5 (Department for Work and Pensions 2006).

In a variety of ways, children who live in poverty tend to have worse health than those who do not. They are more likely to have a low birth weight, to be injured (and killed) in a road accident (because they are more likely to be pedestrians and less likely to have access to a safe play area or garden), to suffer abuse and self-harm or to attempt suicide. Poorer children are also less likely to do well at school and are far more likely to become poor adults (Lister 2004).

As we will see later in the chapter, child poverty is proving to be much more resistant to the social policies of successive governments, with the latest forecasts strongly suggesting that the UK government has missed its own short-term target and is likely to miss the long-term one as well.

Women

As we see at several points throughout this chapter, women are more likely to be poor than men, although their poverty has often been masked behind studies that focused on 'male-headed households' (Ruspini 2000).

The PSE survey carried out by Gordon and his colleagues (2000) found that women comprised 58 per cent of those adults living in poverty. The causes of women's poverty are complex. One important element concerns the gendered division of labour both inside and outside the home. The burden of domestic labour and the responsibility of caring for children and relatives still fall disproportionately on women. This has an important effect on their ambitions and ability to work outside the home. It means that they are far more likely than men to be in part-time, rather than full-time, paid employment and they earn less as a result. Although more women are entering paid work in the UK than ever before, occupational segregation between 'a man's job' and 'women's work' in the labour force remains entrenched. Women are disproportionately represented in less well-paid industries, which has a negative effect on income from private pensions later in life (Flaherty et al. 2004).

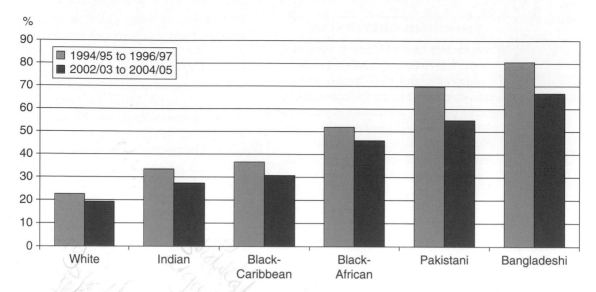

Figure 12.5 Proportion of each group in UK households below 60 per cent median income, after deducting housing costs

Source: From Poverty Among Ethnic Groups: How and Why Does it Differ? by Guy Palmer and Peter Kenway, published in 2007 by the Joseph Rowntree Foundation. Reproduced by permission of the Joseph Rowntree Foundation.

Ethnic minorities

Members of ethnic minority groups are also disproportionately represented among the poor. Pakistani and Bangladeshi people, in particular, are far more likely to have an income of less than 60 per cent of the average than individuals of other ethnicities, though income poverty has fallen across all ethnic groups at roughly the same rate over recent years (see figure 12.5). Part of the reason for such ethnic differences in income poverty levels can be found in the high unemployment and low employment rates for all ethnic minorities in the UK.

Employment rates differ substantially across ethnic minority groups. In 2006, Indian and Black Caribbean groups have relatively high employment rates of 70.2 and 67.8 per cent respectively, while Pakistani and Bangladeshi groups have the lowest employment rates among ethnic minorities; 44.2 and 40.2 per cent respectively. In the same year, the unemployment rate for African and Pakistani/Bangladeshi people, for example, was 11.2 per cent compared to an overall rate of 5.2 per cent,

and ethnic minorities are still twice as likely to be unemployed as white people (Ethnic Minority Employment Taskforce 2006). There is also a high degree of labour market segregation. Pakistani groups are heavily concentrated in the former heavy manufacturing and textile industry areas, such as Yorkshire and Birmingham – industries that fell into recession in the late 1970s and 1980s. Black Caribbean men are over-represented in manual occupations, particularly within the transport and communications industries. Chinese and Bangladeshis are particularly concentrated in the catering industry. There is some evidence to show that some occupational segregation has occurred because ethnic minorities perceive certain industries or employers as 'white', whereas some employers see ethnic minorities as 'outside their recruitment pool' (Performance and Innovation Unit 2002). Ethnic minorities in the UK are also more likely to have poorly paid jobs, struggle at school, live in deprived areas and in poor quality housing and to suffer health problems (Salway et al. 2007).

Ethnic minority people are amongst the poorest in Western societies, often as a result of high unemployment.

Older people

Many people who may have been reasonably well paid during their working lives experience a sharp reduction in income (and status) when they retire, especially if they did not, or could not afford to, invest in a private pension while working. The ageing of the population is putting increasing strain on state pension provision. As life expectancy increases, so too does the number of older people in the population. Between 1961 and 2005, the proportion of people in the UK aged 65 and over more than doubled, to make up 16 per cent of the total population. At the age of 65, men can now expect to live, on average, to 81.6 years and women to 84.4 years, the highest ever levels (Palmer et al. 2007).

In recent years, several studies have shown that poverty amongst pensioners has

> Global life expectancy is discussed in more detail in chapter 8, 'The Life-Course'.

been reducing since 1997. Based on the HBAI measure of 'households below 60 per cent of average income', individual pensioners in poverty decreased from 29.1 per cent (2.9 million) in 1997–8 to 17 per cent (1.8 million) in 2005–6 (Brewer et al. 2007). The number of pensioners on a low income does tend to increase with age, though there are divisions within pensioner groups. For example, those with additional private pension provision are less likely to experience poverty and there is a clear gender dimension to this: only 30 per cent of women have an additional private pension, compared to more than 70 per cent of men (Wicks 2004). In recent decades, older women and those from ethnic minorities are more likely to experience poverty than other pensioner groups.

Explaining poverty

Explanations of poverty can be grouped under two main headings: theories that see poor individuals as responsible for their own poverty, and theories that view poverty as produced and reproduced by structural forces in society. These competing approaches are sometimes described as 'blame the victim' and 'blame the system' theories, respectively. We will briefly examine each in turn.

There is a long history of attitudes that hold the poor as responsible for their own disadvantaged positions. Early efforts to address the effects of poverty, such as the poorhouses of the nineteenth century, were grounded in a belief that poverty was the result of an inadequacy or pathology of individuals. The poor were seen as those who were unable – because of a lack of skills, moral or physical weakness, absence of motivation, or below average ability – to succeed in society. Social standing was taken as a reflection of a person's talent and effort; those who deserved to succeed did so, while others less capable were doomed to fail. The existence of 'winners' and 'losers' was regarded as a fact of life.

As we see in our discussion of the rise of the welfare state below, accounts of poverty that explain it as primarily an individual failing lost popularity during the mid-twentieth century. Beginning in the 1970s and 1980s, they then enjoyed a renaissance, as the political emphasis on entrepreneurship and individual ambition rewarded those who 'succeeded' in society, and held those who did not responsible for the circumstances in which they found themselves. Often, explanations for poverty were sought in the lifestyles of poor people, along with the attitudes and outlooks they supposedly espoused. One influential version of this thesis was put forward by the American sociologist Charles Murray.

Murray (1984) argues that there is an underclass of individual who must take personal responsibility for their poverty. This group forms part of a **dependency culture**. By this term, Murray refers to poor people who rely on government welfare provision rather than entering the labour market. He argues that the growth of the welfare state has created a subculture–that undermines personal ambition and the capacity for self-help. Rather than looking to the future and striving to achieve a better life, the welfare dependent are content to accept handouts. Welfare, Murray argues, has eroded people's incentive to work. He makes a contrast between those individuals who must take personal responsibility for their poverty and those who are poor through 'no fault of their own' – such as widows, orphans or people who are disabled, for example.

> **Murray's work is examined in more detail in chapter 11, 'Stratification and Social Class'.**

Murray's views may resonate among sections of the British population. Many people regard the poor as responsible for their own problems and are suspicious of those who live on 'government hand-outs'. Yet these views are out of line with the reality of poverty for many people. As we have seen, the very oldest and youngest people are often the poorest in society, and are not in a position to work. Many people receiving financial help from the government, such as those receiving tax credits in the UK, are actually in work but not earning enough to bring them over the poverty threshold. Of the remainder, the majority are children under the age of 14, those aged 65 and over, and the ill or disabled. In spite of popular views about the high level of welfare cheating, fewer than 1 per cent of welfare applications involve fraudulent claims – much lower than is the case for income tax returns, where it is estimated that more than 10 per cent of tax is lost through misreporting or evasion.

The second approach to explaining poverty emphasizes larger social processes

The continuing decline of manufacturing industries in the 1970s and '80s eliminated many well-paid jobs, restructuring the urban economy and thus leading to increases in poverty levels.

which produce conditions of poverty that are difficult for individuals to overcome. According to such a view, structural forces within society – factors like class, gender, ethnicity, occupational position, educational attainment and so forth – shape the way in which resources are distributed. Writers who advocate structural explanations for poverty argue that the lack of ambition among the poor, which is often taken for the 'dependency culture', is in fact a *consequence* of their constrained situations, not a *cause* of it.

An early exponent of this type of argument was R. H. Tawney (1964 [1931]), who saw poverty as an aspect of social inequality. For Tawney, social inequality led to extremes of both wealth and poverty and both were dehumanizing. Extreme poverty limited life to mere subsistence, while extreme wealth led to a pampering of the rich. Both were reprehensible, but the key to tackling poverty was therefore to reduce structural social inequality, not simply to

blame individuals for their situation (Hickson 2004). Reducing poverty is not simply a matter of changing individual outlooks, but requires policy measures aimed at distributing income and resources more equally throughout society. Childcare subsidies, a minimum hourly wage and guaranteed income levels for families are examples of policy measures that have sought to redress persistent social inequalities.

Two research studies from the mid-1990s reached similar conclusions on the reasons for contemporary poverty levels, and both use what we can call an 'economic restructuring' hypothesis. In America, sociologist William Julius Wilson put forward one important version in his book *When Work Disappears: The World of the New Urban Poor* (1996), and in Britain, Will Hutton's *The State We're In* (1995), described the emergence of a 'thirty, thirty, forty' society (see below)

Wilson argued that persistent urban poverty stems primarily from the structural transformation of the inner-city economy. The decline of manufacturing industries, the 'suburbanization' of employment and the rise of a low-wage service sector dramatically reduced the number of jobs available to those immediately leaving education that pay wages sufficient to support a family. The high rate of joblessness resulting from economic shifts has led to a shrinking pool of 'marriageable' men – those financially able to support a family. Thus, marriage has become less attractive to poor women, the number of children born out of wedlock has increased and female-headed families have proliferated. New generations of children are born into poverty, and the vicious cycle is perpetuated. Wilson argues that black Americans suffer disproportionately because of past discrimination and because they are concentrated in locations and occupations particularly affected by economic restructuring. He argued that these economic changes were accompanied by an increase in the spatial concentration of poverty within black neighbourhoods in the USA.

In Will Hutton's analysis of the UK, similar processes of economic restructuring during the 1970s and '80s created new divides within the population. Around 30 per cent were *disadvantaged*. That is, they were either out of work (but seeking employment), in irregular part-time and short-term jobs, or 'economically inactive' for other reasons, such as those we discussed above in relation to single parents. The disadvantaged groups live in poverty on the margins of society. Another 30 per cent, the *marginalized insecure*, had jobs and regular work, but because of economic restructuring, which weakened the trade unions and led to many more fixed-term contracts, their income levels were low and the jobs were relatively insecure. This group includes many women in generally poorly paid, part-time jobs (McGivney 2000). Finally, around 40 per cent – the privileged – are in full-time employment or are self-employed. The majority of this group are not rich, but their employment is more secure and their income tends to be higher; compared to the other two groups, therefore, they are relatively advantaged. Like Wilson in the USA, Hutton suggests that it is much harder for those in the disadvantaged and marginalized insecure groups to hold a marriage together, as parenting becomes more stressful and people have to work long hours in several jobs to earn a living wage. Hutton concludes that economic restructuring and the loss of industrial workplaces and well-paid jobs has served to produce a more divided society and perceptions that 'nothing can be done' to redress the issue of poverty.

For both Wilson and Hutton, poverty cannot be explained by reference to individual motivations and personal attitudes. Instead, poverty levels have to be explained with reference to structural changes in society and these do not happen in isolation from developments within the global economy.

Evaluation

Both explanations of poverty, as outlined above, have enjoyed broad support, and variations of each view are consistently encountered in public debates about poverty. Critics of the culture of poverty view accuse its advocates of 'individualizing' poverty and blaming the poor for circumstances largely beyond their control. They see the poor as victims, not as freeloaders who are abusing the system. Yet we should be cautious about accepting uncritically the arguments of those who see the causes of poverty as lying exclusively in the structure of society itself. Such an approach implies that the poor simply passively accept the difficult situations in which they find themselves. This is far from the truth, as we shall see below.

Poverty and social mobility

Most research into poverty in the past has focused on people's entry into poverty and has measured aggregate levels of poverty year by year. Less attention has traditionally been paid to the 'life-cycle' of poverty –

people's trajectories out of (and often back into) poverty over time.

A widely held view of poverty is that it is a permanent condition. Yet being poor does not necessarily mean being mired in poverty. A substantial proportion of people in poverty at any one time have either enjoyed superior conditions of life previously or can be expected to climb out of poverty at some time in the future. Recent research has revealed a significant amount of mobility into and out of poverty: a surprising number of people are successful in escaping poverty, and at the same time a larger number than previously realized live in poverty at some point during their lives.

Statistical findings from the British Household Panel Survey (BHPS) in the decade of the 1990s, showed that just over half of the individuals who were in the bottom fifth (quintile) by income in 1991 were in the same category in 1996. This does not necessarily mean that these people remained consistently in the same position over the five-year period, however. While some of them may have done so, others are likely to have risen out of the bottom quintile and returned to it again during that time. In fact, the BHPS longitudinal panel study, which tracks 16,000 individuals across 9,000 households over a long period, has shown significant social mobility. For example, it shows that relatively large proportions of children experience poverty, but most for quite short periods. However, many families that move out of poverty also have a higher risk of re-entering the category later, during periods of economic change. These findings have led to a new understanding of the quite fluid patterns of poverty, which have also been found in other developed societies (Leisering and Leibfried 1999).

Using data from the UK's New Earnings Survey Panel Dataset and other sources, Abigail McKnight (2000) analysed trends in *earnings* mobility in Britain between 1977 and 1997. By tracking groups of low-paid workers, McKnight found a significant amount of persistence in low pay. Her

survey showed that around a fifth of employees in the lowest earnings quartile (quarter) are still there six years later. She also found that people who are unemployed, who are amongst the poorest group in Britain, are most likely to gain employment in the lowest-paid sections when they do find work; and that low-paid employees are more likely to go on to experience unemployment than are higher-paid employees.

Scholars have stressed that we should interpret such findings carefully, as they can easily be used by those who wish to scale back on welfare provisions or avoid categorizing poverty as a political and social issue altogether. John Hills (1998) at the Centre for Analysis of Social Exclusion has cautioned against accepting a 'lottery model' view of income determination. By this he means that we should be sceptical of arguments which present poverty as a 'one off' outcome that is experienced by people more or less randomly as they move through the income hierarchy. This view suggests that the inequalities between the wealthy and poor in society are not terribly critical; everyone has a chance of being a winner or a loser at some point, so the idea of poverty is no longer a cause for serious concern. Some unlucky individuals may end up having low incomes for several years in a row, the argument goes, but, essentially, low income is a random phenomenon.

As Hills points out, the BHPS does reveal a fair amount of short-range mobility on the part of those living in poverty. For example, among individuals in the poorest decile (tenth), 46 per cent were still there the following year. This suggests that more than half of those in the lowest decile managed to escape from poverty. Yet a closer look shows that 67 per cent of the individuals remain within the bottom two deciles; only one-third progress further than this. Among the bottom fifth of the population by income, 65 per cent were still in the same position a year later; meanwhile, 85 per cent remained in the bottom two-fifths. Such findings suggest that about one-third of low income is 'transient' in nature, while the other two-thirds are not. According to Hills, it is misleading to think that over time the population gradually 'mingles' throughout the income deciles. Rather, many of those who move out of poverty do not advance far, and eventually drift back in again; the 'escape rates' for those who remain at the bottom for more than a year get progressively lower.

While climbing out of poverty is surely fraught with challenges and obstacles, research findings indicate that movement into and out of poverty is more fluid than is often thought. Poverty is not simply the result of social forces acting on a passive population. Even individuals in severely disadvantaged positions can seize on opportunities to better their positions; the power of human agency to bring about change should not be underestimated. Social policy can play an important role in maximizing the action potential of disadvantaged individuals and communities. In our discussion of welfare later in this chapter, we will draw attention to policy measures designed to relieve poverty by strengthening the labour market, education and training opportunities, and social cohesion.

 Social mobility is discussed more fully in chapter 11, 'Stratification and Social Class', and chapter 19, 'Education'.

Social exclusion

What is social exclusion?

The idea of **social exclusion** has been used by politicians in various ways to frame their own social welfare policies. Because of this, the concept has become rather diluted over recent years and its meaning less clear. However, the notion was first introduced by sociologists to refer to new sources of inequality and the concept continues to inform much applied social research, which aims to understand and tackle disadvantage and inequality. Social exclusion refers to ways in which individuals may become cut off from full involvement in the wider soci-

ety. For instance, people who live in a dilapidated housing estate, with poor schools and few employment opportunities in the area, may effectively be denied the opportunities for self-betterment that most people in society have. The concept of social exclusion implies its opposite – *social inclusion* – and attempts to foster inclusion of marginalized groups have now become part of the agenda of modern politics, though *how* this is done differs across societies (Lister 2004).

Social exclusion raises the question of personal responsibility. After all, the word 'exclusion' implies that someone or something is being left out. Certainly, there are instances in which individuals are excluded as a result of decisions that lie outside their own control. Banks might refuse to grant a current account or a credit card to individuals living in a certain postcode area; insurance companies might reject an application for a policy on the basis of an applicant's personal history and background; an employee made redundant later in life may be refused further jobs on the basis of his or her age.

But social exclusion is not only the result of people being excluded; it can also result from people excluding themselves from aspects of mainstream society. Individuals can choose to drop out of education, to turn down a job opportunity and become economically inactive, or to abstain from voting in political elections. In considering the phenomenon of social exclusion, we must once again be conscious of the interaction between human agency and responsibility, on the one hand, and the role of social forces in shaping people's circumstances on the other.

A useful way of thinking about social exclusion is to differentiate between 'weak' and 'strong' versions of the concept (Veit-Wilson 1998). Weak versions of social exclusion see the central issue simply as one of trying to ensure the inclusion of those who are currently socially excluded. Strong versions also seek social inclusion, but, in addition, try to tackle some of the processes through which relatively powerful social groups 'can exercise their capacity to exclude' (Macrae et al. 2003: 90). This is a significant distinction as the version adopted by governments will shape their policies towards social exclusion. For example, in debates on rising levels of school exclusions for bad behaviour, a weak approach would focus on how individual children can be brought back into the mainstream education system, while a strong approach would also look at potential problems of the education system itself and the role of powerful groups within it that have the capacity to exclude.

Social exclusion, then, is a broader concept than poverty, though it does encompass it. It focuses attention on a broad range of factors that prevent individuals or groups from having the same opportunities that are open to the majority of the population. Ruth Lister (2004) concludes that the broad concept of social exclusion is a useful one for social scientists, provided that it is not seen as an alternative to the concept of poverty, which, she contends, remains central to our understanding of inequality and disadvantage.

The 2000 PSE survey distinguished four dimensions to social exclusion: poverty or exclusion from *adequate income* or resources (which we have discussed above), *labour market* exclusion, *service* exclusion and exclusion from *social relations* (Gordon et al. 2000). Next, we look at these last three elements in relation to evidence from the UK, although the patterns identified here are, to varying degrees, repeated in other industrialized countries.

Labour market exclusion

For the individual, work is important not just because it provides an adequate income, but also because involvement in the labour market is an important arena for social interaction. Thus, labour market exclusion can lead to the other forms of social exclusion – poverty, service exclusion and exclusion from social relations. Conse-

quently, increasing the number of people in paid work has been seen by politicians who are concerned about the issue as an important way to reduce social exclusion.

To be in a 'jobless household', however, should not necessarily be associated with unemployment. The 2000 PSE survey found that 43 per cent of adults (50 per cent of women and 37 per cent of men) are not in paid work. By far the largest group of those who are not active in the labour market are retired (24 per cent of all adults). Other groups who are inactive in the labour market include people involved in domestic and caring activities, those unable to work, perhaps because of disability, and students. Overall, we should be cautious about claiming that labour market inactivity is a sign of social exclusion in itself, because of the high proportion of the population that this involves, but we can say that exclusion from the labour market significantly increases the risk of social exclusion.

Service exclusion

An important aspect of social exclusion is lack of access to basic services, whether these are in the home (such as power and water supplies) or outside it (for example, access to transport, shops or financial services). Service exclusion can involve individual exclusion (when an individual cannot use a service because he or she cannot afford to do so) or collective exclusion (when a service is unavailable to the community). The PSE survey found that almost a quarter of people are excluded from two or more basic services and only just over 50 per cent of people had access to the full range of publicly and privately provided services. Table 12.6 shows the levels of collective and individual exclusion from each of the various services.

Exclusion from social relations

There are many ways in which people can be excluded from social relations. First, this type of exclusion can mean that individuals are unable to participate in common social

Table 12.6 Public and private services used by respondents (%)

	Collective exclusion		Individual exclusion		
	Use: adequate	Use: inadequate	Don't use: unavailable or unsuitable	Don't use: can't afford	Don't use: don't want or not relevant
Public services					
Libraries	55	6	3	0	36
Public sports facilities	39	7	5	1	48
Museums and galleries	29	4	13	1	52
Evening classes	17	2	5	3	73
A public or community village hall	31	3	9	0	56
A hospital with accident/ emergency unit	75	13	2	0	10
Doctor	92	6	0	0	2
Dentist	83	5	1	0	11
Optician	78	3	1	1	17
Post office	93	4	0	0	2
Private services					
Places of worship	30	1	2	0	66
Bus services	38	15	6	0	41
Train or tube station	37	10	10	1	41
Petrol stations	75	2	2	1	21
Chemist	93	3	1	0	3
Corner shop	73	7	8	0	12
Medium/large supermarket	92	4	2	0	2
Banks or building societies	87	7	1	0	4
Pub	53	4	2	2	37
Cinema or theatre	45	6	10	5	33

Source: From Poverty and Social Exclusion in Britain by David Gordon et al, published in 2000 by the Joseph Rowntree Foundation. Reproduced by permission of the Joseph Rowntree Foundation.

activities, such as visiting friends and family, celebrating special occasions, spending time on hobbies, having friends round for a meal and taking holidays. Second, people are excluded from social relations if they are isolated from friends and family – the PSE survey (2000) found that 2 per cent of people had no contact with either a family member or a friend outside their own house even a few times a year. A third aspect of exclusion from social relations involves a lack of practical and emotional support in times of need – someone to help with heavy jobs around the house or in the garden or to talk to when depressed or to get advice from about important life changes. Fourth, people are excluded from social relations through a lack of *civic engagement*. Civic engagement includes voting, getting involved in local or national politics, writing a letter to a newspaper or campaigning on an issue one feels strongly about. Lastly, some people are excluded from social relations because they are confined to their home, perhaps due to disability, caring responsibilities or because they feel unsafe on the streets.

Examples of social exclusion

Sociologists have conducted research into the different ways that individuals and communities experience exclusion. Investigations have focused on topics as diverse as housing, education, the labour market, crime, young people and the elderly. We shall now look briefly at three examples of exclusion that have attracted attention in Britain, as well as in other industrialized societies.

Housing and neighbourhoods

The nature of social exclusion can be seen clearly within the housing sector. While many people in industrialized societies live in comfortable, spacious housing, others reside in dwellings that are overcrowded, inadequately heated or structurally unsound. When entering the housing market, individuals are able to secure housing on the basis of their existing and projected resources. Thus, a dual-earning childless couple will have a greater chance of obtaining a mortgage for a home in an attractive area. In countries where people tend to buy rather than rent their home, in recent decades house prices have risen considerably faster than inflation, ensuring that owner-occupiers realize large profits on their property, while those not already on the housing ladder find it increasingly difficult to buy a first home. By contrast, households whose adults are unemployed or in low-paying jobs may be restricted to less desirable options in the rented or public housing sector.

Stratification within the housing market occurs at both the household and the community level. Just as disadvantaged individuals are excluded from desirable housing options, so whole communities can be excluded from opportunities and activities that are norms for the rest of society. Exclusion can take on a spatial dimension: neighbourhoods vary greatly in terms of safety, environmental conditions and the availability of services and public facilities. For example, low-demand neighbourhoods tend to have fewer basic services such as banks, food shops and post offices than do more desirable areas. Community spaces such as parks, sports grounds and libraries may also be limited. Yet people living in disadvantaged places are often dependent on what few facilities are available. Unlike residents of more affluent areas, they may not have access to transport (or funds) which would allow them to shop and use services elsewhere.

In deprived communities, it can be difficult for people to overcome exclusion and to take steps to engage more fully in society. Social networks may be weak; this reduces the circulation of information about jobs, political activities and community events. High unemployment and low-income levels place strains on family life; crime and juvenile delinquency undermine the overall quality of life in the neighbourhood. Low-demand housing areas often experience high household turnover rates as many residents seek to move on to more desirable housing, while new, disadvantaged entrants to the housing market continue to arrive.

Rural areas

Although much attention is paid to social exclusion in urban settings, people living in rural regions can also experience exclusion. Some social workers and caregivers see that the challenges of exclusion in the countryside are as large, if not larger, than those in cities. In small villages and sparsely populated areas, access to goods, services and facilities is not as extensive as in more settled areas. In most industrial societies, proximity to basic services such as doctors,

Run-down housing estates can be sites of intense social exclusion, where many factors combine to prevent full social participation.

schools and government services is considered a necessity for leading an active, full and healthy life. But rural residents often have limited access to such services and are dependent on the facilities available within their local community.

Access to transport is one of the biggest factors affecting rural exclusion. If a household owns or has access to a car, it is easier to remain integrated in society. For example, family members can consider taking jobs in other towns, periodic shopping trips can be arranged to areas that have a larger selection of shops, visits to friends or family in other areas can be organized more readily, and young people can be fetched home from parties. People who do not have access to their own transport, however, are dependent on public transport, and in country areas such services are limited in scope. Some villages might be serviced by a bus only a few times a day or week, with reduced schedules on weekends and holidays, and nothing at all later in the evening.

Homelessness

Homelessness is one of the most extreme forms of exclusion. People lacking a permanent residence may be shut out of many of the everyday activities that others take for granted, such as going to work, keeping a bank account, entertaining friends and even getting letters in the post.

Most homeless people are in some form of temporary accommodation, although there are still many who sleep rough on the street. Some homeless people deliberately choose to roam the streets, sleeping rough, free from the constraints of property and possessions. But the large majority have no such wish at all; they have been pushed over

Homelessness is one of the most complicated and often extreme forms of social exclusion.

the edge into homelessness by factors beyond their control. Once they find themselves without a permanent dwelling, their lives sometimes deteriorate into a spiral of hardship and deprivation.

Who sleeps on the streets in Britain? The answer is very complicated. For example, from the 1960s onwards, people with mental health problems and learning difficulties were discharged from institutions as a result of changes in healthcare policy. Before that, these people would have spent years in what used to be called long-stay psychiatric or mental sub-normality hospitals. This process of deinstitutionalization was prompted by several factors. One was the desire of the government to save money – the cost of residential care in mental health institutions is high. Another, more praiseworthy motive was the belief on the part of leaders of the psychiatric profession that long-term hospitalization often

did more harm than good. Anyone who could be cared for on an outpatient basis therefore should be. The results have not borne out the hopes of those who saw deinstitutionalization as a positive step. Some hospitals discharged people who had nowhere to go and who perhaps had not lived in the outside world for years. Often, little concrete provision for proper outpatient care was in fact made (Social Exclusion Unit 1998a).

Surveys consistently show that about a quarter of people who sleep rough have spent time in mental health institutions, or have had a diagnosis of mental illness. Hence changes in relevant healthcare policy are likely to have a disproportionate effect on the incidence of homelessness. Most people who are homeless, however, have not suffered mental health problems; nor are they alcoholics or regular consumers of illegal drugs. They are people who find themselves on the streets because they have experienced personal disasters, often several at a time. Becoming homeless is rarely the outcome of a direct 'cause–effect' sequence. A number of misfortunes may occur in quick succession, resulting in a powerful downward spiral. A woman may get divorced, for instance, and at the same time lose not only her home but also her job. A young person may have trouble at home and make for the big city without any means of support. Research has indicated that those who are most vulnerable to homelessness are people from lower working-class backgrounds who have no specific job skills and very low incomes. Long-term joblessness is a major indicator. Family and relationship breakdowns also appear to be key influences.

Although the vast majority of people who are homeless manage to sleep in shelters or receive temporary accommodation, those who find themselves sleeping rough are often in danger. Research by the Institute for Public Policy Research (IPPR) into homelessness and street crime in London, Glasgow and Swansea provides the first indication of the extent of victimization suffered by homeless people on the streets. The British Crime Survey, the leading statistical indicator of crime in Britain, does not include homeless people among its respondents. In *Unsafe Streets* (1999), the IPPR revealed that four out of five rough sleepers have been the victims of crime at least once. Almost half of them have been assaulted, yet only one-fifth chose to report the crimes to the police. The picture that emerges is one of homeless people who are victims of high levels of violence on the streets, but who are also excluded from the systems of legal and police protection that might possibly offer some assistance.

Although making homelessness a top priority has been universally praised, there is little consensus on how to get people off the streets into permanent housing and to lead more stable lives. Advocates for homeless people agree that a more long-term approach – including counselling, media-tion services, job training and befriending schemes – is needed. Yet, in the meantime, many charity groups are loath to suspend short-term measures such as delivering soup, sleeping bags and warm clothing to homeless people on the streets. The issue is a controversial one. In trying to shift attention towards the need for permanent solutions, the government's 'homelessness tsar' Louise Casey remarked that 'well-meaning people are spending money servicing the problem on the streets and keeping it there' (quoted in Gillan 1999). Many housing action groups agree. Yet charity and outreach groups such as the Salvation Army take a different approach: as long as there are people living on the streets, they will continue to go to them and offer what assistance they can.

Even though it is not the whole answer, most sociologists who have studied the issue agree that the provision of more adequate forms of housing is of key importance in tackling the multiple problems faced by homeless people, whether the housing is directly sponsored by the government or not. As Christopher Jencks concluded in *The Homeless* (1994): 'Regardless of why people are on the streets, giving them a place to live that offers a modicum of privacy and stability is usually the most important thing we can do to improve their lives. Without stable housing, nothing else is likely to work.'

Others disagree, stressing that homelessness is only 20 per cent about 'bricks and mortar' and 80 per cent about social work and outreach to counter the effects of family breakdown, violence and abuse, drug and alcohol addictions and depression. Mike, a homeless man in his late 50s, concurs: 'I think that for most people the situation is much more complicated than it seems. Often the problem is about their own belief in themselves, their self-worth. A lot of people on the street have low self-esteem. They do not believe they can do anything better' (quoted in Bamforth 1999).

Crime and social exclusion

Some sociologists have argued that in many industrialized societies, there are strong links between crime and social exclusion. There is a trend in modern societies, they argue, away from inclusive goals (based on citizenship rights) and towards arrangements that accept and even promote the exclusion of some citizens (Young 1998, 1999). Crime rates may be reflecting the fact that a growing number of people do not feel valued by – or feel they have an investment in – the societies in which they live.

The American sociologist, Elliott Currie, investigated the connections between social exclusion and crime in the United States, particularly among young people. Currie (1998) argues that in American society, young people are increasingly growing up on their own without the guidance and support they need from the adult population. Faced by the seductive lure of the market and consumer goods, young people are also confronted by diminishing opportunities in the labour market to sustain a livelihood. In fact, the economic restructuring identified by Hutton and Wilson above has led to feelings of a profound sense of relative deprivation amongst young people, and a willingness to turn to illegitimate means of sustaining a desired lifestyle. The standards of economic status and consumption that are promoted within society cannot be met through legitimate means by the socially excluded population. According to Currie, who echoes Merton's earlier ideas about 'strain' (see chapter 21, 'Crime and Deviance'), one of the most troublesome dimensions to this connection between social exclusion and crime is that legitimate channels for change are bypassed in favour of illegal ones. Crime is favoured over alternative means (Currie 1998).

In a more recent ethnographic study of a deprived community in the North of England, Robert McAuley (2006) investigated the links between social exclusion and crime amongst young people. McAuley argues that the dominant explanation for persistent youth crime is that some communities are 'intolerant of work'; that is, many arguments suggest that a growing underclass – or the experience of social exclusion – gives rise to poor communities in which many people are turning to crime to get what they want. However, most of the young people McAuley spoke to still valued work, but felt abandoned by the rest of society and 'victimized' both at school and when applying for jobs, because of the stigma attached to the place in which they lived. McAuley argues that, as Britain's industrial base contracted, service industries provided the main work, and Britain, like many other developed societies, became a consumer society. In fact, says McAuley, it is consumer societies rather than the urban poor that have devalued work, because consumerism promotes the acquisition of material goods rather than a work ethic.

Britain's consumer society defines itself in opposition to the poor estates, whose young people are labelled anti-social and susceptible to crime. These labels follow young people into school and the labour market, thus helping to produce the cheap source of labour on which consumerism depends. Ironically, consumer culture then also uses images of urban gangs and gangsters to sell its global commodities. What McAuley's research points to are some of the consequences for young people growing up in

---

THINKING CRITICALLY

What are the main differences between social exclusion at the 'bottom' and at the 'top' of society? What could or should governments do to deal with the problems created by elite forms of social exclusion? Should governments concentrate on tackling social exclusion at the bottom rather than the top of society?

USING YOUR SOCIOLOGICAL IMAGINATION

12.1 Social exclusion at the top?

The examples of exclusion that we have considered thus far all concern individuals or groups who, for whatever reason, are unable to participate fully in institutions and activities used by the majority of the population. Yet not all cases of exclusion occur among those who are disadvantaged at the bottom of society. In recent years, new dynamics of 'social exclusion at the top' have been emerging. By this, it is meant that a minority of individuals at the very top of society can 'opt out' of participation in mainstream institutions by merit of their affluence, influence and connections.

Such elite exclusion at the top of society can take a number of forms. The wealthy might retreat fully from the realm of public education and healthcare services, preferring to pay for private services and attention. Affluent residential communities are increasingly closed off from the rest of society – the so-called 'gated communities' located behind tall walls and security checkpoints. Tax payments and financial obligations can be drastically reduced through careful management and the help of private financial planners. Particularly in the United States, active political participation among the elite is often replaced by large donations to political candidates who are seen to represent their interests. In a number of ways, the very wealthy are able to escape from their social and financial responsibilities into a closed, private realm largely separate from the rest of society. Just as social exclusion at the 'bottom' undermines social solidarity and cohesion, exclusion at the 'top' is similarly detrimental to an integrated society.

Elite social exclusion can physically separate the rich from the rest of society.

deprived communities of that 'thirty, thirty, forty' society described by Will Hutton (1995), described above. But for McAuley, it is not just a period of economic restructur-ing, but the affluent consumer society itself which effectively 'socially excludes' the poor.

The welfare state

In most industrialized societies, poverty and social exclusion at the bottom are alleviated to some degree by the **welfare state**. Why is it that welfare states have developed in most industrialized countries? How can we explain the variations in the welfare models favoured by different states? The face of welfare is different from country to country, yet industrial societies have on the whole devoted a large share of their resources to addressing public needs.

Theories of the welfare state

Most industrialized and industrializing countries in the world today are welfare states. By this, it is meant that the state plays a central role in the provision of welfare, which it does through a system that offers services and benefits that meet people's basic needs for things such as healthcare, education, housing and income. An important role of the welfare state involves managing the risks faced by people over the course of their lives: sickness, disability, job loss and old age. The services provided by the welfare state and the levels of spending on it vary from country to country. Some have highly developed welfare systems and devote a large proportion of the national budget to them. In Sweden, for example, tax revenues in 2005 represented 51.1 per cent of the gross domestic product (GDP), in Belgium, 45.4 per cent and in Austria, 49.7 per cent. By comparison, other industrialized nations take far less in tax. In the UK, tax revenues are 37.2 per cent of GDP, in Germany, 34.7 per cent and in the USA, just 26.8 per cent (OECD 2006). In this chapter, we have focused on the role of the welfare state in alleviating poverty. However, the role of the welfare state in providing these services and benefits is discussed throughout the book. Chapter 8 looks at the welfare state and the provision of services and benefits for older people, chapter 10 looks at the welfare state and the provision of healthcare and chapter 19 looks at the role of the welfare state in providing education.

Many theories have been advanced to explain the evolution of the welfare state. Marxists have seen welfare as necessary for sustaining a capitalist system, while functionalist theorists held that welfare systems helped to integrate society in an orderly way under the conditions of advanced industrialization. While these and other views have enjoyed support over the years, the writings of the British sociologist T. H. Marshall (1893–1981) and Danish sociologist Gøsta Esping-Andersen have perhaps been the most influential contributions to theories of the welfare state. Marshall's influential arguments are outlined in 'Classic Studies 12.2', and you should look at this before moving on to later arguments about welfare and citizenship.

Gøsta Esping-Andersen: three worlds of welfare

Gøsta Esping-Andersen's *The Three Worlds of Welfare Capitalism* (1990) brings a comparative perspective to the earlier theories of the welfare state. In doing this, Esping-Andersen can be seen to have taken seriously the criticism levelled at Marshall's general evolutionary perspective, namely that different national societies followed different paths towards citizenship rights and, accordingly, created different 'welfare regimes'. In this important work, Esping-Andersen compares Western welfare systems and presents a three-part typology of their welfare regimes.

In constructing this typology, Esping-Andersen evaluated the level of welfare **decommodification** – a term which simply means the degree to which welfare services are free from the market. In a system with high decommodification, welfare is provided publicly and is not in any way linked to one's income or economic resources. In a commodified system, welfare services are treated more like commodities – that is, they are sold on the market like any other good or service. By

Classic Studies 12.2 T. H. Marshall and the evolution of citizenship in Britain

The research problem

You may have been described as a 'citizen' of a particular country, implying a certain 'belonging' to it. But when did the idea of 'citizenship' emerge and how did it develop? What exactly *is* citizenship anyway, and what rights and responsibilities does it confer on citizens? How is citizenship related to the state's provision of welfare? One important theorist who tackled these questions is Thomas Humphrey Marshall, whose ideas have been very influential in shaping debates on welfare and citizenship rights. Writing from the late 1940s, Marshall saw citizenship as emerging alongside industrialization as a fundamental feature of modern society.

Marshall's explanation

Taking an historical approach, Marshall (1973) traced what he described as the 'evolution' of citizenship in Britain (specifically England) and identified three key stages, each one expanding the meaning of 'citizenship'. The eighteenth century, according to Marshall, was the time when *civil rights* were obtained. These included important personal liberties such as freedom of speech, thought and religion, the right to own property, and the right to fair legal treatment. Building on these rights, in the nineteenth century, *political rights* were gained. These included the right to vote, to hold office and to participate in the political process. The third set of rights – *social rights* – were obtained in the twentieth century. These include the right of citizens to economic and social security through education, healthcare, housing, pensions and other services, all of which became enshrined in the welfare state. The incorporation of social rights into the notion of citizenship meant that everyone was entitled to live a full and active life and had a right to a reasonable income, regardless of their position in society. In this respect, the rights associated with social citizenship greatly advanced the ideal of equality for all, and Marshall's account is often described as an optimistic one, seeing a growing range of rights for all citizens.

Critical points

One immediate problem with Marshall's explanation is that it is based on a single case-study – Britain – and critics have shown that his evolutionary approach cannot be applied to other national cases such as Sweden, France or Germany (Turner 1990). Marshall's 'evolutionary' explanation is also not entirely clear. Is it really just a description of *how* citizenship actually developed in Britain, rather than a causal explanation of *why* it did so? Critics argue that Marshall tends to *assume* the progressive development of types of rights but does not explain the links between them or how, say, civil rights lead inevitably to political and then to social rights.

In more recent times, critics have argued that the awareness of globalization makes Marshall's theory– which is based on the influence of the nation-state – rather outdated, as it seems to assume that citizenship develops from the internal dynamics of national societies. Today, however, sociologists are much more sensitive to the relationships and influences between and across the world's societies. Finally – as we will see later in the chapter – Marshall's evolutionism is severely challenged by the crisis of 'welfarism' from the 1970s and the attempt to 'roll back' levels of welfare provision in many developed societies, a development which does not appear to fit his historical thesis.

Contemporary significance

Marshall's views influenced debates about the nature of citizenship and, in recent years, informed political questions and academic research on social inclusion and exclusion. His central idea that rights and responsibilities are tightly intertwined with the notion of citizenship is enjoying renewed popularity in discussions about how to promote an 'active citizenship'. And although his explanation is certainly too state-centred to be entirely satisfactory in a globalizing age, the notion of an evolving expansion of citizenship rights and responsibilities continues to inform our understanding of what citizenship is. For example, a relatively new type of citizenship now seems to be emerging – environmental or ecological – based on the rights and responsibilities of people towards the natural environment (Smith 1998; Dobson and Bell 2006). Hence, despite its flaws, Marshall's general approach may have a little more life left yet.

 The concept of environmental citizenship is discussed in more detail in chapter 5, 'The Environment'.

comparing policies on pensions, unemployment and income support among countries, Esping-Andersen identified the following three types of welfare regime:

1 *Social democratic* Social democratic welfare regimes are highly decommodified. Welfare services are subsidized by the state and available to all citizens (universal benefits). Most Scandinavian states such as Sweden and Norway are examples of social democratic welfare regimes.

2 *Conservative-corporatist* In conservative-corporatist states, such as France and Germany, welfare services may be highly decommodified, but they are not necessarily universal. The amount of benefits to which a citizen is entitled depends on their position in society. This type of welfare regime may not be aimed at eliminating inequalities, but at maintaining social stability, strong families and loyalty to the state.

3 *Liberal* The United States is the best example of a liberal welfare regime. Welfare is highly commodified and sold through the market. **Means-tested benefits** are available to the very needy, but become highly stigmatized. This is because the majority of the population is expected to purchase its own welfare through the market.

The United Kingdom does not fall cleanly into any of these three 'ideal types'. Formerly, it was closer to a social democratic model, but welfare reforms since the 1970s have brought it much closer to a liberal welfare regime with higher levels of commodification, which seem set to continue. This shift from one model to another makes the UK an interesting case study.

The welfare state in the UK

One of the main differences between welfare models is the availability of benefits to the population. In systems that provide universal benefits, welfare is a right to be enjoyed equally by all, regardless of economic status. An example of this in the UK is the provision of child benefit, which goes to the parents or guardians of children under the age of 16 regardless of their income or savings. Welfare systems predicated on universal benefits are designed to ensure that all citizens' basic welfare needs are met on an ongoing basis. The Swedish system has a higher proportion of universal benefits than that of the UK, which depends more on means-tested benefits. 'Means-testing' refers to an administrative process by which the state assesses the actual income (or resources) of an applicant for welfare against its standardized rate, and, if there is a shortfall, makes up the difference as a social security benefit, or provides the service. Examples of means-tested benefits in the UK are income support, housing benefit and working tax credit. Examples of means-tested services are those provided by local authority social services departments as part of packages of care for older people who are living in care homes or in other accommodation within the community.

This distinction between universal and means-tested benefits is expressed at a policy level in two contrasting approaches to welfare. Supporters of an institutional view of welfare argue that access to welfare services should be provided as a right for everyone. Those taking a residualist view argue that welfare should only be available to members of society who truly need help and are unable to meet their own welfare needs.

The debate between those who support an institutional view of welfare and those who support a residualist view is often presented as a dispute about taxation. Welfare services have to be funded through tax. Advocates of the 'safety-net welfare state' approach stress that only the most in need – to be demonstrated through means-testing – should be the recipients of welfare benefits. Supporters of a residual view of welfare see the welfare state as expensive, ineffective and too bureaucratic. On the other hand, some feel that tax levels should be high, because the welfare state needs to be well funded. They argue that the welfare state must be maintained and even expanded in order that the harsh polarizing effects of the market are limited, even though this means a large tax burden. They claim that it is the responsibility of any civilized state to provide for and protect its citizens.

This difference of opinion over institutional and residual welfare models is at the heart of current debates over welfare reform. In all industrialized countries, the future of the welfare state is under intense examination. As the face of society changes – through globalization, migration, changes in the family and work, and other fundamental shifts – the nature of welfare must also change. We will briefly trace the history of the welfare state in Britain and recent attempts to reform it.

The formation of the British welfare state

The welfare state in Britain was created during the twentieth century, yet its roots stretch back to the Poor Laws of 1601 and the dissolution of the monasteries. The monasteries had provided for the poor; without this provision, abject poverty and a near complete absence of care for the sick resulted, which led to the creation of the Poor Laws. With the development of industrial capitalism and the transition from an agricultural to an industrial society, traditional forms of informal support within families and communities began to break down. In order to maintain social order and reduce the new inequalities brought about by capitalism, it was necessary to offer assistance to those members of society who found themselves on the periphery of the market economy. This resulted in 1834 in the Poor Law Amendment Act. Under this Act, workhouses were built, offering a lower standard of living than anything available outside. The idea was that the living conditions in the poorhouses would make people do all they could to avoid poverty. With time, as part of the process of nation-building, the state came to play a more central role in administering to the needy. Legislation which established the national administration of education and public health in the late 1800s was a precursor of the more extensive programmes which would come into being in the twentieth century.

The welfare state expanded further under the pre-First World War Liberal government, which introduced, amongst other policies, pensions, health and unemployment insurance. The years following the Second World War witnessed a further powerful drive for the reform and expansion of the welfare system. Rather than concentrating solely on the destitute and ill, the focus of welfare was broadened to include all members of society. The war had been an intense and traumatic experience for the entire nation – rich and poor. It produced a sense of solidarity and the realization that misfortune and tragedy were not restricted to the disadvantaged alone.

This shift from a selective to a universalist vision of welfare was encapsulated in the Beveridge Report of 1942, often regarded as the blueprint for the modern welfare state. The Beveridge Report was aimed at eradicating the five great evils: Want, Disease,

Ignorance, Squalor and Idleness. A series of legislative measures under the post-war Labour government began to translate this vision into concrete action. Several main acts lay at the core of the new universalist welfare state. The wartime National government had already introduced the Education Act in 1944, which tackled lack of schooling, while the 1946 National Health Act was concerned with improving the quality of health among the population. 'Want' was addressed through the 1946 National Insurance Act, which set up a scheme to protect against loss of earnings due to unemployment, ill health, retirement or widowhood. The 1948 National Assistance Act provided means-tested support for those who were not covered under the National Insurance Act, and finally abolished the old Poor Laws. Other legislation addressed the needs of families (1945 Family Allowances Act) and the demand for improved housing conditions (1946 New Towns Act).

The British welfare state came into being under a set of specific conditions and alongside certain prevailing notions about the nature of society. The premises on which the welfare state was built were threefold. First, it equated work with paid labour and was grounded in a belief in the possibility of full employment. The ultimate goal was a society in which paid work played a central role for most people, but where welfare would meet the needs of those who were located outside the market economy through the mischance of unemployment or disability. Connected to this, the vision for the welfare state was predicated on a patriarchal conception of families – the male breadwinner was to support the family, while his wife tended to the home. Welfare programmes were designed around this traditional family model, with a second tier of services aimed at those families in which a male breadwinner was absent.

Second, the welfare state was seen as promoting national solidarity. It would integrate the nation by involving the entire population in a common set of services. Welfare was a way of strengthening the connection between the state and the population. Third, the welfare state was concerned with managing risks that occurred as a natural part of the life-course. In this sense, welfare was viewed as a type of insurance that could be employed against the potential troubles of an unpredictable future. Unemployment, illness and other misfortunes in the country's social and economic life could be managed through the welfare state.

These principles underpinned the enormous expansion of the welfare state in the three decades following the war. As the manufacturing economy grew, the welfare state represented a successful class 'bargain' that met the needs of the working class as well as those of the economic elite who depended on a healthy, high-performing workforce. But by the 1970s the splintering of political opinion into institutional and residualist welfare camps became increasingly pronounced. In the 1990s both the left and the right acknowledged that the Beveridge vision for welfare was outmoded and in need of significant reform.

Reforming the welfare state: the 1980s

The political consensus on welfare broke down in the 1980s when the administrations of Margaret Thatcher in the UK and Ronald Reagan in the USA attempted to 'roll back' the welfare state. Several main criticisms were at the heart of attempts to reduce welfare. The first concerned mounting financial costs. General economic recession, growing unemployment and the emergence of enormous welfare bureaucracies meant that expenditure continued to increase steadily – and at a rate greater than that of overall economic expansion. A debate over welfare spending ensued, with advocates of a 'roll-back' pointing to the ballooning financial pressure on the welfare system. Policy-makers emphasized the potentially overwhelming impact of the 'demographic time bomb' on the welfare system: the number of people dependent on welfare services was growing as the population aged, yet the number of young people of working age paying into the system was declining. This signalled a potential financial crisis.

> The 'greying' of the global population is discussed in chapter 8, 'The Life-Course'.

A second line of criticism was related to the notion of *welfare dependency*. Critics of existing welfare institutions argued that people become dependent on the very programmes that are supposed to allow them to forge an independent and meaningful life. They become not just materially dependent, but psychologically dependent on the arrival of the welfare payment. Instead of taking an active attitude towards their lives, they tend to adopt a resigned and passive one, looking to the welfare system to support them.

The UK Conservative government implemented a number of welfare reforms that began to shift responsibility for public welfare away from the state and towards the private sector, the voluntary sector and local communities. Services, which were formerly provided by the state at highly subsidized rates, were privatized or made subject to more stringent means-testing. One example of this can be seen in the privatization of council housing in the 1980s. The 1980 Housing Act allowed rents for council housing to be raised significantly, laying the groundwork for a large-scale sell-off of council housing stock. This move towards residualism in housing provision was particularly harmful to those located just above the means-tested eligibility line for housing benefit, as they could no longer get access to public housing, but could ill-afford to rent accommodation at market rates. Critics argue that the privatization of council housing contributed significantly to the growth of homelessness in the 1980s and 1990s.

Another attempt to reduce welfare expenditure and increase its efficiency came through the introduction of market principles in the provision of public services. The Conservative government argued that injecting a degree of competition into welfare services such as healthcare and education would provide the public with greater choice and ensure high-quality service. Consumers could, in effect, 'vote with their feet' by choosing among schools or healthcare providers. Institutions providing substandard services would be obliged to improve or be forced to close down, just like a business. This is because funding for an institution would be based on the number of students, or patients, who chose to use its services. Critics charged that 'internal markets' within public services would lead to lower-quality services and a stratified system of service provision, rather than protecting the value of equal service for all citizens.

To what extent did the Conservative governments of the 1980s succeed in rolling back the welfare state? In *Dismantling the Welfare State?* (1994), Christopher Pierson compared the process of welfare 'retrenchment' in Britain and the USA and concluded that welfare states emerged from the Conservative era relatively intact. Although both administrations came into office with the express intent of slashing welfare expenditure, Pierson argued that the obstacles to rolling back welfare were ultimately more than either government could overcome. The reason for this lies in the way in which social policy had unfolded over time: since its inception, the welfare state and its institutions had given rise to specific constituencies – such as trade unions and voluntary agencies like the Child Poverty Action Group – which actively defended benefits against political efforts to reduce them.

Pierson saw the welfare state as under severe strain, but rejected the notion that it was 'in crisis'. Social spending stayed fairly constant and all the core components of the welfare state remained in place. While not denying the great rise in inequalities as a result of welfare reform in the 1980s, he points out that social policy on the whole was not reformed to the extent that industrial relations or regulatory policy were.

The theory underlying the policies of Margaret Thatcher's and successive Conservative administrations (1979–97) was that cutting tax rates for individuals and corporations would generate high levels of economic growth, the fruits of which would then 'trickle down' to the poor. Similar policies were implemented in the USA. But the evidence does not support the 'trickle-down' thesis. Such an economic policy may generate an acceleration of economic development, but it also tends to expand the differentials between the poor and the wealthy and increase the numbers living in poverty.

THINKING CRITICALLY

From your reading so far, does a comprehensive welfare state system tend to create a dependency culture? With reference to Esping-Andersen's (1990) three types of welfare regime (discussed above), which countries would you expect to have the highest levels of welfare dependency? What evidence is there that these societies have been damaged by state welfare?

Reforming the welfare state: 1997–2008

Welfare reform was a top priority for the Labour government, which came to office in the UK in 1997. Agreeing in some respects with Conservative critics of welfare (and thus breaking with traditional left politics), Labour argued that new welfare policies were needed to cope with poverty and inequality as well as to improve health and education. It saw the welfare state as often part of the problem, creating dependencies and offering a 'hand-out' instead of a 'hand-up'. Instead, Labour wanted to tackle the roots of poverty, arguing that it was pursuing a Third Way, beyond the politics of the

'old' left and that of the Thatcher government's 'new' right. In doing so – initially at least – Labour drew on some of my own ideas (Giddens 1994, 1998), aimed at modernizing the politics of the left for a global age. These included: the strengthening of civil society; decentralization of power away from the nation-state, which should embrace cultural diversity in all of its policies; a focus on social exclusion rather than inequality; and use of the private sector to add a dynamic element into public service provision to create a 'social investment state'.

Initially rejecting the policies of the old left as outdated in an era of individualism, consumerism and globalization, Labour looked to create a 'new left' political position and programme. For example, the party argued that one of the main difficulties with the welfare system was that the conditions under which it had been created no longer existed: it had happened at a time of full employment when many families could rely on men to work and bring in a 'family wage'. However, changes in family structures had, by the 1990s, rendered such a patriarchal view of the male breadwinner inapplicable. An enormous number of women had entered the workforce and the growth of lone-parent households placed new demands on the welfare state. There has also been a distinct shift in the types of risk that the welfare state needs to contend with. For instance, the welfare state had proved to be an inadequate tool for dealing with the harmful consequences of environmental pollution or lifestyle choices such as smoking.

From the outset, Labour focused on a type of 'positive welfare', involving a new 'welfare contract' between the state and citizens based on both rights *and* responsibilities. It saw the role of the state as helping people into work and thereby a stable income, not just supporting them financially through periods of unemployment. At the same time, it expected citizens to take responsibility for trying to change their own circumstances, rather than waiting for welfare hand-outs.

Employment became one of the cornerstones of Labour's social policy, as it was believed that getting people into work was one of the main steps in reducing poverty. Among the most significant welfare reforms introduced under Labour were so-called 'welfare-to-work' programmes (see 'Using your sociological imagination 12.2').

Women are now much more equal in economic, social and cultural terms than in previous generations and the entry of large numbers of women into higher education and the labour market has meant a growing divide between 'work-rich' households, characterized by dual earners, and 'work-poor' households, in which no one is active in the labour market. Women's earnings have become more integral to household income than they were in earlier times and the impact of their earnings can carry enormous weight. Indeed, the success of dual-earner households, particularly those without children, is one of the most important factors in the shifting pattern of income distribution. The differences between two-earner, one-earner and no-earner households are becoming increasingly apparent.

THINKING CRITICALLY

Is it realistic to expect welfare-to-work programmes to succeed in helping *all* social groups to get employment? Is everyone able to work? Why do you think these programmes fail to help the long-term unemployed to find work? List the obstacles facing those who have been unemployed for more than a year, when they are looking for a job. What can governments do to help remove these obstacles?

As well as the welfare-to-work programmes discussed above, Labour has also used welfare measures to raise the income of those in low-paid jobs. A minimum wage was introduced in 1999 and a commitment was made to reduce child poverty by 25 per cent by 2004–5 and to abolish child poverty by 2020. Recent assessments show that the government has had some success in its aim, with child poverty falling by 600,000 by 2006. However, it has also been noted that even if the ten-year target of halving child poverty by 2010 is met, levels will still be higher than in 1979 when Margaret Thatcher became Prime Minister (Flaherty et al. 2004). In 2006, government figures on Households Below Average Income (HBAI) showed that in spite of optimistic forecasts by many commentators, Labour had failed to achieve its interim target of reducing child poverty by 25 per cent between 1998/9 and 2004/5. Projections based on current policies suggest that far more radical measures will be needed than those in place at the moment if child poverty is to be further reduced in a large-scale way.

Even critics accept that some of Labour's welfare policies have had some successes: helping many young people into work, raising levels of funding for public services and helping people like Lisa (featured at the start of this chapter) get into work. However, Labour's approach to welfare has been more harshly judged. The attempt to make welfare benefits dependent on a commitment actively to seek work or attend interviews has been described as a 'creeping conditionality', which erodes the principle of a citizen's 'entitlement' (Dwyer 2004). Labour's work-focused programmes (and others in some European countries) have been promoted through the language of 'social inclusion', as we saw above. However, it is not clear how exclusion relates to underlying problems of social *inequality*, which, historically, have formed the basis of Labour's policy programmes when in government.

In *The Inclusive Society*, Ruth Levitas (2005) studied three main discourses, or ways of discussing and framing welfare policy, used by Labour since 1997. First,

12.2   Evaluating welfare-to-work programmes

Since 1997, the Labour government has put forward a number of policies and targets to move people from welfare into work. 'New Deal' programmes have been set up for certain groups such as the disabled, the long-term unemployed, young people and those aged over 50.

Similar programmes have existed for some time in the United States, and there has been some opportunity to study their implications. Daniel Friedlander and Gary Burtless (1994) studied four different US government-initiated programmes designed to encourage welfare recipients to find paid work. The programmes were roughly similar: they provided financial benefits for welfare recipients who actively searched for jobs, as well as guidance in job-hunting techniques and opportunities for education and training. The target populations were mainly single-parent heads of households who were recipients of Aid to Families with Dependent Children, the largest cash welfare programme in the country. Friedlander and Burtless found that the programmes did achieve results. People involved in them were able either to enter employment or to start working sooner than others who did not participate. In all four programmes, the earnings produced were several times greater than the net cost of the programme. They were least effective, however, in helping those who needed them the most – those who had been out of work for a lengthy period, the long-term unemployed.

Although welfare-to-work programmes have succeeded in reducing American welfare claims by approximately 40 per cent, some statistics suggest that the outcomes are not wholly positive. In the USA, approximately 20 per cent of those who cease to receive welfare do not work and have no source of independent income; nearly one-third who do get jobs return to claim welfare again within a year. Between a third and a half of welfare leavers who are in work find that their incomes are less than their previous benefit levels.

In Wisconsin, the US state which was one of the first to introduce welfare-to-work programmes, two-thirds of welfare leavers live below the poverty line (Evans 2000). Pointing to such findings, critics argue that the apparent success of welfare-to-work initiatives in reducing the absolute number of welfare cases conceals some troublesome patterns in the actual experiences of those who lose their welfare.

Others question the effectiveness of local empowerment 'zones' for combating social exclusion. They argue that poverty and deprivation are not concentrated in those designated areas alone, yet the programmes are targeted as if all the poor live together. In the UK, the findings of the government's own Social Exclusion Unit back this claim: in 1997, when Labour came to power, two-thirds of all unemployed people lived in areas outside the 44 most deprived boroughs of the country. Localized initiatives, sceptics point out, cannot replace a nation-wide anti-poverty strategy, because too many people fall outside the boundaries of the designated empowerment zones.

Labour adopted a *redistributionist* discourse, which viewed social exclusion as a *consequence*, not a cause of poverty and social inequalities. Second, she identified a *moral* discourse on the underclass (as we saw in the discussion of Charles Murray earlier in the chapter). This discourse tends to blame those who are socially excluded, seeing them as responsible for their own situation and, sometimes, as a separate social group with specific characteristics. Third, Levitas notes a

social integrationist discourse that ties social exclusion and inclusion firmly to employment, encouraging labour market participation as a solution to social exclusion.

The main issue for Levitas is that Labour discourse and policy has drifted away from the Labour Party's historically dominant, redistributionist approach to welfare. On this account, Labour's welfare policy has become little different from that of the previous Conservative approach with its

The drug-taking antics of celebrities are often a source of entertainment in the media, while the negative aspects of addiction are associated with the poor and socially excluded.

focus on making those at the bottom of society's hierarchy responsible for their own position and for getting out of it. The problem is that this has separated social exclusion from social inequality and concentrates on the divide between the excluded and the included rather than that between rich and poor, allowing the rich successfully to evade their own responsibilities to the wider society. Susan MacGregor, for example, argues that Labour has, in practice, dealt mainly with the unacceptable behaviour of the poor – separating out the 'deserving' from the 'undeserving' unemployed and the genuine 'asylum seeker' from the 'economic migrant' and so on. She argues that, 'This concentrates on the bad behaviours among the poor, ignoring the drug taking, infidelities, frauds and

deceptions and other human frailties found among the rich, the better off and the not-quite-poor' (2003: 72).

Finally, despite opposing the Conservatives' privatization of railways and other public sector enterprises while in opposition, Labour has not reversed any of them (with the partial exception of Railtrack, which owns tracks but not the trains themselves). Indeed, in government, Labour has relied heavily on market mechanisms, particularly in the partnerships between public and private sectors, in order to raise the level of investment in public services such as the National Health Service without having to resort to raising tax rates.

Poverty and welfare in a changing world

Changes in the occupational structure and the global economy have contributed to the trend towards inequality in Britain, the United States and elsewhere. A decline in the manual workforce had an important effect both on patterns of income distribution and on unemployment. It is often the case that workers in unskilled or semi-skilled jobs have found it difficult to re-enter a rapidly changing labour market where educational qualifications and technological competence are in increasing demand. Although there has been a marked expansion of opportunities in the service sector, much of this has been for positions that are low-paid and with little prospect for advancement.

In the twenty-first century, welfare debates are not simply about material prosperity, but about the overall well-being of the population. Social policy is concerned with promoting social cohesion, fostering networks of interdependence and maximizing people's abilities to help themselves. Rights and responsibilities are taking on new importance – not only for those at the bottom attempting to move off welfare and into work, but also for those at the top whose wealth should not entitle them to evade civic, social and tax obligations. Critics say Labour should have done more to tackle spiralling inequalities at the top. This issue is not as distant from attempts to reduce poverty as it may seem at first sight. For if the rich paid higher levels of taxation, not only would they be living up to their social responsibilities, but that extra money could be used to help the poor – for example, to make more impact on reducing child poverty than the government has so far been able to achieve. In academic and political debates as well as policy-making, issues surrounding social exclusion and inclusion, poverty and wealth creation and material provision and well-being look likely to be the key dilemmas for the next few decades.

Summary points

1. There have been two ways of understanding poverty. Absolute poverty refers to a lack of basic resources needed to maintain health and bodily functioning; relative poverty involves assessing the gaps between the living conditions of some groups and those enjoyed by the majority of a population.

2. Many countries have an official measurement of poverty: a poverty line. This is a level below which people are said to live in poverty. Subjective measurements of poverty are based on people's own understandings of what is needed for an acceptable standard of living.

3. Poverty remains widespread in the wealthy countries. In the 1980s and '90s Britain had one of the worst poverty records in the developed world. Inequalities between the rich and poor widened dramatically as a result of government policies, the transformation of the occupational structure and large-scale unemployment. The poor comprise a diverse group, but individuals who are disadvantaged or discriminated against in other aspects of life have an increased risk of being poor.

4. Two main approaches have been taken to explain poverty. The 'culture of poverty' and 'dependency culture' arguments claim that the poor are responsible for their own situation. The second approach argues that poverty results from larger social processes, which are both reinforced and influenced by the actions of individuals.

5. Social exclusion refers to processes by which individuals may become cut off from full involvement in the wider society. Social exclusion is a wider term than poverty, and includes a lack of resources and income and exclusion from the labour market, services and social relations. Homelessness is one of the most extreme forms of social exclusion. Homeless people lacking a permanent residence may be shut out of many everyday activities which most people take for granted.

6. Welfare states are those in which government plays a central role in reducing inequalities through the provision or subsidizing of certain goods and services. Welfare services vary across countries but often include education, healthcare, housing, income support, disability, unemployment and pensions. The future of welfare provision is being debated in most industrialized countries. On one side are those who think welfare should be well funded and universal; on the other are people who say it should be just a safety net for those who truly cannot get help in any other way.

7. The British welfare state developed in the twentieth century, undergoing periods of expansion during the pre-First World War and post-Second World War periods. It leant towards a broad vision of welfare that included all members of society. By the 1970s, the welfare state was criticized as being ineffective, bureaucratic and too expensive, and concerns were expressed that welfare dependency was preventing people from leading independent lives.

8. Margaret Thatcher's Conservative government sought to roll back the welfare state, shifting responsibility for welfare away from the state and onto the private sector, voluntary sector and local communities. Deinstitutionalization is the process by which individuals cared for by the state (in institutions) are returned to their families and communities.

9. Tony Blair's Labour government carried out a raft of measures for reforming welfare, including welfare-to-work programmes aimed at moving welfare recipients into paid jobs and reducing child poverty.

Further reading

For an introduction to issues of poverty and social exclusion, Pete Alcock's *Understanding Poverty*, 3rd edn (Basingstoke: Palgrave Macmillan, 2006) is very well written, up-to-date and reliable. Ruth Lister's *Poverty* (Cambridge: Polity, 2004) covers all the basics as well as a discussion of social exclusion and inclusion.

The concept of social exclusion can then be further explored in John Hills, David Piachaud and Julian Le-Grand's edited volume, *Understanding Social Exclusion* (Buckingham: Open University Press, 2002), while the practical role that social workers and professionals can play in promoting social inclusion is outlined in John Pierson's *Tackling Social Exclusion* (London: Routledge, 2001).

For a very reliable and widely used account of the development of welfare in Britain, see Derek Fraser's *The Evolution of the British Welfare State*, 3rd rev. edn (Basingstoke: Palgrave Macmillan, 2002). Jet Bussemaker's edited collection of essays in *Citizenship and Welfare State Reform in Europe* (London: Routledge, 1999) is not an easy read, but is useful for those looking for a more comparative European perspective.

Finally, for the more adventurous, a series of analyses of the British Poverty and Social Exclusion (PSE) survey can be found in David Gordon, Ruth Levitas and Christina Pantazis's edited volume, *Poverty and Social Exclusion in Britain: The Millennium Survey* (Bristol: The Policy Press, 2006).

Internet links

Townsend Centre for International Poverty Research based at Bristol University, UK:
www.bristol.ac.uk/poverty/index.html

OECD site for Social and Welfare Issues:
www.oecd.org/topic/0,3373,en_2649_37419_1_1_1_1_37419,00.html

The World Bank's PovertyNet site:
http://go.worldbank.org/33CTPSVDC0

The Poverty Site – UK-based site covering the UK and Europe:
www.poverty.org.uk/intro/index.htm

The Child Poverty Action Group, UK:
www.cpag.org.uk/

UK Social Exclusion Task Force (replaced the Social Exclusion Unit):
www.cabinetoffice.gov.uk/social_exclusion_task_force/

The Social Market Foundation – UK think-tank on state-market relations:
www.smf.co.uk/

13

Global Inequality

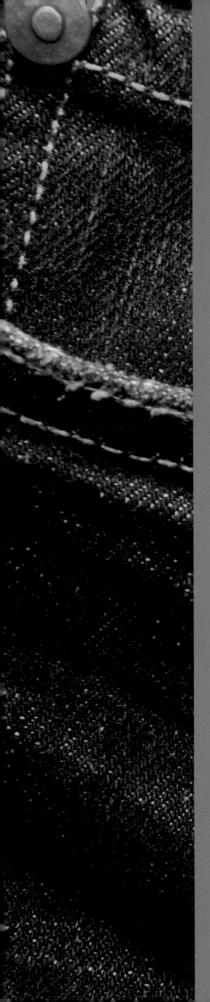

CHAPTER 13

Global Inequality

Bill Gates numbers amongst the world's wealthiest individuals. He is trustee of one of the largest charitable foundations in the world, but his personal wealth still means he is richer than about two thirds of countries.

The past 30 years have seen the creation of more billionaires than ever before in history (a billionaire is defined as someone with wealth of *at least* a thousand million US$). At the start of the twenty-first century there were some 573 billionaires worldwide – 308 in the United States, 114 in Europe, 88 in Asia, 32 in Latin America, 15 in Canada, 13 in the Middle East, and 3 in Australia (Forbes 2000). Their combined assets in mid-2000 were estimated at US$1.1 trillion – greater than the total gross national products of 87 countries representing more than a third of the global world population (calculated from World Bank 2000–1).

In May 2008, Bill Gates, founder of Microsoft Corporation, was finally displaced as the world's wealthiest individual after holding that status for

13 consecutive years. Warren Buffett, an American investor and businessman, was heralded as the world's richest person, with a net personal worth of US$62 billion, primarily based on his stock holding in Berkshire Hathaway, a US-based insurance conglomerate (see table 13.1). Gates's fortune, some US$58 billion, is based largely on ownership of Microsoft's stock and he seems to personify the entrepreneurial spirit: a computer nerd turned capitalist, whose software provides the operating system for the vast majority of personal computers worldwide. During the late 1990s, Gates had a net worth of around US$100 billion, but after reaching this peak, the value of Microsoft's stock began to decline, leaving his personal fortune greatly reduced. Nevertheless, he remains one of the wealthiest individuals in the world and his personal fortune dwarfs that of other well-known entrepreneurs like Richard Branson (Virgin Group) and Roman Abramovich (Russian oil industry).

Among the world's top forty richest individuals and families in 2007 were 16 from North America, 13 from Europe, 5 from the Middle East, 3 from Hong Kong, 2 from India and 1 from Mexico (*Sunday Times* 2007). If Bill Gates typifies the Western, high-tech entrepreneur, then Hong Kong's Li Ka-shing – number 11 on the 2008 list – is the hero in a rags-to-riches story that characterizes the success of many Asian businessmen. Li began his career by making plastic flowers, but by 2007 his US$26.5

Table 13.1 **Twenty richest individuals and families in the world, 2008**

Rank	Name	Citizenship	Age	Net Worth ($bil)	Residence
1	Warren Buffett	United States	77	62.0	United States
2	Carlos Slim Helu & family	Mexico	68	60.0	Mexico
3	William Gates III	United States	52	58.0	United States
4	Lakshmi Mittal	India	57	45.0	United Kingdom
5	Mukesh Ambani	India	50	43.0	India
6	Anil Ambani	India	48	42.0	India
7	Ingvar Kamprad & family	Sweden	81	31.0	Switzerland
8	KP Singh	India	76	30.0	India
9	Oleg Deripaska	Russia	40	28.0	Russia
10	Karl Albrecht	Germany	88	27.0	Germany
11	Li Ka-shing	Hong Kong	79	26.5	Hong Kong
12	Sheldon Adelson	United States	74	26.0	United States
13	Bernard Arnault	France	59	25.5	France
14	Lawrence Ellison	United States	63	25.0	United States
15	Roman Abramovich	Russia	41	23.5	Russia
16	Theo Albrecht	Germany	85	23.0	Germany
17	Liliane Bettencourt	France	85	22.9	France
18	Alexei Mordashov	Russia	42	21.2	Russia
19	Prince Alwaleed Bin Talal Alsaud	Saudi Arabia	51	21.0	Saudi Arabia
20	Mikhail Fridman	Russia	43	20.8	Russia

Source: Forbes Magazine, 'The World's Billionaires', 3 May 2008

billion in personal wealth derived from a wide range of real estate and other investments throughout Asia, including family ownership of STAR TV, a television-transmission satellite whose broadcasts reach half the world.

How have a few individuals and families been able to accumulate such enormous wealth? One reason is that globalization – the increased economic, political, social and cultural interconnectedness of the world – has produced many more opportunities in many more parts of the world, which have enabled some people vastly to increase their wealth.

In the UK, the sixth Duke of Westminster, Major-General Gerald Cavendish Grosvenor, represents an older, aristocratic form of wealth acquisition and transmission down through families. But fewer people today are rich because of such inherited wealth. The sixth Duke's fortune of some £7 billion – largely consisting of property in fashionable areas of London – does not even make him the richest person in the UK. That title belongs to Indian-born steel magnate, Lakshmi Mittal, whose £27.7 billion makes him the richest person in the UK and fourth richest in the world. A glance at the list of the wealthiest people around the world shows that most of them could describe their riches as 'new entrepreneurial wealth', rapidly made during the course of a single individual's life.

Bill Gates and Lakshmi Mittal exemplify this new entrepreneurial wealth. Both of these multi-billionaires were born into relatively modest backgrounds in their respective countries before gaining fantastic economic success. Both men benefited from globalization: Gates through his involvement with some of the new information and communication technologies that drive globalization and Mittal by driving forward the international expansion of his family's India-based steel-making business.

> At this point you may want to refer to chapter 4, 'Globalization and the Changing World', to refresh your understanding of 'globalization'.

Yet the benefits of globalization have been uneven, and are by no means enjoyed by all. Consider, for example, Wirat Tasago, a 24-year-old garment worker in Bangkok, Thailand. Tasago – along with more than a million other Thai garment workers, most of whom are women – labours from 8 a.m. until about 11 p.m. six days a week, earning little more than the equivalent of £2 pounds an hour (Dahlburg 1995). Billions of workers such as Tasago are being drawn into the global labour force, many working in oppressive conditions that would be unacceptable, if not unimaginable, under employment laws, such as the minimum wage, which are taken for granted in the developed world. And these are the fortunate ones: although many countries, such as those in Eastern Europe, have found engagement in the global economy socially and economically difficult, especially

Millions of workers across the world are employed in 'sweatshops', working long hours for little financial reward. Has globalization been beneficial for these workers?

initially, the populations of those societies that have remained outside the world economy, such as North Korea, have typically fared far worse.

Social inequality is one of the issues on which the discipline of sociology was founded, though the focus of the classical sociologists was on inequalities of class, status and power *within* the industrial societies. This generally meant studying the internal processes which produced inequality, disadvantage and exclusion. For example, in chapter 12 we examined poverty, social exclusion and welfare, noting large differences of income, wealth, work chances and quality of life, mainly *within* the industrialized countries. In chapter 11 we looked at types of social stratification, class-based inequality and social status distinctions and why these hierarchical social divisions continue to shape life chances today. Then in chapter 22 we will turn our attention to inequalities of power and explore the spread of democracy across the world with a tendency to reduce very steep power gradients as people gain new political rights.

However, these same crucial issues of class, status and power exist on an even larger scale in the world as a whole. Just as we can speak of the rich and poor, high and low status or powerful and powerless *within a single country*, so we can talk about these inequalities and their causes *within the global system as a whole*. In this chapter, we look at global inequality, primarily in the late twentieth and early twenty-first centuries (see chapter 4 for globalization in a longer time-scale). We begin with a brief discussion of what is understood by the term 'global inequality', and how definitions of the term change the way we think about it. We examine what differences in economic standards of living mean for people throughout the world. We then turn to the newly industrializing countries of the world to understand which countries are improving their fortunes and why. This will lead us to a discussion of theories that attempt to explain why global inequality exists and what can be done about it. We conclude this section by speculating on the future of economic inequality in a global world. From an examination of global inequality, we then move to an account of global population growth, a trend occurring at its greatest pace in some of the poorest countries of the world. The central issue here is how population growth impacts on the prospects for improved life chances and equality across the world.

Economic inequality is a major source of the world's problems with poverty, hunger and health, and for that reason it forms the central focus of this chapter. However, as we noted above, there are also major inequalities of social status and global inequalities of power both within and between nation-states. The latter remains an important source of many entrenched conflicts, some of which are discussed in chapter 23, 'Nations, War and Terrorism'. This chapter will also refer to these forms of inequality where necessary, but for a broader discussion, readers should consult the relevant chapters identified above.

Global economic inequality

Global economic inequality refers primarily to the systematic differences in wealth, incomes and working conditions that exist *between* countries. But there are, of course, many differences *within* countries: even the wealthiest countries today have growing numbers of poor people, while less wealthy nations are producing many of the world's super-rich. Sociology's challenge is not merely to identify such differences, but to explain *why* they occur and *how* they might be overcome.

One way to classify countries in terms of global inequality is to compare their economic productivity. One important measure of economic productivity is **gross domestic product** (GDP). A country's GDP is made up of all the goods and services on record as being produced by a country's economy in a particular year. Income earned abroad by individuals or corporations is not included in GDP. An important alternative measure is **gross national income** (GNI). (GNI was formerly referred to as gross national product or GNP.) Unlike GDP, GNI includes income earned by individuals or corporations outside the country. Measures of economic activity, such as GDP or GNI, are often given per person; this allows us to compare the wealth of an average inhabitant of a country. Also, in order to compare different countries, we need to use a common currency, and most international institutions, such as the World Bank, use the US dollar. We will use both the US dollar and, on occasion, the UK pound.

The World Bank is an international lending organization that provides loans for development projects in poorer countries. It uses per person GNI to classify countries as high-income, upper-middle-income, lower-middle-income or low-income. This system of classification will help us to understand more easily why there are such vast differences in living standards between countries, though, for the sake of simplicity, we will usually merge the upper-middle and lower middle categories.

The World Bank (2003) divides 132 countries, containing nearly 6 billion people, into the three economic classes. There are 74 other economies in the world, encompassing about 178 million people, for whom the World Bank does not provide data, either because it is lacking or because the economies have fewer than 1.5 million people. While 40 per cent of the world's population live in low-income countries, only 15 per cent live in high-income countries. Bear in mind that this classification is based on *average income* for each country, it therefore masks income inequality within each country. Such differences can be significant, although we do not focus on them in this chapter.

For example, the World Bank classifies India as a low-income country, since its per-person GNI in 1999 was just $450. Yet despite widespread poverty, India also boasts a large and growing middle class. China, on the other hand, was reclassified in 1999 from low- to middle-income, since its GNI per capita in that year was $780 (the World Bank's lower limit for a middle-income country is $756). Yet even though its average income now confers middle-income status on China, it nonetheless has hundreds of millions of people living in poverty.

Comparing countries on the basis of income alone, however, may be misleading, since GNI includes only goods and services that are produced for cash sale. Many people in low-income countries are farmers or herders who produce for their own families or for barter, involving non-cash transactions. The value of their crops and animals is not taken into account in the statistics. Further, economic output is not a country's whole story. Countries possess unique and widely differing languages and traditions. Poor countries are no less rich in history and culture than their wealthier neighbours, even though the lives of their people may be much harsher. Social and cultural assets such as social solidarity, strong cultural traditions or systems of familial and community assistance do not lend themselves to statistical measurement with quite the same ease as monetary transactions.

Many environmental campaigners have argued that GDP and GNI are particularly blunt measures of quantity that tell us nothing about the quality of life. Even those economic activities that damage the natural environment and human lives the most are simply counted as part of a country's total output and, thus, are seen to contribute to economic well-being. From the perspective of long-term environmental sustainability, this method is completely irrational. If we took account of some of the social and cultural aspects of life noted above, we may arrive at a radically different view of the apparent 'benefits' of continual increases in GDP/GNI.

Even if we do compare countries solely on the basis of economic statistics, the ones we choose for our comparisons are likely to make a difference to our conclusions. For example, if we choose to study global inequality by comparing levels of household consumption (of, say, food, medicine or other products) rather than GNI, we might reach a different conclusion on global inequality. We could also choose to take into account other factors. A comparison of the GNI of several countries is all very well, but it does not take into account how much things *actually* cost in a country. For example, if two countries have a more or less equal GNI, but in the first, an average family meal costs just pennies, whereas in the second it costs several pounds, then we might conclude that it is misleading to argue that the countries are equally wealthy – after all, in the first country one gets considerably more for one's money. Instead, the researcher might choose to compare *purchasing power parities* (PPP) that eliminate the difference in prices between two countries. *The Economist* magazine uses a famous measure of PPP with its light-hearted 'Big Mac Index', which compares the cost of the hamburger – made with identical ingredients – in different countries. In this chapter we concentrate on comparisons of GNI between countries, but it is important to be aware of the other measures commonly used.

THINKING CRITICALLY

How useful do you find the World Bank's ranking of low-, middle- and high-income countries? Which aspects of life within different countries does the 'average income' measure help us to understand? Which aspects of life is this method likely to miss? How else could we compare the living conditions of countries with such different cultures, social structures and economic standards of living? Why might such comparisons be useful to policy-makers?

High-income countries

The *high-income countries* are generally those that were first to industrialize, starting with the UK some 250 years ago, spreading to Europe, the United States and Canada. It was only some 30 years ago that Japan joined the ranks of such high-income, industrialized nations, while Singapore, Hong Kong and Taiwan moved into this category only in the 1980s and 1990s. The reasons for the success of these Asian late-comers are much debated by sociologists and economists and we will look at these debates later in the chapter.

High-income countries account for only 15 per cent of the world's population (roughly 891 million people) – yet they lay claim to 79 per cent of the world's annual output of wealth (World Bank 2000–1). High-income countries offer decent housing, adequate food, safe water supplies and other comforts unknown in many other parts of the world. Although these countries often have large numbers of poor people, most of their inhabitants enjoy a standard of living unimaginable for the majority of the world's people.

Middle-income countries

The *middle-income countries* are primarily found in East and Southeast Asia, the oil-rich countries of the Middle East and North Africa, the Americas (Mexico, Central America, Cuba and other countries in the Caribbean, and South America) and the once-Communist republics that formerly made up the Soviet Union and its East European allies. Most of these countries began to industrialize relatively late in the twentieth century and are therefore not yet as industrially developed (or wealthy) as the high-income countries. The countries that once comprised the Soviet Union, on the other hand, are highly industrialized, although their living standards have been eroded since the collapse of communism and the shift towards capitalist economies. In Russia itself, for example, the wages of ordinary people dropped by nearly a third between 1998 and 1999, while retirement pensions dropped by almost half: millions of people, many of them elderly, suddenly found themselves destitute (CIA 2000).

In 1999, middle-income countries included 45 per cent of the world's population (2.7 billion people) but accounted for just 18 per cent of the annual wealth produced. Although many people in these countries are substantially better off than their neighbours in low-income countries, most do not enjoy the high standard of living of the high-income countries. The ranks of the world's middle-income countries expanded between 1999 and 2000, according to the World Bank's system of classification, when China – with 1.3 billion people (22 per cent of the world's population) – was reclassified from low- to middle-income because of its rapid economic growth. This reclassification is somewhat misleading, however. China's average per person income of $1,100 per year in 2003 is quite close to the cut-off for low-income countries (at $766), and a large majority of its population are in fact within the low-income category by World Bank standards.

Low-income countries

Finally, the *low-income countries* include much of eastern, western and sub-Saharan Africa; Vietnam, Cambodia, Indonesia and some other East Asian countries; India, Nepal, Bangladesh and Pakistan in South Asia; East and Central European countries such as Georgia and Ukraine; and Haiti and Nicaragua in the western hemisphere. These countries mostly have agricultural economies and only recently began to industrialize.

In 1999, the low-income countries included 40 per cent of the world's population (2.4 billion people) yet produced only 3 per cent of the world's annual output of wealth. What is more, this inequality is increasing. Fertility is much higher in low-income countries than elsewhere, as large families provide additional farm labour or otherwise contribute to family income. In wealthy industrial societies, where children are more likely to be in school than on the farm, the economic benefit of large families declines, and so people tend to have fewer children. Because of this, the populations of low-income countries (with the principal exception of India) are growing more than three times as fast as those of high-income countries (World Bank 2003). In many low-income countries, people struggle with poverty, malnutrition and even starvation. Most people live in rural areas, although this is rapidly changing. Hundreds of millions of people are moving to huge, densely populated cities, where they live either in dilapidated housing or on the open streets.

 See chapter 6, 'Cities and Urban Life', for a wider discussion of urbanization.

Is global economic inequality increasing?

The question of whether global inequality is increasing or diminishing has polarized opinion in recent years. Anti-globalization activists argue that globalization generates more inequality, while defenders argue that it is proving to be a great levelling force between the world's rich and poor. The first dramatic changes in global inequality occurred more than two centuries ago with the Industrial Revolution, as Europe and then other regions underwent rapid economic expansion, leaving the rest of the world far behind in terms of wealth and material goods.

Those who see that global inequality is expanding argue that in the past few decades globalization has exacerbated the trend towards inequality that began with industrialization. Globalization's critics cite statistics of the kind used in the UN Human Development Report 2007/08, which noted that the 40 per cent of the human population living on less than US$2 a day account for just 5 per cent of global income, but the wealthiest 20 per cent account for three-quarters of global income. In particular, sub-Saharan Africa will account for a full one-third of world poverty by 2015, up from one-fifth in 1990 (UNDP 2007a: 25). At the global level as well as within many countries, inequality is increasing along with globalization.

By contrast, others have pointed out that over the past few decades the overall standard of living in the world as a whole has actually risen. Many indicators measuring the living standards of the world's poorest people show improvements. Illiteracy is reduced, infant death rates and malnutrition are falling, people are living longer, and global poverty – commonly defined as the number of people living on less than one US dollar a day – has reduced (see table 13.2 below).

However, there are substantial differences between countries. Many of these gains have been in the high- and middle-income countries, while living standards in many of the poorest countries have declined. Indeed, although the 1990s was a time of economic boom for the world's richest country, the United States, the UN Human Development Report (2003) found that more than 50 countries, located mainly in sub-Saharan Africa, suffered falling living standards during the decade as a result of famine, the global AIDS epidemic, conflicts and failed national economic policies. Atkinson (2003) reminds us that increasing inequality cannot be explained entirely by general reference to rapid globalization, as national taxation and other economic policies continue to play an important role. For example, in Scandinavian countries like Sweden, where the welfare state operates in a redistributive way, global trends towards the widening of social inequality have been more effectively prevented than in other countries, such as the UK, which have adopted a more right-of-centre approach to welfare reform.

See chapter 12, 'Poverty, Social Exclusion and Welfare', for a discussion of welfare state regimes.

As the above dispute shows, the way we chose to measure global inequality makes a big difference to the conclusions that we reach on the issue. The economist, Stanley Fischer, compared two ways of looking at global income inequality: the first simply compares income inequality between countries; the second takes into account the number of people living in those countries as well. The first way of looking at global inequality is shown in the top chart of figure 13.1. This shows the average income of a selection of poor and rich countries between 1980 and 2000, with each country represented on the graph by a uniform dot. The figure shows that during this period the average income of the poorest nations grew much more slowly than the average income

of the world's richest nations. Hence, the trend (shown by the black line) shows inequality increasing as the economies of the richer countries on the right of the graph grow more quickly than those of the poorer countries (on the left). If the poorest countries had grown faster than the richest, the black trends line would slope down from left to right. The gap between the richest and the poorest of the world's countries therefore appears to be growing.

The bottom chart, which takes into account the population size of the countries, presents a rather different view on global inequality. The same chart is shown here, but this time the dots that represent each country have been drawn in proportion to the size of the number of people living in that country. What is particularly noticeable about this graph is that two of the world's biggest countries – India and China, which between them account for well over one-third of the world's population – have increased the sizes of their economies considerably since 1980. Because of the size of these two countries, a population-weighted line of best fit drawn through the second chart would slope downwards, implying that global inequality is falling, as, on average, the populations of the poorest countries catch up.

Once we take account of the fact that China and India have performed so well economically since 1980, and especially since 1990, together with the fact that these two countries account for such a big share of the world's poorest people, global poverty appears to be relatively stable. Those countries that have done best economically in the period since 1980 – like India, China and Vietnam, for example – also tend to be those countries that have integrated most successfully into the global economy. The enormous inequality still found within those countries that have grown economically in recent decades means that some critics have asked at what price integration into the global economy comes.

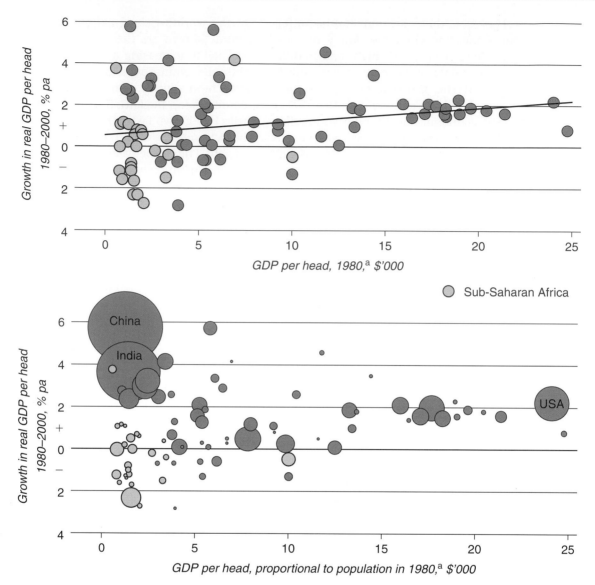

Figure 13.1 Two ways of looking at global income inequality
[a]1996 prices

Source: The Economist, 11 March 2004 © The Economist Newspaper Limited, London

Unequal life chances

Urbanization in developing countries is discussed in more detail in chapter 6, 'Cities and Urban Life'.

An enormous gulf in living standards separates most people in rich countries from their counterparts in poor ones. Wealth and poverty make life different in a host of ways. For instance, about one-third of the world's poor are undernourished, and almost all are illiterate, lacking access to basic primary school education. While most of the world is still rural, within a decade there are likely to be more poor people in urban than in rural areas.

Many of the global poor come from tribes or racial and ethnic groups that differ from the dominant groups of their countries and

Table 13.2 **Global quality of life measures show an improving picture, 1990–2005**

Quality of life indicator	1990–1	2004–5
World		
Enrolment in primary education per 100 children of primary age (%)	82.5	88.8
Literacy rate of 15–24 year olds (%)	83.5	87.4
Mortality rate for under-5s per 1,000 live births	95	76
Infant mortality rate (children under 1) per 1,000 live births	65	52
Births attended by skilled health personnel (%)	47	59
Population using an improved drinking water source (%)	78	83
Developing regions only (%)		
Population living below US$1 a day	31.6	19.2
Poverty gap ratio[1]	9.3	5.4
Prevalence of underweight children under 5 years of age	33.0	27.0
Urban population living in slums	46.5	36.5

[1] The *poverty gap ratio* = average percentage shortfall of poor individuals' incomes below the poverty line. This measure assesses the depth of poverty rather than just the percentage of a population whose income falls below the poverty line.

Source: Data taken from United Nations, *Millennium Development Goals Report,* 2007

their poverty is, at least in part, the result of discrimination. Here we focus on differences between high- and low-income countries in terms of health, starvation and famine, and education and literacy.

Health

People in high-income countries are far healthier than their counterparts in low-income countries. Low-income countries generally suffer from inadequate health facilities, and when they do have hospitals or clinics, these seldom serve the poorest people. People living in low-income countries also lack proper sanitation, drink polluted water and run a much greater risk of contracting infectious diseases. They are more likely to suffer malnourishment, starvation and famine. These factors all contribute to physical weakness and poor health, making people in low-income countries susceptible to illness and disease. There is growing evidence that high rates of HIV/AIDS

infection found in many African countries are due, in part, to the weakened health of impoverished people (Stillwagon 2001).

Because of poor health conditions, people in low-income countries are more likely to die in infancy and less likely to live to old age than people in high-income countries. Infants are 11 times more likely to die at birth in low-income countries than they are in high-income countries, and – if they survive birth – they are likely to live on average 18 years fewer. Children often die of illnesses that are readily treated in wealthier countries, such as measles or diarrhoea. In the mid-1990s in some parts of the world, such as sub-Saharan Africa, a child was statistically more likely to die before the age of 5 than to enter secondary school (World Bank 1996). Still, conditions have improved in low- and middle-income countries since then. For example, between 1990/1 and 2004/5 the global infant mortality rate dropped from 65 (per 1,000 live births) to 52 alongside an increase in the proportion of

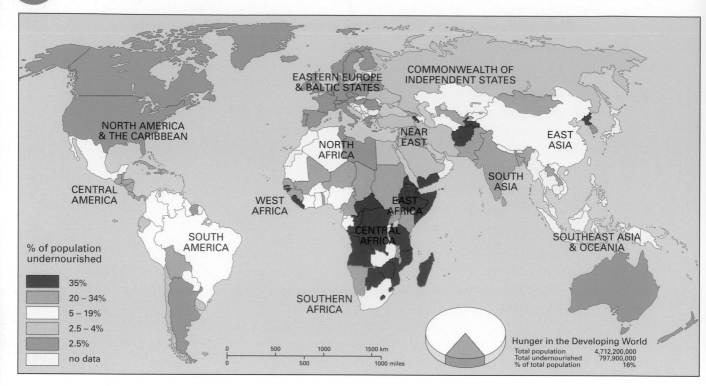

Figure 13.2 Undernourishment – a global problem, unevenly distributed

Source: World Food Programme, 29 June 2007. © 2007, World Food Programme.

births attended by medical personnel from 47 to 59 per cent. A range of other measures also showed marked improvement (see table 13.2)

During the past three decades, many improvements have occurred in most of the middle-income countries of the world and in some of the low-income countries as well. Throughout the world, infant mortality has been cut in half, and average life expectancy has increased by ten years or more. The wider availability of modern medical technology, improved sanitation and rising incomes account for most of these changes.

Hunger, malnutrition and famine

Hunger, malnutrition and famine are major global sources of poor health; they are not new problems, but long-standing issues. What seems to be new is the extent of hunger and undernourishment – the fact that so many people in the world today appear to be on the brink of starvation (see figure 13.2). The United Nations World Food Programme (UNWFP 2001) estimated that 830 million people go hungry every day, 95 per cent of them in developing countries. The UN defines 'hunger' as a diet of 1,800 or fewer calories per day – an amount insufficient to provide adults with the nutrients required for active, healthy lives. According to the World Food Programme study, 200 million of the world's hungry are children under the age of 5, who are underweight because they lack adequate food. Every year hunger kills an estimated 12 million children. As one 10-year-old child from the west African country of Gabon told researchers from the World Bank:

> When I leave for school in the mornings I don't have any breakfast. At noon there is no lunch, in the evening I get a little

supper, and that is not enough. So when I see another child eating, I watch him, and if he doesn't give me something I think I'm going to die of hunger. (Narayan 1999)

Yet more than three-quarters of all malnourished children under the age of 5 in the world's low- and middle-income countries live in countries that actually produce a food surplus (Lappe 1998). It has been estimated that the amount the population of the United States spends on pet food each year ($13 billion) would eradicate much of the world's human hunger (Bread for the World Institute 2005).

Famine and hunger are the result of a combination of natural and social forces. Drought alone affects an estimated 100 million people in the world today. In countries such as Sudan, Ethiopia, Eritrea, Indonesia, Afghanistan, Sierra Leone, Guinea and Tajikistan, the combination of drought and internal warfare has devastated food production, resulting in starvation and death for millions of people. In Latin America and the Caribbean at the start of the twenty-first century, 53 million people (11 per cent of the population) were malnourished, along with 180 million (33 per cent) in sub-Saharan Africa and 525 million (17 per cent) in Asia (UNWFP 2001).

The spread and persistence of HIV/AIDS has also contributed to the problem of food shortages and hunger, killing many working-age adults. A study by the United Nations Food and Agricultural Association (FAO) has predicted that HIV/AIDS-caused deaths in the ten African countries most afflicted by the epidemic will reduce the labour force by 26 per cent by the year 2020. Of the estimated 26 million people worldwide infected with HIV, 95 per cent live in developing countries. According to the FAO, the epidemic can be devastating to nutrition, food security and agricultural production, affecting 'the entire society's ability to maintain and reproduce itself' (UNFAO 2001).

Every year, hunger, resulting from both natural and social causes, kills about 12 million children.

The countries affected by famine and starvation are, for the most part, too poor to pay for new technologies that would increase their food production. Nor can they afford to purchase sufficient food imports from elsewhere in the world. At the same time, paradoxically, as world hunger grows, food production continues to increase. Between 1965 and 1999, for example, world production of grain doubled. Even allowing for the substantial world population increase over this period, the global production of grain per person was 15 per cent higher in 1999 than it was 34 years earlier. This growth, however, is not evenly distributed around the world. In

Global Society 13.1 **What does the world eat? What should the world eat?**

In 2000, photojournalist Peter Menzel and journalist Faith D'Alusio set out to record what a culturally diverse range of families across the world ate in one week. Their 2005 book *Hungry Planet: What the World Eats* was the result. They visited 30 families in 24 countries looking at food purchases, costs and recipes, and photographing families with their typical weekly food items. Two examples from their book are reproduced here:

Republic of Chad: The Aboubakar family of Breidjing Camp
Food expenditure for one week: 685 CFA francs, or $1.23
Favourite foods: soup with fresh sheep meat

USA: The Revis family of North Carolina
Food expenditure for one week: $341.98
Favourite foods: spaghetti, potatoes, sesame chicken

much of Africa, for example, food production per person declined in recent years. Surplus food produced in high-income countries such as the United States is seldom affordable to the countries that need it most.

Education, literacy and child labour

Education and literacy are important routes to economic development. Here, again, lower-income countries are disadvantaged, since they can seldom afford high-quality public education systems. As a consequence, children in high-income countries are much more likely to get schooling than are children in low-income countries, and adults in high-income countries are much more likely to be able to read and write (see figure 13.3). While virtually all secondary school-aged males and females are still in full-time education in high-income countries, in 1997 only 71 per cent were in middle-income countries and only 51 per cent in low-income countries. In low-income countries, 30 per cent of male adults and almost half of female adults are unable to read and write. One reason for these differences is a sizeable gap in public expenditures on education: high-income countries spend a much larger percentage of their gross domestic product on education than do low-income countries (World Bank 2001).

Education is important for several reasons. First, it contributes to economic growth, since people with advanced schooling provide the skilled work necessary for high-wage industries. Second, education offers the only hope of escaping from the cycle of harsh working conditions and poverty, since poorly educated people are condemned to low-wage, unskilled jobs. Finally, educated people are less likely to have large numbers of children, thus slowing the global population explosion that contributes to global poverty.

A further important reason for the relatively low levels of children in primary education in low-income countries is children's involvement in work at the expense of their education. Children are often forced to work because of a combination of family poverty, lack of education provision and traditional indifference to the plight of those who are poor or who belong to ethnic minorities (UNICEF 2000a). Child labour has been legally eliminated in the high-income countries, but still exists in many parts of the world today. According to the United Nations International Labour Organization (ILO) more than 218 million boys and girls between the ages of 5 and 14 are working in developing countries, about one out of every four children in the world. Of these, 126 million are estimated to be working in hazardous conditions (ILO 2004). Child labour is found throughout the developing world, with the highest incidence of children's work in sub-Saharan Africa and the largest number of child workers found in the Asia-Pacific region.

Two-thirds of working children (132 million) labour in agriculture, with the rest in manufacturing, wholesale and retail

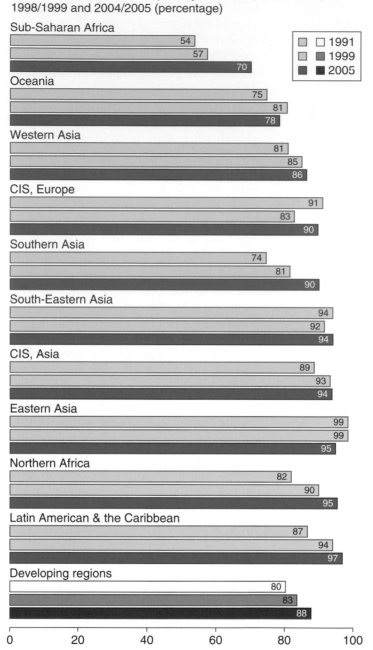

Total net enrolment ratio in primary education, *1990/1991, 1998/1999 and 2004/2005 (percentage)

Legend: 1991, 1999, 2005

Sub-Saharan Africa: 54, 57, 70

Oceania: 75, 81, 78

Western Asia: 81, 85, 86

CIS, Europe: 91, 83, 90

Southern Asia: 74, 81, 90

South-Eastern Asia: 94, 92, 94

CIS, Asia: 89, 93, 94

Eastern Asia: 99, 99, 95

Northern Africa: 82, 90, 95

Latin American & the Caribbean: 87, 94, 97

Developing regions: 80, 83, 88

*Number of pupils of the theoretical school-age group for primary education, enrolled either in primary or secondary education, expressed as a percentage of the total population in that age group.

Figure 13.3   Global inequality in educational enrolment, 1991–2005

Source: Global Monitoring Report 2007 by World Bank. © 2007 by World Bank. Reproduced with permission of World Bank in the format Textbook via Copyright Clearance Center.

Education plays a crucial role in countries' economic development, but low-income nations' schools are often underfunded.

trade, restaurants and hotels and a variety of services, including working as servants in wealthy households (ILO 2007). At best, these children work for long hours with little pay and are therefore unable to go to school and develop the skills that might eventually enable them to escape their lives of poverty. However, simply enforcing an immediate ban on all child labour, even if it were possible, might be counter-productive. Child labour is a better alternative to child prostitution or chronic under-nourishment, for example. The challenge is not just to end child labour, but also to move children from work into education, and to ensure that they are properly provided for during their school years.

One form of child labour that is close to slavery is 'bonded labour'. In this system, children as young as 8 or 9 are pledged by their parents to factory-owners in exchange for small loans. These children are paid so little that they never manage to reduce the debt, condemning them to a lifetime of bondage. One case of bonded labour that attracted international attention was that of Iqbal Masih, a Pakistani child who, at the age of 4, was sold into slavery by his father in order to borrow 600 rupees (roughly US$16) for the wedding of his first-born son. For six years, Iqbal spent most of his time chained to a carpet-weaving loom, tying tiny knots for hours on end. After fleeing the factory at the age of 10, he began speaking to labour organizations and schools about his experience. Iqbal paid a bitter price for his outspokenness: when he was 13, while riding his bicycle in his home-town, he was gunned down by agents believed to be working for the carpet indus-try (Bobak 1996).

Global Society 13.2　Child labour in agriculture

An ILO Report published for their World Day Against Child Labour, on 12 June 2007, focused on child labour in agricultural work settings, where the majority of child labourers work. Much agricultural child labour is not seen as formal employment but simply as 'helping the family', which tends to render it invisible to policy-makers.

The following section is from the ILO Report (2007) and it gives an indication of the risks children face in agricultural child labour.

Seventy per cent of working children are in agriculture – more than 132 million girls and boys aged 5–14 years old. The vast majority of the world's child labourers are not toiling in factories and sweatshops or working as domestics or street vendors in urban areas; they are working on farms and plantations, often from sun up to sun down, planting and harvesting crops, spraying pesticides, and tending livestock on rural farms and plantations. These children play an important role in crop and livestock production, helping supply some of the food and drink we consume, and the fibres and raw materials we use to make other products. Examples include cocoa/chocolate, coffee, tea, sugar, fruits and vegetables, along with other agricultural products like tobacco and cotton.

A large, though uncertain, number of the 132 million girls and boys carry out 'hazardous child labour', which is work that can threaten their lives, limbs, health, and general well-being. Irrespective of age, agriculture – along with construction and mining – is one of the three most dangerous sectors in which to work in terms of work-related fatalities, non-fatal accidents and occupational disease. Child labourers are susceptible to all the hazards and risks faced by adult workers when placed in the same situation. They are at even greater risk from these dangers because their bodies are still growing and their minds and personalities still developing, and they lack work experience. So the effects of poor to non-existent safety and health protection can often be more devastating and lasting for them. Also, a feature of agriculture that sets it apart from most other forms of child labour is that the children usually live on the farms or plantations where they work. This exposes them to additional risks.

Bangladesh is a primarily rural country and for many children working to help grow, harvest, transport or sell farm products is a normal, everyday role from the earliest days of childhood. They are regularly exposed to farm machinery and tools that often result in devastating injuries. About 50 children a day are injured by machines, and three of them are injured so severely that they become permanently disabled.

In Zimbabwe, the wheels of a tractor which had been standing overnight had become bogged down in the mud. The following morning, a 12-year-old boy started the tractor, revved up the engine to free the wheels, trying to move in a forward direction (when the safe procedure would have been to try to reverse out). The wheels remained stuck, that is, resisted movement, and the tractor reared up on its front wheels and overturned backwards, fatally crushing the boy beneath it.

In 2000, an 11-year-old girl, illegally employed on a farm in Ceres, Western Cape, South Africa, fell off a tractor, resulting in the amputation of her left leg.

In 1990, a 15-year-old migrant farm worker in the USA was fatally electrocuted when a 30-foot section of aluminium irrigation pipe he was moving came into contact with an overhead power line. Two other child labourers with him sustained serious electrical burns to their hands and feet.

Source: ILO 2007

Abolishing exploitative child labour will require countries around the world to enact strong laws against the practice and be willing to enforce them. International organizations, such as the UNILO, have outlined a set of standards for such laws to follow. In June 1999, the UNILO adopted Convention 182, calling for the abolition of the 'Worst Forms of Child Labour'. These are defined as including:

- all forms of slavery or practices similar to slavery, such as the sale and trafficking of children, debt bondage and serfdom, and forced or compulsory labour, including forced or compulsory recruitment of children for use in armed conflict;
- the use, procuring or offering of a child for prostitution, for the production of pornography, or for pornographic performances;
- the use, procuring or offering of a child for illicit activities, in particular for the production and trafficking of drugs as defined in the relevant international treaties; and
- work that, by its nature or the circumstances in which it is carried out, is likely to harm the health, safety, or morals of children. (ILO 1999)

Countries must also provide free public education and require that children attend school full time (UNICEF 2000). But part of the responsibility for solving the problem also lies with the global corporations that manufacture goods using child labour, trade unions that organize the workforce, agricultural cooperatives whose values are opposed to child labour and, ultimately, the consumers who buy the goods.

Can poor countries become rich?

By the mid-1970s, a number of low-income countries in East Asia were undergoing a process of industrialization that appeared to threaten the global economic dominance of the United States and Europe (Amsden 1989; also see chapter 4 for a discussion of these developments). This process began with Japan in the 1950s, but quickly extended to the **newly industrializing countries** (NICs), that is, the rapidly growing economies of the world, particularly in East Asia but also in Latin America. The East Asian NICs included Hong Kong in the 1960s and Taiwan, South Korea and Singapore in the 1970s and 1980s. Other Asian countries began to follow in the 1980s and the early 1990s, most notably China, but also Malaysia, Thailand and Indonesia. Today, most are middle-income, and some – such as Hong Kong, South Korea, Taiwan and Singapore – have moved up to the high-income category.

Figure 13.4 compares the average economic growth rates of the low-, middle- and high-income countries of the world. Economists have tended to assume that the developing countries, en bloc, would experience higher average rates of economic growth than the developed, high-income ones, as their development starts to catch up. However, until quite recently this was often not the case and only a few developing countries managed to out-perform the average growth rate of the developed economies.

This has changed since the mid-1990s, though, as the *average* growth rates of low- and middle-income countries have been higher than those in the developed world. Indeed, 13 countries have now been reclassified by the World Bank as 'developed economies' as their economic growth rates have propelled them into the ranks of the relatively wealthy countries: Antigua and Barbuda, Bahrain, Greece, Guam, Isle of Man, Republic of Korea, Malta, New Caledonia, Northern Mariana Islands, Puerto Rico, Saudi Arabia, San Marino and Slovenia (World Bank 2007b). These are all places that were considered to be poor just two generations ago. By 1999, the GDP per person in Singapore was virtually the same as that in the United States, while China, the world's most populous country, has one of the most rapidly growing economies on the planet. At an average annual growth rate of 10 per cent between 1980 and 1999, the Chinese economy doubled in size.

Comparing countries on the basis of their average income level continues to show a wide divergence, particularly between the developed and developing countries. Comparing the incomes of rich and poor people *within* a single country shows that, over recent years, some countries have experienced widening income inequality (USA, UK, Brazil), while others have remained fairly stable (France, Canada). However, measuring global inequality at the *individual* level, regardless of country of residence, shows that since 1970, 'the average global citizen has become richer' and global income distribution has become more equal (Loungani 2003; see figure 13.4). However, this conclusion is heavily influenced by the rapid growth of a small number of large countries, including China, India and Vietnam. Leaving these aside, the 13 countries recategorized by the World Bank as 'developed economies' represent a small minority of all developing countries,

USING YOUR SOCIOLOGICAL IMAGINATION

13.1   Solutions to global inequality?

Poverty

Most of sub-Saharan Africa is in the World Bank's lowest income category of less than US$765 gross national income (GNI) per person per year. Ethiopia and Burundi are the worst off with just US$90 GNI per person. Even middle-income countries like Gabon and Botswana have sizeable sections of the population living in poverty. North Africa generally fares better than sub-Saharan Africa. Here, the economies are more stable, trade and tourism are relatively high and AIDS is less prevalent. Development campaigners continue to urge the G8 to reform the rules on debt, aid and trade to help lift more African nations out of poverty.

Debt

The Heavily Indebted Poor Countries initiative (HIPC) was set up in 1996 to reduce the debt of the poorest countries. Poor countries are eligible for the scheme if they face unsustainable debt that cannot be reduced by traditional methods. They also have to agree to follow certain policies of good governance as defined by the World Bank and the IMF. Once these are established, the country is at 'decision point' and the amount of debt relief is established. Critics of the scheme say the parameters are too strict and more countries should be eligible for HIPC debt relief.

This map shows how much 'decision point' HIPC countries spend on repaying debts and interest. Under a new plan drawn up by the G8 finance ministers, 14 African HIPC countries will have their debts totally written off.

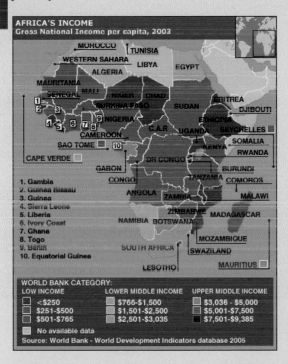

AFRICA'S INCOME
Gross National Income per capita, 2003

1. Gambia
2. Guinea Bissau
3. Guinea
4. Sierra Leone
5. Liberia
6. Ivory Coast
7. Ghana
8. Togo
9. Benin
10. Equatorial Guinea

WORLD BANK CATEGORY:

LOW INCOME	LOWER MIDDLE INCOME	UPPER MIDDLE INCOME
<$250	$766-$1,500	$3,036 - $5,000
$251-$500	$1,501-$2,500	$5,001-$7,500
$501-$765	$2,501-$3,035	$7,501-$9,385
No available data		

Source: World Bank - World Development Indicators database 2005

Source:
http://news.bbc.co.uk/1/shared/spl/hi/africa/05/africa_economy/html/poverty.stm
© bbc.co.uk/news

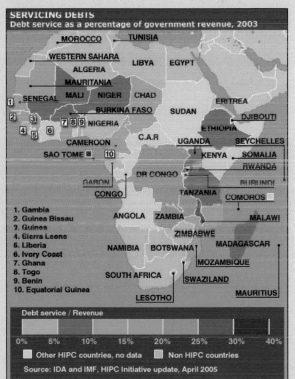

SERVICING DEBTS
Debt service as a percentage of government revenue, 2003

1. Gambia
2. Guinea Bissau
3. Guinea
4. Sierra Leone
5. Liberia
6. Ivory Coast
7. Ghana
8. Togo
9. Benin
10. Equatorial Guinea

Debt service / Revenue

| 0% | 5% | 10% | 15% | 20% | 25% | 30% | 40% |

Other HIPC countries, no data   Non HIPC countries

Source: IDA and IMF, HIPC Initiative update, April 2005

Source:
http://news.bbc.co.uk/1/shared/spl/hi/africa/05/africa_economy/html/debt.stm © bbc.co.uk/news

Aid

Africa receives about a third of the total aid given by governments around the world, according to the Organization for Economic Cooperation and Development (OECD). Most aid has conditions attached, meaning that governments must implement certain policies to receive the aid or must spend the money on goods and services from the donor country. The World Bank, which is reviewing its conditionality policies, argues that aid is far more effective, and less vulnerable to corruption, when coupled with improved governance. There was a sharp drop in rich countries' relative spending on aid in the late 1990s.

In 2005, the 'Make Poverty History' campaign sought to persuade the G8 to raise an extra US$50 billion more in aid per year and to enforce earlier pledges for developed countries to give 0.70 per cent of their annual GDP in aid. The campaign claims success in gaining 'international acceptance of the principle of 100 per cent multilateral debt cancellation; an undertaking at the G8 summit that developing countries have the right to decide, plan and sequence their economic policies to fit with their own development strategies and international support for (as close as possible) universal access to treatment for HIV and AIDS for all who need it by 2010' (www.makepovertyhistory.org/theyearof/).

Source:
http://news.bbc.co.uk/1/shared/spl/hi/africa/05/africa_economy/html/aid.stm © bbc.co.uk/news

Trade

Africa is rich in natural resources such as minerals, timber and oil, but trade with the rest of the world is often difficult. Factors include poor infrastructure, government instability, corruption and the impact of AIDS on the population of working age. Poorer countries and agencies such as Oxfam also argue that international trade rules are unfair and favour the developed world. They say rich countries 'dump' subsidized products on developing nations by undercutting local producers. And they accuse the World Trade Organization (WTO) of forcing developing nations to open their markets to the rest of the world but failing to lower rich countries' tariff barriers in return. The WTO responds that low-income countries receive special treatment, including exemption from some regulations that apply to richer nations.

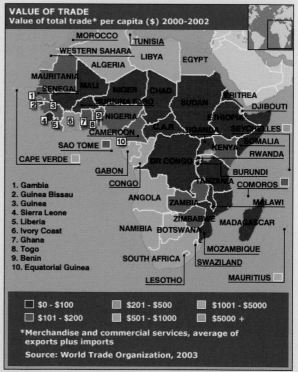

Source:
http://news.bbc.co.uk/1/shared/spl/hi/africa/05/africa_economy/html/trade.stm © bbc.co.uk/news

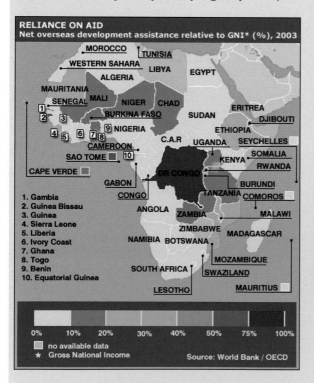

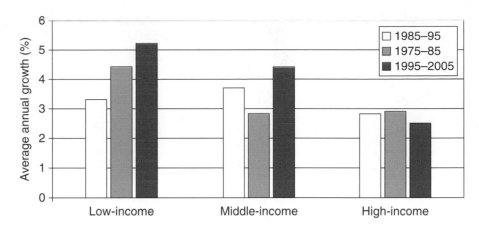

Figure 13.4   Average economic growth in the low-, middle- and high-income countries, 1975–2005

Source: World Bank 2007b

Table 13.3   Cross-country, within-country and global inequalities

Concept of income inequality	Cross-country inequality	Within-country inequality	Global inequality
What it measures	Inequality of *average* incomes across countries	Differences between incomes of the rich and the poor within a country	Differences between incomes of the rich and the poor, ignoring the country to which they belong
What the evidence shows	Divergence	Increasing inequality in many countries (for example, Brazil, China, United States), but low and stable levels in many others (for example, Canada, France, Japan)	Convergence

Source: Loungani 2003

whose combined population totals only around 2 per cent of the global population. Clearly, economic growth rates remain very unevenly distributed. The share of global output over the decade 1995–2005 did not improve for most developing regions, with the notable exception of East Asia and the Pacific (see figure 13.5), which increased its share by some 6 per cent in the period.

The economic expansion in East Asia in particular has not been without its costs. These have included the sometimes violent repression of labour and civil rights, terrible factory conditions, the exploitation of an increasingly female workforce, the exploitation of immigrant workers from impoverished neighbouring countries and widespread environmental degradation. Nonetheless, thanks to the sacrifices of past generations of workers, large numbers of people in these countries are now prospering.

How do social scientists account for the rapid economic growth in the East Asian NICs? The answer to this question may hold some crucial lessons for those low-income countries elsewhere that hope to follow in the steps of the NICs. Although the NICs' success is partly due to historically unique

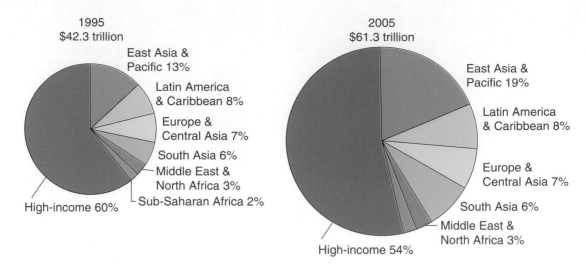

Figure 13.5 Share of global output by region, 1995 and 2005

Source: World Bank, World Development Indicators, 2007. © 2007 by World Bank. Reproduced with permission of World Bank in the format Textbook via Copyright Clearance Center.

factors, it is also the result of factors that could lead to a rethinking about the causes of global inequality. To understand the rapid development of this region, we need to view these countries both historically and within the context of the world economic system today.

The economic success of the East Asian NICs, particularly from the mid-1970s to the mid-1990s, can be attributed to a combination of factors. Some of these are historical, including those that stem from world political and economic shifts. Some are cultural. Still others have to do with the ways these countries have pursued economic growth. Some of the factors that aided their success are as follows:

1   Historically, Taiwan, South Korea, Hong Kong and Singapore were once part of colonial situations that, while imposing many hardships, also helped to pave the way for economic growth. Taiwan and Korea were tied to the Japanese Empire; Hong Kong and Singapore were former British colonies. Japan eliminated large landowners who opposed industrialization, and both Britain and Japan encouraged industrial development, constructed roads and other transportation systems, and built relatively efficient governmental bureaucracies in these particular colonies. Britain also actively developed both Hong Kong and Singapore as trading centres (Gold 1986; Cumings 1987). Elsewhere in the world – for example, in Latin America and Africa – countries that are today poor did not fare so well in their dealings with richer, more powerful nations.

2   The East Asian region benefited from a long period of world economic growth. Between the 1950s and the mid-1970s, the growing economies of Europe and the United States provided a substantial market for the clothing, footwear and electronics that were increasingly being made in East Asia, creating a 'window of opportunity' for economic development. Furthermore, periodic economic slowdowns in the United States and Europe forced businesses to cut their labour costs and spurred the relocation of factories to low-wage East Asian countries (Henderson and Appelbaum 1992). One World Bank study (1995)

From a Weberian perspective, traditions of respect and submission to authority embedded in Japanese culture can be used to explain the country's economic development.

found that between 1970 and 1990, wage increases averaged 3 per cent yearly in developing countries where economic growth was led by exports to wealthier countries, while wages failed to increase elsewhere in the developing world.

3 Economic growth in this region took off at the high point of the Cold War, when the United States and its allies, in erecting a defence against communist China, provided generous economic and military aid. Direct aid and loans fuelled investment in such new technologies as transistors, semiconductors and other electronics, contributing to the development of local industries. Military assistance frequently favoured strong (often military) govern- ments that were willing to use repression to keep labour costs low (Mirza 1986; Cumings 1987, 1997; Castells 1992).

4 Some sociologists argue that the economic success of Japan and the East Asian NICs is due in part to their cultural traditions, in particular, their shared Confucian philosophy (Berger 1986). A century ago, Max Weber (1976 [1904–5]) argued that the Protestant belief in thrift, frugality and hard work partly explained the rise of capitalism in Western Europe. His argument has been applied to Asian economic history. Confucianism, it is argued, inculcates respect for one's elders and superiors, education, hard work and proven accomplishments as the key to advancement, as well as a will- ingness to sacrifice today to earn a

greater reward tomorrow. As a result of these values, the Weberian argument goes, Asian workers and managers are highly loyal to their companies, submissive to authority, hardworking and success-oriented. Workers and capitalists alike are said to be frugal. Instead of living lavishly, they are likely to reinvest their wealth in further economic growth.

This explanation has some merit, but it overlooks the fact that businesses are not always revered and respected in Asia. During the late 1950s, pitched battles occurred between workers and capitalists in Japan – as they did in South Korea in the late 1980s. Students and workers throughout the East Asian NICs have opposed business and governmental policies they felt to be unfair, often at the risk of imprisonment and sometimes even their lives (Deyo 1989; Ho 1990). Furthermore, such central Confucian cultural values as thrift appear to be on the decline in Japan and the NICs, as young people – raised in the booming prosperity of recent years – increasingly value conspicuous consumption over austerity and investment.

5   Many of the East Asian governments followed strong policies that favoured economic growth. Their governments played active roles in keeping labour costs low, encouraged economic development through tax breaks and other economic policies and offered free public education. We shall discuss the role of East Asian government policies later in this chapter.

Whether the growth of these economies will continue is unclear. In 1997–8, a combination of poor investment decisions, corruption and world economic conditions brought these countries' economic expansion to an abrupt halt. Their stock markets collapsed, their currencies fell and the entire global economy was threatened. The experience of Hong Kong was typical: after 37 years of continuous growth, the economy stalled and its stock market – the Hang Seng Index – lost more than half its value. It remains to be seen whether the 'Asian meltdown', as the newspapers called it in early 1998, will have a long-term effect on the region or is merely a blip in its recent growth. Once their current economic problems are solved, many economists argue, the newly industrializing Asian economies will resume their growth, although perhaps not at the meteoric rates of the past. For example, by 2004 economists noted that Hong Kong's economy was again growing and the property market was rising.

Theories of development

What causes global inequality and how can it be overcome? *Can* it ever be overcome? In this section, we shall examine different types of theory that have been advanced over the years to explain development: market-oriented theories, dependency and world systems theories and state-centred theories. These theories have strengths and weaknesses. One shortcoming of all of them is that they frequently give short shrift to the role of women in economic development. By putting them together, however, we should be able to answer a key question facing the 85 per cent of the world's population living outside high-income countries: how can they move up in the world economy?

Market-oriented theories

The most influential theories of global inequality advanced by British and American economists and sociologists 40 years ago were **market-oriented theories**. These assume that the best possible economic consequences will result if individuals are free – uninhibited by any form of governmental constraint – to make their own economic decisions. Unrestricted capitalism, if it is allowed to develop fully, is said to be the avenue to economic growth. Government bureaucracy should not dictate which goods to produce, what prices to charge or how much workers

Classic Studies 13.1 **Walt Rostow and the stages of economic growth**

The research problem

Why have some countries and regions experienced rapid economic development, while others continue to struggle? Is the problem of underdevelopment essentially an internal one (rooted within particular countries), or is it the consequence of external forces? What can we learn about the process of development from the already developed societies? The answers given by Walt Rostow (1916–2003), an economic adviser to former US President John F. Kennedy who became an influential economic theorist, helped to shape US foreign policy towards Latin America during the 1960s.

Rostow's explanation

Rostow's explanation is a market-oriented approach, which came to be described as modernization theory. **Modernization theory** says that low-income societies *can* develop economically, but only if they give up their traditional ways and adopt modern economic institutions, technologies and cultural values, which emphasize savings and productive investment. According to Rostow (1961), the traditional cultural values and social institutions of low-income countries impede their economic effectiveness. For example, he argued that many people in low-income countries lack a strong work ethic; they would rather consume today than invest for the future. Large families are also seen as partly responsible for 'economic backwardness', since a breadwinner with many mouths to feed can hardly be expected to save money for investment purposes.

But for Rostow and other modernization theorists, the problems in low-income countries run much deeper. The *cultures* of such countries tend to support 'fatalism' – a value system that views hardship and suffering as an unavoidable part of normal life. Acceptance of one's lot in life thus discourages people from working hard and being thrifty in order to overcome their fate. On this view, then, a country's economic underdevelopment is due largely to the cultural failings of the people themselves. Such failings are reinforced by government policies that set wages and control prices, generally interfering

in the operation of the economy. So how can low-income countries break out of their poverty? Rostow saw economic growth as moving through several stages, which he likened to the journey of an aeroplane (see figure 13.6):

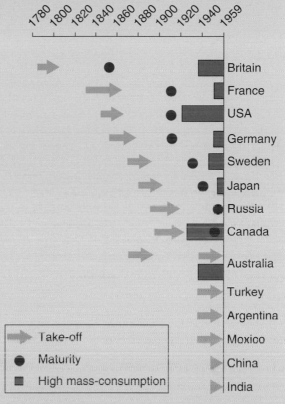

Figure 13.6 Rostow's stages of economic growth for selected countries, 1750–1959

Source: www.agocg.ac.uk/reports/visual/casestud/southall/trajecto.htm

1 *The traditional stage.* This is the stage just described, characterized by low rates of savings, the (supposed) lack of a strong work ethic and the 'fatalistic' value system. We could say that this aeroplane is stuck on the runway.
2 *Take-off to economic growth.* The traditional stage, *can* give way to a second one: economic take-off. This occurs when poor countries begin to jettison their traditional values and institutions, and people start to save and invest money for the future. The role

of wealthy countries is to facilitate and support this take-off. They can do this by financing birth control programmes or providing low-cost loans for electrification, road and airport construction, and starting new industries.

3 *Drive to technological maturity*. According to Rostow, with the help of money and advice from high-income countries, the aeroplane of economic growth would taxi down the runway, pick up speed and become airborne. The country would then approach technological maturity. In the aeronautical metaphor, the plane would slowly climb to cruising altitude, improving its technology, reinvesting its recently acquired wealth in new industries and adopting the institutions and values of the high-income countries.

4 *High mass consumption*. Finally, the country would reach the phase of high mass consumption. Now people are able to enjoy the fruits of their labour by achieving a high standard of living. The aeroplane (country) cruises along on automatic pilot, having entered the ranks of the high-income countries.

Rostow's ideas remain influential. Indeed, neoliberalism, which is perhaps the prevailing view among economists today, is rooted in Rostow's ideas. Neoliberals argue that free-market forces, achieved by minimizing governmental restrictions on business, provide the only route to economic growth, holding that global free trade will enable all the countries of the world to prosper. Eliminating governmental regulation is seen as necessary for economic growth to occur. Neoliberal economists therefore call for an end to restrictions on trade and often challenge minimum wage and other labour laws, as well as environmental restrictions on business.

Critical points

Supporters of modernization theory point to the success of the newly industrializing economies of East Asia as proof that development really is open to all. However, it can be objected that (as we saw above) the reasons for this success is partly accidental, involving Cold War political expediency and the historical legacy of colonialism. Such a conjunction of conditions is unlikely to apply to other low-income countries in the post-Cold War world. Indeed, even in the twenty-first century, many low-income countries, in spite of external assistance, have not passed through Rostow's stages and remain very far from becoming economically developed. A further criticism is that Rostow saw high-income countries playing a key role in helping low-income ones to grow. But this fails to take proper account of the long-term consequences of colonialism, which benefited the militarily powerful European societies at the expense of those in Asia and Latin America, thus dealing the latter's economic development a devastating early blow. Finally, by pointing to 'fatalistic' cultural values as a causal factor in underdevelopment, Rostow can be seen as ethnocentric, holding up Western values, ideals and models of 'progress' as superior. As chapter 5, 'The Environment', shows, the Western pursuit of untrammelled economic growth has, perhaps irrevocably, damaged the global natural environment, leading some to question whether this kind of 'progress' can be sustainable over the long term.

Contemporary significance

Rostow's theory of 'evolutionary' stages towards self-sustaining economic growth has suffered in the light of continued global poverty, hunger and underdevelopment, leading many to abandon it altogether. Certainly any notion of *inevitable* progress through the Rostovian stages finds little support almost half a century later as his 'non-communist manifesto' has probably attracted as much opposition and criticism as Marx and Engels's (1848) original communist version. But as we have already seen in this chapter, recent *global* indicators do present a more positive picture of an improving situation for many, though by no means all, populations in the low- and middle-income countries of the world. This may show that economic development is not exclusive to the high-income societies and that, as Rostow argued, the process of modernization remains a possibility for all in an era of rapid globalization and the intensification of international trade.

should be paid. According to market-oriented theorists, governmental direction of the economies of low-income countries results in blockages to economic development. In this view, local governments should get out of the way of development (Rostow 1961; Warren 1980; Ranis 1996).

THINKING CRITICALLY

Karl Marx said that the industrialized countries showed an image of their own future to the less developed countries. What are the main differences between Marx's version of modernization theory and that of Walt Rostow? Whose version, if any, is best supported by the historical evidence to date?

Dependency and world systems theories

During the 1960s, a number of theorists questioned market-oriented theories of global inequality such as modernization theory. Many of these critics were sociologists and economists from the low-income countries of Latin America and Africa, who drew on Marxist ideas to reject the idea that their countries' economic underdevelopment was due to their own cultural or institutional faults. Instead, they build on the theories of Karl Marx, who argued that world capitalism would create a class of countries manipulated by more powerful countries, just as capitalism within countries leads to the exploitation of workers. The **dependency theorists**, as they are called, argue that the poverty of low-income countries stems from their exploitation by wealthy countries and the multinational corporations that are based in wealthy countries. In their view, global capitalism locked their countries into a downward spiral of exploitation and poverty.

According to dependency theories, this exploitation began with **colonialism**, a political-economic system under which powerful countries established, for their own profit, rule over weaker peoples or countries. Powerful nations have colonized other countries usually to procure the raw materials needed for their factories and to control markets for the products manufactured in those factories. Under colonial rule, for example, the petroleum, copper, iron and food products required by industrial economies are extracted from low-income countries by businesses based in high-income countries. Although colonialism typically involved European countries establishing colonies in North and South America, Africa and Asia, some Asian countries (such as Japan) had colonies as well.

Even though colonialism ended throughout most of the world after the Second World War, the exploitation did not: transnational corporations continued to reap enormous profits from their branches in low-income countries. According to dependency theory, these global companies, often with the support of the powerful banks and governments of rich countries, established factories in poor countries, using cheap labour and raw materials to maximize production costs without governmental interference. In turn, the low prices set for labour and raw materials prevented poor countries from accumulating the profit necessary to industrialize themselves. Local businesses that might compete with foreign corporations were prevented from doing so. In this view, poor countries are forced to borrow from rich countries, thus increasing their economic dependency.

Low-income countries are thus seen not as underdeveloped, but rather as *misdeveloped* (Frank 1966; Emmanuel 1972). With the exception of a handful of local politicians and businesspeople who serve the interests of the foreign corporations, people fall into poverty. Peasants are forced to choose between starvation and working at near-starvation wages on foreign-controlled plantations and in foreign-controlled mines and factories. Since dependency theorists argue that such exploitation has kept their

Transnational corporations have often been accused of exploiting the poorest and reaping the financial rewards. Some argue this means that dependency culture, whereby the economic growth of poorer nations is held back by developed countries, did not die with colonialism.

countries from achieving economic growth, they typically call for revolutionary changes that would push foreign corporations out of their countries altogether (Frank 1969).

While market-oriented theorists usually ignore political and military power, dependency theorists regard the exercise of power as central to enforcing unequal economic relationships. According to this theory, whenever local leaders question such unequal arrangements, their voices are quickly suppressed. Unionization is usually outlawed, and labour organizers are jailed and sometimes killed. When people elect a government opposing these policies, that government is likely to be overthrown by the country's military, often backed by the armed forces of the industrialized countries themselves. Dependency

theorists point to many examples: the role of the CIA in overthrowing the Marxist governments of Guatemala in 1954 and Chile in 1973 and in undermining support for the leftist government in Nicaragua in the 1980s. In the view of dependency theory, global economic inequality is thus backed up by military force: economic elites in poor countries, backed by their counterparts in wealthy ones, use police and military power to keep the local population under control.

Brazilian sociologist, Enrique Fernando Cardoso, once a prominent dependency theorist, argued more than 25 years ago that some degree of dependent development was nonetheless possible – that under certain circumstances, poor countries can still develop economically, although only in

ways shaped by their reliance on the wealthier countries (Cardoso and Faletto 1979). In particular, the governments of these countries could play a key role in steering a course between dependency and development (Evans 1979). As President of Brazil from 1995 to 2003, Cardoso changed his thinking, calling for greater integration of Brazil into the global economy.

During the last quarter of a century, sociologists have increasingly seen the world as a single (although often conflict-ridden) economic system. Although dependency theories hold that individual countries are economically tied to one another, **world-systems theory**, which is strongly influenced by dependency theory, argues that the world capitalist economic system is not merely a collection of independent countries engaged in diplomatic and economic relations with one another, but must instead be understood as a single unit. The world-systems approach is most closely identified with the work of Immanuel Wallerstein and his colleagues (Wallerstein 1974, 1990 and elsewhere).

>> In chapter 4, 'Globalisation and the Changing World', see 'Classic Studies 4.1' for a discussion of Wallerstein's pioneering role in world-systems theory.

Wallerstein showed that capitalism has long existed as a global economic system, beginning with the extension of markets and trade in Europe in the fifteenth and sixteenth centuries. The world system is seen as comprising four overlapping elements (Chase-Dunn 1989):

- a world market for goods and labour;
- the division of the population into different economic classes, particularly capitalists and workers;

- an international system of formal and informal political relations among the most powerful countries, whose competition with one another helps shape the world economy; and
- the carving up of the world into three unequal economic zones, with the wealthier zones exploiting the poorer ones.

World-systems theorists term these three economic zones 'core', 'periphery' and 'semi-periphery'. All countries in the world system are said to fall into one of the three categories. **Core countries** are the most advanced industrial countries, taking the lion's share of profits in the world economic system. These include Japan, the United States and the countries of Western Europe. **Peripheral countries** comprise low-income, largely agricultural countries that are often manipulated by core countries for their own economic advantage. Examples of peripheral countries are found throughout Africa and to a lesser extent in Latin America and Asia. Natural resources, such as agricultural products, minerals and other raw materials, flow from periphery to core – as do the profits. The core, in turn, sells finished goods to the periphery, also at a profit. World-systems theorists argue that core countries have made themselves wealthy with this unequal trade, while at the same time limiting the economic development of peripheral countries. Finally, the **semi-peripheral countries** occupy an intermediate position: these are semi-industrialized, middle-income countries that extract profits from the more peripheral countries and in turn yield profits to the core countries. Examples of semi-peripheral countries include Mexico in North America; Brazil, Argentina and Chile in South America; and the newly industrializing economies of East Asia. The semi-periphery, though to some degree controlled by the core, is thus also able to exploit the periphery. Moreover, the greater economic success of the semi-periphery holds out to the periphery the promise of similar development.

Although the world system tends to change very slowly, once-powerful countries eventually lose their economic power and others then take their place. For example, some five centuries ago the Italian city-states of Venice and Genoa dominated the world capitalist economy. First the Dutch, then the British and currently the United States superseded them. Today, in the view of some world-systems theorists, American dominance is giving way to a more 'multipolar' world where economic power will be shared between the United States, Europe and Asia (Arrighi 1994).

State-centred theories

Some of the most recent explanations of successful economic development emphasize the role of state policy in promoting growth. Differing sharply from market-oriented theories, **state-centred theories** argue that appropriate government policies do not interfere with economic development but rather can play a key role in bringing it about. A large body of research now suggests that in some regions of the world, such as East Asia, successful economic development has been state-led. Even the World Bank, long a strong proponent of free-market theories of development, has changed its thinking about the role of the state. In its 1997 report *The State in a Changing World*, the World Bank concluded that without an effective state, 'sustainable development, both economic and social, is impossible'.

Strong governments contributed in various ways to economic growth in the East Asian NICs during the 1980s and 1990s (Appelbaum and Henderson 1992; Amsden et al. 1994; World Bank 1997):

1 *East Asian governments have sometimes aggressively acted to ensure political stability, while keeping labour costs low.* This has been accomplished by acts of repression, such as outlawing trade unions, banning strikes, jailing labour leaders and, in general, silencing the voices of workers. The governments of

Taiwan, South Korea and Singapore in particular have engaged in such practices.

2 *East Asian governments have frequently sought to steer economic development in desired directions.* For example, state agencies have often provided cheap loans and tax breaks to businesses that invest in industries favoured by the government. Sometimes this strategy has backfired, resulting in bad loans held by the government (one of the causes of the region's economic problems during the late 1990s). Some governments have prevented businesses from investing their profits in other countries, forcing them to invest in economic growth at home. Sometimes governments have owned and therefore controlled key industries. For example, the Japanese government has owned railways, the steel industry and banks; the South Korean government has owned banks; and the government of Singapore has owned airlines and the armaments and ship-repair industries.

3 *East Asian governments have often been heavily involved in social programmes such as low-cost housing and universal education.* The world's largest public housing systems (outside socialist or formerly socialist countries) have been in Hong Kong and Singapore, where government subsidies keep rents extremely low. As a result, workers do not require high wages to pay for their housing, so they can compete more easily with American and European workers in the emerging global labour market. In Singapore, which has an extremely strong central government, well-funded public education and training help to provide workers with the skills they need to compete effectively in the emerging global labour market. The Singaporean government also requires businesses and individual citizen alike to save a large percentage of their income for investment in future growth.

Evaluating theories of development

Each type of theory discussed above has both strengths and weaknesses. But together, they enable us to understand better the causes and cures for global inequality.

Market-oriented theories recommend the adoption of modern capitalist institutions to promote economic development, as the recent example of East Asia attests. They further argue that countries can develop economically only if they open their borders to trade, and they can cite evidence in support of this argument. But market-oriented theories also fail to take into account the various economic ties between poor countries and wealthy ones – ties that can impede economic growth under some conditions and enhance it under others. They tend to blame low-income countries themselves for their poverty rather than looking to the influence of outside factors, such as the business operations of more powerful nations. Market-oriented theories also ignore the ways government can work with the private sector to spur economic development. Finally, they fail to explain why some countries manage to take off economically while others remain grounded in poverty and underdevelopment.

Dependency theories address the market-oriented theories' neglect in considering poor countries' ties with wealthy countries by focusing on how wealthy nations have economically exploited poor ones. However, although dependency theories help to account for much of the economic backwardness in Latin America and Africa, they are unable to explain the occasional success story among such low-income countries as Brazil, Argentina and Mexico or the rapidly expanding economies of East Asia. In fact, some countries, once in the low-income category, have risen economically even in the presence of multinational corporations.

Even some former colonies, such as Hong Kong and Singapore, both once dependent on Great Britain, count among the success stories. World-systems theory sought to overcome the shortcomings of dependency theories by analysing the world economy as a whole. Rather than beginning with individual countries, world-systems theorists look at the complex global web of political and economic relationships that influence development and inequality in poor and rich nations alike.

State-centred theories stress the governmental role in fostering economic growth. They thus offer a useful alternative to both the prevailing market-oriented theories, with their emphasis on states as economic hindrances, and dependency theories, which view states as allies of global business elites in exploiting poor countries. When combined with the other theories – particularly world-systems theory – state-centred theories can explain the radical changes now transforming the world economy.

International organizations and global inequality

There are a number of international organizations whose work impacts on global poverty. The International Monetary Fund (IMF) and the World Bank – together known as the Bretton Woods Institutions (named after the place they were set up: Bretton Woods, New Hampshire, USA) – were established during the Second World War. They are based in Washington, DC, and their membership is made up of governments from across the world. The IMF is an organization of 184 countries. The main work of the IMF is in maintaining stability in the international financial system – most noticeably when it is called in to sort out a large debt crisis, for example as happened in Argentina from 2001 to 2003. It also works with governments across the world to improve their economic management, but it is precisely that advice which is often criticized as causing some of

the problems that poorer countries face (Stiglitz 2002).

The IMF's Structural Adjustment Programmes (SAPs) are essentially sets of conditions aimed at helping countries to balance their economies. These conditions are imposed on governments, primarily in the developing world, in return for new loans or to enable them to make repayments on older loans from commercial banks or from the World Bank. However, although SAPs were meant to target the needs of the specific country, in practice they have focused on the same 'solutions', including privatization programmes, reductions in social welfare spending and free market reforms. Critics argue that in too many cases, structural adjustment has had negative rather than positive effects on developing countries. Some have even suggested leaving the IMF and setting up an alternative bank, specifically for the developing countries of the Southern hemisphere (see 'Global Society 13.3'). Since 1999, the IMF and World Bank have tried to counter such criticisms by requiring loan recipients to produce Poverty Reduction Strategy Papers (PRSPs) outlining country-wide plans to reduce poverty. They hope that this will connect the IMF and World Bank's financial assistance to the Millennium Development Goal of halving 1990 poverty levels by 2015.

The World Bank Group's mission is to fight poverty and improve the living standards of people in the developing world. It is a development bank, which provides loans, policy advice, technical assistance and knowledge-sharing services to low- and middle-income countries to reduce poverty. The World Bank is made up of a number of accounts providing relatively cheap finance – mainly loans – for its member governments. Recently, the Bank has also started giving grants to governments for specific programmes. It also provides technical expertise alongside its loans and grants. Both the World Bank and the IMF have been accused of promoting market-driven

Global Society 13.3 | Why South America wants a new bank

Leaders of several South American nations have signed a founding document to create a new body, the Bank of the South, as an alternative to multilateral credit organizations such as the International Monetary Fund and World Bank.

The idea was first put forward by Venezuelan President Hugo Chavez in December 2006 as part of his battle against the influence of the US and the international financial institutions, which he has described as 'tools of Washington'. Argentina, Brazil, Bolivia, Ecuador, Paraguay, Uruguay and Venezuela have all joined the initiative. Chile and Peru decided to remain on the sidelines, while Colombia, which had expressed interest, has put its decision on hold following recent disagreements between Colombian President Alvaro Uribe and Mr Chavez.

According to Venezuelan finance minister Rodrigo Cabezas, the creation of a new organization is 'a demonstration that times have changed'. The Bank of the South, known as Banco del Sur in Spanish and Banco do Sul in Portuguese, he explains, will be funded and run by South American countries themselves.

Analysts believe the Bank of the South initiative reflects the increased unpopularity of the IMF and the World Bank among many South American countries. Mark Weisbrot, co-director of the Center for Economic and Policy Research in Washington, also sees it as one of many signs of a new independence from institutions such as the IMF and its 'unwanted austerity measures'. 'At the beginning of this decade, scepticism in Latin America was sealed when Argentina disregarded IMF advice by defaulting on its debt and then experienced robust economic recovery', Mr Weisbrot said.

Luis Maldonado, a presidential representative to the government body that helps regulate Ecuador's banking sector, argues that 'Latin America has been impoverished and harassed long enough that we have no other choice [but to] start the Bank of the South'. Venezuela has gone so far as to threaten to leave the IMF – although it has not set any date for such a move. 'If the IMF does not abandon its record of implementing tough policies with regards to emerging countries and being totally benevolent to developed countries, as it was in the last US

mortgage crisis, it will struggle to regain its credibility', said Mr Cabezas. Pulling out of the IMF would amount to a technical default on Venezuela's bonds and would raise the cost of future borrowing in global markets.

Other members of the Bank of the South share many of Venezuela's concerns about the IMF, but have made clear that they do not intend to leave it or other international institutions. Gustavo Guzman, Bolivia's ambassador to Washington, explained to the BBC that the bank would provide a much-needed 'alternative source' of funds. He points out that it has been difficult for Bolivia to get loans from the IMF and international markets since the government's recent moves to renationalise its oil and natural gas industry.

Colombian finance minister Oscar Ivan Zuluaga said at a meeting in New York that the Banco del Sur was seen as an effort to integrate the countries of South America and 'nothing more than that'.

Mixed reactions

The Bank of the South proposition has been greeted with caution by most analysts, although they agree that having more options for countries seeking funding is not a bad idea. Michael Shifter, Latin American expert at the Washington-based Inter-American Dialogue, said that while it was 'tempting to dismiss the Banco del Sur because of the political agenda behind it', he would advise sceptics to wait and see. 'Chavez's political agenda is undeniable, but so is the money he has at his disposal right now', he said. 'Over the longer run, the initiative will have real problems because of politicisation, but in the meantime it would be a mistake to underestimate its possibilities.'

Mr Shifter also feels the timing is fortunate. 'Banco del Sur is taking off precisely when traditional multilateral institutions like the Inter-American Development Bank and World Bank are struggling to redefine their missions and adapt to new circumstances', he said. 'Everything is in flux, so anything can happen.'

Source: Adapted from Lourdes Heredia, BBC News, 10 December 2007 © bbc.co.uk/news

reforms to the detriment of poor countries and people, and both have made an effort in recent years to concentrate more on the elimination of poverty.

One example of the new approach taken by the World Bank and IMF in recent years has been an initiative known as HIPC – Heavily Indebted Poor Countries – to grant debt relief to many of the poorest countries (see 'Using your sociological imagination 13.1' above). Some countries had taken on so many loans over a number of decades, which had attracted so much interest, that they could not afford to pay them back. If they were to pay them back in full, it would probably have wiped out the resources that the countries' governments had available for education, health and other basic services. The HIPC initiative was launched in 1996 to give those countries sufficient relief – funded by governments of rich countries – that they could deal with their debt burden as well as tackle poverty. A key element of the initiative was the requirement for all countries involved to produce and implement a Poverty Reduction Strategy Paper. By 2007, 29 countries had taken part in the HIPC process.

The United Nations, perhaps the best known of the international organizations, includes a series of funds and programmes, which work across the world to tackle the causes and effects of poverty. Examples include the United Nations Development Programme (UNDP) and United Nations Children's Fund, both based in New York, the World Food Programme in Rome and the World Health Organization (WHO) in Geneva. All have country offices across the world. Each aims to tackle different aspects of poverty. UNICEF's work is focused on girls' education, protection of children and immunization, as well as provision of clean water and sanitation. UNDP works with governments in poor countries to improve governance, including the rule of law, justice, state provision of basic services and tackling corruption. Add perhaps another ten UN organizations in any one country

and there is likely to be a complicated mix of organizations covering a number of interrelated issues. One key concern is the spread of HIV and its effects on economic, health, institutional capacity, family and social spheres. At least four UN organizations are therefore involved in tackling this problem. UN organizations generally suffer from low levels of core funding compared to their Bretton Woods cousins. Some, like the WHO, are also involved in setting international standards and undertaking research.

One member of the UN family that has regularly been in the news headlines in recent years is the World Trade Organization (WTO). Based in Geneva, it regulates international trade through negotiations between its 149 member governments and provides a mechanism for resolving trade disputes. The WTO has been the focus for a wave of anti-globalization and anti-capitalist demonstrations since its creation in 1995, replacing the previous General Agreement on Tariffs and Trade (GATT), which had operated since 1948. The protests have involved a varied range of political activists and social movements which view the WTO, along with the World Bank and the IMF, as managing the world economy in the interests of the already wealthy and powerful countries against the interests of the global poor.

 Chapter 22, 'Politics, Government and Social Movements', discusses the anti-globalization movement in more detail.

The round of WTO negotiations launched in Doha in Qatar in 2001 is referred to by some as a 'development round'. There is a widespread view that the current international trading system is not fair to poorer countries and is constraining their economic development. A prime aim of these negotiations is to rectify this through, for example, improved access for these countries' goods and services to others' markets. However, the lack of real progress in negotiations led to the Doha Round being suspended on 27 July 2006. In particular, no agreement could be reached on reducing the huge subsidies which farmers in the USA, Europe and Japan receive, or the restrictive import tariffs imposed by emerging economies including China, Brazil and India. Without some movement on these two issues, developing countries continue to be disadvantaged and denied access to 'fair trade' in international markets (see 'Global Society 13.4').

THINKING CRITICALLY

Look at the evidence presented in 'Global society 13.4' on world trade. How do the four theoretical perspectives we introduced above fare in the light of this evidence? For instance, does it illustrate Rostow's *stages of economic growth*? Can *dependency theory* explain the persistence of such unequal trading relations? Is there evidence here of the threefold typology outlined in Wallerstein's economic *world-system theory*? What explanatory power do *state-centred theories* have in relation to international trade and its obvious inequities? What would the WTO need to do in order to give poorer, developing countries more opportunities to trade across the world and improve their share of world trade? How likely do you think it is that the WTO will achieve this?

All the organizations described above are said to be multilateral, as they involve many, indeed the majority of, countries. So-called bilateral donors are also involved in the reduction of global poverty. In the UK, the government's Department for International Development (DfID), works with specific poor countries to meet the Millennium Development Goals. These goals were set out by the international community in the late 1990s. They include a series of targets, of which two of the most important are halving, between 1990 and 2015, the proportion of people whose income is less than US$1 a day and ensuring that, by 2015, all children will be able to complete a full course of primary schooling. Several of these targets are unlikely to be met. In the UK, the work of DfID includes the provision of grants and expertise in the country, as well as policy and advocacy at the international level to remove some of the structural barriers to the reduction of poverty (for example debt, trade rules and exploitation of resources).

Global economic inequality in a changing world

Today the social and economic forces leading to a single global capitalist economy appear to be irresistible. The principal challenge to this outcome – socialism/communism – ended with the collapse of the Soviet Union in 1991. The largest remaining socialist country in the world today, the People's Republic of China, is rapidly adopting many capitalist economic institutions and is the fastest-growing economy in the world. It is too soon to tell how far the future leaders of China will move down the capitalist road. Will they eventually adopt a complete market-oriented economy or some combination of state controls and capitalist institutions? Most China experts agree on one thing: when China, with its 1.3 billion people, fully enters the global capitalist system, its impact will be felt around the world. China has an enormous workforce, much of which is well trained and educated and now receives extremely low wages – sometimes less than one-twentieth of what workers earn in comparable jobs in the developed countries. Such a workforce will be extremely competitive in a global economy and will force wages down from Los Angeles to London.

What does rapid globalization mean for the future of global inequality? No sociologist knows for certain, but many possible scenarios exist. In one, our world might be dominated by large, global corporations with workers competing against each other for a living wage. Such a scenario might

Global Society 13.4 | **World trade, globalization and the persistence of global inequality, 1950–2002**

The growth in world trade has been unevenly spread. Some developing countries – often in Asia – have increased growth by producing more manufactured goods. But others – often in Africa – have fallen further behind.

The world's poorest countries – the 49 least developed countries – have not shared in the growth of world trade. The 646 million people in the top exporting countries – the US, Germany, Japan, France and UK – have 100 times more trade than their poor counterparts.

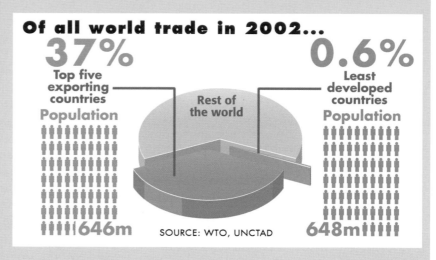

Huge agricultural subsidies by Western countries to their small farm populations far outweigh the aid given to developing countries. The rich countries have repeatedly pledged to reduce the size of their farm supports. So far the amount of such subsidies has changed little in 20 years, while the amount of aid has declined.

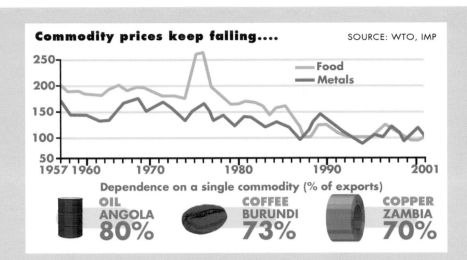

Many poor countries depend on a single primary export like wood, coffee, copper or cotton. But prices for such commodities have been declining. Prices of manufactured goods have, in contrast, risen in relative terms.

Source: BBC News Online, 15 August 2007, 'Trade and the poor: will globalization save or destroy the world?' http://news.bbc.co.uk/1/hi/in_depth/business/2004/world_trade/default.stm#

China is the fastest-growing economy in the world. Despite its communist foundations, the gap between rich and poor is large and arguably widening

predict falling wages for large numbers of people in today's high-income countries and rising wages for more in low-income countries. There might be a general levelling out of average income around the world, although at a level much lower than that currently enjoyed in the industrialized nations. In this scenario, the polarization between the 'haves' and the 'have-nots' within countries would grow, as the whole world would be increasingly divided into those who benefit from the global economy and those who do not. Such a polarization could fuel conflict between ethnic groups, and even nations, as those suffering from economic globalization would blame others for their plight (Hirst and Thompson 1992; Wagar 1992).

On the other hand, a global economy could mean greater opportunity for everyone, as the benefits of modern technology stimulate worldwide economic growth. According to this more optimistic scenario, the more successful East Asian NICs, such as Hong Kong, Taiwan, South Korea and Singapore, are a sign of things to come. Other NICs such as Malaysia and Thailand will soon follow, along with China, Indonesia, Vietnam and other Asian countries. India, the world's second most populous country, already boasts a middle class of some 200 million people, about a quarter of its total population (although roughly the same number live in poverty) (Kulkarni 1993).

A countervailing trend, however, is the technology gap that divides rich and poor countries, which today appears to be widening, making it even more difficult for poor countries to catch up. The global technology gap is a result of the disparity in wealth between nations, but it also reinforces those disparities, widening the gap between rich and poor countries. Poor countries cannot easily afford modern technology – yet, in the absence of it, they face major barriers in overcoming poverty. They are caught in a vicious downward spiral from which it is proving difficult to escape.

Jeffrey Sachs, Director of the Earth Insti-

tute at Columbia University in New York, and a prominent adviser to many East European and developing countries, claims that the world is divided into three classes: technology innovators, technology adopters and the technologically disconnected (Sachs 2000).

Technology innovators are those regions that provide nearly all of the world's technological inventions; they account for no more than 15 per cent of the world's population. Technology adopters are those regions that are able to adopt technologies invented elsewhere, applying them to production and consumption; they account for 50 per cent of the world's population. Finally, the technologically disconnected are those regions that neither innovate nor adopt technologies developed elsewhere; they account for 35 per cent of the world's population. Note that Sachs speaks of regions rather than countries. In today's increasingly borderless world, technology use does not always respect national frontiers. For example, Sachs notes that technologically disconnected regions include 'southern Mexico and pockets of tropical Central America; the Andean countries; most of tropical Brazil; tropical sub-Saharan Africa; most of the former Soviet Union aside from the areas nearest to European and Asian markets; landlocked parts of Asia such as the Ganges valley states of India; landlocked Laos and Cambodia; and the deep-interior states of China' (Sachs 2000). These are impoverished regions that lack access to markets or major ocean trading routes. They are caught in what Sachs terms a 'poverty trap', plagued by 'tropical infectious disease, low agricultural productivity and environmental degradation – all requiring technological solutions beyond their means' (ibid.).

Innovation requires a critical mass of ideas and technology to become self-sustaining. 'Silicon Valley', near San Francisco in the United States, provides one example of how technological innovation tends to be concentrated in regions rich in universities and high-tech firms. Silicon Valley grew up around Stanford University and other educational and research institutions located south of San Francisco. Poor countries are ill-equipped to develop such high-tech regions. Sachs calculates that 48 tropical or partly tropical countries, whose combined population totalled 750 million, accounted for only 47 of the 51,000 patents granted in the USA to foreign inventors in 1997. Most poor countries lack even a science adviser to their government. Moreover, these countries are too poor to import computers, mobile phones, fax machines, computerized factory machinery or other kinds of high technology. Nor can they afford to license technology from the foreign companies that hold the patents.

What can be done to overcome the technological abyss that divides rich and poor countries? Sachs calls on wealthy, high-technology countries to provide much greater financial and technical assistance to poor countries than they now do. For example, lethal infectious diseases such as malaria, measles and diarrhoea claim million of lives each year in poor countries. The modern medical technology necessary to eradicate these illnesses would cost only US$10 billion a year – less than US$15 from every person who lives in a high-income country, if the cost were shared equally.

Sachs urges the governments of wealthy countries, along with international lending institutions, to provide loans and grants for scientific and technological development. He notes that very little money is available to support research and development in poor countries. The World Bank, a major source of funding for development projects in poor countries, spends only US$60 million a year supporting tropical, agricultural or health research and development. By way of comparison, Merck, the giant pharmaceutical corporation, spends 35 times that much (US$2.1 billion) for research and development for its own products. Even universities in wealthy nations could play a role, establishing overseas research and training institutes that would foster collaborative research projects. From computers and the Internet to biotechnology, the 'wealth of nations' increasingly depends on modern information technology. As long as major regions of the world remain technologically disconnected, it seems unlikely that global poverty will be eradicated.

In the most optimistic view, the republics of the former Soviet Union, as well as the formerly socialist countries of Eastern Europe, will eventually advance into the ranks of the high-income countries. Economic growth will spread to Latin America, Africa and the rest of the world. Because capitalism requires that workers be mobile, the remaining caste societies around the world will be replaced by class-based societies. These societies will experience enhanced opportunities for upward mobility.

What is the future of global inequality? It is difficult to be entirely optimistic. Global economic growth has slowed, and many of the once promising economies of Asia now seem to be in trouble. The Russian economy, in its move from socialism to capitalism, has encountered many problems, leaving many Russians poorer than before. It remains to be seen whether the countries of the world will learn from one another and work together to create better lives for their peoples. What is certain is that the past quarter of a century has witnessed a global economic transformation of unprecedented magnitude. The effects of this transformation in the next 25 years will leave few lives on the planet untouched.

If global inequality is one of the most important problems facing people today, then a related issue is the dramatic increase in world population. Global poverty and population growth are tied together today, for it is in some of the world's poorest countries that population growth is greatest, and it is to a discussion of this phenomenon that we now turn.

World population growth and global inequality

It is estimated that the Earth's six-billionth inhabitant was born on 12 October 1999. The world's population is booming – it has more than doubled since 1960. An American expert on population studies, Paul Ehrlich, calculated in the 1960s that if the rate of population growth at that time were to continue, 900 years from now (not a long period in world history as a whole) there would be 60,000,000,000,000,000 (60 quadrillion) people on the face of the earth. There would be 100 people for every square yard of the Earth's surface, including both land and water.

The physicist, J. H. Fremlin, worked out that housing such a population would require a continuous 2,000-storey building covering the entire planet. Even in such a stupendous structure there would only be three or four yards of floor space per person (Fremlin 1964).

Such a picture, of course, is nothing more than nightmarish fiction designed to drive home how cataclysmic the consequences of continued population growth would be. The real issue is what will happen over the next 30 or 40 years. Partly because governments and other agencies heeded the warnings of Ehrlich and others, by introducing population control programmes, there are grounds for supposing that world population growth is beginning to trail off (see figure 13.7). Estimates calculated in the 1960s of the likely world population by the year 2000 turned out to be inaccurate. The World Bank estimated the world population to be just over 6 billion in 2000, compared to some earlier estimates of more than 8 billion. Nevertheless, considering that a century ago there were only 1.5 billion people in the world, this still represents growth of staggering proportions. Can this scale of human population be adequately fed and housed, or will large sections of it be condemned to a life of poverty? What would the spread of current Western lifestyles to the world's population mean for the global environment? Can the planetary ecosystem cope with the pollution and waste of global consumerism? These questions are made more urgent when we realize that the factors underlying population growth are by no means entirely predictable. The population in 40 years' time could be even higher than current forecasts suggest.

Population analysis: demography

The study of population is referred to as **demography**. The term was invented about a century and a half ago, at a time when nations were beginning to keep official statistics on the nature and distribution of their populations. Demography is concerned with measuring the size of populations and explaining their rise or decline. Population patterns are governed by three factors: births, deaths and migrations. Demography is customarily treated as a branch of sociology, because the factors that influence the level of births and deaths in a given group or society, as well as migrations of population, are largely social and cultural.

Demographic work tends to be statistical. All the developed nations today gather and analyse basic statistics on their populations by carrying out censuses (systematic surveys designed to find out about the whole population of a given country). Rigorous as the modes of data collection now are, even in these nations demographic statistics are not wholly accurate. In the United Kingdom, there has been a population Census every ten years since 1801. The Census aims to be as accurate as possible, but for various reasons some people might not be registered in the official population statistics – for example illegal immigrants, homeless people, transients and others who for one reason or another avoided registration. In many developing countries, particularly those with recent high rates of population growth, demographic statistics are much more unreliable.

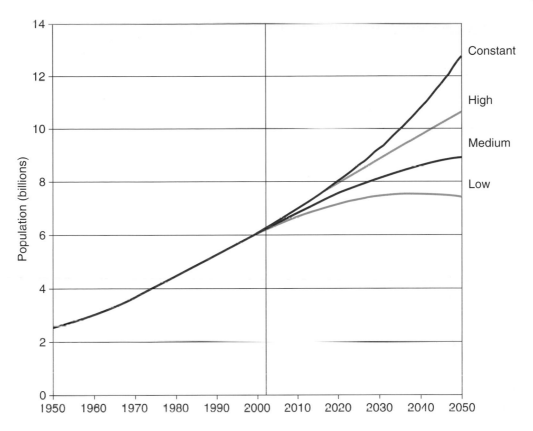

Figure 13.7 Estimated and projected population of the world by projection variant, 1950–2050

Source: UN 2003a

Dynamics of population change

Rates of population growth or decline are measured by subtracting the number of deaths per 1,000 from the number of births per 1,000 – this is usually calculated annually. Some European countries have negative growth rates – in other words, their populations are declining. Virtually all the industrialized countries have growth rates of less than 0.5 per cent. Rates of population growth were high in the eighteenth and nineteenth centuries but have since levelled off. Many developing countries today have rates of between 2 and 3 per cent. These may not seem very different from the rates of the industrialized countries, but in fact, the consequences are enormous.

The reason for this is that growth in population is exponential. There is an ancient Persian myth that helps to illustrate exponential growth. A courtier asked a ruler to reward him for his services by giving him twice as many grains of rice for each service than he had given him the time before, starting with a single grain on the first square of a chess board. Believing that he was onto a good thing, the king commanded grain to be brought up from his storehouse. By the 21st square, the storehouse was empty; the 40th square required ten billion grains of rice (Meadows et al. 1972). In other words, starting with one item and doubling it, doubling the result, and so on, rapidly leads to huge figures – 1:2:4:8:16:32:64:128, and so on. In seven operations, the figure has grown by 128 times. Exactly the same principle applies to population growth. We can measure this effect by means of the **doubling time**, the period of time it takes for the

Global Society 13.5 Demography – the key concepts

Among the basic concepts used by demographers, the most important are crude birth rates, fertility, fecundity and crude death rates. **Crude birth rates** are expressed as the number of live births per year per 1,000 of the population. They are called 'crude' rates because of their very general character. They do not, for example, tell us what proportion of a population is male or female, or what the age distribution of a population is (the relative proportions of young and old people in the population). Where statistics are collected that relate birth or death rates to such categories, demographers speak of 'specific' rather than 'crude' rates. For instance, an age-specific birth rate might specify the number of births per 1,000 women in different age groups.

If we wish to understand population patterns in any detail, the information provided by specific birth rates is normally necessary. Crude birth rates, however, are useful for making overall comparisons between different groups, societies and regions. Thus, in 2006 the crude birth rate in Australia was 12.4 (per year, per 1,000 population), in Nicaragua 24.9, in Mozambique 39.5 and, highest of all, in the Democratic Republic of the Congo it was 49.6 (UN ESA 2006). The industrialized countries tend to have low rates, while in many other parts of the world, crude birth rates are much higher (figure 13.8).

Birth rates are an expression of the fertility of women. **Fertility** refers to how many live-born children the average woman has. A fertility rate is usually calculated as the average number of births per 1,000 women of childbearing age. Fertility is distinguished from **fecundity**, which means the potential number of children women are biologically capable of bearing. It is physically possible for a normal woman to bear a child every year during the period when she is capable of conception. There are variations in fecundity according to the age at which women reach puberty and menopause, both of which differ among countries as well as among individuals. While there may be families in which a woman bears 20 or more children, fertility rates in practice are always much lower than fecundity rates, because social and cultural factors limit breeding.

Crude death rates (also called 'mortality rates') are calculated in the same way as birth rates – the number of deaths per thousand of population per year. Again, there are major variations among countries, but death rates in many societies in the developing world are falling to levels comparable to those in developed nations. The death rate in the United Kingdom in 2002 was 10 per 1,000. In India it was 9 per 1,000; in Ethiopia it was 18 per 1,000. A few countries have much higher death rates. In Sierra Leone, for example, the death rate is 30 per

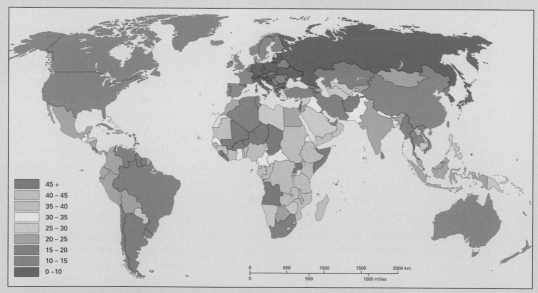

45 +
40 – 45
35 – 40
30 – 35
25 – 30
20 – 25
15 – 20
10 – 15
0 –10

Figure 13.8 Global crude birth rates

Source: Based on *CIA Factbook* 2007

1,000. Like crude birth rates, crude death rates only provide a very general index of **mortality** (the number of deaths in a population). Specific death rates give more precise information. A particularly important specific death rate is the **infant mortality rate**: the number of babies per 1,000 births in any year who die before reaching their first birthday. One of the key factors underlying the population explosion has been reductions in infant mortality rates.

Declining rates of infant mortality are the most important influence on increasing **life expectancy** – that is, the number of years the average person can expect to live. In 2007, life expectancy at birth for women born in the UK was 81.3 years, compared with 76.23 years for men (CIA 2007).

This contrasts with 49 and 45 years respectively at the turn of the twentieth century. This does not mean, however, that most people born in 1901 died when they were in their 40s. When there is a high infant mortality rate, as there is in many developing nations, the average life expectancy – which is a statistical average – is brought down. Illness, nutrition and the influence of natural disasters are other factors that influence life expectancy. Life expectancy has to be distinguished from **life span**, which is the maximum number of years that an individual could live. While life expectancy has increased in most societies in the world, life span has remained unaltered. Only a small proportion of people live to be 100 or more.

population to double. A population growth of 1 per cent will produce a doubling of numbers in 70 years. At 2 per cent growth, a population will double in 35 years, while at 3 per cent it will double in just 23 years. It took the whole of human history until 1850 for the global population to reach 1 billion. But during the next 80 years, by 1930, it had doubled to 2 billion. By 1975 – in just 45 years – the population had doubled again to 4 billion and in 2007, it stood at 6.6 billion.

Malthusianism

In pre-modern societies, birth rates were very high by the standards of the industrialized world today. Nonetheless, population growth remained low until the eighteenth century because there was a rough overall balance between births and deaths. The general trend of numbers was upward, and there were sometimes periods of more marked population increase, but these were followed by increases in death rates. In medieval Europe, for example, when harvests were bad, marriages tended to be postponed and the number of conceptions fell, while deaths increased. These complementary trends reduced the number of mouths to be fed. No pre-industrial society was able to escape from this self-regulating rhythm (Wrigley 1968).

During the period of the rise of industrialism, many looked forward to a new age in which scarcity would be a phenomenon of the past. The development of modern industry, it was widely supposed, would create a new era of abundance. In his celebrated *Essay on the Principle of Population* (1976 [1798]), Thomas Malthus criticized these ideas and initiated a debate about the connection between population and food resources that continues to this day. At the time he wrote, the population in Europe was growing rapidly. Malthus pointed out that while population increase is exponential, food supply depends on fixed resources that can be expanded only by developing new land for cultivation. Population growth therefore tends to outstrip the means of support available. The inevitable outcome is famine, which, combined with the influence of war and plagues, acts as a natural limit to population increase. Malthus predicted that human beings would always live in circumstances of misery and starvation, unless they practised what he called 'moral restraint'. His cure for excessive population growth was for people strictly to limit their frequency of sexual intercourse. The use of contraception he proclaimed to be a 'vice'.

For a while, **Malthusianism** was ignored, since the population development of the

Western countries followed a quite different pattern from that which he had anticipated – as we shall see below. Rates of population growth trailed off in the nineteenth and twentieth centuries. Indeed, in the 1930s there were major worries about population decline in many industrialized countries, including the United Kingdom. The upsurge in world population growth in the twentieth century has again lent some credence to Malthus's views, although few support them in their original version. Population expansion in developing countries seems to be outstripping the resources that those countries can generate to feed their citizens.

The demographic transition

Demographers often refer to the changes in the ratio of births to deaths in the industrialized countries from the nineteenth century onward as the **demographic transition**. This thesis was first outlined by Warren S. Thompson, who described a three-stage process in which one type of population stability would be eventually replaced by another, as a society reached an advanced level of economic development (Thompson 1929).

The prospects for twenty-first-century equality

Fertility remains high in developing world societies partly because traditional attitudes to family size have been maintained. Having large numbers of children is often still regarded as desirable, providing a source of labour on family-run farms. Some religions are either opposed to birth control or affirm the desirability of having many children. Contraception is opposed by Islamic leaders in several countries and by the Catholic Church, whose influence is especially marked in South and Central America. The motivation to reduce fertility has not always been forthcoming even from political authorities. In 1974, contraceptives were banned in Argentina as part of a programme to double the population of the country as fast as possible; this was seen as a means of developing its economic and military strength.

Yet a decline in fertility levels has at last occurred in some large developing countries. An example is China, which currently has a population of about 1.3 billion people – almost a quarter of the world's population as a whole. The Chinese government established one of the most extensive programmes of population control that any country has undertaken, with the object of stabilizing the country's numbers at close to their current level. Incentives were instituted (such as better housing and free healthcare and education) to promote single-child families, while families with more than one child face special hardships (wages are cut for those who have a third child). In some cases the Chinese government's policy has had horrific unintended consequences. A traditional preference for boys, and a belief that males will look after their parents in their old age, whereas females, once married, 'belong to' someone else, has led to some newborn girls being killed by their families in preference to facing the penalties of having a second child. However, there is evidence that China's antenatal policies, however harsh they may appear, have had a substantial impact on limiting the country's population growth.

China's programme demands a degree of centralized government control that is either unacceptable or unavailable in most other developing countries. In India, for instance, many schemes for promoting family planning and the use of contraceptives have been tried, but with only relatively small success. In 1988 India had a population of 789 million. By 2000, its population just topped a billion. And even if its population growth rate does diminish, by 2050 India will be the most populous country in the world, with more than 1.5 billion people.

It is claimed that the demographic changes that will occur over the next 100

Classic Studies 13.2 | **Demographic transition theory**

The research problem

As societies industrialized from the mid-eighteenth century onwards, their populations increased rapidly. But a century or so later, population growth had slowed, and in the twenty-first century, many developed societies are barely replacing their population. Why did this happen? Is there a pattern to such a long-term transformation and, if so, is it likely to be repeated across other industrializing countries? What will happen to the size of the global human population in the future? Warren S. Thompson (1887–1973), an American demographer, was the first to identify a pattern to such developments and his work was developed by later demographers who linked demographic trends to industrialization.

The Demographic Transition Model

Thompson (1929) recognized that although changes to birth and death rates shape population growth and size, there are important *transitions* in a society's birth and death rates, which have a profound impact on their overall population. Later demographers refined and developed his ideas into a model, usually referred to as the *Demographic Transition Model* (DTM), which identifies a series of stages through which societies pass as they go through industrial development (you may wish to refer to the model illustrated in figure 13.9 as you read the next section).

Stage One refers to the conditions characterizing most traditional societies, in which both birth and death rates are high and the infant mortality rate is especially large. Population grows little, if at all, as the high number of births is more or less balanced by the level of deaths. This stage was operative for most of human history as epidemics, disease and natural disasters such as floods and drought kept down human numbers. In *Stage Two*, which began in most of Europe and the United States in the early part of the nineteenth century – with wide regional variations – the death rate fell but fertility remained high. The consequence was a marked phase of long-term population growth. Improvements in food quality and higher crop yields, safe water supplies for drinking and washing, more efficient sewerage and waste disposal; all of these produced a fall in the death

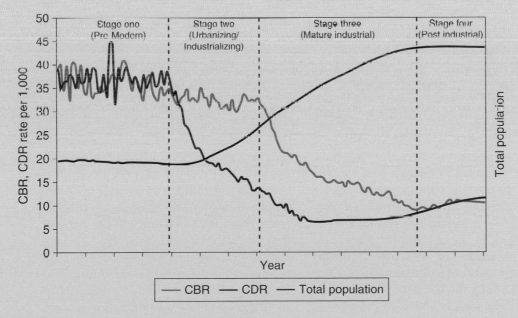

Figure 13.9   The Demographic Transition Model

Source: http://en.wikipedia.org/wiki/Image: Stage5.jpg

rate and subsequent rise in population. In *Stage Three* the birth rate also fell, to a level such that the population gradually became fairly stable, though obviously, at a much higher absolute level than in Stage One. Several possible reasons have been put forward for this change, including increasing literacy levels (particularly amongst women) leading to the challenging of traditional ideas regarding women's primary role as childbearers; compulsory education which removed children from the workforce; and urbanization, which removed the need (in rural areas) for large families to work on the land.

Somewhat later, improved contraceptive technologies also played a major part in enabling people to control their fertility. Some demographers identify a *Stage Four*, in which populations stabilize, thus completing the demographic transition. However, some countries, including Greece, Italy and Japan, have recently been reproducing below replacement levels and we might speculate about a stage in which population levels in the advanced industrial societies may decline. However, so far this stage remains a theoretical possibility rather than reality.

Critical points

Although it is generally accepted that the sequence accurately describes a major transformation in the demographic character of modern societies, there are some considerable differences amongst the industrialized countries. When the model is applied to developing countries, critics have pointed out that the

emergence of HIV/AIDS in the 1980s has been a major factor in slowing or even halting some countries' progress as death rates and infant mortality rates have risen rather than fallen. Sub-Saharan Africa has suffered most as a result of the spread of HIV/AIDS (see chapter 10, 'Health, Illness and Disability').

The DTM has been widely seen as an anti-Malthusian thesis. It suggests that rather than exponential growth leading to mass hunger and widespread famine, human populations are likely to settle into comfortable stability. One objection to the optimism embedded in this view is that the spread of Western-style consumerism to even the existing population would seriously damage the global ecosystem, and on present population forecasts, things can only get worse. Some environmentalists argue we should not be so sanguine about high absolute human numbers but should be aiming for a managed *reduction* in the global population.

Contemporary significance

The DTM has been perhaps the most influential perspective on long-term population trends ever devised and it continues to inform research in the field of demography. Demographers do not agree about how the sequence of change predicted by the model should be interpreted though, nor how long Stage Three is likely to last. Nevertheless, the great virtue of the model is that it encourages us to take a long-term view of human development in a global perspective and provides a point from which to start doing so.

years will be greater than any that have taken place in all of human history. It is difficult to predict with any precision the rate at which the world population will rise, but the United Nations has several fertility scenarios. The 'high' scenario places the world's population at more than 25 billion people by 2150. The 'medium' fertility scenario, which the UN deems most likely, assumes that fertility levels will stabilize at just over two children per woman, resulting in a world population of 11.8 billion people by 2150.

This overall population increase conceals two distinct trends. First, most developing countries will undergo the process of demographic transition described above. This will result in a substantial surge in the population, as death rates fall. India and China are each likely to see their populations reach 1.5 billion people. Areas in Asia, Africa and Latin America will similarly experience rapid growth before the population eventually stabilizes.

The second trend concerns the developed countries that have already undergone demographic transition. These societies will experience very slight population growth, if any at all. Instead, a process of ageing will occur in which the number of young people will decline in absolute terms and the older segment of the population will increase markedly. This will have widespread economic and social implications for developed countries: as the dependency ratio increases, pressure will mount on health and social services. Yet, as their numbers grow, older people will also have more political weight and may be able to push for higher expenditures on programmes and services of importance to them.

> Ageing of the global population is discussed in chapter 8, 'The Life-Course'.

What will be the consequences of these demographic changes for global inequality? Some observers see the makings of widespread social upheaval – particularly in the developing countries undergoing demographic transition. Changes in the economy and labour markets may prompt widespread internal migration as people in rural areas search for work. The rapid growth of cities is likely to lead to environmental damage, new public health risks, overloaded infrastructures, rising crime and impoverished squatter settlements.

Famine and food shortages are another serious concern. As we saw in our discussion of global inequality, there are around 830 million people in the world suffering from hunger or under-nourishment. As the population rises, levels of food output will need to rise accordingly to avoid widespread scarcity. Yet it is difficult to see how this can happen; many of the world's poorest areas are particularly affected by water shortages, shrinking farmland and soil degradation – processes that reduce, rather than enhance, agricultural productivity. It is almost certain that food production will not occur at a level to ensure self-sufficiency. Large amounts of food and grain will need to be imported from areas where there are surpluses. According to the United Nations Food and Agricultural Organization (FAO), by 2010 industrialized countries will be producing 1,614 pounds of grain per person, compared to only 507 pounds per head in the developing world.

Technological advances in agriculture and industry are unpredictable, so no one can be sure how large a population the world might eventually be able to support. Yet even at current population levels, global resources may already be well below those required to create living standards in the less developed world comparable to those of the industrialized countries.

Summary points

1. The countries of the world can be stratified according to their per-person gross national income. Currently, 40 per cent of the world's population live in low-income countries, compared with only 16 per cent in high-income countries.

2. An estimated 1.3 billion people in the world, or nearly one in four people, live in poverty today, an increase since the early 1980s. Many are the victims of discrimination based on race, ethnicity or tribal affiliation.

3. In general, people in high-income countries enjoy a far higher standard of living than their counterparts in low-income countries. They are likely to have more food to eat, less likely to starve or suffer from malnutrition and likely to live longer. They are far more likely to be literate and educated and therefore have higher-skilled, higher-paying jobs. Additionally, they are less likely to have large families, and their children are much less likely to die in infancy of malnutrition or childhood diseases.

4. *Market-oriented theories* of global inequality,

such as modernization theory, claim that cultural and institutional barriers to development explain the poverty of low-income societies. In this view, to eliminate poverty, fatalistic attitudes must be overcome, government meddling in economic affairs ended and a high rate of savings and investment encouraged. *Dependency theories* claim that global poverty is the result of the exploitation of poor countries by wealthy ones. Even though the economic fate of poor countries is ultimately determined by wealthy ones, some development is possible within dependent capitalistic relations. *World-systems theory* argues that the capitalist world system as a whole must be understood if we hope to make sense of global inequality. It focuses on relationships of the core, peripheral and semi-peripheral countries and on long-term trends in the global economy. *State-centred theories* emphasize the role that governments can play in fostering economic development. These theories draw on the experience of the rapidly growing East Asian newly industrializing economies as an example.

5. Population growth is one of the most significant global problems currently faced by humanity. Malthusianism is the idea, first advanced by Thomas Malthus two centuries ago, that population growth tends to outstrip the resources available to support it. Unless people limited their frequency of sexual intercourse, he argued, excessive population growth would ensure a future of misery and starvation.

6. The study of population growth – demography – is primarily statistical, but demographers are also concerned with trying to explain why population patterns take the form they do. The most important concepts in population analysis are birth rates, death rates, fertility and fecundity.

7. Changes in population patterns are usually analysed in terms of stages within the demographic transition. Prior to industrialization, both birth and death rates were high. During the beginning of industrialization, there was population growth, because death rates were reduced while birth rates took longer to decline. Finally, a new equilibrium was reached with low birth rates balancing low death rates.

8. World population is projected to grow to more than 10 billion people by 2150. Most of this growth will occur in the developing world, where countries will undergo a demographic transition and experience rapid growth before the population stabilizes. In the developed world, population will grow only slightly. Instead, a process of ageing will occur and the number of young people will decline in absolute terms. These population trends will have far-reaching implications for labour markets, welfare systems, food and water supplies and the natural environment.

Further reading

Given the wide-ranging subject matter of this chapter, a word of caution is in order. None of the reading for this chapter can legitimately be labelled 'introductory' and all of it makes intellectual demands of the reader. This should be a worthwhile challenge rather than a turn-off though.

Perhaps a good place to begin some additional reading is with Vic George and Robert Page's edited volume, *Global Social Problems* (Cambridge: Polity, 2004) to gain a better view of the range of social problems that demand global solutions. From here, David Held and Ayse Kaya's edited *Global Inequality: Patterns and Explanations* (Cambridge: Polity, 2006) offers exactly what it says: a discussion of patterns of inequality and the explanations and theories which try to account for it.

A good account of what 'development' means today and has meant in the past can be found in Katie Willis's *Theories and Practices of Development* (London and New York: Routledge, 2005), which also looks at attempts to put theory into practice. Alastair Greig, David Hulme and Mark Turner's *Challenging Global Inequality: Development Theory and Practice in the 21st Century* (Basingstoke: Palgrave Macmillan, 2007) presents another up-to-date alternative.

Anyone interested in the issues raised in relation to measurement of inequality, could try Branko Milanovich's *Worlds Apart: Measuring International and Global Inequality* (Princeton, NJ: Princeton University Press, 2007), which is a stimulating read.

Internet links

The Global Site – scholarly writings on global matters, based at the University of Sussex, Brighton, UK:
www.theglobalsite.ac.uk/

International Monetary Fund:
www.imf.org/

Make Poverty History campaign – London-based:
www.makepovertyhistory.org/

United Nations – multilingual site with enormous amount of information on global issues:
www.un.org/

World Bank – globalization pages of the World Bank Group, has lots of briefing papers, research and other data:
www.worldbank.org/

14

Sexuality
and
Gender

CHAPTER 14

Sexuality and Gender

(opposite) Other high-profile individuals to be involved in same-sex civil partnerships include Lissy Groner, a German member of the European Parliament.

'By the power vested in me by the state of Massachusetts as a justice of the peace, and most of all by the power of your own love, I now pronounce you married under the laws of Massachusetts', intoned the city clerk, Margaret Drury, shortly after 9 a.m. on 17 May 2004. 'You may seal this marriage with a kiss.' The couple embraced. Marcia Kadish, who had married her partner of 18 years, was overjoyed: 'I feel all tingly and wonderful', she said. 'So much love. Can't you see it is just bursting out of me?' Her partner said it felt like 'winning the lottery'.

Yet the marriage caused great controversy in the United States. 'The documents being issued across Massachusetts may say "marriage licence" at the top but they are really death certificates for the institution of marriage', said James Dobson, head of the Christian group 'Focus on the Family'. The reason for the controversy was that Marcia Kadish's long-term partner was another woman – Tanya McCloskey. The couple was amongst the first same-sex couples to be married under new laws in the US state of Massachusetts. Throughout the day, one gay couple after another filed out of the local town hall clutching the newly issued papers that would allow them to get married. Outside, thousands of people had gathered to applaud the couples, and to celebrate a right that many of them regarded as self-evident.

The state of Massachusetts has often been at the cusp of liberal reforms in the USA. In May 2004, after months of battles in and out of the state Supreme Court and legislature, Massachusetts became the first state to legalize gay marriage. Although increasing numbers of people in the USA do accept that marriages between homosexuals should be recognized as valid by the law, the majority (55 per cent in May 2004) has consistently been against it (Gallup 2004) and an overwhelming majority of states has laws or constitutional amendments barring 'gay marriage'. Massachusetts joined the Netherlands, Belgium and large parts of Canada as one of the few places in the world where gay marriages *are* legally recognized.

The very possibility of legal gay marriage demonstrates how radically ideas about sexuality have changed in recent decades. After all, it was only in 1967 that male homosexuality was legalized in the UK. Gay marriage also raises questions about sexual orientation: to what extent is sexual orientation inborn and to what extent is it learned? Many of the themes that we examine in this chapter overlap with the questions raised in chapter 9, 'Families and Intimate Relationships'. Human sexuality is tied up with our ideas about love and the question of what makes a good relationship. Increasingly, people argue that a good relationship must

be one between equals. Gay marriage has only become possible through a struggle against discrimination and inequality that is still continuing.

We begin this chapter by discussing human sexuality and examine how sexual behaviour is changing in Western society. We then look more specifically at sexual orientation, and particularly at issues surrounding homosexuality in the West. This leads us to the broader issue of gender, and raises questions of what it means to be a man or a woman in modern society. We close with a discussion of gender inequality and look at how women's equality is increasingly finding a global expression.

Human sexuality

Ideas about **sexuality** are undergoing dramatic changes. Over the last few decades in Western countries, important aspects of people's sexual lives have been altered in a fundamental way. In traditional societies, sexuality was tied tightly to the process of reproduction, but in our current age it has been separated from it. Sexuality has become a dimension of life for each individual to explore and shape. If sexuality once was 'defined' in terms of heterosexuality and monogamy in the context of marital relations, there is now a growing acceptance of diverse forms of sexual behaviour and orientations in a broad variety of contexts, as we saw in the discussion of gay marriage above.

In this section, we explore some of the issues surrounding human sexual behaviour: the importance of biological versus social influences, how society shapes sexual activity and the influence of reproductive technology. We then examine some of the recent trends in human sexual behaviour in Western society.

Biology and sexual behaviour

Sexuality has long been considered a highly personal subject. For this reason it is a challenging area for sociologists to study. Until recently, much of what we have known about sexuality came from biologists, medical researchers and sexologists. Scholars have also looked to the animal world in an attempt to understand more about human sexual behaviour.

There is clearly a biological component to sexuality, because female anatomy differs from that of the male. There also exists a biological imperative to reproduce; otherwise, the human species would become extinct. Some sociobiologists, such as David Barash (1979), have argued that there is an evolutionary explanation for why men tend to be more sexually promiscuous than women. His argument is that men produce millions of sperm during a lifetime and therefore can be seen as biologically disposed to impregnate as many women as possible. However, women only produce a few hundred eggs in a lifetime and have to carry the foetus within their body for nine months, which, says Barash, explains why they focus more on emotional commitment and are not so sexually promiscuous. The biological core of males and females drives their sexual behaviour in society. Barash's argument finds some support in other studies of the sexual behaviour of animals, which claim to show that males are normally more promiscuous than females of the same species.

Many commentators are dismissive of such an evolutionary approach. Steven Rose, for example, argued that, unlike most animals, human behaviour is shaped more by the environment than it is determined by genetically programmed instincts: 'The human infant is born with relatively few of its neural pathways already committed' (Rose et al. 1984). Rose argues that humans have an exceptionally long infancy relative to other animals, which gives them far more time than other species to learn from their experiences.

The claims of sociobiologists such as Barash are fiercely contested, especially as regards any implications for human sexual

behaviour. One thing clearly distinguishes humans from animals, however. Human sexual behaviour is meaningful – that is, humans use and express their sexuality in a variety of ways. For humans, sexual activity is much more than biological. It is symbolic, reflecting who we are and the emotions we are experiencing. As we shall see, sexuality is far too complicated to be wholly attributable to biological traits. It must be understood in terms of the social meanings which humans ascribe to it.

Forms of sexuality

Most people, in all societies, are heterosexual – they look to the other sex for emotional involvement and sexual pleasure. Heterosexuality in every society has historically been the basis of marriage and family. Yet there are many minority sexual tastes and inclinations too. Judith Lorber (1994) distinguishes as many as ten different sexual identities: straight (heterosexual) woman, straight man, lesbian woman, gay man, bisexual woman, bisexual man, transvestite woman (a woman who regularly dresses as a man), transvestite man (a man who regularly dresses as a woman), transsexual woman (a man who becomes a woman), and transsexual man (a woman who becomes a man). Sexual practices themselves are even more diverse.

There are a number of possible sexual practices. For example, a man or woman can have sexual relations with women, with men or with both. This can happen one at a time or with three or more participating. One can have sex with oneself (masturbation) or with no one (celibacy). One can have sexual relations with transsexuals or with people who erotically cross-dress, use pornography or sexual devices, practise sado-masochism (the erotic use of bondage and the inflicting of pain), have sex with animals, and so on (Lorber 1994).

In all societies there are sexual norms that approve of some practices while discouraging or condemning others. Members of a society learn these norms through socialization. Over the last few decades, for example, sexual norms in Western cultures have been linked to ideas of romantic love and family relationships. Such norms, however, vary widely between different cultures. Homosexuality is a case in point. Some cultures have either tolerated or actively encouraged homosexuality in certain contexts. Among the ancient Greeks, for instance, the love of men for boys was idealized as the highest form of sexual love.

Accepted types of sexual behaviour also vary between cultures, which is one way we know that most sexual responses are learned rather than innate. The most extensive study was carried out nearly 60 years ago by Clellan Ford and Frank Beach (1951), who surveyed anthropological evidence from more than 200 societies. Striking variations were found in what is regarded as 'natural' sexual behaviour and in norms of sexual attractiveness. For example, in some cultures, extended foreplay, perhaps lasting hours, is thought desirable and even necessary prior to intercourse; in others, foreplay is virtually non-existent. In some societies, it is believed that overly frequent intercourse leads to physical debilitation or illness. Among the Seniang of the South Pacific, advice on the desirability of spacing out love-making is given by the elders of the village – who also believe that a person with white hair may legitimately copulate every night.

In most cultures, norms of sexual attractiveness (held by both females and males) focus more on physical looks for women than for men, a situation that seems to be gradually changing in the West as women increasingly become active in spheres outside the home. The traits seen as most important in female beauty, however, differ greatly. In the modern West, a slim, small body is admired, while in other cultures a much more generous shape is regarded as most attractive. Sometimes the breasts are not seen as a source of sexual stimulus, whereas in some societies great erotic significance is attached to them. Some societies place great store on the shape of the face, while others emphasize the shape and colour of the eyes or the size and form of the nose and lips.

Sexual orientation

Sexual orientation concerns the direction of one's sexual or romantic attraction. The term 'sexual preference', which is sometimes incorrectly used instead of sexual orientation, is misleading and is to be avoided, since it implies that one's sexual or romantic attraction is entirely a matter of personal choice. As you will see below, sexual orientation in all cultures results from a complex interplay of biological and social factors which are not yet fully understood.

The most commonly found sexual orientation in all cultures is **heterosexuality**, a sexual or romantic attraction for persons of the opposite sex ('hetero' comes from the Greek word meaning 'other' or 'different'). **Homosexuality** involves the sexual or romantic attraction for persons of one's own sex. Today, the term *gay* is used to refer to male homosexuals, **lesbian** for female homosexuals, and *bi* as shorthand for **bisexuals**, people who experience sexual or romantic attraction for persons of either sex.

Orientation of sexual activities or feelings towards others of the same sex exist in all cultures. In some non-Western cultures, homosexual relations are accepted or even encouraged among certain groups. The Batak people of northern Sumatra, for example, permit male homosexual relations before marriage. Boys leave the parental home at puberty and sleep in a dwelling with a dozen or so older males who initiate the newcomers into homosexual practices. In many societies, however, homosexuality is not so openly accepted or practised. In the Western world, for example, sexuality is linked to individual identity, and the prevailing idea of a homosexual (or heterosexual) is of a person whose sexual orientation lies within themselves and is therefore a very personal matter, not something to be shared with many others.

In his studies of sexuality, Michel Foucault has shown that before the eighteenth century in Europe, the notion of a homosexual person seems barely to have existed (Foucault 1978). The act of sodomy was denounced by Church authorities and by the law; in England and several other European countries, it was punishable by death. However, sodomy was not defined specifically as a homosexual offence. It applied to relations between men and women, men and animals, as well as men among themselves. The term 'homosexuality' was coined in the 1860s, and from then on, homosexuals were increasingly regarded as being a separate type of people with a particular sexual aberration (Weeks 1986). Homosexuality became part of a 'medicalized' discourse; it was spoken of in clinical terms as a psychiatric disorder or a perversion, rather than a religious 'sin'. Homosexuals, along with other 'deviants' such as paedophiles and transvestites, were seen as suffering from a biological pathology that threatened the wholesomeness of mainstream society.

The death penalty for 'unnatural acts' was abolished in the United States after independence, and in European countries in the late eighteenth and early nineteenth centuries. Until just a few decades ago, however, homosexuality remained a criminal activity in virtually all Western countries. The shift of homosexuals from the margins of society to the mainstream is not yet complete, but rapid progress has been seen over recent years, as the discussion of gay marriage that opened this chapter shows.

Is sexual orientation inborn or learned?

Most sociologists today argue that sexual orientation of all kinds results from a complex interplay between biological factors and social learning. Since heterosex-

Which body shape is more appealing? The answer differs across cultures.

uality is the norm for most people, a great deal of research has focused on why some people become homosexual. Some scholars argue that biological influences are the most important, predisposing certain people to become homosexual from birth (Bell et al. 1981). Biological explanations for homosexuality have included differences in such things as brain characteristics of homosexuals (Maugh and Zamichow 1991) and the impact on foetal development of the mother's *in utero* hormone production during pregnancy (McFadden and Champlin 2000). Such studies, which are based on small numbers of cases, give highly inconclusive (and highly controversial) results (Healy 2001). It is virtually impossible to separate biological from early social influences in determining a person's sexual orientation.

Studies of twins hold some promise for understanding if there is any genetic basis for homosexuality, since identical twins share identical genes. In two related studies, Bailey and Pillard (1991; Bailey 1993) examined 167 pairs of brothers and 143 pairs of sisters, with each pair of siblings raised in the same family, in which at least one sibling defined him- or herself as homosexual. Some of these pairs were identical twins (who share all genes), some were fraternal twins (who share some genes) and some were adoptive brothers or sisters (who share no genes). The researchers reasoned that if sexual orientation is determined entirely by biology, then all the identical twins should be homosexual, since their genetic make-up is identical. Among the fraternal twins, some pairs would be homosexual, since some genes are shared. The lowest rates of homosexuality were predicted for the adoptive brothers and sisters.

The results of this study seem to show that homosexuality results from a combination of biological and social factors. Among both the men and the women studied, roughly one out of every two identical twins was homosexual, compared with one out of every five fraternal twins, and one out of every ten adoptive brothers and sisters. In other words, a woman or man is five times more likely to be lesbian or gay if her or his identical twin is lesbian or gay than if his or her sibling is lesbian or gay but related only through adoption. These results offer some support for the importance of biological factors, since the higher the percentage of shared genes, the greater the percentage of cases in which both siblings were homosexual. However, since approximately half the identical twin brothers and sisters of homosexuals were not themselves homosexual, a great deal of social learning must also be involved; otherwise one would expect *all* identical twin siblings of homosexuals to be homosexual as well.

It is clear that even studies of identical twins cannot fully isolate biological from social factors. It is often the case that, even in infancy, identical twins are treated more like one another by parents, peers and teachers than are fraternal twins, who in turn are treated more like one another than are adoptive siblings. Thus, identical twins may have more than genes in common: they may share a higher proportion of similar socializing experiences as well.

Sexuality, religion and morality

Attitudes towards sexual behaviour are not uniform across the world's societies, and even within a single country they undergo significant changes throughout history. For example, Western attitudes to sexuality were, for nearly 2,000 years, moulded primarily by Christianity. Although different Christian sects and denominations have held divergent views about the proper place of sexuality in life, the dominant view of the Christian Church has been that all sexual behaviour is suspect except what is needed for reproduction. At some periods, this view produced an extreme prudishness in society at large. But at other times, many people ignored or reacted against the teachings of the Church, commonly engaging in practices (such as adultery) forbidden by religious authorities. The idea that sexual fulfilment can and should be sought only through marriage was rare.

In the nineteenth century, religious presumptions about sexuality became partly replaced by medical ones. Most of the early writings by doctors about sexual behaviour, however, were as stern as the views of the Church. Some argued that any type of sexual activity unconnected with reproduction causes serious physical harm. Masturbation was said to bring on blindness, insanity, heart disease and other ailments, while oral sex was claimed to cause cancer. In Victorian times, sexual hypocrisy abounded. Virtuous women were believed to be indifferent to sexuality, accepting the attentions of their husbands only as a duty. Yet in the expanding towns and cities, where prostitution was rife and often openly tolerated, 'loose' women were seen in an entirely different category from their respectable sisters.

Many Victorian men who were, on the face of things, sober, well-behaved citizens, devoted to their wives, regularly visited prostitutes or kept mistresses. Such behaviour was treated leniently; whereas 'respectable' women who took lovers were

INTERIOR OF A WEST-END BROTHEL.

In Victorian England, a man could keep a mistress or visit prostitutes with impunity. But the sexuality of 'respectable' women was strictly contained within heterosexual marriage.

regarded as scandalous and were shunned in public society if their behaviour came to light. The different attitudes towards the sexual activities of men and women formed a double standard, which has long existed and whose residues still linger on today (Barret-Ducrocq 1992).

In current times, traditional attitudes exist alongside much more liberal attitudes towards sexuality, which developed particularly strongly in the 1960s. In films and plays, scenes are shown that previously would have been completely unacceptable, and pornographic material is readily available to most adults who want it. Some people, particularly those influenced by Christian teachings, believe that pre-marital sex is wrong, and generally frown on all forms of sexual behaviour except heterosexual activity within the confines of marriage – although it is now much more commonly accepted that sexual pleasure is a desirable and important feature. Others, by contrast,

condone or actively approve of pre-marital sex and hold tolerant attitudes towards different sexual practices.

Sexual attitudes have undoubtedly become more permissive over the past 30 years in most Western countries, though as the survey results given below in figure 14.4 demonstrate, there are some significant differences globally. For example, in the Republic of Ireland and the USA around one-third of the sample still thought sex

---

THINKING CRITICALLY

How are your attitudes towards sex and sexuality different from those of your parents and older relations? How do you think such attitudes are related to religious beliefs? Do the changing attitudes of younger generations provide evidence for secularization or are there other ways of explaining these changes?

"We're not doing anything for Gay Pride this year.
We're here, we're queer, we're used to it."

before marriage was 'always wrong' and in the Philippines 60 per cent did so. But in Sweden the figure was just 4 per cent and in the Czech Republic it was 5 per cent (Widmer et al. 1998). Such cultural differences show that religious beliefs and traditional norms relating to sexuality have not simply been swept aside in the modern age, but continue to exert an influence on people's attitudes and values.

Homosexuality

Kenneth Plummer (1975), in a classic study, distinguished four types of homosexuality within modern Western culture. *Casual homosexuality* is a passing encounter that does not substantially structure a person's overall sexual life. Schoolboy crushes and mutual masturbation are examples. *Situated activities* refer to circumstances in which homosexual acts are regularly carried out but do not become an individual's overriding preference. In settings such as prisons or military camps, where men live without women, homosexual behaviour of this kind is common, regarded as a substitute for heterosexual behaviour rather than as preferable.

Personalized homosexuality refers to individuals who have a preference for homosexual activities but who are isolated from groups in which this is easily accepted. Homosexuality here is a furtive activity, hidden away from friends and colleagues. *Homosexuality as a way of life* refers to individuals who have 'come out' and have made associations with others of similar sexual tastes a key part of their lives. Such people usually belong to gay subcultures, in which homosexual activities are integrated into a distinct lifestyle. Such communities often provide the possibility of collective political action to advance the rights and interests of homosexuals.

The proportion of the population (both male and female) who have had homosexual experiences or experienced strong inclinations towards homosexual sex is probably much larger than those who follow an openly *gay* lifestyle. The term 'gay' has been used primarily to refer to male homosexuals, as in the widely used phrase, 'gay and lesbian' people, though it is becoming increasingly used to describe lesbians.

Male homosexuality generally receives more attention than lesbianism – homosexual attachment or activities among women. Lesbian groups tend to be less highly organized than male gay subcultures and include a lower proportion of casual relationships. In campaigns for homosexual rights, lesbian activist groups are often treated as if their interests were identical to those of male organizations. But while there is sometimes close cooperation between male gays and lesbians, there are also differences, particularly where lesbians are actively involved in feminism. Some lesbian women came to feel that the gay liberation movement reflected the interests of men, while liberal and radical feminists were concerned exclusively with the concerns of middle-class, heterosexual women. Thus, a distinctive brand of lesbian feminism emerged which promoted the spread of 'female values' and challenged the established, dominant institution of male heterosexuality (Rich 1981). Many gay women view lesbianism less as a sexual orientation and more as a commitment to and form of solidarity with other women – politically, socially and personally (Seidman 1997).

Attitudes towards homosexuality

Attitudes of intolerance towards homosexuality have been so pronounced in the past that it is only during recent years that some of the myths surrounding the subject have been dispelled. Homosexuality has long been stigmatized in the United Kingdom and around the world. **Homophobia**, a term coined in the late 1960s, refers to an aversion or hatred of homosexuals and their lifestyles, along with behaviour based on such aversion. Homophobia is a form of prejudice that is reflected not only in overt acts of hostility and violence towards lesbians and gays, but also in various forms of verbal abuse. In Britain, for example, terms like 'fag' or 'queer' are used to insult a heterosexual male, as are female-related offensive terms like 'sissy' or 'pansy'. Although homosexuality is becoming more accepted, homophobia remains ingrained in many realms of Western society; antagonism towards homosexuals persists in many people's emotional attitudes. Instances of violent assault and murder of homosexuals remain all too common.

> See also the issues raised in the section 'Crimes against homosexuals', in chapter 21, 'Crime and Deviance'.

Some kinds of male gay behaviour might be seen as attempts to alter the usual connections of masculinity and power – one reason, perhaps, why the heterosexual community so often finds them threatening. Gay men tend to reject the image of the effeminacy popularly associated with them, and they deviate from this in two ways. One is through cultivating outrageous effeminacy – a 'camp' masculinity that parodies the stereotype. The other is by developing a 'macho' image. This also is not conventionally masculine; men dressed as motorcyclists or cowboys are again parodying masculinity, by exaggerating it – think, for example, of the 1970s band the Village People and their globally recognized anthem *YMCA* (Bertelson 1986).

Some sociologists have investigated the effect of the AIDS epidemic on popular attitudes to homosexuality. They suggest that the epidemic has challenged some of the main ideological foundations of heterosexual masculinity. Sexuality and sexual behaviour, for example, have become topics of public discussion, from safe sex campaigns backed by government funds to media coverage of the spread of the epidemic. The epidemic has threatened the legitimacy of traditional ideas of morality by drawing public attention to the prevalence of premarital sex, extramarital affairs and non-heterosexual relations in society. But most of all, in increasing the visibility of homosexuals, the epidemic has called the 'universality' of heterosexuality into question and has demonstrated that alternatives exist to the

The Village People demonstrate a particularly extreme parody of 'macho' forms of masculinity.

traditional nuclear family (Redman 1996). The response has sometimes taken hysterical and paranoid forms, however. Homosexuals are depicted as a deviant threat to the moral well-being of 'normal society'. In order to preserve heterosexual masculinity as the 'norm', it becomes necessary to marginalize and vilify the perceived threat (Rutherford and Chapman 1988).

In many ways, homosexuality has become more normalized – more of an accepted part of everyday society, with many countries passing legislation to protect the rights of homosexuals. When South Africa adopted its new constitution in 1996, it became one of the only countries in the world, at that time, constitutionally to guarantee the rights of homosexuals. Many countries in Europe, including Denmark, the Netherlands and Spain, now permit homosexual partners to register with the state in a civil ceremony and to claim most of the prerogatives of marriage, including social security and pension benefits, tenancy rights, possible parental responsibility for a partner's children, full recognition for life assurance, responsibility to provide reasonable maintenance for partners and children, the same tax treatment as married couples and visiting rights in hospitals. The opportunity to make such a public demonstration of personal commitment has been very popular. For example, in the 12 months following introduction of the UK's civil partnership legislation in 2005, 18,059 gay and lesbian couples became civil partners (figure 14.1)

Nevertheless, as we saw in this chapter's opening example, public attitudes towards equal marriage rights for lesbian and gay people differ widely within societies as well as across the world. Even within one geographical region such as Europe, a wide divergence of national opinion exists (see figure 14.2). A recent Eurobarometer survey (European Commission 2006) asked respondents if they agreed with the statement 'Homosexual marriages should be allowed throughout Europe'. In the Netherlands, 82 per cent agreed, along with 71 per cent of Swedes, 69 per cent of Danes and 62 per cent of Belgians. However, in most of Eastern Europe, only a minority of people

agreed; just 11 per cent in Romania, 15 per cent in Bulgaria and 17 per cent in Poland. In only 8 of the then 25 European Union countries surveyed did 50 per cent or more of those in the survey agree with the statement – an interesting finding in a period when more and more governments are moving in the direction of legally acknowledging homosexual unions. As 'public opinion' on sexuality is really quite diverse, with strong disagreements rooted in religious and political beliefs, legislative change and social policy do not always *follow* public opinion, but can also contribute to *changing* it.

More and more gay activists in Europe, the USA and elsewhere are pushing for homosexual marriage to be fully legalized. Why should they care? After all, as we discuss in chapter 9, marriage between heterosexual couples appears to be in decline. Activists care because they want the same status, rights and obligations as anyone else. Marriage in many societies today is, above all, an emotional commitment, but as recognized by the state it also has definite legal implications, conferring

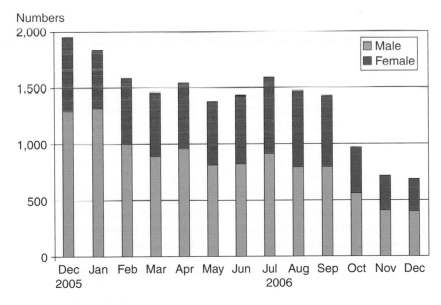

Figure 14.1   Number of UK civil partnerships, December 2005 – December 2006

Source: Office of National Statistics 2006b

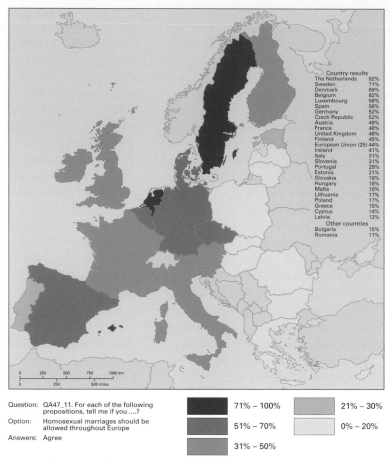

Country results

The Netherlands	82%
Sweden	71%
Denmark	69%
Belgium	62%
Luxembourg	58%
Spain	56%
Germany	52%
Czech Republic	52%
Austria	49%
France	48%
United Kingdom	46%
Finland	45%
European Union (25)	44%
Ireland	41%
Italy	31%
Slovenia	31%
Portugal	29%
Estonia	21%
Slovakia	19%
Hungary	18%
Malta	18%
Lithuania	17%
Poland	17%
Greece	15%
Cyprus	14%
Latvia	12%

Other countries

Bulgaria	15%
Romania	11%

Question: QA47_11. For each of the following propositions, tell me if you ....?

Option: Homosexual marriages should be allowed throughout Europe

Answers: Agree

71% – 100%   21% – 30%

51% – 70%   0% – 20%

31% – 50%

Figure 14.2   European attitudes to 'homosexual marriage', by country, 2006

Source: Eurobarometer 66, European Commission, 2006

upon partners important rights and responsibilities. 'Ceremonies of commitment' – non-legal marriages – have also become popular among both homosexuals and heterosexuals in America, but do not confer these rights and obligations. Conversely, of course, these legal rights and obligations are one reason why many heterosexual couples now decide either to defer marriage or not to get married at all.

Opponents of homosexual marriage condemn it as either frivolous or unnatural. They see it as legitimating a sexual orientation which the state should be doing its best to curb. For example, there are pressure groups in America dedicated to getting homosexuals to change their ways and marry people of the opposite sex. Some still

see homosexuality as a perversion and are violently opposed to any provisions that might normalize it. In other countries, homosexuality remains illegal and carries severe legal penalties including long terms of imprisonment and even execution. In 2005, two Iranian teenagers were convicted and hanged, allegedly for the rape of a 13-year-old boy, though human rights groups argued their crime was having gay sex, with confessions extracted under torture (BBC News, July 2005).

Gay and lesbian civil rights

Until recently, most homosexuals hid their sexual orientation, for fear that 'coming out of the closet' would cost them their jobs, families and friends, and leave them open to verbal and physical abuse. Yet, since the late 1960s, many homosexuals have acknowledged their homosexuality openly, and, as we saw in the discussion of gay marriage above, in some areas the lives of homosexual men and women have to a large extent been normalized (Seidman 1997). Manchester, New York, San Francisco, Sydney and many other large metropolitan areas around the world have thriving gay and lesbian communities. 'Coming out' may be important not only for the person who does so, but for others in the larger society; previously 'closeted' lesbians and gays come to realize they are not alone, while heterosexuals are forced to recognize that people whom they have admired and respected are homosexual.

The current global wave of gay and lesbian civil rights movements began partly as an outgrowth of the social movements of the 1960s, which emphasized pride in racial and ethnic identity. One pivotal event was the Stonewall Riots in June 1969 in the United States, when New York City's gay community – angered by continual police harassment – fought the New York Police Department for two days, a public action that for most people (gay or not) was practically unthinkable (Weeks 1977; D'Emilio 1983). The Stonewall Riots became a symbol of gay pride, heralding the 'coming out' of gays and lesbians, who insisted not only on equal treatment under the law, but also on a complete end to the stigmatization of their lifestyle. In 1994, on the 25th anniversary of the Stonewall Riots, 100,000 people attended the International March on the United Nations to Affirm the Human Rights of Lesbian and Gay People. It is clear that significant strides have been made, although discrimination and outright homophobia remain serious problems for many lesbian, gay, bisexual and transsexual (LGBT) people.

There are enormous differences between countries in the degree to which homosexuality is legally punishable (see figure 14.3). In Africa, for example, male homosexual acts have been legalized in only a handful of countries, while female homosexuality is seldom mentioned in the law at all. In South Africa, the official policy of the former white government was to regard homosexuality as a psychiatric problem that threatened national security. Once it took power, however, the black government legislated full equality. In Asia and the Middle East, the situation is similar: male homosexuality is banned in the vast majority of countries, including all those that are predominantly Islamic. Europe, meanwhile, has some of the most liberal laws in the world: homosexuality has been legalized in nearly all countries, and, as we saw above, several countries legally recognize same-sex marriages.

Today there is a growing movement around the world for the rights of homosexuals. The International Lesbian and Gay Association (ILGA), which was founded in 1978, today has more than 600 member organizations in some 90 countries on every continent (ILGA 2008). It holds international conferences, supports lesbian and gay social movements around the world, and lobbies international organizations. For example, it convinced the Council of Europe to require all its member nations to repeal laws banning homosexuality. In general, active lesbian and gay social movements tend to thrive in countries that emphasize individual rights and liberal state policies (Frank and McEneaney 1999).

The political campaigning of lesbian and gay movements in many parts of the world brought about new debates on gender identities and led to the problematizing of what previously appeared obvious: the gender differences and sexual differences are the same. Gayle Rubin (1975, 1984) argued that the typical Western gender difference is between men and women, while the key difference in sexuality is that between heterosexual and homosexual. However, sexuality is often expressed through *gender* distinctions rather than in its own terms. For example, it is common to talk about 'feminine' gay men or 'masculine' lesbians; the implication of this discourse is that gay men

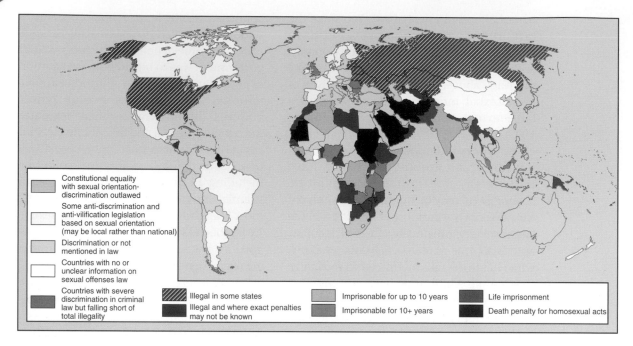

The legend of the map reads:

- Constitutional equality with sexual orientation discrimination outlawed
- Some anti-discrimination and anti-vilification legislation based on sexual orientation (may be local rather than national)
- Discrimination or not mentioned in law
- Countries with no or unclear information on sexual offenses law
- Countries with severe discrimination in criminal law but falling short of total illegality
- Illegal in some states
- Illegal and where exact penalties may not be known
- Imprisonable for up to 10 years
- Imprisonable for 10+ years
- Life imprisonment
- Death penalty for homosexual acts

Figure 14.3   Sexual minorities and the law across the world

Source: © 2000 by New Internationalist, www.newint.org; reprinted by kind permission of New Internationalist.

and lesbians are deviant, because they break the norms of *gender*. Rubin was one of the first to argue that, theoretically, it is possible to separate gender from sexuality altogether. This theoretical move is the starting point for **queer theory**, which marks not only a break with conventional ideas but also from lesbian theory and gay theory, which deal with sexual difference as it relates to female and male gender respectively.

Queer theory builds upon the social constructionist approach to sexuality developed by Gagnon and Simon (1973), and has been heavily influenced by poststructuralist thought, particularly that associated with Judith Butler (1990), Michel Foucault and Jacques Derrida. In particular, queer theorists challenge the very notion of 'identity' as something that is relatively fixed or assigned to people by socializing agents. Following Foucault, queer theorists argue that gender and sexuality, along with all of the other terms that come with these concepts, constitute a specific *discourse* of

sexuality, rather than referring to something objectively real or 'natural'. For example, in his work on the history of sexuality during the 1970s and '80s, Foucault argued that the male homosexual identity that today is associated with gay men, was not part of the dominant discourse on sexuality in the nineteenth century and before. Therefore, this form of identification just did not exist for people until it became part of, or was created within, the discourses of medicine and psychiatry. Identities can then be seen as pluralistic, quite unstable and subject to change over a lifetime.

Queer theorists are also interested in all forms of unconventional sexuality, including prostitution, bisexuality, transgender and so on, many of which are heterosexual rather than, or as well as, homosexual. In this way, queer theory can be viewed as a radical social constructionism that explores the process of *identity creation* and re-creation insofar as this relates to human sexuality and gender. Some queer theorists also argue that every major sociological topic (religion, the body, globalization and so on), as well as other subjects, including literature and even lesbian and gay studies, should bring queer voices to the centre to challenge the heterosexual assumptions that underlie much contemporary thinking (Epstein 2002).

Critics argue that queer theory tends to study cultural texts (film, novels and so on) and currently lacks empirical support. It may well be that many, maybe most people, do not experience their identity as being as fluid and changing as the theory suggests, but, rather, as something quite firm and fixed (Edwards 1998). If so, it may be that the radical constructionism of queer theorists overestimates the degree to which identities are open to change. We can gain an insight into the empirical evidence by looking at how research into sexuality has been conducted and what particular problems can arise when studying this sensitive area of people's lives.

Researching sexuality

When Alfred Kinsey began his research in the United States in the 1940s and 1950s, it was the first time a major investigation of actual sexual behaviour had been undertaken, and many people were shocked and surprised at the divergence between public norms and private sexual behaviour his team discovered (see 'Classic Studies 14.1'). We can speak much more confidently about public values concerning sexuality than we can about private practices, which, by their nature, go mostly undocumented. Still, many other areas of personal life, such as that within families and relationships, is similarly personal, yet has been the subject of many research studies. Why should sexuality be particularly difficult to research sociologically?

Surveys of sexual behaviour are fraught with difficulties. As we saw above, until quite recently sex was a taboo subject, not something to be discussed in either the public or the private realm. Perhaps more so than in any other areas of life, many, perhaps even most, people see sexual behaviour as a purely personal matter and are unwilling to discuss such an intimate subject with strangers. This may mean that those who *are* prepared to come forward to be interviewed are essentially a self-selected sample, which is therefore unrepresentative of the general population.

The social silence in relation to sexual matters has changed somewhat since the 1960s, a time when **social movements** associated with 'hippy' lifestyles and countercultural ideas of 'free love' challenged the existing order of things, including breaking with existing sexual norms. But we must be careful not to exaggerate their impact. Once the movements of the 1960s had become assimilated into mainstream society, it was clear that some of the older norms relating to sex continued to exert an influence. Some have even argued that a 'new fidelity' may be emerging (Laumann 1994), perhaps partly as a result of concerns about the risks associated with the transmission of HIV/AIDS and other sexually transmitted diseases. For example, a 1998 survey of attitudes towards sexual relations in 24 countries (see figure 14.4) showed (with some exceptions) overwhelming majorities to be against extramarital sex, homosexual sex and sex before the age of 16. The survey also found that only a minority were against sex before marriage (Widmer et al. 1998), suggesting that the traditional linkage between marriage and sexual relations has been broken. In this context, sociological research into sexuality today faces the same problem as earlier studies; we simply do not know how far people tell the truth about their sexual lives when asked by a researcher whom they do not know and perhaps do not trust with their highly personal information. However, we must remember the lesson from Kinsey's studies here: such publicly stated attitudes may simply reflect people's understanding of prevailing public norms

Classic Studies 14.1 **Alfred Kinsey discovers the diversity of sexual behaviour**

The research problem

Do public norms of sexuality really govern people's sexual behaviour? Are sexually 'deviant' practices limited to a tiny minority of individuals? Is it possible that many more people engage in such practices in private, and that public norms fail to reflect this fact? To address these issues, Alfred Kinsey (1894–1956) and his research team set out to collect evidence from the white population in 1940s America. They faced condemnation from religious organizations and their work was denounced as immoral in the newspapers and even in Congress. But they persisted and eventually obtained sexual life histories from 18,000 people, a reasonably representative sample of the white American population (Kinsey 1948, 1953).

Kinsey's findings

Kinsey's research findings were surprising to most people and shocking to many, because they did indeed reveal a large difference between the public expectations of sexual behaviour prevailing at that time and actual sexual conduct. The research team found that almost 70 per cent of men had visited a prostitute and 84 per cent had had pre-marital sexual experiences. Yet, following the sexual double standard, 40 per cent of men also expected their wives to be virgins at the time of marriage. More than 90 per cent of males had engaged in masturbation and nearly 60 per cent in some form of oral sexual activity. Among women, around 50 per cent had had pre-marital sexual experiences, although mostly with their prospective husbands. Some 60 per cent had masturbated and the same percentage had engaged in oral-genital contact. The study also showed much higher levels of male homosexuality than expected, revealing that many otherwise heterosexual men had experienced homosexual feelings.

The gap between publicly accepted attitudes and actual behaviour that Kinsey's findings demonstrated was especially great in that particular period, just after the Second World War. A phase of sexual liberalization had begun rather earlier, in the 1920s, when many younger people felt freed from the strict moral codes that had governed earlier generations. Sexual behaviour probably changed a good deal, but issues concerning sexuality were not openly discussed in the way that has now become familiar. People participating in sexual activities that were still strongly disapproved of on a public level concealed them, not realizing the full extent to which many others were engaging in similar practices.

Critical points

Kinsey's research was controversial in the USA and was attacked by conservative and religious organizations. For example, one aspect of the studies explored the sexuality of children under 16 years of age. Many critics objected to their involvement as research subjects. Religious leaders also argued that open discussion of sexual behaviour would undermine Christian moral values. Academic critics argued that Kinsey's **positivist** approach collected much raw data, but failed to grasp the complexity of sexual desire underpinning the diverse behaviour he uncovered, or the meanings people attach to their sexual relationships. Later surveys also found lower levels of homosexual experience than Kinsey, suggesting that his sample may have been less representative than the team first thought.

Contemporary significance

Kinsey is widely seen as a founder of the scientific study of human sexuality and his findings were instrumental in challenging the widespread view at the time, that homosexuality was a form of mental illness requiring treatment. It was only in the more permissive era of the 1960s, which brought openly declared attitudes more into line with the realities of behaviour, that the overall tenor of Kinsey's findings came to be seen as providing a realistic picture of sexual behaviour. Kinsey died in 1956, but the Institute for Sex Research, which he headed, continues its research today and has produced much valuable information about contemporary sexual behaviour. It was renamed the Kinsey Institute for Research in Sex, Gender and Reproduction in 1981 to celebrate his contribution to scientific research in this field.

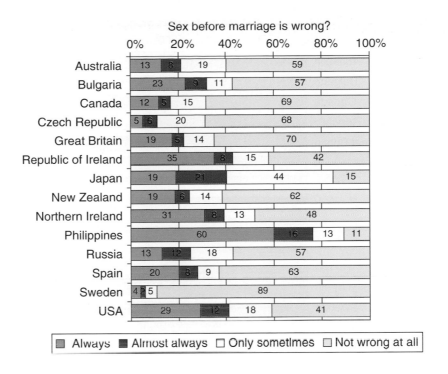

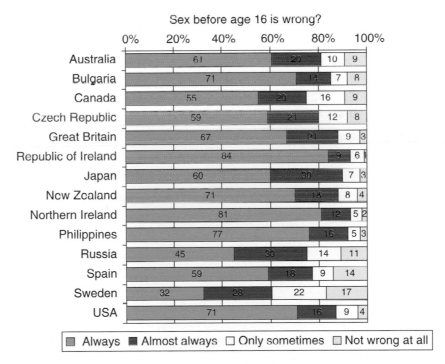

Figure 14.4 Attitudes towards sexual relations, 1998 (selected countries)

Source: Widmer et al. 1998

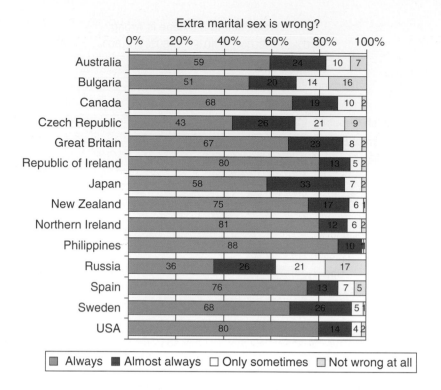

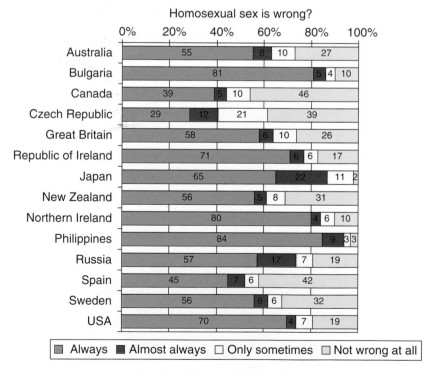

Figure 14.4 (Continued)

rather than accurately describing their private beliefs and sexual behaviours.

The validity of surveys of sexual behaviour has also been the focus of intense debate (Lewontin 1995). Critics have argued that they do not generate reliable information about sexual practices. In one American survey (Rubin 1990), researchers reported that 45 per cent of men aged between 80 and 85 say they have sex with their partner. Critics feel that this is so obviously untrue that it calls into doubt the findings of the whole survey. However, **social gerontologists** suggest that this criticism may itself be based on negative stereotypes of ageing rather than evidence. They point out that in one study of older men living outside institutions, 74 per cent were indeed sexually active, while others have found that most men even in their 90s sustained an interest in sex. When researching sexuality, sociologists need to be acutely aware of their own, sometimes unevidenced, assumptions.

THINKING CRITICALLY

The survey reported in figure 14.4 was carried out over a decade ago. Which countries appear to have the most 'liberal' attitudes towards sexual behaviour? Which seem to be more 'conservative'? Did any of the findings surprise you? Do you think that if the same questions were asked today, the results would be significantly different? If so, in what ways might they differ?

Gathering evidence on sexual behaviour

Many studies of sexual behaviour have taken the form of attitude and behaviour surveys using postal questionnaires or face-to-face interviews. But evidence in this area can also be collected through the analysis and interpretation of documentary materials such as personal diaries, oral history, magazines, newspapers and other published and unpublished historical materials. These research methods are not mutually exclusive of course, and can be combined to produce a richer account of changing forms of sexuality within societies.

An example of a large-scale survey is that of Lillian Rubin (1990), who interviewed 1,000 Americans between the ages of 13 and 48 to discover what changes had occurred in sexual behaviour and attitudes since the Kinsey studies. According to her findings, there had been some significant developments. Sexual activity was typically beginning at a younger age than was characteristic of the previous generation and the sexual practices of teenagers tended to be as varied and comprehensive as those of adults. There was still a double standard, but it was not as powerful as it once had been.

One of the most important changes was that women had come to expect, and actively pursue, sexual pleasure in relationships. They were expecting to receive, not only to provide, sexual satisfaction. Rubin found that women were more sexually liberated than previously, but most men in the survey found such female assertiveness difficult to accept, often saying they 'felt inadequate', were afraid they could 'never do anything right' and found it 'impossible to satisfy women these days' (Rubin 1990). This finding seems to contradict all that we have come to expect about gender relations. Men continue to dominate in most spheres and they are, in general, much more violent towards women than the other way round. Such violence is substantially aimed at the control and continuing subordination of women. Yet a number of authors have begun to argue that masculinity is a burden as well as a source of rewards, and if men were to stop using sexuality as a means of control, not only women, but men too would be beneficiaries.

The use of documentary materials to study changing forms of sexuality is well demonstrated in Dutch sociologist Cas Wouters's *Sex and Manners* (2004), a comparative study of shifting gender relations and sexuality in England, Germany, the Netherlands and the USA. Wouters studied books on 'good manners' from the end of the nineteenth century to the end of the twentieth, particularly as these pertained to relationships between men and women and 'courting behaviour' – the opportunities for and limitations on meetings and 'dating' between men and women. Manners books provide advice on how such meetings should be conducted, providing codes of manners on how to meet and behave in relations with 'the opposite sex'.

For instance, in an English publication from 1902, *Etiquette for Women*, the advice given is: 'It is the man's place to pay for what refreshments are had, if the ladies do not insist on paying their share; and if he invited the ladies with him to go in somewhere and have some, then the case is simple enough.' But by the 1980s, the practice of 'going Dutch' – sharing the cost of a date – was well established. One manners book from 1989, reflecting on the old practice of the man always paying for the woman, noted that, 'some still do, but women can't dine endlessly without offering a crust in return' (Wouters 2004: 25–7). This example seems fairly trivial, but in fact it shows how shifting gender relations in the wider society, with more women moving into paid employment and the public sphere more generally (Walby 1990), were also leading to changing behavioural norms between men and women. Wouters's research provides many such examples in relation to sexual behaviour and courtship. By analysing manners books over the course of a century and relating the advice given in these to sociological theories of social change, Wouters argues that the four countries all exhibit a long-term trend away from very formal and rigid codes of manners, towards much more informal codes that allow for a wider range of acceptable courtship behaviour. Hence, those critics of the 'permissiveness' brought about since the 1960s fail to appreciate that such changes are part of a much longer and deeper process of social transformation.

The two studies reported here have many similarities. Both are concerned with changes in gender relations, norms of sexual behaviour alongside private and public attitudes towards sexuality. While Rubin's study tells us something of how people *today* feel about such changes and what impact they are having on contemporary lifestyles, Wouters's analysis of primary documents sets these contemporary findings into historical and comparative perspective. Bringing together the findings from studies using different methods, which also focus on different aspects of changing sexual behaviour, may give sociologists more confidence in their conclusions in this difficult to research area.

Prostitution and 'sex work'

Prostitution

Prostitution can be defined as the granting of sexual favours for monetary gain. The word 'prostitute' began to come into common usage in the late eighteenth century. In the ancient world, most purveyors of sexuality for economic reward were courtesans, concubines (kept mistresses) or slaves. Courtesans and concubines often had a high position in traditional societies. A key aspect of modern prostitution is that women and their clients are generally unknown to one another. Although men may become 'regular customers', the relationship is not initially established on the basis of personal acquaintance. This was not true of most forms of the dispensing of sexual favours for material gain in earlier times. Prostitution is directly connected to the break-up of small-scale communities, the development of large impersonal urban areas and the commercializing of social relations. In small-scale traditional communities, sexual relations were controlled by their very visibility. In newly developed urban areas, more anonymous social connections were easily established.

A United Nations resolution passed in 1951 condemns those who organize prostitution or profit from the activities of

Amsterdam's Red Light District contains many sex clubs, bars and 'prostitution windows' from which sex is sold. In 2006, city officials announced they were shutting down about one-third of the 'windows' in a crackdown on trafficking and pimping in the area.

prostitutes, but does not ban prostitution as such. A total of 53 member states have formally accepted the resolution, although their legislation on prostitution varies widely. In some countries, prostitution itself is illegal. Other countries prohibit only certain types, such as street soliciting or child prostitution. Some national or local governments license officially recognized brothels or sex parlours – such as the 'Eros centres' in Germany or the sex houses in Amsterdam. In October 1999 the Dutch Parliament turned prostitution into an official profession for the estimated 30,000 women who work in the sex industry. All venues where sex is sold can now be regulated, licensed and inspected by local authorities. However, only a few countries license male prostitutes.

Legislation against prostitution rarely punishes clients. Those who purchase sexual services are not arrested or prosecuted, and in court procedures their identities may be kept hidden. There are far fewer studies of clients than of those selling sex, and it is rare for anyone to suggest – as is often stated or implied about prostitutes – that the clients are psychologically disturbed. The imbalance in research surely expresses an uncritical acceptance of orthodox stereotypes of sexuality according to which it is 'normal' for men to actively seek a variety of sexual outlets, while those who cater for these needs are condemned.

Sex work

Today, prostitution is more widely seen by sociologists as just one form of **sex work**. Sex work can be defined as the provision of sexual services in a financial exchange between consenting adults, though, of course, children (and adults) have historically been – and still are – forced into sex work in both developed and developing countries. Sex workers, like prostitutes, are mostly female, and sex work includes at least all of the following: actors in pornographic films, nude modelling, striptease and lap dancers, live sex show workers, providers of erotic massage, phone sex workers and home-based 'webcam sex' via the Internet, if this involves a financial exchange (Weitzer 2000).

The original 1970s concept of the sex worker aimed to destigmatize the working practices of prostitutes and other women working in the sex industry. Provided that sexual services were exchanged between freely consenting adults, it was argued that such work should be treated like any other type of work and prostitution, in particular, should be decriminalized. Prostitutes around the world today come mainly from poorer social backgrounds, as they did in the past, but they have now been joined by considerable numbers of middle-class women working across the range of sex work described above and many see their work as providing useful and respectable sexual services. As 'Rona', a sex worker with ten years' experience insists:

> Yes, it is a profession – I believe a perfectly respectable profession, and should be viewed as such in the same way as a teacher, accountant or anyone else. I believe that the first step is to obtain recognition for sex workers as legitimate workers in a legitimate industry and profession. . . . Why should the fact that I have chosen to work as a prostitute be considered any different from that of being a nurse, which I once was? There should be no social stigma attached. I work in clean comfortable surroundings, have regular medical check-ups and pay taxes like anyone else. ('Rona' 2000)

The idea of a trade union for sex workers may appear strange, but in the context of ensuring health and safety at work, legal support in disputes over pay and conditions and access to training or retraining (for those who wish to leave the sex industry), these issues lie at the centre of mainstream trade union activity. Sex workers point out that union collectivization may help to root out exploitation and abuse within the sexual services industry. For example, formed in 2000, the International Union of Sex Workers (IUSW), based in London, sees unionization as the first step towards the professionalization of sex work and in 2002 it became affiliated to the GMB, a large general trade union in the UK. The IUSW campaigns for:

- the decriminalization of all aspects of sex work involving consenting adults;
- the right to form and join professional associations or unions;
- the right to work on the same basis as other independent contractors and employers and to receive the same benefits;
- no taxation without such rights and representation;
- zero tolerance of coercion, violence, sexual abuse, child labour, rape and racism;
- legal support for sex workers who want to sue those who exploit their labour;
- the right to travel across national boundaries;
- clean and safe places to work;
- the right to choose whether to work on our own or cooperatively
- the absolute right to say no;
- access to training – our jobs require very special skills and professional standards;
- access to health clinics where we do not feel stigmatized;
- retraining programmes for sex workers who want to leave the industry;
- an end to social attitudes which stigmatise those who are or have been sex workers. (IUSW: www.iusw.org/start/index.html)

Nevertheless, the concept of sex work remains controversial, as many feminists actively campaign against the sex industry, seeing it as degrading to women, strongly linked to sexual abuse and drug addiction, and ultimately rooted in women's subordination to men. More recently, though, sex work has been reappraised by some feminists who argue that many, though by no means all, women sex workers earn a good living, enjoy their work and do not fit the stereotype of the poor, sexually abused drug addict forced into prostitution by their circumstances (O'Neill 2000). For these women, sex work provides worthwhile jobs that are relatively well paid. Many sex workers see themselves as independent women who have taken control of their lives, which makes them little different from successful women working in other employment sectors (Chapkis et al. 1997).

> ### THINKING CRITICALLY
>
> Why does prostitution continue to thrive into the twenty-first century? How might functionalist theorists explain its persistence over such a long time period? What would an explanation rooted in Marxism focus on? Could either perspective satisfactorily account for the strongly gendered character of prostitution and expansion of sex work? What would a feminist approach add to our understanding of sex work today?

Explaining prostitution and sex work

Why do prostitution and other forms of sex work still exist? Certainly, prostitution is an enduring phenomenon, which resists the attempts of governments to eliminate it. It is also almost always a matter of women selling sexual favours to men, rather than the reverse – although there are some instances, as in Hamburg, Germany, where 'houses of pleasure' exist to provide male sexual services to women. And of course, boys or men also sell sex to other men.

No single factor can explain the persistence of prostitution or sex work. It might seem that men simply have stronger, or more persistent, sexual needs than women, and therefore require the outlets that the sex industry provides. But this explanation is implausible. Most women seem capable of developing their sexuality in a more intense fashion than men of comparable age. Moreover, if prostitution existed simply to serve sexual needs, there would surely be many male prostitutes catering for women.

One possible conclusion to be drawn is that sex work expresses, and to some extent helps perpetuate, the tendency of men to treat women as objects who can be 'used' for sexual purposes. Prostitution expresses in a particular context the inequalities of power between men and women. Of course, many other elements are also involved. Prostitution offers a means of obtaining sexual satisfaction for people who, because of their physical shortcomings or the existence of restrictive moral codes, cannot find other sexual partners. Prostitutes and sex workers often cater for men who are away from home, desire sexual encounters without commitment or have unusual sexual tastes that other women will not accept. Of course, such a 'negative' conclusion ignores the possibility that many female sex workers, like many of the men who also profit from the sex industry, are active social agents who are adept at selling sexual services to men who need and benefit from them. Certainly, that is the way that some sex workers describe themselves and the services they provide.

The global sex industry

'Sex tourism' exists in several areas of the world, including Thailand and the Philippines. Sex tourism in the Far East has its origins in the provision of prostitutes for American troops during the Korean and Vietnam wars. 'Rest and recreation' centres were built in Thailand, the Philippines, Vietnam, Korea and Taiwan. Some still remain, particularly in the Philippines, catering to regular shipments of tourists as well as to the military stationed in the region.

Today, package tours oriented towards prostitution draw men to these areas from Europe, the United States and Japan, often in search of sex with minors – although these tours are illegal in more than 30 countries including the UK, Australia, Canada, Japan and the USA, under laws dealing with the 'extraterritorial accountability' of their citizens. Enforcement is patchy though, and in 2004 a UN report noted that Japan had made no prosecutions under its legislation, whereas the USA had made at least 20 prosecutions for sex tourism (Svensson 2004).

A report published in 1998 by the International Labour Organization (ILO) found that prostitution and the sex industry in Southeast Asia have taken on the dimensions of a fully fledged commercial sector, having grown rapidly over recent decades. For example, it is estimated that there are up to 2 million female prostitutes in Thailand alone. Cheaper global travel and the large differential in the exchange rate between Asian and international currencies have made sex tourism more affordable and attractive to foreigners. Furthermore, the sex industry is linked to economic hardship. Some desperate families force their own children into prostitution; other young people are unwittingly lured into the sex trade by responding innocently to advertisements for 'entertainers' or 'dancers'. Migration patterns from rural to urban areas are an important factor in the growth of the sex industry, as many women eager to leave their traditional and constraining home towns grasp at any opportunity to do so. Sex tourism has serious implications for the spread of AIDS and sexually transmitted diseases and is often associated with violence, criminality, the drug trade and violations of human rights (Lim 1998).

The trafficking of people, mostly women and girls, across the world has become a much more significant issue in recent years. For example, the trafficking of women into Western Europe to become prostitutes and sex workers is expanding rapidly. Although it is impossible to know exactly how many people become victims of human trafficking, the UN Refugee Agency's (2006) best estimate is that between 100,000 and 500,000 people are trafficked into Europe annually. As EU borders expand with the entry of new countries such as Bulgaria and Romania, more transit routes become available for entry into wealthy Western European countries or the new border countries become final destinations themselves for a growing sex industry.

Governments are moving to legislate against trafficking. In the UK, the Nationality, Immigration and Asylum Act 2002 made trafficking for prostitution a criminal offence for the first time (extended to trafficking for domestic servitude and forced labour in 2004). Clearly, globalization enables the more rapid movement of people across national boundaries and new patterns of movement are emerging. In relation to sex tourism and trafficking for prostitution, these patterns are related to the huge disparities in wealth across the world's countries and to gendered power relations. Relatively rich Westerners make short trips into developing countries to buy sex from relatively poor people, while relatively powerless Eastern European women are being forced into 'sex work' in Western Europe by organized gangs of, mostly male, people traffickers. The lives of many victims of the global sex industry are very far removed from those of the liberated and empowered sex workers described by 'Rona' above.

Gender

'Sex' is an ambiguous term. It can mean, as in the previous sections, 'sexual activity'. However, it can also refer to the physical characteristics that separate men and women. You might think that being a man or a woman is simply associated with the sex of the physical body we are born with. But, like many questions of interest to sociologists, the nature of maleness and femaleness is not so easily classified. This section examines the origins of the differences between men and women. Before we go on, though, we need to make an important distinction, between **sex** and **gender**.

In general, sociologists use the term 'sex' to refer to the anatomical and physiological differences that define male and female bodies. Gender, by contrast, concerns the psychological, social and cultural differences between males and females. Gender is linked to socially constructed notions of masculinity and femininity; it is not necessarily a direct product of an individual's biological sex. Some people, for example, feel that they have been born into the wrong bodies and seek to 'put things right' by switching gender part way through life, or following the lifestyles or dress of the other sex. The distinction between sex and gender is a fundamental one, since many differences between males and females are not biological in origin. Contrasting approaches have been taken to explain the formation of gender identities and the social roles based on those identities. The debate is really one about how much learning there is; some scholars allow more prominence than others to social influences in analysing gender differences.

Sociological interpretations of gender differences and inequalities have taken contrasting positions on this question of sex and gender. Three broad approaches will be explored below. First we will look at arguments for a biological basis to behavioural differences between men and women. Next, attention will turn to theories placing central importance on socialization and the learning of gender roles. Finally, we will consider the ideas of scholars who argue that neither gender nor sex have a biological basis, but are both entirely socially constructed.

Gender and biology: natural differences?

How far are differences in the behaviour of women and men the result of sex rather than gender? In other words, how much are they the result of biological differences? As we saw above, some authors hold that aspects of human biology – ranging from hormones to chromosomes to brain size to genetics – are responsible for innate differences in behaviour between men and women. These differences, they claim, can be seen in some form across all cultures, implying that natural factors are responsible for the inequalities between genders which characterize most societies. Such researchers are likely to draw attention to the fact, for example, that in almost all cultures, men rather than women take part in hunting and warfare. Surely, they argue, this indicates that men possess biologically based tendencies towards aggression that women lack?

Many researchers remain unconvinced by this argument. The level of aggressiveness of males, they say, varies widely between different cultures, and women are expected to be more passive or gentle in some cultures than in others (Elshtain 1987). Critics point out that theories of 'natural difference' are often grounded in data on animal behaviour rather than in anthropological or historical evidence about human behaviour, which reveal variation over time and place. Moreover, they add, because a trait is more or less universal, it does not follow that it is biological in origin; there may be cultural factors of a general kind that produce such characteristics. For instance, in the majority of cultures, most women spend a significant part of their lives caring for children and could not readily take part in hunting or war.

Although the hypothesis that biological factors determine behaviour patterns in men and women cannot be dismissed out of hand, nearly a century of research to identify the physiological origins of such an influence has been unsuccessful. There is no evidence of the mechanisms which would link such biological forces with the complex social behaviour exhibited by human men and women (Connell 1987). Theories that see individuals as complying with some kind of innate predisposition neglect the vital role of social interaction in shaping human behaviour.

Gender socialization

Another route to take in understanding the origins of gender differences is the study of **gender socialization**, the learning of gender roles with the help of social agencies such as the family and the media. Such an approach makes a distinction between biological sex and social gender – an infant is born with the first and develops the second. Through contact with various agencies of socialization, both primary and secondary, children gradually internalize the social norms and expectations which are seen to correspond with their sex. Gender differences are not biologically determined, they are culturally produced. According to this view, gender inequalities result because men and women are socialized into different roles.

Theories of gender socialization have been favoured by functionalists who see boys and girls as learning 'sex roles' and the male and female identities – masculinity and femininity – which accompany them. They are guided in this process by positive and negative sanctions, socially applied forces which reward or restrain behaviour. For example, a small boy could be positively sanctioned in his behaviour ('What a brave boy you are!'), or be the recipient of negative sanction ('Boys don't play with dolls'). These positive and negative reinforcements aid boys and girls in learning and conforming to expected sex roles. If an individual develops gender practices which do not correspond to his or her biological sex – that is, they are deviant – the explanation is seen to reside in inadequate or irregular socialization. According to this functionalist view,

socializing agencies contribute to the maintenance of social order by overseeing the smooth gender socialization of new generations.

This rigid interpretation of sex roles and socialization has been criticized on a number of fronts. Many writers argue that gender socialization is not an inherently smooth process; different 'agencies' such as the family, schools and peer groups may be at odds with one another. Moreover, socialization theories ignore the ability of individuals to reject, or modify, the social expectations surrounding sex roles. As Connell has argued:

> 'Agencies of socialization' cannot produce mechanical effects in a growing person. What they do is invite the child to participate in social practice on given terms. The invitation may be, and often is, coercive – accompanied by heavy pressure to accept and no mention of an alternative. . . . Yet children do decline, or more exactly start making their own moves on the terrain of gender. They may refuse heterosexuality . . . they may set about blending masculine and feminine elements, for example girls insisting on competitive sport at school. They may start a split in their own lives, for example boys dressing in drag when by themselves. They may construct a fantasy life at odds with their actual practice, which is perhaps the commonest move of all. (1987)

It is important to remember that humans are not passive objects or unquestioning recipients of gender 'programming', as some sociologists have suggested. People are active agents who create and modify roles for themselves. While we should be sceptical of any wholesale adoption of the sex roles approach, many studies have shown that to some degree gender identities are a result of social influences.

Social influences on gender identity flow through many diverse channels; even parents committed to raising their children in a 'non-sexist' way find existing patterns of gender learning difficult to combat (Statham 1986). Studies of parent–child

Gendered learning does not take place simply through formal instruction but also occurs in many everyday activities.

interactions, for example, have shown distinct differences in the treatment of boys and girls even when the parents believe their reactions to both are the same. The toys, picture books and television programmes experienced by young children all tend to emphasize differences between male and female attributes. Although the situation is changing somewhat, male characters generally outnumber females in most children's books, television programmes and films. Male characters tend to play more active, adventurous roles, while females are portrayed as passive, expectant and domestically oriented (Weitzman 1972; Zammuner 1987; Davies 1991). Feminist researchers have demonstrated how cultural and media products marketed to young audiences embody traditional attitudes towards gender and towards the sorts of aims and ambitions girls and boys are expected to have.

 A more detailed discussion of gender socialization is in chapter 8, 'The Life-Course'.

Reproductive technologies

For hundreds of years, childbirth and child-rearing dominated the lives of most women. In traditional societies, contraception was ineffective or, in some societies, unknown. As late as the eighteenth century in Europe and the United States, it was common for women to experience as many as 20 pregnancies, often involving miscarriages and infant deaths. In many parts of the developing world today, it is still commonplace for women to have a large number of pregnancies over a lifetime. For example, the total fertility rate in sub-Saharan Africa is 5.6, which is double the global average. When researchers asked what was people's ideal number of children, the average was 4.1 in Kenya and 8.5 in Chad and

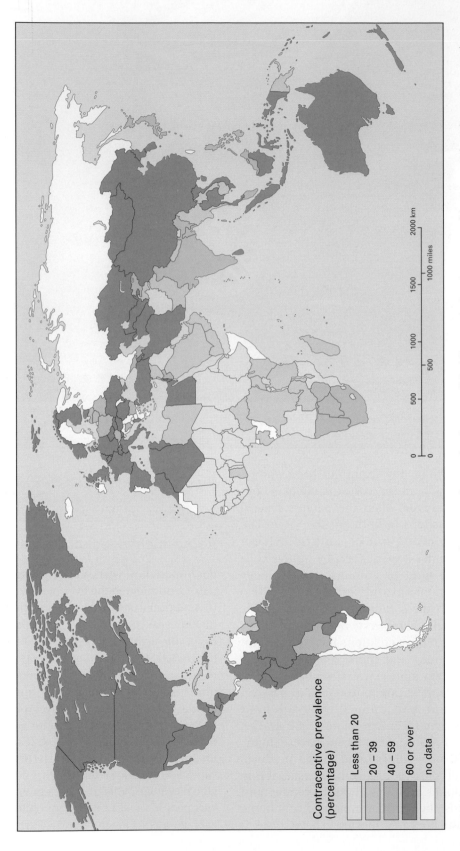

Contraceptive prevalence (percentage)

- Less than 20
- 20 – 39
- 40 – 59
- 60 or over
- no data

NB: 'Contraceptive prevalence' is the percentage of women of reproductive age (15–49), married or in partnerships, currently using contraception.

Figure 14.5 Global contraceptive prevalence, October 2005 estimates

Source: United Nations Population Division, 2005. Reprinted by permission of the United Nations Population Division.

Niger, with men reporting a higher 'ideal number' than women.

In many parts of the world, improved methods of contraception have changed this situation in a fundamental way. Far from any longer being natural, it is almost unknown in the industrial countries for women to undergo so many pregnancies. Advances in contraceptive technology enable most women and men around the world to control whether and when they choose to have children, though this also depends on social acceptance and whether they are made available. In many African countries, for example, contraceptive prevalence in 2003 (see figure 14.5) was below 20 per cent; a significant factor in the continuing HIV/AIDS epidemic in those countries.

 See chapter 10, 'Health, Illness and Disability', for more discussion of HIV/AIDS as a global issue.

However, contraception is only one example of a **reproductive technology**. Some other examples of the social shaping of natural processes are described below.

Childbirth

Medical science has not always been involved with the major life transitions from birth to death. The medicalization of pregnancy and childbirth developed slowly, as local physicians and midwives were displaced by paediatric specialists. Today in the industrialized societies, most births occur in a hospital with the help of a specialized medical team, and infant mortality rates are historically low, more than ten times lower than rates in developing countries. However, childbirth is still fraught with danger in many parts of the developing world, where a combination of uneven provision of medical services, a high risk of infection – particularly HIV/AIDS – and very high teenage pregnancy rates make giving birth to new lives a major cause of death for young women as well. Globally, only 10 per cent of all births (13 million per year) are to

women under the age of 20, but more than 90 per cent of these births are in the developing world. Hence, complications arising in pregnancy are the leading cause of death in young women aged between 15 and 19 in developing countries (Mayor 2004).

> Medicalization of the body is discussed in chapter 10, 'Health, Illness and Disability'.

In the past, new parents had to wait until the day of birth to learn the sex of their baby and whether it would be healthy. Today, prenatal tests such as the sonogram (an image of the foetus produced by using ultrasonic waves) and amniocentesis (which draws off some of the amniotic fluid from around the foetus) can be used to discover structural or chromosomal abnormalities before the baby's birth. Such new technology presents couples and modern societies with new ethical and legal decisions. When a disorder is detected, the couple are faced with the decision of whether or not to have the baby, knowing it may be seriously disabled throughout its life.

The development of *assisted reproductive technologies* since the late 1970s – particularly *in vitro* fertilization (IVF) techniques – have enabled many cases of human infertility to be overcome, though success rates decline rapidly for women over the age of 40 who use their own eggs. IVF involves egg cells from a woman being fertilized outside the womb in a fluid medium, before being returned to the womb where pregnancy occurs. The first successful IVF births were known as 'test-tube babies' because of this laboratory fertilization process. IVF, as with pre-natal tests, turns what was previously thought to be a natural fate into a social choice. An individual's biology is no longer the absolute determinant of whether they can have children. Instead, social factors such as income levels and the availability and accessibility of specialist IVF facilities determine whether biological infertility is such an obstacle.

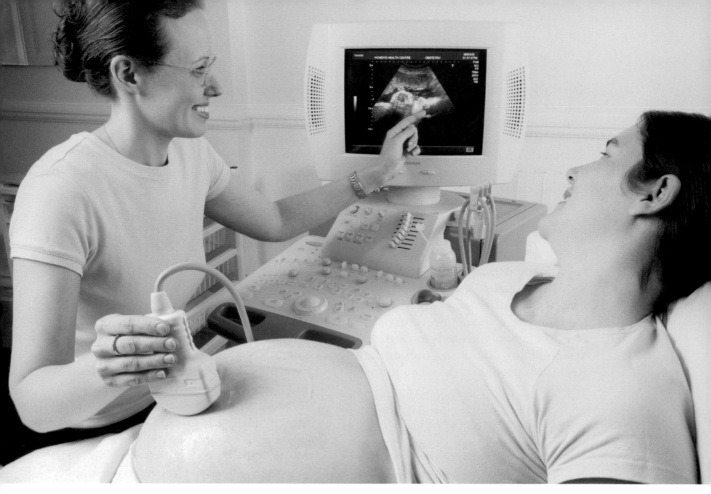

Modern medical technologies have helped to transform the experience of pregnancy and childbirth for women in the developed world.

Genetic engineering: designer babies?

A great deal of scientific endeavour these days is being devoted to the expansion of genetic engineering; that is, intervening in the genetic make-up of the foetus so as to influence its subsequent development. The likely social impact of genetic engineering is starting to provoke debates almost as intense as those that surround the issue of abortion. According to its supporters, genetic engineering will bring us many benefits. It is possible, for example, to identify the genetic factors that make some people vulnerable to certain diseases. Genetic reprogramming will ensure that these illnesses are no longer passed on from generation to generation. It will be possible to 'design' bodies before birth in terms of colour of skin, hair and eyes, weight and so on.

There could be no better example of the mixture of opportunities and problems that the increasing socialization of nature creates for us than genetic engineering. What choices will parents make if they can design their babies, and what limits should be placed on those choices? Genetic engineering is unlikely to be cheap. Will this mean that those who can afford to pay will be able to programme out from their children any traits they see as socially undesirable? What will happen to the children of more deprived groups, who will continue to be born naturally?

Some sociologists have argued that differential access to genetic engineering might lead to the emergence of a 'biological underclass'. Those who do not have the physical advantages that genetic engineering can bring might be subject to prejudice and discrimination by those who do enjoy these advantages. They might have difficulty finding employment and life or health insurance (Duster 1990).

The abortion debate

Perhaps the most controversial ethical dilemma created by modern reproductive technologies in modern societies is this: under what conditions should abortion be available to women? The abortion debate has become so intense in many countries precisely because it centres on basic ethical issues to which there are no easy solutions. Those who are 'pro-life' believe that abortion is always wrong except in extreme circumstances, because it is equivalent to murder. For them, ethical issues are above all subject to the value that must be placed on human life. Those who are 'pro-choice' argue that the mother's control over her own body – her own right to live a rewarding life – must be the primary consideration.

The debate in the USA has led to numerous episodes of violence; for example, in 2003 an anti-abortion campaigner was executed in Florida following his conviction for the murder of two people, one of them a doctor who performed abortions. Can such an emotionally polarized issue ever be resolved? At least one prominent social and legal theorist, Ronald Dworkin (1993), has suggested that it can. The intense divisions between those who are pro-life and those who are pro-choice, he argues, hide deeper sources of agreement between the two sides, and in this there is a source of hope. At previous periods of history, life was often relatively cheap. In current times, however, we have come to place a high value on the sanctity of human life. Each side agrees with this value, but they interpret it differently, the one emphasizing the interests of the child, the other the interests of the mother. If the two sides can be persuaded that they share a common ethical value, Dworkin suggests, a more constructive dialogue may be possible.

This young Wodaabe man, from the Gerewol in Niger, is taking part in a formal dance. The kohl on his lips and eyes, and his eye rolling and grinning are thought to give him extra sex appeal to the young women of the Wodaabe.

The social construction of gender and sex

In recent years, socialization and gender role theories have been criticized by a growing number of sociologists. Rather than seeing sex as biologically determined and gender as culturally learned, they argue that we should view both sex and gender as socially constructed products. Not only is gender a purely social creation that lacks a fixed 'essence', but the human body itself is subject to social forces which shape and alter it in various ways. We can give our bodies meanings which challenge what is usually thought of as 'natural'. Individuals can choose to construct and reconstruct their bodies as they please – ranging from exercise, dieting,

There is a gender dimension to everyday social interaction. Even the way people sit demonstrates gendered socialization. It can be quite disturbing, for example, when men and women break the rules.

piercing and personal fashion, to plastic surgery and sex-change operations.

Technology is blurring the boundaries of our physical bodies. Thus, the argument goes, the human body and biology are not 'givens', but are subject to human agency and personal choice within different social contexts.

 For a discussion of the social construction of bodies, see chapter 10, 'Health, Illness and Disability'.

According to such a perspective, writers who focus on gender roles and role learning implicitly accept that there is a biological basis to gender differences. In the socialization approach, a biological distinction between the sexes provides a framework which becomes 'culturally elaborated' in society itself. In contrast to this, some strict social constructionist theorists reject any biological basis for gender differences.

Gender identities emerge, they argue, in relation to perceived sex differences in society and in turn help to shape those differences. For example, a society in which ideas of masculinity are characterized by physical strength and 'tough' attitudes will encourage men to cultivate a specific body image and set of mannerisms. In other words, gender identities and sex differences are inextricably linked within individual human bodies (Connell 1987; Scott and Morgan 1993; Butler 1990)

Masculinities and gender relations

Considering feminists' concern with women's subordination in society, it is perhaps not surprising that most early research on gender concerned itself almost exclusively with women and concepts of femininity. Men and masculinity were regarded as relatively straightforward and

unproblematic. Little effort was made to examine masculinity, the experience of being a man or the formation of male identities. Sociologists were more concerned with understanding men's oppression of women and their role in maintaining patriarchy.

Since the late 1980s, however, greater attention has been devoted to critical studies of men and masculinity. The fundamental changes affecting the role of women and family patterns in industrialized societies have raised questions about the nature of masculinity and its changing role in society. What does it mean to be a man in late modern society? How are the traditional expectations and pressures on men being transformed in a rapidly changing age? Is masculinity in crisis?

In recent years, sociologists have become increasingly interested in the positions and experience of men within the larger order that shapes them. This shift within the sociology of gender and sexuality has led to new emphasis on the study of men and masculinity within the overarching context of **gender**

relations, the societally patterned interactions between men and women. Sociologists are interested to grasp how male identities are constructed and what impact socially prescribed roles have on men's behaviour.

The gender order

In *Gender and Power* (1987), *The Men and the Boys* (2001) and *Masculinities* (2005), R. W. Connell sets forth one of the most complete theoretical accounts of gender, which has become something of a 'modern classic' (see 'Classic Studies 14.2'). Her approach has been particularly influential in sociology because she integrates the concepts of patriarchy and masculinity into an overarching theory of gender relations. According to Connell, masculinities are a critical part of the gender order and cannot be understood separate from it, or from the femininities which accompany them.

Connell is concerned with how the social power held by men creates and sustains gender inequality. She stresses that empirical evidence on gender inequality is not simply a 'shapeless heap of data', but reveals the basis of an 'organized field of human practice and social relations' through which women are kept in subordinate positions to men (Connell 1987). In Western capitalist societies, gender relations are still defined by patriarchal power. From the individual to the institutional level, various types of masculinity and femininity are all arranged around a central premise: the dominance of men over women.

According to Connell, gender relations are the product of everyday interactions and practices. The actions and behaviour of average people in their personal lives are directly linked to collective social arrangements in society. These arrangements are continuously reproduced over lifetimes and generations, but are also subject to change.

Connell sets forth three aspects which interact to form a society's **gender order** – patterns of power relations between masculinities and femininities that are widespread throughout society – namely, labour, power and cathexis (personal/sexual relationships). These three realms are distinct but interrelated parts of society that work together and change in relation to one other. They represent the main sites in which gender relations are constituted and constrained. *Labour* refers to the sexual division of labour both within the home (such as domestic responsibilities and childcare) and in the labour market (issues like occupational segregation and unequal pay). *Power* operates through social relations such as authority, violence and ideology in institutions, the state, the military and domestic life. *Cathexis* concerns dynamics within intimate, emotional and personal relationships, including marriage, sexuality and childrearing.

Gender relations, as they are enacted in these three areas of society, are structured on a societal level in a particular gender order. Connell uses the term **gender regime** to refer to the play of gender relations in smaller settings, such as a specific institution. Thus, a family, a neighbourhood and a state all have their own gender regimes. (The formation of masculinities in one such gender regime is explored by Máirtín Mac an Ghaill in 'Using your sociological imagination 14.1' below.)

Change in the gender order: crisis tendencies

Although Connell has set forth a clearly organized gender hierarchy, she rejects the view that gender relations are fixed or static. On the contrary, she suggests that they are the outcome of an ongoing process and are therefore open to change and challenge. She sees the gender order in dynamic terms. If sex and gender *are* socially constructed, Connell argues, then people can change their gender orientations. By this she does not necessarily mean that people can switch their sexuality from homosexual to heterosexual and vice versa, although this does occur in some cases, but that people's gender identities and outlooks are constantly being adjusted. Women who once subscribed to 'emphasized femininity' might develop a feminist consciousness, for example. This constant possibility of change makes patterns of gender relations open to disruption and subject to the power of human agency.

While some sociologists suggest that Western society is undergoing a 'gender crisis', Connell suggests that we are simply in the presence of powerful tendencies towards crisis. These crisis tendencies take three forms. First, there is the *crisis of institutionalization*. By this, Connell means that institutions that have traditionally supported men's power – the family and the state – are gradually being undermined. The legitimacy of men's domination over women is being weakened through legislation on divorce, domestic violence and rape, and economic questions such as taxation and pensions. Second, there is a *crisis of sexuality*, in which hegemonic heterosexuality is less dominant than it once was. The growing strength of women's sexuality and gay sexuality put traditional hegemonic masculinity under

Classic Studies 14.2 R. W. Connell on the dynamics of the gender order

The research problem

Why do some people become male and female role models? What characteristics and actions do role models display and how do those characteristics and actions (and not others) come to be widely seen as desirable? R. W. Connell (1987, 2001, 2005) explored such questions in her studies of the 'gender order' in societies. In particular, she developed a theory of the *gender hierarchy*.

Connell's explanation

Connell argues that there are many different expressions of masculinity and femininity. At the level of society, these contrasting versions are ordered in a hierarchy which is oriented around one defining premise – the domination of men over women (figure 14.6). She uses stylized 'ideal types' of masculinities and femininities in her hierarchy.

At the top of the hierarchy is **hegemonic masculinity**, which is dominant over all other masculinities and femininities in society. 'Hegemonic' refers to the concept of hegemony – the social dominance of a certain group, exercised not through brute force, but through a cultural dynamic which extends into private life

and social realms. Thus, the media, education, ideology, even sports and music can all be channels through which hegemony is established. According to Connell, hegemonic masculinity is associated first and foremost with heterosexuality and marriage, but also with authority, paid work, strength and physical toughness. Examples of men who embody hegemonic masculinity include film stars such as Arnold Schwarzenegger, rappers like 50 Cent and the entrepreneur Donald Trump.

Although hegemonic masculinity is held up as an ideal form of masculinity, only a few men in society can live up to it. A large number of men, however, still gain advantage from hegemonic masculinity's dominant position in the patriarchal order. Connell refers to this as the 'patriarchal dividend' and to those who benefit from it as embodying **complicit masculinity**.

Existing in a subordinated relationship to hegemonic masculinity are a number of subordinated masculinities and femininities. Among subordinated masculinities, the most important is that of **homosexual masculinity**. In a gender order dominated by hegemonic masculinity, the homosexual is seen as the opposite of the 'real man'; he does not measure up to the hegemonic masculine ideal and often embodies many of the 'cast off' traits of hegemonic masculinity. Homosexual masculinity is stigmatized, and ranks at the bottom of the gender hierarchy for men.

Connell argues that femininities are all formed in positions of subordination to hegemonic masculinity. One form of femininity – **emphasized femininity** – is an important complement to hegemonic masculinity. It is oriented to accommodating the interests and desires of men and is characterized by 'compliance, nurturance and empathy'. Among young women it is associated with sexual receptivity, while among older women it implies motherhood. Connell refers to Marilyn Monroe as both 'archetype and satirist' of emphasized femininity and stresses that images of emphasized femininity remain highly prevalent in the media, advertising and marketing campaigns.

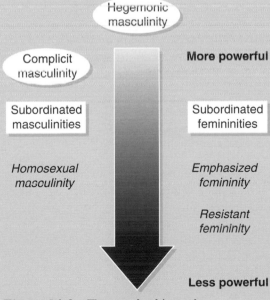

Figure 14.6   The gender hierarchy

Finally, there are subordinated femininities, which reject the version of emphasized femininity outlined above. But on the whole, the overwhelming attention devoted to maintaining emphasized femininity as the conventional norm in society means that other subordinated femininities which resist convention are not given voice. Women who have developed non-subordinated identities and lifestyles include feminists, lesbians, spinsters, midwives, witches, prostitutes and manual workers. The experiences of these resistant femininities, however, are largely 'hidden from history'.

Critical points

Several critics have argued that although hegemonic masculinity appears to be fairly obvious, Connell does not really present a satisfactory account of it. This is because she does not specify what would count as 'counter-hegemonic'. For example, with more men now involved in childcare and parenting, is this part of or a trend against hegemonic masculinity? Unless we know what actions would challenge hegemonic masculinity, how can we know what actions constitute it in the first place? Some social psychologists also wonder *how* men come to 'embody' complicit masculinity; if they do not live up the hegemonic masculine ideal themselves, what does this failure mean for them psychologically and what do they actually do? In short, 'What is missing is more fine-grain work on what complicity and resistance look like in practice' (Wetherell and Edley 1999: 337). Finally, Connell did not theorize the gender order at the global level, though this was the subject of a later work.

Contemporary significance

Given that Connell's work is relatively recent, sociologists are still working through all of its implications. The early work is notable for its wider focus on men and masculinities as well as women in the field of gender studies. However, so far her ideas have been enormously influential in shaping gender studies and particularly in our understanding of how particular gender regimes are stabilized and, potentially, destabilized. As Connell's ideas show that the gender order is never fixed or static, they have influenced not just sociologists, but also political activists within LGBT social movements.

pressure. Finally, there is a *crisis of interest formation*. Connell argues that there are new foundations for social interests that contradict the existing gender order. Married women's rights, gay movements and the growth of 'anti-sexist' attitudes among men all pose threats to the current order. Of course, threats to the gender order do not have to be negative for men. More men today are becoming fully involved in childrearing and a minority have enthusiastically embraced the relatively new social role of 'house-husband', as their wives and partners are able to establish careers and bring in a 'family wage'. Similarly, the idea of the 'new man', who self-consciously rejects the older forms of behaviour associated with hegemonic masculinity in favour of a more caring and emotionally open disposition, brings with it the possibility of new types of relationship. Connell argues that such positive actions of individuals and groups can bring about change in the gender order. The crisis tendencies already in evidence within the existing order could be exploited in order to bring about the eradication of gender inequality (Connell 1987, 2005).

See chapter 9, 'Families and Intimate Relationships', for a more detailed discussion of changes to gender roles within family life.

More recently, Connell has begun to examine the effects of globalization on the gender order. She argues that gender itself has become globalized. This involves interaction between previously distinct, local gender orders as well as the creation of new arenas of gender relations beyond individual localities.

Connell argues that there are several crucial new arenas of gender relations that play a part in the globalization of gender:

14.1 Education and the formation of masculinities and sexualities

In *The Making of Men* (1994), Máirtín Mac an Ghaill presented the findings from a piece of ethnographic research at a British state secondary school, which explored its 'gender regime' – the way gender relations play out within the confines of the school. Drawing on Connell's work, Mac an Ghaill was interested in how schools actively create a range of masculinities and femininities among students. Although he was particularly curious about the formation of heterosexual masculinities, he also investigated the experiences of a group of gay male students. His findings revealed that the school itself is an institution characterized by gendered and heterosexual patterns.

The prevailing 'regime' encourages the construction of gender relations among students which coincide with the larger gender order – that is, a hierarchy of dominant and subordinate masculinities and femininities could be detected within the confines of the school. Social influences and practices as diverse as disciplinary procedures, subject allocation, teacher–student and student–teacher interactions, and surveillance all contribute to the formation of heterosexual masculinities.

Mac an Ghaill notes four emergent types of masculinity in the school setting. The *macho lads* are a group of white, working-class boys who are defiant of school authority and disdainful of the learning process and student achievers. Mac an Ghaill concludes that the macho lads are undergoing a 'crisis of masculinity', as the manual and unskilled/semi-skilled jobs which they once saw as defining their future identities are no longer available. This leaves the lads in a psychological and practical dilemma about

their futures which is difficult for them to comprehend and even harder to resolve.

The second group is made up of *academic achievers*, who see themselves as future professionals. These boys are stereotyped by the 'macho lads' (and teachers) as effeminate, 'dickhead achievers'. The most common route taken by the achievers in handling the vicious stereotyping, according to Mac an Ghaill, is to retain confidence that their hard work and academic credentials will grant them a secure future. This forms the basis of their masculine identities.

The third group, the *new enterprisers*, are boys who gravitate towards subjects in the new vocational curriculum, such as computer science and business studies. Mac an Ghaill sees them as children of the new 'enterprise culture' which was cultivated during the Thatcher years. For these boys, success in A-level exams is relatively useless for their emphasis on the market and their instrumental planning for the future.

The *real Englishmen* make up the final group. They are the most troublesome of the middle-class groups, as they maintain an ambivalent attitude towards academic learning, but see themselves as 'arbiters of culture', superior to anything their teachers can offer. Because they are oriented towards entry into a career, masculinity for the 'real Englishmen' involves the appearance of effortless academic achievement.

In his study of homosexual male students, Mac an Ghaill found that a distinctly heterosexual set of norms and values – based on traditional relationships and nuclear families – is taken for granted in all classroom discussions that touch on gender or sexuality. This leads to difficult 'confusions and contradictions' in the construction of gender and sexual identities for young gay men, who can simultaneously feel ignored and categorized by others.

transnational and multinational corporations, which tend to have a strong gendered division of labour and a masculine management culture; international non-governmental organizations, such as the UN agencies, which are also gendered and mainly run by men; the international media, which again has a strong gender division of labour and disseminates particular understandings of gender through its output; and, lastly, global markets (in capital, commodities, services and labour) which tend to be strongly gender-structured and can increasingly reach into local economies.

THINKING CRITICALLY

Do you recognise any of the school-based groups in Mac an Ghaill's study ('Using your sociological imagination 14.1') from your own experiences in education? How difficult would it be to change such a school culture? Why do you think the bulk of such school-based studies have focused attention on boys and masculine norms rather then the experiences of girls?

To Connell, the globalization of gender has resulted in interaction between local gender orders and the new arenas of gender relations discussed above, so that it is now possible to talk of a 'world gender order'. She argues that globalization provides the context in which we must now think about the lives of men and the construction and enactment of masculinities in the future.

Theories of gender inequality

We have seen that gender is a socially created concept which attributes differing social roles and identities to men and women. Yet gender differences are rarely neutral – in almost all societies, gender is a significant form of **social stratification**. Gender is a critical factor in structuring the types of opportunities and life chances faced by individuals and groups, and strongly influences the roles they play within social institutions from the household to the state. Although the roles of men and women vary from culture to culture, there is no known instance of a society in which females are more powerful than males. Men's roles are generally more highly valued and rewarded than women's roles: in almost every culture, women bear the primary responsibility for childcare and domestic work, while men have traditionally borne responsibility for providing the family livelihood. The prevailing division of labour between the sexes has led to men and

women assuming unequal positions in terms of power, prestige and wealth.

Despite the advances that women have made in countries around the world, gender differences continue to serve as the basis for social inequalities. Investigating and accounting for **gender inequality** has become a central concern of sociologists. Many theoretical perspectives have been advanced to explain men's enduring dominance over women – in the realm of economics, politics, the family and elsewhere. In this section we shall review the main theoretical approaches to explaining the nature of gender inequality at the level of society, leaving our discussion of gender inequality in specific settings and institutions to other chapters of the book.

 Evidence on gender inequality is introduced and discussed in chapter 11, 'Stratification and Social Class', and chapter 13, 'Global Inequality'.

Functionalist approaches

As we saw in chapter 1, 'What is Sociology?', the functionalist approach sees society as a system of interlinked parts which, when in balance, operate smoothly to produce social solidarity. Thus, functionalist and functionalist-inspired perspectives on gender seek to show that gender differences contribute to social stability and integration. While such views once commanded great support, they have been heavily criticized for neglecting social tensions at the expense of consensus and for promulgating a conservative view of the social world.

Writers who subscribe to the 'natural differences' school of thought tend to argue that the division of labour between men and women is biologically based. Women and men perform those tasks for which they are biologically best suited. Thus, the anthropologist George Murdock saw it as both practical and convenient that women should concentrate on domestic and family responsibilities while men work outside the home. On the basis of a cross-cultural study of more than 200 societies, Murdock (1949) concluded that the sexual division of labour is present in all cultures. While this is not the result of biological 'programming', it is the most logical basis for the organization of society.

Talcott Parsons, a leading functionalist thinker, concerned himself with the role of the family in industrial societies (Parsons and Bales 1956). He was particularly interested in the socialization of children, and argued that stable, supportive families are the key to successful socialization. In Parsons's view, the family operates most efficiently with a clear-cut sexual division of labour in which females act in *expressive* roles, providing care and security to children and offering them emotional support. Men, on the other hand, should perform *instrumental* roles – namely, being the breadwinner in the family. Because of the stressful nature of this role, women's expressive and nurturing tendencies should also be used to stabilize and comfort men. This complementary division of labour, springing from a biological distinction between the sexes, would ensure the solidarity of the family.

Another functionalist perspective on childrearing was advanced by John Bowlby (1953), who argued that the mother is crucial to the primary socialization of children. If the mother is absent, or if a child is separated from the mother at a young age – a state referred to as **maternal deprivation** – the child runs a high risk of being inadequately socialized. This can lead to serious social and psychological difficulties later in life, including anti-social and psychopathic tendencies. Bowlby argued that a child's well-being and mental health can be best guaranteed through a close, personal and continuous relationship with its mother. He did concede that an absent mother can be replaced by a 'mother-substitute', but suggested that such a substitute should also be a woman – leaving little doubt about his view that the mothering role is a distinctly female one. Bowlby's maternal deprivation thesis has been used by some to argue that working mothers are neglectful of their children.

Feminists have sharply criticized claims to a biological basis to the sexual division of labour, arguing that there is nothing natural or inevitable about the allocation of tasks in society. Women are not prevented from pursuing occupations on the basis of any biological features; rather, humans are socialized into roles that are culturally expected of them.

There is a steady stream of evidence to suggest that the maternal deprivation thesis is questionable – studies have shown that children's educational performance and personal development are in fact enhanced when both parents are employed at least part of the time outside the home. Parsons's view on the 'expressive' female has similarly been attacked by feminists and other sociologists who see such views as condoning the domination of women in the home. There is no basis to the belief that the 'expressive' female is necessary for the smooth operation of the family – rather, it is a role which is promoted largely for the convenience of men.

Feminist approaches

The feminist movement has given rise to a large body of theory which attempts to explain gender inequalities and set forth agendas for overcoming those inequalities. Feminist theories in relation to gender inequality contrast markedly with one another. Competing schools of feminism have sought to explain gender inequalities through a variety of deeply embedded social processes, such as sexism, patriarchy and capitalism. We begin by looking at the major strands of feminism in the West during the twentieth century: liberal, socialist (or Marxist) and radical feminism. The distinction between the different strands of feminism has never been clear-cut, although it provides a useful introduction. The tripartite categorization has become less useful in recent decades with the introduction of new forms of feminism that draw upon, and cut across, the earlier strands (Barker 1997). We will conclude this section with a brief examination of two important newer theories: black and postmodern feminism.

Liberal feminism

Liberal feminism looks for explanations of gender inequalities in social and cultural attitudes. An important early contribution to liberal feminism came from the English philosopher John Stuart Mill in his essay *The Subjection of Women* (1869), which called for legal and political equality between the sexes, including the right to vote. Unlike radical and socialist feminists, whose work we examine below, liberal feminists do not see women's subordination as part of a larger system or structure. Instead, they draw attention to many separate factors which contribute to inequalities between men and women. For example, in recent decades liberal feminists have campaigned against sexism and discrimination against women in the workplace, educational institutions and the media. They tend to focus their energies on establishing and protecting equal opportunities for women through legislation and other democratic means. In the UK, legal advances such as the Equal Pay Act (1970) and the Sex Discrimination Act (1975) were actively supported by liberal feminists, who argued that enshrining equality in law is important to eliminating discrimination against women. Liberal feminists seek to work through the existing system to bring about reforms in a gradual way. In this respect, they are more moderate in their aims and methods than many radical and socialist feminists, who call for an overthrow of the existing system.

While liberal feminists have contributed greatly to the advancement of women over the past century, critics charge that they are unsuccessful in dealing with the root causes of gender inequality and do not acknowledge the systemic nature of women's oppression in society. By focusing on the independent deprivations which women suffer – sexism, discrimination, the 'glass ceiling', unequal pay – liberal feminists draw only a partial picture of gender inequality. Radical feminists accuse liberal feminists of encouraging women to accept an unequal society and its competitive character.

Socialist and Marxist feminism

Socialist feminism developed from Marx's conflict theory, although Marx himself had little to say about gender inequality. It has been critical of liberal feminism for its perceived inability to see that there are powerful interests in society hostile to equality for women (Bryson 1993). Socialist feminists have sought to defeat both patriarchy and capitalism (Mitchell 1966). It was Marx's friend and collaborator Friedrich Engels who did more than Marx to provide an account of gender equality from a Marxist perspective.

Engels argued that under capitalism, material and economic factors underlay women's subservience to men, because **patriarchy** (like class oppression) has its roots in private property. Engels argued that capitalism intensifies patriarchy – men's domination over women – by concentrating wealth and power in the hands of a small number of men. Capitalism intensifies patriarchy more than earlier social systems because it creates enormous wealth compared to previous eras which confers power on men as wage-earners as well as possessors and inheritors of property. Second, for the capitalist economy to succeed, it must define people – in particular women – as consumers, persuading them that their needs will only be met through ever-increasing consumption of goods and products. Last, capitalism relies on women to labour for free in the home, caring and cleaning. To Engels, capitalism exploited men by paying low wages and women by paying no wages.

 Payment for housework is an important component of many feminists' belief, and is discussed further in chapter 20, 'Work and Economic Life'.

Socialist feminists have argued that the reformist goals of liberal feminism are inadequate. They have called for the restructuring of the family, the end of 'domestic slavery' and the introduction of some collective means of carrying out childrearing, caring and household maintenance. Following Marx, many argued that these ends would be achieved through a socialist revolution, which would produce true equality under a state-centred economy designed to meet the needs of all.

Radical feminism

At the heart of **radical feminism** is the belief that men are responsible for and benefit from the exploitation of women. The analysis of patriarchy – the systematic domination of females by males – is of central concern to this branch of feminism. Patriarchy is viewed as a universal phenomenon that has existed across time and cultures. Radical feminists often concentrate on the family as one of the primary sources of women's oppression in society. They argue that men exploit women by relying on the free domestic labour that women provide in the home. As a group, men also deny women access to positions of power and influence in society.

Radical feminists differ in their interpretations of the basis of patriarchy, but most agree that it involves the appropriation of women's bodies and sexuality in some form. Shulamith Firestone (1971), an early radical feminist writer, argues that men control women's roles in reproduction and childrearing. Because women are biologically able to give birth to children, they become dependent materially on men for protection and livelihood. This 'biological inequality' is socially organized in the nuclear family. Firestone speaks of a 'sex class' to describe women's social position and argues that women can be emancipated only through the abolition of the family and the power relations which characterize it.

Other radical feminists point to male violence against women as central to male supremacy. According to such a view, domestic violence, rape and sexual harassment are all part of the systematic oppression of women, rather than isolated cases with their own psychological or criminal roots. Even interactions in daily life – such as non-verbal communication, patterns of listening and interrupting, and women's sense of comfort in public – contribute to gender inequality. Moreover, the argument goes, popular conceptions of beauty and sexuality are imposed by men on women in order to produce a certain type of femininity. For example, social and cultural norms that emphasize a slim body and a caring, nurturing attitude towards men help to perpetuate women's subordination. The 'objectification' of women through the media, fashion and advertising turns women into sexual objects whose main role is to please and entertain men. Radical feminists do not see any strong evidence that women can be liberated from sexual oppression through reforms or gradual change. Because patriarchy is a systemic phenomenon, they argue, gender equality can only be attained by overthrowing the patriarchal order.

The use of patriarchy as a concept for explaining gender inequality has been popular with many feminist theorists. In asserting that 'the personal is political', radical feminists have drawn widespread attention to the many linked dimensions of women's oppression. Their emphasis on male violence and the objectification of women has brought these issues into the heart of mainstream debates about women's subordination.

Many objections can be raised, however, to radical feminist views. The main one, perhaps, is that the concept of patriarchy as it has been used is inadequate as a general explanation for women's oppression. Radical feminists have tended to claim that patriarchy has existed throughout history and across cultures – that it is a universal phenomenon. Critics argue, however, that such a conception of patriarchy does not leave room for historical or cultural variations. It also ignores the important influence that race, class or ethnicity may have on the nature of women's subordination. In other words, it is not possible to see patriarchy as a

14.2 Theorizing patriarchy

The idea of **patriarchy** has been central to many feminist interpretations of gender inequality. But as an analytical tool, it has also been criticized for failing to explain the changes to and diversity in gender inequalities. Surely, critics argue, we cannot speak of one uniform and unchanging system of oppression for all of history? Sylvia Walby is one theorist who believes that the concept of patriarchy is essential to any analysis of gender inequality. But she agrees that many criticisms of it are valid. In *Theorizing Patriarchy* (1990), Walby presents a way of understanding patriarchy that is more flexible than its predecessors. It allows room for change over historical time, and for consideration of ethnic and class differences.

For Walby, patriarchy is 'a system of social structures and practices in which men dominate, oppress and exploit women' (1990: 20). She sees patriarchy and capitalism as distinct systems which interact in different ways – sometimes harmoniously, sometimes in tension – depending on historical conditions. Capitalism, she argues, has generally benefited from patriarchy through the *sexual division of labour*. But at other times, capitalism and patriarchy have been at odds with one another. For example, in wartime, when women have entered the labour market in great numbers, the interests of capitalism and patriarchy have not been aligned.

Walby identifies six structures through which patriarchy operates. She recognizes that a weakness of early feminist theory was the tendency to focus on one 'essential' cause of women's oppression, such as male violence or women's role in reproduction. Because Walby is concerned with the depth and interconnectedness of gender inequality; she sees patriarchy as composed of six structures that are independent, but interact with one another.

1 *Production relations in the household.* Women's unpaid domestic labour, such as housework and childcare, is expropriated by her husband (or cohabitee).
2 *Paid work.* Women in the labour market are excluded from certain types of work,

receive lower pay, and are segregated in less skilled jobs.
3 *The patriarchal state.* In its policies and priorities, the state has a systematic bias towards patriarchal interests.
4 *Male violence.* Although male violence is often seen as composed of individualistic acts, it is patterned and systematic. Women routinely experience this violence, and are affected by it in standard ways. The state effectively condones the violence with its refusal to intervene, except in exceptional cases.
5 *Patriarchal relations in sexuality.* This is manifested in 'compulsory heterosexuality' and in the sexual double standard between men and women, in which different 'rules' for sexual behaviour apply.
6 *Patriarchal cultural institutions.* A variety of institutions and practices – including media, religion and education – produce representations of women 'within a patriarchal gaze'. These representations influence women's identities and prescribe acceptable standards of behaviour and action.

Walby distinguishes two distinct forms of patriarchy. *Private patriarchy* is domination of women which occurs within the household at the hands of an individual patriarch. It is an exclusionary strategy, because women are essentially prevented from taking part in public life. *Public patriarchy*, on the other hand, is more collective in form. Women are involved in public realms, such as politics and the labour market, but remain segregated from wealth, power and status.

Walby contends that, at least in Britain, there has been a shift in patriarchy – both in degree and form – from the Victorian era to the present day. She notes that the narrowing of the wage gap and the gains in women's education demonstrate a shift in the degree of patriarchy, but do not signal its defeat. If at one time women's oppression was found chiefly in the home, it is now located throughout society as a whole – women are now segregated and subordinated in all areas of the public realm. In other words, patriarchy has shifted in form from the private to the public realm. As Walby quips: 'Liberated from the home, women now have the whole of society in which to be exploited.'

universal phenomenon; doing so risks biological reductionism – attributing all the complexities of gender inequality to a simple distinction between men and women.

Sylvia Walby has advanced an important reconceptualization of patriarchy (see 'Using your sociological imagination 14.2'). She argues that the notion of patriarchy remains a valuable and useful explanatory tool, providing that it is used in certain ways.

THINKING CRITICALLY

Taking each of Walby's six 'structures of patriarchy' in turn ('Using your sociological imagination 14.2'), what evidence is there of a shift towards public forms of patriarchy? Has this shift intensified the subordination of women within society? What evidence is there that the movement of women into the public sphere has actually been largely *beneficial* for the majority of women?

Black feminism

Do the versions of feminism outlined above apply equally to the experiences of both white and non-white women? Many black feminists, and feminists from developing countries, claim they do not. They argue that ethnic divisions among women are not considered by the main feminist schools of thought, which are oriented to the dilemmas of white, predominantly middle-class women living in industrialized societies. It is not valid, they claim, to generalize theories about women's subordination as a whole from the experience of a specific group of women. Moreover, the very idea that there is a 'unified' form of gender oppression that is experienced equally by all women is problematic.

Dissatisfaction with existing forms of feminism has led to the emergence of a strand of thought which concentrates on the particular problems facing black women. In the foreword to her personal memoirs, American black feminist bell hooks (1997; her name is always written in lower-case letters) argues:

Many feminist thinkers writing and talking about girlhood right now like to suggest that black girls have better self-esteem than their white counterparts. The measurement of this difference is often that black girls are more assertive, speak more, appear more confident. Yet in traditional southern-based black life, it was and is expected of girls to be articulate, to hold ourselves with dignity. Our parents and teachers were always urging us to stand up right and speak clearly. These traits were meant to uplift the race. They were not necessarily traits associated with building female self-esteem. An outspoken girl might still feel that she was worthless because her skin was not light enough or her hair the right texture. These are the variables that white researchers often do not consider when they measure the self-esteem of black females with a yardstick that was designed based on values emerging from white experience.

Black feminist writings tend to emphasize history – aspects of the past which inform the current problems facing black women. The writings of American black feminists emphasize the influence of the powerful legacy of slavery, segregation and the civil rights movement on gender inequalities in the black community. They point out that early black suffragettes supported the campaign for women's rights, but realized that the question of race could not be ignored: black women were discriminated against on the basis of their race and gender. In recent years, black women have not been central to the women's liberation movement in part because 'womanhood' dominated their identities much less than concepts of race did.

hooks has argued that explanatory frameworks favoured by white feminists – for example, the view of the family as a mainstay of patriarchy – may not be applicable in black communities, where the family represents a main point of solidarity against racism. In other words, the oppression of black women may be found in different locations compared with that of white women.

Black feminists contend, therefore, that any theory of gender equality which does

Can the concept of patriarchy adequately explain the diverse experiences of women across social classes and ethnic groups, for instance in the work environment?

not take racism into account cannot be expected to explain black women's oppression adequately. Class dimensions form another factor that cannot be neglected in the case of many black women. Some black feminists have held that the strength of black feminist theory is its focus on the interplay between race, class and gender concerns. Black women are multiply disadvantaged, they argue, on the basis of their colour, their sex and their class position. When these three factors interact, they reinforce and intensify one another (Brewer 1993).

Postmodern feminism

Like black feminism, **postmodern feminism** challenges the idea that there is a unitary basis of identity and experience shared by all women. This strand of feminism draws on the cultural phenomenon of postmodernism

in the arts, architecture, philosophy and economics. Some of the roots of postmodern feminism are found in the work of Continental theorists like Derrida (1978, 1981), Lacan (1995) and de Beauvoir (1949). Postmodern feminists reject the claim that there is a grand theory that can explain the position of women in society, or that there is any single, universal essence or category of 'woman'. Consequently, these feminists reject the accounts given by others to explain gender inequality – such as patriarchy, race or class – as 'essentialist' (Beasley 1999).

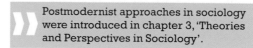 Postmodernist approaches in sociology were introduced in chapter 3, 'Theories and Perspectives in Sociology'.

Instead, postmodernism encourages the acceptances of many different standpoints as equally valid. Rather than there existing an essential core to womanhood, there are many individuals and groups, all of whom have very different experiences (heterosexuals, lesbians, black women, working-class women, etc.). The 'otherness' of different groups and individuals is celebrated in all its diverse forms. Emphasis on the positive side of 'otherness' is a major theme in postmodern feminism, and symbolizes plurality, diversity, difference and openness: there are many truths, roles and constructions of reality. Hence, the recognition of difference (of sexuality, age and race, for example) is central to postmodern feminism.

As well as the recognition of difference between groups and individuals, postmodern feminists have stressed the importance of 'deconstruction'. In particular, they have sought to deconstruct male language and a masculine view of the world. In its place, postmodern feminists have attempted to create fluid, open terms and language which more closely reflect women's experiences. For many postmodern feminists, men see the world in terms of pairs or binary distinctions ('good versus bad', 'right versus wrong', 'beautiful versus ugly', for example). Men, they argue, have cast the male as normal, and female as a deviation from it. The founder of modern psychiatry Sigmund Freud, for example, saw women as men who lacked a penis and argued that they envied males for possessing one. In this masculine worldview, the female is always cast in the role of the 'other'. Deconstruction involves attacking binary concepts and recasting their opposites in a new and positive manner.

> Women's movements are discussed in chapter 22, 'Politics, Government and Social Movements'.

Postmodern feminism is said to have the most difficult relationship with the previous strands of feminism discussed above (Carrington 1995, 1998). This is largely because of its belief that many feminists may be misled in assuming that it is possible to provide overarching explanations for women's oppression and to find steps towards its resolution.

Women's movements

The influence of feminist ideas and women's movements has been profound in Western societies, but increasingly, such movements are challenging gender inequality in other areas of the world. Feminism is not merely an academic exercise, nor is it restricted to Western Europe and North America. In today's increasingly globalized world, there is a good chance that those who become active in the British women's movement will come into contact with women pursuing other feminist struggles overseas.

 Freud's views on gender socialization are debated in chapter 8, 'The Life-Course'.

Although participants in women's movements have, for many years, cultivated ties to activists in other countries, the number and importance of such contacts has increased with globalization. A prime forum for the establishment of cross-national contacts has been the United Nation's Conference on Women, held four times since 1975 with a fifth conference to be held before 2010. Approximately 50,000 people – of whom more than two-thirds were women – attended the most recent conference, held in Beijing, China, in 1995. Delegates from 181 nations attended, along with representatives from thousands of non-governmental organizations. One attendee, Mallika Dutt, wrote in the journal *Feminist Studies*: 'For most women from the United States, Beijing was an eye-opening, humbling, and transformative experience. US women were startled by the sophisticated analysis and well-organized and powerful voices of women from other parts of the world' (Dutt 1996).

The Platform for Action finally agreed to by the conference participants called on the countries of the world to address such issues as:

- the persistent and increasing burden of poverty on women;
- violence against women;
- the effects of armed or other kinds of conflict on women;
- inequality between men and women in the sharing of power and decision-making;
- stereotyping of women;
- gender inequalities in the management of natural resources;
- persistent discrimination against and violation of the rights of the girl child.

The 1995 conference heard that in China, for example, women are working to secure equal rights, employment, a role in production and participation in politics; and that South African women played a major role in the fight against apartheid and are now working to improve conditions for the poorest groups of people in the country. Peruvian activists told delegates that they have been working for decades to create more opportunities for women to participate in public life; and in Russia, women's protest was responsible for blocking the passage of legislation that encouraged women to stay home and perform 'socially necessary labour' (Basu 1995). According to Dutt, having heard of many such campaigns across the world, conference participants left Beijing with a 'sense of global solidarity, pride, and affirmation' (1996).

> **THINKING CRITICALLY**
>
> Do you consider yourself to be a feminist? What does such a label mean in the twenty-first century? Given the very different social situations of women in the developed and developing countries, how realistic is the idea of a global feminism?

Gender and globalization

In this chapter, most of our discussion has focused on notions of gender within Western industrialized societies. We have seen how the women's movement has given rise to a powerful body of sociological theory to make sense of persistent gender inequalities and to advance agendas for overcoming them. We have also seen how the changing gender order is beginning to transform the dominant form of masculinity, bringing with it new men's organizations and campaigning groups.

In a global age, women's movements are forging international networks and a more global orientation in order to remain effective, though an obstacle to this lies in the different material interests of women in very different national situations. What feminism means to people differs across the world. In parts of the developing world, feminism means working to alleviate absolute poverty and to change traditional male attitudes, which favour large families and dislike contraception, while in the developed countries, feminism means continuing campaigns for equality in employment, adequate childcare provision and the ending of male violence towards women. Bringing together such diverse interests will be a key issue for a twenty-first century global feminism.

Summary points

1. While there is a biological component in human sexuality, most sexual *behaviour* seems to be learned rather than innate. Sexual practices vary widely between and within cultures. In the West, Christianity has been important in shaping sexual attitudes. In societies with rigid sexual codes, the gulf between norms and actual practice can be large, as studies of sexual behaviour have shown. In the West, repressive attitudes to sexuality gave way to a more permissive outlook in the 1960s, the effects of which are still obvious today.

2. Most people in the world are heterosexual, but there are many minority sexual tastes and inclinations. Homosexuality seems to exist in all cultures and in recent years attitudes towards homosexuals have become more relaxed. In some countries, laws have been passed which recognize homosexual unions and grant gay couples the same rights as married people.

3. Sociologists distinguish between sex and gender. Sex refers to the biological differences between male and female bodies, while gender concerns the psychological, social and cultural differences between men and women. There is no conclusive evidence to suggest a biological basis to gender differences.

4. Gender socialization refers to the learning of gender roles with the help of agencies such as the family, schools and the media. Gender socialization begins as soon as an infant is born; children learn and internalize the norms and expectations that correspond to their biological sex. They therefore adopt 'sex roles' and the male and female identities (masculinity and femininity) that accompany them.

5. Some sociologists argue that sex and gender are *both* socially constructed, and can be shaped and altered in various ways. Not only does gender lack a fixed 'essence', but the human body can also be changed through social influences and technological interventions.

6. Gender inequality refers to the differences in status, power and prestige enjoyed by women and men in various contexts. In explaining gender inequality, functionalists emphasized that gender differences and the sexual division of labour contribute to social stability and integration. Feminist approaches reject the idea that gender inequality is somehow 'natural'. Liberal feminists have explained gender inequality in terms of social and cultural attitudes, such as sexism and discrimination. Radical feminists argue that men are responsible for the exploitation of women through patriarchy – the systematic domination of females by males. Black feminists have seen factors such as class and ethnicity, in addition to gender, as essential for understanding the oppression experienced by non-white women.

7. Gender relations refer to societally patterned interactions between men and women in society. Some sociologists have argued that a gender order exists in which expressions of masculinity and femininity are organized in a hierarchy that promotes the domination of men over women.

8. In recent years, more attention has been paid to the nature of masculinity. Some argue that wide economic and social transformations are provoking a crisis of masculinity in which men's traditional roles are being eroded.

Further reading

A good introduction to the issues around sexualities is Joe Bristow's *Sexuality* (London: Routledge, 2006), the second edition of which brings debates right up to date. A similarly reliable introduction to the study of gender in sociology is R. W. Connell's *Gender* (Cambridge: Polity, 2002).

If you decide to pursue these themes further, then two more challenging books are Jeffrey Weeks, Janet Holland and Matthew Waites's edited volume, *Sexualities and Society: A Reader* (Cambridge: Polity, 2002), which contains many interesting chapters, and Chris Beasley's *Gender and Sexuality: Critical Theories, Critical Thinkers* (London: Sage, 2005), which provides a good overview of some challenging theories.

Amy S. Wharton's *The Sociology of Gender: An Introduction to Theory and Research* (Malden, MA: Blackwell Publishing, 2005) looks at gender through individual, interactional and institutional perspectives. A very good review of the masculinities field is Chris Haywood and Máirtín Mac an Ghaill's *Men and Masculinities: Theory, Research and Social Practice* (Buckingham: Open University Press, 2007).

Finally, anyone looking for a reference work in these areas could consult Jane Pilcher and Amanda Whelehan's *50 Key Concepts in Gender Studies* (London: Sage Publications, 2004), which contains exactly what it says.

Internet links

Intute: UK academic social science gateway for gender and sexuality:
www.intute.ac.uk/socialsciences/
cgi-bin/browse.pl?id=120918&gateway=%

The Women's Library – has lots of electronic and other resources:
www.londonmet.ac.uk/thewomenslibrary/

Queer Resource Directory – a gateway to many resources:
www.qrd.org/qrd/

Eldis – gender issues in developing countries:
www.eldis.org/gender/

Voice of the Shuttle – many gender and sexuality studies resources:
http://vos.ucsb.edu/browse.asp?id=2711

A BBC debate on same-sex marriage:
www.bbc.co.uk/religion/ethics/
samesexmarriage/

ILGA –International Lesbian and Gay Association:
www.ilga.org/

15
....
Race, Ethnicity and Migration

CHAPTER 15

· ·

Race, Ethnicity and Migration

(opposite) Townships, such as Soweto (pictured here), were home to millions of black and 'coloured' South Africans under the apartheid system.

Until the first free multiracial elections, held in 1994, South Africa was governed by apartheid – a system of forced racial segregation. Under apartheid, every South African was classified into one of four categories: *white* (descendants of European immigrants), *coloured* (people whose descent is traced from members of more than one race), *Asian* and *black*. The white South African minority – around 13 per cent of the population – ruled over the non-white majority. Non-whites had no vote and no representation in the central government. Segregation was enforced at all levels of society, from public places like washrooms and railway carriages, to residential neighbourhoods and schools. Millions of blacks were herded into so-called 'homelands', well away from the main cities, and worked as migrant labourers in gold and diamond mines.

Apartheid was encoded in law, but enforced through violence and brutality. The National Party, which formalized apartheid in 1948, used law enforcement and security services to suppress all resistance to the new regime. Opposition groups were outlawed and political dissidents detained without trial and often tortured. Peaceful demonstrations frequently ended in violence. After years of international condemnation, economic and cultural sanctions, and growing domestic resistance, the apartheid regime began to weaken. When F. W. de Klerk became President in 1989, he inherited a country already deep in crisis and virtually ungovernable.

In 1990, de Klerk lifted the ban on the African National Congress (ANC), the main opposition party and, in a historic decision, freed the ANC leader, Nelson Mandela, who had been in prison for 27 years. A series of complex negotiations followed, paving the way for South Africa's first national election involving both whites and non-whites. On 27 April 1994, the ANC received an overwhelming 62 per cent of the vote and Nelson Mandela became South Africa's first post-apartheid president.

The task facing Mandela and the ANC was enormous. In a country of 38 million people, 9 million were impoverished and 20 million lived without electricity. Unemployment was widespread. More than half the black population was illiterate and infant mortality rates were more than ten times higher amongst blacks than whites. South Africa was a highly divided society. Decades of white rule, premised on ideas of racial superiority, had left the country scarred and in desperate need of reconciliation for the atrocities of the apartheid regime. Ethnic tensions within the African population flared up in violent outbreaks and civil war threatened.

Mandela's presidency laid the foundations for the emergence of an equitable, multiethnic society before he stood down in 1999. The 1996 constitution is one of the most progressive in the world, outlawing all discrimination on the basis of race, ethnic or social origin, religion and belief, sexual orientation, disability and pregnancy. Mandela's repeated calls for a 'new patriotism' sought to rally 'nervous whites' and 'impatient blacks' into a common nation-building project. Dissenting political groups, such as the Zulu-based Inkatha Freedom Party (IFP), were brought into government to reduce ethnic and political tensions. Beginning in April 1996 and ending in July 1998, the Truth and Reconciliation Commission (TRC) held hearings across South Africa to examine the abuses of human rights which had occurred under apartheid. The Nobel laureate, Archbishop Desmond Tutu, headed the TRC's investigations. More than 21,000 testimonies were given and recorded and the TRC hearings were designed to uncover the realities of the apartheid era – from the most horrific to the most banal – for all to see; they were not intended to serve as trials or to mete out punishments. Those who committed crimes under apartheid were offered amnesty in return for their honest testimonies and the 'full disclosure' of all relevant information. Not surprisingly, the apartheid government was identified as the main perpetrator of human rights abuses, although transgressions committed by other organizations, including the ANC, were also noted. Some have criticized the TRC for its inability to 'right the wrongs' that had occurred. Many others believe that the process of gathering testimonies brought into focus the injustices of the old era. South Africa remains a fractured society and continues to struggle against bigotry and intolerance. In 2000, 'hate speech' was outlawed and new 'equality courts' established to hear charges of racial discrimination.

In this chapter we investigate the ideas of race and ethnicity and question why racial and ethnic divisions so frequently produce social conflicts – as in South Africa and many other societies. After considering the

Nelson Mandela being sworn in as President of South Africa in 1994, after 27 years in prison.

ways that social scientists understand and use the concepts of race and ethnicity, we shall turn to the topics of prejudice, discrimination and racism and discuss sociological theories that help to explain their persistence. From there, we will address models of ethnic integration and explore examples of ethnic conflict. In the final sections, we will turn to issues of migration, ethnic diversity and ethnic relations, paying particular attention to trends in immigration and patterns of ethnic inequality, before examining migration on a global level.

Key concepts

Race

Race is one of the most complex concepts in sociology, not least because of the contra-diction between its widespread, everyday usage and its supposedly 'scientific' basis. Many people today believe, mistakenly, that humans can be readily separated into biologically different races. This is not surprising considering the numerous attempts by scholars and governments, such as that of South Africa before the ending of apartheid, to establish racial cate-gorizations of the peoples of the world. Some authors have distinguished four or five major races, while others have recog-nized as many as three dozen.

In many ancient civilizations, distinc-tions were often drawn between social groups on visible skin colour differences, usually between lighter and darker skin tones. However, before the modern period, it was more common for perceived distinc-tions between human groupings to be based on tribal or kinship affiliations. These groups were numerous and the basis of their classification was relatively unconnected to modern ideas of race, with its biological or genetic connotations. Instead, classification rested on cultural similarity and group membership.

Scientific theories of race arose in the late eighteenth and early nineteenth centuries. They were used to justify the emerging social order, as England and other European nations became imperial powers ruling over subject territories and populations. Count Joseph Arthur de Gobineau (1816–82), sometimes called the father of modern racism, proposed the existence of just three races: white (*Caucasian*), black (*Negroid*) and yellow (*Mongoloid*). According to de Gobineau, the white race possesses superior intelligence, morality and will-power, and it is these inherited qualities that underlie the spread of Western influence across the world. The blacks, by contrast, are the least capable, marked by an animal nature, a lack of morality and emotional instability. The ideas of de Gobineau and other proponents of scientific racism later influenced Adolf Hitler, who transformed them into the ideology of the German Nazi party, and other white supremacist groups, such as the Ku-Klux-Klan in the United States.

In the years following the Second World War, 'race science' was thoroughly discredited. In biological terms, there are no clear-cut races, only a range of physical variations in human beings. Differences in physical type between groups of human beings arise from population inbreeding, which varies according to the degree of contact between different social or cultural groups. Human population groups are a continuum. The genetic diversity *within* populations that share visible physical traits is as great as the diversity *between* them. In the light of this evidence, the scientific community has virtually abandoned the concept of race. Many social scientists concur, arguing that race is nothing more than an ideological construct whose use in academic circles

perpetuates the commonly held (false) belief that it has a grounding in reality (Miles 1993). Other social scientists disagree, claiming that, as a concept, 'race' still has meaning for many people, even if its scientific basis has been discredited; for sociological analysis, they argue, it remains a vital, if highly contested concept. Some scholars therefore choose to use the word 'race' in inverted commas to reflect its problematic, but commonplace, usage.

Nevertheless, racial ideas in science have a habit of recurring. Debates on the scientific basis of race continue in the field of genetic research, for example, and in parts of the USA, law enforcement has made use of racial profiling (as part of the wider trend towards offender profiling), which assesses the likelihood of individuals in specific racial or ethnic groups committing particular types of offence. Hence, it is probably too early to suppose that we have seen the end of scientific racial theories just yet.

> **THINKING CRITICALLY**
>
> If 'race' can only be discussed by using 'scare quotes', should it now be abandoned as a concept altogether? Are there any compelling reasons to carry on using the concept of race in modern social science research?

What, then, is 'race', if it does not refer to biological categories? There are some clear physical differences between human beings, some of which are inherited. But the question of why some differences and not others become matters of discrimination and prejudice has nothing to do with biology. Racial differences, therefore, should be understood as physical variations singled out by the members of a community or society as socially significant. Differences in skin colour, for example, are treated as socially significant, whereas differences in colour of hair are not. Race can be understood as a set of social relationships, which allow individuals and groups to be located, and various attributes or competencies assigned, on the basis of biologically grounded features. Racial distinctions are more than ways of describing human differences – they are also important factors in the reproduction of patterns of power and inequality within society.

The process by which understandings of race is used to classify individuals or groups of people is called **racialization**. Historically, racialization meant that certain groups of people came to be labelled as distinct biological groups on the basis of naturally occurring physical features. During the period from the fifteenth century onwards, as Europeans came increasingly into contact with people from different regions of the world, attempts were made to categorize and explain both natural and social phenomena. Non-European populations were racialized in opposition to the European 'white race'. In some instances, this racialization took on codified institutional forms, as in the case of slavery in the American colonies and apartheid in South Africa. More commonly, however, everyday social institutions became racialized in a de facto manner. Racialization has also occurred *within* Europe, for example in relation to the discrimination against and exclusion of Roma populations within European nation-states. Within a racialized system, aspects of individuals' daily lives – employment, personal relations, housing, healthcare, education and legal representation – are shaped and constrained by their own positions within that system. Race may be a thoroughly discredited scientific concept, but its material consequences throughout

THINKING CRITICALLY

Reflect on your own use of the term 'race' in the past; what did you understand it referred to? Given the discussion above, should sociologists now stop using the term at all? How might the concept of 'race' still be used, if at all, in sociological research?

history is a telling illustration of W. I. Thomas's (1928) famous theorem that 'if men define situations as real, they are real in their consequences'.

Ethnicity

While the idea of race mistakenly implies something fixed and biological, the concept of ethnicity is one that is purely social in meaning. Ethnicity refers to the cultural practices and outlooks of a given community of people which sets them apart from others. Members of ethnic groups see themselves as culturally distinct from other groups and are seen by them, in return, as different. Different characteristics may serve to distinguish ethnic groups, but the most usual ones are language, history or ancestry (real or imagined), religion and styles of dress or adornment. Ethnic differences are wholly learned, a point that seems self-evident until we remember how often some groups are regarded as 'born to rule' or 'naturally lazy', 'unintelligent' and so on. In fact, there is nothing innate about ethnicity; it is a purely social phenomenon that is produced and reproduced over time. Through socialization, young people assimilate the lifestyles, norms and beliefs of ethnic communities. However, what marks out ethnic groups is often the use of 'exclusionary devices', such as the prohibiting of intermarriage, which serve to sharpen and maintain culturally established boundaries.

For many people, ethnicity is central to individual and group identity, but its significance does vary amongst individuals. It can provide an important thread of continuity with the past and is often kept alive through the practices of cultural traditions. Every year, for instance, the excitement and virtuoso displays of Carnival evoke the Caribbean on the streets of Notting Hill in London, while third-generation Americans of Irish descent may proudly identify themselves as Irish-American despite having lived their entire lives in the United States. Irish traditions and customs are often

Global Society 15.1 | Reclaiming black identities

The use of the term 'black' to describe individuals and populations has undergone fundamental transformations over the years and remains highly contested. For a long time, 'black' was a derogatory label assigned by whites. Only in the 1960s did Americans and Britons of African descent 'reclaim' the term and apply it to themselves in a positive way. The term then became a source of pride and identity, rather than a racial slur. The slogan 'black is beautiful' and the motivational concept of 'black power' were central to the black liberation movement. These ideas were used to counter the symbolic domination of 'whiteness' over 'blackness'. As the term 'black' became more accepted within British society, it began to be applied to non-whites who were not of African descent – particularly Asians. It was more than simply a label, however; it also contained an underlying political message. Because black people had all experienced racism and exclusion at the hands of the white population, there was a call for them to mobilize around their common black identity in pushing for change.

In the late 1980s some scholars and members of ethnic minority groups began to challenge the use of the term 'black' to refer to the non-white population as a whole. While acknowledging that non-whites have shared a common oppression, they argue that the term 'black' obscures the differences between ethnic groups.

According to opponents of the term, more attention should be paid to the distinctive experiences of individual ethnic minority groups, rather than presuming a shared experience. Tariq Modood has been one of the leading critics, arguing that the term 'black' is used too loosely – sometimes meaning only people of African descent, and other times referring collectively to Asians as well. He believes that the term over-emphasizes oppression based on skin colour and neglects the large amount of racism that is culturally based. According to Modood, Asians tend not to see themselves as black because of the powerful connotations between the term 'black' and the experience of people of African origin. Finally, Modood points out that 'black' implies an essential identity which is inherently false. Non-white populations possess many diverse identities, just as do groups within the so-called white population (Modood 1994). Nonetheless, the black power movement showed that such essentialist ideas can be a powerful motivator for political activism as well as promoting prejudice and discrimination.

There is no clear consensus about the use of the term 'black' in sociology. While the criticisms raised by Modood and others are surely valid, the term remains a useful way to speak about the shared experience of white racism that most non-whites have encountered. Recent trends within sociology, however, seem to support Modood's concerns. Writers associated with the postmodern school tend to highlight the differences between various ethnic minority groups, rather than dwell on the significance of a collective 'black' identity.

passed down through generations of families and in the larger Irish community. Although it is maintained within tradition, ethnicity is not static and unchanging. Rather, it is fluid and adaptable to changing circumstances. In the case of Irish-Americans, it is possible to see how popular customs from Ireland have been maintained but transformed in the context of American society. The boisterous St Patrick's Day parades in many US cities are one example of how Irish heritage has been recast with a distinctly American flair. Similar examples can be found around the globe in cases where populations – as a result of migration, war, shifting labour markets or other factors – have mixed to produce ethnically diverse communities.

Sociologists favour the term 'ethnicity' over 'race' because it is a social concept with no biological meaning to cause confusion. However, references to ethnicity and ethnic differences can also be problematic, especially if they suggest a contrast with some 'non-ethnic' norm. In Britain, for example, ethnicity is commonly used in the press and amongst the wider white population, to refer to cultural practices and traditions that differ from 'indigenous' (non-ethnic) British practices. The term 'ethnic' is applied in this way to cuisine, clothing, music and neighbourhoods to designate practices that are 'non-British'. Using ethnic labels in this manner risks producing divisions between an 'us' and a 'them', where certain parts of the population are seen as 'ethnic', while others are not. In fact, ethnicity is an attribute possessed by *all* members of a population, not just certain segments of it. Yet, as we shall see, in practice, ethnicity is most often associated with minority groups within a population.

> The concept of 'identity' is introduced and discussed in chapter 7, 'Social Interaction and Everyday Life'.

Minority groups

The notion of **minority groups** (often 'ethnic minorities') is widely used in sociology and is more than a merely numerical distinction. There are many minorities in a statistical sense, such as people over six feet tall or those wearing shoes bigger than size 12, but these are not minorities according to the sociological concept. In sociology, members of a minority group are disadvantaged when compared with the dominant group – a group possessing more wealth, power and prestige – and have some sense of *group solidarity*, of belonging together. The experience of being the subject of prejudice and discrimination tends to heighten feelings of common loyalty and interests.

Thus sociologists frequently use the term 'minority' in a non-literal way to refer to a group's subordinate position within society, rather than its numerical representation. There are many cases in which a 'minority' is in fact in the majority. In some geographical areas such as inner cities, ethnic minority groups make up the majority of the population, but are nonetheless referred to as 'minorities'. This is because the term 'minority' captures their disadvantaged positions. Women are sometimes described as a minority group, while in many countries of the world they form the numerical majority. Yet because women tend to be disadvantaged in comparison with men (the 'majority'), the term is applied to them as well.

Members of minority groups often tend to see themselves as a people apart from the majority. They are sometimes physically and socially isolated from the larger community. They tend to be concentrated in certain neighbourhoods, cities or regions of a country. Traditionally there has been little intermarriage between those in the majority and members of the minority group, or between minority groups, though this is changing as more African Caribbean men and women marry white Britons. People within the minority sometimes actively promote **endogamy** (marriage within the group) in order to keep alive their cultural distinctiveness. It is also the case that some white Britons actively oppose all interracial relationships on racialist grounds.

Some scholars have favoured speaking of 'minorities' to refer collectively to groups that have experienced prejudice at the hands of the 'majority' society. The term 'minorities' draws attention to the pervasiveness of discrimination by highlighting the commonalities between experiences of various subordinate groups within society. As an example, disablist attitudes, anti-Semitism, homophobia and racism share many features in common and reveal how oppression against different groups can take similar forms. At the same time, however, speaking collectively of 'minorities' can result in generalizations about discrimination and oppression that do not accurately reflect the experiences of specific groups. Although homosexuals and Pakistanis are both minority groups in London, the way in which they experience subordination in society is far from identical.

Many minorities are both ethnically and physically distinct from the rest of the population. This is the case with West Indians and Asians in Britain, for example, and with African Americans, Chinese and other groups in the United States. As we noted above, in practice the designation of a group or a set of traditions as 'ethnic' occurs somewhat selectively. While West Indians in Britain and African Americans in the United States are clear examples of ethnic minorities, Britons and Americans of Italian or Polish descent are less likely to be considered ethnic minorities. Frequently, physical differences such as skin colour are the defining factor in designating an ethnic minority. As we shall see in this chapter, ethnic distinctions are rarely neutral, but are commonly associated with inequalities of wealth and power, as well as with antagonisms between groups.

Prejudice and discrimination

The concept of race is relatively modern, but prejudice and discrimination have been widespread in human history, and we must first clearly distinguish between them. **Prejudice** refers to opinions or attitudes held by members of one group towards another. A prejudiced person's preconceived views are often based on hearsay rather than on direct evidence, and are resistant to change even in the face of new information. People may harbour favourable prejudices about groups with which they identify and negative prejudices against others. Someone who is prejudiced against a particular group will not deal with its members impartially.

Prejudices are often grounded in **stereotypes**, fixed and inflexible characterizations of a group of people. Stereotypes are often applied to ethnic minority groups, such as the notion that all black men are naturally athletic or that all East Asians are hardworking, diligent students. Some stereotypes contain a grain of truth; others are simply a mechanism of **displacement**, in which feelings of hostility or anger are directed against objects that are not the real origin of those feelings. Stereotypes become embedded in

cultural understandings and are difficult to erode, even when they are gross distortions of reality. The belief that single mothers are dependent on welfare and refuse to work is an example of a persistent stereotype that lacks basis in fact. A great number of single mothers do work, and many who receive welfare benefits would prefer to work but have no access to childcare. **Scapegoating** is common when two deprived ethnic groups come into competition with one another for economic rewards. People who direct racial attacks against ethnic minorities, for example, are often in an economic position similar to theirs. A recent poll found that half of all people who felt 'hard done by' believed that immigrants and ethnic minorities were getting priority over them (Stonewall 2003; *The Economist* 2004). They blame ethnic minorities for grievances whose real causes lie elsewhere.

Scapegoating is normally directed against groups that are distinctive and relatively powerless, because they make an easy target. Protestants, Catholics, Jews, Italians, black Africans, Muslims, gypsies and others have played the unwilling role of scapegoat at various times throughout Western history. Scapegoating frequently involves projection, the unconscious attribution to others of one's own desires or characteristics. Research has consistently demonstrated that when the members of a dominant group practice violence against a minority and exploit it sexually, they are likely to believe that the minority group itself displays these traits of sexual violence. For instance, in apartheid South Africa, the belief that black males are exceptionally potent sexually and that black women are promiscuous was widespread among whites. Black males were thought to be highly dangerous sexually to white women, while, in fact, virtually all criminal sexual contact was initiated by white men against black women (Simpson and Yinger 1986).

If prejudice describes attitudes and opinions, **discrimination** refers to actual behaviour towards another group or individual. Discrimination can be seen in activities that disqualify members of one group from opportunities open to others, as when a black Briton is refused a job made available to a white person. Although prejudice is often the basis of discrimination, the two may exist separately. People may have prejudiced attitudes that they do not act on. Equally important, discrimination does not necessarily derive directly from prejudice. For example, white house-buyers might steer away from purchasing properties in predominantly black neighbourhoods, not because of attitudes of hostility they might have towards those who live there, but because of worries about declining property values. Prejudiced attitudes in this case influence discrimination, but in an indirect fashion.

A recent report by the European Union Fundamental Rights Agency on racism and xenophobia (EUFRA 2007) listed numerous examples of continuing discrimination in some European societies, including poor housing provision for ethnic minority groups, a lack of adequate educational provision for Romany children and rising levels of racist violence and crime in eight European member states – Denmark, Germany, France, Ireland, Poland, Slovakia, Finland and England and Wales. A key problem identified in the report is the 'paucity of adequate comparable official statistical or quantitative research data' on which anti-discriminatory policy could be founded. Such evidence covers a range of types of discrimination: direct (racist attacks), indi-

In 1992 the models, Iman and Bethann Hardison, founders of The Black Girls Coalition (a coalition of fashion models promoting aid for the homeless), spoke out about the under-representation of African Americans in all areas of the fashion industry. Sudanese model Alex Wek still represents a relatively rare example of black people in the Western fashion industry.

rect (inappropriate education) and structural (a lack of adequate housing). The EUFRA report outlines the range of measures taken by EU countries to combat all of these forms of discrimination.

What is racism?

One widespread form of prejudice is **racism** – prejudice based on socially significant

---

THINKING CRITICALLY

How satisfactory is the distinction between prejudice and discrimination? For example, is it possible for people to hold prejudiced attitudes and yet not behave in discriminatory ways? Are there any examples of this in your own experience? Should we accept prejudice provided it does not turn into discrimination?

An anti-Semitic attack on a Jewish cemetery in Germany.

physical distinctions. A racist is someone who believes that some individuals are superior or inferior to others on the basis of racialized differences. Racism is commonly thought of as behaviour or attitudes held by certain individuals or groups. An individual may profess racist beliefs or may join in with a group, such as a white supremacist organization, which promotes a racist agenda. Yet many have argued that racism is more than simply the ideas held by a small number of bigoted individuals.

The concept of **institutional racism** was developed in the USA in the late 1960s by civil rights campaigners who saw that racism underpinned American society, rather than merely representing the opinions of a small minority of people (Omi and Winant 1994). The concept suggests that racism pervades all of society's structures in a systematic manner. According to this view, institutions such as the police, the health service and the education system all promote policies that favour certain groups, while discriminating against others. A highly significant investigation into the practices of the London Metropolitan Police Service (the Stephen Lawrence Inquiry – see 'Classic Studies 15.1') used and built on a definition of institutional racism devised by Stokely Carmichael, a USA civil rights campaigner in the 1960s:

> [Institutional racism is] the collective failure of an organisation to provide an appropriate and professional service to people because of their colour, culture or ethnic origin which can be seen or detected in processes; attitudes and behaviour which amount to discrimination through unwitting prejudice, ignorance, thoughtlessness and racist stereotyping

which disadvantages minority ethnic people. (Macpherson 1999)

The Lawrence Report found that institutional racism did exist within the police force and the criminal justice system (ibid.). In culture and the arts, institutional racism has also been revealed in spheres such as television broadcasting (negative or limited portrayal of ethnic minorities in programming) and the international modelling industry (industry-wide bias against non-white fashion models).

From 'old' to 'new' forms of racism'

Just as the concept of biological race has been discredited, so too is old-style 'biological' racism, based on differences in physical traits, rarely openly expressed in society today. The end to legalized segregation in the United States and the collapse of apartheid in South Africa were important turning points in the rejection of biological racism. In both these cases, racist attitudes were proclaimed by directly associating physical traits with biological inferiority. Such blatantly racist ideas are rarely heard today, except in the cases of violent hate crimes or the platforms of certain extremist groups. But this is not to say that racist attitudes have disappeared from modern societies. Rather, as some scholars argue, they have been replaced by a more sophisticated new racism (or *cultural racism*), which uses the idea of cultural differences to exclude certain groups (Barker 1981).

Those who argue that a 'new racism' has emerged claim that cultural arguments are now employed instead of biological ones in order to discriminate against certain segments of the population. According to this view, hierarchies of superiority and inferiority are constructed according to the values of the majority culture. Those groups that stand apart from the majority can become marginalized or vilified for their refusal to assimilate. It is alleged that new racism has a clear political dimension.

Prominent examples of new racism can be seen in the efforts by some American politicians to enact official English-only language policies and in the conflicts in France over girls who wish to wear Islamic headscarves to school. The fact that racism is increasingly exercised on cultural rather than biological grounds has led some scholars to suggest that we live in an age of 'multiple racisms', where discrimination is experienced differently across segments of the population (Back 1995).

The persistence of racism

Why has racism persisted into the twenty-first century? There are several reasons. One important factor leading to modern racism was simply the invention and diffusion of the concept of race itself. Quasi-racist attitudes have been known to exist for hundreds of years. But the notion of race as a set of fixed traits emerged with the rise of 'race science', discussed above. Belief in the superiority of the white race, although completely without value factually, remains a key element of white racism.

A second reason for the rise of modern racism lies in the exploitative relations that Europeans established with non-white peoples. The slave trade could not have been carried on had it not been widely believed by Europeans that blacks belonged to an inferior, even subhuman, race. Racism helped justify colonial rule over non-white peoples and denied them the rights of political participation that were being won by whites in their European homelands. Some sociologists argue that exclusion from citizenship remains a central feature of modern-day racism as well.

A third reason concerns the large-scale migration of ethnic minorities to Britain, Europe and North America – regions which were previously predominantly white (with the exception of indigenous people of North America). As the post-war economic boom faltered in the mid-1970s, and most Western economies moved from being short of labour (and having relatively open

Classic Studies 15.1 | **Institutional racism in the Stephen Lawrence Inquiry**

The research problem

The overwhelming majority of 'Classic Studies' chosen for this book are pieces of research or theoretical studies conducted by professional sociologists. Sometimes, however, research conducted by public bodies or investigators on behalf of government has such a far-reaching impact that it takes on the status of a classic. The Stephen Lawrence Inquiry Report (1999) carried out by Sir William Macpherson is a good example. In 1993, a black teenager, Stephen Lawrence, was murdered in a racially motivated attack by five white youths as he was waiting at a bus stop with a friend in south-east London. The attackers stabbed him twice and left him on the pavement to die. That no one has been convicted of his murder has been seen as a gross miscarriage of justice. Why was no one convicted of such a brutal crime?

Macpherson's explanation

The commission which inquired into the case concluded that the investigation into Lawrence's murder had been mishandled from the very start (Macpherson 1999). Police arriving on the scene made little effort to pursue Lawrence's attackers and displayed a lack of respect for his parents, denying them access to information about the case to which they were entitled. An erroneous assumption was made that Lawrence had been involved in a street brawl, rather than being an innocent victim of an unprovoked racist attack. Police surveillance of the suspects was poorly organized and conducted with a 'lack of urgency'; searches of the suspects' dwellings, for example, were not performed thoroughly, despite tips describing where weapons might be concealed. Senior officers who were in a position to intervene in the case to correct such mistakes failed to do so. During the course of the investigation and subsequent inquiries into it, police withheld vital information, protected one another and refused to take responsibility for mistakes.

As a result of the perseverance of Stepehen Lawrence's parents, three of the suspects were brought to trial in 1996, but the case collapsed when a judge ruled that the evidence presented

by one witness was inadmissible. Jack Straw, then Home Secretary, announced a full inquiry into the Lawrence case in 1997; the findings of the inquiry were published in 1999 in the Macpherson Report. The authors of the report were unequivocal in their findings: '

> The conclusions to be drawn from all the evidence in connection with the investigation of Stephen Lawrence's racist murder are clear. There is no doubt but that there were fundamental errors. The investigation was marred by a combination of professional incompetence, institutional racism and a failure of leadership by senior officers.

The charge of *institutional racism* was one of the most important outcomes of the inquiry. The authors of the report concluded that not only the Metropolitan Service, but many other institutions, including the criminal justice system, were also implicated in a 'collective failure … to provide an appropriate and professional service to people because of their colour, culture or ethnic origin. It can be seen or detected in processes, attitudes and behaviour which amount to discrimination through unwitting prejudice, ignorance, thoughtlessness, and racist stereotyping which disadvantage minority ethnic people'. The Report concluded that 'it is incumbent upon every institution to examine their policies and the outcome of their policies' to ensure that no segment of the population be disadvantaged. Seventy recommendations were set forth for improving the way in which racist crimes are policed. These included 'race-awareness' training for police officers, stronger disciplinary powers to remove racist officers, clearer definitions of what constitutes a racist incident, and a commitment to increasing the total number of black and Asian officers in the police force.

Critical points

Although the Macpherson Report's conclusions were welcomed by many people, some thought it did not go far enough. Stephen Lawrence's mother, Doreen Lawrence, said at the time that the police had investigated her son's murder like 'white masters during slavery' and although she was positive about the Report's honest appraisal of police failings, it had 'only scratched the surface' of racism within the police force. The most contentious part of the report was its central finding, that not just the Metropolitan Police Service but the criminal justice system as a whole was 'institutionally racist'. The Police Complaints Commission (PCC) found 'no evidence' of racist conduct by the police, and the idea of 'unwitting racism' in the report's definition of institutional racism has been criticized as being too general. Echoing the PCC's conclusions, historian Michael Ignatieff wrote that the real issues from the case were not 'race' and 'race awareness', but

'institutionalized incompetence' and 'equal justice before the law' (in Green 2000).

Contemporary significance

The Lawrence Inquiry Report did not deliver justice for Stephen Lawrence. However, it did help to change the way that people in the UK and elsewhere think about racially motivated crime and its prosecution. The concept of institutional racism, which was devised in the civil rights struggles of late 1960s America, was accepted in an official report commissioned by government. In this way, the Lawrence Inquiry not only imposed new demands on the criminal justice system; it also marked a significant change in discourses of race in British society.

borders) to having large numbers of people unemployed, some members of the native population began to believe that immigrants were filling limited jobs and claiming welfare that they believed they were entitled to. Immigrants became an easy scapegoat for dissatisfied natives, often encouraged by the media. In practice, this widely held fear is largely a myth. Immigrant workers tend not to displace local workers, but are more likely to complement them by doing the work that local people reject, by providing valuable additional skills or creating jobs. Similarly, once they are allowed to work, immigrants are likely to make a net contribution to the government budget as taxpayers.

Sociological theories of racism

Some of the concepts that are discussed above – such as stereotypical thinking, displacement and projection – help explain prejudice and discrimination through psychological mechanisms. They provide an account of the nature of prejudiced and racist attitudes and why ethnic differences matter so much to people, but they tell us

little about the social processes involved in racism. To study such processes, we must call on sociological ideas.

Ethnocentrism, group closure and allocation of resources

Sociological concepts relevant to ethnic conflicts on a general level are those of ethnocentrism, ethnic group closure and resource allocation. Ethnocentrism is a suspicion of outsiders combined with a tendency to evaluate the culture of others in terms of one's own culture. Virtually all cultures have been ethnocentric to some degree, and it is easy to see how ethnocentrism combines with stereotypical thought discussed above. Outsiders are thought of as aliens, barbarians or morally and mentally inferior. This was how most civilizations viewed the members of smaller cultures, for example, and the attitude has fuelled innumerable ethnic clashes in history.

Ethnocentrism and **group closure**, or ethnic group closure, frequently go together. 'Closure' refers to the process whereby groups maintain boundaries separating themselves from others. These boundaries are formed by means of exclusion devices, which sharpen the divisions between one ethnic group and another (Barth 1969). Such devices include limiting or prohibiting intermarriage between the groups, restrictions on social contact or economic relationships like trading, and the physical separation of groups (as in the case of ethnic ghettos). Black Americans have experienced all three exclusion devices: racial intermarriage has been illegal in some states, economic and social segregation was enforced by law in the South, and segregated black ghettos still exist in most major cities.

Sometimes, groups of equal power mutually enforce lines of closure: their members keep separate from each other, but neither group dominates the other. More commonly, however, one ethnic group occupies a position of power over another. In these circumstances, group closure coincides with **resource allocation**, instituting inequalities in the distribution of wealth and material goods.

Some of the fiercest conflicts between ethnic groups centre on the lines of closure between them precisely because these lines signal inequalities in wealth, power or social standing. The concept of ethnic group closure helps us understand both the dramatic and the more insidious differences that separate communities of people from one another – not just why the members of some groups get shot, lynched, beaten up or harassed, but also why they do not get good jobs, a good education or a desirable place to live. Wealth, power and social status are scarce resources – some groups have more of them than others. To hold onto their distinctive positions, privileged groups sometimes undertake extreme acts of violence against others. Similarly, members of underprivileged groups may also turn to violence as a means of trying to improve their own situation.

Conflict theories

Conflict theories, by contrast, are concerned with the links between racism and prejudice on the one hand and relationships of power and inequality on the other. Early conflict approaches to racism were heavily influenced by Marxist ideas, which saw the economic system as the determining factor for all other aspects of society. Some Marxist theorists held that racism was a product of the capitalist system, arguing that the ruling class used slavery, colonization and racism as tools for exploiting labour (Cox 1959).

Later, neo-Marxist scholars saw these early formulations as too rigid and simplistic and suggested that racism was not the product of economic forces alone. A set of articles published in 1982 by the Birmingham Centre for Contemporary Cultural Studies, *The Empire Strikes Back*, takes a broader view of the rise of racism. While agreeing that the capitalist exploitation of labour is one factor, contributors to the volume, John Solomos, Paul Gilroy and others, point to a variety of historical and political influences which led to the emergence of a specific brand of racism in Britain in the 1970s and 1980s. They argue that racism is a complex and multifaceted phenomenon involving the interplay of ethnic minority and working-class identities and beliefs. In their eyes, racism is much more than simply a set of oppressive ideas enacted against the non-white population by powerful elites (Hall et al. 1982).

> **THINKING CRITICALLY**
>
> Given the persistence of racism over long periods of time, which of the theories discussed above would best explain its longevity? Give some contemporary examples of how racism may be related to group closure, ethnocentrism, resource allocation or social class. Can these theories be combined to explain a specific instance of racism?

Ethnic integration, diversity and conflict

Many states in the world today are characterized by multiethnic populations. Often they have evolved in this way over the course of centuries. Some Middle Eastern and Central European states, for example, like Turkey or Hungary, are ethnically diverse as a result of long histories of changing borders, occupations by foreign powers and regional migration. Other societies have become multiethnic more rapidly, as a result of deliberate policies encouraging migration, or by way of colonial and imperial legacies.

In an age of globalization and rapid social change, the rich benefits and complex challenges of ethnic diversity are confronting a growing number of states. International migration is accelerating with the further integration of the global economy; the movement and mixing of human populations seems sure to intensify in years to come. Meanwhile, ethnic tensions and conflicts continue to flare in societies around the world, threatening to lead to the disintegration of some multiethnic states and hinting at protracted violence in others. How can ethnic diversity be accommodated and the outbreak of ethnic conflict averted? Within multiethnic societies, what should be the relation between ethnic minority groups and the majority population? There are three primary models of ethnic integration that have been adopted by multiethnic societies in relation to these challenges: assimilation, the 'melting pot' and, finally, cultural pluralism or multiculturalism. It is important to realize that these three models are ideal types, and are not in practice easy to achieve.

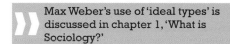

Max Weber's use of 'ideal types' is discussed in chapter 1, 'What is Sociology?'

Models of ethnic integration

The first model is **assimilation**, meaning that immigrants abandon their original customs and practices, moulding their behaviour to the values and norms of the majority. An assimilationist approach demands that immigrants change their language, dress, lifestyles and cultural outlooks as part of integrating into a new social order. In the United States, which was formed as a 'nation of immigrants', generations of immigrants were subjected to pressure to become 'assimilated' in this way, and many of their children became more or less completely 'American' as a result. Most official policies in the UK have been aimed at assimilating immigrants into British society. Of course, even if minorities try to assimilate, many are unable to do so if they are racialized or if their attempts are rebuffed – whether it be in employment or dating or any other context.

A second model is that of the **melting pot**. Rather than the traditions of the immigrants being dissolved in favour of those dominant among the pre-existing population, they become blended to form new, evolving cultural patterns. With its attractions for a diverse range of ethnic groups, the USA is often said to best exhibit the pattern associated with the idea of a melting pot. Not only are differing cultural values and norms 'brought in' to a society from the outside, but diversity is also created as ethnic groups adapt to the wider social environments in which they find themselves. One often-cited literal example of a melting-pot culture is the chicken tikka masala, a meal said to have been invented by Bangladeshi chefs in Indian restaurants in the UK. The chicken tikka is an Indian dish, but the masala sauce was then added. In 2001, the dish was described by former Foreign Secretary, Robin Cook (1946–2005), as a 'British national dish'.

Many have believed that the melting pot model is the most desirable outcome of ethnic diversity. Traditions and customs of immigrant populations are not abandoned, but contribute to and shape a constantly transforming social milieu. Hybrid forms of cuisine, fashion, music and architecture are manifestations of the melting pot approach. To a limited degree, this model is an accurate expression of aspects of American cultural development. Although the 'Anglo' culture has remained the pre-eminent one, its character in some part reflects the impact of the many different groups that now compose the American population.

The third model is that of cultural pluralism, in which ethnic cultures are given full validity to exist separately, yet participate in the larger society's economic and political life. A recent and important outgrowth of pluralism is multiculturalism, which refers to policies that encourage cultural or ethnic groups to live in harmony with each other. The United States and other Western countries are pluralistic in many senses, but ethnic differences have for the most part been associated with inequalities rather than equal but independent membership in the national community. It does seem at least possible to create a society in which ethnic groups are distinct but equal, as is demonstrated by Switzerland, where French, German and Italian groups coexist in the same society, though multiculturalism has its critics.

One advocate of multiculturalism, political scientist Bhikhu Parekh (2000: 67), puts forward its central argument, arguing:

> The cultural identity of some groups ('minorities') should not have to be confined to the private sphere while the language, culture and religion of others ('the majority') enjoy a public monopoly and are treated as the norm. For a lack of public recognition is damaging to people's self-esteem and is not conducive to encouraging the full participation of everyone in the public sphere.

Parekh (2000) argues that there are three 'insights' within multicultural thinking. First, human beings are embedded within a culturally structured world, which provides them with a system of meanings. And though individuals are not entirely determined by their cultures, they are 'deeply shaped' by them. Second, cultures also contain visions of what constitutes 'a good life'. But if they are not to stagnate or become irrelevant, each culture needs other, different cultures with alternative visions, which encourage critical reflection and the expansion of horizons. Finally, cultures are not monolithic, but are internally plural with continuing debates between different traditions. The crucial task for multicultural societies in the twenty-first century, according to Parekh, is 'the need to find ways of reconciling the legitimate demands of unity and diversity, of achieving political unity without cultural uniformity, and cultivating among its citizens both a common sense of belonging and a willingness to respect and cherish deep cultural differences' (2000: 78).

Amartya Sen (2007) argues against a 'solitarist approach' to understanding human identities. Solitarism, such as that found in some religious and civilizationist approaches, which perceive a person's national, civilizational or religious adherence to be their primary form of identity, assumes that it is possible to understand people by placing them into just one 'identity group'. However, Sen argues that this approach generates much mutual misunderstanding. In the different contexts of everyday life, we see ourselves and each other as belonging to a variety of identity groups and have little problem doing so:

> The same person can be, without any contradiction, an American citizen, of Caribbean origin, with African ancestry, a Christian, a liberal, a woman, a vegetarian, a long-distance runner, a historian, a schoolteacher, a novelist, a feminist, a heterosexual, a believer in gay and lesbian rights, a theater lover, an environmental activist, a tennis fan, a jazz musician, and someone who is deeply committed to the view that there are intelligent beings in outer space with whom it is extremely urgent to talk (preferably in English). Each

of these collectivities to all of which this person simultaneously belongs, gives her a particular identity. None of them can be taken to be the person's only identity or singular membership category. (2007: xii)

The assumption that people have one, unique identity which dominates all others breeds mistrust and often violence, as solitarist identities, which generate an 'illusion of destiny' – such as that of a national people's unique identity that gives them an ancient right to hold territory – come into conflict. Sen argues that a more widespread recognition of the plurality of individual identities holds out the hope of a genuine multiculturalism, set against the divisiveness of a model based on the imposition of singular identities.

Critics of multiculturalism raise concerns about the potential for segregation of ethnic groups if states enable, for example, separate schooling and curricula. Some countries, including France, Norway and Denmark, have drawn back from recognizing multiculturalism as official policy and there does seem to be a backlash against the idea within some sections of most Western societies. We must remember though, that all of these societies are already 'multicultural', in the sense that they are constituted by a diversity of cultures. What is currently being debated is really 'political multiculturalism' – that is, whether multiculturalism should become official state policy and therefore be encouraged and facilitated.

In many developed societies, the leaders of most ethnic minority groups have increasingly emphasized the path of pluralism. To achieve 'distinct but equal' status will demand major struggles, and, as yet, this is a distant option. Ethnic minorities are still perceived by many people as a threat: to their job, their safety and to the 'national culture'. The scapegoating of ethnic minorities is a persistent tendency. With many young people quite often still holding similar prejudices to those of older generations, ethnic minorities in most countries face a future of continued discrimination. This is likely in a social climate characterized by tensions and anxiety, heightened by the invasion of Iraq by USA and UK forces in 2003 and recent terrorism in the name of Islam across the world, along with governments' reactions to it.

Many commentators in the media and politics have turned against the idea of multiculturalism. In the UK and other Western countries, some people, fearful of militant Islam and rising immigration, now argue that multiculturalism risks tearing societies apart, undermining the way of life for the predominantly white majority. In Britain, for example, the tabloid newspapers often report that, in the name of multiculturalism, local councils have attempted to 'ban' Christmas, by forbidding schoolchildren to put on nativity plays or send each other Christmas cards. Whether or not these reports are accurate, they reflect a general feeling that multiculturalism has gone too far, and needs to be reigned in.

However, the meaning of multiculturalism has actually become very confused. People often confuse multiculturalism with *cultural diversity* – they talk about living in a 'multicultural society' when, in reality, they mean that society is made up of people from many different ethnic backgrounds. Others think that multiculturalism is about separatism, or cultural relativism. But this is a very naive way of thinking about multiculturalism. According to this view, we simply have to accept that there are many different cultures across the world and within societies and that none can have primacy over others. This implies leaving all groups to follow whatever norms they like, regardless of the consequences for wider society.

An alternative view is what I will call *sophisticated multiculturalism*. This perspective emphasizes the importance of national identity and national laws, but also the fostering of connections between different social and ethnic groups. This form of multiculturalism is concerned with social solidarity, not separateness as some people claim.

In this form of multiculturalism, different groups have equality of status and we should value diversity and openly respect and interact with other cultures. But equality of status does not mean that we accept uncritically the practices of other groups. The philosopher, Charles Taylor (1992), has written about the need for all people in society to have equal rights and respect, but if they have equal rights they also have responsibilities, and one fundamental responsibility is to obey the laws of the land. Thus, practices such as having several wives, female circumcision or carrying out honour killings may occur within some rural, tribal groups and amongst some sections of South Asian communities, but they are illegal in the UK, Europe and many other regions of the world. Not all the issues are as clear-cut as this, as they are not dealt with fully in law, and have to be worked out on a case-by-case basis. For example, is it appropriate for women to be completely veiled so that their faces are covered in the classroom? Such matters will need to be worked out through open debate with different cultural groups. It is precisely the fostering of this kind of dialogue that is itself an important part of multiculturalism.

THINKING CRITICALLY

What are your own assumptions about multiculturalism? Is it inevitable in a globalizing world or does it bring new problems that mean it should be resisted? Could Amartya Sen's idea of recognizing multiple identifications as 'normal' provide the basis for a more multicultural education? Why do some forms of identification – such as national or religious identity – seem more powerful than others?

Terrorism is discussed in more detail in chapter 23, 'Nations, War and Terrorism'.

Ethnic diversity

Ethnic minority groups make up almost 8 per cent of the overall British population (HMSO 2004), but it is important to note that immigration is now responsible for a declining proportion of the minority ethnic population. For every ethnic group, children are much more likely to have been born in Britain, marking an important shift away from an 'immigrant population' to a non-white British population with full citizenship rights. Since the 1991 Census was the first to ask respondents to classify themselves in ethnic terms, comparing data across studies can be difficult (Mason 1995). The number of people belonging to the largest ethnic minority groups, according to the 2001 Census, is shown in figure 15.1, though it is necessary to be cautious about the accuracy of official statistics. For example, respondents' understandings of their own ethnicity may be more complex than the options offered (Moore 1995). This is particularly true in the case of individuals of mixed ethnic and racial backgrounds, which are growing considerably. The 2001 Census estimated around 670,000 mixed race individuals and the UK has one of the fastest growing mixed race populations in the world.

The 2001 Census showed that Britain's ethnic minority population of 4.6 million people was concentrated primarily in the most densely populated urban areas of England. More than 75 per cent of ethnic minorities live in Greater London, the West Midlands, Yorkshire and Humberside, and the north-west and Merseyside (Strategy Unit 2003). In London, 29 per cent of all residents are non-white. By contrast, the more rural regions such as the north-east, south-west, Wales, Scotland and Northern Ireland have an ethnic minority population of less than 2 per cent (ONS 2002b). Many members of ethnic minorities do not live in the inner city by choice; they moved there because such areas were least favoured by the white population.

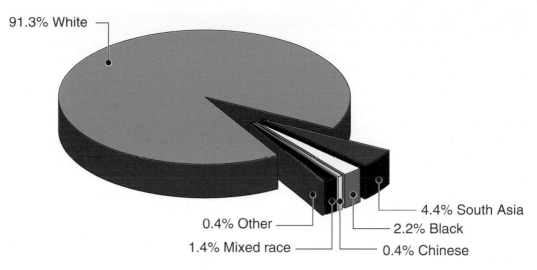

91.3% White

0.4% Other

1.4% Mixed race

4.4% South Asia

2.2% Black

0.4% Chinese

Figure 15.1 Ethnic groups in England and Wales

Source: Census 2001

The 2001 Census also showed that people from the non-white ethnic groups had a younger age structure than the white population in the UK. The 'Mixed' group were the youngest, with half under the age of 16. 'Bangladeshi', 'Other Black' and 'Pakistani' groups also had young age structures, with more than a third of each of these groups being under the age of 16 (ONS 2003a). In terms of gender, the composition of most ethnic minority groups is more balanced between the sexes than in previous times. In earlier years, the bulk of immigrants, particularly from New Commonwealth countries, such as India and the Caribbean, were men. Later policies favoured immigration for family reunification, which helped to equalize the proportions of men and women in many ethnic minority groups. Increasingly, sociologists are emphasizing the need to focus on differences between Britain's ethnic minority groups, rather than speaking generally about the experience of 'ethnic minorities'. For example, black and Asian people in Britain are disadvantaged in comparison with the white population, but there is much differentiation among ethnic minority groups.

Ethnic minorities in labour markets

Employment is a crucial area for monitoring the effects of social and economic disadvantages that result from factors such as gender, age, class and ethnicity. Studies on the position of ethnic minorities in the labour market have revealed patterns of disadvantage in terms of occupational distribution, wage levels, discrimination in hiring and promotional practices, and unemployment rates. We shall consider some of these themes in this section.

Trends in occupational patterns

The earliest national survey of ethnic minorities in Britain, conducted by the Policy Studies Institute (PSI) in the 1960s, found that most recent immigrants were clustered disproportionately in manual occupations within a small number of industries. Even those recent arrivals who possessed qualifications from their countries of origin tended to work in jobs incommensurate with their abilities. Discrimination on the basis of ethnic background was a common and overt practice, with some employers refusing to hire non-

15.1 Ethnic diversity versus social solidarity?

In a controversial article published in February 2004, David Goodhart, the editor of *Prospect* magazine, argued that there is a trade-off between an ethnically diverse society and one that has the solidarity amongst citizens that allows it to have a decent welfare system to protect those in need. To Goodhart, people are willing to pay taxes – to go towards pensions or unemployment benefit, for example – if they believe that they are paying to help people who are in some way like themselves: people who share at least common values and assumptions. Goodhart called this trade-off 'the progressive dilemma' which faces all those who want both a diverse and a solidaristic society.

As evidence of this trade-off, Goodhart pointed to the Scandinavian countries, such as Sweden and Denmark, which historically have the world's most generous welfare states. He argued that it has been possible to build large welfare systems in these countries because they are fairly socially and ethnically homogeneous, so people are prepared to pay more in taxes. In contrast, welfare states have been weaker in ethnically more divided countries such as the United States.

Goodhart asked if there is a 'tipping point' that occurs somewhere between the proportion of the population in Britain that belongs to an ethnic minority group (fewer than one in ten people) and that of the United States (which is nearer one in three), where a wholly different US-style society is created – that is, one with sharp ethnic divisions and a weak welfare state. He suggested that for this tipping point to be avoided and for feelings of solidarity towards incomers not to be overstretched, it is important that there are limits to the number of people allowed to enter the country and that the process of asylum and immigration is seen to be transparent and under control (Goodhart 2004).

Goodhart's thesis has been heavily criticized. The sociologist Saskia Sassen has argued that, in the long run, integration of immigrants does happen, and that, broadly speaking, immigrants face the same sort of difficulties in becoming accepted today as they did in previous centuries. Historically, all European societies have over time incorporated many, if not all, the major foreign immigrant groups. Past experience shows that it has often taken no more than a couple of generations to turn 'them' into 'us' – the community that can experience solidarity in Goodhart's analysis (Sassen 2004).

The political theorist, Bhikhu Parekh (2004), has also attacked Goodhart's thesis. One of the arguments that Parekh puts forward is that Goodhart gets the relationship between solidarity and the redistribution of the welfare state the wrong way round. Goodhart is convinced that solidarity is a necessary precondition of redistribution. That is a half truth, argues Parekh; one could just as plausibly say that redistribution generates loyalty, creates common life experiences and so on, and therefore paves the way for solidarity. The relation between the two is far more complex than Goodhart suggests in his article.

Bernard Crick (2004), another political theorist, asked Goodhart: 'Solidarity of what?' Goodhart discusses solidarity in *Britain*, but, Crick noted, if he had talked of the 'United Kingdom', it might have reminded him that the UK has been a multinational and a multiethnic state for a long time. Today, the dual status of being British and Scottish, Welsh, Irish or English is an established fact. The question then does not concern either solidarity *or* loss of identity: identity lies partly in being a member of more than one group.

white workers, or agreeing to do so only when there was a shortage of suitable white workers.

By the 1970s, employment patterns had shifted somewhat. Members of ethnic minority groups continued to occupy semi-skilled or unskilled manual positions, but a growing number were employed in skilled manual jobs. Few ethnic minorities were represented in professional and managerial positions. Regardless of changes in legislation to prevent racial discrimination in

THINKING CRITICALLY

In your experience, is Crick right (see 'Using your sociological imagination 15.1'). Are dual identities widely accepted within the UK and Europe? What evidence is there that people in the UK accept and celebrate their 'British' identity? Does the recent devolution of power to a Welsh Assembly and Scottish Parliament show that 'Britishness' is waning in parts of the UK? Might these lead to the break-up of Britain? What might we learn about the concept of a dual identity from other countries such as Canada and the USA?

hiring practices, research found that whites were consistently offered interviews and job opportunities in preference to equally qualified non-white applicants.

The third PSI survey in 1982 found that, with the exception of African-Asian and Indian men, ethnic minorities were suffering rates of unemployment twice as high as whites, due to the general economic recession, which had a strong impact on the manufacturing sector. Qualified non-whites with fluent English, however, were increasingly entering white-collar positions, and on the whole there was a narrowing in the wage gap between ethnic minorities and whites. A growing number of ethnic minorities took up self-employment, contributing to higher earnings and lower levels of unemployment, especially among Indians and African Asians.

Many observers have suggested that de-industrialization has had a disproportionate impact on ethnic minorities. The shift of the British economy from one based on industry to one driven by technology and the service sector has been harmful to ethnic minority workers who are less well equipped to make the transition into new occupations. However, this conventional view was challenged by findings from the PSI surveys and comparisons of Labour Force Survey and Census statistics (Iganski and Payne 1999). These studies demonstrated that certain non-white groups have in fact attained high levels of economic and occupational success in recent decades, in much the same way as successful white workers. The process of economic restructuring has actually contributed to reducing the gap between ethnic minority and white populations in the labour market. Using data from three decades of Labour Force Surveys and Censuses (1971, 1981 and 1991), Iganski and Payne found that, as a whole, ethnic minority groups experienced *lower* levels of job loss than did the rest of the industrial labour force. The move towards service sector employment had tended to 'sweep up' non-whites and whites alike in a way that narrowed the gap between them.

However, the substantial gains made by certain ethnic minority groups should not be mistaken for the end of occupational disadvantage. Such 'collective social mobility' demonstrates that the forces of post-industrial restructuring are stronger than those of racial discrimination and persistent disadvantage.

Recent investigations of ethnic minorities in the UK have revealed more than ever before the divergent employment trajectories of different ethnic groups. For example, the government's Strategy Unit found that Indians and Chinese are, on average, outperforming whites in the labour market. However, other groups are doing less well: Pakistanis, Bangladeshis and black Caribbeans experience, on average, significantly higher unemployment and lower earnings than whites (Strategy Unit 2003). The fourth PSI survey in 1997 also found employment patterns that vary among non-white women. Caribbean women are much less likely to be in manual work than white women, while Indian women, like Pakistanis, tend to occupy primarily manual jobs. There is a much higher level of economic activity among Caribbean and Indian women, but Pakistani and Bangladeshi women are less active in the labour market. On average,

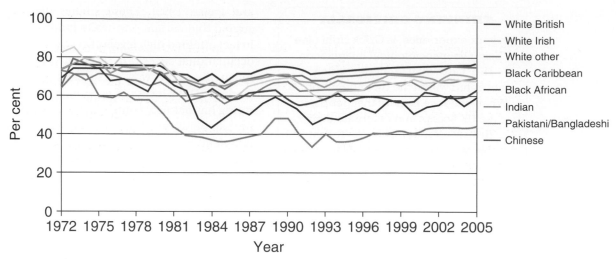

Figure 15.2 Probability of *employment* by ethnic group, UK, 1972–2005 (men aged 16–64; women aged 16–59)

Source: Li and Heath 2007

Caribbean and Indian women tend to have slightly higher full-time earnings than do white women, although among Indian women there is a sharp polarization between those on relatively high incomes and those who are on low incomes (Modood et al. 1997). Figure 15.2 shows how much these employment rates for men and women vary across different ethnic backgrounds.

The most successful non-whites, as measured in terms of level of income, are those South Asians who are self-employed or small employers. The proportion of people in this category has risen steadily over the past 25 years: Indian men and women are now more than twice as likely to be self-employed than whites. Studies indicate that discrimination among wage and salary employers is one reason for the overrepresentation of ethnic minorities in self-employment (Clark and Drinkwater 1998). Asian corner shops and other forms of Asian-run business have become such a prominent aspect of British society that some have suggested that they could lead an economic revival of inner-city areas.

It is important not to overstate the pros-

perity and potential impact of South Asian small businesses, however. Many self-employed Asians work extremely long hours – up to 60 or 80 hours per week – for relatively low levels of overall income. They are registered as self-employed, but are in effect employed by other members of the family who run the business; and they do not have the usual advantages that employees enjoy of sick pay, paid holidays and employer contributions to National Insurance.

Advances within the occupational structure are not always matched by increased representation at the top levels of power. Despite the fact that a higher number of ethnic minorities occupy white-collar professional positions than was the case previously, there appears to be a 'glass ceiling' which prevents all but a few people from the ethnic minorities from advancing to the top positions within large companies and organizations. This is particularly pronounced within the large public sector organizations. In general, ethnic minority men – even the most highly qualified – are only half as likely as white men to be represented among the top 10 per cent of jobs by power, status and earnings (Modood et al. 1997).

Housing

Ethnic minorities in Britain, as elsewhere, tend to experience discrimination, harassment and material deprivation in the housing market. Since the early calls for immigration controls, housing has been at the forefront of struggles over resources between groups and tendencies towards ethnic closure. One reason for this may be that housing is a highly symbolic matter – it indicates status, provides security and interweaves with overall livelihood. As with employment patterns, differentials in the quality and type of housing vary across ethnic groups. Although the non-white population as a whole is more disadvantaged than whites in terms of housing, this is far from a unified picture. Certain groups, such as those of Indian origin, have attained very high levels of home ownership, while others are clustered disproportionately in substandard accommodation or the social housing sector (Ratcliffe 1999).

A number of factors contribute to housing differentials between non-white and white populations, and among non-white groups. Racial harassment or violent attacks, which are still frequent not only in Britain but across Europe, are likely to encourage a certain degree of ethnic segregation in housing patterns. In many European countries, recent evidence shows that Roma communities face the worst discrimination in relation to available and affordable housing (EUFRA 2007). Non-white families with the means to move into more affluent, predominantly white neighbourhoods may be dissuaded from doing so because of ethnic hostility.

Another factor relates to the physical condition of housing. In general, housing occupied by ethnic minority groups tends to be in greater disrepair than that of the white population. A high proportion of Pakistanis and Bangladeshis live in accommodation that is overcrowded (because of the large average size of their households); their housing also tends to be more susceptible to damp and more likely to lack central heating.

People of Indian origin, by contrast, are as likely as whites to occupy detached or semi-detached homes and are less likely than other ethnic groups to reside in inner-city neighbourhoods. African-Caribbean households, on the other hand, are much more likely to rent accommodation in the social housing sector, rather than become home-owners. This may be related to the high proportion of lone-parent families within this ethnic group.

How can ethnic differentials in housing be understood? In a classic study, John Rex and Robert Moore (1967) argued that, as a result of the competitive processes in the housing market, ethnic minorities have emerged as a distinct 'housing class'. According to such an approach, the challenges facing minority groups – from economic disadvantage to racial discrimination – mean that they have few options and little chance to exert control over their housing position. Ethnic minorities are essentially forced to make do with inadequate housing because they have few or no choices in the matter. While there are certainly many constraining circumstances which disadvantage ethnic minorities in the housing market, it would be wrong to imply that they are simply passive victims of discriminatory or racist forces. Patterns and practices change over time through the choices made by social actors.

Poor housing is a significant factor leading to higher levels of poor health amongst some ethnic minority groups, though such health inequalities are strongly correlated with social class position (Cockerham 2007).

 See also chapter 10, 'Health, Illness and Disability', for a wider discussion of health inequalities

Understanding the intersecting social inequalities of class, ethnicity and gender have formed the basis for much recent sociological research, and this work has informed attempts to improve public services for ethnic minorities. Awareness of discrimination can also become an impetus for creative action. This is important, as one independent health service report argued: 'At present, people from the black and minority ethnic … are not getting the service they are entitled to. Putting it bluntly, this is a disgrace' (Blofeld 2003: 58). An additional factor for ethnic minority groups is racist attitudes within society, which, as the Macpherson Report (1999) discussed above shows, are also institutionally embedded in many public services (Karlsen 2007). We can see this in relation to the operation of the criminal justice system.

The criminal justice system

Since the 1960s, members of ethnic minority groups have been represented in ever greater numbers within the criminal justice system, both as offenders and victims. Compared to their distribution in the overall population, ethnic minorities are over-represented in prisons. In 2002, 16 per cent of male prisoners in England and Wales were from an ethnic minority group (HMSO 2004). There is reason to believe that members of ethnic minority groups suffer from discriminatory treatment once they are within the criminal justice system. There is a higher rate of custodial sentencing among non-whites, even in cases where there are few or no previous convictions. Ethnic minorities are also more likely to experience discrimination or racial attacks once imprisoned. Some scholars have pointed out that the administration of the criminal justice system is overwhelmingly dominated by whites. A small percentage of practising lawyers are black, and blacks make up less than 2 per cent of the police force (Denney 1998).

Non-white groups are all vulnerable to racism of one kind or another – including racially motivated attacks. Most escape such treatment, but for a minority the experience can be disturbing and brutal. It has been estimated that racially motivated incidents represented 12 per cent of all crime against minority ethnic people (compared with 2 per cent for white people) (ONS 2002b). The British Crime Survey also found that emotional reactions to racially motivated incidents were generally more severe than for non-racially motivated incidents.

How can we account for these patterns of crime and victimization? Crime is not evenly distributed among the population. There appears to be a distinct spatial element to patterns of crime and victimization. Areas that suffer from material deprivation generally have higher crime rates and individuals living in such regions run a greater risk of falling victim to crime.

The deprivations to which people exposed to racism are subject both help to produce, and are produced by, the decaying environment of the inner cities (see chapter 6, 'Cities and Urban Life'). Here, there are clear correlations between 'race', unemployment and crime, which tend to centre on the position of young males from ethnic minority backgrounds. Through the political and media creations of **moral panic** about crime, a public link has been established between 'race' and crime.

>> The theory of moral panic is discussed in chapter 21, 'Crime and Deviance'.

Yet the experience of many people from ethnic minorities, and particularly young men, is that it is precisely they who are the 'objects of violent exploitation' in their encounters with whites and to some extent also, unfortunately, the police. Sociological studies have been instrumental in revealing racist attitudes among police officers. In the 1980s, a study of police by Roger Graef (1989) concluded that police were 'actively hostile to all minority groups'. He noted the frequency with which officers would use stereotypes and racial slurs when speaking about ethnic minorities. During the 1990s, several high-profile incidents in Britain and the United States raised awareness about police racism in ways that no study ever could. The racist murder of Stephen Lawrence in 1993 has significantly altered the nature of the debate over racism in Britain by demonstrating that it is not restricted to certain individuals, but can pervade entire institutions (see 'Classic Studies 15.1' above). For example, in the first year after the report, more than one-third of police forces had not hired any additional black or Asian officers and the number of ethnic minority officers had fallen in 9 out of 43 forces in England and Wales.

Ethnic minorities are in the greatest need of protection by police and the criminal justice system because they are more likely to be victims of crime, but there are some indications that law-enforcement policies seem to have a racial character that targets non-whites: so-called 'stop-and-search' policies, for example, tend to target non-whites disproportionately. The number of 'stop-and-search' procedures against ethnic minorities fell after the publication of the Macpherson Report in 1999, but has since risen as police forces became more sensitive to the risk of terrorism in the name of Islam. This has led to a rise in the number of cases where British Asians, some of whom are Muslim, have been stopped and searched, with police using new powers granted to them under the 2000 Terrorism Act.

Ethnic conflict

Ethnic diversity can greatly enrich societies. Multiethnic states are often vibrant and dynamic places that are strengthened by the varied contributions of their inhabitants. But such states can also be fragile, especially in the face of internal upheaval or external threat. Differing linguistic, religious and cultural backgrounds can become fault-lines that result in open antagonism between ethnic groups. Sometimes societies with long histories of ethnic tolerance and integration can rapidly become engulfed in ethnic conflict – hostilities between different ethnic groups or communities.

This was the case in the former Yugoslavia in the 1990s, a region renowned for its rich multiethnic heritage. The Balkans have long been the crossroads of Europe. Centuries of migration and the rule of successive empires have produced a diverse, intermixed population composed predominantly of Slavs (such as the Eastern Orthodox Serbs), Croats (Catholic), Muslims and Jews. After 1991, alongside major political and social transformations following the fall of communism, deadly conflicts broke out between ethnic groups in several areas of the former Yugoslavia.

The conflicts in the former Yugoslavia involved attempts at **ethnic cleansing**, the creation of ethnically homogeneous areas through the mass expulsion of other ethnic populations. Croatia, for example, has become an independent 'mono-ethnic' state after a costly war in which thousands of Serbs were expelled from the country. A war that broke out in Bosnia in 1992, between Serbs, Croats and Muslims, involved the ethnic cleansing of the Bosnian Muslim population at the hands of the Serbs: thousands of Muslim men were forced into internment camps and a campaign of systematic rape was carried out against Muslim women. The war in Kosovo in 1999 was prompted by charges that Serbian forces were intent on ethnic cleansing by forcing the Kosovar Albanian (Muslim) population from the province.

In both Bosnia and Kosovo, ethnic conflict became internationalized. Hundreds of thousands of refugees spilled over into neighbouring areas, further destabilizing the region. Western states intervened both diplomatically and militarily to protect the human rights of ethnic groups which had become targets of ethnic cleansing. In the short term, such interventions succeeded in quelling the systematic violence. Yet they had unintended consequences as well. The fragile peace in Bosnia was maintained, but only through the presence of peacekeeping troops and the partitioning of the country into separate ethnic enclaves. In Kosovo, a process of 'reverse ethnic cleansing' ensued after the NATO bombing campaign in 1999. Ethnic Albanian Kosovars began to drive the local Serb population out of Kosovo; the presence of UN-led 'Kfor' troops proved to be inadequate to prevent ethnic tensions from reigniting.

Ethnic cleansing involves the forced relocation of ethnic populations through targeted violence, harassment, threats and campaigns of terror. Genocide, by contrast, describes the systematic elimination of one ethnic group at the hands of another. The term 'genocide' has often been used to describe the process by which indigenous populations in North and South America were decimated after the arrival of European explorers and settlers. Disease, forced relocation and campaigns of violence destroyed many native populations, although the extent to which this was systematically planned remains contested.

The twentieth century witnessed the emergence of 'organized' genocide and carries the dubious distinction of being the most 'genocidal' century in history. In the Armenian genocide of 1915–23, more than a million Armenians were killed at the hands of the Ottoman Turks. The Nazi Holocaust resulted in the death of more than six million Jews and remains the most horrific example of the planned extermination of one ethnic group by another. The ethnic Hutu majority in Rwanda launched a genocidal campaign against the ethnic Tutsi minority in 1994, claiming the lives of more than 800,000 individuals within a span of three months. More than two million Rwandan refugees spilled over into neighbouring states, heightening ethnic tensions in countries such as Burundi and Zaire (now the Democratic Republic of Congo). More recently, government-backed Arab militias have been accused of ethnic cleansing in Sudan, after an uprising by some of the black population of the Western Sudanese region of Darfur in 2003. Reprisals by the militia led to the loss of at least 70,000 lives and left around two million people homeless.

It has been noted that violent conflicts around the globe are increasingly based on ethnic divisions, as the examples of Rwanda and Sudan show. Only a tiny proportion of wars now occur between states; the vast majority of conflicts are civil wars with ethnic dimensions. In a world of increasing interdependence and competition, international factors become even more important in shaping ethnic relations, while the effects of 'internal' ethnic conflicts are felt well outside national borders. As we have seen, ethnic conflicts attract international attention and have sometimes provoked physical intervention. International war crimes tribunals have been convened to investigate and try those responsible for the ethnic cleansing and genocide in Yugoslavia and Rwanda. Responding to and preventing ethnic conflict have become key challenges facing both individual states and international political structures. Although ethnic tensions are often experienced, interpreted and described at the local level, they are increasingly taking on national and international dimensions.

Migration in a global age

While we may think of immigration as a phenomenon of the twentieth century, it is a process whose roots stretch back to the earliest stages of written history and beyond. For example, the considerable number of Irish, Welsh and Scottish names scattered across England today is a reminder of the traditional flow of people from the so-called 'Celtic fringes' to the urban centres of England. In the early nineteenth century, long before the advent of major immigration from the British Empire's distant colonies, developing English cities attracted migrants from the less prosperous areas within the British Isles. In this section we recount the experience of immigration in Britain, which has played a crucial role in the movement of people around the world, during the period

Global Society 15.2 Genocide in Rwanda

Between April and June 1994, an estimated 800,000 Rwandans were killed in the space of 100 days. Most of the dead were Tutsis – and most of those who perpetrated the violence were Hutus. Even for a country with such a turbulent history as Rwanda, the scale and speed of the slaughter left its people reeling.

The genocide was sparked by the death of the Rwandan president Juvenal Habyarimana, a Hutu, when his plane was shot down above Kigali airport on 6 April 1994. A recent French official report blamed current Rwandan President, Paul Kagame. The report – extracts of which appeared in the daily newspaper *Le Monde* – said French police had concluded that Mr Kagame gave direct orders for the rocket attack. Rwanda has rejected the report, describing it as a 'fantasy'.

Within hours of the attack, a campaign of violence spread from the capital throughout the country, and did not subside until three months later. But the death of the president was by no means the only cause of Africa's largest genocide in modern times.

History of violence

Ethnic tension in Rwanda is nothing new. There have been always been disagreements between the majority Hutus and minority Tutsis, but the animosity between them has grown substantially since the colonial period. The two ethnic groups are actually very similar – they speak the same language, inhabit the same areas and follow the same traditions.

But when the Belgian colonists arrived in 1916, they saw the two groups as distinct entities, and even produced identity cards classifying people according to their ethnicity. The Belgians considered the Tutsis as superior to the Hutus. Not surprisingly, the Tutsis welcomed this idea, and for the next 20 years they enjoyed better jobs and educational opportunities than their neighbours. Resentment among the Hutus gradually built up, culminating in a series of riots in 1959. More than 20,000 Tutsis were killed, and many more fled to the neighbouring countries of Burundi, Tanzania and Uganda. When Belgium relinquished power and granted Rwanda independence in 1962, the Hutus took their place. Over subsequent decades, the Tutsis were portrayed as the scapegoats for every crisis.

Building up to genocide

This was still the case in the years before the genocide. The economic situation worsened and the incumbent president, Juvenal Habyarimana, began losing popularity. At the same time, Tutsi refugees in Uganda – supported by some moderate Hutus – were forming the Rwandan Patriotic Front (RPF). Their aim was to overthrow Habyarimana and secure their right to return to their homeland. Habyarimana chose to exploit this threat as a way to bring dissident Hutus back to his side, and Tutsis inside Rwanda were accused of being RPF collaborators.

In August 1993, after several attacks and months of negotiation, a peace accord was signed between Habyarimana and the RPF, but it did little to stop the continued unrest. When Habyarimana's plane was shot down at the beginning of April 1994, it was the final nail in the coffin. Exactly who killed the president – and with him the president of Burundi and many chief members of staff – has not been established. Whoever was behind the killing, its effect was both instantaneous and catastrophic.

Mass murder

In Kigali, the presidential guard immediately initiated a campaign of retribution. Leaders of the political opposition were murdered, and almost immediately, the slaughter of Tutsis and moderate Hutus began. Within hours, recruits were dispatched all over the country to carry out a wave of slaughter. The early organizers included military officials, politicians and businessmen, but soon many others joined in the mayhem.

Encouraged by the presidential guard and radio propaganda, an unofficial militia group called the Interahamwe (meaning 'those who attack together') was mobilized. At its peak, this group was 30,000-strong. Soldiers and police officers encouraged ordinary citizens to take part. In some cases, Hutu civilians were forced to murder their Tutsi neighbours by military personnel. Participants were often given incentives, such as money or food, and some were even told they could appropriate the land of the Tutsis they killed.

On the ground at least, the Rwandans were largely left alone by the international community. UN troops withdrew after the murder of ten of their soldiers. The day after Habyarimana's death, the RPF renewed their assault on government forces,

The ethnic Hutu majority in Rwanda claimed the lives of more than 800,000 Tutsis during the genocide of 1994.

and numerous attempts by the UN to negotiate a ceasefire came to nothing.

Aftermath

Finally, in July, the RPF captured Kigali. The government collapsed and the RPF declared a ceasefire. As soon as it became apparent that the RPF was victorious, an estimated two million Hutus fled to Zaire (now the Democratic Republic of Congo). Back in Rwanda, UN troops and aid workers then arrived to help maintain order and restore basic services.

On 19 July a new multiethnic government was formed, promising all refugees a safe return to Rwanda. But although the massacres are over, the legacy of the genocide continues, and the search for justice has been a long and arduous one. About 500 people have been sentenced to death, and another 100,000 are still in prison. But some of the ringleaders have managed to evade capture, and many who lost their loved ones are still waiting for justice.

Source: Adapted from BBC News, 1 April 2004

both of imperialist expansion and of the demise of the British Empire.

Although migration is not a new phenomenon, it is one that seems to be accelerating as part of the process of global integration. Worldwide migration patterns can be seen as one reflection of the rapidly changing economic, political and cultural ties between countries. It has been estimated that around 175 million people currently reside in a country other than where they were born, equivalent to around

Across Europe, fears about 'bogus asylum-seekers' have been linked to concerns about national security, especially in the years after 11 September 2001. This picture shows sub-Saharan Africans waiting to be driven to a police holding centre after arriving on a beach in Fuerteventura, Spain.

....

3 per cent of the world's population (DESA 2002), prompting some scholars to label this the 'age of migration' (Castles and Miller 2003).

Immigration, the movement of people into a country to settle, and emigration, the process by which people leave a country to settle in another, combine to produce global migration patterns linking countries of origin and countries of destination. Migratory movements add to ethnic and cultural diversity in many societies and help to shape demographic, economic and social dynamics. The intensification of global migration since the Second World War, and particularly in more recent decades, has transformed immigration into an important political issue in many countries. Rising immigration rates in many Western societies have challenged commonly held notions of national identity and have forced a re-examination of concepts of citizenship.

Scholars have identified four models of migration to describe the main global population movements since 1945. The *classic model* of migration applies to countries such as Canada, the United States and Australia, which have developed as 'nations of immigrants'. In such cases, immigration has been largely encouraged and the promise of citizenship has been extended to newcomers, although restrictions and quotas help to limit the annual intake of immigrants. The colonial model of immigration, pursued by countries such as France and the United Kingdom, tends to favour immigrants from former colonies over those from other countries. The large number of immigrants to Britain in the years after the Second World War from

Immigration brings about new ideas of what it means to be British, at all levels of society, as this image of a black Queen Elizabeth suggests.

Commonwealth countries, such as India or Jamaica, reflected this tendency.

Countries such as Germany, Switzerland and Belgium have followed a third policy – the *guest workers model*. Under such a scheme, immigrants are admitted into the country on a temporary basis, often in order to fulfil demands within the labour market, but do not receive citizenship rights even after long periods of settlement.

Finally, *illegal forms* of immigration are becoming increasingly common as a result of tightening immigration laws in many industrialized countries. Immigrants who are able to gain entry into a country either secretly or under a 'non-immigration' pretence are often able to live illegally outside the realm of official society. Examples of this can be seen in the large number of Mexican 'illegal aliens' in many Southern American states, or in the growing international business of smuggling refugees across national borders.

The spread of industrialization dramatically transformed migration patterns in the industrializing societies. The growth of opportunities for work in urban areas coupled with the decline of household production in the countryside encouraged a trend towards rural–urban migration. Demands within the labour market also gave new impetus to immigration from abroad. In Britain, Irish, Jewish and black communities had existed long before the Industrial Revolution, but the surge of new opportunities altered the scale and scope of international immigration. New waves of Dutch, Chinese, Irish and black immigrants transformed British society.

In more recent times, a large wave of immigration to Britain occurred when the 1930s Nazi persecutions sent a generation of European Jews fleeing westwards to safety. It has been estimated that some 60,000 Jews settled in the UK between 1933 and 1939, but the real figure may well have been higher. In the same period, around 80,000 refugees also arrived from Central Europe, and a further 70,000 arrived during the war itself. By May 1945, Europe faced an unprecedented refugee problem: millions of people had become refugees and many settled in Britain.

Following the Second World War, Britain experienced immigration on a large scale as people from Commonwealth countries were encouraged and facilitated to come to the UK, which had a marked shortage of labour. In addition to rebuilding the country and economy following the destruction of the war, industrial expansion provided British workers with unprecedented mobility, creating a need for labour in unskilled and manual positions. Government, influenced by ideas of Britain's imperial heritage, encouraged people from the West

Indies, India, Pakistan and other former colonies in Africa to settle in Britain. The 1948 British Nationality Act granted favourable immigration rights to citizens of Commonwealth countries.

With each wave of immigration, the religious make-up of the UK changed. British cities, in particular, are now multiethnic and religiously diverse. In the nineteenth century, immigrants from Ireland swelled the number of Catholics in cities like Liverpool and Glasgow, where many settled. In the post-war period, large-scale immigration from Asia increased the number of Muslims, many from the largely Muslim countries of Pakistan and Bangladesh, and Hindus mainly from India. Immigration brought new questions about what it means to be British and how ethnic and religious minorities can integrate fully into British society.

>> Religious diversity is discussed in more detail in chapter 16, 'Religion'.

Migration and the decline of empire: Britain since the 1960s

The 1960s marked the start of a gradual rolling back of the idea that inhabitants of the British Empire had the right to settle in Britain and claim citizenship. Although changing labour markets played a role in the new restrictions, they were also the response to a backlash against immigrants by groups of white Britons. In particular, working people living in poorer areas, to which the new immigrants gravitated for their work, were sensitive to the 'disruption' to their own lives. Attitudes to the newcomers were often hostile. The 1958 Notting Hill riots, in which white residents attacked black immigrants, were testament to the strength of racist attitudes. In an infamous phrase from a 1962 speech in Birmingham, Enoch Powell, a Conservative front-bench minister at the time, envisaged an extraordinary growth in the non-white population in Britain: 'Like the Romans, I seem to see "the River Tiber flowing with much blood".'

However, a Gallup poll showed that 75 per cent of the population were broadly sympathetic to Powell's views.

Many anti-racist campaigners have argued that British immigration policy is racist and discriminatory against non-white groups. Since the Commonwealth Immigrants Act 1962, a series of legislative measures have been passed, gradually restricting entry and settlement rights for non-whites, while protecting the ability of whites to enter Britain relatively freely. For example, among citizens of Commonwealth states, immigration laws discriminated against the predominantly non-white 'New Commonwealth' states, while preserving the rights of mainly white immigrants from 'old Commonwealth' countries such as Canada and Australia. The British Nationality Act of 1981 separated 'British citizenship' from citizenship of British dependent territories. Legislation introduced in 1988 and 1996 increased these restrictions even further.

Britain, like other European countries, has also reduced the possibility of asylum-seekers gaining entry. To be granted asylum, individuals must claim that being forced to leave the country would break obligations that the government has under the United Nations 'Convention and Protocol relating to the Status of Refugees' (1951). The agreement obliges signatory nations to protect refugees who are fleeing persecution and treat them as well as other foreign nationals on their territory. Since 1991, there have been more stringent checks on people claiming refugee status, including fingerprinting, reduced access to free legal advice and the doubling of fines levied on airlines which bring in passengers not holding valid visas. As more measures were introduced, an increased number of refusals resulted in a larger number of asylum-seekers being held in detention centres for long periods of time.

In the last 15 years or so, issues of 'race' and immigration have become more important in public opinion surveys across Europe and other developed societies. For

There was a rise in Commonwealth immigrants coming to Britain after the Second World War in response to a national labour shortage, but they often faced racism. Immigration was later restricted.

example, as figure 15.3 shows, race and immigration barely registered in UK surveys from the early 1990s, but the twenty-first century has witnessed an enormous rise in the salience of these issues amongst the public. More than one-third of people in a 2006 Ipsos/MORI poll said that race and immigration, were amongst 'the most important issues facing Britain today'. This placed 'race' and immigration second only to the NHS as the most important issue. Of course, key events can also affect public opinion and although migration issues were rising in opinion surveys in the late 1990s, so-called 'race riots' in parts of the UK also played a part; following the al-Qaeda attacks

on the USA in September 2001, the trend has been towards rising concerns about race and ethnicity (see figure 15.4), not just in Britain but across the developed world.

In Europe, concerns over 'race' and immigration have generally followed a similar pattern, but with some interesting differences. Research reported by the Pew Global Attitudes Project (2005) found that in Germany only a minority, 34 per cent, thought immigration from the Middle East and North Africa was 'a good thing', 57 per cent thought it was 'a bad thing' and two-thirds of Germans in the survey disapproved of immigration from Eastern Europe. Public opinion in the Netherlands

Q. What are the most/other important issues facing Britain today? % mentioning 'race/immigration'

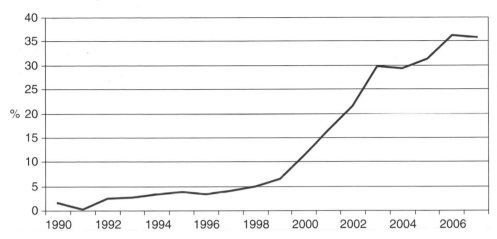

Figure 15.3   Rise in British public concern about race/immigration, 1990–2007

Source: Ipsos/MORI, Sept 2007

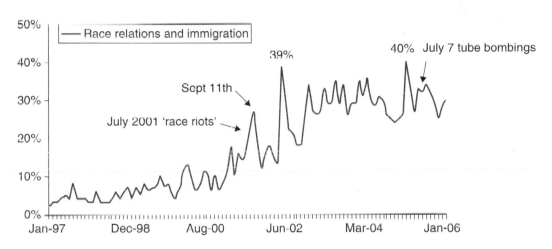

Figure 15.4   Concern about race relations and immigration, 1997–2006

Source: Ipsos/MORI, March 2006

is rather more split, with roughly equal percentages approving and disapproving of immigration from the Middle East and North Africa and Eastern Europe (50 per cent and 47 per cent). In France, a small majority actually approved of immigration from these areas, and in Spain, 67 per cent saw immigration from the Middle East and North Africa as a good thing and 72 per cent approved of Eastern European immigra-tion. Approval is even higher in Canada, with 77 per cent approving of Asian immi-gration and 78 per cent saying the same of Mexican and Latin American immigration (Pew Global Attitudes Project, June 2005).

As opportunities for immigrants to enter Britain were cut off, there was a sharp rise in the number of people seeking asylum. Depictions, particularly in tabloid newspa-pers, of 'bogus' asylum-seekers 'swamping'

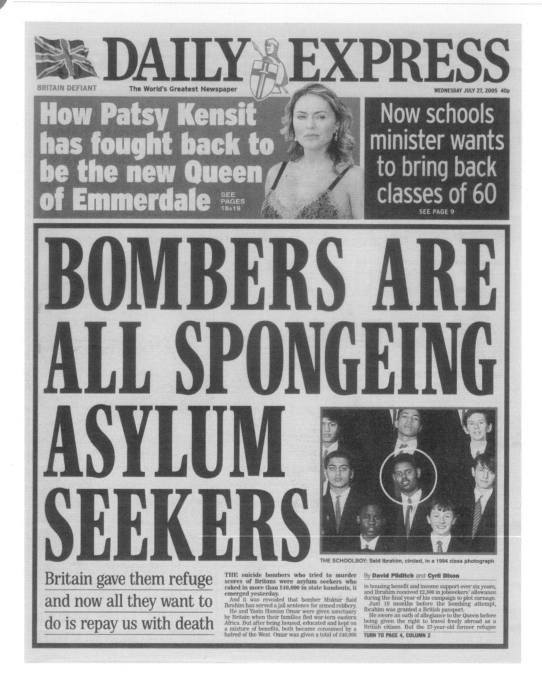

BRITAIN DEFIANT   The World's Greatest Newspaper   WEDNESDAY JULY 27, 2005 40p

DAILY EXPRESS

How Patsy Kensit has fought back to be the new Queen of Emmerdale SEE PAGES 18&19

Now schools minister wants to bring back classes of 60 SEE PAGE 9

BOMBERS ARE ALL SPONGEING ASYLUM SEEKERS

THE SCHOOLBOY: Said Ibrahim, circled, in a 1994 class photograph

Britain gave them refuge and now all they want to do is repay us with death

By **David Pilditch** and **Cyril Dixon**

THE suicide bombers who tried to murder scores of Britons were asylum seekers who raked in more than £40,000 in state handouts, it emerged yesterday.

And it was revealed that bomber Muktar Said Ibrahim has served a jail sentence for armed robbery.

He and Yasin Hussan Omar were given sanctuary by Britain when their families fled war-torn eastern Africa. But after being housed, educated and kept on a mixture of benefits, both became consumed by a hatred of the West. Omar was given a total of £40,000

in housing benefit and income support over six years, and Ibrahim received £2,300 in jobseekers' allowance during the final year of his campaign to plot carnage.

Just 10 months before the bombing attempt, Ibrahim was granted a British passport.

He swore an oath of allegiance to the Queen before being given the right to travel freely abroad as a British citizen. But the 27-year-old former refugee

TURN TO PAGE 4, COLUMN 2

the UK, have helped to create a distorted image of immigration and asylum. The coordinated terrorist suicide bombings in London on 7 July 2007, which killed 52 civilians and injured 700 others, followed by failed attempts on 21 July, promoted lurid headlines in some British newspapers (see *Daily Express* front page illustrated), suggesting a direct link between such types of terrorism and those seeking asylum, even though the identities and status of the bombers were not even known for sure at the time.

Several surveys have also found that the public grossly overestimates the number of asylum-seekers and refugees coming to the UK and the benefits they receive (for instance, MORI, 17 June 2002). The 2002 Nationality, Immigration and Asylum Act, which built on the government's White Paper *Secure Borders, Safe Haven: Integration with Diversity* (2002), set new requirements for people wanting British citizenship, including a basic knowledge of life in the UK, citizenship ceremonies and a pledge of allegiance. The Act also provided for the housing of asylum-seekers in specially built accommodation centres dispersed around the country, a measure widely criticized by refugee groups as stigmatizing refugees.

Thinking critically

Is the rising public concern with migration issues really justified? Look at the questions asked in the survey results presented above. What criticisms would you make about the way these questions are phrased? How might sociologists investigate public attitudes towards migration, without creating a similar problem?

Migration and the European Union

As part of the move towards European integration, many of the earlier barriers to the free movement of commodities, capital and employees have been removed. This has led to a dramatic increase in regional migration among European countries. Citizens of countries in the European Union – including the ten new member states, largely from Eastern Europe, that joined the EU in May 2004 – now have the right to work in any other EU country. Professionals with highly developed skills and qualifications have joined the ranks of asylum-seekers and economic migrants as the largest groups of European migrants. With this shift, scholars have noted a growing polarization within the migrant population between the 'haves' and the 'have-nots'.

Migration into the EU from non-EU countries has become one of the most pressing issues on the political agenda in a number of European states. As the process of European integration continues, a number of countries have dissolved internal border controls with neighbouring states as part of the Schengen agreement, which came into force in 1995. The agreement has been signed by 31 countries and implemented by 26, which means the latter now only monitor their external borders and allow free entry from neighbouring member states (see figure 15.5). This reconfiguration of European border controls has had an enormous impact on illegal immigration into the EU and on cross-border crime. Illegal immigrants able to gain access to a Schengen state can move unimpeded throughout the entire Schengen zone.

Since most EU states have now limited legal immigration to cases of family reunification, instances of illegal immigration have been on the increase. Some illegal migrants enter the EU legally as students or visitors and overstay their visas, but a growing number of illegal immigrants are smuggled across borders. The International Centre for Migration Policy Development estimates that 400,000 people are smuggled into the EU annually. Italy's long coastal border has been considered one of the most porous in Europe, attracting illegal immigrants from nearby Albania, the former Yugoslavia, Turkey and Iraq. Since joining the Schengen agreement, Italy has tightened its external border significantly. Germany, which receives a disproportionate share of illegal immigrants and applications from asylum-seekers, has been working with the governments in Poland and the Czech Republic to strengthen controls on their eastern borders.

The racism that is associated with anti-immigration sentiment has produced some explosive incidents in Europe, and the 1990s saw a revival in the electoral fortunes of far right parties in several European countries, including France, Switzerland, Italy, Austria, Denmark and the Netherlands. In the UK, the first-past-the-post system to elect Members of Parliament, where only one candidate is returned in each constituency, prevents minor parties from winning seats

Figure 15.5 The Schengen Zone

in the House of Commons. However, support for the far right British National Party is at its highest point since the 1970s, and the party has several seats on local councils. The anti-immigration UK Independence Party has also seen a surge in popular support, winning 12 seats in the 2004 elections for the European Parliament.

The risks that migrants take in search of a better life often have tragic consequences, for example when 58 Chinese people suffocated in a lorry in Dover off the English coast in June 2000, or when at least 26 people died on an overcrowded Libyan boat attempting to land in Sicily, off the coast of southern Italy, in August 2004. Because of the illegal nature of most of this migration, the number of people who actually die attempting to enter the West is difficult to gauge, but one recent survey estimated that up to 4,000 migrants drown at sea every year as they attempt to flee persecution or poverty. The research suggests that around 2,000 people die annually in the Mediterranean trying to reach Europe, and similar numbers are thought to die on crossings to Australia and the United States – the two other main destinations for 'boat people' (*Guardian*, 9 October 2004).

The tightening of control over the 'new migrants' is not taking place in a vacuum, however. Informal responses to changes in immigration policies occur in the trafficking and smuggling networks. Trade in human migrants has become one of the fastest growing categories of organized crime in Europe. Just as such criminal groupings manage to shuttle drugs, weapons and stolen goods across borders, they are also capable of smuggling illegal immigrants by various means. Migrants and smugglers join together in drawing on the knowledge and experience of other migrants in making choices about their own movements. In this sense, policy restrictions seem to be provoking new forms of resistance (Koser and Lutz 1998).

Migration and ethnic relations

Like Britain, most other European countries have been profoundly transformed by migration during the twentieth century. Large-scale migrations took place in Europe during the first two decades after the Second World War. The Mediterranean countries provided the nations in the North and West with cheap labour. Migrants moving from areas like Turkey, North Africa, Greece and southern Spain and Italy were for a period actively encouraged by host countries facing acute shortages of labour. Switzerland, Germany, Belgium and Sweden all have considerable populations of migrant workers. At the same time, countries that used to be colonial powers experienced an influx of immigrants from their former colonies: this applied primarily to France (Algerians) and the Netherlands (Indonesians), as well as the UK.

Labour migration into and within Western Europe slowed down appreciably as the post-war boom turned into a recession in the late 1970s. But since the fall of the Berlin Wall in 1989 and the transformations occurring in the countries of Eastern Europe and the former Soviet Union, Europe has witnessed the birth of what has been termed the **new migration**. This 'new migration' has been marked by two main events. First, the opening of borders between East and West led to the migration of some five million people in Europe between 1989 and 1994. Second, war and ethnic strife in the former Yugoslavia has resulted in a surge of approximately five million refugees into other regions of Europe (Koser and Lutz 1998). The geographical patterns of European migration have also shifted, with the lines between countries of origin and countries of destination becoming increasingly blurred. Countries in Southern and Central Europe have become destinations for many migrants, a notable departure from earlier immigration trends.

Another feature of the 'new migration' is that of ethnic 'unmixing'. In the former Soviet Union, the former Yugoslavia and in some Central European states, shifting borders, changing political regimes or the outbreak of conflict have led to migrations on the principle of 'ethnic affinity'. A clear illustration of this can be seen in the case of the thousands of ethnic Russians who found themselves living in newly independent countries – such as Latvia, Kazakhstan and Ukraine – following the break-up of the Soviet Union. Many of them are choosing to migrate back to Russia as part of a process of ethnic unmixing (Brubaker 1998).

Globalization and migration

So far we have concentrated on recent immigration into Europe, but European expansionism centuries ago initiated a large-scale movement of populations,

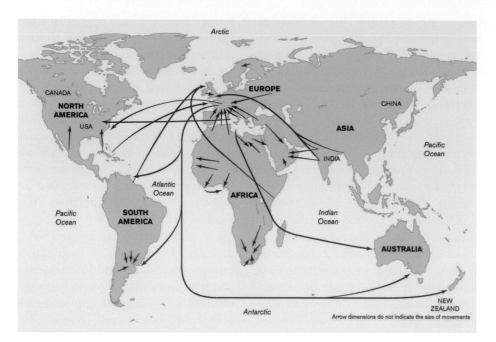

Figure 15.6   Global migrations, 1945–73

Source: Castles and Miller 1993: 67. Reproduced with permission of Palgrave Macmillan.

which formed the basis of many of the world's multiethnic societies today. Since these initial waves of global migration, human populations have continued to interact and mix in ways that have fundamentally shaped the ethnic composition of many countries. In this section we shall consider concepts related to global migration patterns.

What are the forces behind global migration and how are they changing as a result of globalization? Many early theories about migration focused on so-called **push and pull factors**. 'Push factors' referred to dynamics within a country of origin which forced people to emigrate, such as war, famine, political oppression or population pressures. 'Pull factors', by contrast, were those features of destination countries which attracted immigrants: prosperous labour markets, better overall living conditions and lower population density, for example, could 'pull' immigrants from other regions.

More recently 'push and pull' theories of migration have been criticized for offering overly simplistic explanations of a complex and multifaceted process. Instead, scholars of migration are increasingly looking at global migration patterns as 'systems' which are produced through interactions between macro- and micro-level processes. While this idea may sound complicated, it is actually quite simple. Macro-level factors refer to overarching issues such as the political situation in an area, the laws and regulations controlling immigration and emigration, or changes in the international economy. Micro-level factors, on the other hand, are concerned with the resources, knowledge and understandings that the migrant populations themselves possess.

> See chapter 14, 'Sexuality and Gender', for a discussion of sex tourism and sex work.

The intersection of macro and micro processes can be seen in the case of Germany's large Turkish immigrant community. On the macro level are factors such as Germany's economic need for

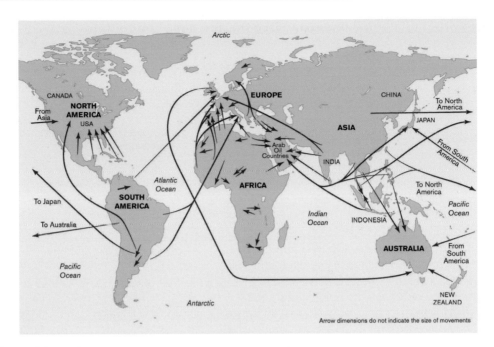

Figure 15.7 Global migratory movements from 1973

Source: Castles and Miller 1993: 6. Reproduced with permission of Palgrave Macmillan.

labour, its policy of accepting foreign 'guest workers' and the state of the Turkish economy which prevents many Turks from earning at the level they would wish. At the micro level are the informal networks and channels of mutual support within the Turkish community in Germany and the strong links to family and friends who have remained in Turkey. Among potential Turkish migrants, knowledge about Germany and 'social capital' – human or community resources that can be drawn on – help to make Germany one of the most popular destination countries. Supporters of the migration systems approach emphasize that no single factor can explain the process of migration. Rather, each particular migratory movement, like that between Turkey and Germany, is the product of an interaction of macro- and micro-level processes.

Global diasporas

Another way to understand global migration patterns is through the study of **diaspo-** ras. This term refers to the dispersal of an ethnic population from an original homeland into foreign areas, often in a forced manner or under traumatic circumstances. References are often made to the Jewish and African diasporas to describe the way in which these populations have become redistributed across the globe as a result of slavery and genocide. Although members of a diaspora are by definition scattered geographically, they are held together by factors such as shared history, a collective memory of the original homeland or a common ethnic identity which is nurtured and preserved.

Although today we are most familiar with the diaspora as the involuntary movement of people resulting from persecution and violence, Robin Cohen argues that, in fact, the dominant meaning associated with the term has changed over time. In *Global Diasporas* (1997), Cohen adopts a historical approach to the dispersal of people and identifies five different categories of diaspora. The ancient Greeks used the word to

Classic Studies 15.2 | Understanding the new age of migration

The research problem

People have always moved around the world for better job prospects, or to flee persecution. But today, as globalization takes hold, patterns of migration have changed as people take advantage of global transport and travel systems and new opportunities for tourism. How can we characterize and explain these new patterns? How will global migration affect the composition and solidarities within the societies of the twenty-first century? A book on the 'new migration' by Stephen Castles and Mark Miller (1993) was into its third edition just a decade later and has been through many reprintings in the meantime. This suggests that the authors have successfully framed and redefined the field of migration studies to strike a chord with a global audience. In short, their analysis of 'the new migration' has become a modern classic.

Castles and Miller's explanation

Castles and Miller acknowledge that international migration is certainly not new; it has existed from the earliest times. What have changed today though are the sheer size, speed and scope of migration, which have the potential to transform societies. Examining recent trends in global migration patterns, they identify four tendencies, which they claim will characterize migration in the coming years.

First, a tendency towards the *acceleration* of migration across borders as people move in greater numbers than ever before. Second is the tendency towards *diversification*. Most countries now receive immigrants from many different places with a variety of motivations, in contrast with earlier times when particular forms of immigration, such as labour immigration or refugees fleeing persecution, were predominant. Third, there is a tendency towards *globalization*. Migration has become global in character, involving a larger number of countries both as 'senders' and 'recipients' of migrants. Finally, there is a tendency towards the *feminization* of migration. A growing number of migrants are women, making contemporary migration much less male-dominated than in previous times.

Such an increase in women migrants is closely related to changes in the global labour market, including the growing demand for domestic workers, the expansion of sex tourism and 'trafficking' in women and the 'mail-order brides' phenomenon.

 Sex tourism in discussed in chapter 14, 'Sexuality and Gender'.

Taken together, Castles and Miller argue that in the 'new age of migration', there will be much more people movement, much more of it will involve women and particular countries will experience a more diverse range of immigrant groups. Migration is also very likely to become normalized as a central feature of the global world we live in; people, governments and international bodies (such as the United Nations) will have to find new ways of managing it.

Critical points

Some have suggested that the analysis presented by Castles and Miller remains quite conventional and does not do enough to link with emerging and potentially overlapping fields, such as the new studies of mobilities (see Sheller and Urry 2004; Larsen et al. 2006). Others argue that their book is centred on states and their fate in the age of mass migration, rather than moving beyond states to explore urban regions. Finally, the inclusion of terrorist activity in the latest edition, has been seen by some critics as rather forced, rather than flowing from their general analytical framework.

Contemporary significance

Castles and Miller have made a significant contribution to the new migration studies by effectively showing how globalization influences patterns of migration and how migration has much greater potential to reshape societies. They have also helped to reshape the field of migration studies by adopting a more comparative perspective than usual and exploring migration from the developed to the developing countries as well as in the other direction. They also manage to link migration patterns to theories of globalization, thus bringing the study of migration into the mainstream of sociology.

describe the dispersal of populations, which resulted from *colonization*. *Victim* diasporas, such as those of the African slave trade, along with Jewish and Armenian population movements, are those in which people suffer forced exile and long to return back to their homelands. *Labour* diasporas are typified by the indentured labour of Indian workers during British colonialism. Cohen sees movements of Chinese people to Southeast Asia during the creation of a *trading* diaspora as an example of a voluntary movement for the buying and selling of goods, not the result of some traumatic event. *Imperial* diasporas are those where imperialist expansion into new lands takes with it people who subsequently make new lives; the British Empire would be the most well-known example. Finally, Cohen makes a case for viewing the movement of people from the Caribbean as an instance of *cultural* diaspora; 'cemented as much by literature, political ideas, religious convictions, music and lifestyles as by permanent migration' (Cohen 1997). In reality though, as Cohen admits, these categories are overlapping and diasporas occur for a variety of reasons.

Despite the diversity of forms, however, all diasporas share certain key features. Cohen suggests that they all meet the following criteria:

- a forced or voluntary movement from an original homeland to a new region or regions;
- a shared memory about the original homeland, a commitment to its preservation and belief in the possibility of eventual return;
- a strong ethnic identity sustained over time and distance;
- a sense of solidarity with members of the same ethnic group also living in areas of the diaspora; a degree of tension in relation to the host societies;
- the potential for valuable and creative contributions to pluralistic host societies.

Although Cohen's typology is a simplification (which he readily admits) and may therefore be criticized for being imprecise for the analysis he undertakes, the study is valuable because it shows how the meaning of diaspora is not static, but relates to the ongoing processes of maintaining collective identities and preserving ethnic cultures in the context of a rapid period of globalization.

Conclusion

In our global age, ideas, goods and people are flowing across borders in greater volumes than ever before in history. These processes are profoundly altering the societies in which we live. Many societies are becoming ethnically diverse for the first time; others are finding that existing patterns of multiethnicity are being transformed or intensified. In all societies, however, individuals are coming into regular contact with people who think differently, look different and live differently from themselves. These interactions are happening in person, as a result of global migration, as well as through the images that are transmitted through the media and Internet.

Some welcome this new ethnic and cultural complexity as a vital component of a cosmopolitan, yet cohesive, society. Others find it dangerous and threatening. One of the main challenges facing our globalizing world is how to generate societies that are more cosmopolitan in character. As the patient efforts of the Truth and Reconciliation Commission in South Africa have shown, creating a forum for open and respectful communication is a difficult, but effective, first step in initiating ethnic reconciliation.

Summary points

1. 'Race' refers to physical and other characteristics, such as skin colour and intelligence, treated by members of a community or society as socially significant. Many popular beliefs about race are mythical. There are no clear-cut characteristics by means of which human beings can be allocated to different races.

2. Sections of a population form ethnic groups by virtue of sharing common cultural characteristics, which separate them from others in that population. Ethnicity refers to cultural differences that set one group apart from another and exclusionary devices, which reinforce cultural boundaries. The main distinguishing characteristics of an ethnic group are language, history or ancestry, religion and styles of dress or adornment. Ethnic differences are wholly learned.

3. A minority group is one whose members are discriminated against by the majority population in a society. Members of minority groups often have a strong sense of group solidarity, deriving in part from the collective experience of exclusion.

4. Racism means falsely ascribing inherited characteristics of personality or behaviour to individuals of a particular physical appearance. A racist is someone who believes that a biological explanation can be given for characteristics of inferiority supposedly possessed by people of one physical stock or another.

5. Institutional racism refers to patterns of discrimination that have become embedded within social institutions.

6. 'New racism' describes racist attitudes that are expressed through notions of cultural difference, rather than biological inferiority.

7. Three models of ethnic integration have been adopted by multiethnic societies. In the model of assimilation, new immigrant groups adopt the attitudes and language of the dominant community. In a melting pot, the different cultures and outlooks of the ethnic groups in a society are merged together. Pluralism means that ethnic groups exist separately but are seen as equal participants in economic and political life.

8. Multiethnic states can be fragile and sometimes experience episodes of ethnic conflict. Ethnic cleansing is a form of conflict in which ethnically homogeneous areas are created through the mass expulsion of other ethnic groups. Genocide describes the systematic elimination of one ethnic group at the hands of another.

9. Immigration has led to the existence of numerous different ethnic groups within the developed countries, which are now described as multicultural societies. In Britain, as elsewhere, many ethnic minority groups experience disadvantages in relation to the white population – in areas such as employment, income, housing and crime. However, patterns of inequality have been shifting and there are now many differences between ethnic minority groups.

10. Migration is the movement of people from one region or society to another for the purpose of settlement. Global migration, the movement of individuals across national borders, has increased in the years following the Second World War and is further intensifying with globalization. Diaspora refers to the dispersal of an ethnic population from an original homeland into foreign areas, often in a forced manner or under traumatic circumstances.

Further reading

A good place to start your reading is with Steve Fenton's *Ethnicity* (Cambridge: Polity, 2003), which is an introductory text pitched at the right level. In a similar vein you could then try Khalid Koser's *International Migration: A Very Short Introduction* (Oxford: Oxford University Press, 2007), which is exactly what you might expect.

From these, you can move on to Stephen E. Cornell and Douglas Hartmann's *Ethnicity and Race: Making Identities in a Changing World*, 2nd edn (Pine Forge Press, 2007), an American book which covers a lot of ground and is right up to date. For debates and issues around multiculturalism, see Tariq Modood's *Multiculturalism* (Cambridge: Polity, 2007).

Stephen Castles and Mark J. Miller's *The Age of Migration: International Population Movements in the Modern World* (Basingstoke: Palgrave Macmillan, 2003) is very accessible, and though not an 'easy read', it is worth the effort.

If you need reference works, then Les Back and John Solomos's *Theories of Race and Racism* (London and New York: Routledge, 2007) is an excellent edited collection covering theories, while David Theo Goldberg and John Solomos's *A Companion to Racial and Ethnic Studies* (Oxford: Blackwell Publishing, 2002) is another very useful and comprehensive edited collection.

Internet links

Origination – UK Channel 4 site covering British immigrant cultures:
www.blackhistorymap.com/

CRER – Centre for Research in Ethnic Relations at the University of Warwick:
www.warwick.ac.uk/CRER/index.html

EUCM – European Monitoring Centre on Racism and Xenophobia – very useful publications and surveys on discrimination and anti-discrimination measures in Europe:
http://fra.europa.eu/fra/index.php?fuseaction=content.dsp_cat_content&catid=1

Intute – Social Science Gateway for 'Racial and Ethnic Minorities':
www.intute.ac.uk/socialsciences/cgi-bin/browse.pl?id=120585&gateway=%

UNHCR – the United Nations Refugee Agency:
www.unhcr.org/home.html

The Institute of 'Race' Relations, UK site:
www.irr.org.uk/index.html

ICAR – Information Centre about Asylum and Refugees in the UK:
www.icar.org.uk/

Politeia – network for citizenship and democracy in Europe, based in Amsterdam – links on Roma people:
www.politeia.net/newsletter/politeia_newsletter_45_may_2007/quarterly_theme_roma_in_europe

**16
Religion**

CHAPTER 16

•••

Religion

(opposite) Mother Theresa became famous for her work amongst India's poorest people.
•••••••••••••••••••••••••••••••••••

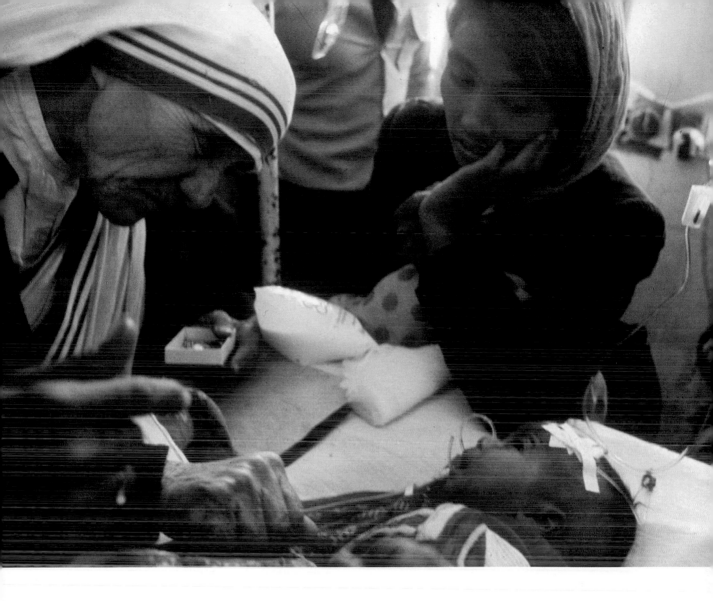

When Monica Besara, an illiterate mother of five from North Bengal in India, visited the Catholic nuns at the Missionaries of Charity in Calcutta it was to seek their blessing before she died. She had what she thought was a malignant tumour in her stomach that modern medical treatment had failed to cure. It was 5 September 1998, exactly one year after the death of Mother Teresa, the nun awarded the Nobel Prize for her work with the sick and poor and the founder of the Missionaries of Charity. The nuns prayed for Besara and placed a medallion on her stomach that had been blessed by Mother Teresa. The lump disappeared overnight.

Besara recalls that she had been suffering with a 'splitting headache, day and night, and the lump in the stomach was unbearably painful'. She remembers a service at the church to commemorate the anniversary of Mother Teresa's death. 'It is there', she said, 'I had the vision. Mother's death-picture was lying next to the altar. I saw a light like this [she points at a camera flash] coming out of the picture. Only I saw it. At 1 a.m. I got up and found that the lump had disappeared, as had the headache. I walked the next morning like a normal person.'

To Monica Besara and the nuns at the Missionaries of Charity, this was a miracle. A medical team sent out by the Catholic Church to investigate agreed. The nuns issued a statement saying: 'God has worked his miracle through Mother [Teresa] and we are so very happy.' The Pope, as head of the Catholic Church, accepted that a miracle had taken place and ordered the beatification of Mother Teresa, the final step before sainthood – normally attained after the Pope's approval of a second miracle. The beatification went ahead to celebrations around the world in October 2003. In Albania, Mother Teresa's country of origin, the day was observed as a national holiday and 2004 was declared Mother Teresa Year. In her adopted country of India, priests celebrated special masses across the country, children paraded on Calcutta's streets, and the ceremony, held at the Vatican in Italy, was broadcast live on national television. In Rome, films, musicals, cartoons and exhibitions were shown celebrating Mother Teresa's life, and her relics have been put on display.

Despite the Catholic Church's insistence, not everyone is convinced that Monica Besara's recovery was a miracle. Probir Ghosh is founder of India's Science and Rationalists' Society, which specializes in exposing holy men who dupe ordinary Indians into paying for miracle cures. His organization claims a membership of more than 20,000 people and has a mandate to 'free poor and illiterate Indians from superstition'. Ghosh has a simple solution for Besara's dramatic recovery: 'The medication had started having effect, when the so-called "miracle" happened.' Doctors who treated Besara at various hospitals in Bengal made similar statements, and questioned whether the growth was actually a cancerous tumour or something more benign. Ghosh argued: 'Mother Teresa was a great soul and I think it is an insult to her legacy to make her sainthood dependent on bogus miracles. It should be linked to her great work among the poor.'

At times, religion and science seem to be at odds with one another. The debate around the miracle of Monica Besara shows that a religious outlook and modern rationalist thought exist in an uneasy state of tension. With the deepening of modernity, a rationalist perspective has conquered many aspects of our existence; its hold seems unlikely to be weakened in the foreseeable future. Yet there will always be reactions against science and rationalist thought, for they remain silent on such fundamental questions as the meaning and purpose of life. It is these matters which have always been at the core of religion and have fuelled the idea of faith, an emotional leap into belief.

Religion has had a strong hold over the lives of human beings for thousands of years. In one form or another, religion is found in all known human societies. The earliest societies on record, of which we have evidence only through archaeological remains, show clear traces of religious symbols and ceremonies. Cave drawings suggest that religious beliefs and practices existed more than 40,000 years ago. Throughout subsequent history, religion has continued to be a central part of human experience, influencing how we perceive and react to the environments in which we live.

Why has religion been such a pervasive aspect of human societies? How is its role changing in late modern societies? Under what conditions does religion unite communities, and under what conditions does it divide them? How can religion have such a purchase on individuals' lives that they are prepared to sacrifice themselves for its ideals? These are the questions that we shall try to answer in this chapter. In order to do so, we shall have to ask what religion really is, and look at some of the different forms that religious beliefs and practices take. We shall also consider the main sociological theories of religion and analyse the various types of religious organization that can be distinguished. Throughout, we will consider the fate of religion primarily though not exclusively in relation to the developed countries, for it has seemed to many observers that, with the rise of science and modern industry, religion today has become a less central force in social life than it was prior to the modern age. A key question is whether the developed world really is a secular place, or put another way, can religion survive modernity?

The sociological study of religion

What is religion?

The study of religion is a challenging enterprise which places quite special demands on the sociological imagination. In analysing religious practices, we have to make sense of the many different beliefs and rituals found in the various human cultures. We must be sensitive to ideals that inspire profound conviction in believers, yet at the same time take a balanced view of them. We have to confront ideas that seek the eternal, while recognizing that religious groups also promote quite mundane goals – such as acquiring finance or soliciting for followers. We need to recognize the diversity of religious beliefs and modes of conduct, but also probe into the nature of religion as a general phenomenon.

Sociologists define **religion** as a cultural system of commonly shared beliefs and rituals that provides a sense of ultimate meaning and purpose by creating an idea of reality that is sacred, all-encompassing and supernatural (Durkheim 1976 [1912]; Berger 1967; Wuthnow 1988). There are three key elements in this definition:

1. *Religion is a form of culture.* Culture consists of the shared beliefs, values, norms and ideas that create a common identity among a group of people. Religion shares all these characteristics.
2. *Religion involves beliefs that take the form of ritualized practices.* All religions thus have a behavioural aspect – special activities in which believers take part and that identify them as members of the religious community.
3. *Perhaps most important, religion provides a sense of purpose* – a feeling that life is ultimately meaningful. It does so by explaining coherently and compellingly what transcends or overshadows everyday life, in ways that other aspects of culture (such as an educational system or a belief in democracy) typically cannot (Geertz 1973; Wuthnow 1988).

What is absent from the sociological definition of religion is as important as what is included: nowhere is there mention of God. We often think of *theism*, a belief in one or more supernatural deities (the term originates from the Greek word for God), as basic to religion, but this is not necessarily the case. As we shall see later, some religions, such as Buddhism, believe in the existence of spiritual forces rather than a particular God.

How sociologists think about religion

When sociologists study religion, they do so as sociologists and not as believers (or disbelievers) in any particular faith. This stance has several implications for the sociological study of religion:

1. *Sociologists are not concerned with whether religious beliefs are true or false.* From a sociological perspective, religions are regarded not as being decreed by God but as being socially constructed

by human beings. As a result, sociologists put aside their personal beliefs when they study religion. They are concerned with the human rather than the divine aspects of religion. Sociologists ask: How is the religion organized? What are its principal beliefs and values? How is it related to the larger society? What explains its success or failure in recruiting and retaining believers? The question of whether a particular belief is 'good' or 'true', however important it may be to the believers of the religion under study, is not something that sociologists are able to address as sociologists. (As individuals, they may have strong opinions on the matter, but one hopes that as sociologists they can keep these opinions from biasing their research.)

2 *Sociologists are especially concerned with the social organization of religion.* Religions are among the most important institutions in society. They are a primary source of the most deep-seated norms and values. At the same time, religions are typically practised through an enormous variety of social forms. Within Christianity and Judaism, for example, religious practice often occurs in formal organizations, such as churches or synagogues. Yet this is not necessarily true of such Asian religions as Hinduism and Buddhism, where religious practices are likely to occur in the home or some other natural setting. The sociology of religion is concerned with how different religious institutions and organizations function. The earliest European religions were often indistinguishable from the larger society, as religious beliefs and practices were incorporated into daily life. This is still true in many parts of the world today. In modern industrial society, however, religions have become established in separate, often bureaucratic, organizations, and so sociologists focus on the organizations through which religions must operate in order to

survive (Hammond 1992). As we shall see below, this institutionalization has even led some sociologists to view religions in the United States and Europe as similar to business organizations, competing with one another for members (Warner 1993).

3 *Sociologists often view religions as a major source of social solidarity.* To the extent that religions provide believers with a common set of norms and values, they are an important source of social solidarity. Religious beliefs, rituals and bonds help to create a 'moral community' in which all members know how to behave towards one another (Wuthnow 1988). If a single religion dominates a society, it may be an important source of social stability. If a society's members adhere to numerous competing religions, however, religious differences may lead to destabilizing social conflicts. Recent examples of religious conflict within a society include struggles between Sikhs, Hindus and Muslims in India; clashes between Muslims and Christians in Bosnia and other parts of the former Yugoslavia; and 'hate crimes' against Jews, Muslims and other religious minorities in the United States.

4 *Sociologists tend to explain the appeal of religion in terms of social forces rather than in terms of purely personal, spiritual or psychological factors.* For many people, religious beliefs are a deeply personal experience, involving a strong sense of connection with forces that transcend everyday reality. Sociologists do not question the depth of such feelings and experiences, but they are unlikely to limit themselves to a purely spiritual explanation of religious commitment. A person may claim that he or she became religious when God suddenly appeared in a vision, but sociologists are likely to look for more earthly explanations. Some researchers argue that people often 'get religion' when their fundamental sense of a

social order is threatened by economic hardship, loneliness, loss or grief, physical suffering, or poor health (Berger 1967; Schwartz 1970; Glock and Bellah 1976; Stark and Bainbridge 1980). In explaining the appeal of religious movements, sociologists are more likely to focus on the problems of the social order than on the psychological response of the individual.

Religion in classical sociological theory

Sociological approaches to religion are still strongly influenced by the ideas of the three classical sociological theorists: Marx, Durkheim and Weber. None of the three was religious, and all thought that the significance of traditional religions would decrease in modern times. The advocates of different faiths may be wholly persuaded of the validity of the beliefs they hold and the rituals in which they participate, yet the very diversity of religions and their obvious connection to different types of society, the three thinkers held, make these claims inherently implausible. An individual born into an Australian society of hunters and gatherers would plainly have different religious beliefs from someone born into the caste system of India or the Catholic Church of medieval Europe. However, as we shall see below, although the classical sociologists agreed in this respect, they developed very different theories when it came to studying the role of religion in society.

THINKING CRITICALLY

Should the sociology of religion be a secular enterprise? If it is, does the absence of a *spiritual* dimension mean that its results can only ever be partial? If it is not, can religious sociologists ever approach their research in a properly scientific manner?

Karl Marx: religion and inequality

In spite of his influence on the subject, Karl Marx never studied religion in any detail. His ideas mostly derived from the writings of several early nineteenth-century theological and philosophical authors. One of these was Ludwig Feuerbach, who published a famous work, translated as *The Essence of Christianity* (1957 [1853]). According to Feuerbach, religion consists of ideas and values produced by human beings in the course of their cultural development, but mistakenly projected on to divine forces or gods. Because human beings do not fully understand their own history, they tend to attribute socially created values and norms to the activities of gods. Thus the story of the ten commandments given to Moses by God is a mythical version of the origin of the moral precepts which govern the lives of Jewish and Christian believers.

So long as we do not understand the nature of the religious symbols we ourselves have created, Feuerbach argues, we are condemned to be prisoners of forces of history we cannot control. Feuerbach uses the term **alienation** to refer to the establishing of gods or divine forces distinct from human beings. Humanly created values and ideas come to be seen as the product of alien or separate beings – religious forces and gods. While the effects of alienation have in the past been negative, the understanding of religion as alienation, according to Feuerbach, promises great hope for the future. Once human beings realize that the values projected on to religion are really their own, those values become capable of realization on this earth, rather than being deferred to an afterlife. Human beings themselves can appropriate the powers believed to be possessed by God in Christianity. Christians believe that while God is all-powerful and all-loving, human beings themselves are imperfect and flawed. However, the potential for love and goodness and the power to control our own lives, Feuerbach argued, are present in human social institutions and can be brought to fruition once we understand their true nature.

Marx accepted the view that religion represents human self-alienation. It is often believed that Marx was dismissive of religion, but this is far from true. Religion, he writes, is the 'heart of a heartless world' – a haven from the harshness of daily reality. In Marx's view, religion in its traditional form will, and should, disappear; yet this is because the positive values embodied in religion can become guiding ideals for improving the lot of humanity on this earth, not because these ideals and values themselves are mistaken. We should not fear the gods we ourselves have created, and we should cease endowing them with values we ourselves can realize.

Marx declared, in a famous phrase, that religion has been the 'opium of the people'. Religion defers happiness and rewards to the afterlife, teaching the resigned acceptance of existing conditions in this life. Attention is thus diverted away from inequalities and injustices in this world by the promise of what is to come in the next. Religion has a strong ideological element: religious beliefs and values often provide justifications of inequalities of wealth and power. For example, the teaching that 'the meek shall inherit the earth' suggests attitudes of humility and non-resistance to oppression.

> **THINKING CRITICALLY**
>
> Was Marx right about the role of religion in capitalist societies? Can you think of any examples from across the world where religions have opposed rather than supported the dominant social order? Can religions also be a force for political and social change and if so, does this effectively show that Marx was wrong?

Emile Durkheim: functionalism and religious ritual

In contrast to Marx, Emile Durkheim spent a good part of his later intellectual career studying religion, though he admitted that in his earlier work he had not appreciated its enduring social significance. In the twentieth century, the founder of structural functionalism, Talcott Parsons, was also concerned with the role and fate of religion in modern societies.

> **THINKING CRITICALLY**
>
> How accurate has been Durkheim's forecast that 'the old Gods are dead', in relation to the demise of the traditional world religions? What examples can you think of which may suggest that the 'old Gods' have survived rather better than he thought they would?

Max Weber: world religions and social change

Durkheim based his arguments on a very small range of examples, even though he claims his ideas apply to religion in general. Max Weber, by contrast, embarked on an enormous project to study the major religions of the world. No scholar before or since has undertaken a task of such scope. Most of his attention was concentrated on what he called the *world religions* – those that have attracted large numbers of believers and decisively affected the course of global history. He made detailed studies of Hinduism, Buddhism, Taoism and ancient Judaism (1951, 1952, 1958, 1963), and in *The Protestant Ethic and the Spirit of Capitalism* (1976 [1904–5]) and elsewhere, he wrote extensively about the impact of Christianity on the history of the West. He did not, however, complete his projected study of Islam, which was taken up by later Weber scholars (Turner 1974).

Weber's writings on religion differ from those of Durkheim in that they concentrate on the connection between religion and social change, something to which Durkheim gave little attention. They contrast with the work of Marx because Weber argues that religion is not necessarily a conservative force; on the contrary, reli-

The research problem

There are many religions across the world, some very old, such as Christianity and Hinduism, and some more recently developed, such as Scientology, which dates only from the 1950s. What, if anything, do they all have in common? What is it that allows us to discuss them as 'religions' rather than, say, philosophies? And how should we try to answer such questions sociologically? Emile Durkheim (1976 [1912]) posed just such questions and suggested that the most productive method for discovering the essential character of religion was to investigate it in its simplest form, in small-scale, traditional societies. Hence the title of his classic study, *The Elementary Forms of the Religious Life*, which is one of the most influential studies in the sociology of religion.

Durkheim's explanation

Unlike Marx, Durkheim does not connect religion primarily with social inequalities or power, but instead relates it to the overall nature of the institutions of a society. He bases his work on a study of **totemism** as practised by Australian Aboriginal societies, as he argues that totemism represents religion in its most 'elementary' form. In this uncluttered form, he argued, it becomes easier to discern the crucial defining features of religion.

A 'totem' was originally an animal or plant taken as having particular symbolic significance for a group. It is a sacred object, regarded with veneration and surrounded by various ritual activities. Durkheim defines religion in terms of a distinction between the **sacred** and the **profane**. Sacred objects and symbols, he holds, are treated as apart from the routine aspects of existence, which are the realm of the profane. Eating the totemic animal or plant, except on special ceremonial occasions, is usually forbidden, and as a sacred object the totem is believed to have divine properties which separate it completely from other animals that might be hunted, or crops gathered and consumed.

But why is the totem sacred? According to Durkheim, it is because it is the symbol of the group itself; it stands for the values central to the group or community. The reverence which people

Durkheim argues that rituals like the Puja ceremonies in Calcutta mark out the spiritual from the ordinary, but in doing so reinforce key social values.

feel for the totem derives from the respect they hold for central social values. In religion, the object of worship is actually society itself.

Durkheim strongly emphasized that religions are never just a matter of belief. All religions involve regular ceremonial and ritual activities in which a group of believers meets together. In collective ceremonials, a sense of group solidarity is affirmed and heightened in what Durkheim called collective effervescence – the heightened feeling of energy generated in collective gatherings and events. Ceremonials take individuals away from the concerns of profane social life into an elevated sphere, in which they feel in contact with higher forces. These higher forces, attributed to totems, divine influences or gods, are really the expression of the influence of the collectivity over the individual. Nonetheless, people's religious *experience* should not be dismissed as mere self-delusion. Rather, it is the *real* experience of social forces.

Ceremony and ritual, in Durkheim's view, are essential to binding the members of groups together. This is why they are found not only in regular situations of worship, but also in the various life crises when major social transitions are experienced – for example, birth, marriage and death. In virtually all societies, ritual and ceremonial procedures are observed on such occasions. Durkheim reasons that collective ceremonials reaffirm group solidarity at a time when people are forced to adjust to major changes in their lives. Funeral rituals demonstrate that the values of the group outlive the passing of particular individuals, and so provide a means for bereaved people to adjust to their altered circumstances. Mourning is not the spontaneous expression of grief – or, at least, it is only so for those personally affected by the death. Mourning is a duty imposed by the group.

In small, traditional cultures, Durkheim argued, almost all aspects of life are permeated by religion. Religious ceremonials both originate new ideas and categories of thought, and reaffirm existing values. Religion is not just a series of sentiments and activities; it actually conditions the modes of thinking of individuals in traditional cultures. Even the most basic categories of thought, including how time and space are thought of, were first framed in religious terms. The concept of 'time', for instance, was originally derived from counting the intervals involved in religious ceremonials.

With the development of modern societies, Durkheim saw, the influence of traditional religion wanes. Scientific thinking increasingly replaces religious explanation, and ceremonial and ritual activities come to occupy only a small part of individuals' lives. Durkheim agrees with Marx that older forms of religion involving divine forces or gods are on the verge of disappearing. 'The old gods are dead', Durkheim writes. Yet he also says that religion, in altered forms, is likely to continue. Even modern societies depend for their cohesion on rituals that reaffirm their values; new ceremonial activities can thus be expected to emerge to replace the old. Durkheim is vague about what these might be, but it seems that he has in mind the celebration of humanist and political values such as freedom, equality and social cooperation.

Critical points

One strand of criticism of Durkheim's thesis focuses on the notion that it is possible to understand the essential character of all religions by generalizing from a few small-scale societies. For example, it seems unlikely that Aboriginal totemism is typical of the large-scale, multinational world religions, which casts doubt on what can be learned about the latter from studying the former. Over the course of the twentieth century, many of the world's societies have become more multicultural with a diverse range of religions existing within a single national society. Durkheim's thesis of religion as a source of the continual recreation of social solidarity may be less persuasive in multi-faith societies and does not properly account for intra-society conflicts around different religious beliefs. Finally, we may take issue with the basic idea that religion is essentially the worship of society rather than deities or spirits. This can be seen as a reductionist argument; that religious experience can be reduced to social phenomena, thus rejecting even the possibility of a 'spiritual' level of reality. For people with strong religious beliefs and commitment, Durkheim's argument will probably always appear inadequate.

Contemporary significance

Durkheim's sociological theory of religion, like his work on suicide (see chapter 1), was of immense significance in establishing the discipline of sociology. It demonstrated that any subject could be approached from a sociological perspective. But he went further; without a sociological perspective we are likely to misunderstand social life and its institutions. By locating religions firmly *within* the social realm rather than outside it, Durkheim effectively demystified religious experience and encouraged the empirical study of religions. As we will see later in the chapter, the emergence of new religious movements and alternative forms of spirituality bear out the functionalist theory that although the old Gods may well be dead or dying, new ones will have to be created as societies undergo significant change. We might well agree with Durkheim that 'there is something eternal in religion which is destined to survive all the particular symbols in which religious thought has successively enveloped itself' (1976 [1912]: 427).

Hinduism is the oldest of the major world religions, dating back some 6,000 years.

giously inspired movements have often produced dramatic social transformations. Thus Protestantism – particularly Puritanism – was the source of the capitalistic outlook found in the modern West. The early entrepreneurs were mostly Calvinists. Their drive to succeed, which helped initiate Western economic development, was originally prompted by a desire to serve God. Material success was for them a sign of divine favour.

Weber saw his research on the world religions as a single project. His discussion of the impact of Protestantism on the development of the West is part of a comprehensive attempt to understand the influence of religion on social and economic life in varying cultures. Analysing the Eastern religions, Weber concluded that they provided insuperable barriers to the development of industrial capitalism, such as took place in the West. This is not because the non-Western

civilizations are backward; they have simply accepted values different from those which came to predominate in Europe.

In traditional China and India, Weber pointed out, there was at certain periods a significant development of commerce, manufacture and urbanism, but these did not generate the radical patterns of social change involved in the rise of industrial capitalism in the West. Religion was a major influence in inhibiting such change. For example, Hinduism is what Weber called an 'other-worldly' religion. That is to say, its highest values stress escape from the toils of the material world to a higher plane of spiritual existence. The religious feelings and motivations produced by Hinduism do not focus on controlling or shaping the material world. On the contrary, Hinduism sees material reality as a veil hiding the true concerns to which humankind should be oriented. Confucianism also acted to direct effort away from economic development, as this came to be understood in the West, emphasizing harmony with the world rather than promoting active mastery of it. Although China was for a long while the most powerful and culturally most developed civilization in the world, its dominant religious values acted as a brake on a strong commitment to economic development for its own sake.

Weber regarded Christianity as a salvation religion, involving the belief that human beings can be 'saved' if they adopt the beliefs of the religion and follow its moral tenets. The notions of sin and of being rescued from sinfulness by God's grace are important here. They generate a tension and an emotional dynamism essentially absent from the Eastern religions. Salvation religions have a 'revolutionary' aspect. While the religions of the East cultivate an attitude of passivity in the believer towards the existing order, Christianity involves a constant struggle against sin, and hence can stimulate revolt against the existing order of things. Religious leaders – like Jesus – arise, who reinterpret existing doctrines in such a way as to challenge the prevailing power structure.

Critical assessment of the classical theories

Marx, Durkheim and Weber each identified some important general characteristics of religion, and in some ways their views complement one another. Marx was right to claim that religion often has ideological implications, serving to justify the interests of ruling groups at the expense of others: there are innumerable instances of this in history. Take as an example the influence of Christianity on the European colonialists' efforts to subject other cultures to their rule. The missionaries who sought to convert 'heathen' peoples to Christian beliefs were no doubt sincere, yet the effect of their teachings was to reinforce the destruction of traditional cultures and the imposition of

white domination. The various Christian denominations almost all tolerated, or endorsed, slavery in the United States and other parts of the world up to the nineteenth century. Doctrines were developed that claimed slavery was based on divine law, disobedient slaves being guilty of an offence against God as well as their masters.

Yet Weber was certainly correct to emphasize the unsettling, and often revolutionary, impact of religious ideals on pre-established social orders. Despite the churches' early support for slavery in the United States, many church leaders later played a key role in the fight to abolish it. Religious beliefs have prompted many social movements seeking to overthrow unjust systems of authority, playing a prominent part, for instance, in the civil rights movements of the 1960s in the United States. Religion has also influenced social change – often provoking much bloodshed – through the armed clashes and wars fought for religious motives.

These divisive influences of religion, so prominent in history, find little mention in Durkheim's work. Durkheim emphasized above all the role of religion in promoting social cohesion. Yet it is not difficult to redirect his ideas towards explaining religious division, conflict and change as well as solidarity. After all, much of the strength of feeling which may be generated against other religious groups derives from the commitment to religious values generated within each community of believers.

Among the most valuable aspects of Durkheim's writings is his stress on ritual and ceremony. All religions involve regular assemblies of believers, at which ritual prescriptions are observed. As he rightly points out, ritual activities also mark the major transitions of life – birth, entry to adulthood (rituals associated with puberty are found in many cultures), marriage and death (also see van Gennep 1977 [1908]).

In the rest of this chapter we shall make use of ideas developed by all three authors. First, we shall outline the major world religions and the different types of religious organization. Then we will go on to discuss the sociological debate over secularization, the idea that religion is becoming less significant in industrial societies. From there we will then consider some of the developments in world religion which challenge the idea of secularization – namely the rise of new religious movements and the power of religious fundamentalism.

Religions in the real world

In traditional societies, religion usually plays a central part in social life. Religious symbols and rituals are often integrated with the material and artistic culture of the society – music, painting or carving, dance, storytelling and literature. In small cultures, there is no professional priesthood, but there are always certain individuals who specialize in knowledge of religious (and often magical) practices. Although there are various sorts of such specialists, one common type is the shaman (a word originating among North American Indians). A shaman is an individual believed to be able to direct spirits or non natural forces through ritual means. Shamans are sometimes essentially magicians rather than religious leaders, however, and are often consulted by individuals dissatisfied with what is offered in the religious rituals of the community.

Totemism and animism

Two forms of religion found frequently in smaller cultures are **totemism** and **animism**. The word 'totem' originated among North American Indian tribes, but has been widely used to refer to species of animals or plants believed to have supernatural powers (see 'Classic Studies 16.1'). Usually, each kinship group or clan within a society has its own particular totem, with which various ritual activities are associated. Totemic beliefs might seem alien to those living in industri-alized societies, yet in certain relatively minor contexts, symbols similar to those of totemism are familiar – as when a sports team has an animal or plant for its emblem: mascots are totems.

Animism is a belief in spirits or ghosts, thought to populate the same world as human beings. Such spirits may be seen as either benign or malevolent, and may influence human behaviour in numerous respects. In some cultures, for example, spirits are believed to cause illness or madness, and may also possess or take over individuals in such a way as to control their behaviour. Animistic beliefs are not confined to small cultures, but are found to some degree in many religious settings. In medieval Europe, those believed to be possessed by evil spirits were frequently persecuted as sorcerers or witches.

Small, seemingly 'simple' societies frequently have complex systems of religious belief. Totemism and animism are more common among these societies than in larger ones, but some small societies have far more complex religions. The Nuer of southern Sudan, for instance, described by E. E. Evans-Pritchard (1956), have an elaborate set of theological ideas centred on a 'high god' or 'sky spirit'. Religions which incline towards **monotheism** (belief in one god), however, are found relatively infrequently among smaller traditional cultures. Most are **polytheistic** – there is a belief in many gods.

Judaism, Christianity and Islam

The three most influential monotheistic religions in world history are Judaism, Christianity and Islam. All originated in the Middle East and each has influenced the others.

Judaism

Judaism is the oldest of the three religions, dating from about 1000 BCE. The early Hebrews were nomads, living in and around ancient Egypt. Their **prophets**, or religious leaders, partly drew their ideas from existing religious beliefs in the region, but differed in their commitment to a single, almighty God. Most of their neighbours were polytheistic. The Hebrews believed that God demands obedience to strict moral codes, and insisted on their claim to a monopoly of truth, seeing their beliefs as the only true religion (Zeitlin 1984, 1988).

Until the creation of Israel, not long after the end of the Second World War, there was no state of which Judaism was the official religion. Jewish communities survived in Europe, North Africa and Asia, although they were frequently persecuted – culminating in the murder of millions of Jews by the Nazis in concentration camps during the war.

Christianity

Many Judaic views were taken over and incorporated as part of Christianity. Jesus was an Orthodox Jew, and Christianity began as a sect of Judaism; it is not clear that Jesus wished to found a distinctive religion. His disciples came to think of him as the Messiah – a Hebrew word meaning 'the anointed', the Greek term for which was 'Christ' – awaited by the Jews. Paul, a Greek-speaking Roman citizen, was a major initiator of the spread of Christianity, preaching extensively in Asia Minor and Greece. Although the Christians were at first savagely persecuted, the Emperor Constantine eventually adopted Christianity as the official religion of the Roman Empire. Christianity spread to become a dominant force in Western culture for the next 2,000 years.

Christianity today commands a greater number of adherents, and is more generally spread across the world, than any other religion. More than a thousand million individuals regard themselves as Christians, but there are many divisions in terms of theology and church organization, the main branches being Roman Catholicism, Protestantism and Eastern Orthodoxy.

Islam

The origins of Islam, today the second largest religion in the world (see figure 16.1), overlap with those of Christianity. Islam derives from the teachings of the prophet Muhammad in the seventh century CE. The single God of Islam, Allah, is believed to hold sway over all human and natural life. The Pillars of Islam refer to the five essential religious duties of Muslims (as believers in Islam are called). The first is the recitation of the Islamic creed: 'There is no god but Allah, and Muhammad is the apostle of Allah.' The second is the saying of formal prayers five times each day, preceded by ceremonial washing. The worshipper at these prayers must always face towards the holy city of Mecca in Saudi Arabia, no matter how far away that is. The third is the giving of alms (money to the poor), set out in Islamic law, which has often been used as a source of taxation by the state. The fourth is the observance of Ramadan, a month of fasting during which no food or drink may be taken during daylight. Finally, there is the expectation that every believer will attempt, at least once, to make a pilgrimage to Mecca.

Muslims believe that Allah spoke through earlier prophets – including Moses and Jesus – before Muhammad, whose teachings most directly express his will. Islam has come to be very widespread, having some thousand million adherents throughout the world. The majority are concentrated in North and East Africa, the Middle East and Pakistan.

The religions of the Far East

Hinduism

There are major contrasts between Judaism, Christianity and Islam, and the religions of the Far East. The oldest of all the great religions still prominent in the world today is Hinduism, the core beliefs of which date back some 6,000 years. Hinduism is a polytheistic religion. It is so internally diverse that some scholars have suggested that it

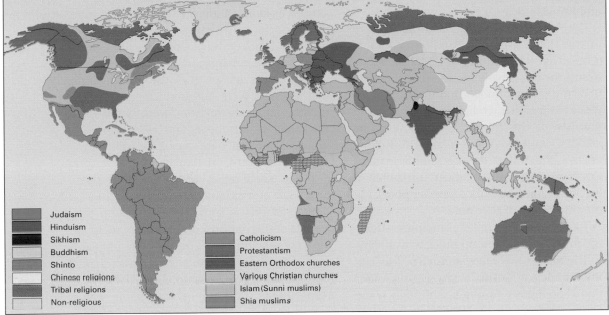

Figure 16.1 Religion and religious belief around the world, 2003

Source: Encyclopaedia Britannica, 2003

should be regarded as a cluster of related religions rather than a single religious orientation; many local cults and religious practices are linked by a few generally held beliefs.

Most Hindus accept the doctrine of the cycle of reincarnation – the belief that all living beings are part of an eternal process of birth, death and rebirth. A second key feature is the caste system, based on the belief that individuals are born into a particular position in a social and ritual hierarchy, according to the nature of their activities in previous incarnations. A different set of duties and rituals exists for each caste, and one's fate in the next life is governed mainly by how well these duties are performed in this one. Hinduism accepts the possibility of numerous different religious standpoints, not drawing a clear line between believers and non-believers. There are more than 750 million Hindus, virtually all living on the Indian subcontinent. Hinduism does not seek to convert others into 'true believers', unlike Christianity and Islam.

Buddhism, Confucianism, Taoism

The **ethical religions** of the East encompass Buddhism, Confucianism and Taoism. These religions have no gods. Rather, they emphasize ethical ideals that relate the believer to the natural cohesion and unity of the universe.

Buddhism derives from the teachings of Siddhartha Gautama, the Buddha ('enlightened one'), who was a Hindu prince in a small kingdom in south Nepal in the sixth century BCE. According to the Buddha, human beings can escape the reincarnation cycle by the renunciation of desire. The path of salvation lies in a life of self-discipline and meditation, separated from the tasks of the mundane world. The overall objective of Buddhism is the attainment of Nirvana, complete spiritual fulfilment. The Buddha rejected Hindu ritual and the authority of the castes. Like Hinduism, Buddhism tolerates many local variations, including belief in local deities, not insisting on a single view. Buddhism today is a major influence in several states in the Far East, including

Thailand, Burma, Sri Lanka, China, Japan and Korea.

Confucianism was the basis of the culture of the ruling groups in traditional China. 'Confucius' (the Latinized form of the name K'ung Fu-tzu), lived in the sixth century BCE, the same period as Buddha. Confucius was a teacher, not a religious prophet in the manner of the Middle Eastern religious leaders. Confucius is not seen by his followers as a god, but as 'the wisest of wise men'. Confucianism seeks to adjust human life to the inner harmony of nature, emphasizing the veneration of ancestors.

Taoism shares similar principles, stressing meditation and non-violence as means to the higher life. Like Confucius, Lao-tzu, the founder of Taoism, was a teacher rather than a religious prophet. Although some elements survive in the beliefs and practices of many Chinese, both Confucianism and Taoism have lost much of their influence in China as a result of determined opposition from the government.

Religious organizations

The sociology of religion has concerned itself with non-European religions since its origins in the writings of Durkheim and Weber. Nonetheless, there has frequently been a tendency to view all religions through concepts and theories that grew out of the European experience. For example, notions like *denomination* or *sect* presuppose the existence of formally organized religious institutions; they are of questionable utility in the study of religions that emphasize ongoing spiritual practice as a part of daily life or that pursue the complete integration of religion with civic and political life. In recent decades, there has been an effort to create a more comparative sociology of religion, one that seeks to understand religious traditions from within their own frames of reference (Wilson 1982; Van der Veer 1994).

Early theorists such as Max Weber (1963), Ernst Troeltsch (1981 [1931]) and Richard

Niebuhr (1929) described religious organizations as falling along a continuum, based on the degree to which they are well established and conventional: churches lie at one end (they are conventional and well established), cults lie at the other (they are neither) and sects fall somewhere in the middle. These distinctions were based on the study of European and US religions. There is much debate over how well they apply to the non-Christian world.

Today, sociologists are aware that the terms *sect* and *cult* have negative connotations, and this is something they wish to avoid. For this reason, contemporary sociologists of religion sometimes use the phrase *new religious movements* to characterize novel religious organizations that lack the respectability that comes with being well established for a long period of time (Hexham and Poewe 1997; Hadden 1997).

> **THINKING CRITICALLY**
>
> Why should sociologists avoid using terms such as 'cult' or 'sect', which have acquired a negative meaning in society? How might the use of these terms influence their research? Is it *possible* for sociologists to avoid making value judgements during the research process? *Should* sociologists try to avoid making such value judgements?

Churches and sects

All religions involve communities of believers, but there are many different ways in which such communities are organized. One mode of classifying religious organizations was first put forward by Max Weber and his colleague, the religious historian Ernst Troeltsch. Weber and Troeltsch distinguished between churches and sects. A church is a large, well-established religious body – like the Catholic Church or the Church of England. A **sect** is a smaller, less highly organized grouping of committed believers, usually setting itself up in protest against what a church has become – as Calvinists or Methodists did. Churches normally have a formal, bureaucratic structure, with a hierarchy of religious officials, and tend to represent the conservative face of religion, since they are integrated into the existing institutional order. Most of their adherents are like their parents in being church members.

Sects are comparatively small; they usually aim at discovering and following 'the true way', and tend to withdraw from the surrounding society into communities of their own. The members of sects regard established churches as corrupt. Most have few or no officials, all members being regarded as equal participants. A small proportion of people are born into sects, but most actively join them in order to further their beliefs.

Denominations and cults

Other authors have further developed the church/sect typology as originally set out by Weber and Troeltsch. One of these is Howard Becker (1950), who added two further types: the **denomination** and the **cult**. A denomination is a sect which has 'cooled down' and become an institutionalized body rather than an active protest group. Sects which survive over any period of time inevitably become denominations. Thus Calvinism and Methodism were sects during their early formation, when they generated great fervour among their members; but over the years they have become more 'respectable'. Denominations are recognized as more or less legitimate by churches and exist alongside them, quite often cooperating harmoniously with them.

Cults resemble sects, but have different emphases. They are the most loosely knit and transient of all religious organizations, being composed of individuals who reject what they see as the values of the outside society. Their focus is on individual experience, bringing like-minded individuals together. People do not formally join a cult, but rather follow particular theories or prescribed ways of behaviour. Members are usually allowed to maintain other religious connections. Like sects, cults quite often form around an inspirational leader. Instances of cults in the West today would include groups of believers in spiritualism, astrology or transcendental meditation.

A tragic example of a cult built around an inspirational leader came to light in the USA in 1993. David Koresh, who led the Branch Davidian religious cult, claimed to be a messiah. He was also allegedly stockpiling illegal weapons, practising polygyny and having sex with some of the children living in the group's compound in Waco, Texas. Up to 80 members of the cult (including 19 children) burned to death as a fire engulfed their complex when it came under assault by officials from the US government after a lengthy armed stand-off. Controversy remains over whether the fire was ordered by Koresh, who reportedly preferred mass suicide to surrender, or whether the actions of the federal authorities caused the tragedy.

It should be obvious that what is a cult in one country may well be an established religious practice in another. When Indian gurus (religious teachers) bring their beliefs into the United Kingdom, what might be considered an established religion in India is regarded as a cult in the UK. Christianity began as an indigenous cult in ancient Jerusalem, and in many Asian countries today Evangelical Protestantism is regarded as a cult imported from the West, and particularly the United States. Thus, cults should not be thought of as 'weird'. A leading sociologist of religion, Jeffrey K. Hadden, points out (1997) that all the approximately 100,000 religions that humans have devised were once new; most, if not all, were initially despised cults from the standpoint of respectable religious belief of the times. Jesus was crucified because his ideas were so threatening to the established order of the Roman-dominated religious establishment of ancient Judaea.

Religious movements

Religious movements represent a subtype of social movements in general. A religious movement is an association of people who join together to spread a new religion or to promote a new interpretation of an existing religion. Religious movements are larger than sects and less exclusivist in their membership – although like churches and sects, movements and sects (or cults) are not always clearly distinct from one another. In fact, all sects and cults can be classified as religious movements. Examples of religious movements include the groups that originally founded and spread Christianity in the first century, the Lutheran movement that split Christianity in Europe about 1,500 years later and the groups involved in the more recent Islamic Revolution (discussed in more detail later in the chapter).

Religious movements tend to pass through certain definite phases of development. In the first phase, the movement usually derives its life and cohesion from a powerful leader. Max Weber classified such leaders as *charismatic* – that is, having inspirational qualities capable of capturing the imagination and devotion of a mass of followers. (Charismatic leaders in Weber's formulation could include political as well as religious figures – revolutionary China's Mao Tse-tung, for example, as well as Jesus and Muhammad.) The leaders of religious movements are usually critical of the religious establishment and seek to proclaim a new message. In their early years, religious movements are fluid; they do not have an established authority system. Their members are normally in direct contact with the charismatic leader, and together they spread the new teachings.

The second phase of development occurs following the death of the leader. Rarely does a new charismatic leader arise from the masses, so this phase is crucial. The movement is now faced with what Weber termed the 'routinization of charisma'. To survive, it has to create formalized rules and procedures, since it can no longer depend on the central role of the leader in organizing the followers. Many movements fade away when their leaders die or lose their influence. A movement that survives and takes on a permanent character becomes a church. In other words, it becomes a formal organization of believers with an established authority system and established symbols and rituals. The church might itself at some later point become the origin of other movements that question its teachings and either set themselves up in opposition or break away completely.

> Social movements are discussed in more detail in chapter 22, 'Politics, Government and Social Movements'.

New religious movements

Although traditional churches have been experiencing a decline in membership in recent decades, we see below in table 16.1 and figure 16.3 (pages 697, 700) that other forms of religious activity have been increasing. Sociologists use the term **new religious movements** to refer collectively to the broad range of religious and spiritual groups, cults and sects that have emerged in Western countries alongside the larger mainstream religions. New religious movements encompass an enormous diversity of groups, from spiritual and self-help groups within the **New Age movement** to exclusive sects such as the Hare Krishnas (International Society for Krishna Consciousness).

Many new religious movements are derived from the major religious traditions which we discussed above, Hinduism, Christianity and Buddhism, while others have emerged from traditions that were almost unknown in the West until recently. Some new religious movements are essentially new creations of the charismatic leaders who head their activities. This is the case, for example, with the Unification Church led by the Reverend Sun Myung Moon, who is seen by his supporters as a messiah, and whose church claims 4.5 million members.

Membership in new religious movements mostly consists of converts rather than individuals brought up in a particular faith. Members more often than not are well educated and from middle-class backgrounds.

Most new religious movements in Britain originated in the United States or the East, although a few, such as the Aetherius Society (founded in 1955) and the Emin Foundation (founded in 1971), were established in Britain. Since the Second World War, the United States has witnessed a far greater proliferation of religious movements than at any previous time in its history, including an unprecedented series of mergers and divisions between denominations. Most have been short-lived, but a few have achieved remarkable followings.

Various theories to explain the popularity of new religious movements have been advanced. Some observers have argued that they should be seen as a response to the process of liberalization and secularization within society and even within traditional churches. People who feel that traditional religions have become ritualistic and devoid of spiritual meaning may find comfort and a greater sense of community in smaller, less impersonal new religious movements.

Others have pointed to new religious movements as an outcome of rapid social change (Wilson 1982). As traditional social norms are disrupted, people search for both explanations and reassurance. The rise of groups and sects that emphasize personal spirituality, for example, suggest that many individuals feel a need to reconnect with their own values or beliefs in the face of instability and uncertainty.

A further factor may be that new religious movements appeal to people who feel alienated from mainstream society. The collective, communal approaches of sects and cults, some authors argue, can offer support and a sense of belonging. For example, middle-class youths are not marginalized from society in a material sense, but they may feel isolated emotionally and spiritu-

ally. Membership in a cult can help to overcome this feeling of alienation.

New religious movements can be understood as falling into three broad categories: world-affirming, world-rejecting and world-accommodating movements (Wallis 1984). Each is based on the relationship of the individual group to the larger social world and, though relatively small compared to the world religions, the rise of new religious movements can be seen as reflecting some aspects of wider social changes such as the decline of deference to experts and established authorities amongst younger generations. Sociological interest in new religious movements stems from the 1960s and '70s, when they were seen as challenging mainstream social values. In particular, the fact that young people tended to be disproportionately attracted to some new movements was associated with ideas of religious 'brainwashing', in a moral panic about the future of youth, which was similar in tone to the panics around spectacular youth subcultures.

> See chapter 8, 'The Life Course', for more on youth culture.

World-affirming movements

World-affirming movements are more akin to self-help or therapy groups than to conventional religious groups. They are movements that often lack rituals, churches and formal theologies, turning their focus on members' spiritual well-being. As the name suggests, world-affirming movements do not reject the outside world or its values. Rather, they seek to enhance their followers' abilities to perform and succeed in that world by unlocking human potential.

The Church of Scientology is one example of such a group, widely known of today as a result of the involvement of US actor Tom Cruise. Founded by L. Ron Hubbard in the early 1950s, the Church of Scientology has grown from its original base in California to include a large membership in countries around the world. Scientologists believe we are all spiritual beings, but have neglected our spiritual nature. Through training that makes them aware of their real spiritual capacities, people can recover forgotten supernatural powers, clear their minds and reveal their full potential.

Many strands of the so-called **New Age movement** fall under the category of world-affirming movements. The New Age movement emerged from the counterculture of the 1960s and '70s and encompasses a broad spectrum of beliefs, practices and ways of life. Pagan teachings (Celtic, Druidic, Native American and others), shamanism, forms of Asian mysticism, Wiccan rituals and Zen meditation are only a few of the activities that are thought of as 'New Age'.

On the surface, the mysticism of the New Age movement appears to stand in stark contrast to the modern societies in which it is favoured. Followers of New Age movements seek out and develop alternative ways of life in order to cope with the challenges of modernity. Yet New Age activities should not be interpreted as simply a radical break with the present. They should also be seen as part of a larger cultural trajectory that exemplifies aspects of mainstream culture. In late modern societies, individuals possess unparalleled degrees of autonomy and freedom to chart their own lives. In this respect, the aims of the New Age movement coincide closely with the modern age: people are encouraged to move beyond traditional values and expectations and to live their lives actively and reflexively.

World-rejecting movements

As opposed to world-affirming groups, **world-rejecting movements** are highly critical of the outside world. They often demand significant lifestyle changes from their followers – members may be expected to live ascetically, to change their dress or hairstyle, or to follow a certain diet. World-rejecting movements are frequently exclusive, in contrast to world-affirming movements, which tend to be inclusive in nature. Some world-rejecting movements display characteristics of total institutions; members are expected to subsume their individual identities in that of the group, to adhere to strict ethical codes or rules and to withdraw from activity in the outside world.

Most of the world-rejecting movements place far more demands on their members, in terms of time and commitment, than do older established religions. Some groups have been known to use the technique of 'love bombing' to gain the individual's total adherence. A potential convert is overwhelmed by attention and constant displays of instant affection until he or she is drawn emotionally into the group. Some new movements, in fact, have been accused of brainwashing their adherents – seeking to control their minds in such a way as to rob them of the capacity for independent decision-making.

Many world-rejecting cults and sects have come under the intense scrutiny of state authorities, the media and the public. Certain extreme cases of world-rejecting cults have attracted much concern. For example, the Japanese group Aum Shinrikyo released deadly sarin gas into the Tokyo subway system in 1995, injuring thousands of commuters and killing 12 people. (The cult's leader, Shoko Asahara, was sentenced to death for ordering the attacks by the Japanese courts in February 2004.) The Branch Davidian cult in the United States (discussed above) also grabbed the world media's attention when it became embroiled in a deadly confrontation with US authorities in 1993 after accusations of child abuse and weapons stock-piling.

World-accommodating movements

The third type of new religious movement is the one most like traditional religions. **World-accommodating movements** tend to emphasize the importance of inner religious life over more worldly concerns. Members of such groups seek to reclaim the spiritual purity that they believe has been lost in traditional religious settings. Where followers of world-rejecting and world-affirming groups often alter their lifestyles in accordance with their religious activity, many adherents of world-accommodating movements carry on in their everyday lives and careers with little visible change. One example of a world-accommodating movement is Pentecostalism. Pentecostalists believe that the Holy Spirit can be heard through individuals who are granted the gift of 'speaking in tongues'.

THINKING CRITICALLY

How do you think *religious* movements, such as those discussed above, differ from *secular* social movements, such as socialism, feminism and environmentalism? Are there any 'religious' elements within secular social movements? Can religious movements be analysed using the concepts and theories that were designed for studying secular social movements?

Christianity, gender and sexuality

Churches and denominations, as the preceding discussion has indicated, are religious organizations with defined systems of authority. In these hierarchies, as in other areas of social life, women are mostly excluded from power. This is very clear in Christianity, but it is also characteristic of all the major religions.

More than 100 years ago, Elizabeth Cady Stanton, an American campaigner for women's rights, published a series of commentaries on the Scriptures, entitled *The Woman's Bible*. In her view, the deity had created women and men as beings of equal value, and the Bible should fully reflect this fact. Its 'masculinist' character, she believed, reflected not the authentic word of God, but the fact that the Bible was written by men. In 1870, the Church of England established a Revising Committee to revise and update the biblical texts; but, as Stanton pointed out, the committee contained not a

single woman. She asserted that there was no reason to suppose that God is a man, since it was clear in the Scriptures that all human beings were fashioned in the image of God. When a colleague opened a women's rights conference with a prayer to 'God, our Mother', there was a virulent reaction from the church authorities. Yet Stanton pressed ahead, organizing a Women's Revising Committee in America, composed of 23 women, to advise her in preparing *The Woman's Bible*, which was published in 1895.

A century later the Anglican Church is still largely dominated by men, although recently this has begun to change. In the Church of England between 1987 and 1992 women were allowed to be deacons, but not permitted to be priests. Although they were officially part of the laity, they were not allowed to conduct certain basic religious rituals, like pronouncing blessings or solemnizing marriages. In 1992, after increasing pressure, particularly from women inside the Church of England, the Synod (governing assembly) voted to make the priesthood open to women with the first women priests ordained in 1994. The decision is still opposed by many conservatives in the Anglican Church, who argue that the full acceptance of women is a blasphemous deviation from revealed biblical truth and a move away from eventual reunification with the Catholic Church. As a result of the decision to allow women priests, some people decided to withdraw from the Church of England, often converting to Catholicism. Ten years later around a fifth of priests in the Church of England are women, and it is expected that there will soon be more women priests than men priests. In July 2005, the Church of England voted to begin the process that would allow women to become bishops, a decision strongly opposed by several senior figures in the Church. In July 2008, the ruling General Synod rejected proposals for separate structures aimed at accommodating traditionalists and instead agreed to introduce a national statutory code of practice which would include ordaining women bishops.

The Catholic Church has been more conservative in its attitude to women than the Church of England, and persists in formally supporting inequalities of gender. Calls for the ordination of women have been consistently turned down by the Catholic authorities. In 1977 the Sacred Congregation for the Doctrine of the Faith, in Rome, declared formally that women were not admissible to the Catholic priesthood. The reason given was that Jesus did not call a woman to be one of his disciples. In January 2004, seven women, who had been ordained as priests by rebel Argentinean Bishop, Romulo Antonio Braschi, were

Opening up the priesthood to women was a controversial step for many in the Anglican Church.

excommunicated from the Church and their ordinations overturned by the Vatican. Pope John Paul II (1920–2005) encouraged women to recall their roles as wives and mothers, attacked feminist ideologies which assert that men and women are fundamentally the same and supported policies prohibiting abortion and the use of contraception which place further limitations on women's freedom (Vatican 2004).

Controversy in the Anglican Church in recent years has shifted away from gender to the issue of homosexuality and the priesthood. Homosexuals have long served in the Christian Church, but with their sexual inclinations either suppressed, ignored or unobserved. (The Catholic Church still holds to the position set out in 1961 that those 'affected by the perverse inclination' towards homosexuality must be barred from taking religious vows or being ordained.) Other Protestant denominations have introduced liberal policies towards homosexuals and openly gay clergy have been admitted to the priesthood in some of the smaller denominations. The Evangelical Lutheran Church in the Netherlands was the first European Christian denomination to decide that lesbians and gays could serve as pastors in 1972. Other denominations, such as the United Church of Canada (in 1988) and the Norwegian Church (in 2000), have also followed suit.

The controversy over the admission of homosexuals to the priesthood came to the fore in the UK in June 2003 when Dr Jeffrey John, an acknowledged homosexual living a celibate life, was appointed Bishop of Reading. He eventually declined to take the post after his appointment caused a bitter row within the international Anglican Church. In August 2003 the rank and file of the Anglican Church in America voted to elect an openly gay bishop, Reverend Canon Gene Robinson of New Hampshire. A conservative lobby group, Anglican Mainstream, was created to lobby against the appointment of gay clergy and the issue remains unresolved.

See chapter 14, 'Sexuality and Gender', for a wider discussion of sexuality and identities.

Secularization and religious revival

Secularization

As we have seen, one view shared by early sociological thinkers was that traditional religion would become more and more marginal to the modern world. Marx, Durkheim and Weber all theorized that a process of secularization was bound to occur as societies modernized and became more reliant on science and technology to control and explain the social world. **Secularization** describes the process whereby religion loses its influence over the various spheres of social life. For example, figure 16.2 uses data from surveys of ten West European countries in which secularization took hold relatively early. It shows that weekly church attendance in these countries dropped significantly over the twentieth century, but seems to have stabilized at around 5 per cent. The survey also shows that the drop in religious belief has not been as dramatic as church attendance, which tends to support the picture of Western Europe as a region of 'belief without belonging' (Davie 1994).

As we will see though, the debate over the secularization thesis is one of the most complex areas in the sociology of religion. In the most basic terms, there is disagreement between supporters of the thesis – who agree with sociology's founding fathers and see religion as diminishing in power and importance in the modern world – and opponents of the concept, who argue that religion remains a significant force, albeit often in new and unfamiliar forms.

The enduring popularity of new religious movements presents a challenge to the secularization thesis. Opponents of the thesis point to the diversity and dynamism of new religious movements and argue that religion and spirituality remain a central facet of modern life. As traditional religions lose their hold, religion is not disappearing, but is being channelled in new directions. Not all scholars agree, however. Proponents of the idea of secularization point out that

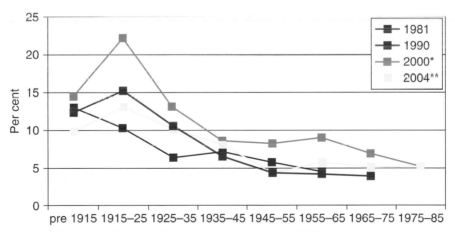

* Data for 2000 uses Norway responses from 1997
** Data for 2004 from ESS which uses same question but different methodolgy

Figure 16.2   Weekly attendance by cohort and generation in 10 West European countries, 1981, 1990, 2000, 2004

Source: Kaufman 2007

these movements remain peripheral to society as a whole, even if they make a profound impact on the lives of their individual followers. New religious movements are fragmented and relatively unorganized; they also suffer from high turnover rates as people are attracted to a movement for some time and then move on to something new. Compared to a serious religious commitment, they argue, participation in a new religious movement appears little more than a hobby or lifestyle choice.

The sociological debate

Secularization is a complex sociological concept, in part because there is little consensus about how the process should be measured. Moreover, many sociologists employ definitions of religion which do not coincide – while some argue that religion is best understood in terms of the traditional church, others argue that a much broader view must be taken to include dimensions such as personal spirituality and deep commitment to certain values. These differences in perception will necessarily influence arguments for or against secularization.

Secularization can be evaluated according to a number of aspects or dimensions. Some of them are objective in nature, such as the *level of membership* of religious organizations. Statistics and official records can show how many people belong to a church or other religious body and are active in attending services or other ceremonies. As we shall see, with the exception of the USA, most of the industrialized countries have experienced considerable secularization according to this index. The pattern of religious decline seen in Britain is found in most of Western Europe, including Catholic countries such as France or Italy. More Italians than French attend church regularly and participate in the major rituals (such as Easter communion), but the overall pattern of declining religious observance is similar in both cases.

A second dimension of secularization concerns how far churches and other religious organizations maintain their *social influence*, *wealth* and *prestige*. In earlier times, religious organizations could wield considerable influence over governments and social agencies, and commanded high respect in the community. How far is this still the case? The answer to the question is clear. Even if we confine ourselves to the last century, we see that religious organizations have progressively lost much of the social and political influence they previously had – and the trend is worldwide, although there are some exceptions. Church leaders can no longer automatically expect to be influential with the powerful. While some established churches remain very wealthy by any standards, and new religious movements may rapidly build up fortunes, the material circumstances of many long-standing religious organizations are insecure. Churches and temples have to be sold off, or are in a state of disrepair.

The third dimension of secularization concerns beliefs and values. We can call this the dimension of *religiosity*. Levels of church-going and the degree of social influence of churches are obviously not necessarily a direct expression of the beliefs or ideals people hold. Many who have religious beliefs do not regularly attend services or take part in public ceremonies; conversely, regularity of such attendance or participation does not always imply the holding of strong religious views – people may attend out of habit or because it is expected of them in their community.

As in the other dimensions of secularization, we need an accurate understanding of the past to see how far religiosity has declined today. Supporters of the secularization thesis argue that, in the past, religion was far more important to people's daily lives than it is today. The church was at the heart of local affairs and was a strong influence within family and personal life. Yet critics of the thesis contest this idea, arguing that just because people attended

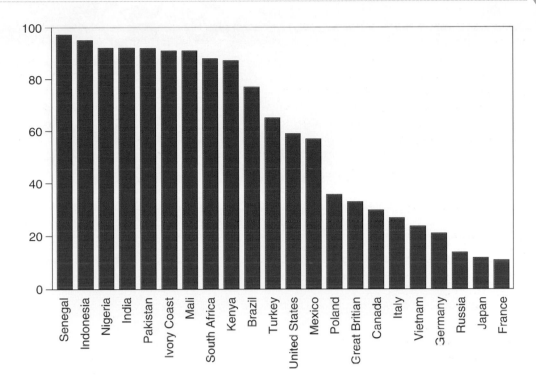

Figure 16.3 The importance given to religion in selected countries (percentage of adult population saying religion is 'very important' in their lives)

Source: Pew Forum on Religion and Public Life 2002

church more regularly does not necessarily prove that they were more religious. In many traditional societies, including medieval Europe, commitment to religious belief was less strong and less important in day-to-day life than might be supposed. Research into English history, for example, shows that lukewarm commitment to religious beliefs was common among the ordinary people. Religious sceptics seem to have been found in most cultures, particularly in the larger traditional societies (Ginzburg 1980).

Yet there can be no doubt at all that the hold of religious ideas today is less than was generally the case in the traditional world – particularly if we include under the term 'religion' the whole range of the supernatural in which people believed. Most of us simply do not any longer experience our environment as permeated by divine or spiritual entities. Some of the major tensions in the world today – like those afflicting the Middle East, Chechnya and Sudan – derive primarily, or in some part, from religious differences. But the majority of conflicts and wars are now mainly secular in nature – concerned with divergent political creeds or material interests.

Nonetheless, if we take Durkheim's characterization of religion as the representation of society's moral rules and collective existence, then an alternative view of secularization emerges. Drawing on Durkheim's ideas, French sociologist Michel Maffesoli (1995) has theorized that we live in the 'time of the tribes'.

Arguing against theories of a growing individualization (such as in the work of Giddens and Beck) and those older theories of a mass society which brings uniformity and the loss of difference, Maffesoli suggests that modern societies are in fact characterized by the rapid growth of small

Skateboarding has become a popular activity amongst young people, but according to Maffesoli, the subculture it generates can also be seen as a 'neo-tribe', which fulfils the members' need for sociability.

groupings of people who band together on the basis of shared musical tastes, ideas, consumer preferences, leisure pursuits and so on. These groups he calls 'neo-tribes' or 'new' tribes. They are like traditional tribes because their existence is based on a shared identity, but they are unlike traditional tribes because they do not have the same longevity. People's commitment to neo-tribes tends to be quite weak, short-lived and they are therefore quite fluid and fragile social entities.

However, Maffesoli's point is that the creation of neo-tribes demonstrates that there remains a very strong human need and quest for social contact and interaction, which does not support either theories of excessive individualization or those of mass society. And this underlying and continual search for human sociability is, in Durkheim's terms at least, a religious search. The old Gods may well be in decline, but there may (still) be 'something eternal in religion'.

> ### THINKING CRITICALLY
>
> The theory of secularization is 'essentially contested'; sociologists still disagree about its real extent and future prospects. If you were to design a research study aimed at resolving this disagreement, what would be your main research questions and what kind of empirical evidence would you collect, which both pro- and anti-secularization theorists might accept as legitimate?

Bearing in mind these three dimensions of secularization, let us review some recent trends in religion in Europe and the United States and consider how they support or contradict the idea of secularization.

Religion in Europe

The influence of Christianity was a crucial element in the evolution of Europe as a political unit. One possible border to what we now define as Europe is down the line of the first great split in European Christian thought in the eleventh century, between Catholic and Eastern Orthodox forms of Christianity. Orthodox Christianity is still the dominant religion in many East European countries, including Bulgaria, Belarus, Cyprus, Georgia, Greece, Romania, Russia, Serbia and Ukraine.

In Western Europe the division of the continent into Catholic and Protestant in the sixteenth century marked a second great rupture in Christian thought. This process, known as the Reformation, is inseparable from the division of Western Europe into the relatively stable patchwork of modern nation-states that we still see on the map today. Very broadly, Western Europe divided itself into a Protestant North (Scandinavia and Scotland), a Catholic South (which includes Spain, Portugal, Italy and France, as well as Belgium and Ireland further north) and several more or less denominationally mixed countries (including Britain and Northern Ireland, the Netherlands and Germany).

The Reformation took different forms in different countries, but was unified by the attempt to escape the influence of the Pope and the Catholic Church. A variety of denominations of Protestantism, and relations between Church and State, emerged in Europe. Below we give a brief sketch of religion in some of the major Western European nations.

The Nordic countries (Sweden, Norway, Denmark, Finland and Iceland) have a state church (the Lutheran State Church of Northern Europe). The population is characterized by a high rate of church membership, but a low level of both religious practice and acceptance of Christian beliefs. These countries have been described as 'belonging without believing'. Particularly in Sweden the close relationship between Church and State is now being questioned. Many people find the idea of a church that is specially privileged by the state inappropriate in an increasingly ethnically and culturally diverse country.

Germany can still be characterized as being divided between Catholicism and Protestantism. However, this is now challenged – first, by a growing Muslim population and, second, by an increase in the number of people who claim no religious allegiance. This second point is partly explained by the reunification of East and West Germany after the fall of the Berlin Wall in 1989, and the suppression of Christianity in the former Communist countries of Eastern Europe, including East Germany.

France is largely a Catholic country, but it is far more like the Protestant countries of Northern Europe in demonstrating low levels of religious belief and practices (see table 16.1). Of all the countries of Western Europe, France has the strictest separation between Church and State. The French state is strictly secular and refuses to privilege any religion or denomination. This takes in the exclusion of discussion of religion in all state institutions, including a ban on religious education in state-run schools. This strict separation between Church and State also led to the controversial ban on 'conspicuous' religious items in French school which came into place in September 2004, and particularly affected those Muslim girls who wore headscarves.

The *United Kingdom* is a predominantly Protestant country and the 2001 Census reported that some 72 per cent of people described themselves as Christians. Islam is the next most common faith, with almost 3 per cent of the population describing themselves as Muslims. Other significant groups include Hindus, Sikhs, Jews and Buddhists, each accounting for less than 1 per cent of the total population. The extent to which people identified with a religion varied around the UK, with 86 per cent identifying with a religion in Northern

Table 16.1	Adult (aged 15+) attendance at religious services, selected European countries 2002
Country	**%**
Poland	75.5
Ireland	67.2
Greece	54.6
Portugal	46.9
Italy	44.1
Austria	35.3
Slovenia	30.0
Spain	28.9
Netherlands	20.9
Germany	20.1
Belgium	18.9
UK	18.6
Hungary	18.2
France	14.2
Denmark	9.3

Source: Compiled from Ashworth and Farthing 2007

Ireland, 77 per cent in England and 67 per cent in Scotland. Some 16 per cent – mainly atheists and agnostics – said they had no religion.

Although over 70 per cent of the UK population describe themselves as Christian, a far smaller number attend church regularly. The 1851 Census of religion found about 40 per cent of adults in England and Wales attended church each Sunday, but by 1900 this had dropped to 35 per cent, by 1950 to 20 per cent and by 2000 to just 8 per cent. There are now signs that this trend is slowing, and the general decline in church attendance is unevenly spread. Among ethnic minority populations, attendance at church and religious services has been rising and a number of 'new religious movements' have also attracted followers in Britain.

In the UK, older people are more religious than those in younger age groups. Church-going among young people reaches a peak at the age of 15, after which average levels of attendance slump until people reach their 30s and 40s and enthusiasm is revived; church-going thereafter rises with increasing age. Women are more likely to be involved in organized religion than men. In Anglican churches this is only marginally the case, but in Christian Science churches, for example, women outnumber men by four to one. Religious participation also varies widely according to where people live: 35 per cent of adults in Merseyside and 32 per cent in Lancashire are church members, compared with only 9 per cent in Humberside and 11 per cent in Nottinghamshire. One reason for this is immigration – Liverpool has a large population of Irish Catholics, just as North London is a focus for Jews and Bradford for Muslims and Sikhs.

Italy, *Spain* and *Portugal* are largely Catholic. They demonstrate higher levels of religious belief and practice than most other European countries, especially those in the north. The Catholic Church, based inside Italy, enjoys a high level of influence in all these countries. In Italy, Catholicism is privileged above other denominations and religions. In Spain, the Catholic Church was instrumental in supporting the political right in the civil war which led to General Franco's dictatorship between 1939 and 1975. There is no official link between State and Church in Spain, although the Catholic Church is privileged by its dominance in terms of numbers. In Portugal, despite some constitutional reform in the 1970s, the Catholic Church still has a degree of influence in law (Davie 2000).

Religious minorities

Europe is also home to sizeable non-Christian religious minorities. Although Jews have been present in Europe for centuries, their recent history has been bound up

Global Society 16.1 | In Poland, a Jewish revival thrives – minus Jews

Krakow, Poland. There is a curious thing happening in this old country, scarred by Nazi death camps, raked by pogroms and blanketed by numbing Soviet sterility: Jewish culture is beginning to flourish again.

'Jewish-style' restaurants are serving up platters of pirogis, klezmer bands are playing plaintive Oriental melodies, derelict synagogues are gradually being restored. Every June, a festival of Jewish culture here draws thousands of people to sing Jewish songs and dance Jewish dances. The only thing missing, really, are Jews.

'It's a way to pay homage to the people who lived here, who contributed so much to Polish culture', said Janusz Makuch, founder and director of the annual festival and himself the son of a Catholic family.

Jewish communities are gradually reawakening across Eastern Europe as Jewish schools introduce a new generation to rituals and beliefs suppressed by the Nazis and then by Communism. At summer camps, thousands of Jewish teenagers from across the former Soviet bloc gather for crash courses in Jewish culture, celebrating Passover, Hanukkah and Purim – all in July.

Even in Poland, there are now two Jewish schools, synagogues in several major cities and at least four rabbis. But with relatively few Jews, Jewish culture in Poland is being embraced and promoted by the young and the fashionable.

Before Hitler's horror, Poland had the largest Jewish population in Europe, about 3.5 million souls. One in ten Poles was Jewish. More than three million Polish Jews died in the Holocaust. Post-war pogroms and a 1968 anti-Jewish purge forced out most of those who survived.

Probably about 70 per cent of the world's European Jews, or Ashkenazi, can trace their ancestry to Poland — thanks to a fourteenth-century king, Casimir III, the Great, who drew Jewish settlers from across Europe with his vow to protect them as 'people of the king'. But there are only 10,000 self-described Jews living today in this country of 39 million.

Source: Adapted from the *New York Times*, 12 July 2007

The Hasidic 'dance of happiness', pictured here at a wedding in Jerusalem, is one of the mainstays of the annual Jewish festival in Krakow. This celebrates the traditions of the 3.5 million Jews who lived in Poland before the Holocaust. In June 2007, 20,000 people attended, though few of them were Jewish.

with anti-Semitic discrimination and genocide.

In the years after the Second Word War, many Jews who had survived the holocaust left Europe for the newly created state of Israel. These factors meant that the number of Jews living in Europe fell dramatically during the twentieth century from 9.6 million in 1937 to fewer than 2 million by the mid-1990s (as table 16.2 shows).

> Racism and discrimination are discussed in more detail in chapter 15, 'Race, Ethnicity and Migration'.

In the twentieth century, global migration, partly shaped by Europe's colonial history, has also led to the development of sizeable non-Judeo-Christian minorities across the whole of the European continent for the first time. Of these, Islam is by far the largest non-Christian faith, with some 20 million members in the European Union (eumap.org, 2007). The colonial links between France and North Africa account for a sizeable French Muslim population of three to four million. Germany, by contrast, has large numbers of Muslim migrant workers from Turkey and South-East Europe. Britain's Muslim population, as we shall see below, comes largely from the former British Empire countries of the Indian subcontinent (Davie 2000; figure 16.4 shows the migration of Muslims into Europe and their country of origin).

Religion in the United States

Compared to the citizens of other industrial nations, Americans are unusually religious. With few exceptions, 'the United States has been the most God-believing and religion-adhering, fundamentalist, and religiously traditional country in Christendom [where] more new religions have been born . . than [in] any other country' (Lipset 1991). According to public opinion polls, around three out of every five Americans say that religion is 'very important' in their own life, and at any given time around 40 per cent will have been to church in the previous week (Gallup 2004). The overwhelming majority of Americans reportedly believe in God and claim they regularly pray one or more times a day (Pew Forum on Religion and Public Life 2002). Seven out of ten Americans report that they believe in an afterlife (Roof and McKinney 1990; Warner 1993).

About 52 per cent of Americans identify themselves as Protestants and 24 per cent as Catholics. Other significant religious groups include Mormons, Muslims and Jews (Pew Forum on Religion and Public Life 2002). The Catholic Church has shown by far the largest increase in membership, partly because of the immigration of Catholics from Mexico and Central and South America. Yet the growth in Catholic Church membership has also slowed in recent years, as some followers have drifted away. The papal encyclical of 1968, which reaffirmed the ban on the use of contraceptives among Catholics, appears to have pushed many Catholics, especially women, to question the Church's authority. For example, one survey found that 50 per cent of American Catholics now reject the notion that the Pope is infallible when he teaches on matters of morals, such as birth control and abortion (Gallup 2004).

In recent decades, the composition of the Protestant Church in America has also changed. Membership of the liberal or mainstream American churches, such as the Lutherans, Episcopalians (Anglicans), Methodists and Presbyterians, is in decline. But there has been an increase in the membership of conservative, non-traditional, Protestant churches, such as Pentecostalists and the Southern Baptists (Roof and McKinney 1990; Jones et al. 2002). This shows the growing strength of conservative Protestants in the United States.

Conservative Protestants emphasize a literal interpretation of the Bible, morality in daily life and conversion through evangelizing. Twice as many people belong to conservative Protestant groups as they do to liberal

Table 16.2 Jewish populations in Europe, 1937–94

	1937	1946	1967	1994
Austria	191,000	31,000[a]	12,500	7,000
Belgium	65,000	45,000	40,500	31,800
Bulgaria	49,000	44,200	5,000	1,900
Czechoslovakia	357,000	55,000	15,000	7,600[b]
Denmark	8,500	5,500	6,000	6,400
Estonia[c]	4,600	–	–	3,500
Finland	2,000	2,000	1,750	1,300
France	300,000	225,000	535,000	530,000
Germany	500,000	153,000[a]	30,000	55,000
Great Britain	330,000	370,000	400,000	295,000
Greece	77,000	10,000	6,500	4,800
Hungary	400,000	145,000	80,000	56,000
Ireland (Republic)	5,000	3,900	2,900	1,200
Italy	48,000	53,000[a]	35,000	31,000
Latvia	95,000	–	–	18,000
Lithuania[c]	155,000	–	–	6,500
Luxembourg	3,500	500	500	600
Netherlands	140,000	28,000	30,000	25,000
Norway	2,000	750	1,000	1,000
Poland	3,250,000	215,000	21,000	6,000
Portugal	n/a	4,000	1,000	300
Romania	850,000	420,000	100,000	10,000
Spain	n/a	6,000	6,000	12,000
Sweden	7,500	15,500	13,000	16,500
Switzerland	18,000	35,000	20,000	19,000
Turkey[d]	50,000	48,000	35,000	18,000
USSR/CIS[d]	2,669,000	1,971,000	1,715,000	812,000
Yugoslavia	71,000	12,000	7,000	3,500[e]
Total	9,648,100	3,898,350	3,119,650	1,980,900

Note: These figures, collated from many sources, are of varying reliability and in some cases are subject to a wide margin of error and interpretation. This warning applies particularly to the figures for 1946, a year in which there was considerable Jewish population movement. It must also be borne in mind that the boundaries of many European countries changed between 1937 and 1946.

n/a = not available.

[a] Includes 'Displaced Persons'. [b] Total for Czech Republic and Slovakia. [c] Baltic States included in USSR between 1941 and 1991. [d] Excludes Asiatic regions. [e] Total for former Yugoslavia.

Source: Wasserstein 1996; reproduced in Davie 2000: 123

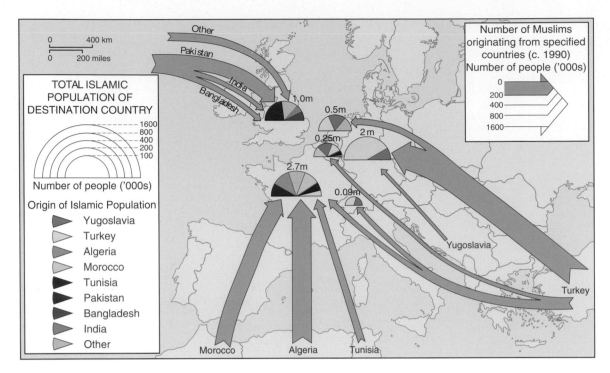

Figure 16.4   Number of European Muslims originating from specified countries and total Islamic population of European destination countries, *c.* 1990

Source: Vertovec and Peach 1997; reproduced in Davie 2000: 128. Reproduced with permission of Palgrave Macmillan

ones, and conservative Protestants may soon outnumber moderates as well (Roof and McKinney 1990). The ageing members of the liberal Protestant denominations have not been replaced by new young followers, commitment is low and some current members are switching to other faiths. Black Protestant churches also continue to thrive in the United States, as their members move into the middle class and gain a degree of economic and political prominence (Roof and McKinney 1990; Finke and Stark 1992).

The Protestant Church in the USA has also seen a huge rise in **evangelicalism**, the belief in spiritual rebirth (being 'born again'). Evangelicalism can be seen in part as a response to growing secularism, religious diversity and, in general, the decline of once core Protestant values in American life (Wuthnow 1988). In recent years, there has been an enormous growth in evangelical denominations, paralleled by a decline in the more mainstream Protestant religious affiliations. Many Protestants are clearly seeking the more direct, personal and emotional religious experience promised by evangelical denominations. President George W. Bush is a born-again Christian and has said that his faith helped him to overcome a drink problem earlier in life and to start afresh. Bush's born-again Christianity is reflected in his conservative views on gay marriage and abortion. His evangelical religious values were vital in helping him to win a second term as President in November 2004, when he gained the support of the majority of evangelical Christians in the USA who saw these moral issues as crucial.

Evangelical organizations are good at mobilizing resources to help achieve their

The USA has witnessed a dramatic growth in evangelicalism. The support of evangelical Christians helped George W. Bush into power in 2000 and 2004.

religious and political objectives, as the 2004 presidential election demonstrated. In the business-like language used by the religious economists, they have proved to be extremely competitive 'spiritual entrepreneurs' in the 'religious marketplace' (Hatch 1989; also see 'Using your sociological imagination 16.1'). Radio and television have provided important new marketing technologies, used by some evangelicals to reach a much wider audience than was previously possible. Called 'televangelists' because they conduct their evangelical ministries via television, these ministers depart from many earlier evangelicals by preaching a 'gospel of prosperity': the belief that God wants the faithful to be financially prosperous and satisfied, rather than to sacrifice and suffer. This approach differs considerably from the austere emphasis on hard work and self-denial ordinarily associated with traditional conservative Protestant beliefs (Hadden and Shupe 1987; Bruce 1990). Luxurious houses of worship, epitomized by Robert H. Schuller's Crystal Cathedral in Garden Grove, California, provide the televised settings for electronic churches, whose congregants are geographically dispersed and are united primarily by means of electronic technology. Theology and fundraising are the staples of televangelism, which must support not only the television ministries themselves, but also schools, universities, theme parks and sometimes the lavish lifestyles of its preachers.

The electronic preaching of religion has become particularly prevalent in Latin

America, where North American television programmes are shown. As a result, Protestant movements, most of them of the Pentecostal kind, have made a dramatic impact on such countries as Chile and Brazil, which are predominantly Catholic (Martin 1990).

THINKING CRITICALLY

The religious economy approach suggests that religion is continually renewed through competition. How could such an approach help us to understand the process of secularization in the industrialized world? What does religious economy tell us, if anything, about the role of spirituality in human affairs?

Although some evangelicals combine a thoroughly modern lifestyle with traditional religious beliefs, others strongly reject many contemporary beliefs and practices. Fundamentalists are evangelicals who are anti-modern in many of their beliefs, calling for strict codes of morality and conduct. These frequently include taboos against drinking, smoking and other 'worldly evils', a belief in biblical infallibility and a strong emphasis on Christ's impending return to earth (Balmer 1989). Their 'old-time religion' clearly distinguishes good from evil and right from wrong (Roof and McKinney 1990).

In the debate on secularization, the United States represents an important exception to the view that religion is generally declining in Western societies. While, on the one hand, the USA is one of the most thoroughly 'modernized' countries, it is, on the other, characterized by some of the highest levels of popular religious belief and membership in the world. How can we account for this American exceptionalism?

Steve Bruce (1996), one of the leading advocates of the secularization thesis, has argued that the persistence of religion in the USA can be understood in terms of cultural transition. In cases where societies undergo rapid and profound demographic or economic change, Bruce suggests, religion can play a critical role in helping people adjust to new conditions and survive instability. Industrialization came relatively late to the United States and proceeded very quickly, he argues, among a population that was composed of a great diversity of ethnic groups. In the USA, religion was important in stabilizing people's identities and allowed a smoother cultural transition into the American 'melting pot'.

Evaluating the secularization thesis

There is little question among sociologists that, considered as a long-term trend, religion in the traditional church has declined in most Western countries – with the notable exception of the USA. The influence of religion has diminished along each of the three dimensions of secularization, much as nineteenth-century sociologists predicted it would. Should we conclude that they and later proponents of the secularization thesis were correct? Has the appeal of religion lost its grasp with the deepening of modernity? Such a conclusion would be questionable for a number of reasons.

First, the present position of religion in Britain and other Western countries is much more complex than supporters of the secularization thesis suggest. Religious and spiritual belief remain powerful and motivating forces in many people's lives, even if they do not choose to worship formally through the framework of the traditional church. Some scholars have suggested that there has been a move towards 'believing without belonging' (Davie 1994) – as we have seen in our discussion of religious belief in the UK, people maintain a belief in God or a higher force, but practise and develop their faith outside institutionalized forms of religion.

USING YOUR SOCIOLOGICAL IMAGINATION

16.1 Competition in the religious economy?

One of the most recent and influential approaches to the sociology of religion is tailored to Western societies, and particularly the United States, which offers many different faiths from which to pick and choose. Taking their cue from economic theory, sociologists who favour the religious economy approach argue that religions can be fruitfully understood as organizations in competition with one another for followers (Stark and Bainbridge 1987; Finke and Stark 1988, 1992; Moore 1994).

Like contemporary economists who study businesses, these sociologists argue that competition is preferable to monopoly when it comes to ensuring religious vitality. This position is exactly opposite to those of the classical theorists. Marx, Durkheim and Weber assumed that religion weakens when it is challenged by different religious or secular viewpoints, whereas the religious economists argue that competition increases the overall level of religious involvement in modern society. Religious economists believe this to be true for two reasons. First, competition makes each religious group try that much harder to win followers. Second, the presence of numerous religions means that there is likely to be something for just about everyone. In culturally diverse societies a single religion will probably appeal to only a limited range of followers, while the presence of Indian gurus and fundamentalist preachers, in addition to more traditional churches, is likely to encourage a high level of religious participation.

This analysis is adapted from the business world, in which competition presumably encourages the emergence of highly specialized products that appeal to the very specific markets. In fact, the religious economists borrow the language of business in describing the conditions that lead to the success or failure of a particular religious organization. According to Roger Finke and Rodney Stark (1992), a successful religious group must be well organized for competition, have eloquent preachers who are effective

Many 'televangelists' preach a gospel of prosperity rather than austerity, departing from traditional Protestant beliefs. They have proved to be particularly effective businesspeople in selling their religious products.

'sales reps' in spreading the word, offer beliefs and rituals that are packaged as an appealing product, and develop effective marketing techniques. Religion, in this view, is a business much like any other.

Thus religious economists such as Finke and Stark do not see competition as undermining religious beliefs and thus contributing to secularization. Rather, they argue that modern religion is constantly renewing itself through active marketing and recruitment. Although there is a growing body of research that supports the notion that competition is good for religion (Stark and Bainbridge 1980, 1985; Finke and Stark 1992), not all research comes to this conclusion (Land et al. 1991).

The religious economy approach overestimates the extent to which people rationally pick and choose among different religions, as if they were shopping around for a new car or pair of shoes. Among deeply committed believers, particularly in societies that lack religious pluralism, it is not obvious that religion is a matter of rational choice. In such societies, even when people are allowed to choose among different religions, most are likely to practise their childhood religion without ever questioning whether or not there are more appealing alternatives. Even in the United States, where the religious economy approach originated, sociologists may overlook the spiritual aspects of religion if they simply assume that religious buyers are always on spiritual shopping sprees. A study of baby boomers in the USA (the generation born in the two decades after the end of the Second World War) found that a third had remained loyal to their childhood faith, while another third had continued to profess their childhood beliefs although they no longer belonged to a religious organization. Thus only a third were actively looking around for a new religion, making the sorts of choice presumed by the religious economy approach (Roof 1993).

Second, secularization cannot be measured according to membership in mainstream Trinitarian churches alone. To do so discounts the growing role of non-Western faiths and new religious movements, both internationally and within industrialized societies. In Britain, for example, active membership within traditional churches is falling, yet participation among Muslims, Hindus, Sikhs, Jews, evangelical 'born-again' believers and Orthodox Christians remains dynamic.

Third, there seems to be little evidence of secularization in non-Western societies. In many areas of the Middle East, Asia, Africa and India, a vital and dynamic Islamic fundamentalism challenges Westernization. When the Pope toured South America, millions of Catholics there enthusiastically followed his progress. Eastern Orthodoxy has been enthusiastically re-embraced by citizens in parts of the former Soviet Union after decades of repression of the Church by the Communist leadership. This enthusiastic support for religion around the globe is, unfortunately, mirrored by religiously inspired conflicts as well. Just as religion can be a source of solace and support, it has also been – and continues to be – at the origin of intense social struggles and conflicts.

One can point to evidence both in favour of and against the idea of secularization. It seems clear that, as a concept, it is most useful in explaining changes that are occurring within the traditional churches today – both in terms of declining power and influence and in regard to internal secularizing processes affecting, for example, the role of women and gays. Modernizing forces in society at large are being felt within many traditional religious institutions.

> **THINKING CRITICALLY**
>
> Why do you think many migrant groups display higher levels of religiosity and church attendance than the rest of the population? What factors can you identify which might explain the 'alarming decline in the number of children and young people in church'? What social changes have led to young people not attending churches in large numbers?

Above all, however, religion in the late modern world should be evaluated against a backdrop of rapid change, instability and diversity. Even if traditional forms of religion are receding to a degree, religion still remains a critical force in our social world. The appeal of religion, in its traditional and novel forms, is likely to be long-lasting. Religion provides many people with insights into complex questions about life and meaning that cannot be answered satisfactorily with rationalist perspectives.

It is not surprising, then, that during these times of rapid change, many people look for – and find – answers and calm in religion. Fundamentalism is perhaps the clearest example of this phenomenon. Yet, increasingly, religious responses to change are occurring in new and unfamiliar forms: new religious movements, cults, sects and 'New Age' activities. While these groups may not 'look like' forms of religion on the surface, many critics of the secularization hypothesis argue that they represent transforma-

USING YOUR SOCIOLOGICAL IMAGINATION

16.2 Migration and religion

The rate of decline in church attendance has been slowed by an unexpected factor – the influx of Christians from Africa and Europe. One of the biggest surveys among Britain's 37,000 churches, published today, finds that the growth of immigrant-led churches has partly offset dwindling congregations elsewhere [Brierly 2006]. The news will cheer Church leaders. The Archbishop of Canterbury, Dr Rowan Williams, said the phenomenon was having a healthy impact on mainstream churches.

But the survey also shows that congregations are getting older as young people continue to abandon the pews, which could have a devastating impact in a decade. The 2005 English Church Census, carried out by the independent Christian Research Organization, finds that, between 1998 and 2005, half a million people stopped going to a Christian church on Sunday. The figure is lower than expected because a million left in the previous nine years.

The survey finds that black led Pentecostal churches in immigrant communities gained about 100,000 worshippers since 1998.

Although churches of all denominations and sizes have stemmed their losses, most growth has occurred in the larger charismatic and evangelical churches. The research shows that black people now make up 10 per cent of all Sunday churchgoers in England, while other non-white ethnic groups add a further 7 per cent. In inner London, fewer than half the worshippers are white, with black Christians accounting for 44 per cent of churchgoers and non-white ethnic groups 14 per cent. The impact of Roman Catholic Croatians and Poles and Orthodox Russians and Greeks has been significant.

The findings will give the churches hope that they are pulling out of the decline they have been in for decades. Overall, however, they are losing far more than they are gaining. While 1,000 new people are joining a church each week, 2,500 are leaving. Just 6.3 per cent of the population goes to church on an average Sunday, compared with 7.5 per cent in 1998, although more people are going midweek.

Dr Williams, who wrote the foreword to the research, said one of its most striking findings was the number of thriving churches started by immigrant communities. 'This is having a big impact on our major cities, where the black majority churches are growing fast', he said. 'People from ethnic minorities are also bringing new life and energy into churches from established denominations such as the Church of England. This is one of the reasons why the Anglican Diocese of London, for example, is now growing steadily.' However, the Archbishop acknowledged that the mainstream denominations faced serious problems as the average worshipper was getting older.

The research, based on questionnaires from 19,000 churches, finds that 29 per cent of church-goers are 65 or over compared with 16 per cent of the population. It also finds that 9 per cent of churches have no one under the age of 11 in their congregations. 'The last English Church Census, carried out in 1998, showed an alarming decline in the number of children and young people in church', said Dr Williams. 'These latest results suggest we have yet to reverse this, but at least the rate of change has slowed.'

Source: Jonathan Petre, *Daily Telegraph*, 19 September 2006

tions of religious belief in the face of profound social change.

Religious fundamentalism

The strength of religious fundamentalism is another indication that secularization has not triumphed in the modern world. The term **fundamentalism** can be applied in many different contexts to describe strict adherence to a set of principles or beliefs. Religious fundamentalism describes the approach taken by religious groups, which call for the literal interpretation of basic scriptures or texts and believe that the doctrines which emerge from such readings should be applied to all aspects of social, economic and political life.

Religious fundamentalists believe that only one view – their own – of the world is possible, and that this view is the correct one: there is no room for ambiguity or multiple interpretations. Within religious fundamentalist movements, access to the exact meanings of scriptures is restricted to a set of privileged 'interpreters' – such as priests, clergy or other religious leaders. This gives these leaders a great amount of authority – not only in religious matters, but in secular ones as well. Religious fundamentalists have become powerful political figures in opposition movements, within mainstream political parties and as heads of state.

Religious fundamentalism is a relatively new phenomenon – it is only in the last two to three decades that the term has entered common usage. It has arisen largely in response to globalization. As the forces of modernization progressively undermine traditional elements of the social world – such as the nuclear family and the domination of women by men – fundamentalism has arisen in defence of traditional beliefs. In a globalizing world which demands rational reasons, fundamentalism insists on faith-based answers and references to ritual truth: fundamentalism is tradition defended in a traditional way. It has more to do with how beliefs are defended and justified than with the content of the beliefs themselves.

Although fundamentalism sets itself in opposition to modernity, it also employs modern approaches in asserting its beliefs. Christian fundamentalists in the United States, for example, were among the first to use television as a medium for spreading their doctrines; Islamic fundamentalists fighting Russian forces in Chechnya have developed websites to set forth their views; Hindutva militants in India have used the Internet and email to promote a feeling of 'Hindu identity'.

In this section we will examine two of the most prominent forms of religious fundamentalism: Islamic and Christian. In the past 30 years, both have grown in strength, shaping the contours of national and international politics.

Islamic fundamentalism

Of the early sociological thinkers, only Weber might have suspected that a traditional religious system like Islam could undergo a major revival and become the basis of important political developments in the late twentieth century; yet this is exactly what occurred in the 1980s in Iran. In recent years, Islamic revivalism has spread, with a significant impact on other countries, including Egypt, Syria, Lebanon, Algeria, Afghanistan and Nigeria. What explains this large-scale renewal of Islam?

To understand the phenomenon, we have to look both to aspects of Islam as a traditional religion and to secular changes that have affected modern states where its influence is pervasive. Islam, like Christianity, is a religion that has continually stimulated activism: the Koran – the Islamic holy scripture – is full of instructions to believers to 'struggle in the way of God'. This struggle is against both unbelievers and those who introduce corruption into the Muslim community. Over the centuries there have been successive generations of Muslim reformers, and Islam has become as internally divided as Christianity.

Shiism split from the main body of orthodox Islam early in its history and has remained influential. Shiism has been the official religion of Iran (earlier known as Persia) since the sixteenth century, and was the source of the ideas behind the Iranian revolution. The Shiites trace their beginnings to Imam Ali, a seventh-century religious and political leader who is believed to have shown qualities of personal devotion to God and virtue outstanding among the worldly rulers of the time. Ali's descendants came to be seen as the rightful leaders of Islam, since they were held to belong to the prophet Muhammad's family, unlike the dynasties in power. The Shiites believed that the rule of Muhammad's rightful heir would eventually be instituted, doing away with the tyrannies and injustices associated with existing regimes. Muhammad's heir would be a leader directly guided by God, governing in accordance with the Koran.

There are large Shiite populations in other Middle Eastern countries, including Iraq, Turkey and Saudi Arabia, as well as in India and Pakistan. Islamic leadership in these countries, however, is in the hands of the majority, the *Sunni*. The Sunni Muslims follow the 'Beaten Path', a series of traditions deriving from the Koran which tolerate a considerable diversity of opinion, in contrast to the more rigidly defined views of the Shiites.

Islam and the West

During the Middle Ages, there was a more or less constant struggle between Christian Europe and the Muslim states, which controlled large sections of what became Spain, Greece, Yugoslavia, Bulgaria and Romania. Most of the lands conquered by the Muslims were reclaimed by the Europeans, and many of their possessions in North Africa were in fact colonized as Western power grew in the eighteenth and nineteenth centuries. These reverses were catastrophic for Muslim religion and civilization, which Islamic believers held to be the highest and most advanced possible, transcending all others. In the late nineteenth century, the inability of the Muslim world effectively to resist the spread of Western culture led to reform movements seeking to restore Islam to its original purity and strength. A key idea was that Islam should respond to the Western challenge by affirming the identity of its own beliefs and practices (Sutton and Vertigans 2005).

This idea has been developed in various ways in the twentieth century, and formed a backdrop to the Islamic revolution in Iran of 1978–9. The revolution was fuelled initially

The three most prominent leaders of the Islamic revolution in Iran – Ayatollah Khomeini (in the foreground), Ayatollah Ali Khamenei and the then President Hashemi Rafsanjani – look down from a poster over a street in Tehran.

by internal opposition to the Shah of Iran, who had accepted and tried to promote forms of modernization modelled on the West – for example, land reform, extending the vote to women and developing secular education. The movement that overthrew the Shah brought together people of diverse interests, by no means all of whom were attached to Islamic fundamentalism, but a dominant figure was the Ayatollah Khomeini, who provided a radical reinterpretation of Shiite ideas.

Following the revolution, Khomeini established a government organized according to traditional Islamic law. Religion, as specified in the Koran, became the

Was the conflict in the former Yugoslavia in the 1990s an example of 'civilizational conflict' rooted in religious beliefs and cultures?

direct basis of all political and economic life. Under Islamic law – sharia – as it was revived, men and women were kept rigorously segregated, women were obliged to cover their bodies and heads in public, practising homosexuals were sent to the firing squad and adulterers were stoned to death. The strict code is accompanied by a very nationalistic outlook, which sets itself especially against Western influences.

The aim of the Islamic Republic in Iran was to Islamicize the state – to organize government and society so that Islamic teachings would become dominant in all spheres. The process was by no means completed, however, and forces emerged to act against it. Zubaida (1996) has distinguished three sets of groups now engaged in struggle with one another. The radicals want to carry on with and deepen the Islamic

revolution; they also believe that the revolution should be actively exported to other Islamic countries. The conservatives are made up mostly of religious functionaries, who think that the revolution has gone far enough; it has given them a position of power in society which they wish to hold onto. The pragmatists favour market reforms and the opening up of the economy to foreign investment and trade; they oppose the strict imposition of Islamic codes on women, the family and the legal system.

The death of the Ayatollah Khomeini in 1989 was a blow to radical and conservative elements in Iran; his successor, Ayatollah Ali Khamenei, retains the loyalty of Iran's powerful mullahs (religious leaders), but is increasingly unpopular with average Iranian citizens, who resent the repressive regime and persistent social ills. The fault-lines within Iranian society between pragmatists and others came to the surface quite clearly under the reform-minded presidency of Mohammad Khatami (1997–2005). Khatami's administration was characterized by disputes with conservatives who largely managed to hamper Khatami's attempts at reform of Iranian society. In 2005, the election as President of Tehran's deeply conservative mayor, Mahmond Ahmadinejad, decreased tensions between the country's religious and political leadership, but increased tensions with the West.

The spread of Islamic revivalism

Although the ideas underlying the Iranian revolution were supposed to unite the whole of the Islamic world against the West, governments of countries where the Shiites are in a minority have not aligned themselves closely with the situation in Iran. Yet Islamic fundamentalism has achieved significant popularity in most of these other states, and various forms of Islamic revivalism elsewhere have been stimulated by it.

Though Islamic fundamentalist movements have gained influence in many countries in North Africa, the Middle East and South Asia over the past 10–15 years, they have succeeded in coming to power in only two other states: Sudan has been ruled since 1989 by the National Islamic Front; the fundamentalist Taliban regime consolidated its hold on the fragmented state of Afghanistan in 1996 but was ousted from power at the end of 2001 by Afghan opposition forces and the US military. In many other states, Islamic fundamentalist groups have gained influence but have been prevented from rising to power. In Egypt, Turkey and Algeria, for example, Islamic fundamentalist uprisings have been suppressed by the state or the military.

Many have worried that the Islamic world is heading for a confrontation with those parts of the world that do not share its beliefs. The political scientist Samuel Huntington (1996) argued that struggles between Western and Islamic views might become part of a worldwide 'clash of civilizations' with the ending of the Cold War and with increasing globalization. According to Huntington, the nation-state is no longer the main influence in international relations; rivalries and conflicts will therefore occur between larger cultures or civilizations.

Possible examples of such conflicts were seen during the 1990s in the former Yugoslavia, in Bosnia and in Kosovo, where the Bosnian Muslims and Albanian Kosovars fought against the Serbs, who represent an Orthodox Christian culture. Such events have heightened awareness of Muslims as a world community; as observers have noted: 'Bosnia has become a rallying point for Muslims throughout the Muslim world. . . [It] has created and sharpened the sense of polarization and radicalization in Muslim societies, while at the same time increasing the sense of being a Muslim' (Ahmed and Donnan 1994).

 The wars in the former Yugoslavia are discussed in more detail in chapter 23, 'Nations, War and Terrorism'.

In the same way, the American-led war in Iraq became a rallying point for radical Muslims after the invasion in 2003. As an explanation of the causes of the terrorist attacks on New York and Washington on 11 September 2001, the American decision to oust the Islamic regime in Afghanistan and the revival of religious resistance to the US presence in Iraq after 2003, Huntington's thesis gained widespread media attention.

However, critics point out that there are many political and cultural divisions *within* civilizations and the forecast of conflict between entire civilizations is unlikely and alarmist. For example, in 1990 Saddam Hussein's Sunni regime in Iraq invaded Kuwait, which also has a majority Sunni population, and between 1980 and 1988,

Iraq and Iran (with a majority Shi'a population) were engaged in armed conflict with each other. The number of 'civilizational conflicts' in the past can also be too easily exaggerated, as many apparently culturally defined conflicts have been more centrally focused on access to scarce resources and the struggles for political power and military dominance (Russett et al. 2000; Chiozza 2002). In such conflicts, it has been, and still is, much more common to see alliances forming across the borders of Huntington's large-scale civilizations.

At the start of the twenty-first century, Islamic opposition is still building up in states such as Malaysia and Indonesia, several provinces within Nigeria have recently implemented sharia law, and the war in Chechnya has attracted the participation of Islamic militants who support the establishment of an Islamic state in the Caucasus. Members of Osama bin Laden's al-Qaeda terrorist network come from all over the Muslim world. Islamic symbolism and forms of dress have become important markers of identity for the growing number of Muslims living outside the Islamic world. Events such as the Gulf War and the 9/11 terrorist attacks in New York and Washington have provoked variable but intense reactions within the Islamic world, either against or in response to the West.

> The phenomenon of terrorism is discussed further in chapter 23, 'Nations, War and Terrorism'.

Islamic revivalism plainly cannot be understood wholly in religious terms; it represents in part a reaction against the impact of the West and is a movement of national or cultural assertion. It is doubtful whether Islamic revivalism, even in its most fundamentalist forms (which remain a small minority of the revival as a whole), should be seen only as a renewal of traditionally held ideas. What has occurred is something more complex. Traditional prac-

tices and modes of life have been revived, but they have also been combined with concerns that relate specifically to modern times.

Christian fundamentalism

The growth of Christian fundamentalist religious organizations in Europe and, particularly, in the United States, is one of the most notable features of the past few decades. Fundamentalists believe that 'the Bible, quite bluntly, is a workable guidebook for politics, government, business, families, and all of the affairs of mankind' (Capps 1990). The Bible is taken as infallible by fundamentalists – its contents are expressions of the Divine Truth. Fundamentalist Christians believe in the divinity of Christ and in the possibility of the salvation of one's soul through the acceptance of Christ as personal saviour. Fundamentalist Christians are committed to spreading their message and converting those who have not yet adopted the same beliefs.

Christian fundamentalism is a reaction against liberal theology and supporters of 'secular humanism' – those who 'favour the emancipation of reason, desires and instincts in opposition to faith and obedience to God's command' (Kepel 1994). Christian fundamentalism sets itself against the 'moral crisis' wrought by modernization – the decline of the traditional family, the threat to individual morality and the weakening relationship between man and God.

In the United States, beginning with the Reverend Jerry Falwell's Moral Majority in the 1970s, some fundamentalist groups became increasingly involved in what has been termed the 'New Christian Right' in national politics, particularly in the conservative wing of the Republican Party (Simpson 1985; Woodrum 1988; Kiecolt and Nelson 1991). Falwell noted 'five major problems that have political consequences, that moral Americans should be ready to face: abortion, homosexuality, pornography, humanism, the fractured family' (in

Kepel 1994). Taking concrete action, the New Christian Right aimed first at the nation's schools, lobbying law-makers on the content of school curricula and trying to overturn the ban on prayer in school, and moved quickly to support Operation Rescue, the militant organization which blockades abortion clinics. Fundamentalist religious organizations are a powerful force in the USA and have helped to shape Republican Party policies and rhetoric during the Reagan and both Bush administrations.

Falwell initially blamed the 9/11 terrorist attacks against New York and Washington on 'sinners' in the USA. He commented on live television:

> I really believe that the pagans, and the abortionists, and the feminists, and the gays and the lesbians who are actively trying to make that an alternative lifestyle, the [American Civil Liberties Union], People For the American Way [both liberal organizations], all of them who have tried to secularize America. I point the finger in their face and say 'you helped this happen'. (CNN, 14 September 2001)

Although he later apologized for these remarks, he caused further controversy by stating that 'Mohammad was a terrorist. I read enough by both Muslims and non-Muslims [to decide] that he was a violent man, a man of war' (BBC, 13 October 2002). Again, he apologized for the remark, but it was too late to stop sectarian rioting between Hindus and Muslims reacting against his claims in Solapur, Western India, which left at least eight people dead. Not surprisingly, his comments led to widespread condemnation from Islamic leaders around the world.

Prominent preachers on the New Christian Right have founded a number of universities in the United States to produce a new generation 'counter-elite', schooled in fundamentalist Christian beliefs and able to take up prominent positions in the media, academia, politics and the arts. Liberty University (founded by Jerry Falwell), Oral Roberts University, Bob Jones University and others confer degrees in standard academic disciplines, taught within the framework of biblical infallibility. On campus, strict ethical standards are maintained within students' private lives and sexuality is channelled towards marriage alone. Giles Kepel (1994) says:

> To anybody who has spent some time on the Liberty campus, it is a striking spectacle. The dormitories are single-sex, and strict surveillance, a mixture of coercion and self-discipline, is practised. French kissing is forbidden, and any sexual relations between unmarried students are punished by expulsion. (Married couples live in town.) But kissing on the cheek is permitted, and couples are free to hold hands, though not to put an arm round the partner's waist. Students willingly defend this sexual self-discipline when questioned about it by a visiting stranger; they maintain total repression would be bound to lead to deviant practices, in particular to homosexuality, which (they say) is rife in a rival Fundamentalist university in which all flirting is forbidden. On the other hand, the expression of sexual desire would go against the spirit of the educational aims of the university.

The Christian fundamentalist movement in the United States draws support from across the country, but there is a strong regional element. The American South has become known as the 'Bible Belt' – a swath of land located below the agricultural 'cattle belt', 'maize belt' and 'cotton belt'. Many of America's best-known and most influential evangelists are based in the southern and mid-western states of Virginia, Oklahoma and North Carolina. The most influential fundamentalist groups in the United States are the Southern Baptist Convention, the Assemblies of God and the Seventh-Day Adventists.

THINKING CRITICALLY

Religious fundamentalism appears to have increased during a period of rapid globalization. How might these two phenomena be related? What evidence is there that fundamentalist religion will not be temporary, but may become a permanent feature of our increasingly global human society?

Conclusion

In a globalizing age that is in desperate need of mutual understanding and dialogue, religious fundamentalism can be a destructive force. Fundamentalism is edged with the possibility of violence – in the cases of Islamic and Christian fundamentalism, examples of violence inspired by religious allegiance are not uncommon. There have been a number of violent clashes over the past few years between Islamic and Christian groups in Lebanon, Indonesia and other countries. Yet in an increasingly cosmopolitan world, people of contrasting traditions and beliefs are coming into contact with one another more than ever before (Beck 2006). As the unquestioning acceptance of traditional ideas declines, we must all live in a more open and reflective way – discussion and dialogue are essential between people of differing beliefs. They are the main way in which violence can be controlled or dissolved.

Summary points

1. Religion exists in all known societies, although religious beliefs and practices vary from culture to culture. All religions involve a set of symbols, involving feelings of reverence, linked to rituals practised by a community of believers.

2. Sociological approaches to religion have been most influenced by the ideas of the 'classical' thinkers: Marx, Durkheim and Weber. All held that traditional religions would decline, though each viewed the role of religion in society very differently. To Marx, religion contains a strong ideological element: religion provides justification for the inequalities of wealth and power found in society. For Durkheim, religion is important because of the cohesive functions it serves, especially in ensuring that people meet regularly to affirm common beliefs and values. For Weber, religion is important because of the role it plays in social change, as seen in the development of Western capitalism.

3. Totemism and animism are common types of religion in smaller cultures. In totemism, a species of animal or plant is perceived as possessing supernatural powers. Animism means a belief in spirits or ghosts, populating the same world as human beings, sometimes possessing them.

4. The three most influential monotheistic religions (religions in which there is only one God) in world history are Judaism, Christianity and Islam. Polytheism (belief in several or many gods) is common in other religions such as Hinduism. In other religions, like Confucianism, there are no gods or supernatural beings.

5. Churches are large and established religious bodies, normally with a formal bureaucratic structure and a hierarchy of religious officials. Sects are smaller, less formal groups of believers, usually set up to revive an established church. If a sect survives over a period of time and becomes institutionalized, it is called a denomination. Cults resemble sects, but are more loosely knit groups, which follow similar practices, but not within formal organizations.

6. Secularization refers to the declining influence of religion. Measuring the level of secularization is complicated, because several dimensions of change are involved: level of membership, social status and personal religiosity. Although the influence of religion

has definitely declined, religion is certainly not on the verge of disappearing, and continues to unite as well as divide people in the modern world.

7. Rates of regular church attendance in most European countries are low, particularly compared to the United States, where a much higher proportion of the population goes to church regularly. Far more people in Europe and the USA say they believe in God than attend church regularly – they 'believe but do not belong'.

8. Although traditional churches have experienced a decline in membership, many new religious movements have emerged. New religious movements encompass a broad range of religious and spiritual groups, cults and sects. They can be broadly divided into world-affirming movements, world-rejecting movements and world-accommodating movements.

9. Fundamentalism has become common among some believers in different religious groups across the world. 'Fundamentalists' believe in returning to the fundamentals of their religious doctrines. Islamic fundamentalism has affected many countries in the Middle East following the 1979 revolution in Iran, which set up a religiously inspired government. Christian fundamentalism in the United States is a reaction against secular values and a perceived moral crisis in American society. In their efforts to convert non-believers, fundamentalist Christians have pioneered the 'electronic church' – using television, radio and new technologies to build a following.

Further reading

The sociology of religion is a well-established field and there are many good introductions to it. Alan Aldridge's *Religion in the Contemporary World: A Sociological Introduction.* 2nd edition (Cambridge: Polity, 2007) is very well written, as is Malcolm Hamilton's *The Sociology of Religion: Theoretical and Comparative Perspectives* (London: Routledge, 2001), which is also a second edition. Both books cover the main issues discussed in this chapter and take readers deeper into the subject. After these, Grace Davie's *The Sociology of Religion* (London: Sage, 2007) is a very good critical assessment of the sociology of religion by a renowned expert.

Steve Bruce's *God is Dead: Secularization in the West* (Oxford: Blackwell Publishing, 2002) presents a staunch argument in support of the secularization thesis and for an alternative view you could try Peter Berger's *Questions of Faith: A Skeptical Affirmation of Christianity* (Oxford: Blackwell Publishing, 2003). Given Berger's earlier support for the secularization thesis (which he now sees as a mistake), this is an interesting book by a sociologist with a religious faith.

Finally, two useful, if large, edited collections of essays by scholars of religion are Richard K. Fenn's *Blackwell Companion to the Sociology of Religion* (Oxford: Blackwell Publishing, 2003) and James Beckford and N. Jay Demerath III, *The SAGE Handbook of the Sociology of Religion* (London: Sage, 2007).

Internet links

Academic Info Religion Gateway – US-based site with lots of information on many faiths: www.academicinfo.us/religindex.html

Hartford Institute for Religion Research, Connecticut – US-based Institute that carries out and disseminates research on religions: www.hirr.hartsem.edu/

The Association of Religion Data Archives – American site aiming to 'democratize access to the best data on religion': www.thearda.com/

Journal for Cultural and Religious Theory (online) – Peer-reviewed journal with some interesting articles. www.jcrt.org/

BBC, Religion and Ethics – BBC's UK-based site on all things religious, includes message boards: www.bbc.co.uk/religion/

Religious Tolerance – Canadian-based site, which 'promotes religious freedom, and diversity as positive cultural values': www.religioustolerance.org/

17

The Media

CHAPTER 17

• •

The Media

(opposite) Since the late nineteenth century, the character of modern communication technology has been radically transformed. Here, New Yorkers in Times Square watch the terrorist attacks against the World Trade Center in real time.

In 1865, the actor John Wilkes Booth assassinated US President Abraham Lincoln in a Washington theatre. It took 12 days before the news reached London. A smaller boat off the south coast of Ireland met the ship carrying the message from the United States and the news was telegraphed to London from Cork, beating the ship by three days. It was not until the 1950s that a dedicated trans-oceanic cable existed to carry telegraphs instantly across the Atlantic – although long-wave radio transmission between continents became possible in the early twentieth century. On 11 September 2001, terrorists hijacked three planes and used them to attack sites in Washington and New York. When the second plane crashed into the Twin Towers in New York, some 20 minutes after the first tower had been struck, it is estimated that a global audience of two billion people watched the attack on television in real time.

In the twenty-first century, communication technologies enable information to be shared instantaneously and simultaneously with many millions of people almost anywhere around the world. **Communication** – the transfer of information from one individual or group to another, whether in speech or through the mass media in modern times – is crucial to any society. In this chapter, we will study the transformations affecting the **mass media** of communications as part of globalization. The mass media includes a wide variety of forms, such as television, newspapers, films, radio, video games and the Internet. These are referred to as 'mass' media, because they communicate to a mass audience comprised of very large numbers of people.

Canadian media theorist, Marshall McLuhan (1964), argued that different types of media have very different effects on society. His famous dictum is that, 'the medium is the message'. That is to say, society is influenced much more by the *type* of the media than by its content, or the messages, which are conveyed by it. A society in which satellite television plays an important part, for example, is obviously a very different society from one that relies on the printed word carried aboard an ocean liner. Everyday life is experienced differently in a society in which television, relaying news instantaneously from one side of the globe to the other, plays an important role, to one that relies on horses, ships or the telegraph wire. According to McLuhan, the electronic media tends to create a **global village** in which people throughout the world see major events unfold and hence participate in them together. For billions of people around the world, the images of celebrities like Paris Hilton or Madonna are more instantly recognizable to them than that of their neighbours.

We live today in an interconnected world in which people experience the same events from many different places. Thanks to the process of globalization and the power of communications technology to effectively shrink large distances, people from Caracas to Cairo are able to receive the same popular music, news, films and television programmes. Twenty-four-hour news channels report on stories as they occur and broadcast coverage of unfolding events for the world to watch. Films made in Hollywood or Hong Kong reach audiences around the world, while sporting celebrities such as David Beckham and Maria Sharapova have become household names on every continent.

For several decades, we have been witnessing a process of convergence in the production, distribution and consumption of information. Even 30 years ago, ways of communicating, such as print, television and film, were still relatively self-contained spheres, but today they have become intertwined to a remarkable degree. The divisions between forms of communication are no longer as dramatic as they once were: television, radio, newspapers and telephones are undergoing profound transformations as a result of advances in technology and the rapid spread of the Internet. While newspapers remain central to our lives, the way they are organized and deliver their services are changing. Newspapers can be read online, mobile telephone use is exploding, and digital television and satellite broadcasting services allow an unprecedented diversity of choice for viewing audiences. With the expansion of technologies such as voice recognition, broadband transmission, web casting and cable links, the Internet threatens to erase the distinctions between traditional forms of media and to become the primary conduit for the delivery of information, entertainment, advertising and commerce to media audiences.

We begin our study by looking at the recent digital revolution in communications, focusing on the Internet and World

Wide Web, which are impacting on societies across the world. We then provide a brief account of other important forms of mass media, including film, television, music and newspapers, before considering some of the main theoretical approaches to studying the media and its role in society. Media representations of different social groups and the effects of mass media on the audience follow, and the chapter ends with a discussion of the ownership and political control of the global media and the resistance to it.

Media in a global age

For most of human history the main means of communication was speech, with face-to-face communication being the norm. In such oral cultures, information, ideas and knowledge were transmitted across generations by word of mouth and the kind of repositories of useful knowledge we are used to – such as books and libraries – just did not exist. Once speech could be written down and stored, initially on stone, the first writing cultures began to emerge, initially in China around 3,000 years ago. Religions have played a major part in the development of flexible communications by finding ways of producing manuscripts and religious texts for study and transportation, such as on papyrus and parchment, to literally 'spread the word'.

An important precursor to the modern mass media was the invention of the Gutenberg movable type printing press in the mid-fifteenth century, which enabled texts to be reproduced. Gutenberg made use of existing technologies – paper and wood-block printing – that originated in Asia much earlier. Yet, although technological advances and new uses of older technologies played a crucial part in the development of the mass media, the influence of social, cultural and economic factors must also be taken into account. For instance, mass forms of printed media could only develop in societies with relatively cheap

How many of your friends around the world would *not* know who these people are?
....

access to them, and an educated population that was able to take advantage and use them.

In the late twentieth century, new digital technologies, such as the mobile phone, video games, digital television and the Internet, have revolutionized the mass media. We will look first at this 'digital revolution' in communications, and especially the Internet and World Wide Web. We then examine the ways in which globalization impacts on other mass media, taking film, television, music and newspapers as our case studies, noting how the digital revolution is also transforming these older forms.

 For more on the Internet and mobile phones, see chapter 4, 'Globalization and The Changing World'.

The digital revolution

In his book *Being Digital* (1995), the founder of the media laboratory at the Massachusetts Institute of Technology, Nicholas Negroponte, analyses the profound importance of digital data in current communications technologies. Any piece of information, including pictures, moving images and sounds, can be translated through a binary system into 'bits'. A bit can be a 1 or a 0. For instance, the digital representation of 1, 2, 3, 4, 5, is 1, 10, 11, 100, 101, etc. Digitization – and speed – is at the origin of the development of multimedia: what used to be different media needing different technologies (such as visuals and sound) can now be combined on a single medium (such as DVDs and PCs). In recent years the processing power of computers has doubled every 18 months and Internet speeds have become much faster, making it possible to watch films and listen to music via the Internet. Digitization also permits the development of interactive media, allowing individuals actively to participate in, or structure, what they see or hear. In this section we examine the profound impact that this digitization process has had on the mass media.

One of the most fundamental aspects of the media concerns the very infrastructure through which information is communicated and exchanged. Some important technological advances during the second half of the twentieth century have completely transformed the face of telecommunications – the communication of information, sounds or images at a distance through a technological medium.

New communications technologies stand behind profound changes in the world's money systems and stock markets. Money is no longer gold or the cash in your pocket. More and more, money has become electronic, stored in computers in the world's banks. The value of whatever cash you do happen to have in your pocket is determined by the activities of traders on electronically linked money markets. Such markets have been created only over the last few decades, the product of a marriage between computers and satellite communication technology.

Four technological trends have contributed to these developments: first, the constant improvement in the *capabilities of computers*, together with declining costs; second, *digitization of data*, making possible the integration of computer and telecommunications technologies; third, *satellite communications* development; and fourth, *fibre optics*, which allow many different messages to travel down a single small cable. The dramatic communications explosion of recent years shows no signs of slowing down. Indeed, such a rapid pace of development means that our discussion below of digital technologies and their applications and consequences, may well be starting to date by the time you read this book, as new applications are created and the process of digitization continues.

The Internet and the World Wide Web

By the early 1990s, it was clear that the future lay not with the individual personal computer (PC) but with a global system of interconnected computers – the Internet. Although many computer users may not have realized it at the time, the PC was quickly to become little more than a point of access to events happening elsewhere – events happening on a network stretching across the planet, a network that is not owned by any individual or company.

 The potential of the Internet for the growth of international political activism is explored in chapter 22, 'Politics, Government and Social Movements'.

The Internet originated during the Cold War period before 1989. The 'Net' developed out of a system used in the Pentagon, the headquarters of the American military, from 1969. This system was first of all

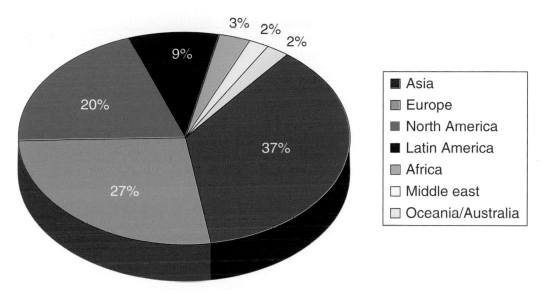

Figure 17.1 Global Internet use, by world region, 2007

Source: Internet World Stats 2007

named the ARPA net, after the Pentagon's Advanced Research Projects Agency. The ARPA sought to allow scientists working on military contracts in different parts of America to pool their resources and to share the expensive equipment they were using. Almost as an afterthought, its originators thought up a way of sending messages too – thus electronic mail, 'email', was born. Until the early 1980s, the Pentagon Internet consisted of 500 computers, all of which were located in military laboratories and university computer science departments. Other people in universities then started catching on, and began using the system for their own purposes. By 1987, the Internet had expanded to include 28,000 host computers, at many different universities and research labs.

The spread of commercial Internet service providers (ISPs) which offered dial-up, and later broadband, access through modems has fuelled the growing proportion of households with online capabilities. Online services, electronic bulletin boards, chatrooms and software libraries were put onto the net by a bewildering variety of people, initially mainly situated in the United States, but now all over the world. Corporations also got in on the act. In 1994 companies overtook universities as the dominant users of the network.

The best-known use of the Internet is the World Wide Web. 'The web' is in effect a global multimedia library. It was invented by a software engineer, Tim Berners-Lee, at a Swiss physics lab in 1990, and the software that popularized it across the world was written by an undergraduate at the University of Illinois. Users generally navigate the web with the help of a 'web browser' – a software program that allows individuals to search for information, locate particular sites or web pages, and mark those pages for future reference. Through the web, it is possible to download a wide variety of documents and programs, from government policy papers to anti-virus software to computer games. Websites have grown in sophistication and many are adorned with intricate graphics and photographs, or contain video and audio files. The web also serves as the main interface for 'e-commerce' – business transactions conducted online.

With the spread of cheaper home-based personal computers, access to the Internet continues to grow. According to a survey by the UK National Office of Statistics (HMSO 2004), the most common use of the Internet among adults who used it during the previous three months was for email (85 per cent) and finding information about goods or services (82 per cent). The most frequent place of access was the person's own home (82 per cent), followed by their workplace (42 per cent). The survey also found that even in an advanced industrial country like the UK, 37 per cent of adults had *never* used the Internet, a sizeable proportion of the population.

How many people are connected to the Internet globally is not known with any accuracy, but the UN estimated around 10 per cent of the global population were Internet users in 2000. By 2007, this figure had risen to around 18 per cent and it continues to grow. Although user numbers are rising fast, the evidence above shows that Internet access is geographically very uneven. Just 4 per cent of the population of Africa are Internet users, 10 per cent in the Middle East and 12 per cent in Asia, compared with almost 70 per cent in North America, 54 per cent in Australia/Oceania and 40 per cent in Europe (Internet World Stats 2007; see figure 17.2).

The impact of the Internet

In a world of quite stunning technological change, no one can be sure what the future holds. Many see the Internet as exemplifying the new global order emerging at the close of the twentieth century. Exchanges on the Internet take place in the new virtual world of cyberspace. **Cyberspace** means the space of interaction formed by the global network of computers that compose the Internet. In cyberspace, we cannot know with any certainty details about other people's identity, whether they are male or female, or where in the world they are.

Opinions on the effects of the Internet on social interaction fall into two broad categories. On the one hand are those observers who see the online world as fostering new forms of electronic relationship that either enhance or supplement existing face-to-face interactions. While travelling or working abroad, individuals can use the Internet to communicate regularly with friends and relatives at home. Distance and separation become more tolerable. The Internet also allows the formation of new types of relationship: 'anonymous' online users can meet in 'chatrooms' and discuss topics of mutual interest. These cyber contacts sometimes evolve into fully fledged electronic friendships or even result in face-to-face meetings. Many Internet users become part of lively online communities that are qualitatively different from those they inhabit in the physical world. Scholars who see the Internet as a positive addition to human interaction argue that it expands and enriches people's social networks.

On the other hand, not everyone takes such an enthusiastic outlook. As people spend more and more time communicating online and handling their daily tasks in cyberspace, it may be that they spend less time interacting with one another in the physical world. Some sociologists fear that the spread of Internet technology will lead to increased social isolation and atomization. They argue that one effect of increasing Internet access in households is that people are spending less 'quality time' with their families and friends. The Internet is encroaching on domestic life as the lines between work and home are blurred: many employees continue to work at home after hours – checking email or finishing tasks that they were unable to complete during the day. Human contact is reduced, personal relationships suffer, traditional forms of entertainment such as the theatre and books fall by the wayside, and the fabric of social life is weakened.

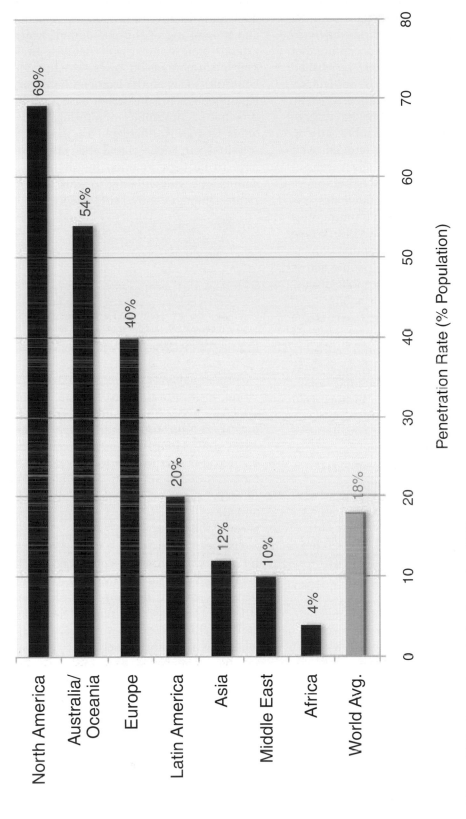

Figure 17.2 Internet penetration by region, 2007

Source: Internet World Stats 2007

In *The Virtual Community* (2000), Howard Rheingold acknowledges both the positive potential of *computer-mediated communications* whilst also accepting that its darker side cannot simply be wished away. Rheingold (2000: 5) is particularly interested in **virtual communities,** which he defines as, 'social aggregations that emerge from the Net when enough people carry on . . . public discussions long enough, with sufficient human feeling, to form webs of personal relationships in cyberspace'. Rheingold provides an extended description and analysis of a virtual community – a parenting conference – on the WELL (Whole Earth 'Lectronic Link), a computer conferencing system that enables people across the world to engage in open public discussions and to exchange private emails.

Rheingold says that being a part of the WELL is very much like being part of the real physical world, but in disembodied form. Members help each other to solve problems, exchange information and, sometimes, disagree and fall out. As Rheingold says:

> People in virtual communities use words on screens to exchange pleasantries and argue, engage in intellectual discourse, conduct commerce, exchange knowledge, share emotional support, make plans, brainstorm, gossip, feud, fall in love, find friends and lose them, play games, flirt, create a little high art and a lot of idle talk. People in virtual communities do just about everything people do in real life, but we leave our bodies behind. You can't kiss anybody and nobody can punch you in the nose, but a lot can happen within those boundaries. To the millions who have been drawn into it, the richness and vitality of computer-linked cultures is attractive, even addictive.
> (www.rheingold.com/vc/book/intro.html)

Nevertheless, he also acknowledges the less palatable potential of the Internet. For example, it is possible that the Internet will come to be dominated by business corporations who see members of virtual communities simply as commodities, gathering and selling their details for profit to anyone who wants it. The Internet also offers new opportunities for intensified surveillance and monitoring of the population, which extends state control over people's lives. This 'nightmare vision' owes something to Foucault's ideas on the eighteenth-century Panopticon, a prison design based on the principle of continuous monitoring of prisoners by guards. Rheingold has no magic solutions, but suggests that such criticisms have to be kept in mind by all Internet enthusiasts, who will have to work hard to create a human-centred virtual world.

See chapter 18, 'Organizations and Networks', for a discussion of the Panopticon.

Questions about personal identity, new forms of community and possibilities for democratic participation are discussed in chapter 7, 'Social Interaction and Everyday Life'.

Very similar fears were expressed as television burst onto the media scene. In *The Lonely Crowd* (1961), an influential sociological analysis of American society in the 1950s, David Riesman and his colleagues expressed concern about the effects of TV on family and community life. While some of their fears were well placed, television and the mass media have also enriched the social world in many ways.

Manuel Castells (2001) argues that the Internet will continue to grow because it allows networks to flourish. For Castells, networks are the defining organizational structure of our age. The inherent flexibility and adaptability of networks give them enormous advantages over older types of rational, hierarchical organizations. Castells argues that the Internet gives businesses the capability for global coordination of decentralized and highly complex activities. For individuals, the Internet will enable new combinations of work and self-employment, individual expression, collaboration and sociability, and for political activists it will make it possible for networks of individuals to combine and cooperate and spread their message around the world. For example, recent social networking sites such as Bebo, MySpace and Facebook, along with video sharing sites such as YouTube, show just how popular web-based communications are becoming for all age groups. Playing on McLuhan's idea that 'the medium is the message', Castells argues that, now, 'the network is the message'.

Castells' work is discussed in more detail in chapter 18, 'Organizations and Networks'.

THINKING CRITICALLY

How important do you think the Internet is likely to become in the emerging global society? In what ways is it becoming built into the everyday routines of individuals, businesses, workplaces and retailing? On balance, is the Internet a positive development for both individuals and societies?

Film

The first film to be shown to paying customers was in 1895 in Paris, France, where the Lumière brothers' *Arrival of the Train in La Ciotat Station* caused viewers to flee from their seats as the screen slowly filled with an oncoming steam engine heading towards them. While the print media developed slowly over many decades, film and the cinema arrived much faster. The first cinema in the UK opened in 1896 and by 1914 there were more than 500 in London alone. Cinema tickets could be afforded by all classes and the decline in working hours and rise in unemployment in the late 1920s meant the cinema-goers soon formed a mass audience in developed countries.

Audience demands were soon leading cinemas to screen two new programmes a week, each consisting of two films, a B-movie and the main feature. The demand for new films led studios to churn out productions to tight schedules. These films tended to be formulaic and created by bureaucratic organizations with a high degree of specialization and division of labour. As the industry became more commercialized a 'star system' emerged, with studios encouraging interest in the personal lives of actors like Mary Pickford and Rudolf Valentino, whose appearance in a film would ensure a box-office hit.

By 1925, the vast majority of commercially successful films were American in origin. They still are, as table 17.1 demonstrates. Cinemas were increasingly controlled by the American studios, which owned the distribution rights to films. The studios could oblige cinemas to bulk-buy future productions, effectively freezing out competitors. As with the print media, ownership had become largely concentrated amongst a few large corporations. The obvious dominance of American film production raises questions about 'cultural imperialism', as American values, products and culture are promoted through the worldwide distribution of film, especially pronounced in an age of globalization.

There are different ways to assess the globalization of cinema. One is to consider *where* films are produced and the sources of financing that support them. By such criteria, there has unquestionably been a process of globalization in the cinema industry. According to studies by the United Nations Educational, Scientific and Cultural Organization (UNESCO), many nations possess the capacity to produce films. In the 1980s approximately 25 countries were producing 50 or more films a year, while a small handful of countries – the United States, Japan, South Korea, Hong Kong and India – led all the others in producing more than 150 films a year (Held et al. 1999).

Another way to assess the globalization of cinema is to consider the extent to which nationally produced films are *exported* to other countries. In the 1920s, when feature films first saw the light of day, Hollywood made four-fifths of all films screened in the world. Today, India, with its growing

Table 17.1 Top-grossing films of all time worldwide at (non-US) box office, 2007

Rank	USA Films	Year	Country of origin	Total gross revenue (US $ millions)
1	*Titanic*	1997	USA	1,235
2	*The Lord of the Rings: The Return of the King*	2003	USA	752
3	*Harry Potter and The Sorcerer's Stone*	2001	USA	651
4	*Pirates of the Caribbean: At World's End*	2007	USA	649
5	*Harry Potter and the Order of the Phoenix*	2007	USA	642
6	*Pirates of the Caribbean: Dead Man's Chest*	2006	USA	637
7	*Harry Potter and the Chamber of Secrets*	2002	USA	604
8	*Harry Potter and the Goblet of Fire*	2005	USA	602
9	*The Lord of the Rings: The Two Towers*	2002	USA	581
10	*Jurassic Park*	1993	USA	563
	Non-USA films			
69	*Spirited Away*	2001	Japan	254
90	*Howl's Moving Castle*	2004	Japan	227
103	*The Full Monty*	1997	UK	211
106	*Bridget Jones's Diary*	2001	UK	210
125	*Four Weddings and a Funeral*	1994	UK	191

Source: Internet Movie Database 2007

Bollywood film productions, produces more films than any other country (more than 1,100 per year), with the United States next (with around 800 per year). However, many Indian films are not shown internationally and although governments of many countries provide subsidies to aid their own film industries, the USA continues to be the largest exporter of film (Hong Kong is the second largest and hence exerts more influence in the global cinema industry. As table 17.1 shows, the top-grossing films of all time at the international (non-US) box office were all US films. In 2003, for instance, US films dominated the UK box office, accounting for almost 62 per cent of takings; films solely originating in the UK, by contrast, accounted for just 2.5 per cent of money taken (UK Film Council, 2003).

Hollywood studios generate well over half of their revenues from the overseas distribution of films. In an effort to increase the size of foreign audiences further, these studios are involved in building multiplex cinemas around the world. Global box office revenues are forecast to rise to $25.6 billion (£14 billion) by 2010, nearly double the 1995 total, as the audiences increase. The spread of video and more recently DVD players has also increased the number of people across the world who are now able regularly to watch films.

Television

The interaction between television and the audience is different from that between the cinema and its audience. Television enters the household in a way that the cinema cannot and does not demand the same level of attention that film does. Television also has an immediacy which film does not: it can report events, as in the attacks in the USA in September 2001, from almost anywhere in the world to a mass audience as they happen.

Bollywood – one part of the Indian cinema industry – produces more films than Hollywood and about a billion more tickets a year are sold for Indian films than for Hollywood blockbusters. Yet US films are still better known around the world and can take in about fifty times as much revenue.

The number of television sets in the developed countries and the amount of time that people spend viewing them increased dramatically from the 1950s onwards. If current trends in TV watching continue, the average child born today will have spent more time watching television by the age of 18 than in any other activity except sleep. Virtually every household now possesses a TV set. Most people will watch television at some point every day and the average set is switched on for between three and six hours per day. Individuals aged 4 and over in the UK watch an average of 25 hours of television a week. Older people watch more than twice as much television as children, perhaps because they are not in school and go to bed later in the evening, and people from lower social classes watch more than those from the top three social classes (see figure 17.3 for UK figures).

Television and social life

Television has become ubiquitous and is now so ingrained into the routines of everyday life, that most people now simply take it for granted as a constitutive part of social life as such. We watch TV, talk about programmes with friends and family and organize our leisure time around TV schedules. The 'box in the corner' is switched on whilst we get on with other things and appears to provide an essential backdrop to out lives. As Roger Silverstone explains:

> Television accompanies us as we wake up, as we breakfast, as we have our tea and as we drink in bars. It comforts us when we are alone. It helps us sleep. It gives us

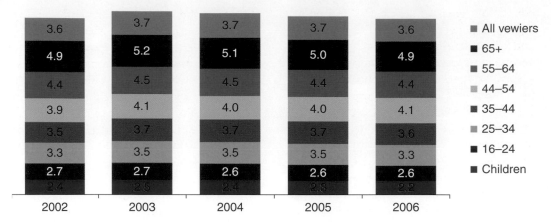

Figure 17.3 Number of hours of television viewed, by age group, 2002–6, UK

Source: Ofcom, *Public Service Broadcasting: Annual Report*, March 2007

pleasure, it bores us and sometimes it challenges us. It provides us with opportunities to be both sociable and solitary. Although, of course, it was not always so and although we have had to learn how to incorporate the medium into out lives we now take television entirely for granted. (1994: 3)

It is the way that television contributes to people's emotional and cognitive needs, and assists in designing the routines and habits that create a stronger sense of trust in others, or 'ontological security' (Giddens 1991), that helps to explain its all-pervading existence. However, none of this means that the dominant position of TV is inevitable or unassailable; the technological dimension of television does not determine its social and cultural reception. As 'Using your sociological imagination 17.1' shows, young people's everyday routines and habits today may well be significantly different from those of their parents, with significant consequences for the medium of television.

Several media theorists have been highly critical about the effects of a seemingly ever-increasing diet of television: two influential accounts have been provided by Robert Putnam's work on social capital and Neil Postman (1931–2003), in his tellingly titled *Amusing Ourselves to Death: Public Discourse in the Age of Show Business* (1986).

To Postman, television presents serious issues as entertainment because, in his phrase, 'the form excludes the content'. By this, he means that television as 'the form' is a medium that is incapable of sustaining serious 'content'. For Postman, rational argument is best carried on in the form of the printed word, which is capable of sustaining complex and serious content. He harks back to the nineteenth century as an 'age of reason', when the written word was dominant. Postman's argument contains some similarities with Marshall McLuhan's claim that 'the medium is the message', although Postman is much more sceptical than McLuhan about the benefits of electronic media. To Postman, the medium of print creates a rational population, whereas the medium of television creates an entertained one. In a society dominated by the television, news, education and politics are all reduced to entertainment, so that we are, as the title of his book indicates, doing nothing more than 'amusing ourselves to death'.

In a similar vein, Robert Putnam (1995) has argued that in the USA, the significant decline in social capital – mutual obligations and trust – correlates pretty well with the rise of the television. In 1950, around the time measures of social capital peaked, barely 10 per cent of Americans had a television set; by 1959, this figure had risen to 90 per cent. Taking other facts into consideration, such as education, age and gender, TV viewing is strongly and negatively related to social trust and group membership. Using the same criteria, the correlation of newspaper reading to social trust and group membership is positive. One reason Putnam suggests for why TV viewing erodes social capital is the effect of programme content on viewers. For example, studies suggest that heavy watchers of TV are unusually sceptical about the benevolence of other people – by overestimating crime rates for example. Putnam concludes: 'Just as the erosion of the ozone layer was detected only many years after the proliferation of the chlorofluorocarbons that caused it, so too the erosion of America's social capital became visible only several decades after the underlying process had begun' (1995).

However, in recent years, the evidence is growing that television watching habits are changing, particularly amongst young people, as 'on-demand' services become more popular, Internet use increases and video sharing websites such as YouTube provide new, interactive ways of viewing. Many of the new social networking websites such as MySpace and Facebook, which have grown enormously in recent years, may also show that Putnam's thesis is too pessimistic. There is some evidence that young people are beginning to abandon the relatively passive medium of television in favour of more interactive media. If so, then this is highly likely to lead to changes in television production and output as well.

> Putnam's thesis on the decline of social capital is examined in more detail in chapter 18, 'Organizations and Networks'.

On the other hand, Sonia Livingstone and Moira Bovill's (1999) survey of children's media use in the UK – the first such survey for 40 years – found a developing 'bedroom culture' in the UK, with two out of three working-class children and 54 per cent of middle-class children having a TV in their bedroom. By contrast, in other parts of Europe, TV ownership by children is much lower. In the UK, 72 per cent of working-class and 61 per cent of middle-class children also had a TV-linked games machine and young people spent around five hours a day using various media, with TV being the form they would 'miss most', taking up around half of their media time. By contrast, 55 per cent of children had a home PC with just 7 per cent using the Internet. Twice as many boys (16 per cent) as girls had a PC in their bedroom and just 2 per cent of working-class children had Internet access at home, compared with 14 per cent of middle-class children.

The Internet generated some initial excitement as a means of establishing 'pen-pal' type relationships in other countries, but young people reported much frustration at the difficulties involved in accessing useful information and said it was expensive. Books fared even worse; they were seen as boring, old-fashioned and not trendy, and required too much effort – the sort of things 'your parents approve of'. Much has happened in the ten years since this report, of course, not least the continuing growth in the number of Internet users and the expansion of PC and mobile phone ownership. However, the continuing popularity of TV, the researchers suggest, appears to be rooted in its ability to provide a broad range of 'gratifications': 'excitement', to overcome boredom, for relaxation and to overcome the threat of feeling 'left out'.

THINKING CRITICALLY

Think of your own TV viewing habits. Where do you watch TV? Do you do other things while 'watching' and if so, what? How do you see your viewing habits changing in the next few years? What could TV executives do to make their programmes more attractive to young people?

Digital television

Since the beginning of the twenty-first century, television broadcasting technology has been undergoing a revolution, with the

17.1: The threat of young viewers turning off?

Broadcasting body says that fewer of us are watching TV, and those that do are not giving it their full attention. Predictions of television's demise may be as commonplace as faked TV phone-ins these days, but when the UK's Royal Television Society warns that viewing habits are changing, it is time for executives to take notice.

The RTS, whose members include every major broadcaster, has commissioned research from OC&C Consultants, which shows that young people in particular are switching off in huge numbers. It found that the under-30s now watch 40 per cent of their 'television' by downloading it over the Internet or viewing it 'on demand' rather than watching it as it is broadcast. More than 10 per cent of viewing by young people is already online, with the youngest groups (under 24) spending the most time on the Internet.

Unsurprisingly, perhaps, 73 per cent of the under-30s surveyed are using the Internet more than they did three years ago, and 43 per cent of them are watching less TV. The number of viewers engaging in other activities while they tune in seems to be higher than previously estimated: 81 per cent of under-30s do something else while watching TV; among 15–17-year-olds, the figure is 86 per cent. That suggests that TV is not getting 100 per cent of younger viewers' attention, which could worry advertisers, who pay a premium based on an assumption that they do, according to OC&C.

Young viewers typically use social networking sites or talk on the phone while the TV is on rather than using 'competing forms of entertainment' like a PC console or radio. Fewer people under 30 – 71 per cent – do other activities while using the Internet, although 86 per cent of 15–17-year-olds do so.

The younger the viewer, the more likely they are to complain about the number of repeats, soaps and reality shows, and they moan that there are too many adverts. But it's not all bad news. While most people say having children made them consume less TV, moving in with a partner boosts consumption: those who marry or cohabit spend

Are young people deserting television for more interactive media?

35 per cent of their free time in front of the box. More importantly, older age groups still watch the way their parents did: on the sofa.

It also seems likely that greater choice encourages more viewing, which is good news for broadcasters as the number of homes with multi-channel access increases. By 2012, when the analogue signal is due to be turned off, every household will have digital TV. The research found that under-30s who already have a bigger choice of channels are viewing more TV than their peers.

Under-30s with Freeview, Sky or Cable watch 5 per cent more TV than those with terrestrial only, and ownership of a personal video recorder like Sky Plus or Tivo increases viewing by 7 per cent. Under-30s with multi-channel TV also express greater satisfaction with the programmes on offer.

What can broadcasters and programme-makers do to accentuate this trend, besides boosting their presence on the Internet or posting clips on YouTube? One answer is to create shorter content that is easier to consume online and many broadcasters are starting to experiment with this.

'The industry should be very worried indeed about teenage viewing habits in particular', claims OC&C director Paul Zwillenberg. 'If they don't respond they won't be able to deliver eyeballs to their advertisers. There has been a dramatic and rapid shift in the media consumption habits of under-20s and they need to start doing today what they should have done yesterday but plan to do tomorrow. They've got to throw away the old commissioning handbook and use all the platforms out there.' Reports of TV's demise may be exaggerated, but it must evolve in order to survive.

Source: Observer, 30 September 2007

transfer of programme transmission from analogue to digital. Analogue TV is the 'old' system of broadcasting that has been used to transmit signals to television sets around the country since the 1940s. It converts sound and pictures into waves, which are transmitted through the air and picked up by the aerial on the roof of the house or on top of the television.

Digital TV works by transforming pictures and sound into information that is understood by a computer. Digital transmissions are received in three ways: through the TV aerial and a decoder (often a set-top box), via a satellite dish or via cable. The television acts like a computer and converts this information back into pictures and sound. Broadcasters and service providers argue that digital television not only means more channels, but also a better quality of sound and pictures and additional services. Digital TV offers the possibility of, for instance, interactive television, the Internet, home shopping and home banking. The arrival of digital TV has also created the possibility of single units that merge the personal computer with the television, although these are not yet widely in use.

Once digital take-up has reached a tipping point, the transmission of television on analogue frequencies is expected to stop and has already been agreed in the USA and UK. All transmissions from then on will be digital and this will mark the end of a particular stage in the history and development of television. The number of television channels available has been increasing massively as a result of advances in satellite, cable and digital technology. It is now not unusual to see digital service providers offering monthly subscription packages that give viewers the choice of a staggering 200+ TV and radio channels. Analogue TV in the UK offered just five. Such an increase in digital output offers many more opportunities for TV content providers and, crucially, for

---

THINKING CRITICALLY

'The introduction of digital television genuinely represents more choice for viewers.' In what ways do you think this statement can be said to be true? What evidence and arguments are there, which suggest that this 'choice' is illusory rather than real?

advertisers, while the advent of pay-per-view and monthly subscriptions is likely vastly to increase the amount that consumers spend on television watching in the future. Of course, the originality, creativity and quality of what they will be watching is another matter entirely.

Music

Music is as old as human societies and its use within societies pre-dates the development of complex languages. The first music is assumed to have come from the human voice, with instruments developing later along with different forms of material culture. Some of the oldest musical instruments have been found in parts of India and China and some of the earliest functional uses of music were within religious rituals and practices. But as these rituals and practices have tended to diminish in modern societies, music has continued to flourish.

Theodore Adorno (1976) of the Frankfurt School of critical theory agued that musical forms tend to reflect the society within which they exist.

> See chapter 3, 'Theories and Perspectives in Sociology', for discussion of this school.

Many musical forms in capitalist societies, for example, take on predictable structures and offer an easy gratification. They train people to expect uniformity and repetition, and require little effort on the part of listeners to be enjoyed. In his own time, Adorno saw jazz and other popular music as guilty of this. However, although music can promote conformity, it can also foster critical enlightenment and is therefore, at least potentially, an active force in social life. Some forms of 'progressive' music (such as the experimental music of Schoenberg) defy standard musical conventions and, in 'breaking the rules', challenge people's assumptions and force them to think more critically.

Like Adorno, music theorist Jacques Attali's *Noise: The Political Economy of Music* (1985), argues that music holds up a mirror to society as its social organization and forms reflect society's own mode of organization. For example, in industrialized societies, music is listened to primarily as recordings, via vinyl records, cassette tapes and, latterly, CDs. Music's hallmark in such societies is therefore repetitive mass production and the erosion of difference. Music becomes background noise in supermarkets, railway stations, restaurants and many other public and private spaces. Echoing Max Weber's comments on music in the bureaucratic age, Attali notes that this endless repetition of recorded music reflects the industrial society that enabled it, which tends to produce uniform products.

However, Attali's thesis goes one step further. He argues that music not only *mirrors* social organization, it also carries a *prophecy* of the future. Music can do this, he says, because musicians rapidly explore and exhaust all the possibilities within a given code (the 'rules of the game', as it were) much more quickly than other forms of cultural output. Music is not bound so much to material things such as projectors or TV sets, but can be passed on and change more quickly. As musical organization is pushed to its internal limits, it is forced to break the bounds of the existing system in order to continue moving forward. An example would be the current battles over downloading and free sharing of copyrighted music. The commercial element of music-making is now desperately struggling to keep pace with an emergent form of music, which continually pushes and breaks the existing commercial 'rules of the game'.

What Attali saw emerging from industrialized music was a form of music-making based on the erosion of boundaries between the composer, the performer and the audience. Instead, people were starting to make music for their own and their friends' pleasure, with little or no commercial motivation. Music was becoming, once again, localized and made for smaller communities of people. The paradox of Attali's argument is that the movement towards the localization of music is occurring at a time when we seem to be caught up in a much more rapid globalization of the world's societies.

In contrast to such large-scale social structural theories, the 1970s and '80s saw the emergence of a new approach, known as the 'production of culture' perspective (Peterson 1976; Becker 1982). Here, music and other cultural products are viewed as social activities that have to be analysed in relation to the processes and contexts in which they are produced.

For example, Peterson and Berger (1975) studied pop music by looking at 'Number 1' hits in the USA between 1948 and 1973, comparing the number of performers and lyrics. They found that competition between large and small recording companies in the production of music was a key factor in explaining innovations in pop music. In periods of high market concentration (when just four companies produced some 75 per cent of all hit singles), there was little innovation because there was no need to look for novelty or to introduce new products. However, as the large companies lost their monopoly on radio promotion of music and smaller companies were able to gain a foothold, innovation increased. What Peterson and Berger were able to show through their careful analysis of how pop music is *actually produced* (the production of culture) is that innovation and increasing diversity in pop music *followed* changes in market concentration, they did not lead it. Thus, musical innovations in pop music were less to do with creative individual genius or powerful consumers demanding new music and more to do with the prevailing conditions of the music industry, within which pop music was being produced (see also Negus 1999).

This culture of production approach opened the way for more empirical studies of music in society. For example, Tia Denora's *Music in Everyday Life* (2000) is an empirical study that adopts an interaction-ist approach to explore the way individuals use music in the construction of the self and personal experience. But music is not only something to be used, she argues, it can also influence people's actions in use. For instance, a routine car journey to the shops can easily become a secondary aim to listening to music on the car radio. Hearing a particular opening chord or melody can reorientate people's actions, turning them away from their previous course.

Denora argues that people often behave rather like disc jockeys to their own selves, choosing music to create or change their mood and to alter the way they experience social life. And though sociology has lagged behind other disciplines, such as psychology, in the academic study of music, Denora argues that music is, 'a dynamic material, a medium for making, sustaining and changing social worlds and activities' (2000: x), though this cannot be understood in the abstract and has to be explored within the different contexts in which music is used. In this way, empirical studies could bring together the structural sociological theories of music and individual experience of it, to enhance our understanding of music's 'social powers'. Denora's own book is based on in-depth interviews with women in the USA and UK and participant observation of 'music in action' in an aerobics class, karaoke evenings and music therapy sessions in retail settings, but it also contributes to theories of music in society.

Globalization and the digitization of music

As David Held and colleagues have noted in their investigation into the globalization of media and communications, 'the musical form is one that lends itself to globalization more effectively than any other' (1999: 351). This is because music is able to transcend the limitations of written and spoken language to reach and appeal to a mass audience. The global music industry, dominated by a small number of multinational corporations, has been built on its ability to find, produce, market and distribute the musical abilities of thousands of artists to audiences around the world. The growth of technology – from personal stereo systems to music television (such as MTV) to the compact disc – have provided newer, more sophisticated ways for music to be distributed globally. Over recent decades, an 'institutional complex' of companies has developed as part of the global marketing and distribution of music.

The global industry in recorded music is one of the most concentrated. The four largest firms – Universal (which absorbed PolyGram in 1998), Time Warner, Sony BMG and EMI – control between 80 and 90 per cent of all music sales internationally (Herman and McChesney 1997). Until January 2000, when it announced a merger with Time Warner, EMI was the only company among the top five that was not part of a larger media conglomerate. The global music industry experienced substantial growth during the mid-1990s, with sales in developing countries particularly strong, prompting many of the top companies to sign up more local artists in anticipation of further market growth.

However, the music industry has been challenged by the arrival of the Internet, which allows users to (illegally) share music for free more easily and extensively than before and to produce and disseminate their own music without the need for large media corporations and marketing drives. This is the kind of development that Attali (1985) forecast would become much more common.

THINKING CRITICALLY

How significant a challenge do you think Internet downloads and file-sharing are likely to be to the mainstream music industry? Are Held and colleagues right to say that music 'lends itself to globalization' more than other media? Why should that be so?

The growth of the global music industry in the post-war period has been due primarily to the success of popular music – originating mainly in America and Britain – and the spread of the youth cultures and subcultures that identify with it (Held et al. 1999). Processes of globalization have therefore been one of the main forces in the diffusion of American and British styles and music genres to international audiences. The USA and the UK are the world leaders in the export of popular music, with other countries having much lower levels of domestic music production. While some critics argue that the domination of the music industry by these two countries undermines the success of local musical sounds and traditions, it is important to remember that globalization is a contested concept. The growing popularity of 'world music' – such as the phenomenal success of Latin-inspired sounds in the United States – shows that globalization may lead to cultural diffusion in more than one direction.

Although the music industry is becoming ever more concentrated in the hands of a few international conglomerates, some observers think that it is the most vulnerable link within the 'culture industry'. This is because the Internet allows music to be shared and downloaded digitally, rather than purchased from local music stores. The global music industry is currently mainly comprised of a complex network of factories, distribution chains, music shops and sales staff. If the Internet removes the need for all these elements by allowing music to be marketed and downloaded directly, what will be left of the music industry? Jacques Attali, whose ideas were discussed above, has argued that the increasing battles over illegal downloading and free sharing of music are a sign of things to come, as the mass production and consumption system of industrialized music begins to break down.

But the music industry is attempting to come to terms with the effects of digitization. Global music sales have been falling, with annual record sales down from $40 billion (£22 billion) to $30 billion (£17 billion) between 2000 and 2004. The sector has undergone large-scale redundancies and has been forced to restructure. Many in the music industry claim that the swapping of music files, such as MP3s, over the Internet is one of the major causes of this loss of revenue. Research by the British Phonographic Industry (BPI) found that eight million people in the UK claim to be downloading music, 92 per cent of them using illegal sites (BBC 2004c). Although attempts are being made to impose tight controls on the replication of legally purchased music, the pace of technological change is eclipsing the ability of the industry to curtail piracy.

One case that attracted much attention in 2000 was the Napster case. Napster is a software program that allows people to trade files over the Internet – including music copied to files on other sharers' computers. The record industry filed several lawsuits against the small company behind Napster, eventually forcing it to stop providing the file-sharing software. However, since the victory over Napster the music industry has had mixed fortunes in its court actions against the companies that support file-swapping on the Internet. In 2003, a US judge ruled that two file-swapping networks, Grokster and Morpheus, were not responsible for the legal status of files traded on their systems, but the legal battle continues.

As well as attacking the companies that create file-sharing software, the music industry has also taken action against individual computer users. In 2004, the BPI issued a statement claiming it would sue individual music fans who swapped song files over the Internet. This follows similar action by the Recording Industry Association of America (RIAA), which by 2004 had sued more than 5,700 downloaders. In 2003, the RIAA took action against a college student in Michigan, USA, who ran a network offering more than 650,000 files – the equivalent of more than 43,000 albums (BBC 2004c).

The music industry has also begun to adapt to the challenges of the Internet by offering *legal* download services. The downloading is legal because royalties are paid on the songs to record labels and artists. The Internet has seen a large increase, catalysed by the advent of the portable MP3 player, particularly Apple's iPod, and by the rise in the number of online companies offering songs that can be legally purchased and downloaded. By the end of 2004, more than 125 million legal downloads of songs had been purchased and an official 'music download chart' had been established. After initial rejection of the Internet by the music industry, by the mid-2000s its successful adaptation to selling music through legal downloading was perceived by many in the industry to be crucial to its future (BBC 2004b).

Newspapers

The development of the press during the nineteenth century occurred at a time of political and social unrest in Europe. The UK government, for example, exerted its control over the emerging newspaper industry through strict laws on libel and sedition, which prevented political agitation; at the same time, a stamp tax was imposed to ensure that newspapers were only affordable by the well off. The stamp tax had unintended consequences, as illegal and inexpensive pamphlets emerged, spreading radical views amongst the newly industrial working class. The biggest of these pamphlets, such as William Cobbett's weekly *Political Register*, outsold the official, 'stamped' press many times over (Hall et al. 1982).

The stamp tax – condemned by its opponents as a 'tax on knowledge' – was finally repealed in 1855 after a series of reductions, leading many writers to hail a golden era of British journalism marked by a 'transition from official to popular control' (Koss 1973). An alternative view was put forward by James Curran and Jean Seaton

Despite the prevalence of digital media in today's society, newspapers remain extremely popular.

who challenged this view in their historical account of the British press, *Power Without Responsibility* (2003). They argue that the repeal of the stamp tax was an attempt to break the popularity of the radical press and to boost the sales of more 'respectable' newspapers. For Curran and Seaton, the repeal of the stamp tax did not introduce a new era of press freedom, but a time of repression and ideological control, this time by market forces rather than government.

The newspaper was a fundamentally important development in the history of modern media, because it packaged many different types of information in a limited and easily reproducible format. Newspapers contained in a single package information on current affairs, entertainment and consumer goods. The cheap daily press was pioneered in the United States with the 'one-cent daily' paper in New York. The invention of cheap newsprint was the key to the mass diffusion of newspapers from the late nineteenth century onwards.

Curran and Seaton have noted that extra revenue from advertising enabled the cover prices to fall dramatically during this period, making the newspaper affordable for all. They also argue that advertising undermined the radical press as advertisers tended to place announcements in papers to which they were politically sympathetic, and to select papers with a smaller circulation and a wealthy readership, rather than radical papers with a higher circulation which sold to readers who would be unlikely to afford the product advertised.

By the early twentieth century, ownership of much of the UK newspaper industry was concentrated amongst a handful of rich entrepreneurs. By the 1930s, Lords Beaverbrook, Camrose, Kemsley and Rothermere owned 50 per cent of British national and local daily papers and 30 per cent of the Sunday papers. Critics have argued that the 'press barons', as they became known, used their ownership of national newspapers to promote their own political causes and ambitions (Curran and Seaton 2003).

For half a century or more, newspapers were the chief way of conveying information quickly and comprehensively to a mass public. But their influence has waned with the rise of radio, cinema and – much more important – television and, increasingly, the Internet. Figures for newspaper readership suggest that the proportion of people who read a national daily paper in Britain has declined since the early 1980s. Among men, the proportion of daily newspaper readers dropped from 76 per cent in 1981 to 60 per cent in 1998–9; readership levels are somewhat lower among women, but a similar drop – from 68 per cent to 51 per cent – has taken place (HMSO 2000).

Newspapers, particularly the tabloid press, have become less focused on providing news and more oriented towards reporting, creating and sustaining modern celebrity culture (Cashmore 2006). The role of newspapers and television in creating a climate in which celebrity culture can flourish alerts us to what some sociologists have called, following the 'production of culture' approach (discussed below), the 'celebrity industry' (Turner 2004). But what is a celebrity? In the early 1960s, Daniel Boorstin (1961: 58) noted that 'the celebrity is a person who is well known for their well-knownness'. Although many celebrities today are film stars or sportspeople, they may be known more for their media personalities and private lives than for their achievements. Others become celebrities just by regularly making it into magazines and newspapers (Paris Hilton) or appearing on television (*Big Brother* and other reality show contestants).

> **THINKING CRITICALLY**
>
> Do you think that paper-based newspapers will survive the Internet revolution? How could the newspaper business change, what new practices could it adopt, to maximize its opportunities of gaining and holding on to readers? What does the decline in newspaper sales tell us about recent social change?

Of course, the production of celebrity culture in newspapers and on television requires an appreciative and demanding audience. As consumers, we also participate in the production of celebrity culture and we do it in knowing ways (Gamson 1994). We know that many of our celebrities have no major achievements to offer and that their fame will probably be short-lived. When we get bored with them, we simply move on to the next one. In this way, celebrities have become commodities for our consumption – not literally, but via their representations in the mass media. Nonetheless, despite the apparent public addiction to celebrity, the decline in newspaper sales seems to indicate that celebrity news, in itself, will not be enough to insulate the paper-based newspaper industry from its media competitors.

Indeed, online communication might well bite further into newspaper circulation. News information and celebrity gossip is now available online via numerous websites almost instantaneously and is constantly updated during the course of the day. Many newspapers themselves can also be accessed and read online free of charge to consumers. In the longer term it would seem that the age of paper-based newspapers may be drawing to a close, but newspaper companies are already diversifying their output into new media forms in order to survive.

Theorizing the media

In this section we examine four influential theoretical approaches to the study of the mass media: functionalism, conflict theory, symbolic interactionism and recent postmodern media theory. As we will see, there are widely divergent views on the role and functions of the media within societies and our fourfold categorization here is not an exhaustive one in the field of Media Studies.

Functionalism

In the mid-twentieth century, functionalist theorists such as Charles Wright (1960) focused on the ways in which the media helps to integrate and bind societies together. Following the media theorist Denis McQuail (2000), we can identify several important social functions of the media that may work to stabilize the social system.

1 *Information* The media provides us with a continuous flow of information about our society and the world, from webcams and radio reports alerting us to traffic jams, to rolling weather reports, the stock market and news stories about issues that might affect us personally.

2 *Correlation* The media explains, and helps us to understand the meaning of the information it gives us. In this way the media provides support for established social norms and has an important role in the socialization of children, providing a shared framework for the interpretation of events.

3 *Continuity* The media has a certain function in expressing the dominant culture, recognizing new social developments and forging common values.

4 *Entertainment* The media provides amusement, a diversion from the rigours of work and acts to reduce social tensions. This is essentially the function of a release valve for society, allowing people to set aside their problems and conflicts, at least temporarily.

5 *Mobilization* The media can be used to encourage people to contribute to economic development, to support and uphold moral rules and to mobilize the population in times of war. This can be through very direct public campaigns, but also in much more subtle ways, such as the moral tales within soap operas or films, for example.

In recent decades, functionalist theories of the media – along with the functionalist approach in general – have fallen into decline. There are several reasons why sociologists have moved decisively away from functionalism. First, the theory appears to do little more than describe the media's current roles rather than explaining why they are necessary. Second, functionalist accounts have had little or nothing to say about the audience reception of media products, tending to assume that people are relatively passive recipients, rather than active interpreters of media messages. Third, the functions above appear wholly positive, but others have seen the media as a much less benign force within societies. In particular, conflict approaches influenced by Marxism see the modern mass media as destructive of society's cultural vitality.

> Functionalism was introduced in chapter 1, 'What is Sociology?', and discussed in chapter 3, 'Theories and Perspectives in Sociology'.

Conflict theories

In Europe, conflict approaches to the mass media have had more impact than functionalism. Below, we look at two of the most important theories of the media from a broadly Marxist standpoint: the political economy approach, which concentrates on the ownership and control of media forms, and the 'culture industry' approach of the Frankfurt School of critical theory. The important research of the Glasgow Media

17.2   Media bias in the Iraq dossier affair?

To rally support for [the 2003 Iraq] war, the Prime Minister's office published a dossier of charges against Iraq in September 2002. It claimed, among other things, that Iraq could deploy weapons of mass destruction (WMD) within 45 minutes.

Yet with no WMD used by Iraqi forces in the ensuing war and none found, the dossier's veracity came under suspicion. One of its allegations, which George Bush made part of his 2003 state-of-the-union address, was discredited by intelligence sources. Then, in June 2003, a BBC journalist accused Alistair Campbell, Tony Blair's chief spin-doctor, of having 'sexed up' the dossier against the wishes of Britain's security services (in particular, inserting the '45-minute' claim).

A parliamentary investigation cleared Mr Campbell of this charge (he resigned in August 2003). But the BBC refused to back

down, sparking a furious row with the government. This took a tragic turn when a government scientist [Dr David Kelly], who'd been exposed as the main source of the BBC's story, committed suicide. An inquiry into his death, which reported in January 2004, cleared the government of 'sexing up' the dossier and largely – but not wholly – vindicated the scientist's employers, the Defence Ministry. Criticism was instead heaped on the BBC, prompting the resignations of its director-general and chairman of governors.

A related inquiry into intelligence failures, headed by Lord Butler, in July 2004 cleared the government of any deliberate attempt to mislead Parliament. But it did suggest that Mr Blair was prepared to exaggerate what turned out to be fairly thin evidence to bolster the case for a war.

Source: © *The Economist* Newspaper Limited, London, 5 April 2005

Group is also rooted in Marxist theory and is discussed below.

Political economy approaches

Political economy approaches view the media as an industry and examine the way in which the major means of communication have come to be owned by private interests. The ownership of the media has often been concentrated in the hands of a few wealthy media magnates. In the era of mass newspaper readership for example, a few so-called 'press barons' owned a majority of the pre-war press in many countries and were able to set the agenda for news and its interpretation. In our increasingly global age, the ownership of media crosses national borders and media magnates now own transnational media corporations, giving them international recognition and influence. Perhaps the best known of these is Australian-born Rupert Murdoch, the owner of Sky Digital, Fox Broadcasting Company and other media institutions.

Advocates of a political economy view argue that, as in other industries, economic interests in media ownership work to exclude those voices that lack economic power. Moreover, the voices that *do* survive are those that are least likely to criticize the prevailing distribution of wealth and power (Golding and Murdock 1997). This view was famously advanced by the American linguist and radical writer Noam Chomsky, in *Media Control: The Spectacular Achievement of Propaganda* (1991). Chomsky is

---

THINKING CRITICALLY

What does the Iraq dossier episode tell us, if anything, about bias in the media? In times of war and conflict, is it the job of a public service broadcaster like the BBC to support the government or to be critical of it? As a non-commercial company, who should the BBC ultimately be responsible to, TV licence payers or the government of the day?

highly critical of the dominance of large corporations over the American and global media, which results in the tight control of information provided to the public. During the Cold War, for example, these corporations controlled information to create a climate of fear in the West about the Soviet Union. Since the collapse of the USSR in 1991, Chomsky argues that the corporately owned media have exaggerated fears of global terrorism, which prevents the airing of other issues that are, arguably, more significant such as the unaccountability of corporations or the lack of democracy from being properly discussed. Chomsky sees the mass media as disseminating propaganda in support of the ruling groups in society.

Ideology and bias in the media

The study of the media is closely related to the impact of ideology in society. Ideology refers to the influence of ideas on people's beliefs and actions. The concept has been widely used in media studies, as well as in other areas of sociology, but it has also long been controversial. The word was first coined by a French writer, Destutt de Tracy, in the late 1700s. He used it to refer to a 'science of ideas', which he thought would be a branch of knowledge. De Tracy's view has been seen as a 'neutral' conception of ideology. Neutral conceptions discuss phenomena as being ideological, but this does not imply they are misleading or biased in favour of particular social classes or groups.

In the hands of later authors, however, 'ideology' was used in a more critical way. Karl Marx, for example, saw ideology as important in the reproduction of relations of class domination. Powerful groups are able to control the dominant ideas circulating in a society so as to justify their own position. Thus, according to Marx, religion is often ideological: it teaches the poor to be content with their lot. The social analyst should uncover the distortions of ideology so as to allow the powerless to gain a true perspective on their lives – and take action to improve their conditions of life. Critical notions of ideology 'convey a negative, critical or pejorative sense' and carry within them 'an implicit criticism or condemnation' (Thompson 1990: 53–4).

John Thompson argues that the critical notion is to be preferred, because it links ideology with power. Ideology is about the exercise of symbolic power – how ideas are used to hide, justify or legitimate the interests of dominant groups in the social order. In their studies, members of the Glasgow Media Group (discussed in the 'Classic Studies 17.1') in effect, analyse the ideological aspects of TV news reporting and how it systematically generates bias. For example, when reporting on industrial disputes, news reports tend to favour government and management at the expense of striking workers. In general, Thompson argues that mass media – including not only the news but also all varieties of programme content and genre – greatly expand the scope of ideology in modern societies. They reach mass audiences and are, in his terms, based on 'quasi-interaction' – that is, audiences cannot answer back in a direct way.

In media and communication studies, a particular type of analysis – **discourse analysis** – has been widely used in the study of media products. Discourse analysts begin from the premise that language is a fundamental part of social life which is related to all other aspects and, in that sense, all social science has to take account of language and its use (Fairclough 1992). Discourse analysis is used to examine texts of many kinds, though there are different versions of it (van Dijk 1997). For example, some studies engage in a detailed analysis of texts and documents, while others, drawing on Foucault's ideas, connect texts to social theories of society, exploring the way that discourses construct and shape social life itself. Fairclough argues that, 'text analysis is an essential part of discourse analysis, but discourse analysis is not merely the linguistic analysis of texts' (2000: 3).

Classic Studies 17.1 **The Glasgow University Media Group brings 'bad news'**

The research problem

As we have seen, a substantial proportion of the population no longer reads newspapers. However, for many people, TV news is their key source of information about what goes on in the world. Can it be trusted to give a true and accurate picture of events? Why would the news *not* provide accurate information? And what are the consequences for our understanding of the world around us if it does not? Some of the best-known – and most controversial – research studies concerned with television news have been those carried out by the Glasgow University Media Group in the UK. Over the last three decades, the group has published a series of studies that are highly critical of the presentation of the news. Their early studies, including *Bad News* (1976), *More Bad News* (1981), *Really Bad News* (1983) and *War and Peace News* (1985), were very influential, setting out a research strategy for critical content analysis. Their research strategies were essentially similar in each of these studies, though they altered the focus of their investigations.

The Glasgow Group's explanation

Bad News (Glasgow Media Group 1976), their first and most influential book, was based on an analysis of TV news broadcasts on the three UK terrestrial channels available at that time, between January and June 1975. The objective was to provide a systematic and dispassionate analysis of the content of the news and the ways in which it was presented. *Bad News* concentrated on the portrayal of industrial disputes, whilst the later books concentrated more on political coverage, including the Falklands War of 1982.

The conclusion of *Bad News* was that news reporting of industrial relations was typically presented in a selective and biased fashion. Terms like 'trouble', 'radical' and 'pointless strike' suggested anti-union views. The effects of strikes, causing disruption for the public, were much more likely to be reported on than their underlying or immediate causes. Film material that was used, very often made the activities of

protesters appear irrational and aggressive. For example, film of strikers stopping people entering a factory would focus on any confrontations that occurred, even if they were infrequent.

Bad News also pointed out that those who construct the news act as 'gatekeepers' for what gets on the agenda – in other words, what the public hears about at all. Strikes in which there were active confrontations between workers and management, for instance, might get widely reported, while more consequential and long-lasting industrial disputes might be largely ignored. The view of news journalists, the Glasgow Media Group suggested, tends to reflect their middle-class backgrounds and supports the views of the dominant groups in society, who inevitably see strikers as dangerous and irresponsible.

In recent years, members of the Glasgow Media Group have carried out a range of further research studies. The latest edition of the *Bad News* series, *Bad News From Israel* (Philo and Berry 2004), examined television news reporting of the Israeli-Palestinian conflict. The study was carried out over a two-year period and was supported by several senior television news broadcasters and journalists who were involved in panel discussions with members of an 800-person sample audience. As well as looking at the television coverage of the conflict and its production, the authors were interested in how the coverage related to the understanding, beliefs and attitudes of the audience.

The study concluded that the television news coverage of the conflict confused viewers and substantially featured Israeli government views. There was little coverage devoted to the history or origins of the conflict for example, which would have contextualized the conflict. The study found a bias towards official 'Israeli perspectives', particularly on BBC 1, where Israelis were interviewed or reported more than twice as much as Palestinians. In addition, American politicians who supported Israel were often featured. The study also found that the news gave a strong emphasis to Israeli casualties, relative to Palestinians (although two to three times more Palestinians than Israelis died). There were also differences in the language used by journalists to describe Israeli and Palestinian attacks. For example, journalists would often describe Palestinian acts as 'terrorism', but when an Israeli group was reported as trying to bomb a Palestinian school, they were referred to as 'extremists' or 'vigilantes' (Philo and Berry 2004). The message of this body of work is that news reporting can never be thought of as neutral or 'objective'. Rather, news reporting reflects the unequal societies within which it exists and as such, should be seen as systematically biased.

Critical points

The work of the Glasgow Media Group are much discussed in media circles as well as in the academic community. Some news producers accused the researchers of simply exercising their own biases, which they thought lay with workers and strikers rather than government and management. They pointed out that, while *Bad News* contained a chapter entitled 'The trade unions and the media', there was no chapter on management and the media. This should have been discussed, because news journalists are often accused by management of bias against them in disputes, rather than against the strikers.

Academic critics made similar points. Martin Harrison (1985) gained access to transcripts of ITN news broadcasts for the period covered by the original 1976 study and argued that the five months analysed in the study were not typical. There was an abnormal number of days lost because of industrial action over the period and, as it would have been impossible for the news to report all of these, the tendency to focus on the more dramatic episodes was understandable.

In Harrison's view, the Glasgow Media Group was wrong to claim that news broadcasts concentrated too much on the effects of strikes. After all, many more people are affected by strikes than take part in them. Sometimes millions of people find their lives disrupted by the actions of just a handful of people. Finally, according to Harrison's analysis, some of the assertions made by the Media Group were simply false. For example, contrary to what the Group stated, the news reports did normally name the unions involved in disputes and did say whether or not the strikes were official or unofficial.

Contemporary significance

The central point made in the GMG studies holds that the news is never just a description of what 'actually happened'. The news is a complex construction and the process of construction regularly influences what 'the news' is. For example, when a politician appears on a news programme and makes a comment about a controversial issue – say, the state of the economy and what should be done about it – that comment itself becomes 'news' in subsequent programmes.

John Eldridge (1993), editor of one volume of GMG research, points out that what counts as objectivity in news reporting will always be difficult. Against those postmodernists who say that the idea of objectivity is irrelevant, Eldridge affirms the importance of continuing to look at media products with a critical eye. Accuracy in news reporting can and must be studied. After all, when the football results are reported, we expect them to be accurate. The work of the GMG forcefully reminds us that issues of truth and truthfulness are always involved in news reporting and the latter is certainly a worthy subject for sociological research.

Texts can be newspaper articles and personal diaries, but they can also be transcripts of interviews, ethnographic conversations and focus groups, films, television programmes and web pages. *Discourses* are 'systems of thought' or ways of thinking about and discussing the world within a particular framework. Discourses erect boundaries around subjects, which limit what can sensibly be said about them.

For example, the recent discourse on 'Islamic terrorism' sets the terms of debate for discussion of this phenomenon, ruling out alternative conceptions of the actions of

Does mass reproduction equal cultural destruction?

the people involved, as 'freedom fighters' for example. In *critical discourse analysis*, such discursive practices are linked to wider social structures of inequality and power relations, so that the ideological aspects of discourses can be identified and opened up for examination. Fairclough argues that, '. . . language connects with the social through being the primary domain of ideology, and through being both a site of, and a stake in, struggles for power' (1989: 15). As we see in 'Classic Studies 17.1', the continuing work of the Glasgow Media Group shows what critical content analysis can add to our understanding of the ideological character of news reporting in conflict situations.

The culture industry

Members of the Frankfurt School of critical theory (see chapter 3, page 76) such as Theodore Adorno (1903–69), were highly critical of the effects of mass media on the population and culture. The Frankfurt School was established in the 1920s and '30s, consisting of a loose group of theorists inspired by Marx who nevertheless saw that Marx's views needed radical revision. Among other things, they argued that Marx had not given enough attention to the influence of culture in modern capitalist societies.

Members of the Frankfurt School argued that leisure time had effectively been industrialized. Their extensive studies of what they called the 'culture industry' – such as the entertainment industries of film, TV, popular music, radio, newspapers and magazines – have been very influential in the field of cultural studies (Horkheimer and Adorno 2002 [1947]). They argued that in mass societies, the production of culture had become just as standardized and dominated by the desire for profit as other

Classic Studies 17.2 | **Jürgen Habermas on the rise and fall of the public sphere**

The research problem

Modern democracies developed alongside the mass media, particularly newspapers and other types of publication. In a very real sense, the mass media enabled and encouraged democracy. And yet today, the mass media is often seen negatively, as trivializing the democratic process and creating a climate of general hostility to politics itself. How did such a radical shift happen? Could it be reversed or is the mass media today inevitably failing democracies? German philosopher and sociologist, Jürgen Habermas, has been widely seen as the last influential intellectual from the Frankfurt School and he took up these questions in a series of important works.

Habermas's explanation

Habermas (1981, 1985, 1989 [1962]) developed themes from the Frankfurt School in different directions, based on his abiding interest in language and he process of democracy. He analysed the emergence and development of the mass media from the early eighteenth century to the present day, tracing the creation and subsequent decay of the 'public sphere'. For Habermas, the **public sphere** is an arena of public debate in which issues of general concern can be discussed and opinions formed, which is necessary for effective democratic participation and oils the wheels of the democratic process.

According to Habermas, the public sphere developed first in the salons and coffee houses of seventeenth- and eighteenth-century London, Paris and other European cities (see the depiction of a salon in chapter 1). People would meet to discuss issues of the moment, with political debate becoming a matter of particular importance. Although only small numbers of the population were involved in the salon cultures, Habermas argues that they were vital to the early development of democracy, primarily because the salons introduced the idea of resolving political problems through public discussion. The public sphere – at least in principle – involves individuals coming together as equals in a forum for public debate.

However, the promise offered by the early development of the public sphere has not been fully realized. Democratic debate in modern societies is now stifled by the development of the culture industry. The spread of mass media and mass entertainment causes the public sphere to become largely a sham. Politics is stage-managed in Parliament and the mass media, while commercial interests triumph over those of the public. 'Public opinion' is not formed through open, rational discussion any longer, but through manipulation and control – as, for example, in advertising. On the one hand, the spread of global media can put pressure on authoritarian governments to loosen their hold over state-controlled broadcasting outlets and many 'closed' societies such as China are discovering that the media can become a powerful force in support of democracy. Yet, as the global media become increasingly commercialized, they encroach on the public sphere in the way described by Habermas. Commercialized media are beholden to the power of advertising revenue and compelled to favour content that guarantees high ratings and sales. As a result, entertainment will necessarily triumph over controversy and debate, weakening citizen participation in public affairs and shrivelling the public sphere. The media, which promised so much, has now become part of the problem with democracy. Yet Habermas remains optimistic. He argues that it is still possible to envisage a political community beyond individual nation-states in which issues can be openly debated and where public opinion will influence governments.

Critical points

Habermas's ideas have been subject to an important critique. The salon culture that he holds up as an arena of civilized, rational debate was strictly limited to the higher social classes and was beyond the reach of the working class. In short, it was an elitist pastime that bore little real resemblance to the needs of mass democratic participation. Habermas's view that the modern mass media are destructive of the public sphere has also been seen as misguided. As we will see below, John Thompson (1995) argues that the media actually enables *more* public debate by airing a variety of public matters and encouraging a wider discussion. The Internet, with its innumerable forums and chatrooms, is just the latest example of this.

Contemporary significance

Habermas's ideas have provoked a good deal of debate and much controversy. Currently, it appears that they have lost some ground in the wake of critique from those who defend the mass media as, on balance, a positive force in society, but also from postmodern thinkers who see Habermas as working within the older Frankfurt tradition, with its fear and mistrust of the 'mass' public. There is some truth in such critiques. And yet, Habermas is a powerful reminder that the rational, modernist project that we can trace back to the Enlightenment still has much to offer sociological or social theory. In particular, Habermas's work is scholarly, full of dense research material and serious-minded. As a model for all new students of sociology, it remains a very positive one.

industries. The concept of a mass society suggests that cultural differences have become levelled down in the densely populated developed societies, where cultural products are targeted at the largest possible audience. In a mass society, the leisure industry was used to induce appropriate values amongst the public: leisure was no longer a break from work, but a preparation for it.

Members of the Frankfurt School argued that the spread of the culture industry, with its undemanding and standardized products, undermined the capacity of individuals for critical and independent thought. Art disappears, swamped by commercialization – 'Mozart's Greatest Hits', for example, or student posters of the great works of art – and culture is replaced by simple entertainment. As Lazarsfeld and Merton commented on the USA in the 1950s: 'Economic power seems to have reduced direct exploitation and to have turned to a subtler type of psychological exploitation' (cited in Curran and Seaton 2003).

Conflict theories remain popular in media studies, though they are subject to some of the same criticisms as functionalist theories. There is a tendency to assume that people are unable to resist media propaganda and fall easy prey to it. Like functionalism, the early critical theorists paid little or no attention to audiences and the reception of media messages, focusing

> ### THINKING CRITICALLY
>
> Do you think that the mass reproduction of great works of art devalues them? Why should a wall poster of, say, the *Mona Lisa*, be described as 'undemanding' when the original is not? Is there a positive side to mass reproduction of this kind – who benefits from it, if anyone?

instead on the production of culture. The Frankfurt School's damning critique of mass culture has also been seen as linked to their defence of the high culture – classical music, opera, painting and the arts – favoured by social elites (Swingewood 1977). This is somewhat ironic, of course, given the Marxist origins of critical theory. As we will see later, this distinction between high and 'low' or popular culture was seized upon and attacked by postmodern media theorists in the 1980s and '90s.

Habermas and Herman and McChesney are not the only ones to notice that the public sphere was in trouble. In *The Fall of Public Man* (2003 [1977]) Richard Sennett argued that the private and public spheres have become separated, both physically – with the separate development of residential housing estates, workplaces and leisure developments (including shopping arcades) – and philosophically, in the way we think about our distinct private lives, for example. However, the private sphere has tended to canalize – or take over – the public sphere, so that, for instance, politicians are now judged more on their personal characteristics such as honesty and sincerity, rather than their ability to perform public roles. And the advent of modern visual media, especially television, has led to a highly developed presentation of self by political figures aimed at matching such expectations of their personalities. Sennett sees this as destructive of an effective political life and representative of the fall of the dedicated public official.

However, there are some problems with the way the 'the public sphere' is presented and idealized in these various accounts. The public sphere was constituted by excluding certain social groups including women, ethnic minorities and non-property owners. Even though essentially limited in this way, the notion of a public sphere allowed middle-class men to perceive themselves and their role and to present it to others as universal. Feminist scholars argue that Habermas did not pay enough attention to the *gendered* nature of the public sphere. In separating the public sphere from the domestic, private sphere, many issues that were important for women were simply excluded. As Nancy Fraser argues, 'The view that women were excluded from the public sphere turns out to be ideological; . . . In fact, . . . the bourgeois public was never *the* public' (1992: 116).

This alerts us to another important point, namely that some 'publics' – such as women – were *intentionally* blocked from participating, demonstrating that conflictual social relations underpinned the idealized conception of a common public sphere. What critics suggest therefore, is that the 'bourgeois concept' of the public sphere was a male-dominated one that helped to legitimize systematic social inequalities.

Symbolic interactionism

Interactionist media studies have not been as numerous as functionalism and conflict theories, though they have become more popular in recent years. Herbert Blumer's 1930s study of the impact of cinema on the audience was an early attempt to allow people themselves to inform sociological understandings of media influence. Blumer asked 1,500 American high school and college students to record their experiences of watching films in 'autobiographies', presenting these in his book, *Movies and Conduct* (1970 [1933]). Although pioneering in some ways, the study has been seen as rather naive, both in believing that the respondents' views could 'speak for themselves' and in its rather simple approach to cinematic 'texts'.

Perhaps the most influential interactionist approach to the media is moral panic theory, which emerged out of the labelling perspectives of Charles Lemert and Howard Becker. Stan Cohen's (2003 [1972]) famous study of clashes between Mods and Rockers in the UK showed how exaggerated and sensational media representations contribute to recurring moral panics in society. Such panics serve to scapegoat social groups, including youth cultures and ethnic minorities, taking attention away from structural problems like unemployment and economic recession.

 See chapter 21, 'Crime and Deviance', for a discussion of the labelling perspective and also for a detailed discussion of moral panic theory, which you may want to refer to.

THINKING CRITICALLY

In what ways are social networking sites such as Bebo or MySpace similar to and different from the kind of salon culture discussed by Sennett and Habermas above? Is the conversation and discussion on such sites part of the contemporary public sphere? If it is, how representative of 'the public' are such sites? Who is likely to be excluded?

More recently, and drawing partly on the work of Habermas, John Thompson has analysed the relation between the media and the development of industrial societies (1990, 1995). From early forms of print through to electronic communication, Thompson argues, the media have played a central role in the development of modern institutions. The main founders of sociology, including Marx, Weber and Durkheim gave too little attention to the role of media in shaping even the early development of modern society.

Sympathetic to some of the ideas of Habermas, Thompson is also critical of him, as he is of the Frankfurt School and of Baudrillard's postmodern position. The Frankfurt School's attitude to the culture industry was too negative. The modern mass media, Thompson thinks, do not deny us the possibility for critical thought; in fact, they provide us with many forms of information to which we could not have had access previously. In common with the Frankfurt School, he says, too often Habermas tends to treat people as the passive recipients of media messages rather than active agents:

> Media messages are commonly discussed by individuals in the course of reception and subsequent to it. . . . [They] are transformed through an ongoing process of telling and retelling, interpretation and

reinterpretation, commentary, laughter and criticism. . . . By taking hold of messages and routinely incorporating them into our lives . . . we are constantly shaping and reshaping our skills and stocks of knowledge, testing our feelings and tastes, and expanding the horizons of our experience. (1995: 42–3)

Thompson's theory of the media depends on a distinction between three types of interaction (see table 17.2). *Face-to-face* interaction, such as people talking at a party,

Table 17.2 Types of interaction

Interactional characteristics	Face-to-face interaction	Mediated interaction	Mediated quasi-interaction
Space–time constitution reference system	Context of co-presence; shared spatial-temporal time and space	Separation of contexts; extended availability in time and space	Separation of contexts; extended availability in time and space
Range of symbolic cues	Multiplicity of symbolic cues	Narrowing of the range of symbolic cues	Narrowing of the range of symbolic cues
Action orientation	Oriented towards specific others	Oriented towards specific others	Oriented towards an indefinite range of potential recipients
Dialogical/ monological	Dialogical	Dialogical	Monological

Source: Thompson 1995: 465

is rich in the cues used by individuals to make sense of what others say (see chapter 7, 'Social Interaction and Everyday Life'). *Mediated interaction* involves the use of a media technology – paper, electrical connections, electronic impulses. Characteristic of mediated interaction is that it is stretched out in time and space – it goes well beyond the contexts of ordinary face-to-face interaction. Mediated interaction takes place between individuals in a direct way – for instance, two people talking on the telephone – but there is not an opportunity for the same variety of non-verbal cues.

A third type of interaction is *mediated quasi-interaction*. This refers to the sort of social relations created by the mass media. Such interaction is stretched across time and space, but does not link individuals directly: hence the term 'quasi-interaction'. The two previous types are 'dialogical': individuals communicate in a direct way. Mediated quasi-interaction is 'monological': a TV programme, for example, is a one-way form of communication. People watching the programme may discuss it, and perhaps address some remarks to the TV set – but, of course, it does not answer back.

Thompson's point is that all three types of interaction intermingle in our lives today. The mass media, he suggests, changes the balance between the public and the private in our lives. Unlike Sennett and Habermas, though, Thompson argues that this shift brings *more* into the public domain than before, not less, and often leads to more debate and controversy than previously. Postmodern theorists see things rather differently and some argue that mediated quasi-interaction has come to dominate the other two types, with dramatic and negative consequences for social life.

It is the case that more people today are appearing on television to discuss moral and political issues on audience discussion shows such as Oprah Winfrey and Ricki Lake, and in so-called 'reality television' shows, such as *Big Brother*, *Wife Swap* and many others. In addition, millions of people watch these programmes at home and discuss their content at work, in pubs and other social gathering places. In the case of the global phenomenon *Big Brother*, audiences interact with the show, taking part in voting for televised evictions of participants (which often attract more votes than are cast in national elections) and commenting in online forums and spin-off shows. But are such programmes really providing new public spaces for citizens to engage in moral and political debates on key issues of the day or are they just cheap and trashy TV for the masses?

In an empirical study of *audience discussion programmes*, Livingstone and Lunt (1993) used a multi-method approach involving focus group discussions, individual interviews, textual analysis of the programmes and a survey questionnaire to gather the views of studio audiences and home viewers. They argue that such programmes deal with current issues as they affect people's everyday experiences, use experts, but are not really documentaries and tend to construct viewers as community members (Signes 2000). Hence, audience discussion programmes do not easily fit into any existing TV genre. As types of participation largely depend on the conventions of the genre involved, these programmes are particularly open and undefined. Some involve both lay people and experts sitting together while the host moves around with a microphone. In these shows, experts can be questioned and challenged, and thus made accountable. In this sense, they are public spaces for the exercise of democracy and this is reinforced through the systematic prioritization of the lay rather than the expert perspective (Livingstone and Lunt 1993).

However, this positive conclusion can be questioned, as the study did not explore the 'interactional dynamics' of the actual discussions within the programmes (Hutchby 2005). This is an important criticism because the issue of who speaks and when is a fundamental part of the shaping of conversations in particular directions. For example, audience discussions follow a certain formulaic progression, usually dominated and steered by the host, which means that these programmes may not be quite such open, public forums as they appear in audience and participants' accounts of them (Tolson 2005). There have also been allegations of actors being hired and paid to take part in discussion programmes, such as Jerry Springer in the USA and Vanessa Feltz's show in the UK. The latter was cancelled in 1999 when it was revealed that an agency had been used to source several audience members. Such episodes are reminders of Neil Postman's argument that TV is primarily an *entertainment* medium, to which all of its other potentially useful functions are subordinated. No consensus has yet emerged amongst media scholars on which side of this debate is most strongly supported by the evidence.

THINKING CRITICALLY

How satisfactory is Thompson's threefold schema? Is television still 'monological', for example, or is it becoming more 'dialogical'? In what ways? Is Thompson's optimistic conclusion justified or is the mass media, on the whole, damaging to social life? Give specific reasons for your answer.

Postmodern theory

Since the publication of Jean-François Lyotard's *The Postmodern Condition* (1985), sociology has had to contend with a set of ideas about science, knowledge and culture that seem to be at odds with the progressive, modernist ideas and ideals of modern life since the Enlightenment period. Lyotard argued that the great metanarratives of modernity, scientific truths, progress and history, are now in decline.

Science continues, but in the wake of global warming and the loss of global biodiversity, who now believes that it leads inexorably to a better life for all? Technologies develop and many of us can have camera phones, digital TVs and personal games consoles at home, but in the light of continuing undernourishment, famine and wars, does anyone really still believe that we are witnessing human progress in history? For postmodern thinkers like Zygmunt Bauman (1992, 1997), the demise of such metanarratives is a positive development. It means that we live in a period when people are forced to face our modernity head-on and with no more grand illusions. We live in a time of 'self-conscious modernity', which Bauman (and others) describe as **postmodernity**.

The postmodern world is one marked by a lack of certainty, a mixing and matching of styles and genres and a playfulness in relation to cultural products. In pop music, there is the advent of sampling, the mixing of original tracks with new rhythms and rap. In film, David Lynch's seminal *Blue Velvet* (1986), merged time periods and historical eras seamlessly, with vehicles from the 1950s, '60s and '70s driving the same 1980s streets. And in art, postmodern trends reject the idea of a progressive 'avant-garde', instead mixing high and popular forms in playful 'post-progressive' ways. Lyotard saw such playful mixing as marking the end of specific modern genres. At the end of a progressive Western culture, he said, all that is left to do is to 'play with the pieces'.

Baudrillard and hyperreality

One of the most influential contemporary media theorists is the French postmodernist thinker Jean Baudrillard (1929–2007), whose work has been strongly influenced by the ideas of Marshall McLuhan. Baudrillard regards the impact of modern mass media as being quite different from, and very much more profound than, that of any previous media technology. The coming of the mass media, particularly electronic media such as

Was the 2003 invasion of Iraq a hyperreal event? How?

television, has transformed the very nature of our lives. TV does not just 'represent' the world to us; it increasingly defines what the world in which we live actually is.

Baudrillard's postmodern ideas can be hard to grasp, but a relatively simple way of doing so is as follows. There was a time – not so long ago – when it was possible to separate reality, or the real world and its events, from media representations of that world. So, for instance, in the real world there may be a war with real and terrible consequences for the combatants and civilians caught up in it. The media report on this war and inform us of what is happening; how many casualties there are, who is winning and so on. These two aspects – the reality and the representations – were seen as quite separate things.

But Baudrillard's (1983) theory argues that the border between reality and repre-

sentation has collapsed; we can no longer separate out representations from reality. Why not? After all, there are still wars and there are still reporters sending back images and reports on them. Baudrillard argues that the media representations are in fact, *part of* the hyperreal world and cannot be seen as separate from it. As the vast majority of people only ever 'know' about wars via media representations of them, their reality is shaped, determined even, by the media. Hyperreality is a world in which the ultimate guarantor of authenticity and reality is to be seen on TV and in the media – to be 'more real than the real'. This may be one part of an explanation for the growth of our celebrity culture, where the only genuinely acceptable sign of success and significance is to appear on TV or in glossy magazines.

Just before the outbreak of hostilities in the first Gulf War in 1991, Baudrillard wrote a newspaper article entitled 'The Gulf War cannot happen'. When war was declared and a bloody conflict took place, it might seem obvious that Baudrillard got it wrong. Not a bit of it. After the end of the war, Baudrillard (2004 [1991]) then wrote *The Gulf War Did Not Take Place*. What did he mean? He meant that the war was not like other wars that have happened in history. It was a war of the media age, a televisual spectacle, in which, along with other viewers throughout the world, George Bush Senior and former President of Iraq, Saddam Hussein, watched the coverage by CNN to see what was actually 'happening'.

Baudrillard argues that, in an age where the mass media are everywhere, in effect a new reality – hyperreality – is created, composed of the intermingling of people's behaviour and media images. The world of hyperreality is constructed of simulacra – images which only get their meaning from other images and hence have no grounding in an 'external reality'. A famous series of advertisements for Silk Cut cigarettes, for example, did not refer to the cigarettes at all, but only to previous ads which had appeared in a long series. No political leader today can win an election if he or she does not appear constantly on television: the TV image of the leader is the 'person' most viewers know, however misleading such an image may be.

Baudrillard's theory is seductive in an age of the global mass media and it certainly has to be taken seriously. However, it can be objected that, once again, it tends to treat the mass of people as passive recipients of media messages and forms, rather than being able to engage with and even to resist them. Many media-savvy social movement organizations such as Greenpeace do try to compete with the mass media to create an alternative (hyper)reality which will motivate the uncommitted to environmental activism. It also remains the case that many real-world conflicts fail to attract sufficient Western media interest, such as the ongoing conflict in the Darfur region of Sudan, and therefore fall outside Baudrillard's hyperre-

ality, but the outcome of the conflict will still shape that country's future and its relations internationally. There is still a real world beyond the media-saturated hyperreality of postmodern theory.

> ### THINKING CRITICALLY
>
> List as many examples of 'hyperreality' as you can think of. Explain in your own words exactly what makes each one 'hyperreal'. Why should it matter that we can only understand the world through the lens of the mass media? Could it ever be any other way in our global age?

Audiences and media representations

The effect that ideological bias has on the audience depends upon the theoretical position one takes over the position of the audience for mass media. Here, we turn to the question through a relatively brief analysis of audience studies and media representations of social groups.

Audience studies

One of the earliest, and the most straightforward, models of audience response is the *hypodermic model*. This compares the media message to a drug injected by syringe. The model is based on the assumption that the audience (patient) passively and directly accepts the message and does not critically engage with it in any way. The hypodermic model also assumes that the message is received and interpreted in more or less the same way by all members of society. The concept of narcotization, associated with the Frankfurt School, draws on the hypodermic model. Under this view, the media is seen as 'drugging' the audience, destroying its ability to think critically about the wider world (Marcuse 1964). The hypodermic model is now out of fashion, and was often little more than an unstated

The hypodermic model assumes that media messages are passively received by viewers. Such ideas are often implicit in arguments about the effects of television on children.

assumption in the works of early writers on the mass media. However, the model's assumptions about the media can still be found in the works of contemporary writers who are sceptical about the effects of the mass media on modern society.

Critics of the hypodermic model have pointed out that it takes no account of the very different responses that different audiences have to the media, treating them as homogenous and passive. Most theorists now argue that audience responses go through various stages. In their work on audience response, Katz and Lazarsfeld (1955) drew on studies of political broadcasts during US presidential elections, and argued that audience response is formed through a two-step flow: the first step is when the media reaches the audience; the second comes when the audience interprets the media through their social interaction with influential people – 'opinion leaders' – who further shape audience response.

Later models assume a more active role for an audience in response to the media. The *gratification model* looks at the ways in which different audiences use the media to meet their own needs (Lull 1990). Audiences may use the media to learn more about the world they live in – finding out about the weather or stock market, for example. Others may use the media to help with their relationships, to feel part of a fictional community (from watching TV soaps, for example), or to get on with friends and colleagues who also watch the same programme. Critics of this model have argued that it assumes that the needs of the audience already exist, not that they are created by the media.

Later theories of audience response have looked at the ways in which people actively interpret the media. Stuart Hall's account of *reception theory* (1980) focuses on the way in which an audience's class and cultural background affects the way in which it makes sense of different media 'texts' – a term that is used to encompass various forms of media from books and newspapers to films and CDs. Some members of an audience may simply accept the preferred reading 'encoded' in a text – such as a news bulletin – by its producer. This preferred reading, Hall argues, is likely to reflect the dominant or mainstream ideology (as the Glasgow Media Group found). However, Hall argues that the understanding of a text also depends on the cultural and class background of the person interpreting it. Other members of an audience may take an 'oppositional' reading of a text, because their social position places them in conflict with the preferred reading. For example, a worker involved in strike action or a member of an ethnic minority is likely to take an oppositional reading of a text such as a news story on industrial or race relations, rather than accept the dominant reading encoded in the text by its producer.

Recent theories have also focused on the way in which audiences filter information through their own experience (Halloran 1970). The audience may link different media 'texts' (programmes or genres, for example) or use one type of media to engage with another – questioning what they are told on the television compared to the newspaper (Fiske 1988). Here the audience has a powerful role, far removed from the hypodermic model. The *interpretative model* views audience response as shaping the media through its engagement or rejection of its output.

What we can see in this brief sketch of audience studies is the movement away from an overly simplistic understanding of the relationship between media output and the audience, towards increasingly more sophisticated models that place much more emphasis on the active audience. We can also see a shift away from one-way models (from media to the audience) in favour of two-way models that allow room for audiences to shape media output rather than simply being passive sponges soaking up whatever comes their way.

Representing class, gender, ethnicity and disability

An issue that has received much attention in media studies is the problem of media representations, particularly in television fiction. Which social groups should the mass media represent and which groups are absent from our TV screens? What effects might this have on the audience? We briefly look at the way that representations of social class, gender, ethnicity and disabled people serve to reinforce stereotypes, though there is some evidence that this may now be changing in some cases.

Representations of the working class on UK television appear to be ubiquitous (Kendall 2005). From soap operas such as the UK's long-running *Coronation Street* (from 1960 to the present) and *EastEnders* (1985 to the present), to films exploring working-class life such as *Saturday Night and Sunday Morning* (1960) or *Billy Elliott* (2000) and drama series like *Boys from the Black Stuff* (1982) and *Auf Wiedersehen Pet* (1983); there seems to be no shortage of representations of working-class lives on TV and film.

This may well be true, but some have argued that the majority of such representations reflect a middle-class version of what working-class life is like. This is mainly because the production of TV and film is dominated by middle-class professionals and consequently presents a somewhat distorted view. The working class tends to be shown in northern industrial cities and environments; people work with their hands in manual jobs (or are unemployed) and are seldom shown as making livings in other ways. The environments they live in are usually presented as hard and unforgiving, but, paradoxically, also as strong communities exhibiting social solidarity. This stereotypical presentation has been remarkably enduring and persists today.

Research studies have repeatedly demonstrated that representations of girls and women in the mass media overwhelmingly use traditional stereotypes of gender roles. Women are conventionally seen in domestic roles as housewives and homemakers, objects of male sexual desire or in working situations that extend the domestic role – such as nurses, carers or office workers. Generally, such representations have been fairly consistent across news reports, drama and entertainment programming, leading Gaye Tuchman (1978) to refer to 'the symbolic annihilation of women' on television. For example, between 1973 and 1993, of all characters on American prime time television, 68.5 per cent were male; the proportion went down from 72 per cent in 1973 to 65 per cent by 1993 (Gerbner 1997).

However, more recent research has concluded that things are changing, albeit slowly, with an increasing variety of portrayals, including that of the strong, independent woman (Glascock 2001; Meyers 1999). New female heroines such as Buffy the Vampire Slayer, La Femme Nikita and Lara Croft, alongside female characters such as high-powered lawyers (*The Practice*), police chiefs (*Prime Suspect*) and other professions in TV drama, all attest to some changing representations of women.

> See chapter 14, 'Sexuality and Gender', for a detailed discussion of gender issues.

Things are not quite so simple though. Many of these strong female characters still conform to other feminine norms. Buffy and Lara Croft are still young, slim and attractive women who appeal to the 'male gaze', and many health professionals and researchers see the persistent media portrayal of ideal female bodies as a contributory factor in the problem of eating disorders, particularly amongst young women. Many of the older successful, professional women also tend to have disastrous or empty personal lives, which illustrates Susan Faludi's (1991) argument of a subtle backlash (both in reality and fictional accounts) against women who break with conventional gender roles – it will all end in tears eventually!

> **THINKING CRITICALLY**
>
> Do you watch soap operas? If so, which ones? Why do you find them attractive? If you do not, what do you think other people, who do watch, actually get out of the experience? How might soap operas be analysed by neo-Marxist critical theorists as being part of the 'culture industry' and is that type of explanation convincing? What criticisms could be levelled at it?

Media representations of ethnic minorities and disabled people have also been seen as reinforcing rather than challenging stereotypes. Black and Asian people were noticeably absent from mainstream television until quite recently, and even when they were present, for example in news reports and documentaries, this tended to be as problematic social groups. For example, media coverage of the 1970s moral panic around 'mugging' (Hall at al. 1978), or the inner-city riots of the 1980s and early twenty-first century, was extensive.

Jack Shaheen's *TV Arabs* (1984) and *Reel Bad Arabs: How Hollywood Vilifies a People* (2001) examined the portrayal of Arabs on television and in Hollywood films (mostly American made) respectively. The 1984 study looked at more than 100 television shows featuring Arab characters between 1975 and 1984. Shaheen argues that TV depictions depend on four myths: '[Arabs] are all fabulously wealthy; they are barbaric and uncultured; they are sex maniacs with a penchant for white slavery; they revel in acts of terrorism' (1984: 179). They are

17.3   Real life and soap operas

A genre created by radio and television came to be called 'soap opera' – now TV's most popular type of programme. Of the most watched TV shows in Britain each week, almost all are soaps – *EastEnders, Coronation Street, Emmerdale* and several others. Soap operas fall into various different types, or sub-genres, at least on British TV. Soaps produced in the UK, like *Coronation Street*, tend to be gritty and down to earth, often concerned with the lives of poorer people. Second, there are American imports, many of which, like *Dallas* in the 1980s, portray more glamorous lives. A third category is made up of Australian imports, such as *Neighbours*. These tend to be low-budget productions, featuring middle-class homes and lifestyles.

Soaps are like TV as a whole: continuous. Individual stories may come to an end, and different characters appear and disappear, but the soap itself has no ending until it is taken off the air completely. Tension is created between episodes by so-called 'cliff-hangers'. The episode stops abruptly just before some key event happens and the viewer has to wait until the next episode to see how things turn out.

A basic part of the genre of soap opera is that it demands regular viewing on the part of whoever watches it. A single episode makes very little sense. Soap operas presume a history, which the regular viewer knows – he or she becomes familiar with the characters, with their personalities and their life experiences. The threads, which are linked to create such a history, are above all personal and emotional – soaps for the most part do not look at larger social or economic frameworks, which impinge only from the outside.

Sociologists have put different views forward as to why soap operas are so popular – and they are popular across the world, not only in Britain or America, but also in Africa, Asia and Latin America. Some think that they provide a means of escape, particularly where women (who watch soaps in greater numbers than men) find their own lives dull or oppressive. Such a view is not particularly convincing, though, given that many soaps feature people whose lives are just as problematic. More plausible is the idea that soap operas address universal properties of personal and emotional life. They explore dilemmas anyone may face, and perhaps they even help some viewers to think more creatively about their own lives. In her book *Soap Opera* (2002), the sociologist Dorothy Hobson argues that soaps work not because they are escapist, but 'because the audience has intimate familiarity with the characters and their lives. Through its characters the soap opera must connect with the experience of its audience, and its content must be stories of the ordinary.'

usually dressed strangely, reinforcing the view that Arabs do not look or act like Americans. Such portrayals were just as easy to find in children's cartoons and many educational programmes, though some more recent documentaries had attempted to provide more accurate accounts.

In the overwhelming majority of Hollywood film characterizations, Shaheen found that Arab characters were the 'bad guys'. In fact, out of around 1,000 films, just 12 involved positive depictions, 52 were quite balanced and the other 900+ portrayed Arabs this way. This was the case irrespective of whether the film was a block-buster or low-budget feature, and whether the character was central to the plot or played a minor part. Shaheen shows that Arab stereotypes have existed in film since 1896 and generally depict Arab people as, 'brutal, heartless, uncivilized religious fanatics and money-mad cultural "others" bent on terrorizing civilized Westerners, especially Christians and Jews'. He argues that such stereotypes are useful for writers and film-makers as they make their jobs that much easier. Shaheen suggests this situation will only change when the Arab American community is powerful enough to exert an influence on the film industry in the same way that women and African Americans have done in the past.

Ethnic minorities have also been commonly presented as different from an indigenous white British culture and often, as presenting problems for it (Solomos and Back 1996). Recent attempts to produce more representative imagery, for instance, in soaps (or 'serial dramas') such as *East-Enders*, may offer a way forward. The serial drama provides a format which allows a variety of ethnic groups to be shown as ordinary members of society with similar lives and personal troubles to everyone else. Perhaps it is through such mundane representations that stereotypes can be avoided?

If ethnic minorities have been defined as *culturally* different, then the representations of disabled people in the media have routinely been as *physically* or *bodily* different, based on the 'personal tragedy' model of disability (Oliver 1990; also see chapter 10). News stories involving disabled people are much more likely to get an airing if the story can be fitted into this dominant framing and typically, this means showing disabled people as dependent, rather than living independent lives (Karpf 1988).

Disabled people have been all but invisible in TV drama and entertainment and, when they are included, are over-represented amongst criminals and mentally unstable characters or amongst 'the bad, mad and sad'. This situation has a very long history. Think of the evil Captain Hook in *Peter Pan*, the tragic Quasimodo in *The Hunchback of Notre Dame* or John Merrick in *The Elephant Man*. Disabled characters are never incidental to a storyline, but are included precisely because of their disability. In a content analysis of six weeks of UK television, Cumberbatch and Negrine (1992) found just 0.5 per cent of fictional characters were disabled people and almost all of these were wheelchair users – not an accurate representation of disabled people in the UK, the overwhelming majority of whom are not wheelchair users.

A 1992 report by sociologist and disability activist, Colin Barnes, on media representa-tions of disabled people found some positive changes, particularly in American drama series, which tried to present disabled people as 'normal', playing down the characters' disabilities. However, Barnes sees that simply ignoring disability is not the answer. Instead, he argues:

> The only solution with any hope of success is for all media organisations to provide the kind of information and imagery which; firstly, acknowledges and explores the complexity of the experience of disability and a disabled identity and; secondly, facilitates the meaningful integration of all disabled people into the mainstream economic and social life of the community. (1991: 19)

Media representations are not the *cause* of discrimination or exclusion of disabled people from mainstream society. Nevertheless, stereotypical representations can *reinforce* existing negative ideas of social groups and in doing so can be seen as part of the wider social problem. Despite some signs of a growing awareness of the issue and some positive change in recent years, the examples above show that it will be some time yet before media representations make any significant contribution to challenging social stereotypes.

Controlling the global media

Sociological theories of the various forms of media show us that they can never be assumed to be politically neutral or socially beneficial. For many people, a key problem is the increasing concentration of ownership of different types of media within large conglomerates that have come to be known as 'supercompanies'. If politicians were alarmed at the ownership of a single national newspaper by one of the big press barons, then how much more serious is ownership of transnational media companies? As we have seen throughout this book, the Internet is one of the main

The dramatic increase in mobile-phone coverage around the world is one way in which globalization continues to compress time and space.

contributors to – and manifestations of – current processes of globalization. Yet globalization is also transforming the international reach and impact of other forms of media as well. In this section we will consider some of the changes affecting the mass media under conditions of globalization.

Although the media have always had international dimensions – such as the gathering of news stories and the distribution of films overseas – until the 1970s most media companies operated within specific domestic markets in accordance with regulations from national governments. The media industry was also differentiated into distinct sectors – for the most part, cinema, print media, radio and television broadcasting all operated independently of one another.

In the past three or four decades, however, profound transformations have taken place within the media industry. National markets have given way to a fluid global market, while new technologies have led to the fusion of forms of media that were once distinct. By the start of the twenty-first century, the global media market was dominated by a group of about 20 multinational corporations whose role in the production, distribution and marketing of news and entertainment could be felt in almost every country in the world.

In their work on globalization, David Held and his colleagues (1999) point to five major shifts that have contributed to bringing about the global media order:

1 *Increasing concentration of ownership.* The global media is now dominated by a

small number of powerful corporations. The small-scale, independent media companies have gradually been incorporated into highly centralized media conglomerates.

2 *A shift from public to private ownership.* Traditionally, media and telecommunications companies in almost all countries were partially or fully owned by the state. In the past few decades, the liberalization of the business environment and the relaxing of regulations have led to the privatization (and commercialization) of media companies in many countries.

3 *Transnational corporate structures.* Media companies no longer operate strictly within national boundaries. Likewise, media ownership rules have been loosened to allow cross-border investment and acquisition.

4 *Diversification over a variety of media products.* The media industry has diversified and is much less segmented than in previous times. Enormous media conglomerates, such as Time Warner Inc. (profiled below), produce and distribute a mix of media content, including music, news, print media and television programming.

5 *A growing number of corporate media mergers.* There has been a distinctive trend towards alliances between companies in different segments of the media industry. Telecommunications firms, computer hardware and software manufacturers, and media 'content' producers are increasingly involved in corporate mergers as media forms become increasingly integrated.

The globalization of the media has thrust 'horizontal' forms of communications to centre stage. If traditional media forms ensured that communication occurred within the boundaries of nation-states in a 'vertical' fashion, globalization is leading to the horizontal integration of communica-

tions. Not only are people making connections with one another at a grass-roots level, but also media products are being disseminated widely due to new harmonized regulatory frameworks, ownership policies and transnational marketing strategies. Communications and media can now more readily extend themselves beyond the confines of individual countries (Srebrerny-Mohammadi et al. 1997).

Yet like other aspects of global society, the new information order has developed unevenly and reflects divisions between the developed societies and less developed countries. Some commentators have suggested that the new global media order would be better described as 'media imperialism'.

Media imperialism?

The paramount position of the industrialized countries, above all the United States, in the production and diffusion of media has led many observers to speak of **media imperialism** (Herman and McChesney 2003). According to this view, a cultural empire has been established. Less developed countries are held to be especially vulnerable, because they lack the resources to maintain their own cultural independence.

However, others argue that American media domination is not as simple as the above sketch suggests. What *exactly* is media imperialism? Does it exist when people from other cultures watch, and perhaps come to accept as superior, Western cultural products – the content of TV programmes, film and music, for example – that are imbued with Western cultural values? Or does media imperialism lie in the export of particular technologies such as television and mobile phones, which disrupt local cultures and transform them? Or does it exist when one country or region's media industries become so powerful they take over or force out of existence the local media outlets? And can we even speak of domination at all, when people across the world have chosen to purchase TV sets and mobile phones and actually claim to find use and pleasures in them (Tomlinson 1991)?

The headquarters of the world's 20 largest media conglomerates are all located in industrialized nations; the majority of them are in the United States. Media empires such as Time Warner, Disney/ABC and Viacom are all US-based. Other large media corporations – apart from the Murdoch empire profiled in the 'Global Society 17.1' – include Sony BMG (one of the 'big 4' music companies), a joint venture between Sony Music Group and Bertelsmann Music Group, which owns numerous record labels including Arista and Columbia Records and distributes many independent labels; and Mondadori, a publishing house controlled by the television corporation owned by Silvio Berlusconi, the Italian Prime Minister.

Through the electronic media, Western cultural products have certainly become widely diffused round the globe. As we have seen, American films are available around the world, as is Western popular music. A new Disney theme park in Hong Kong was opened in 2005, which replicates largely American attractions, rather than reflecting local culture. For example, the 'themed lands' in Hong Kong are Main Street (USA), Adventureland, Fantasyland and Tomorrowland, with all the usual characters, including Mickey Mouse, Donald Duck, Winnie the Pooh and Buzz Lightyear. And, as the chairman of Disney theme parks indicated, this may be just the beginning: 'If there is only one Disney theme park in a country with 1.3 billion people, that doesn't compare very well to five theme parks in the US with only a population of 280 million' (quoted in Gittings 1999).

It is not only the more popular entertainment forms that are at issue, however. Control of the world's news by the major Western agencies, it has been suggested, means the predominance of a 'First World outlook' in the information conveyed. Thus it has been claimed that attention is given to the developing world in news broadcasts mainly in times of disaster, crisis or military confrontation, and that the daily files of other types of news kept on the industrialized world are not maintained for developing world coverage.

Nonetheless, there are also some counter-trends which may support a more pluralistic theory of the media at a global level. One such is that of 'reverse flows', where media products in, for example, former colonial countries become popular and can be sold to former colonizers. Reverse flows suggest that media imperialism is not absolute or unchallengeable. A well-known example of a reverse-flow is the increasingly international success of the Mumbai-based, Hindi language, Indian film industry: Bollywood. Bollywood is the largest producer of films in the world and, though many have in the past only been seen by a domestic audience, this is changing as global migration patterns lead to South Asian communities around the world. Bollywood films are also becoming more popular in the UK (the former colonial power), the USA and Russia, and come second only to Hollywood films in Australia.

A second criticism is that the thesis of media imperialism rests implicitly on the 'hypodermic needle' model (discussed earlier), which tends to assume that Western cultural products carry with them Western values that are 'injected' into passive consumers around the globe. However, the growth of audience studies has alerted us to the fact that consumers are active, not passive, watchers and listeners, and may reject, modify or reinterpret the messages in media products. Ien Ang's (1985) study of the American series *Dallas* showed that, in the Netherlands, people reported enjoying the series and its colourful characters, but also expressed their disapproval of its cut-throat capitalistic values.

In a similar vein, Roland Robertson (1995) has argued that a better concept for understanding global processes is *glocalization* (the mixture of globalizing and localizing forces) rather than globalization (see chapter

4 for discussion). This is because American corporations have to take cognizance of local cultures if they are to market their products successfully in other countries. They certainly cannot ignore them. In this process, the products are often significantly altered. The thesis of glocalization suggests that the simple one-way flow process suggested by media imperialism is likely to be the exception rather than the rule. In two studies, 30 years apart, Jeremy Tunstall's book titles tell a similar story. In *The Media Are American* (1977), he argued that the industrialization of mass media in America enabled it to dominate global media production. But in *The Media Were American* (2007), Tunstall's thesis is that the USA has lost its global dominance. The rise of India and China as media producers and consumers, along with stronger national cultures and media systems has transformed and weakened the position of America in relation to the rest of the world.

Even so, as Hackett and Zhao argue, the logic of capital accumulation continues to spread across the world: 'In the global media system, it is as if anything can be said, in any language, at any location, as long as it can be said profitably' (2005: 22). In that sense, it is capitalistic values rather than American national values, which characterizes the exchange of media products.

Ownership of media 'supercompanies'

In January 2000, two of the world's most influential media companies joined together in what was the largest corporate merger the world had ever seen. In a deal worth $337 billion, the world's biggest media company, Time Warner, and the world's largest Internet service provider, America Online (AOL), announced their intention to create the 'world's first fully integrated media and communications company for the Internet Century'. The merger brought together the enormous media 'content' owned by Time Warner – including newspapers and maga-

> ### THINKING CRITICALLY
>
> Is 'media imperialism' an accurate description of the global influence of Western media and culture? Are there any examples of media and cultural products moving the other way, to exert an influence on the development of Western culture? How does media imperialism fit with Lyotard's postmodern thesis of the collapse of Western culture? Which view is best supported by the evidence?

zines, film studios and TV stations – with the powerful Internet distribution capabilities of AOL, whose subscription base exceeded 25 million people in 15 countries at the time of the merger.

The merger generated enormous excitement in financial markets, as it created the world's fourth largest company. But even more than its size, the deal attracted great attention as the first major union between 'old media' and 'new media'. The origins of Time Warner date back to 1923 when Henry Luce founded *Time* magazine, a weekly publication that summarized and interpreted the voluminous amount of information contained in daily newspapers. The overwhelming success of *Time* was soon followed by the creation of the business magazine *Fortune* in 1930 and the photographic magazine *Life* in 1936. Over the course of the twentieth century, Time Inc. grew into a media corporation embracing TV and radio stations, the music industry, the vast Warner Brothers movie and cartoon empire, and the world's first 24-hour news channel, CNN. At the time of the merger, Time Warner's annual turnover was US$26 billion; 120 million readers read its magazines each month and the company owned the rights to an archive of 5,700 films, as well as some of the most popular network television programmes.

If the history of Time Warner closely mirrored the general development of communications in the twentieth century,

Global Society 17.1 **Media empires – news corporation**

Rupert Murdoch is an Australian-born entrepreneur who is the head of one of the world's largest media empires. News Corporation's holdings include nine different media operating on six continents. By 2001 News Corporation's turnover was £16.5 billion and it employed 34,000 staff (BBC 2001). In October 2004, ABC News reported the annual turnover as £29 billion.

Murdoch established News Corporation in Australia before moving into the British and American markets in the 1960s. His initial purchases of the UK *News of the World* and the *Sun* in 1969 and the US *New York Post* in the mid-1970s paved the way for a dramatic expansion in later acquisitions. In the USA alone, News Corporation's holdings now include more than 130 newspapers. Murdoch turned many of these newspapers towards sensationalistic journalism, building on the three themes of sex, crime and sport. The *Sun*, for example, became highly successful, with the highest circulation of any daily English-language newspaper in the world, standing at around 3.4 million copies daily in mid-2004.

In the 1980s Murdoch started to expand into television, establishing Sky TV, a satellite and cable chain that, after initial reverses, proved commercially successful. He also owns 64 per cent of the Star TV network based in Hong Kong. Its declared strategy is to 'control the skies' in satellite transmission over an area from Japan to Turkey, taking in the gigantic markets of India and China. It transmits five channels, one of which is BBC World News.

In 1985, Murdoch bought a half interest in Twentieth Century Fox, a film company that owns the rights to more than 2,000 films. His Fox Broadcasting Company started up in 1987 and has become the fourth major television network in the United States after ABC, CBS and NBC. Murdoch now owns 22 US television stations, which account for over 40 per cent of TV households in the United States. He controls 25 magazines, including the popular TV Guide, and acquired the US-based publishers, Harper and Row – now renamed HarperCollins – in 1987.

In recent years Murdoch has invested heavily in the profitable digital satellite television industry, particularly through his ownership of Sky and coverage of live sporting events such as basketball and live premiership football. According to Murdoch, sports coverage is News Corporation's 'battering ram' for entering new media markets (Herman and McChesney 1997). Because sporting events are best viewed live, they lend themselves to the 'pay-per-view' format that is profitable both for Murdoch and for advertisers. Competition for broadcasting rights to key fixtures is intense between News Corporation and other media empires as the global demand for sport eclipses other kinds of events.

Governments can cause trouble for Murdoch, because, at least within their own boundaries, they can introduce legislation limiting media cross-ownership – that is, a situation where the same firm owns several newspapers and TV stations. The European Union has also expressed concern about the dominant position of very large media companies. Yet Murdoch's power is not easily contained, given its global spread. He is weighty enough to influence governments, but it is in the nature of the telecommunications business that it is everywhere and nowhere. Murdoch's power base is very large, but also elusive.

In a speech given in October 1994, Murdoch took on those who see his media empire as a threat to democracy and freedom of debate: 'Because capitalists are always trying to stab each other in the back, free markets do not lead to monopolies. Essentially, monopolies can only exist when governments support them. . . . We at News Corporation are enlightened.' He discovered that in India, where Star television transmissions could be picked up, thousands of private operators had invested in satellite dishes and were selling Star programming illegally. Well, what we should do, Murdoch argued, is applaud! News Corporation, he concluded, looks forward to 'a long partnership with these splendid entrepreneurs' (Murdoch 1994).

Murdoch was, for a while, head of the largest media organization the world has known. In 1995, however, he was overtaken when the Disney Company and ABC merged. The Disney Chairman at the time, Michael Eisner, made it clear that he wanted to compete with Murdoch in the rapidly expanding markets of Asia. Murdoch's response to the merger was: 'They are twice as big as me now.' Then he added: 'A bigger target.' The merger of

AOL and Time Warner presented another target for Murdoch, but it seems clear that he will not shrink from the challenge. The chief executives of Disney, Time Warner and Viacom have all noted that Murdoch is the media executive they respect and fear the most – and whose moves they study most carefully (Herman and McChesney 1997).

the rise of America Online is typical of the 'new media' of the information age. Founded in 1982, AOL initially offered dial-up Internet access charged at an hourly rate. By 1994, it had 1 million subscribed users; after introducing unlimited Internet use for a standard monthly fee in 1996, its membership soared to 4.5 million. As the number of users continued to grow – 8 million people were using AOL by 1997 – the company embarked on a series of mergers, acquisitions and alliances, which consolidated its position as the pre-eminent Internet service provider. CompuServe and Netscape were both purchased by AOL, a joint venture with the German company Bertelsmann in 1995 led to the creation of AOL Europe, and an alliance with Sun Microsystems has allowed AOL to enter the realm of e-commerce.

The merger between the two companies was set to create a US$350 billion multinational, AOL-Time Warner, bringing 24 million AOL subscribers, 120 million magazine readers and the television channels CNN, HBO and Warner Brothers all under one corporate roof. Yet the merger suffered grave difficulties. In particular, AOL was never able to meet its ambitious subscriber or revenue targets and the technological spin-offs from combining film and Internet technologies were slow to materialize. As investors adjusted their expectations of what the corporation could achieve, the media giant looked in imminent danger of being forced into a break-up. In 2002, the company posted a loss of almost $100 billion, resulting in the company dropping 'AOL' from the company name in 2003. Plans to sell off AOL were mooted in 2007 and on 1 March 2008, support for the Netscape Navigator web browser was ended.

The implications of the AOL/Time Warner merger will not be clear for some time, yet already the lines have been drawn between those who see the deal as unleashing exciting new technological potentials and those who are concerned about the domination of the media by large corporations. The enthusiasts see the merger as an important step towards the creation of media 'supercompanies' that can deliver direct to people's homes, through the Internet, all the news shows, TV programmes, films and music they want, when they want them.

Not everyone agrees, however, that the idea of media supercompanies is one that should be aspired to. Where enthusiasts see a dream, critics sense a nightmare. As media corporations become ever more concentrated, centralized and global in their reach, there is reason to be concerned that the important role of the media as a forum for free speech, expression and debate will be curtailed. A single company that controls both the content – TV programmes, music, films, news sources – and the means of distribution is in a position of great power. It can promote its own material (the singers and celebrities it has made famous), it can exercise self-censorship (omitting news stories that might cast its holdings or corporate supporters in a negative light) and it can 'cross-endorse' products within its own empire at the expense of those outside it.

The vision of the Internet in the hands of several media conglomerates stands in stark contrast to the idea of a free and unrestricted electronic realm held out by Internet enthusiasts just a few years ago. In its early years, the Internet was viewed by many as an individualistic realm where users could roam freely, searching for and sharing information, making connections and interacting outside the realm of corporate power. The looming presence of corporate media giants and advertisers has threatened this, however. Critics worry that the rise of corporate power on the Internet will drown out everything but the 'corporate message' and may lead to the Internet becoming a restricted domain accessible only to subscribers.

It is important to remember that there are few inevitabilities in the social world. Attempts at total control of information sources and distribution channels rarely succeed, either because of anti-trust legislation aimed at preventing monopolies, or through the persistent and creative responses of media users who seek out alternative information routes. Media consumers are not 'cultural dopes' who can be manipulated effortlessly by corporate interests; as the scope and volume of media forms and content expand, individuals are becoming more, not less, skilled in interpreting and evaluating the messages and material they encounter.

Anti-monopoly measures

As the Glasgow University Media Group pointed out, those who construct the news act as 'gatekeepers' for what gets on the agenda. News stories that are successfully broadcast or published are not always chosen according to some simple criterion of newsworthy-ness. Journalists are well aware that they must find stories that fit with the agenda of the organization they work for, and these news organizations may have political agendas of their own – they are not just in the business of selling goods but of influencing opinions. For this reason, the rise and influence of the media entrepreneurs and the large media companies worries many. The proprietors of such corporations, like Rupert Murdoch, make no secret of their political views, which

inevitably are a cause of concern to political parties and other groups holding different political positions.

Recognizing this, all countries have provisions that seek to control media ownership. But how tight should these be? And given the global character of media enterprises, can national governments in any case have much hope of controlling them?

The issue of media regulation is more complex than might appear at first sight. It seems obvious that it is in the public interest that there should be a diversity of media organizations, since this is likely to ensure that many different groups and political perspectives can be listened to. Yet placing limits on who can own what, and what forms of media technology they can use, might affect the economic prosperity of the media sector. A country that is too restrictive might find itself left behind – the media industries are one of the fastest growing sectors of the modern economy.

Critics of media concentration say that the large media companies wield excessive power. Businesses, on the other hand, argue that if they are subject to regulation, they cannot make effective commercial decisions and will lose out in global competition. Moreover, they ask, who is to do the regulating? Who is to regulate the regulators?

One guiding thread of media regulation policy might be the recognition that market dominance by two or three large media companies simultaneously threatens both proper economic competition and democracy – since the media-owners are unelected. Existing anti-monopoly legislation can be brought into play here, although it differs widely across Europe and other industrial countries.

Competitiveness means pluralism – or should do – and presumably pluralism is good for democracy. Yet is pluralism enough? Many point to the USA in arguing that having a plurality of media channels does not guarantee quality and accuracy of content. Some see the maintenance of a strong public broadcasting sector as of key importance in blocking the dominance of the large media companies. Yet public broadcasting systems create their own problems. In most countries they themselves used to be a monopoly and in many countries were effectively used as a means of government propaganda. The question of who is to regulate the regulators comes up here with particular force.

One issue that complicates the question of media regulation is the very rapid rate of technological change. The media are constantly being transformed by technical innovations, and forms of technology, which were once distinct, are now fusing together. If television programmes are watched via the Internet, for example, what type of media regulation applies? Among member states of the European Union, the question of media and telecommunications convergence is at the forefront of debate. While some see the need for coordinated legislation that would harmonize telecommunications, broadcasting and information technology across Europe, this has been difficult to bring about. The role of the EU in media regulation remains weak. The current (2005) policy document, the 'Audio-Visual Services Directive', remains the subject of much debate and some governments see it as either unjustified, because member states already have their own safeguards in place, or unworkable.

Political control

In most countries the state has been directly involved with the administration of television broadcasting. In Britain the British Broadcasting Corporation, which initiated the first television programmes ever produced, is a public organization, funded by licence fees paid by every household that owns a TV set. For some years the BBC was the only organization permitted to broadcast either radio or television programmes in Britain, but today there also exist three terrestrial commercial television channels. Only the BBC is funded by the licence fee;

the commercial channels rely on revenue generated by advertising. The frequency and duration of advertising is controlled by law, with a maximum of six minutes per hour. These regulations also apply to satellite channels, which became widely available to subscribers in the 1980s.

In the USA the three leading television organizations are all commercial networks – the American Broadcasting Company (ABC), Columbia Broadcasting System (CBS) and the National Broadcasting Company (NBC). Networks are limited by law to owning no more than five licensed stations, which, in the case of these three organizations, are in the biggest cities. The 'big three' together reach over a quarter of all households through their own stations. Some 200 affiliated stations are also attached to each network, comprising 90 per cent of the 700 or so TV stations in the country. The networks depend for their income on selling advertising time. The National Association of Broadcasters, a private body, lays down guidelines about the proportion of viewing time per hour to be devoted to advertising: 9.5 minutes per hour during 'prime time' and 16 per hour at other periods. TV companies use regularly collected statistics (ratings) of how many people watch specific programmes in setting advertising fees. The ratings also, of course, strongly influence decisions on which programmes to continue to show.

The power of publicly run television stations has been reduced since the advent of multi-channel TV, DVD and video, and the arrival of services such as Sky+ (which combines a digital video recorder and satellite receiver to find and record programmes the viewer has expressed an interest in, effectively creating a personalized channel). In return for a subscription fee or one-off payment for a digital set-top box, today's television watcher can select from a multiplicity of channels and programmes. In such circumstances people increasingly do their own 'programming', constructing personal viewing schedules rather than

Global Society 17.2 Censoring the Internet in China

The contradictory nature of globalization is illustrated clearly in China, a country that is undergoing rapid cultural and economic transformation under the Chinese Communist Party.

In the 1980s, the Chinese government oversaw the expansion of a national television system and encouraged the purchase of televisions by its citizens. The government saw television broadcasting as a means of uniting the country and promoting party authority. Television, however, can be a volatile medium. Not only is it not possible for television broadcasting to be tightly controlled in an age of satellite based channels, but Chinese audiences have demonstrated their willingness to interpret TV content in ways that run contrary to government intentions (Lull 1997).

In interviews with 100 Chinese families, James Lull found that Chinese audiences, like other populations under Communist regimes, were 'masters of interpretation, reading between the lines in order to pick up the less obvious messages'. In his interviews, Lull noted that his respondents would describe not only what they watched, but how they watched it: 'Because viewers know that the government often bends and exaggerates its reports, they become skilled at imagining the true situation. What is presented, what is left out, what is given priority, how things are said – all these modes are noticed and interpreted sensitively.'

Lull concluded that many of the messages seen by Chinese audiences on TV – primarily in imported films and commercials – run contrary to the way of life and opportunities available in their own society. Seeing television content emphasizing individuality and the consumer society, many Chinese viewers felt their own options were constrained in real life. Television conveyed to Chinese audiences that other social systems seemed to function more smoothly and offer greater freedom than their own.

More recently, the Internet and other new communication technologies have posed fresh challenges for the Chinese government. While some people contend that these new media will help people to circumvent state controls, others maintain that the state censors are likely to keep pace with technological advances. In 2006, leading Internet company Google announced that, in order to gain access to China's vast market, it would censor search results to satisfy the Chinese authorities. Reporters using the new site reported that the BBC website was inaccessible and critics warn that sensitive subjects, such as the 1989 Tiananmen Square massacre and sites promoting independence for Taiwan, will be restricted. Google's cooperation with the Chinese authorities supports those arguments suggesting that profit-making rather than spreading American values drives US media companies.

The great firewall of China

The Chinese effort to censor the Internet is a feat of technology, legislation and manpower. According to the BBC, which is almost completely blocked within the 'great firewall of China' (as it is known among techies), 50,000 different Chinese authorities 'do nothing but monitor traffic on the Internet'. No single law exists to permit this mass invasion of privacy and proscription of free speech. Rather, hundreds of articles in dozens of pieces of legislation work to obfuscate the mandate of the government to maintain political order through censorship.

According to *Internet Filtering in China in 2004–2005: A Country Study*, the most rigorous survey of Chinese Internet filtering to date, China's censorship regime extends from the fatpipe backbone [the Internet or computer network] to the street cyber-café. Chinese communications infrastructure allows packets of data to be filtered at 'choke points' designed into the network, while on the street liability for prohibited content is extended onto multiple parties – author, host, reader – to chilling effect. All this takes place under the watchful eye of machine and human censors, the latter often volunteers.

The ramifications of this system, as the Open Net Initiative's John Parley stressed when he delivered a report to the US-China Economic and Security Review Commission in April, 'should be of concern to anyone who believes in participatory democracy'. The ONI found that 60 per cent of sites relating to opposition political parties were blocked, as were 90 per cent of sites detailing the Nine Commentaries, a series of columns about the Chinese Communist Party published by the Hong Kong-based Epoch

Times and associated by some with the banned spiritual movement Falun Gong.

The censorship does not end at the World Wide Web. New internet-based technologies, which looked to lend hope to free speech when ONI filed its last report on China in 2002, are also being targeted. Although email censorship is not as rampant as many (including the Chinese themselves) believe, blogs, discussion forums and bulletin boards have all been targeted through various measures of state control.

What then, of China's 94 million web-surfers? One discussion thread at Slashdot, the well-respected and popular discussion forum for techno-libertarians, is telling. When a well-meaning Westerner offered a list of links prefaced with 'assuming that you can read Slashdot, here are a few web pages that your government would probably prefer you not to read', one poster, Hung Wei Lo responded: 'I have travelled to China many times and work with many H1-B's [temporary workers from outside US] from all parts of China. All of them are already quite knowledgeable about all the information provided in the links above, and most do not hesitate to engage in discussions about such topics over lunch. The fact that you feel all 1.6 billion Chinese are most certainly blind to these pieces of information is a direct result of years of indoctrination of Western (I'm assuming American) propaganda.'

Indeed, anti-Japanese protests [in 2005] have been cited by some as an example of how the Chinese people circumvent their state's diligent censorship regime using networked technologies such as mobile text messages (SMS), instant messaging, emails, bulletin boards and blogs to communicate and organize. The argument here of course is that the authorities were ambivalent towards these protests – one blogger reports that the state sent its own SMS during the disturbances: 'We ask the people to express your patriotic passion through the right channel, following the law and maintaining order.'

China will have to keep up with the slew of emerging technologies making untapped networked communication more sophisticated by the day. . . . Judging by the past record, it cannot be assumed that the state censorship machinery will not be able to meet these future challenges.

Source: Hogge 2005. This article was originally published on the independent online magazine: www/opendemocracy.net/. Reprinted by permission of openDemocracy

depending on the presupplied network scheduling. Digital, satellite and cable are altering the nature of television almost everywhere. As these make inroads into the domains of the orthodox terrestrial television channels, it will become yet more difficult for governments to control the content of TV, as they have characteristically done in the past. For example, the reach of Western media seems to have played a part in the circumstances that produced the revolutions of 1989 in Eastern Europe.

Resistance and alternatives to the global media

While the power and reach of the global media are undeniable, there are forces within all countries that can serve to slow down the media onslaught and shape the nature of media products in a way that reflects local traditions, cultures and priorities. Religion, tradition and popular outlooks are all strong brakes on media globalization, while local regulations and domestic media institutions can also play a role in limiting the impact of global media sources. The case of new media in the Middle East is an interesting one.

Ali Mohammadi (2002) investigated the response of Islamic countries to the forces of media globalization. The rise of international electronic empires that operate across state borders is perceived as a threat to the cultural identity and national interests of many Islamic states. According to

In spite of incurring suspicion and being banned in some Middle East countries and American military attacks on its broadcast centres in Afghanistan and Iraq, Al Jazeera continues to expand and prosper in the digital age.

Mohammadi, resistance against the incursion of outside media forms has ranged from muted criticism to the outright banning of Western satellites. The reaction to media globalization and the action taken by individual countries in large part reflect their overall responses towards the legacy of Western colonialism and the encroachment of modernity. In analysing Islamic responses to media globalization, Mohammadi divides states into three broad categories: modernist, mixed and traditional.

Until the mid-1980s, most television programming in the Islamic world was produced and distributed within national borders or through Arabsat – the pan-Arab satellite broadcasting network composed of 21 states. The liberalization of broad-

casting and the power of global satellite TV have transformed the contours of television in the Islamic world. The events of the 1991 Gulf War made the Middle East a centre of attention for the global media industry and significantly affected television broadcasting and consumption within the region as well. Satellites spread rapidly, with Bahrain, Egypt, Saudi Arabia, Kuwait, Dubai, Tunisia and Jordan all launching satellite channels by 1993. By the end of the decade, most Islamic states had established their own satellite channels, as well as accessing global media programmes.

Al Jazeera is the largest Arabic news channel in the Middle East, offering news coverage 24 hours a day. Founded in 1996, and based in Qatar, the Al Jazeera is the fastest growing news network among Arab communities and Arabic-speaking people around the world. Some Western critics have argued that Al Jazeera is overly sensational, and shows too much violent and emotionally charged footage from war zones, as well as giving disproportionate coverage to fundamentalist and extremist groups (Sharkey 2004). Its political programmes are most popular, but other shows covering culture, sport and health help to increase the channel's audience share. However, many, perhaps most, TV stations use sensational stories to capture audiences and it may be objected that Al Jazeera is simply reflecting its audience in the same way that Western stations also do.

Recent academic studies argue that Al-Jazeera has played an influential role in breaking open state control of the Middle East media, encouraging open debate on important issues such as the invasion of Iraq, the situation in Palestine and Arab identities (Lynch 2006; Zayani 2005; Miles 2005). The news channel has helped to change political and social debates, not only in the Middle East, but also in the West, where digital viewers can tune in for an alternative perspective on global events. (Al-Jazeera now broadcasts from London and Washington, DC, as well as Doha and Kuala Lumpur.)

In some Islamic states, the themes and material dealt with on Western television have created tensions. Programmes relating to gender and human rights issues are particularly controversial; Saudi Arabia, for example, no longer supports BBC Arabic because of concerns over its coverage of human rights issues. Three Islamic states – Iran, Saudi Arabia and Malaysia – have banned satellite access to Western television. Iran has been the staunchest opponent of the Western media, branding it a source of 'cultural pollution' and the promotion of Western consumer values.

Such strong responses are in the minority, however. Mohammadi (2002) concluded that, although Islamic countries have responded to media globalization by attempting to resist or provide an alternative, most have found it necessary to accept certain modifications to their culture in order to maintain their own cultural identity. The 'traditionalist approach', such as that favoured by Iran and Saudi Arabia, is losing ground to responses based on adaptation and modernization.

Conclusion

As individuals, we do not control technological change, and some critics perceive that the sheer pace of such change threatens to swamp our lives. The often cited notion of an 'information superhighway' suggests an orderly road map, whereas the impact of the new technologies often feels chaotic and disruptive. Yet the arrival of the wired-up world, thus far at any rate, has not produced any of the overwhelmingly negative scenarios predicted by some sceptics. 'Big Brother' has not emerged as a result of the Internet: on the contrary, it has promoted decentralization and new forms of global social networking. In spite of the enormous hype surrounding the potential collapse of the global computer infrastructure in 2000 – from the so-called 'Y2K bug' – the moment passed relatively uneventfully. Books and other 'pre-electronic' media look unlikely to disappear. Bulky as it is, this book is handier to use than a computerized version would be and is much more flexible and portable, requiring no power source.

The modern mass media now consists of a complex variety of different types from print and newspapers, to radio, television and film, new digital media and interactive cyberspace. Understanding the impact of the new digital media forms will be an important task for the next generation of sociologists, who will have experienced a socialization process that incorporates them. However, this task will still require the same struggle for sociological detachment and methodological rigour that characterizes the discipline's best research studies.

Summary points

1. The mass media are media of communication – newspapers, magazines, television, radio, cinema, videos, CDs and other forms – which reach mass audiences, and their influence on our lives is considerable. The media not only provide entertainment, but also provide and shape much of the information we act on in our daily lives.

2. Newspapers were among the most important of early mass media and continue to be significant, but newer media, particularly television and the Internet, have supplemented them. Until the emergence of digital technology, television was probably the most important media development. Satellite and cable technology are altering the nature of television and public television broadcasting is losing audience share as a multiplicity of channels become available.

3. In recent years, advances in new communications technology have transformed telecommunications – the communication of text, sounds or images at a distance through a technological medium. Digitization, fibre optics and satellite systems work together to facilitate multimedia – the combination of several media forms in a single medium – and interactive media, which allow individuals actively to participate in what they see or hear.

4. The Internet is allowing unprecedented levels of interconnectedness and interactivity. The number of worldwide Internet users has been growing rapidly and the range of activities that can be completed online continues to expand. The Internet is also transforming other media. For instance, television programmes and newspapers are increasingly available online, changing the very character of the press and TV. Some people also worry that the Internet's exciting new possibilities bring with them an undermining of human relationships and communities by encouraging social isolation.

5. A range of different theories of the media have been developed including functionalist, symbolic interactionist, conflict and postmodern perspectives. McLuhan coined the phrase, 'the medium is the message', focusing attention on the type of media rather than the content it carries. The Frankfurt School saw modern mass media as part of the culture industry which threatened to stifle creativity and reduce the quality of cultural products.

6. Other recent media theorists include Habermas, Baudrillard and Thompson. Habermas points to the role of the media in creating and diminishing the public sphere of opinion and debate. Baudrillard argues that the new media, particularly television, creates a new hyperreality, which comprises both the real world and its representations. Thompson argues that the mass media have created a new form of social interaction – 'mediated quasi-interaction' – that is more limited, narrow and one-way than everyday social interaction.

7. Audience research has made a significant contribution to our understanding of the way media messages are received and moved sociologists away from simple ideas of viewer passivity. Messages always have to be interpreted. Media representations tend to reinforce stereotypes rather than challenge them, though there have been some signs of change in recent years.

8. The media industry has become globalized over the past three decades. The ownership of media is increasingly concentrated in the hands of large media conglomerates; private ownership of media is eclipsing public ownership; media companies operate across national borders; media companies have diversified their activities; and media mergers have become more frequent.

9. The sense today of inhabiting one world, is in large part a result of the international scope of media and communications. Given the paramount position of the industrial countries in the world information order, some argue that developing countries are subject to a new form of media imperialism, though critics suggest that cultural products flow in more than one direction.

10. The globalizing influence of the Internet is proving hard for nation states to control and regulate, though it is not yet clear whether they will be able to do so in future. The emergence of Al Jazeera shows that alternatives to the Western global media can not only survive, but also thrive in the new digital media environment.

Further reading

John Thompson's *The Media and Modernity: A Social Theory of the Media* (Cambridge: Polity, 1995) is an excellent account of the history of mass media and their role in the emergence of modernity. For the new forms of media, you could try Martin Lister, Kieran Kell, John Dovey, Seth Giddings and Iain Grant's *New Media: A Critical Introduction* (London: Routledge, 2003), which does exactly what it says. James Slevin's *The Internet and Society* (Cambridge: Polity, 2000) is also a useful book on the impact of the Internet.

On media theories, a good place to start reading would be Kevin Williams's *Understanding Media Theory* (London: Hodder Arnold, 2003), which is very clear and is aimed at an introductory level. A broader discussion of the media can then be found in Graeme Burton's *Media and Society: Critical Perspectives* (Buckingham: Open University Press, 2004), which also covers a range of theoretical perspectives.

Audience research has been important for understanding media influence and Marie Gillespie's *Media Audiences* (Buckingham:

Open University Press, 2005) is a worthwhile edited collection that shows what can be learned from this research. James Watson's *Media Communication: An Introduction to Theory and Process*, 3rd edn (Basingstoke: Palgrave Macmillan, 2003) is a good addition.

On the difficult problems created by global media ownership, Gillian Doyle's *Media Ownership: The Economics and Politics of Convergence and Concentration in the UK and European Media* (London: Sage, 2002) does an excellent job of helping us to understand the developing situation in Europe.

Finally, for those looking to pursue media studies further, you could try Gill Branston and Roy Stafford's *The Media Student's Book, Fourth Edition* (London: Routledge, 2006). Then, David Deacon, Michael Pickering, Peter Golding and Graham Murdock's *Researching Communications: A Practical Guide to Methods in Media and Cultural Analysis*, 2nd edn (London: Hodder Arnold, 2007) provides many insights into the methods used to study the media and should be a helpful guide for anyone looking to carry out their own piece of media research.

Internet links

Foundation for Information Policy Research – studies the interaction between ICT and society:
www.fipr.org/

NewsWatch.org – a media watchdog website:
www.newswatch.org/

OECD, ICT Homepage – lots of comparative data on information technology:
www.oecd.org/topic/0,2686,en_2649_37441_1_1_1_1_37441,00.html

Theory.org – playful postmodern site on links between media and identities:
www.theory.org.uk/

Ofcom – UK Office of Communications:
www.ofcom.org.uk/

BARB, Broadcasters' Audience Research Board – lots of UK research and surveys here:
www.barb.co.uk/

18

Organizations and Networks

CHAPTER 18

Organizations and Networks

Do you ever eat in a McDonald's restaurant? If you do, then next time you are there, study how the restaurant is organized. Compared to other restaurants, one of the most obvious differences you will notice is how efficient the whole process is, or at least appears to be – you can go in hungry and leave full in almost no time at all. Instead of having a waiter to show you to your table and take your order, you go straight to the counter and are given your food there. If you chose to eat in, there are no tablecloths and a minimum of cutlery. Aside from the tray, anything you need to eat your food, and the wrapping that the food arrives in, is disposable. At the end of the meal, you take your packaging to the bin and throw it away yourself – even though you are not a paid employee. In fact, the food and service at McDonald's can be easily quantified and calculated. McDonald's aims to give 'more bang for the buck' – you buy 'value meals', 'Big Macs' or 'large fries'. And the service is measurably fast too. The founder of McDonald's, Ray Kroc, aimed to get a burger and milkshake to customers in less than 50 seconds.

If you look behind the counter, you are likely to see that each member of staff works on a specialized and quite straightforward job: one makes the fries, another flips the burgers, a third puts the burger in a bun and adds the salad. You might also notice how much of the process is automated – milkshakes are made at the press of a button, the deep fryers work at set temperatures and timers let the staff know when the food is ready; even the tills have buttons for each item, so staff do not have to learn prices.

If you have visited a McDonald's restaurant abroad, as well as at home, you will have noticed that there are many similarities between them. The interior decoration may vary, the language spoken will differ from country to country, but the layout, the procedure for ordering, staff uniforms, the tables, the packaging and the 'service with a smile' are essentially similar. The McDonald's experience was designed to be uniform and predictable whether it is in London or Lima. No matter where they are located, visitors to McDonald's know that they can expect quick service and a product that is filling and consistent in any of the more than 31,000 restaurants in 120 countries worldwide.

The American sociologist George Ritzer (1983, 1993, 1998) argues that McDonald's provides a vivid metaphor of the transformations taking place in industrialized societies. He argues that what we are witnessing is the 'McDonaldization' of society. According to Ritzer, McDonaldization is 'the process by which the principles of the fast-food restaurants are coming to dominate more and more sectors of American society as well as the rest of the world'. Ritzer uses the four guiding principles for McDon-

ald's restaurants – *efficiency*, *calculability*, *uniformity* and *control through automation* – to show that our society is becoming ever more 'rationalized' with time. He is keen to point out that he has no special desire to pick on McDonald's; it is simply the best exemplar of this process. Besides, he notes: 'McDonaldization' is catchier than 'Burger Kingization' or 'Starbuckization'.

Ritzer, like the classical sociologist Max Weber before him, is fearful of the harmful effects of **rationalization**. As we will see later in the chapter, Weber saw the increasingly rationalized modern world giving rise to irrational outcomes as bureaucracies took on a life of their own and spread throughout social life. Similarly, Ritzer argues that the apparently rationalized process of McDonaldization spawns a series of irrationalities – which he calls the 'irrationality of rationality'. These include damage to our health (from a 'high calorie, fat, cholesterol, salt, and sugar content' diet) and to the environment – think of all the packaging that is thrown away with each meal. But most of all, Ritzer argues, McDonaldization is 'dehumanizing'. We file forward in queues to get a burger as if on a conveyer belt, while staff on the other side of the counter repeat the same specialized task again and again, like robots on an assembly line. Ritzer's thesis has been very influential in sociology, but, as we will see later in this chapter, not only has it received some significant criticisms, but also McDonald's Corporation itself has been forced to change its practices to survive in the global economy.

There is a difference between the customer's experience, described so eloquently by Ritzer and that of the McDonald's staff. Customers are only ever likely to experience the 'public face' of McDonald's and form their opinion of the company from this. However, staff at various levels of the company may see things very differently from the inside of the organization. While customers experience an efficient, highly organized restaurant, staff may be more aware of the inefficiencies and internal problems of, and external pressures on, what is, after all, a multinational capitalist organization aimed at maximizing profits. Understanding organizations demands an investigation of their internal arrangements and management practices, and their roles within the wider society and this requires both empirical research and theoretical development.

The study and theory of organizations is an important aspect of sociology, which was a central concern of the classical sociologist Max Weber (whose ideas Ritzer drew upon) and, consequently, Weber will be a central figure in this chapter. We examine what Weber and other sociologists have to say about organizations, and ask whether theories of organizations are still relevant. This is a pertinent issue today, as we seem to be witnessing the rapid growth of technologically advanced, loose social networks, which some have argued, may be replacing some of the previous functions of formal organizations. Thus, the second part of the chapter explores the emergence of global social networks and the argument that we are witnessing the rise of the 'network society' (Castells 1996).

Organizations

People frequently band together to pursue activities that they could otherwise not readily accomplish by themselves. A principal means for accomplishing such cooperative actions is the **organization**, a group with an identifiable membership that engages in concerted collective actions to achieve a common purpose (Aldrich and Marsden 1988). An organization can be a small group of people who know each other face to face, but it is more likely to be a larger, impersonal one: universities, religious bodies and business corporations, are all examples of organizations. Such organizations are a central feature of all societies.

Organizations tend to be highly formal in modern industrial and post-industrial societies. A formal organization is one that is rationally designed to achieve its objectives, often by means of explicit rules, regulations and procedures. The modern bureaucratic organization, discussed later in this chapter, is a prime example of a formal organization. As Max Weber first recognized in the 1920s (see 1979 [1925]), there has been a long-term trend in Europe and North America towards formal organizations. This is in part the result of the fact that formality is often a requirement for legal standing. For a college or university to be legally accredited, for example, it must satisfy explicit written standards governing everything from grading policy to faculty performance to fire safety. Today, formal organizations remain the dominant form of organization throughout the entire world.

Most social systems in the traditional world developed over lengthy periods as a result of custom and habit. Organizations, on the other hand, are mostly designed – established with definite aims in view and housed in buildings or physical settings specifically constructed to help realize those aims. The edifices in which hospitals, colleges or business firms carry on their activities are generally custom built. Organizations can therefore be said to have a regulative function; they influence and shape people's behaviour in particular ways and some are representative of society's values. For example, as we will see below, Michel Foucault argued that clinics, schools, hospitals and prisons all share a similar principle of physical organization, which tells us something about the power relationships in society and helps to constrain the behaviour of the 'inmates'.

In current times, organizations play a much more important part in our everyday lives than was previously the case. Besides delivering us into this world, they also mark our progress through it and see us out of it when we die. Even before we are born, our mothers, and probably our fathers too, are involved in classes, pregnancy check-ups and so forth, carried out within hospitals and other medical organizations. Every child born today is registered by a government organization, which collects information on us from birth to death. Most people in developed countries today die in a hospital, not at home as was once the case – and each death must be formally registered with the government too.

It is easy to see why organizations are so important to us today. In the pre-modern world, families, close relatives and neighbours provided for most needs – food, the instruction of children, work and leisure-time activities. In modern times, the mass of the population is much more interdependent than was ever the case before. People we never meet and who indeed might live many thousands of miles away supply many of our requirements. A tremendous amount of coordination of activities and resources – which organizations provide – is needed in such circumstances.

The tremendous influence organizations have come to exert over our lives cannot be seen as wholly beneficial. Organizations often have the effect of taking things out of our own hands and putting them under the control of officials or experts over whom we have little influence. For instance, we are all required to do certain things the government tells us to do – pay taxes, abide by laws, go off to fight wars – or face punishment. As sources of social power, organizations can thus subject the individual to dictates she or he may be powerless to resist.

Organizations as bureaucracies

The word **bureaucracy** was coined by a Monsieur de Gournay in 1745, who added the word 'bureau', meaning both an office and a writing table, to 'cracy', a term derived from the Greek verb meaning 'to rule'. Bureaucracy is thus 'the rule of officials'. The term was first applied only to government officials, but it was gradually extended to refer to large organizations in general.

From the beginning, the concept was used in a disparaging way. De Gournay spoke of the developing power of officials as 'an illness called bureaumania'. The French novelist Honoré de Balzac saw bureaucracy as, 'the giant power wielded by pygmies'. The Czech author, Franz Kafka, gave a nightmarish depiction of an impersonal and unintelligible bureaucracy in his novel *The Trial*, first published in 1925. This sort of view has persisted into current times: bureaucracy is frequently associated with red tape, inefficiency and wastefulness. However, sociological studies of organizations as bureaucracies have been dominated by the work of Max Weber (see 'Classic Studies 18.1').

Formal and informal relations

Weber's analysis of bureaucracy gave prime place to **formal relations** within organizations – the relations between people as stated in the rules of the organization. Weber had little to say about the informal connections and small-group relations that may exist in all organizations. But in bureaucracies, informal ways of doing things often allow for a flexibility that could not otherwise be achieved.

In a classic study, Peter Blau (1963) looked at **informal relations** in a government agency whose task was to investigate possible income-tax violations. Agents who came across problems they were unsure how to deal with were supposed to discuss them with their immediate supervisor; the rules of procedure stated that they should not consult colleagues working at the same level as them. Most officials were wary of approaching their supervisors, however, because they felt this might suggest a lack of competence on their part and could reduce their promotion chances. Hence, they usually consulted one another, violating the official rules. This not only helped to provide concrete advice; it also reduced the anxieties involved in working alone. A cohesive set of loyalties often found in small groups developed among those working at the same level. The problems these workers faced, Blau concludes, were probably coped

Classic Studies 18.1 **Max Weber: modernity as bureaucratic domination**

The research problem

Modern life needs some kind of formal organization if things are to run smoothly. But many people now see organizations in a negative light as stifling individual creativity, or as obstructive when we need them to help us. Why should this be so? How can organizations be perceived as necessary but at the same time as unhelpful? Is this a relatively minor problem of perceptions or something much more deep-rooted and therefore serious?

The German sociologist, Max Weber, developed the first systematic interpretation of the rise of modern organizations. He saw them as ways of coordinating the activities of human beings in a fairly stable way across space and time. Weber emphasized that organizations depend on the control of information, and he stressed the central importance of writing in this process: an organization needs *written* rules to function and files in which its 'memory' is stored. However, Weber also detected a clash, as well as a connection between modern organizations and democracy, which has far-reaching consequences for social life.

Weber's explanation

All large-scale modern organizations, according to Weber, tend to be bureaucratic in nature. A limited number of bureaucratic organizations existed in traditional civilizations. For example, there was a bureaucratic officialdom in imperial China that was responsible for the overall affairs of government. But it is only in modern times that bureaucracies have developed fully.

According to Weber, the expansion of bureaucracy is inevitable in modern societies; bureaucratic authority is the only way of coping with the administrative requirements of large-scale social systems. However, Weber also argued that bureaucracy exhibits a number of major failings, which have important implications for the nature of modern social life.

In order to study the origins and nature of the expansion of bureaucratic organizations, Weber constructed an ideal type of bureaucracy. 'Ideal' here refers not to what is most desirable, but to a 'pure' form of bureaucratic organization. An

ideal type is an abstract description constructed by accentuating certain features of real cases so as to pinpoint their most essential characteristics (see chapter 1). Weber (1979 [1925]) listed several characteristics of the ideal type of bureaucracy:

1 There is a clear-cut hierarchy of authority, such that tasks in the organization are distributed as 'official duties'. A bureaucracy looks like a pyramid, with the positions of highest authority at the top. There is a chain of command stretching from top to bottom, thus making coordinated decision-making possible. Each higher office controls and supervises the one below it in the hierarchy.
2 Written rules govern the conduct of officials at all levels of the organization. This does not mean that bureaucratic duties are just a matter of routine. The higher the office, the more the rules encompass a wide variety of cases and demand flexibility in their interpretation.
3 Officials are full time and salaried. Each job has a definite and fixed salary attached to it. Individuals are expected to make a career within the organization. Promotion is possible based on capability, seniority, or a mixture of the two.
4 There is a separation between the tasks of an official within the organization and his life outside. The home life of the official is distinct from his activities in the workplace and is also physically separated from it.
5 No members of the organization own the material resources with which they operate. The development of bureaucracy, according to Weber, separates workers from the control of their means of production. In traditional communities, farmers and craft workers usually had control over their processes of production and owned the tools they used. In bureaucracies, officials do not own the offices they work in, the desks they sit at, or the office machinery they use.

Weber argued that the more an organization approaches the ideal type of bureaucracy, the more effective it will be in pursuing the objectives for which it was established. He often likened bureaucracies to sophisticated machines operating by the principle of **rationality**. But he recognized that bureaucracies could be inefficient and he accepted that many bureaucratic jobs are dull, offering little opportunity for the exercise of creative capabilities. While Weber feared that the rationalization of society could have negative consequences, he concluded that bureaucratic routine and the authority of officialdom over our lives are prices we pay for the technical effectiveness of bureaucratic organizations.

The diminishing of democracy with the advance of bureaucratic organization was something that worried Weber a great deal. What especially disturbed him was the prospect of rule by faceless bureaucrats. How can democracy be anything other than a meaningless slogan in the face of the increasing power that bureaucratic organizations are wielding over us?

Critical points

Some of the critics of Weber's views on bureaucratic organizations are discussed throughout the rest of this chapter; their criticisms fall into several main areas. Some argue that Weber's account is a *partial* one. It concentrates on the formal aspects of organizations and has little to say about the informal life of organizations, which tends to introduce a welcome flexibility into otherwise rigid systems. Others argue that Weber let bureaucracy off too lightly; that its consequences are actually *more* damaging than he thought. For example, in different ways, both George Ritzer's thesis of the McDonaldization of society (discussed above)

and Zygmunt Bauman's account of the mass murder of Jews and other groups during the Second World War (see page 790) show that bureaucratic systems have been and still are much more damaging and potentially destructive than Weber had considered. Finally, some see Weber's perspective as *too negative*. Many problems commonly attributed to an abstract concept of 'bureaucracy' are really caused by specific attempts to *bypass* or circumvent the rules and guidelines of bureaucratic management. Bureaucratic rules, if adhered to, may actually contain some important safeguards which prevent, rather than facilitate, abuses of power by political leaders. In summary, Weber was, at least in part, wrong.

Contemporary significance

Of course, Weber could not have been expected to foresee all of the consequences of bureaucratization, and some of the criticisms of the direction of social change can be conceded. But there are two main reasons why we should continue to read and learn from Max Weber's ideas. First, a majority of later studies of bureaucratic organizations have been forced to engage in debates with his influential interpretation, or attempt to take his ideas further. This probably demonstrates that he managed to put his finger on a crucial aspect of what it is like to live in the modern world. Second, Weber was clear that bureaucratic organization was an important contributor to the continuing rationalization of society, spreading to more and more areas of social life. Although we may quibble with parts of his analysis, the global spread of capitalism and modern bureaucracies means that the general thrust of Weber's argument still has to be taken seriously.

with much more effectively as a result. The group was able to evolve informal procedures allowing for more initiative and responsibility than was provided for by the formal rules of the organization.

Informal networks tend to develop at all levels of organizations. At the very top, personal ties and connections may be more important than the formal situations in

which decisions are supposed to be made. For example, meetings of boards of directors and shareholders supposedly determine the policies of business corporations. In practice, a few members of the board often really run the corporation, making their decisions informally and expecting the board to approve them. Informal networks of this sort can also stretch across different corporations. Business leaders from different firms frequently consult one another in an informal way and may belong to the same clubs and leisure-time associations.

John Meyer and Brian Rowan (1977) argue that formal rules and procedures in organizations are usually quite distant from the practices actually adopted by the organizations' members. Formal rules, in their view, are often 'myths' that people profess to follow but that have little substance in reality. They serve to legitimate – to justify – ways in which tasks are carried out, even while these ways may diverge greatly from how things are 'supposed to be done' according to the rules.

Formal procedures, Meyer and Rowan point out, often have a ceremonial or ritual character. People will make a show of conforming to them in order to get on with their real work using other, more informal procedures. For example, rules governing ward procedure in a hospital help justify how nurses act towards patients: a nurse will faithfully fill in a patient's chart hanging at the end of the bed, but will also check the patient's progress by means of other, informal criteria – how well the person is looking and whether he or she seems alert and lively. Rigorously keeping up the charts impresses the patients and keeps the doctors happy, but is not always essential to the nurse's assessments.

Deciding how far informal procedures generally help or hinder the effectiveness of organizations is not a simple matter. Systems that resemble Weber's ideal type tend to give rise to a forest of unofficial ways of doing things. This is partly because the flexibility that is lacking ends up being achieved by unofficial tinkering with formal rules. For those in dull jobs, informal procedures often also help to create a more satisfying work environment. Informal connections between officials in higher positions may be effective in ways that aid the organization as a whole. On the other hand, these officials may be more concerned about advancing or protecting

In the business world, and in other organizations, informal networks may be created by people who get together during out-of-work hours.

their own interests than furthering those of the overall organization.

The dysfunctions of bureaucracy

Robert Merton, a functionalist sociologist, examined Weber's bureaucratic ideal type and concluded that several elements inherent in bureaucracy could lead to harmful consequences for the smooth functioning of the bureaucracy itself (Merton 1957). He referred to these as 'dysfunctions of bureaucracy'.

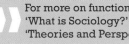
For more on functionalism, see chapter 1, 'What is Sociology?', and chapter 3, 'Theories and Perspectives in Sociology'.

First, Merton noted that bureaucrats are trained to rely strictly on written rules and procedures. They are not encouraged to be flexible, to use their own judgement in making decisions or to seek creative solutions; bureaucracy is about managing cases according to a set of objective criteria. Merton feared that this rigidity could lead to bureaucratic ritualism, a situation in which the rules are upheld at any cost, even in cases where another solution might be a better one for the organization as a whole.

A second concern of Merton's is that adherence to the bureaucratic rules could eventually take precedence over the underlying organizational goals. Because so much emphasis is placed on the correct procedure, it is possible to lose sight of the big picture. A bureaucrat responsible for processing insurance claims, for example, might refuse to compensate a policyholder for legitimate damages, citing the absence or incorrect completion of a form. In other words, processing the claim correctly could come to take precedence over the needs of the client who has suffered a loss.

Merton foresaw the possibility of tension between the public and bureaucracy in such cases. This concern was not entirely misplaced. Most of us interact with large bureaucracies on a regular basis – from insurance companies to local government to the Inland Revenue. Not infrequently, we encounter situations in which public servants and bureaucrats seem to be unconcerned with our needs. One of the major weaknesses of bureaucracy is the difficulty it has in addressing cases that need special treatment and consideration.

Organizations as mechanistic and organic systems

Can bureaucratic procedures be applied effectively to all types of task? Some scholars have suggested that bureaucracy makes logical sense for carrying out routine tasks, but that it can be problematic in contexts where the demands change unpredictably.

In their research on innovation and change in electronics companies, Tom Burns and G. M. Stalker (1996) found that bureaucracies are of limited effectiveness in industries where flexibility and being on the cutting edge are prime concerns.

Burns and Stalker distinguished between two types of organization: mechanistic and organic. Mechanistic organizations are bureaucratic systems in which there is a hierarchical chain of command, with communication flowing vertically through clear channels. Each employee is responsible for a particular task; once the task is completed, responsibility passes onto the next employee. Work within such a system is anonymous, with people at the top and those at the bottom rarely in communication with one another.

Organic organizations, by contrast, are characterized by a looser structure in which the overall goals of the organization take precedence over narrowly defined responsibilities. Communication flows and directives are more diffuse, moving along many trajectories, not simply vertical ones. Everyone involved in the organization is seen as possessing legitimate knowledge and input that can be drawn on in solving problems; decisions are not the exclusive domain of people at the top.

According to Burns and Stalker, organic organizations are much better equipped to handle the changing demands of an innovative market, such as telecommunications, computer software or biotechnology. The more fluid internal structure means that they can respond more quickly and appropriately to shifts in the market and can come up with solutions more creatively and rapidly. Mechanistic organizations are better suited to more traditional, stable forms of production that are less susceptible to swings in the market. Although their study was first published 40 years ago, it is highly relevant to present-day discussions of organizational change. Burns and Stalker foreshadowed many of the issues that have taken centre stage in recent debates over globalization, flexible specialization and de-bureaucratization.

Bureaucracy versus democracy?

Even in democratic countries, government organizations hold enormous amounts of information about people, from records of our dates of birth, schools and universities attended and jobs held, to data on income used for tax collecting, and information used for issuing drivers' licences and allocating National Insurance numbers. Since we do not always know what information is held on us, and which agencies are holding it, people fear that such surveillance activities can infringe on the principle of democracy. These fears formed the basis of George Orwell's famous novel, *1984*, in which the state, 'Big Brother', uses surveillance of its citizens to suppress internal criticism and the difference of opinion normal in any democracy.

Proposals to introduce identity cards in many countries, partly to help tackle global terrorism and protect citizens against identity theft, have focused these concerns. Such cards usually contain a photograph of the card-holder, their name, address, gender and date of birth, but now also a microchip which would hold biometric information, such as the person's fingerprints, iris image or facial dimensions. Critics have expressed concerns that national central databases, which contain information about people's identities, will not be secure and will pose a threat to people's rights to privacy and freedom from discrimination. Supporters of identity cards argue that some types of surveillance may actually protect the principle of democracy, by allowing easier surveillance of those who are trying to destroy it.

Weber's student, Robert Michels (1967), invented a phrase, which has since become famous, to refer to this loss of power: in large-scale organizations, and more generally a society dominated by organizations, he argued, there is an **iron law of oligarchy** ('oligarchy' means 'rule by the few'). According to Michels, the flow of power towards the top is simply an inevitable part of an increasingly bureaucratized world – hence the term 'iron law'.

Was Michels right? It surely is correct to say that large-scale organizations involve the centralizing of power. Yet there is good reason to suppose that the 'iron law of oligarchy' is not quite so hard and fast as Michels claimed. The connections between oligarchy and bureaucratic centralization are more ambiguous than he supposed.

We should recognize first that unequal power is not just a function of size, as Michels presumed. In modest-sized groups there can also be very marked differences of power. In a small business, for instance, where the activities of employees are directly visible to the directors, much tighter control might be exerted than in offices in larger organizations. As organizations expand in size, power relationships often in fact become looser. Those at the middle and lower levels may have little influence over general policies forged at the top. On the other hand, because of the specialization and expertise involved in bureaucracy, people at the top also lose control over many administrative decisions, which are handled by those lower down.

In many modern organizations, power is also quite often openly delegated

---

THINKING CRITICALLY

Think of a time when you have had to deal with a bureaucratic system, maybe the health service, welfare benefits office or local government, and list all the *negative* aspects of the encounter. Were you satisfied with the way the staff communicated with you and did you think it was an efficient process? Now, list all the *positive* aspects of the encounter. Do you think the relatively formal, rule-directed character of bureaucracies is the only way to deal with large numbers of people? Based on your experiences, how might such bureaucratic systems be improved?

18.1 Can bureaucracy be defended?

As the sociologist Paul du Gay admits, 'These are not the best days for bureaucracy'. As we have seen, since the term 'bureaucracy' was coined, it has been used in a negative way. In an influential book, *In Praise of Bureaucracy* (2000), du Gay resists this attack. Whilst recognizing that bureaucracies can and do, of course, have flaws, he seeks to defend bureaucracy against the most common lines of criticism directed against it.

First, du Gay argues against the claim that there are ethical problems with the idea of bureaucracy. He singles out the sociologist Zygmunt Bauman's book, *Modernity and the Holocaust* (1989), as an important account of this view. Bauman believes that it was only with the development of the bureaucratic institutions associated with modern society that horrendous acts like the holocaust in the Second World War became possible. The planned genocide of millions of people by the Nazis in the Final Solution could only

happen once institutions were in place that distanced people from taking moral responsibility for their actions. Rather than being a barbaric explosion of violence, Bauman argues that the holocaust was only possible because rational bureaucratic institutions had emerged that separated discrete tasks from their consequences. German bureaucrats, and particularly the SS, would focus on carrying out their allotted tasks to the best of their abilities, and on following orders – for example, making sure that a railway line had been built, or that a group of people was moved from one part of the country to another – rather than questioning the whole rationale behind mass murder.

As we have seen, Bauman argues that responsibility is diluted in a bureaucracy, but du Gay argues quite the opposite. For the holocaust to happen, du Gay contends, the Nazis had to *overcome* the legitimate and ethical procedures integral to bureaucracy. One aspect of this was in the promotion of unquestioning allegiance to the

Was Auschwitz the ultimate expression of bureaucratic organization?

Führer, Adolf Hitler, rather than to the objective codes of bureaucracies. Du Gay argues that bureaucracies have an important ethos, which includes the equal and impartial treatment of all citizens regardless of their values. For du Gay, the holocaust came about when the racist convictions of Nazis overcame the impartial application of rules that is essential to a bureaucracy.

Du Gay also seeks to defend bureaucracy against a second line of attack, by rejecting what he sees as the current fashionable talk of the need for entrepreneurial reform of bureaucracies, especially public services. He stresses that the ethos of bureaucratic impartiality is being undermined by an increasingly politicized civil service, which is enthusiastic to get the job done in the way that pleases politicians, rather than to follow a bureaucratic framework that ensures administrative responsibility for the public interest and constitutional legitimacy.

downward from superiors to subordinates. In many large companies, corporate heads are so busy coordinating different departments, coping with crises, and analysing budget and forecast figures that they have little time for original thinking. They hand over consideration of policy issues to others below them, whose task is to develop proposals. Many corporate leaders frankly admit that, for the most part, they simply accept the conclusions given to them.

The physical setting of organizations

Most modern organizations function in specially designed physical settings. A building that houses a particular organization possesses specific features relevant to the organization's activities, but it also shares important architectural characteristics with buildings of other organizations. The architecture of a hospital, for instance, differs in some respects from that of a business firm or a school. The hospital's separate wards, consulting rooms, operating rooms and offices give the overall building a definite layout, while a school may consist of classrooms, laboratories and a gymnasium. Yet there is a general resemblance: both are likely to contain hallways with doors leading off and to use standard decoration and furnishings throughout. Apart from the different dress of the people moving through the corridors, the buildings in which modern organizations are usually housed have a definite sameness to them. And they often look similar from the outside as well as within their interiors. It would not be unusual to ask, on driving past a building, 'Is that a school?' and receive the response, 'No, it's a hospital.'

Organizations and the control of time and space

Michel Foucault (1971, 1978) showed that the architecture of an organization is directly involved with its social make-up

The physical organization of this 1940s typing pool means that the workers are kept under close surveillance. In modern organizations, surveillance tends to take new forms.

and system of authority. By studying the physical characteristics of organizations, we can shed new light on the problems analysed by Weber. The offices he discussed abstractly are also architectural settings – rooms, separated by corridors. The buildings of large firms are sometimes actually constructed physically as a hierarchy, in which the more elevated one's position in the hierarchy of authority, the nearer to the top of the building one's office is; the phrase 'the top floor' is sometimes used to mean those who hold ultimate power in the organization.

In many other ways, the geography of an organization will affect its functioning, especially in cases where systems rely heavily on informal relationships. Physical proximity makes forming groups easier, while physical distance can polarize groups, resulting in a 'them' and 'us' attitude between departments.

Surveillance in organizations

The arrangement of rooms, hallways and open spaces in an organization's buildings can provide basic clues to how its system of authority operates. In some organizations, groups of people work collectively in open settings. Because of the dull, repetitive nature of certain kinds of industrial work, like assembly-line production, regular supervision is needed to ensure that workers sustain the pace of labour. The same is often true of other types of routine work, such as that carried out by customer service operators in call centres, who often have their calls and activities monitored by their supervisors. Foucault laid great emphasis on how visibility, or lack of it, in the architectural settings of modern organizations influences and expresses patterns of authority. Their level of visibility determines how easily subordinates can be subject to what Foucault calls **surveillance**, the supervision of activities in organizations. In modern organizations, everyone, even in relatively high positions of authority, is subject to surveillance; but the lowlier a person is, the more his or her behaviour tends to be closely scrutinized.

Surveillance takes several forms. One is the direct supervision of the work of subordinates by superiors. Consider the example of a school classroom. Pupils sit at tables or desks, often arranged in rows, all in view of the teacher. Children are supposed to look alert or otherwise be absorbed in their work. Of course, how far this actually happens in practice depends on the abilities of the teacher and the inclinations of the children to conform to what is expected of them.

A second type of surveillance is more subtle but equally important. It consists of keeping files, records and case histories about people's work lives. Weber saw the importance of written records (nowadays often computerized) in modern organizations, but did not fully explore how they can be used to regulate behaviour. Employee records usually provide complete work histories, registering personal details and often giving character evaluations. Such records are used to monitor employees' behaviour and assess recommendations for promotion. In many business firms, individuals at each level in the organization prepare annual reports on the performance of those in the levels just below them. School records

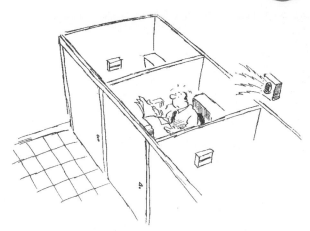

'Sensors indicate that No. 2 cubicle has been occupied for eighteen minutes. Do you require assistance?'

and college transcripts are also used to monitor individuals' performance as they move through the organization. Records are kept on file for academic staff, too.

Lastly, there is self-surveillance, where assumptions about the surveillance by others change ones behaviour and limit what one does. Think of the example used above of the telephone operator in a call centre. The operator will often have no way of knowing whether calls are being monitored, or how often supervisors listen in to phone conversations. Yet, operators are likely to assume that they are under surveillance from management and so keep calls short, efficient and formal, in line with the company guidelines.

Organizations cannot operate effectively if employees' work is haphazard. In business

THINKING CRITICALLY

Reflect on your experience of schools, workplaces and public areas. In what ways are these becoming subject to more surveillance? What type of surveillance is being introduced in each? Why might people welcome an increase in surveillance? What are the positive aspects of increasing surveillance?

Classic Studies 18.2 | **Michel Foucault, the Panopticon and surveillance**

The research problem

We have already seen that schools look a bit like hospitals and there is a similarity to the design of many other modern organizations. But why is this? The function of schools is very different to hospitals, so why are their designs not radically different? How did it happen that the physical structures of so many modern organizations came to bear such a strong resemblance to each other? The French social philosopher, Michel Foucault, investigated the origins of modern forms of organization and reached a surprising conclusion – many have their roots in the same underlying principles as prisons.

Foucault's explanation

Foucault's work covers a wide range of subjects, but he paid a great deal of attention to organizations such as prisons and 'asylums' (institutions for the mentally ill), in which individuals are physically separated for long periods from the outside world. In such

A prison built following Bentham's model of the Panopticon.

organizations, people are incarcerated – kept hidden away – from the external social environment. A prison illustrates in clear detail the nature of surveillance, because it seeks to maximize control over inmates' behaviour. But controlling behaviour is also a central feature of most other organizations and Foucault asks, 'Is it surprising that prisons resemble factories, schools, barracks, hospitals, which all resemble prisons?' (1975: 228).

In *Discipline and Punish* (1975), Foucault argues that the modern prison has its origins in the Panopticon, an organization planned according to principles designed around 1787 by the philosopher and social reformer Jeremy Bentham. 'Panopticon' was the name Bentham gave to his ideal model of a prison, which he tried to sell to the British government. And though the design never was fully implemented, some of its main principles were incorporated into prisons built in nineteenth-century Europe and the USA. The Panopticon was circular in shape, with the cells built around the outside edge. In the centre was an inspection tower. Two windows were placed in every cell, one facing the inspection tower and the other facing outside. The aim of the design was to make prisoners visible to guards at all times. The windows in the tower itself were equipped with Venetian blinds, so that while the prison staff could keep the prisoners under constant observation, they themselves could be invisible. Even today, most prisons look remarkably like the Panopticon, with viewing holes in cell doors, for example, ensuring that the principle of prisoners not knowing when they might be seen remains intact. Foucault argues that this compels inmates to behave well all the time, as they never know when they will be observed.

For Foucault, such principles of surveillance, observation and correcting unwanted behaviour do not stop at the prison gates. In fact, they are part and parcel of modernity itself. The principles of surveillance and discipline run throughout modern life, into the organization of schools, hospitals and businesses, making for a 'carceral society' – one which effectively incarcerates its members under a managerial gaze.

Critical points

Foucault's work has been enormously influential in the social sciences, but it has also drawn much criticism. The notion that modern life constitutes incarceration seems exaggerated, particularly compared to previous societies. It is hard to see workers as prisoners, for example. As Marx pointed out, even in the nineteenth century capitalism was based on wage labour not slavery, and workers had private lives outside the organization. There is also reason to see even those 'closed' organizations discussed by Foucault as in long-term decline. Since the late 1960s, many societies have witnessed a process of 'decarceration', as institutions for disabled people and 'asylums' have been closed down, in favour of integration into the wider community. Similarly, community penalties rather than imprisonment have become routinely used as punishment for some categories of offender. Critics say that Foucault's thesis does not adequately account for such trends. Finally, even on his own terms, Foucault's argument that prisons and other organizations were designed for maximum efficiency is open to criticism. Direct supervision may work tolerably well when the people involved, as in prisons, are hostile to those in authority and do not want to be where they are. But in other organizations, where managers need to cooperate with staff in reaching common goals, the situation is different. Too much direct supervision alienates employees, who then feel they are denied opportunities for involvement and may well rebel or do the minimum required (Sabel 1982; Grint 2005). That does not seem to be the most efficient form of organization.

People in the wider society are also prone to resist rather than submit to high levels of surveillance. People in the former Soviet-styled communist societies were routinely spied on and governments kept detailed information on citizens to clamp down on possible opposition. The whole society did indeed come almost to resemble a gigantic prison. But this also brought the same discontents, conflicts and opposition that prisons generate, ultimately leading to widespread disenchantment, rebellion and the collapse of Soviet-style communist societies.

Contemporary significance

Foucault added a new twist to our understanding of what modern life is like. He reminded us that it is not simply about progress, technological invention and increasing material wealth. There is also a dark side to modernity that has always accompanied its progressive face, which can be found in prisons, asylums and disciplinary techniques. In this sense, his work remains significant, because it has made social scientists (and others) more realistic about the balance of benefits and dangers of modernization.

Foucault's focus on surveillance has become much more important today because of the growing impact of information and communications technologies (ICT). We may not accept that we live in Foucault's carceral society, but some sociologists argue that we do now live in a **surveillance society** (Lyon 1994). A society in which information about our lives is gathered and shared by different types of organizations, where urban CCTV cameras follow all of our movements and where the technologies we love and feel we cannot do without – such as the Internet and mobile phones – also enable our physical and virtual movements to be tracked more accurately and systematically than ever before.

firms, as Weber pointed out, people are expected to work regular hours. Activities must be consistently coordinated in time and space, something promoted both by the physical settings of organizations and by the precise scheduling of detailed timetables. Timetables regularize activities across time and space – in Foucault's words, they 'efficiently distribute bodies' around the organization. Timetables are a condition of organizational discipline, because they slot the activities of large numbers of people together. If a university did not strictly observe a lecture timetable, for example, it would soon collapse into complete chaos. A timetable makes possible the intensive use of time and space: each can be packed with many people and many activities.

Transnational organizations

For the first time in history, organizations have become truly global in scale. Information technologies have rendered national borders less meaningful, since they can no longer contain key economic, cultural and environmental activities. As a consequence, international organizations are expected to continue to grow in number and importance, providing a measure of predictability and stability in a world where nations are no longer the all-powerful actors they once were.

Sociologists therefore study international organizations in order to understand better how it is possible to create institutions that span national borders and what their effects will be. Some sociologists even argue that global organizations will push the world's countries to become more and more alike (Thomas 1987; Scott and Meyer 1994; McNeely 1995).

International organizations are not new, however. For example, organizations concerned with managing trade across borders have existed for centuries. The Hanseatic League, a business alliance among German merchants and cities, was one such organization, dominating trade in the North and Baltic Seas from the middle of the thirteenth century to the middle of the seventeenth century. But it was not until the creation of the short-lived League of Nations in 1919 that truly global organizations, with elaborate bureaucracies and member nations around the world, were formed. The United Nations, created in 1945, is perhaps the most prominent modern example of a global organization.

Sociologists have divided international organizations into two principal types: international governmental organizations comprise national governments, while international non-governmental organizations comprise private organizations. We will consider each of these separately.

International governmental organizations

The first type of global organization is the **international governmental organization** (IGO), a type of international organization established by treaties between governments for purposes of conducting business between the nations making up its membership. Such organizations emerge for reasons of national security (both the League of Nations and the United Nations were created after highly destructive world wars), the regulation of trade (for example, by the World Trade Organization), social welfare or human rights or, increasingly, environmental protection.

Some of the most powerful IGOs today were created to unify national economies into large and powerful trading blocks. One of the most advanced IGOs is the European Union (EU), whose rules since May 2004 have governed 25 European member states. The EU was formed to create a single European economy, in which businesses could operate freely across borders in search of markets and labour and workers could move freely in search of jobs. EU members have common economic policies and, since 2002, 12 of them even share a single currency (the euro). Not all Europeans welcome this development, however, arguing that it means that member countries will eventually surrender most of their economic decision-making to the EU as a whole.

IGOs can also wield considerable military power, provided that their member nations are willing to do so. The North Atlantic Treaty Organization (NATO) and the UN, for example, used the full weight of their members' combined military might against Iraq during the first Gulf War in 1991, and again in Kosovo, in the former Yugoslavia, in 1999. Yet, since nations ultimately control their own use of military force, there are limits to the authority of even the most powerful military IGOs, whose strength derives from the voluntary participation of their member nations. In the face of violent civil strife in Bosnia and the African countries of Somalia, Rwanda and the Darfur region of Sudan, for example, UN peacekeeping efforts have proved largely ineffective.

IGOs often tend to reflect inequalities in power among their member nations. For example, the UN Security Council is responsible for maintaining international peace and security and is therefore the most powerful organization within the UN. Its five permanent members include Britain, the United States, China, France and Russia, giving these countries significant control over the Security Council's actions. The remaining ten countries are elected by the UN General Assembly for two-year terms and therefore have less ongoing power than the permanent members.

At the beginning of the twentieth century, there were only about three dozen IGOs in the world, although data for that time are sketchy. By 1981, when consistent reporting criteria were adopted, there were 1,039 and by 2006 there were as many as 7,350 IGOs, though some are no longer active (Union of International Organizations 2007).

International non-governmental organizations

The second type of global organization is the international non-governmental organization (INGO), which consists of international organizations established by agreements between the individuals or private organizations making up their membership. Examples include the International Sociological Association, the International Council of Women and the environmental group Greenpeace. As with IGOs, the number of INGOs has increased explosively in recent years – from fewer than 200 near the beginning of the twentieth century to about 15,000 in the mid-1990s (Union of International Associations 1996–7). By 2006 there were around 51,509 INGOs, though more than a third of these were apparently inac-

tive (Union of International Organizations 2006).

In general, INGOs are primarily concerned with promoting the global interests of their members, largely through influencing the UN, other INGOs or individual governments. They also engage in research and education and spread information by means of international conferences, meetings and journals. INGOs have succeeded in shaping the policies of powerful nations.

One prominent (and highly successful) example of an INGO is the International Campaign to Ban Landmines (ICBL). The campaign, along with its founder Jody Williams, was awarded the Nobel Peace Prize in 1997 for its success in getting a majority of the world's countries to agree to a treaty banning the devastating use of landmines. The Nobel Prize committee commended the campaign for changing 'a vision to a feasible reality', adding that 'this work has grown into a convincing example of an effective policy for peace that could prove decisive in the international effort for disarmament' (ICBL 2001).

The ICBL is affiliated with more than 1,000 other INGOs in some 60 countries. Together they have focused public attention on the dangers posed to civilians of the more than 100 million anti-personnel mines that are a deadly legacy of former wars fought in Europe, Asia and Africa. These mines are unlike other weapons. They can remain active for decades after a war, terrorizing and trapping whole populations. In Cambodia, for example, fertile croplands have been mined, threatening with starvation farmers who are not willing to risk action that could reduce them or their families to a shower of scraps. The campaign's efforts resulted in a treaty banning the use, production, stockpiling and transfer of anti-personnel landmines. The treaty is supported by 150 countries, and became international law in March 1999.

Although they are far more numerous than IGOs and have achieved some successes, INGOs have far less influence, since legal power (including enforcement) ultimately lies with governments. In the effort to ban landmines, for instance, although most of the major powers in the world signed the treaty, the United States, citing security concerns in Korea, refused to do so, as did Russia. Some INGOs, like Amnesty International and Greenpeace, have nonetheless achieved considerable influence.

Economic organizations

Modern societies are, in Marx's term, capitalistic. **Capitalism** is a way of organizing economic life that is distinguished by the following important features: private ownership of the means of production; profit as incentive; free competition for markets to sell goods, acquire cheap materials and utilize cheap labour; and restless expansion and investment to accumulate capital. Capitalism, which began to spread with the growth of the Industrial Revolution in the early nineteenth century, is a vastly more dynamic economic system than any other that preceded it in history. While the system has had many critics, like Marx, it is now the most widespread form of economic organization in the world.

So far in this chapter, we have been looking at work mostly from the perspective of occupations and employees. We have studied patterns of work and the factors influencing the development of trade unions. Here, we concern ourselves with the nature of the business firms in which the workforce is employed. (It should, however, also be recognized that many people today are employees of government organizations, although we shall not consider these here.) What is happening to business corporations today, and how are they run?

Corporations and corporate power

Since the turn of the twentieth century, modern capitalist economies have been increasingly influenced by the rise of large business **corporations**. A recent survey of the world's top 200 corporations showed that between 1983 and 1999 their combined sales grew from the equivalent of 25 per cent to 27.5 per cent of world GDP. During the same period, the profits of these corporations grew 362.4 per cent, while the number of people they employ grew by only 14.4 per cent (Anderson and Cavanagh 2000).

Of course, there still exist thousands of smaller firms and enterprises within the British economy. In these companies, the image of the **entrepreneur** – the boss who owns and runs the firm – is by no means obsolete. The large corporations are a different matter. Ever since Adolf Berle and Gardiner Means published their celebrated study *The Modern Corporation and Private Property* in the 1930s, it has been accepted that most of the largest firms are not run by those who own them (Berle and Means 1997 [1932]). In theory, the large corporations are the property of their shareholders, who have the right to make all-important decisions. But Berle and Means argued that since share-ownership is so dispersed, actual control has passed into the hands of the managers who run firms on a day-to-day basis. Ownership of the corporations is thus separated from their control.

Whether run by owners or managers, the power of the major corporations is very extensive. When one or a handful of firms dominate in a given industry, they often cooperate in setting prices rather than freely competing with one another. Thus, the giant oil companies normally follow one another's lead in the price charged for gasoline. When one firm occupies a commanding position in a given industry, it is said to be in a **monopoly** position. More common is a situation of **oligopoly**, in which a small group of giant corporations predominate. In situations of oligopoly, firms are able more or less to dictate the terms on which they buy goods and services from the smaller firms that are their suppliers.

Types of corporate capitalism

There have been three general stages in the development of business corporations, although each overlaps with the others and all continue to coexist today. The first stage, characteristic of the nineteenth and early twentieth centuries, was dominated by **family capitalism**. Large firms were run either by individual entrepreneurs or by members of the same family and then passed on to their descendants. The famous corporate dynasties, such as the Sainsburys in the UK or the Rockefellers in the USA, belong in this category. These individuals and families did not just own a single large corporation, but held a diversity of economic interests and stood at the apex of economic empires.

Most of the big firms founded by entrepreneurial families have since become public companies – that is, shares of their stock are traded on the open market – and have passed into managerial control. But important elements of family capitalism remain, even within some of the world's largest corporations, such as the Ford car company, whose Chief Executive is William Clay Ford, Jr., the great-grandson of Henry Ford who founded the company. Among small firms, such as local shops run by their owners, small plumbing and house-painting businesses and so forth, family capitalism continues to dominate. Some of these firms, such as shops that remain in the hands of the same family for two or more generations, are also dynasties on a minor scale. However, the small business sector is a highly unstable one, and economic failure is very common; the proportion of firms owned by members of the same family for extended periods is minuscule.

In the large corporate sector, family capitalism was increasingly succeeded by **managerial capitalism**. As managers came to have more and more influence through the growth of very large firms, the entrepreneurial families were displaced. The result has been described as the replacement of the family in the company by the company itself. The corporation emerged as a more defined economic entity. In a study of the 200 largest manufacturing corporations

in the United States, Michael Allen (1981) found that in cases where profit showed a decline, family-controlled enterprises were unlikely to replace their chief executive, but manager-controlled firms did so rapidly.

There is no question that managerial capitalism has left an indelible imprint on modern society. The large corporation drives not only patterns of consumption but also the experience of employment in contemporary society – it is difficult to imagine how different the work lives of many people in the developed societies would be in the absence of large factories or corporate bureaucracies. Sociologists have identified another area in which the large corporation has left a mark on modern institutions. **Welfare capitalism** refers to a practice that sought to make the corporation – rather than the state or trade unions – the primary shelter from the uncertainties of the market in modern industrial life. Beginning at the end of the nineteenth century, large firms began to provide certain services to their employees, including child-care, recreational facilities, profit-sharing plans, paid holidays, unemployment insurance and life insurance. These programmes often had a paternalistic bent, such as that sponsoring 'home visits' for the 'moral education' of employees. Viewed in less benevolent terms, a major objective of welfare capitalism was coercion, as employers deployed all manner of tactics – including violence – to avoid unionization.

In his study of the US labour movement, Sanford Jacoby (1997) argues that conventional histories typically suggest that welfare capitalism met its demise in the Depression years of the 1930s, as trade unions achieved unprecedented levels of influence and as President Franklin Roosevelt's New Deal administration began to guarantee many of the benefits provided by firms. In contrast to this standard interpretation, Jacoby argues that welfare capitalism did not die, but instead went underground during the apex of the labour movement. In firms that avoided unionization during the period between the 1930s and 1960s – like the US-based companies Kodak, Sears and Thompson Products – welfare capitalism was modernized, shedding blatantly paternalistic aspects and routinizing benefit programmes. When the union movement began to weaken after 1970, these companies offered a model to many other firms, which were now able to press their advantage against flanking unions, reasserting the role of the firm as 'industrial manor'.

Despite the overwhelming importance of managerial capitalism in shaping the modern economy, many scholars now see emerging the contours of a third, different phase in the evolution of the corporation. They argue that managerial capitalism has today partly ceded place to **institutional capitalism**. This term refers to the emergence of a consolidated network of business leadership, concerned not only with decision-making within single firms, but also with the development of corporate power beyond them. Institutional capitalism is based on the practice of corporations holding shares in other firms. In effect, interlocking boards of directors exercise control over much of the corporate landscape. This reverses the process of increasing managerial control, since the managers' shareholdings are dwarfed by the large blocks of shares owned by other corporations. One of the main reasons for the spread of institutional capitalism is the shift in patterns of investment that has occurred over the past 30 years. Rather than investing directly by buying shares in a business, individuals now invest in money market, trust, insurance and pension funds that are controlled by large financial organizations, which in turn invest these grouped savings in industrial corporations.

Transnational corporations

With the intensifying of globalization, most large corporations now operate in an international economic context. When they establish branches in two or several countries, they are referred to as multinational or **transnational corporations**. 'Transnational' is the preferred term, indicating that these companies operate across many different national boundaries.

The largest transnationals are gigantic; their wealth outstrips that of many countries. Half of the 100 largest economic units in the world today are nations; the other half are transnational corporations. The scope of these companies' operations is staggering. The 600 largest transnationals account for more than a fifth of the total industrial and agricultural production in the global economy; about 70 are responsible for half of total global sales (Dicken 1992). The revenues of the largest 200 companies rose tenfold between the mid-1970s and the 1990s, reaching $9.5 trillion in 2001. In 2003 it was estimated that the world's top ten pharmaceutical companies controlled over 53 per cent of the global market share. Over the past 20 years, the transnationals' activities have become increasingly global: only three of the world's largest companies in 1950 had manufacturing subsidiaries in more than 20 countries; some 50 do so today. These are still a small minority; most of the transnationals have subsidiaries in two to five countries.

Of the top 200 companies in the year 2000, US corporations dominated the list, with 82 slots (41 per cent of the total); Japanese firms came second, with 41 slots (Anderson and Cavanagh 2000). However, the proportion of American companies in the top 200 has fallen significantly since 1960, when just five Japanese corporations were included in that list. Contrary to common belief, three-quarters of all foreign direct investment is between the industrialized countries. Nevertheless, the involvement of transnationals in developing countries is extensive, with Brazil, Mexico and India showing the highest levels of foreign investment. The most rapid rate of increase in corporate investment by far has been in the Asian newly industrializing countries (NICs) of Singapore, Taiwan, Hong Kong, South Korea and Malaysia.

The reach of the transnationals in recent decades would not have been possible without advances in transport and communications. Air travel now allows people to move around the world at a speed that would have seemed inconceivable even 60 years ago. The development of extremely large ocean-going vessels (superfreighters), together with containers that can be shifted directly from one type of carrier to another, makes possible the easy transport of bulk materials.

Telecommunications technologies now permit more or less instantaneous communication from one part of the world to another. Satellites have been used for commercial telecommunications since 1965, when the first one in use could carry 240 telephone conversations at once. Current satellites can carry at least 12,000 simultaneous conversations. The larger transnationals now have their own satellite-based communications systems. The Mitsubishi Corporation, for instance, has a massive network, across which five million words are transmitted to and from its headquarters in Tokyo each day.

Types of transnational corporations

The transnationals came to assume an increasingly important place in the world economy over the course of the twentieth century. They are of key importance in the international **division of labour** – the specialization in producing goods for the world market that divides regions into zones of industrial or agricultural production or high- or low-skilled labour (McMichael 1996). Just as national economies have become increasingly concentrated – dominated by a limited number of very large companies – so too has the world economy. In the case of the United Kingdom and several of the other leading industrialized countries, the firms that dominate nationally also have a very wide-ranging international presence. Many sectors of world production (such as agribusiness) are oligopolies – production is

controlled by three or four corporations that dominate the market. Over the past two or three decades, international oligopolies have developed in the automobile, microprocessor and electronics industries, and in the production of some other goods marketed worldwide.

H. V. Perlmutter (1972) divided transnational corporations into three types. One consists of **ethnocentric** transnationals, in which company policy is set and, as far as possible, put into practice from a headquarters in the country of origin. Companies and plants that the parent corporation owns around the world are cultural extensions of the originating company – its practices are standardized across the globe. A second category is that of **polycentric** transnationals, where overseas subsidiaries are managed by local firms in each country. The headquarters in the country or countries of origin of the main company establish broad guidelines within which local companies manage their own affairs. Finally, there are geocentric transnationals, which are international in their management structure. Managerial systems are integrated on a global basis, and higher managers are very mobile, moving from country to country as needs dictate.

Of all transnationals, Japanese companies tend to be the most strongly ethnocentric in Perlmutter's terms. Their worldwide operations are usually controlled tightly from the parent corporation, sometimes with the close involvement of the Japanese government. The Japanese Ministry of International Trade and Industry (MITI) plays a much more direct part in the overseeing of Japanese-based foreign enterprise than Western governments do. MITI has produced a series of development plans coordinating the overseas spread of Japanese firms over the past two decades. One distinctive Japanese type of transnational consists of the giant trading companies or *sogo shosha*. These are colossal conglomerates whose main concern is with the financing and support of trade. They provide

Advertising for Pepsi and Coca-Cola in Tripoli, Lebanon.

financial, organizational and information services to other companies. About half of Japanese exports and imports are routed through the ten largest *sogo shosha*. Some, like Mitsubishi, also have large manufacturing interests of their own.

Global-scale planning

The global corporations have become the first organizations able to plan on a truly world scale. Pepsi and Coca-Cola adverts, for example, reach billions of people across the globe. A few companies with developed global networks are able to shape the commercial activities of diverse nations. Richard Barnet and John Cavanagh (1994) argue that there are four webs of interconnecting commercial activity in the new world economy: the Global *Cultural Bazaar*, the Global *Shopping Mall*, the Global *Workplace* and the Global *Financial Network*. The Global Cultural Bazaar is the newest of the four, but is already the most extensive. Global images and global dreams are diffused through movies, TV programmes, music, videos, games, toys and T-shirts, sold on a worldwide basis. All over the earth, even in the poorest developing world countries, people are using the same electronic devices to see or listen to the same commercially produced songs and shows.

The Global Shopping Mall is a 'planetary supermarket with a dazzling spread of things to eat, drink, wear and enjoy'. It is more exclusive than the Cultural Bazaar because the poor do not have the resources to participate – they have the status only of window shoppers. Of the 5.5 billion people who make up the world's population, 3.5 billion lack the cash or credit to purchase any consumer goods.

The third global web, the Global Workplace, is the increasingly complex global division of labour that affects all of us. It consists of the massive array of offices, factories, restaurants and millions of other places where goods are produced and consumed or information is exchanged. This web is closely bound up with the Global Financial Network, which it fuels and is financed by. The Global Financial Network consists of billions of bits of information stored in computers and portrayed on computer screens. It entails almost endless currency exchanges, credit card transactions, insurance plans, and the buying and selling of stocks and shares.

The transformation of large corporations?

There are big differences between the large corporation of the first decade of the twenty-first century and its counterpart of the mid-twentieth century. Many of the names are the same – General Motors, Ford and IBM, for example – but these have been joined by other giant firms, largely unknown in the 1950s, such as Microsoft and Intel. They all wield great power, and their top executives still inhabit the large buildings that dominate so many city centres.

But below the surface of similarities between today and half a century ago, some profound transformations have taken place. The origin of these transformations lies in that process we have encountered often in this book: globalization. Over the past 50 years, the giant corporations have become more and more caught up in global competition; as a result, their internal composition, and in a way their very nature, has altered.

Former US Labour Secretary, Robert Reich (1991) wrote:

> Underneath, all is changing. America's core corporation no longer plans and implements the production of a large volume of goods and services; it no longer invests in a vast array of factories, machinery, laboratories, inventories, and other tangible assets; it no longer employs armies of production workers and middle-level managers. . . . In fact, the core corporation is no longer even American. It is, increasingly, a façade, behind which teems an array of decentralised groups and subgroups continuously contracting with similarly diffuse working units all over the world.

The large corporation is less and less a big business and more an 'enterprise web' – a central organization that links smaller firms together. IBM, for example, which used to be one of the most jealously self-sufficient of all large corporations, in the 1980s and early 1990s joined with dozens of US-based companies and more than 80 foreign-based firms to share strategic planning and cope with production problems.

Some corporations remain strongly bureaucratic and are often centred in the country in which they first became established. However, most are no longer so clearly located anywhere. The old transnational corporation used to work mainly from its national headquarters, from where its overseas production plants and subsidiaries were controlled. Now, with the transformation of space and time (discussed in chapter 7, 'Social Interaction and Everyday Life'), groups situated in any region of the world are able, via telecommunications and computers, to work with others. Nations still try to influence flows of information, resources and money across their borders. But modern communications technologies make this increasingly difficult, if not impossible. Knowledge and finances can be transferred across the world as electronic blips moving at the speed of light.

The products of the transnational companies similarly have an international character. When is something 'Made in Britain' or any other country and when is it not? There is no longer any clear answer. In chapter 4, 'Human History and Globalization', we

"That was a fine report, Barbara. But since the sexes speak different languages, I probably didn't understand a word of it."

looked at the example of Barbie, the 'all-American' doll, whose packaging says she is 'Made in China'. But as we saw, the origin of her body and wardrobe span the globe, from the Middle to the Far East, before she is eventually sold in the USA or shipped on again for sale elsewhere.

Women and the corporation

Until three decades or so ago, organizational studies did not devote very much attention to the question of gender. Weber's theory of bureaucracy and many of the influential responses to it, were written by men and presumed a model of organizations that placed men squarely at the centre. The rise of feminist scholarship in the 1970s, however, led to examinations of gender relations in all the main institutions of society, including organizations and bureaucracy. Feminist sociologists not only focused on the imbalance of gender roles within organizations, they also explored the ways in which modern organizations had developed in a specifically gendered way.

Feminists have argued that the emergence of the modern organization and the bureaucratic career was dependent on a particular gender configuration. They point to two main ways in which gender is embedded in the very structure of modern organizations. First, bureaucracies are characterized by occupational gender segregation. As women began to enter the labour market in greater numbers, they tended to be segregated into *categories of occupations* that were low paying and involved routine work. These positions were subordinate to those occupied by men and did not provide opportunities for women to be promoted. Women were used as a source of cheap, reliable labour, but were not granted the same opportunities as men to build careers.

Second, the idea of a bureaucratic career was, in fact, a male career in which women played a crucial supporting role. At the workplace, women performed routine tasks – as clerks, secretaries and office managers – thereby freeing up men to advance their careers. Men could concentrate on obtaining promotions or landing big accounts because the female support staff handled much of the busy work. In the domestic sphere, women also supported the bureaucratic career by caring for the home, the children and the man's day-to-day wellbeing. Women serviced the needs of the male bureaucrat by allowing him to work long hours, travel and focus solely on his work without concerning himself with personal or domestic issues.

As a result of these two tendencies, early feminist writers argued, modern organizations have developed as male-dominated preserves in which women are excluded from power, denied opportunities to advance their careers and victimized on the basis of their gender through sexual harassment and discrimination. Although most early feminist analysis focused on a common set of concerns – unequal pay, discrimination, and the male hold on power – there was no consensus about the best approach to take in working for women's equality. Two of the leading feminist works on women and organizations exemplified the split between liberal and radical feminist perspectives.

One early and important liberal perspective was Rosabeth Moss Kanter's *Men and Women of the Corporation* (1977). Kanter investigated the position of women in corporations and analysed the ways in which they were excluded from gaining power. She focused on 'male homosociability' – the way in which men successfully kept power within a closed circle and allowed access only to those who were part of the same close group. Women and ethnic minorities were effectively denied opportunities for advancement and were shut out of the social networks and personal relationships that were crucial for promotion.

Although Kanter was critical of such gender imbalances, she was not entirely pessimistic about the future. She saw the problem as one of power, not gender. Women were in a disadvantaged position, not because they were women, but because they did not wield sufficient power within organizations. As greater numbers of women came to assume powerful roles, the power imbalances would be swept away.

An alternative approach was presented by the radical feminist Kathy Ferguson, in her book *The Feminist Case Against Bureaucracy* (1984). Ferguson did not see the gender imbalance within organizations as something that could be resolved simply with the promotion of more women to positions of power. In her view, modern organizations were *fundamentally* tainted by male values and patterns of domination and women would always be relegated to subordinate roles within such structures. The only real solution was for women to build their own organizations on principles very different from those designed by and for men. Ferguson argued that women have a better capacity than men to organize in a way that is more democratic, participatory and cooperative; men are prone to authoritarian tactics, inflexible procedures and an insensitive management style.

What impact have feminist ideas on organizations had on studies in this area? The answer appears to be a quite limited one. In spite of a large body of scholarship on gender and organizations, for example, a comprehensive *Handbook of Organizational Culture and Climate*, published in 2000 (Ashkanasy et al.) still contained only a single chapter on gender and organizations, thus restricting 'gender' to one specific issue, rather than seeing the gendered character of organizations as a crucial matter for the whole field of organization studies. This suggests that feminist theories have yet to become part of the mainstream of this subdiscipline. However, the renewal of interest in Marxism and critical theory through Critical Management Studies (CMS) (which we discuss below), may present feminist scholars with new opportunities to transform the current status of debates about conflict, power and gender within organizations in the future (Aaltio and Mills 2002).

 Gender inequality in the workplace is discussed in more detail in chapter 20, 'Work and Economic Life'.

Beyond bureaucracy?

Sociologists such as George Ritzer, whose thesis on the McDonaldization of society we looked at at the start of this chapter, argue that bureaucracy and rationalization remain key characteristics of most organizations, particularly in the developed world, where the modern form of bureaucracy has existed longest. However, others argue that although Weber's model of bureaucracy, mirrored by that of Foucault, may once have held good, it is now starting to look rather tired and may be less effective in explaining the changes to organizations of all kinds. Numerous organizations are overhauling themselves to become less, rather than more, hierarchical and, in the process, are becoming more informal and loosely organized.

In the 1960s, Burns and Stalker concluded that traditional bureaucratic structures can stifle innovation and creativity in cutting-edge industries; in today's electronic

Global Society 18.1 The changing face of the McDonald's corporation

In 2003, the then Chairman and Chief Executive of McDonald's, Jim Cantalupo, said, 'The world has changed. Our customers have changed. We have to change, too', promising investors that the company no longer wanted to be bigger than everybody else, just better. His speech came at a time when McDonald's had announced its first quarterly loss since 1965 and faced increasingly public attacks from environmental activists and health specialists. McDonald's' reputation for good service was also flagging, with the company ranked the worst for customer satisfaction in America, below health insurers and banks. All this resulted in the share price falling from more than US$48 in 1999, to a ten-year low of US$12 in 2003.

The article below illustrates how McDonald's has had to move away from its founder's original philosophy in order to adapt to local contexts in an age of globalization.

Adapt or die

The wind of change is blowing through the empire of fast food. The vision of endless growth through new markets across the planet for fast food companies now looks unsustainable when it's not what people want anymore. When fashions, styles and tastes change, it's time to adapt or die. As the fast food companies have expanded around the world, they have had to adapt to local sensitivities. In the old days, no franchise holder could deviate from the 700-page McDonald's operations manual known as 'the Bible'. But that policy may be changing.

In the 34 restaurants in India, the 'Maharaja Mac' is made of mutton, and the vegetarian options contain no meat or eggs. There were disturbances in India when it was learned that McDonald's French fries were precooked in beef fat in the USA, because Hindus revere cows and cannot eat beef.

Likewise, McDonald's in Pakistan offers three spicy 'McMaza meals': Chatpata Chicken Roll, Chicken 'n' Chutni Burger and Spicy Chicken Burger. All three are served 'with Aaloo fingers and a regular drink'.

In the USA itself, the taste for the food of the Eisenhower-era brightly coloured takeaway has

McDonald's has been trying to reinvent itself in recent years, following a fall in sales. This new-look London branch is now virtually indistinguishable from a bar or coffee shop.

changed over 50 years too. What the market is meant to offer is more choice, not less. In the heartland of America, at Evansville, Indiana, there's now a McDonald's With the Diner Inside, where waitresses serve 100 combinations of food, on china. This is not Ray Kroc's vision of stripping out choice to save time and money.

At the end of 2002, McDonald's began closing 175 outlets in ten countries. Some were branches in cities like London, but the company pulled out altogether from certain countries that were not giving appropriate financial returns. The reasons for these corporate changes may not be just to do with fast food.

One of Ray Kroc's partners once admitted that McDonald's was not really in the food business at all, but in real estate. McDonald's actually makes most of its money from rent, because it owns more retail property than any other company on earth. Land is more valuable than appetite, and the sites are more valuable an asset than what they sell.

Will McDonald's mutate into another business entirely, in order to survive?

Source: BBC WorldService.com, 'Fast Food Factory': www.bbc.co.uk/worldservice/specials/1616_fast food/page9.shtml (accessed 28/07/07)

economy, few would dispute the importance of these findings. Departing from rigid vertical command structures, many organizations are turning to 'horizontal', collaborative models in order to become more flexible and responsive to fluctuating markets. In this section, we shall examine some of the main forces behind these shifts, including globalization and the growth of information technology, and consider some of the ways in which late modern organizations are reinventing themselves in the light of the changing circumstances.

> ### THINKING CRITICALLY
>
> What does the recent experience of the McDonald's corporation tell us about the impact of globalization on large companies? Does the changing face of McDonald's invalidate Ritzer's thesis of 'MacDonaldization'? In what ways might Roland Robertson's concept of glocalization (see chapter 4) be the best guide to understanding the reality of global businesses today?

Organizational change: the Japanese model

Many of the changes now witnessed in organizations around the world were first pioneered amongst some of the large Japanese manufacturing corporations, such as Nissan and Panasonic. Although the Japanese economy suffered in the 1990s, it has been phenomenally successful during most of the post-war period. This economic success was often attributed to the distinctive characteristics of large Japanese corporations – which differed substantially from most business firms in the West. As we shall see, many of the organizational characteristics associated with Japanese corporations have been adapted and modified in other countries in recent years.

Japanese companies have diverged from the characteristics that Weber associated with bureaucracy in several ways:

1 *Bottom-up decision-making*. The big Japanese corporations do not form a pyramid of authority as Weber portrayed it, with each level being responsible only to the one above. Rather, workers low down in the organization are consulted about policies being considered by management, and even the top executives regularly meet them.

2 *Less specialization*. In Japanese organizations, employees specialize much less than their counterparts in the West. Young workers entering a firm in a management training position will

spend the first year learning generally how the various departments of the firm operate. They will then rotate through a variety of positions in both local branches and national headquarters in order to gain experience in the many dimensions of the company's activities. By the time employees reach the peak of their careers, some 30 years after having begun as a trainee, they will have mastered all the important tasks.

3 *Job security*. The large corporations in Japan are committed to the lifetime employment of those they hire; the employee is guaranteed a job. Pay and responsibility are geared to seniority – how many years a worker has been with the firm – rather than to a competitive struggle for promotion.

4 *Group-oriented production*. At all levels of the corporation, people are involved in small cooperative 'teams', or work groups. The groups, rather than individual members, are evaluated in terms of their performance. Unlike their Western counterparts, the 'organization charts' of Japanese companies – maps of the authority system – show only groups, not individual positions.

5 *Merging of work and private lives*. In Weber's depiction of bureaucracy, there is a clear division between the work of people within the organization and their activities outside. This is in fact true of most Western corporations, in which the relation between firm and employee is an economic one. Japanese corporations, by contrast, provide for many of their employees' needs, expecting in return a high level of loyalty to the firm. Workers receive material benefits from the company over and above their salaries. The electrical firm Hitachi, for example, studied by Ronald Dore (1973), provided housing for all unmarried workers and nearly half of its married male employees. Company loans were available for the education of children and to help with the cost of weddings and funerals.

Studies of Japanese-run plants in Britain and the United States indicate that 'bottom-up' decision-making does work outside Japan. Workers seem to respond positively to the greater level of involvement these plants provide (White and Trevor 1983). It seems reasonable to conclude, therefore, that the Japanese model does carry some lessons relevant to the Weberian conception of bureaucracy. Organizations that closely resemble Weber's ideal type are probably much less effective than they appear on paper, because they do not permit lower-level employees to develop a sense of involvement and autonomy in relation to their work tasks.

Until recently, many British and US business writers looked to the Japanese corporation as a model that Anglo-American companies should follow (Hutton 1995). The slowdown in the Japanese economy during the 1990s has led many experts to question this assumption. The commitment and sense of obligation that many Japanese companies traditionally had towards their staff may have encouraged loyalty, but it has also been criticized as inflexible and uncompetitive. As we have seen, during much of the post-war period core workers in Japanese companies could expect to be with the same company their entire working lives, dismissals or redundancies were rare and ambition for promotion was not particularly encouraged. The economic problems facing the country from the early 1990s, which only now appear to be easing, have meant that the future of Japanese business is torn between traditionalists, seeking to preserve the old system, and radical capitalists supporting reform towards a more competitive, individualistic model of business (Freedman 2001).

Transforming management practices

Most of the components of the 'Japanese model' described above come down to issues of management. While it is impossible to ignore specific production-level practices developed by the Japanese, a large part of the Japanese approach focused on management–worker relations and ensured that employees at all levels felt a personal attachment to the company. The emphasis on teamwork, consensus-building approaches and broad-based employee participation were in stark contrast to traditional Western forms of management that were more hierarchical and authoritarian.

In the 1980s, many Western organizations introduced new management techniques in order to boost productivity and competitiveness. Two popular branches of management theory – human resource management and the corporate culture approach – indicated that the Japanese model had not gone unnoticed in the West. The first of these, human resource management (HRM), is a style of management which regards a company's workforce as vital to economic competitiveness: if the employees are not completely dedicated to the firm and its product, the firm will never be a leader in its field. In order to generate employee enthusiasm and commitment, the entire organizational culture must be retooled so that workers feel they have an investment in the workplace and in the work process. According to HRM, human resources issues should not be the exclusive domain of designated 'personnel officers', but should be a top priority for all members of company management.

HRM is based on the assumption that there is no serious conflict within the company between workers and employers and there is therefore little need for trade unions to represent the workforce. Instead, HRM presents the company as an integrated whole, the only rivalry being that with its competitor firms. Instead of dealing with its workers through negotiation with trade unions, companies using the techniques of HRM seek to individualize their workforce by providing individual contracts and performance-related pay. Recent studies have shown that whilst workers may

comply with the dictates of HRM at work, many are privately cynical about the assumption of corporate unity that underlies it (Thompson and Findlay, 1999).

> **THINKING CRITICALLY**
>
> Think about workplaces that you have either worked in or seen in action. How widespread was the use of information technology and what, exactly, was it used for? Was management surveillance of employees seen as an issue by workers themselves? Do you think the potential dangers facing workers are real, or is the impact of information technology on their working lives essentially benign? What steps, if any, do you think can be taken to counter these trends?

The second management trend – creating a distinctive corporate culture – is closely related to human resource management. In order to promote loyalty to the company and pride in its work, the company's management works with employees to build an organizational culture involving rituals, events or traditions unique to that company alone. These cultural activities are designed to draw together all members of the firm – from the most senior managers to the newest employee – so that they make common cause with each other and strengthen group solidarity. Company picnics or 'fun days', 'casual Fridays' (days on which employees can 'dress down') and company-sponsored community service projects are examples of techniques for building a corporate culture.

In recent years, a number of Western companies have been founded according to the management principles described above. Rather than constructing themselves according to a traditional bureaucratic model, companies like the Saturn car company in the United States have organized themselves along these new managerial lines. At Saturn, for example, employees

18.2 Computers versus workers?

For businesses competing in the global economy, investment in information technology – computer and communications equipment – is a necessity. Firms in the financial sector rely heavily on computers to engage in transactions in international financial markets; manufacturing firms depend on communications equipment to coordinate global production processes; and the customers of consumer services firms demand 24-hour-a-day access to their accounts by telephone or the Internet. In short, information technology has become part of the basic infrastructure of business.

While some of these technologies have made workers' lives easier, there is reason to think that the new high-tech workplace may erode their power and rights. First, business reliance on information technology may undermine coalitions amongst workers. There is great demand today for employees with high-tech skills, whereas those who finish school or further education with few such skills find themselves eligible only for a limited

number of positions. Increasingly, there are coming to be two 'classes' of employees in firms: a privileged class with high-tech skills and another class relegated to lower-status work. But when employees negotiate with management over such issues as wages, hours and benefits, employee unity is essential for securing concessions. Will high-tech workers side with lower-skilled employees in workplace disputes, or will they be more likely to side with management? The status of worker rights and benefits in the future may well hinge on the answer to this question.

Second, in part because new communications technologies allow the branch offices and production facilities of multinational firms to communicate easily with one another, a higher proportion of manufactured goods is coming to be produced on a transnational basis – a situation that may make individual workers more easily replaceable. Robert Reich, who served as US Labour Secretary under President Clinton, provides the following example of a global production process:

In modern open-plan offices like these, employers can still keep workers under close surveillance.

Precision ice-hockey equipment is designed in Sweden, financed in Canada, and assembled in Cleveland and Denmark for distribution in North America and Europe, respectively, out of alloys whose molecular structure was researched and patented in Delaware and fabricated in Japan. An advertising campaign is conceived in Britain; film footage is shot in Canada, dubbed in Britain, and edited in New York. (Reich 1991)

Although high-tech, high-skilled workers will be needed to carry out many aspects of the production process, these skills may no longer give workers the same bargaining power that skilled craftsmanship carried with it in previous eras. Because the manufacturing process has been broken down into many small components, with each carried out at a different production facility, the number of skills that any one worker must have is more limited than was the case in previous times, making it easier for companies to replace 'difficult' workers. Communication technologies may therefore contribute to the process that Marxist scholar Harry Braverman (1974) called, 'the deskilling of labour'.

Third, the nature of workplace surveillance is likely to change as information technology becomes even more important for business. Employers have always watched their employees closely, monitoring performance, seeking to improve efficiency and checking that they do not steal. But as a greater proportion of work is done using computers, the capacity of managers to scrutinize the behaviour of their employees increases with computerized performance evaluations, scrutiny of emails and enhanced management access to personal employee information. Such an Orwellian scenario becomes ever more likely as the role of information technology in the workplace expands.

at all levels have the opportunity to spend time in positions in other areas of the company in order to gain a better sense of the operation of the firm as a whole. Shop-floor workers work alongside the marketing team, sharing insights into the way in which the vehicles are made; sales staff rotate through the servicing department to become more aware of common maintenance problems that might concern prospective buyers; representatives from both sales and the shop floor are involved in product design teams in order to discuss shortcomings, which the management may not have been aware of in earlier models. A corporate culture focused on friendly and knowledgeable customer service unifies company employees and enhances the sense of company pride.

Studying management practices

Academic research into management and business today takes place, largely, within multidisciplinary business and management schools. Here, organizations have tended to be analysed as 'systems', containing a series of integrated parts, such as different departments and groups of people. However, theoretical perspectives are also treated with some suspicion as management practices are seen as more-or-less rational responses to the changing economic, political and social context that organizations find themselves in. On this view, management is a neutral activity undertaken in the interests of organizations and understanding management practices is a commonsense activity requiring no special theoretical perspectives (Knights and Willmott 2007: 7–8). The recourse to 'common sense' (discussed in chapter 2) tends to rely on overly general 'explanations' that are often found wanting when faced with empirical research findings. This is why, as sociologists, we need theories that connect organizations and management practices to the wider society of which they are part.

Since the 1980s, there have been several new approaches to the study of management, with two theoretical perspectives emerging from theoretical perspectives developed within the social sciences and social theory. For this reason, critical management studies (CMS) and actor-network theory (ANT) are arguably of most interest to sociologists of organizations.

Critical management studies

Critical management studies (CMS) – as the name suggests – adopts a critical approach to mainstream management studies (Alvesson and Willmott 2003) and has risen to prominence since the mid-1990s. Conventionally, the mainstream of management studies tends to assume that the management of organizations is positive and necessary and that scientific studies of organizations should be of interest primarily to managers, who may then manage more effectively and efficiently. In short, management is seen as a relatively neutral activity, which is good for workers, consumers and society as a whole, while managers perform a socially useful function. In practice, this has meant that management studies has become a site primarily for the training of people who are seeking careers within the management of organizations.

CMS questions whether management really is such a neutral activity and takes a more critical approach to the whole subject, drawing on the ideas of Marx and particularly the neo-Marxist critical theory of the Frankfurt School (see chapter 3 for more detail on the Frankfurt School). However, CMS also uses the work of Foucault as well as insights gleaned from feminist theory and postmodernism in its studies of management and organizations.

Chris Grey and Hugh Willmott (2005) argue that CMS challenges the ingrained assumptions of management studies, that organizational hierarchies are 'natural' or 'normal' and that the evaluation of management has to be in terms of the internal goals of the organization itself. Instead, CMS encourages wider reflection on the social impact of managerial strategies and on the way that graduates are trained in management studies itself. In doing so, CMS is alert to the ecological dimensions of organizations – how does their design affect and influence the experience of workers and how does the organization impact on the natural environment? By bringing these types of question into the field of management studies, CMS encourages a constant reflexivity amongst students of management on their own assumptions and practices. But therein lies the main problem facing CMS: how to turn its social-theoretical arguments into practical measures to transform real organizations and businesses within the context of capitalist economies. After all, existing businesses embody exactly the assumptions that CMS theorists are critical of and they often pay for and certainly employ graduates from management schools. Will they welcome (and be prepared to pay for) a new generation of managers schooled in Marxism and critical theory? If not, then CMS may be restricted to those working on the margins of management studies.

Actor-network theory

Actor-network theory (or ANT) is a theoretical approach to the study of human–non-human relationships, with its origins in sociological studies of natural science and scientific research. In particular, the approach has been popularized by the French scholar Bruno Latour (1993, 2005). ANT is notable for (and controversial because of) its insistence on the agency or active involvement of non-human 'things'. For example, in an important early study of the French fishing industry, Michel Callon (1986) argued that the scallops being farmed were, in a real sense, also *active agents* in the process rather than simply passive recipients of human actions. The fishermen had to adapt their farm management strategies to the behaviour of the scallops, which were, in this sense, independent actors. To understand the whole process of scallop-farming, therefore, we need to

How useful is ANT's insistence that all the elements within situations such as this can be thought of as actors?

understand not just the fishermen's managerial policies and strategy, but also the way that scallops behave in their environment. In short, we need to be able to grasp the whole 'actor-network' situation.

In the study of organizations, ANT similarly looks to bring 'the missing masses' (Latour 1992) – machines, documents, artefacts and so on – into the picture, so that organizations can be understood in a more coherent and comprehensive way than in previous approaches. Think of a company, for instance: what exactly is it? how is it constituted? ANT would suggest that a business company is not just the sum of its physical buildings and human workforce. In fact, it is constituted by its buildings, people, textual materials, machinery and much more, all of which are connected as a network of actors (hence 'actor-network'

theory). ANT has been used to study a variety of organizational features from general studies of organization (Czarniawska and Hernes 2005) to consultancy work (Legge 2002) and the implementation of information technologies in businesses (Doorewaard and Van Bijsterveld, 2001).

What makes ANT controversial is its insistence that all the elements above – people, documents, machines and so on – are 'actors' and none of them has priority over the others. ANT advocates often use the term 'actants' to differentiate their position from the Weberian perspective, which sees only self-conscious human individuals as capable of social action. Conventionally, sociology has seen *human intentions* as a significant point of difference from the objects studied by natural scientists. People's actions are intentional or 'thought through', while most animals rely on instinct, and inanimate objects, such as machines, surely cannot 'act' in the same way as humans. ANT rejects this basic divide, instead seeing all actors in a network as essentially equal partners, a position known as 'ontological equality'. Which actor is more powerful or influential within a given network is something that has to be determined by research. We cannot assume that human actors will always be dominant or the ones that exercise power over the others. Hence, Durkheim was wrong; social phenomena cannot be explained by reference only to other social phenomena, but must also take into account the technical phenomena that jointly build actor-networks.

ANT may well appear strange to students of sociology who are used to dealing only with people. Surely it is human beings that design, build and use machines, so how can machines exercise power over people? A simple example is the moving production line or conveyor belt, introduced by Ford Motors to produce and assemble cars in the early twentieth century (see chapter 20 for a discussion of Fordist production methods). Of course, this was designed, built and used by people, but once in use, the conveyor belt (a simple machine) becomes an actor within the whole actor-network within the factory. Workers 'using' the belt have to become attuned to its speed and rhythm in order for the system to work and, in a real sense, the belt exerts power over the workers who use it. Similarly, when we think of the rules and company policies which exist within organizations, it is clear that these texts have also been designed, written and used by people, but again, once in use as part of a whole actor-network, they exert a certain control over the people who agree to be bound by them. ANT makes us aware of the way that the combination of different actors form organizations, and there are some similarities with Michel Foucault's ideas on the power of physical buildings (such as prisons, schools and hospitals) and discourses (particular ways of thinking and

speaking about a subject) to shape people's behaviour (see chapter 3 for more on Foucault's ideas).

What ANT suggests, therefore, is that fully to understand contemporary management practices and organizations may require the expertise of a whole series of currently separate academic disciplines, from sociology and psychology to economics, business studies, architecture, environmental sciences and the arts. Arguably, this is necessary because sociologists are not, for instance, trained engineers who understand the workings of machinery, or literary experts who regularly analyse the structural elements of texts. In this way, although ANT has its roots in social theory, in practice it tends to encourage an *interdisciplinary* approach to organizational research and has gained some ground in the study of management and organizations.

Critics of the ANT approach have been unimpressed with the amount of theoretical jargon used in ANT studies, which seems to generate unnecessarily complex accounts of organizations and management practices that would not be recognized by the people being studied. This could be worthwhile if it were to produce genuinely novel theoretical explanations, but critics argue that most ANT-based research studies are largely descriptive rather than explanatory. Many ANT studies of organizations also tend to take a management perspective, which plays down or ignores the sociological issues of social inequalities and power, leading some to see the theory as lacking a critical edge (Whittle and Spicer 2008).

So far, the chapter has concentrated on some significant aspects and recent theories of formal organizations. This is important because, as noted above, organizations have been a central feature of modern societies and many scholars have studied them. However, in recent years, attention has shifted somewhat towards the study of networks and their roles in society. And though all formal organizations quite clearly involve networks, the advent of information technologies seems to be lending loose, relatively informal social networks a greater prominence in the organization of society than previously, facilitating the creation of more effective, global networks of individuals, groups and organizations (Lilley et al. 2004).

The study of networks

Social networks

There is an old saying: 'It's not what you know, it's who you know.' This adage expresses the value of having 'good connections'. Sociologists refer to such connections as **networks** – all the direct and indirect connections that link a person or a group with other people or groups. Your personal networks thus include people you know directly (such as your friends) as well as people you know indirectly (such as your friends' friends). Personal networks often include people of similar race, class, ethnicity and other types of social background, although there are exceptions. For example, if you subscribe to an online mailing list, you are part of a network that consists of all the people on the list, who may be of different racial or ethnic backgrounds and genders. Because groups and organizations can also be networked – for example, all the alumni of a particular university – belonging to such groups can greatly extend your reach and influence.

Social groups are an important source for acquiring networks; but not all networks are social groups. Many networks lack the shared expectations and common sense of identity that are the hallmark of social groups. For example, you are not likely to share a sense of identity with the subscribers to an online mailing list, nor will you probably even know the neighbours of most of your co-workers at the office, even though they would form part of your social network.

Networks serve us in many ways. The American sociologist Mark Granovetter

(1973) demonstrated that there can be enormous strength in *weak* ties, particularly among higher socio-economic groups. Granovetter showed that upper-level professional and managerial employees are likely to hear about new jobs through connections such as distant relatives or remote acquaintances. Such weak ties can be of great benefit because relatives or acquaintances tend to have very different sets of connections from those of closer friends, whose social contacts are likely to be similar to one's own. Among lower socio-economic groups, Granovetter argued, weak ties are not necessarily bridges to other networks and so do not really widen opportunities (Marsden and Lin 1982; Wellman et al. 1988; Knoke 1990). After graduation from college, you may rely on a good degree and a strong CV to find a job. But it may prove more beneficial if it happens that your friend at college went to school with the interviewer in the organization where you are seeking work.

Most people rely on their personal networks in order to gain advantages, but not everyone has equal access to powerful networks. Some sociologists argue, for example, that women's business and political networks are weaker than men's, so that women's power in these spheres is reduced (Brass 1985). Several of the best-known fee-paying schools in England, such as Eton and Harrow, only admit boys, thereby denying women access to powerful connections formed by pupils during their school years. In general, sociologists have found that when women look for work, their job market networks comprise fewer ties than do men's, meaning that women know fewer people in fewer occupations (Moore 1990). Meagre networks tend to channel women into female-typical jobs, which usually offer less pay and fewer opportunities for advancement (Roos and Reskin 1992; Drentea 1998). Still, as more and more women move up into higher-level positions, the resulting networks can foster further advancement. One study found that women are more likely to be hired or promoted into job levels that already have a high proportion of women (Cohen et al. 1998).

Networks confer more than economic advantage. You are likely to rely on your networks for a broad range of contacts, from obtaining access to your Member of Parliament to finding a date. Similarly, when you visit another country, your friends, school or religious organization may steer you to their overseas connections, which can then help you to find your way around in the unfamiliar environment. When you graduate from school or further education, your alumni group can further extend your network of social support.

Networks and information technology

As we have seen, networks are very old forms of human practice. But for the sociologist Manuel Castells, networks, powered by the development of information technology and particularly of the Internet, are the defining organizational structure of our age. The inherent flexibility and adaptability of networks gives them enormous advantages over older types of organization. In the past, rational, hierarchical bureaucracies of the kind Weber described proved to be highly successful at using resources to meet the organization's goals. Networks, in contrast, were unable to coordinate functions, focus on specific goals or accomplish given tasks as successfully as bureaucracies. To Castells, the enormous advances in computing and technology during the last quarter of the twentieth century, which created what he calls the 'Internet Galaxy' (2001), changed all that. The arrival of the Internet means that data can now be processed instantaneously in almost any part of the world; there is no need for physical proximity between those involved. As a result, the introduction of new technology has allowed many companies to 're-engineer' their organizational structure, becoming more decentralized, and reinforcing the tendency

towards smaller, more flexible types of enterprises, including homeworking.

Traditionally, identifying the boundaries of organizations has been fairly straightforward. Organizations were generally located in defined physical spaces, such as an office building, a suite of rooms or, in the case of a hospital or university, a whole campus. The mission or tasks an organization aimed to fulfil were also usually clear-cut. A central feature of bureaucracies, for example, was adherence to a defined set of responsibilities and procedures for carrying them out. Weber's view of bureaucracy was that of a self-contained unit that intersected with outside entities at limited and designated points.

We have already seen how the physical boundaries of organizations are being worn away by the capacity of new information technology to transcend countries and time zones. But the same process is also affecting the work that organizations do and the way in which it is coordinated. Many organizations no longer operate as independent units, as they once did. A growing number are finding that their operations run more effectively when they are linked into a web of complex relationships with other organizations and companies. No longer is there a clear dividing line between the organization and outside groups. Globalization, information technology and trends in occupational patterns all mean that organizational boundaries are more open and fluid than they once were.

In *The Rise of the Network Society* (1996), Castells argues that the 'network enterprise' is the organizational form best suited to a global, information economy. By this, he means that it is increasingly impossible for organizations – be they large corporations or small businesses – to survive if they are not part of a network. What enables the process of networking to occur is the growth of information technology: organizations around the world are able to locate each other, enter readily into contact and coordinate joint activities through an electronic

Organizations and Networks

medium. Castells cites several examples of organizational networking and emphasizes that they have originated in diverse cultural and institutional contexts. According to Castells, however, they all represent 'different dimensions of a fundamental process' – the disintegration of the traditional, rational bureaucracy.

Although there are many examples of organizations as networks, let us consider an illustrative case. The sociologist Stewart Clegg studied the clothing retailers Benetton. At first glance, you might not think that Benetton, with its 5,000 outlets around the world, is particularly different from any other global fashion brand. But in fact, Benetton is an example of a particular type of network organization that is made possible by advances in information technology. The Benetton outlets around the world are licensed franchises run by individuals who are not employed by Benetton directly, but who are part of a larger complex devoted to making and selling Benetton products.

The entire operation is based on a network principle: the central Benetton firm in Italy subcontracts orders for products to a variety of manufacturers based on demand from its franchises round the globe. Computers link the various parts of the network, so that, at the touch of a till button at, for example, the Moscow outlet, information is relayed back to the headquarters in Italy about the shipments it needs. Whereas other international fashion retailers introduce identical sets of products into all their shops worldwide, Benetton's structure allows it to customize orders for individual franchises. Rather than entering into regular contracts with suppliers, Benetton can react to the market and call on its loose network of collaborating partners to provide services when needed (Clegg 1990).

Is the combination of information technology with networks taking us completely away from Weber's pessimistic vision of the future of bureaucracy? We should be cautious about such a view. Bureaucratic systems are more internally fluid than

Weber suggested and are increasingly being challenged by other, less hierarchical, forms of organization. But, as Ritzer shows in his thesis on the McDonaldization of society, they probably will not disappear altogether. In the near future, there is likely to be a continuing push and pull between tendencies towards large size, impersonality and hierarchy in organizations on the one hand, and opposing influences on the other.

Social capital: the ties that bind

One of the principal reasons people join organizations is to gain connections and increase their influence. The time and energy invested in an organization can bring welcome returns. Parents who belong to a Parent–Teacher Association, for example, are more likely to be able to influence school policy than those who do not belong. The members know who to call, what to say and how to exert pressure on school officials.

Sociologists call these fruits of organizational membership **social capital**, the social knowledge and connections that enable people to accomplish their goals and extend their influence. Although the idea of social capital can be traced back to antiquity, the expression entered mainstream academic discussion in the late 1980s. In Europe, the concept was particularly associated with the French sociologist Pierre Bourdieu. The last decade has seen an explosion in the use of the term 'social capital', sparked by the influential work of the American political scientist Robert Putnam (1995, 2000).

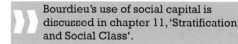
Bourdieu's use of social capital is discussed in chapter 11, 'Stratification and Social Class'.

Social capital includes useful social networks, a sense of mutual obligation and trustworthiness, an understanding of the norms that govern effective behaviour and, in general, other social resources that enable people to act effectively. For example, university students often become active

What benefits do these members of a Parent–Teacher Association stand to gain?

in the student union or newspaper partly because they hope to learn social skills and make connections that will pay off when they graduate. They may, for example, get to interact with lecturers and administrators, who then will support them when they are looking for a job or applying for postgraduate courses.

Differences in social capital mirror larger social inequalities. In general, for example, men have more capital than women, whites more than non-whites, the wealthy more than the poor. The social capital gained from being educated at a fee-paying school is an important reason why some parents make this choice for their children. Attendance at such schools can give pupils access to powerful social, political and business resources later in life, helping to extend their wealth and influence. Differences in social capital can also be found among countries. According to the World Bank (2001), countries with high levels of social capital, where business people can effectively develop the 'networks of trust' that foster healthy economies, are more likely to experience economic growth. An example is the rapid growth experienced by many East Asian economies in the 1980s – a growth some sociologists have argued was fuelled by strong business networks.

Robert Putnam completed an extensive study of social capital in the United States and distinguished two types of social capi-

tal: *bridging social capital*, which is outward-looking and inclusive, and *bonding social capital*, which is inward-looking and exclusive. Bridging social capital unifies people across social cleavages. The capacity to unify people can be seen in such examples as the civil rights movement, which brought blacks and whites together in the struggle for racial equality, and interfaith religious organizations. Bonding social capital reinforces exclusive identities and homogeneous groups; it can be found in ethnic fraternal organizations, church-based women's reading groups and fashionable country clubs (Putnam 2000).

People who actively belong to organizations are more likely to feel 'connected'; they feel engaged, able to 'make a difference'. From the standpoint of the larger society, social capital, the bridging form in particular, provides people with a feeling that they are part of a wider community, and one that includes people who are different from themselves. Democracy flourishes when social capital is strong. Indeed, cross-national survey evidence suggests that levels of civic engagement in the United States, where Putnam's research was based, are among the highest in the world (Putnam 1993, 2000). But there is equally strong evidence that during the past 30 or so years, the ties of political involvement, club membership and other forms of social and civic engagement that bind Americans to one another have significantly diminished. Could it be that democracy is being eroded as a result?

Bowling alone: an example of declining social capital?

Putnam argued that participation in organizations provides many Americans with such social capital as the ability to cooperate with others for mutual benefit, a sense of trust and a feeling of belonging to the larger society. This kind of social capital is essential for effective citizenship. Yet, according to Putnam, these social ties are rapidly lessening in American society. One subtle but significant sign of this decline is seen in American bowling alleys: more and more people are bowling alone these days (Putnam 1995, 2000). Putnam points out that league bowlers consume three times more beer and pizza than solo bowlers, a fact which suggests to him that the former spend more time socializing, perhaps even discussing civic issues. Bowling alone, according to Putnam (2000), is symptomatic of the loss of community today:

> The most whimsical yet discomfiting evidence of social disengagement in contemporary America that I have discovered is this: more Americans are bowling today than ever before, but bowling in organized leagues has plummeted in the last decade or so. Between 1980 and 1993 the total number of bowlers in America increased by 10 percent, while league bowling decreased by 40 percent. (Lest this be thought a wholly trivial example, I should note that nearly 80 million Americans went bowling at least once in 1993, nearly a third more than voted in the 1994 Congressional elections and roughly the same number as claim to attend church regularly. . . .) . . . Without at first noticing, we have been pulled apart from one another and from our communities over the last third of the century.

Putnam points out that not only has bowling in organized leagues declined, but

organizational memberships of all sorts have dropped by as much as 25 per cent since the 1970s. In the USA, parent–teacher associations, the National Federation of Women's Clubs, the League of Women Voters and the Red Cross have all experienced membership declines of roughly 50 per cent since the 1960s. Putnam reports that in 1974, about one in four adults regularly volunteered his or her time to such associations; today, the number is closer to one in five. Along with these organizational declines, fewer people in the USA report that they socialize with their neighbours or feel that most people can be trusted. Such declines in organizational membership, neighbourliness and trust in general have been paralleled by a decline in democratic participation. Voter turnout in presidential and parliamentary elections in the USA fell considerably since its peak in the late 1960s, although it rose again during a highly polarized presidential election between George Bush Junior and John Kerry in 2004.

There are undoubtedly many reasons for such decline. For one thing, women, who were traditionally active in voluntary organizations, are more likely to hold a job than ever before. For another, people are increasingly disillusioned with government and less likely to think that their vote counts. Furthermore, people now spend more time commuting and so use up time and energy that might have been available for civic activities. But the principal source of declining civic participation, according to Putnam, is simple: television. The many hours people spend at home alone in the USA watching TV has replaced social engagement in the community.

Is the rest of the world also suffering the same decline in social capital? David Halpern (2000) found that Sweden, the Netherlands and Japan show stable or rising levels of social capital, whereas for Germany and France the indicators are more mixed. However, Halpern concludes that social capital in the UK, along with Australia and the USA, has declined significantly in the last few decades. Looking at Europe and elsewhere, the evidence for a decline in social capital is far more mixed than in the USA.

Similarly, if voter turnout really is an indicator of low social capital (and there are many other reasons why voter turnout differs), then some recent elections demonstrate that many developed countries may not be suffering anything like the same decline as in the USA. For example, in the 2007 French presidential elections, a record voter turnout of 84 per cent was recorded in both first and second rounds of voting. Indeed, since 1945, Western Europe has had the highest average turnout, at 77 per cent, with Latin America recording the lowest, at 53 per cent (IDEA 2007). The International Institute for Democracy and Electoral Assistance (IDEA) notes that, globally, voter turnout actually rose steadily between 1945 and 1990, increasing from 61 per cent in the 1940s to 68 per cent in the 1980s with the post-1990 average slipping back to 64 per cent. Nevertheless, this is not a simple picture of continuous decline as Putnam's study suggests.

New social ties?

Putnam's study raises some important issues about social participation and solidarity, but are its conclusions too negative? In many ways, such studies carry more than an echo of the concerns and anxieties raised by late nineteenth-century sociologists such as Ferdinand Tönnies and Emile Durkheim. Tönnies, in particular, saw industrial culture and urbanization in Germany as destructive of long-lasting social bonds, creating an aggregate of dislocated individuals with few real connections to each other. And yet, the early modernizing society that so worried Tönnies is now held up as a model of strong social solidarity by Putnam when seen in the light of recent social changes. Is Putnam missing something? Some sociologists who have studied

the new information communication technologies (ICTs) think he may well be.

> **Thinking critically**
>
> Based on the survey opposite, why do young people use social networking sites? How would you interpret the evidence from this report? Does it support the 'loss of community' thesis or does it suggest that online communities are being formed? Can such virtual relationships ever be considered the equivalent of face-to-face friendship relations?

The rapid growth of new information technologies is startling (as we saw in chapter 2), and they are becoming built-in to people's everyday routines, both at home and work (Kraut et al. 2006). This is also the conclusion from a 2007 MTV Networks/ Nickelodeon survey of 18,000 young people aged 8–24 years across 16 countries, including China, Japan, the UK, the USA, Canada and Mexico. The survey found that, 'Young people don't see "tech" as a separate entity – it's an organic part of their lives. . . . Talking to them about the role of technology in their lifestyle would be like talking to kids in the 1980s about the role the park swing or the telephone played in their social lives – it's invisible' (Reuters 2007).

Information technologies are no longer restricted to the relatively rich, developed world either. For example, mobile phone use topped 3.25 billion in 2007, equivalent to half of the world's population, with demand currently booming in China, India and Africa (www.telecomasia.net – 2007). Indeed, the fastest growing mobile phone market is in Africa (see figure 18.1). From a relatively low base, the 'penetration rate' (the number of phone connections compared to the size of population) in Africa reached 21 per cent in early 2007, with more than 200 million cellular connections. In 2007 alone, the number of cellular connections grew by 38 per cent, a larger annual rise than in the Middle East (33 per cent)

Global Society 18.2 **The decline or reinvention of 'community'?**

Researchers working on the Pew Research Center's 'Internet and American Life Project' conducted a telephone survey in October and November 2006, including a random sample of 935 American young people between the ages of 12 and 17 years, asking about their use of social networking websites (SNS) such as MySpace and Facebook – interactive online networking environments. Some of the survey's main findings from the report are shown below.

MySpace dominates the social networking world

Fully 85% of teens who use social networking sites say the profile they use or update most often is on MySpace, while 7% update a profile on Facebook. Another 1% tend to a primary profile on Xanga. Smaller numbers told us they have profiles at places like Yahoo, Piczo, Gaiaonline and Tagged.com.

While the vast majority of social networking website users update MySpace profiles most often, there are some differences between boys and girls in the sites they choose to use. Young men are more likely than young women to say they use MySpace most often (90% of social networking boys use the site, compared with 81% of social networking girls). Conversely, teen girls are more likely than boys to say they use Facebook most often: just 4% of boys use Facebook as their primary account compared with 9% of girls. Among older social networking girls (age 15–17), the per cent using Facebook rises to 12%.

Teens & Friends on Social Networking Sites

What are the different ways you use social networking sites? Do you ever use those sites to   ?

	Yes	No
Stay in touch with friends you see a lot	91%	9%
Stay in touch with friends you rarely see in person	82	18
Make plans with your friends	72	28
Make new friends	49	50
Flirt with someone	17	83

Teens say social networking sites help them manage their friends

- 91% of all social networking teens say they use the sites to stay in touch with friends they see frequently, while 82% use the sites to stay in touch with friends they rarely see in person.
- 72% of all social networking teens use the sites to make plans with friends; 49% use the sites to make new friends.
- Older boys who use social networking sites (age 15–17) are more likely than girls of the same age to say that they use social networking sites to make new friends (60% vs. 46%).
- Just 17% of all social networking teens use the sites to flirt.
- Older boys who use social networking sites are more than twice as likely as older girls to say they use the sites to flirt; 29% report this compared with just 13% of older girls.

How Teens Communicate with Friends Using Social Networking

The percentage of teen SNS users who . . .

Post messages to a friend's page or wall	84%
Send private messages to a friend within the social networking system	82
Post comments to a friend's blog	76
Send a bulletin or group message to all of your friends	61
Wink, poke, give "e-props" or kudos to your friends	33

Source: Pew Internet & American Life Project, January 2007.
http://www.pewinternet.org/pdfs/pip_sns_data_memo_jan_2007.pdf

Facebook only opened its site to users who were not affiliated to a high school, college or employer on 26 September 2006. Previously it was a relatively 'closed' system, which partly explains the dominance of the open access MySpace in this report. However, in July 2007, *The Economist* reported that Facebook membership had already risen to at least 31 million members, suggesting that it may be 'the next big thing' in social networking.

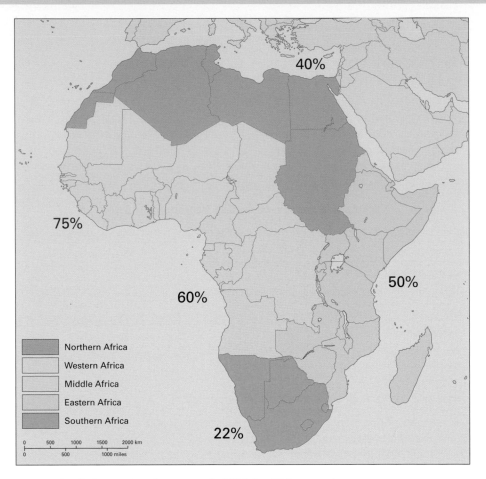

Figure 18.1 Annual cellular connections growth 2006, by African region

Source: © Wireless Intelligence 2007

and Asia-Pacific (29 per cent) regions. What will be the impact of these technologies on the social life of societies?

In a recent study of how people make use of ICT such as mobile phones, the Internet, email and social networking websites, Deborah Chambers (2006) investigated the social changes identified by Putnam, from the fairly stable and fixed ties of families, neighbourly relations and communities towards more voluntaristic and fluid ties. Chambers argues that new patterns of association and social ties are emerging based around ideals of 'friendship', some of which are sustained through ICT networks. She also argues that other forms are forged through creating new social identities amongst previously marginalized groups, such as those created within 'queer communities', creating safe spaces for the exploration of 'self'.

The creation of 'virtual', online communities and friendship networks via constant mobile phone communication certainly look very different from traditional communities based on face-to-face contact, but does that make them less effective in the building of social ties via 'bridging social capital'? Many environmental protests, for example, are organized and set in motion through information on websites, text messaging or email. Many contemporary social movements also engage in direct actions rather than relying on conventional political lobbying through mainstream channels. Perhaps then, what we are witnessing is not the end of democracy, but the emergence of a new type of politics based on the principle of *participatory* rather than *representative* democracy. If so, then this may partly explain the low voter turnout that Putnam saw as evidence of declining social capital.

> Social movement activity and environmentalism are discussed in chapter 22, 'Politics, Government and Social Movements', and chapter 5, 'The Environment'.

The informality, sheer speed of communication and the geographical distances involved in virtual relationships have led to concerns and anxieties amongst academics and governments, but this new 'collapse of community' thesis may be somewhat exaggerated. Chambers sees the quest for friendship relations as one indicator that people are pursuing new social ties based on equality and mutual respect, rather than giving up on community altogether.

Of course, the new ICTs bring with them potentially new social problems. Chambers notes that in spite of the positive aspects of social networking, these forms of social relationship may not provide an adequate basis for ensuring relationships of care and caring, most of which do need regular face-to-face contact and long-term commitment. Many schools and parents are also concerned about social networking and mobile phones in relation to fears about the abuse of children by adults as well as the provision of new opportunities for children to bully each other, for instance by text messaging or the filming of attacks to be shown online. Such fears are not completely unfounded. The leading SNS provider, MySpace, admitted in 2007 that it had found more than 29,000 registered sex offenders amongst its 180 million members (Media-Guardian 2007). Although a very small number compared to the overall membership, it is clear that the fast-changing and relatively anonymous online environment does present regulators and police forces with some very different problems, which they could not have foreseen.

Researchers will need to analyse these emerging 'communities of friendship' with the detached eye that marks out sociological work from journalism and other forms of social commentary, if they are to arrive at a better understanding of why Putnam's touchstone activity of bowling is losing out to online social networking as crucibles for building and maintaining friendships and relationships.

> Friendship and relationships are discussed in more detail in chapter 9, 'Families and Intimate Relationships'.

Conclusion

The organizations and networks that people belong to exert an enormous influence over their lives. As we have seen in this chapter, conventional groups appear to be losing ground in people's daily lives. For example, today's students are less likely to join civic groups and organizations – or even vote – than were their parents, a decline that may well signal a lower commitment to their communities. Some sociologists worry that this signals a weakening of society itself, which could bring about social instability.

As we have also seen, the global economy and information technology are redefining group life in ways that are now beginning to be felt. For instance, the older generations of workers are likely to spend much of their careers in a relatively small handful of long-lasting, bureaucratic organizations; the younger generation is much more likely to be part of a larger number of networked, 'flexible' ones. Many of today's group affiliations will be created through the Internet or through other forms of communication, which continue to develop. It will become increasingly easy to connect with like-minded people anywhere on the planet, creating geographically dispersed groups around the world, whose members may never meet each other face-to-face.

How will these trends affect the quality of social relationships? For nearly all of human history, most people have interacted exclusively with others who are close at hand. The Industrial Revolution, which facilitated the rise of large, impersonal bureaucracies where people knew one another poorly if at all, changed the nature of social interaction. Today, the Information Revolution is doing so once again. Tomorrow's groups and organizations could provide a renewed sense of communication and social intimacy, or they could spell further isolation, social distance and social problems.

Summary points

1. Many modern organizations are to some degree bureaucratic in nature. Bureaucracy is characterized by a clearly defined hierarchy of authority; written rules governing the conduct of officials and a separation between the tasks of the official within the organization and life outside it. Members of the organization do not own the material resources with which they operate. Max Weber argued that modern bureaucracy is a highly effective means of organizing large numbers of people, ensuring that decisions are made according to general criteria.

2. Informal networks tend to develop at all levels both within and between organizations. The study of these informal ties is as important as the more formal characteristics on which Weber concentrated his attention.

3. The physical settings of organizations strongly influence their social features. The architecture of modern organizations is closely connected to surveillance as a means of securing obedience to those in authority. Surveillance refers to the supervision of people's activities, as well as to the keeping of files and records about them. Self-surveillance refers to the way people limit their behaviour because of the assumption that they are under surveillance.

4. Modern organizations have evolved as gendered institutions. Women have traditionally been segregated into certain occupational categories that support the ability of men to advance their careers. In recent years, women have been entering professional and managerial positions in greater numbers, but it has been argued that women have to adopt a traditionally male management style to succeed at top levels.

5. Large organizations have started to restructure themselves over recent years to become less bureaucratic and more flexible. Many firms have adopted aspects of Japanese management systems: more consultation of lower-level workers by managerial executives; pay and responsibility linked to seniority; and groups, rather than individuals, evaluated for their performance.

6. Two important forms of global organization are international governmental organizations (IGOs) and international non-governmental organizations (INGOs). Both play an increasingly important role in the world today, and IGOs – particularly the United Nations – may become key organizational actors in the future.

7. The modern economy is dominated by the

large corporations. When one firm has a commanding influence in a given industry, it is in a monopoly position. When a cluster of firms wields such influence, a situation of oligopoly exists. The giant corporations have a profound effect on people's lives. Multinational or transnational corporations operate across national boundaries. The largest of them exercise tremendous economic power. Half of the 100 largest economic units are not countries, but privately owned companies.

8. The study of organizations and management practices has been relatively under-theorized. However, critical management studies (CMS) and actor-network theory (ANT) are two recently developed theoretical perspectives that have their roots is social theory and social science and have led to different ways of thinking about management and organization.

9. New information communications technology (ICT) is changing the way that organizations work. Many tasks can now be completed electronically, which allows organizations to transcend time and space. Many organizations now work as loose networks, rather than as self-contained independent units.

10. Social capital refers to the knowledge and connections that enable people to cooperate with one another for mutual benefit and extend their influence. Some social scientists have argued that social capital has declined since the 1970s, a process they worry indicates a decline in commitment to civic engagement. However, scholars of new ICTs suggest that these may be giving rise to new forms of sociability and new social relations, which should be analysed on their own terms.

Further reading

This chapter covers a diverse range of material, but the following books should provide useful introductions to some key areas.

For a guide to the changing meanings and evaluation of bureaucracies, see David Beetham's *Bureaucracy*, 2nd edn (Buckingham: Open University Press, 1996). This is getting rather old now, but remains a short and reliable introduction to the concept of bureaucracy. A more up-to-date text covering organizations and management is Stewart Clegg, Martin Kornberger and Tyrone Pitsis's *Managing and Organizations: An Introduction to Theory and Practice*, 2nd edn (London: Sage, 2008), which is well organized (well, it should be!) and informative.

Some of the main arguments and issues in relation to the impact of information technologies can be found in David Lyon's *Surveillance Society: Monitoring Everyday Life* (Cambridge: Polity, 2007). If you are feeling adventurous, then you could try Manuel Castells in his own words in his *The Internet Galaxy: Reflections on the Internet, Business and Society* (Oxford: Oxford University Press, 2002).

The concept of social capital is explored in John Field's *Social Capital* (London: Routledge, 2002), which is another quite short, but very well-written book. Then, a useful companion to this would be Yair Amichai-Hamburger's *The Social Net: Human Behaviour in Cyberspace* (Oxford: Oxford University Press, 2005) – an accessible edited collection of chapters looking at how people behave when using information technologies.

Finally Stewart Clegg, Cynthia Hardy, Thomas Lawrence and Walter R. Nord's *The Sage Handbook of Organization Studies* (London and New York: Sage, 2006), contains numerous useful pieces for your studies. Be warned, though, it is a large volume.

Internet links

The Centre for the Sociology of Organisations (CSO), based in Paris, France:
www.cso.edu/home.asp

Social Science Information System resources on organizations – based at the University of Amsterdam, the Netherlands:
www.sociosite.net/topics/organization.php

The International Sociological Association's Research Committee on organizations:
www.isa-sociology.org/rc17.htm

Electronic Journal of Radical Organisational Theory (EJROT), based at the University of Waikato, New Zealand:
www.mngt.waikato.ac.nz/cjrot/

A site with everything you need to know about Michel Foucault, hosted by Queensland University of Technology, Brisbane:
www.michel-foucault.com/

A gateway for resources on social capital, hosted by the Universities of Siena and Rome, Italy:
www.socialcapitalgateway.org/

19
....
Education

CHAPTER 19

Education

Sakina, who was about 12 years old in 2007 (she is not entirely sure), did not attend primary school at all in the remote village of Tudun Kose in north-west Nigeria. Families in Tudun Kose generally do not send daughters to school and Sakina's reading and writing skills are poor: she can barely write her own name. Sakina's life is spent collecting water and making grain for the family meal; her parents are preparing for her to get married soon. Sakina would like to go to secondary school, but her parents cannot afford to send her; anyway, it is a long way from the village. Sakina says that when she is older, she hopes to be able to read the holy Koran.

Hawwau, Sakina's younger sister, has had a very different experience. Since

of girls is not worthwhile because they won't be able to bring the economic return to the household that boys will, and also because they're likely to get married and leave the family home. There are also issues around early pregnancy, fears of violence towards girls on the way to and at school, inappropriate teaching and an absence of basic facilities like toilets for girls. It's a gamble sending a child to school when you are poor and need support in the household, and its often girls who lose out. (*Independent*, 17 October 2007)

Sakina and Hawwau's story shows how the value attributed to 'getting a good education' is both culturally and socially variable. What kind of education is appropriate in the context of agricultural communities and high levels of rural poverty? Should education systems be expected to challenge traditional gender divisions or do they help to reproduce them?

In relatively rich industrialized countries like Britain, the situation is very different. In 1998, Shaun had two years left at his primary school in the UK. He was hardworking, poor, white and working class, and had clear ideas about secondary education: 'I'm gonna go to Westbury because my mate Mark's going there and my girlfriend. . . . Sutton Boys is like one of the worst schools around here; only tramps go there.' A year later though, Shaun was not so certain: 'I might not get into Westbury 'cos it's siblings and how far away you live and I haven't got any siblings there and I live a little way out so I might have to go on a waiting list. . . . I might go to Sutton Boys instead 'cos all my mates are going there.'

Shaun's headteacher, Mrs Whitticker, had told him that Westbury would be far too risky a choice as he lived on the edge of its catchment area, so Shaun and his mother resigned themselves to applying to Sutton Boys. Shaun's mother was bitterly disappointed, but she accepted the advice: 'I could have wept at the thought of him going to Sutton, but what choice did we have 'cos Mrs Whitticker said we didn't have any?'

2005 she has been able to attend the village primary school and is proud of her school uniform. She says, 'I feel very happy when I am at school, and when I grow up I want to be a doctor.' Hawwau has benefited from a project created by the charity, ActionAid, which tries to persuade parents in the village that it is worthwhile educating their daughters. The project began in 2004 – too late for Sakina – and by 2007 had seen the primary school attendance of girls increase in every year.

According to ActionAid, Nigeria has the highest proportion of children not in education of any country in the world, some eight million in total. Rural families in very poor situations educate boys rather than girls, and the consequence is that some 60 per cent of all young people not in school are girls. David Archer at ActionAid explains:

There are a lot of different reasons why parents don't send their girls to school. Some are to do with traditional attitudes, which hold that investing in the education

Shaun and his mother worried about the reputation of Sutton Boys. As Shaun said: 'My mum and I think the standards might be too low because people just bunk and everything at Sutton.'

Over the next few years Shaun faced constant tension between being tough in the playground and working hard in the classroom. He was suspended twice from his primary school for fighting, and had a local reputation for being 'tough', which he saw as vital to sustain if he was to survive at Sutton Boys. Yet in order to succeed academically, he deliberately had to set himself apart from the rest of his peer group. At the same time, to avoid being reclassified as a 'geek', he had continually to prove to his peers that he was still really 'a lad'. As a result, on the estate and in the playground, Shaun resurrected his old self, in contrast to his displays of hard-working, non-conformity in the classroom. He reclaimed a very different identity as 'tough' and as 'a skilful footballer', which redeemed – most of the time – his 'geekiness' in the classroom. This brought Shaun into conflict with his mother, who worried about him hanging out with the wrong crowd. Shaun's story was told in a series of interviews with sociologist Diane Reay between 1997 and 2001, and his account of the transition from primary to secondary school raises the issue of what links exist between education and wider social structures, such as social class and gender (Reay 2002).

The situations of the children discussed above are very different. In rural Nigeria, the crucial issue is whether Sakina and Hawwau will gain access to formal education at all, while in the UK, the problem exercising Shaun and his mother is *what kind* of schooling he will receive. But despite these very different national contexts, the connection between education and social inequality is central to both situations, and has been the subject of much debate in sociology.

Education was one of sociology's founding subjects, seen as important in socialization processes for the transmission of society's values and moral rules. Indeed, Emile Durkheim's first professorial post was as a Professor of Education at the Sorbonne in Paris. As one of the oldest sociological subjects, education has a huge body of research and scholarship behind it. We cannot hope to cover this body of work here, but this chapter offers an overview of some of the most important themes and recurring issues that have helped to shape the field of the sociology of education.

The chapter begins with the initial and crucial question: What is education for? The answer to this question is not as simple as it may seem. Is education simply the same thing as formal schooling, for instance? How is it linked to the economy? Not surprisingly, there have been are several ways to answer these questions and we look at some influential sociological theories of education. We then explore the links between the major social divisions – class, gender and ethnicity – and education systems, and evaluate debates on IQ, which have proved to be highly contentious. The final section examines the impact of globalization on education systems and that of new technologies in the classroom. The section covers global literacy levels and suggestions for their improvement as well as recent developments in higher education that seem set to change the face of education across the world to meet the demands of the global knowledge economy. The chapter concludes with some thoughts on the notion of 'lifelong learning' and its practical feasibility.

Theorizing the significance of education

Education, like health, is often seen as an unproblematic social good to which everyone is entitled as a right. Who would not be in favour of it? Indeed, most people who have been through an education system and emerged literate, numerate and reasonably knowledgeable would probably agree that education has been beneficial for them. However, there is a difference between education and schooling. **Education** can be defined as a *social institution*, which enables and promotes the acquisition of skills, knowledge and the broadening of personal horizons. Education can take place in many social settings. **Schooling** on the other hand, refers to the formal process through which certain types of knowledge and skills are delivered, normally via a predesigned curriculum in specialized settings: schools. Schooling in most countries is typically divided into stages such as those in primary and secondary schools, and in many societies is a mandatory requirement for all young people up to a specified age.

As we will see in this section, some theorists see education as crucial for individuals to fulfil their potential, but they also argue that education is not confined to or defined by that which is delivered in schools. Mark Twain is reported to have said: 'I never let my schooling get in the way of my education' – the implication being that schools are not the best educators and may even be obstacles to much useful learning, such as that to be gained from wise adults, within families or from personal experience. In this chapter we will deal with both education and schooling and will often refer to the latter as taking place within organized 'education systems', to reflect common usage.

Also like health, education is a complex political, economic, social and cultural issue. How should education be delivered and who should pay for it? Should education systems be paid for by the state via taxation and delivered free to all, or should we expect to pay directly for our own family's education? These are important *political and economic* decisions, which are matters of continuing public debate. What *kind* of education should be delivered and how? Should it cover history, politics, astrology or sociology, for example? Should we aim for the same basic education for all, regardless of inequalities of wealth, gender or ethnicity in comprehensive education systems? Or should the wealthy be allowed to buy their children's education outside the state system? These *social* issues combine with the political and economic in increasingly complex arguments. Should education involve the compulsory teaching of religion? Should faith-based education in separate schools be allowed? What kinds of values should underpin education systems? These *cultural* issues are of enormous significance in multicultural societies, and have become contentious matters of political debate.

Education has become an important site for a whole range of debates, which are not simply about what happens within schools. They are debates about the direction of society itself and how we can best equip young people for life in the increasingly globalized modern world. Sociologists have been involved in debates about education ever since the work of Emile Durkheim in the late nineteenth century and this is where we begin our review of theories of education.

Education as socialization

For Emile Durkheim, education plays an important role in the socialization of children because, particularly by learning history, for example, children gain an understanding of the common values in society, uniting a multitude of separate individuals. These common values include religious and moral beliefs and a sense of self-discipline. Durkheim argues that schooling enables children to internalize the social rules that contribute to the functioning of society. Durkheim was particularly concerned with upholding moral guidelines, because in late nineteenth-century France, an increasing individualism was developing that threatened social solidarity. Durkheim saw a key role for schools in teaching mutual responsibility and the value of the collective good. As a 'society in miniature', the school also teaches discipline and respect for authority.

In industrial societies, Durkheim argues (1961 [1925]), education also has another socialization function: it teaches the skills needed to perform roles in increasingly specialized occupations. In traditional societies, occupational skills could be learnt within the family, but as social life became more complex and an extended division of labour emerged in the production of goods, an education system developed that could pass on the skills required to fill the various specialized, occupational roles.

>> Durkheim's functionalist approach to sociology was introduced in chapter 1, 'What is Sociology?', and chapter 3, 'Theories and Perspectives in Sociology'.

American sociologist, Talcott Parsons, outlined a somewhat different structural functionalist approach to education. Durkheim was concerned with the way in which nineteenth-century French society was becoming increasingly individualistic and looked for ways to mitigate its possible harmful effects. But, writing somewhat later, in mid-twentieth-century America, Parsons argued that a central function of education was to instil in pupils the value of individual achievement. This value was crucial to the functioning of industrialized societies, but it could not be learned in the family. A child's status in the family is ascribed – that is, fixed from birth. By contrast, a child's status in school is largely achieved, and in schools children are assessed according to universal standards, such as exams. For Parsons, the function of education is to enable children to move from the particularistic standards of the family to the universal standards needed in a modern society. According to Parsons, schools, like the wider society, largely operate on a meritocratic basis: children achieve their status according to merit (or

Education systems in developed societies celebrate individual achievement.
....

worth) rather than according to their sex, race or class (Parsons and Bales 1956). However, as we shall see, Parsons's view that schools operate on meritocratic principles has been subject to much criticism.

There is little doubt that functionalist theory does tell us something significant about education systems; they do try to provide individuals with the skills and knowledge needed to participate in societies, and schools do teach children some of the values and morals of wider society. However, functionalist theory appears to overstate the case for a set of society-wide values. There are many cultural differences within a single society and the notion of a set of central values that should be taught to all may not be accurate or well received. This highlights a recurring problem within functionalist accounts, namely the concept of 'society' itself. Functionalists see education systems as serving several functions for society as a whole, but the problem is that this assumes that society is relatively homogeneous and that all social groups share similar interests. Is this really true? Critics from the conflict tradition in sociology point out that in a society marked by major social inequalities, an education system that supports that society must reinforce social inequalities. In that sense, schooling works in the interests of the ruling groups in societies.

The importance of education and peer relations in socialization is discussed further in chapter 8, 'The Life-Course'.

Schooling for capitalism

In a highly influential study of education in the USA, Bowles and Gintis (1976) argued that schools are involved in socialization, but only because this helps to produce the right kind of workers for capitalist companies. Their Marxist thesis argued that this close connection between the productive sphere and education was not simply a matter of the school curriculum involving the kinds of knowledge and skills, which employers needed. The American education system, they argued, in fact helped to shape whole personalities.

> The structure of social relations in education not only inures the student to the discipline of the workplace, but also develops the types of personal demeanour, modes of self-presentation, self-image, and social class identifications, which are the crucial ingredients of job adequacy. Specifically, the social relationships of education – the relationships between administrators and teachers, teachers and students, and students and students, and students and their work – replicate the hierarchical divisions of labor. (Bowles and Gintis 1976: 131)

Bowles and Gintis argue that the structure of schooling is based on a 'correspondence principle'. That is, the structures of school life *correspond* to the structures of working life. In both school and work, conformity to rules leads to success, teachers and managers dictate tasks, pupils and workers perform these tasks, school staff are organized hierarchically, as is company management, and this has to be accepted as inevitable. Bowles and Gintis's theory challenged the existing and widespread idea that education could be 'a great leveller', treating people equally and enabling everyone to achieve. Instead, they proposed that education under capitalism was, in fact, a great divider.

In some ways this orthodox Marxist theory represents a kind of 'conflict functionalism'. It is clearly a theory based on the idea of society as riven with conflict, but the education system within this society also performs certain functions for the system as a whole. Marxist critics saw the main flaw in the thesis as its correspondence principle, which was too simple and reductionist. For example, it relied on the social structure shaping and determining individuals and did not give enough significance to the possibility of active pupil and student resistance (Giroux 1983; Brown and Lauder 1997). The thesis is also rather too generalized and was not borne of empirical research within schools themselves. Later researchers found a diversity of practice within schools and, in many cases, it may be possible for school heads and teachers to generate an ethos that encourages working-class pupils to be

---

THINKING CRITICALLY

Thinking of your own experience of schools, what attitudes and behaviour have you acquired and how might these 'fit' the needs of employers? On Bowles and Gintis's account, are successful middle-class children also subject to the 'hierarchical division of labour' in schools? In what ways do you think the 'correspondence principle' works in schools based in middle-class areas?

more ambitious than the theory allows for. After all, it is the case that in many capitalist countries today, employers complain that schools are *failing* to produce workers with the skills they need.

The hidden curriculum

In focusing on the *structure* of schooling rather than simply its content, Bowles and Gintis showed that a hidden curriculum exists within education systems, through which pupils learn discipline, hierarchy and passive acceptance of the status quo. John Taylor Gatto (2002), a retired schoolteacher with 30 years' experience, reached a similar conclusion from a non-Marxist perspective, arguing that the hidden curriculum in the USA teaches seven basic lessons.

The curriculum involves a quite random mix of information on a variety of subjects, which produces *confusion* rather than genuine knowledge and understanding. Schools teach children to accept the status quo, to know their place within the *class hierarchy* and to defer to their betters. The rule of the class bell at the start and end of lessons teaches *indifference*; for example, no lesson is ever so important that it can carry on after the bell sounds. Students are taught to be both emotionally and intellectually *dependent* on authority figures, in the form of teachers who tell them what to think and how to feel. They also learn that their own *self-esteem is provisional*, relying on the opinion that officials have of them and that opinion is based on a battery of tests, report cards and grades. The final lesson is that being under *constant surveillance* is normal, as evidenced by the culture of homework, which effectively transfers school discipline into the home environment. Gatto concludes that the compulsory state school system in the USA (and, by implication, everywhere else) delivers 'compulsory subordination for all' and is 'structurally unreformable'. Instead, he argues for home education where children themselves can take control of their own learning, using parents and other adults as 'facilitators', rather than teachers.

One of the most controversial and interesting theorists of education to explore the consequences of the hidden curriculum is Austrian anarchist and philosopher, Ivan Illich (1926–2002). Illich is noted for his staunch opposition to the culture of industrial capitalism, which he sees as gradually deskilling the population as they come to rely more and more on the products of industry and less and less on their own creativity and knowledge. In the sphere of health, for example, traditional remedies and practices are lost as bureaucratic health systems push people to rely on doctors and hospitals to look after their health needs, and this pattern is repeated in all areas of life, including education.

Illich (1971) argued that the very notion of compulsory schooling – now accepted throughout the world – should be questioned. Like Bowles and Gintis, he stressed the connection between the development of education and the requirements of the economy for discipline and hierarchy. He argued that schools have developed to cope with four basic tasks: the provision of custodial care, the distribution of people within occupational roles, the learning of dominant values and the acquisition of socially approved skills and knowledge. Schools, like prisons, have become custodial organizations because attendance is compulsory and young people are therefore 'kept off the streets' between early childhood and their entry into work.

Much is learned in school that has nothing to do with the formal content of lessons. Schools tend to inculcate what Illich called 'passive consumption' – an uncritical acceptance of the existing social order – by the nature of the discipline and regimentation they involve. These lessons are not explicitly taught, but are implicit in school procedures and organization. The hidden curriculum teaches young people that their role in life is 'to know their place and to sit still in it' (ibid.).

Does compulsory schooling inculcate passive consumption?

Illich advocated what he called the *deschooling of society*. Compulsory schooling, he pointed out, is a relatively recent invention, and there is no reason why it should be accepted as inevitable. Since schools do not promote equality or the development of individual creative abilities, why not do away with them altogether in their current form? Illich did not mean by this that all forms of educational organization should be abolished. Everyone who wants to learn should be provided with access to available resources – at any time in their lives, not just in their childhood or adolescent years. Such a system should make it possible for knowledge to be widely diffused and shared, not confined to specialists. Learners should not have to submit to a standard curriculum, and they should have personal choice over what they study.

What all this means in practical terms is not wholly clear. In place of schools, however, Illich suggested several types of educational framework. Material resources for formal learning would be stored in libraries, rental agencies, laboratories and information storage banks, available to any student. 'Communications networks' would be set up, providing data about the skills possessed by different individuals and whether they would be willing to train others or engage in mutual learning activities. Students would be provided with vouchers, allowing them to use educational services as and when they wished.

Are these proposals wholly utopian? Many think so. Yet if, as looks possible, paid work is substantially reduced or restructured in the future, they may appear much more realistic and perhaps even attractive. If paid employment becomes less central to social life, people might instead engage in a wider variety of pursuits. Against this backdrop, some of Illich's ideas make good sense. Education would not be just a form of early training, confined to special institutions, but would become available to whoever wished to take advantage of it. Illich's ideas from the 1970s became interesting again with the rise of new communications technologies and ideas of 'lifelong learning' throughout the life-course. We will return to these recent developments towards the end of this chapter.

Education and cultural reproduction

As we saw from the individual cases at the start of this chapter, education and inequality are clearly related. Shaun came from a poor background, and did not get into the school his mother wanted him to. He then had to struggle to get on in class, when most of his friends were uninterested or even hostile to academic achievement. This section reviews a number of different ways in which sociological theorists have attempted to account for social inequalities in education systems. Basil Bernstein's classic study emphasizes the significance of language (see 'Classic Studies 19.1'), Paul Willis looks at the effects of cultural values in shaping pupil attitudes to education and work, while Pierre Bourdieu examines the relationship between the cultures of school and home. What all of these key studies are concerned with is **cultural reproduction** – the generational transmission of cultural values, norms and experience and the mechanisms and processes through which this is achieved.

Learning to labour – by failing in school

A second classic study in the sociology of education is the discussion of cultural reproduction provided in the report of a fieldwork study carried out by Paul Willis (1977) in a school in the city of Birmingham in the UK. Although this study was conducted more than 30 years ago, it remains a classic of sociological investigation.

The research problem Willis set out to investigate was how cultural reproduction occurs – or, as he put it, 'how working-class kids get working-class jobs'. It is often thought that, during the process of schooling, young people from lower-class or ethnic minority backgrounds simply come to see that they 'are not clever enough' to expect to get highly paid or high-status jobs in their future work lives. In other words, the experience of academic failure teaches them to recognize their intellectual limitations and, having accepted their 'inferiority', they move into occupations with limited career prospects.

As Willis's explanation pointed out, this interpretation does not conform at all to the reality of people's lives and experiences. The 'street wisdom' of those from poor neighbourhoods may be of little or no relevance to academic success, but involves as subtle, skilful and complex a set of abilities as any of the intellectual skills taught in school. Few if any young people leave school thinking, 'I'm so stupid that it's fair and proper for me to be stacking boxes in a factory all day.' If children from less privileged backgrounds accept such manual jobs, but without feeling themselves throughout life to be a failure, there must be other factors involved.

Willis concentrated on a particular group of boys in the school, spending a lot of time with them. The members of the gang, who called themselves 'the lads', were white, though the school also contained many young people from West Indian and Asian backgrounds. Willis found that the lads had an acute and perceptive understanding of the school's authority system – but used this to fight that system rather than work with it. They saw the school as an alien environment, but one they could manipulate to their own ends. They derived positive pleasure from the constant conflict – which they kept mostly to minor skirmishes – they

Classic Studies 19.1 | **Basil Bernstein on social class and language codes**

The research problem

It is a well-established finding that working-class children tend not to do as well in school as their middle-class peers. But this is a deceptively bald statement, which demands an answer. Why do working-class children not do so well? Are they, on average, less intelligent? Are they lacking motivation to do well at school? Do they not get enough support from their parents? Or is there something about education systems that prevents working-class children from doing well?

Bernstein's explanation

British sociologist, Basil Bernstein (1924–2000), was interested in the way in which education reproduces class inequalities in society. Drawing on conflict theory, Bernstein (1975) examined the problem through an analysis of linguistic skills. In the 1970s, Bernstein argued that children from varying backgrounds develop different *language codes*, or forms of speech, during their early lives, which affect their subsequent school experience. He was not concerned with differences in vocabulary or verbal skills, as these are usually thought of; rather, his interest was in systematic differences in ways of using language, particularly in the contrast between poorer and wealthier children.

The speech of working-class children, Bernstein contended, represents a restricted code – a way of using language containing many unstated assumptions that speakers expect others to know. A restricted code is a type of speech tied to its own cultural setting. Many working-class people live in a strong familial or neighbourhood culture, in which values and norms are taken for granted and not expressed in language. Parents tend to socialize their children directly by the use of rewards or reprimands to correct their behaviour. Language in a restricted code is more suitable for communication about practical experience than for discussion of more abstract ideas, processes or relationships. Restricted code speech is thus

Children who have been given reasons and explanations for their behaviour are more likely to be able to master the elaborate language codes used in school, which is the key to academic success.

characteristic of children growing up in lower-class families, and of the peer groups in which they spend their time. Speech is oriented to the norms of the group, without anyone easily being able to explain why they follow the patterns of behaviour they do.

The language development of middle-class children, by contrast, according to Bernstein, involves the acquisition of an elaborated code – a style of speaking in which the meanings of words can be individualized to suit the demands of particular situations. The ways in which children from middle-class backgrounds learn to use language are less bound to particular contexts; the child is able more easily to generalize and express abstract ideas. Thus middle-class mothers, when controlling their children, frequently explain the reasons and principles that underlie their reactions to the child's behaviour. While a working-class mother might tell a child off for wanting to eat too many sweets by simply saying 'No more sweets for you!', a middle-class mother is more likely to explain that eating too many sweets is bad for one's health and the state of one's teeth.

Children who have acquired elaborated codes of speech, Bernstein proposes, are more able to deal with the demands of formal academic education than those confined to restricted codes. This does not imply that working-class children have an 'inferior' type of speech, or that their codes of language are 'deprived'. Rather, the way in which they use speech clashes with the academic culture of the school. Those who have mastered elaborated codes fit much more easily into the school environment.

Joan Tough (1976) studied the language of working-class and middle-class children and found some systematic differences which support Bernstein's thesis. She found that working-class children had less experience of having their questions answered at home and were less able to ask questions in classroom situations. A later study by Barbara Tizard and Martin Hughes (1984) came to similar conclusions and it is generally accepted that Bernstein's thesis has been a productive one (Morais et al. 2001). His ideas help us to understand why those from certain socio-economic backgrounds tend to be 'under achievers' at school. Working-class children find the classroom situation difficult to cope with, especially when middle-class children appear so comfortable with it. The majority of teachers are from middle-class backgrounds and much of what they say is likely to be incomprehensible, as they use language in ways the child is just not accustomed to. The child may attempt to cope with this by translating the teacher's language into something she or he is familiar with – but may then fail to grasp the principles the teacher intends to convey. And while working-class children experience little difficulty with rote or 'drill' learning, they may have major difficulties grasping conceptual distinctions involving generalization and abstraction.

Critical points

Some critics of Bernstein's thesis argue that it is one of several 'deficit hypothesis' theories, which see working-class culture as lacking something essential (Boocock 1980; Bennett and LeCompte 1990) – in this case, the elaborated language code which enables middle-class children to express themselves more fully. For these critics, Bernstein takes the middle-class code to be superior to that of the working-class code; it can be seen therefore as an elitist theory. It is not just that the working class *perceives* the higher social classes as somehow their betters – as in many theories of ideological dominance; in Bernstein's theory, the elaborate code is *objectively* superior to the restricted code. Finally, critics argue that the theory of language codes is not supported by enough empirical research to be accepted and does not tell us enough about what happens inside schools.

Contemporary significance

Basil Bernstein's theory of language codes has been enormously influential in the sociology of education and many research studies have been conducted which draw heavily on his methods (Jenkins 1990). More recent studies have also taken his ideas into new areas such as the study of gender and pedagogy and his reputation as an educational theorist has spread internationally (Sadovnik 1995; Arnot 2001). Bernstein's work successfully linked language and speech with education systems and wider power relations in society as a whole and he rejected the critics' assessment of his thesis as 'elitist'. His code theory, 'draws attention to the relations between macro power relations and micro practices of transmission, acquisition and evaluation and the positioning and oppositioning to which these practices give rise' (1990: 118–19). By understanding these relations better, he always hoped to find ways of preventing the wastage of the educational potential of working-class children and he did succeed in providing a deeper insight into the social processes at work in the production of educational inequalities.

19.1 Learning *not* to labour?

More than two decades after Paul Willis conducted his study on 'the lads' in Birmingham, another sociologist, Máirtín Mac an Ghaill, investigated the experiences of young working-class men at the Parnell School in the West Midlands (1994). Mac an Ghaill was particularly interested in how male students develop specific forms of masculinity in school as part of their passage to manhood. He was intent on understanding how working-class boys in the early 1990s viewed their own transitions to adult life and prospects for the future. Unlike Willis's lads, the boys at the Parnell School were growing up in the shadow of high unemployment, the collapse of the manufacturing base in the region and cutbacks in government benefits for young people.

Mac an Ghaill found that the transition to adulthood for young men at the Parnell School was much more fragmented than that experienced by Willis's lads 25 years earlier. There was no longer a clear trajectory stretching from school into wage labour. Many of the boys in the school saw the post-school years as characterized by dependency (on family in particular), 'useless' government training schemes and an insecure labour market not favourable to young manual workers. There was widespread confusion among many of the students as to how education was relevant to their futures. This confusion manifested itself in very different responses to schooling – while some of the male peer groups tried to chart upwardly mobile paths for themselves as academic achievers or 'new enterprisers', others were openly hostile to schooling altogether.

Of the four peer groups Mac an Ghaill identified at the school, the 'macho lads' were the most traditionally working-class group in the school. The macho lads had coalesced as a group by the time they became teenagers; the group's members were in the bottom two academic 'sets' for all subjects. Their attitudes towards education were openly hostile – they shared a common view that the school was part of an authoritarian system that placed meaningless study demands on its captive students. Where Willis's 'lads' had found ways to manipulate the school environment to their

advantage, the macho lads were defiant about their role within it.

The macho lads were seen by the school administration as the most 'dangerous' anti-school peer group at Parnell School. Teachers were encouraged to deal with them using more overtly authoritarian means than they might with other students. The macho lads' symbolic displays of working-class masculinity – such as certain clothing, hairstyles and earrings – were banned by the school administration. Teachers were involved in the 'surveillance' of students, by constantly monitoring them in the hallways, instructing them to 'look at me when I'm talking to you' and telling them to 'walk properly down the corridor'.

Secondary school for the macho lads was their 'apprenticeship' in learning to be tough. School was not about the 3 R's (reading, writing and arithmetic), but about the 3 F's (fighting, fucking and football). 'Looking after your mates' and 'sticking together' were key values in the macho lads' social world. School became a contested territory, much like the streets. The macho lads regarded teachers in the same way they did law-enforcement (with open disdain) and believed that they were the main source of conflict within the school. They refused to affirm the teachers' authority within the school setting, and were convinced that they were constantly being 'set up' to be punished, disciplined or humiliated.

Like Willis's 'lads', the macho lads also associated academic work and achievement with something inferior and effeminate. The students who excelled scholastically were labelled 'dickhead achievers'. Schoolwork was rejected out of hand as inappropriate for men. As one macho lad, Leon, commented: 'The work you do here is girls' work. It's not real work. It's just for kids. They [the teachers] try to make you write down things about how you feel. It's none of their fucking business' (Mac an Ghaill 1994: 59).

Mac an Ghaill's work demonstrates how the 'macho lads', more than other male peer groups, were undergoing a particular 'crisis of masculinity'. This is because they were actively developing an 'outdated' working-class masculinity that centred around manual waged labour – at a time when a secure future in manual labour had all but disappeared. According to Mac an Ghaill, the macho lads continued to fantasize about the 'full employment' society which their fathers and uncles had inhabited. Although some of their behaviours came across as hypermasculine and therefore defensive, they were grounded squarely in a working-class world-view which had been inherited from older generations.

 The changing forms of masculinity are discussed in chapter 14, 'Sexuality and Gender'.

carried on with teachers. They were adept at seeing the weak points of the teachers' claims to authority, as well as where they were vulnerable as individuals.

In class, for instance, the young people were expected to sit still, be quiet and get on with their work. But the lads were forever on the move, except when the teacher's stare might freeze one of them momentarily; they would gossip surreptitiously, or pass open remarks that were on the verge of direct insubordination but could be explained away if challenged.

The lads recognized that work would be much like school, but they actively looked forward to it. They expected to gain no direct satisfaction from the work environ-

ment, but were impatient for wages. Far from taking the jobs they did – in tyre fitting, carpet-laying, plumbing, painting or decorating – from feelings of inferiority, they held an attitude of dismissive superiority towards work, as they had towards school. They enjoyed the adult status that came from working, but were not interested in 'making a career' for themselves. As Willis points out, work in blue-collar settings often involves quite similar cultural features to those the lads created in their counter-school culture – banter, quick wit and the skill to subvert the demands of authority figures when necessary.

In this way, what Willis shows us is that the lads' subculture, created in an active process of engagement with school norms and disciplinary mechanisms, mirrors the shop-floor culture of the work they expect to move into. Only later in their lives might they come to see themselves as trapped in arduous, unrewarding labour. By the time they have families, they might perhaps look back on education retrospectively, and see it – hopelessly – as having been the only escape. Yet if they try to pass this view on to their own children, they are likely to have no more success than their own parents did.

THINKING CRITICALLY

Both Willis and Mac an Ghaill's studies focused on the experience of working-class 'lads', but in your experience, are there also girl subcultures? How would you explain the lack of studies dealing with the subcultures of girls? From your own school experience, is it likely that similar processes of exclusion and gang formation could be found amongst girls and young women?

Willis's study shows that educational sociological research can be both empirically oriented and at the same time, theoretically informed, and this is one of the main reasons why it has been so influential. However, its focus is quite explicitly on the educational experiences of white, working-class boys and it is not possible to generalize from this to the experiences of other social classes, girls or ethnic minorities.

Ethnicity, aspiration and class in the USA

In a 1987 study in the USA – *Ain't No Makin' It: Aspirations and Attainment in a Low-Income Neighborhood* – Jay MacLeod investigated the attitudes and aspirations of two gangs of young men who lived on the same public housing project: 'Clarendon Heights' in Boston. MacLeod followed this up eight years later, tracking the young people into adulthood to see whether their hopes had materialized.

In the original study, MacLeod looked at two subcultural groups from the same housing project. One was a mainly white group of older teenagers, called the Hallway Hangers as they spent much time just 'hanging around' in the halls of the housing project, and a second, mostly black group, the Brothers. MacLeod found that the Hallway Hangers were overwhelmingly despondent about their prospects for the future. They held anti-school attitudes based on their awareness of older family members who had either failed at school in spite of trying hard, or had actually done well in school but had still failed to move into decent jobs afterwards. By contrast, and perhaps surprisingly, the Brothers tended to express more support for the education system as the means to get a job and move up the social ladder. Such attitudes appeared to be based on widely publicized attempts to improve opportunities for African Americans in the USA.

What MacLeod's study seems to show is that although material circumstances are important in shaping attitudes, the latter are also dependent on peoples' subjective assessment of how likely it is that they can succeed through education.

MacLeod revisited both groups some eight years later, and a revised edition with three new chapters was published in 1995. What he found was that, in spite of their very different assessments of their likely futures, in fact, *neither* group had done well in school and both were struggling in the labour market. The previously pessimistic Hallway Hangers, having failed in school and facing unemployment and poverty, had turned to the underground economy – what MacLeod call 'cocaine capitalism', and expressed strongly racist and sexist attitudes. The more optimistic Brothers had also become unemployed or were in insecure, low-paid, part-time work. They had been forced to adjust their attitudes towards education and their own aspirations for the future downwards in the light of their real-world experiences. MacLeod's

1995 update shows, therefore, that the material realities of life in poor, inner-city neighbourhoods present very significant structural obstacles, which serve to reproduce social inequalities over generations, in spite of the aspirations and hopes of individuals.

Reproducing gender divisions

Until the 1970s, the issue of gender was not central to the sociology of education and research on the experience of girls was very limited in scope (Gilligan 1982). This situation was not uncommon, as most other sociological subjects lacked a female perspective, including, for instance, crime and deviance studies (Heidensohn 1985). Sociologists working from a feminist theoretical perspective in the 1970s explored the socialization of girls into feminine norms from very early on in life, including during their school careers, and a series of studies established that schools systematically disadvantaged girls.

Angela McRobbie (1991) and Sue Lees (1993) argued that schooling in the UK helped to reproduce 'appropriate' feminine norms amongst girls. Schools saw their task as preparing girls for family life and responsibilities and boys for future employment, thus reinforcing the traditional gender stereotypes within the wider society (Deem 1980). Michelle Stanworth (1983) studied the classroom experiences of a mixed group of children in comprehensive school and discovered that, although comprehensives were intended to provide equal opportunities, girls tended to receive less attention from the teachers than did boys. She concluded that this differential pattern of teaching undermined the girls' confidence in their own abilities and contributed to their under-achievement. This is an example of a typical self-fulfilling prophecy, in which teachers' initial expectations (boys will do better than girls) shape their behaviour towards the pupils, which then brings about the outcome they (perhaps wrongly) assumed at the start.

The culture of schools has been found to be permeated with a general heterosexual sexism, particularly in the playground, corridors and other spaces outside the classroom (Wood 1984). As Willis (1977) also found, boys routinely use sexist language and refer to girls via derogatory categories. This creates an atmosphere of aggressive masculinity that degrades girls and women while corralling boys' acceptable identities into a very narrow range. One consequence is that homosexuality is made invisible and gay and lesbian young people find that the school environment does not allow them openly to express their emerging identities. If they do, they run the risk of teasing, harassment and physical assault (Burbridge and Walters 1981; see chapter 14, 'Sexuality and Gender' for a wider discussion of sexuality in society).

Feminist scholars have also investigated the *content* of the school curriculum. For example, Australian sociologist Dale Spender (1982) reported that many subjects were thoroughly imbued with an unwitting sexism, which made them unattractive to girls. Science texts, for example, routinely ignored the achievements of female scientists, making them invisible to students. In this way, science offers girls no positive role models and fails to engage them with the subject. Sue Sharpe (1994) also saw schools steering girls' subject choices towards the more 'feminine' subjects like health studies and the arts and away from the more 'masculine' ones such as mathematics and ICT (information communication technologies).

Nonetheless, as we will see later, in recent years there have been some significant changes to such traditional patterns of disadvantage and exclusion, one of the most striking being the way that girls and young women now outperform boys and young men in almost every subject area and at every level of education. This development has seen new debates emerging on the problems boys face amidst an apparent 'crisis of masculinity' (Connell 2005).

Education, cultural capital and the formation of habitus

The most systematic general theory of cultural reproduction to date is, arguably, that of the French sociologist Pierre Bourdieu (1930–2002). Bourdieu (1986, 1988; Bourdieu and Passeron 1977) devised a broad theory of cultural reproduction, which connects economic position, social status and symbolic capital with cultural knowledge and skills. Education is a central feature of this theoretical perspective, but it is necessary to outline Bourdieu's theory of forms of capital in order to grasp the significance of his perspective for educational sociology.

The central concept in Bourdieu's theory is *capital*, which he takes from Marx's ideas on the development of capitalism. Marx saw the ownership of the means of production as the crucial division in society, conferring social advantage on capitalists who are able to subordinate the workers. But for Bourdieu, such economic capital is just one of several forms of capital which individuals and social groups can use to gain advantage. Bourdieu identifies social capital, cultural capital and symbolic capital in addition to economic capital. Social capital refers to membership of and involvement in elite social networks or moving within social groups which are well connected. Cultural capital is that form which is gained within the family environment and through education, usually leading to certificates such as degrees and other credentials, which are forms of symbolic capital. Symbolic capital refers to the prestige, status and other forms of social honour, which enable those with high status to dominate those with lower status.

The important aspect of this scheme is that forms of capital can be exchanged. For example, those with high *cultural capital* may be able to trade it for *economic capital*: for example, during interviews for well-paid jobs, their superior knowledge and credentials can give them an advantage over other applicants. Those with high *social capital* may 'know the right people' or 'move in the right social circles' and be able to effectively exchange this *social capital* for *symbolic capital* – respect from others and increased social status – which increases their power chances in dealings with other people.

The second concept that Bourdieu introduces is that of fields – various social sites or arenas within which the competitive struggles rooted in forms of capital take place. It is through fields that social life is organized and power relationships operate and each field has its own 'rules of the game' that may not be transferred to other fields. For example, in the field of art and aesthetics, cultural capital is most highly prized and those who are able to converse knowledgeably about the history of art or music and so on become powerful within the field – hence the power of the critics in literature or cinema to make or break a book or film with their reviews, for example. But such criteria do not apply in the field of production, where economic capital holds sway.

Finally, Bourdieu uses the concept of habitus, which can be described as the learned dispositions such as bodily comportment, ways of speaking or ways of thinking and acting which are adopted by people in relation to the social conditions in which they exist and move through. Examples of aspects of habitus would include Bernstein's language codes and Mac an Ghaill's macho boys' displays of working-class masculinity. The concept of habitus is important, as it allows us to analyse the links between social structures and individual actions and personalities.

The issue for us at this point is: what has all of this to do with education? Bourdieu's (1986) concept of cultural capital is at the heart of the matter, and he identifies three forms in which it can exist. Cultural capital can exist in an *embodied state* – that is, we carry it around with us in our ways of thinking, speaking and bodily movement. It can also exist in material form – an *objectified state* – for example in the possession of works of art, books or clothes. Finally, cultural capital is found in *institutionalized forms* such as those held in educational qualifications, which are nationally accepted and easily translated into economic capital in the labour market. It is easy to see how the embodied and institutionalized forms are acquired through education, forming resources to be used in the specific fields of social life. In this way, education can be a rich source of cultural capital, which potentially benefit many people.

However, as Bernstein, Willis and Mac an Ghaill all saw, the education system itself is *not* just a neutral field divorced from the wider society. Rather, the culture and standards within the education system reflect that society and, in doing so, schools systematically advantage those who have already acquired cultural capital in their family and through the social networks in which it is embedded (a crucial form of social capital). Middle-class children fit into the culture of schools with ease; they speak correctly, they have the right manners and they do better when it comes to exams. But because the education system is portrayed and widely perceived as being open to all on the basis of talent, many working-class children come to see themselves as intellectually inferior and accept that they, rather than the system itself, are to blame for their failure. In this way, the education system is able to play a key role in the cultural reproduction of social inequalities.

Acquiring cultural capital

In an ethnographic study of twelve diverse families in the USA, Annette Lareau (2003) drew on Bourdieu's ideas, particularly the concept of cultural capital, to conduct an 'intensive "naturalistic" observation' of parenting styles in the different cultures of family life of social classes. In the working class and poorer families, as discussed by Bernstein above, parents did not try to reason with children but told them what to do. Children were also expected to find their own forms of recreation and not to rely on

parents to create it for them. Lareau says that children from working-class backgrounds did not talk back and accepted that their financial situation imposed limits on their aspirations. Working-class parents saw a clear difference between adults and children and did not see a need to engage with children's feelings and opinions, preferring to facilitate the 'accomplishment of natural growth'. This parenting style, says Lareau, is 'out of synch' with the current standards of social institutions. But working-class parents and children still come into contact with social institutions like schools, and children therefore begin to develop a growing sense of 'distance, distrust and constraint'.

On the other hand, the middle-class children in the study were talkative, good at conversation and adept at social mores such as shaking hands and making eye contact when talking. They were also very good at getting other family members, especially parents, to serve their needs, and were comfortable with adults and authority figures, seeing themselves as their equals. Lareau argues that middle-class parents are constantly interested and involved in their children's feelings and opinions and jointly organize their leisure activities, rather than leaving them to make their own. Continual discussion between parents and children marks out the middle-class parenting style, which is based on a *concerted cultivation* of the child. The result is that the middle-class children had a clear sense of personal entitlement rather than feeling distant and constrained. What Lareau's study shows us are some of the practical ways in which cultural capital is passed on across generations and how styles of parenting are strongly linked to social class.

Lareau says that both parenting methods have their advantages, but, interestingly, some of the middle-class families she studied were exhausted by their constant efforts to fulfil their children's demands and the children themselves were more anxious and stressed than the working-class children, whose family ties were closer and who experienced much less sibling rivalry. Lareau's conclusion is that parenting methods tend to vary much more by social class than by ethnicity and that, as several other studies have also found, the middle-class children in the study were much better prepared for success at school than were the children from working-class families.

Summary

Bourdieu's theory has been very influential in stimulating sociological research into education, inequality and the study of cultural reproduction. However, it has its critics. One criticism is that it appears almost impossible for the working classes to succeed in a middle-class education system, but, of course, a fair number do succeed. In an age of mass higher education, many more working-class people are finding their way into universities and acquiring the kinds of institutionalized cultural capital that enables them to compete with the middle classes. They do remain in the minority though. We should also not mistake the resigned acceptance by working-class children of their situation with a positive legitimation of schools and their outcomes. After all, there is ample evidence of resistance and rebellion amongst working-class pupils through truancy, bad behaviour in classrooms and the formation of school gangs which generate alternative standards of success. Nevertheless, Bourdieu's theoretical framework remains the most systematic synthesis yet produced for understanding the role of schooling in the reproduction of social inequality.

Bourdieu's view on class and social capital are discussed in more detail in chapter 11, 'Stratification and Social Class'.

Evaluation

The sociological theories explored in this chapter illustrate two important aspects of

> **THINKING CRITICALLY**
>
> Do you think the public school system (see opposite) is likely to survive in its present form in the age of mass higher education and the opening up of educational opportunities? If not, how might public schools have to change? Drawing on Bourdieu's theory described above, what kinds of cultural capital do the British public schools transmit to their students?

education. On the one hand, a good quality education is something that can change people's lives for the better and in many parts of the world, children like Sakina and Hawwau are desperate to gain access to schooling as the route to a better life. In this sense, education is highly sought after and has often had to be fought for against opposition. However, on the other hand, sociological research consistently finds that education systems not only create new opportunities for advancement, but are also experienced differently by a range of social groups. Education systems cannot stand apart from the society within which they are embedded, and when society is riven with inequalities schools also help reproduce them, even against the best intentions of the people who work in them. As Bernstein, Wills and Bourdieu's works (amongst others) demonstrate, cultural reproduction in unequal societies leads to patterns of educational inequality. The next section looks at such patterns and how the changes they have undergone in recent times.

Social divisions and education

Much of our discussion of inequality so far has focused on social class, but in this section, we turn to other inequalities. We begin with an outline of a long-standing and highly contentious debate on IQ and human intelligence, before moving on to

19.2 The British public schools

The public schools in Britain are an oddity in more ways than one. They are not 'public' at all, but, on the contrary, private, fee-paying institutions. The degree of independence they have from the rest of the education system and the key role they play in the society at large marks them out from the systems of other countries. There are some private schools, often linked to religious denominations, in all Western societies, but in no other society are private schools either so exclusive or so important as in the UK.

The public schools are nominally subject to state supervision, but in fact few major pieces of educational legislation have affected them. They were left untouched by the 1944 Act, as they were by the setting up of the comprehensive schools; and the large majority stayed single-sex schools until relatively recently. There are about 2,300 fee-paying schools in England, educating some 6 per cent of the population. They include a diversity of different organizations, from prestigious establishments such as Eton, Rugby or Charterhouse, through to so-called minor public schools whose names would be unknown to most people.

The term 'public school' is limited by some educationalists to a group of the major fee-paying schools. These include those schools that are members of the Headmasters' Conference (HMC), originally formed in 1871. Initially there were only 50 schools in the Conference; the number has now expanded to more than 240. Schools like those listed above – Eton, Rugby and the rest – are members. Individuals who have attended HMC schools tend to dominate the higher positions in British society. A study by Ivan Reid and others, for example, published in 1991, showed that 84 per cent of judges, 70 per cent of bank

Eton College boys in their very traditional school uniform.

directors and 49 per cent of top civil servants had attended an HMC school (Reid 1991).

Following the 1988 Education Reform Act, all state schools have to follow a standard national curriculum, which involves testing pupils at the ages of 7, 11, 14 and 16. Representatives from the fee-paying schools were involved in the creation of the national curriculum. Yet these schools do not have to follow it. The fee-paying schools can teach whatever they wish and have no obligation to test children. Most have opted to follow the national curriculum, but some have simply ignored it.

look at educational inequalities involving gender and ethnicity. This will help us to see how education systems may be changing as societies themselves undergo significant economic restructuring.

The IQ debate in education

For many years, psychologists have debated whether there exists a single human ability, which can be called *intelligence*, and, if so, how far it rests on innately determined differences. Intelligence is difficult to define, because it covers many different, often unrelated, qualities. We might suppose, for example, that the 'purest' form of intelligence is the ability to solve abstract mathematical puzzles. However, people who are very good at such puzzles sometimes have low ability in other areas, such as grasping the narrative of history or understanding works of art. Since the concept has proved so resistant to a generally accepted definition, some psychologists have proposed (and many educators have by default accepted) that intelligence can simply be regarded as 'what IQ tests measure' (IQ simply means 'intelligence quotient'). The unsatisfactory nature of this is obvious enough, because the definition of intelligence then becomes wholly circular – IQ tests measure intelligence and intelligence is what IQ tests say it is.

Most IQ tests consist of a mixture of conceptual and computational problems. You may have taken one yourself. The tests are constructed so that the average score is 100 points: anyone scoring less is labelled as 'below-average intelligence', and anyone scoring above has 'above-average intelligence'. In spite of the fundamental difficulty in measuring intelligence, IQ tests are still widely used in research studies, as well as in schools and businesses.

'The bell curve'

Scores on IQ tests do in fact correlate well with academic performance, which is not surprising, since the tests were originally developed to predict success in school. They therefore also correlate closely with social, economic and ethnic differences, since these are associated with variations in levels of educational attainment. White students score better, on average, than black students or members of other disadvantaged minorities. Such results have led some, such as Arthur Jensen (1967, 1979) to suggest that IQ differences between blacks and whites are, in part, due to genetic variation. Of course,

as we have already seen in this chapter, pinning down the reasons for educational under-achievement have to take into account the role of education systems in reproducing social inequalities and we should not consider the latter to be neutral sites where those with the highest intelligence simply do better on account of higher inherited intelligence.

More recently, psychologist Richard J. Herrnstein and the sociologist Charles Murray reopened the debate about IQ and education in a controversial way. They argued in their book, *The Bell Curve: Intelligence and Class Structure in American Life* (1994), that the accumulated evidence linking IQ to genetic inheritance has become overwhelming. The significant differences in intelligence between various racial and ethnic groups, they say, must in part be explained in terms of heredity. According to Herrnstein and Murray, evidence from the USA indicates that some ethnic groups have, on average, a higher IQ than others. Asian Americans, particularly Japanese and Chinese Americans tend to possess a higher IQ than whites, though the difference is not large. The average IQ of Asians and whites, however, is substantially higher than that of blacks. The authors argue that such differences in inherited intelligence contribute in an important way to social divisions in society. The more intelligent an individual is, the greater the chance that she or he will rise in the social scale. Those at the top are there partly because they are more intelligent than the rest of the population – from which it follows that those at the bottom remain there because, on average, they are not so clever.

Critics deny that IQ differences between racial and ethnic groups are genetic in origin. They argue that differences in IQ result from social and cultural differences. For example, IQ tests pose questions to do with abstract reasoning that are just more likely to be part of the experience of more affluent white students than of blacks and ethnic minorities. Scores on IQ tests may also be influenced by factors that have nothing to do with the abilities supposedly being measured, such as whether the testing is experienced as stressful. Some research has demonstrated that African Americans score six points lower on IQ tests when the tester is white than when the tester is black (Kamin 1977).

Recent social psychological research studies carried out in the USA show that the 'stereotype threat' – the fear of confirming a negative social stereotype as a self-characteristic – can impair people's performance in intelligence and ability tests (Steele and Aronson 1995; Steele 1997). Steele and Aronson conducted a test involving both white and African American students, in which half of each ethnic group was told that their intelligence was being measured. While the white students' performance was not noticeably affected, African American students who thought their IQ was being tested performed well below their previous achievement level. The researchers concluded that the stereotype threat (that African Americans have a lower IQ than whites) raised students' anxiety levels, leading to poorer performance on the test. Other research on the effects of gender stereotyping on performance found physiological evidence indicating increased stress and anxiety (such as changes in surface skin temperature and diastolic blood pressure) in a sample of girls who were told that girls did consistently worse than boys on a particular maths test (Osborne 2007). Studies such as these lend support to the argument that social and cultural stereotypes can play a large part in people's performance in test situations, including IQ tests.

Observations of deprived ethnic minority groups in other countries – such as the 'untouchables' in India, the Maoris in New Zealand and Burakumin of Japan – also strongly suggest that the variations in IQ between African Americans and whites in the United States result from social and cultural differences. Children in all these groups score an average of 10–15 points below children belonging to the ethnic majority. Similar differences can be seen across generations, with average IQ scores rising substantially over the past half century for whole populations. When old and new versions of IQ tests are given to the same group of people, they score significantly higher on the old tests. There is no evidence that young people today are innately superior in intelligence to their parents or grandparents; the better scores are therefore more likely to result from increasing prosperity and social advantage. The notion that some entire racial groups are on average more intelligent than others remains unproven and improbable.

In *The Bell Curve Wars* (Fraser 1995), a number of noted scholars explored the ideas of Herrnstein and Murray. The editor described *The Bell Curve*, as 'the most incendiary piece of social science to appear in the last decade or more'. The claims and assertions in the work 'have generated flash floods of letters to the editor in every major magazine and newspaper, not to mention the over-the-air commentary on scores of radio and television shows' (Fraser 1995: 3). The contributors saw Herrnstein and Murray's work as 'racist pseudoscience' and attacked almost every facet of their argument.

For example, biologist Stephen Jay Gould (1941–2002) argued that Herrnstein and Murray are wrong on four major counts. A single IQ score cannot describe intelligence; people cannot be meaningfully ranked along a single intelligence scale; intelligence does not derive substantially from genetic inheritance; and 'intelligence' can be altered and does improve with age. Howard Gardner argued that a century of research has dispelled the notion of 'intelligence' as a general category. There are only 'multiple intelligences' – practical, musical, spatial, mathematical and so forth. Gould concluded:

> We must fight the doctrine of *The Bell Curve* both because it is wrong and because it will, if activated, cut off all

possibility of proper nurturance for everyone's intelligence. Of course, we cannot all be rocket scientists or brain surgeons, but those who can't might be rock musicians or professional athletes (and gain far more social prestige and salary thereby). (In Fraser 1995: 22)

The new IQ'ism'

David Gillborn and Deborah Youdell (2001) argue that although measures of IQ are rarely used explicitly in education today, educationalists now use the term 'ability' in a very similar way. They claim that the use of the term 'ability' systematically disadvantages black and working-class students in schools.

The authors carried out surveys in two London schools over two years in the mid-1990s. They interviewed and observed teachers, and pupils in their third and final years at secondary school. At both schools they surveyed, teaching was heavily shaped around 'the A-to-C economy'. By this phrase, they meant that schools were aiming to get as high a proportion of pupils as possible to obtain five or more A–C grades at GCSE level (exams taken at 16 years of age). This is because the proportion of pupils meeting this benchmark is one key criterion on which schools are rated in the government's annually published official league tables. As the headmaster of one school noted in a memo to staff: 'The best thing we can do is to get the greatest possible proportion achieving the five high-grade benchmark.'

Although this seems a legitimate aim, Gillborn and Youdell found that it put teachers under pressure to spend more time on those pupils they think are able to achieve five or more GCSEs at grade C or above. The effect of this was that 'both schools are increasingly rationing the time and effort they expend on different groups of pupils'. Teachers had to make a choice over which pupils have the ability to get the five good GCSE grades – and they gave these pupils most attention. In both schools teachers' notions of a pupil's 'ability' determined whether they saw that pupil as a likely candidate to gain five or more GCSEs. From their interviews and observations, Gillborn and Youdell found that 'ability' was viewed by teachers as something fixed, which determined the potential of different pupils. As one headteacher remarked: 'You can't give someone ability can you? You can't achieve more than you're capable of, can you?'

It was also found that teachers often believed that ability could be measured objectively. At one school, pupils were given a 'cognitive ability' test when they arrived, which teachers took as a good indication of GCSE performance later on. Not surprisingly, given the findings of Bernstein, Wills and Bourdieu discussed above, pupils with highest 'ability' tended to be white and middle class. The authors also noted that they 'observed many occasions when black pupils seemed to be dealt with more harshly or to face lower expectations than their peers of other ethnic backgrounds'. These beliefs about which pupils had ability constituted an unwitting discrimination against black and working-class children.

The consequence of this 'new IQ'ism' was that fewer black and working-class pupils gained five GCSEs above grade C, thus reinforcing the teacher's assessment of their 'fixed ability'. In one school, 16 per cent of black pupils attained five or more GCSEs above C level, compared to 35 per cent of white pupils. These results are typical of the UK national pattern, which sees black and working-class pupils doing worse academically than the average.

Gillborn and Youdell's conclusion is that, although most educationalists would disagree strongly with the idea that intelligence is inherited, 'in one sense at least, the hereditarians have won. Without any genuine debate, the British education system is increasingly returning to policy and practice that takes for granted the assumptions proposed by IQ'ists like Herrnstein and Murray.' To Gillborn and Youdell, the familiar social divisions (especially those of race and class) are reappearing through language that appears to stress the individual 'ability' of pupils, but actually relies on unstated prejudices about group identities.

> ### THINKING CRITICALLY
>
> Critics of IQ tests say that they do not really measure 'intelligence'. If this is true, what are they actually measuring and why do they get such diverse results? Are IQ theorists who carry out research into possible racial differences in intelligence behaving in a racist manner?

Emotional intelligence

Since the 1990s, there have been many popular books and psychological studies that have sought to include emotional awareness and competence in our general understanding of what 'intelligence' means. The idea was popularized by the best-selling book, *Emotional Intelligence* (1996) by Daniel Goleman. Goleman argued that emotional intelligence can be at least as important as IQ in determining people's life chances. Emotional intelligence (or EI) refers to how people use their emotions, and is thought of as the ability or skill to recognize emotions, evaluate them when they arise and manage them both in themselves and in others. Unlike IQ theorists though, EI qualities are not inherited, and the more that children can be taught them, the more chance they have of making use of their intellectual capabilities. According to Goleman, 'The brightest among us can founder on shoals of unbridled passion and unruly impulses; people with high IQs can be stunningly poor pilots of their private lives' (1996: 34).

Theories of emotional intelligence have become more popular amongst educationalists through the idea of 'emotional literacy', which, as the term implies, is something that can be taught in schools as a way

> ### THINKING CRITICALLY
>
> On reflection, do you recognize emotional intelligence in yourself and other people? How convincing is the idea that we possess or can learn *emotional intelligence*? If one element of being emotionally intelligent is the ability to *manage* our own emotions and those of others, does this mean that emotions can be brought completely under rational control? Or are human emotions essentially spontaneous and uncontrollable?

to build resilience and give pupils the emotional resources to cope with a range of emotional pressures (see 'Using your sociological imagination 19.3'). To the extent that other forms of 'intelligence' such as emotional intelligence or interpersonal intelligence are brought into our understanding of people's abilities, then we will have to revise our ideas to include the diverse range of factors that contribute towards success in life. Similarly, schooling is becoming more than just a stage preparing people for work. As society and technologies change, the necessary skills also change, and even if education is seen from a purely vocational point of view – as providing skills relevant to work – most observers agree that access to education throughout the life-course will be needed in the future.

Gender and schooling

As we saw earlier, in the past, education and the formal school curriculum in the developed societies were differentiated along gendered lines. For example, in late nineteenth-century Britain, girls were taught the skills to prepare them for domesticity, while boys took basic mathematics and were expected to gain the skills needed for work. Women's entry into higher education was very slow and they were not able to gain degree level qualifications until 1878. Even so, the number of women studying for degrees remained low; a situation that only

19.3   Emotional literacy in schools?

'Emotional literacy' to be taught

'Emotional literacy' is to be taught in secondary schools in England.

A pilot scheme, involving about 50 schools, is expected to test the benefits of lessons helping pupils to talk about their feelings. This could involve introducing ideas such as 'worry boxes' in which pupils could send letters expressing any particular concerns.

Such lessons promoting emotional intelligence have already been running in primary schools.

These lessons for younger children are seen by the government as having been a success – and it is now expected that they will be extended into secondary schools.

'Anger management'

Teaching 'emotional literacy' is intended to help pupils' behaviour – with lessons in subjects such as anger management to defuse confrontations and classroom aggression. There have been ongoing concerns about bullying in schools – and violence between pupils – and such lessons will encourage children to talk about their anxieties. In primary schools, this has involved approaches such as 'circle time', where children discuss worries or disagreements that might be troubling or upsetting them.

Among the areas that might be covered will be self-awareness, friendships, empathy and self-motivation. 'Social, emotional and behavioural skills need to be regularly reinforced and practised and also developed as children grow older', said a spokesperson for the Department for Education and Skills. 'These skills are vital to continuing to promote positive behaviour and they are also vital skills for learning, both of which continue to be of key importance.'

Source: BBC News, 28 November 2005

---

began to change significantly in the 1960s and '70s. As we will see later, this state of affairs has been utterly transformed in the present period.

Today, the secondary school curriculum no longer distinguishes between boys and girls in any systematic way (apart from participation in sports). However, there are various other 'points of entry' for the development of gender differences in education. These include teacher expectations, school rituals and other aspects of the hidden curriculum. Although rules are gradually loosening, regulations which compel girls to wear dresses or skirts in school form one of the most obvious ways in which gender-typing occurs. The consequences go beyond mere appearance. As a result of the clothes she wears, a girl lacks the freedom to sit casually, to join in rough-and-tumble games or sometimes to run as fast as she is able.

Although this is changing, school textbooks also help to perpetuate gender images. Until recently, it was common for storybooks in primary schools to portray boys as showing initiative and independence, while girls, if they appeared at all, were more passive and watched their brothers. Stories written especially for girls often have an element of adventure in them, but this usually takes the form of intrigues or mysteries in a domestic or school setting. Boys' adventure stories are more wide-ranging, having heroes who travel off to distant places or who are sturdily independent in other ways. At the secondary level, females have tended to be 'invisible' in most science and maths textbooks, perpetuating the view that these are 'male subjects'.

Gender differences in education are also very obvious when one looks at subject choice in schools. The view that some subjects are more suited to boys or to girls is a common one. Sociologist Becky Francis (2000) has argued that girls are more likely to be encouraged into less academically prestigious subjects than boys. There is

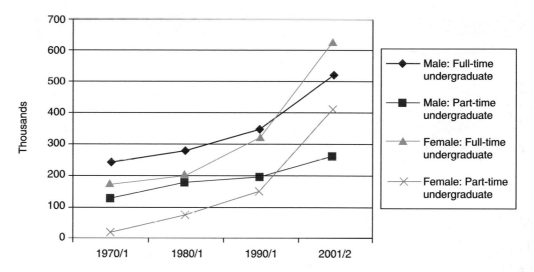

Figure 19.1 Students in higher education: by sex, 1970/1–2001/2

Source: HMSO Social Trends 2004, 44

certainly a marked difference in the subjects they choose to pursue. In 2001/2, around 75 per cent of young people aged 16–18 who entered for an A-level or equivalent (the standard entry qualification for a university degree) in physics and in computer studies in the UK, and 60 per cent of those entered for maths, were male. By comparison, around 70 per cent of entries for social studies and English literature, and 95 per cent of entries for home economics, were female (figure 19.1). Nonetheless, the achievement of girls in many education systems around the world has now surpassed that of boys at all levels.

Gender and achievement

Throughout the twentieth century, girls tended to outperform boys in terms of school results until they reached the middle years of secondary education. They then fell behind and by the ages of 16 and 18, as well as at university, boys did much better. For example, in the UK until the late 1980s, girls were less likely than boys to attain the three A levels necessary for admission to university and were entering higher education in smaller numbers than boys. Concerned

about such unequal outcomes, feminist researchers conducted a number of important studies into how gender influences the learning process. They found that school curricula were often male-dominated and that teachers were devoting more attention to boys than to girls in the classroom.

In recent years though, the debate around gender in schools has undergone a dramatic and unexpected reversal. 'Under-achieving boys' are now one of the main subjects of conversation amongst educators and policy-makers. Since the early 1990s, girls began consistently to outperform boys in all subject areas (including science and mathematics) and at all levels of the British educational system (see table 19.1 for figures for England). Similar findings have been reported in America and elsewhere. Young women in the USA are more likely than young men to go further in school, get a college education and go on to do a postgraduate degree (as figure 19.2 shows).

The problem of 'failing boys' has been seized on, as it is seen to be linked to a host of social problems such as crime, unemployment, drug abuse and lone parenthood. In combination, these factors have

Girls are outperforming boys at every level of education, and in most subjects.

amounted to what has been described as a 'crisis in masculinity' (discussed in chapter 14, 'Sexuality and Gender') that was explored above by Máirtín Mac an Ghaill. Boys who leave school early or with poor educational results are less likely to find good jobs and create stable families, because, in the post-industrial economies of the developed world, fewer unskilled manual jobs are available for young men with weak educational backgrounds. Meanwhile, a large proportion – up to 70 per cent – of jobs that are being created in the rapidly growing service sector are now being filled by women. However, Mac an Ghaill (1996) also points out that although many women are entering into employment, the jobs they are moving into are by no means all professional careers. In fact, women still make up the overwhelming majority of part-time workers and the service-based work they do

is often relatively poorly paid and low in status.

Explaining the gender gap

A variety of explanations have been advanced to account for the dramatic turnaround in gender performance in schools. One factor that must be taken into account in explaining girls' achievement is the influence of the women's movement on their self-esteem and expectations. Many girls presently in school have grown up surrounded by examples of working women – indeed, many of their own mothers work outside the home. Exposure to these positive role models increases girls' awareness of career opportunities and challenges traditional stereotypes of women as housewives. Another result of feminism is that teachers and educationalists have become more aware of gender discrimination within

Table 19.1 **Students reaching or exceeding expected standards in England, teacher assessment by key stage and sex, 1996 and 2006**

England				Percentages
	1996		2006	
	Boys	Girls	Boys	Girls
Key Stage 1				
English				
Reading	73	83	80	89
Writing	71	82	76	87
Mathematics	80	83	89	92
Science	83	85	88	91
Key Stage 2				
English	53	68	72	82
Mathematics	58	62	78	78
Science	64	67	83	85
Key Stage 3				
English	51	70	64	78
Mathematics	60	64	74	77
Science	59	61	70	73

Source: Department for Education and Skills

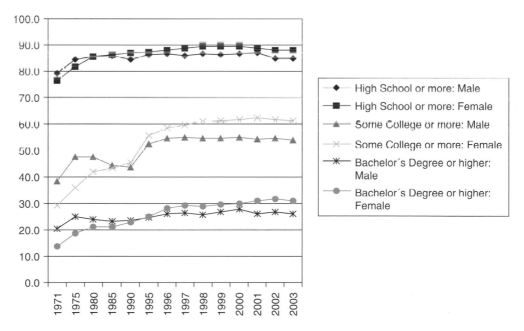

Figure 19.2 Percentage of 25–29-year-olds by level of education completed in the USA by gender, selected years, 1971–2003

Source: Child Trends: www.childtrendsdatabank.org/pdf/6_PDF.pdf

the educational system. In recent years, many schools have taken steps to avoid gender stereotyping in the classroom, to encourage girls to explore traditionally 'male' subjects and to promote educational materials that are free of gender bias.

Some theories centre on the difference in learning styles between boys and girls. Girls are often regarded as more effectively organized and motivated than boys; they are also seen as maturing earlier. One manifestation of this is that girls tend to relate to one another by talking and using their verbal skills – one aspect of emotional intelligence perhaps. Boys, on the other hand, socialize in a more active manner – through sport, computer games and hanging out in the school playground – and tend to be more disruptive in the classroom. These broad patterns of behaviour seem to be reaffirmed by teachers in the classroom, who may have lower expectations for boys than for girls, and indulge boys' disruptions by paying more attention to them.

Another line of reasoning focuses on 'laddism' – a set of attitudes and outlooks shared by many boys that is anti-education and anti-learning. The research of Willis and Mac an Ghaill provides some evidence for these theories. Many see high rates of exclusion and truancy among boys as rooted in their belief that learning is not 'cool'.

Other scholars question the enormous amount of attention and resources being directed at under-achieving boys. They argue that the gender gap in language skills is one that can be found the world over. Differences that used to be ascribed to boys' 'healthy idleness' are now provoking a firestorm of controversy and frantic attempts to improve boys' results. As national performance targets, league tables and international literacy comparisons proliferate – drawing differences out into the open for all to see – 'equal outcomes' in education have become a top priority.

All the attention give to boys, critics argue, serves to hide other forms of inequality within education. Although girls have forged ahead in many areas, they are still less likely than boys to choose subjects in school leading to careers in technology, science or engineering. Boys pull ahead in science by about the age of 11 and continue to outperform girls through to university: in subjects such as chemistry and computer science, which are central to economic growth in the present economy, they continue to dominate. Although women may be entering higher education in greater numbers, they continue to be disadvantaged in the job market in comparison with men who hold the same levels of qualification (Epstein 1998).

More than gender, factors such as class and ethnicity produce the greatest inequalities within the educational system. For example, UK comparisons in achievement by pupils across social classes reveal that 70 per cent of children from the top professional class receive five or more pass grades, compared with only 14 per cent from working-class backgrounds. Concentrating upon 'failing boys' is misleading, critics contend, since men continue to dominate positions of power in society. The under-achievement of working-class boys, they argue, may have less to do with their gender than with the disadvantages of their social class.

Gender and higher education

One significant aspect of the expansion in higher education is the increase in the number of female students. For example, since the 1970s, UK higher education has seen much faster growth rates for women entering further and higher education than for men (table 19.2). By 1990/1, there were more women than men in further education and by 2005/5, the same was true of higher education. This is a reversal of the position in the 1970s, when there were far more male than female students. By 2004/5 there were seven times as many female students in further and higher education than there had been in 1970/1, but only around two and a half times as many male students. However, evidence from the USA suggests that choice

Table 19.2 **UK students in further and higher education, by type of course and sex, 1970–2005**

	Men				Women			
								Thousands
	1970/71	1980/81	1990/91	2004/05	1970/71	1980/81	1990/91	2004/05
Further education								
Full-time	116	154	219	532	95	196	261	551
Part-time	891	697	768	1,534	630	624	986	2,429
All further education	1,007	851	986	2,066	725	820	1,247	2,981
Higher education								
Undergraduate								
Full-time	241	277	345	549	173	196	319	680
Part-time	127	176	148	267	19	71	106	458
Postgraduate								
Full-time	33	41	50	113	10	21	34	114
Part-time	15	32	46	139	3	13	33	172
All higher education	416	526	588	1,068	205	301	491	1,420

Source: HMSO Social Trends 37. 2007

of subjects is still marked by conventional gender norms.

The previous pattern of subject choice in American higher education, as in many other developed countries, saw women pursuing degrees in education and the health professions, which led into somewhat lower-paid careers than those following from computer science and engineering subjects, which were dominated by male students. Women have made some inroads into these latter subjects, but they remain male-dominated today. This is the case at postgraduate levels too. On the other hand, many degree subjects that were previously dominated by men, including those in the social sciences, history, life sciences and business management, have seen a broad gender parity achieved (Freeman 2004). What does *not* appear to be happening is a move by men into the university subjects that were previously female dominated.

Women's organizations have often attacked sex discrimination in school and higher education. Women still find themselves heavily under-represented among the teaching staff in colleges and universities, especially in senior posts. In 2002/3, for example, although women made up 39 per cent of academic staff in the UK, only 26 per cent of senior lecturers and researchers were women and there were 1,860 women professors, accounting for just over 14 per cent of the total. However, there is a trend towards greater gender equality in higher education. The figures quoted here mark a 5.7 per cent rise in the number of female academics and a 10.4 per cent leap in the number of female professors over the preceding year (HESA 2004).

With men occupying more of the senior positions in higher education institutions, women, on average, are paid significantly less. A recent survey found that average pay for women is lower than for men at every university in the UK. Across the university sector as a whole, women earn on average more than £5,000 less than men, and the gender difference in pay is significantly larger at some institutions (*THES*, 3 September 2004).

What we may conclude from this brief survey is that girls and women have made significant headway within education systems over the past 40 years. In terms of sheer numbers, they now outperform boys both in qualifications gained and attendance at higher education institutions. But there remain significant inequalities once highly educated women move into the workforce, with men maintaining their traditionally better rates of pay and improved promotional prospects. It is unclear whether such gendered advantages will survive long into the twenty-first century.

THINKING CRITICALLY

List all of the reasons you can think of as to why the achievement of boys in the developed countries is now falling behind that of girls. What social consequences might there be for communities in future and should we really be concerned? If we should, what can be done to change the situation?

Ethnicity and education

Sociologists have carried out a good deal of research into the educational fortunes of ethnic minorities. Governments have also sponsored their own investigations, such as *Education for All* in the UK, the report of the 1985 Swann Committee. The Swann report found significant differences in average levels of educational success between groups from different ethnic backgrounds. Children from black Caribbean families tended to fare worst in school, as measured by formal academic attainments. They had improved from ten years earlier, however. Asian children did as well as white children, in spite of the fact that, on average, the families from which they came were economically worse off than white families (Swann Committee 1985).

Subsequent research indicates that the picture has changed somewhat. Trevor Jones carried out research in the UK, which indicated that young people from all minority group backgrounds were more likely than white children to continue into full-time education from the age of 16–19. Only 37 per cent of white children stayed on in education in 1988–90, compared to 43 per cent from West Indian backgrounds, 50 per cent of South Asians and 77 per cent of Chinese. In spite of this apparently improving picture for minority ethnic groups, Jones suggested something of a negative explanation for it. Many members of ethnic minority groups may be staying on in education because of their particular problems in finding a decent job. (Jones 1993)

On the whole, members of ethnic minority groups are not under-represented in British higher education. People from Indian and Chinese backgrounds are, on average, significantly more likely to have a degree qualification or higher than those from other ethnic backgrounds. However, men who defined themselves as 'mixed race' and women who defined themselves as 'black/black British' and 'Asian/Asian British' were slightly less likely to have gained a degree or higher qualification than the national average (HMSO 2004).

School exclusions and ethnicity

Social exclusion has become a topic of great interest for sociologists over the past decade. One specific area of concern has been the growing number of young people outside the formal education system, many of whom are children from minority ethnic groups. Within the sociology of education, connections are often drawn between the exclusion of students from school and other phenomena such as truancy, delinquency, poverty, limited parental supervision and a weak commitment to education.

 See chapter 12, 'Poverty, Social Exclusion and Welfare', for a wider discussion of social exclusion.

Rates per 10,000 pupils

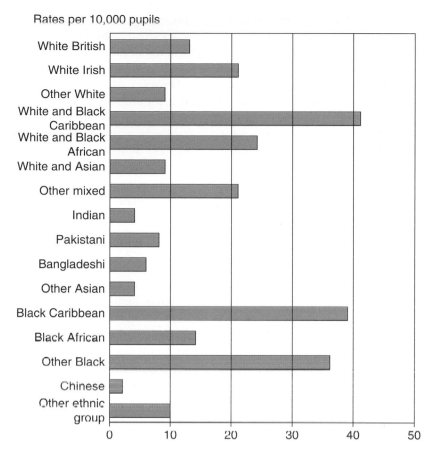

Figure 19.3 Permanent exclusion rates in England by ethnic group, 2004–5

Source: HMSO Social Trends 37, 2007

School exclusion rates have been increasing in recent years in many developed countries, though in England rates have actually fallen by 23 per cent since 1997/8 to 12 per 10,000 pupils in 2004/5. Some 12,300 pupils were permanently excluded from school in 1997/8, but this was down to 9,440 in 2004/5 (HMSO 2007: 29) when the number of boys permanently excluded outnumbered girls by nearly four to one. Exclusion rates also differ according to ethnicity (see figure 19.3). In 2004/5 the highest permanent exclusion rates in England were among pupils of mixed white and black Caribbean origin, while black African pupils were far less likely to be permanently excluded. Rates were lowest for Chinese pupils, with just two in every 10,000 being permanently excluded.

Findings from American schools reflect a similar disparity in exclusion rates between black pupils and students from other ethnic backgrounds. Following a series of school shootings in the USA, more than 80 per cent of American schools have adopted 'zero tolerance' policies towards disruptive students. A nationwide investigation revealed that black students are being excluded from schools at rates disproportionate to their representation within student populations and at a rate unlikely to be due simply to disruptiveness in school. For example, in San Francisco, black students accounted for 52 per cent of exclusions, yet made up only 16 per cent of school enrolment. In Phoenix, where the black population was 4 per cent, black students made up 21 per cent of exclusions. How can the high rate of exclusions among black male pupils be explained? A number of factors are likely to be involved, but it is possible that stricter exclusion policies are being applied in a racially discriminatory way.

It is important also to consider how rates of school exclusion may reflect much broader patterns of exclusion and disadvantage within society. As we have seen elsewhere, many young people are growing up under very challenging conditions, with a relative lack of adult guidance and support. Traditional notions of masculinity are under threat and there is no stable vision of the future. For young people growing up against this turbulent backdrop – particularly boys and young men from disadvantaged groups – schools may appear irrelevant or too authoritative, rather than a site for opportunity and advancement.

A significant aspect of education systems and school exclusions which has to be considered is the potential for **institutional racism** within them (Rattansi 1992). In education systems, the concept is used to refer to the way that school life is structured, the dress codes deemed to be appropriate and the curriculum adopted. Therefore, teachers may often interpret the behaviour and dress styles of black pupils as evidence of their 'disruptive' behaviour, leading to more temporary and permanent exclusions. It has to be borne in mind, though, that some non-white ethnic groups have relatively low rates of school exclusion and the concept of **ethnocentrism** – a concern with one's own culture and a

> The concept of institutional racism was introduced in chapter 15, 'Race, Ethnicity and Migration', in relation to the UK Metropolitan Police Service's inadequate handling of the racist murder of Stephen Lawrence (Macpherson 1999).

consequent lack of interest in others – may be a more accurate description of the roots of much discrimination in schools (Mason 2000).

However, racism within schools may be a contributory factor in the high rates of exclusion found specifically amongst black pupils. In a research study carried out in the UK, which explored race relations in primary schools, Cecile Wright (1992) studied relationships within four inner-city primary schools over a three-year period. She found that teachers tended to assume that African Caribbean boys were disruptive, and they were quick to reprimand and control their behaviour. Asian pupils were perceived as likely to struggle with language skills but were perceived as willing to learn and compliant with the teachers' instructions. Social stereotypes were leading to a certain level of fear amongst staff, which then fed into the reinforcement of stereotypes. Even so, Wright acknowledged that the teachers were committed to equal treatment for all, but were caught up in wider social processes that led to discrimination.

Such processes were present in relations amongst the pupils too. Racial harassment was part of the daily experience of black pupils and Asian pupils were very often victimized by white children. The staff's failure to deal with these issues led to problems between staff and parents and a marked lack of satisfaction amongst black children's' parents compared with those of the white pupils. This often led to parental complaints of injustice, which staff interpreted as attempts to play down their children's' bad behaviour. Wright's research showed that the processes leading to racism and discrimination in the wider society were also found within schools and, she explains, 'staff, like most other people, do treat people differently on the basis of perceived "racial" characteristics. Further, many nursery and primary staff are still reluctant to accept that younger children can hold incipient racist attitudes and

Social stereotypes may impact in the way teachers treat children from different ethnic groups. For example, African Caribbean children are often assumed to be disruptive.

exhibit hostility towards members of other groups' (1992: 103).

Findings such as these have led some to advocate multicultural forms of education, which would need curriculum changes to bring currently ignored national histories, religions and cultures into schools. This has happened to a limited extent, for example within religious education where pupils are introduced to the diversity of religious beliefs and practices. There are some problems with such multicultural initiatives however. For example, historical facts can never speak for themselves and history still has to be interpreted. How should the history of colonialism and imperial expansion be taught, for instance, and where should the emphasis of interpretation lie? Would a multiculturalist approach to education threaten to dilute national identities? Wright's finding of racism at work even within primary schools seems to indicate that some form of anti-racist education may be more effective. Ant-racist education would involve multicultural teaching but would also go further, to challenge inequalities by helping both staff (during staff training) and young people to understand how racist attitudes and stereotypes develop and how they can deal with them when they arise. Anti-racism in schools would not ignore or play down racism within the school, but would attempt to actively identify and challenge discriminatory language, actions and policies. The main issue raised by critics is the potential for such teaching to reinforce divisions and to contribute to the 'racialization' of conflicts within the school community. Whilst multiculturalist and anti-racist approaches are in many ways quite different, it has been suggested that a 'critical multiculturalist' approach may offer the best way to preserve the best of each (May 1999).

> ### THINKING CRITICALLY
>
> Thinking about your own school experience, is there any evidence that schools are *institutionally* racist or is it more accurate to say that there is racism within schools? Did your school(s) have an anti-racist curriculum? If it did, how did this help to combat racism? If it did not, should it develop one?

Evaluation

Inequalities within education systems have proved remarkably persistent, particularly in relation to social class divisions. However, as we have seen in relation to gender inequalities, there can also be quite radical changes. The educational opportunities for women have opened up considerably over the latter half of the twentieth century, though these do take time to become firmly established. Economic restructuring – which has reduced the need for heavy, manual work and workers in favour of post-industrial employment in the service sector – has been a major structural factor favouring a better trained and educated female workforce. Nonetheless, differences in the educational experiences of ethnic groups also show us that inequality of education is strongly linked to cultural factors as much as to economic ones.

Education in global context

Until around a century and a half ago, and even more recently in some regions, the children of the wealthy were educated by private tutors. Some still are. Most people had no formal schooling whatsoever until the first few decades of the nineteenth century, when in European countries and the United States, systems of primary schools began to be constructed. The process of industrialization and the expansion of cities served to increase the demand for specialized schooling. People worked in many different occupations, and work skills could no longer be passed on directly from parents to children. The acquisition of knowledge became increasingly based on abstract learning in subjects like maths, science, history, literature and so on, rather than on the practical transmission of specific skills. In modern societies, people have to be furnished with basic skills, such as reading, writing and calculating, as well as a general knowledge of their physical, social and economic environment. It is also important that they know *how to learn*, so they are able to master new and often very technical, forms of information.

Most modern educational systems first took shape in most Western societies in the early part of the nineteenth century, though England was more reluctant than most other countries to establish an integrated national system. By the mid-1800s, Holland, Switzerland and the German states had achieved more or less universal enrolment in elementary schools, but England and Wales fell far short of such a target; education in Scotland was somewhat more developed at an earlier stage. The USA, by contrast, already had around 50 per cent of its 5–19 year olds in education by 1850.

When we look at education today in our increasingly global context, what is striking is the diversity of educational provision across the world. As we saw through the individual examples of Sakina, Hawwau and

Shaun in the chapter introduction, many people in the developing world struggle to gain access to education and illiteracy remains widespread, while in developed countries, issues of choice and consumerism are more likely to exercise parents and governments. If inequalities *within* countries are proving difficult to tackle, then the global inequalities *between* the countries of the developed and developing worlds are even more of a challenge.

One way of comparing the world's nationally based education systems is to look at government spending on education. Given the diversity of local currencies, this is not a simple task. In order to compare cost per student and the size of national education budgets, local currencies have to be converted into one standard measure, usually the US dollar at the market exchange rate. However, according to UNESCO Institute for Statistics (2008), 'purchasing power parities' (PPP$) better reflect the real value of educational investments by governments and families. PPPs are rates of currency conversion that eliminate differences in price levels among countries. So, a given sum of money, when converted into US dollars at PPP rates, will buy the same basket of goods and services in all countries.

Table 19.3 uses PPPs in its comparison of world regions. The table shows that the governments of the world spent 4.4 per cent of global GDP on education in 2004. The highest levels of education spending were in North America and Western Europe, with 5.6 per cent of their regional GDP. The Arab States (4.9 per cent), sub-Saharan Africa (4.5 per cent) and Latin America and the Caribbean (4.4 per cent) also spend at or above the global average. But the lowest levels of spending by far were in Central Asia (2.8 per cent) and East Asia and the Pacific (2.8 per cent), though the latter is based on estimates for China and may therefore not be so reliable. Within these broad regions are some large national differences. For example, the United Arab Emirates spends

1.3 per cent, Indonesia 0.9 per cent and Equatorial New Guinea just 0.6 per cent. Conversely, the USA, which has only 4 per cent of global population, spends more than one-quarter of the global public education budget (28 per cent). North America and Western Europe, with just 8 per cent of global population, spends 55 per cent of global public education expenditure.

> ### THINKING CRITICALLY
>
> Education spending seems to be directly linked to literacy levels and educational achievement. In such a grossly unequal world situation, what can be done to raise the level of educational spending in the poorest countries? How might it be argued that today's wealthy countries benefit from the high illiteracy rates of the poor countries?

Global primary school enrolment

An important aspect of global education is the number of children of primary school age actually in some form of primary education (see figure 19.5). A useful measure of this is primary school enrolments. Between 1999 and 2004, primary school enrolment increased globally to around 86 per cent, with the largest increases in sub-Saharan Africa (27 per cent) and South and West Asia (19 per cent), the two regions that were furthest away from universal provision (UNESCO 2008). However, in 2004 there were still 77 million primary age children not in any form of primary education, three-quarters of these in sub-Saharan Africa and South and West Asia. This is inevitably an underestimate however, as not all those who are enrolled actually attend regularly or at all, as Michael Bruneforth's (2006) analysis in figure 19.6 shows in relation to some of the countries facing the biggest challenge in 2004.

An analysis of factors contributing to being out of school revealed that slightly more boys than girls were out of school, but

Table 19.3 Public education expenditure by world region, 2004

| Region | Education expenditure | | | | |
| | as % of GDP | | PPP$ (in billions) | | % of regional |
	Total	Primary level	Total	Primary level	Total
Arab States	4.9	1.7	77.8	27.0	3.2
Central and Eastern Europe	4.2	1.1	164.0	41.2	6.7
Central Asia	2.8	0.6	7.7	1.8	0.3
East Asia and the Pacific	2.8	1.0	441.7	149.8	17.9
Latin America and Western Europe	5.6	1.5	1,355.6	372.3	55.1
South and West Asia	3.6	1.2	169.1	54.6	6.9
Sub-Saharan Africa	4.5	2.1	59.9	27.9	2.4
WORLD	4.4	1.3	2,462.2	741.1	100.0

Source: © UNESCO Institute for Statistics (UIS); more data are available at: www.uis.unesco.org

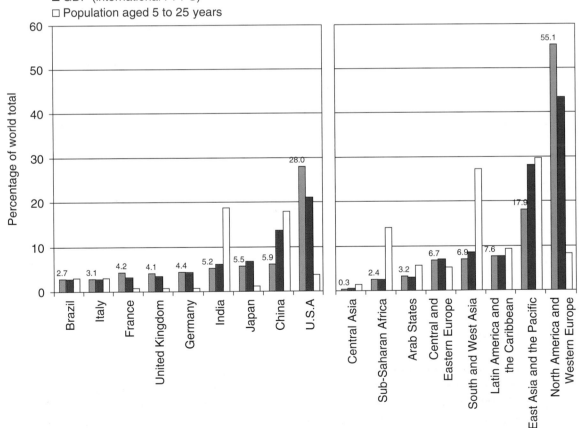

Figure 19.4 Global distribution of public education expenditure, GDP and population aged 5–25, by selected countries and world regions

Source: © UNESCO Institute for Statistics (UIS); more data are available at www.uis.unesco.org

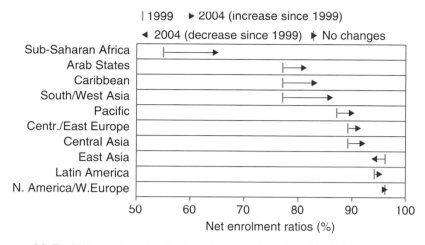

Figure 19.5 Net enrolment ratios in primary education, 1999–2004

Source: UNESCO EFA Global Monitoring Report, 2008

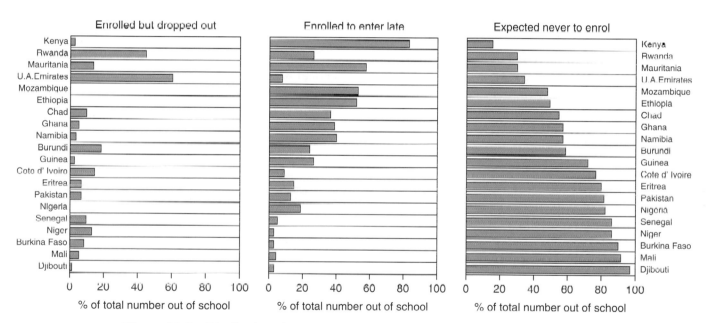

Figure 19.6 Distribution of out-of-school children in selected countries with most difficulties in enrolment

Source: UNESCO EFA Global Monitoring Report, 2008

gender was not the key factor. Residence was important: 18 per cent of primary age children were out of school, but almost a third (30 per cent) of rural children were not in primary school. Household wealth was also significant: 38 per cent of children in the poorest fifth of households were not in primary education compared to 25 per cent of the middle fifth and just 1 per cent of the wealthiest fifth. Once again, we can see the issue of social class and educational inequality arising, but this time at the global level. The final factor that seems to be significant is whether mothers had been involved

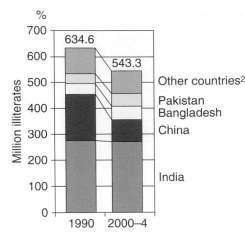

	Number of illiterates			Literacy rates		
	1990	2000–4[1]	Change 1990 to 2000–4	1990	2000–4[1]	Change 1990 to 2000–4
	(000)	(000)	(%)	(%)	(%)	(Percentage points)
Morocco	9,140	10,106	10.6	38.7	52.3	13.6
Iran, Isl. Rep.	11,501	10,509	−8.6	63.2	77.0	13.8
Egypt	17,411	14,210	−18.4	47.1	71.4	24.3
Brazil	17,369	15,052	−13.3	82.0	88.6	6.6
Indonesia	23,791	15,100	−36.5	79.5	30.4	10.9
Ethiopia	19,815	23,554	18.9	28.6	45.2	16.6
Pakistan	40,817	48,818	19.6	35.4	49.9	14.5
Bangladesh	40,405	52,530	30.0	34.2	42.6	8.4
China	181,331	87,019	−52.0	78.3	90.9	12.6
India	273,066	266,426	−1.7	49.3	61.0	11.7

[1] Data are for the most recent year available during the period specified.
[2] Brazil, Egypt, Ethiopia, Indonesia, Morocco, Islamic Republic of Iran.

Figure 19.7 Changes in adult literacy (15+) between 1990 and 2004 in countries with more than 10 million illiterate adults

Source: UNESCO EFA Global Monitoring Report, 2008

in education themselves. Whereas just 16 per cent of children whose mothers had had some education were not in primary school, 38 per cent of those whose mothers who had had no education were not in school (UNESCO 2008). This may indicate that the value families place on education and the existence of positive role models are crucial elements in raising primary school attendance levels. Clearly, primary school attendance is fundamental if global levels of basic literacy are to be improved.

Literacy and illiteracy

In 2007, some 781 million adults across the world did not have even basic literacy skills and 64 per cent of these were women (UNESCO 2008). The majority live in sub-Saharan Africa, South and West Asia and East Asia, though illiteracy exists in every society including those in the developed world. National literacy rates below 60 per cent are recorded in 22 countries, 14 of which are in sub-Saharan Africa. In each of the 10 countries listed in figure 19.7, there are more than 10 million illiterate adults, and these account for some 70 per cent of the world's illiterate population. In Morocco, Ethiopia, Pakistan and Bangladesh, although literacy *rates* have increased, the absolute *number* of illiterate adults has increased, due to the growth of their populations, while India has remained fairly static. With growing populations and large numbers of illiterate adults, these countries face a major literacy challenge in the twenty-first century which presents a formidable obstacle in the competitive global economy.

The global adult literacy rate actually rose between 1990 and 2004, from 75 per cent to 82 per cent, though again, there are many national differences. Some have also suggested that a new kind of illiteracy may be emerging, as information technology becomes commonplace in work environments. This could see large numbers of people without regular access to information technology, or to training for its use and familiarity with the specialized language of computing, being disadvantaged in new ways. We will return to this issue in the final part of this chapter.

 See chapter 4, 'Globalization and the Changing World', for more detail on the global spread of ICT.

Global Society 19.1 **The threat of literacy in colonial regimes**

Literacy is the 'baseline' of education. Without it, schooling cannot proceed. We take it for granted in the West that the majority of people are literate, but, as has been mentioned, this is only a recent development in Western history, and in previous times no more than a tiny proportion of the population had any literacy skills.

In some countries only a small minority of the population has any reading or writing skills. This can be partially explained by the absence of universal education in some countries. Yet even if the provision of primary schooling were to increase with the level of population growth, illiteracy will not be much reduced for many years, because a high proportion of illiterates are adults. The absolute number of those who cannot read or write is actually rising.

Illiteracy has a strong gender dimension, especially in the poorest countries of the world. High rates of female illiteracy are linked strongly to poverty, infant mortality, high fertility rates and low levels of economic development. A combination of traditional culture and economic pressures keep many girls out of school: rural families tend to be more traditional and less supportive of women's education. But in large families, it is expensive to educate all the children, so girls' schooling is often sacrificed in favour of educating boys.

Although many countries have instituted literacy programmes, these have made only a small contribution to a problem of large-scale dimensions. Television, radio and the other electronic media can be used, where they are available, to skip the stage of learning literacy skills and convey educational programmes directly to adults. But educational programmes are usually less popular than commercialized entertainment.

During the period of colonialism, the colonial governments regarded education with some trepidation. Until the twentieth century, most believed indigenous populations to be too primitive to be worthy of educating. Later, education was seen as a way of making local elites responsive to European interests and ways of life. But to some extent, the result was to foment discontent and rebellion, since the majority of those who led anti-colonial and nationalist movements were from educated elites who had attended schools or colleges in Europe. They were able to compare at first hand the democratic institutions of the European countries with the absence of democracy in their lands of origin.

The education that the colonizers introduced usually pertained to Europe, not to the colonial areas themselves. Educated Africans in the British colonies knew about the kings and queens of England, read Shakespeare, Milton and the English poets, but knew next to nothing about their own countries' history or past cultural achievements. Policies of educational reform since the end of colonialism have not completely altered the situation even today.

Partly as a result of the legacy of colonial education, which was not directed towards the majority of the population, the educational system in many developing countries is top-heavy: higher education is disproportionately developed, relative to primary and secondary education. The result is a correspondingly overqualified group who, having attended colleges and universities, cannot find white-collar or professional jobs. Given the low level of industrial development, most of the better-paid positions are in government, and there are not enough of those to go around.

In recent years, some developing countries, recognizing the shortcomings of the curricula inherited from colonialism, have tried to redirect their educational programmes towards the rural poor. They have had limited success, because usually there is insufficient funding to pay for the scale of the necessary innovations. As a result, countries such as India have begun programmes of self-help education. Communities draw on existing resources without creating demands for high levels of finance. Those who can read and write and who perhaps possess job skills are encouraged to take others on as apprentices, whom they coach in their spare time.

The links between literacy and development are discussed in chapter 13, 'Global Inequality'.

THINKING CRITICALLY

In what ways would the restriction of educational opportunity under colonial regimes have affected future economic development? How should the former colonial powers help their former colonies to catch up in today's global economy? What practical assistance could they offer?

Creating literate environments

There are clear links between educational expenditure, primary school attendance and literacy. Levels of government and other expenditure on education not only bring children and young people into free schooling, but can also help to create 'literate environments'. Literate environments are those spaces which provide numerous opportunities for the newly literate to exercise their skills. These opportunities include a range of printed and visual materials such as newspapers, magazines and books, easy access to continuing education such as in schools and training centres, opportunities to be involved in organizations where literacy skills can be used, such as local government or agricultural cooperatives, and opportunities to work in businesses or non-for-profit organizations that allow the exercise of literate skills (Easton 2006). Primary schools and other schools are obviously literate environments, which benefit very young children and young people, but literate environments can also be created in libraries and other public spaces, as well as in workplaces and even private homes.

Apart from providing opportunities for the exercise of literacy skills, the main significance of literate environments may be in their impact on people's *motivation* to become literate or improve their levels of literacy. What is clearer today, however, is that literate environments will have to be able to provide access to electronic forms of communication, as well as more conventional forms, if they are to be successful in tackling illiteracy in the future.

The changing face of education

Education systems across the world today are changing quite quickly. One reason for this is the continuing spread and development of information communication technologies (ICTs), which we explore in our final section below. However, education systems face other challenges as well, not least the question of how they should be funded in the future, an issue that has been particularly contentious in higher education as universities are gradually opened up to larger numbers of people from a variety of social backgrounds. To get a sense of the way that education systems in the developed countries have changed over the twentieth century, we will take a brief look at British education and its development. Although education systems are diverse, a single case can reveal some of the key general issues arising at different historical moments.

The development of UK education

Between 1870 (when compulsory education was first established in Britain) and the Second World War, successive governments increased expenditure on education. The minimum school-leaving age rose from 10 to 14, and more and more schools were built, but education was not really considered to be a major area for government intervention. Private or church authorities under the supervision of local government boards ran most schools. The Second World War changed this attitude. Recruits to the armed forces were given ability and learning tests; the results startled the authorities by showing a low level of educational skills. Concerned about prospects for post-war recovery, the government began to rethink the existing education system (Halsey 1997).

By the 1960s, it was clear that the results of those selecting pupils who were considered to be more intelligent for grammar schools at the age of 11 had not come up to expectations. Only 12 per cent of pupils continued in school until the age of 17, and early leaving was shown to be more closely related to class background than to academic performance (Crowther Report 1959). Since the early 1970s, UK state education has been strongly affected by the jolting transition from a situation in which labour power was in short supply to one in which there was too much – leading to a time of rising unemployment and reduced government revenue. Educational expansion, which characterized the whole of the postwar period, was suddenly replaced by contraction and efforts to reduce government expenditure. The percentage of general government expenditure on education rose steadily and, with the exception of a drop in the mid-1980s, education spending as a share of the government total has remained at around 12 per cent ever since.

Education has long been a political battleground, and one protracted debate has centred on the impact of comprehensive schooling and its results. The architects of comprehensive education believed that the new schools would provide for more equality of opportunity than was possible in selective education. The 1979 Conservative government criticized comprehensive schooling, believing that selective grammar schools should not have been allowed more or less to disappear. In the late 1980s, the government sought to dismantle the giant comprehensive system and reduce the power of the local education authorities that were responsible for running them. The 1988 Education Act introduced a universal national curriculum for the state sector. This was resisted by some in the teaching profession (involving a strike in 1993) who opposed standardized testing and saw the new curriculum as unnecessarily confining.

The 1988 Act also introduced local management of schools, devolving their administration to balance the inevitable centralization involved in the national curriculum. A new group of City Technology Colleges (CTCs) and grant-maintained schools was also to be established. The latter could 'opt out' of local authority control and receive funding directly from the state – effectively becoming a business funded from central government. They would also have the right to select up to 50 per cent of their student intake on the basis of ability. The government hoped 'that over time all schools will have become grant-maintained' – in other words, would have opted out.

By 1995, however, only 1,000 schools had done so out of a total number of 23,000 state schools. A study by Gewirtz et al. (1995) found that, for many parents, the choice of school was severely limited (as we saw in Shaun's case at the start of this chapter) as the extent of real school choice largely depended on parents' social class and cultural capital and was therefore likely to reinforce educational inequalities.

The New Labour government elected in 1997 put 'education, education, education' at the top of its agenda. In a White Paper, *Excellence in Schools*, Labour committed itself to defending and modernizing comprehensive schools. The White Paper also called for intervention in the case of schools with chronically sub-standard performance, and a variety of approaches has been used to raise educational standards. Labour has emphasized the importance of good teaching methods and strong leadership by heads as the keys to educational reform. In primary schools, literacy and numeracy strategies were introduced, which have now been extended to form a primary strategy, which sets out standards in English, mathematics and science. Grant-maintained schools have become 'Foundation Schools', retaining a high degree of independence and focusing on technology, arts or maths, for example. These schools are allowed to select up to 10 per cent of their intake according to a pupil's ability in these specialist areas.

City Academies have also been created in deprived areas and are heavily oversubscribed. Sponsors from the private or charitable sector provide 20 per cent of the start-up costs, up to a maximum of two million pounds. The state then pays the rest. Sponsors then run the academy, which is funded by the taxpayer. Critics claim that the generous funding of academies drains resources from other schools. Labour has also been rigorous in its policy of school inspections. Where schools are deemed to be failing, government agencies intervene directly to take over the running of the school. In some cases, failing schools have reopened as City Academies. Education Action Zones were created in areas of high deprivation. In these zones, money from government and the private sector could be used to attract more teachers through offers of higher pay, to tackle the wider problems associated with social exclusion. By 2004 there were 47 Education Action Zones across England.

The system of higher education in Britain has, like many others, expanded rapidly in the past 30 years or so. There were 21 universities in Britain in the immediate pre-war period. Most of the universities at that time were very small by today's standards. Between 1945 and 1970 the UK higher education system grew to be four times larger. The older universities expanded and new universities, such as at Sussex, Kent, Stirling and York – labelled 'red-brick' – were built. A binary system was set up with the creation of polytechnics, which concentrated more on vocational courses than the universities did. Today, UK higher education has a 'standard coinage' – a degree from Leicester or Leeds, at least in theory, is of the same standard as one from Cambridge, Oxford or London. Yet Oxford and Cambridge are noted for their highly selective intake, about half of whom come from fee-paying schools. An Oxford or Cambridge degree confers a greater chance of a profitable career than a qualification from most other universities. Major social divisions, discussed earlier in the chapter, are not confined to the compulsory education sector.

In 1900/1 there were a mere 25,000 students in full-time higher education in the UK. But by 1971, this had increased to 457,000 and by 2001/2 there were almost 1.2 million. Social class background influences the likelihood of participation in higher education and though working-class involvement has increased, it remains well below that of students from non-manual classes. The debate about access to education for the children of working-class parents has been central to the debates about how higher education is funded.

While the number of students in higher education has expanded massively, government spending has not grown at the same rate. The result has been a crisis in funding for higher education. Funding per student fell by 29 per cent in real terms between 1976 and 1989, and by a further 38 per cent between 1989 and 1999. The National Committee of Inquiry into Higher Education (1997) concluded that the expansion and improvement of higher education would be impossible under existing funding arrangements. But who should pay?

The two main sources of large-scale investment into universities are the general taxpayer and those who experience and benefit from higher education: students. Some argue that, given the social and economic benefits that higher education provides for society, university funding should be met by the taxpayer. Where would we be without university-trained medical professionals and teachers, for example? Others counter that those taxpayers who do not go to university should not have to pay for those who do. Graduates enjoy many career advantages – financial and non-financial – that non-graduates do not. For example, graduates, on average, earn significantly more over a lifetime than non-graduates from similar backgrounds, though the difference has narrowed over the past 15 years, partly as a result of the rising cost of course fees and, subsequently, higher levels of graduate debt. It has become largely accepted that students should pay a greater share of their university costs.

One problem with such a policy may be that it will act as a deterrent to currently under-represented groups, such as working-class students, who will see the prospect of incurring a large debt as unacceptable. However, university grants have been reinstated for the poorest third of students in order to tackle this problem. A second is the impact on universities. Prestigious universities will be able to charge more in fees, attract better staff and get better facilities, and a two-tier system may well develop.

What we can see in the example of the British case is something of the changing face of education systems. The twentieth century saw compulsory schooling become established across the developed world and years spent in education rise for all social classes. Strict selection on the basis of testing gave way in the 1960s and '70s to more comprehensive models of schooling, but by the 1990s, new forms of selection were emerging. In higher education, universities have very slowly opened their doors to a wider section of the population, but as the elite system has become a mass higher education system, the thorny problem of who pays has become a serious problem. The next big challenge for education systems will be how to make effective use of the new possibilities created by information technology and we now turn to this issue.

Technology in the classroom

The spread of information technology is already influencing education in schools in a number of different ways. The knowledge economy demands a computer literate workforce and it is increasingly clear that education can, and must, play a critical role in meeting this need. While household computer ownership has risen sharply in recent years, many children still do not have access to a computer at home. For this reason, schools are a crucial forum for young people to learn about and become comfortable with the capabilities of computers and online technology.

As we saw earlier in this chapter, the rise of education in its modern sense was connected with a number of other major changes happening in the nineteenth century. One was the development of printing and the arrival of 'book culture'. The mass distribution of books, newspapers and other printed media was as distinctive a feature of the development of industrial society as were machines and factories. Education provided the skills of literacy and numeracy, giving access to the world of printed media. Nothing is more characteristic of the school than the schoolbook or textbook.

In the eyes of many, all this is set to change with the growing use of computers and multimedia technologies in education. Will the digital media increasingly replace the schoolbook? And will schools still exist in anything like the form in which they do today if children turn on their computers in order to learn, rather than listening to a teacher? The new technologies, it is said, will not just add to the existing curriculum; they will undermine and transform it. For young people now are already growing up in an information- and media-related society and are much more familiar with its technologies than most adults are – including their teachers.

A 2003 OECD study assessed the educational performance of 15-year-old students and found that regular computer use led to better scores, particularly in mathematics. The report found that students who had used computers for several years generally performed better at maths than the OECD average, while those with infrequent access to computers or who had only used them for a short time tended to lag behind their class year group (OECD 2005). Of the sample of students, 10 per cent had used computers for less than a year and their average score was well below the OECD average in mathematics. Almost three out of four students in the OECD countries frequently used a computer at home, but only 44 per cent did so at school. This is the kind of data which

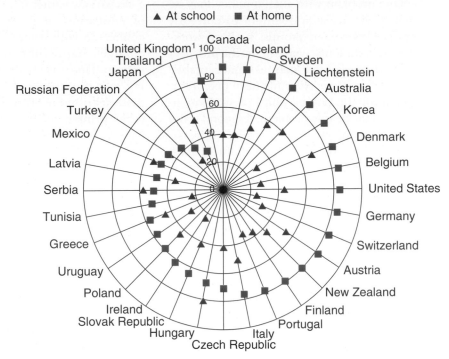

Countries are ranked in descending order of percentage of students frequently using computers at school.
[1] Response rate too low to ensure comparability.

Figure 19.8 Percentage of students who frequently use a computer at home or school, OECD countries, from 2003 data

Source: OECD 2005

some social scientists see as evidence of the growing divide between IT-rich and IT-poor households. If schools do not provide better access to computing, then the social class divide in education systems looks likely to become wider.

Over recent years, the use of technology in education has been utterly transformed. In most of the developed countries, education systems have been modernized and computerized. Some observers now talk of a 'classroom revolution' – the arrival of 'desktop virtual reality' and the classroom without walls. There is little question that computers have expanded opportunities in education. They provide the chance for children to work independently, to research topics with the help of online resources, and to benefit from educational software that allows them to progress at their own pace. Yet the vision (or nightmare) of classrooms of children learning exclusively through individual computers has not yet come to pass. In fact, the 'classroom without walls' looks some way off.

Even if there were enough computers to go around at school or in the home, most teachers see computers as a supplement to traditional lessons, rather than as a replacement for them. And though the number of students with regular access to a computer is rising, the picture is quite an uneven one, even across the relatively wealthy countries of the OECD (see figure 19.8). Pupils can use computers to complete tasks within the standard curriculum, such as producing a research project or investigating current events. But few educators see information technology as a medium that can substitute for learning from and interacting with human teachers. The challenge for teachers is learning how to integrate the new information technologies into lessons in a way that is meaningful and educationally sound.

Higher education in an information age

There are large differences between societies in the organization of higher education. In some countries, all universities and colleges are public agencies, receiving their funding directly from government sources. Higher education in France, for instance, is organized nationally, with centralized control being almost as marked as in primary and secondary education. All course structures have to be validated by a national regulatory body responsible to the minister of higher education. Two types of degree can be gained, one awarded by the individual university, the other by the state. National degrees are generally regarded as more prestigious and valuable than those of specific universities, since they are supposed to conform to guaranteed uniform standards. A certain range of occupations in government departments are only open to the holders of national degrees, which are also favoured by most industrial employers. Virtually all teachers in schools, colleges and universities in France are themselves state employees. Rates of pay and the broad framework of teaching duties are fixed centrally.

The United States is distinctive among developed countries in terms of the high proportion of colleges and universities that are in the private sector. Private organizations make up 54 per cent of organizations of higher education in the United States. These include some of the most prestigious universities, such as Harvard, Princeton and Yale. The distinction between public and private in American higher education, however, is not as clear-cut as is the case in other countries. Students at private universities are eligible for public grants and loans,

and these universities receive public research funding. Public universities often possess substantial endowments, and may be given donations by private firms. They also often obtain research grants from private industrial sources.

The British system of higher education is considerably more decentralized than that of France, but more unitary than that of the USA. Universities and colleges are government financed, and teachers at all levels of the educational system have their salaries determined according to national wage scales. Yet there is considerable diversity in the organization of institutions and curricula.

E-universities

Back in 1971, Britain's Open University pioneered the use of television in higher education distance learning. Its programmes were broadcast by the BBC in the early morning and late at night. Students combined these with written materials, work by correspondence, meetings with a personal tutor and summer courses with other students. In this way they could take high-quality degree courses from home – and often while still doing a job. The OU has become the UK's largest university, and increasingly it is adding the Internet to its range, though it remains committed to a mix of encounters with its students. Today many, perhaps most, universities offer some distance learning courses, which depend on the Internet for email communication, course-based chatrooms, online assessment or web-based course materials such as podcasts and online videos.

The Internet now appears to be transforming education in an even more profound way than television did more than three decades ago. This approach was, and is, being pioneered by the University of Phoenix in the United States. Founded in 1989, it is the largest accredited university in the USA. Yet, unlike most large US universities, it cannot boast a grassy campus, a sprawling library, a football team or a student centre. The 68,000 students enrolled at the university meet and interact predominantly across the Internet – the University of Phoenix's 'online campus' – or at one of more than 50 'learning centres' located in large cities throughout North America.

The University of Phoenix offers more than a dozen degree programmes which can be completed entirely online, making students' actual geographical location irrelevant. Online 'group mailboxes' substitute for physical classrooms: rather than making presentations or discussing ideas in person, students post their work in the electronic classroom for other students and the instructor to read. An electronic library is available for students to complete their research and reading assignments. At the start of each week, the course instructor distributes the week's reading list and discussion topics electronically. Students complete the required work according to their own schedules – they can access the 'electronic classroom' at any hour of day or night – and instructors mark assignments and return them to students with comments.

It is not simply the medium of learning that is distinctive at the University of Phoenix. The university only admits students who are over 23 years of age and who are employed at a workplace. Both the structure and the content of the university's offerings are aimed at adult professionals who want new skills and qualifications, but need to complete this continuing education in a way that does not conflict with their busy personal and professional lives. For this reason, courses are taught in intensive five- to eight-week blocks and are run continuously throughout the year, rather than according to an academic calendar.

There is one more important way in which the University of Phoenix is different from traditional universities – it is a for-profit institution owned by a corporation called Apollo Communications. A decade after its creation, the University of Phoenix was making an average profit of US$12.8 million a quarter. A growing number of educational institutions are drawing on private rather than public management. Outside organizations with expertise in management, or in the production and distribution of technology, are becoming involved in the educational system as consultants or administrators.

The flexibility and convenience of Internet-based learning cannot be denied, but the approach is not without its critics. Many argue that there is no substitute for face-to-face learning in a truly interactive environment with other students. Will future generations of learners be little more than networks of anonymous students known only by their online user names? Will skills-oriented, practical studies undermine the importance of abstract reasoning and learning 'for learning's sake'?

Globalization and technological advance have also enabled the creation of a global market in higher education. Although higher education has always had an international dimension – thanks to overseas students, cross-national research projects and international scholarly conferences – radically new opportunities are emerging for collaboration among students, academics and educational institutions scattered round the globe. Through Internet-based learning and the formation of 'e-universities', education and qualifications are becoming more accessible to a global audience. Credentials, certificates and degrees can now be acquired outside the world of physical classrooms and traditional educational establishments. A range of competing institutions and companies – some commercially based – are rapidly entering the global education market. More than ever before, knowledge and learning are 'up for grabs'.

Even conventional universities are taking steps to become 'e-universities' as well – consortia of institutions are sharing their academic resources, research facilities, teaching staff and students online. Universities around the world are acknowledging the benefits of these partnerships with other institutions whose offerings complement their own. As scholarship and technological innovation proliferate, it is impossible for even the most elite institutions to stay on top of advances in all disciplines. Through online partnerships, they can pool their expertise and make it available to students and researchers within the consortium. Students in Brisbane, for example, can access online libraries in San Francisco, email specialized academic staff elsewhere to have questions clarified, and collaborate on research projects.

The future of education

New communication technologies create enormous new possibilities in education. They allow the possibility that formal education can escape the confines of the classroom or lecture hall and reach new students anywhere in the world, regardless of age, gender or class. However, rather than being a liberating and egalitarian force, critics have pointed out that new information and communication technologies may act to reinforce educational inequalities. Information poverty might be added to the material deprivations and inequalities that education can serve to reproduce, and which have been discussed in this chapter. The sheer pace of technological change and the demand of employers for computer-literate workers may mean that those who are technologically competent 'leapfrog' over people who have little experience with computers. This threat of a divide between those who are technologically qualified and those who are not reinforces the importance of lifelong learning to cope with the new challenges of life in the information age.

Some already fear the emergence of a 'computer underclass' within Western soci-

> **THINKING CRITICALLY**
>
> How realistic is the suggestion that formal schooling will give way to a less formal and structured form of lifelong learning? What current evidence is there to support this forecast? Will employers really support the concept of lifelong learning and facilitate it? What benefits could accrue for them if they do?

eties. As the global economy becomes increasingly knowledge-based, there is a real danger that poorer countries will become even more marginalized because of the gap between the information rich and information poor. Similarly, in the developed countries information technology may well increase the gap in performance between the middle and working classes, given the financial investment and space needed for home PC use.

Internet access has, arguably, already become the new line of demarcation between the rich and the poor. Internet users made up less than 4 per cent of the population of Latin America, East Asia, Eastern Europe, the Arab states and sub-Saharan Africa in 2000. In the same year, 54 per cent of the US population were Internet users (UNDP 2001).

IT enthusiasts argue that computers need not result in greater national and global inequalities – that their very strength lies in their ability to draw people together and to open up new opportunities. Schools in Asia and Africa that are lacking textbooks and qualified teachers can benefit from the Internet, it is claimed. Distance learning programmes and collaboration with colleagues overseas could be the key to overcoming poverty and disadvantage. When technology is put in the hands of smart, creative people, they argue, the potential is limitless.

Global Society 19.2 · The lifelong learning environment

New technologies and the rise of the knowledge economy are transforming traditional ideas about work and education. The sheer pace of technological change is creating a much more rapid turnover of jobs than once was the case. As we have seen in this chapter, training and the attainment of qualifications is now occurring throughout people's lives, rather than just once early in life. Mid-career professionals are choosing to update their skills through continuing education programmes and Internet-based learning. Many employers now allow workers to participate in on-the-job training as a way of enhancing loyalty and improving the company skills base.

As societies continue to change, the traditional beliefs and institutions that underpin it are also undergoing transformation. The idea of schooling, as a structured transmission of knowledge within formal institutions for a limited period, is giving way to a broader notion of 'learning' that takes place in a diversity of settings and at different times. The shift from 'education' to 'learning' is not an inconsequential one. Learners are active, curious social actors who can derive insights from a multiplicity of sources, not just within an institutional setting. Emphasis on learning acknowledges that skills and knowledge can be gained through all types of encounters – with friends and neighbours, at seminars and museums, in conversations at the local pub, through the Internet and other media, and so forth.

The shift in emphasis towards lifelong learning can already be seen within schools themselves, where there is a growing number of opportunities for pupils to learn outside the confines of the classroom. The boundaries between schools and the outside world are breaking down, not only via cyberspace, but in the physical world as well. 'Service learning', for example, has become a mainstay of many American secondary schools. As part of their graduation requirements, pupils devote a certain amount of time to volunteer work in the community. Partnerships with local businesses have also become commonplace in many countries, fostering interaction and mentor relationships between adult professionals and pupils.

Continuing professional development (CPD) and lifelong learning can continue over a person's lifetime.

Lifelong learning should play a role in the move towards a knowledge society (Longworth 2003). Not only is it essential to a well-trained, motivated workforce, but learning should also be seen in relation to wider human values. Learning is both a means and an end to the development of a rounded and autonomous self-education in the service of self-development and self-understanding. There is nothing utopian in this idea; indeed, it reflects the humanistic ideals of education developed by educational philosophers. An example already in existence is the 'university of the third age', which provides retired people with the opportunity to educate themselves as they choose, developing whatever interests they care to follow (see the weblink at the end of this chapter).

Conclusion

While new technologies can open important doors for some people, it has to be recognized that there is no such thing as an easy 'techno-fix' for the problems facing education systems across the world. Many developing countries are struggling with high levels of illiteracy and lack telephone lines and electricity. They will need an improved educational infrastructure before they can truly benefit from new technologies that enable distance learning programmes. And, as we have seen throughout this chapter, there is a strong body of evidence which shows that education systems reproduce and reinforce social inequalities based on class, gender and ethnicity. New information and communication technologies may serve to exacerbate these divisions, while also creating new ones. However, if managed properly, they may also offer some exciting, liberating and egalitarian possibilities for education systems around the world.

Is a new 'computer underclass' emerging in poorer countries?

Summary points

1. Education in its modern form, involving the instruction of pupils in specially designated schools, began to emerge with the spread of printed materials and higher levels of literacy. Knowledge could be retained, reproduced and consumed by more people in more places. With industrialization, work became more specialized, and more people acquired abstract knowledge in addition to the practical skills of reading, writing and calculating.

2. Functionalist theories see education as primarily part of the socialization process. Conflict theories, including Marxism, view education as helping to reproduce class inequality through the hidden curriculum, which trains children and young people to accept authority and discipline in readiness for accepting their place in the workforce.

3. Theories of cultural reproduction see schooling as reproducing class-based cultures. Basil Bernstein argued that this is partly achieved through elaborated and restricted language codes, which favoured middle-class children in the school environment. Pierre Bourdieu's more general theory connects the cultural capital that people acquire within families to other forms of capital, such as the symbolic capital of credentials and status, in order to link education systems with the wider social process of social exclusion and the production of inequalities.

4. Social inequalities are evident in education systems, as they are in the wider society, though in much of the developed world, girls are now doing better at all levels of education than boys, which is a dramatic turnaround from the early twentieth century. Inequalities related to ethnic group persist, though some argue that these are closely tied to social class position, with the latter explaining more of the ethnic inequality that exists than 'race'. Racism is a persistent issue within schools and multicultural education is thought to be relatively ineffective unless it is linked to explicit anti-racist initiatives.

5. The 'IQ debate' around inherited intelligence continues to exercise academics, with some arguing that there is a racial basis to intelligence, whilst others criticize the reliance on IQ testing and measurement as ethnocentric and culturally biased. A 'new IQ-ism' seems to be emerging based on the notion of fixed ability rather than intelligence and this has been found amongst schoolteachers.

6. Globally, illiteracy rates have reduced, though some national rates are still increasing. In the developing world, illiteracy in rural areas has a clear gender dimension with the majority of illiterate individuals being women. Education spending worldwide is concentrated in a very few countries and regions, particularly North America and Western Europe.

7. With the move towards a knowledge economy, education will become even more important. As opportunities for unskilled manual workers decrease, the labour market will require workers who are comfortable with new information technology, can acquire new skills and are able to work creatively.

8. Higher education has expanded significantly since the Second World War and many societies now have mass higher education with large student numbers. There is a funding crisis, however and many more students have to make a financial contribution to their higher education.

9. New technologies and the knowledge economy are changing our understandings of education and schooling: formal education is giving way to the notion of lifelong learning. There are growing opportunities for individuals, throughout their lifetimes, to engage in learning activities and training outside the traditional classroom.

10. Information technology is being integrated into educational processes – in the classroom, through the establishment of 'e-universities' and with the expansion of Internet-based learning. There are concerns that those who are not computer literate, or who do not have access to new technology, may suffer from a form of 'information poverty'.

Further reading

To take your reading on the sociology of education further, you could begin with a good introductory text such as Rob Moore's *Education and Society: Issues and Explanations in the Sociology of Education* (Cambridge: Polity, 2004), which provides a comprehensive guide to the field. Amanda Coffey's *Education and Social Change* (Buckingham: Open University Press, 2001) focuses on the challenges facing UK education, but its arguments apply beyond the UK

The sociology of education is a well-established field within the discipline, so consulting one or two edited collections on specific topics is a good idea. To this end you could try Stephen Ball's *The Routledge Falmer Reader in the Sociology of Education* (London: Routledge Falmer, 2003), which contains a very comprehensive range of subjects from

theories to masculinities and inequalities. Alan Sadovnik's *Sociology of Education: A Critical Reader* (London and New York: Routledge, 2007) is a complementary collection which includes many excellent original source readings from Durkheim to Bourdieu.

For more on the transformation of education in the global age, Hugh Lauder, Phillip Brown, Jo-Anne Dillabough and A. H. Halsey's edited *Education, Globalization and Social Change* (Oxford: Oxford University Press, 2006) provides an effective mix of classic and contemporary readings. And if you are interested in the idea and practices of lifelong learning, you could start with Norman Longworth's *Lifelong Learning in Action: Transforming Education in the 21st Century* (London: Routledge Falmer, 2003), which includes both the theory and many real-world examples.

Internet links

Global Campaign for Education, based in South Africa. Lots of useful education resources here:
www.campaignforeducation.org/resources/resources_latest.php

UNESCO Education Homepage:
http://unesco.org/education/

Encyclopaedia of Philosophy of Education – a searchable encyclopaedia:
www.vusst.hr/ENCYCLOPAEDIA/main.htm

21st Century Learning Initiative – UK-based campaign for new ideas on education:
www.21learn.org/

Department for Children, Schools and Families (UK):
www.dfes.gov.uk/

UK Lifelong Learning site:
www.lifelonglearning.co.uk/

The University of the Third Age, UK – 'a self-help organization for people no longer in full time employment providing educational, creative and leisure opportunities in a friendly environment':
www.u3a.org.uk/

20

Work and Economic Life

CHAPTER 20

••

Work and Economic Life

(opposite) Work in a factory environment such as this one is a much less common experience for workers in developed countries today.

Jockey made his first bronze mushroom at five past six on a Monday morning in January 1885. The foreman showed him how: 'Now get thee belly well set up against t'lathe bed,' he said, 'feet planted solid on t'floor, an' rip into 'em.' Jockey ripped into them. The machinery sparked and screeched and a bronze mushroom valve for a steam-driven engine dropped into a box. ''Ow many do I 'ave to do?' Jockey asked innocently. ''Ow many stars in 'eaven?' said the foreman, and walked away.

Jockey was 15 then. The job was a promotion – a step up from making tea and running errands round the factory in Salford, near Manchester. Jockey never did another job for 61 years. After his first few years he joined the trade union.

When he was 25 his feet went through the floorboards below him. The joiner came to fix them. Jockey excused himself: 'I gotta press down yer see – it wears.' 'Don't apologize', said the joiner. 'It's not my bleedin' floor.' The boards broke again in 1907 and then in 1916. In 1918 Jockey had three days off – 'Spanish 'flu', he apologized; 'couldn't 'old my 'ead up' – and he took two more in 1935, when his wife died. During 61 years with the company, he missed five days of work.

When he was 76, shortly after the end of the Second World War and a week after making his millionth valve, the worn out floor collapsed under him once more. 'That's all I was waiting for', he said. He flicked off the lathe and went over to the foreman, a man young enough to be his grandson. 'I'm finishin' up at the weekend, George', he called over the noise of the machinery. The men bought him an armchair when he left: 'An' when you've worn t'seat out o' that,' they said, 'we'll send the joiner to put some boards in!' Late Friday afternoon the foreman introduced him to the new apprentice: 'Just put him in the way of it, will yer?' he asked. Jockey smiled: 'Sithee,' he said to the boy, 'there's not much to it. Get thee belly well set against t'lathe bed now, feet solid on t'floor, an' rip into 'em!'

The nature of work has changed massively since Robert Roberts (1971) described Jockey's working life in his classic, first-hand account of life in a Salford slum during the first quarter of the twentieth century. For most people in the developed countries, Jockey's work life is unrecognizably different from their own. This chapter explores the development of work in modern societies and looks at the structure of modern economies. From here, we examine some recent trends in work. First, however, we must look more closely at what is actually understood when we use the term 'work'.

What is work?

We can define **work**, whether paid or unpaid, as being the carrying out of tasks requiring the expenditure of mental and physical effort, which has as its objective the production of goods and services that cater to human needs. An **occupation**, or job, is work that is done in exchange for a regular wage or salary. In all cultures, work is the basis of the **economy**. The economic system consists of institutions that provide for the production and distribution of goods and services.

> **THINKING CRITICALLY**
>
> Thinking about your own choices, what type of paid work do you do or what type of career are you aiming for? What is attractive about that kind of work? Why do *you* find these aspects attractive? Is your choice of work or career influenced more by its status in the wider society or its intrinsic satisfaction?

We often tend to think of work as equivalent to having a paid job, as the notion of being 'out of work' implies, but in fact this is an oversimplified view. Non-paid labour (such as housework or repairing one's own car) looms large in many people's lives and makes an enormous contribution to the continuation of societies.

Voluntary work, for charities or other organizations, is another form of work, which has an important social role, often filling the gaps ignored by official and commercial goods and services providers and enhancing people's quality of life.

Many types of work just do not conform to orthodox categories of paid employment. Much of the work done in the informal economy, for example, is not recorded in any direct way in the official employment statistics. The term **informal economy** refers to transactions outside the sphere of regular employment, sometimes involving the exchange of cash for services provided, but also often involving the direct exchange of goods or services. Someone who comes round to mend a leaking pipe, for example, may be paid in cash, without any receipt being given or details of the job recorded. People exchange 'cheap' – that is to say, stolen – goods with friends or associates in return for other favours. The informal economy includes not only 'hidden' cash transactions, but also many forms of self-provisioning, which people carry on inside and outside the home. Do-it-yourself activities, domestic machinery and household tools, for instance, provide goods and services which would otherwise have to be purchased (Gershuny and Miles 1983).

If we take a *global* view of the experience of work, then there are large differences between the developed world and developing countries. One major difference is that agriculture remains the main source of employment in most of the developing world, while only a tiny proportion of people work in agriculture in the industrialized countries. In fact, as we will see later in the chapter, the description 'industrialized countries' is fast losing currency as the shift towards service employment continues in these societies. Clearly, the lived experience of paid work is very different in the rural settings of developing countries from the office environments that are typical of the developed world. Similarly, whilst a series of employment laws in developed countries have protected the working hours, health, safety and rights of workers over many years, 'sweatshops', in which people (including many children) work very long hours for very little pay, operate in the less tightly-regulated environments of developing countries (Louie 2001). This global division of labour means that most of the goods they produce so cheaply are sold to the relatively rich workers in the industrialized countries.

See chapter 13, 'Global Inequality', for more on child labour.

Employment patterns are also very different across the world. In most developed countries, the informal economy (sometimes called the 'black economy' or 'parallel economy') is relatively small compared to that of the formal paid employment sector, though many recent migrant workers earn their livings in it. However, this pattern is reversed in the developing countries, where the informal economy thrives on the cheap labour and enforced flexibility of workers. In many developing countries, most people's main experience of work is in the informal sector, which is often seen as the norm (see 'Global Society 20.1'). Though many people rely on such informal work to survive, governments' spending plans are constrained by the consequent loss of tax revenues and, some argue, economic development is therefore made more difficult. Again, not just the experience of work, but what work means for people is potentially very different in different regions of the world.

Having a paid job is important for all the reasons listed above, particularly in the developed world – but the category of 'work' stretches much more widely to include that in the informal economy. Housework, which has traditionally been carried out mostly by women, is usually unpaid, even though it is often very hard and exhausting work. It is worth exploring housework in more detail through Ann Oakley's classic studies of housework (see 'Classic Studies 20.1').

THINKING CRITICALLY

What is your own childhood experience of the gendered domestic division of labour? What memories do you have of parents, aunts and uncles, grandparents and their performance of domestic tasks? Have things changed much with the younger generation? What aspects do you think have seen most change – housework, childcare, paying bills, looking after ill relatives, and so on? Which aspects have been most resistant to change and why do you think that is?

Global Society 20.1 **Nigeria's reliance on an informal economy**

Nigeria 'fuelled' by black economy

Nigeria's economy is estimated to be worth about US$42 billion, making it one of the largest in Africa. But this figure doesn't include much of the country's economic activity, which takes place in the informal economy or the black market. The informal economy is where most Nigerians make their living, as street hawkers, minibus drivers, money-changers or market traders.

The Nigerian government – which has seen its export dollars hit by the falling price of oil – is thought to see many more tax dollars slip through the net in the unregulated black economy. These untaxed and unregulated revenues – by some estimates – account for between 40% and 45% of gross domestic product (GDP).

Job lifeline

Fewer than half of Nigeria's young population have 'proper' jobs and many of these earn their living within the black economy. 'Most of the employment in this country does come from the informal sector', a Nigerian-based analyst told the BBC's World Business Report. 'Most of what keeps people going comes from work that they do in the informal sector.'

Apart from providing people with work, the black economy is usually the only place people can buy goods they need. A Lagos-based banker told the BBC's World Business Report: 'The customers are the everyday person in Nigeria. Supermarkets, shopping malls are really not that widespread, so most people shop in the markets.'

'The informal economy really is the backbone of the Nigerian economy. It is the backbone because most services that Nigerians require to keep things running come from the informal sector', the Nigerian-based analyst added.

Source: BBC News, 3 December 2001
(http://news.bbc.co.uk/1/hi/business/1689165.stm)

Street traders are a commonplace right in Nigeria.

Classic Studies 20.1 Ann Oakley on housework and the housewife role

The research problem

You may think 'work' is exclusively what goes on in the world of business, agriculture and industrial manufacturing. Before the 1970s, sociological studies of work did focus on paid employment in this, the public sphere. But this ignored the domestic sphere and simply assumed that what happened within families was a private matter. However, such ingrained assumptions were thoroughly shaken by second-wave feminism, which challenged the idea that personal life was not relevant to sociologists. But how had such assumptions become so widespread in the first place? What is the relationship between paid work and domestic tasks? Why has the latter been seen as exclusively a female preserve? Ann Oakley explored these issues in two related books published in 1974, *The Sociology of Housework* and *Housewife*.

Oakley's explanation

Oakley (1974b) argued that housework, in its current form in the West, came into existence with the separation of the home from the workplace. With industrialization, 'work' came to take place away from the home and family, and the home became a place of consumption rather than a place for the production of goods. Domestic work then became largely 'invisible', as 'real work' was increasingly defined as that which receives a direct wage; significantly, housework was seen as the 'natural' domain of women, while the realm of 'real work' outside the home was reserved for men. In this conventional model, the domestic division of labour – the way in which responsibilities at home are shared by household members – was quite straightforward. Women (housewives) shouldered most, if not all, of the domestic tasks, while men 'provided' for the family by earning a 'family wage'.

Women often work a 'double shift', at home and in paid employment.

The period of the development of a separate 'home' also saw other changes. Before the inventions and facilities provided by industrialization, work in the household was hard and exacting. The weekly wash, for example, was a heavy and demanding task. The introduction of hot and cold running water into homes eliminated many time-consuming tasks; previously, water had to be carried to the home and heated there, as it still is in much of the developing world. The piping of electricity and gas made coal and wood stoves obsolete, and chores such as the regular chopping of wood, carrying of coal and constant cleaning of the stove were largely eliminated.

Yet, Oakley argues, the average amount of time spent on domestic work by women has not declined markedly, even since the introduction of labour-saving equipment. The amount of time British women not in paid employment spend on housework remained quite constant as homes now had to be cleaned more thoroughly than before. Household appliances eliminated some of the heavier chores, but new tasks were created in their place. Time spent on childcare, stocking up the home with purchases, and meal preparation all increased. This unpaid domestic labour is of enormous significance to the economy. For instance, it has been estimated that housework accounts for between 25 and 40 per cent of the wealth created in the industrialized countries. One UK study of time-use estimated that if housework were paid, it would be worth £700 billion to the economy (ONS 2002a). Oakley argued that such unacknowledged and unrewarded domestic work actually props up the rest of the economy by providing free services on which many of those in paid work depend.

Women's full-time devotion to domestic tasks can also be very isolating, alienating and lacking in intrinsic satisfaction. Housewives in Oakley's study (1974a) found domestic tasks highly monotonous and had difficulty escaping the self-imposed psychological pressure to meet certain standards which they established for their work. Because housework is not paid and brings no direct monetary reward, women gain satisfaction and psychological rewards from meeting standards of cleanliness and order, which feel like externally imposed rules. Unlike male workers though, women cannot leave their 'workplace' at the end of the day.

Forms of paid and unpaid work are closely interrelated, as housework's contribution to the overall economy demonstrates. And though some of the women interviewed said they were 'their own boss' at home, Oakley argued that this was illusory. While men work fixed hours and avoided additional domestic duties, all extra domestic duties, such as caring for sick children, partners or older relatives, means that the working hours of women, who are seen as the 'natural carers' in the home, are increased. This means that men tend to divide work and leisure quite sharply and see extra duties as impinging on their protected leisure time, but for women this makes little sense as they do not experience such a clear division of time. Oakley also saw that paid work brings an income, which in turn creates an unequal power relationship by making housewives dependent on male partners for their own and their family's economic survival.

Critical points

Some critics took issue with Oakley's argument that patriarchy rather than social class was the most significant factor in explaining the gendered division of household labour. Critics argued that this neglected important differences between working-class and middle-class households in relation to decision-making and sharing of resources. Recent social changes have also raised the question of whether working women really do carry a greater 'double burden' than men, having to combine paid work with housework. Gershuny (1992), for example, argues that real changes have occurred which have, to a degree, equalized the amount of work in many households. He found that the amount of housework done by men has been increasing, and if we measure the *total* amount of work (paid and domestic) carried out by men and women, then a real process of equalization is taking place, though society's adaptation to more working women has lagged behind somewhat. Therefore, we can also expect the attitudes of younger generations to change as socialization takes place within more egalitarian family situations. Sullivan's (2000) study of UK time-budget data supports Gershuny's optimistic conclusion. She discovered that, since the late 1950s, women's share of domestic duties had fallen by about one-fifth across all social class groups, and the more women worked in paid employment, the lower was their time-commitment to domestic tasks. What such studies suggest is that perhaps Oakley was too pessimistic about the prospects for change in household gender relations.

Contemporary significance

Ann Oakley's work was immensely influential in the 1970s and '80s when feminist studies were opening up the sociological study of gender and household relations. And despite the legitimate points made by more recent critics, her ideas remain important. Even the work of Gershuny, Sullivan and others have conceded that, although social changes are in train, generally women continue to do more housework than men. This supports Oakley's contention that Western societies have deeply embedded attitudes and assumptions about what constitutes women's 'proper place' within the domestic sphere.

More recently, Crompton et al. (2005) have found that, as global economic pressures increase competition and push firms to demand more commitment from their (mostly male) workers, the process of equalization has 'stalled'. Attitudes towards the domestic division of labour *were* becoming less traditional, but the real *practices* within households had in some countries, including the UK, actually reverted to a more traditional pattern.

Clearly there is more comparative research to be done on the impact of global economic change on the household division of labour, but what Ann Oakley's research did in the 1970s was to convince sociologists that understanding societies and social change must involve an analysis of relations within domestic situations every bit as much as those in the public sphere of work and paid employment.

One of the main questions of interest to sociologists is how the growing involvement of women in the labour market has affected the domestic division of labour. If the quantity of domestic work has not diminished but fewer women are now full-time housewives, it follows that the domestic affairs of households must be arranged rather differently today.

Transforming the social organization of work

One of the most distinctive characteristics of the economic system of modern societies is the existence of a highly complex **division of labour**: work has become divided into an enormous number of different occupations in which people specialize. In traditional societies, non-agricultural work entailed the mastery of a craft. Craft skills were learned through a lengthy period of apprenticeship, and the worker normally carried out all aspects of the production process from beginning to end. For example, a metalworker making a plough would forge the iron, shape it and assemble the implement itself. With the rise of modern industrial production, most traditional crafts have disappeared altogether, replaced by skills that form part of larger-scale production processes. Jockey, whose life story we discussed at the beginning of this chapter, is an example. He spent his whole working career on one highly specialized task; other people in the factory dealt with other specific tasks.

Modern society has also witnessed a shift in the location of work. Before industrialization, most work took place at home and was completed collectively by all the members of the household. Advances in industrial technology, such as machinery operating on electricity and coal, contributed to the separation of work and home. Factories owned by entrepreneurs became the focal points of industrial development: machinery and equipment were concentrated within them and the **mass production** of goods began to eclipse small-scale artisanship based in the home. People seeking jobs in factories, like Jockey, would be trained to perform a specialized task and would receive a wage for this work. Managers, who concerned themselves with implementing techniques for enhancing worker productivity and discipline, oversaw employee performance.

The contrast in the division of labour between traditional and modern societies is truly extraordinary. Even in the largest traditional societies, there usually existed no more than 20 or 30 major craft trades, together with such specialized roles as merchant, soldier and priest. In a modern industrial system, there are literally thousands of distinct occupations. For example, the UK Census lists some 20,000 distinct jobs in the British economy. In traditional communities, most of the population worked on farms and were economically self-sufficient. They produced their own food, clothes and other necessities of life. One of the main features of modern societies, by contrast, is an enormous expansion of **economic interdependence**. We are all dependent on an immense number of other workers – today stretching right across the world – for the products and services that sustain our lives. With few exceptions, the vast majority of people in modern societies do not produce the food they eat, the houses they live in or the material goods they consume.

Early sociologists wrote extensively about the potential consequences of the division of labour – both for individual workers and for society as a whole. Karl Marx was one of the first writers to speculate that the development of modern industry would reduce many people's work to dull, uninteresting tasks. According to Marx, the division of labour alienates human beings from their work. For Marx, **alienation** refers to feelings of indifference or hostility not only to work,

but also to the overall framework of industrial production within a capitalist setting. In traditional societies, he pointed out, work was often exhausting – peasant farmers sometimes had to toil from dawn to dusk. Yet peasants held a real measure of control over their work, which required much knowledge and skill. Many industrial workers, by contrast, have little control over their jobs, only contributing a fraction to the creation of the overall product, and they have no influence over how or to whom it is eventually sold. Marxists would argue that for workers like Jockey, work appears as something alien, a task that must be carried out in order to earn an income but that is intrinsically unsatisfying.

Durkheim had a more optimistic outlook about the division of labour, although he too acknowledged its potentially harmful effects. According to Durkheim, the specialization of roles would strengthen social solidarity within communities. Rather than living as isolated, self-sufficient units, people would be linked together through their mutual dependency. Solidarity would be enhanced through multidirectional relationships of production and consumption. Durkheim saw this arrangement as a highly functional one, although he was also aware that social solidarity could be disrupted if change occurred too rapidly. He referred to this resulting sense of normlessness as anomie.

 You may find it useful to look at the overview of Durkheim and Marx's writings in chapter 1, 'What is Sociology?'

Taylorism and Fordism

Writing some two centuries ago, Adam Smith, one of the founders of modern economics, identified advantages that the division of labour provides in terms of increasing productivity. His most famous work, *The Wealth of Nations* (1776), opens with a description of the division of labour in a pin factory. A person working alone could perhaps make 20 pins per day. By breaking down that worker's task into a number of simple operations, however, ten workers carrying out specialized jobs in collaboration with one another could collectively produce 48,000 pins per day. The rate of production per worker, in other words, is increased from 20 to 4,800 pins, each specialist operator producing 240 times more than when working alone.

More than a century later, these ideas reached their most developed expression in the writings of Frederick Winslow Taylor (1865–1915), an American management consultant. Taylor's approach to what he called 'scientific management' involved the detailed study of industrial processes in order to break them down into simple operations that could be precisely timed and organized. Taylorism, as scientific management came to be called, was not merely an academic study; it was a system of production designed to maximize industrial output, and it had a widespread impact not only on the organization of industrial production and technology, but also on workplace politics. In particular, Taylor's time-and-motion studies wrested control over knowledge of the productions process from the worker and placed such knowledge firmly in the hands of management, eroding the basis on which craft workers maintained autonomy from their employers (Braverman 1974). As such, **Taylorism** has been widely associated with the deskilling and degradation of labour.

The principles of Taylorism were appropriated by the industrialist Henry Ford (1863–1947). Ford designed his first auto plant at Highland Park, Michigan, in 1908 to manufacture only one product – the Model T Ford – involving the introduction of specialized tools and machinery designed for speed, precision and simplicity of operation. One of Ford's most significant innovations was the introduction of the assembly line, said to have been inspired by Chicago slaughterhouses, in which animals were disassembled section by section on a moving line. Each worker on Ford's assembly line was assigned a specialized task, such as fitting the left-side door handles as the car bodies moved along the line. By 1929, when production of the Model T ceased, more than 15 million cars had been produced.

Ford was among the first to realize that mass production requires mass markets. He reasoned that if standardized commodities such as the automobile were to be produced on an ever-greater scale, the presence of consumers who were able to buy those commodities must also be assured. In 1914, Ford took the unprecedented step of unilaterally raising wages at his Dearborn, Michigan, plant to US$5 for an eight-hour day – a very generous wage at the time and one that ensured a working-class lifestyle that included owning such an automobile. As David Harvey remarks: 'The purpose of the five dollar, eight-hour day was only in part to secure worker compliance with the discipline required to work the highly productive assembly-line system. It was coincidentally meant to provide workers with sufficient income to consume the mass-produced products the corporations were about to turn out in ever vaster quantities' (1989: 126). Ford also enlisted the services of a small army of social workers who were sent into the homes of workers in order to educate them in the proper habits of consumption.

Fordism is the name given to designate the system of mass production tied to the cultivation of mass markets. In certain contexts, the term has a more specific meaning, referring to a historical period in the development of post-Second World War capitalism, in which mass production was associated with stability in labour relations and a high degree of unionization. Under Fordism, firms made long-term commitments to workers, and wages were tightly linked to productivity growth. As such, collective bargaining agreements – formal agreements negotiated between firms and unions that specified working conditions such as wages, seniority rights, benefits and so on – closed a virtuous circle that ensured worker consent to automated work regimes and sufficient demand for mass-produced commodities. The system is generally understood to have broken down in the 1970s, giving rise to greater flexibility and insecurity in working conditions.

The reasons for the demise of Fordism are complex and intensely debated. As firms in a variety of industries adopted Fordist production methods, the system encountered certain limitations. At one time, it looked as though Fordism represented the likely future of industrial production as a whole. But this has not proved to be the case. The system can only be applied successfully in those industries, such as car manufacture, that produce standardized products for large markets. To set up mechanized production lines is enormously expensive, and once a Fordist system is established, it is quite rigid; to alter a product, for example, substantial reinvestment is needed. Fordist production is easy to copy if sufficient funding is available to set up the plant. But firms in countries where labour power is expensive find it difficult to compete with those where wages are cheaper. This was one of the factors originally leading to the rise of the Japanese car industry (although Japanese wage levels today are no longer low) and subsequently that of South Korea.

The difficulties with Fordism and Taylorism extend beyond the need for expensive equipment, however. Fordism and Taylorism are what some industrial sociologists call **low-trust systems**. Jobs are set by management and are geared to machines. Those who carry out the work tasks are closely supervised and are allowed little autonomy of action. In order to maintain discipline and high-quality production standards, employees are continuously monitored through various surveillance systems.

> Surveillance within work and other organizations is discussed in chapter 18, 'Organizations and Networks'.

This constant supervision, however, tends to produce the opposite of its intended result: the commitment and morale of workers is often eroded because they have little say in the nature of their jobs or in how they are carried out. In workplaces with many low-trust positions, the level of worker dissatisfaction and absenteeism is high, and industrial conflict is common.

A **high-trust system**, by contrast, is one in which workers are permitted to control the pace, and even the content, of their work, within overall guidelines. Such systems are usually concentrated at the higher levels of industrial organizations. As we shall see, high-trust systems have become more common in many workplaces in recent decades, transforming the very way we think about the organization and execution of work.

Globalization and post-Fordism

In recent decades, flexible practices have been introduced in a number of spheres, including product development, production techniques, management style, the working environment, employee involvement and marketing. Group production, problem-solving teams, multi-tasking and niche marketing are just some of the strategies that have been adopted by companies attempting to restructure themselves to take advantage of the opportunities presented in the global economy. Some commentators have suggested that, taken collectively, these changes represent a radical departure from the principles of Fordism; they contend that we are now operating in a period that can best be understood as **post-Fordism**. The phrase was popularized by Michael Piore and Charles Sabel in *The Second Industrial Divide* (1984), and describes a new era of capitalist economic production in which flexibility and innovation are maximized in order to meet market demands for diverse, customized products.

The idea of post-Fordism is problematic, however. The term is used to refer to a set of overlapping changes that are occurring not only in the realm of work and economic life, but throughout society as a whole. Some writers argue that the tendency towards post-Fordism can be seen in spheres as diverse as party politics, welfare programmes and consumer and lifestyle choices. While observers of contemporary society often point to many of the same changes, there is no consensus about the precise meaning of post-Fordism or, indeed, if this is even the best way of understanding the phenomenon we are witnessing.

Despite the confusion surrounding the term, several distinctive trends within the world of work have emerged in recent decades that seem to represent a clear departure from earlier Fordist practices. These include the decentralization of work into non-hierarchical team groups, the idea of flexible production and mass customization, the spread of global production and the introduction of a more open occupational structure. We shall first consider examples of the first three of these trends, before looking at some criticisms of the post-Fordist thesis.

Group production

Group production – collaborative work groups in place of assembly lines – has sometimes been used in conjunction with automation as a way of reorganizing work. The underlying idea is to increase worker motivation by letting groups of workers collaborate in team production processes rather than requiring each worker to spend the whole day doing a single repetitive task, like inserting the screws in the door handle of a car.

An example of group production is **quality circles** (QCs): groups of between five and twenty workers who meet regularly to study and resolve production problems. Workers who belong to QCs receive extra training, enabling them to contribute technical knowledge to the discussion of production issues. QCs were initiated in the United States, taken up by a number of Japanese companies, and then repopularized in Western economies in the 1980s. They represent a break from the assumptions of Taylorism, since they recognize that workers possess the expertise to contribute towards the definition and method of the tasks they carry out.

The positive effects of group production on workers can include the acquisition of new skills, increased autonomy, reduced managerial supervision and growing pride in the goods and services that they produce. However, studies have identified a number of negative consequences of team production. Although direct managerial authority is less apparent in a team process, other forms of monitoring exist, such as supervision by other team workers. The American sociologist Laurie Graham went to work on the assembly line at the Japanese-owned Subaru-Isuzu car plant based in Indiana, in the USA, and found that peer pressure from other workers to achieve greater productivity was relentless.

 For more on Japanese models of business organization, see chapter 18, 'Organizations and Networks'.

One co-worker told her that after initially being enthusiastic about the team concept, she found that peer supervision was just a new means of management trying to work people 'to death'. Graham (1995) also found that Subaru-Isuzu used the group-production concept as a means of resisting trade unions, their argument being that if management and workers were on the same 'team', then there should be no conflict between the two. In other words, the good 'team player' does not complain. At the Subaru-Isuzu plant that Graham worked in, demands for higher pay or reduced responsibilities were viewed as a lack of employee cooperativeness. Studies like Graham's have led sociologists to conclude that while team-based production processes provide workers with opportunities for less monotonous forms of work, systems of power and control remain the same in the workplace.

Flexible production and mass customization

One of the most important changes in worldwide production processes over the past few years has been the introduction of computer-aided design and *flexible production*. While Taylorism and Fordism were successful at producing mass products (that were all the same) for mass markets, they were unable to produce small orders of goods, let alone goods specifically made for an individual customer. The limited ability of Taylorist and Fordist systems to customize their products is reflected in Henry Ford's famous quip about the first mass-produced car: 'People can have the Model T in any colour – so long as it's black.' Computer-aided designs, coupled to other types of computer-based technology, have altered this situation in a radical way. Stanley Davis speaks of the emergence of 'mass customizing': the new technologies allow the large-scale production of items designed for particular customers. Five thousand shirts might be produced on an assembly line each day. It is now possible to customize every one of the shirts just as quickly as, and at no greater expense than, producing five thousand identical shirts (Davis 1988).

While flexible production has produced benefits for consumers and the economy as a whole, the effect on workers has not been wholly positive. Though workers do learn new skills and have less monotonous jobs, flexible production can create a completely new set of pressures, which result from the need to coordinate the complex production process carefully and to produce the results quickly. Laurie Graham's study of the Subaru-Isuzu factory documented instances when workers were left waiting until the last minute for critical parts in the production process. As a result, employees were forced to work longer and more intensely to keep up with the production schedule, without additional compensation.

Technology such as the Internet can be used to solicit information about individual consumers and then manufacture products to their precise specifications. Enthusiastic proponents argue that **mass customization** offers nothing short of a new Industrial Revolution, a development as momentous as the introduction of mass production techniques in the previous century. Sceptics, however, are quick to point out that, as currently practised, mass customization only creates the illusion of choice – in reality, the options available to the Internet customer are no greater than those offered by a typical mail-order catalogue (Collins 2000).

One of the manufacturers that has taken mass customization the farthest is Dell Computer. Consumers who want to purchase a computer from the manufacturer must go online – the company does not maintain retail outlets – and navigate Dell's website. Customers can select the precise mix of features they desire. After the order is placed, a computer is custom built according to specifications and then shipped – typically within days. In effect, Dell has turned traditional ways of doing business upside down: firms used to build a product first, then worry about selling it; now, mass customizers like Dell sell first and build second. Such a shift has important consequences for industry. The need to hold stocks of parts on hand – a major cost for manufacturers – has been dramatically reduced. In addition, an increasing share of production is outsourced. Thus, the rapid transfer of information between manufacturers and suppliers – also facilitated by Internet technology – is essential to the successful implementation of mass customization.

Global production

Changes in industrial production include not only *how* products are manufactured,

Even when production has become customized, such as in the electronics industry, elements of the production line can still exist.

but also *where* products are manufactured, as we saw with the example of the Barbie doll in chapter 4. For much of the twentieth century, the most important business organizations were large manufacturing firms that controlled both the making of goods and their final sales. Giant automobile companies such as Ford and General Motors in the USA typify this approach. Such companies employ tens of thousands of factory workers, making everything from individual components to the final cars, which are then sold in the manufacturers' showrooms. Such manufacture-dominated production processes are organized as large bureaucracies, often controlled by a single firm.

During the past 20 or 30 years, however, another form of production has become important – one that is controlled by giant retailers. In retailer-dominated production, firms such as the American retailer Wal-Mart – which in 2000 was the world's second largest corporation – buy products from manufacturers, who in turn arrange to have their products made by independently owned factories.

The American sociologists Edna Bonacich and Richard Appelbaum (2000) show that in clothing manufacturing, most manufacturers actually employ no garment workers at all. Instead, they rely on thousands of factories around the world to make their clothing, which they then sell in department stores and other retail outlets. Clothing manufacturers do not own any of these factories and therefore are not responsible for the conditions under which the clothing is made. Two-thirds of all clothing sold in America is made in factories outside the United States, where workers are paid a fraction of US wages. (In China, workers are lucky to make US$40 – just over £20 – a month.) Bonacich and Appelbaum argue that such competition has resulted in a global 'race to the bottom', in which retailers and manufacturers will go to any place on earth where they can pay the lowest wages possible. One result is that much of the clothing we buy today is likely to have been made in sweatshops by young workers – often teenage girls – who get paid mere pennies for making clothing or athletic shoes that sell for tens, if not hundreds, of pounds.

Criticisms of post-Fordism

While acknowledging that transformations are occurring in the world of work, some commentators reject the label 'post-Fordism'. One common criticism is that post-Fordist analysts are exaggerating the extent to which Fordist practices have been abandoned. What we are witnessing is not a wholesale transformation, as advocates of post-Fordism argue, but the integration of some new approaches into traditional Fordist techniques. This argument has been adopted by those who claim we are actually experiencing a period of 'neo-Fordism' – that is, modifications to the traditional Fordist techniques (Wood 1989).

It has been suggested that the idea of a smooth linear transition from Fordist to post-Fordist techniques overstates the true nature of work at both ends. Anna Pollert (1988) has argued that Fordist techniques were never as entrenched as some have suggested. It is also an exaggeration, she contends, that the age of mass production has passed in favour of total flexibility. She points out that mass production techniques still dominate in many industries, especially those that are aimed at consumer markets. According to Pollert, economic production has always been characterized by a diversity of techniques rather than a standard, unified approach.

The changing nature of work and working

The occupational structure across all industrialized countries has changed very substantially since the beginning of the twentieth century. At the start of the twentieth century the labour market was dominated by blue-collar manufacturing jobs, but over time the balance has shifted towards white-collar positions in the service sector. Table 20.1 shows the gradual decline of manufacturing work and the rise of the service sector in the UK since 1981. In 1900, more than three-quarters of the employed population of the UK was in manual (blue-collar) work. Some 28 per cent of these were skilled workers, 35 per cent semi-skilled and 10 per cent unskilled. White-collar and professional jobs were relatively few in number. By the middle of the century, manual workers made up less than two-thirds of the population in paid labour, and non-manual work had expanded correspondingly. Between 1981 and 2006, manufacturing jobs were reduced from 31 per cent to just 17 per cent (male) and 18 per cent to 6 per cent (female).

There is considerable debate over why such changes have occurred, but there seem to be several reasons. One is the continuous introduction of labour-saving machinery, culminating in the spread of information technology in industry in recent years. Another is the rise of manufacturing industry outside the West, particularly in the Far East. The older industries in Western societies have experienced major cutbacks because of their inability to compete with the more efficient Far Eastern producers, whose labour costs are lower.

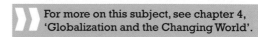
For more on this subject, see chapter 4, 'Globalization and the Changing World'.

The globalizing of economic production, together with the spread of information technology, is altering the nature of the jobs most people do. As discussed in chapter 11,

Table 20.1	UK employee jobs by gender and industry, 1981–2006 (%)							
	Men				Women			
	1981	1991	2001	2006	1981	1991	2001	2006
Distribution, hotels and restaurants	16	19	22	22	26	26	26	26
Banking, finance and Insurance	11	16	20	21	12	16	19	19
Manufacturing	31	25	21	17	18	12	8	6
Public administration, education and health	13	14	14	15	34	36	36	39
Transport and communication	10	10	9	9	2	2	3	3
Construction	9	8	8	8	2	2	1	2
Agriculture and fishing	2	2	1	1	1	1	1	1
Energy and water	4	3	1	1	1	1	–	–
Other services[1]	3	4	5	5	5	5	5	5
All employee jobs (=100%) (millions)	13.1	12.0	13.1	13.5	10.2	11.8	12.9	13.3

[1] Community, social and personal services including sanitation, dry cleaning, personal care, and recreational, cultural and sporting activities.

Source: HMSO Social Trends 37, 2007.

'Stratification and Social Class', the proportion of people working in blue-collar jobs in industrial countries has progressively fallen and one major consequence is a decline in the membership of trades unions.

Trade-unionism in decline?

Although their levels of membership and the extent of their power vary widely, union organizations exist in most countries of the world. Where unions do exist, governments legally recognize the right of workers to withdraw their labour – to 'go on strike' – in pursuit of economic objectives. Why have unions become a basic feature of modern societies? Why does union–management conflict seem to be a more or less ever-present possibility in industrial settings?

In the early development of modern industry, workers in most countries had no political rights and little influence over the conditions of work in which they found themselves. Unions developed as a means of redressing the imbalance of power between workers and employers. Whereas workers had virtually no power as individuals, through collective organization their influence was considerably increased. An employer can do without the labour of any particular worker, but not without that of all or most of the workers in a factory or plant. Unions were originally mainly 'defensive' organizations, providing the means whereby workers could counter the overwhelming power that employers wielded over their lives.

Workers today have voting rights in the political sphere, and there are established forms of negotiation with employers, by means of which economic benefits can be pressed for and grievances expressed.

However, union influence exists primarily in the form of a veto power, both at the level of the local plant and nationally. In other words, using the resources at their disposal, including the right to strike, unions can only block employers' policies or initiatives, not help formulate them in the first place. There are exceptions to this, for instance where unions and employers negotiate periodic contracts covering conditions of work.

The post-Second World War period witnessed a dramatic reversal in the positions of unions in advanced industrial societies. In most developed countries, the period from 1950 to 1980 was a time of steady growth in union density, a statistic that represents the number of union members as a percentage of the number of people who could potentially be union members. In the late 1970s and early '80s over 50 per cent of the British workforce was unionized. High union density was common in Western countries for several reasons. First, strong working-class political parties created favourable conditions for labour organization. Second, bargaining between firms and trade unions was coordinated at the national level rather than occurring in decentralized fashion at sectoral or local levels. Third, unions rather than the state directly administered unemployment insurance, ensuring that workers who lost their jobs did not leave the labour movement. Countries in which some combination but not all three of these factors were present had lower rates of union density, ranging from between two-fifths to two-thirds of the working population.

From a peak in the 1970s, unions began to suffer a decline across the advanced industrial countries. There are several prominent explanations for the difficulties confronted by unions since 1980. Perhaps the most common is the decline of the older manufacturing industries and the rise of the service sector. Traditionally, manufacturing has been a stronghold for labour, whereas jobs in services are more resistant to unionization.

However, this explanation has come under scrutiny. The sociologist Bruce Western (1997) argued that such an explanation cannot account for the experience of the 1970s, which was generally a good period for unions (although not in the United States) and yet was also characterized by a structural shift from manufacturing to services. Similarly, a significant share of growth in service sector employment has occurred in social services – typically public sector union jobs. As such, Western argued that declines in unionization within manufacturing may be more significant than declines across sectors.

Several explanations are consistent with the fall in union density within, as well as between, industries. First, the recession in world economic activity, associated with high levels of unemployment, particularly during the 1980s, weakens the bargaining position of labour. Second, the increasing intensity of international competition, particularly from Far Eastern countries, where wages are often lower than in the West, also weakens unions' bargaining powers. Third, the rise to power in many countries of right-wing governments, such as the British Conservatives in 1979 led to an aggressive assault on unions throughout the 1980s. The unions came out second-best in several major strikes, including the crushing of the National Union of Miners in the UK in 1984–5. Union-protected working conditions and wages have been eroded in several major industries over the past 25 years.

Decline in union membership and influence is a general phenomenon in the industrialized countries and is not to be explained wholly in terms of political pressure applied by right-wing governments against unions. Unions usually become weakened during periods when unemployment is relatively high, as was the case in the UK in the 1980s and 1990s, though union membership for UK employees continues to fall, from 29 per cent in 2005 to 28.4 per cent in 2006 (ONS 2007). Trends

USING YOUR SOCIOLOGICAL IMAGINATION

20.1 Industrial conflict and strikes

There have long been conflicts between workers and those in economic and political authority over them. Riots against conscription and high taxes, and food riots at periods of harvest failure were common in urban areas of Europe in the eighteenth century. These 'pre-modern' forms of labour conflict continued up to not much more than a century ago in some countries. For example, there were food riots in several large Italian towns in 1868 (Geary 1981). Such traditional forms of confrontation were not just sporadic, irrational outbursts of violence: the threat or use of violence had the effect of limiting the price of grain and other essential foodstuffs (Rudé 1964; Booth 1977).

Industrial conflict between workers and employers at first tended to follow these older patterns. In situations of confrontation, workers would quite often leave their places of employment and form crowds in the streets; they would make their grievances known through their unruly behaviour or by engaging in acts of violence against the authorities. Workers in some parts of France in the late nineteenth century would threaten disliked employers with hanging (Holton 1978). Use of the strike as a weapon, today commonly associated with organized bargaining between workers and management, developed only slowly and sporadically.

Strikes

We can define a **strike** as a temporary stoppage of work by a group of employees in order to express a grievance or enforce a demand (Hyman 1984). All the components of this definition are important in separating strikes from other forms of opposition and conflict. A strike is temporary, since workers intend to return to the same job with the same employer; where workers quit altogether, the term strike is not appropriate. As a stoppage of work, a strike is distinguishable from an overtime ban or 'slowdown'. A group of workers has to be involved, because a strike involves *collective action*, not the response of one individual worker. That those involved are employees serves to separate strikes from protests such as may be conducted by tenants or students. Finally, a strike involves seeking to make known a grievance or press a demand; workers who miss work to go to a soccer match could not be said to be on strike.

Strikes represent only one aspect or type of conflict in which workers and management may become involved. Other closely related expressions of organized conflict are lock-outs (where the employers rather than the workers bring about a stoppage of work), output restrictions and clashes in contract negotiations. Less-organized expressions of conflict may include high labour turnover (where employers regularly replace old staff with new), absenteeism and interference with production machinery.

Workers choose to go out on strike for many specific reasons. They may be seeking to gain higher wages, forestall a proposed reduction in their earnings, protest against technological changes that make their work duller or lead to lay-offs, or obtain greater security of employment. However, in all these circumstances the strike is essentially a mechanism of power: a weapon of people who are relatively powerless in the workplace and whose working lives are affected by managerial decisions over which they have little or no control. It is usually a weapon of 'last resort', to be used when other negotiations have failed, because workers on strike either receive no income or depend on union funds, which might be limited.

towards more flexible production tend to diminish the force of unionism, which flourishes more extensively where there are many people working together in large factories. Still, trade unions have worked hard to stabilize their position and remain a significant force in most Western countries. Given the relatively weak power chances of individual workers in relation to powerful employers, the collective strength afforded by trades unions is unlikely to disappear altogether.

THINKING CRITICALLY

Why should strikes be less common amongst 'white-collar' occupational groups than 'blue-collar' industrial workers? In Western 'post-industrial' economies dominated by office work and service employment, are strikes likely to become a thing of the past? What are the implications of such a transformation of work for the Marxist theory of social class revolution? Could workers in the industrializing economies of the developing world fulfil Marx's prediction without the help of those in the developed economies?

Gender and the 'feminization of work'

Fewer people in the developed world now work in factories than they did in the twentieth century. Most of the new jobs have been created in offices and service centres such as supermarkets, call centres and airports and many of these new jobs are being filled by women. This 'feminization of the workforce' is not only a major historical shift in employment patterns that is transforming the experience of paid work, but is also transforming gender relations in every area of society, including education and the domestic sphere. This is why it demands special attention here.

Throughout history, men and women have contributed to producing and reproducing the social world around them, both on a day-to-day basis and over long periods of time. Yet the nature of this partnership and the distribution of responsibilities within it have taken different forms over time. Until recently, paid work in Western countries was predominantly the sphere of men. Over the past few decades, though, this situation has changed radically as more and more women have moved into the labour force in what has been described as the 'feminization' of work (Caraway 2007).

In most regions of the world today, women make up at least half of the workforce (see figures 20.1 and 20.2), though the types of employment they are engaged in differ widely. For example, in the developed regions and the European Union, Central and Eastern Europe and the Commonwealth of Independent States, Latin America as well as in the Middle East and North Africa, women are predominantly employed in the service sector, while in sub-Saharan Africa, where more than 60 per cent of the workforce is female, women work largely in agriculture. The ILO (2007) reports that women also have a higher share of agricultural employment than men in East Asia, South Asia, sub-Saharan Africa and the Middle East and North Africa. Globally, the overwhelming majority of workers are now employed in either services or agriculture with less than one quarter in industrial manufacture. In 2005, for the first time, a higher percentage of the global workforce was employed in services compared to either agriculture or industry (figure 20.1). It seems likely that this trend towards service employment will continue.

It is also the case that the *nature* of women's employment is different from that of men. Reports from the UK suggest that three-quarters of the working female population are engaged in part-time, low-paid work: clerical, cleaning, cashiering and catering and this pattern is repeated in many other developed economies (Women and Equality Unit 2004). In the following sections, we look at the origins and implications of this phenomenon – one of the most important transformations at the present time.

Women and the workplace: the historical view

For the vast majority of the population in pre-industrial societies (and many people in the developing world), productive activities and the activities of the household were not separate. Production was carried on either in the home or nearby, and all

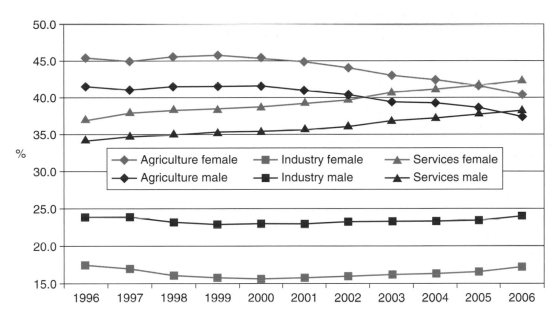

Figure 20.1 Global female and male sectoral shares as a percentage of total employment, 1996–2006

Source: © International Labour Organization, 2007

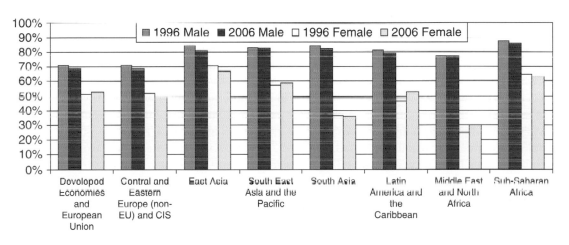

Figure 20.2 The global workforce by gender and region, 1996 and 2006

Source: ILO 2007

members of the family participated in work on the land or in handicrafts. Women often had considerable influence within the household as a result of their importance in economic processes, even if they were excluded from the male realms of politics and warfare. Wives of craftsmen and farm-ers often kept business accounts and widows quite commonly owned and managed businesses.

Much of this changed with the separation of the workplace from the home brought about by the development of modern industry. The movement of production into mechanized factories was probably the largest single factor. Work was done at the machine's pace by individuals hired specifically for the tasks in question, so employers gradually began to contract workers as individuals rather than families. With time and the progress of industrialization, an increasing division was established between home and workplace. The idea of separate spheres – public and private – became entrenched in popular attitudes. Men, by merit of their employment outside the home, spent more time in the public realm and became more involved in local affairs, politics and the market. Women came to be associated with 'domestic' values and were responsible for tasks such as childcare, maintaining the home and preparing food for the family. The idea that 'a woman's place is in the home' had different implications for women at varying levels in society. Affluent women enjoyed the services of maids, nurses and domestic servants. The burdens were harshest for poorer women, who had to cope with the household chores as well as engaging in industrial work to supplement their husband's income.

Rates of employment of women outside the home, for all classes, were quite low until well into the twentieth century. Even as late as 1910, in Britain, more than a third of gainfully employed women were maids or house servants. The female labour force consisted mainly of young single women, whose wages, when they worked in factories or offices, were often sent by their employers direct to their parents. Once married, they generally withdrew from the labour force and concentrated on family obligations.

The growth in women's economic activity

Women's participation in the paid labour force has risen more or less continuously over the last century. One major influence was the labour shortage experienced during the First World War. During the war years, women carried out many jobs previously regarded as the exclusive province of men. On returning from the war, men again took over most of those jobs, but the pre-established pattern had been broken.

In the years since the Second World War, the gender division of labour has changed dramatically. The UK employment rate – that is, the proportion of working-age people who are in employment – rose from 56 per cent to 70 per cent for women between 1971 and 2006. In contrast, the UK employment rate for men fell from 92 per cent to 79 per cent in the same period. Thus the gap between men and women's employment rates narrowed significantly from 35 per cent in 1971 to just 9 per cent in 2006 (see figure 20.3). This narrowing of the gender gap looks likely to continue in the years to come, though much of the increase in women's economic activity has been the result of a growth in part-time work.

There are a number of reasons why the gap in economic activity rates between men and women have been closing in recent decades. First, there have been changes in the scope and nature of the tasks that have traditionally been associated with women and the 'domestic sphere'. As the birth rate has declined and the average age of childbirth has increased, many women now take on paid work before having children and return to work afterwards. Smaller families have meant that the time many women previously spent at home caring for young children has been reduced. The mechanization of many domestic tasks has also helped to cut down the amount of time that needs to be spent to maintain the home. Automatic dishwashers, vacuum cleaners and washing machines have made the domestic workload less labour-intensive. There is also evidence that the domestic division of labour between men and women is being steadily eroded over time, although women certainly still carry out more domestic tasks than men.

There are also financial reasons why a growing number of women have entered the labour market. The traditional nuclear family model – composed of a male bread-

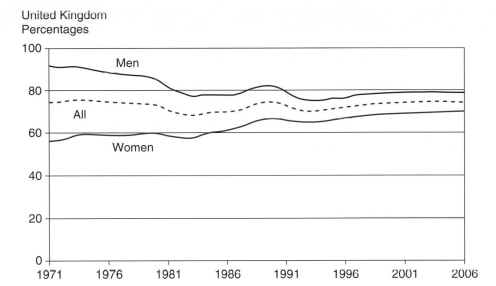

United Kingdom
Percentages

Figure 20.3   UK Employment rates by gender, 1971–2006

Source: HMSO Social Trends 37, 2007

winner, female housewife and dependent children – now accounts for only a quarter of families in Britain. Economic pressures on the household, including a rise in male unemployment, have led more women to seek paid work. Many households find that two incomes are required in order to sustain a desired lifestyle. Other changes in household structure, including high rates of singlehood and childlessness as well as a growth in lone-mother households, has meant that women outside traditional families have also been entering the labour market – either out of choice or necessity. Additionally, recent efforts to reform welfare policies, both in Britain and the United States, have aimed to support women – including lone mothers and married women with small children – in entering paid work.

Finally, it is important to note that many women have chosen to enter the labour market out of a desire for personal fulfilment and in response to the drive for equality propelled forward by the women's movement of the 1960s and '70s. Having gained legal equality with men, many women have seized on opportunities to realize these rights in their own lives. As we have already noted, work is central in contemporary society and employment is almost always a prerequisite for living an independent life. In recent decades women have made great strides towards parity with men and increasing economic activity has been central to this process (Crompton 1997).

Gender and inequalities at work

Despite possessing formal equality with men, women still experience a number of inequalities in the labour market. In this section we will look at three of the main inequalities for women at work: occupational segregation, concentration in part-time employment and the wage gap.

Occupational segregation

Women workers have traditionally been concentrated in poorly paid, routine occupations. Many of these jobs are highly gendered – that is, they are commonly seen as 'women's work'. Secretarial and caring jobs (such as nursing, social work and child care) are overwhelmingly held by women

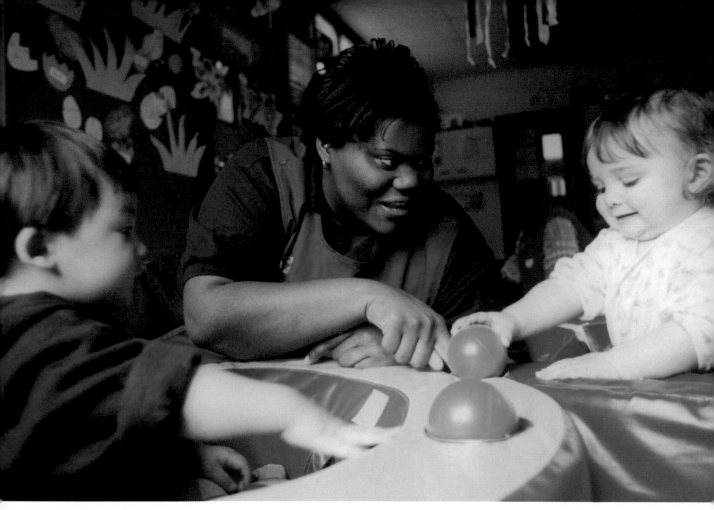

Occupations dominated by women tend to be the lowest paid.

and are generally regarded as 'feminine' occupations. Occupational gender segregation refers to the fact that men and women are concentrated in different types of jobs, based on prevailing understandings of what is appropriate 'male' and 'female' work.

Occupational segregation has both vertical and horizontal components. Vertical segregation refers to the tendency for women to be concentrated in jobs with little authority and room for advancement, while men occupy more powerful and influential positions. Horizontal segregation refers to the tendency for men and women to occupy different categories of job. For example, women largely dominate in domestic and routine clerical positions, while men are clustered in semi-skilled and skilled manual positions. Horizontal segregation can be pronounced. More than 50 per cent of women's employment (compared to 17 per cent of men's) in the UK in 1991 fell into four occupational categories: clerical, secretarial, personal services and 'other elementary'

THINKING CRITICALLY

Do you think there are any 'natural' barriers to women entering the male dominated occupations above in larger numbers? What other factors could account for the dominance of men in higher paid occupations as plumbers, car mechanics, police officers and others? What would you predict might happen to pay rates and male participation if women did start to enter such occupations? What conclusions do you draw from your answers about the underlying reasons for gender divisions in occupations?

USING YOUR SOCIOLOGICAL IMAGINATION

20.2 'The 5 deadly Cs'

Jobs traditionally done by women are poorly paid and undervalued. Low-paid jobs dominated by women are found in each of the five 'Cs' – cleaning, catering, caring, cashiering and clerical work. It is the concentration of women in these roles that particularly contributes to their poor rewards. Sometimes women are doing jobs they love, but almost certainly they are low-paid. Historically described as working for 'pin money', one could also describe them as 'labourers of love' doing tasks 'naturally' associated with women, because of what is regarded as their 'innate' attributes rather than their skills. As a result this undervaluation of women's work is often not taken seriously, so women in these roles have been largely overlooked by policy makers.

Source: UK Equal Opportunity Commission 2007

What do they earn?

Average hourly earnings of full-time employees, UK, 2006

Occupation	£ per hour
Car mechanics	9.27
Childminders	7.64
Care assistants & home carers	7.61
Plumbers	11.51
Medical secretaries	9.78
Nurses	13.44
Police officers	15.91

Source: ONS 2006, Annual survey of hours and earnings 2006

(Crompton 1997). In 1998, 26 per cent of women were in routine white-collar work, compared with only 8 per cent of men, while 17 per cent of men were in skilled manual work, compared with only 2 per cent of women (HMSO 1999).

Changes in the organization of employment as well as sex-role stereotyping have contributed to occupational segregation. Alterations in the prestige and the work tasks of 'clerks' provide a good example. In 1850, 99 per cent of clerks in the UK were men. To be a clerk was often to have a responsible position, involving knowledge of accountancy skills and sometimes carrying managerial responsibilities. Even the lowliest clerk had a certain status in the outside world.

The twentieth century has seen a general mechanization of office work (starting with the introduction of the typewriter in the late nineteenth century), accompanied by a marked downgrading of the skills and status of 'clerk' – together with another related occupation, that of 'secretary' – into a low-status, low-paid occupation. Women came to fill these occupations as the pay and prestige associated with them declined and by 1998 nearly 90 per cent of clerical workers and 98 per cent of all secretaries in the UK were women. However, the proportion of people working as secretaries has fallen over the past two decades. Computers have replaced typewriters and many managers now do much of their letter-writing and other tasks directly onto the computer.

Part-time work and the 'wage gap'

Although increasing numbers of women now work full time outside the home, a large number are concentrated in part-time employment. In recent decades, opportunities for part-time work have grown enormously, partly as a result of labour market reforms to encourage flexible employment policies and partly due to the expansion of the service sector (Crompton 1997).

Part-time jobs are seen as offering much greater flexibility for employees than full-time work. For this reason they are often favoured by women who are attempting to balance work and family obligations. In many cases this can be done successfully, and women who might otherwise forgo employment become economically active. Yet part-time work carries certain disadvantages, such as low pay, job insecurity and limited opportunities for advancement. Part-time work is attractive to many women and much of the growth in women's economic activity in the post-war period can be attributed to this.

Some scholars have argued that there are different 'types' of women – those who are committed to work outside the home and those who are uncommitted to work, viewing the traditional sexual division of labour as unobjectionable (Hakim 1996). According to such an approach, many women happily choose to work part time in order to fulfil traditional domestic obligations. However, there is an important sense in which women have little choice. Men, by and large, do not assume prime responsibility for the rearing of children. Women who have that responsibility as well as other domestic duties, but still want, or need, to work in paid jobs, inevitably find part-time work a more feasible option.

The average pay of employed women in Britain, as elsewhere, is well below that of men, although the difference has narrowed somewhat over the past 30 years. In 1970 women in full-time employment earned 63 pence for every pound earned by a man working full-time; by 1999 it had risen to 84 pence. Among women working part-time, the gap reduced from 51 pence to 58 pence over the same period of time. This general tendency towards closing the 'wage gap' has rightly been seen as a significant step in the move towards equality with men.

Several processes have affected these trends. One significant factor is that more women are moving into higher-paying professional positions than was earlier the case. Young women with good qualifications are now as likely as their male counterparts to land lucrative jobs. Girls are regularly outperforming boys at school, and in many university subjects women now outnumber men. The improved educational qualifications of women seems to lead inexorably towards more women finding their way into the professions looking for a long career that will include promotion to the higher levels. Yet this progress at the top of the occupational structure is offset by the enormous increase in the number of women in low-paid part-time jobs within the rapidly expanding service sector.

Occupational segregation by gender is one of the main factors in the persistence of a wage gap between men and women. Women are over-represented in the more poorly paid job sectors: more than 45 per cent of women earn less than £100 pounds per week, compared to just over 20 per cent of men. Despite some gains, women also remain under-represented at the top of the income distribution: 10 per cent of men earn more than £500 per week, compared to only 2 per cent of women (Rake 2000).

The introduction of a national minimum wage in 1999 (in 2007 this was £5.35 per hour for workers over the age of 22) also helped to narrow the pay gap between men and women, since many women are concentrated in occupations such as hairdressing and waitressing, which for a long time have paid below the level at which the minimum wage was set. It was estimated that nearly 2 million people enjoyed a pay raise of approximately 30 per cent after the minimum wage was first introduced. Regular rises to the minimum wage since its introduction have further benefited women in low-paid jobs. The benefits of the minimum wage, however, do not negate the fact that a large proportion of women still work in jobs which pay at or slightly above the minimum wage, and there are still many men and women who are employed (illegally) to work for less than the minimum wage – earnings on which it is exceedingly difficult to live, especially with dependent children.

One manifestation of this is the fact that a substantial proportion of women in the UK live in poverty. This is particularly true of women who are heads of households. The percentage of women among the poor has risen steadily in recent years. Poverty tends to be especially acute for women with very small children who need constant care. There is a vicious circle here: a woman who can obtain a reasonably well-paid job may be financially crippled by having to pay for childcare, yet if she starts working part time, her earnings drop, whatever career prospects she may have had disappear, and she also loses other economic benefits – such as pension rights – which full-time workers receive.

For more on women in poverty in the UK, see chapter 12, 'Poverty, Social Exclusion and Welfare'.

Taken over a woman's lifetime, the wage gap produces striking differences in overall earnings. One UK study carried out in the 1990s (Rake 2000) found that a mid-skilled woman, for example, would experience a 'female forfeit' of more than £240,000 over her lifetime. The female forfeit refers to how much less a woman will earn over a lifetime than a man with similar qualifications, even if she has no children. Rake showed that the amount a woman will earn varies with her qualifications. For example, a childless women with no qualifications was expected to earn £518,000 during her working life; a graduate could expect to earn more than double that amount – her 'female forfeit'

would be relatively low and she would not suffer the 'mother gap', the gap between the earnings of a woman with no children and a woman with children. In 2006, the UK Office for National Statistics released figures showing that the gender pay gap remained at 17.2 per cent. This means that the average woman working full-time will lose out on some £330,000 over the course of a working life. The EOC (2007) points out that such a loss of earnings is the equivalent of any one of the following:

- 19 house down-payments (deposits);
- paying off a student debt 21 times over;
- 29 years of childcare;
- 15 new cars;
- 525 extra holidays;
- 10,500 nights out – including dinner and drinks – with friends.

Being on the wrong side of the gender pay gap has serious consequences for people's quality of life and long-term life chances.

Gender inequality in the workplace is discussed further in chapter 18, 'Organizations and Networks'.

Changes in the domestic division of labour

One of the results of more women entering paid work is that certain traditional family patterns are being renegotiated. The 'male breadwinner' model has become the exception rather than the rule, and women's growing economic independence has meant that they are better placed to move out of gendered roles at home if they choose to do so. Both in terms of housework and financial decision-making, women's traditional domestic roles are undergoing significant changes. There appears to be a move towards more egalitarian relationships in many households, although women continue to shoulder the main responsibility for most housework. The exception to this seems to be small household repairs,

which men are more likely to carry out. Surveys have found that women still spend nearly 3 hours a day on average on housework (excluding shopping and child care). This compares with the 1 hour 40 minutes spent by men (ONS 2003c).

Married women employed outside the home do less domestic work than others, although they almost always bear the main responsibility for care of the home. The pattern of their activities is of course rather different. They do more housework in the early evenings and for longer hours at weekends than do those who are full-time housewives.

> This issue is examined in more detail in chapter 9, 'Families and Intimate Relationships'.

There is evidence that even this pattern may be changing, however. Men are contributing more to domestic work than they have in the past, although scholars who have investigated the phenomenon argue that the process is one of 'lagged adaptation' (Gershuny 1994). By this, it is meant that the renegotiation of domestic tasks between men and women is proceeding more slowly than women's entry into the labour market. Research has found that the division of labour within households varies according to factors such as class and the amount of time the woman spends in paid work. Couples from higher social classes tend to have a more egalitarian division of labour, as do households in which the woman is working full time. On the whole, men are taking on a greater amount of responsibility around the home, but the burden is still not equally shared.

A survey conducted by Warde and Heatherington (1993) in Manchester revealed that the domestic division of labour was more egalitarian among young couples than among those of older generations. The authors concluded that over time, gender stereotypes are loosening. Young people who were raised in households with parents who attempted to share domestic tasks were more likely to implement such practices in their own lives.

Vogler and Pahl (1994) examined a different aspect of the domestic division of labour – that of household financial 'management' systems. Their study sought to understand whether women's access to money and to control over spending decisions had become more egalitarian with the increase in female employment. Through interviews with couples in six different British communities, they found the distribution of financial resources to be, on the whole, done more fairly than in the past, but that it remained interlinked with class issues. Among higher income couples, 'pooled' finances tended to be managed jointly and there was a greater degree of equality in accessing money and making spending decisions. The more a woman contributes to the household financially, the greater the level of control she exercises over financial decisions.

In families with lower income, women were often responsible for the day-to-day management of household finances, but were not necessarily in charge of strategic decisions about budgeting and spending. In these cases, Vogler and Pahl noted a tendency for women to protect their husbands' access to spending money while depriving themselves of the same right. In other words, there appeared to be a disjunction between women's everyday control over finances and their access to money.

Automation and the 'skills' debate

The relationship between technology and work has long been of interest to sociologists. How is our experience of work affected by the type of technology that is involved? As industrialization has progressed, technology has assumed an ever-greater role at the workplace – from factory automation to the computerization of office work. The current information technology revolution has attracted renewed interest in this question. Technology can lead to greater efficiency and productivity, but how does it affect the way work is experienced by those who carry it out? For sociologists, one of the main questions is how the move to more complex systems influences the nature of work and the institutions in which it is performed.

The concept of automation, or programmable machinery, was introduced in the mid-1800s, when Christopher Spencer, an American, invented the Automat, a programmable lathe that made screws, nuts and gears. Automation has thus far affected relatively few industries, but with advances in the design of industrial robots, its impact is certain to become greater. A robot is an automatic device that can perform functions ordinarily done by human workers. The term 'robot' comes from the Czech word *robota*, or serf, popularized about 50 years ago by the playwright Karel Čapek.

The majority of the robots used in industry worldwide are to be found in automobile manufacture, though the electronics industries for CD/DVD players, iPods, mobile phones and so on, are also heavily 'robotized'. The usefulness of robots in production thus far is relatively limited, because their capacity to recognize different objects and manipulate awkward shapes is still at quite a rudimentary level. Yet it is certain that automated production will spread rapidly in coming years; robots are becoming more sophisticated, while their costs are decreasing. The spread of automation provoked a heated debate among sociologists and experts in industrial relations over the impact of the new technology on workers, their skills and their level of commitment to their work.

In his influential book, *Alienation and Freedom* (1964), Robert Blauner examined the experience of workers in four different industries with varying levels of technology. Using the ideas of Durkheim and Marx, Blauner operationalized the concept of

Classic Studies 20.2 | **Harry Braverman on the degradation of work in capitalist economies**

The research problem

Blauner's (1964) exploration of workers' *experience* of alienation had argued that increasing automation could help to reduce such feelings. But can technology really have such an influence on the labour process? Why are some technologies more widely adopted than others in the production process? Blauner's academic sociological approach was rejected by the American Marxist writer Harry Braverman, in his famous book *Labor and Monopoly Capital* (1974), which set out a very different evaluation of automation and Fordist methods of production and management, which he saw as part of a general **deskilling** of the workforce.

Braverman's explanation

Braverman did not come to the study of capitalist production as a sociologist. He had been (amongst other things) an apprentice coppersmith, pipe-fitter, sheet-metal worker and office worker, and had become a socialist in his teenage years, later helping to found the Socialist Union, a splinter group from the American Socialist Workers Party. Hence, he approached the problem of technology, automation and human skills having experienced at first hand some of the effects of technological change. This highly involved and committed perspective comes through clearly in Braverman's account.

Drawing on Marx's theory of alienation, Braverman argued that far from improving the lot of workers, automation, combined with Taylorist management methods, actually intensified workers' estrangement from the production process and 'deskilled' the industrial labour force. By imposing Taylorist organizational techniques and breaking up the labour process into specialized tasks, managers were able to exert more control over the workforce. In both industrial settings and modern offices, the introduction of new technology contributed to this overall degradation of work by limiting the need for creative human input. Instead, all that was required was an unthinking, unreflective body capable of endlessly carrying out the same unskilled task.

Braverman rejected the idea that technologies were somehow 'neutral' or inevitable. Instead, he argued that they are developed and introduced to serve the needs of capitalists. Similarly, he did not see any point in blaming machines or technologies themselves for worker alienation; the problem lay in the social class divisions which determined how such machinery was used. In particular, Braverman argued that since the late nineteenth century, an era of 'monopoly capitalism' had developed. As smaller firms were swallowed up or put out of business by larger and larger companies, these new monopolistic businesses were able to afford a whole tier of technicians, scientists and managers whose task was to find better, more effective ways of controlling workers – scientific management or Taylorism discussed above is a good example.

Some industrial sociologists had seen technological development and automated processes as leading to the need for a better educated, better trained and more involved workforce, something that remains a commonsense assumption of modern politics today. Braverman disagreed. In fact, he argued that exactly the reverse was true. While 'average skill levels' may well be higher than in previous times, like all averages, this conceals the fact that workers have actually been largely deskilled. As he caustically put it, 'to then say that the ''average'' skill has been raised is to adopt the logic of the statistician who, with one foot in the fire and the other in ice water, will tell you that ''on the average'', he is perfectly comfortable (1974: 424).

Paradoxically, the more that scientific knowledge becomes embedded into the labour process, the less the workers need to know and the less they understand about the machinery and the process itself. Instead, an increasing divide emerges as the control by managers of workers intensifies. Braverman saw monopoly capitalism as a stronger form of capitalism that would be much more difficult to overthrow.

Critical points

Several objections have been raised to Braverman's thesis. First, he overstates the spread of Taylorism, assuming that it will become the dominant form of management. Industrial sociologists have argued that it never did become fully implemented widely, which leaves Braverman arguing against something of a 'straw man'. Second, some feminists have argued that the thesis is really focused on male workers and largely fails to explain the particular nature of women's oppression. Others suggest that he does not provide an adequate account of changing family structures and their impact on working life. Finally, it may be argued that Braverman's thesis of deskilling tends to romanticize earlier, especially craft-based, forms of production, which are then contrasted with modern mass manufacture. Such a view could be said to be ahistorical – not properly taking into account historical development.

influenced many later sociologists working in this field. The book was also a popular success, selling some 125,000 copies by the year 2000. However, arguably Braverman's main aim was to contribute to the renewal of Marxist theory itself, which he thought had failed to adapt to the radically different form of capitalism that had developed in the twentieth century. And though some Marxists have criticized his thesis as too pessimistic, failing to leave enough room for workers to effectively resist monopolistic capitalism, it could be argued that the decreasing number of workers joining trades unions along with the widespread introduction of information technology into workplaces and the wider society, show that his central argument retains much of its force in the twenty-first century.

Contemporary significance

Braverman's thesis had a major impact. It challenged the dominant functionalist perspectives within industrial sociology and

> Strong echoes of Braverman's deskilling thesis can be heard in George Ritzer's account of low-skill 'McJobs', discussed in chapter 18, 'Organizations and Networks'.

alienation and measured the extent to which workers in each industry experienced it in the form of powerlessness, meaninglessness, isolation and self-estrangement. He concluded that workers on assembly lines were the most alienated of all, but that levels of alienation were somewhat lower at workplaces using automation. In other words, Blauner argued that the introduction of automation to factories was responsible for reversing the otherwise steady trend towards increased worker alienation. Automation helped to integrate the workforce and gave workers a sense of control over their work that had been lacking with other forms of technology.

The American sociologist, Richard Sennett (1998), studied the people who worked in a bakery that had been bought by a large food conglomerate and automated with the introduction of high-tech machinery. Computerized baking radically altered the way that bread was made. Instead of using their hands to mix the ingredients and

knead the dough, and their noses and eyes to judge when the bread was baked, the bakery's workers had no physical contact with the materials or the loaves of bread. In fact, the entire process was controlled and monitored via computer screen. Computers decided the temperature and baking time of the ovens. While at times the machines produced excellent-quality bread, at other times the results were burnt, blackened loaves. The workers at this bakery (it would be erroneous to call them bakers) were hired because they were skilled with computers, not because they knew how to bake bread. Ironically, these workers used very few of their computer skills. The production process involved little more than pushing buttons on a computer. In fact, when at one point the computerized machinery broke down, the entire production process was halted because none of the bakery's 'skilled' workers was trained or empowered to repair the problem. The workers whom Sennett observed wanted to

Global Society 20.2 | **The impact of information technology**

The opposing perspectives of Blauner and Braverman, discussed above, on the effects of automation are echoed today in debates over the impact of information technology (IT) in the workplace. Certainly there is little question that the Internet, email, teleconferencing and e-commerce are changing the way in which companies do business. But they are also affecting the way in which employees work on a daily basis. Those who take an optimistic approach, as Blauner did, argue that information technology will revolutionize the world of work by allowing new, more flexible ways of working to emerge. These opportunities will permit us to move beyond the routine and alienating aspects of industrial work into a more liberating informational age, giving workers greater control over and input into the work process. Enthusiastic advocates of technological advances are sometimes referred to as 'technological determinists', because they believe in the power of technology to determine the nature and shape of work itself.

Others are not convinced that information technology will bring about an entirely positive transformation of work. As Shoshana Zuboff (1988) concluded in her research into the use of IT in firms, management can choose to use IT towards very different ends. When embraced as a creative, decentralizing force, information technology can help to break down rigid hierarchies, engage more employees in decision-making and involve workers more closely in the day-to-day affairs of the company. On the other hand, it can just as easily be used as a way to strengthen hierarchies and surveillance practices. The adoption of IT in the workplace can cut down on face-to-face interactions, block channels of accountability and transform an office into a network of self-contained and isolated modules. Such an approach sees the impact of information technology as influenced by the uses to which it is put and the way in which those using the technology understand its role.

The spread of information technology will certainly produce exciting and heightened

Is Blauner right? Do these workers experience less alienation than those working on mass production lines in industrial factories?

opportunities for some segments of the labour force. In the fields of media, advertising and design, for example, IT both enhances creativity in the professional realm and introduces flexibility into personal work styles. It is well-qualified, valued employees in responsible positions for whom the vision of wired workers and telecommuting comes closest to being realized. Yet at the other end of the spectrum are thousands of low-paid unskilled individuals working in call centres and data-entry companies. These positions, which are largely a product of the telecommunications explosion in recent years, are characterized by degrees of isolation and alienation that rival those of Braverman's deskilled workers. Employees at call centres that process travel bookings and financial transactions work according to strictly standardized formats where there is little or no room for employee discretion or creative input. Employees are closely monitored and their interactions with customers are tape-recorded for 'quality assurance'. The information revolution also seems to have produced a large number of routine, unskilled jobs on a par with those of the industrial economy.

be helpful, to make things work again, but they could not, because automation had diminished their autonomy. The introduction of computerized technology in the workplace has led to a general increase in all workers' skills, but has also led to a bifurcated workforce composed of a small group of highly skilled professionals with a high degree of flexibility and autonomy in their jobs and a larger group of clerical, service and production workers who lack autonomy in their jobs.

> ### THINKING CRITICALLY
>
> Call-centre workers in developing countries – such as in New Delhi, India, depicted opposite – tend to be young, single and relatively well paid. Are they becoming more skilled or deskilled? To what extent does your evaluation depend on the *social context* within which information technology is introduced? How do call centres in the developed countries differ from this one?

The skills debate is very difficult to resolve, however. Both the conceptualization and measurement of skill are problematic. As feminist researchers have argued, what constitutes 'skill' is socially constructed (Steinberg 1990). As such, conventional understandings of 'skilled' work tend to reflect the social status of the typical incumbent of the job, rather than the difficulty of the task in an objective sense. The history of occupations is rife with examples of jobs in which the very same task was assigned a different skill level (and even renamed) once women entered the field (Reskin and Roos 1990). The same, of course, holds for other low-status workers, such as racial minorities. Even where gender and racial biases are not in operation, skill has multiple dimensions; the same job may be downgraded on one dimension while simultaneously upgraded on another (Block 1990). Thus, opinions as to whether automation has deskilled work depend on which dimension of skill is examined. In his comprehensive review of the skill debate, Spenner (1983) notes that studies that have examined skill in terms of the substantive complexity of tasks have tended to support the 'upskilling' position, whereas those that have examined skill in terms of the autonomy and/or control exercised by the worker have tended to find that work has in fact been 'deskilled' through automation (Zuboff 1988; Vallas and Beck 1996).

 Economic growth and development are discussed in chapter 12, 'Poverty, Social Exclusion and Welfare'.

The knowledge economy

Some observers have suggested that what is occurring today is a transition to a new type of society that is no longer based primarily on industrialism. We are entering, they claim, a phase of development beyond the industrial era altogether. A variety of terms have been coined to describe this new social order, such as the post-industrial society, the information age and the new economy. The term that has come into most common usage, however, is the **knowledge economy**.

A precise definition of the knowledge economy is difficult to formulate, but in general terms, it refers to an economy in which ideas, information and forms of knowledge underpin innovation and economic growth. A knowledge economy is one in which much of the workforce is involved not in the physical production or distribution of material goods, but in their design, development, technology, marketing, sale and servicing. These employees can be termed knowledge workers. The knowledge economy is dominated by the constant flow of information and opinions, and by the powerful potentials of science and technology. As Charles Leadbeater has observed:

> Most of us [knowledge workers] make our money from thin air: we produce nothing that can be weighed, touched or easily measured. Our output is not stockpiled at harbours, stored in warehouses or shipped in railway cars. Most of us earn our livings providing service, judgement, information and analysis, whether in a telephone call centre, a lawyer's office, a government department or a scientific laboratory. We are all in the thin-air business. (1999: vii)

How widespread is the knowledge economy at the start of the twenty-first century? A 1999 study by the Organization for Economic Cooperation and Development (OECD) attempted to gauge the extent of the knowledge economy among developed nations by measuring the percentage of each country's overall business output that can be attributed to knowledge-based industries. Knowledge-based industries are understood broadly to include high technology, education and training, research and development, and the financial and investment sector. Among OECD countries as a whole, knowledge-based industries accounted for more than half of all business output in the mid-1990s. Western Germany had a high figure of 58.6 per cent, and the United States, Japan, Britain, Sweden and France were all over 50 per cent. In 2006, The Work Foundation produced a report for the EU, which assessed data from 2005. The authors found that over 40 per cent of European Union workers were employed in the knowledge-based industries, with Sweden, Denmark, the UK and Finland leading the way (see table 20.2). Education and health services constituted the largest group with recreational and cultural services next; together these sectors employed almost 20 per cent of European Union workers. Market-based sectors including financial services, business and communication services accounted for a further 15 per cent.

Investments into the knowledge economy – in the form of public education, spending on software development, and research and development – now comprise a significant part of many countries' budgets. Admittedly, the knowledge economy remains a difficult phenomenon to investigate – both quantitatively and qualitatively. It is easier to measure the value of physical things than 'weightless' ideas, research and knowledge. Yet it is undeniable that the generation and application of knowledge is becoming increasingly central to modern economic life.

Multi-skilling

One of the arguments of post-Fordist commentators is that new forms of work allow employees to increase the breadth of their skills by engaging in a variety of tasks, rather than performing one specific task over and over again. Group production and teamwork are seen as promoting a 'multi-

Table 20.2 Employment in knowledge-based industries, European countries, 2005

	Manufacturing	Services	Total
Sweden	6.5	47.8	54.3
Denmark	6.3	42.8	49.1
UK	5.6	42.4	48.0
Finland	6.8	40.5	47.3
Netherlands	3.3	41.9	45.2
Belgium	6.5	38.3	44.8
Germany	10.4	33.4	43.8
France	6.3	36.3	42.6
Ireland	6.0	33.9	39.9
Austria	6.5	31.0	37.5
Italy	7.4	29.8	37.2
Spain	4.7	27.0	31.7
Greece	2.1	24.5	26.6
Portugal	3.3	22.7	26.0

Source: Brinkley and Lee 2007 © The Work Foundation

skilled' workforce capable of carrying out a broader set of responsibilities. This in turn leads to higher productivity and better quality goods and services; employees who are able to contribute to their jobs in multiple ways will be more successful in solving problems and coming up with creative approaches.

The move towards 'multi-skilling' has implications for the hiring process. If at one time these were made largely on the basis of education and qualifications, many employers now look for individuals who are adaptable and can learn new skills quickly. Thus, expert knowledge of a particular software application might not be as valuable as a demonstrable ability to pick up ideas easily. Specializations are often assets, but if employees have difficulty in applying narrow skills creatively in new contexts, they may not be seen as a benefit in a flexible, innovative workplace.

A Joseph Rowntree Foundation study on The Future of Work (Meadows 1996) investigated the types of skill that are now sought by employers. The authors of the study concluded that in both skilled and unskilled occupational sectors, 'personal skills' are increasingly valued. The ability to collaborate and to work independently, to take the initiative and to adopt creative approaches in the face of challenges are among the best skills an individual can bring to a job. In a market in which consumers' individual needs are increasingly catered for, it is essential that employees in a range of settings from the service sector to financial consulting be able to draw on 'personal skills' at the workplace. This 'downgrading' of technical skills, according to the authors of the study, may be most difficult for workers who have long worked in routine, repetitive work in which 'personal skills' had no place.

Training on the job

Multi-skilling is closely tied up with the idea of employee training and retraining. Rather

Global Society 20.3 'Offshoring' and its discontents

The changing occupational structure today has to be viewed in a global perspective. One good reason for this is because production and the delivery of many services now involve people working collectively across several national boundaries. In general, this is the result of firms in the developed world moving certain jobs to the developing world where the work can be done more cheaply, thus maintaining or improving profitability. India – which has many English speakers – has become a centre for banking transactions and call centres; China is a major producer of toys, clothing and consumer goods; and Taiwan produces many of the electronic components needed in the information age. This process has been called 'offshoring' (sometimes 'outsourcing') and although it is by no means a recent development, there is much debate today on the future of offshoring and its consequences, particularly for the industrialized countries.

Systematic studies of offshoring are not numerous, but two views have emerged. On one view, offshoring is simply another extension of international trade – it is just that there are now more things to trade and more places in which to trade. There is nothing special to be concerned about. On the second view, offshoring could in future be a major world-historical force that transforms the global economy and may be particularly worrying for the developed countries. A leading exponent of the second view is the American economist, Alan S. Blinder (2006), who explains exactly why governments such as that in the USA should be planning for the future.

Blinder argues that manufacturing workers and firms in the relatively rich countries are used to competing with workers and firms in developing countries, but well-educated service sector workers are not. Yet in future, these service sector workers will, Blinder forecasts, face the biggest challenge. A major divide is now emerging, which Blinder describes as that between those types of work that are 'easily deliverable down an electronic wire (or via wireless connections)' without a loss of quality and those that are not'. For example, it is impossible to see German or American taxi drivers or airline pilots losing out to offshoring, but it is possible to envisage typing services, security analysis, radiology services, accountancy, higher education, research and development, computer programming, banking services and many, many more doing so. Blinder notes that the big change here is that jobs requiring high levels of education are not 'safe' anymore, so the oft-repeated government mantra, that developing a highly educated workforce is the key to the economy of the future, could be mistaken. What may be required is to invest in those 'personal services' that have to be delivered face-to-face and thus can escape offshoring (so far). All other 'impersonal services' that can be delivered electronically are fair game. Because of this, Blinder suggests that the main challenge to developed countries today is not China, which specializes in manufacturing, but India, which is better placed to take advantage of the movement of services offshore. As the article immediately below demonstrates though, China is already aware of this and is taking steps to be able to compete in the future.

Blinder admits that his thesis is a form of speculation or 'futurology' and that much more research and evidence of current patterns is required, but the process he describes is clearly already under way. Given the present period of rapid globalization, it seems that offshoring is here to stay.

Offshore boost for finance sector

The shifting of UK financial services jobs to developing countries such as India and China has saved the sector about £1.5 billion a year, a study suggests. Accountants Deloitte said the number of financial jobs going overseas over the past four years had increased 18-fold. More than 75 per cent of major financial institutions have operations overseas, compared with fewer than 10 per cent in 2001.

But the trade union Unite said an effective case for offshoring had not been made, and pointed to growing staff turnover. It says that many companies are having to retrain an entire workforce over the course of a year and that wages are rising.

China vs India

Offshoring has spread across nearly all business functions, with significant growth around transaction processing, finance and human resources. India has kept the top spot for firms looking to move processes overseas, with about two-thirds of global offshored staff employed there. But it is in danger of losing its crown to China, with one-third of financial institutions now having back-office – mainly IT – processes there. Some 200 million Chinese people are currently learning English, providing a potential pool of skilled workers that may compete with India in coming years.

'Complexities'

Chris Gentle, associated partner for financial services at Deloitte and author of the study, said: 'Financial institutions need to re-engineer business processes, or risk simply transferring offshore the legacy inefficiencies of older, onshore processes.'

The typical financial services firm now has 6 per cent of its staff outside the host country, with the proportion having doubled in the past year.

However David Fleming, national officer at Unite, said the human and social costs of moving jobs 'have been absolutely huge, and customer dissatisfaction is widespread'. He added: 'Unite still believes that organizations are overlooking the complexities of offshoring and are still failing to make a sound business case for exporting work overseas.'

Source: BBC News, 22 June 2007

THINKING CRITICALLY

Blinder notes that the Industrial Revolution did not end agriculture 'we still eat' – but it did fundamentally transform it. Similarly, the Information Revolution has not ended industry – we still use machines – but with far fewer human workers. What consequences might follow for the developed societies from the large-scale offshoring of services? What types of paid work will workers in these societies actually do to earn their livings?

---

than employing narrow specialists, many companies would prefer to hire capable non-specialists who are able to develop new skills on the job. As technology and market demands change, companies retrain their own employees as needed instead of bringing in expensive consultants or replacing existing staff with new employees. Investing in a core of employees who may become valuable lifelong workers is seen as a strategic way to keep up with rapidly changing times.

Some companies organize on-the-job training through job-sharing teams. This technique allows skills training and mentoring to take place at the same time as work is getting done: an IT specialist might be paired for several weeks with a company manager in order for each to learn some of the other's skills. This form of training is cost-effective, as it does not significantly lessen working hours and allows all employees involved to broaden their skills base.

Training on the job can be an important way for workers to develop their skills and career prospects. But it is important to note that training opportunities are not equally available to all workers. The Economic and Social Research Council (ESRC) cohort studies of young people born in 1958 and 1970 found that employees already possessing qualifications were much more likely to receive training on the job than their counterparts who were without qualifications. Such studies suggest that there is more continuing investment in those who are already the most highly qualified, while those without qualifications suffer from fewer opportunities. Training also has an impact on wage levels: among the 1970 cohort, work-based training increased employee earnings by an average of 12 per cent.

Homeworking

Homeworking allows employees to perform some or all of their responsibilities from home, often via a computer connected to the Internet. In jobs that do not require regular contact with clients or co-workers, such as computer-based graphic design work or copy-writing for advertisements, employees find that working from home allows them to balance non-work responsibilities and perform more productively. The phenomenon of 'wired workers' seems sure to grow in the years to come, as technology radically changes the way we work.

> See the Helsinki 'virtual village' featured in 'Global Society 6.2', in chapter 6, 'Cities and Urban Life'.

Although working at home has become more accepted in recent years, it is by no means favoured by all employers. It is much more difficult to monitor an employee's work when they are out of the office; for this reason, new types of control are often placed on homeworkers in order to ensure that they do not abuse their 'freedom'. Workers might be expected to check in regularly with the office, for example, or to submit updates on their work more frequently than other employees.

> For a wider discussion of surveillance in the workplace, see chapter 18, 'Organizations and Networks'.

While there is great enthusiasm about the potential of 'home offices', some scholars have cautioned that a significant polarization is likely to emerge between professional homeworkers who pursue challenging, creative projects, and largely unskilled homeworkers who perform routine jobs such as typing or data entry. Were such a schism to develop, women would be most likely to be concentrated among the lower ranks of homeworkers (Phizacklea and Wolkowitz 1995).

The end of the career for life and the rise of the portfolio worker

In light of the impact of the global economy and the demand for a 'flexible' labour force, some sociologists and economists have argued that more and more people in the future will become **portfolio workers**. They will have a 'skill portfolio' – a number of different job skills and credentials – which they will use to move between several jobs and kinds of job during the course of their working lives. Only a relatively small proportion of workers will have continuous 'careers' in the current sense. Indeed, proponents argue, the idea of a 'job for life' is becoming a thing of the past.

Some see this move to the portfolio worker in a positive light: workers will not be stuck in the same job for years on end and will be able to plan their work lives in a creative way (Handy 1994). Others hold that 'flexibility' in practice means that organizations can hire and fire more or less at will, undermining any sense of security their workers might have. Employers will only have a short-term commitment to their workforces and will be able to minimize the paying of extra benefits or pension rights.

A recent study of Silicon Valley, California, claims that the economic success of the area is already founded on the portfolio skills of its workforce. The failure rate of firms in Silicon Valley is very high: about 300 new companies are established every year, but an equivalent number also goes bust. The workforce, which has a very high proportion of professional and technical workers, has learned to adjust to this. The result, the authors say, is that talents and skills migrate rapidly from one firm to another, becoming more adaptable on the way. Technical specialists become consultants, consultants become managers, employees become venture capitalists – and back again (Bahrami and Evans 1995).

Among young people, especially consultants and specialists in information technology, there does seem to be a growing tendency towards portfolio work. By some estimates, young graduates can expect to work in 11 different jobs using three different skill bases over the course of their working lives. Yet such a situation still remains the exception rather than the rule. Employment statistics have not shown the great rise in employee turnover that one would expect with a large-scale shift towards portfolio work. Surveys carried out in the 1990s revealed that full-time workers in Britain and the USA – which have the most deregulated labour markets among industrial countries – spent as long in each job as they were doing ten years before (*The Economist*, 21 May 1995). The reasons seem to be that managers recognize that a high degree of turnover among workers is costly and bad for morale, and that they prefer to retrain their own employees rather than bring in new ones, even if this means paying above the market rate. In their book, *Built to Last* (1994), James Collins and Jerry Porras analysed 18 American companies which had continuously outperformed the stock market average since 1926. They found that these companies, far from hiring and firing at will, had followed highly protective policies towards their staff. Only two of these companies over the period studied brought in a chief executive from the outside, compared to 13 of the less successful corporations included in the research.

These findings do not disprove the ideas of those who speak of the arrival of the portfolio worker. Organizational downsizing is a reality, throwing many thousands of workers who may have thought they had a lifetime job onto the labour market. To find work again, they may be forced to develop and diversify their skills. Many, particularly older people, might never be able to find jobs comparable to those they held before, or perhaps even paid work at all.

Job insecurity, unemployment and the social significance of work

While new ways of working present exciting opportunities for many people, they can also produce deep ambivalence on the part of others who feel that they are caught up in

a runaway world. As we have seen in this chapter, the labour market is undergoing profound change as part of the shift from a manufacturing to a service-oriented economy. The widespread introduction of information technology is also provoking transformations in the way organizations structure themselves, the type of management style that is used and the manner in which work tasks are delegated and carried out. Rapid change can be destabilizing; workers in many different types of occupation now experience job insecurity and a sense of apprehension about both the future safety of their work position and their role within the workplace.

In recent decades, the phenomenon of job insecurity has become an important topic of debate within the sociology of work. Many commentators and media sources have suggested that there has been a steady increase in job insecurity for some 30 or more years and that this insecurity has now reached unprecedented heights in industrialized countries. Young people can no longer count on a secure career with one employer, they claim, because the rapidly globalizing economy is leading to ever more corporate mergers and corporate 'downsizings', where employees are laid off. The drive for efficiency and profit means that those with few skills – or the 'wrong' skills – are relegated to insecure, marginal jobs that are vulnerable to shifts in the global markets. Despite the benefits of flexibility at the workplace, the argument continues, we now live in a 'hire-and-fire' culture where the idea of a 'job for life' no longer applies.

The social significance of work

For most of us, work occupies a larger part of our lives than any other single type of activity. We often associate the notion of work with drudgery – with a set of tasks that we want to minimize and, if possible, escape from altogether. Work has more going for it than drudgery, however, or people would not feel so lost and disoriented when they

20.3 The declining importance of work?

Persistent unemployment, job insecurity, downsizing, portfolio careers, part-time work, flexible employment patterns, job sharing: it seems that, more than ever, people are working in non-standard ways, or are not in formal paid work at all. Perhaps it is time to rethink the nature of work and in particular the dominant position it often has in people's lives.

Because we so closely associate 'work' and 'paid employment', it is sometimes difficult to see what options might exist outside this view. The French sociologist and social critic André Gorz is one analyst who has argued that in the future paid work will play a less and less important part in people's lives. Gorz bases his views on a critical assessment of Marx's writings. Marx argued that the working class – to which more and more people would supposedly belong – would lead a revolution that would bring about a more humane type of society, in which work would be central to the

satisfactions life has to offer. Although writing as a socialist, Gorz rejects this view. Rather than the working class becoming the largest grouping in society (as Marx suggested) and leading a successful revolution, it is actually shrinking. Blue-collar workers have now become a minority – and a declining minority – of the labour force.

It no longer makes much sense, in Gorz's view, to suppose that workers can take over the enterprises of which they are a part, let alone seize state power. There is no real hope of transforming the nature of paid work, because it is organized according to technical considerations that are unavoidable if an economy is to be efficient. 'The point now', as Gorz puts it, 'is to free oneself from work' (1982: 67). This is particularly necessary where work is organized along Taylorist lines, or is otherwise oppressive or dull.

Rising unemployment, together with the spread of part-time work, Gorz argues, has already created what he calls a 'non-class of non-workers',

Investment in information technology is just as likely to lead to job losses as it is to new 'high-skill' jobs. What happened to the workers?

alongside those in stable employment. Most people, in fact, are in this 'non-class', because the proportion of the population in stable paid jobs at any one time is relatively small – if we exclude the young, the retired, the ill and housewives, together with people who are in part-time work or unemployed. The spread of information technology, Gorz argues, will further reduce the numbers of full-time jobs available. Investment in production technology has traditionally led to more full-time jobs, but investment in information technologies now leads to fewer jobs as the technology effectively allows fewer workers to produce the same or more products. The result is likely to be a swing towards rejecting the 'productivist' outlook of Western society, with its emphasis on wealth, economic growth and material goods. A diversity of lifestyles, followed outside the sphere of permanent, paid work, will be pursued by the majority of the population in coming years.

According to Gorz, we are moving towards a 'dual society'. In one sector, production and political administration will be organized to maximize efficiency. The other sector will be a sphere in which individuals occupy themselves with a variety of non-work pursuits offering enjoyment or personal fulfilment. Perhaps more and more individuals will engage in life planning, by which they arrange to work in different ways at different stages of their lives.

How valid is this viewpoint? That there are major changes going on in the nature and organization of work in the industrialized countries is beyond dispute. It does seem possible that more and more people will become disenchanted with 'productivism' – the stress on constant economic growth and the accumulation of material possessions. It is surely valuable, as Gorz has suggested, to see unemployment not wholly in a negative light, but as offering opportunities for individuals to pursue their interests and develop their talents. Yet, thus far at least, progress in this direction has been slight; we seem to be far from the situation Gorz envisages. With women pressing for greater job opportunities, there has been a rise, not a fall, in the numbers of people actively interested in securing paid employment. Paid work remains for many the key to generating the material resources necessary to sustain a varied life.

THINKING CRITICALLY

How important is paid work in your life? Gorz (1985) argues that the declining significance of work potentially opens up new 'paths to paradise', as people spend less time in the formal economy, leaving more time for them to engage in creative activities and enjoy their relationships with others. Can such a utopian society really emerge from within capitalist economies? How does Gorz's 'post-industrial socialist' vision differ from traditional socialist and communist political programmes for social change?

and the tasks dull, work tends to be a structuring element in people's psychological make-up and the cycle of their daily activities. Several characteristics of work are relevant here.

1 *Money*. A wage or salary is the main resource many people depend on to meet their needs. Without an income, anxieties about coping with day-to-day life multiply.

2 *Activity level*. Work often provides a basis for the acquisition and exercise of skills and capacities. Even where work is routine, it offers a structured environment in which a person's energies may be absorbed. Without it, the opportunity to exercise such skills and capacities may be reduced.

3 *Variety*. Work provides access to contexts that contrast with domestic surroundings. In the working environment, even

become unemployed. How would you feel if you thought you would never get a job? In modern societies, having a job is important for maintaining self-esteem. Even where work conditions are relatively unpleasant, when the tasks are relatively dull, people may enjoy doing something different from home chores.

4 *Temporal structure.* For people in regular employment, the day is usually organized around the rhythm of work. While this may sometimes be oppressive, it provides a sense of direction in daily activities. Those who are out of work frequently find boredom a major problem and develop a sense of apathy about time.

5 *Social contacts.* The work environment often provides friendships and opportunities to participate in shared activities with others. Separated from the work setting, a person's circle of possible friends and acquaintances is likely to dwindle.

6 *Personal identity.* Work is usually valued for the sense of stable social identity it offers. For men in particular, self-esteem is often bound up with the economic contribution they make to the maintenance of the household.

Against the backdrop of this formidable list, it is not difficult to see why being without work may undermine individuals' confidence in their social value.

The rise in job insecurity

In 1999 the Joseph Rowntree Foundation published the results of the Job Insecurity and Work Intensification Survey (JIWIS), which drew on in-depth interviews with 340 working Britons from shop-floor workers to senior managers. The study was designed to assess the extent of job insecurity and to gauge its impact both in the workplace and in families and communities. The authors of the study found that job insecurity had been on the rise in Britain since 1966, with the most intensive period of growth occurring among blue-collar workers in the late 1970s and 1980s. Despite a general economic recovery beginning in the mid-1980s, however, job insecurity continued to grow. The study concluded that job insecurity had

reached its highest point since the Second World War (Burchell et al. 1999).

The survey also examined the types of worker who had experienced greater or lesser levels of insecurity with the passing of time. The authors found that in the mid-1990s the greatest increase in job insecurity occurred among non-manual workers. From 1986 to 1999, professionals shifted from the most secure occupational group to the least secure, while manual workers experienced somewhat lower levels of job insecurity. One of the main sources of this insecurity appeared to be a lack of trust in management. When asked if management looked out for the employees' best interests, 44 per cent of respondents claimed that they did so 'only a little' or 'not at all' (Burchell et al. 1999).

Most scholars agree that job insecurity is not a new phenomenon. The disagreement surrounds the extent to which it has become more pronounced in recent years and, more importantly, which segments of the working population experience job insecurity most acutely. Some critics argue that studies like the JIWIS project are nothing more than an unwarranted response to perceived job insecurity among the middle classes.

The 'insecure middle': is job insecurity exaggerated?

In the late 1970s and '80s Britain experienced an economic recession that proved to be particularly harmful to traditional manufacturing industries. Roughly one million jobs were lost during this time in sectors such as steel, shipbuilding and coal-mining. It was not until the 1980s and into the 1990s that professional and managerial workers had their first large-scale exposure to job insecurity. Corporate take-overs and lay-offs have affected the banking and finance sector; the spread of the information age has cost many civil servants their jobs, as systems are streamlined through the use of computer technology.

If manufacturing workers had become accustomed to living with the threat of

Older ideas of 'a job for life' proved mythical for workers at the Ravenscraig Steelworks in Scotland, which closed in 1992. The works has now been demolished and the site is undergoing redevelopment.

redundancy, white-collar workers were less prepared for the changes affecting their occupations. This anxiety among professionals led some to speak of 'the insecure middle'. The term was used to describe white-collar workers whose faith in the stability of their jobs meant that they had taken on significant financial commitments such as sizeable mortgages, private education for children or expensive hobbies. Because redundancy had never crossed their minds before, the sudden spectre of unemployment caused them to experience enormous anxiety and insecurity. Job insecurity soon became a 'buzz' topic in the media and in professional circles – although some argue that this was an overreaction when compared to the more chronic insecurity experienced by the working classes.

The harmful effects of job insecurity

The *Job Insecurity and Work Intensification* survey (Burchell et al. 1999) found that for many workers job insecurity is much more than a fear of redundancy. It also encompasses anxieties about the transformation of work itself, and the effects of that transformation on employees' health and personal life.

The study revealed that workers are being asked to take on more and more responsibility at work as organizational structures become less bureaucratic and decision-making is spread throughout the workplace. Yet at the same time that the demands on them are increasing, many workers see their chances of promotion decreasing. This combination leads workers to feel that they are 'losing control' over important features

USING YOUR SOCIOLOGICAL IMAGINATION

20.4   Living to work or working to live?

For some analysts, the end of the millennium should have witnessed a colossal change in patterns of work – or rather the lack of work – to the point where there would be no economic stimulus to immigration. As Jenkins and Sherman insisted in 1979: 'It is impossible to over-dramatize the forthcoming crisis. . . . Now we have inflation, a slump and rising unemployment. In fifteen or twenty years time we shall have a boom, minimal inflation, high growth and the largest unemployment in our history . . . a jobs holocaust' (1979: 182). . . .

Well we certainly have not reached the workerless economy – but have we instead arrived in a place where the kind of relationship we have to work has changed beyond all recognition? . . .

While it is easy to scoff at the pessimism of [authors such as Jenkins and Sherman], it remains the case that the contemporary perception of job insecurity appears to be almost as high as the unreality of job insecurity they predicted. Smith (1997: 39), for instance, compared the relative insignificance of newspaper stories about insecurity in 1986

(when unemployment in Britain was much higher than a decade later) with its preponderant presence in 1996, by which time stories about job insecurity had increased 100-fold. According to the *Observer* (16 June 1996), 40 per cent of British employees feared for their jobs, while 60 per cent argued that insecurity had been rising. . . .

Yet, despite claims to the contrary, job tenure in Britain only marginally decreased between 1975 and 2000 (from 6 to 5.5 years), with women's tenure actually increasing (Gregg and Wadsworth 1999; Nolan 2000: 3; Green (2000) suggests that in the 1970s the average job tenure was 10 years and it remained stuck at 9.5 in 2000). Indeed, in the allegedly worst period of the 'neurotic nineties', tenure actually increased over the rate of the 'erratic eighties'. . . . 80 per cent of British employees remain in permanent jobs, and 28 per cent of employees have remained with the same employer for more than ten years. Indeed, most people can probably look forward to staying with the same employer for, at the very least, four or five years.

Source: Grint 2005: 325–7

---

of their job, such as the pace of work and confidence in their overall career progression.

The sociologist Paul du Gay argues for the importance of bureaucracy in providing accountability and moral responsibility against increasingly entrepreneurial and flexile work practices (see chapter 18, 'Organizations and Networks').

A second harmful dimension to job security can be seen in workers' personal lives. Burchell et al.'s study found a strong correlation between job insecurity and poor overall health. This link is substantiated by data from the British Household Panel Survey, which showed that people's mental and physical health continues to deteriorate with episodes of prolonged job insecurity. Rather than adjusting to the insecure conditions, workers remain anxious and under

constant stress. This pressure from work seems to transfer into the home environment: those workers reporting high levels of job insecurity also tended to experience tensions at home (Burchell et al. 1999).

Unemployment

Rates of **unemployment** have fluctuated considerably over the course of this century. In the developed economies, unemployment reached a peak during the economic depression of the early 1930s, with some countries experiencing 20 per cent of the labour force out of work. The ideas of the economist John Maynard Keynes (1883–1946) strongly influenced public policy in Europe and the United States during the post-war period. Keynes argued that unemployment results from a lack of sufficient purchasing power to buy goods, so that production is not stimulated and fewer workers are needed; but governments can intervene to increase the level of demand in an economy, leading to the creation of new jobs. With state management of economic life, many came to believe that high rates of unemployment belonged in the past. Commitment to full employment became part of government policy in virtually all of the developed societies. Until the 1970s, these policies appeared to be successful and economic growth was more or less continuous.

During the 1970s and '80s, though, unemployment rates proved more difficult to control and Keynesianism was largely abandoned as a means of trying to regulate economic activity. For example, for about a quarter of a century after the Second World War, the British unemployment rate was less than 2 per cent. It rose as high as 12 per cent in the early 1980s, then fell, increasing again at the end of the decade. From the mid- to late 1990s, unemployment in Britain once again began to decline, and by 2005 it stood at just under 5 per cent.

Globally, unemployment rates remain historically high at around 6.3 per cent or some 200 million in 2006, though we also have to bear in mind that much of informal work, particularly in developing countries, falls outside such official statistics and it is probably the case that many people who are 'officially' unemployed are, in reality, working in some capacity. Young people aged 15–24 made up 44 per cent of the unemployed population, and a persistent gender gap in employment exists: just 48.9 percent of women over the age of 15 were working compared to 74 per cent of men. Unemployment rates differ widely too, with East Asia averaging 3.6 per cent, sub-Saharan Africa 9.8 per cent and the Middle East and North Africa highest at 12.2 per cent (Europaworld 2007). Such regional statistics also mask very different national economic situations. In Southern Africa, for instance, unemployment rates range from around 80 per cent in

Zimbabwe to 50 per cent in Zambia, 21 per cent in Mozambique to just 5.3 per cent in Namibia (CIA 2007).

Analysing unemployment

Interpreting official unemployment statistics, however, is not straightforward (see figure 20.4). Unemployment is not easy to define. It means 'being out of work'. But 'work' here means 'paid work', and 'work in a recognized occupation'. People who are properly registered as unemployed may engage in many forms of productive activity, like painting the house or tending the garden. Many people are in part-time paid work, or only in paid jobs sporadically; the retired are not counted as 'unemployed'.

Many official statistics are calculated according to the definition of unemployment used by the International Labour Organization (ILO). The ILO's measure of unemployment refers to individuals who are without a job, who are available to start work within two weeks and who have attempted to look for a job within the previous month. Many economists think this standard unemployment rate should be supplemented by two other measures. 'Discouraged workers' are those who would like a job, but who despair of getting one and thus have given up looking. 'Involuntary part-time workers' are people who cannot find a full-time job even though they want one.

General unemployment statistics are also complicated by the fact that they encompass two different 'types' of unemployment. Frictional unemployment, sometimes called 'temporary unemployment', refers to the natural, short-term entry and exit of individuals into and out of the labour market for reasons such as switching jobs, searching for a position after graduation, or a period of poor health. Structural unemployment, by contrast, describes joblessness, which results from large shifts in the economy, rather than circumstances affecting particular individuals. The decline of heavy industries in the 1970s and '80s, for

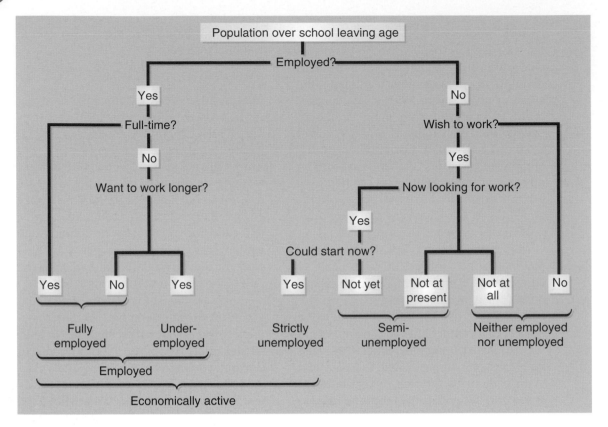

Figure 20.4 A taxonomy of possible employment, unemployment and non-employment states

Source: Sinclair 1987: 2

example, contributed to higher levels of structural unemployment in many industrialized economies.

Trends in unemployment

Variations in the distribution of government-defined unemployment within Britain are well documented. Unemployment is higher for men than for women. At the end of 2006 there were 975,000 men unemployed, compared to 702,000 women, as figure 20.5 shows. Unemployed men were almost twice as likely as women to have previously been in work. Women registering for unemployment were ten times more likely than men to have been at home caring for children or the household.

On average, ethnic minorities have higher unemployment rates than whites. Ethnic minorities also have much higher rates of long-term unemployment than the rest of the population. However, these general trends hide a large amount of diversity in unemployment rates among ethnic minority groups (see figure 20.6). Unemployment among the white population stood at less than 5 per cent in 2004. For Indians, the rate was only slightly higher than this, at around 7 per cent – one of the factors which leads some to suggest that the British Indian population has nearly attained socio-economic parity with the white population. For all other minority ethnic groups, unemployment rates were between two and three times higher than those for white men. In 2004, the unemployment rate among Pakistani women was the highest in the UK at 20 per cent, five times that of white British and white Irish women. For men, black Caribbean, black African, Bangladeshi and

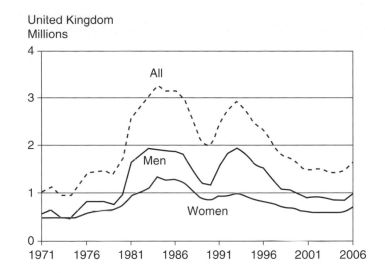

Figure 20.5   UK unemployment by gender, 1971–2006

Source: HMSO Social Trends 37, 2007: 42

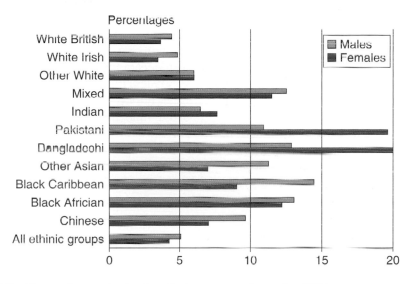

Figure 20.6   Unemployment rates by ethnic group and gender, 2004

Source: Office for National Statistics 2004a

mixed ethnic groups had the highest rates at between 13 and 14 per cent, almost three times higher than the 5 per cent unemployment of white British and white Irish men.

Young people, particularly in minority ethnic groups, are especially affected by unemployment. Over 40 per cent of Bangladeshi men in the UK under the age of 25 were unemployed in 2001–2. Amongst the other ethnic minority groups, the unemployment rate for young men ranged between 25 and 31 per cent. This compared with a rate of 12 per cent for white men of the same age.

A substantial proportion of young people are among the long-term unemployed, especially members of minority groups; and more than half the male teenage unemployment involves those out of work for six months or more. The long-term unemployed are now offered skills training, assistance in searching for jobs and opportunities for subsidized work.

Social class and unemployment rates are correlated. According to the ESRC cohort study for young people born in 1970, those people whose fathers were from social classes I or II experienced the lowest rates of unemployment. Those whose fathers were from social class V, or who were raised by lone mothers, had the highest rates of unemployment, including a high proportion of people who had never been in work at all.

Unemployment rates are also linked to educational qualifications. Surveys in the UK have shown that the higher the level of qualification, the lower the unemployment rate. In spring 2003 the unemployment rate among those with no qualifications was over three times that of those with a degree or equivalent (Regional Trends 38, 2003).

The experience of unemployment

The experience of unemployment can be very disturbing to those accustomed to having secure jobs. Obviously, the immediate consequence is a loss of income. The effects of this vary between countries, because of contrasts in the level of unemployment benefits. In countries where there is guaranteed access to healthcare and other welfare benefits, unemployed individuals may experience acute financial difficulties but remain protected by the state. In some Western countries, such as the United States, unemployment benefits last a shorter time and healthcare is not universal, making the economic strain on those without work correspondingly greater.

Studies of the emotional effects of unemployment have noted that people who are unemployed often pass through a series of stages as they adjust to their new status. While the experience is of course an individual one, the newly unemployed often experience a sense of shock, followed by optimism about new opportunities. When that optimism is not rewarded, as is often the case, individuals can slip into periods of depression and deep pessimism about themselves and their employment prospects. If the period of unemployment stretches on, the process of adjustment is eventually completed, with individuals resigning themselves to the realities of their situation (Ashton 1986).

The strength of communities and social ties can be undermined by high levels of unemployment. In a classic sociological study in the 1930s, Marie Jahoda and her colleagues investigated the case of Marienthal, a small town in Austria experiencing mass unemployment after the closure of the local factory (Jahoda et al. 1972 [1933]). The researchers noted how the long-term experience of unemployment eventually undermined many of the community's social structures and networks. People were less active in civic affairs, spent less time socially with one another and even visited the town library less frequently.

It is important to note that the experience of unemployment also varies by social class. For those at the lower end of the income scale, the consequences of unemployment may be felt mostly financially. It has been suggested that middle-class individuals find unemployment damaging primarily in terms of their social, rather than their finan-

> **THINKING CRITICALLY**
>
> Have you ever been unemployed? If so, how did it make you feel? Is there a gender dimension to the experience of unemployment? What social and psychological effects might unemployment have on the traditional 'breadwinners' – men – and on the traditional 'housewives' – women? Given that many more women are also now in paid employment, is unemployment potentially a more disruptive social problem today than in the past?

cial, status. A 45-year-old lecturer who is made redundant may have acquired enough assets to get by comfortably during the initial phases of unemployment, but may struggle to make sense of what unemployment means for their future career and worth as a professional.

Conclusion: the 'corrosion of character'?

In 1970, as part of his study of blue-collar workers in Boston, USA, the sociologist Richard Sennett drew up a profile of Enrico, an Italian immigrant who spent his working years as a janitor in a downtown office building. Although Enrico did not enjoy the poor conditions and meagre pay, his job provided him with a sense of self-respect and an 'honest' way to provide for his wife and children. He cleaned toilets and mopped floors day in and day out for 15 years before being able to afford a house in a suburb of the city. Although it was not glamorous, his work was secure, his job was protected by a union and Enrico and his wife could confidently plan their future and that of their children. Enrico knew well in advance exactly when he would retire and how much money he would have at his disposal. As Sennett says, Enrico's work 'had one single and durable purpose, the service of his family'. Although Enrico was proud of his honest hard work, he did not want the same future for his children. It was important to Enrico that he create the conditions for his children to be upwardly mobile.

Sennett discovered 15 years later, in a chance meeting with Enrico's son Rico, that the children *did* become more mobile. Rico finished his first degree in engineering before going on to business school in New York. In the 14 years following his graduation, he built up a highly lucrative career and rose to within the top 5 per cent of the wage scale. Rico and his wife Jeanette have moved no fewer than four times during their marriage in order to advance their respective careers. In taking risks and being open to change, Rico and Jeanette have adapted to the turbulent times and have become affluent as a result. Yet, despite their success, the story is not an entirely happy one. Rico and his wife worry that they are close to 'losing control of their lives'. As a consultant, Rico feels a lack of control over time and his work: contracts are vague and always changing, he has no fixed role, and his fate is largely dependent on the fortunes and pitfalls of networking. Jeanette similarly feels that she has only a tenuous hold on her job. She manages a team of accountants who are geographically divided: some work at home, some at the office and some thousands of miles away in a different branch of the company. In managing this 'flexible' team, Jeanette cannot rely on face-to-face interactions and personal knowledge of an individual's work. Instead, she manages from afar, using email and phone calls.

In moving around the country, Rico and Jeanette's meaningful friendships have fallen by the wayside; new neighbours and communities know nothing about their pasts, where they come from or who they are as people. Sennett (1998) writes: 'The fugitive quality of friendship and local community form the background to the most important of Rico's inner worries, his family.' At home, Rico and Jeannette find that their work lives interfere with their ability to fulfil their goals as parents. Hours are long and they worry that they neglect their children. But more troublesome than juggling time and schedules, however, is the concern that they are setting a disorienting example. While trying to teach their children the value of hard work, commitment and long-term goals, they fear that their own lives tell a different story. Rico and Jeanette are examples of the short-term, flexible approach to work that is increasingly favoured in contemporary societies. Their work histories are characterized by constant movement, temporary commitments and short-term investments in what they are doing. The couple realize that, in our current runaway society, 'the qualities of good work are not the qualities of good character'.

To Sennett, such experiences illustrate some of the consequences of the flexible approach to work for employees' personal lives and characters. In *The Corrosion of Character* (1999) he argues that the growing emphasis on flexible behaviour and working styles can produce successful results, but inevitably leads also to both confusion and harm. This is because the expectations placed on workers today directly contradict many of the core features of strong character: loyalty, the pursuit of long-term goals, commitment, trust and purpose. Sennett suggests that these tensions are inevitable in the new era of flexibility. Rather than committing to a life career, workers are now expected to work fluidly in teams, entering and exiting, moving from task to task. Loyalty becomes a liability rather than an asset. When life becomes a series of discrete jobs rather than a coherent career, long-term goals are eroded, social bonds fail to develop and trust is fleeting. People can no longer judge which risks will pay off in the end and the old 'rules' for promotions, dismissals and reward no longer seem to apply. For Sennett, the central challenge for adults in the present era is how to lead a life with long-term goals in a society, which emphasizes the short term.

Summary points

1. Work is the carrying out of tasks, involving the expenditure of mental and physical effort, which have as their objective the production of goods and services catering for human needs. Many important kinds of work – like housework or voluntary work – are unpaid and much work in developing countries takes place in the informal economy. An occupation is work, which is done in exchange for a regular wage. Work is in all cultures the basis of economic systems.

2. A distinctive characteristic of modern capitalist economies is the development of a highly complex and diverse division of labour. The division of labour means that work is divided into different occupations requiring specialization. This brings economic interdependence: we are all dependent on each other to maintain our livelihoods.

3. Industrial production was made more efficient with the introduction of Taylorism, or scientific management – the theory and practice of dividing all industrial processes into simple tasks that can be timed and organized. Fordism extended the principles of scientific management to mass production tied to mass markets. Fordism and Taylorism can be seen as low-trust systems that increase worker alienation. A high-trust system allows workers control over the pace and content of their work.

4. Union organizations, together with recognition of the right to strike, are characteristic features of economic life in all developed and most developing countries. Unions emerged as defensive organizations, concerned to provide a measure of control for workers over their conditions of labour. Today, union leaders quite often play an important role in formulating national economic policies.

5. In recent years Fordist practices have been replaced by more flexible operating techniques in many industrialized countries. The term 'post-Fordism' is favoured by some to describe the current period of economic production in which flexibility and innovation are maximized in order to meet market demands for diverse, customized products.

6. Some speak of the 'death of the career' and the arrival of the 'portfolio' worker – the worker who has a portfolio of different skills and will be able to move readily from job to job. Such workers do exist, but for many people in the workforce, 'flexibility' is more likely to be associated with poorly paid jobs with few career prospects.

7. Unemployment is a recurrent problem in the industrialized world. As work is a structuring element in a person's life, the psychological experience of unemployment is often extremely disorienting, disturbing people's perceptions of their self-identity.

8. The effects of job insecurity can be as debilitating as the actual experience of being unemployed. Job insecurity is a sense of apprehension felt about the future safety of jobs and workplace roles. Job insecurity has risen sharply even amongst the middle classes, although some argue that anxiety over job insecurity is greatly exaggerated.

Further reading

One of the most widely used and referenced textbooks on the sociology of work is Keith Grint's excellent *The Sociology of Work: An Introduction*, 3rd edn (Cambridge: Polity, 2005). Tony Watson's *Sociology, Work and Industry* (London: Routledge, 2003) is also a very good introduction to this field.

Stephen Edgell's *The Sociology of Work: Continuity and Change in Paid and Unpaid Work* (London: Sage, 2005) does exactly what you might think it should – namely, it tries to make sociological sense of paid and unpaid work such as housework. On the same theme, Rosemary Crompton's *Employment and the Family: The Reconfiguration of Work and Family Life in Contemporary Societies* (Cambridge: Cambridge University Press, 2006) assesses recent social change in work and employment and family life.

Contemporary debates are then well served in Lynne Pettinger, Jane Parry, Rebecca Taylor and Miriam Glucksmann's *A New Sociology of Work?* (Oxford: Blackwell Publishing, 2006).

Finally, for a comprehensive reference work covering many of the issues introduced in this chapter, dip into Neil J. Smelser and Richard Swedberg's edited *The Handbook of Economic Sociology*, 2nd edn (Princeton: Princeton University Press, 2005).

Internet links

The International Labour Organization – campaigns for decent work for all. Site contains many useful resources:
www.ilo.org/global/lang–en/index.htm

The Work Foundation, UK – a not-for-profit organization promoting 'mutual respect and motivation' for all those in paid work:
www.theworkfoundation.com/

Intute: Social Sciences – UK (mostly) academic resources on work and employment:
www.intute.ac.uk/socialsciences/cgi-bin/browse.pl?id=120793&gateway=%

European Commission – Directorate General for Employment and Social Affairs, containing many helpful resources and statistics on work and working life:
http://ec.europa.eu/employment_social/index_en.html

21

Crime and Deviance

CHAPTER 21

· ·

Crime and Deviance

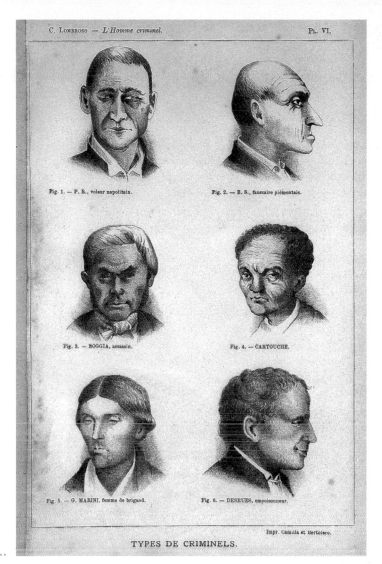

Fig. 1. — P. R., voleur napolitain.

Fig. 2. — B. S., faussaire piémontais.

Fig. 3. — BOGGIA, assassin.

Fig. 4. — CARTOUCHE.

Fig. 5. — G. MARINI, femme de brigand.

Fig. 6. — DESRUES, empoisonneur.

Impr. Camilla et Bertolero.

TYPES DE CRIMINELS.

Criminal types, as presented in his book *L'Homme criminel*, by Cesare Lombroso (1836–1909): a robber from Naples, a forger from Piedmont, an assassin, Cartouche, whose criminal tendency is not specified, a robber's wife and a poisoner.

Why do people commit crimes? A century ago, many people who thought about the issue believed that criminals were born, not made, and that criminal tendencies were biologically given, not learned. The Italian criminologist, Cesare Lombroso, working in the 1870s, even argued that criminal types could be identified by a collection of anatomical features. He investigated the appearance and physical characteristics of convicted criminals, such as the shape of the skull and forehead, jaw size and arm length, and concluded that criminals displayed signs of atavism. That is, they had traits held over from earlier stages of human evolution. Some of Lombroso's images showing the physical characteristics he thought were linked to certain types of criminal are shown here. Could you identify criminals from the way they look, from just their physical features?

Lombroso's ideas became thoroughly discredited through lack of evidence and seem almost comical to us today, although biological explanations of crime have continually resurfaced over the last century. One later theory distinguished three main types of human physique, each linked to a type of personality, claiming that one body type was directly associated with delinquency. Muscular active types (mesomorphs), the theory went, tend to be more aggressive and physical, and therefore more likely to become delinquent than those of thin physique (ectomorphs) or more round, fleshy people (endomorphs) (Sheldon 1949; Glueck and Glueck 1956).

Again, such views have been widely criticized. Even if there were an overall relationship between bodily type and delinquency, this would not necessarily show the determining influence of heredity. People of the muscular type may be drawn towards criminal activities because these offer opportunities for the physical display of their athleticism. Moreover, nearly all studies in this field have been restricted to delinquents in reform schools, and it may just be that the tougher, athletic-looking delinquents are more liable to be sent to such schools than fragile-looking, skinny ones. Some individuals might be inclined towards irritability and aggressiveness and this could be reflected in crimes of physical assault on others. Yet there is no decisive evidence that any traits of personality are inherited in this way, and even if they were, their connection to criminality would at most be only a distant one.

If biological approaches do not satisfactorily answer our question: 'Why do people commit crimes?', perhaps psychology is more successful? Psychological approaches to criminality have searched for explanations within the individual, not society. But whereas biological approaches focus on physical features that predispose individuals to crime, psychological views concentrate on personality types. Much early criminological research was carried out in prisons and other institutions, such as asylums, and in these settings, psychiatric ideas were especially influential. Emphasis was placed on the distinctive traits of criminals – including 'feeble-mindedness' and 'moral degeneracy'. The psychologist, Hans Eysenck (1964), for example, has suggested that abnormal mental states are inherited; these can either predispose an individual to crime or create problems during the process of socialization.

Some have suggested that in a minority of individuals, an amoral, or psychopathic, personality develops. Psychopaths are withdrawn, emotionless characters who act impulsively and rarely experience feelings of guilt. Some psychopaths delight in violence for its own sake. Individuals with psychopathic traits do sometimes commit violent crimes, but there are major problems with the concept of the psychopath. It is not at all clear that psychopathic traits lead inevitably to criminal acts. Nearly all studies of people said to possess these traits have been of convicted prisoners and their personalities inevitably tend to be presented negatively. If we describe the same traits positively, the personality type sounds quite different, and there seems no reason why people of this sort should be inherently criminal.

Psychological theories of criminality can at best explain only some aspects of crime. While some criminals may possess personality characteristics distinct from the remainder of the population, it is highly improbable that the majority of criminals do so. There are many different types of crime, from violent and aggressive murders and assaults, to the calculated and well-planned fraud, which makes it implausible to suppose that those who commit crimes share the same psychological characteristics.

Both biological and psychological approaches to criminality presume that deviance is a sign of something 'wrong' with the individual, rather than with society.

They see crime as caused by factors outside an individual's control, embedded either in the body or the mind. Therefore, if scientific criminology could successfully identify the causes of crime, it would be possible to treat those causes and prevent criminal behaviour. In this respect, both biological and psychological theories of crime are positivist in nature. As we learned in chapter 1, positivism is the belief that applying natural scientific methods to the study of the social world can reveal its basic truths. In the case of positivist criminology, this led to empirical research aimed at pinpointing the individual causes of crime in order to make recommendations about how to eradicate it. Perhaps this promise of an easy solution is why such theories keep on emerging.

Early positivist criminology came under great criticism from later generations of scholars. They argued that any satisfactory account of the nature of crime must be sociological, because what crime actually is depends on the social institutions of a society. Over time, attention shifted away from individualistic explanations to sociological theories that stress the social and cultural context in which crime and deviance take place. Any full answer to our question: 'Why do people commit crimes?', must be sociological, and it is most likely to start by questioning the terms implicit in our question. For example, what exactly do we mean by 'crime' and 'deviance'?

In this chapter we look at several sociological explanations for criminal and deviant behaviour. First, however, we look more closely at what terms such as deviance and crime mean. Later in the chapter we examine crime in the UK and elsewhere, before turning to some important issues concerning the victims as well as the perpetrators of crime.

The basic concepts

Deviance may be defined as non-conformity to a given set of norms that are accepted by a significant number of people in a community or society. No society can be divided up in a simple way between those who deviate from norms and those who conform to them. Most of us, on some occasions, transgress generally accepted rules of behaviour. We generally follow social norms because, as a result of socialization, we are used to doing so. All social norms are accompanied by sanctions promoting conformity and protecting against non-conformity. A sanction is any reaction from others to the behaviour of an individual or group that is meant to ensure compliance with a given norm. Sanctions may be positive (offering rewards for conformity) or negative (punishing behaviour that does not conform). Sanctions can be levied informally or formally. Informal sanctions are less organized and more spontaneous reactions to non-conformity. A studious pupil who is teased by classmates for working too hard, or who is accused of being a 'nerd' when he or she refuses to go out in the evenings, experiences a type of informal sanctioning. Informal sanctioning might also occur, for example, when an individual who makes a sexist or racist comment is met with disapproving responses from friends or work colleagues.

Formal sanctions are applied by a specific body of people or an agency to ensure that a particular set of norms is followed. The main types of formal sanction in modern societies are those represented by the courts and prisons. A law is a formal sanction defined by government as a rule or principle that its citizens must follow; it is used against people who do not conform.

Many of us may, for example, have committed minor acts of theft, shoplifted in our youth or taken small items from the workplace – such as office notepaper and pens – for personal use. At some point in our lives, we may have exceeded the speed limit, made prank phone calls or smoked marijuana.

Deviance and crime are not synonymous, although in many cases they overlap. The concept of deviance is much broader than that of crime, which refers only to non-conformist conduct that breaks a law. Many forms of deviant behaviour are not sanctioned by law. Thus, studies of deviance might examine phenomena as diverse as naturism, rave culture and New Age travellers.

The concept of deviance can be applied both to individual behaviour and to the activity of groups. An illustration is the Hare Krishna cult, a religious group whose beliefs and mode of life are different from those of the majority of the population. The cult was first established in the 1960s, when Sril Prabhupada came to the West from India to spread the word of Krishna consciousness. He aimed his message particularly at young people who were drug-users, proclaiming that one could 'stay high all the time, discover eternal bliss' by following his teachings. The Hare Krishnas became a familiar sight, dancing and chanting in the streets, running vegetarian cafés and distributing literature about their beliefs. They are generally regarded in a tolerant light by most people, even if their views seem somewhat eccentric.

The Hare Krishnas represent an example of a deviant subculture. Although their membership today has declined from its peak some years ago, they have been able to survive fairly easily within the wider society. The organization is wealthy, financed by donations from members and sympathizers. Their position diverges from that of another deviant subculture, which might be mentioned by way of contrast: that of the permanently homeless – people who live on the streets by day, spending their time in parks or in public buildings. They may sleep outside or find refuge in shelters. Most of the permanently homeless eke out a precarious existence on the fringes of society.

Two distinct, but related disciplines are engaged in the study of crime and deviance. Criminology is an interdisciplinary subject, concerned mainly with forms of behaviour that are sanctioned by criminal law. Criminologists are often interested in techniques for measuring crime, trends in crime rates and policies aimed at reducing crime. The sociology of deviance draws on criminological research, but also investigates conduct which lies beyond the criminal law. Sociologists studying deviant behaviour seek to understand *why* certain behaviours are widely regarded as deviant in the first place and how these notions of deviance are applied to groups of people within society.

The study of deviance therefore directs our attention to the issue of power as well as the influence of social class – the divisions between rich and poor. When we look at deviance from or conformity to social rules or norms, we always have to bear in mind the question, *whose* rules are they? As we shall see, social norms are strongly influenced by divisions of power and class.

Explaining crime and deviance: sociological theories

In the sociology of deviance, no single theory has emerged as dominant; instead, many theoretical perspectives remain relevant and useful. Having looked briefly at biological and psychological explanations, we will now turn to the four sociological approaches that have been most influential within the sociology of deviance: *functionalist theories, interactionist theories, conflict theories and control theories.*

Hare Krishna devotees dancing and singing in the streets of London.

Functionalist theories

Functionalist theories see crime and deviance resulting from structural tensions and a lack of moral regulation within society. If the aspirations held by individuals and groups do not coincide with society's available rewards, the disparity between desires and their fulfilment will be seen in the deviant motivations of some of its members.

Crime and anomie: Durkheim and Merton

As we saw in chapter 1, the concept of **anomie** was first introduced by Emile Durkheim, who suggested that in modern societies, traditional norms and standards become undermined without being replaced by new ones. Anomie exists when there are no clear standards to guide behaviour in a given area of social life. Under such circumstances, people can feel disoriented and anxious; Durkheim saw anomie as one of the social factors influencing dispositions to suicide.

Durkheim saw crime and deviance as social facts; arguing that both were inevitable and necessary elements of modern societies. According to Durkheim, people in the modern age are less constrained than those in traditional societies. Because there is more room for individual choice, it is inevitable that there will be some non-conformity or deviance. There would never be a complete consensus in any society about the norms and values which govern it.

Durkheim also argued that deviance is necessary for society, as it fulfils two important functions. First, deviance has an *adaptive* function; it can introduce new ideas and challenges into society and therefore can be an innovative force, bringing about social and cultural change. Second, deviance promotes *boundary maintenance* between 'good' and 'bad' behaviours; a deviant or criminal act can provoke a collective response that heightens group solidarity and clarifies social norms. For example, residents of a neighbourhood facing a problem with drug-dealers might join together in the aftermath of a drug-related shooting and commit themselves to maintaining the area as a drug-free zone. Durkheim's ideas on crime and deviance were influential in shifting attention from individual explanations to social forces and relations.

Subcultural explanations

Following Merton's work, Albert Cohen also saw the contradictions within American society as the main cause of crime. But while Merton emphasized individual deviant responses, Cohen saw such adaptive responses as occurring collectively through the formation of subcultures. In *Delinquent Boys* (1955), Cohen argued that boys in the lower working class who are frustrated with their positions in life often join together in delinquent subcultures, such as gangs. These subcultures reject middle-class values and replace them with norms that celebrate defiance, such as delinquency and other acts of non-conformity.

Richard A. Cloward and Lloyd E. Ohlin (1960) agreed with Cohen that most delinquent youths emerge from the lower working class. But they argue that the boys most 'at risk' are those who have internalized middle-class values and been encouraged, on the basis of ability, to aspire towards a middle-class future. When such boys find they are unable to realize their goals, they become particularly prone to delinquent activity. In their study of boys' gangs, Cloward and Ohlin found that delinquent gangs arise in subcultural communities where the chances of achieving success legitimately are small, such as among deprived ethnic minorities in inner city areas.

Defining deviance

Many people take it for granted that a well-structured society is designed to prevent deviant behaviour from occurring. However, as we have seen, Emile Durkheim argued that deviance has an important part to play in a well-ordered society. By defining what is deviant, we become aware of what is not deviant and thereby learn the standards we share as members of a society. It is not necessarily the case that we should aim to eliminate deviance completely. It is more likely, Durkheim thought, that society needs to keep it within acceptable limits.

Seventy years after Durkheim's work appeared, the sociologist Kai Erikson published *Wayward Puritans* (1966), a study of deviance in New England in the United States during the seventeenth century. Erikson sought 'to test [Durkheim's] notion that the number of deviant offenders a community can afford to recognize is likely to remain stable over time'. His research led him to conclude that 'a community's capacity for handling deviance, let us say, can be roughly estimated by counting its prison cells and hospital beds, its policemen and psychiatrists, its courts and clinics. . . . The agencies of control often seem to define their job as that of keeping deviance within bounds rather than obliterating it altogether.' Erikson advanced the hypothesis that societies need their quotas of deviance and that they function in such a way as to keep them intact.

But what does a society do when the amount of deviant behaviour gets too high? In 'Defining Deviance Down' (1993), a controversial article by American academic and politician, Daniel Patrick Moynihan, it was argued that levels of deviance in America had increased beyond the point that society could accept. As a result, society had been, 'redefining deviance so as to exempt much conduct previously stigmatised', and also quietly raising the 'normal' level, so that behaviour seen as abnormal by an earlier standard is no longer considered to be so. One example was the deinstitutionalization

Classic Studies 21.1 **Robert Merton and the failing American dream**

The research problem

Why do people commit crimes? Why are crime rates still high in the relatively rich societies? To answer these questions, the American sociologist, Robert K. Merton, used Durkheim's concept of anomie to construct an influential theory that found the sources of crime within the social structure of American society (Merton 1957). Merton tried to explain the well-established observation from official statistics, that a high proportion of crimes for immediate financial gain are committed by the 'lower working class' – those from manual, blue-collar families. But why should this be so?

Merton's explanation

Merton used the concept of 'anomie' to describe the *strain* put on individuals' behaviour when widely accepted cultural values conflict with their lived social reality.

In American society – and by implication in similar industrial societies – generally held values emphasize material success, with the means of achieving this as self-discipline and hard work. Accordingly, people who work hard can succeed, no matter what their starting point in life – an idea known in the USA as 'The American Dream', because it has proved so attractive to many immigrant groups. Controversially at the time, Merton argued that for many social groups it really is just a dream, because most disadvantaged groups have only limited conventional opportunities for advancement or none at all. Yet those who do not 'succeed' find themselves condemned for their apparent inability to make material progress. In this situation, there is great pressure to try to get ahead by any means, legitimate or illegitimate. Deviance and crime are then products of the strain between people's cultural values and the unequal distribution of legitimate opportunities within society.

Merton identifies five possible responses to the tensions between socially endorsed values

The idea of the American Dream – an open society where people will always succeed by their own efforts – has motivated people from across the world to live and work in the USA.

and the limited means of achieving them (see table 21.1). *Conformists* accept both generally held values and the conventional means of realizing them, whether or not they meet with success. A majority of the population fall into this category. *Innovators* also accept socially approved values but turn to illegitimate or illegal means to follow them. Criminals who acquire wealth through illegal activities exemplify this type. *Ritualists* conform to social values, though they have lost sight of the values behind these standards. Rules are followed for their own sake without a wider end in view, in a compulsive way. A ritualist would be someone who dedicates herself to a boring job, even though it has no career prospects and provides few rewards. *Retreatists* have abandoned the values and the legitimate means, effectively 'dropping out' of mainstream society.

Examples would be the members of self-supporting communes or people with addictions who play no part in the functioning of society. Finally, *rebels* reject both the existing values and the legitimate means, but instead of dropping out, work actively to substitute new values and reconstruct the social system. Members of radical political groups fall into this category.

Critical points

Critics pointed out that in focusing on individual responses, Merton failed to appreciate the significance of **subcultures** in sustaining deviant behaviour. His reliance on official statistics is also problematic, because these have since been shown to be flawed and unreliable. It has also been noted that Merton's thesis seems to overestimate the amount of 'lower working-class' criminality – it implies that everyone in this class group should experience the strain towards crime. But as the majority of this class group never become involved in crime, we have to ask, why not?

Contemporary significance

Merton's study retains its significance because it addresses a central research problem in the study of crime and deviance: when society as a whole is becoming more affluent, why do crime rates continue to rise? In emphasizing the social strain between rising aspirations and persistent structural social inequalities, Merton points to the sense of *relative deprivation* amongst manual working-class groups as an important motivator for deviant behaviour. His research was also an effective sociological critique of earlier biological and psychological explanations of crime and deviance. He demonstrates that individual choices and motivations are always made within a wider social context, which shapes those decisions according to the place of social groups and the differential opportunities available to them.

 The idea of relative deprivation is discussed in chapter 12, 'Poverty, Social Exclusion and Welfare'.

Table 21.1	**Adaptive responses to social strain**	
	Approved Values	Approved Means
Conformity	+	+
Innovation (crime)	+	—
Ritualism	—	+
Retreatism	—	—
Rebellion	replacement	replacement

of mental health patients that began in the 1950s. Instead of being forced into institutions, the mentally ill were treated with tranquillizers and then released. As a result, the number of psychiatric patients in New York dropped from 93,000 in 1955 to just 11,000 by 1992.

What happened to all those psychiatric patients? Many of them became homeless, sleeping rough across New York. By 'defining deviance down', people sleeping on the street were thus redefined, not as insane, but as persons lacking affordable housing. At the same time, the 'normal' acceptable level of crime had risen. Moynihan points out that after the St Valentine's Day massacre in 1929, in which seven gangsters were murdered, America was outraged. Today, violent gang murders are so common there is hardly a reaction. Moynihan also sees the under-reporting of crime as another way in which it becomes 'normalized'. He concludes: 'We are getting used to a lot of behaviour that is not good for us.'

Evaluation

Functionalist theories rightly emphasize connections between conformity and deviance in different social contexts. Lack of opportunity for success is a key differentiating factor between those who engage in criminal behaviour and those who do not. But we should be cautious about the idea that people in poorer communities aspire to the same level of success as more affluent groups. Most tend to adjust their aspirations to what they see as the reality of their situation and only a minority turn to crime. Merton, Cohen and Cloward and Ohlin can all be criticized for presuming that middle-class values have been accepted throughout society. It would also be wrong to suppose that a mismatch of aspirations and opportunities is confined to the less privileged. There are pressures towards criminal activity among other groups too, as indicated by the 'white-collar crimes' of embezzlement, fraud and tax evasion, which we will deal with later.

Interactionist theory

Sociologists studying crime and deviance in the interactionist tradition focus on deviance as a socially constructed phenomenon. They reject the idea that there are types of conduct that are inherently 'deviant'. Rather, interactionists ask how behaviours come to be defined as deviant and why certain groups and not others are labelled as deviant.

Labelling perspectives

One of the most important interactionist approaches to understanding crime and deviance is the **labelling perspective**. Labelling theorists interpret deviance not as a set of characteristics of individuals or groups, but as a process of interaction between deviants and non-deviants. Therefore, we must discover why some people come to be tagged with a 'deviant' label if we are to understand the nature of deviance itself.

People who represent the forces of law and order, or are able to impose definitions of conventional morality on others, do most of the labelling. The labels that create categories of deviance thus express the power structure of society. By and large, the rules in terms of which deviance is defined are framed by the wealthy for the poor, by men for women, by older people for younger people, and by ethnic majorities for minority groups. For example, many children wander into other people's gardens, steal fruit or play truant. In an affluent neighbourhood, these might be regarded by parents, teachers and police alike as innocent pastimes of childhood. In poorer areas, they might be seen as evidence of tendencies towards juvenile delinquency. Once a child is labelled a delinquent, he or she is stigmatized and is likely to be considered untrustworthy by teachers and prospective employers. In both instances the acts are the same, but they are assigned different meanings.

Howard Becker is one of the sociologists most closely associated with labelling perspectives. His work showed how deviant identities are produced through labelling processes rather than through deviant motivations or behaviour. Becker argued that 'deviant behaviour is behaviour that people so label'. He was highly critical of criminological approaches which saw a clear distinction between the 'normal' and the 'deviant'. For Becker, deviant behaviour is not the determining factor in why people become 'deviants'. Rather, there are processes unrelated to the behaviour itself, which are more influential in determining whether or not someone is labelled as deviant. A person's dress, manner of speaking or country of origin could be the key factors that determine whether or not a deviant label is applied.

Labelling theory came to be associated with Becker's studies of marijuana smokers (Becker 1963). In the early 1960s, smoking marijuana was a marginal activity within subcultures rather than the lifestyle choice it has become today. Becker found that becoming a marijuana smoker depended on one's acceptance into the subculture, close association with experienced users and one's attitudes towards non-users.

Labelling not only affects how others see an individual, but also influences the individual's sense of self-identity. Edwin Lemert (1972) advanced a model for understanding how deviance can either coexist with or become central to one's identity. He argued that, contrary to what some might think, deviance is actually quite commonplace and people usually get away with it. For example, deviant acts, such as traffic violations, rarely come to light, while others, such as small-scale theft from the workplace, are often 'overlooked'. Lemert called the initial act of transgression **primary deviance**. In most cases, these acts remain 'marginal' to the person's self-identity and a process occurs through which the deviant act is 'normalized'. In some cases though,

---

THINKING CRITICALLY

Which of these unconventional acts is more likely to be labelled as 'deviant'? What explanation can you offer as to why one of these people is more likely to be labelled as 'a deviant' than the other? List the consequences for the individual that may follow from being so labelled.

normalization does not occur and the person is labelled a criminal or delinquent. Lemert used the term **secondary deviance** to describe cases where individuals come to accept the label and see themselves as deviant. In these cases, the label can become central to a person's self-identity and lead to a continuation or intensification of the deviant behaviour.

In an influential study, 'The Saints and the Roughnecks' by William Chambliss (1973), the labelling process was linked to the wider social class structure. Chambliss studied two groups of delinquents in an American school, one from upper-middle-class families – the Saints – the other from poor families – the Roughnecks. Although the Saints were constantly involved in petty crimes such as drinking, vandalism, truancy and theft, none of their members was ever arrested. The Roughnecks were involved in similar activities, yet they were constantly in trouble with the police. Chambliss concluded that neither group was more delinquent than the other and looked to other factors for an explanation of the different reactions of the police and the broader community towards the two groups.

He found that the upper-class gang had cars and were able physically to remove themselves from the eyes of the community. The lower-class boys, through necessity, congregated in a public area where they were frequently on view. Chambliss concluded that differences of this sort were indicative of the class structure of society, which gave wealthier groups advantages in avoiding being labelled as deviant. For instance, the parents of the Saints saw their sons' crimes as harmless pranks, while the parents of the Roughnecks acquiesced to the police's labelling of their sons' behaviour as criminal. The community as a whole also seemed to share these different labels.

The boys went on to have lives consistent with the labels, the Saints living out a conventional middle-class existence, while the Roughnecks had continuing problems with the law. As we saw earlier, such outcomes are linked to what Lemert called 'secondary deviance', which prevents people from carrying on as 'normal' once they have been labelled as 'deviant'. Chambliss's study demonstrates the connections between macrosociological factors like social class and microsociological phenomena, such as how people become labelled as deviant. The research therefore shows why we need a sociological imagination that links micro- and macro-level factors.

The process of 'learning to be deviant', which the Roughnecks went through, tends to be accentuated by prisons and social agencies, the very organizations that are set up to correct deviant behaviour. For labelling theorists, this is a clear demonstration of the 'paradox of social control', described by Leslie Wilkins (1964) as **deviancy amplification**.

Wilkins was interested in how deviant identities are 'managed' and integrated into daily life. He suggested that the outcome of this process is often deviancy amplification. This refers to the unintended consequence of labelling a behaviour as deviant, when an agency of control actually provokes more of that same deviant behaviour. If the labelled person incorporates the label into his or her identity through secondary deviance, this is likely to provoke more responses from agencies of control. In other words, the behaviour that was seen as undesirable becomes more prevalent, and those labelled as deviant become more resistant to change.

Evaluation

Labelling perspectives have been important, because they begin from the assumption that no act is intrinsically 'deviant' or 'criminal'. Such definitions are established by the powerful, through the formulation of laws and their interpretation by police, courts and correctional institutions. Critics of labelling have argued that certain acts are universally and consistently prohibited across virtually all societies, such as murder, rape and robbery. But this view is surely incorrect. Killing, for example, is not

Classic Studies 21.2 | **Stan Cohen's folk devils and moral panics**

The research problem

Youth subcultures are colourful, spectacular and, for some, quite frightening. You may be or have been part of one. But how are youth subcultures actually created? And how do societies react to such youthful deviance? What role does the mass media play in its reporting of, say, skinheads, punk rockers or rave culture? The process of *deviancy amplification* was examined in a highly influential study conducted by Stanley Cohen, published as *Folk Devils and Moral Panics* in 1972. In this classic study, Cohen examined labelling processes in relation to the emergence and control of youth cultures in the UK. As a young postgraduate student, Cohen observed some of the minor clashes between 'Mods' and 'Rockers' in the seaside town of Clacton in 1964, but could not reconcile what he saw with newspaper reports the following day. Had he just missed the violence they all reported or was there another explanation?

Cohen's explanation

Lurid headlines such as 'Day of Terror by Scooter Groups' and 'Wild Ones Invade the Seaside' described youths as 'out of control'. Cohen notes that although these reports were wide of the mark, they set the tone for future reporting. In carefully sifting the documentary evidence from newspapers, court reports and arrest records, Cohen was able to reconstruct the events at Clacton and show that, apart from a few minor skirmishes, nothing out of the ordinary had happened. In fact, far worse disturbances had occurred in the years before the Mods and Rockers emerged. Cohen argued that, in presenting young people's activities in such a sensationalist way, the press contributed to a climate of fear and a panic that society's moral rules were under threat. In doing so, they inadvertently helped to *construct* new forms of youth identities rather than just reporting on them.

Attempts to control certain youth subcultures in the UK during the 1960s only succeeded in drawing attention to them and made them more popular. The process of labelling a group as outsiders – or 'folk devils' – in an attempt to

control them, backfired. Future seaside gatherings attracted much larger crowds, including some youths just looking for a fight, potentially creating larger problems for law-enforcement – a classic instance of the paradox of social control we noted above. Exaggerated media coverage was part of a new **moral panic** – a concept used by sociologists to describe societal over-reaction towards a certain social group or type of behaviour. Moral panics often emerge around public issues that are taken as symptomatic of general social disorder.

Critical points

Critics argued that the main problem with the theory was how to differentiate between an exaggerated moral panic and a serious social problem. For example, would the societal response to recent terrorist acts in the name of Islam be part of a moral panic, or is this such a serious matter that extensive media coverage and new laws are appropriate? Where does the boundary lie between an unnecessary panic and a legitimate response? Who decides? A further criticism is that, in recent years, moral panics have arisen over matters such as youthful crime and drug-use and 'bogus' asylum-seekers. This has led some sociologists to argue that such moral panics are not confined to short bursts of intense activity, but have become chronic features of everyday life in modern societies and, as such, have become 'normalized'.

Contemporary significance

Cohen's early study is particularly important because it successfully combined theories of deviant labelling with ideas of social control and the creation of deviant identities. In doing so, it created the framework for a very productive research agenda in the sociology of deviance which continues today. It also reminds us that, as sociologists, we cannot take events at face value or accept journalists' reports as accurate. Instead, we have to dig beneath the surface if we are better to understand societies and social processes.

always regarded as murder. In times of war, killing the enemy is positively approved and rewarded. Until recently, the laws in Britain did not recognize as rape sexual intercourse forced on a woman by her husband, which also shows that labelling changes over time.

However, we can criticize labelling perspectives on more convincing grounds. First, in focusing so heavily on secondary deviance, labelling theorists neglect the processes that lead people to commit acts of primary deviance. The labelling of certain activities as deviant is not completely arbitrary; differences in socialization, attitudes and opportunities all influence how far people are likely to engage in behaviour labelled as deviant. For instance, children from deprived backgrounds are more likely than richer children to steal from shops. It is not being labelled that leads them to steal in the first place, but the backgrounds from which they come.

Second, it is not clear whether labelling actually does have the effect of increasing deviant conduct. Delinquent behaviour tends to increase following conviction, but is this really the result of labelling? Other factors, such as increased interaction with other delinquents or learning about new criminal opportunities, may also be involved.

Conflict theories and the 'new criminology'

Publication of *The New Criminology* by Taylor, Walton and Young in 1973 marked an important break with earlier theories of crime and deviance. Its authors drew on elements of Marxist thought to argue that deviance is deliberately chosen and often political in nature. They rejected the idea that deviance is 'determined' by factors such as biology, personality, anomie, social disorganization or labelling. Rather, people actively choose to engage in deviant behaviour in response to the inequalities of the capitalist system. Thus, members of countercultural groups regarded as 'deviant' – such as supporters of the Black Power or gay liberation movements – were engaging in political acts which challenged the social order. Theorists of the **new criminology** framed their analysis in terms of the structure of society and the protection of the power of the ruling class.

This broad perspective was developed in specific directions by other sociologists. Stuart Hall and others at the Birmingham Centre for Contemporary Cultural Studies (BCCCS) conducted an important study on a phenomenon which had attracted enormous attention in the early 1970s in Britain – the crime of 'mugging'. Several high-profile muggings were publicized, fuelling widespread popular concerns of an explosion in violent street crime. Muggers were overwhelming portrayed as black, contributing to the view that immigrants were primarily responsible for the breakdown of society. In *Policing the Crisis* (1978), Hall and his colleagues argued that this was a moral panic, encouraged by both the state and the media as a way of deflecting attention away from rising unemployment, declining wages and other deep structural flaws within society. As we will see in the section on victimization below, a notable feature of the patterning of crime and deviance is that some social groups, such as young people within black and south Asian communities, are much more likely to be victims of crime or seen as a social problem, than others.

Around the same time, other criminologists examined the formation and use of laws in society, arguing that laws are tools used by the powerful to maintain their own privileged positions. They rejected the idea that laws are 'neutral', to be applied evenly across the population. Instead, they claimed that as inequalities increase between the ruling class and the working class, law becomes a more important instrument which the powerful use to maintain order. This dynamic can be seen in the workings of the criminal justice system, which had become increasingly oppressive towards working-class 'offenders'; or in tax legislation which disproportionately favoured the wealthy. This power imbalance is not restricted to the creation of laws. The powerful also break laws, but are rarely monitored and caught. These crimes are, on the whole, much more harmful than the everyday crime and delinquency which attracts most attention. But, fearful of the implications of pursuing 'white-collar' criminals, law-enforcement focuses its efforts on less powerful members of society, such as prostitutes, drug-users and petty thieves (Pearce 1976; Chambliss 1978; Box 1983).

These studies and others associated with the 'new criminology' were important in widening the debate about crime and deviance to include questions of levels of harm, social justice, power and politics. They emphasized that crime occurs at all levels of society and must be understood in the context of inequalities and competing interests.

THINKING CRITICALLY

Imagine you have been paid to carry out a research study (a pleasant thought!) into drug-use and harm. How would you measure the level of harm to individuals, communities and society caused by the following legal and illegal substances: tobacco, alcohol, prescription tranquillisers, ecstasy (MDMA), cocaine, heroin. What consequences would you foresee, if *all* of these substances were: (a) made legal or (b) made illegal? Based on your conclusions, what recommendations would you give to government policy-makers?

Left Realism

In the 1980s, a strand of criminology emerged which became known as 'New Left' or 'Left Realism'. This strand also drew on ideas from the 'new criminology'

discussed above, but distanced itself from so-called 'left idealists', whom they saw as romanticizing deviance and downplaying the real problem of crime, particularly within working-class communities. For quite some time, many criminologists had minimized the importance of rises in official crime rates arguing that the mass media created unnecessary public disquiet about the figures, or that most crime was a disguised form of protest against inequality. Left Realism moved away from this position, emphasizing that there was reliable evidence that increases in crime had occurred and that the public was right to be worried. Left Realists argued that criminology needed to engage more with the 'real' issues of crime control and social policy, rather than debate them abstractly (Lea and Young 1984; Matthews and Young 1986).

Left Realism drew attention to the victims of crime, arguing that victim surveys provide a more valid picture of the extent of crime than official statistics (Evans 1992). Victim surveys revealed that crime was a serious problem, particularly in impoverished inner-city areas. Left Realists pointed out that rates of crime and victimization were concentrated in marginalized neighbourhoods and that deprived groups in society were at a much greater risk of crime than others.

This approach draws on Merton, Cloward and Ohlin and others to suggest that, in the inner cities, criminal subcultures develop. Such subcultures do not derive from poverty as such, but from political marginalization and relative deprivation – people's experience of being deprived of things they and everyone else is entitled to. In recent times, these ideas have been increasingly discussed using the concept of social exclusion – the processes that operate to effectively deny some social groups full citizenship within society. Criminalized youth groups, for example, operate at the margins of 'respectable society' and pit themselves against it. The fact that rates of crime carried out by blacks have risen over recent years is attributed to the fact that policies of racial integration have failed.

> The ideas of relative deprivation and social exclusion are discussed in chapter 12, 'Poverty, Social Exclusion and Welfare'.

To address these trends in crime, Left Realism advanced 'realistic' proposals for changes in policing procedures. Law-enforcement needs to become more responsive to communities, it is claimed, rather than relying on 'military policing' techniques which alienate public support. Left Realists proposed 'minimal policing', whereby locally elected police authorities would be accountable to citizens, who would have a larger say in setting policing priorities for their area. Furthermore, by spending more time investigating and clearing up crimes and less time on routine or administrative work, the police can regain the trust of local communities. On the whole, Left Realism represents a more pragmatic and policy-oriented approach than many of the criminological perspectives which preceded it.

Critics of Left Realism accept the importance of their stress on victimization, but criticize their focus on individual victims only within the narrow confines of the political and media-driven discussions of 'the crime problem'. Such narrow definitions of crime focus on the most visible forms of criminality, such as street crimes, while neglecting other offences, such as those carried out by the state or large corporations (Walton and Young 1998). In this sense, many Marxists argued, the Left Realists had conceded too much ground to mainstream criminology with its focus on changing policies and this had blunted the radical edge of the new criminology.

Control theories

Control theories posit that crime occurs as a result of an imbalance between impulses towards criminal activity and the social or

Left Realists emphasize the real and very harmful effects of crime on the lives of the poorest people and communities in society.

physical controls that deter it. It is less interested in individuals' motivations for carrying out crimes, assuming that people act rationally so that, given the opportunity, everyone would engage in deviant acts. Many types of crime, it is argued, are the result of 'situational decisions' – a person sees an opportunity and is motivated to act to take advantage of it.

An early control theorist, Travis Hirschi, argued that humans are fundamentally selfish beings who make calculated decisions about whether or not to commit crime by weighing the potential benefits against the risks of doing so. In *Causes of Delinquency* (1969), Hirschi's research argued that there are four types of social bond linking people to society and hence, law-abiding behaviour: attachment, commitment, involvement and belief. When sufficiently strong, these bonds help to maintain social control and conformity by tying people into bonds of conformity. But if these bonds with society are weak, delinquency and deviance may result. Hirschi's approach suggests that delinquents are often individuals whose low levels of self-control are a result of inadequate socialization at home or in school (Gottfredson and Hirschi 1990).

Right Realism

The late-1970s election successes of Margaret Thatcher in Britain and Ronald Reagan in the United States led to vigorous 'law-and-order' approaches to crime in both countries, often described as **Right Realism**. This approach remains influential today, particularly in the USA under the presidency of George W. Bush. The perceived escalation of crime and delinquency were said to be linked to moral degeneracy, the decline of individual responsibility due to dependence on the welfare state and liberal education, the collapse of the nuclear family and communities and the wider erosion of traditional values (Murray 1984). Public debates and extensive media coverage centred on the crisis of violence and lawlessness which threatened society.

For Right Realists, deviance was portrayed as an individual pathology – a set of destructive lawless behaviours, actively chosen and perpetrated by individual selfishness and a lack of self-control and morality. They were dismissive of other 'theoretical' approaches discussed in this chapter, especially those that linked crime to poverty and class-based inequalities. Conservative governments in the UK and USA began to intensify law-enforcement activities. Police powers were extended, funding for the criminal justice system expanded and long prison sentences were increasingly relied on as the most effective deterrent against crime. In the USA, 'thee strikes laws' were introduced by state governments in the 1990s to tackle 'habit-ual' offenders. If a person commits three separate serious offences, then the third offence carries a mandatory extended term of imprisonment with no room for judges to exercise their discretion. It is argued that three-time offenders are demonstrably incorrigible and public safety from their activities should be the priority. Of course, one major consequence of this policy has been the enormous growth of the prison population in the USA.

Crime prevention involving target hardening and surveillance systems has been a popular approach to 'managing' the risk of crime (Vold et al. 2002). Such techniques are often favoured by policy-makers because they are relatively simple to introduce alongside existing policing techniques, and they reassure citizens by giving the impression that decisive action against crime is being taken. Yet critics argue that because such techniques do not engage with the underlying causes of crime – such as social inequalities, unemployment and poverty – their greatest success lies in protecting certain segments of the population against crime and displacing delinquency into other areas.

One illustration of this process can be seen in the physical exclusion of certain categories of people from common spaces in an attempt to reduce crime and the perceived risks of crime. In response to feelings of insecurity among the population at large, public spaces in society, such as libraries, parks and even street corners, are increasingly being transformed into 'security bubbles'. Risk-management practices, such as police monitoring, private security teams and surveillance systems, are aimed at protecting the public against potential risks. In shopping precincts, for example, security measures are becoming more prominent as part of a 'contractual bargain' between businesses and consumers. In order to attract and maintain a customer base, businesses must ensure the safety and comfort of their clients. Young people tend to be excluded from such spaces disproportionately because they are perceived as a greater threat to security and are statistically more likely to offend than adults. As part of creating 'locations of trust' for consumers, young people find that the number of public spaces open to them is shrinking.

Police forces have also expanded in response to increasing crime. When crime rates are rising, there is a public clamour for more police 'on the street'. Governments eager to appear decisive on crime tend to favour increasing the number and resources of the police in an attempt to prevent crime. The popularly held view of policing is that it is the cornerstone of maintaining law and order. But what is the role of the police in controlling crime? It is not clear that having more police necessarily translates into lower crime rates. In the United Kingdom, official statistics on the crime rate and number of police cast doubt on the link between the two. This raises some puzzling questions. If increased policing does not prevent offending, why does the public demand a visible police presence? What role does policing really play in our society?

Controlling crime

Some control theorists see growing crime as an outcome of the increasing number of opportunities and targets for crime in modern societies. As the population becomes more affluent, consumerism becomes more central to people's lives and goods such as televisions, DVD players, computers, cars and designer clothing – favourite targets for thieves – are owned by more and more people. Residential homes are increasingly left empty during the daytime as more women take on employment outside the home. 'Motivated offenders', interested in committing crimes, can select from a broad range of 'suitable targets'.

In response, official policies on crime prevention in recent years have focused on limiting the opportunities for the commission of crimes in an approach known as **situational crime prevention** (SCP) (Hughes 1998; Colquhoun 2004). Central to such policies are the ideas of *surveillance* and *target hardening*. Surveillance involves communities 'policing' themselves via Neighbourhood Watch schemes and often includes the installation of closed circuit television (CCTV) systems in city centres and public spaces to deter criminal activity. Modifying the local environment has also become a more widespread technique, making it more difficult for crimes to take place by intervening directly into potential 'crime situations' – this is one type of 'environmental criminology', the name given to several approaches based on the idea of intervening in environments to prevent criminal activity.

Although environmental criminologies may seem to be novel, in fact they are best seen as modern versions of the 'ecological approach' of the Chicago School of Sociology in 1920s and '30s America. Chicago School sociologists mapped the social patterns of urban environments from the official statistics, showing how cities developed over time. They identified particular areas associated with a range of social problems, such as crime, and related these to the distribution of social groups within the city. Modern cities were seen as productive of 'social disorganization' – the weakening of primary social relations through poverty and transient populations, with a consequent loss of social solidarity and community cohesion. Crime, they argued, flourished in such an environment, as neighbourhoods were not able effectively to defend themselves. An echo of this basic approach to urban crime problems can be heard in the modern environmental criminologies.

 The Chicago School's ideas are discussed in chapter 6, 'Cities and Urban Life'.

Target hardening involves strengthening the security of potential targets, making

Physical signs of social disorder can lead to more serious crime, according to the 'broken windows' thesis.

them more difficult to steal. For example, factory-fitted vehicle immobilizers, alarms and better locks are intended to reduce the opportunities for car thieves, and public telephones have been fitted with tougher coin boxes to deter opportunistic vandals. SCP theorists based their ideas on a widespread feeling that previous policies which had tried to reform criminals had all failed. Rather than changing the criminal, they argue that the most effective policy is to take practical measures to control the environment within which criminals are able to commit crime.

Target hardening techniques, combined with zero tolerance policing, have gained favour among politicians in recent years and have been successful in reducing crime in some contexts. Zero tolerance policing targets petty crime and forms of disruptive conduct, such as vandalism,

loitering and public drunkenness. Police crackdowns on such low-level deviance are thought to have a positive effect in reducing more serious forms of crime. But criticisms of such an approach can also be made. Target hardening and zero tolerance policing do not address the underlying causes of crime, but protect and defend certain social groups from crime's reach. The growing popularity of private security services, car alarms, house alarms, guard dogs and gated communities has led some people to feel that we are heading towards an 'armoured' society, where segments of the population feel compelled to defend themselves against others. This tendency is occurring not only in Britain and the United States as the gap between the wealthiest and most deprived widens, but is particularly marked in the former Soviet Union, South Africa and Brazil, where a 'fortress mentality' has emerged among the privileged (Davis 2006).

There is another unintended consequence of such policies: as popular crime targets are 'hardened', patterns of crime may shift from one domain to another. For example, strengthening the security of new cars left older models relatively more vulnerable. The result was that the occurrence of car thefts shifted from newer models to older ones. Target hardening and zero tolerance approaches run the risk of displacing criminal offences from better protected areas into more vulnerable ones and, as Left Realists point out, victimization is likely to fall even more disproportionately on poorer communities. Neighbourhoods that are poor or lacking in social cohesion may well experience a growth in crime and delinquency as affluent regions defend themselves.

Target hardening and zero tolerance policing are based on a theory known as 'broken windows' (Wilson and Kelling 1982) which is rooted in a 1960s study by the American social psychologist, Philip Zimbardo, who abandoned cars without licence plates and with their hoods up in two entirely different social settings: the wealthy community of Palo Alto, California and a poor neighbourhood in the Bronx, New York. In both places, as soon as passersby, regardless of class or race, sensed that the cars were abandoned and that 'no one cared', the cars were vandalized (Zimbardo 1969). Extrapolating from this study, the authors of the 'broken windows' theory argued that any sign of social disorder in a community, even the appearance of a broken window, will encourage more serious crime to flourish. One unrepaired broken window is a sign that no one cares, so breaking more windows – that is, committing more serious crimes – is a rational response by criminals to the situation. As a result, minor acts of deviance can lead to a spiral of crime and social decay (Felson 1994).

Since the late 1980s, the 'broken windows' theory has served as the basis for new policing strategies, focused on 'minor' crimes such as drinking or using drugs in public, and traffic violations.

However, one important flaw in the 'broken windows' theory is that the police are left to identify what constitutes 'social disorder'. Without a systematic definition, the police are authorized to see almost anything as a sign of disorder and anyone as a potential threat. In fact, as crime rates fell throughout the 1990s, the number of complaints of police abuse and harassment went up, particularly by young, urban, black men who fit the 'profile' of a potential criminal and prison populations expanded.

Theoretical conclusions

What can we conclude from this survey of theories of crime? First, we must recall a point made earlier: even though crime is only one type of deviant behaviour, it covers such a variety of activities – from shoplifting a bar of chocolate to mass murder – that it is highly unlikely that a single theory would ever account for all criminal conduct.

Sociological theories of crime are significant for two reasons. First, they correctly emphasize the continuities between criminal and 'normal' behaviour. The contexts in which particular types of activity are seen as criminal and punishable by law vary widely and are linked to wider questions of power and inequality within society. Second, all agree that social context is important in criminal activities. Whether someone engages in a criminal act or comes to be regarded as a criminal is influenced fundamentally by social learning and social surroundings.

In spite of its deficiencies, labelling perspectives are perhaps the most widely used in studies of crime and deviant behaviour. The labelling approach desensitizes us to the ways in which some activities come to be defined as punishable in law, and the power relations that form such definitions, as well as to the interaction process through

"We find that all of us, as a society, are to blame, but only the defendant is guilty."

which particular individuals may come to take on a deviant identity.

The way in which crime is understood directly affects the policies developed to combat it. For example, if crime is seen as the product of deprivation or social disorganization, policies might be aimed at reducing poverty and strengthening social services. If criminality is seen as opportunistic and freely chosen by individuals, attempts to counter it may concentrate more on changing environments. We shall now examine recent crime trends in the UK and elsewhere, considering some of the policy responses to them.

Patterns of crime in the United Kingdom

As measured by statistics of crimes reported to the police, rates of crime in the developed countries of the world increased enormously over the twentieth century. For example, prior to the 1920s, there were fewer than 100,000 offences recorded each year in England and Wales; this number had reached 500,000 by 1950, and peaked at 5.6 million in 1992. Levels of recorded crime more than doubled between 1977 and 1992.

Since the mid-1990s, the overall number of crimes committed in England and Wales appears to have levelled off, with additional measures, such as the British Crime Survey, showing a considerable fall in the overall amount of crime (see figure 21.1). This is consistent with trends in most European countries. According to recent data, the risk of becoming a victim of crime in England and Wales is at its lowest for more than 20 years (Clegg et al. 2005). The end of rising crime figures has taken many experts by surprise. The causes behind it and whether the trend is sustainable are still uncertain.

Despite such recent falls in the crime statistics, there remains a widespread perception that, over time, crime in developed countries has grown more prevalent and become more serious (Nicholas et al. 2007). It has been reported that levels of

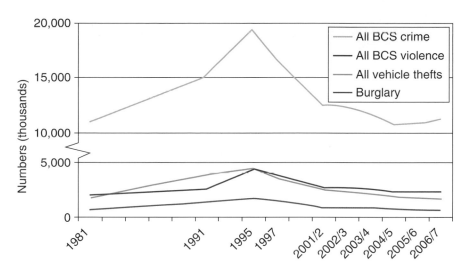

Figure 21.1   Trends in British crime surveys, 1981–2006/7

Source: Nicholas et al. 2007: 6

worry about the main types of crime have been falling, but anxiety about anti-social behaviour remains more stable (Clegg et al. 2005). If at one time crime was seen as something marginal or exceptional, in recent decades it has become a more prominent concern in many people's lives. Surveys now show that people are much more fearful of crime than in earlier periods and are experiencing heightened anxiety about going out after dark, about their homes being burgled or about becoming victims of violence. People are reportedly also more worried about more low-level types of disorder, such as graffiti, drunken rowdiness and groups of teenagers hanging about on the streets – in fact, the very offences that situational crime prevention policies discussed above were introduced to tackle.

So how much crime actually exists and how vulnerable are people to becoming its victims? What is being done to curb crime? These questions have become highly contested in the last few decades as media coverage of crime has risen along with public outrage, and as successive governments have promised to 'get tough on crime'. Untangling the nature and distribu-

tion of crime, let alone designing policies to address it, has proved to be far from straightforward.

Crime and crime statistics

To determine the extent of crime and the most common forms of criminal offence, one approach is to examine the official statistics on the number of crimes which the police actually record. Since such statistics are published regularly, there would seem to be no difficulty in assessing crime rates – but this assumption is quite erroneous. Statistics about crime and delinquency are probably the least reliable of all officially published figures on social issues. Criminologists have emphasized that we cannot take official crime statistics at face value.

First, the most basic limitation of statistics based on reported crime is that the majority of crimes never get reported to the police at all. There are many reasons why people decide not to report a crime (see table 21.2). Even when a victim is wounded, more than half the cases are not reported to the police; victims claim, for example, that it is a private affair or something they have dealt with themselves. Crime may go

Table 21.2 Reasons for not reporting crime, 2007

Percentages

	Vandalism	Burglary	Thefts from vehicles & attempts	Other household theft	Other personal theft	BCS violence	2006/07 BCS All BCS
Trivial/no loss/police would not/could not do anything	83	70	84	81	66	46	72
Private/dealt with ourselves	10	17	10	13	13	34	16
Inconvenient to report	5	6	7	5	6	4	6
Reported to other authorities	2	2	1	2	14	8	5
Common occurrence	3	2	2	1	3	4	3
Fear of reprisal	3	4	0	2	1	7	33
Dislike or fear of the police/previous bad experience with the police or courts	2	1	1	1	2	2	2
Other	3	9	5	3	9	10	6
Unweighted base	*2,805*	*352*	*1,323*	*1,414*	*504*	*933*	*8,252*

Source: Nicholas et al. 2007

unreported for other reasons. Some forms of criminal violence, for example, are more 'hidden' than others. Physical and sexual abuse often takes place behind closed doors in the home, or in care institutions and prisons. Victims may fear that they won't be believed by the police, or that the abuse will get worse if they tell. As we will see below, the victims of domestic violence are often extremely reluctant to report the crime to police. Some people assume that the crime is too trivial to be reported, or that the police wouldn't be able to do anything about it anyway. A large proportion of car theft is reported, however, because the owner needs to have done so in order to claim on an insurance policy.

Second, of the crimes that *are* reported to the police, many do not get recorded in the statistics. It has been estimated that in the UK, although 43 per cent of crimes get *reported* to the police, just 29 per cent are *recorded*; this figure does, however, vary depending on the crime (Simmons and Dodds 2003). The police may be sceptical of the validity of some information about purported crimes that comes their way, or the victim may not want to lodge a formal complaint.

The overall effect of such partial reporting and recording of crimes is that the official crime statistics reflect only a portion of overall criminal offences. The offences not captured in official statistics are referred to as the *hidden figure* of unrecorded crime.

Perhaps a more accurate picture of crime in England and Wales comes from the annual British Crime Survey (BCS), which measures levels of crime by asking people directly about crimes which they have experienced. As a result, the BCS includes crimes that are not reported to or recorded by the police, and it can be seen as an important addition to police records. The survey is based on interviews with people living in private households, who are asked about their experiences of crime in the last twelve months. Each year, the survey involves a representative survey of about 40,000 adults across England and Wales. Although there are differences in the rates of growth and decline for varying types of offences, with some figures suggesting a recent rise in violent crime, the overall trend in both the BCS and the figures for recorded crimes has been downwards since the mid-1990s.

> ### THINKING CRITICALLY
> Study figure 21.2, which estimates the percentage of types of crime known to the police in England and Wales. Taking each in turn, give some reasons for why some types of crime are almost always reported and others are not. What factors would influence people's decision to report or not to report? How might such differential reporting of offences impact on the reliability of the police recorded crime statistics? How could we improve the reporting of these crimes?

Surveys such as the BCS are known as **victimization studies**. While they are valuable indicators, the data from victimization studies must also be treated with some caution. In certain instances, the methodology of the study itself may result in significant under-reporting. The BCS is conducted by means of interviews in respondents' homes. This might result, for example, in a victim of domestic violence not reporting violent incidents in the presence of the abuser, or where the abuse has taken place. What is more, the survey does not include people under the age of 16, or those who are homeless or live in some kind of institution, such as a care home. This is particularly important, as other research has shown that these groups can be particularly prone to being victims of crime, as we discover below.

Another important source of information about crime is self-report studies, in which people are asked to admit anonymously if they have *committed* any offences. The Offending, Crime and Justice Survey (OCJS) was introduced for England and Wales in

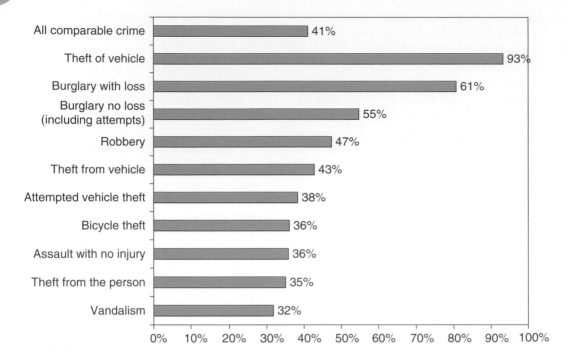

Figure 21.2 Estimate of crimes known to the police, 2006/7

Source: Nicholas et al. 2007: 39

2003 and aims to uncover the extent of offending, anti-social behaviour and drug-use, especially amongst young people aged 10–25. Such surveys are a useful addition to victimization surveys and police records. Of course, these studies could also suffer from under-reporting, as participants might be unwilling to report an offence for fear of the consequences. Over-reporting could also take place, perhaps because of a bad memory or through a desire to show off.

Victims and perpetrators of crime

Are some individuals or groups more likely to commit crimes, or to become the victims of crime? The evidence tells us that, indeed, they are. Social science research and crime statistics show that crime and victimization are not randomly distributed across the population. For example, men are more likely than women to commit crimes and the young are more often involved in crime than older people.

The likelihood of someone becoming a victim of crime is closely linked to the area in which they live. Areas suffering from greater material deprivation generally have higher crime rates and higher proportions of ethnic minority groups tend to live in such areas. People living in inner-city neighbourhoods have a much greater risk of becoming victims of crime than do residents of more affluent suburban areas. That ethnic minorities are concentrated disproportionately in inner-city areas also appears to be a significant factor in their higher rates of victimization.

Gender, sexuality and crime

Before the 1970s, criminological studies had generally ignored half the population. Feminists correctly criticized criminology for being a male-dominated enterprise in which women were largely 'invisible', both

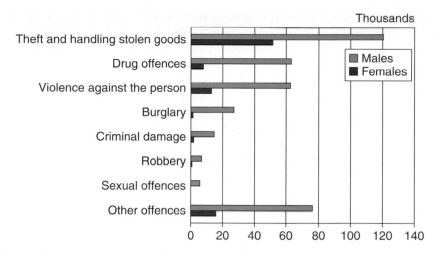

Note: 'Other offences' include fraud, forgery and indictable motoring offences

Figure 21.3   Offenders found guilty of, or cautioned for, indictable offences 2004, England and Wales

Source: National Statistics 2006c

in theoretical considerations and empirical studies. Since the 1970s, many important feminist studies have drawn attention to the way in which criminal transgressions by women occur in different contexts from those of men, and how women's experiences with the criminal justice system are influenced by certain gendered assumptions about appropriate male and female roles. Feminists have also played a critical role in highlighting the prevalence of violence against women, both at home and in public.

Male and female crime rates

Crime statistics on gender and crime show the most striking and long-established pattern of crime and deviance across all developed and developing countries. For instance, according to recent data, only some 19 per cent of all known offenders in England and Wales are female (Home Office 2003). There is also an enormous imbalance in the ratio of men to women in prison, not only in Britain but in all the industrialized countries. In recent years, the number of women in UK prisons has risen rapidly, from an average of 1560 in 1993 to an all

time high of 4672 in May 2004. However, despite this rise, women still constitute a tiny percentage of prisoners overall: just 5.6 per cent of the total prison population of 75,030 in England and Wales (HM Prison Service 2006). There are also sharp contrasts between the types of crime that men and women commit. As figure 21.3 illustrates, women are much more likely to commit theft, usually from shops, than violent crime.

Of course, the real gender difference in crime rates could be much less than the official statistics show. Otto Pollak (1950) suggested as much, contending that certain crimes perpetrated by women tend to go unreported. He saw women's predominantly domestic role as providing them with the opportunity to commit crimes, such as poisoning, in the home. Pollak regarded women as naturally deceitful and highly skilled at covering up their crimes. This was grounded in biology, as women had learned to hide the pain and discomfort of menstruation from men and were also able to fake interest in sexual intercourse in a way that men could not. Pollak also argued that female offenders are treated more leniently because male police officers tend to adopt a 'chivalrous' attitude towards them.

Although Pollak cannot be accused of ignoring female criminality, his stereotypical portrayal of women as conniving and deceptive has no basis in any evidence from research studies. However, his suggestion that women are treated more leniently by the criminal justice system has prompted much debate and examination. This 'chivalry thesis' has been applied in two ways. First, it is possible that police and other officials regard female offenders as less dangerous than men and ignore some activities for which males would be arrested. Second, in sentencing for criminal offences, women tend to be much less likely to be imprisoned than male offenders. A number of empirical studies have been undertaken to test the chivalry thesis, but the results remain inconclusive. For example, one reason for differential sentencing may simply be that, as figure 21.3 shows, women commit less serious offences than men. If so, then a gender dimension clearly exists, but it is unrelated to the 'chivalry' of officials. Another major difficulty is assessing the relative influence of gender compared to other factors such as age, class and race. For example, it appears that older women offenders tend to be treated less forcefully than their male counterparts. Other studies have shown that black women receive worse treatment than white women at the hands of the police.

Another perspective adopted by feminists examines how social understandings of 'femininity' affect women's experiences in the criminal justice system. Frances Heidensohn (1995) has argued that women are treated more harshly in cases where they have allegedly deviated from feminine norms. For example, young girls who are perceived to be sexually promiscuous are more often taken into custody than boys. In such cases, women are seen as 'doubly deviant' – not only have they broken the law, but they have also flouted 'appropriate' norms of female behaviour. They are judged

less on the nature of the offence and more on their 'deviant' lifestyle choice. Heidensohn and others have pointed out the double standard within the criminal justice system: male aggression and violence are seen as natural phenomena, while explanations of female offences are sought in 'psychological' imbalances.

In an effort to make female crime more visible, feminists have conducted a number of detailed investigations on female criminals – from girl gangs to female terrorists and women in prison. Such studies have shown that violence is not exclusively a characteristic of male criminality. Women *are* much less likely than men to participate in violent crime, but women *do* commit similar acts of violence.

Why, then, are female rates of criminality so much lower than those of men? There is some evidence that female lawbreakers are quite often able to escape coming before the courts because they are able to persuade the police or other authorities to see their actions in a particular light. They invoke what has been called the 'gender contract' – the implicit assumption that to be a woman is to be erratic and impulsive, on the one hand, and in need of protection on the other (Worrall 1990). On this view, it is argued that the police and courts do act chivalrously, and do not seek to punish women for behaviour which would be considered unacceptable in men. Other research suggests that particular women, such as those who do not live up to the norms of femininity, may end up being treated more harshly than men. Women perceived as 'bad mothers', for example, may receive more severe penalties from the courts (Carlen 1983).

Yet differential treatment could hardly account for the vast difference between male and female rates of crime. Reasons for this are almost certainly the same as those that explain gender differences in other spheres. There are, of course, certain specifically 'female crimes' – most notably prostitution, for which women are convicted while their male clients are not. 'Male crimes' remain 'male' because of differences in socialization and because men's activities and involvements are still more non-domestic than those of most women. As we saw with Pollak's approach, gender difference in crime often used to be explained by supposedly innate biological or psychological differences such as differential strength, passivity or a preoccupation with reproduction. Today, 'womanly' qualities are seen as largely socially generated, in common with the traits of 'masculinity'. Many women are socialized to value different qualities in social life (caring for others and the fostering of personal relationships) from those valued by males. Equally important, through the influence of ideology and other factors – such as ideas of what it means to be a 'nice girl' – women's behaviour is often kept confined and controlled in ways that male activities are not.

Ever since the late nineteenth century, criminologists have predicted that gender equalization would reduce or eliminate the differences in criminality between men and women, but, so far, crime remains a robustly gendered phenomenon.

Crime and the 'crisis of masculinity'

The high levels of crime found in poorer areas of large cities are associated particularly with the activities of young men. But why should so many young men in these areas turn to crime? As we saw earlier in the chapter, sociologists and criminologists have provided us with some ideas. Boys are often part of gangs from an early age, a subculture in which some forms of crime become a way of life. Once gang members are labelled as criminals by the authorities, they may embark on regular criminal activities. Although today there are girl gangs too, such subcultures tend to be fundamentally masculine and are infused with 'male' values of adventure, excitement and comradeship.

At one time, young men could look forward confidently to a lifetime career and a stable role as the family breadwinner, but this role has become much more elusive. Major shifts in the labour market have made unemployment and job insecurity a tangible threat, while women are growing increasingly independent financially, professionally and otherwise. Connell's work on 'hegemonic masculinity', discussed in chapter 14, has been drawn on by many sociologists and criminologists to explain how violence and aggression can be seen as an acceptable facet of masculine identities.

> In chapter 14, 'Sexuality and Gender', we discussed the notion that modern societies are witnessing a 'crisis of masculinity'.

Crimes against women

There are certain categories of crime where men are overwhelmingly the aggressors and women the victims. Domestic violence, sexual harassment, sexual assault and rape are crimes in which males use their superior social or physical power against women. While each of these has been practised by women against men, they nevertheless remain almost exclusively crimes carried out by men against women. It is estimated that 25 per cent of women in the developed world have been a victim of violence at some point in their lives, but all women face the threat of such crimes either directly or indirectly.

For many years, these offences were ignored by the criminal justice system; victims had to persevere tirelessly to gain legal recourse against offenders. Even today, the prosecution of crimes of intimate violence against women remains far from straightforward, though feminist criminology has done much to raise awareness and to integrate such offences into mainstream debates on crime. In this section we shall examine the crime of rape in the UK context, leaving discussions of domestic violence and sexual harassment to other chapters.

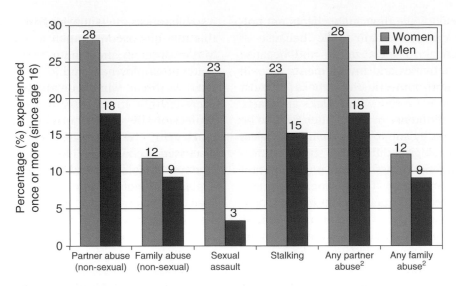

Figure 21.4   Prevalence of intimate violence since the age of 16, England and Wales 2004–5

Source: Finney 2006

> See chapter 9, 'Families and Intimate Relationships', for a wider discussion of domestic violence.

The extent of rape is very difficult to assess with any real accuracy. Only small numbers of rapes are actually reported to, and recorded by, the police and, hence, show up in official statistics. In 1999 the police recorded 7,809 offences as rape, but a detailed analysis of the 2001 British Crime Survey estimated around 47,000 female victims of rape or attempted rape in the previous year (Walby and Allen 2004). For the reasons discussed above, it is likely that the BCS also underestimates the real incidence of rape.

Until 1991, rape within marriage was not recognized as an offence in Britain. In a ruling delivered in 1736, Sir Matthew Hale declared that a husband 'cannot be guilty of rape committed by himself upon his lawful wife, for by their mutual matrimonial consent and contract the wife hath given up herself in this kind unto her husband which she cannot retract' (quoted in Hall et al. 1984: 20). This formulation remained the law in England and Wales until 1994, when an amendment brought 'marital rape' (and

'male rape') within the legislative framework, thus ending the previous assumption that a husband had the right to force himself on his wife.

There are many reasons why a woman might choose not to report sexual violence to the police. The majority of women who are raped either wish to put the incident out of their minds, or are unwilling to participate in what can be a humiliating process of medical examination, police interrogation and courtroom cross-examination. The legal process often takes a long time and can be intimidating. Courtroom procedure is public and the victim must come face to face with the accused. Proof of penetration, the identity of the rapist and the fact that the act occurred without the woman's consent all have to be forthcoming. A woman may feel that *she* is the one on trial, particularly if her own sexual history is examined publicly, as often happens in such cases.

Over recent years, women's groups have pressed for change in both legal and public thinking about rape. They have stressed that rape should not be seen as a sexual offence, but as a type of violent crime. It is not just a physical attack but an assault on an individual's integrity and dignity. Rape is clearly related to the association of masculinity with power, dominance and toughness. It is not for the most part the result of overwhelming sexual desire, but of the ties between sexuality and feelings of power and superiority. The sexual act itself is less significant than the debasement of the woman. The campaign has had some real results in changing legislation and rape is today generally recognized in law to be a specific type of criminal violence.

There is a sense in which all women are victims of rape. Women who have never been raped often experience anxieties similar to those who have. They may be afraid to go out alone at night, even on crowded streets, and may be almost equally fearful of being on their own in a house or flat. Emphasizing the close connection between rape and orthodox male sexuality, Susan Brownmiller (1975) argued that rape is part of a system of male intimidation that keeps all women in fear. Those who are not raped are still affected by the anxieties provoked and by the need to be much more cautious in everyday aspects of life than men have to be.

Crimes against homosexuals

Feminists have pointed out that understandings of violence are highly gendered and are influenced by 'common-sense' perceptions about risk and responsibility. Because women are generally seen as less able to defend themselves against violent attack, common sense holds that they should alter their behaviour in order to reduce the risk of becoming a victim of violence. For example, not only should women avoid walking in 'unsafe' neighbourhoods alone and at night, but they should be careful not to dress provocatively or to behave in a manner that could be misinterpreted by men. Women who fail to do so can be accused of 'asking for trouble'. In a court setting, their behaviour can be taken as a mitigating factor in considering the perpetrator's violent act (Dobash and Dobash 1992; Richardson and May 1999).

It has been suggested that a similar 'common-sense' logic applies in the case of violent acts against gay men and lesbians. Victimization studies reveal that homosexuals experience a high incidence of violent crime and harassment. A UK national survey of 4,000 gay men and women found that, in the previous five years, 33 per cent of gay men and 25 per cent of lesbians had been the victim of at least one violent attack. In all, a third had experienced some form of harassment, including threats or vandalism, and an overwhelming 73 per cent had been verbally abused in public (Mason and Palmer 1996).

Diane Richardson and Hazel May (1999) have argued that because homosexuals remain stigmatized and marginalized in many societies, there is a greater tendency for them to be seen as 'deserving' of crime, rather than as innocent victims. Homosexual relationships are still seen as belonging to the private realm, while heterosexuality is the overwhelming norm in public spaces. According to Richardson and May, lesbians and gay men who deviate from this private–public contract by displaying their homosexual identities in public are often blamed for making themselves vulnerable to crime. There is still a sense that introducing homosexuality into the public sphere represents a form of provocation. Crimes against homosexuals in the UK have led to calls by many social groups for the adoption of 'hate crime' legislation to protect the human rights of groups that remain stigmatized in society. These calls were acted upon in the Criminal Justice Act of 2003, which allowed judges in England and Wales to increase a sentence if an assault was motivated by 'homophobia' – the hatred or fear of homosexuals. Similar legislation has been introduced in Scotland and Northern Ireland.

Youth and crime

Popular fears about crime in many developed countries centres on offences such as

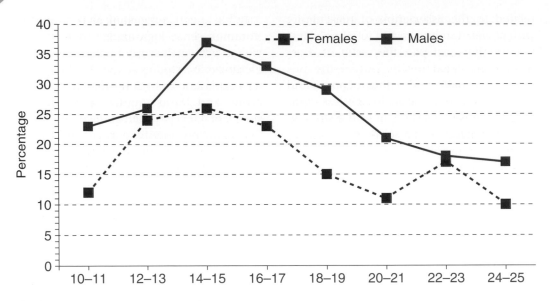

Figure 21.5 Prevalence of offending by age and sex (%)

Source: Home office 2004

theft, burglary and assault – 'street crimes' that are largely seen as the domain of young working-class males. Media coverage of rising crime rates often focuses on 'moral breakdown' amongst young people and highlights such issues as vandalism, school truancy and drug-use to illustrate the increasing 'permissiveness' in society. This equation of youth with criminal activity is not a new one. Young people have often been taken as an indicator of the health and welfare of society itself. Why should that be so?

Official statistics about crime rates do reveal high rates of offending among young people. According to self-report studies, fewer girls than boys admit to ever having committed an offence, as figure 21.5 illustrates for England and Wales (but remember that self-reported data can be unreliable). For boys, the peak age of offending tends to be around 18 and for girls, around 15.

According to this data, it might seem that offending by young people is a big problem. Yet we must be cautious in making such an assumption. As John Muncie has noted (1999), 'moral panics' about youth criminal-

ity may not accurately reflect social reality. An isolated event involving young people and crime – such as the 1964 Mods and Rockers episode discussed above – can be transformed symbolically into a full-blown 'crisis of childhood' demanding tough law and order responses. In Britain, the high-profile murder of 2-year-old James Bulger in 1993, by two 10-year-old boys, is an example of how moral outrage can deflect attention away from larger social issues. In the Bulger case, CCTV cameras in a shopping centre captured the image of the older boys leading the small child by the hand, which etched the case into the public consciousness. According to Muncie, the brutal murder was a watershed event in political and media portrayals of youth crime. Even very young children were seen as potentially violent threats. The 10-year-old boys were labelled 'demons', 'monsters' and 'animals'. Less attention was paid to the personal histories of the offenders or to the fact that, despite early indications of a propensity to violence and self-aggression in one of the boys, no interventions had been made (Muncie 1999).

Similar caution can be expressed about the popular view that most youth crime in developed countries is drug-related. There is a common assumption that robberies, for example, are committed by young people in order to finance their drug habits. Recent studies reveal that drug and alcohol use among young people has become relatively 'normalized' (Parker et al. 1998). A 2003 survey of more than 10,000 school children aged between 11 and 15, conducted for the UK Department of Health, revealed that 9 per cent were regular smokers, 25 per cent had drunk alcohol in the past week, 21 per cent had taken drugs in the past year, and 4 per cent had used 'Class A' drugs, such as cocaine or heroin (DoH 2006).

Trends in drug-use have shifted away from 'hard' drugs, such as heroin, towards combinations of substances such as amphetamines, alcohol and Ecstasy. Ecstasy in particular has become a 'lifestyle' drug associated with the rave and club subcultures, rather than the basis of an expensive, addictive habit pushing young people into lives of crime. The so-called 'war on drugs' only serves to criminalize large segments of the youth population who are otherwise generally law-abiding (Muncie 1999).

Analysis of youth criminality is rarely straightforward. Where crime implies a transgression of law, youth criminality is often associated with activities that, strictly speaking, are not crimes. Anti-social behaviour, subcultural activity and non-conformity in young people may be regarded as delinquency, but none of these is in fact *criminal* conduct. Critics argue that the recent introduction of Anti-Social Behaviour Orders (ASBOs) will criminalize ordinary, borderline nuisance behaviour that, for many, is a normal part of growing up.

White-collar crime

Although there is a tendency to associate crime with young people, especially young males in the lower classes, involvement in criminal activity is by no means confined to this part of the population. The world's largest energy trading company, Enron, collapsed in 2001 after the discovery that false accounting was disguising huge debts. The company's bankruptcy caused the loss of thousands of jobs around the world. Several of its senior staff, including the company's founder Kenneth Lay, were arrested. A similar scandal at communications giant WorldCom, in 2002, shows that wealthy and powerful people carry out crimes whose consequences can be much more far-reaching and damaging than the often petty crimes of the poor.

The term **white-collar crime** was first introduced by Edwin Sutherland in 1949. It refers to crime that is carried out by those in the more affluent sectors of society, often against the interests of the companies they work for. White-collar crime therefore covers many types of criminal activity, including tax fraud, illegal sales practices, securities and land frauds, embezzlement, the manufacture or sale of dangerous products, as well as straightforward theft. Of course, most white-collar crime is not as grand as that which occurred at Enron or WorldCom. The distribution of white-collar crimes is even harder to measure than that of other types of crime and much of it does not appear in the official statistics at all. We can distinguish between white-collar crime and crimes of the powerful. White-collar crime mainly involves the use of a middle-class or professional position to engage in illegal activities for personal gain. Crimes of the powerful are those in which the authority conferred by a position is used in criminal ways – as when an official accepts a bribe to favour a particular policy.

Although it is regarded by the authorities in a much more tolerant light than crimes of the less privileged (several of those convicted in the Enron scandal avoided serving time in gaol), the cost of white-collar crime is enormous. Far more research has been carried out on white-collar crime in the United States than in Britain and

Powerful men like Kenneth Lay, founder of Enron, rarely find themselves in the dock, even though their actions potentially have much more serious consequences than the types of crime usually dealt with by the courts.

Europe. In America, it has been calculated that the amount of money involved in white-collar crime (defined as tax fraud, insurance frauds, home improvement frauds and car repair frauds) is 40 times as great as that in ordinary crimes against property (robberies, burglaries, larceny, forgeries and car thefts).

Corporate crime

Some criminologists have referred to corporate crime to describe the types of offence which are committed by large corporations in society. Pollution, mislabelling and violations of health and safety regulations affect much larger numbers of people than does petty criminality. The increasing power and influence of large corporations, and their rapidly growing global reach, means that our lives are touched by them in many ways. Corporations are involved in producing the cars we drive and the food we eat. They also have an enormous impact on the natural environment and financial markets, aspects of life which affect all of us. Crime cannot be seen as something committed exclusively by individuals against other individuals, criminal and anti-social acts can also be committed collectively by corporations causing harm to individuals, social groups and society as a whole.

Stephen Box (1983) argued that in capitalist economies where companies are in competition against each other, corporations are inherently 'criminogenic' – that is, they are forced to consider criminal acts to gain a competitive advantage and tend to see the harm they cause as a simple calculation of financial risk. Gary Slapper and Steve Tombs (1999) reviewed both quantitative and qualitative studies of corporate crime and concluded that a large number of corporations do not adhere to the legal regulations which apply to them. Like Box, they argue that corporate crime is not confined to a few 'bad apples', but is pervasive and widespread. Other studies have revealed six types of violation linked to large corporations: administrative (paperwork or non-compliance), environmental (pollution, permits violations), financial (tax violations, illegal payments), labour (working conditions, hiring practices), manufacturing (product safety, labelling) and unfair trade practices (anti-competition, false advertising).

Victimization patterns in corporate crime are not straightforward. Sometimes there are 'obvious' victims, as in cases of environmental disasters like the gas poisoning of workers and residents in and around the Bhopal chemical plant in India (1984), or the health dangers posed to women by silicone breast implants. Recently, those injured in rail crashes or relatives of those who were killed have called for the company executives responsible for the track and trains to be brought to trial, where the companies have shown negligence. But very often victims of corporate crime do not see themselves as victims at all. This is because, in 'conventional' crimes, the physical proximity between victim and offender is much closer – it is difficult not to recognize that you have been mugged. But in the case of corporate crime, greater distances in time and space mean that victims may not realize they have been victimized, or may not know how to seek redress for the crime. It is also more difficult to know who to blame when harmful decisions are made by groups of boardroom executives rather than single individuals. For legal systems founded on

'Kickbacks, embezzlement, price fixing, bribery . . . this is an extremely high-crime area.'
(Reproduced by permission of Sidney Harris)

the principle of individual responsibility, corporate offences pose specific problems that are very difficult to solve.

> **THINKING CRITICALLY**
>
> Why do you think that corporate offenders are so hard to prosecute? List as many factors as you can think of which make the monitoring, detection and prosecution of corporate criminality so difficult for police forces. Based on your list, what suggestions would you make to the police on how they could improve the policing of corporate crime?

The effects of corporate crime are often experienced unevenly within society. Those who are disadvantaged by other types of socio-economic inequalities tend to suffer disproportionately. For example, safety and health risks in the workplace tend to be concentrated most heavily in low-paying occupations. Many of the risks from healthcare products and pharmaceuticals have had a greater impact on women than on men, as is the case with contraceptives or fertility treatments with harmful side-effects (Slapper and Tombs 1999).

The violent aspects of corporate crime are less visible than in cases of homicide or assault, but are just as real and may on occasion be much more serious in their consequences. Flouting regulations concerning the preparation of new drugs, ignoring safety in the workplace or environmental pollution may cause physical harm or death to large numbers of people. Deaths from hazards at work far outnumber murders, although precise statistics about job accidents are difficult to obtain. Of course, we cannot assume that all, or even the majority, of these deaths and injuries are the result of employer negligence in relation to safety factors for which they are legally liable. Nevertheless, there is some basis for supposing that many are due to the neglect of legally binding safety regulations by employers or managers.

Crime in global context

Organized crime

Organized crime refers to forms of activity that have many of the characteristics of orthodox business, but are illegal. Organized crime embraces smuggling, illegal gambling, the drug trade, prostitution, large-scale theft and protection rackets, among other activities. It often relies on violence or the threat of violence to conduct its activities. While organized crime has traditionally developed within individual countries in culturally specific ways, it has become increasingly transnational in scope.

The reach of organized crime is now felt in many countries throughout the world, but historically it has been particularly strong in a handful of nations. In America, for example, organized crime is a massive business, rivalling any of the major orthodox sectors of economic enterprise, such as the car industry. National and local criminal organizations provide illegal goods and services to mass consumers. Illicit gambling on horse races, lotteries and sporting events represents the greatest source of income generated by organized crime in the United States. Organized crime has probably become so significant in American society because of an early association with – and in part a modelling on – the activities of the industrial 'robber barons' of the late nineteenth century. Many of the early industrialists made fortunes by exploiting immigrant labour, largely ignoring legal regulations on working conditions and often using a mixture of corruption and violence to build their industrial empires.

Although we have little systematic information on organized crime in the UK, it is known that extensive criminal networks exist in areas of London and other large cities. Some of these have international connections. London in particular is a centre for criminal operations based around the world. 'Triads' (Chinese gangsters, originally from Hong Kong and Southeast Asia) and 'Yardies' (drug dealers with links to the Caribbean) are two of the largest criminal networks, but other organized crime groups from Eastern Europe, South America and West Africa are involved in money-laundering, drug-trafficking and fraud schemes.

Organized crime is much more complex than it was even 30 years ago. There is no single national organization linking different criminal groups, but such crime has become more sophisticated than ever before. For example, some of the larger criminal organizations find ways of laundering money through the big clearing banks, in spite of the procedures intended to foil them; using their 'clean' money, they then invest in legitimate businesses. Police believe that between £2.5 and £4 billion of criminally generated money passes through UK banks each year.

Global Society 21.1 **Transnational drug-trafficking**

How easy is it to purchase marijuana or ecstasy? Is there ever a drug-free music festival? Lamentable as it may seem to some, most young people in Britain have relatively easy access to illegal drugs.

What factors determine the availability of illegal drugs in your community? The level of police enforcement is important, of course, as is the extent of local demand. But no less important is the existence of networks of traffickers able to transport the drugs from the countries where they are grown to your home town. These networks have been able to flourish, in part, because of globalization.

While the cultivation of marijuana may be just a matter of someone's back garden, almost all of the world's coca plants and opium poppies are grown in the Third World. Billions are spent each year to assist Third World nations with eradication efforts, but, despite this massive expenditure, there is little evidence that eradication or interdiction efforts

have significantly decreased the supply of illegal drugs in Britain and other European countries. Why have these efforts failed'?

One answer is that the profit motive is simply too great. Farmers struggling to scratch out a living for themselves in Bolivia or Peru, members of the Colombian drug cartels and low-level dealers on our streets and in our clubs all receive substantial monetary rewards for their illegal activities. These rewards create a strong incentive to devise ways around anti-drug efforts, and to run the risk of being caught.

Another answer is that drug-traffickers have been able to take advantage of globalization. First, in their attempts to evade the authorities, traffickers make use of all the communications technologies that are available in a global age. As one commentator put it, drug traffickers 'now use sophisticated technology, such as signal interceptors, to plot radar and avoid monitoring . . .

Customs officials spend a lot of their time tracking and attempting to intercept the movement of drugs across national borders.

[and] they can use faxes, computers and mobile phones to coordinate their activities and make their business run smoothly'. Second, the globalization of the financial sector has helped create an infrastructure in which large sums of money can be moved around the world electronically in a matter of seconds, making it relatively easy to 'launder' drug money (that is, to make it appear to have come from a legitimate business venture). Third, recent changes in the policies of governments designed to allow the freer flow of persons and legitimate goods across international borders have increased the opportunities for smuggling.

At the same time, globalization may create new opportunities for governments to work together to combat drug-trafficking. Indeed, world leaders recently called for greater international cooperation in narcotics enforcement, stressing the need for information sharing and coordinated enforcement efforts.

The changing face of organized crime

In *End of Millennium* (1998), Manuel Castells argues that the activities of organized crime groups are becoming increasingly international in scope. He notes that the coordination of criminal activities across borders – with the help of new information technologies – is becoming a central feature of the new global economy. Involved in activities ranging from the narcotics trade to counterfeiting to smuggling immigrants and human organs, organized crime groups are now operating in flexible international networks rather than within their own territorial realms.

According to Castells, criminal groups set up strategic alliances with one another. The international narcotics trade, weapons-trafficking, the sale of nuclear material and money-laundering have all become 'linked' across borders and crime groups. Criminal organizations tend to base their operations in 'low-risk' countries where there are fewer threats to their activities. In recent years, the former Soviet Union has been one of the main points of convergence for international organized crime. The flexible nature of this networked crime makes it relatively easy for crime groups to evade the reach of law-enforcement initiatives. If one criminal 'safe haven' becomes more risky, the 'organizational geometry' can shift to form a new pattern.

The international nature of crime has been felt in the United Kingdom. Japanese Yakuza gangs and Italian and American mafia operators have established themselves in Britain. Among the newest arrivals are criminals from the former Soviet Union. Some commentators believe that the new Russian mafia is the world's most dangerous organized crime syndicate. The Russian criminal networks are deeply involved in money-laundering, linking up their activities with Russia's largely unregulated banks. Some think the Russian groups may come to be the world's largest criminal networks. They have their basis in a mafia-riddled Russian state, where underworld 'protection' is now routine for many businesses. The most worrying possibility is that Russia's new mobsters are smuggling nuclear materials on an international scale, materials taken from the Soviet nuclear arsenal.

Despite numerous campaigns by governments and police forces, the narcotics trade is one of the most rapidly expanding international criminal industries, having an annual growth rate of more than 10 per cent in the 1980s and early 1990s and an extremely high level of profit. Heroin networks stretch across the Far East, particularly South Asia, and are also located in North Africa, the Middle East and Latin America. Supply lines also pass through Paris and Amsterdam, from where drugs are commonly supplied to Britain.

Cybercrime

Not only is international organized crime greatly facilitated by recent advances in information technology, the information and telecommunications revolution is changing the face of crime in fundamental ways. Advances in technology have provided exciting new opportunities and benefits, but they also heighten vulnerability to crime. While it is difficult to quantify the extent of cybercrime – criminal acts committed with the help of information technology – it is possible to outline some of the major forms it appears to be taking. P. N. Grabosky and Russell Smith (1998) identified nine main types of technology-based crime:

1 Illegal interception of telecommunications systems means that eavesdropping has become easier, with implications ranging from 'spouse-monitoring' to espionage.

2 Heightened vulnerability to electronic vandalism and terrorism, as interference with computerized systems – from hackers or computer viruses – could pose serious security hazards.

3 The ability to steal telecommunications services means that people can conduct illicit business without being detected or simply manipulate telecom and mobile phone services in order to receive free or discounted telephone calls.

4 Telecom privacy is a growing problem. It has become relatively easy to violate copyright rules by copying materials, software, films and CDs.

5 It is difficult to control pornography and offensive content in cyberspace. Sexually explicit material, racist propaganda and instructions for making incendiary devices can all be placed on, and downloaded from, the Internet. 'Cyberstalking' can pose not only virtual, but very real threats to online users.

6 A growth in telemarketing fraud has been noted. Fraudulent charity schemes and investment opportunities are difficult to regulate.

7 There is an enhanced risk of electronic funds-transfer crimes. The widespread use of cash machines, e-commerce and 'electronic money' heightens the possibility that such transactions will be intercepted.

8 Electronic money-laundering can be used to 'move' the illegal proceeds from a crime in order to conceal their origins.

9 Telecommunications can be used to further criminal conspiracies. Because of sophisticated encryption systems and high-speed data transfers, it is difficult for law-enforcement agencies to intercept information about international criminal activities.

There are indications that cybercrime is rising, though, as with all crime statistics, it is difficult to reach firm conclusions. A 2005 YouGov poll of UK Internet users found that 1 in 20 had lost money in online scams, while a 2001 survey revealed that 52 per cent of companies interviewed said Internet fraud posed real problems for them (Wall 2007). Identity theft has also become a larger part of all credit and other plastic card losses (see table 21.3).

David Wall (2007) argues that there have been three successive phases of cybercrime, closely tied to the development of communications technology. *First-generation cybercrimes* are those that make use of computers to assist traditional types of offending. Drug dealers, for instance, make use of whatever forms of communication exist and, even in the absence of computers, would continue to buy and sell drugs. Similarly, finding information on how to build weapons or bombs may be easier on the Internet, but there have been, and still are, conventional sources available. *Second-generation cybercrimes* are those where the Internet has opened up new global opportunities for fairly conventional crimes. Examples include the global trade in online pornography, international fraud and theft

Table 21.3 **Annual plastic card fraud losses on UK-issued cards 1997–2007. All figures in £ millions**

Fraud type	1997	1998	1999	2000	2001	2002	2003	2004	2005	2006	2007
Card-not-present	10.0	13.6	29.3	72.9	95.7	110.1	122.1	150.8	183.2	212.7	290.5
Counterfeit	20.3	26.8	50.3	107.1	160.4	148.5	110.6	129.7	96.8	98.6	144.3
Lost/stolen	66.2	65.8	79.7	101.9	114.0	108.3	112.4	114.5	89.0	68.5	56.2
Card ID theft	13.1	16.8	14.4	17.4	14.6	20.6	30.2	36.9	30.5	31.9	34.1
Mail non-receipt	12.5	12.0	14.6	17.7	26.8	37.1	45.1	72.9	40.0	15.4	10.2
Total	122.0	135.0	188.4	317.0	411.5	424.6	420.4	504.8	439.4	427.0	535.2

Source: APACS 2008

and deception via Internet auction sites. Second-generation cybercrimes are therefore 'hybrids' – traditional offences but within a new global networked environment. *Third-generation* or *'true' cybercrimes* are those crimes that are solely the product of the Internet and which can take place only within cyberspace. Examples include the illegal downloading of music and film, vandalism of virtual environments and spam email containing virus attachments. The latter is an example of the automation of cybercrime, where 'botnets' can enable control over the infected computer, thus allowing the personal information to be gathered for future identity theft. Third-generation cybercrimes have been greatly facilitated by faster and cheaper broadband Internet access, which allows people to remain online for much longer periods and opens up new criminal opportunities.

The global reach of telecommunications crime poses particular challenges for law-enforcement. Criminal acts perpetrated in one country have the power to affect victims across the globe and this has troubling implications for detecting and prosecuting crimes. It becomes necessary for police from the countries involved to determine the jurisdiction in which the act occurred and to agree on extraditing the offenders and providing the necessary evidence for prosecution. Although police cooperation across national borders may improve with the growth of cybercrime, at present, cyber-criminals have a great deal of room to manoeuvre.

At a time when financial, commercial and production systems in countries around the world are being integrated electronically, rising levels of Internet fraud and unauthorized electronic intrusions and the constant threat of computer viruses are serving as potent warnings of the vulnerability of existing computer security systems. From the US Federal Bureau of Investigation (FBI) to the Japanese government's new anti-hacker police force, governments are scrambling to contend with new and elusive forms of cross-national computer activity.

Prisons and punishment

From our discussion of control theories and recent preventative criminologies, it can be seen that much effort is now being expended in an attempt to control and

---

THINKING CRITICALLY

Place each of Grabosky and Smith's (1998) nine types of cybercrime, listed above, into one of David Wall's (2007) 3 stages of cybercrime. How many of the nine types are genuinely 'pure' or 'third-generation' cybercrimes? How might an increase in third-generation cybercrimes change the way that police forces operate in the future?

21.1 The future of crime?

Imagine a world in which physical cash no longer exists, all personal possessions are tagged with electronic chips and your personal identity is your most valuable asset. According to a report, *Just Around the Corner*, published by the British Department of Trade and Industry (DTI 2000), crime will soon be thoroughly transformed by advances in technology. Within two decades, the report suggests, many goods such as cars, cameras and computers will become less attractive targets for theft because they will be programmed to operate only in the hands of their legal owners. Personalized 'identities' – such as computer chips, PIN numbers and security codes – will become ubiquitous. They will be essential for conducting online transactions, using 'smart cards' (virtual cash) and passing through security systems.

According to the report, cases of 'identity fraud' and thefts of personal identities will proliferate as more and more aspects of life become based in high technology.

A dramatic example came to light in March 2007 when US retailer, TJX – which owns the fashion outlet TK Maxx – announced that computer hackers had stolen information from at least 45.7 million payment cards used by their customers. TJX said that it did not know the full extent of the theft or its effect on customer accounts, but revealed that information had been accessed over a 16-month period since July 2005. With the recent introduction and roll-out of replacement 'chip-and-pin' cards, many of the stolen details of UK cards would be worthless as the physical cards no longer exist. However, the case highlights the potentially huge scale of 'virtual' theft and identity fraud in the global information age.

reduce offending behaviour. However, when prevention fails, societies punish offenders and, in most legal systems, imprisonment remains a widely used method of formal punishment, during which offenders are deprived of the freedoms they previously enjoyed. This section explores the use of prisons as institutions for the control and reform of criminals.

The underlying principle of modern prisons is to 'improve' individuals and prepare them to play a fit and proper part in society once released. Prison, with a reliance on long prison sentences, is also seen as a powerful deterrent to crime. For this reason, many politicians eager to 'get tough' on rising crime rates have favoured a more punitive justice system and the expansion of prison facilities. Do prisons have the intended effect of 'reforming' convicted criminals and preventing new crimes from being committed? It is a complex question, as we shall see, but evidence seems to suggest that they do not.

The criminal justice system of England and Wales has become more punitive in recent years. On 30 March 2007, there were 80,303 people in prison service facilities in England and Wales – an all-time high. England and Wales have a greater proportion of their population imprisoned – 148 per 100,000 – than any other country in Western Europe, though this is far less than some Eastern European countries: Poland imprisons 230 per 100,000 and Russia 611 per 100,000. By contrast, Germany has a prison population of just 95 per 100,000 and France has 85 per 100,000 (see table 21.4). English and Welsh courts also tend to assign longer prison sentences to offenders than do courts in other European countries. Some critics fear that Britain is following too closely in the path of the United States – by far the most punitive nation among industrial countries.

Prisoners are no longer routinely physically maltreated, as was once common practice, but they do suffer many other types of deprivation. They are deprived not only of their freedom, but also of a proper income, the company of their families and previous friends, heterosexual relationships, their

Table 21.4 **World prison population 2006, selected countries**

Continent	Country	Prison population total (including pre-trial detainees)	Prison population rate (per 100,000 of national population)
Africa	South Africa	157,402	335
	Zimbabwe	18,033	139
	Kenya	47,036	130
	Algeria	42,000	127
	Uganda	26,126	95
	Niger	5,709	46
	Burkina Faso	2,800	23
Americas	USA	2,186,230	738
	Puerto Rico	14,239	356
	Mexico	214,450	196
	Brazil	361,402	191
	Jamaica	4,913	182
	Colombia	62,216	134
	Haiti	3,670	43
Asia	Kazakhstan	49,292	340
	Iran	147,926	214
	Lebanon	5,971	168
	China	1,548,498*	118*
	India	332,112	30
	Nepal	7,135	26
Europe	Russian Federation	869,814	611
	Poland	87,901	230
	England & Wales	79,861	148
	Netherlands	21,013	128
	Germany	78,581	95
	France	52,009**	85
	Sweden	7,450	82
	Denmark	4,198	77
	Norway	3,048	66
	Færoe Islands	7	15
Oceania	New Zealand	7,620	186
	Fiji	1,113	131
	Australia	25,353	126
	Samoa	223	123
	Tonga	128	114
	Papua New Guinea	4,056	69
	Nauru	3	23

* Sentenced prisoners only
** Metropolitan France, excluding departments and territories in Africa, the Americas and Oceania

Source: adapted from Walmsley 2007

own clothing and other personal items. They frequently live in overcrowded conditions, and have to accept strict disciplinary procedures and the regimentation of their daily lives (Stern 1989).

Living in these conditions tends to drive a wedge between prison inmates and the outside society; they cannot adjust their behaviour to the norms of that society. Prisoners have to come to terms with an environment quite distinct from 'the outside', and the habits and attitudes they learn in prison are quite often exactly the opposite of those they are supposed to acquire. For instance, they may develop a grudge against ordinary citizenry, learn to accept violence as normal, gain contacts with seasoned criminals which they maintain when freed, and acquire criminal skills about which they previously knew little. For this reason prisons are sometimes referred to as 'universities of crime'. It is therefore not surprising that rates of recidivism – repeat offending by those who have been in prison before – are disturbingly high. More than 60 per cent of all men set free after a serving prison sentence in the UK are rearrested within four years of their original crimes.

While the evidence seems to show that prisons do not succeed in rehabilitating prisoners, there remains enormous pressure to increase the number of prisons and to toughen prison sentences for many crimes. The prison system is overcrowded, prompting calls for the construction of new facilities. Yet critics argue that not only are prison-building programmes an unreasonably expensive burden for taxpayers to bear, in addition they will have little impact on the crime rate.

Some campaigners for penal reform argue that there should be a shift away from punitive justice towards forms of restorative justice. Restorative justice seeks to raise awareness among offenders of the effects of their crimes through 'sentences' served within the community. Offenders might be required to contribute to community service projects or to engage in mediated reconciliation sessions with victims. Rather than being separated from society and shielded from the aftermath of their criminal acts, criminals need to be exposed to the costs of crime in a meaningful way that helps to reintegrate them back into mainstream of social relationships.

There are no easy answers to the debate over whether or not prisons 'work'. Although prisons do not seem to succeed in rehabilitating prisoners, it is possible that they deter people from committing crimes. While those who are actually imprisoned have not been deterred, the unpleasantness of prison life might well deter others. There is an almost intractable problem here for prison reformers: making prisons thoroughly unpleasant places to be in probably helps deter potential offenders, but it makes the rehabilitating goals of prisons extremely difficult to achieve; on the other hand, the less harsh that prison conditions are, the more imprisonment loses its deterrent effect.

> ### THINKING CRITICALLY
>
> Do you think that prison is the best option for vulnerable young offenders? What other punishments would you suggest might be considered as an alternative to prison for this group? Would the alternatives also protect the public from repeat offending?

While prisons certainly do keep some dangerous individuals off the streets, evidence suggests that we need to find other means to deter crime. A sociological interpretation of crime makes it clear that there are no quick fixes. The causes of crime are bound up with structural conditions of society, including poverty, the condition of the inner cities and the deteriorating life circumstances of many young men. While short-term measures, such as reforms that make prisons places of rehabilitation rather than simply incarceration, and experiments with alternatives to prison, such as

21.2 Self-harm and suicide in an English prison: the death of Joseph Scholes

Joseph had an unsettled childhood and became a disturbed young boy. He had allegedly been sexually abused from an early age and was seeing a psychiatrist and taking medication at the time of his arrest. Joseph was depressed, had begun to self-harm and to have periodic suicidal thoughts.

On 30 November 2001, he was voluntarily taken into the care of social services and placed in a children's home. Six days later, he went out with a group of children from the home and was involved in a series of mobile phone robberies. He was subsequently arrested and charged with robbery. Both victims and other witnesses accepted that Joseph's involvement in these incidents was peripheral; there was no suggestion that he had used or threatened violence.

As the robbery trial date drew nearer, Joseph became more depressed and agitated. Two weeks before his court appearance he slashed his face with a knife more than 30 times. The deepest wound, across his nose, cut right down to the bone. The walls in his room had to be completely repainted as they were covered in blood. Prior to Joseph's sentencing, the judge at Manchester Crown Court was alerted to Joseph's vulnerability, his experience of sexual abuse and history of suicidal and self-harming behaviour.

Joseph was unfortunate to be tried at a time of heightened public anxiety over street crime. The Lord Chief Justice had issued sentencing guidelines, which were widely interpreted as requiring an automatic custodial sentence for such crimes. On 15 March 2002, Joseph was sentenced to a two-year detention and training order. The judge stated in open court that he wanted the warnings about Joseph's self-harming and history of sexual abuse 'most expressly drawn to the attention of the authorities'.

After sentencing, the responsibility for Joseph's care transferred to the Youth Justice Board (YJB), which was informed of Joseph's history – most notably, his suicide attempt and

Some people believe that regimes in prison and young offender institutions, such as the Feltham Youth Offender Institute pictured here, are too 'soft'. However, the induction process described below fits Erving Goffman's picture of a total institution well (see Classic Studies 7.2).

self-harming behaviour. People involved in Joseph's care urged the YJB to place him in local authority secure accommodation where he would have access to the necessary intensive care and support. Despite his vulnerability, the YJB placed him in prison service accommodation at Stoke Heath Young Offender Institution (YOI), claiming that no suitable alternative placement was available. Joseph's mother Yvonne subsequently telephoned Stoke Heath YOI to inform them that he had been a victim of sexual abuse, was depressed and unstable with a history of self-harm and suicidal behaviour.

On arrival at Stoke Heath YOI, Joseph was stripped of his clothing, including his underwear, and placed in a garment like a horse blanket with stiff Velcro fastenings. At the inquest, members of the jury and the coroner were visibly shocked when the garment was shown in court and the strip of clothing was described by one childcare expert as 'dehumanizing'.

During his short time in Stoke Heath YOI he was kept in virtual seclusion and was not offered any meaningful activity. He was told that he would later be put on the main wing with other prisoners, a prospect that horrified him because of his history of sexual abuse. Joseph took his own life in March 2002. A lack of close observation and unsafe conditions in Joseph's cell meant that he was able to hang himself from a sheet tied to the bars of his window. He was just nine days into his prison sentence. . . .

A two-week inquest into Joseph's death was held in April 2004. . . . [Investigators] into Joseph's death were unanimous in their opinion that prison service accommodation was completely unsuitable for Joseph as it did not have the resources and facilities to cope with someone so vulnerable [Inquest 2004].

The Howard League for Penal Reform, a charity working for the reform of the penal system, carries out research on criminal justice issues, including analysis of prison conditions. During 2003 it found that 94 men and women took their own lives in prison in England and Wales. Anita Dockley, the Assistant Director at the Howard League said: 'It is shameful that so many men and women in prison take their own lives. Yet sadly the Howard League does not anticipate the numbers falling while the prison population continues to surge and the system remains under such stress. The number of prison suicides will only fall when the numbers in prison are radically reduced and the strategies for dealing with suicide and self-harm are properly realized. We call on the government to act immediately to reduce the number of people behind bars.'

Source: Howard League for Penal Reform 2004

community work schemes, need to be further explored, for solutions to be effective they must address the long term (Currie 1998).

Conclusion: deviance, crime and social order

It would be a mistake to regard crime and deviance wholly in a negative light. Any society which recognizes that human beings have diverse values and concerns must find space for individuals or groups whose activities do not conform to the norms followed by the majority. People who develop new ideas, in politics, science, art or other fields, are often regarded with suspicion or hostility by those who follow orthodox ways. The political ideals developed in the American Revolution, for example – freedom of the individual and equality of opportunity – were fiercely resisted by many people at the time, yet they have now become accepted across the world. To deviate from the dominant norms of a society takes courage and resolution, but it is often crucial in securing processes of change which are later seen to be in the general interest.

Is 'harmful deviance' the price a society must pay when it allows considerable leeway for people to engage in non-conformist pursuits? For example, are high rates of criminal violence a cost which is exacted in a society in exchange for the individual liberties its citizens enjoy? Some have certainly suggested as much, arguing that crimes of violence are inevitable in a society where rigid definitions of conformity do not apply. But this view does not hold much water when examined closely. In some societies that recognize a wide range of individual freedoms and tolerate deviant activities (such as Holland), rates of violent crime are low. Conversely, countries where the scope of individual freedom is restricted (like some Latin American societies) show higher levels of violence.

Global Society 21.2 | **Punitive justice in the United States**

The United States has by far the most punitive justice system in the world. The world's total prison population is around 9.25 million, more than 2 million of whom are presently incarcerated in American prisons. In the USA, for every 1000,000 of the population, 738 people are in prison (see figure 21.6 for a global comparison).

The American prison system employs more than 500,000 people and costs $35 billion annually to maintain. It has also become partially privatized, with private companies now able to win government contracts to build and administer prisons to accommodate the growing inmate population. Critics charge that a 'prison-industrial complex' has emerged: large numbers of people – including bureaucrats, politicians and prison employees – have vested interests in the existence and further expansion of the prison system.

Support for capital punishment (the death penalty) is high in the United States. A 2004 survey found that 71 per cent of adults said that they believed in capital punishment; 26 per cent opposed it. This represents a significant shift from 1966, when 42 per cent of those surveyed supported the death penalty and 47 per cent were opposed (Gallup 2004). The number of individuals

awaiting execution climbed steadily from 1977, when the Supreme Court upheld state capital punishment laws (see figure 21.6). At the end of 1998, more than 3,3000 prisoners were on 'death row' (US Bureau of Justice 1998). Since 2003, however, numbers have decreased very slowly year on year, standing at 3,228 at the end of 2006. Of these, 1,802 were white, 1,352 were black and 358 were Hispanic. Of the 3,228 people under sentence of death, just 54 were women.

Proponents of tough sentencing point to the overall drop in crime in the United States over the past decade as proof that prisons work. Critics disagree, claiming that the reduction in crime can be explained by other factors, such as the strong economy and low unemployment. They argue that high rates of incarceration are breaking up families and communities unnecessarily. More than a quarter of African-American men are either in prison or under the control of the penal system. Some 60 per cent of individuals imprisoned in the United States are serving sentences for non-violent drug-related crimes. Critics charge that such gross imbalances prove that incarceration is no longer a measure of 'last resort' – prison is now turned to as the solution for all social problems.

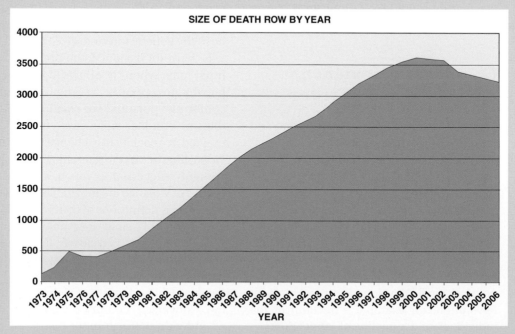

Figure 21.6 Prisoners on death row in the USA, 1954–2006

Source: US Bureau of Justice 2005

A society that is tolerant towards deviant behaviour need not suffer social disruption. A good outcome can probably only be achieved, however, where individual liberties are joined to social justice – in a social order where inequalities are not glaringly large and in which everyone has a chance to lead a full and satisfying life. If freedom is not balanced with equality, and if many people find their lives largely devoid of self-fulfilment, deviant behaviour is likely to be channelled towards socially destructive ends.

Summary points

1. Deviant behaviour refers to actions which transgress commonly held norms. What is defined as deviant differs across time and place. The concept of deviance is broader than that of crime, which is restricted to law-breaking. 'Normal' behaviour in one period or cultural setting may be labelled 'deviant' in another.

2. Early theories sought a biological explanation for criminal behaviour, but these have been largely discredited. Sociologists have successfully argued that inequalities of wealth and power in society strongly influence the opportunities available to different social groups and what kinds of activities are regarded as criminal. Criminal activities are learned in much the same way as law-abiding ones, and tend to be directed towards meeting the same needs.

3. Functionalist theories show us that some crime and deviance is produced by structural tensions and a lack of moral regulation within society. Robert Merton's strain theory helps to account for some types of individualistic, acquisitive crime. Later subcultural theories showed how social groups such as gangs, in replacing mainstream norms with alternatives celebrating defiance and delinquency, can also provide rewards for deviant behaviour.

4. Labelling perspectives are important because they remind us that no act is intrinsically criminal or normal, so we have to investigate how some behaviours come to be defined as deviant, why certain groups are labelled as deviant and what consequences such labels have on an individual's self-identity.

5. Conflict theories locate crime and deviance within the structure of society and have opened up new areas of crime studies linked to questions of social class, gender, ethnicity and the crimes of powerful groups. The 'new' criminologists expanded the field of crime and deviance studies into much wider debates on the relative harm caused by a diverse range of criminal and deviant activities.

6. Control theories demonstrate that the growth of crime may be linked to the growing number of targets and opportunities for committing crimes. Recent 'environmental criminologies' have shifted the emphasis away from reforming criminals, towards the design of 'crime-resistant' areas. Sociologists will have to study and evaluate such initiatives and explore their social consequences in the future.

7. The extent of crime in any society is difficult to assess, as not all crimes are reported. The 'hidden figure' of unrecorded crime can be made a little more visible through victimization studies, but we must always handle these carefully when sociological research involves the use of official statistics.

8. Rates of criminality are much lower for women than for men, probably because of general socialization differences between men and women and the greater involvement of men in public, non-domestic spheres of life. Female crime has increased in recent years and there are now more women in prison, but as a percentage of total crime,

female crime remains a relatively unusual phenomenon.

9. Popular fear about crime often focuses on street crimes, such as theft, burglary and assault, that are largely the domain of young, working-class males, but it is now clear that there is a large amount of white-collar and corporate crime which is not as well policed or as easily prosecuted as street crime. This realization should make us reflect again on whether official statistics can ever present a 'true' picture of crime.

10. Organized crime is likely to become more prevalent as globalization facilitates the rapid transfer of people, goods and transactions across the globe. Sociologists may well need to design new theories if they are to have useful things to say about the connections between organized crime and information technologies, such as electronic money-laundering and internet fraud.

11. Prisons were developed partly to protect society and partly to reform criminals. Prisons *may* sometimes protect society but do *not* seem routinely to reform criminals. Although alternatives to prison have been suggested and tried, there remains a popular perception that prison is appropriate for offenders. For sociologists, the crime and imprisonment debate has to be seen as a long-term problem, requiring the social causes of crime to be tackled as well as criminal activities themselves.

Further reading

A good place for beginners to the subject is Robert D. White and Fiona Haines's *Crime and Criminology: An Introduction* (Oxford: Oxford University Press, 2004) or Sandra Walklate's *Understanding Criminology* (Buckingham: Open University Press, 2007). These are very lively and readable introductions. Roger Hopkins Burke's *An Introduction to Criminological Theory*, 2nd edn (Devon: Willan Publishing, 2005) is a useful textbook dealing with criminological theories. Taken together, these three books cover most of the theoretical perspectives you will need.

For crime in the British context, John Muncie and Eugene McLaughlin's edited volume, *The Problem of Crime*, 2nd edn (London: Sage, 2001), is a clear example of what criminology has to offer, while Eamonn Carrabine at al.'s *Criminology: A Sociological Introduction* (London: Routledge, 2004) is an equally strong text covering the USA and Europe.

If you intend to pursue crime and deviance studies further, then David Downes and Paul Rock's *Understanding Deviance*, 5th edn (Oxford: Oxford University Press, 2007) is very good, though not an easy read. There are also two reference works you should consider: *The Sage Dictionary of Criminology*, 2nd edn (London: Sage, 2005) edited by Eugene McLaughlin and John Muncie, is exactly what it says it is; and the most authoritative text is Mike Maguire, Rod Morgan and Robert Reiner's indispensable collection of essays in *The Oxford Handbook of Criminology*, 4th edn (Oxford: Oxford University Press, 2007) – which runs to a mere 1,200 pages!

Internet links

The British Journal of Criminology – one of the world's top criminology journals:
http://bjc.oxfordjournals.org

UK Home Office, Crime Reduction Unit – official statistics and crime prevention:
www.crimereduction.gov.uk/statistics/statistics26.htm

Critical Criminology (USA) – for the 'new' criminology and its later development:
www.critcrim.org/

Site created by the Centre for Crime and Justice Studies, King's College London UK:
www.crimeinfo.org.uk/

Howard League for Penal Reform – a UK penal reform charity:
www.howardleague.org

NACRO – UK charity concerned with crime prevention and the welfare of offenders:
www.nacro.org.uk

United Nations Office on Drugs and Crime – coverage of crime internationally:
www.unodc.org/unodc/crime_cicp_sitemap.html

22

Politics,
Government
and Social
Movements

CHAPTER 22

Politics, Government and Social Movements

(opposite) In February 2003, millions of people around the world – shown here in London – took to the streets to protest against the planned invasion of Iraq.

In February 2003, global protests took place against the impending invasion of Iraq by the USA and its allies, particularly the UK. In London, more than one million people took to the streets: the country's largest ever demonstration. Similar sized demonstrations took place in Rome and Barcelona, with smaller marches taking place in cities around the world from New York to Bangladesh. Rough estimates put the total number of protestors globally at up to ten million, in 60 countries (*Guardian*, 13 February 2003).

What made the coordination of millions of people marching on the same day in cities all over the world possible was the global spread of the mass media. Discussion of the likelihood of war dominated the television and newspapers for months before the event, and the media circulated plans of the anti-war demonstration in advance. Anti-war groups were able to mobilize supporters from a range of different backgrounds through emails and announcements on websites.

The people who marched in February 2003 were brought together by a variety of concerns. Some argued that although democracy is the best model, exporting Western-style democracy to the Middle East by force contradicted its basic values. Others saw the basis for the invasion on the grounds that Iraq's president, Sadam Hussein, had developed 'weapons of mass destruction' as unproven and a thinly veiled excuse for the West to get hold of a stable source of oil. In the UK, many feared that involvement in a US-led war would make Britain more, not less, likely to be the target of terrorist attacks – like the ones suffered a couple of years later by Londoners on 7 July 2005. Another issue that mobilized support against the war was the failure of the pro-war governments to persuade the United Nations to pass a resolution explicitly allowing them to use force against Iraq for its non-compliance with earlier UN resolutions. When the invasion of Iraq eventually began in March 2003, without explicit authorization from the United Nations, critics argued that it was illegitimate, even illegal.

This chapter discusses many of the themes that emerged out of these protests and the subsequent war. In particular, in this and the final chapter we look at the ways in which globalization processes are transforming politics and government and, with it, the theories and concepts used by political sociologists to make sense of the increasingly global arena of politics. We begin with a discussion of important, but contested, concepts in political sociology; in particular we examine the concept of power. We then look at the remarkable global spread of democracy over the past couple of decades, the demise of communism and the end of the Cold War, and the impact of such momentous changes on

national party politics. Questions of global governance are then raised before the chapter focuses on social movements, such as those behind the anti-war protests discussed above, which have become more widespread and significant in the past 30 years or so. We look at how sociologists have tried to explain these. In chapter 23, we then move on to explore nationhood and the rise of nationalism alongside sociological studies of war, genocide and the impact of and responses to terrorist activity of various kinds – an increasingly important development in recent years.

Basic concepts in political sociology

Politics, government and the state

Many people find politics remote and uninteresting, viewing it as the preserve, most often, of middle-aged men in Parliaments and Assemblies around the world. On this view, **politics** concerns the means whereby power is used to affect the scope and content of governmental activities. Yet politics is a contested concept and the sphere of the political may range well beyond that of government itself. The anti-war movement, with which we began this chapter, is a social movement with political goals, as are many of the groups, networks and organizations (such as those composed of environmentalists or feminists) that are discussed elsewhere in this book.

Whether we like it or not, however, all our lives are touched by what happens in the political sphere – even in the narrow sense of governmental activity. Governments influence quite personal activities and, in times of war, can even order us to lay down our lives for aims they deem necessary. The sphere of **government** is the sphere of political power. All political life is about power: who holds it, how they achieve it and what they do with it. Below, the concept of power is examined more closely.

Where there is a political apparatus of government (institutions like a parliament or congress, plus civil service officials) ruling over a given territory, whose authority is backed by a legal system and by the capacity to use military force to implement its policies, we can say that a **state** exists. All modern societies are **nation-states**. That is, they are states in which the great mass of the population consists of citizens who regard themselves as part of a single nation. Nation-states have come into existence at various times in different parts of the world; for example, the United States in 1776 and the Czech Republic in 1993. Their main characteristics contrast rather sharply with those of non-industrial or traditional civilizations, such as those described in chapter 4, 'Human History and Globalization'. These characteristics are:

- *Sovereignty*. The territories ruled by traditional states were always poorly defined, the level of control wielded by the central government being quite weak. The notion of sovereignty – that a government possesses authority over an area with a clear-cut border, within which it is the supreme power – had little relevance. All nation-states, by contrast, are sovereign states.
- *Citizenship*. In traditional states, most of the population ruled by the king or emperor showed little awareness of, or interest in, those who governed them. Neither did they have any political rights or influence. Normally, only the dominant classes or more affluent groups felt a sense of belonging to an overall political community. In modern societies, by contrast, most people living within the borders of a political system are citizens, having common rights and duties and regarding themselves as part of a nation. While there are some people who are political refugees or are 'stateless', almost everyone in the world today is a member of a definite national political order.

- *Nationalism*. Nation-states are associated with the rise of nationalism, which can be defined as a set of symbols and beliefs providing the sense of being part of a single political community. Thus, individuals feel a sense of pride and belonging in being British, American, Canadian, Russian, or whatever. These are the feelings that gave impetus to the quest of the East Timorese for independence. Probably people have always felt some kind of identity with social groups of one form or another – their family, village or religious community. Nationalism, however, made its appearance only with the development of the modern state. It is the main expression of feelings of identity with a distinct sovereign community.

 We explore the phenomenon of nationalism in greater detail in chapter 23, 'Nations, War and Terrorism'.

Power

The meaning, nature and distribution of **power** are central issues for political sociologists. One of sociology's founding figures, Max Weber, gave a general definition of power as 'the chance of a man or a number of men to realize their own will in a command action even against the resistance of others who are participating in the action' (Gerth and Mills 1948). To Weber, power is about getting your own way, even against the opposition of others.

Many sociologists have followed Weber in making a distinction between forms of power that are *coercive* and those that have *authority*. Sceptics about the 2003 war in Iraq, for example, often criticized the American-led invasion because it did not have explicit authority from the United Nations, so they viewed the war as illegitimate – a coercive use of power. Most forms of power are not based solely on force, but are legitimated by some form of authority.

THINKING CRITICALLY

Is Weber's definition of power satisfactory? Provide some examples of situations where this definition helps to explain events. Think of other examples where power is exercised *without* the use of force. Can people and groups be said to be 'powerful', even if they have no means of force and violence?

Max Weber's discussion of power focused on distinguishing between different categories – or 'ideal types' – of authority. For Weber, there were three sources of authority: traditional, charismatic and rational-legal. *Traditional authority* is power legitimized through respect for long-established cultural patterns. Weber gives the example of hereditary family rule of nobles in medieval Europe.

By contrast, *charismatic authority* tends to disrupt tradition. It is drawn from the devotion felt towards a leader by his or her subordinates who believe that the leader possesses exceptional qualities that inspire devotion. 'Charisma', to Weber, is a trait of personality. Jesus Christ and Adolf Hitler are often given as examples of individuals with charismatic authority. Yet charismatic authority can be exercised in more mundane ways too: the authority of certain teachers, for example, may be in part charismatic. In Weber's view, most societies in the past were characterized by traditional authority structures, which were periodically punctuated by bursts of charisma.

In the modern world, Weber argued, rational-legal authority was increasingly replacing traditional *authority*. This is power that is legitimated through legally enacted rules and regulations. It is found in modern organizations and bureaucracies (discussed in chapter 18, 'Organizations and Networks'), and in government, which Weber described as the formal organizations that direct the political life of a society (Gerth and Mills 1948).

Foucault and power

The French sociologist Michel Foucault (1926–84) has also developed a highly influential account of power, far removed from Weber's more formal definition. Foucault argued that power was not concentrated in one institution, such as the state, or held by any one group of individuals. He argued that these older models of power, including that of Stephen Lukes, relied on fixed identities. Power was held by groups that were easily identifiable: for example, the ruling class (for Marxists) or men (for feminists). Instead, Foucault argued power operates at all levels of social interaction, in all social institutions, by all people.

Foucault's ideas were introduced in chapter 3, 'Theories and Perspectives in Sociology', and his account of power in organizations can be found in chapter 18, 'Organizations and Networks'.

To Foucault, power and knowledge are closely tied together, and serve to reinforce one another. The claims to knowledge of a doctor, for example, are also claims to power, as they are put into practice in an institutional context, such as a hospital. The increase in knowledge about health and illness gave power to doctors who could claim authority over patients. Foucault describes the development of 'discourses', which provide ways of discussing power and knowledge – a 'Foucauldian' (someone who supports Foucault's arguments) might talk about 'medical discourses', for example.

Foucault's ideas have gained popularity as political sociology has shifted away from straightforward conflict theories, especially economic interpretations of Marxism, towards forms of political struggle based on identity, such as gender or sexuality (Foucault 1967, 1978). Foucault's account breaks down the simple division introduced above, between authoritative and coercive forms of power, as power is understood as something found in all social relations

Classic Studies 22.1 Stephen Lukes offers a 'radical view' of power

The research problem

Some research problems in sociology are theoretical rather than empirical. Often, sociologists need systematically to think through their key concepts in order to clarify them and expand their reach. The concept of power, for example, has been contested, provoking much disagreement. Is power something people can hold, like other material possessions? Is it something that can be shared? Or is it more indirectly observed, only existing in the relationships between people? Stephen Lukes attempted to think through the concept of power in order to cover all of its possible empirical instances.

Lukes's explanation

Weber's perspective on power remains a valuable starting point for political sociologists, but an alternative and 'radical' view of power has been proposed by the sociologist Stephen Lukes (1974). In his classic account, Lukes offers what he calls a 'three-dimensional view' of power. One-dimensional studies of power focus on the ability to make decisions to go one's own way in observable conflicts: for example, if the government had changed its support for military intervention in Iraq in response to the anti-war protests in February 2003, it would be evidence that the protestors had power. One-dimensional analyses look at the behaviour of participants in the making of decisions, particularly where there is a conflict of interests. When decisions are made, it then becomes observable which side is 'powerful' when decisions go their way. Lukes argues that this is a somewhat restricted view of power.

A two-dimensional perspective on power builds on this. Two-dimensional analyses also look at the ability of social actors and groups to control which issues are decided upon. By this, Lukes means that groups or individuals with power can exercise it, not just by making decisions in their own interests, but by limiting the alternatives available to others. For example, one way in which authoritarian governments (such as the 'soft authoritarianism of the Asian nation of Singapore) exert their power is by

placing restrictions on what the press can report. In doing so, they are often able to prevent certain grievances – such as international condemnation of their use of judicial corporal punishment – from becoming issues within the political process. On the two-dimensional view of power, we should examine not simply observable decisions and policies, but also how the decision-making agenda itself is created. Which issues are kept *off* the agenda?

Lukes (1974) argues that, building on the previous two types, there is also a three-dimensional perspective, which makes for a 'radical view' of power. He calls this the 'manipulation of desires'. He asks: 'Is it not the supreme exercise of power to get another or others to have the desires you want them to have – that is, to secure their compliance by controlling their thoughts and desires?' He points out that this does not necessarily mean that people are brainwashed. Our desires can also be manipulated in much more subtle ways. Neo-Marxists, such as Herbert Marcuse and the Frankfurt School of Critical Theory, have argued, for example, that capitalists exercise power over workers by shaping their desires through the media and other means of socialization, to take on the role of worker and mass consumer. Lukes's point here is that this 'ideological' exercise of power is not explicitly observable or measurable, but can be inferred when people act in ways that are against their own interests. In his theoretical analysis of power, Lukes is able to arrive at a wider definition than that offered by Weber. He argues: 'A exercises power over B when A affects B in a manner contrary to B's interests.'

 See chapter 3, 'Theories and Perspectives in Sociology', for a discussion of critical theory.

Critical points

Lukes's work has had a large influence on the way sociologists approach issues of power and its exercise, which continues today. However, it is not without its critics. One problem with Lukes's radical view of power is that it leaves open the question of how we, as sociologists, can know what people's interests really are. The adequacy of the radical view rests on how we address this question, but it has proved a very difficult one to answer in any conclusive way. A second, related problem is that the three-dimensional perspective asks us to study non-decisions and the unobservable influence of ideologies on people's desires. But how can sociologists study things that do *not* happen or they cannot observe? Finally, it may be objected that Lukes's three-dimensional view of power is not really a theory of power at all, but an acknowledgement of the influence of social structures on individuals. If this is so, then this amounts to a theory of structural determination rather than the exercise of power.

Contemporary significance

Lukes's 1974 work was quite a short analytical piece and in 2004 a second edition was published which contained two new essays, to bring his arguments up to date. In particular, Lukes discusses Foucault's theory of power, defending the three-dimensional view against more general (Foucauldian) ideas of power as running through all social relations in equal measure. However, following feminist theories of how male domination is established through the closing down of women's expectations and Amartya Sen's (1999) work on the concept of 'development' as lying in the *capacities* of people to 'live the kind of lives they value – and have reason to value', Lukes argues in the later edition that power is similarly a 'capacity' or set of human 'capabilities', drawing attention to the way in which these can be denied or enhanced. His influential argument in favour of a radical view of power seems set to continue as the standard reference point for debates on the subject.

rather than something exercised by dominant groups. Foucault's conception of power therefore widens the conception of 'the political'. Critics of Foucault, however, argue that although he provided a highly subtle account of the way in which power operates in everyday social interactions, his hazy conception of the term underestimates the concentration of power in structures such as the military or social classes.

Having looked at rival conceptions of power, we now concentrate on the way in which power is exercised in formal politics. In the next section we turn from discussions of political power to their exercise, by examining two forms of political system.

Authoritarianism and democracy

Throughout history, societies have relied on a variety of political systems. Even today, at the start of the twenty-first century, countries around the world continue to organize themselves according to different patterns and configurations. While most societies now claim to be democratic – that is to say, they are ruled by the people – other forms of political rule continue to exist. In this section we shall profile democracy and authoritarianism, two of the basic types of political system.

Authoritarianism

If democracy, which we examine below, encourages the active involvement of citizens in political affairs, in *authoritarian states* popular participation is denied or severely curtailed. In such societies, the needs and interests of the state are prioritized over those of average citizens and no legal mechanisms have been established for opposing government or for removing a leader from power.

Authoritarian governments exist today in many countries, some of which profess to be democratic. Iraq, under the leadership of Saddam Hussein until 2003, was an example of an authoritarian state where dissent was smothered and an inordinate share of national resources was diverted for the

A show of military strength at a May Day parade in North Korea. The country is perhaps the most politically isolated in the world, and its leader one of the most authoritarian. Head of State Kim Jong-il has recently decreed that men's hair may be no more than five centimetres in length. Balding men over the age of 50 are allowed an additional two centimetres for a 'comb-over'.

benefit of a select few. The powerful monarchies in Saudi Arabia and Kuwait and the leadership of Myanmar (Burma) strictly curtail citizens' civil liberties and deny them meaningful participation in government affairs.

The Asian nation of Singapore is often cited as an example of so-called 'soft authoritarianism'. This is because the ruling People's Action Party maintains a tight grip on power but ensures a high quality of life for its citizens by intervening in almost all aspects of society. Singapore is notable for its safety, its civil order and the social inclusion of all citizens. Singapore's economy is successful, the streets are clean, people are

employed and poverty is virtually unknown. However, despite the high standard of living in material terms, even minor transgressions such as dropping litter or smoking in public are punishable by stiff fines; there is tight regulation of the media, access to the Internet and on the ownership of satellite dishes; the police possess extraordinary powers to detain citizens for suspected offences and the use of corporal and capital judicial punishments is common. Despite this authoritarian control, popular satisfaction with the government has been high and social inequalities are minimal in comparison with many other countries. Although Singapore may be lacking in democratic freedoms, the country's brand of authoritarianism is different from those of more dictatorial regimes, leading the writer William Gibson to describe the island as 'Disneyland with the death penalty'.

Democracy

The word **democracy** has its roots in the Greek term *demokratia*, the individual parts of which are *demos* ('people') and *kratos* ('rule'). Democracy in its basic meaning is therefore a political system in which the people, not monarchs or aristocracies, rule. This sounds straightforward enough, but it is not. Democratic rule has taken contrasting forms at varying periods and in different societies, depending on how the concept is interpreted. For example, 'the people' has been variously understood to mean all men, owners of property, white men, educated men, and adult men and women. In some societies the officially accepted version of democracy is limited to the political sphere, whereas in others it is extended to broader areas of social life.

The form that democracy takes in a given context is largely an outcome of how its values and goals are understood and prioritized. Democracy is generally seen as the political system which is most able to ensure political equality, protect liberty and freedom, defend the common interest, meet citizens' needs, promote moral self-development and enable effective decision-making which takes everyone's interests into account (Held 2006). The weight that is granted to these various goals may influence whether democracy is regarded first and foremost as a form of popular power (self-government and self-regulation) or whether it is seen as a framework for supporting decision-making by others (such as a group of elected representatives).

Participatory democracy

In **participatory democracy** (or direct democracy), decisions are made communally by those affected by them. This was the original type of democracy practised in ancient Greece. Those who were citizens, a small minority of the society, regularly assembled to consider policies and make major decisions. Participatory democracy is of limited importance in modern societies, where the mass of the population has political rights, and it would be impossible for everyone actively to participate in the making of all the decisions that affect them.

Yet some aspects of participatory democracy do play a part in modern societies. Small communities in New England, in the north-eastern part of the United States, continue the traditional practice of annual 'town meetings'. On these designated days, all the residents of the town gather together to discuss and vote on local issues that do not fall under state or federal government jurisdiction. Another example of participatory democracy is the holding of referenda, when the people express their views on a particular issue. Direct consultation of large numbers of people is made possible by simplifying the issue down to one or two questions to be answered. Referenda are regularly used at the national level in some European countries to inform important policy decisions. There were referenda in several European countries in 2005 over whether they should sign up to the proposed European Constitution. The UK also agreed to hold a vote, but the defeat of the proposal in France and the Netherlands in May 2005 led to the abandonment of the Constitution and the suspension of plans for a British referendum. The rejection of an

---

THINKING CRITICALLY

How feasible is participatory democracy in large-scale modern societies? Could more use be made of referenda to make decisions or are there reasons to think that they would lead to a populist form of politics? Are there ways in which information technologies could facilitate this, and what might be the pitfalls in practice?

alternative 'Reform Treaty' in the Republic of Ireland in June 2008 destroyed any immediate hopes of this amended treaty being adopted. Referenda have also been used to decide contentious issues of secession in ethnic nationalist regions such as Quebec, the predominantly French-speaking province of Canada.

Representative democracy

Practicalities render participatory democracy unwieldy on a large scale, except in specific instances such as a special referendum. More common today is **representative democracy**, political systems in which decisions affecting a community are taken, not by its members as a whole, but by people they have elected for this purpose. In the area of national government, representative democracy takes the form of elections to congresses, parliaments or similar national bodies. Representative democracy also exists at other levels where collective decisions are taken, such as in provinces or states within an overall national community, cities, counties, boroughs and other regions. Many large organizations choose to run their affairs using representative democracy by electing a small executive committee to take key decisions.

Countries in which voters can choose between two or more parties and in which the mass of the adult population has the right to vote are usually called liberal democracies. Britain and the other Western European countries, the USA, Japan, Australia and New Zealand all fall into this category. Many countries in the developing world, such as India, also have liberal democratic systems, and, as we shall see, this number is growing.

The global spread of democracy

When political sociologists of the future look back on the 1980s and 1990s, one historical development in particular is likely to stand out: the democratization of many of the world's nations. Since the early 1980s, a number of countries in Latin America, such as Chile, Bolivia and Argentina, have undergone the transition from authoritarian military rule to a thriving democracy. Similarly, with the collapse of the Communist bloc in 1989, many East European states – Russia, Poland and Czechoslovakia, for example – have become democratic. And in Africa, a number of previously undemocratic nations – including Benin, Ghana, Mozambique and South Africa – have come to embrace democratic ideals.

In the mid-1970s, more than two-thirds of all societies in the world could be considered authoritarian. Since that time, the situation has shifted markedly – now less than a third of societies are authoritarian in nature. Democracy is no longer concentrated primarily in Western countries, but is endorsed, at least in principle, as the desired form of government in many areas of the world. As David Held (2006) has noted, 'democracy has become the fundamental standard of political legitimacy in the current era'.

In this section we will consider the global spread of liberal democracy and advance some possible explanations for its popularity. We will then move on to examine some of the main problems democracy faces in the contemporary world.

The fall of communism

For a long time, the political systems of the world were divided between liberal democracy and communism, as found in the former Soviet Union and Eastern Europe (and which still exists in China and a few other countries). For much of the twentieth century, a large proportion of the world's population lived under political systems that were communist or socialist in orientation. The 100 years following Marx's death in 1883 seemed to bear out his prognosis of the spread of socialism and workers' revolutions around the globe.

The tearing down of the Berlin Wall in 1989 was a symbolic moment in the rapid dismantling of communism in the East, giving way to an unprecedented spread of liberal democratic institutions.

Communist states regarded themselves as democracies, although the systems in these countries differed greatly from what people in the West understand by democracy. Communism was essentially a system of one-party rule. Voters were given a choice not between different parties but between different candidates of the same party – the Communist Party; there was often only one candidate running. There was thus no real choice at all. The Communist Party was easily the most dominant power in Soviet-style societies: it controlled not just the political system but the economy as well.

Almost everyone in the West, from trained scholars to average citizens, believed that the communist systems were deeply entrenched and had become a permanent feature of global politics. Few people, if any, predicted the dramatic course of events that began to unfold in 1989 as one communist regime after another collapsed in a series of 'velvet revolutions'. What had seemed like a solid and pervasively established system of rule throughout Eastern Europe was thrown off almost overnight. The Communists lost power in an accelerating sequence in the countries they had dominated for half a century: Hungary, Poland, Bulgaria, East Germany, Czechoslovakia and Romania. Eventually, the Communist Party within the Soviet Union itself lost control of power. When the 15 constituent republics of the USSR declared their independence in 1991, Mikhail Gorbachev, the last Soviet leader, was rendered a 'president without a state'.

USING YOUR SOCIOLOGICAL IMAGINATION

22.1 Politics at the 'end of history'?

The writer whose name has come to be synonymous with the phrase 'the end of history' is Francis Fukuyama (1989). Fukuyama's classic and highly contested conception of the end of history is based on the worldwide triumph of capitalism and liberal democracy. In the wake of the 1989 revolutions in Eastern Europe, the dissolution of the Soviet Union and a movement towards multiparty democracy in other regions, Fukuyama argued, the ideological battles of earlier eras are over. The end of history is the end of alternatives. No one any longer defends monarchism, and fascism is a phenomenon of the past. So is communism, which had been for so long the major rival of Western democracy. Capitalism has won in its long struggle with socialism, contrary to Marx's prediction, and liberal democracy now stands unchallenged. We have reached, Fukuyama asserts, 'the end

point of mankind's ideological evolution and [the] universalization of Western democracy as the final form of human government'.

Fukuyama's thesis has provoked critical responses, yet in some sense he has highlighted a key phenomenon of our time. At present, there is no sizeable electorate or mass movement able to envisage forms of economic and political organization beyond that of the market and liberal democracy. Although this currently seems to be the case, however, it seems very doubtful that history has come to a stop in the sense that we have exhausted all alternatives open to us. Who can say what new forms of economic, political or cultural order may emerge in the future? Just as the thinkers of medieval times had no inkling of the industrial society that was to emerge with the decline of feudalism, so we cannot at the moment anticipate how the world will change over the coming century.

Even in China, the students and others protesting in Tiananmen Square in 1989 seemed to shake the Communist Party's grip on power until they were brutally dispersed by the army.

THINKING CRITICALLY

What evidence is there from party politics that Fukuyama may be right (see 'Using your sociological imagination 22.1') that the old ideological battles around capitalism, communism and socialism are now over? Have any new political ideologies arisen to replace these? Is there any evidence around the world that suggests that Western-style democracy will *not* be the 'final form' of human government?

Since the fall of the Soviet Union and its allied governments, processes of democratization have continued to spread. Even among what were some of the world's most authoritarian states, signs of democratiza-

tion can be detected. Afghanistan was controlled by the Soviet Union after their troops invaded in 1979. The USSR occupation ended ten years later, after fierce resistance from the mujahidin (Muslim guerrilla warriors). During the early 1990s the country was the site of infighting between warlords composed of mujahidin factions. By 1996 the Taliban had seized control of most of the country and began the creation of a 'pure Islamic state'. They introduced an extreme interpretation of Islamic law, bringing in public executions and amputations, forbidding girls from going to school and women from working, and banning 'frivolous' entertainment. Following the events of 11 September 2001, the USA successfully led efforts to topple the Taliban, which it linked to the terrorist attacks. In late 2001, Hamid Karzai was chosen as Chairman of the Afghan Interim Authority, becoming President in June 2002, and he set about gaining approval for a new constitution. The constitution was signed in January 2004 and provides a strong executive branch, a moderate role for Islam and basic protections for human rights. The first elections in Afghanistan were held in October 2004 and resulted in Karzai winning a five-year mandate as President. However, by 2007 the Taliban had regrouped, leading to a large increase in the number of attacks against US and other foreign troops that were, and still are, in the country, as well as against the Afghan government and its officials. Outside the capital, Kabul, the situation remains extremely difficult for the bulk of the population. The country continues to struggle with problems such as widespread poverty and large-scale illegal opium production, which forms a large part of the economy. Hence, in spite of its fledgling democracy, it is not yet clear whether Afghanistan will become a viable and stable state.

In China, which contains about a fifth of the world's population, the Communist government is facing strong pressures to become more democratic. Thousands of people remain in prison in China for the non-violent expression of their desire for democracy. But there are still groups, resisted by the Communist government, working actively to secure a transition to a democratic system. In recent years, other authoritarian Asian states, such as Myanmar, Indonesia and Malaysia, have also witnessed growing democratic movements. Some of these calls for greater freedoms have been met with violent responses. Nonetheless, the 'globalization of democracy' continues apace around the world.

This general trend towards democracy is not inevitable. For some countries in the former Soviet bloc, such as Poland, the Czech Republic, Hungary and the Baltic states, liberal democracy appears to be taking a firm hold, while in others, such as the former Central Asian republics of the Soviet Union, Yugoslavia and even Russia, democracy remains fragile. Indeed, democratic political institutions have been shown to be fragile and vulnerable at various points in history. In Iran, for example, one of the world's most militant Islamic states, popular discontent with the powerful mullahs (religious leaders) led to the election of reformist president Mohammed Khatami in 1997 with over 70 per cent of the vote. It seemed as if democracy was coming to Iran. Khatami was likened to former Soviet leader Mikhail Gorbachev, as a leader who recognized that popular yearnings for democracy – if left unaddressed – would result in the collapse of the system itself. However, after religious conservatives regained control of parliament, Khatami only succeeded in introducing limited reforms and, in June 2005, one of their members, Mahmoud Ahmadinejad, was elected President, leaving prospects for further democratic reform highly unlikely. The recent history of Iran shows that we should not assume that democratization is an irreversible process. Yet the fact that democratization is tied to larger globalizing forces is reason for optimism about the future of democracy.

Democratization and its discontents

Why has democracy become so widespread? One explanation is that other types of political rule have been attempted and have failed – that democracy has proved itself to be the 'best' political system. It seems clear that democracy is a better form of political organization than authoritarianism, but this alone does not adequately explain the recent waves of democratization. While a full explanation for these developments would require a detailed analysis of the social and political situations in each country that led up to the transition to democracy, there can be little doubt but that globalizing processes have played an important role in this trend.

First, the growing number of cross-national cultural contacts that globalization has brought with it has invigorated democratic movements in many countries. A

Global Society 22.1 | **Does the Internet promote democratization?**

The Internet is a powerful democratizing force. It transcends national and cultural borders, facilitates the spread of ideas around the globe and allows like-minded people to find one another in the realm of cyberspace. More and more people in countries around the world access the Internet regularly and consider it to be important to their lifestyles. Yet the dynamic spread of the Internet is perceived as a threat by governments – especially authoritarian ones – that recognize the potential of online activity to subvert state authority. Although the Internet has been allowed to exist more or less freely in most countries, some states have begun to take steps to curb its usage by citizens.

By the end of 2007 – that is, 12 years after the Internet became commercially available – the number of Internet users in China had reached 162 million, some 11 per cent of China's population, more than double that of 2003. This total continues to rise rapidly. In the eyes of the Chinese Communist leadership, the Internet presents a dangerous threat to state security by allowing political opposition groups to coordinate their activities.

In response to the rapid growth of the Internet, the Chinese government has introduced scores of regulations, closed thousands of Internet cafés, blocked emails, search engines, foreign news and politically sensitive websites, and introduced a filtering system for web searches on a list of prohibited key words and terms. Nevertheless, it appears that Internet activism is continuing to grow in China as fast as the controls are tightened.

In 2004, Amnesty International reported:

> Signing online petitions, calling for reform and an end to corruption, planning to set up a pro-democracy party, publishing 'rumours about [the disease] SARS', communicating with groups abroad, opposing the persecution of the [religious movement] Falun Gong and calling for a review of the 1989 crackdown on the democracy protests are all examples of activities considered by the authorities to be 'subversive' or to 'endanger state security'. Such charges almost always result in prison sentences.

In an earlier report, Amnesty estimated that '30,000 state security personnel are reportedly monitoring websites, chat rooms and private email messages' (2002).

Other governments have reached similar conclusions. The Burmese government has introduced a ban on the dissemination of information 'detrimental to government' through the Internet or email. Malaysian authorities demanded that cyber cafés keep lists of all individuals who use their computers. Religious conservatives in the Iranian government forced the closure of hundreds of Internet cafés in late 2003 and introduced new rules requiring proprietors to restrict customers' access to a long list of 'immoral and anti-Islamic sites'.

globalized media, along with advances in communications technology, has exposed inhabitants of many non-democratic nations to democratic ideals, increasing internal pressure on political elites to hold elections. Of course, such pressure does not automatically result from the diffusion of the notion of popular sovereignty. More important is that, with globalization, news of democratic revolutions and accounts of the mobilizing processes that lead to them are quickly spread on a regional level. News of the revolution in Poland in 1989, for example, took little time to travel to Hungary, providing pro-democracy activists there with a useful, regionally appropriate model around which to orient their work.

THINKING CRITICALLY

What do you think makes the Internet so different from older types of media in acting as a force for the spread of democracy? If the Internet is helping to spread democratic ideals, is it also promoting Western cultural values? How likely is it that the prohibitions described in 'Global Society 22.1' will be effective in the long term?

Second, international organizations such as the United Nations and the European Union – which, in a globalized world, come to play an increasingly important role – have put external pressure on non-democratic states to move in democratic directions. In some cases, these organizations have been able to use trade embargoes, the conditional provision of loans for economic development and stabilization, and diplomatic manoeuvres of various kinds to encourage the dismantling of authoritarian regimes. For example, the United Nations Development Programme (UNDP) and UN Mission in the Democratic Republic of Congo supported a new Independent Electoral Commission to monitor and administer the 2006 national election, achieving an 80 per cent participation rate. This was a real achievement in a society that had experienced around four million deaths as a result of civil war and had not held democratic elections for 40 years. The UN's assistance is not limited to technical and administrative expertise. The organization also provides support for developing a democratic culture by assisting the groups and organizations in civil society, such as trade unions and human rights monitoring groups, as well as promoting the value of a free media as part of the democratic process. In recent years, UNDP has focused particularly on improving the participation rates of women in elections, both as voters and candidates, in, for example, Kuwait, Morocco and Mauritania (UNDP 2007b).

Third, democratization has been facilitated by the expansion of world capitalism. Although transnational corporations are notorious for striking deals with dictators, corporations generally prefer to do business in democratic states – not because of an inherent philosophical preference for political freedom and equality, but because democracies tend to be more stable than other kinds of state, and stability and predictability are essential for maximizing profits. Because political, economic and military elites, particularly in the develop-

ing world and in the former Soviet Union, are often anxious to increase levels of international trade and to encourage transnationals to set up shop in their countries, they have sometimes pursued a democratic agenda of their own, leading to what the political sociologist Barrington Moore (1966), once called 'revolutions from above'.

It is true that if globalization were the sole cause of the most recent wave of democratization, all countries today would be democratic. The persistence of authoritarian regimes in such countries as China, Cuba and Nigeria suggests that globalizing forces are not always sufficient to force a transition to democracy. But democratic moves are afoot even in several of these countries, leading some sociologists to argue that, under the influence of globalization, many more nations will become democratic in the years to come.

Democracy in trouble?

Between 1974 and the end of the century, largely as a result of countries gaining independence and introducing democratic systems, the proportion of democracies to non-democracies in the world increased from 27 per cent to 62 per cent (Linz 2000). As democracy is becoming so widespread, we might expect it to be working in a highly successful way. Yet this appears not to be the case. Almost everywhere, established democracies are in some difficulty. This is not only because it is proving difficult to set up a stable democratic order in Russia and other former communist societies; democracy also seems to be in trouble in its main countries of origin, of which the UK is a good example. In Britain, like other Western countries, the number of people who vote in European, general and local elections has declined considerably since the early 1990s (see table 22.1).

It has been argued that the decline in voting shows that people in the West seem to have lost trust in those in power: some academics and politicians have talked about a wider 'crisis of trust' in society. The

Table 22.1 **UK general elections: electorates and turnout, 1945–2005**

Year	Turnouts %[a]
1945	72.8
1950	83.9
1951	82.6
1955	76.8
1959	78.7
1964	77.1
1966	75.8
1970	72.0
Feb 1974	78.8
Oct 1974	72.8
1979	76.0
1983	72.7
1987	75.3
1992	77.7
1997	71.5
2001	59.4
2005	61.3

[a] Total valid vote as a percentage of the electorate

Source: www.electoral-reform.org.uk/ publications/statistics/turnouts.htm

(Accessed 30.6.05)

philosopher Onora O'Neill (2002) sums up this view:

> Mistrust and suspicion have spread across all areas of life, and supposedly with good reason. Citizens, it is said, no longer trust governments, or politicians, or ministers, or the police, or the courts, or the prison service. Consumers, it is said, no longer trust business, especially big business, or their products. None of us, it is said, trusts banks, or insurers, or pension providers. Patients, it is said, no longer trust doctors . . . and in particular no longer trust hospitals or hospital consultants. 'Loss of trust' is, in short, a cliché of our times.

Evidence seems to confirm a loss of trust, at least when it comes to party politics. In the UK, for example, surveys have been carried out in general election years that ask voters if they trust the government to put national interests above party interests 'all or most of the time'; the number of people who said they did not trust the government on this issue fell from 47 per cent in 1987 to 33 per cent in 1992 to 28 per cent in 2001 (cited in Skidmore and Harkin 2003).

Some have argued that trends like these indicate that people are increasingly sceptical of traditional forms of authority. Connected to this has been a shift in political values in democratic nations from 'scarcity values' to 'post-materialist values' (Inglehart 1997). This means that after a certain level of economic prosperity has been reached, voters become concerned less with economic issues than with the

What explains increasing voter apathy?

quality of their individual (as opposed to collective) lifestyles, such as the desire for meaningful work. As a result, voters are generally less interested in national politics, except for issues involving personal liberty.

The past few decades have also been a period in which, in several Western countries, the welfare state has come under attack. Rights and benefits, fought for over long periods, have been contested and cut back. Right-wing parties, such as the Conservatives in the UK or the Republicans in the USA, have attempted to reduce levels of welfare expenditure in their countries. One reason for this governmental retrenchment is the declining revenues available to governments as a result of the general world recession that began in the early 1970s. Yet there also seems to have developed an increasing scepticism, shared not only by some governments, but also by many of their citizens, about the effectiveness of relying on the state for the provision of many essential goods and services. This scepticism is based on the knowledge that the welfare state is also bureaucratic, alienating and inefficient, and that welfare benefits can create perverse consequences that undermine what they were designed to achieve.

The global picture of voter turnout is quite varied and it has been suggested that the type of voting system may explain this variety (see table 22.2). For example, it may be argued that election turnout tends to be highest in those countries with compulsory voting and lowest where voting in elections is entirely voluntary. This seems to be an effective argument in some parts of Western Europe, where Lichtenstein's average turnout of almost 93 per cent since 1945 can be partly attributed to that country's compulsory voting system, compared to, say, Switzerland's low average of just 56.5 per cent. However, this can only be a partial explanation of cross-national voting patterns. This becomes evident when we look, for example, at the Bahamas, which averages almost a 92 per cent turnout since 1945 in a *non-compulsory* system. Clearly there must be other factors at work here.

This shows that comparative statistics on voter turnout, in themselves, tell us very little about the state of democracy *within* particular countries. What are not revealed in such bald figures are the different national contexts within which the turnout figures were achieved. This is a particularly pertinent critical point when comparisons are made between the 'new' and 'old' democracies, which are often very different political environments. For example, in many established democracies, such as the USA, there are other means through which people's interests can be represented, such as in the courts under equal rights legislation (Pintor and Gratschew 2002), which may partly explain low voter turnout in elections. So, although voter turnout gives us a

Table 22.2 Vote/registration ratio (%), league table by world region, selected countries: ranking of average turnout since 1945

Oceania		Central & South America	
Australia (22)	94.5	Guyana (7)	88.5
New Zealand (19)	90.8	Chile (11)	78.9
Fiji (3)	81.0	Nicaragua (6)	75.9
Tonga (4)	56.3	Colombia (18)	47.6
Average	*83.1*	*Average*	*71.5*
Western Europe		Asia	
Liechtenstein (17)	92.8	Singapore (8)	93.5
Sweden (17)	87.1	Japan (22)	69.6
United Kingdom (16)	75.2	India (13)	59.4
Switzerland (14)	56.5	Pakistan (6)	45.3
Average	*82.6*	*Average*	*74.0*
North America		Middle East	
Bahamas (6)	91.9	Israel (15)	80.3
Canada (18)	73.9	Iran (1)	77.3
United States of America (17)	66.5	Jordan (3)	51.8
Haiti (3)	47.1	Lebanon (3)	39.5
Average	*69.6*	*Average*	*72.2*
Africa		Central & Eastern Europe	
Burundi (1)	91.4	Uzbekistan (3)	93.5
Morocco (5)	71.2	Czech Republic (4)	82.8
Zimbabwe (3)	48.7	Russia (3)	58.4
Mali (2)	21.3	Poland (5)	50.3
Average	*64.5*	*Average*	*71.9*

Note: Number of elections in brackets

Source: Reproduced with permission of International IDEA from Pintor R., and Gratschew M. (2002), *Voter Turnout Since 1945*, (International IDEA), Fig.11, p.70. © The International Institute for Democracy and Electoral Assistance (IDEA) 2002.

basic guide to the proportions of people voting in elections across the world, it may be more informative to look at the changing voting patterns over time within particular national contexts, as in our UK example in table 22.1 above. Addressing the important question of *why* people do or do not vote requires statistical evidence to be related to the societal context within which politics takes place.

In the next section, we look at the impact of voter disaffection with mainstream politics and the historic demise of communist systems on national party politics, taking the UK, which has a particularly strong tradition of class-based politics, as our case study.

Old and new party politics

As in other industrialized countries, British electoral politics has changed significantly over the past 25 years or so. The Labour and Conservative parties have come under increasing pressure from dwindling membership numbers, fewer financial resources and a loss of voting support. The Labour Party managed successfully to reinvent itself and return to power in 1997, repeating its general election success in 2001 and 2005, while the Conservative Party continues to face declining membership levels and an ageing base of supporters.

Several factors are important for understanding the changing experience of the main parties. The first factor is structural: the proportion of the economically active population involved in traditional blue-collar occupations has dropped considerably. There is little doubt that this has eroded some traditional sources of support for Labour, such as cohesive working-class communities and trade unions.

A second factor is the split that occurred in the Labour Party at the beginning of the 1980s, which led to the founding of the Social Democratic Party (SDP), which, in turn, merged with the Liberal Party in 1988 to form the Liberal Democrats. In recent general elections, Britain's 'third party' has achieved significant support and drawn votes away from the two main parties. For much of the post-war period, the Liberal Party had only a small number of seats in Parliament (ranging from a low of 6 to a peak of 23 in 1983). Since 1997 this figure has risen. In the general election of 2005, the Liberal Democrats won 62 seats in the House of Commons (out of a total of 646) and gained over 21 per cent of the popular vote. This seems to indicate that a three-party system is now operating in the UK.

A third influence was that of the then Conservative prime minister, Margaret Thatcher, who was in post from 1979 to 1990. The vigorous programme of change initiated by Thatcher and her cabinets expressed a significant move away from earlier Tory philosophy. 'Thatcherism' gave prime emphasis to restricting the role of the state and made faith in market forces the basis of both individual liberties and economic growth. One way in which the

state withdrew from the economy was through the privatization of public companies, many of which had been nationalized after the Second World War. The sale of shares in British Telecom, British Gas, British Steel, British Airways and British Petroleum divided public opinion. Privatization of this sort is claimed to reintroduce healthy economic competition in place of unwieldy and ineffective public bureaucracies, reduce public expenditure and end political interference in managerial decisions. The privatization policies begun by the Conservatives have had an enduring impact. At first, they were hotly contested by the Labour Party, but it later abandoned its hostile stance and came to accept that much of this trend was irreversible in a society that increasingly embraced individualism and difference rather than collectivity and uniformity.

After winning a crushing election victory in 1987, Margaret Thatcher's popularity began to decline sharply. Key factors were an unpopular 'poll tax' (the Community Charge) – based not on income or property, but 'per head' – and the slide of the economy into recession. In 1990 John Major replaced Thatcher and continued to privatize state enterprises, including the controversial sale of British Rail, until he resigned in the wake of Labour's landslide victory in the 1997 general election.

A fourth factor was the emergence of Tony Blair's **New Labour** in the mid-1990s. Although the New Labour project was started under Neil Kinnock and John Smith in the mid-1980s, it was under Tony Blair from 1994 that some far-reaching internal reforms of the party took place. For example, New Labour saw through the abolition of Clause 4 of the party constitution, which had committed it to widespread public ownership of industry. The central importance of the market economy was thus formally recognized and old style socialist economics eschewed. This brought the party into line with many others in Western Europe. A decisive influence here had been the dissolution of communism in the Soviet Union and Eastern Europe. Most people accepted that the disintegration of Soviet communism was a signal that less extreme ideas of socialist politics also needed to be radically overhauled. The idea that a modern economy could be 'managed' directly by the state – central both to communism and to 'Old' Labour socialism – now appears obsolete for the foreseeable future.

The election of 1997, which brought New Labour to power, represented one of the largest electoral shifts in twentieth-century British politics, putting an end to 18 years of Conservative Party rule. The Labour Party captured 419 parliamentary seats, giving them their largest ever majority of 179 seats. The Conservatives' share of the UK vote was their lowest since 1832, at just 30.7 per cent, marking a steep drop from previously fairly stable levels of support. In 2001, Labour won again with another landslide majority of 166 seats, but this time on a much lower voter turnout – just 59.4 per cent of those eligible to vote (Watkins 2004). Tony Blair pledged to continue the programme of revitalizing public services begun in 1997. However, much of British political debate, as well as that around the world, revolved around the controversial decision to support, both morally and militarily, the US-led invasion of Iraq. Blair's popularity and that of New Labour fell during this term.

> See chapter 23, 'Nations, War and Terrorism', for a wider discussion of war and terrorism.

Labour did win for a historic third time in the general election of May 2005, but with a much reduced majority of 65. Turnout remained low, at just 61.5 per cent, and the signs were that the large-scale demonstrations and opposition to the invasion of Iraq had cost the party many seats. Labour's share of the vote fell significantly in constituencies with high Muslim populations, which, as a group, were particularly opposed to the war. Often these votes went to the Liberal Democrats, the only main party that had opposed military action in Iraq. In Bethnal Green and Bow, former Labour MP, George Galloway, overturned a large Labour majority to win the seat on an anti-war agenda for a newly formed 'Respect Party'. The Conservative Party polled just 32.3 per cent and, in 2005, David Cameron became the party's fourth leader in just over eight years. Labour's vote also fell in nine out of the ten constituencies with the highest student populations, reflecting opposition amongst many students to the Iraq war and higher education tuition fees (Mellows-Facer et al. 2005). In 2007, Blair stood down enabling Gordon Brown to become prime minister, pledging to 'learn the lessons' from mistakes made in Iraq. Nonetheless, amidst rising global energy, fuel and food prices, and following a series of by-election defeats in 2008, Labour's opinion poll ratings fell even further. A defeat by the SNP in Glasgow East was particularly worrying for Labour MPs, as it had been a solid Labour seat for nearly 60 years.

Some commentators described New Labour's project as part of a 'third way' in politics (Giddens 1998). New Labour embarked on an ambitious course of political reform and modernization. While maintaining a commitment to the values of social justice and solidarity, the government sought to engage with the realities of the new global order. It recognized that the Old Labour politics was out of line with the challenges of the new era. Like more than a dozen other European governments, New Labour wanted to move beyond traditional political categories of left and right and embark on a new brand of centre-left politics. It is because this approach tries to avoid customary political divides that it is often referred to as third way politics.

There are six main dimensions to third way politics:

1   *Reconstruction of government.* Active government is required to meet the

needs of a rapidly changing world, yet government should not be exclusively associated with top-down bureaucracies and national policies. Dynamic forms of management and administration, such as those sometimes found in the business sector, can work with government in defending and revitalizing the public sphere.

2 *The cultivating of civil society*. Government and the market alone are not enough to solve the many challenges in late modern societies. Civil society – the realm outside the state and market – must be strengthened and joined up with government and business. Voluntary groups, families and civic associations can play vital roles in addressing community issues from crime to education.

3 *Reconstruction of the economy*. The third way envisages a new mixed economy characterized by a balance between government regulation and deregulation. It rejects the neoliberal view that deregulation is the only way to ensure freedom and growth.

4 *Reform of the welfare state*. While it is essential to protect the vulnerable through the provision of effective welfare services, the welfare state must be reformed in order to become more efficient. Third way politics looks towards a 'society of care', while acknowledging that old forms of welfare were often unsuccessful in reducing inequalities, and controlled, rather than empowered, the poor.

5 *Ecological modernization*. Third way politics rejects the view that environmental protection and economic growth are incompatible. There are many ways that a commitment to defending the environment can generate jobs and stimulate economic development.

6 *Reform of the global system*. In an era of globalization, third way politics looks to new forms of global governance. Transnational associations can lead to

democracy above the level of the nation-state and can allow greater governance of the volatile international economy.

Third way politics emerged against the backdrop of a double political crisis. The revolutions of 1989 revealed that socialism was not a viable approach to economic organization, yet the unchecked enthusiasm for the free market favoured by neoliberal conservatives was also flawed. The modernizing agenda of third way politics adopted in Britain and elsewhere was an attempt to renew social democracy by responding creatively to the forces of globalization. It sought to harness the energy behind these transformations to revitalize the workings of government and democracy.

This idea of finding a third way in politics, however, has been widely criticized. Many Conservatives see the new politics as largely empty of content – political posturing rather than a policy programme with real bite. Some on the traditional left, on the other hand, argue that the third way does too little to deal with problems of social inequality and insecurity. They hold that 'Old Labour', with its focus on maintaining close links with the trade unions and opposition to the privatization of state-owned industries, represents a more grounded form of labour politics over the long term (for an account of the third way, see Giddens 1998, 2001, 2002).

THINKING CRITICALLY

New Labour and third way politics were attempts to get to grips with globalization and the collapse of 'actually existing socialism'. Thinking back to Francis Fukuyama's (1989) argument above regarding the 'end of history', in what ways can third way politics be seen as supportive of his central claims? Is communism/socialism now a moribund political ideology?

In early 2008, the 'global credit crunch' almost led to the collapse of a well-known high-street bank in the UK. Thousands of customers queued to withdraw their money. Such crises lend weight to arguments in favour of global financial regulation, one example of global governance.

Global governance

The American sociologist Daniel Bell (1997) observed that national government is *too small* to respond to the big questions – such as the influence of global economic competition or the destruction of the world's environment – but it has become *too big* to deal with the small questions – issues that affect particular cities or localities. The suggestion is that national politics is caught in a pincer movement of globalization and localization, which partly explains why many people, as we noted above, are just not enthused enough to participate.

National governments have little power over the activities of giant business corporations, the main actors within the global economy. For instance, a British corporation may decide to shut down its production plants in the UK and shift production to Malaysia, as vacuum-cleaner manufacturer Dyson did in 2002, in order to lower costs and compete more effectively with other corporations. The result was that British workers lost their jobs and, in such cases, they are likely to want the government to do something. But national governments are unable to control the globalizing processes bound up with the world economy. All they can do is try to soften the blow by, for example, providing unemployment benefits or job retraining.

Globalization has created new risks: the spread of weapons of mass destruction, pollution, terrorism and international financial crises, for example. These issues cannot be managed by nation-states alone and international governmental organizations (IGOs), like the World Bank, World Trade Organization and the United Nations, have been created as a way of pooling global risks. These organizations form the basis for discussions about **global governance**. Global governance is not about creating government on a global level. Instead it is concerned with the framework of rules needed to tackle global problems, and the diverse set of institutions, including both international organizations and national governments, needed to guarantee this framework of rules. Many of the global organizations already in place to tackle these problems lack democratic accountability. For example, the UN Security Council has 15 members, of which five are permanent: the USA, Britain, France, China and Russia – some of the world's most powerful countries. For any resolution to be passed, the Council requires nine votes, including the votes of all five permanent members. The UN did not back a resolution explicitly allowing force against Iraq in 2003, for example, because France threatened to veto it. This was one of the main grounds cited by critics of the war, who condemned it as an illegitimate use of power, as we saw at the start of this chapter. The views of the vast majority of the world's poorer countries were largely irrelevant to the debate.

We discuss the emergence of IGOs in chapter 18, 'Organizations and Networks'.

THINKING CRITICALLY

Why might institutions like the EU be better equipped to deal with politics in a global age than the nation-state? If nation-states promoted national identities, will the EU have to challenge national identities if it is ultimately to be successful? What benefits does the EU confer on its member states that they could not otherwise achieve?

What, then, is the fate of democracy in an age when democratic governance on a nation-state level seems ill-equipped to deal with the flow of events? Some observers suggest that there is little to be done, that governments cannot hope to control the rapid changes occurring around us, and that the most prudent course of action is to reduce the role of government and allow market forces to guide the way.

David Held (2004) contests this view. He argues that in a global age we are in need of *more*, not less, government. Yet effective governing in our present era demands a deepening of democracy, at the level of the nation-state as well as above and below it. Held maintains that a global social democracy is needed to face the new challenges brought about by globalization. This involves making global organizations accountable, in the same way that democratically elected governments are accountable to their electorate in national elections. Held argues that the foundations are already in place for a global social democracy. The International Criminal Court, which was set up to prosecute and bring to justice those responsible for the worst global crimes (such as genocide, crimes against humanity and war crimes), and the United Nations both provide good foundations, although the latter needs to be made more democratically accountable. These institutions foster a vision of a world in which basic human rights are protected and a peaceful process for resolution of difference is agreed upon. The existence of these organizations marks the entrenchment of the values of the equal dignity and worth of all humans.

In Held's view, global social democracy will be achieved through multi-layer governance in which many organizations operate together at different levels: local, national and global. Where states were once the main actors in international politics, through their heads and foreign ministers, the primary actors now include administrative agencies, courts and legislatures as well.

22.2 The European Union in a global age

The historical roots of the European Union lie in the Second World War. The idea of European integration was conceived to prevent such destruction from ever happening again. The British wartime prime minister, Winston Churchill, called for a 'United States of Europe' in 1946. The first practical moves towards European unity were proposed by the French foreign minister, Robert Schuman, in a speech on 9 May 1950. This date, the 'birthday' of what is now the European Union (EU), is celebrated annually as 'Europe Day'.

Initially, the EU consisted of just six countries: Belgium, Germany, France, Italy, Luxembourg and the Netherlands. Denmark, Ireland and the United Kingdom joined in 1973, Greece in 1981, Spain and Portugal in 1986, Austria, Finland and Sweden in 1995. In 2004 the biggest ever enlargement took place when ten new countries joined, mainly from Eastern Europe. Bulgaria and Romania joined in 2007, and membership talks are under way with Turkey.

In the early years, much of the cooperation between EU countries was about trade and the economy, but now the EU also deals with many other subjects of direct importance for our everyday life. EU agencies deal with areas as diverse as citizens' rights, security, job creation, regional development and environmental protection. EU member countries are democratic, and must be committed to working together for peace and prosperity.

Some people, especially in the UK, are concerned that membership of the EU undermines national sovereignty – that is, the independence and ability for self-government – of existing states, while others argue that the EU is not much more than another international body like the United Nations or the World Trade Organization.

Defenders of the EU argue that both the accounts above are inaccurate. They argue that the EU is an organization whose member states have set up common institutions to which they delegate some of their power so that decisions on specific matters of joint interest can be made democratically at European level. All EU decisions and procedures are based on the treaties, which are agreed by all the EU countries. This pooling of sovereignty is also called 'European integration'.

There are five EU institutions, each playing a specific role:

- the European Parliament (elected by the peoples of the member states);
- the Council of the European Union (representing the governments of the member states);
- the European Commission (driving force and executive body);
- the Court of Justice (ensuring compliance with the law);
- the Court of Auditors (controlling sound and lawful management of the EU budget).

These are flanked by five other important bodies:

- the European Economic and Social Committee (expresses the opinions of organized civil society on economic and social issues);
- the Committee of the Regions (expresses the opinions of regional and local authorities);
- the European Central Bank (responsible for monetary policy and managing the euro);
- the European Ombudsman (deals with citizens' complaints about maladministration by any EU institution or body);
- the European Investment Bank (helps achieve EU objectives by financing investment projects).

A number of agencies and other bodies complete the system.

The growth of the EU gave European leaders the opportunity to overhaul the organization's basic documents. In 2002 a constitutional convention was launched, chaired by former French president Valéry Giscard d'Estaing. The EU constitution, or 'constitutional treaty', which it produced pulled together various treaties into a single document and committed members to closer cooperation on defence and immigration, amongst others things, and to stewardship under a single EU president. Defeat of the constitution in referenda in France and the Netherlands in 2005 [and rejection of the Reform Treaty in Ireland, 2008] seems to have ended the hopes of those in favour of closer European political integration for the time being.

Supporters of the EU argue that it has delivered half a century of stability, peace and prosperity. It has helped to raise living standards, built a single Europe-wide market, launched the single European currency, the euro, and strengthened Europe's voice in the world. The EU fosters cooperation among the peoples of Europe, promoting unity while preserving diversity and ensuring that decisions are taken as close as possible to the citizens. In the increasingly interdependent world of the twenty-first century, it will be even more necessary for every European citizen to cooperate with people from other countries in a spirit of curiosity, tolerance and solidarity.

Sources: European Union 2005; *The Economist* 2005b

Former Secretary-General of the UN, Kofi Annan, has been highly influential in international politics, for example. Held also argues that non-governmental organizations, such as Oxfam and Amnesty International, as well as social movements can also play an important role in the creation of global social democracy. Below, we look in more detail at the increasing significance of social movements in society and how sociologists have understood their emergence and growth.

Social movements and social change

Political life, as our discussion above shows, is by no means carried on only within the orthodox framework of political parties, voting systems and representation in legislative and governmental bodies. It often happens that groups find that their objectives or ideals cannot be achieved within, or are actively blocked by, this framework. Despite the spread of democracy we explored earlier, the persistence of authoritarian regimes in many countries – such as China, Turkmenistan and Cuba – reminds us that effecting change within existing political structures is not always possible. Sometimes political and social change can only be brought about through recourse to non-orthodox forms of political action such as revolutions or social movements.

What are social movements?

The most dramatic and far-reaching example of non-orthodox political action is revolution – the overthrow of an existing political order by means of a mass movement, using violence. Revolutions are tense, exciting and fascinating events; understandably, they attract great attention. Yet for all of their high drama, revolutions occur relatively infrequently.

See chapter 2, 'Asking and Answering Sociological Questions', for a discussion of Theda Skocpol's work on social revolutions.

The most common type of non-orthodox political activity takes place through **social movements** – collective attempts to further a common interest or secure a common goal through action outside the sphere of established institutions. A wide variety of social movements besides those leading to revolution have existed in modern societies, some enduring and some transient. Social movements come in all shapes and sizes. Some are very small, numbering no more than a few dozen members; others may include thousands or even millions of people. While some social movements carry on their activities within the laws of the society in which they exist, others operate as illegal or underground groups. It is characteristic of protest movements, however, that they operate near the margins of what is defined as legally permissible by governments at any particular time or place.

Social movements often arise with the aim of bringing about change on a public issue, such as expanding civil rights for a segment of the population. In response to social movements, counter-movements sometimes arise in defence of the status quo. The campaign for women's right to abortion, for example, has been vociferously challenged by anti-abortion ('pro-life') activists, who argue that abortion should be illegal.

Often, laws or policies are altered as a result of the action of social movements. These changes in legislation can have far-reaching effects. For example, it used to be illegal for groups of workers to call their members out on strike, and striking was punished with varying degrees of severity in different countries. Eventually, however, the laws were amended, making the strike a permissible tactic of industrial conflict. Similarly, lesbian and gay movements have been largely successful in raising the issue of equal rights and many countries around the world have equalized their laws on the legal age of sexual activity for heterosexuals and homosexuals.

Social movements are among the most powerful forms of collective action. Well-organized, persistent campaigns can bring about dramatic results. The American civil rights movement, for example, succeeded in pushing through important pieces of legislation outlawing racial segregation in schools and public places. The feminist movement scored important gains for women in terms of economic and political equality. In recent years, environmental movements have campaigned in highly unconventional ways to promote sustainable forms of development and change attitudes towards the natural environment.

> See chapter 5, 'The Environment', for a much wider discussion of environmental issues.

Social movements are as evident a feature of the contemporary world as are the formal, bureaucratic organizations they often oppose, and some scholars suggest that we may be moving towards a global 'social movement society', which provides fertile ground for this type of collective action. For this reason, we need to explore sociological theories of social movements.

Theories of social movements

For most of the twentieth century, social movements were seen as rather unusual phenomena by sociologists. As with other forms of collective behaviour, such as the study of riots, crowds and revolutions, they seemed to be marginal to the practice of mainstream sociology (Tarrow 1998). This began to change with the emergence of a new wave of movements from the 1960s, which attracted a fresh generation of sociologists looking to understand and explain them. When they did so, they found the existing theories of social movements to be inadequate for the task. To see why, we must take a brief tour through some of the earlier social movement theories.

Collective behaviour and social unrest

The Chicago School of Sociology is often seen as the first to systematically chart forms of collective behaviour and to turn these into a specialist field of inquiry in sociology from the 1920s (Della Porta and Diani 2006). Scholars in the Chicago tradition, including Robert E. Park, Ernest W. Burgess and Herbert Blumer, saw social movements as *agents* of social change, not merely as *products* of it. In this sense, they began to theorize social movements in more productive ways.

Herbert Blumer (1969) was the foremost social movement analyst in the Chicago tradition of symbolic interactionism. He devised a theory of social unrest to account for the unconventional protest activities of social movements outside the sphere of formal party politics and interest representation. Essentially, Blumer saw social movements of all kinds as motivated by dissatisfaction with some aspects of current society, which they sought to rectify. In doing so, they were trying to build a 'new order of life'. Blumer argued:

> Social movements can be viewed as collective enterprises to establish a new order of life. They have their inception in a condition of unrest, and derive their motive power on the one hand from dissatisfaction with the current form of life, and on the other hand, from wishes and hopes for a new scheme of living. The career of a social movement depicts the emergence of a new order of life. In its beginning, a social movement is amorphous, poorly organized, and without form; the collective behavior is on the primitive level. . . . As a social movement develops, it takes on the character of a society. It acquires organization and form, a body of customs and traditions, established leadership, an enduring division of labor, social rules and social values – in short, a culture, a social organization, and a new scheme of life. (1969: 8)

Blumer's theory of social movements as social unrest makes some important points. For example, he saw that movements can be 'active' or outwardly directed, aiming to transform society, or they can be 'expressive' or inwardly directed, trying to change the people who become involved. An example of the former would be the labour movement, which aimed to radically change capitalist societies in egalitarian ways, while the latter would include 'New Age' movements, which encourage people to transform their inner selves. In practice, most social movements involve both active and expressive elements as movement activists and supporters undergo changes in their self-identity as a result of campaigns to change society. Many environmental campaigns, for example, are explicitly aimed at preventing environmental damage, but in the process they often generate an increasing self-identification with the natural world, thereby transforming people's perception of self.

Blumer also argued that social movements have a 'life-cycle', many of which involve four consecutive stages. First. there is 'social ferment', when people are agitated about some issue but this is relatively unfocused and disorganized. This develops into a stage of 'popular excitement' during which the sources of people's dissatisfaction are more clearly defined and understood. In the third stage, formal organizations are normally created which are able to bring about a higher level of coordination to the emerging movement and a more effective campaigning structure is put in place. Finally comes 'institutionalization', in which the movement, which was originally outside mainstream politics, comes to be accepted as part of the wider society and political life. Of course, some movements partly succeed, while others completely fail. Some endure over quite long periods of time, while others simply run out of finances or enthusiasm, thus ending their life-cycle. This idea of a life-cycle has proved to be extremely productive and has been central to many more recent studies, particularly in the USA, which shows that Blumer's work continues to have an influence in social movement studies (Goodwin and Jasper 2002).

One problem with this interactionist approach is that, although it treats movements as meaningful phenomena – which was a clear breakthrough at the time – its studies tended not to explore the rational decisions and strategies of movement activists. This aspect was left for later scholars to pursue. Second, although the approach produced some very detailed case studies of particular movements, critics argued that these were largely descriptive accounts that did not really pay enough attention to explanations that were able to connect social movement activity to changes in the social structure (Della Porta and Diani 2006).

Resource mobilization

Traditions of social movement research in the USA and Europe have tended to be quite

The research problem

Social movements have become very common and you yourself may well be part of one, if not more than one. They often appear unannounced, taking sociologists by surprise. But they can also collapse in much the same way. Does this mean that their emergence is entirely random, the product of chance and unpredictable circumstances? How might they be linked to wider social changes? Can we develop a general theory of movement emergence and development that would help us to understand the process better? Sociologist, Neil J. Smelser, worked with Talcott Parsons and studied collective behaviour from a structural functionalist perspective, aiming for just such a theory of social movements.

Smelser's explanation

Smelser (1962) devised a theory of *structural strain* to account for the emergence of social movements, though one thing that marks out his perspective is that it amounts to a '**value-added model**' of movement emergence. This idea is taken from economic theory and suggests that social movements emerge through a process with identifiable stages, with each successive stage 'adding value' to the emerging movement. In the case of social movements, this model sees each stage making an addition to the probability that collective behaviour or a social movement will be created. In this sense, Smelser's argument is multi-causal, rejecting all notions of a single cause of social movements. This was a very important moment in the study of social movements.

Smelser argued that six 'value-added' elements are necessary for a social movement to develop:

1 *Structural conduciveness.* All social movements take place within a wider social context and this structural context has to be conducive to movement formation. For example, in authoritarian societies there may be very little scope for people to gather together in large groups or to demonstrate legally against things they oppose. Therefore,

opponents of the regime may have to find other, less open, ways to pursue change. The situation is not structurally conducive to social movement activity. In recent years, social movement scholars have used the concept of 'political opportunity structure' to describe the ways in which political systems create or deny opportunities for movements to develop (Tarrow 1998) and this concept clearly owes much to Smelser's earlier idea (Crossley 2002).

2 *Structural strain.* If the social structure is conducive to collective behaviour, then there needs to be a strain between people's expectations and social reality. When people expect or have been led to expect certain things from society and these expectations are not met, frustrations arise and people look for other ways to meet them. Robert Merton made use of strain theory in his account of high levels of working-class acquisitive crime, which, he argued, was the product of a mismatch between the cultural goal of material success and the limited means to achieve this legitimately (see chapter 21, 'Crime and Deviance').

3 *Generalized beliefs.* Smelser argues that if the first two conditions are met, then it is necessary for generalized beliefs about the causes of strain to develop and spread in order to convince people of the need to join or form a social movement. He sees such generalized beliefs as often quite primitive and based on wish fulfilment, rather than rationally thought through.

4 *Precipitating factors.* These are essentially events that act as sparks to ignite the flame of protest action. A good example of this would be the removal of Rosa Parks from a racially segregated bus in the USA in 1955, which triggered protests and became a key event in the black civil rights movement. Precipitating factors help to make social strains more immediately visible for potential supporters. Without them, the process of movement formation may be stalled for a long period.

5 *Mobilization for action.* Having witnessed a precipitating event, the next value-added

The response of governments and authorities to social movement protests can be instrumental in encouraging or discouraging further activism.

element is effective communication via the formation of an active social network which allows activists to perform some of the functions necessary for successful protest and organization-building; writing and distributing pamphlets, organizing demonstrations, taking membership fees and so on. All of this activity requires a higher level of networking and social networking.

6 *Failure of social control*. The final causal factor in Smelser's model is the response of the forces of social control. The response of authorities can be crucial in closing down an emergent social movement or creating opportunities for it to develop. Sometimes an over-reaction by authorities can encourage others to support the movement, especially in our media-dominated age. For example, the widespread media reports of heavy-handed treatment of Greenpeace activists aboard the *Greenpeace III* in 1972, served to create the impression of a David and Goliath

confrontation that attracted many onto the side of the underdog. However, severe repressive measures can sometimes bring emergent social networking to a halt if people perceive the risks of continuing to be too great.

Critical points

Smelser's theory was subjected to critical attacks. In focusing attention on generalized beliefs, Smelser's model implied that individuals are motivated to start social movements for irrational reasons, rooted in misleading ideas about their situation. This fell back into an older tradition that saw movements as unusual or marginal phenomena. Social movement studies since Smelser have moved towards seeing activists as rational actors who weigh the costs and benefits of their actions (see Olson 1965) and social movements are seen as part and parcel of social life rather than marginal to it. Smelser's theory was also structural functionalist in orientation, setting social movements in the context of their adaptive function during periods of rapid social change. Movements reassure people that something is being done to deal with their concerns. But the theory suffered indirectly from attacks on Parsonian functionalism and, probably unfairly, was not built on until quite recently.

Contemporary significance

Smelser's work on social movements has deservedly received more attention in recent years and is undergoing something of a resurgence. It still offers a multi-causal model of movement formation and even critics have extracted elements from it – such as ideas within resource mobilization theory, political opportunity structures and frame analysis – which have proved very productive (Crossley 2002). Similarly, his model connects movement activism to social structures and may provide insights into the rise of new social movements. Revisiting these stimulating ideas is long overdue.

different. In the USA, social movements have been studied using some form of rational choice theory, which assumes that individuals make rational decisions, based on weighing up the choices facing them at any particular time. In Europe, though, as we will see later, the focus has tended to be much more on the connections between social movements and social classes within theories of broad social change. It has been suggested that American approaches mainly (though by no means exclusively) focus on the question of *how* movements become organized, while European approaches focus on *why* social movements emerge when they do (Melucci 1989).

One of the most influential American perspectives in social movement studies is **resource mobilization theory** (RMT). RMT developed in the late 1960s and 1970s, partly as a reaction to social unrest theories, which appeared to portray social movements as 'irrational' phenomena. Against this view, advocates of RMT argued that movement participants behaved in rational ways and movements themselves were purposeful, not chaotic (Oberschall 1973; Tilly 1978; Zald and McCarthy 1987). RMT theorists argued that capitalist societies produce chronic discontent amongst sections of the public, which renders social unrest theories problematic. Social unrest is always present and movements therefore cannot be explained by reference to it. What turns this chronic discontent into effective mobilizations and social movements, they argue, is the availability of the necessary *resources* to mount effective campaigns that challenge the established order. This point is nicely illustrated by Merl Storr:

> The central insight of resource mobilization theory is actually very basic: social movements need resources. Suppose you and I are members of a social movement. If we want to call a meeting, we need to have somewhere to hold it. If we want to publicize a protest action such as a demonstration, we need to be able to make leaflets, posters or fliers and to reproduce large numbers of them, and to distribute them widely. If we want to book our meeting space or contact our printer, we are probably going to need a telephone – and some money to pay for it all. As well as these material resources, we are more likely to be successful if we can call on other, less tangible resources – an address book full of useful contacts, practical know-how in poster design or web-site construction, and even just the time and energy to devote to our activism. According to resource mobilization theory, the more of these resources we can mobilize, the more likely we are to be successful in our pursuit of social change. (2002: 182)

In RMT, political dissatisfaction is not enough, in itself, to bring about social change. Without resources, such dissatisfaction does not become an active force in society. RMT does have something of an economistic feel, drawing similarities between social movements and the competitive market economy. That is, the theory pictures social movements as operating within a competitive field of movements – a 'social movement industry' (SMI) – within which they compete for scarce resources, not least members and activists. Social movement organizations (SMOs) therefore find themselves in competition with other SMOs, some of which may appear to share their aims.

Although RMT has helped to fill the gap left by social unrest theories, by producing very detailed studies of how movements and movement organizations acquire resources and mobilize their campaigns, critics still see these as partial accounts. In particular, RMT underplays the effects on social movements of broad social changes such as the trend towards post-industrialism or globalization processes. These may change the context of movement struggles. For example, the increasingly global political context has meant that traditional UK conservation organizations such as the National Trust have come under pressure from the new international environmental organizations such as Greenpeace, whose ideology and campaigns seem to fit the changing context more closely.

It may also be objected that RMT has little explanation for social movements that achieve success with very limited access to resources. Piven and Cloward (1977) analysed 'poor people's movements' in the USA, such as unemployed workers in the 1930s, black civil rights in the 1950s and welfare movements of the late 1960s and '70s . Surprisingly, they found that the main successes of these movements were achieved during their formative stage, before they became properly organized. This was because activists in the early stages

were very enthusiastic and took part in many direct actions such as strikes and sit-ins. But once they became more effectively organized, direct actions became fewer and the 'dead hand of bureaucracy', as described by Max Weber and Robert Michels, took over as the movements lost momentum and impact. This is quite the reverse of what we would expect according to RMT and shows that, sometimes, a lack of resources can be turned to a movement's advantage.

 See chapter 18, 'Organizations and Networks', for discussions about Weber's and Michels's work on bureaucracy.

THINKING CRITICALLY

Choose a social movement from the ones discussed so far in the chapter and research its history, development and successes. Analyse this material using RMT, showing what the theory can tell us about *how* the movement became organized and *why* it succeeded or failed in its aims. What aspects of the movement, if any, does RMT *not* address?

New social movements

Since the late 1960s there has been an explosion of social movements in many countries around the globe. These new movements include student movements in the 1960s, civil rights and feminist movements of the 1960s and '70s, anti-nuclear and ecological movements of the 1980s, gay rights campaigns of the 1990s – and many more. Collectively, this group of movements is often referred to by European scholars as **new social movements** (NSMs). This is because the late 1960s is seen as ushering in a new *type* of social movement that diverges from previous forms (Touraine 1971, 1981). Sociological theories of NSMs try to address the question of why this has happened when it did and, in some ways, this approach complements the general focus of RMT on how movements garner resources and make use of them.

However, 'new' in this context means more than just 'contemporary'. There are four main ways in which NSMs are said to differ from 'old' movements, which we will now outline.

New issues

NSMs have introduced some new issues into political systems, many of which are relatively unrelated to simple material self-interests. Instead, these issues are concerned with the 'quality of life', including the state of the global environment, animal welfare and animal rights, peaceful (non-nuclear) energy production and the 'identity politics' associated with gay rights and disabled people's movements.

For NSM theorists, these movements reflect a very broad social transformation from an industrial to a post-industrial society. While industrial politics centred on wealth creation and its distribution, post-industrial politics centres on postmaterial issues. Ronald Inglehart (1977, 1990) conducted surveys of social values in more than 25 industrialized countries and found that younger generations exhibited postmaterial values. That is, they took for granted a certain material standard of well-being and were more likely to be concerned with the quality rather than the quantity of life. This 'glacial', generational shift in values, Inglehart argued, could be explained by several factors. The post-1945 generation did not experience the depression and hardship of their parents' generation, nor did they have personal experience of war. Rather, they became used to post-war peace and affluence, being raised in the context of a 'post-scarcity socialization', in which the historic obstacle of food scarcity at least appeared to have been solved for good. This generation also had a different experience of work as a growing service sector took over from the old industrial workplaces. These enormous social changes led to the demise of an 'old' politics, which was rapidly giving way to a 'new', post-industrial form of politics.

New organizational forms

NSMs also appeared to be different in the way they organized. Many of them adopted a loose organizational form that rejected the formal organization that earlier social movement theorists argued was necessary for success. NSMs looked much more like loose networks of people. In addition, they seemed to have no single centre or headquarters, preferring a polycephalous, or 'many-headed', structure. This meant that should one local group break the law and face prosecution, the rest of the network could carry on, but this structure also suited the emotional needs of activists, who tended to be younger and imbued with postmaterial values and identities.

Alberto Melucci (1989) saw that this organizational form itself carried a message, namely the symbolic rejection of the aggressively masculine, bureaucratic power politics of the industrial age, typified by some trade unions and party politics. The first President of the Czech Republic, Vaclav Havel (1988) described this as a form of anti-hierarchical and 'anti-political politics', insofar as it opposed mainstream party politics, but was itself a new type of cultural politics rooted in social movements. What marked out this new form of politics was a self-imposed limitation. NSMs did not seek to take over the state and use the levers of state power to change society; instead, they looked to appeal directly to the public by working at the cultural level. This strategy has been described as a 'self-limiting radicalism' that contrasts sharply with the state-centred politics of socialism and the labour movement (Papadakis 1988).

New action repertoires

Like all other social movements, NSMs use a range of protest actions, from political lobbying, to sit-ins and alternative festivals, but one thing that characterizes their 'action repertoire' is non-violent, symbolic direct actions. Like the rejection of bureaucratic organization, the adoption of non-violence is an attempt by NSMs to practise in the present the changes they would like to see within society in the future. In this way, non-violent protest allows NSMs to take a high moral stance in relation to the forces of the state, such as the military and police. Many NSM actions aim to present aspects of society to the public that were previously unseen and unknown. For example, campaigns against nuclear and toxic waste dumping in the UK, the culling of seal pups in Newfoundland, animal cruelty, the destruction of woodlands for road-building or the presence of disabling environments all showed people things of which they may not previously have been aware. Of course, these issues are presented in ways that support the campaigners. We always know whose side we should be on: the plucky, defenceless underdog against the violence of big business and the state.

NSMs tend to make extensive use of the mass media to generate support – filming their own protests, showing videos on the Internet, organizing campaigns using text messaging and email and creating a perspective on politics that encourages ordinary people to become empowered to participate. Such efforts illustrate well the point made by Melucci (1985) that NSMs are forms of communication: 'messages' to society which present symbolic challenges to the existing political system.

New social constituencies

Finally, many studies of NSM activists have shown a predominance of the 'new' middle class that works in the post-1945 welfare state bureaucracies, creative and artistic fields and education (including many students). This finding led some to describe NSM activism as a form of 'middle-class radicalism' (Cotgrove and Duff 1980). Many of the large demonstrations – against nuclear weapons, or in favour of animal welfare, and so on – attract a 'rainbow coalition' of retired people, students, first-time protesters, feminists, anarchists, socialists,

traditional conservatives and many more. However, it seems that the working classes are not involved in significant numbers in NSM politics. Again, this marks a significant change from the industrial period with its working-class-based movements.

Some have argued that the postmaterial politics of the NSMs is not a self-interested politics on behalf of middle-class interests, but seeks to improve the quality of life for everyone (Eckersley 1989).

> **THINKING CRITICALLY**
>
> What evidence is there in Peter Tatchell's account (opposite) of his experiences with the UK Gay Liberation Front, which suggests that this organization was part of a NSM? How did the GLF learn from and adapt some of the tactics and campaigning methods of other social movements? Thinking back to Blumer's distinction between 'active' and expressive movements, how would you characterize the gay and lesbian movement?

As should be clear from this characterization, many observers argue that NSMs are a unique product of late modern society and are profoundly different in their methods, motivations and orientations from forms of collective action in earlier times. We can view new social movements in terms of a 'paradox of democracy'. While faith in traditional politics seems to be waning, the growth of NSMs is evidence that citizens in late modern societies are not apathetic or uninterested in politics, as is sometimes claimed. Rather, there is a belief that direct action and participation is more useful than reliance on politicians and political systems. More than ever before, people are supporting social movements as a way of highlighting complex moral issues and putting them at the centre of social life. In this respect, NSMs are helping to revitalize democracy in many countries. They are at the heart of a strong civic culture or civil society – the sphere between the state and

22.3   The birth of gay liberation

The formation of the Gay Liberation Front (GLF) in London in 1970 was the defining watershed moment in queer history. For the first time ever, thousands of lesbians and gays stopped hiding in the closet and suffering in silence. We came out and marched in the streets, proclaiming that we were proud to be gay and demanding nothing less than total equality.

That had never happened before. Lots of gay people in 1970 were ashamed of their homosexuality and kept it hidden. They wished they were straight. Some went to quack doctors to get 'cured'. Many accepted the bigot's view that being 'queer' was second rate.

Until the 1970s, the state branded gay sex as 'unnatural, indecent and criminal', the Church condemned homosexuality as 'immoral and sinful' and the medical profession classified us as 'sick' and in need of 'treatment'.

Queers were routinely sacked from their jobs, arrested for kissing in the street, denied custody of their children, portrayed in films and plays as limp-wristed figures of ridicule, and only ever appeared in the news as murderers, traitors and child molesters.

Straights vilified, scapegoated and invisibilised us – with impunity. And very few gay people dared question heterosexual supremacy.

Indeed, prior to GLF, most gay rights campaigners masqueraded as straight, and pleaded for 'tolerance' rather than acceptance. Some argued that we needed 'help', not criminalisation. They urged heterosexuals to show 'compassion' for those 'afflicted' by the 'homosexual condition'.

This apologetic, defensive mentality was shot to pieces by GLF. It transformed attitudes towards homosexuality – among both gay and straight people.

Inspired by the Black Power slogan 'Black is Beautiful', GLF came up with a little slogan of its own, which also had a huge impact: 'Gay Is Good!'. Back

GLF

then, it was absolutely outrageous to suggest there was anything good about being gay.

Even liberal-minded heterosexuals mostly supported us out of 'sympathy' and 'pity'. Many reacted with revulsion and horror when GLF proclaimed: '2–4–6–8! Gay is just as good as straight.' Those words – which were so empowering to queers everywhere – frightened the life out of smug, arrogant straight people who had always assumed they were superior.

This challenge to heterosexual supremacism kick-started a still ongoing revolution in cultural values. GLF overturned the conventional wisdom on matters of sex and human rights. Its joyous celebration of gayness contradicted the straight morality that had ruled the world for centuries. The common-sense, unquestioned assumption had always been that queers were bad, mad and sad.

All that prejudiced nonsense was turned upside down in 1970. While politicians, doctors, priests and journalists saw homosexuality as a social problem, GLF said the real problem was society's homophobia. Instead of us having to justify our existence, we forced the gay-haters to justify their bigotry.

Like many others of my generation, GLF changed me for the better – and forever. When I heard about the formation of the Gay Liberation Front, I could not wait to get involved.

Within five days of my arrival in London from Australia, I was at my first GLF meeting. A month later I was helping organise many of its witty, irreverent, defiant protests. Being part of GLF was a profound personal liberation – arguably the most exciting, influential period of my life.

GLF's unique style of 'protest as performance' was not only incredibly effective, but also a lot of fun. We had a fabulous collection of zany props and costumes, including a whole wardrobe of police uniforms and bishop's cassocks and mitres.

Imaginative, daring, humorous, stylish and provocative, our demonstrations were both educative and entertaining. We mocked and ridiculed homophobes with wicked satire, which made even the most hard-faced straight people realise the stupidity of bigotry.

A 12 foot papier-mache cucumber was delivered to the offices of Pan Books in protest at the publication of Dr David Reuben's homophobic sex manual, *Everything You Always Wanted To Know About Sex*, which implied that gay men were obsessed with shoving vegetables up their arses.

Christian morality campaigner Mary Whitehouse had her Festival of Light rally in Central Hall Westminster invaded by a posse of gay nuns, who proceeded to kiss each other when one of the speakers, Malcolm Muggeridge, disparaged homosexuals, saying 'I just don't like them' (the feeling was mutual).

On the night of the Miss World contest at the Royal Albert Hall, GLF's legendary street theatre group staged an alternative pageant on the pavement outside, starring 'Miss Used', 'Miss Conceived' and 'Miss Represented', plus a starving 'Miss Bangladesh' and a bloody bandaged 'Miss Ulster'.

There were also more serious acts of civil disobedience to confront the perpetrators of discrimination. We organised freedom rides and sit-ins at pubs that refused to serve 'poofs' and 'dykes'. A lecture by the psychiatrist, Professor Hans Eysenck, was disrupted after he advocated electric-shock aversion therapy to 'cure' homosexuality.

As well as its feisty protests, GLF pioneered many of the gay community institutions that we now take for granted. It set up the first help-line run by and for gay people (which later became Gay Switchboard); the first pro-gay psychiatric counselling service (Icebreakers), and the first gay newspaper (Gay News). These and many other trail-blazing institutions helped shape the gay community as we know it today, making a huge positive difference to the lives of lesbians and gay men.

Thirty years on, we've come a long way baby! As we look back at the giant strides for freedom that lesbian and gay people have made since 1970, let us also remember with pride that GLF was where it all started.

Source: Peter Tatchell, QX Mardi Gras Day Guide, 1 July 2000; www.petertatchell.net/

the marketplace occupied by family, community associations and other non-economic institutions (Habermas 1981).

However, NSM theory has come in for some sharp criticism. All the supposedly 'new' features identified above have been found in 'old' social movements. For example, postmaterial values were evident in some small-scale communes in the nineteenth century (D'Anieri et al. 1990). A focus on identity creation was also a crucial, perhaps defining, aspect of all nationalist movements and early women's movements. Such historical evidence led Craig Calhoun (1993) to describe these old movements, ironically, as 'new social movements of the early nineteenth century'.

Others saw NSM theorists as too quick to draw radical conclusions from little empirical evidence. Over time, some NSMs have developed formal organizations and these have become more bureaucratic than the theory allows for. Greenpeace is the most notable example. Originally a loose network of like-minded individuals involved in numerous direct actions, over time Greenpeace has become a very large business-like organization with a mass membership and huge financial resources. Indeed, it seems to conform much more to the long-term process of change identified by Blumer and RM theorists which Claus Offe called, 'the institutional self-transformation' of the NSMs. Finally, even some of the apparently 'new' issues have been seen as rather older. Environmental politics, for instance, can be traced back to the European and North American nature defence organizations of the mid-nineteenth century and is perhaps best understood as an enduring social movement which has passed through various stages of growth and decay (Lowe and Goyder 1983; Paehlke 1989).

Globalization and the 'social movement society'

Despite the critical barrage aimed at NSM theory, it is apparent that social movements now operate in a very different set of historical circumstances from those of earlier movements. In particular, processes of globalization mean that systematic and much more immediate connections across national boundaries become possible and, with this, the possibility of genuinely global social movements.

The rise of NSMs also reflects some of the changing risks now facing human societies. The conditions are ripe for social movements, as increasingly traditional political institutions find it harder to cope with the challenges before them. They find it impossible to respond creatively to the negative risks facing the natural environment from nuclear energy, the burning of fossil fuels or experimentation in bio- or nanotechnology. These new problems and challenges are ones that existing democratic political institutions cannot hope to fix, and as a result they are frequently ignored or avoided until it is too late and a full-blown crisis is at hand.

The cumulative effect of these new challenges and risks may be a growing sense that people are 'losing control' of their lives in the midst of rapid change. Individuals feel less secure and more isolated – a combination that leads to a sense of powerlessness. By contrast, corporations, governments and the media appear to be dominating more and more aspects of people's lives, heightening the sensation of a runaway world (Giddens 2002). There is a growing sense that, left to its own logic, globalization will present ever greater risks to citizens' lives.

In our current information age, social movements around the globe are able to join together in huge regional and international networks comprising non-governmental organizations, religious and humanitarian groups, human rights associations, consumer protection advocates, environmental activists and others who campaign in the public interest. These electronic networks now have the unprecedented ability to respond immediately to events as they occur, to access and share sources of information, and to put pressure on corporations, governments and international bodies as part of their campaigning strategies. The enormous protests against the war in Iraq in cities around the world in February 2003, for example, were organized in large part through Internet-based networks, as were the protests outside the meeting of world leaders in Genoa in 2001, and the protests that took place in Seattle in 1999 against the World Trade Organization. Similarly, the emergence of the World Social Forum in Porto Alegre, Brazil in 2001 was one element of an 'even newer social movement' (Crossley 2003) that aims to provide a global space for debates on what progressive politics really means and can offer in the twenty-first century (see 'Global Society 22.2').

The Internet has been at the forefront of these changes, although mobile phones, fax machines and satellite broadcasting have also hastened their evolution. With the press of a button, local stories are disseminated internationally. Grass-roots activists from Japan to Bolivia can meet online to share informational resources, exchange experiences and coordinate joint action.

While rejecting some of the claims to novelty of the NSMs, Sidney Tarrow argues: 'What *is* new is that they have greater discretionary resources, enjoy easier access to the media, have cheaper and faster geographic mobility and cultural interaction, and can call upon the collaboration of different types of movement-linked organizations for rapidly organized issue campaigns' (1998: 207–8). Acknowledging these changes raises the possibility that we may be moving towards a 'social movement society' (Meyer and Tarrow 1997) in which the nationally bounded social movements of the past give way to movements without borders. The World Social Forums with their democratic principles (see 'Global Society 22.2') give us one example of such a prospect, though it is important to recognize that the global networks of al-Qaeda – a social movement terrorist organization – give us another

(Sutton and Vertigans 2006). There is no certainty that an emerging movement society will see the widespread adoption of the non-violence that characterized the wave of NSMs in the 1960s and '70s in the industrialized world. Indeed, the more ready access to weapons and the information needed to build them holds out the more terrifying prospect of a more violent social movement society.

> See chapter 23, 'Nations, War and Terrorism', for a wider discussion of violence in human affairs.

THINKING CRITICALLY

In 'Global Society 22.2', the World Social Forums (WSFs) are said to have been more successful in protesting and networking than proposing solutions. Why should this be the case? What obstacles do such global forums face when trying to bring new voices into democratic debates? What evidence is there that WSFs may be early harbingers of a more global form of democracy beyond national state systems?

The last dimension discussed above – the ability to coordinate international political campaigns – is the one that is the most worrying for governments and the most inspiring to participants in social movements. In the last two decades, the number of 'international social movements' has grown steadily with the spread of the Internet. From global protests in favour of cancelling Third World debt to the international campaign to ban landmines (which culminated in a Nobel Peace Prize), the Internet has proved its ability to unite campaigners across national and cultural borders. Some observers argue that the information age is witnessing a 'migration' of power away from nation-states into new non-governmental alliances and coalitions.

Global Society 22.2 | The three faces of the World Social Forum

The World Social Forum (WSF) is about three things, a young Frenchman told me. We were coming back from Kenya together. He had been to most of them since they first began in Porto Alegre in Brazil in January 2001. They are, he said, about protesting, networking and proposing.

Protesting power

When they began, before 9/11, the protest was against the World Economic Forum (WEF) at Davos, which appeared to celebrate the end of government and the triumph of market-driven, 'neoliberal' capitalism and its rampant inequality. It was in the wake of the battle of Seattle in November 1999 that disrupted the world trade talks. The creation of the WSF as anti-Davos ensured that the new century began with a multinational stand in the name of the peoples of the world against the presumptions of the world economic order.

Since 2001, until this year [2007], the WSFs have grown and, undoubtedly, shifted the agenda, making sure that the big battalions have not had it all their own way. It has been a remarkable achievement. In 2004 the WSF was held in Mumbai with an enormous mobilisation of Indian organisations. In 2005 it returned to Porto Alegre. In 2006 it went regional or 'polycentric': to Caracas in Venezuela, Karachi in Pakistan and Bamako in Mali. One reason for this was that the decision had been taken to hold the next full world forum in Kenya, giving the organisers plenty of time to prepare against the backdrop of poor infrastructure.

Thus, this year, global civil society and Africa were planned to come together for the seventh World Social Forum in Nairobi (20–25 January 2007), close to the great rift valley from which the human species first emerged in triumph on its own two legs. The hope was that in 2007 the social movements of the world would inspire African civil society to stand up and show its strength, wisdom and the music of its needs.

For, unlike the mere protest mobilisations such as Seattle in 1999 (or the one being planned for the G8 meeting in June 2007 in Germany's remote Baltic resort of Heiligendamm), WSFs are designed as a form of positive protest, exemplary sites of solidarity with the struggles of the poor, to give voice to the 'have-nots'.

Networking Africa

In its second role, as an event for networking, I was impressed. In his account of his disappointment with what he felt was a lack of politics, Firoze Manji in Pambazuka News considers whether Nairobi's WSF was 'just another NGO fair'. But where else can the far-flung universe of all those who are working for a better world come together? In advance, the organisers boasted that 150,000 would attend. When it opened, they claimed 50,000. I doubt if more than 20,000 participated, including Kenyans (but not including the water-vendors).

But still, to get 20,000 people from around the world to equatorial Africa is an achievement. A wonderful, friendly variety of views, arguments, dress, interests, beliefs and backgrounds came together in many conversations – such as Susan Richards and Solana Larsen described in their openDemocracy reports and blogs from previous WSFs.

Below the radar of the public platforms, from the Habitat International Coalition to the network on water resources, and women's rights to human rights, new connections were being made and a younger generation was assessing the intercontinental scene. Patricia Daniel in her blog described this energy and intensity among the women's networks that were a large part of the forum.

Thinking beyond

This brings us to the third role of the WSF. After the protests and the networking, what does it propose? Thomas Ponniah (who gave an interview to openDemocracy on the nature of the WSF in February 2003) put this question to a small session on the future of politics: 'For seven years we have built a global consciousness. The question is, what next?'

The last meeting I attended was a gathering of all the social movements, organised by Christophe Aguiton of Attac. Trevor Ngwane of the South African anti-privatisation forum led the proceedings. About a thousand people initially thronged the spacious double tent. Being of the greying dreadlocks generation, I enjoyed chanting 'Down with Bush' (but drew the line at 'Viva Chávez'). There was much condemnation of the commercialisation of the forum, about which a Brazilian speaker said: '[It] is not enough that our cause be pure and just, purity and justice must also be within us'.

But an answer to Ponniah's question came there none. In the different specialist areas there was strategic thinking. In smaller sessions there were arguments for engagement. Emira Woods of the Institute for Policy Studies in Washington, DC insisted that 'grassroots campaigns, national campaigns and global campaigns can influence government'. In a dedicated session on implementing United Nations resolution 1325 to enhance the role of women (which I blogged), Cora Weiss called for 'participation, critical thinking and a holistic approach that engages with the issues'.

There was participation in Nairobi. The holistic approach was often just knee-jerk, 'oppose all forms of exploitation'. At that overall, movement level, there was little if any strategic thinking.

As a result, this year Davos won. Since that first WSF in 2001 China has doubled its wealth and output; India, and Turkey, have grown theirs by more than half. Then, Google had only recently got its initial funding. Today, the argument on climate change is over. For all the glitz and its versions of hot air, these huge changes are being seriously mapped and assessed at Davos. In Nairobi they were addressed only peripherally, if at all.

Larry Elliott, the economics editor of the *Guardian*, sensed at Davos 'more than a hint of a return to the future: a scramble for Africa, a sidelining of civil society, and geopolitical concerns trumping human rights'. If so, there needs to be a World Social Forum that continues to set out its different claim on the global future in a way the world notices. Its international committee should be very concerned that this is slipping away.

Source: Anthony Barnett, 30 January 2007; www.opendemocracy.net/globalization-protest/wsf_faces_4297.jsp

Policy advisers in think-tanks such as the RAND Corporation (in the United States) have spoken of 'netwars' – large-scale international conflicts in which it is information and public opinion that are the stakes in the contest, rather than resources or territory. Participants in netwars use the media and online resources to shape what certain populations know about the social world. These online movements are often aimed at spreading information about corporations, government policies or the effects of international agreements to audiences who may otherwise be unaware of them. For many governments – even democratic ones – netwars are a frightening and elusive threat. As a US Army report has warned: 'A new generation of revolutionaries, radicals and activists are beginning to create information age ideologies in which identities and loyalties may shift from the nation state to the transnational level of global civic society' (quoted in the *Guardian*, 19 January 2000).

Are such fears misplaced? There are reasons to think that social movements have indeed been radically transformed in recent years. In *The Power of Identity* (1997), Manuel Castells examined the cases of three social movements which, while completely dissimilar in their concerns and objectives, all attracted international attention to their cause through the effective use of information technology. The Mexican Zapatista rebels, the American 'militia' movement and the Japanese Aum Shinrikyo cult have all used media skills in order to spread their message of opposition to the effects of globalization and to express their anger at losing control over their own destinies.

According to Castells, each of these movements relies on information technologies as its organizational infrastructure. Without the Internet, for example, the Zapatista rebels would have remained an isolated guerrilla movement in southern Mexico. Instead, within hours of their armed uprising in January 1994, local, national and international support groups had emerged online to promote the cause of the rebels and to condemn the Mexican government's brutal repression of the rebellion. The Zapatistas used telecommunications, videos and media interviews to voice their objections to trade policies, such as the North American Free Trade Agreement (NAFTA), which further exclude impoverished Indians of the Oaxaca and Chiapas areas from the benefits of globalization. Because their cause was thrust to the forefront of the online networks of social campaigners, the Zapatistas were able to force negotiations with the Mexican government and to draw international attention to the harmful effects of free trade on indigenous populations.

Conclusion

Political life has clearly been undergoing some major changes in recent decades. Democracy has become much more widespread around the world, but in many of the established representative democracies voters seem to be less than enthusiastic participants. On the other hand, social movements are thriving, bringing new issues and campaigning methods into the mainstream. The conventional left–right political division now looks much less clear-cut. Is opposing road-building on environmental grounds a right-wing or left-wing position? Are those who propose that animals have rights that should be protected on the political left or right? Such issues seem to cut across the old political distinctions, but, particularly in the case of environmentalism, they are becoming more relevant to younger generations than the older materialist politics rooted in the workplace.

For political sociologists, understanding political systems now means getting to grips with social movements, which increasingly organize internationally, can mount large protests anywhere in the world and link the central issues of the industrialized nations with those that exercise activism in developing countries. In this century, sociologists may have to work across disciplinary boundaries and specialist subjects if they are to better understand where the 'new' politics is taking us.

Summary points

1. The term 'government' refers to a political apparatus in which officials enact policies and make decisions. 'Politics' is the means by which power is used and contested to affect the scope and content of government activities.

2. A state exists where there is a political apparatus, ruling over a given territory, whose authority is backed by a legal system and by the ability to use force to implement its policies. Modern states are nation-states, characterized by the idea of citizenship, a recognition that people have common rights and duties and belong to a broader, unifying political community.

3. Power, according to Max Weber, is the capacity to achieve one's aims even against the resistance of others, and often involves the use of force. Steven Lukes devised a three-dimensional view of power which sees power as residing in non-decisions and agenda-setting as well as meeting self-interests against others. A government is said to have authority when its use of power is legitimate; legitimacy derives from the consent of those being governed. The most common form of legitimate government is democratic, but other legitimate forms are also possible.

4. In authoritarian states, popular participation is denied or severely curtailed. The needs and interests of the state are prioritized over those of average citizens and there are no

legal mechanisms in place for opposing government or for removing a leader from power.

5. Democracy is a political system in which the people rule. In participatory democracy (or direct democracy), decisions are made by those affected by them. A liberal democracy is a representative democracy where all citizens have the vote and can choose between at least two parties.

6. The number of countries with democratic governments has rapidly increased in recent years, due in large part to the effects of globalization, mass communications and the collapse of communist regimes. But democracy is not without its problems: people everywhere have begun to lose faith in the capacity of politicians and governments to solve problems and to manage economies, and political participation in established electoral systems is decreasing.

7. Party politics has been changed in many industrialized countries, away from an older class-based system to a multi-party system in which political parties have become less class-oriented. Socialist parties, such as the UK Labour Party, have undergone major changes in the wake of the demise of communism, dropping their commitments to socialist notions, including nationalization and planned economies. This new brand of centre-left politics is often referred to as 'third way' politics.

8. Social movements involve collective attempts to further common interests through collaborative action outside the sphere of established political institutions. Social movements are many and varied, from old labour and trades union movements to feminism, lesbian and gay movements and environmentalism.

9. Sociological theories of social movements have focused on how movements form as a result of periods of social unrest or frustrations associated with the social strain between expectations and reality. Movements are seen as having 'life-cycles' from emergence and development to eventual institutionalization. In the USA, theories of resource mobilization explore how movements garner the resources needed for effective organization.

10. The term 'new social movements' is applied to a set of social movements that have arisen in Western countries since the 1960s. They bring new issues into the political domain, tend to be more loosely organized, involve the new middle class and adopt symbolic direct actions as their main campaigning tactic. Some scholars suggest that globalization and information technologies are facilitating the move towards a global 'movement society' in which social movements increasingly organize across national boundaries.

Further reading

A good introductory text which should give a feel for political sociology is Kate Nash's *Contemporary Political Sociology: Globalization, Politics and Power* (Oxford: Blackwell Publishing, 1999). Keith Faulks's *Political Sociology: A Critical Introduction* (Edinburgh: Edinburgh University Press, 1999) is also a useful book which provides exactly what it says.

For up-to-date coverage of political ideologies including environmentalism, Andrew Heywood's *Political Ideologies: An Introduction*, 4th edn (Basingstoke: Palgrave Macmillan, 2007) is a tried and trusted work.

For those interested in democratization, Bernard Crick's *Democracy: A Very Short Introduction* (Oxford: Oxford University Press, 2002) is a good place to begin your reading, and David Held's *Models of Democracy*, 3rd edn (Cambridge: Polity, 2006) is a much more involved book, looking at the history of the concept and its reality.

Donatella Della Porta and Mario Diani's *Social Movements: An Introduction* (Oxford: Blackwell Publishing, 2006) covers a lot of ground and includes reference to many social movements. An excellent book dealing with theories of social movements is Nick Crossley's *Social Movements: An Introduction* (Buckingham: Open University Press, 2002), which carefully dissects older as well as recent theories for useful insights. Jeff Goodwin and James M. Jasper's *The Social Movements Reader: Cases and Concepts* (Oxford: Blackwell Publishing, 2003) is an edited collection covering a range of movements that is engagingly organized according to the process of a movement life-cycle.

Finally, another edited collection by Thomas Janoski, Robert Alford, Alexander Hicks and Mildred Schwartz, *The Handbook of Political Sociology: States, Civil Societies, and Globalization* (Cambridge: Cambridge University Press, 2005), is a useful resource with a broad coverage.

Internet links

Foreign Policy – Washington, DC, US-based site with lots of political articles and comment:
www.foreignpolicy.com/

International Institute for Democracy and Electoral Assistance – based in Stockholm, Sweden, provides information and analysis in support of democratization:
www.idea.int/

Intute: Social Sciences, Politics – UK-based gateway for political sociology resources:
www.intute.ac.uk/socialsciences/politics/

World Politics Review – 'a daily foreign policy, national security and international affairs Web publication':
www.worldpoliticsreview.com/

openDemocracy – London, UK-based site which 'aims to ensure that marginalized views and voices are heard' on issues of global importance:
www.opendemocracy.net/

The World Social Forum – 'another world is possible':
www.wsf2008.net/

United Nations Research Institute for Social Development – some good materials on 'Democracy, Governance and Well Being' and 'Civil Society and Social Movements':
www.unrisd.org/

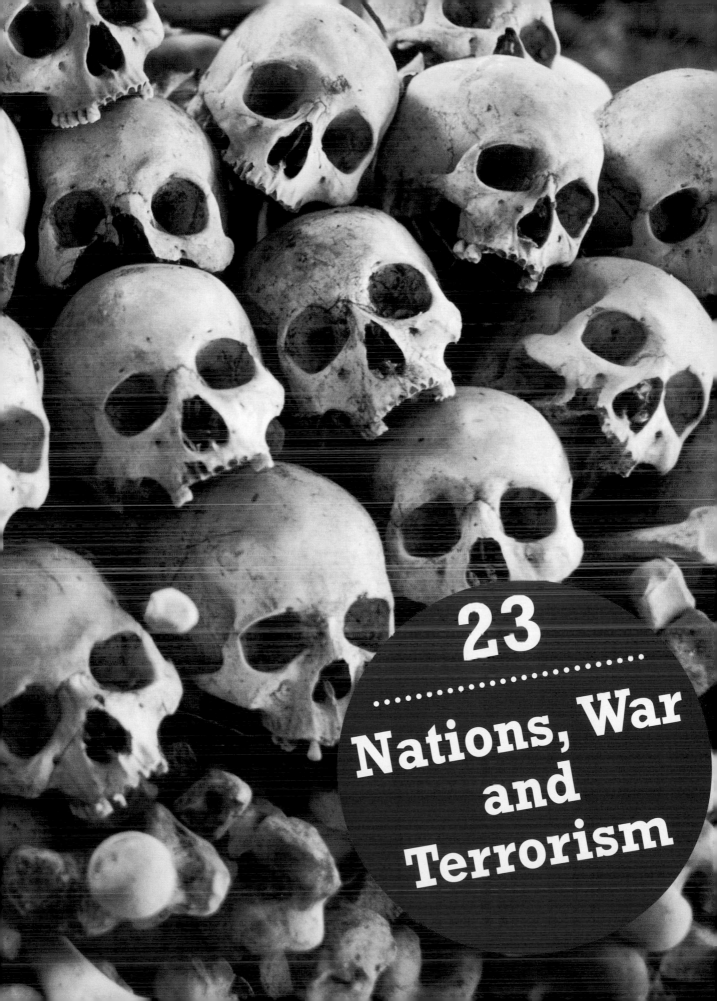

23

Nations, War
and
Terrorism

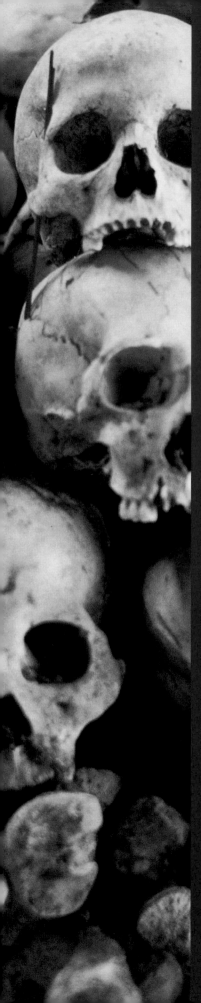

CHAPTER 23

•••

Nations, War and Terrorism

(opposite) Celebrations in the Kosovo capital, Pristina, on the declaration of independence, 17 February 2008. Two regions of the former Soviet state of Georgia, South Ossetia and Abkhazia, immediately announced they too would be seeking full independence.
•••

On the morning of 17 February 2008, tens of thousands of people filled the streets of Pristina, the capital of Kosovo, in anticipation of an historic announcement. When the Kosovan Parliament unanimously endorsed a motion declaring independence from Serbia, it triggered wild scenes of national celebration. Later in the evening, a monument to national independence was unveiled and the prime minister, Hashim Thachi, said: 'We have waited for this day for a very long time . . . from today, we are proud, independent and free.' He also promised that Kosovo would have a democratic system that respected the rights of all ethnic minorities in the country; an important statement in a country where some 88 per cent of the population is ethnic Albanian and 7 per cent Serbian, with fewer Bosniak (1.9 per cent), Roma (1.7 per cent) and Turkish (1 per cent) and smaller numbers of Ashkali, Egyptian and Gorani people.

Kosovo had previously been part of Serbia, a country itself formed by the break-up of Yugoslavia. The latter experienced a savage civil war after the fall of communism in 1989. The Serbian government strongly opposed the breakaway of Kosovo, which it regarded as an integral part of Serbia. The ten ethnic Serbian MPs in the Kosovo Parliament boycotted the parliamentary session in protest. The Serbian prime minister, Vojislav Kostunica, blamed America, which he said was 'ready to violate the international order for its own military interests', describing independent Kosovo as 'a false state'. The US president, George W. Bush, strongly supported Kosovo, declaring: 'The Kosovars are now independent.' In the ethnic Serbian area of Mitrovica, an ethnically diverse city close to the border between Kosovo and Serbia (see figure 23.1), hand grenades were thrown at a UN court and a proposed EU office, while in Belgrade, the capital city of Serbia, demonstrators broke windows at the US embassy and gangs of youths attacked symbols of the USA, including a McDonald's restaurant. In the view of many Serbians, Kosovo's hundreds of mediaeval churches, monasteries and shrines form part of Serb history and heritage, and should remain in Serbian territory. The Serbian president, Boris Tadic, expressed this in an appeal to the United Nations Security Council to declare Kosovo's announcement null and void because it violated Security Council Resolution 1244, which reaffirms Serbia's sovereignty and territorial integrity. Tadic said: 'Serbia will never recognize the independence of Kosovo. We shall never renounce Kosovo and we shall not give up the struggle for our legitimate interests. For the citizens of Serbia and its institutions, Kosovo will forever remain a part of Serbia' (UN Interim Administration Mission in Kosovo

(UNMIK), 18 February 2008). On 20 February, NATO troops temporarily closed the border between Serbia and Kosovo following the burning of UN and Kosovo customs and police posts at Jarinje and Brnjak.

The Kosovo declaration of independence also demonstrated divisions within the international community of nation-states. The USA, UK, Turkey, France, Albania, Costa Rica and Afghanistan immediately recognized an independent Kosovo, with many others, including Australia, Germany, Denmark, Italy and Peru intending to recognize it after due process had taken place. However, many others, such as Russia, China, Spain, Serbia and Argentina, refused to recognize Kosovo as an independent country.

For some, Kosovo's unilateral declaration set a very dangerous precedent, which other separatist movements would seek to follow, thus destabilizing the system of states with potentially disastrous consequences. Indeed, two regions within the former Soviet state of Georgia – South Ossetia and Abkhazia – announced that they would be seeking independent status as soon as possible. China also opposes the independence claim of Taiwan; Israel is involved in protracted negotiations with neighbouring Palestine, which seeks an independent Palestinian state; and Spain has a long-standing opposition to the independence claims of the Basque movement. For others, though, Kosovo is a unique case and its legitimate independence is the inevitable consequence of Kosovan history, which thereby sets no precedent for any other country to follow. Although Kosovan independence, arguably, has deep roots in the rise and fall of the Ottoman Empire between the early fourteenth century and the end of the First World War in 1918, recent history has generated some very bitter enmities, which helps to explain such strongly worded reactions.

At the end of the Second World War in 1945, Kosovo became an autonomous province of Serbia, the largest republic of the Communist

Figure 23.1 Population distribution of ethnic Albanians and Serbians in Kosovo, 2007

Source: BBC 2008: OSCE/US Institute of Peace

Federal People's Republic of Yugoslavia. In 1974 under a new constitution, Kosovo gained more wide-ranging self-governing powers. However, in the tumultuous year of 1989, with Soviet communism collapsing across Eastern Europe, the Serbian nationalist, Slobodan Milosevic, came to power promising to scrap Kosovo's autonomous powers. In protest, the Kosovan Parliament declared Kosovo independent from Serbia on 2 July 1990, but the international community of states did not recognize this and Milosevic dissolved the Parliament. A period of non-violent resistance followed, until, in 1998, the separatist Kosovo Liberation Army began attacks on the police, military and Serb civilians.

Milosevic's security apparatus used massive force in a crackdown that began a war in Kosovo in 1998. When NATO intervened by bombing Serbia in 1999, Milosevic launched an intensive terror campaign, killing around 10,000 and displacing about one million ethnic Albanians, and leading to accusations of attempted genocide. NATO stepped up its bombing campaign (in which close to 1,000 Serbians died) and, after 78 days, Serbian troops were ordered out of Kosovo and a NATO-led peacekeeping mission of 45,000 troops entered, but on condition (under Resolution 1244) that Serbia retained sovereignty over Kosovo. Many thousands of Serbians fled, fearing that Kosovars would retaliate against them. More than 10,000 ethnic Albanians and 3,000 Serbians died in the conflict, with accusations of attempted genocide levelled at Serbia. UNMIK was formed to oversee the building of democratic institutions, to which powers gradually passed. However, in March 2004, violence broke out again, this time in riots by ethnic Albanians across Kosovo, which led to the burning of hundreds of houses and many churches, and 19 people were killed. Negotiations that

were aimed at finding a solution to Kosovo's future status ended in failure in November 2007, with Russia refusing to agree that Kosovo should be released from Serbian sovereignty. Finally, with the support of the USA and others, Kosovo declared independence in February 2008.

This chapter deals with some of the broader themes emerging from the recent history of Kosovo, including nationalism, the use of physical violence, and warfare. Why is the desire for national independence in the form of a nation-state such a powerful force in history? How is nationalism related to conflict and wars within and between nations? And what exactly is war?

We begin with a discussion of nations and nationalism, asking how globalization might be changing people's sense of their own national identity. We then move on to look at human conflict, especially war and its close relation, genocide, focusing particularly on those conflicts involving the modern nation-state. Then we explore a phenomenon that seems to have become an ever-present danger in the modern world – terrorism – before drawing some tentative conclusions about violence, war and terrorism in the twenty-first century.

Nations and nationalism

Some of the most important social movements in the contemporary world are nationalist movements. The sociological thinkers of the nineteenth and early twentieth centuries displayed little interest in, or concern with, nationalism. Marx and Durkheim saw it as, above all, a destructive tendency. Durkheim argued that the increasing economic integration produced by modern industry would cause its rapid decline, while Marx argued that nationalism would fade away under socialism. Only Max Weber spent much time analysing nationalism or was prepared to declare himself a nationalist. But even Weber failed to estimate the importance that nationalism and

---

THINKING CRITICALLY

Is it likely that Kosovo will be a stable nation-state? Should unilateral national declarations of independence be encouraged? How might an increase in the number of smaller nation-states be a positive development for the international states systems and what risks and dangers would this scenario present?

the idea of the nation would have in the twentieth century.

At the start of the twenty-first century, nationalism is not only alive, but – in some parts of the world, at least – flourishing. Although the world has become more interdependent, especially over the past 30 or 40 years, this interdependence has not meant the end of nationalism. In some respects, it has probably even helped to intensify it.

> The resurgence of nationalism in former Yugoslavia is discussed in chapter 15, 'Race, Ethnicity and Migration'.

Recent thinkers have come up with contrasting ideas about why this is so. There are also disagreements about the stage of history at which nationalism, the nation and the nation-state came into being. Some say they have much earlier origins than others.

Nationalism and modern society

Perhaps the leading theorist of nationalism is Ernest Gellner (1925 95). Gellner (1983) argued that nationalism, the nation and the nation-state are all products of modern civilization, whose origins lie in the Industrial Revolution of the late eighteenth century. Nationalism, and the feelings or sentiments associated with it, do not have deep roots in human nature. They are the products of the new large-scale society that industrialism creates. According to Gellner, nationalism as such is unknown in traditional societies, as is the idea of the nation.

There are several features of modern societies that have led to the emergence of these phenomena. First, a modern industrial society is associated with rapid economic development and a complex division of labour. Gellner points out that modern industrialism creates the need for a much more effective system of state and government than existed before. Second, in the modern state, individuals must interact all the time with strangers, since the basis of society is no

Flags are one of the most potent symbols of national communities and often a source of national pride. However, they are also burned in anger by opponents as a way of symbolically attacking a nation. Here, Muslims in Karachi, Pakistan, are burning the Danish flag after a Danish newspaper published controversial cartoons of the Prophet Muhammad.

longer the local village or town, but a very much larger unit. Mass education, based on an 'official language' taught in the schools, is the main means whereby a large-scale society can be organized and kept unified.

Gellner's theory has been criticized in more than one respect. It is a functionalist theory, critics say, which argues that education functions to produce social unity. As with the functionalist approach more generally, this view tends to underestimate the role of education in producing conflict and division. Gellner's theory does not really explain the passions that nationalism can, and often does, arouse. The power of nationalism is probably related not just to education, but also to its capacity to create an identity for people – something that individuals cannot live without. In that sense, perceived threats to national interests can also be perceived as threats to the integrity of people's self-identity.

The need for *identity* is certainly not just born with the emergence of modern industrial society. Critics therefore argue that Gellner is wrong to separate nationalism and the nation so strongly from premodern times. Nationalism is in some ways quite modern, but it also draws on sentiments and forms of symbolism that go back much further into the past. According to one of the best-known current scholars of nationalism, Anthony Smith (1986), nations tend to have direct lines of continuity with earlier ethnic communities – or what he calls **ethnies**. An ethnie is a group that shares ideas of common ancestry, a common cultural identity and a link with a specific homeland.

Many nations, Smith points out, do have pre-modern continuities, and at previous periods of history there have been ethnic communities that resemble nations. The Jews, for example, have formed a distinct ethnie for more than 2,000 years. At certain periods, Jews clustered in communities that had some of the characteristics of nations. In 1948, following the genocide of Jews during the Second World War, the state of Israel was founded, marking the culmination of the Zionist movement, whose aim was to create a homeland for Jews scattered around the world. Like most other nationstates, Israel was not formed from just a single ethnie. The Palestinian minority in Israel traces its origins to a quite different ethnic background and claims that the creation of the Israeli state has displaced the Palestinians from their ancient homelands – hence their persistent tensions with Jews in Israel and the tensions between Israel and most surrounding Arab states.

Different nations have followed divergent patterns of development in relation to ethnies. In some, including most of the

> ### THINKING CRITICALLY
>
> What evidence is there from recent wars and conflicts that the civilizing process identified by Elias (opposite) is continuing in the twenty-first century? Whilst Elias shows how state *formation* influences individual personalities, what could be the consequences of the slow *demise* of the nation-state, in the face of increasingly rapid globalization?

nations of Western Europe, a single ethnie expanded so as to push out earlier rivals. Thus in France up to the nineteenth century, several other languages were spoken to which different ethnic histories were linked. The French state forced schoolchildren to learn French – they would be punished if they spoke their home language – so that by the early twentieth century French became the dominant language, and most of the rival languages largely disappeared. Yet remnants of them have persisted, and many of them are officially encouraged again. One is the Basque language, from the area that overlaps the French and Spanish frontiers. The Basque language is quite different from either French or Spanish, and the Basques claim a separate cultural history of their own. Some Basques want their own nationstate, completely separate from France and Spain. While there has been nothing like the level of violence seen in other areas – such as East Timor, or Chechnya in southern Russia – separatist groups in the Basque country have sporadically used bombing campaigns to further their goal of independence.

Nations without states

The persistence of well-defined ethnies within established nations leads to the phenomenon of **nations without states**. In these situations, many of the essential characteristics of the nation are present, but those who comprise the nation lack an

Classic Studies 23.1 Norbert Elias on state-formation and the civilizing process

The research problem

How have some nations come to see themselves as 'civilized' and others as 'uncivilized'? How can self-styled 'civilized nations' conduct wars involving extreme violence and mass killing, yet still maintain their civilized self-image? Is there a relationship between nation-states, violence and civilization? The German-born sociologist Norbert Elias (1897–1990) studied these issues in a two-volume book, *The Civilizing Process* (2000), first published in 1939. That year was not the time to be talking about 'civilized behaviour', just as war was breaking out in Europe for the second time in just 25 years. Consequently, it was only when *The Civilizing Process* was published in English in 1969 that sociologists began to take account of the book's wide-ranging significance.

Elias's explanation

Elias begins *The Civilizing Process* with an observation: the concept of civilization, 'expresses the self-consciousness of the West. One could even say: the national consciousness'; he continues:

> It sums up everything in which Western society of the last two or three centuries believes itself superior to earlier societies or 'more primitive' contemporary ones. By this term, Western society seeks to describe what constitutes its special character and what it is proud of: the level of *its* technology, the nature of *its* manners, the development of *its* scientific knowledge or view of the world, and much more. (2000 [1939]: 5)

In short, people in modern Western nations have come to understand their societies as setting the standard for civilized conduct and therefore, as being superior to other types of society.

Comparing and contrasting England, France and Germany, the first volume of *The Civilizing Process* looks at the development of typically modern psychic structures and codes of manners. Elias uses many historical examples from etiquette and manners books to show how standards of behaviour in relation to table manners, bodily functions (such as spitting and toileting), sexual expression and violence slowly

changed. In particular, Elias shows that the direction of change since the medieval period was towards increasing thresholds of repugnance and shame, with many behaviours previously considered 'normal' gradually coming to be seen as unacceptable. People developed stronger internalized self-restraints and exhibited increasing control over their emotions.

In the second volume, Elias develops a theory to explain these changes. He finds the key factors to be the process of state-formation and the increasingly long and complex webs of interdependent relations in the early modern period. As courtiers vied with each other for prestige and influence in the European royal courts, new codes of conduct imposed on them a tighter and more even control of their emotions and violent outbursts. With this, a more individualized personality type developed amongst courtiers, making them the first 'modern people' (Korte 2001: 29). The cultivated and refined manners of courtiers set the standard for rising bourgeois classes and eventually spread to other social groups too. This more even, balanced and tightly regulated type of self-control, which became 'second-nature' in modern, industrialized societies, can appear to others as rather detached and calculating. Today, socialization processes routinely shape personalities in this direction.

The absolutist monarchies of seventeenth- and eighteenth-century Europe exemplified the increasing centralization of societies. The competition for power amongst rival regions, towns and social groups often led to violent conflicts and the elimination of the weakest or less well organized. As a result, fewer but larger social units developed via the logic of what Elias calls this 'monopoly mechanism'. This mechanism led to 'a state in which all opportunities are controlled by a single authority: a system with open opportunities has become a system with closed opportunities'. Thus, Elias explains the emergence of the modern nation-state, with its monopolization of the means of physical force and taxation (Elias cited in van Krieken 1998: 101). What Elias shows in *The Civilizing Process* is that the formation of nation-states, alongside increasingly denser webs of social relations, is intimately tied to the emergence of the typically modern personality type. Only where the state monopolization of physical force is relatively stable and secure can individuals, from infancy onwards, become attuned to a new, higher level of self-control, which then becomes 'second nature' to them.

Critical points

Elias's work has attained the status of a modern classic today, but it has also been criticized on several grounds. First, some have suggested that Elias overplays the differences between the modern individual and people in other societies. German ethnologist, Hans-Peter Duerr, argues that the notion of the civilizing process is 'a myth'. Human beings today are essentially similar to human beings of the past; there have been no 'uncivilized' or 'primitive' people. Duerr argues that public 'nakedness' has always been a cause of shame and is not the product of 'civilization'. Second, Elias sees social processes as essentially the unplanned outcome of many intentional actions. But critics point out that this assumption needs to be tested against the evidence in particular cases and seems to ignore 'civilizing offensives', such as those carried out by powerful social elites (van Krieken 1998). Third, Elias's focus on civilizing processes may be criticized for neglecting or under-theorizing the 'dark side' of such processes. Western civilization was not a painless process and, as Foucault shows, can feel far from 'civilized' for many social groups.

Contemporary significance

Elias's ideas have been influential in many fields, not least historical sociology, sociology of the body and the study of human emotions. What continues to attract scholars to Elias's work is the way it allows macro- and micro-levels to be linked, through a central focus on dynamic social processes. Given current concerns about levels of violence in society, terrorism and genocide, it is likely that the study of civilizing and *decivilizing* processes will be one important aspect of sociology's attempts to understand why the recourse to physical violence continues to produce so much human suffering.

independent political community. Separatist movements, like those in Chechnya and the Basque country, as well as those in many other areas of the world – such as in Kashmir in northern India – are driven by the desire to set up an autonomous, self-governing state.

Several different types of nation without states can be recognized, depending on the relationship between the ethnie and the larger nation-state in which it exists (Guibernau 1999). First, in some situations, a nation-state may accept the cultural differences found among its minority or minorities and allow them a certain amount of active development. Thus, in Britain, both Scotland and Wales are recognized as having histories and cultural features that are partly divergent from the rest of the UK,

to some extent as having their own institutions. The majority of Scots, for instance, are Presbyterians, and Scotland has long had a separate educational system from that of England and Wales. Scotland and Wales achieved further autonomy within the UK as a whole with the setting up of a Scottish Parliament and a Welsh Assembly in 1999; the Scottish National Party, which is committed to independence, was elected to government in 2007. Similarly, the Basque country and Catalonia (the area around Barcelona in northern Spain) are both recognized as 'autonomous communities' within Spain. They possess their own parliaments, which have a certain number of rights and powers. In both Britain and Spain, however, much power still remains in the hands of the national governments and

Chechen rebels were responsible for the hostage siege at the school in Beslan, in Russia, which resulted in massive loss of life.

parliaments, located in London and Madrid respectively.

A second type of nations without states consists of those that have a higher degree of autonomy. In Quebec (the French-speaking province of Canada) and Flanders (the Dutch-speaking area including the south west of the Netherlands), regional political bodies have the power to take major decisions, without actually being fully independent. As in the cases mentioned under the first type, they also contain nationalist movements agitating for complete independence.

Third, there are some nations which more or less completely lack recognition from the state that contains them. In such cases, the larger nation-state uses force in order to deny recognition to the minority. The fate of the Palestinians is one example of such a group. Others include the Tibetans in China and the Kurds, whose homeland overlaps parts of Turkey, Syria, Iran and Iraq.

The Tibetans and Kurds date their cultural history back over many centuries. The history of Tibet is strongly bound up with particular forms of Buddhism that have flourished there. The Tibetan leader in exile, the Dalai Lama, is at the centre of movements outside Tibet which aim to achieve a separate Tibetan state through non-violent means. Among the Kurds, on the other hand, several independence movements, mostly located abroad, proclaimed violence as the means of achieving their ends and the Kurds have a 'parliament in exile', based in Brussels. However, after the first Gulf War of 1990–1, allied forces established a 'safe haven' and a level of autonomy for Kurds in Northern Iraq which was extended and consolidated following the overthrow of Saddam Hussein's regime in Iraq in 2003.

In the case of the Tibetans, there is little chance of achieving even limited autonomy unless the Chinese government decides at some point to change its existing policies. But in other instances, it is possible that national minorities might opt for autonomy within, rather than complete independence from, the states in which they are located. In the Basque country, Catalonia and Scotland, for example, a minority of the populations currently support complete independence. In Quebec, a provincial referendum in 1995 on independence from Canada was defeated when it failed to gain the necessary popular votes.

THINKING CRITICALLY

Nations have been described as 'imagined communities' (Anderson 2006 [1983]) – as no one can know all of the people within a nation and its unity is therefore assumed or imagined. What practical actions keep such imagined communities alive over generations, even when no state exists?

National minorities and the European Union

In the case of national minorities in Europe, the European Union has a significant part to play. The EU was formed through allegiances created by the major nations of Western Europe. Yet a key element of the philosophy of the EU is the devolution of power to localities and regions. One of its explicit goals is to create a 'Europe of the regions'. This emphasis is strongly supported by most Basques, Scots, Cata-

lans and other national minority groups. Members of these groups often feel resentment about the ways in which parts of their culture or institutions have been lost, and they wish to retrieve them. They look to the EU as a means of fostering their distinct identities. Their right to relate directly to EU organizations, such as the European Parliament or European courts of law, might give them sufficient autonomy to be satisfied that they are in control of their own destinies. Hence it is at least conceivable that the existence of the EU will mean that national minorities might give up on the ideal of complete independence in favour of a cooperative relationship both with the larger nations of which they are a part and with the EU.

 The basic roles and functions of the EU are introduced in chapter 22, 'Politics, Government and Social Movements'.

Nations and nationalism in developing countries

In most of the countries of the developing world, the course followed by nationalism, the nation and the nation-state has been different compared with that of the industrial societies. Most developing countries were once colonized by Europeans and achieved independence at some point in the second half of the twentieth century. In many of these countries, boundaries between colonial administrations were agreed arbitrarily in Europe and did not take into account existing economic, cultural or ethnic divisions among the population. The colonial powers defeated or subjugated the kingdoms and tribal groupings existing on the African subcontinent, in India and other parts of Asia, and set up their own colonial administrations or protectorates. As a consequence, each colony was 'a collection of peoples and old states, or fragments of these, brought together within the same boundaries' (Akintoye 1976: 3). Most colonized areas contained a mosaic of ethnies and other groups.

Global Society 23.1 | Free market democracy and ethnic hatred

Many commentators have argued that the best way to reduce ethnic conflicts, such as those discussed above, is to establish democracy and introduce free markets. They argue that this would promote peace by giving everyone a say in running the country and by giving them access to the prosperity that comes from trading with others. In an influential book, *World on Fire: How Exporting Free Market Democracy Breeds Ethnic Hatred and Global Instability* (2003), Amy Chua, a professor at Yale University, contests this view.

Chua's starting point is that in many developing countries, a small ethnic minority enjoys disproportionate economic power. One obvious example is the white minority that exploited the non-white ethnic groups in apartheid South Africa. Chua argues that the massacre of Tutsis by Hutus in Rwanda in 1994 and the hatred felt by Serbs towards Croats in former Yugoslavia were also partly related to the economic advantage enjoyed by the Tutsis and the Croats in their respective countries. Another example that Chua often uses concerns the Chinese ethnic minority in Indonesia.

The pro-market reforms of the former Indonesian dictator, General Suharto, particularly benefited the country's small Chinese minority. In turn, Chinese-Indonesians tended to support the Suharto dictatorship. In 1998, the year that mass pro-democracy demonstrations forced Suharto out of office, Chinese-Indonesians controlled 70 per cent of Indonesia's private economy, but made up just 3 per cent of its population. The end of Suharto's regime was accompanied by violent attacks against the Chinese minority, who were perceived as 'stealing' the country's indigenous wealth. Chua writes: 'The prevailing view among the pribumi [ethnic] majority was that it was worthwhile to lose 10 years of growth to get rid of the Chinese problem once and for all.'

As General Suharto's dictatorship collapsed, the USA and other Western countries called for the introduction of democratic elections. Yet, Chua argues that introducing democracy to countries with what she calls 'market dominant minorities', such as the Chinese in Indonesia, is not likely to bring peace. Instead, Chua argues that the competition for votes in a democracy is likely to lead to a backlash from the country's ethnic majority. Political leaders will emerge who seek to scapegoat the resented minority and encourage the ethnic majority to 'reclaim' the country's wealth for the 'true' owners of the nation, as the pribumi majority in Indonesia did against the Chinese minority.

Chua's account shows us that although democracy and the market economy are in principle beneficent forces, they must be grounded in an effective system of law and civil society. Where they are not, as in many parts of the developing world, new and acute ethnic conflicts can emerge.

When erstwhile colonies achieved their independence, they often found it difficult to create a sense of nationhood and national belonging. Although nationalism played a great part in securing the independence of colonized areas, it was largely confined to small groups from the urban elites and intellectuals. Nevertheless, nationalist ideas did influence large numbers of people, though political differences often crystallized around ethnic differences, such as those in Rwanda or Kenya. Even today, many postcolonial states are continually threatened by internal rivalries and competing claims to political authority.

The continent that was most completely colonized was Africa. Nationalist movements promoting independence in Africa following the Second World War sought to free the colonized areas from European domination. Once this had been achieved, the new leaders everywhere faced the challenge of trying to create national unity. Many of the leaders in the 1950s and '60s had been educated in Europe or the USA, and there was a vast gulf between them and their citizens, most of whom were illiterate, poor and unfamiliar with the rights and obligations of democracy. Under colonialism, some ethnic groups had prospered more than others; these groups had different interests and goals and legitimately saw each other as enemies.

Civil wars broke out in a number of post-colonial states in Africa, such as Sudan, Zaire and Nigeria, while ethnic rivalries and antagonisms characterized many others both in Africa and Asia. In the case of Sudan, about 40 per cent of the population claimed Arabic ethnic origins, while in other regions of the country, particularly in the south, most of the population was black, and Christian or animist in their religious beliefs. Once the nationalists took power, they set up a programme for national integration based on Arabic as the national language. The attempt was only partly successful, and the stresses and strains it produced are still visible (as we saw in our discussion of ethnic conflicts, such as those in Rwanda or Darfur in Western Sudan, in chapter 15). Many of the wars that have taken place on the African continent since independence are a direct result of difficulties like these.

Nigeria is another example of the issues involved. The country has a population of some 120 million people: roughly one out of every four Africans is a Nigerian. Nigeria was formerly a British colony and achieved its independence on 1 October 1960. The country is made up of three main ethnic groups: Yoruba, Ibo and Hausa. Soon after independence in 1966, armed struggles developed in the country between different ethnic groups. A military government was set up and since then periods of civilian government have alternated with phases of military rule. In 1967 a civil war broke out in which one area, Biafra, sought independence from the rest of the country. The separatist movement was suppressed by the use of military force, with much loss of life. Successive governments have attempted to build up a clearer sense of national identity around the theme of 'motherland Nigeria', but creating a sense of national unity and purpose remains difficult. The country possesses large reserves of oil and petro-

leum, but remains largely mired in poverty and still in the grip of authoritarian rule.

In summary, most states in the developing world came into being as a result of different processes of nation-formation from those that occurred in the industrialized world. States were imposed externally on areas that often had no prior cultural or ethnic unity, sometimes resulting in civil war after independence. Modern nations have arisen most effectively either in areas that were never fully colonized, or where there was already a great deal of cultural unity – such as Japan, China, Korea or Thailand.

The nation-state, national identities and globalization

How does globalization affect nationalism and national identity? The sociologist Andrew Pilkington has examined this question (2002). He argues that nationalism is actually quite a new phenomenon, despite the fact that many of its supporters claim to be members of nations with histories stretching back into the mists of time. Until relatively recently in historical terms, humans survived in small settlements, largely unaware of what goes on outside their own groups, and the idea of being members of a larger nation would have seemed alien to them. Pilkington has argued that it was only later, from the eighteenth century onwards, with the development of mass communications and media, that the idea of a national community developed and spread. To Pilkington it was during this period that national identities were 'constructed'.

 Social constructionism is discussed in more detail in chapter 2 'Asking and Answering Sociological Questions', chapter 5 'The Environment', and chapter 7, 'Social Interaction and Everyday Life.

Crucial in developing a sense of nation-hood, for Pilkington, was the existence of some 'Other', against which national identity was formed. For instance, central to the shaping of a (Protestant) British identity, Pilkington argued, was the existence of (Catholic) France. Pilkington documents how a sense of Britishness spread downwards from the country's elite to the rest of society as levels of literacy spread throughout the whole population and as communications technology enabled the spread of ideas.

If national identity is socially constructed, as Pilkington argues, then it is possible that it will change and develop. One of the main factors in changing national identity today, Pilkington contends, is globalization. In his view, globalization creates conflicting pressures between centralization and decentralization. On the one hand, the powers of some business organizations and political units (such as multinational corporations or transnational organizations like the EU) become more concentrated, while, on the other, there is pressure for decentralization, such as the collapse and fragmentation of the Soviet Union or the desire for a separate Basque nation in Spain. As a result, Pilkington argues, globalization creates a dual threat to national identity: centralization creates pressures from above, particularly with the growing powers of the European Union, and decentralization creates pressures from below, through the strengthening of ethnic minority identities. In the UK, one response to this has been to reassert a narrow understanding of Britishness. Pilkington cites the example of John Townsend, a former Conservative Party MP, who advanced a strongly anti-European, white, English-speaking view of English national identity. Another is the recent limited local electoral success of the racist British National Party, particularly in some deprived areas of north-west England. Pilkington argues that a parallel response is also found amongst some members of ethnic minority groups within the UK, who, feeling excluded from a British identity, have strengthened their local identities and asserted their differences from other ethnic groups.

THINKING CRITICALLY

Can national identities survive in an age of globalization? What reasons are there for suggesting that national identities may well become stronger rather than weaker in the future? Are there any examples of larger regional identifications that are growing in strength?

A second response to globalization, which Pilkington clearly thinks is a healthier one, is to accept that there are multiple identities – to argue, for example, that it is possible to be English, British and European all at the same time. Pilkington sees evidence of this approach in the new 'hybrid identities' of ethnic minority groups in the UK, whose identities merge different cultures. According to Pilkington, we must challenge the first nationalist response to globalization – which often leads to the retreat into religious fundamentalism or cultural racism – by representing the nation in an ethnically inclusive way and encouraging hyphenated identities, such as British-Asian. Globalization, he argues, leads to contradictory pressures and contradictory responses for national identity.

In some parts of Africa, nations and nation-states are not fully formed. Yet in other areas of the world some writers are already speaking of the 'end of the nation-state' in the face of globalization. According to the Japanese writer Kenichi Ohmae (1995), as a result of globalization we increasingly live in a 'borderless world' in which national identity is becoming weaker.

How valid is this point of view? All states are certainly being affected by globalizing processes. The very rise of 'nations without states', as discussed above, is probably

Hybrid social identities, such as British-Asian, may offer the best way of constructing national identities in multicultural societies whose diversity continues to develop with processes of globalization.

bound up with globalization. As globalization progresses, people often react by reviving local identities, in an effort to achieve security in a rapidly changing world. Nations have less economic power of their own than they used to have, as a result of the spread of the global marketplace.

Yet it would not be accurate to say that we are witnessing the end of the nation-state. In some ways, the opposite is the case. Today, every country in the world is a nation-state or aspires to be one – the nation-state has become a universal political form. Until quite recently, it still had rivals. For most of the twentieth century, colonized areas and empires existed alongside nation-states. Many sociologists have argued that the last empire only disap-

peared in 1990 with the collapse of Soviet communism, and others still see the United States as an empire (Ferguson 2004). The Soviet Union was effectively at the centre of an empire embracing its satellite states in Eastern Europe. Now all of these have become independent nations, as have many areas inside what was formerly the Soviet Union. There are actually far more sovereign nations in the world today than there were 20 years ago.

During much of the last century, nationalism and issues surrounding nations without states were often associated with the use of terrorism as a political weapon. Below, we discuss terrorism, and look at how the concept has changed in recent years.

Human conflict, war and genocide

One major theoretical tradition in sociology is the conflict tradition, which includes important research by Marxists, feminists and Weberian scholars (see chapter 1). However, much of this work concentrates on social conflicts *within* particular societies such as those involving social classes, gender relations and ethnic conflicts. Even when sociologists investigate cross-national conflicts, these are often seen in similar terms. For example, the 2003 invasion of Iraq has been explained by some Marxists in essentially economic terms, as an attempt to establish secure oil supplies for the US and its allies. Such studies and explanations have much to tell us about conflict, but, as a discipline, sociology has not given the study of war as much prominence as it could and should have, preferring to leave it to military theorists and strategists.

One main reason for this is the widely held view that war is not a 'normal' state of affairs and is therefore not central to the development of sociological theories and explanations. After all, it does not make much sense to base general social theories on highly unusual and very specific events. But is this assumption correct? Probably not. Not only is human warfare as old as human societies, but also, in the twentieth century alone, more than 100 million people were killed in wars. Several billion human beings have been killed in more than 14,000 wars over the course of recorded history (Roxborough 2004). From a global perspective, a very good case could be made for the opposite assumption: that the existence of wars is normal in human affairs, while periods of peace have been quite rare. In the developed countries, the period since 1945 has been just such a period, and perhaps it is this that has contributed to the idea that war is somehow abnormal (Inglehart 1977). As the figures above show, however, such massive loss of life and human suffering surely demands that sociologists bring their expertise to bear on understanding the causes of war to try to mitigate its consequences.

Theorizing war and genocide

What is war? Martin Shaw defines it as 'the clash of two organized armed forces that seek to destroy each other's power and especially their will to resist, principally by killing members of the opposing force' (2003: 5). This definition makes organized killing central to the actual practice of war, a fact that was borne out in the enormous loss of life in two twentieth-century world wars, in which a large number of the world's societies became involved. The definition also makes clear that the central aim of war is to 'destroy the enemy's power', thus rendering it unable to resist. As we will see in 'Classic Studies 23.2', this notion was expressed in Carl von Clausewitz's classic statement that, 'war is the continuation of political intercourse by other means' (1993 [1832]).

Although it is tempting to see war – like aggression as a natural part of the human condition that is inevitable and requires no further explanation, Clausewitz's formulation suggests otherwise. Wars are engaged in by organized social groups and are fought because political calculations are made about the likelihood of success and decisions taken by leaders. They require economic resources to be committed, and they usually play on real, perceived or created cultural differences in order to mobilize populations emotionally. War is therefore a social phenomenon, whose nature has changed over time.

In practice, those killed in war have tended to be the armed combatants rather than civilians, which shows that war is not simply chaotic, random killing – hence the idea of the 'rules of war' that regulate what opposing forces can legitimately do in combat and afterwards. Nevertheless, such rules have often been broken in battle conditions, and in recent years there has

23.1 Using the atomic bomb

Hiroshima bomb pilot dies aged 92

The commander of the B-29 plane that dropped the first atomic bomb, on Hiroshima in Japan, has died. Paul Warfield Tibbets Jr died at his home in Columbus, Ohio, aged 92.

The five-ton 'Little Boy' bomb was dropped on the morning of 6 August 1945, killing about 140,000 Japanese, with many more dying later. On the 60th anniversary of the bombing, the three surviving crew members of the Enola Gay – named after Tibbets' mother – said they had 'no regrets'.

'No headstone'

A friend of the retired brigadier-general told AP news agency that Paul Tibbets had died after a two-month decline in health. Gen. Tibbets had asked for no funeral nor headstone as he feared opponents of the bombing may use it as a place of protest, the friend, Gerry Newhouse, said.

The bombing of Hiroshima marked the beginning of the end of the war in the Pacific. Japan surrendered shortly after a second bomb was dropped, on Nagasaki, three days later.

On the 60th anniversary of Hiroshima, the surviving members of the Enola Gay crew – Gen. Tibbets, Theodore J. 'Dutch' Van Kirk (the navigator) and Morris R. Jeppson (weapon test officer) said: 'The use of the atomic weapon was a necessary moment in history. We have no regrets'.

Gen. Tibbets said then: 'Thousands of former soldiers and military family members have expressed a particularly touching and personal gratitude suggesting that they might not be alive today had it been necessary to resort to an invasion of the Japanese home islands to end the fighting.'

Source: BBC News, 1 November 2007
© bbc.co.uk/news

been much deliberate targeting of civilian populations as another means of 'destroying the enemy's will to resist'. Shaw describes the deliberate extension of targets to unarmed civilians as a form of illegitimate or 'degenerate war', seen in the Japanese massacres of more than 260,000 Chinese civilians in 1937, the British fire-bombing of German cities, including Hamburg in 1943 and Dresden in 1945, and the American nuclear bombing of the Japanese cities of Hiroshima and Nagasaki in 1945.

THINKING CRITICALLY

Was the use of nuclear weapons by the USA in 1945 an illegitimate extension of warfare to the unarmed civilian population and therefore an example of 'degenerate war'? Given the justification for the use of such weapons – that it brought Japanese resistance to a swifter end, which may have saved many combatants lives – can any episode of degenerate war ever be considered legitimate?

The changing nature of war

Prior to the twentieth century, most wars made extensive use of mercenary armies or conscripted men into armed forces. Weaponry consisted of swords and, latterly, firearms, and military transport was based on horses, horse-drawn carriages and sailing boats. Even during the First World War (1914–18), horses remained a major form of transport. By the time of the Second World War, weapons and transport had changed considerably. Machine guns, tanks, chemical weapons and aeroplanes made it much easier for armies to engage in the mass killing that characterizes war. A common-sense view would perhaps see wars as conflicts between nation-states for dominance. Until quite recently, many social scientists might have agreed. However, interstate wars seem to be becoming less common. Of 80 conflicts that took place around the world between 1989 and 1992, just three were interstate wars; the remainder were conflicts within countries (Malcolm 1996). On the other hand, internal conflicts seem to be increasing. Of 213 civil wars that took place in the 181 years between 1816 and 1997, 104 of them took place in just 43 years, between 1944 and 1997 (Hironaka 2005). The balance between *inter*state and *intra*state wars seems to have shifted significantly.

In addition, Shaw (2005) has argued that in many contemporary wars involving Western states – such as those involving the USA and its allies in Iraq and Afghanistan – attempts are now made to protect the lives of soldiers on the ground in order to avoid potentially damaging media coverage leading to negative political and electoral consequences for governments at home. This is one reason why recent Western involvement often takes the preferred form of massive air strikes, which minimizes the risk to armed forces. But, in effect, this amounts to the transference of the risks of warfare onto civilian populations below, whose deaths become 'collateral damage' or 'unavoidable accidents of war'. And this new mode of 'risk transfer' war has the potential to damage the older rule-governed type of war and thus opens Western states and everyone else to even more risks. When civilians are intentionally targeted, the question of whether 'genocide' has been committed is now commonly raised.

> ### THINKING CRITICALLY
>
> War is, 'the clash of two organized armed forces that seek to destroy each other's power and especially their will to resist, principally by killing members of the opposing force'. Are 'risk transfer wars' actually wars at all on this definition? Explain your answer fully with reference to the definition's main elements. If they *are* still wars, can they be justified? If they are *not* wars, how should we describe them?

Genocide is a term that has been used with increasing regularity in the mass media and political discourse. It has recently been used to describe Serbian

> ### THINKING CRITICALLY
>
> How do Clausewitz's main arguments stand up today, especially in relation to the development and spread of nuclear weapons? Which aspects of his ideas are undermined by nuclear weapons and the doctrine of 'mutually assured destruction' (MAD), which has, arguably, helped to ensure that there has been no war between nuclear powers since the Second World War?

attacks on ethnic Albanians in Kosovo and Hutu attacks on Tutsis in Rwanda. Originally used by Raphael Lemkin in his book *Axis Rule in Occupied Europe* (1944), it was adopted in 1948 by the United Nations Convention on the Prevention and Punishment of the Crime of Genocide (Article 2), which says:

> Genocide means any of the following acts committed with intent to destroy, in whole or in part, a national, ethnic, racial or religious group, as such:

(a) killing members of the group;
(b) causing serious bodily or mental harm to members of the group;
(c) deliberately inflicting on the group conditions of life calculated to bring about its physical destruction in whole or in part;
(d) imposing measures intended to prevent births within the group;
(e) forcibly transferring children of the group to another group.

This was amongst the first attempts to define genocide and is clearly rooted in the Nazi racial policies against many sections of the European population, including the attempt to exterminate the Jewish people, in the Second World War (1939–45). Genocide is seen here as separate from war. Whereas killing in war can be considered legitimate (if the rules of war are not broken), genocide is, by definition, always wrong. The UN definition makes intention central to genocide. A particular social

Classic Studies 23.2 | Carl von Clausewitz, *On War* (1832)

Carl von Clausewitz (1780–1831) is the classic modern theorist of war. A Prussian army officer who fought in the revolutionary and Napoleonic wars (1793–1815), he taught at the military academy, where he wrote the book published posthumously as *On War*. If social scientists fully recognized the centrality of war in modern society, this work of Clausewitz would figure in canons of social thought alongside those of near contemporaries such as the philosophers Immanuel Kant and Georg Wilhelm Friedrich Hegel, the sociologist Auguste Comte and the revolutionary Karl Marx.

Clausewitz's book contained a number of seminal ideas:

1 His most famous maxim is that 'war is the continuation of political intercourse [also translated as either policy or politics] by other means'. This is often interpreted as meaning that the course of war is determined by its political objectives. However, Clausewitz's real originality lay in his exploration of the 'otherness' of military means.

2 He emphasized that war is 'an act of force' designed to compel an enemy to submit, and hence has 'no logical limit'. He concludes from this that escalation is a law of war, and that there is a general tendency for war to become absolute. Restricted political objectives can limit escalation, only partially, since the clash of arms is always likely to surpass preordained political limits and so is intrinsically unpredictable.

3 War was as likely to be contained by *friction* – i.e., the obstacles to escalation created by inhospitable climate and terrain together with the logistical difficulties of deploying armies over long distances.

4 War can be compared as a social process to commerce. In this light, battle is the moment of realization – the end to which all activity is geared – in war in the same way as exchange in commerce.

5 War is a *trinity* of policy (the province of government), military craft (the business of generals) and raw violence (supplied by the people). Thus the involvement of the people (the nation in arms) is partly responsible for the peculiarly destructive character of modern war compared to earlier periods.

Modern war is sometimes described as 'Clausewitzian'. The main problem with this description is that industrial society gave war enormously more powerful means of destruction – not only weaponry, but also military and political organization – than Clausewitz could foresee. Modern *total war* combined total social mobilization with absolute destructiveness. From the middle of the nineteenth century, this radically expanded the scope for slaughter beyond Clausewitzian conditions. The logical conclusion of this process was the truly total, simultaneous and mutual destruction threatened by nuclear war.

Source: Shaw 2003: 19–20

group need not *actually be* exterminated for genocide to be deemed to have taken place; what matters is that the perpetrator's *intention* was to exterminate the enemy. A problem here, though, is demonstrating intention in order to prove that genocide has taken place. Orders to kill may never be written down, evidence may be incomplete or non-existent and many things can be achieved by acts of omission as well as acts of commission. That is, the destruc-

tion of a social group can be brought about by neglect and indifference as well as by deliberate attacks.

Shaw (2003, 2007) rejects the separation of genocide and war. As he notes, most genocides occur in interstate or civil wars. In most historical cases of genocide, states (or power centres within states) were the perpetrators, state armies, police forces and party organizations carried them out and they took place within the context of

Global Society 23.2 **Cambodia's brutal 'Khmer Rouge' regime**

The Khmer Rouge was the ruling party in Cambodia from 1975 to 1979, but during this short time it was responsible for one of the worst mass killings of the twentieth century. The brutal regime claimed the lives of more than a million people – and some estimates say up to 2.5 million perished.

Under the Marxist leader Pol Pot, the Khmer Rouge tried to take Cambodia back to the Middle Ages, forcing millions of people from the cities to work on communal farms in the countryside. But this dramatic attempt at social engineering had a terrible cost, and whole families died from execution, starvation, disease and overwork.

Communist philosophy

The Khmer Rouge had its origins in the 1960s, as the armed wing of the Communist Party of Kampuchea – the name the Communists used for Cambodia. Based in remote jungle and mountain areas in the north-east of the country, the group initially made little headway.

But after a right-wing military coup toppled the head of state, Prince Norodom Sihanouk, in 1970, the Khmer Rouge entered into a political coalition with him and began to attract increasing support. In a civil war that continued for nearly five years, it gradually increased its control in the countryside.

Khmer Rouge forces finally took over the capital, Phnom Penh, and therefore the nation as a whole in 1975. During his time in the remote north-east, Pol Pot had been influenced by the surrounding hill tribes, members of whom were self-sufficient in their communal living, had no use for money and were 'untainted' by Buddhism.

When he came to power, Pol Pot and his henchmen quickly set about transforming Cambodia – now renamed Kampuchea – into what they hoped would be an agrarian utopia. Declaring that the nation would start again at 'Year Zero', Pol Pot isolated his people from the rest of the world and set about emptying the cities, abolishing money, private property and religion, and setting up rural collectives.

Anyone thought to be an intellectual of any sort was killed. People were often condemned for wearing glasses or for knowing a foreign language. Hundreds of thousands of the educated middle classes were tortured and executed in special centres. The most notorious of these centres was the S21 jail in Phnom Penh, where more than 17,000 men, women and children were imprisoned during the regime's four years in power.

Hundreds of thousands of others died from disease, starvation or exhaustion as members of the Khmer Rouge – often just teenagers themselves – forced people to do back-breaking work.

Opening up

The Khmer Rouge government was finally overthrown in 1979 by invading Vietnamese troops, after a series of violent border confrontations. The higher echelons of the party retreated to remote areas of the country, where they remained active for a while but gradually became less and less powerful.

In the years that followed, as Cambodia began the process of reopening to the international community, the full horrors of the regime became apparent. Survivors told their stories to shocked audiences, and in the 1980s the Hollywood movie *The Killing Fields* brought the plight of the Khmer Rouge victims to worldwide attention.

Pol Pot was denounced by his former comrades in a show trial in July 1997, and was sentenced to house arrest in his jungle home. But less than a year later he was dead – denying the millions of people who were affected by this brutal regime the chance to bring him to justice.

Source: BBC News, 19 September 2007
© bbc.co.uk/news

war. Hence, it may be more accurate to define genocide as, 'a form of war in which social groups are the enemy' (Shaw 2003: 44–5). And if genocide *is* a form of war, this raises the question of whether the dominant form of war is changing.

Old and new wars

Warfare is always based on the available resources, social organization and level of technological development of societies. In this way, it is clear that methods of waging

23.2 Modernity and the Holocaust

'The Holocaust' is a phrase used to describe a specific instance of genocide: the attempt by German National Socialists, led by Adolf Hitler, systematically to exterminate Jews in Europe during the Second World War, 1939–45. Jewish populations in Germany and other countries that were invaded by German troops were persecuted, crowded into ghettos and transported to extermination camps, where mass killing took place in gas chambers. Approximately six million Jewish people were murdered in these few short years as part of the Nazis' 'Final Solution of the Jewish Question'. Although many other social groups, including East European Roma, disabled people, gay men and communists, were also singled out for persecution, conventionally these have not been included in definitions of the Holocaust.

Zygmunt Bauman (1989) discovered that, as with the study of war, sociologists have had very little to say about the Holocaust or its consequences for social science. He suggests that part of the reason for this is that the Holocaust is seen as a specific aspect of Jewish history, which holds no general lessons for social morality in other times and places. Second, there exists a widely accepted interpretation of the Holocaust, which sees it as an aberration, a dreadful and unique episode of barbarism in the otherwise peaceful flow of social life in civilized, modern societies. Bauman argues that we cannot let modern societies off the hook so lightly; the Holocaust, he says, is the ultimate *test of modernity*.

In fact, says Bauman, it was the characteristically modern elements that made the Holocaust possible at all. Modern technology was deployed to speed up the process of mass killing, bureaucratic systems of administration ensured the most efficient method of processing 'human bureaucratic objects' and the bureaucratic mentality dehumanized Jewish people and allowed individuals to avoid moral responsibility for

their actions. Bauman also explores the role of modern racist ideology and the way that victims were led into acquiescence with the extermination process through their rational calculation of survival chances at every stage of the process. All of these elements – modern technology, bureaucracies, racism and rational calculation – are 'normal' or common aspects of modern societies, which by themselves are unremarkable.

However, in the Holocaust these elements were brought together in a unique way. Bauman argues that this became possible as the German state systematically set about dismantling and destroying the voluntary organizations, trade unions and other tissues that make for a strong civil society. This left the modern, centralized nation-state, with its monopolization of the means of violence, free to pursue its social-engineering projects without any controls or countervailing power sources. In short, modernity provided the *necessary* resources that made the Holocaust possible, but this was not *sufficient* without the state's emancipation from the restrictions placed on it by society at large.

For Bauman, there are two main lessons from the Holocaust. The first is 'the facility with which most people, put into a situation that does not contain a good choice, or renders such a good choice very costly, argue themselves away from the issue of moral duty (or fail to argue themselves towards it), adopting instead the precepts of rational interest and self-preservation. *In a system where rationality and ethics point in opposite directions, humanity is the main loser*' (1989: 206).

But the second lesson is: '*It does not matter how many people chose moral duty over the rationality of self-preservation – what does matter is that some did. Evil is not all-powerful. It can be resisted*' (ibid.; italics in original). Of course we may agree with Bauman that people's actions aimed at self-preservation rather than moral duty were indeed a choice rather than an inevitability, the context in which such choices were made did largely shape the overall outcome. As the historian E. H. Carr once argued, 'numbers count in history' (1961: 62).

There were numerous resistance attempts by Jewish people during the war, including a 1943 rebellion in the Treblinka concentration camp and several in Jewish ghettoes. The most serious (for the Nazi regime) was the Warsaw ghetto uprising of January 1943, during which several thousand Jewish people fought the Nazi SS, killing hundreds of German soldiers. However, they were eventually overwhelmed by the superior force of the German army, and 13,000 Jewish people were killed in the insurgency.

THINKING CRITICALLY

Does Jewish resistance in the face of overwhelmingly more powerful forces support Bauman's point about moral duty being a choice we *all* face, even in the worst of times? Should more Jewish people have resisted the Nazis? What factors and considerations could have prevented them from doing so? Why might the apparent choice between individual self-preservation and moral duty to others not be quite as simple as Bauman's conclusion above suggests?

war are never fixed, but change over time alongside the economic, social and political development of societies. The industrialized, *total wars* of the early twentieth century, with their mobilization of entire national populations in the war effort, were quite radically different from earlier wars involving much smaller armies, which took place without the participation of large parts of civilian populations, many of which were unaffected by them. However, some scholars of war have argued that the nature of war has again changed quite dramatically over the past 30 years or so, as a new type of war has come to the fore. This position has come to be known as the Revolution in Military Affairs (RMA), which posits that information technologies are moving to the centre of military strategy. Thinking about the role played by satellite systems and computers in the two recent conflicts in Iraq (1990/91 and 2003) illustrates the force of this argument. We will look at one highly influential account of RMA: Mary Kaldor's *New and Old Wars* (2007).

Kaldor argues that in Africa and Eastern Europe from the late twentieth century, a new type of war began to emerge. One way of describing this has been to see it as 'low-intensity conflict', essentially similar to small-scale guerrilla warfare, or even terrorism. Low-intensity conflicts involve localized violence and many could be called civil wars within particular nation-states. However, Kaldor rejects this label for new wars. She points out that, although they are usually localized conflicts, they also involve many transnational connections, which makes the old distinction between external aggression and internal repression impossible to sustain. New wars also erode the boundaries between warfare (between states), organized crime and violations of basic human rights.

For example, in the Bosnian war in 1992–5, in former Yugoslavia, a genocidal conflict between Serbians (Orthodox Christians), Croatians (Catholics) and Bosniaks (Muslims) resulted in at least 100,000 deaths. On all sides, human rights violations took place in attempts to create ethnically 'pure' areas. Bosnian Serbs received financial and logistical support from Serbia (which, at that time covered much of the Federal Republic of Yugoslavia) and during the conflict embarked on a campaign of 'ethnic cleansing' (attempts to displace an ethnic group from a specific area) against non-Serbians, involving many human rights abuses against civilians, including the systematic mass rape of women, and civilian massacres. The massacre of some 8,000 boys and men at Srebrenica in July 2005 was declared genocide by an International Criminal Tribunal at The Hague. The Tribunal reported:

> By seeking to eliminate a part of the Bosnian Muslims, the Bosnian Serb forces committed genocide. They targeted for extinction the forty thousand Bosnian Muslims living in Srebrenica, a group which was emblematic of the Bosnian Muslims in general. They stripped all the male Muslim prisoners, military and civilian, elderly and young, of their personal belongings and identification, and deliberately and methodically killed them solely on the basis of their identity.

However, in 2007, the International Court of Justice declared that the state of Serbia did not directly commit the genocide (some individuals have been charged with genocide), though it had broken international law by failing to stop it. This was the first time a state had faced genocide charges. Kaldor argued that the large-scale violation of human rights makes new wars illegitimate and that ways must be found to prevent them.

As new wars appear to have increased in the wake of the ending of the Cold War, it may be that the close of an old world order has created a climate in which new war has flourished. The collapse of communist regimes has left a legacy of surplus weaponry as well as a power vacuum, so the argument goes, which localized militia groups and armies can use to their advantage. Kaldor argues that the end of the Cold War is one factor in the rise of new war. But more significant is the increasingly rapid process of globalization that began in the 1970s, carried along on the wave of new information technologies. The latter, she says, lies at the heart of new wars:

> The impact of globalization is visible in many of the new wars. The global presence in these wars can include international reporters, mercenary troops and military advisers, and diaspora volunteers as well as a veritable 'army' of international agencies ranging from non-governmental organizations (NGOs) such as Oxfam, Save the Children, Médecins

Global Society 23.3 **Life after genocide – Srebrenica and the Bosnian war**

Shattered lives in massacre town

Fadila Efendic shows me her house – there's a balcony to look out over the stream and colourful window boxes. In the garden, there are roses and a cherry tree and a cat soaking up the sun on a wooden bench by the tomato plants. You can see lush green mountains in the distance. But everywhere you look beyond this pretty house, there are empty homes, with smashed-up roofs or broken windows.

This is Srebrenica, the town which gave its name to the worst single atrocity in Europe since World War II. Fadila lost her son, Feizo, in the massacre here 10 years ago. She tells me the mornings are the hardest. She still wants to go and wake him up, but his room is empty.

She says it's easier during the day, because she can imagine he's at school. He was just 19 when she last saw him. She cannot even be sure whether he made it past his 20th birthday. Her husband was killed too.

'I will never be able to forgive the criminals: those who ordered or carried out the killings. I know my religion demands forgiveness, but I can't forgive. It would be easier to leave the religion.'

Bitterness

During Bosnia's bitter and bloody war, Srebrenica was declared a United Nations protected safe haven. But in July 1995, Serb troops entered the town and over the following days, thousands of Muslim men and boys were killed.

'The mind of Srebrenica was destroyed. The intellectuals were killed: 200 teachers, engineers, doctors. It can't recover without people', says Fadila. 'I don't have a future. I only have a past. But I still think the town has a future, maybe in 70 years. . . . The mine, the factory, the woods and tourism. We still have all of that. But it needs to be repaired.'

There is only one mosque in Srebrenica now. Before the war, there were five. There were also around 27,000 Muslims living in the town and its many outlying areas. Now they number just 4,000, among them 73-year-old Sija Mustafic, who lost her husband and one of her sons.

One by one, she points to the empty houses around hers, where other Muslims once lived. She tells me life is normal here again, and she has a normal relationship with her Serb neighbours. But that's 'normal' in Srebrenica terms. She says Serbs can never be her friends.

'I will never love the Serbs, and I don't wish them well, because of my child and this catastrophe. But you have to live together', she says. 'Serb friends of my son come and ask after him, and they start crying and say: "Mother, forgive us!" – they call me mother – and they leave crying. But it's all in vain.'

Bitterness and resentment remain on both sides

Goran Rakic, a Bosnian Serb, takes me to see a memorial to his people at a cemetery in the mountains. He believes the number of Muslims who were killed in July 1995 has been exaggerated. He says the Serbs who died here during the war are the forgotten victims.

'They simply attacked the village and killed them all. The attackers were our neighbours, our contemporaries, from Srebrenica and Potocari. My father and brother were killed and my uncle, all on the same day.'

He thinks the world has a slanted picture of what happened in and around Srebrenica, and that the suffering of the Serbs goes unnoticed.

Source: Jon Manel, BBC News, 11 July 2005
© bbc.co.uk/news

Sans Frontières, Human Rights Watch and the International Red Cross to international institutions such as the United Nations High Commissioner for Refugees (UNHCR), the European Union (EU), the United Nations Children's Fund (UNICEF), the Organization for Security and Cooperation in Europe (OSCE), the African Union (AU) and the United Nations (UN) itself, including peacekeeping troops. Indeed, the wars epitomize a new kind of global/local divide between those members of a global class who can speak English, have access to faxes, the Internet and satellite televisions, who use dollars or euros or credit cards, and who can travel freely, and those who are excluded from global processes, who live off what they can steal or barter or what they receive in humanitarian aid, whose movement is restricted by roadblocks, visas and the cost of travel, and who are prey to sieges, forced famines, landmines etc. (2007: 5)

Whereas old wars were fought by nation-states against each other, new war threatens to undermine the nation-state by challenging one of its central characteristics: the state monopoly of organized violence. The transnational connections involved in new wars challenge the state monopoly 'from above', while the 'privatization of violence' in paramilitary groups and involvement of organized crime threatens the state monopoly 'from below'. Kaldor's argument seems to be that we may be witnessing a reversal of the state-formation processes identified by Norbert Elias and Max Weber. During the emergence of the modern state, *centripetal* forces were in the ascendancy as the means of violence became increasingly centralized. However, since the late twentieth century, *centrifugal* forces are gaining the upper hand as the means of violence become distributed more widely amongst populations.

Critics of the new war thesis argue that some of its key arguments are exaggerated and that nation-states are likely to remain the key actors in wars and conflict. One group of critics argue that the apparently new elements of recent warfare can be found in previous times. For example, the historian Antony Beevor (2007) argues that the targeting of civilian populations can be seen in previous conflicts. In particular, during the Second World War, the targeting of civilians by all sides was a significant aspect of operations on the Eastern Front. Paul Hirst (2001) sees the activities of armed militias in the Greek/Turkish war of 1921–2 and the Spanish Civil War, 1936–9, as essentially similar to the recent low-intensity conflicts identified by Kaldor. Similarly, contemporary wars in the developing world can be seen as closer to conventional warfare than to low-intensity conflict.

Earlier European wars also similarly involved the use of famine as part of warfare as well as the plundering of resources and guerrilla tactics avoiding direct confrontations; all features described in the new war thesis as recent developments (Angstrom 2005).

Kaldor's reliance on the thesis of rapid globalization has also been criticized. Hirst argues that the new war thesis underplays the continuing significance of 'old' interstate wars, such as those between Iran and Iraq or the Arab/Israeli wars. For Hirst, the new war theory is far too dependent on the notion that 'globalization changes everything', when the evidence is that the nation-state is still the institution in which people invest their loyalty and ultimately rely on to protect their interests. This is an important point as it undermines the importance placed by Kaldor on international institutions in resolving conflicts. International humanitarian interventions, such as the UN's role in the Bosnian war (discussed above), are just as likely to reactivate old problems as they are to produce long-lasting solutions, given the involvement of 'old' nation-states with their historical alliances and enmities.

Perhaps it is too early to be sure that new wars will become the dominant type of war in the future. But assuming that the present trend towards the new war pattern continues, should we welcome the purported slow demise of interstate warfare? Certainly, it is unlikely that new wars will produce the sheer scale of death and destruction that the interstate wars of the twentieth century did. But in their place may arise a much more insidious privatization of the means of violence, which threatens to 'decivilize' societies by challenging the assumption that the state can guarantee a relatively pacified internal space for its citizens. The modern world will have to find ways of dealing with the more localized, but chronically destabilizing, conflicts of the future.

THINKING CRITICALLY

The conflicts in former Yugoslavia shocked 'civilized' Europeans, who had thought such genocidal violence was a thing of the past. Is there any evidence that contemporary 'nations without states' may be heading in a similar direction? What policies could nations and international bodies adopt that would help to prevent more 'new wars' in the future?

Terrorism

At around 8.45 a.m. on 11 September 2001, a passenger plane making a routine flight across the United States was hijacked by terrorists and flown into the North Tower of the World Trade Center in New York. Minutes later, another hijacked plane hit the South Tower, within an hour causing both buildings to collapse and killing thousands of people at the start of their working day. Approximately an hour later, a third plane was flown into the Pentagon, the headquarters of the US military near Washington, DC, killing hundreds more people. A fourth plane, said to be heading for the White House in Washington, DC, the seat of executive power in the USA, crashed into a field in rural Pennsylvania after passengers took on their hijackers. All the planes hijacked on 11 September were owned by one of two American companies: United or American Airlines. The targets selected by the hijackers – the World Trade Center, the Pentagon and the White House – were chosen for a purpose: to strike symbolically at the heart of American economic, military and political power.

President George W. Bush's response to the attacks was to declare a 'war on terror'. A month later came the first major military response in this 'war': an attack by a coalition of countries on Afghanistan in Asia in October 2001. Afghanistan, as we have seen above, was at the time ruled by a fundamentalist Islamic government, the Taliban, which had often supported the actions of al-Qaeda, the terrorist organization that carried out the 11 September attacks; it was also where many of the al-Qaeda members had trained.

The years following the attacks on New York and Washington saw numerous brutal acts of terrorism for which al-Qaeda claimed responsibility. An attack on a nightclub on the Indonesian island of Bali in October 2002 killed more than 200 people, many of them young tourists on holiday from nearby Australia. Bombs on a train in Madrid, Spain, during the morning rush hour killed around 200 commuters in March 2004. In London, 52 people died and several hundred more were injured after a coordinated series of explosions occurred on three underground trains and a bus in July 2005. Terrorism after 11 September 2001 reflects a new security environment in which a different form of terrorism, potentially more deadly than any before, became possible. It is to the concept of 'terrorism' that we now turn.

What is terrorism?

The word **terrorism** has its origins in the French Revolution of 1789. Thousands of people – originally aristocrats, but later many more ordinary citizens – were hunted down by the political authorities and executed by the guillotine. The term 'terror' was not invented by the revolutionaries themselves, but by the counter-revolutionaries: the people who despised the French Revolution and what it stood for, and who believed that the blood-letting which went on was a form of terrorizing the population (Laqueur 2003). 'Terror', in the sense of the use of violence to intimidate, was used extensively in the twentieth century – for example, by the Nazis in Germany or the Russian secret police under Stalin. However, this kind of use of violence also predates the origins of the term in the French Revolution.

Although the term 'terror' was not coined until the eighteenth century, the phenomenon of terrorizing people through violence

Al-Qaeda terrorists were responsible for attacks in the USA in 2001 and London in 2005. The group operates through a global activist network.

is a very old one. In ancient civilizations, when one army invaded a city held by the enemy, it was not at all uncommon for them to raze the entire city to the ground and kill all the men, women and children in the city. The point of this was not just physically to destroy the enemy, but also to create terror in those living in other cities and demonstrate the power which that terror represented. So the phenomenon of using violence with the idea of terrifying populations, especially civilian populations, is obviously older than the term.

Social scientists disagree over whether the term 'terrorism' can be a useful concept – that is, whether it can be used in a reasonably objective way; it is a notoriously difficult term to define. One issue concerns the shifting moral assessments that people make of terrorism and terrorists. It is often said that 'one person's terrorist is another person's freedom fighter'. It is also well known that people who were terrorists at one point themselves can later come to condemn terror just as violently as they practised it. It could be argued, for example, with some reservations, that the early history of the state of Israel was punctuated by terrorist activity; but in the twenty-first century the Israeli leadership is self-declaredly part and parcel of the 'war on terror', and regards terrorism as its primary enemy. It is only a few decades since the former South African leader Nelson Mandela was wildly reviled as a potentially violent terrorist, but he is now one of the most revered political figures of recent times. For terrorism to be a useful term, therefore, it must be freed as far as possible from moral valuations that shift across time and with the perspective of the observer.

A second issue in looking for a useful conception of terrorism concerns the role of the state. Can states be said to practise terrorism? Is there such a thing as 'state terrorism' or is this a contradiction in terms? After all, states have been responsible for far more deaths in human history than any other type of organization. States have brutally murdered civilian populations; in modern times, states have carried out something comparable to the razing of cities that occurred in traditional civilizations. For example, as we saw earlier, towards the end of the Second World War systematic fire bombing largely destroyed the German city of Dresden, where hundreds of thousands of civilians were killed. Many historians argue that the attack on Dresden happened at a point in the war when it was of no strategic advantage to the Allies. Critics of the Allies' action argue that the purpose of the destruction of Dresden was precisely to create terror and fear in German society and thereby weaken the resolve of its citizens to carry on the war. Is this terrorism?

Nonetheless, it is sensible to restrict the concept of terrorism to groups and organizations working *outside* the state. Otherwise, the concept becomes too close to that of war more generally. So, in spite of the problems noted above, many argue that a neutral definition can be found. For instance, a good attempt is, 'any action [by a non-state organization] . . . that is intended to cause death or serious bodily harm to civilians or non-combatants, when the purpose of such an act, by its nature or context, is to intimidate a population, or to compel a government or an international organization to do or to abstain from doing any act' (Panyarachun et al. 2004). In other words, terrorism concerns attacks on civilians designed to persuade a government to alter its policies, or to damage its standing in the world.

Old and new terrorism

Terrorism, as described above, can be distinguished from acts of violence designed to terrorize in previous periods of history, such as the ancient razing of cities. Terrorism is connected to changes in communications technology. To terrorize populations on a fairly wide spectrum, information about the violence has to reach those populations affected quite quickly. It was not until the rise of modern communications in the late nineteenth century that this became possible. With the invention of the electronic telegraph, instantaneous communication became possible, transcending time and space. Before this time, information could take days or even months to spread. For example, as we saw in the introduction to chapter 17 on the media, news of Abraham Lincoln's assassination took many days to reach the UK. Once instantaneous communication is possible, symbolic acts of terrorist violence can occur that can be projected at distance – it is not only the local population that knows about them.

Old terrorism

We can draw a distinction between old- and new-style terrorism. Old terrorism was dominant for most of the twentieth century and still exists today. This kind of terrorism is largely associated with the rise of nationalism and with the establishment of nations as sovereign, territorially bonded entities, which predominantly occurred from the late eighteenth century onwards in Europe, as we discussed above.

In all nations, boundaries are fixed somewhat arbitrarily, either as lines on a map, as they were by Western colonizers in Africa and Asia, or through conquest, battle and struggle. Ireland, for example, was brought into the United Kingdom in 1800, leading to independence struggles, which resulted in the partition of the country into North and South in the early 1920s. A patchwork of nations mapped out by colonial administrators, or founded on force, has led in various cases to nations that do not have their own state – that is, nations with a claim to having a common cultural identity, but without the territorial and state apparatus which normally belongs to a nation. Most forms of old-style terrorism are linked to nations without states.

The point of old-style terrorism is to establish states in areas where nations do not have control of the territory's state apparatus. This is true, for example, of Irish nationalists, such as the Irish Republican Army (IRA), and Basque nationalists, such as ETA, in Spain. The main issues are territorial integrity and identity in the formation of a state. Old-style terrorism is found where there are nations without states and where terrorists are prepared to use violence to achieve their ends. Old-style terrorism is fundamentally local because its ambitions are local. It wants to establish a state in a specific national area.

In the wake of the events of 11 September 2001, the Houses of Parliament in London installed permanent anti-terrorist barriers.

In recent years, old-style terrorism has also often had an international component to it as it draws on support from outside countries. For example, Libya, Syria and some Eastern European countries, as well as groups within the United States, have, in varying degrees, supported the terrorist acts of the IRA in Northern Ireland and Basque separatists in Spain. But although old-style terrorism might involve a wider global network of supporters for its funding or in filtering arms or drugs to buy weaponry, its ambitions are local.

As well as being limited in its ambitions, old-style terrorism is also limited in its use of violence. For example, although many people have lost their lives as the result of the conflict in Northern Ireland, the proportion of people killed as a result of terrorism since the 'Troubles' recommenced in the 1970s, including British soldiers, is on average less than those who have died in road accidents. With old-style terrorism, although the numbers of people maimed and killed are significant, the use of violence is limited, because the aims of this kind of terrorism are also relatively limited (fearsome and horrific though this violence still is).

In addition, the strong moral compulsion generated by national identity makes old-style terrorism difficult to combat, as British governments found over the conflict in Northern Ireland. Nationalism, as we have seen, has a strong energizing component to it. The myth of national identity can continue to fuel devotees of a movement that seeks to establish a state in cases where a nation exists without one. In cases where there are contested claims on the same territory, historical experience reveals that a settlement is often especially difficult to reach. This was true of the long struggle in Northern Ireland, where there were conflicting pressures from unionists who wanted to remain part of the UK and nationalist groups that wanted to be part of Ireland.

A fundamental distinction can be drawn between old- and new-style terrorism (Tan and Ramakrishna 2002). New-style terrorism is made possible by the changes in communications technology that are driving globalization, and it has a global spread. This type of terrorism is most famously associated with the Islamic fundamentalism of al-Qaeda (see 'Global Society 23.4'), although it is by no means limited to it. It is to a discussion of new-style terrorism that we now turn.

New terrorism

New terrorism differs from old terrorism in several ways – first, in respect of the scope of its claims. One of the distinguishing features of al-Qaeda's view of the world, for example, is that it has global geopolitical aims: it seeks to restructure world society. Parts of the al-Qaeda leadership have wanted to reconstruct an Islamic society stretching from the Indian subcontinent into Europe. This would involve establishing Islamic governments throughout the Middle East and the recapture of North Africa. Al-Qaeda's supporters argue that over the last millennium the West has expelled Islamic groups from those areas to which it has a legitimate claim. These areas include the Balkans and those parts of Spain that were previously ruled by the Moors (Muslims originally from North Africa who controlled much of Spain between the eighth and the fifteenth century). Large expanses of what we now regard as Europe were previously Islamic, ruled either by the Ottoman Empire or from North Africa. Al-Qaeda aims to re-establish the global role of Islam in these regions and areas. So whereas old-style terrorism is local and linked to particular states – normally quite small states – new-style terrorism is global in its ambitions. It wants to reverse the tide of world power.

There is a characteristic tension between modernism and anti-modernism in the world-view of al-Qaeda and similar terrorist organizations. In attempting to re-establish the Islamic dominance of large parts of Europe, the Middle East and Asia that existed in an earlier age, they make

Global Society 23.4   What is al-Qaeda?

Al-Qaeda's origins and links

Al-Qaeda, meaning 'the base', was created in 1989 as Soviet forces withdrew from Afghanistan and Osama Bin Laden and his colleagues began looking for new jihads (a term loosely translated as holy struggle or war). The organization grew out of the network of Arab volunteers who had gone to Afghanistan in the 1980s to fight under the banner of Islam against Soviet communism. During the anti-Soviet jihad, Bin Laden and his fighters received American and Saudi funding. Some analysts believe Bin Laden himself had security training from the CIA. The 'Arab Afghans', as they became known, were battle-hardened and highly motivated.

In the early 1990s, al-Qaeda operated in Sudan. After 1996, its headquarters and about a dozen training camps moved to Afghanistan, where Bin Laden forged a close relationship with the Taliban. The US campaign in Afghanistan, which started in late 2001, dispersed the organization and drove it underground as its personnel were attacked and its bases and training camps destroyed.

Cells across the world

The organization is thought to operate in 40–50 countries, not only in the Middle East and Asia but also in North America and Europe. In Western Europe there have been known or suspected cells in London, Hamburg, Milan and Madrid. These have been important centres for recruitment, fundraising and planning operations.

For training, the group favours lawless areas where it can operate freely and in secret. These are believed to have included Somalia, Yemen and Chechnya, as well as mountainous areas of Afghanistan. There have also been reports of a secret training camp on one of the islands of Indonesia.

Unlike the tightly-knit groups of the past, such as the Red Brigades in Italy or the Abu Nidal group in the Middle East, al-Qaeda is loosely knit. It operates across continents as a chain of interlocking networks. Individual groups or cells appear to have a high degree of autonomy, raising their own money, often through petty crime, and making contact with other groups only when necessary.

Defining al-Qaeda?

This loose connection between groups has raised a question of definition. When we talk about al-Qaeda, do we refer to an actual organization or are we now talking about something closer to an idea?

Attacks like the May 2003 bombings in Riyadh and the attack on Israeli tourists in Mombasa in 2002 are widely attributed to al-Qaeda. But were these attacks in any way planned or financed or organized by Bin Laden or the organization he is still believed to lead?

Some analysts have suggested that the word 'al-Qaeda' is now used to refer to a variety of groups connected by little more than shared aims, ideals and methods. We do, however, know that several radical groups are or have been formally affiliated with al-Qaeda. The most important is the radical wing of the Egyptian group Islamic Jihad, whose members took refuge in Afghanistan and merged with al-Qaeda. Its leader is Ayman al-Zawahri, a ruthless Egyptian believed to be the brains behind al-Qaeda and the mastermind of many of its most infamous operations. These include the attacks on two US embassies in Africa in 1998 and the 9/11 attacks in New York and Washington.

There are also believed to be links with militant Kashmiri groups; the Islamic Movement of Uzbekistan, or IMU; the Abu Sayyaf group in the Philippines; and the GIA, or Armed Islamic Group, in Algeria and its radical offshoot known as the Salafist group, or GSPC.

Source: BBC News, 20 July 2004 © bbc.co.uk/news

great use of modern communications in order to criticize modernity, and attempt to reverse what they see as the moral degeneracy of modern Western society (Gray 2003).

Second, new-style terrorism differs from old-style terrorism in terms of its organizational structure. Although careful not to take this parallel too far, the sociologist Mary Kaldor has pointed out several similarities between the infrastructure of new terrorist groups, notably al-Qaeda, and international non-governmental organizations (NGOs), such as Oxfam or Friends of the Earth.

 NGOs are discussed in more detail in chapter 18, 'Organizations and Networks'.

In its organizational structure, al-Qaeda deploys the same global forms of organization as do many NGOs. Both new terrorist organizations and NGOs like Friends of the Earth are driven by a sense of mission and commitment that allows a fairly loose global organization to flourish (Glasius et al. 2002).

Both NGOs and new terrorist organizations are based on networks, of the kinds discussed by Manuel Castells (see chapter 18). They are highly decentralized structures. There is a lot of autonomy in local cells and these can reproduce without necessarily having any strong direction from the centre. The US attacks on Afghanistan in 2001 substantially weakened al-Qaeda's leadership, but the organization remains strong because of its adherents' moral convictions. This drives a sense of mission that can keep cells functioning even when some aspects of the overall organization have been weakened or broken.

Terrorist organization and NGOs also have a global spread of supporters in many countries. Experts on terrorism disagree over the extent to which al-Qaeda survived the American-led attack on Afghanistan in 2001, but it has been estimated that there are still al-Qaeda cells in around 60 countries, drawing on approximately 20,000 people who are willing to die violently for the cause, most of whom exist semi-autonomously from the centre.

It can also be noted that both new terrorist groups and NGOs work with states. No NGO could flourish completely as a non-state organization. They all have some contacts and support from states and this is also true, Kaldor argues, of new-style terror-

ist organizations. The Libyan involvement in the bombing of a passenger plane that landed on the Scottish village of Lockerbie in 1988 provides one example of this. Of course, the analogy between new terrorist organization and NGOs cannot be taken too far; but in their organizational structures and shared sense of admittedly very different missions, al-Qaeda could be seen as a malign kind of NGO.

Sutton and Vertigans (2006) have argued that, in fact, al-Qaeda exhibits many organizational similarities with the new social movements (NSMs) of the 1970s and '80s. In particular, its loose forms of organization and transnational networks bear comparison with non-violent NSMs such as environmentalism and recent anti-globalization movements. The extreme violence used by al-Qaeda has often been targeted at highly symbolic sites as a way of demonstrating that the West, and the USA in particular, is weak. These attacks also encourage others to join their fight. Whilst NSMs have made use of symbolic, non-violent direct actions, al-Qaeda has instead used symbolic violence to further their cause.

 See chapter 22, 'Politics, Government and Social Movements', for more on NSMs.

The third and last way in which old- and new-style terrorism differ is over means. Old-style terrorism, as we saw above, had relatively limited objectives, and as a result the violence involved was normally fairly limited too. New-style terrorism seems much more ruthless in the means it is prepared to use. Al-Qaeda websites, for example, talk in extremely destructive language of 'the enemy' – that is, principally the United States, but to some extent the West as a whole. These will often explicitly say that terrorist acts should be carried out that kill as many people as possible. This ruthlessness is evident, for example, in the founding statement of al-Qaeda from 1998:

The ruling to kill the Americans and their allies – civilians and military – is an individual duty for every Muslim who can do it in any country in which it is possible to do it, in order to liberate the [Muslim holy sites of the] al-Aqsa Mosque and the Holy Mosque [Mecca] from their grip, and in order for their armies to move out of all the lands of Islam, defeated and unable to threaten any Muslim. (Cited in Halliday 2002: 219)

This is very different from the more limited use of violent means characteristic of old-style terrorism. There are some cases where the two overlap, as in Chechnya in the former Soviet Union, for example, which turned from a separatist struggle to a recruiting ground for newer forms of terrorism.

THINKING CRITICALLY

It has been suggested that al-Qaeda is, at its roots, an ideology rather than an organization or group of people. If this is true, what is the likelihood that the 'war on terror' will be successful? In what ways could the emergence of al-Qaeda and its associated groups be seen as evidence of an impending 'clash of civilizations (Huntington 1996)? Refer to chapter 16, 'Religion', for Huntington's ideas.

War and terrorism in a global age

How should we respond to the threat of new-style terrorism and the localized new wars, which clearly raise difficult questions for political sociologists? The coalition that attacked Afghanistan in 2001 did destroy some of the al-Qaeda terrorist networks. Yet despite some successes against new-style terrorism through conventional warfare, critics are surely right to argue that in many cases the levels of violence, aims and organizational structure of new-style terrorist groups differentiate them from conventional enemies such as hostile nation-states. This has led some sociologists and political scientists to question the concept of a 'war on terrorism'. The war on Iraq launched in 2003 was in part justified, especially in the USA, by concerns that Iraq was developing weapons that would be used to supply terrorist organizations. However, the conventional military approach to the Iraq invasion has come up against the new forms of war and terrorism, with no immediate sign that the older approach will be able to achieve a decisive victory in the way that wars were previously concluded.

The debate about whether terrorism can be tackled through conventional warfare raises further difficult questions regarding the relationship between terrorism and nation-states, like Afghanistan, that have supported it. In turn, this leads to questions about global governance. In a global age, what international support and proof is needed in order to act to prevent a perceived threat? And what are the best institutions to deal with a global terrorist threat?

Mary Kaldor (2007), like Ulrich Beck and others, argues for a 'cosmopolitan' approach to the problems associated with new wars. Cosmopolitan thinkers argue that all individuals should ideally be treated in equal ways, regardless of where they live in the world. Of course, this was considered a utopian dream in an age of strong nation-states, which enforced national boundaries against potential threats. However, as the nation-state begins to lose its central place, it becomes possible to see international institutions emerging that may, in time, be able to make the vision of a cosmopolitan democracy a reality. In her study of new wars, Kaldor sees some evidence of this in the involvement of the United Nations, African Union, European Union and others in peacekeeping missions, relief work and as mediators in negotiations between warring parties. However, such efforts are still in their historically early stages and, so far, have tended to be engaged in only *after* conflicts have started or ended. The goal of making use of such institutions to *prevent* new wars and terrorism remains a long way off.

Summary points

1. Nationalism refers to a set of symbols and beliefs that provide the sense of being part of a single political community: a nation. It emerged alongside the development of the modern state. Although the founders of sociology believed that nationalism would disappear in industrial societies, at the start of the twenty-first century it seems to be flourishing.

2. 'Nations without states' refers to cases in which a national population lacks political sovereignty over the area it claims as its own. In many nations, the desire to create a state often becomes a political ambition, which, when refused or thwarted, can take the form of a guerrilla campaign to force a separation.

3. War is the clash of two organized armed forces that seek to destroy each other's power and especially their will to resist, principally by killing members of the opposing force. Wars have often erupted between politically bounded nation-states, and in the twentieth century, total wars involved the mobilization of entire populations.

4. 'New' war is a type of war that developed in the late twentieth century. New wars are localized conflicts that also involve transnational connections, internationally organized criminal networks and large-scale violations of basic human rights. New wars threaten to destabilize societies and they also challenge the nation-state's monopolization of the means of physical violence.

5. Genocide can be defined as a form of war in which civilian social groups are the enemy, rather than armed forces, so that a state or other armed power organization attempts to destroy social groups by violent and coercive means The attempt by the Nazis to exterminate Jewish populations from Europe – known as the Holocaust – is the most well-known example, though there have been a number in recent years including genocides in the Rwandan civil war of 1990–3 and the Bosnian war of 1992–5. In the era of new wars, episodes of genocide may be set to increase.

6. Terrorism is any action by a non-state organization that is intended to cause death or serious bodily harm to civilians or non-combatants, aimed at intimidating a population or forcing a government or international organization to do or not do something.

7. Old terrorism is most often associated with nations without states, in which groups seeking to force independence in a new nation-state adopt violent methods as part of their campaign. New terrorism is shaped by globalization and differs from old-style terrorism in its scope, organization structure and means. New terrorism aims to restructure global society and is exemplified by the international network, al-Qaeda.

8. Cosmopolitanism views the displacement of the nation-state as presenting an opportunity for international institutions to play more active roles in conflict prevention and resolution. Ultimately, their goal is a global cosmopolitan democracy of equal citizens. However, this has to be seen as a long-term project.

Further reading

An excellent entry point into debates on nations and nationalism is Steve Grosby's *Nationalism: A Very Short Introduction* (Oxford: Oxford University Press, 2005), which sets national identities in their historical contexts. Jyoti Puri's *Encountering Nationalism* (Oxford: Blackwell Publishing, 2003) is also a very good student textbook. A more theoretical approach can then be tackled with Graham Day and Andrew Thompson's *Theorizing Nationalism* (Basingstoke: Palgrave Macmillan, 2004).

On war and genocide, sociological studies are not numerous. However, some of the best work in this area is written with great clarity. Hence, Martin Shaw's comprehensive *War and Genocide: Organized Killing in Modern Society* (Cambridge: Polity, 2003) is hard to better and covers a range of historical examples. Mary Kaldor's *New and Old Wars: Organized Violence in a Global Era*, 2nd edn (Cambridge: Polity, 2007) makes the case that globalization is radically changing the practice of war.

By way of contrast, books on terrorism, especially on al-Qaeda and its so-called, 'Islamic terrorism', could fill many shelves. For newcomers to sociology, though, it is probably better to begin with a general introduction to the phenomenon of terrorism such as Gus Martin's *Understanding Terrorism: Challenges, Perspectives, and Issues, Second Edition* (London and New York: Sage Publications, 2007). Then the arguments around old and new terrorism can be explored in a very good collection edited by Andrew Tan and Kumar Ramakrishna, *The New Terrorism: Anatomy, Trends and Counter-Strategies* (Singapore: Eastern Universities Press, 2002).

Internet links

Internet Modern History – Historical view of nationalism:
www.fordham.edu/halsall/mod/modsbook17.html

The Nationalism Project – contains some good scholarly resources on nations and national-ism):
www.nationalismproject.org/what.htm

Web Genocide Documentation Centre – based at the University of the West of England; the site offers resources on genocide, war crimes and episodes of mass killing:
www.ess.uwe.ac.uk/genocide.htm

CSTPV – Centre for the Study of Terrorism and Political Violence at the University of St Andrew in Scotland, established in 1994; many links here to terror-related websites:
www.st-andrews.ac.uk/~cstpv/

The Terrorism Research Centre – based in Northern Virginia, USA; founded in 1996, an independent research centre on terrorism and security:
www.terrorism.com/

Oxford Research Group – UK-based, this site has lots of useful academic material and commentaries on global security issues:
www.oxfordresearchgroup.org.uk/

The Bulletin Online – global security news and analysis:
www.thebulletin.org/

References

Aaltio, I. and Mills, A. J. (eds) (2002) *Gender, Identity and the Culture of Organizations* (London: Routledge).

Abbott, D. (2001) 'The Death of Class?'. *Sociology Review* 11 (November).

Abeles, R. and Riley, M. W. (1987) 'Longevity, Social Structure and Cognitive Aging', in C. Schooler and K. W. Schaie (eds), *Cognitive Functioning and Social Structure Over the Lifecourse* (Norwood, NJ: Ablex).

Abel-Smith, B. and Townsend, P. (1965) *The Poor and the Poorest: A New Analysis of the Ministry of Labour's Family Expenditure Survey of 1953–54 and 1960* (London: Bell).

Adorno, T. (1976 [1950]) *Introduction to the Sociology of Music* (New York: The Seabury Press).

Agyeman, J., Bullard, R. D. and Evans, B. (2003) *Just Sustainabilities: Development in an Unequal World* (London: Earthscan).

Ahmed, A. S. and Donnan, H. (1994) 'Islam in the Age of Postmodernity', in A. S. Ahmed and D. Hastings (eds), *Islam, Globalization and Postmodernity* (London: Routledge).

Akintoye, S. (1976) *Emergent African States: Topics in Twentieth Century African History* (London: Longman).

Alatas, S. F. (2006) 'Ibn Khaldun and Contemporary Sociology', *International Sociology*, 21(6).

Albrow, M. (1997) *The Global Age: State and Society Beyond Modernity* (Stanford, CA: Stanford University Press).

Aldrich, H. E and Marsden, P. V. (1988) 'Environments and Organizations', in N. J. Smelser (ed.), *Handbook of Sociology* (Newbury Park, CA: Sage).

Alexander, J. C. (1985) *Neofunctionalism* (London: Routledge).

Alexander, J. C. (ed.) (1997) *Neofunctionalism and After: Collected Readings* (Oxford: Blackwell).

Alexander, Z. (1999) *The Department of Health Study of Black, Asian and Ethnic Minority Issues* (London: Department of Health).

Allen, M. P. (1981) 'Managerial Power and Tenure in the Large Corporation', *Social Forces*, 60.

Alvesson, M. and Willmott, H. (eds) (2003) *Studying Management Critically* (London: Sage).

Amnesty International (2002) 'State Control of the Internet in China', 27 February.

Amnesty International (2004) 'People's Republic of China Controls Tighten as Internet Activism Grows', 28 January.

Amsden, A. H. (1989) *Asia's Next Giant: South Korea and Late Industrialization* (New York: Oxford University Press).

Amsden, A. H., Kochanowicz, J. and Taylor, L. (1994) *The Market Meets Its Match: Restructuring the Economies of Eastern Europe* (Cambridge, MA: Harvard University Press).

Anable, J. (2005) 'Complacent Car Addicts or Aspiring Environmentalists? Identifying Travel Behaviour Segments Using Attitude Theory', *Transport Policy*, 12(1).

Anderson, B. (2006) *Imagined Communities: Reflections on the Origin and Spread of Nationalism*, rev. edn (London: Verso Books).

Anderson, E. (1990) *Streetwise: Race, Class, and Change in an Urban Community* (Chicago, IL: University of Chicago Press).

Anderson, F. S. (1977) 'TV Violence and Viewer Aggression: Accumulation of Study Results 1956–1976', *Public Opinion Quarterly*, 41.

Anderson, S. and Cavanagh, J. (2000) *Top 200: The Rise of Corporate Global Power*, 4 December (Institute for Policy Studies).

Andrews, D. and Leigh, A. (2007) *More Inequality, Less Social Mobility* (Available at the Social Science Research Network: http://ssrn.com/abstract=1011695).

Ang, I. (1985) *Watching Dallas: Soap Opera and the Melodramatic Imagination* (London: Methuen).

Angstrom, J. (2005) 'Introduction: Debating the Nature of Modern War', in I. Duyvesteyn and J. Angstrom (eds), *Rethinking the Nature of War* (London and New York: Frank Cass).

Anheier, H., Glasius, M. and Kaldor, M. (eds) (2002) *Global Civil Society 2002* (Oxford: Oxford University Press).

Annenberg Center (2003) 'Parents' Use of the V-Chip to Supervise Children's Television Use' (University of Pennsylvania).

APACS (2008) (UK) *Fraud: The Facts 2008* (London: APACS (Administration) Ltd).

Appadurai, A. (1986) 'Introduction: Commodities and the Politics of Value', in A. Appadurai (ed.), *The Social Life of Things* (Cambridge: Cambridge University Press).

Appelbaum, R. P. and Christerson, B. (1997) 'Cheap Labor Strategies and Export-Oriented Industrialization: Some Lessons from the East Asia/Los Angeles Apparel Connection', *International Journal of Urban and Regional Research*, 21(2).

Appelbaum, R. P. and Henderson, J. (eds) (1992) *States and Development in the Asian Pacific Rim* (Newbury Park, CA: Sage).

Apter, T. (1994) *Working Women Don't Have Wives: Professional Success in the 1990s* (New York: St Martin's Press).

Arber, S. and Ginn, J. (2004) 'Ageing and Gender: Diversity and Change', *Social Trends* 34 (London: HMSO).

Arber, S. and Thomas, H. (2005) 'From Women's Health to a Gender Analysis of Health', in W. Cockerham (ed.), *The Blackwell Companion to Medical Sociology* (Oxford: Blackwell).

Arber, S., Davidson, K. and Ginn, J. (eds) (2003) *Gender and Ageing: Changing Roles and Relationships* (Buckingham: Open University Press).

Ariès, P. (1965) *Centuries of Childhood* (New York: Random House).

ARIS (2001) *American Religious Identification Survey 2001* (The Graduate Center of the City University of New York).

Arnot, M. (2001) 'Bernstein's Sociology of Pedagogy: Female Dialogues and Feminist Elaborations', in K. Weiler (ed.), *Feminist Engagements: Reading, Resisting and Revisioning Male Theorists in Education and Cultural Studies* (New York: Routledge).

Arrighi, G. (1994) *The Long Twentieth Century: Money, Power, and the Origin of Our Times* (New York: Verso).

Ashkanasy, N. M., Wilderom, C. P. M. and Peterson, M. F. (eds) (2000) *The Handbook of Organizational Culture and Climate* (Thousand Oaks, CA: Sage Publishing).

Ashton, D. N. (1986) *Unemployment Under Capitalism: The Sociology of British and American Labour Markets* (London: Wheatsheaf).

Ashworth, A. E. (1980) *Trench Warfare, 1914–1918* (London: Macmillan).

Ashworth, J. and Farthing, I. (2007) *Churchgoing in the UK: A Research Report from Tearfund on Church Attendance in the UK* (Teddington: Tearfund).

Askwith, R. (2003) 'Contender', *Observer*, 6 April.

Atchley, R. C. (2000) *Social Forces and Aging: An Introduction to Social Gerontology* (Belmont, CA: Wadsworth).

Atkinson, A. B. (2003) *Income Inequality in OECD Countries: Data and Explanations*, CESifo Working Paper No. 881 (Hamburg: Centre for Economic Studies/Institute for Economic Research).

Attali, J. (1985) *Noise: The Political Economy of Music* (Minneapolis: University of Minnesota Press).

Baali. F. (2005) *The Science of Human Social Organization: Conflicting Views on Ibn Khaldun's (1332–1406) Ilm al-umran* (Lewiston/NY: Edwin Mellen Press).

Back, L. (1995) *Ethnicities, Multiple Racisms: Race and Nation in the Lives of Young People* (London: UCL Press).

Bahrami, H. and Evans, S. (1995) 'Flexible Recycling and High-Technology Entrepreneurship', *California Management Review*, 22.

Bailey, J. M. (1993) 'Heritable Factors Influence Sexual Orientation in Women', *Archives of General Psychiatry*, 50.

Bailey, J. M. and Pillard, R. C. (1991) 'A Genetic Study of Male Sexual Orientation', *Archives of General Psychiatry*, 48.

Baker, D. and Weisbrot, M. (1999) *Social Security: The Phony Crisis* (Chicago, IL: University of Chicago Press).

Bales, K. (1999) *Disposable People: New Slavery in the Global Economy* (Berkeley and London: University of California Press).

Balmer, R. (1989) *Mine Eyes Have Seen the Glory: A Journey into the Evangelical Subculture in America* (New York: Oxford University Press).

Balswick, J. O. (1983) 'Male Inexpressiveness', in K. Soloman and N. B. Levy (eds), *Men in Transition: Theory and Therapy* (New York: Plenum Press).

Baltes, P. B. and Schaie, K. W. (1977) 'The Myth of the Twilight Years', in S. Zarit (ed.), *Readings in Aging and Death: Contemporary Perspectives* (New York: Harper and Row).

Bamforth, A. (1999) 'The Restive Season', *Guardian*, 15 December.

Barash, D. (1979) *The Whisperings Within* (New York: Harper and Row).

Barker, M. (1981) *The New Racism: Conservatives and the Ideology of the Tribe* (Frederick MD: University Publications of America).

Barker, R. (1997) *Political Ideas in Modern Britain* (London and New York: Routledge).

Barnes, C. (1991) *Disabled People in Britain and Discrimination* (London: Hurst and Co).

Barnes, C. (2002) *Disability Studies* (Cambridge: Polity).

Barnes, C. (2003) *Disability Studies: What's the Point?* (Lancaster: University of Lancaster).

Barnet, R. J. and Cavanagh, J. (1994) *Global Dreams: Imperial Corporations and the New World Order* (New York: Simon and Schuster).

Barnett, A. (2007) *Global Society: The Three Faces of the World Social Forum*, 30 January. Available at: www.opendemocracy.net/globalization-protest/wsf_faces_4297.jsp.

Barret-Ducrocq, F. (1992) *Love in the Time of Victoria: Sexuality and Desire Among Working-Class Men and Women in Nineteenth-Century London* (Harmondsworth: Penguin).

Barry, A. -M. and Yuill, C. (2007) *Understanding the Sociology of Health: An Introduction* (London: Sage).

Barth, F. (1969) *Ethnic Groups and Boundaries* (London: Allen and Unwin).

Basu, A., (ed.) (1995) *The Challenge of Local Feminisms: Women's Movements in Global Perspective* (Boulder, CO: Westview).

Baudrillard, J. (1983) *Simulations* (New York: SemioTex(e)).

Baudrillard, J. (1988) *Selected Writings* (Cambridge: Polity).

Baudrillard, J. (2004 [1991]) *The Gulf War Did Not Take Place* (Power Publications).

Bauman, Z. (1989) *Modernity and the Holocaust* (Cambridge: Polity).

Bauman, Z. (1992) *Intimations of Postmodernity* (London: Routledge).

Bauman, Z. (1997) *Postmodernity and its Discontents* (Cambridge: Polity.

Bauman, Z. (2000) *Liquid Modernity* (Cambridge: Polity).

Bauman, Z. (2003) *Liquid Love: On the Frailty of Human Bonds* (Cambridge: Polity).

Bauman, Z. (2007) *Liquid Times: Living in an Age of Uncertainty* (Cambridge: Polity).

BBC (2001) 'Murdoch Heads Media Power List', 16 July. Available at http://news.bbc.co.uk/1/hi/entertainment/1441094.stm.

BBC (2002) 'Falwell "Sorry" for Mohammed Remark', 13 October. Available at http://news.bbc.co.uk/1/hi/world/americas/2323897.stm.

BBC (2004a) 'Mauritania's "wife-fattening" farm', 26 January. Available at: http://news.bbc.co.uk/1/hi/world/africa/3429903.stm.

BBC (2004b) 'Official Downloads Chart Launches', 28 June. Available at: http://news.bbc.co.uk/1/hi/entertainment/music/3846455.stm.

BBC (2004c) 'Q&A: Will I Be Sued for Music-Swapping?', 7 October. Available at: http://news.bbc.co.uk/1/hi/entertainment/music/3722622.stm.

BBC (2004d) 'UK Music to Sue Online "Pirates"', 7 October. Available at: http://news.bbc.co.uk/1/hi/entertainment/music/3722428.stm.

BBC (2005) 'Violent Crime "Rise" Sparks Row', 21 April. Available at: http://news.bbc.co.uk/1/hi/uk_politics/vote_2005/frontpage/4467569.stm.

BBC (2006) 'China Braced for Pensioner Boom', 16 October. Available at: http://news.bbc.co.uk/1/hi/world/asia-pacific/6048074.stm.

BBC (2008) 'Kosovo MPs Proclaim Independence', 17 February. Available at: http://news.bbc.co.uk/1/hi/world/europe/7249034.stm.

Beall, J. (1998) 'Why Gender Matters', *Habitat Debate*, 4(4).

Beasley, C. (1999) *What Is Feminism?* (Thousand Oaks, CA, and London: Sage).

Beck, U. (1992) *Risk Society: Towards a New Modernity* (London: Sage).

Beck, U. (1999) *World Risk Society* (Cambridge: Polity).

Beck, U. (2002) *Ecological Politics in an Age of Risk* (Cambridge: Polity).

Beck, U. (2006) *Cosmopolitan Vision* (Cambridge: Polity).

Beck, U. and Beck-Gernsheim, E. (1995) *The Normal Chaos of Love* (Cambridge: Polity).

Beck, U. and Grande, E. (2007) *Cosmopolitan Europe* (Cambridge: Polity).

Becker, H. (1950) *Through Values to Social Interpretation* (Durham, NC: Duke University Press).

Becker, H. S. (1963) *Outsiders: Studies in the Sociology of Deviance* (New York: Free Press).

Becker, H. S. (1982) *Art Worlds* (Berkeley: University of California Press).

Beevor, A. (2007) *Berlin: The Downfall 1945* (London: Penguin Books).

Bell, A., Weinberg, M. and Hammersmith, S. (1981) *Sexual Preference: Its Development in Men and Women* (Bloomington: Indiana University Press).

Bell, D. (1997) 'The World and the United States in 2013', *Daedelus*, 115 (Summer).

Bell, M. M. (2004) *An Invitation to Environmental Sociology*, 2nd edn (Newbury Park, CA: Pine Forge Press).

Benhabib, S. (2006) *Another Cosmopolitanism: Hospitality, Sovereignty and Democratic Iterations* (New York: Oxford University Press).

Bennett, K. and LeCompte, M. (1990) *How Schools Work: A Sociological Analysis of Education* (New York: Longman).

Benton, T. (1994) *Natural Relations: Ecology, Animal Rights and Social Justice* (London: Verso Press).

Beresford, P. and Wallcraft, J. (1997) 'Psychiatric System Survivors and Emancipatory Research: Issues, Overlaps and Differences', in C. Barnes and G. Mercer (eds), *In Doing Disability Research* (Leeds: The Disability Press).

Berger, P. L. (1963) *Invitation to Sociology* (Garden City, NY: Anchor Books).

Berger, P. L. (1967) *The Sacred Canopy: Elements of a Sociological Theory of Religion* (Garden City, NY: Anchor Books).

Berger, P. L. (1986) *The Capitalist Revolution: Fifty Propositions about Prosperity, Equality, and Liberty* (New York: Basic Books).

Berger, P. L. and Luckmann, T. (1966) *The Social Construction of Reality: A Treatise in the Sociology of Knowledge* (Garden City, NY: Doubleday).

Berle, A. and Means, G. C. (1997 [1932]) *The Modern Corporation and Private Property* (Buffalo, NY: Heim).

Berman, M. (1983) *All That Is Solid Melts Into Air: The Experience of Modernity* (London: Verso Books).

Bernstein, B. (1975) *Class, Codes and Control* (London: Routledge).

Bernstein, B. (1990) *Class, Codes and Control*. Vol. 4: *The Structuring of Pedagogic Discourse* (London: Routledge).

Bertelson, D. (1986) *Snowflakes and Snowdrifts: Individualism and Sexuality in America* (Lanham, MD: University Press of America).

Berthoud, R. (1998) *The Incomes of Ethnic Minorities* (Colchester: University of Essex, Institute for Social and Economic Research).

Birren, J. E. and Schaie, K. W. (eds) (2001) *Handbook of the Psychology of Aging*, 5th edn (San Diego, CA, and London: Academic Press).

Blackburn, R. (2002) *Banking on Death* (London: Verso).

Blair, T. (2004) Speech by the Prime Minister at the Launch of the Climate Group, 1 August 2005. Available at: www.number-10.gov.uk/output/page5716.asp.

Blanden, J., Goodman, A., Gregg, P., et al. (2002) *Changes in Intergenerational Mobility in Britain* (London: Centre for the Economics of Education, London School of Economics and Political Science).

Blankenhorn, D. (1995) *Fatherless America* (New York: Basic Books).

Blau, P. M. (1963) *The Dynamics of Bureaucracy* (Chicago, IL: University of Chicago).

Blau, P. M. and Duncan, O. D. (1967) *The American Occupational Structure* (New York: Wiley).

Blauner, R. (1964) *Alienation and Freedom* (Chicago, IL: University of Chicago Press).

Blinder, A. S. (2006) 'Fear of Offshoring', *Foreign Affairs*, 85(2), March/April.

Block, F. (1990) *Postindustrial Possibilities: A Critique of Economic Discourse* (Berkeley: University of California Press).

Blofeld, J. (2003) *The Independent Inquiry into the Death of David Bennett* (Norfolk, Suffolk and Cambridgeshire Strategic Health Authority).

Blondet, C. (1995) 'Out of the Kitchen and Onto the Streets: Women's Activism in Peru', in A. Basu (ed.), *The Challenge of Local Feminisms* (Boulder, CO: Westview).

Blumer, H. (1933) *Movies and Conduct* (New York, NY: Macmillan).

Blumer, H. (1969) *Symbolic Interactionism: Perspective and Method* (Englewood Cliffs, NJ: Prentice Hall).

Bobak, L. (1996) 'India's Tiny Slaves', *Ottawa Sun*, 23 October.

Boden, D. and Molotch, H. (1994) 'The Compulsion of Proximity', in D. Boden and R. Friedland (eds), *Nowhere Space, Time, and Modernity* (Berkeley: University of California Press).

Bonacich, E. and Appelbaum, R. P. (2000) *Behind the Label: Inequality in the Los Angeles Garment Industry* (Berkeley: University of California Press)

Bonney, N. (1992) 'Theories of Social Class and Gender', *Sociology Review*, 1.

Boocock, S. (1980) *Sociology of Education: An Introduction*, 2nd edn (Boston, MA: Houghton Mifflin).

Bookchin, M. (1986) *The Modern Crisis* (Philadelphia: New Society Publishers).

Boorstin, D. (1961) *The Image: A Guide to Pseudo-Events in America* (New York: Vintage).

Booth, A. (1977) 'Food Riots in the North-West of England, 1770–1801', *Past and Present*, 77.

Borja, J. and Castells, M. (1997) *Local and Global: The Management of Cities in the Information Age* (London: Earthscan).

Born, G. (2004) *Uncertain Vision: Birt, Dyke and the Reinvention of the BBC* (London: Secker & Warburg).

Boswell, J. (1995) *The Marriage of Likeness: Same-Sex Unions in Pre-Modern Europe* (London: Fontana).

Bourdieu, P. (1986) *Distinction: A Social Critique of the Judgements of Taste* (London: Routledge and Kegan Paul).

Bourdieu, P. (1988) *Language and Symbolic Power* (Cambridge: Polity).

Bourdieu, P. (1990) *The Logic of Practice* (Cambridge: Polity).

Bourdieu, P. (1992) *An Invitation to Reflexive Sociology* (Chicago, IL: University of Chicago Press).

Bourdieu, P. (2001) *Masculine Domination* (Cambridge: Polity).

Bourdieu, P. and Passeron, J.-C. (1977) *Reproduction in Education, Society and Culture* (London: Sage).

Bowlby, J. (1953) *Child Care and the Growth of Love* (Harmondsworth: Penguin).

Bowles, S. and Gintis, H. (1976) *Schooling in Capitalist America: Educational Reform and Contradictions of Economic Life* (New York: Basic Books).

Box, S. (1983) *Power, Crime and Mystification* (London: Tavistock).

Boyer, R. and Drache, D. (1996) *States against Markets: The Limits of Globalization* (London: Routledge).

Brannen, J. (2003) 'The Age of Beanpole Families', *Sociology Review*, 13(1).

Brass, D. J. (1985) 'Men's and Women's Networks: A Study of Interaction Patterns and Influence in an Organization', *Academy of Management Journal*, 28.

Braun, B. and Castree, N. (eds) (1998) *Remaking Reality: Nature at the Millennium* (London: Routledge).

Braverman, H. (1974) *Labor and Monopoly Capital: The Degradation of Work in the Twentieth Century* (New York: Monthly Review Press).

Bread for the World Institute (2005) Hunger Basics. Available at: www.bread.org/learn/hunger-basics/.

Breen, R. and Goldthorpe, J. H. (1999) 'Class Inequality and Meritocracy: A Critique of Saunders and an Alternative Analysis', *British Journal of Sociology*, 50.

Brennan, T. (1988) 'Controversial Discussions and Feminist Debate', in N. Segal and E. Timms (eds), *The Origins and Evolution of Psychoanalysis* (New Haven, CT: Yale University Press).

Brewer, M., Browne, J. and Sutherland, H. (2006) *Micro-simulating Child Poverty in 2010 and 2020* (York: Joseph Rowntree Foundation).

Brewer, M., Goodman, A., Muriel, A. and Sibieta, L. (2007) *Poverty and Inequality in the UK, 2007* (London: Institute for Fiscal Studies).

Brewer, R. M. (1993) 'Theorizing Race, Class and Gender: The New Scholarship of Black Feminist Intellectuals and Black Women's Labor', in S. M. James and A. P. A. Busia (eds), *Theorizing Black Feminisms: The Visionary Pragmatism of Black Women* (New York: Routledge).

Brierly, P. (2006) 'Pulling Out of the Nosedive: 2005 English Church Census', *Religious Trends*, 6.

Brinkley, I. and Lee, N. (2007) *The Knowledge Economy in Europe – A Report Prepared for the 2007 EU Spring Council* (London: The Work Foundation).

Brisenden, S. (2005) Poems for Perfect People. Available at: www.leeds.ac.uk/disability-studies/archiveuk/brisenden/Poems.pdf.

Brookes, G. and Barfoot, P. (2005) 'GM Crops: The Global Economic and Environmental Impact – The First Nine Years, 1996–2004', *AgBioForum* 8(2&3).

Brown, C. and Jasper, K. (eds) (1993) *Consuming Passions: Feminist Approaches to Eating Disorders and Weight Preoccupations* (Toronto: Second Story Press).

Brown, P and Lauder, H. (1997). *Education: Culture, Economy, Society* (Oxford: Oxford University Press).

Browne, K. (2005) *An Introduction to Sociology*, 3rd edn (Cambridge: Polity).

Browne, K. and Bottrill, I. (1999) 'Our Unequal, Unhealthy Nation', *Sociology Review*, 9.

Brownmiller, S. (1975) *Against Our Will: Men, Women and Rape* (London: Secker and Warburg).

Brubaker, R. (1998) 'Migrations of Ethnic Unmixing in the "New Europe"', *International Migration Review*, 32.

Bruce, S. (1990) *Pray TV: Televangelism in America* (New York: Routledge).

Bruce, S. (1996) *Religion in the Modern World from Cathedrals to Cults* (Oxford: Oxford University Press).

Brumberg, J. J. (1997) *The Body Project* (New York: Vintage).

Brundtland, C. (1987) *Our Common Future* (New York: United Nations).

Bruneforth, M. (2006) 'Interpreting the Distribution of Out-of-School Children by Past and Expected Future School Enrolment'. Background Paper for *EFA Global Monitoring Report* 2007 (Paris: UNESCO Publications).

Bryman, A. (2008) *Social Research Methods*, 3rd edn (Oxford: Oxford University Press).

Bryson, V. (1993) 'Feminism', in R. Eatwell and A. Wright (eds), *Contemporary Political Ideology* (London: Pinter).

Buckingham, D. (2000) *After the Death of Childhood: Growing up in the Age of Electronic Media* (Cambridge: Polity).

Bull, P. (1983) *Body Movement and Interpersonal Communication* (New York: Wiley).

Burbridge, M. and Walters, J. (1981) *Breaking The Silence: Gay Teenagers Speak For Themselves* (London: Joint Council for Gay Teenagers).

Burchell, B. et al. (1999) *Job Insecurity and Work Intensification: Flexibility and the Changing Boundaries of Work* (York: YPS).

Burgoon, J. et al. (1996) *Nonverbal Communication: The Unspoken Dialogue*, 2nd edn (New York: McGraw-Hill).

Burkitt, I. (1999) *Bodies of Thought: Social Relations, Activity and Embodiment* (London: Sage Publications).

Burleigh, M. (1994) *Death and Deliverance* (Cambridge: Cambridge University Press).

Burns, T. and Stalker, G. M. (1966) *The Management of Innovation* (London: Tavistock).

Butler, J. (1990) *Gender Trouble: Feminism and the Subversion of Identity* (London: Routledge).

Butler, J. (1997) *Excitable Speech: A Politics of the Performative* (London and New York: Routledge).

Butler, J. (2004) *Undoing Gender* (London: Routledge).

Butler, T. and Savage, M. (1995) *Social Change and the Middle Classes* (London: UCL Press).

Bynner, J., Ferri, E. and Shepherd, P. (eds) (1997) *Twenty-Something in the 1990s: Getting on, Getting by, Getting Nowhere* (Aldershot: Ashgate Publishing).

Bytheway, B. (1995) *Ageism* (Buckingham and Bristol, PA: Open University Press).

Cabinet Office (1999) *Sharing the Nation's Prosperity. Variation in Economic and Social Conditions across the UK* (London: HMSO).

Cabinet Office (2003) *Ethnic Minorities and the Labour Market: Final Report*, March (London: HMSO).

Cahill, S. (2004) 'The Interaction Order of Public Bathrooms', in Cahill (ed.), *Inside Social Life: Readings in Sociological Psychology and Microsociology*, 4th edn (Los Angeles: Roxbury Publishing Company).

Cahill, S. E., Distler, W., Lachowetz, C., Meaney, A., Tarallo, R. and Willard, T. (1985) 'Meanwhile Backstage Public Bathrooms and the Interaction Order', *Journal of Contemporary Ethnography*, 14(1).

Calhoun, C. (1993) '"New Social Movements" of the Early Nineteenth Century', *Social Science History*, 17(3).

Callon, M. (1986) 'Some Elements of a Sociology of Translation. Domestication of the Scallops and Fishermen of St. Brieuc Bay', in J. Law (ed.), *Power, Action and Belief: A New Sociology of Knowledge?* (London: Routledge).

Campbell, C. (1992) *The Romantic Ethic and the Spirit of Modern Consumerism* (Oxford: Basil Blackwell).

Cantle, T. (2001) *Independent Report of the Community Cohesion Review Team* (London: Home Office).

Capps, W. H. (1990) *The New Religious Right: Piety, Patriotism, and Politics* (Columbia: University of South Carolina Press).

Caraway, T. L. (2007) *Assembling Women: The Feminization of Global Manufacturing* (Ithaca, NY: ILR Press).

Cardoso, F. H. and Faletto, E. (1979) *Dependency and Development in Latin America* (Berkeley: University of California Press).

Carlen, P. (1983) *Women's Imprisonment: A Study in Social Control* (London and Boston: Routledge & Kegan Paul).

Carrington, K. (1995) 'Postmodernism and Feminist Criminologies: Disconnecting Discourses', *International Journal of the Sociology of Law*, 22.

Carrington, K. (1998) 'Postmodernism and Criminologies: Fragmenting the Criminological Subject', in P. Walton and J. Young (eds), *The New Criminology Revisited* (London: Macmillan).

Carsten, J. (ed.) (2000) *Cultures of Relatedness: New Approaches to the Study of Kinship* (Cambridge: Cambridge University Press).

Cashmore, E. (2006) *Celebrity Culture* (London: Routledge).

Castells, M. (1983) *The City and the Grass Roots: A Cross-Cultural Theory of Urban Social Movements* (London: Edward Arnold).

Castells, M. (1991) *The Informational City: Economic Restructuring and Urban Development* (Oxford: Blackwell Publishing).

Castells, M. (1992) 'Four Asian Tigers with a Dragon Head: A Comparative Analysis of the State, Economy, and Society in the Asian Pacific Rim', in R. P. Appelbaum and J. Henderson (eds), *States and Development in the Asian Pacific Rim* (Newbury Park, CA: Sage).

Castells, M. (1996) *The Rise of the Network Society* (Oxford: Blackwell).

Castells, M. (1997) *The Power of Identity* (Oxford: Blackwell).

Castells, M. (1998) *End of Millennium* (Oxford: Blackwell).

Castells, M. (2000) 'Information Technology and Global Capitalism', in W. Hutton and A. Giddens (eds), *On the Edge: Living with Global Capitalism* (London: Cape).

Castells, M. (2001) *The Internet Galaxy: Reflections on the Internet, Business, and Society* (Oxford: Oxford University Press).

Castells, M. (2006) *The Network Society: From Knowledge to Policy* (Baltimore: Johns Hopkins University).

Castles, S. and Miller, M. J. (2003) *The Age of Migration: International Population Movements in the Modern World* (Basingstoke: Palgrave Macmillan).

Cayton, H. (2000) 'Alzheimer's: Looking Ahead in the Twenty-First Century', from personal correspondence, Buckingham Palace.

Census (2001) *The Census in England and Wales, 2001* (London: Office of National Statistics).

Chamberlain, M. (1999) 'Brothers and Sisters, Uncles and Aunts: A Lateral Perspective on Caribbean Families', in E. B. Silva and C. Smart (eds), *The New Family?* (London: Sage).

Chambers, D. (2006) *New Social Ties: Contemporary Connections in a Fragmented Society* (Basingstoke: Palgrave Macmillan).

Chambliss, W. J. (1973) 'The Saints and the Roughnecks', *Society*, November.

Chambliss, W. J. (1978) *On the Take: From Petty Crooks to Presidents* (Bloomington: Indiana University Press).

Chapkis, W., Sprinkle, A., Posener, J. and Buurman, G. (1997) *Live Sex Acts: Women Performing Erotic Labour* (London: Routledge).

Charlton, J. I. (1998) *Nothing About Us Without Us: Disability Oppression and Empowerment* (Berkeley: University of California Press).

Charters, A. (ed.) (2001) *Beat Down to Your Soul: What was the Beat Generation?* (New York: Penguin Books).

Chase-Dunn, C. (1989) *Global Formation: Structures of the World Economy* (Oxford: Blackwell).

Cherlin, A. (1999) *Public and Private Families: An Introduction* (New York: McGraw Hill).

Chiozza, G. (2002) 'Is there a Clash of Civilizations? Evidence from Patterns of International Conflict Involvement, 1946–97', *Journal of Peace Research*, 39(6).

Chodorow, N. (1978) *The Reproduction of Mothering* (Berkeley: University of California Press).

Chodorow, N. (1988) *Psychoanalytic Theory and Feminism* (Cambridge: Polity).

Chomsky, N. (1991) *Media Control: The Spectacular Achievements of Propaganda* (New York: Seven Stories Press).

Chua, A. (2003) *World on Fire: How Exporting Free Market Democracy Breeds Ethnic Hatred and Global Instability* (New York: Doubleday).

Church of England (1985) *Faith in the City: The Report of the Archbishop of Canterbury's Commission on Urban Priority Areas* (London: Christian Action).

CIA (2007) *The World Factbook*. Available at: www.cia.gov/library/publications/the-world-factbook/index.html.

Cicourel, A. V. (1968) *The Social Organization of Juvenile Justice* (New York: Wiley).

Cisneros, H. G. (1993) *Interwoven Destinies: Cities and the Nation* (New York: Norton).

Cixous, H. (1976) 'The Laugh of the Medusa', *Signs*, 1(4), Summer.

Clark, D. (ed) (1993) *The Sociology of Death: Theory, Culture, Practice* (Oxford: Blackwell Publishing).

Clark, K. and Drinkwater, S. (1998) 'Self-Employment and Occupational Choice', in D. Leslie (ed.), *An Investigation of Racial Disadvantage* (Manchester: Manchester University Press).

Clark, T. N. and Hoffman-Martinot, V. (1998) *The New Political Culture* (Boulder, CO: Westview).

Clegg, M., Finney, A. and Thorpe, K. (2005) *Crime in England and Wales: Quarterly Update to December 2004* (London: Home Office).

Clegg, S. (1990) *Modern Organizations: Organization Studies in the Postmodern World* (London: Sage).

Cloward, R. and Ohlin, L. (1960) *Delinquency and Opportunity* (New York: Free Press).

CNN (2001) 'Falwell Apologizes to Gays, Feminists, Lesbians', 14 September. Available at: http://archives.cnn.com/2001/US/09/14/Falwell.apology/.

Cockerham, W. (2007) *Social Causes of Health and Disease* (Cambridge: Polity)

Cohen, A. (1955) *Delinquent Boys* (London: Free Press).

Cohen, L. E., Broschak, J. P. and Haveman, H. A. (1998) 'And Then There Were More? The Effect of Organizational Sex Composition on the Hiring and Promotion of Managers', *American Sociological Review*, 63(5).

Cohen, R. (1997) *Global Diasporas: An Introduction* (London: UCL Press).

Cohen, S. (2003 [1972]) *Folk Devils and Moral Panics: The Creation of the Mods and Rockers* (Oxford: Martin Robertson).

Cole, T. R. (1992) *The Journey of Life: A Cultural History of Aging in America* (Cambridge: Cambridge University Press).

Collins, J. and Porras, J. (1994) *Built to Last* (New York: Century).

Collins, J. (2000) 'Quality by Other Means'. Unpublished manuscript, Department of Sociology, University of Wisconsin-Madison.

Colquhoun, I. (2004). *Design Out Crime: Creating Safe and Sustainable Communities* (Amsterdam: Elsevier).

Connell, R. W. (1987) *Gender and Power: Society, the Person and Sexual Politics* (Cambridge: Polity).

Connell, R. W. (2001) *The Men and the Boys* (Berkeley and Los Angeles: Allen and Unwin).

Connell, R. W. (2005) *Masculinities* (Cambridge: Polity).

Coontz, S. (1992) *The Way We Never Were: American Families and the Nostalgia Trap* (New York: Basic Books).

Corbin, J. and Strauss, A. (1985) 'Managing Chronic Illness at Home: Three Lines of Work', *Qualitative Sociology*, 8.

Corrigan, P. (1997) *The Sociology of Consumption: An Introduction* (London: Sage).

Corsaro, W. (1997) *The Sociology of Childhood* (Thousand Oaks, CA: Pine Forge Press).

Coser, L. A. (1977) *Masters of Sociological Thought: Ideas in Historical and Social Context* (New York: Harcourt, Brace, Jovanovich, Inc).

Cotgrove, S. and Duff, A. (1980) 'Environmentalism, Middle Class Radicalism and Politics', *The Sociological Review*, 28(1).

Coward, R. (1984) *Female Desire: Women's Sexuality Today* (London: Paladin).

Cox, O. C. (1959) *Class, Caste and Race: A Study in Social Dynamics* (New York: Monthly Review Press).

Crick, B. (2004) 'Is Britain Too Diverse? The Responses'. Available at: www.prospect-magazine.co.uk/HtmlPages/replies.asp.

Crompton, R. (1993) *Social Stratification: An Introduction to Current Debates* (Cambridge: Polity).

Crompton, R. (1997) *Women and Work in Modern Britain* (Oxford: Oxford University Press).

Crompton, R. (2008) *Class and Stratification: An Introduction to Current Debates*, 3rd edn (Cambridge: Polity).

Crompton, R., Brockmann, M. and Lyonette, C. (2005) 'Attitudes, Women's Employment and the Domestic Division of Labour: A Cross-National Analysis in Two Waves', *Work, Employment and Society*, 19(2).

Crossley, N. (2002) *Making Sense of Social Movements* (Buckingham: Open University Press).

Crossley, N. (2003) 'Even Newer Social Movements? Anti-Corporate Protests, Capitalist Crises and the Remoralization of Society', *Organization*, 10(2).

Crow, G. and Hardey, M. (1992) 'Diversity and Ambiguity Among Lone-Parent Households in Modern Britain', in C. Marsh and S. Arber (eds), *Families and Households: Divisions and Change* (London: Macmillan).

Crowther Report (1959) *Fifteen to Eighteen* (London: Central Advisory Council for Education/HMSO).

Cumberbatch, G. and Negrine, R. (1992) *Images of Disability on Television* (London: Routledge).

Cumings, B. (1987) 'The Origins and Development of the Northeast Asian Political Economy: Industrial Sectors, Product Cycles, and Political Consequences', in F. C. Deyo (ed.), *The Political Economy of the New Asian Industrialism* (Ithaca, NY: Cornell University Press).

Cumings, B. (1997) *Korea's Place in the Sun: A Modern History* (New York: Norton).

Cumming, E. and Henry, W. E. (1961) *Growing Old: The Process of Disengagement* (New York: Basic Books).

Curran, J. and Seaton, J. (2003) *Power Without Responsibility: The Press, Broadcasting and New Media in Britain* (London: Routledge).

Currie, D. and Siner, M. (1999) 'The BBC Balancing Public and Commercial Purpose', in *Public Purpose in Broadcasting Funding the BBC* (Luton: University of Luton Press).

Currie, E. (1998) 'Crime and Market Society Lessons from the United States', in P. Walton and J. Young (eds), *The New Criminology Revisited* (London: Macmillan).

Cylke, F. K. (1993) *The Environment* (New York: Harper Collins).

Czarniawska, B. and Hernes, T. (eds) (2005) *Actor Network Theory and Organizing* (Copenhagen: CBS Press).

Dahlburg, J.-T. (1995) 'Sweatshop Case Dismays Few in Thailand', *Los Angeles Times*, 27 August.

Dahrendorf, R. (1959) *Class and Class Conflict in Industrial Society* (London: Routledge).

D'Anieri, P., Ernst, C. and Kier, E. (1990) 'New Social Movements in Historical Perspective', *Comparative Politics*, 22(4).

Davie, G. (1994) *Religion in Britain Since 1945: Believing without Belonging* (Oxford: Blackwell).

Davie, G. (2000) *Religion in Modern Europe: A Memory Mutates* (Oxford: Oxford University Press).

Davies, B. (1991) *Frogs and Snails and Feminist Tales* (Sydney: Allen and Unwin).

Davis, K. (1949) *Human Society* (New York: Macmillan).

Davis, M. (1990) *City of Quartz: Excavating the Future in Los Angeles* (London: Vintage).

Davis, M. (2006) *City of Quartz: Excavating the Future in Los Angeles*, 2nd edn (London: Verso Books).

Davis, S. M. (1987) *Future Perfect* (Reading, MA: Addison-Wesley).

Davis, S. M. (1988) *2001 Management: Managing the Future Now* (London: Simon and Schuster).

De Beauvoir, S. (1949) *Le Deuxième Sex* (Paris: Gallimard).

D'Emilio, J. (1983) *Sexual Politics, Sexual Communities: The Making of a Homosexual Minority in the United States, 1940–1970* (Chicago, IL: University of Chicago Press).

De Swaan, A. (2001) *Words of the World: The Global Language System* (Cambridge: Polity).

De Witt, K. (1994) 'Wave of Suburban Growth Is Being Fed by Minorities', *New York Times*, 15 August.

Deem, R. (ed.) (1980) *Schooling for Women's Work* (London: Routledge & Kegan Paul).

Delbès, C., Gaymu, J. and Springer, S. (2006) 'Women Grow Old Alone, but Men Grow Old with a Partner. A European Overview', *Population & Societies*, 419 (January).

Della Porta, D. and Diani M. (2006) *Social Movements: An Introduction* (Oxford: Basil Blackwell).

Denney, D. (1998) 'Anti-Racism and the Limits of Equal Opportunities Policy in the Criminal Justice System', in C. J. Finer and M. Nellis (eds), *Crime and Social Exclusion* (Oxford: Blackwell).

Dennis, N. and Erdos, G. (1992) *Families without Fatherhood* (London: IEA Health and Welfare Unit).

Denora, T. (2000) *Music in Everyday Life* (Cambridge: Cambridge University Press).

Department for Education and Skills (2003) *Survey of Information and Communications Technology in Schools* (London: HMSO).

Department for Work and Pensions (2002) *Disabled for Life? Attitudes Towards, and Experiences of, Disability in Britain* (London: HMSO).

Department for Work and Pensions (UK) (2005) *Family Resources Survey, 2004–5* (London: HMSO).

Department for Work and Pensions (2006) *Households Below Average Income, 2004/5* (London: HMSO).

Department for Work and Pensions (2007) *The Pensioners' Income Series, 2005–6* (London: HMSO).

Department of Social Security (1998) *New Ambitions for Our Country: A New Contract for Welfare* (London: HMSO).

Derrida, J. (1976) *Of Grammatology* (Baltimore: Johns Hopkins Press).

Derrida, J. (1978) *Writing and Difference* (London: Routledge & Kegan Paul).

Derrida, J. (1981) *Positions* (London: Athlone Press).

DESA (Department of Economic and Social Affairs) (2002) *International Migration Report 2002* (New York: United Nations).

Devall, B. (1990) *Simple in Means, Rich in Ends: Practising Deep Ecology* (London: Green Print).

Devault, M. L. (1991) *Feeding the Family: The Social Organization of Caring as Gendered Work* (Chicago, IL: University of Chicago Press).

Deyo, F. C. (1989) *Beneath the Miracle: Labor Subordination in the New Asian Industrialism* (Berkeley: University of California Press).

DHSS (1980) *Inequalities in Health* (London: DHSS).

Dicken, P. (1992) *Global Shift: The Internationalization of Economic Activity* (London: Chapman).

Dickens, P. (1996) *Reconstructing Nature: Alienation, Emancipation and the Division of Labour* (London: Routledge).

Dickens, P. (2004) *Society and Nature: Changing Nature, Changing Ourselves* (Cambridge: Polity).

Diehl, M. and Dark-Freudeman, A. (2006) 'The Analytic Template in the Psychology of Aging' in D. J. Sheets, D. B. Bradley and J. Hendricks (eds), *Enduring Questions and Changing Perspectives in Gerontology* (New York: Springer).

Disability Rights Commission (2005) Briefing, June.

Dlugokencky, E. J., Myers, R. C. Lang, P. M., Masarie, K. A., Crotwell, A. M., Thoning, K. W., Hall, B. D., Elkins, J. W. and Steele, L. P. (2005) 'Conversion of NOAA atmospheric dry air CH_4 mole fractions to a gravimetrically prepared standard scale', *Journal of Geophysical Research*, 110.

Dobash, R. E. and Dobash, R. P. (1992) *Women, Violence and Social Change* (London: Routledge).

Dobson, A. and Bell, D. (eds) (2006). *Environmental Citizenship* (Cambridge, MA: The MIT Press).

DoH (2006) *Smoking, Drinking and Drug Misuse among Young People in England in 2002* (London: Department of Health).

Doorewaard, H. and van Bijsterveld, M. (2001) 'The Osmosis of Ideas: An Analysis of the Integrated Approach to IT Management from a Translation Theory Perspective', *Organization*, 8(1).

Dore, R. (1973) *British Factory, Japanese Factory: The Origins of National Diversity in Industrial Relations* (London: Allen and Unwin).

Douglas, M. (1994) *Risk and Blame* (London: Routledge).

Doyal, L. (1995) *What Makes Women Sick: Gender and the Political Economy of Health* (London: Macmillan).

Drentea, P. (1998) 'Consequences of Women's Formal and Informal Job Search Methods for Employment in Female-Dominated Jobs', *Gender and Society*, 12.

Drentea, P. and Moren-Cross, J. L. (2005) 'Social Capital and Social Support on the Web: The case of an Internet Mother Site', *Sociology of Health and Illness*, 27.

Drexler, K. E. (1992) *Engines of Creation* (Oxford: Oxford University Press).

DTI (2000) *Just Around the Corner* (London: Department of Trade and Industry).

Du Gay, P. (2000) *In Praise of Bureaucracy: Weber, Organization, Ethics* (London: Sage).

Duncombe, J. and Marsden, D. (1993) 'Love and Intimacy. The Gender Division of Emotion and "Emotion Work"': A Neglected Aspect of Sociological Discussion of Heterosexual Relationships', *Sociology*, 27.

Duneier, M. (1999) *Sidewalk* (New York: Farrar, Straus and Giroux).

Duneier, M. and Molotch, H. (1999) 'Talking City Trouble: Interactional Vandalism, Social Inequality, and the "Urban Interaction Problem"', *American Journal of Sociology*, 104.

Dunlap, R. E., Buttel, F. H., Dickens, P. and Gijswijt, A. (eds) (2002) *Sociological Theory and the Environment: Classical Foundations, Contemporary Insights* (Lanham, MD and Oxford: Rowman & Littlefield Publishers Inc).

Durkheim, E. (1952 [1897]) *Suicide: A Study in Sociology* (London: Routledge and Kegan Paul).

Durkheim, E. (1961 [1925]) *L'Éducation morale* (Paris: Alcan).

Durkheim, E. (1965 [1912]) *The Elementary Forms of the Religious Life* (New York: The Free Press).

Durkheim, E. (1982 [1895]) *The Rules of Sociological Method* (London: Macmillan).

Durkheim, E. (1984 [1893]) *The Division of Labour in Society* (London: Macmillan).

Duster, T. (1990) *Backdoor to Eugenics* (New York: Routledge).

Dutt, M. (1996) 'Some Reflections on US Women of Color and the United Nations Fourth World Conference on Women and NGO Forum in Beijing, China', *Feminist Studies*, 22.

Duyvesteyn, I. and Angstrom, J. (eds) (2005) *Rethinking the Nature of War* (London: Frank Cass).

Dworkin, R. M. (1993) *Life's Dominion: An Argument About Abortion, Euthanasia, and Individual Freedom* (New York: Knopf).

Dwyer, P. (2004) 'Creeping Conditionality in the UK: from Welfare Rights to Conditional Entitlements?', *Canadian Journal of Sociology*, 29(2).

Dyer, C. (1999) 'Let's Stay Together', *Guardian*, 25 October.

Eating Disorders Association (2007) 'Eating Disorders in the United Kingdom: Review of the Provision of Health Care Services for Men with Eating Disorders'. Available at www.b-eat.co.uk/AboutEatingDisorders/Mengeteatingdisorderstoo.

Eberstadt, N. and Satel, S. (2004) *Health and the Income Inequality Hypothesis: A Doctrine in Search of Data* (Washington DC: AEI Press).

Eckersley, R. (1989) 'Green Politics and the New Class: Selfishness or Virtue?' *Political Studies*, 37(2).

The Economist (1995) 'Book Review of David Blankenhorn, *Fatherless America*', April.

The Economist (2000a) 'All-Clear?', 13 April.

The Economist (2000b) 'Paradise Regained', 21 December.

The Economist (2002) 'Trouble in Nanoland', 5 December.

The Economist (2004) 'The Kindness of Strangers?', 26 February.

The Economist (2005a) 'Backgrounder: The EU Constitution', 3 June.

The Economist (2005b) 'Backgrounder: EU Enlargement', 23 June.

The Economist (2005c) 'Backgrounder: The Iraq Dossier Row', 5 April.

Edwards, T. (1998) 'Queer Fears: Against the Cultural Turn', *Sexualities*, 1(4).

Efron, S. (1997) 'Eating Disorders Go Global', *Los Angeles Times*, 18 October.

Ehrenreich, B. and Ehrenreich, J. (1979) 'The Professional-Managerial Class', in P. Walker (ed.), *Between Labour and Capital* (Hassocks: Harvester Press).

Eibl-Eibesfeldt, I. (1973) 'The Expressive Behaviour of the Deaf-and-Blind Born', in M. von Cranach and I. Vine (eds), *Social Communication and Movement* (New York: Academic Press).

Ekman, P. and Friesen, W. V. (1978) *Facial Action Coding System* (New York: Consulting Psychologists Press).

Elder, G. H. J. (1974) *Children of the Great Depression: Social Change in Life Experience* (Chicago and London: University of Chicago Press).

Electoral Reform Society (2005) *UK General Elections: Electorates and Turnout 1945–2005*, 1 August.

Elias, N. (1985) *The Loneliness of the Dying* (London: Continuum).

Elias, N. (1987) 'On Human Beings and their Emotions: A Process-Sociological Essay', *Theory, Culture and Society*, 4.

Elias, N. (2000 [1939]) *The Civilizing Process: Sociogenetic and Psychogenetic Investigations, Revised Edition* (Oxford: Blackwell).

Ell, K. (1996) 'Social Networks, Social Support and Coping with Serious Illness: The Family Connection', *Social Science and Medicine*, 42.

Elshtain, J. B. (1987) *Women and War* (New York: Basic Books).

Elstein, D., Cox, D., Donoghue, B. et al. (2004) *Beyond the Charter: The BBC after 2006* (London: The Conservative Party).

Emmanuel, A. (1972) *Unequal Exchange: A Study of the Imperialism of Trade* (New York: Monthly Review Press).

Employers' Forum on Disability (2003) *Briefing for CSR Practitioners*. Available online at: www.employers-forum.co.uk/www/guests/info/csr/disability-online/employ/employ1.htm.

EOC (Equal Opportunities Commission) (2007) 'Labourers of Love?' The Cost of Undervaluing Women's Work (Manchester: EOC).

Epley, N. S., Hillis, K. and Petit, M. (eds) (2006) *Everyday eBay: Culture, Collecting and Desire* (New York: Routledge).

Epstein, D. (1998) *Failing Boys: Issues in Gender and Achievement* (Buckingham: Open University Press).

Epstein, S. (2002) 'A Queer Encounter: Sociology and the Study of Sexuality', in C. L. Williams and A. Stein (eds), *Sexuality and Gender* (Oxford: Blackwell).

Erikson, K. (1966) *Wayward Puritans: A Study in the Sociology of Deviance* (New York: Wiley).

Erikson, R. and Goldthorpe, J. (1993) *The Constant Flux: A Study of Class Mobility in Industrial Societies* (Oxford: Clarendon Press).

Esping-Andersen, G. (1990) *The Three Worlds of Welfare Capitalism* (Cambridge: Polity).

Estes, C. L. and Minkler, M. (eds) (1991) *Critical Perspectives on Aging: The Political and Moral Economy of Growing Old* (Amityville: Baywood).

Estes, C. L., Binney, E. A. and Culbertson, R. A. (1992) 'The Gerontological Imagination: Social Influences on the Development of Gerontology, 1945-Present', *Aging and Human Development*, 35.

Estes, C., Biggs, S. and Phillipson, C. (2003) *Social Theory, Social Policy and Ageing* (Buckingham: Open University Press).

Etheridge, D. M, Steele, L. P, Langenfelds, R. J. et al. (1998) 'Historical CO2 records from the Law Dome DE08, DE08–2, and DSS ice cores', in *Trends: A Compendium of Data on Global Change* (Oak Ridge, TN: US Department of Energy).

Ethnic Minority Employment Taskforce (2006) *Ethnic Minorities in the Labour Market, Spring 2006* (London: HMSO).

EUFRA (European Union Fundamental Rights Agency) (2007) *Trends and Developments in Racism, Xenophobia and Anti-Semitism, 1997–2005* (Vienna: FRA).

Europaworld (2007) *Global Unemployment Remains At Historic High Despite Strong Economic Growth*. Available at: www.europaworld.org/week292/global26107. html.

European Commission (2006) *Eurobarometer 66: Public Opinion in the European Union* (Luxembourg: European Commission).

European Union (2005) *The European Union at a Glance*. Available at: http://europa.eu/ abc/index_en.htm.

European Union (2006) The Impact of Ageing on Public Expenditure: Projections for the EU25 Member States on Pensions, Healthcare, Long-term Care, Education and Unemployment Transfers (2004–2050), *European Economy Special Report* No. 1. Available at: http://ec.europa.eu/economy_finance/epc/documents/2006/ ageingreport_en.pdf.

Eurostat (2007) *Europe in Figures: Eurostat Yearbook 2006–7* (Luxembourg: European Commission).

Evans, D. J. (1992) 'Left Realism and the Spatial Study of Crime', in *Crime, Policing and Place: Essays in Environment Criminology* (London: Routledge).

Evans, M. (2000) 'Poor Show', *Guardian*, 6 March.

Evans, M. (2002) *Love: An Unromantic Discussion* (Cambridge: Polity).

Evans, P. (1979) *Dependent Development* (Princeton: Princeton University Press).

Evans-Pritchard, E. E. (1956) *Nuer Religion* (Oxford: Oxford University Press).

Eysenck, H. (1964) *Crime and Personality* (London: Routledge & Kegan Paul).

Fairclough, N. (1989) *Language and Power* (London: Longman Press).

Fairclough, N. (1992) *Critical Language Awareness* (London: Longman Press)

Fairclough, N. (2000) *Language and Power*, 2nd edn (London: Longman Press).

Faludi, S. (1991) *Backlash: The Undeclared War Against Women* (London: Chatto and Windus).

Faludi, S. (2000) *Stiffed: The Betrayal of the Modern Man* (London: Chatto and Windus).

FEASTA (2008) *Using Cap and Share to Control Emissions from the EU Transport Sector*. Available at: www.capandshare.org/pdfs/Transport2.pdf.

Featherstone, M. and Renwick, A. (eds) (1995) *Images of Aging: Cultural Representations of Later Life* (London; New York: Routledge).

Felson, M. (1994) *Crime and Everyday Life: Insights and Implications for Society* (Thousand Oaks, CA: Pine Forge Press).

Ferguson, K. E. (1984) *The Feminist Case Against Bureaucracy* (Philadelphia: Temple University Press).

Ferguson, N. (2004) *Colossus: The Rise and Fall of the American Empire* (London: Allen Lane).

Feuerbach, L. (1957 [1853]) *The Essence of Christianity* (New York: Harper and Row).

Fielder, H. G. (1946) *Textual Studies of Goethe's Faust* (Oxford: Blackwell).

Finke, R. and Stark, R. (1988) 'Religious Economies and Sacred Canopies: Religious Mobilization in American Cities, 1906', *American Sociological Review*, 53.

Finke, R. and Stark, R. (1992) *The Churching of America, 1776–1990: Winners and Losers in Our Religious Economy* (New Brunswick, NJ: Rutgers University Press).

Finkelstein, V. (1980) *Attitudes and Disabled People* (New York: World Rehabilitation Fund).

Finkelstein, V. (1981) 'To Deny or Not to Deny Disability', in A. Brechin et al. (eds), *Handicap in a Social World* (Sevenoaks: Hodder and Stoughton).

Finncy, Λ. (2006) *Domestic Violence, Sexual Assault and Stalking: Findings from the 2004/05 British Crime Survey*, Home Office online report 12/06 (London: Home Office).

Firestone, S. (1971) *The Dialectic of Sex: The Case for Feminist Revolution* (London: Cape).

Firth, R. W. (ed.) (1956) *Two Studies of Kinship in London* (London: Athlone Press).

Fischer, C. S. (1984) *The Urban Experience*, 2nd edn (New York: Harcourt).

Fischer, S. (2004) 'Penn World Tables', *The Economist*, 11 March.

Fiske, J. (1989) *Reading the Popular* (London: Unwin Hyman).

Fitzgerald, M. (2001) 'Ethnic Minorities and Community Safety', in R. Matthews and J. Pitts (eds), *Crime, Disorder and Community Safety: A New Agenda* (London: Routledge).

Flaherty, J., Veit-Wilson, J. and Dornan, P. (2004) *Poverty: The Facts*, 5th edn (London: Child Poverty Action Group).

Flour Advisory Bureau (1998) *Pressure to Be Perfect Report: Bread for Life Campaign* (London: Flour Advisory Bureau).

Flouri, E. (2005) *Fathering and Child Outcomes* (Chichester, West Sussex: John Wiley & Sons).

Forbes (2000) 'The World's Richest People', 29 June. Available at: www.forbes.com/lists/.

Forbes (2004) 'The World's Billionaires'. Available at: www.forbes.com/billionaires/.

Forbes (2008) *The World's Billionaires*. Available at: www.forbes.com/lists/2008/10/billionaires08_The-Worlds-Billionaires_Rank.html

Ford, C. S. and Beach, F. A. (1951) *Patterns of Sexual Behaviour* (New York: Harper and Row).

Foucault, M. (1967) *Madness and Civilization: A History of Insanity in the Age of Reason* (London: Tavistock Publications).

Foucault, M. (1971) *The Order of Things: An Archaeology of the Human Sciences* (New York: Pantheon).

Foucault, M. (1973) *The Birth of the Clinic: An Archaeology of Medical Perception* (London: Tavistock Publications).

Foucault, M. (1975) *Discipline and Punish* (Harmondsworth: Penguin).

Foucault, M. (1978) *The History of Sexuality* (London: Penguin).

Foucault, M. (1988) 'Technologies of the Self', in L. H. Martin, H. Gutman and P. H. Hutton (eds), *Technologies of the Self: A Seminar with Michel Foucault* (Amherst: University of Massachusetts Press).

Foundation for the Economics of Sustainability (2007) *Briefing: Using Cap and Share to Control Emissions from the EU Transport Sector*. Available at: www.capandshare.org/pdfs/Transport2.pdf.

Fox, O. C. (1964) 'The Pre-Industrial City Reconsidered', *Sociological Quarterly*, 5.

Francis, B. (2000) *Boys, Girls and Achievement: Addressing the Classroom Issues* (London: Routledge).

Frank, A. G. (1966) 'The Development of Underdevelopment', *Monthly Review*, 18.

Frank, A. G. (1969) *Capitalism and Underdevelopment in Latin America: Historical Studies of Chile and Brazil* (New York: Monthly Review Press).

Frank, D. J. and McEneaney, E. H. (1999) 'The Individualization of Society and the Liberalization of State Policies on Same-Sex Sexual Relations, 1984–1995', *Social Forces*, 7(3).

Fraser, N. (1989) *Unruly Practices: Discourse and Gender in Contemporary Social Theory* (Cambridge: Polity).

Fraser, N. (1992) *Revaluing French Feminism: Critical Essays on Difference, Agency and Culture* (Indianapolis: Indiana University Press).

Fraser, S. (1995) *The Bell Curve Wars Race, Intelligence and the Future of America* (New York: Basic Books).

Free the Children (1998) (Available online at: www.freethechildren.com/aboutus/index.html.

Freedman, C. (ed.) (2001) *Economic Reform in Japan: Can the Japanese Change?* (Cheltenham: Edward Elgar).

Freeman, C. E. (2004) 'Trends in Educational Equity of Girls and Women' (NCES 2005–16)', *Education Statistics Quarterly*, 6(4).

Freidson, E. (1970) *Profession of Medicine: A Study of the Sociology of Applied Knowledge* (New York: Dodd, Mead).

Fremlin, J. H. (1964) 'How Many People Can The World Support?', *New Scientist*.

Friedan, B. (1963) *The Feminine Mystique* (London: Victor Gollancz).

Friedlander, D. and Burtless, G. (1994) *Five Years After: The Long-Term Effects of Welfare-to-Work Programs* (New York: Russell Sage).

Fries, J. F. (1980) 'Aging, Natural Death, and the Compression of Morbidity', *New England Journal of Medicine*, 303.

Fukuyama, F. (1989) 'The End of History?' *National Interest*, 16.

Gagnon, J. H. and Simon, W. (1973) *Sexual Conduct: The Social Sources of Human Sexuality* (Chicago: Aldine).

Gallie, D. (1994) 'Are the Unemployed an Underclass? Some Evidence from the Social Change and Economic Life Initiative', *Sociology*, 28.

Gallup (2004) *Poll Topics and Trends: Religion*, 1 August.

Gamble, A. (1999) *Marxism after Communism: The Interregnum. Controversies in World Politics 1989–1999* (Cambridge: Cambridge University Press).

Gamson, J. (1994) *Claims to Fame: Celebrity in Contemporary America* (Berkeley, CA: University of California Press).

Gans, H. J. (1962) *The Urban Villagers: Group and Class in the Life of Italian-Americans*, 2nd edn (New York: Free Press).

Gardner, C. B. (1995) *Passing By: Gender and Public Harassment* (Berkeley: University of California Press).

Garfinkel, H. (1963) 'A Conception of, and Experiments with, "Trust" as a Condition of Stable Concerted Actions', in O. J. Harvey (ed.), *Motivation and Social Interaction* (New York: Ronald Press).

Gatto, J. T. (2002) *Dumbing Us Down: The Hidden Curriculum of Compulsory Schooling* (Philadelphia, PA: New Society Publishers).

Geary, D. (1981) *European Labor Protest, 1848–1939* (New York: St Martin's Press).

Geertz, C. (1973) *The Interpretation of Cultures* (New York: Basic Books).

Gelder, L. van (1996) 'The Strange Case of the Electronic Lover', in R. Kling (ed.), *Computerization and Controversy* (San Diego, CA: Academic Press, Inc.).

Gelles, R. and Cornell, C. P. (1990) *Intimate Violence in Families* (Newbury Park, CA: Sage).

Gellner, E. (1983) *Nations and Nationalism* (Oxford: Blackwell).

Gerbner, G. (1979) 'The Demonstration of Power: Violence Profile No. 10', *Journal of Communication*, 29.

Gerbner, G. (1980) 'The "Mainstreaming" of America: Violence Profile No. 11', *Journal of Communication*, 30.

Gerbner, G. (1997) 'Gender and Age in Prime-time Television' in S. Kirschner and D. A. Kirschner (eds), *Perspectives on Psychology and the Media* (Washington, DC: American Psychological Association).

Gereffi, G. (1995) 'Contending Paradigms for Cross-Regional Comparison: Development Strategies and Commodity Chains in East Asia and Latin America', in P. H. Smith (ed.), *Latin America in Comparative Perspective: New Approaches to Methods and Analysis* (Boulder, CO: Westview Press).

Gershuny, J. (1992) 'Change in the Domestic Division of Labour in the UK, 1975–87: Dependent Labour versus Adaptive Partnership', in N. Abercrombie and A. Warde (eds), *Social Change in Contemporary Britain* (Cambridge: Polity).

Gershuny, J. (1994) 'The Domestic Labour Revolution: A Process of Lagged Adaptation', in M. Anderson, F. Bechofer and J. Gershuny (eds), *The Social and Political Economy of the Household* (Oxford: Oxford University Press).

Gershuny, J. I. and Miles. I. D. (1983) *The New Service Economy: The Transformation of Employment in Industrial Societies* (London: Frances Pinter).

Gerth, H. H. and Mills, C. W. (eds) (1948) *From Max Weber: Essays in Sociology* (London: Routledge & Kegan Paul Ltd).

Gewirtz, S., Ball, S, and Bowe, R. (1995) *Markets, Choice, and Equity in Education* (Buckingham: Open University Press).

Gibbons, J. H. (1990) *Trading around the Clock Global Securities Markets and Information Technology* (Washington DC: US Congress).

Gibbs, L. (2002) 'Citizen Activism for Environmental Health: The Growth of a Powerful New Grassroots Health Movement', *The Annals of the American Academy*, AAPSS, 584 (November).

Giddens, A. (1984) *The Constitution of Society* (Cambridge: Polity).

Giddens, A. (1991) *Modernity and Self-Identity: Self and Society in the Late Modern Age* (Cambridge: Polity).

Giddens, A. (1991a) *The Consequences of Modernity* (Cambridge: Polity).

Giddens, A. (1993) *The Transformation of Intimacy: Love, Sexuality and Eroticism in Modern Societies* (Cambridge: Polity).

Giddens, A. (1994) *Beyond Left and Right: The Future of Radical Politics* (Cambridge: Polity Press).

Giddens, A. (1998) *The Third Way: The Renewal of Social Democracy* (Cambridge: Polity).

Giddens, A. (2002) *Runaway World: How Globalisation Is Reshaping Our Lives* (London: Profile).

Giddens, A., (ed.) (2001) *The Global Third Way Debate* (Cambridge: Polity).

Gillan, A. (1999) 'Shelter Backs Rethink on Homeless', *Guardian*, 15 November.

Gillborn, D. and Youdell, D. (2001) 'The New IQism: Intelligence, "Ability" and the Rationing of Education', in J. Demaine (ed.), *Sociology of Education Today* (London: Palgrave).

Gilleard, C. and Higgs, P. (2005) *Contexts of Ageing: Class, Cohort and Community* (Cambridge: Polity).

Gilligan, C. (1982) *In a Different Voice: Psychological Theory and Women's Development* (Cambridge, MA: Harvard University Press).

Gillon, S. (2004) *Boomer Nation: The Largest and Richest Generation Ever, and How it Changed America* (New York: Free Press)

Ginn, J. and Arber, S. (2000) 'Ethnic Inequality in Later Life: Variation in Financial Circumstances by Gender and Ethnic Group', *Education and Ageing*, 15(1).

Ginzburg, C. (1980) *The Cheese and the Worms* (London: Routledge & Kegan Paul).

Giroux, H. (1983) *Theory and Resistance in Education: A Pedagogy for the Opposition* (South Hadley, MA: Bergin and Garvey).

Gittings, D. (1999) 'Mickey Mouse Invasion', *Guardian*, 3 November.

Gittins, D. (1993) *The Family in Question: Changing Households and Familiar Ideologies* (Basingstoke: Macmillan).

Glascock, J. (2001) 'Gender Roles on Prime-time Network Television: Demographics and Behaviors', *Journal of Broadcasting & Electronic Media*, 45(4).

Glaser, B. G. and Strauss, A. L. (1965) *Awareness of Dying* (Chicago: Aldine Publishing Company).

Glasgow Media Group (1976) *Bad News* (London: Routledge).

Glasius, M., Kaldor, M. and Anheier, H. (eds) (2002) *Global Civil Society 2002* (Oxford: Oxford University Press).

Glass, D. (1954) *Social Mobility in Britain* (London: Routledge & Kegan Paul).

Glock, C. Y. and Bellah, R. N. (eds) (1976) *The New Religious Consciousness* (Berkeley: University of California Press).

Glueck, S. and Glueck, E. (1956) *Physique and Delinquency* (New York: Harper Brothers).

Goffman, E. (1959) *The Presentation of Self in Everyday Life* (London: Penguin Books).

Goffman, E. (1963) *Stigma* (Englewood Cliffs, NJ: Prentice-Hall).

Goffman, E. (1967) *Interaction Ritual* (New York: Doubleday/Anchor).

Goffman, E. (1968 [1961]) *Asylums. Essays on the Social Situation of Mental Patients and Other Inmates* (Harmondsworth: Penguin).

Goffman, E. (1971) *Relations in Public: Microstudies of the Public Order* (London: Allen Lane).

Goffman, E. (1973) *The Presentation of Self in Everyday Life* (New York: Overlook Press).

Goffman, E. (1981) *Forms of Talk* (Philadelphia: University of Pennsylvania Press).

Gold, T. (1986) *State and Society in the Taiwan Miracle* (Armonk, NY: M. E. Sharpe).

Golding, P. and Murdock, G. (eds) (1997) *The Political Economy of the Media* (Cheltenham: Edward Elgar Ltd).

Goldscheider, F. K. and Waite, L. J. (1991) *New Families, No Families? The Transformation of the American Home* (Berkeley: University of California Press).

Goldthorpe, J. H. (1968–9) *The Affluent Worker in the Class Structure*, 3 vols (Cambridge: Cambridge University Press).

Goldthorpe, J. H. (1983) 'Women and Class Analysis in Defence of the Conventional View', *Sociology*, 17.

Goldthorpe, J. H. (2000) *On Sociology* (Oxford: Oxford University Press).

Goldthorpe, J. H. and Marshall, G. (1992) 'The Promising Future of Class Analysis', *Sociology*, 26.

Goldthorpe, J. H. and Payne, C. (1986) 'Trends in Intergenerational Class Mobility in England and Wales 1972–1983', *Sociology*, 20.

Goldthorpe, J. H., Llewellyn, C. and Payne, C. (1980) *Social Mobility and Class Structure in Modern Britain* (Oxford: Clarendon Press; 2nd edn 1987).

Goleman, D. (1996) *Emotional Intelligence: Why It Can Matter More Than IQ* (London: Bloomsbury).

Goode, W. J. (1963) *World Revolution in Family Patterns* (New York: Free Press).

Goode, W. J. (1971) 'Force and Violence in the Family', *Journal of Marriage and the Family*, 33.

Goodhart, D. (2004) 'Too Diverse? Is Britain Becoming Too Diverse to Sustain the Mutual Obligations Behind a Good Society and the Welfare State?' *Prospect Magazine*, February.

Goodwin, J. and Jasper, J. (eds) (2002) *The Social Movements Reader: Cases and Concepts* (Oxford: Blackwell).

Gordon, D., Levitas, R., Pantazis, C. et al. (2000) *Poverty and Social Exclusion in Britain* (York: Joseph Rowntree Foundation).

Gorz, A. (1982) *Farewell to the Working Class* (London: Pluto Press).

Gorz, A. (1985) *Paths to Paradise: On the Liberation from Work* (London: Pluto Press)

Gottfredson, M. R. and Hirschi, T. (1990) *A General Theory of Crime* (Stanford CA: Stanford University Press).

Goudsblom, J. (1992) *Fire and Civilization* (London: Allen Lane).

Grabosky, P. N. and Smith, R. G. (1998) *Crime in the Digital Age: Controlling Telecommunications and Cyberspace Illegalities* (New Brunswick, NJ: Transaction).

Graef, R. (1989) *Talking Blues* (London: Collins).

Graham, H. (1987) 'Women's Smoking and Family Health', *Social Science and Medicine*, 25.

Graham, H. (1994) 'Gender and Class as Dimensions of Smoking Behaviour in Britain: Insights from a Survey of Mothers', *Social Science and Medicine*, 38.

Graham, L. (1995) *On the Line at Subaru-Isuzu* (Ithaca, NY: Cornell University Press).

Granovetter, M. (1973) 'The Strength of Weak Ties', *American Journal of Sociology*, 78.

Gray, J. (2003) *Al Qaeda and What It Means to Be Modern* (Chatham, Kent: Faber and Faber).

Greed, C. (1994) *Women and Planning: Creating Gendered Realities* (London: Routledge).

Green, D. G. (2000) *Institutional Racism and the Police: Fact or Fiction?* (London: CIVITAS).

Green, F., Felstead, A. and Burchell, B. (2000) 'Job Insecurity and the Difficulty of Regaining Employment: An Empirical Study of Unemployment Expectations', *Oxford Bulletin of Economics and Statistics*, 62 (Special Issue).

Gregg, P. and Wadsworth, J. (1999) 'Job Tenure, 1975–98', in P. Gregg and J. Wadsworth (eds), *The State of Working Britain* (Manchester: Manchester University Press).

Grey, C. and Willmott, H. (eds) (2005) *Critical Management Studies: A Reader* (Oxford: Oxford University Press).

Grint, K. (2005) *The Sociology of Work*, 3rd edn (Cambridge: Polity).

Grossberg, L., Wartella, E. and Whitney, D. C. (1998) *Mediamaking* (Thousand Oaks, CA: Sage Publications).

Grusky, D. B. and Hauser, R. M. (1984) 'Comparative Social Mobility Revisited: Models of Convergence and Divergence in 16 Countries', *American Sociological Review*, 49.

Guardian (2003) '10 million join world protest rallies', 13 February. Available at: www.guardian.co.uk/uk/2003/feb/13/politics.world.

Guardian (2004) 'Refugees in Britain', 9 October. Available at: www.guardian.co.uk/Refugees_in_Britain/Story/0,2763,1323311,00.html.

Gubrium, J. (1986) *Oldtimers and Alzheimer's: The Descriptive Organization of Senility* (Greenwich, CT; London: Jai).

Guibernau, M. (1999) *Nations without States: Political Communities in a Global Age* (Cambridge: Polity).

Gunter, B. (1985) *Dimensions of Television Violence* (London: Gower).

Habermas, J. (1981) 'New Social Movements', *Telos*, 49 (Fall).

Habermas, J. (1983) 'Modernity – An Incomplete Project', in H. Foster (ed.), *The Anti-Aesthetic* (Port Townsend, WA: Bay Press).

Habermas, J. (1985) *The Philosophical Discourse of Modernity* (Cambridge: Polity).

Habermas, J. (1986–8) *The Theory of Communicative Action*, 2 vols (Cambridge: Polity).

Habermas, J. (1989 [1962]) *The Structural Transformation of the Public Sphere* (Cambridge, MA: MIT Press).

Hackett, R. A. and Zhao, Y. (2005) *Democratizing Global Media: One World, Many Struggles* (Lanham, MD and Oxford: Rowman and Littlefield).

Hadden, J. (1997) *New Religious Movements Mission Statement.* Available at: http://religiousmovements.lib.virginia.edu/welcome/welcome.htm.

Hadden, J. and Shupe, A. (1987) 'Televangelism in America', *Social Compass*, 34(1).

Hajer, M. A. (1996) 'Ecological Modernisation as Cultural Politics', in S. Lash, B. Szerszynski and B. Wynne (eds), *Risk, Environment and Modernity: Towards a New Ecology* (London: Sage).

Hakim, C. (1996) *Key Issues in Women's Work: Female Heterogeneity and the Polarisation of Women's Employment* (London: Athlone Press).

Hall, E. T. (1969) *The Hidden Dimension* (New York: Doubleday).

Hall, E. T. (1973) *The Silent Language* (New York: Doubleday).

Hall, R., James, S. and Kertesz, J. (1984) *The Rapist Who Pays the Rent*, 2nd edn (Bristol: Falling Wall Press).

Hall, S. (1980) *Culture, Media, Language: Working Papers in Cultural Studies, 1972–79* (London: Hutchinson, in association with the Centre for Contemporary Cultural Studies, University of Birmingham).

Hall, S. and Jacques, M. (1988) 'New Times', *Marxism Today*.

Hall, S. et al. (1978) *Policing the Crisis: Mugging, the State, and Law and Order* (London: Macmillan).

Hall, S. et al. (1982) *The Empire Strikes Back* (London: Hutchinson).

Halliday, F. (2002) *Two Hours That Shook the World: September 11, 2001: Causes and Consequences* (London: Saqi Books).

Halloran, J. D. (ed.) (1970) *The Effects of Television* (London: Panther).

Halpern, C. T. (2000) 'Smart Teens Don't Have Sex (or Kiss Much Either)', *Journal of Adolescent Health*, 26(3).

Halpern, D. (2005) *Social Capital* (Cambridge: Polity).

Halsey, A. H. (ed.) (1997) *Education: Culture, Economy, and Society* (Oxford: Oxford University Press).

Halsey, A. H. and Webb, J. (eds) (2000) *Twentieth-Century British Social Trends* (New York: Macmillan).

Hammond, P. E. (1992) *Religion and Personal Autonomy: The Third Disestablishment in America* (Columbia, SC: University of South Carolina Press).

Handy, C. (1994) *The Empty Raincoat: Making Sense of the Future* (London: Hutchinson).

Hannigan J. A. (2006) *Environmental Sociology: A Social Constructionist Perspective*, 2nd edn (London: Routledge).

Haraway, D. (1989) *Primate Visions: Gender, Race and Nature in the World of Modern Science* (New York: Routledge).

Haraway, D. (1991) *Simians, Cyborgs and Women: The Reinvention of Nature* (New York; Routledge).

Harkin, J. and Skidmore, P. (2003) *Grown up Trust* (London: Demos).

Harris, J. R. (1998) *The Nurture Assumption: Why Children Turn out the Way They Do* (New York: Free Press).

Harris, M. (1978) *Cannibals and Kings: The Origins of Cultures* (New York: Random House).

Harrison, M. (1985) *TV News: Whose Bias?* (Hermitage: Policy Journals).

Harrison, P. (1983) *Inside the Inner City: Life under the Cutting Edge* (Harmondsworth: Penguin).

Hartley-Brewer, J. (1999) 'Gay Couple Will Be Legal Parents', *Guardian*, 28 October.

Harvard Magazine (2000) 'The World's Poor: A Harvard Magazine Roundtable', *Harvard Magazine*, 103(2).

Harvey, D. (1973) *Social Justice and the City* (Oxford: Blackwell).

Harvey, D. (1982) *The Limits to Capital* (Oxford: Blackwell).

Harvey, D. (1985) *Consciousness and the Urban Experience: Studies in the History and Theory of Capitalist Urbanization* (Oxford: Blackwell).

Harvey, D. (1989) *The Condition of Postmodernity* (Oxford: Blackwell).

Harvey, D. (1993) 'The Nature of Environment: The Dialectics of Social and Environmental Change', *The Socialist Register*.

Harvey, D. (2006) *Spaces of Global Capitalism: Towards a Theory of Uneven Geographical Development* (London: Verso).

Hasler, F. (1993) 'Developments in the Disabled People's Movement', in J. Swain (ed.), *Disabling Barriers, Enabling Environments* (London: Sage).

Hatch, N. (1989) *The Democratization of American Christianity* (New Haven, CT: Yale University Press).

Havel, V. (1988) 'Anti-Political Politics', in J. Keane (ed.), *Civil Society and the State: New European Perspectives* (London and New York: Verso Press).

Hawley, A. H. (1950) *Human Ecology: A Theory of Community Structure* (New York: Ronald Press).

Hawley, A. H. (1968) *Human Ecology* (Glencoe: Free Press).

Healy, M. (2001) 'Pieces of the Puzzle', *Los Angeles Times*, 21 May.

Heaphy, B., Donovan, C. and Weeks, J. (1999) 'Sex, Money and the Kitchen Sink: Power in Same-Sex Couple Relationships', in J. Seymour and P. Bagguley (eds), *Relating Intimacies: Power and Resistance* (Basingstoke: Macmillan).

Heath, A. (1981) *Social Mobility* (London: Fontana).

Heath, S. and Cleaver, E. (2003) *Young, Free and Single? Twenty-somethings and Household Change* (Basingstoke: Palgrave Macmillan).

Hebdige, D. (1997) *Cut 'n' Mix: Culture, Identity, and Caribbean Music* (London: Methuen).

Heidensohn, F. (1985) *Women and Crime* (London: Macmillan).

Heise, D. R. (1987) 'Sociocultural Determination of Mental Aging', in C. Schooler and K. Warner Schaie (eds), *Cognitive Functioning and Social Structure over the Life-Course* (Norwood, NJ: Ablex).

Held, D. (2004) *Global Covenant: The Social Democratic Alternative to the Washington Consensus* (Cambridge: Polity).

Held, D. (2006) *Models of Democracy*, 3rd edn (Cambridge: Polity).

Held, D. et al. (1999) *Global Transformations: Politics, Economics and Culture* (Cambridge: Polity).

Henderson, J. and Appelbaum, R. P. (1992) 'Situating the State in the Asian Development Process', in R. P. Appelbaum and J. Henderson (eds), *States and Development in the Asian Pacific Rim* (Newbury Park, CA: Sage).

Hendricks, J. (1992) 'Generation and the Generation of Theory in Social Gerontology', *Aging and Human Development*, 35.

Henslin, J. M. and Biggs, M. A. (1971) 'Dramaturgical Desexualization: The Sociology of the Vaginal Examination', in J. M. Henslin (ed.), *Studies in the Sociology of Sex* (New York: Appleton-Century-Crofts).

Henslin, J. M. and Biggs, M. A. (1997) 'Behaviour in Public Places: The Sociology of the Vaginal Examination', in J. M. Henslin (ed.), *Down to Earth Sociology: Introductory Readings*, 9th edn (New York: Free Press).

Hepworth, M. (2000) *Stories of Ageing* (Buckingham: Open University Press).

Heritage, J. (1985) *Garfinkel and Ethnomethodology* (New York: Basil Blackwell).

Herman, E. (1998) 'Privatising Public Space', in D. K. Thussu (ed.), *Electronic Empires Global Media and Local Resistance* (London: Arnold).

Herman, E. S. and McChesney, R. W. (1997) *The Global Media the New Missionaries of Global Capitalism* (London: Cassell).

Herman, E. S. and McChesney, R. W. (2003) 'Media Globalization: The US Experience and Influence', in R. C. Allen and A. Hill (eds), *The Television Studies Reader* (London: Routledge).

Hernandez, M., Pudney, S. E. and Hancock, R. M. (April 2006) 'The Welfare Cost of Means-Testing: Pensioner Participation in Income Support', ISER Working Paper 2006–12 (Colchester: University of Essex).

Herrnstein, R. J. and Murray, C. (1994) *The Bell Curve: Intelligence and Class Structure in American Life* (New York: Free Press).

HESA (2004) *Increase in Female Academics*, Higher Education Statistics Agency. Available at: www.hesa.ac.uk/press/pr76/pr76.htm.

Hexham, I. and K. Poewe (1997) *New Religions as Global Cultures* (Boulder, CO: Westview Press).

Hickson, K. (2004) 'Equality', in R. Plant, M. Beech and K. Hickson (eds), *The Struggle for Labour's Soul: Understanding Labour's Political Thought Since 1945* (London: Routledge).

Hills, J. (1998) 'Does Income Mobility Mean That We Do Not Need to Worry About Poverty?' in A. B. Atkinson and J. Hills (eds), *Exclusion, Employment and Opportunity* (London: Centre for the Analysis of Social Exclusion).

Hironaka, A. (2005) *Neverending Wars: The International Community, Weak States, and the Perpetuation of Civil War* (Cambridge, MA: Harvard University Press:).

Hirschi, T. (1969) *Causes of Delinquency* (Berkeley: University of California Press).

Hirst, P. (1997) 'The Global Economy: Myths and Realities', *International Affairs*, 73.

Hirst, P. (2001) *War and Power in the 21st Century: The State, Military Conflict and the International System* (Cambridge: Polity).

Hirst, P. and Thompson, G. (1992) 'The Problem of "Globalization": International Economic Relations, National Economic Management, and the Formation of Trading Blocs', *Economy and Society*, 24.

Hirst, P. and Thompson, G. (1999) *Globalization in Question: The International Economy and the Possibilities of Governance*, rev. edn (Cambridge: Polity).

Hite, S. (1994) *The Hite Report on the Family: Growing up under Patriarchy* (London: Bloomsbury).

HM Prison Service (2006) 'Female Prisoners'. Available at: www.hmprisonservice.gov.uk/adviceandsupport/prison_life/femaleprisoners/.

HMSO (1992) Social Trends 22 (London: HMSO).

HMSO (1999) Social Trends 29 (London: HMSO).

HMSO (2000) Social Trends 30 (London: HMSO).

HMSO (2004) Social Trends 34 (London: HMSO).

HMSO (2005) Social Trends 35 (London: HMSO).

HMSO (2007) Social Trends 37 (London: HMSO).

Ho, S. Y. (1990) *Taiwan: After a Long Silence* (Hong Kong: Asia Monitor Resource Center).

Hobson, D. (2002) *Soap Opera* (Cambridge: Polity).

Hochschild, A. (1983) *The Managed Heart: Commercialization of Human Feeling* (Berkeley: University of California Press).

Hochschild, A. (1989) *The Second Shift: Working Parents and the Revolution at Home* (New York: Viking).

Hodge, R. and Tripp, D. (1986) *Children and Television: A Semiotic Approach* (Cambridge: Polity).

Hofman, D. J. (2007) *USA National Oceanic and Atmospheric Administration*. Available at: www.esrl.noaa.gov/gmd/aggi/(accessed 31 March 2008).

Hogge, B. (2005) 'Great Firewall of China'. Available at: www.opendemocracy.net/media-edemocracy/china_internet_2524.jsp.

Holton, R. J. (1978) 'The Crowds in History: Some Problems of Theory and Method', *Social History*, 3.

Homans, H. (1987) 'Man-Made Myth: The Reality of Being a Woman Scientist in the NHS', in A. Spencer and D. Podmore (eds), *A Man's World: Essays on Women in Male-Dominated Professions* (London: Tavistock).

Home Office (2002) *Secure Borders, Safe Haven: Integration with Diversity in Modern Britain* (London: Home Office).

Home Office (2003) *World Prison Population List*, 4th edn (London: Home Office).

Home Office (2004) *Criminal Statistics: England and Wales 2003* (London: Home Office).

hooks, b. (1997) *Bone Black: Memories of Girlhood* (London: Women's Press).

Hopkins, T. H. and Wallerstein, I. (1996) *The Age of Transition: Trajectory of the World-System, 1945–2025* (London: Zed Books).

Horkheimer, M. and Adorno, T. W. (2002 [1947]) *Dialectic of Enlightenment: Philosophical Fragments* (Stanford, CA: Stanford University Press).

Hotz, R. L. (1998) 'Boomers Firing Magic Bullets at Signs of Aging', *Los Angeles Times*.

Howard League for Penal Reform (2004). Available at: www.howardleague.org/press/2004/060104a.htm.

Howard, J. H. (1986) 'Change in "Type A" Behaviour a Year after Retirement', *Gerontologist*, 26.

Howard, M., Garnham, A., Fimister, G. and Veit-Wilson, J. (2001) *Poverty: The Facts*, 4th edn (London: Child Poverty Action Group).

Howarth, G. (2006) *Death and Dying: A Sociological Introduction* (Oxford: Blackwell Publishing).

Hughes, E. C. (1945) 'Dilemmas and Contradictions of Status', *American Journal of Sociology*, 50.

Hughes, G. (1991) 'Taking Crime Seriously? A Critical Analysis of New Left Realism', *Sociology Review*, 1.

Hughes, G. (1998) *Understanding Crime Prevention. Social Control, Risk and Late Modernity* (Buckingham: Open University Press).

Humphreys, L. (1970) *Tearoom Trade: A Study of Homosexual Encounters in Public Places* (London: Duckworth).

Hunt, P. (ed.) (1966) *Stigma: The Experience of Disability* (London: Geoffrey Chapman).

Huntington, S. P. (1996) *The Clash of Civilizations and the Remaking of World Order* (New York: Simon and Schuster).

Huston, A. C., Donnerstein, E., Fairchild, H. et al. (1992) *Big World, Small Screen: The Role of Television in American Society* (Lincoln: University of Nebraska Press).

Hutchby, I. (2005) *Media Talk: Conversation Analysis and the Study of Broadcasting* (Buckingham: Open University Press).

Hutton, W. (1995) *The State We're in* (London: Jonathan Cape).

Hyman, R. (1984) *Strikes*, 2nd edn (London: Fontana).

ICBL (2001) *International Campaign to Ban Land Mines*. Available at: www.icbl.org.

IDEA (Institute for Democracy and Electoral Assistance) (2007) *Voter Turnout in Western Europe*. Available at: www.idea.int/vt/western.cfm.

Iganski, P. and Payne, G. (1999) 'Socio-Economic Restructuring and Employment: The Case of Minority Ethnic Groups', *British Journal of Sociology*, 50.

ILGA (International Lesbian and Gay Association) (2008). Available at: www.ilga.org/aboutilga.asp.

Illich, I. (1975) *Medical Nemesis: The Expropriation of Health* (London: Calder and Boyars).

Illich, I. D. (1971) *Deschooling Society* (Harmondsworth: Penguin).

ILO (1999) *C182 Worst Forms of Child Labour Convention, International Labour Organization*. Available at: www.ilocarib.org.tt/childlabour/c182.htm.

ILO (2000) *Statistical Information and Monitoring Programme on Child Labour (SIMPOC): Overview and Strategic Plan 2000–2002* (International Programme on the Elimination of Child Labour (IPEC) and Bureau of Statistics (STAT)).

ILO (2004) *Global Employment Trends for Women* Available at: www.ilo.org/public/english/employment/strat/download/trendsw.pdf.

ILO (2007) *Global Employment Trends for Women, Brief – March 2007*. Available at: www.ilo.org/public/english/employment/strat/download/getw07.pdf.

Inglehart, R. (1977) *The Silent Revolution: Changing Values and Political Styles Among Western Publics* (Princeton: Princeton University Press).

Inglehart, R. (1990) 'Values, Ideology, and Cognitive Mobilization' in R. J. Dalton and M. Kuechler (eds), *Challenging the Political Order: New Social and Political Movements in Western Democracies* (Oxford: Basil Blackwell).

Inglehart, R. (1997) *Modernization and Postmodernization: Cultural, Economic and Political Change in 43 Societies* (Princeton, NJ: Princeton University Press).

Innis, H. A. (1951) *The Bias of Communication* (Toronto: Toronto University Press).

Inquest (2004) *Why Are Children Dying in Custody? Call for a Public Inquiry into the Death of Joseph Scholes*. Available at: http://inquest.gn.apc.org/pdf/Joseph%20Scholes%20inquiry%20briefing%2004.pdf.

Institute for Child and Family Policy (2004) 'Lone Parents/Lone Mother Families with Children'. Available at: www.childpolicyintl.org/.

International Bank for Reconstruction and Development/World Bank (2007) *Millennium Development Goals: Global Monitoring Report* (Washington DC: World Bank).

International Centre for Prison Studies (2007) *World Prison Population List*, 7th edn (King's College London).

International Telecommunications Union (2005) *Global Internet Connectivity*. Available at: www.itu.int/ITU-D/icteye/Indicators/Indicators.aspx#>.

Internet Movie Database (2007) *Top Grossing Films to 2007*. Available at: www.imdb.com/boxoffice/alltimegross?region=non us.

Internet World Stats (2007) *World Internet Users, 2007*. Available at: www.internetworld-stats.com/stats.htm.

IPCC (2007) *Intergovernmental Panel on Climate Change*, 4th Assessment Report. Available at: www.ipcc.ch/ipccreports/ar4-syr.htm.

IPPR (1999) *Unsafe Streets: Street Homelessness and Crime* (London: Institute for Public Policy Research).

IPSOS/MORI (2007) *The Most Important Issues Facing Britain Today*. Available at: www.ipsospublicaffairs.co.uk/polls/2007/mpm070425.shtml.

Irwin, A. (2001) *Sociology and the Environment, A Critical Introduction to Society, Nature and Knowledge* (Cambridge: Polity).

ISSA (2003) 'Global Status of Commercialized Transgenic Crops: 2003' (International Service for the Acquisition of Agri-Biotech Applications). Available at: www.isaaa.org/kc/CBTNews/press_release/briefs30/es_b30.pdf>.

Jackson, M. and Goldthorpe, J. H. (2007) 'Intergenerational Class Mobility in Contemporary Britain: Political Concerns and Empirical Findings', *British Journal of Sociology*, 58(4), December.

Jacoby, S. (1997) *Modern Manors: Welfare Capitalism Since the New Deal* (Princeton: Princeton University Press).

Jahoda, M., Lazarsfeld, P. F. and Zeisel, H. (1972 [1933]) *Marienthal: The Sociography of an Unemployed Community* (London: Tavistock).

James, A., Jenks, C. and Prout, A. (1998) *Theorizing Childhood* (Cambridge: Polity).

James, C. (2003) *Global Status of Commercialized Transgenic Crops* (International Service for the Acquisition of Agri-Biotech Applications).

Jamieson, L. (1998) *Intimacy: Personal Relationships in Modern Societies* (Cambridge: Polity).

Jary, D. and Jary, J. (1999) *Dictionary of Sociology* (Glasgow: HarperCollins Publishers).

Jencks, C. (1994) *The Homeless* (Cambridge, MA: Harvard University Press).

Jenkins, C. (1990) 'The Professional Middle Class and the Origins of Progressivism: A Case Study of the New Education Fellowship 1920–1950', *CORE* 14(1).

Jenkins, C. and Sherman, B. (1979) *The Collapse of Work* (London: Eyre Methuen).

Jenkins, R. (1996) *Social Identity* (London: Routledge; 2nd edn 2004).

Jenks, C. (2005) *Childhood*, 2nd edn (London: Routledge).

Jensen, A. (1967) 'How Much Can We Boost IQ and Scholastic Achievement?' *Harvard Educational Review*, 29.

Jensen, A. (1979) *Bias in Mental Testing* (New York: Free Press).

Jobling, R. (1988) 'The Experience of Psoriasis Under Treatment', in M. Bury and R. Anderson (eds), *Living with Chronic Illness: The Experience of Patients and their Families* (London: Unwin Hyman).

John, M. T. (1988) *Geragogy: A Theory for Teaching the Elderly* (New York: Haworth).

Johnson, M. P. (1995) 'Patriarchal Terrorism and Common Couple Violence: Two Forms of Violence against Women in US Families', *Journal of Marriage and the Family*, 57.

Johnston, C. (2004) 'Women Suffer £5k Pay Gap', *Times Higher Education Supplement*, 3 September.

Jones, D. E., Doty, S., Grammich, C. et al. (2002) *Religious Congregations & Membership in the United States 2000: An Enumeration by Region, State and the County Based on Data Reported for 149 Religious Bodies* (Nashville, TN: Glenmary Research Centre).

Jones, T. (1993) *Britain's Ethnic Minorities* (London: Policy Studies Institute).

Joy, B. (2000) 'Why the Future Doesn't Need Us', *Wired*, 8(4).

Judge, K. (1995) 'Income Distribution and Life Expectancy: A Critical Appraisal', *British Medical Journal*, 311.

Kaldor, M. (2007) *New and Old Wars: Organized Violence in a Global Era*, 2nd edn (Cambridge: Polity).

Kamin, L. J. (1977) *The Science and Politics of IQ* (Harmondsworth: Penguin).

Kanter, R. M. (1977) *Men and Women of the Corporation* (New York: Basic Books).

Karlsen, S. (2007) 'Ethnic Inequalities in Health: The Impact of Racism', *Better Health Briefing 3* (London: Race Equality Foundation).

Karpf, A. (1988) *Doctoring the Media: The Reporting of Health and Medicine* (London: Routledge).

Kasarda, J. D. and Janowitz, M. (1974) 'Community Attachment in Mass Society', *American Sociological Review*, 39.

Katz, E. (1959) 'The Functional Approach to the Study of Attitudes', *Public Opinion Quarterly*, (24).

Katz, E. and Lazarsfeld, P. (1955) *Personal Influence* (New York: The Free Press).

Katz, J., Rice, R. E. and Aspden, P. (2001) 'The Internet, 1995–2000: Access, Civic Involvement, and Social Interaction', *American Behavioral Scientist*, 45(3).

Katz, S. (1996) *Disciplining Old Age: The Formation of Gerontological Knowledge* (Charlottesville and London: University Press of Virginia).

Kaufman, E. (2007) 'The End of Secularization in Europe? A Demographic Perspective'. Working Paper, Birkbeck College, University of London.

Kautsky, J. (1982) *The Politics of Aristocratic Empires* (Chapel Hill: University of North Carolina Press).

Keith, M. (1993) *Race, Riots, and Policing: Lore and Disorder in a Multi-Racist Society* (London: UCL Press).

Kelly, M. P. (1992) *Colitis* (London: Tavistock).

Kemp, A. et al. (1995) 'The Dawn of a New Day: Redefining South African Feminism', in A. Basu (ed.), *The Challenge of Local Feminisms* (Boulder, CO: Westview).

Kendall, D. (2005) *Framing Class: Media Representations of Wealth and Poverty in America* (Lanham, MD: Rowman and Littlefield).

Kepel, G. (1994) *The Revenge of God: The Resurgence of Islam, Christianity and Judaism in the Modern World* (Cambridge: Polity).

Kerr, A. and Shakespeare, T. (2002) *Genetic Politics: From Eugenics to Genome* (Cheltenham: New Clarion).

Kiecolt, K. J. and Nelson, H. M. (1991) 'Evangelicals and Party Realignment, 1976–1988', *Social Science Quarterly*, 72.

Kiernan, K. (2004) 'Unmarried Cohabitation in Britain and Europe' *Law and Policy*, 26:1.

Kinsey, A. C. (1948) *Sexual Behaviour in the Human Male* (Philadelphia, PA: W. B. Saunders).

Kinsey, A. C. (1953) *Sexual Behaviour in the Human Female* (Philadelphia, PA: W. B. Saunders).

Kirkwood, T. (2001) *Ageing Vulnerability: Causes and Interventions* (Chichester: Wiley).

Knights, D. and Willmott, H. (2007) *Introducing Organizational Behaviour and Management* (London: Thomson Learning).

Knoke, D. (1990) *Political Networks: The Structural Perspective* (New York: Cambridge University Press).

Knorr-Cetina, K. and Cicourel, A. V. (1981) *Advances in Social Theory and Methodology: Towards an Interpretation of Micro- and Macro-Sociologies* (London: Routledge & Kegan Paul).

Kohn, M. (1977) *Class and Conformity* (Homewood, IL: Dorsey Press).

Kolakowski, L. (2005) *Main Currents of Marxism: The Founders, the Golden Age, the Breakdown* (New York: W. W. Norton & Co).

Kollock, P. (1999) 'The Production of Trust in Online Markets', *Advances in Group Processes* (16).

Korte, H. (2001) 'Perspectives on a Long Life: Norbert Elias and the Process of Civilization', in T. Salumets (ed.), *Norbert Elias and Human Interdependencies* (Montreal and Kingston: McGill-Queen's University Press).

Koser, K. and Lutz, H. (1998) 'The New Migration in Europe: Contexts, Constructions and Realities', in K. Koser and H. Lutz (eds), *The New Migration in Europe: Social Constructions and Social Realities* (Basingstoke: Macmillan).

Koss, S. E. (1973) *Fleet Street Radical: A. G. Gardiner and the Daily News* (London: Allen Lane).

Kraut, R., Brynin, M. and Kiesler, S. (eds) (2006) *Computers, Phones and the Internet: Domesticating Internet Technology* (Buckingham: Open University Press).

Krieken, R. van (1998) *Norbert Elias* (London: Routledge).

Kristeva, J. (1974) *La Révolution du langage poétique* (Paris: Seuil).

Kristeva, J. (1977) *Polylogue* (Paris: Seuil).

Krupat, E. (1985) *People in Cities: The Urban Environment and Its Effects* (Cambridge: Cambridge University Press).

Kulkarni, V. G. (1993) 'The Productivity Paradox: Rising Output, Stagnant Living Standards', *Business Week*, 8 February.

Kuznets, S. (1955) 'Economic Growth and Income Inequality', *Economic Review*, XLV(1).

Lacan, J. (1995) *Lacan's Four Fundamental Concepts of Psychoanalysis* (New York: SUNY Press).

Lamb, M. E. (2002) 'Nonresidential Fathers', in C. S. Tamis-LeMonda and N. Cabrera (eds), *Handbook of Father Involvement* (Mahway, NJ: Lawrence Erlbaum).

Laming (Lord) (2003) *The Victoria Climbie Inquiry*, January.

Land, K. C., Deane, G. and Blau, J. R. (1991) 'Religious Pluralism and Church Membership', *American Sociological Review*, 56.

Landes, D. S. (1969) *The Unbound Prometheus* (New York: Cambridge University Press).

Lappe, F. M. (1998) *World Hunger: 12 Myths* (New York: Grove Press).

Laqueur, W. (2003) *No End to War: Terrorism in the Twenty-First Century* (New York: Continuum).

Lareau, A. (2003) *Class, Race and Family Life* (Berkeley: University of California Press).

Larsen, J., Urry, J. and Axhausen, K. (2006) *Social Networks and Future Mobilities.* Report for Department for Transport, UK, Lancaster.

Lask B. and Bryant-Waugh, R. (eds) (2000) *Anorexia Nervosa and Related Eating Disorders in Childhood and Adolescence* (Hove: Psychology Press).

Laslett, P. (1996) *A Fresh Map of Life: The Emergence of the Third Age* (Basingstoke: Macmillan).

Laswell, H. (1948) *The Structure and Function of Communication and Society* (New York: Harper & Brothers).

Latour, B. (1992) 'Where are the Missing Masses? The Sociology of a Few Mundane Artifacts', in Bijker, W. E. and Law, J. (eds), *Shaping Technology/Building Society: Studies in Sociotechnical Change* (Cambridge, MA: MIT Press).

Latour, B. (1993) *We Have Never Been Modern* (Cambridge, MA: Harvard University Press).

Latour, B. (2005) *Reassembling the Social: An Introduction to Actor-Network Theory* (Oxford and New York: Oxford University Press).

Laumann, E. O. (1994) *The Social Organization of Sexuality: Sexual Practices in the United States* (Chicago, IL: University of Chicago Press).

Lazarsfeld, P. F., Berelson, B. and Gaudet, H. (1948) *The People's Choice?* (New York: Columbia University Press).

Le Roux, B., Rouanet, H., Savage, M. and Warde, A. (2007) 'Class and Cultural Division in the UK'. Working Paper No. 40 (CRESC, The University of Manchester).

Lea, J. and Young, J. (1984) *What Is To Be Done about Law and Order?* (London: Penguin).

Leadbeater, C. (1999) *Living on Thin Air: The New Economy* (London: Viking).

Lee S. (2001) 'Fat Phobia in Anorexia Nervosa: Whose Obsession Is It?' in M. Nasser, M. Katzman and R. Gordon (eds), *Eating Disorders and Cultures in Transition* (New York: Brunner-Routledge).

Lee, D. and Newby, H. (1983) *The Problem of Sociology* (London: Routledge).

Lee, R. B. (1968) 'What Hunters Do for a Living, or How to Make out on Scarce Resources', in R. B. Lee and I. De Vore (eds), *Man the Hunter* (Chicago: Aldine Press).

Lee, R. B. (1969) '!Kung Bushman Subsistence: An Input-Output Analysis', in A. P. Vayda (ed.), *Environment and Cultural Behavior* (New York: Natural History Press).

Lee, R. B. and I. De Vore (eds) (1968) *Man the Hunter* (Chicago: Aldine Press).

Lees, S. (1993) *Sugar and Spice: Sexuality and Adolescent Girls* (London: Penguin).

Legge, K. (2002) 'On Knowledge, Business Consultants and the Selling of Total Quality Management' in T. Clark and R. Fincham (eds), *Critical Consulting: New Perspectives on the Management Advice Industry* (Oxford: Blackwell Publishing).

Leisering, L. and Leibfried, S. (1999) *Time and Poverty in Western Welfare States* (Cambridge: Cambridge University Press).

Lelkes, O. (2007) *Poverty Among Migrants in Europe* (Vienna: European Centre for Social Welfare Policy and Research).

Lemert, E. (1972) *Human Deviance, Social Problems and Social Control* (Englewood Cliffs, NJ: Prentice Hall).

Lemkin, R. (1944) *Axis Rule in Occupied Europe: Laws of Occupation, Analysis of Government, Proposals for Redress* (New York: Carnegie Endowment for International Peace).

Levin, W. C. (1988) 'Age Stereotyping: College Student Evaluations', *Research on Aging*, 10.

Levitas, R. (2005) *The Inclusive Society: Social Exclusion and New Labour*, 2nd edn (Basingstoke: Palgrave Macmillan).

Li, Y. and Heath, A. (2007) *Minority Ethnic Groups in the British Labour Market: Exploring Patterns, Trends and Processes of Minority Ethnic Disadvantage* (ESRC: UPTAP).

Liebert, R. M., Sprafkin, J. N. and Davidson, M. A. S. (1982) *The Early Window Effects of Television on Children and Youth* (London: Pergamon Press).

Lilley, S., Lightfoot, G. and Paulo Amaral, M. N. (eds) (2004) *Representing Organization: Knowledge, Management and the Information Age* (Oxford: Oxford University Press).

Lim, L. L. (1998) *The Sex Sector: The Economic and Social Bases of Prostitution in Southeast Asia* (Geneva: International Labour Organization).

Linz, J. J. (2000) *Totalitarian and Authoritarian Regimes* (Boulder, CO: Lynne Reinner Publishers).

Lipset, S. M. (1991) 'Comments on Luckmann', in P. Bourdieu and J. S. Coleman (eds), *Social Theory in a Changing Society* (Boulder, CO: Westview).

Lipset, S. M. and Bendix, R. (1959) *Social Mobility in Industrial Society* (Berkeley: University of California Press).

Lister R. (2004) *Poverty* (Cambridge: Polity).

Lister, R. (ed.) (1996) *Charles Murray and the Underclass: The Developing Debate* (London: IEA Health and Welfare Unit, in association with *The Sunday Times*).

Livi-Bacci, M. (1992) *A Concise History of World Population.* (Oxford: Blackwell).

Livingstone, S. and Bovill, M. (1999) *Young People, New Media* (London: London School of Economics).

Livingstone, S. and Lunt, P. (1993) *Talk on Television: Audience Participation and Public Debate* (London: Routledge).

Lloyd-Sherlock, P. (2004) *Living Longer* (London: Zed Books).

Locke, J. and Pascoe, E. (2000) 'Can a Sense of Community Flourish in Cyberspace?' *Guardian*, 11 March.

Logan, J. R. and Molotch, H. L. (1987) *Urban Fortunes: The Political Economy of Place* (Berkeley: University of California Press).

The London Plan (2004) *Spatial Development Strategy* (London: Mayor of London).

Longworth, N. (2003) *Lifelong Learning in Action: Transforming Education in the 21st Century* (London: Routledge Falmer).

Lorber, J. (1994) *Paradoxes of Gender* (New Haven, CT: Yale University Press).

Louie, M. C. Y. (2001) *Sweatshop Warriors: Immigrant Women Workers Take on the Global Factory* (Boston: South End).

Loungani, P. (2003) 'Inequality: Now You See it, Now You Don't', in *Finance and Development* (Washington, DC: International Monetary Fund).

Lowe, P. and Goyder, J. (1983) *Environmental Groups in Politics* (London: Allen and Unwin).

Lukes, S. (1974) *Power: A Radical View* (London: Macmillan).

Lukes, S. (2004) *Power: A Radical View*, 2nd edn (Basingstoke: Macmillan).

Lull, J. (1990) *Inside Family Viewing: Ethnographic Research on Television's Audiences* (London: Routledge).

Lull, J. (1997) 'China Turned on Revisited Television, Reform and Resistance', in A. Sreberny-Mohammadi (ed.), *Media in Global Context: A Reader* (London: Arnold).

Lupton, D. (ed.) (1999) *Risk and Sociocultural Theory: New Directions and Perspectives* (Cambridge: Cambridge University Press).

Lynch (2006) *Voice of the New Arab Public: Iraq, Al Jazeera and Middle East Politics Today* (New York: Columbia University Press).

Lyon, C. and de Cruz, P. (1993) *Child Abuse* (London: Family Law).

Lyon, D. (1994) *The Electronic Eye: The Rise of Surveillance Society* (Cambridge: Polity).

Lyotard, J.-F. (1985) *The Postmodern Condition* (Minneapolis: University of Minnesota Press).

Mac an Ghaill, M. (1994) *The Making of Men: Masculinities, Sexualities and Schooling* (Buckingham: Open University Press).

MacGregor, S. (2003) 'Social Exclusion', in N. Ellison and C. Pierson (eds), *Developments in British Social Policy 2* (Basingstoke: Palgrave Macmillan).

MacGregor, S. and Pimlot, B. (1991) 'Action and Inaction in the Cities', in *Tackling the Inner Cities: The 1980s Reviewed. Prospects for the 1990s* (Oxford: Clarendon Press).

Mack, J. and Lansley, S. (1985) *Poor Britain* (London: George Allen and Unwin).

Mack, J. and Lansley, S. (1992) *Breadline Britain 1990s: The Findings of the Television Series* (London: London Weekend Television).

MacLeod, J. (1995) *Ain't No Makin' It: Aspirations and Attainment in a Low-Income Neighbourhood* (Boulder, CO: Westview Press).

Macnaghten, P. and Urry, J. (1998) *Contested Natures* (London: Sage Publications).

Macpherson, S. W. (1999) *The Stephen Lawrence Inquiry* (London: HMSO).

Macrae, S., Maguire, M. and Milbourne, M. (2003) 'Social Exclusion: Exclusion from School', *International Journal of Inclusive Education* 7(2).

Maffesoli, M. (1995) *The Time of the Tribes: The Decline of Individualism in Mass Society* (London: Sage Publications).

Makino, M., Tsuboi, K. and Dennerstein, L. (2004) 'Prevalence of Eating Disorders: A Comparison of Western and Non-Western Countries', *Medscape General Medicine*, 6(3).

Malcolm, N. (1996) *Bosnia: A Short History* (New York: New York University Press).

Malthus, T. (1976 [1798]) *Essay on the Principle of Population* (New York: Norton).

Mannheim, K. (1972 [1928]) 'The Problem of Generations', in P. Kecskemeti, ed., *Essays on the Sociology of Knowledge* (London: Routledge & Kegan Paul).

Marcuse, H. (1964) *One-Dimensional Man: Studies in the Ideology of Advanced Industrial Society* (London: Routledge & Kegan Paul).

Marcuse, H. and van Kempen, R. (eds) (2000) *Globalizing Cities: A New Spatial Order?* (Oxford: Blackwell).

Marin, L., Zia, H. and Soler, E. (1998) *Ending Domestic Violence: Report from the Global Frontlines* (San Francisco, CA: Family Violence Prevention Fund).

Marsden, P. (1987) 'Core Discussion Networks of Americans', *American Sociological Review*, 52.

Marsden, P. and Lin, N. (1982) *Social Structure and Network Analysis* (Beverly Hills, CA: Sage).

Marshall, G. and Firth, D. (1999) 'Social Mobility and Personal Satisfaction Evidence from Ten Countries', *British Journal of Sociology*, 50.

Marshall, G. (1988) *Social Class in Modern Britain* (London: Hutchinson).

Marshall, T. H. (1973) *Class, Citizenship and Social Development* (Westport, CN: Greenwood).

Martell, L. (1994) *Ecology and Society: An Introduction* (Cambridge: Polity).

Martin, D. (1990) *Tongues of Fire: The Explosion of Protestantism in Latin America* (Oxford: Blackwell).

Martineau, H. (1962 [1837]) *Society in America Garden City* (New York: Doubleday).

Marx, K. (1978 [1875]) *Critique of the Gotha Programme* (Moscow: Progress Publishers).

Marx, K. and Engels, F. (2001 [1848]) *The Communist Manifesto* (London: Electric Book Co.).

Mason, A. and Palmer, A. (1996) *Queer Bashing: A National Survey of Hate Crimes against Lesbians and Gay Men* (London: Stonewall).

Mason, D. (1995) *Race and Ethnicity in Modern Britain* (Oxford: Oxford University Press).

Massey, D. (2007) *World City* (Cambridge: Polity).

Matsuura, J. H. (2004) 'Commercial Tools, Processes and Materials Anticipating the Public Backlash: Public Relations Lessons for Nanotechnology from the Biotechnology Experience', *Nanotech*, 2004 3.

Matthews, R. and Young, J. (1986) *Confronting Crime* (London: Sage).

Maugh, T. H. and Zamichow, N. (1991) 'Medicine: San Diego's Researcher's Findings Offer First Evidence of a Biological Cause for Homosexuality', *Los Angeles Times*, 30 August.

Mauthner, M. L. (2005) *Sistering: Power and Change in Female Relationships* (Basingstoke: Palgrave Macmillan).

May, S. (ed.) (1999) *Critical Multiculturalism: Rethinking Multicultural and Anti-racist Education* (London: The Falmer Press)

May-Chahal, C. and Herczog, M. (2003) *Child Sexual Abuse in Europe* (Council of Europe Publishing).

Mayor, S. (2004) 'Pregnancy and Childbirth are Leading Causes of Death in Teenage Girls in Developing Countries', *British Medical Journal*, 328.

McAuley, R. (2006) *Out of Sight: Crime Youth and Exclusion in Modern Britain* (Cullompton: Willan)

McFadden, D. and Champlin, C. A. (2000) 'Comparison of Auditory Evoked Potentials in Heterosexual, Homosexual, and Bisexual Males and Females', *Journal of the Association for Research in Otolaryngology*, 1.

McGivney, V. (2000) *Working with Excluded Groups: Guidelines on Good Practice for Providers and Policy-makers in Working with Groups Under-represented in Adult Learning* (Leicester, NIACE).

McKeown, T. (1979) *The Role of Medicine: Dream, Mirage or Nemesis?* (Oxford: Blackwell).

McKnight, A. (2000) 'Earnings Inequality and Earnings Mobility, 1977–1997: The Impact of Mobility on Long Term Inequality', Employment Relations Research Series No. 8 (London: Department of Trade and Industry).

McLuhan, M. (1964) *Understanding Media* (London: Routledge & Kegan Paul).

McMichael, P. (1996) *Development and Social Change: A Global Perspective* (Thousand Oaks, CA: Pine Forge).

McNeely, C. L. (1995) *Constructing the Nation-State: International Organization and Prescriptive Action* (Westport, CT: Greenwood).

McQuail, D. (2000) *Mcquail's Mass Communication Theory* (London: Sage).

McRobbie, A. (1991) *Feminism and Youth Culture: From* Jackie *to* Just Seventeen (Cambridge, MA: Unwin Hyman).

McRobbie, A. and Garber, J. (1975) 'Girls and Subcultures', in S. Hall and T. Jefferson (eds), *Resistance Through Rituals. Youth Subcultures in Post-War Britain* (London: Hutchinson).

Mead, G. H. (1934) *Mind, Self and Society, From the Standpoint of a Social Behaviorist* (Chicago, IL: University of Chicago Press).

Meadows, D. H. et al. (1972) *The Limits to Growth* (New York: Universe Books).

Meadows, D. H., Meadows, D. L. and Randers, J. (1992) *Beyond the Limits: Global Collapse or a Sustainable Future?* (London: Earthscan)..

Meadows, D. H., Meadows, D. L. and Randers. J. (2004) *Limits to Growth: The 30-Year Update* (White River Junction, VT: Chelsea Green).

Meadows, P. (1996) *The Future of Work: Contributions to the Debate* (York: YPS).

MediaGuardian (2007) 'Families of Abused Teenagers Sue MySpace', 19 January. Available at: www.guardian.co.uk/media/2007/jan/19/digitalmedia.usnews.

Mellows Facer, A., Young, R. and Cracknell, R. (2005) *General Election 2005, 17 May* (London: House of Commons Library).

Melton, J. G. (1989) *The Encyclopedia of American Religions* (Detroit: Gale Research).

Melucci, A. (1985) 'The Symbolic Challenge of Contemporary Movements', *Social Research*, 52.

Melucci, A. (1989) *Nomads of the Present: Social Movements and Individual Needs in Contemporary Society* (London: Hutchinson Radius).

Mennell, S. (1990) *Norbert Elias: An Introduction* (Oxford: Blackwell).

Menzel, P. (photographs) and D'Alusio, F. (text) (2005) *Hungry Planet: What the World Eats* (Berkeley, CA: Ten Speed Press)

Merton, R. K. (1957) *Social Theory and Social Structure*, rev. edn (Glencoe: Free Press).

Metropolitan Police Authority (2004) *Report of the MPA Scrutiny on MPS Stop and Search Practice*, May (London: MPA).

Meyer, D. S. and Tarrow, S. (eds) (1997) *The Social Movement Society: Contentious Politics for a New Century* (Lanham, MD: Rowman and Littlefield).

Meyer, J. W. and Rowan, B. (1977) 'Institutionalized Organizations: Formal Structure as Myth and Ceremony', *American Journal of Sociology*, 83.

Meyers, M. (1999) *Mediated Women: Representations in Popular Culture* (Cresskill, NJ: Hampton Press).

Michels, R. (1967 [1911]) *Political Parties* (New York: Free Press).

Miles, H. (2005) *Al Jazeera: The Inside Story of the Arab News Channel that is Challenging the West* (New York: Grove Press).

Miles, R. (1993) *Racism after 'Race Relations'* (London: Routledge).

Miles, S. (2000) *Youth Lifestyles in a Changing World* (Buckingham: Open University Press).

Mill, J. S. (1869) *The Subjection of Women* (New York: D. Appleton).

Mills, C. W. (1970) *The Sociological Imagination* (Harmondsworth: Penguin).

Milne, A. E. H. and Harding, T. (1999) *Later Lifestyles: A Survey by Help the Aged and Yours Magazine* (London: Help the Aged).

Mirza, H. (1986) *Multinationals and the Growth of the Singapore Economy* (New York: St Martin's Press).

Mission Frontiers (2000) *An Overview of the World by Religious Adherents.* Available at: www.missionfrontiers.org/2000/03/overview.htm.

Mitchell, J. (1966) *Women: The Longest Revolution. Essays in Feminism and Psychoanalysis* (London: Virago).

Mitchell, J. (1975) *Psychoanalysis and Feminism* (New York: Random House).

Modood, T. (1991) 'The Indian Economic Success', *Policy and Politics*, 19.

Modood, T. (1994) 'Political Blackness and British Asians', *Sociology*, 28.

Modood, T. (2007) *Multiculturalism: A Civic Idea* (Cambridge: Polity)

Modood, T. et al. (1997) *Ethnic Minorities in Britain: Diversity and Disadvantage* (London: Policy Studies Institute).

Mohammadi, A. (1998) 'Electronic Empires: An Islamic Perspective', in D. K. Thussu (ed.), *Electronic Empires Global Media and Local Resistance* (London: Arnold).

Mohammadi, A. (ed.) (2002) *Islam Encountering Globalization* (London: Routledge).

Mol, A. P. J. (2001) *Globalization and Environmental Reform: The Ecological Modernization of the Global Economy* (Cambridge, MA: The MIT Press).

Mol, A. P. J. and Sonnenfeld, D. A. (2000) 'Ecological Modernisation Around the World: An Introduction', *Environmental Politics*, 9(1).

Moore, B. (1966) *Social Origins of Dictatorship and Democracy: Lord and Peasant in the Making of the Modern World* (Boston, MA: Beacon Press).

Moore, G. (1990) 'Structural Determinants of Men's and Women's Personal Networks', *American Sociological Review*, 55.

Moore, L. R. (1994) *Selling God: American Religion in the Marketplace of Culture* (New York: Oxford University Press).

Moore, R. (1995) *Ethnic Statistics and the 1991 Census* (London: Runnymede Trust).

Morais, A., Neves, I., Davies, B. and Daniels, H. (eds) (2001) *Towards a Sociology of Pedagogy* (New York: Peter Lang).

Morgan, P. (1999) *Family Policy, Family Changes* (London: CIVITAS).

Morgan, R. (1994) *The Word of a Woman: Feminist Dispatches* (New York: Norton).

MORI (2000) 'Britain Today: Are We An Intolerant Nation?' 23 October. Available at: www.ipsos-mori.com/polls/2000/rd-july.shtml.

MORI (2002) 'Attitudes Towards Asylum Seekers for "Refugee Week", 17 June. Available at: www.ipsos-mori.com/polls/2002/refugee.shtml.

MORI (2004) 'Can We Have Trust and Diversity?' 19 January. Available at: www.mori.com/polls/2003/community.shtml.

Morris, L. (1993) *Dangerous Classes: The Underclass and Social Citizenship* (London: Routledge).

Morris, L. (1995) *Social Divisions: Economic Decline and Social Structural Change* (London: Routledge).

Mouzelis, N. P. (1995) *Sociological Theory: What Went Wrong? Diagnosis and Remedies* (London: Routledge).

Moynihan, D. P. (1993) 'Defining Deviancy Down', *The American Spectator*, 62(1), Winter.

Mullan, P. (2002) *The Imaginary Time Bomb: Why an Ageing Population Is Not a Social Problem* (London: I. B. Tauris).

Mumford, L. (1973) *Interpretations and Forecasts* (London: Secker and Warburg).

Muncie, J. (1999) *Youth and Crime: A Critical Introduction* (London: Sage).

Murdoch, R. (1994) 'The Century of Networking'. Eleventh Annual John Bonython Lecture. Australia, Centre for Independent Studies.

Murdock, G. P. (1949) *Social Structure* (New York: Macmillan).

Murphy, R. (1997) *Sociology and Nature: Social Action in Context* (Boulder, CO: Westview).

Murray, C. (1990) *The Emerging British Underclass* (London: Institute of Economic Affairs).

Murray, C. A. (1984) *Losing Ground: American Social Policy 1950–1980* (New York: Basic Books).

Najam, A., Huq, S. and Sokona, Youbal (2003) 'Climate Negotiations Beyond Kyoto: Developing Countries Concerns and Interests, Climate Policy, 3.

Narayan, D. (1999) *Can Anyone Hear Us? Voices from 47 Countries* (Washington, DC: World Bank Poverty Group, PREM).

Nasser, M. (2006) 'Eating Disorders across Cultures' *Psychiatry*, 5(11), November, pp 392–5.

Nasser, M., Katzman, M. and Gordon, R. (2001) *Eating Disorders and Cultures in Transition* (Brunner-Routledge, London).

National Committee of Inquiry into Higher Education (1997) *Report* (London: Department for Education and Employment).

National Statistics (2004) 'Internet Access'. Available at: www.statistics.gov.uk/cci/nugget.asp?id=8.

National Statistics (2006a) 'Ageing'. Available at: www.statistics.gov.uk/cci/nugget.asp?ID=949.

National Statistics (2006b) 'Civil Partnerships'. Available at: www.statistics.gov.uk/CCI/nugget.asp?ID=1685

National Statistics (2006c) 'Crime: Gender'. Available at: www.statistics.gov.uk/CCI/nugget.asp?ID=1661.

National Statistics (2006d) 'Wealth distribution'. Available at: www.statistics.gov.uk/CCI/nugget.asp?ID=2&Pos=4&ColRank=1&Rank=176

National Statistics (2007) *Households Below Average Income: An Analysis of the Income Distribution, 1994/5–2006/7* (London: Department for Work and Pensions).

National Survey of Family Growth (1995), 'Centers for Disease Control and Prevention', *National Center for Health Statistics* (Washington, DC: Government Printing Office).

Nature (2000) 'Atlas of a Thirsty Planet: Percentage of Population with Access to Safe Water by Country 2000'. Available at: www.nature.com/nature/focus/water/map.html.

Negroponte, N. (1995) *Being Digital* (London: Hodder and Stoughton).

Negus, K. (1999) *Music Genres and Corporate Cultures* (London: Routledge).

Neighbourhood Renewal Unit (2004) Available at: www.neighbourhood.gov.uk/.

Nettleton, S. (2006) *The Sociology of Health and Illness*, 2nd edn (Cambridge: Polity).

New Internationalist (2000) 'Love, Hate and the Law', *New Internationalist*, 328.

New Scientist (2003) 'Global Warming "Kills 160,000 a Year"', 1 October. Available at: www.newscientist.com/article/dn4223-global-warming-kills-160000-a-year.html.

Newman, K. S. (2000) *No Shame in My Game: The Working Poor in the Inner City* (New York: Vintage).

Nicholas, S., Kershaw, C. and Walker, A. (2007). *Crime in England and Wales 2006/07*. Home Office Statistical Bulletin 11/07 (London: Home Office).

Niebuhr, H. R. (1929) *The Social Sources of Denominationalism* (New York: Henry Holt).

Nielson, F. (1994) 'Income Inequality and Industrial Development: Dualism Revisited', *American Sociological Review*, 59 (October).

Nolan, P. (2000) 'Labouring Under an Illusion', *THES Millennium Magazine*, 22(29), December.

Nunn, A., Johnson, S., Monro, S., Bickerstaffe, T. and Kelsey, S. (2007) *Factors Affecting Social Mobility*, Research Report No 450, (London: Department of Work and Pensions).

Oakley, A. (1974a) *Housewife* (London: Allen Lane).

Oakley, A. (1974b) *The Sociology of Housework* (Oxford: Martin Robertson).

Oakley, A. et al, (1994) 'Life Stress, Support and Class Inequality: Explaining the Health of Women and Children', *European Journal of Public Health*, 4.

Oberschall, A. (1973) *Social Conflict and Social Movements* (Englewood Cliffs, NJ: Prentice Hall).

OECD (2005) *OECD Factbook, 2005*. Available at: http://miranda.sourceoecd.org/vl=7951621/cl=16/nw=1/rpsv/factbook/11-04-02.htm.

OECD (2006) *Environment at a Glance, Environmental Indicators 2006* (Paris:OECD Publishing)

OECD (2007) *Municipal Waste Generation in kg per Capita, OECD Countries, 2003*. Available at: www.oecd.org/dataoecd/16/35/38331999.pdf.

OFCOM (2003) *Hours Viewed Per Household Per Day by Age, Social Class and Platform*. Available at: www.ofcom.org.uk/static/archive/itc/research/industry_info_march03.pdf.

OFCOM (2007) *Public Service Broadcasting: Annual Report 2007*. Available at: www.ofcom.org.uk/tv/psb_review/annrep/psb07/psb07.pdf.

Ohmae, K. (1990) *The Borderless World: Power and Strategy in the Industrial Economy* (London: Collins).

Ohmae, K. (1995) *The End of the Nation State: The Rise of Regional Economies* (London: Free Press).

Oliver, M. (1983) *Social Work with Disabled People* (Basingstoke: Macmillan).

Oliver, M. (1990) *The Politics of Disablement* (Basingstoke: Macmillan).

Oliver, M. (1996) *Understanding Disability: From Theory to Practice* (Basingstoke: Macmillan).

Oliver, M. and Zarb, G. (1989) 'The Politics of Disability: A New Approach', *Disability, Handicap & Society*, 4.

Olson, M. (1965) *The Logic of Collective Action* (Cambridge, MA: Harvard University Press).

Omi, M. and Winant, H. (1994) *Racial Formation in the United States from the 1960s to the 1990s*, 2nd edn (New York: Routledge).

O'Neil, M. (2000) *Prostitution and Feminism: Towards a Politics of Feeling* (Cambridge: Polity).

O'Neill, O. (2002) *The Reith Lectures: A Question of Trust*. Available at: www.bbc.co.uk/radio4/reith2002/.

O'Neill, R. (2002) *Experiments in Living: The Fatherless Family*, September (London: CIVITAS).

ONS (2001) *Geographic Variations in Health – Decennial Supplement* (London: Office of National Statistics).

ONS (2002a) *Labour Force Survey*, Spring (London: Office of National Statistics).

ONS (2002b) *Focus on Ethnicity and Identity* (London: Office of National Statistics).

ONS (2003a) *Ethnicity: Population Size: 7. 9% from a Minority Ethnic Group* (London: Office of National Statistics).

ONS (2003b) *Focus on London* (London: Office of National Statistics).

ONS (2003c) *A Century of Labour Market Change* (London: Office of National Statistics).

ONS (2004a) *Focus on the Labour Market 2002* (London: Office of National Statistics).

ONS (2004b) *Travel Trends*, 17 December (London: Office of National Statistics).

ONS (2004c) *Focus on Gender* (London: Office of National Statistics).

ONS (2004d) *Social Focus in Brief: Ethnicity 2002* (London: Office of National Statistics).

ONS (2005a) *Focus on Ethnicity and Identity*, March (London: Office of National Statistics).

ONS (2005b) *Focus on Families* (London: Office of National Statistics).

ONS (2007) *The Pensioners' Income Series 2005/6*, rev. edn (London: Office of National Statistics).

Osborne, J. W. (2007) 'Linking Stereotype Threat and Anxiety', *Educational Psychology*, 27(1), February.

Paehlke, R. (1989) *Environmentalism and the Future of Progressive Politics* (New Haven, CT and London: Yale University Press).

Pahl, J. (1989) *Money and Marriage* (Basingstoke: Macmillan).

Pakulski, J. and Waters, M. (1996) *The Death of Class* (London: Sage).

Palmer, G. and Kenway, P. (2007) *Poverty Among Ethnic Groups: How and Why Does it Differ?* (York: Joseph Rowntree Foundation).

Palmer, G., MacInnes, T. and Kenway, P. (2006) *Monitoring Poverty and Social Exclusion 2006* (York: Joseph Rowntree Foundation).

Palmer, G., MacInnes, T. and Kenway, P. (2007) *Monitoring Poverty and Social Exclusion 2007* (York: Joseph Rowntree Foundation).

Palmore, E. B. (1985) *Retirement: Causes and Consequences* (New York: Springer).

Panyarachun, A. et al. (2004) *A More Secure World: Our Shared Responsibility: Report of the High-Level Panel on Threats, Challenges and Change* (New York: United Nations).

Papadakis, E. (1988) 'Social Movements, Self-Limiting Radicalism and the Green Party in West Germany', *Sociology*, 22(3), August.

Parekh, B. (2000) *Rethinking Multiculturalism: Cultural Diversity and Political Theory* (Basingstoke: Palgrave Macmillan).

Parekh, B. (2004) *Is Britain Too Diverse? The Responses*. Available at: www.prospect-magazine.co.uk/HtmlPages/replies.asp.

Park, R. E. (1952) *Human Communities: The City and Human Ecology* (New York: Free Press).

Parker, H., Aldridge, J. and Measham, F. (1998) *Illegal Leisure: The Normalization of Adolescent Recreational Drug Use* (London and New York: Routledge).

Parry, N. and Parry, J. (1976) *The Rise of the Medical Profession* (London: Croom Helm).

Parsons, T. (1952) *The Social System* (London: Tavistock).

Parsons, T. (1960) 'Towards a Healthy Maturity', *Journal of Health and Social Behavior*, 1.

Parsons, T. and Bales, R. F. (1956) *Family Socialization and Interaction Process* (London: Routledge & Kegan Paul).

Parsons, T. and Smelser, N. J. (1956) *Economy and Society* (London: Routledge & Kegan Paul).

Pearce, F. (1976) *Crimes of the Powerful: Marxism, Crime and Deviance* (London: Pluto Press).

Pearson, G. (1983) *Hooligan: A History of Respectable Fears* (London: Macmillan).

Performance and Innovation Unit, UK (2002) *Ethnic Minorities and the Labour Market: Interim Analytical Report* (London: Cabinet Office).

Perlmutter, H. V. (1972) 'Towards Research on and Development of Nations, Unions, and Firms as Worldwide Institutions', in H. Gunter (ed.), *Transnational Industrial Relations* (New York: St Martin's Press).

Peterson, P. G. (1999) *Gray Dawn: How the Coming Age Wave will Transform America – and the World* (New York: Random House).

Peterson, R. A. (ed.) (1976) *The Production of Culture* (London: Sage).

Peterson, R. A. and Berger, D. G. (1975) 'Cycles in Symbol Production: The Case of Popular Music', *American Sociological Review*, 40.

Pew Forum on Religion and Public Life (2002) *Americans Struggle with Religion's Role at Home and Abroad*, 20 March (Washington, DC: The Pew Research Center).

Pew Global Attitudes Project (2005) (Washington, DC: Pew Research Center).

Pew Research Center (2007) *Pew Internet and American Life Project: Parents and Teens Survey* (Washington, DC: Pew Research Center).

Philo, G. and Berry, M. (2004) *Bad News From Israel* (London: Pluto Press).

Phizacklea, A. and Wolkowitz, C. (1995) *Homeworking Women: Gender, Racism and Class at Work* (London: Sage).

Piachaud, D. (1987) 'Problems in the Definition and Measurement of Poverty', *Journal of Social Policy*, 16(2).

Piachaud, D. and Sutherland, H. (2002) *Changing Poverty post 1997* (London: Centre for Analysis of Social Exclusion, London School of Economics).

Pierson, C. (1994) *Dismantling the Welfare State? Reagan, Thatcher and the Politics of Retrenchment* (Cambridge: Cambridge University Press).

Pilkington, A. (2002) 'Cultural Representations and Changing Ethnic Identities in a Global Age', in M. Holborn (ed.), *Developments in Sociology* (Ormskirk: Causeway Press).

Pintor R. and Gratschew M. (2002) *Voter Turnout Since 1945* (International IDEA). Available at: www.idea.int/publications/vt/upload/VT_screenopt_2002.pdf.

Piore, M and Sabel, C.F. (1984) *The Second Industrial Divide: Possibilities for Prosperity* (New York: Basic Books).

PISA (2000) *Student Achievement in England: Results in Reading, Mathematical and Scientific Literacy among 15-Year-Olds* (London: Programme for International Student Assessment. OECD).

Piven, F. F. and Cloward, R. A. (1977) *Poor People's Movements: Why they Succeed, How they Fail* (New York: Pantheon Books).

Plummer, K. (1975) *Sexual Stigma: An Interactionist Account* (London: Routledge & Kegan Paul)

Pollak, O. (1950) *The Criminality of Women* (Philadelphia: University of Pennsylvania Press).

Pollert, A. (1988) 'Dismantling Flexibility', *Capital and Class*, 34.

Postman, N. (1986) *Amusing Ourselves to Death: Public Discourse in the Age of Show Business* (London: Heinemann).

Postman, N. (1995) *The Disappearance of Childhood* (New York: Vintage Books).

President's Commission on Organized Crime (1986) *Records of Hearings, June 24–26, 1985* (Washington, DC: US Government Printing Office).

Prout, A. (ed.) (2004) *The Future of Childhood* (London: Routledge Falmer).

Putnam, R. (1993) 'The Prosperous Community: Social Capital and Public Life', *American Prospect*, 13.

Putnam, R. (1995) 'Bowling Alone: America's Declining Social Capital', *Journal of Democracy*, 6.

Putnam, R. (1995) 'The Strange Disappearance of Civic America'. Available at: http://sociology.ucdavis.edu/people/xshu/soc-106–1/106assignment5article.pdf.

Putnam, R. (2000) *Bowling Alone: The Collapse and Revival of American Community* (New York: Simon and Schuster).

Quah, D. (1999) *The Weightless Economy in Economic Development* (London: Centre for Economic Performance).

Radway, J. A. (1984) *Reading the Romance* (Chapel Hill: University of North Carolina Press).

Rake, K. (ed.) (2000) *Women's Incomes over the Lifetime* (London: HMSO).

Ranis, G. (1996) *Will Latin America Now Put a Stop to 'Stop-and-Go?'* (New Haven, CT: Yale University, Economic Growth Center).

Rapoport, R. N., Fogarty, M. P. and Rapoport, R. (eds) (1982) *Families in Britain* (London: Routledge & Kegan Paul).

Ratcliffe, P. (1999) 'Housing Inequality and "Race": Some Critical Reflections on the Concept of "Social Exclusion"', *Ethnic and Racial Studies*, 22.

Rattansi, A. (1992) 'Changing the Subject? Racism, Culture and Education', in J. Donald and A. Rattansi (eds), *'Race', Culture and Difference* (London: Sage).

Rawstorne, S. (2002) 'England and Wales', in R. W. Summers and A. M. Hoffman (eds), *Domestic Violence: A Global View* (Westport, CT: Greenwood Press).

Reay, D. (2002) 'Shaun's Story: Troubling Discourses of White Working-Class Masculinities', *Gender & Education*, 14.

Redman, P. (1996) 'Empowering Men to Disempower Themselves: Heterosexual Masculinities, HIV and the Contradictions of Anti-Oppressive Education', in M. Mac an Ghaill (ed.), *Understanding Masculinities* (Buckingham: Open University Press).

Rees, M. (2003) *Our Final Century: Will the Human Race Survive the Twenty-First Century?* (London: William Heinemann).

Regional Trends 38 (2003) *Unemployment: By Highest Qualification*. Available at: www.statistics.gov.uk/StatBase/ssdataset.asp?vlnk=7705&More=Y.

Reich, R. (1991) *The Work of Nations: Preparing Ourselves for 21st-Century Capitalism* (New York: Knopf).

Reid, I. (1991) 'The Education of the Elite', in G. Walford (ed.), *Private Schooling Tradition, Change and Diversity* (Oxford: Chapman).

Reisman, D. (1961) *The Lonely Crowd. A Study of the Changing American Character* (New Haven: Yale University Press).

Reskin, B. and Roos, P. A. (1990) *Job Queues, Gender Queues: Explaining Women's Inroads into Male Occupations* (Philadelphia: Temple University Press).

Reuters (2007) 'Technology: Young People Like What it Does, Not What it is', 28 July. Available at: www.usabilitynews.com/news/article4077.asp.

Rex, J. and Moore, R. (1967) *Race, Community and Conflict: A Study of Sparkbrook* (Oxford: Oxford University Press).

Rheingold, H. (2000) *The Virtual Community* (Cambridge, MA: MIT Press).

Rich, A. (1981) *Compulsory Heterosexuality and Lesbian Existence* (London: Onlywomen Press).

Richardson, D. and May, H. (1999) 'Deserving Victims? Sexual Status and the Social Construction of Violence', *Sociological Review*, 47.

Riesman, D. (1961) *The Lonely Crowd* (New Haven, CT: Yale University Press).

Riley, M. W., Foner, A. and Waring, J. (1988) 'Sociology of Age', in N. J. Smelser (ed.), *Handbook of Sociology* (Newbury Park, CA: Sage).

Riley, M. W., Kahn, R. L. and Foner, A. (1994) *Age and Structural Lag: Changes in Work, Family, and Retirement* (Chichester: J. Wiley).

Ritzer, G. (1983) 'The McDonaldization of Society', *Journal of American Culture*, 6(1).

Ritzer, G. (1993) *The McDonaldization of Society* (Newbury Park, CA: Pine Forge Press).

Ritzer, G. (1998) *The McDonaldization Thesis: Explorations and Extensions* (London: Sage).

Roberts, R. (1971) *The Classic Slum: Salford Life in the First Quarter of the Century* (Manchester: Manchester University Press).

Robertson, R. (1992) *Globalization: Social Theory and Global Culture* (London: Sage).

Robertson, R. (1995) 'Glocalization: Time–Space and Homogeneity–Heterogeneity', in M. Featherstone, S. Lash and R. Robertson (eds), *Global Modernities* (London: Sage).

'Rona' (2000) 'Why We Need a Union', *Respect: Journal of the International Union of Sex Workers* (London: IUSW).

Roof, W. C. (1993) *A Generation of Seekers: The Spiritual Journeys of the Baby Boom Generation* (San Francisco, CA: Harper San Francisco).

Roof, W. C. and McKinney, W. (1990) *American Mainline Religion: Its Changing Shape and Future Prospects* (New Brunswick, NJ: Rutgers University Press).

Roos, P. and Reskin, B. (1992) 'Occupational Desegregation in the 1970s: Integration and Economic Equity', *Sociological Perspectives*, 35.

Rootes, C. 2005. 'A Limited Transnationalization? The British Environmental Movement' in D. della Porta and S. Tarrow (eds), *Transnational Protest and Global Activism* (Lanham, MD: Rowman and Littlefield).

Rose, S. (2003) *Lifelines: Life Beyond the Gene* (Oxford: Oxford University Press).

Rose, S., Kamin, L. and Lewontin, R. C. (1984) *Not in Our Genes: Biology, Ideology and Human Nature* (Harmondsworth: Penguin).

Rosenau, J. N. (1997) *Along the Domestic-Foreign Frontier: Exploring Governance in a Turbulent World* (Cambridge: Cambridge University Press).

Rossi, A. (1973) 'The First Woman Sociologist: Harriet Martineau', in *The Feminist Papers: From Adams to De Beauvoir* (New York: Columbia University Press).

Rostow, W. W. (1961) *The Stages of Economic Growth* (Cambridge: Cambridge University Press).

Rowling, J. K. (1998) *Harry Potter and the Philosopher's Stone* (London: Bloomsbury).

Roxborough (2004) 'Thinking About War' (Review Essay), *Sociological Forum*, 19(3).

Rubin, G. (1975) 'The Traffic in Women: Notes on the "Political Economy" of Sex', in R. Reiter (ed.), *Toward an Anthropology of Women* (New York, Monthly Review Press).

Rubin, G. (1984) 'Thinking Sex: Notes for a Radical Theory of the Politics of Sexuality', in C. Vance (ed.), *Pleasure and Danger* (New York: Routledge & Kegan Paul).

Rubin, L. (1990) *The Erotic Wars: What Happened to the Sexual Revolution?* (New York: Farrar).

Rubin, L. B. (1994) *Families on the Fault Line* (New York: Harper Collins).

Rudé, G. (1964) *The Crowd in History: A Study of Popular Disturbances in France and England, 1730–1848* (New York: Wiley).

Ruspini, E. (2000) 'Longitudinal Research in the Social Sciences', *Social Research Update*, 28.

Russett, B. M, Oneal, J. R and Cox, M. (2000) 'Clash of Civilizations or Realism and Liberalism Déjà Vu? Some Evidence', *Journal of Peace Research* 37(5).

Rusting, R. L. (1992) 'Why Do We Age?' *Scientific American*, 267.

Rutherford, J. and Chapman, R. (1988) 'The Forward March of Men Halted', in R. Chapman and J. Rutherford (eds), *Male Order: Unwrapping Masculinity* (London: Lawrence and Wishart).

Sabel, C. F. (1982) *Work and Politics: The Division of Labour in Industry* (Cambridge: Cambridge University Press).

Sachs, J. (2000) 'A New Map of the World', *The Economist*, 22 June.

Sadovnik, A. R. (ed.) (1995) *Knowledge and Pedagogy: The Sociology of Basil Bernstein* (Norwood, NJ: Ablex Publishing Company).

Saks, M. (1992) *Alternative Medicine in Britain* (Oxford: Clarendon Press).

Salter, H. (1998) 'Making a World of Difference: Celebrating 30 Years of Development Progress', 25 June, US AID Press Release.

Salway, S., Platt, S., Chowbey, P., Harriss, K. and Bayliss, E. (2007) *Long-term Ill Health, Poverty and Ethnicity* (York: Joseph Rowntree Foundation).

Sandilands, C. (1999) *The Good-Natured Feminist: Ecofeminism and the Quest for Democracy* (Minneapolis: University of Minnesota Press).

Sassen, S. (1991) *The Global City: New York, London, Tokyo* (Princeton: Princeton University Press).

Sassen, S. (1998) *Globalization and Its Discontents: Essays on the Mobility of People and Money* (New York: New Press).

Sassen, S. (2001) *The Global City: New York, London, Tokyo*, 2nd edn (Princeton: Princeton University Press).

Sassen, S. (2004) *Is Britain Too Diverse? The Responses*, 23 November. Available at: www.prospect-magazine.co. uk/HtmlPages/replies.asp.

Saunders, P. (1990) *Social Class and Stratification* (London: Routledge).

Saunders, P. (1996) *Unequal But Fair? A Study of Class Barriers in Britain* (London: IEA Health and Welfare Unit).

Savage, J. (2007) *Teenage: The Creation of Youth Culture* (New York: Viking Books).

Savage, M. et al. (1992) *Property, Bureaucracy and Culture: Middle Class Formation in Contemporary Britain* (London: Routledge).

Sayers, J. (1986) *Sexual Contradiction: Psychology, Psychoanalysis and Feminism* (London: Tavistock).

Scarman, L. G. (1982) *The Scarman Report* (Harmondsworth: Penguin).

Schaie, K. W. (1979) 'The Primary Mental Abilities in Adulthood: An Exploration in the Development of Psychometric Intelligence', in P. B. Baltes and O. G. Brim (eds), *Lifespan Development and Behavior*, vol. 2 (New York: Academic Press).

Schaie, K. W. (1990) 'Handbook of the Psychology of Aging', in J. E. Birren and K. W. Schaie (eds), *Handbook of the Psychology of Aging*, 5th edn (San Diego, CA, and London: Academic Press, 2001).

Schnaiberg, A. (1980) *The Environment: From Surplus to Scarcity* (New York: Oxford University Press).

Schumacher, E. F. (1977) *Small Is Beautiful: A Study of Economics As If People Mattered* (London: Abacus).

Schwartz, G. (1970) *Sect Ideologies and Social Status* (Chicago, IL: University of Chicago Press).

Schwartz, P. and Randall, D. (2003) *An Abrupt Climate Change Scenario and Its Implications for United States National Security*, October (New York: Pentagon).

Schwarz, J. and Volgy, T. (1992) *The Forgotten Americans* (New York: Norton).

Scott, A. (2000) 'Risk Society or Angst Society? Two Views of Risk, Consciousness and Community', in B. Adam, U. Beck and J. van Loon (eds), *The Risk Society and Beyond: Critical Issues for Social Theory* (London: Sage).

Scott, J. (1991) *Who Rules Britain?* (Cambridge: Polity).

Scott, S. and Morgan, D. (1993) 'Bodies in a Social Landscape', in S. Scott and D. Morgan (eds), *Body Matters: Essays on the Sociology of the Body* (London: Falmer Press).

Scott, W. R. and J. W. Meyer (1994) *Institutional Environments and Organizations: Structural Complexity and Individualism* (Thousand Oaks, CA: Sage).

Sedlak, A. and Broadhurst, D. (1996) *Third National Incidence Study of Child Abuse and Neglect* (Washington, DC: US Department of Health and Human Services).

Segura, D. A. and J. L. Pierce (1993) 'Chicana/o Family Structure and Gender Personality: Chodorow, Familism, and Psychoanalytic Sociology Revisited', *Signs*, 19.

Seidman, S. (1997) *Difference Troubles: Queering Social Theory and Sexual Politics* (Cambridge: Cambridge University Press).

Sen, A. (1999) *Development as Freedom* (New York: Random House).

Sen, A. (2007) *Identity and Violence: The Illusion of Destiny* (London: Penguin Books).

Sennett, R. (1993) *The Conscience of the Eye: The Design and Social Life of Cities* (London: Faber and Faber).

Sennett, R. (1998) *The Corrosion of Character: The Personal Consequences of Work in the New Capitalism* (London: Norton).

Sennett, R. (2003 [1977]) *The Fall of Public Man* (Cambridge: Cambridge University Press).

Seymour-Ure, C. (1998) 'Leaders and Leading Articles: Characterization of John Major and Tony Blair in the Editorials of the National Daily Press', in I. Crewe, B. Gosschalk and J. Bartle (eds), *Political Communications: Why Labour Won the General Election of 1997* (London: Frank Cass).

Shaheen J. (1984) *The TV Arab* (Bowling Green, OH: Bowling Green State University Press).

Shaheen J. (2001) *Reel Bad Arabs: How Hollywood Vilifies a People* (New York: Olive Branch Press).

Shakespeare, T. and Watson, N. (2002) 'The Social Model of Disability: An Outdated Ideology?' *Research in Social Science and Disability*, 2.

Sharkey H. J. (2004) 'Globalization, Migration and Identity: Sudan 1800–2000', in B. Schaebler and L. Stenberg (eds), *Globalization and the Muslim World: Culture, Religion and Modernity* (Syracuse, NY: Syracuse University Press).

Sharma, U. (1992) *Complementary Medicine Today: Practitioners and Patients* (London: Routledge).

Sharma, U. (1999) *Caste* (Buckingham: Open University Press).

Sharpe, S. (1994) *Just Like a Girl: How Girls Learn to be Women. From the '70s to the '90s* (London: Penguin).

Shaw, M. (2003) *War and Genocide: Organized Killing in Modern Society* (Cambridge: Polity).

Shaw, M. (2005) *The New Western Way of War: Risk-Transfer and its Crisis in Iraq* (Cambridge: Polity).

Shaw, M. (2007) *What is Genocide? A New Social Theory* (Cambridge: Polity).

Shaw, W. (2001) 'In Helsinki: Virtual Village', *Wired*, March.

Sheldon, W. A. (1949) *Varieties of Delinquent Youth* (New York: Harper).

Sheller, M. and Urry, J. (2004) *Tourism Mobilities: Places to Stay, Places in Play* (London: Routledge).

Shelton, B. A. and John, D. (1993) 'Does Marital Status Make a Difference? Housework among Married and Cohabiting Men and Women', *Journal of Family Issues*, 14(3).

Shelton, B. A. (1992) *Women, Men, and Time: Gender Differences in Paid Work, Housework, and Leisure* (Westport, CT: Greenwood).

Shiva, V. (1993) *Ecofeminism* (London: Zed Books).

Siegel, L. (2007) *Not Remotely Controlled: Notes on Television* (New York: Basic Books).

Signes, C. (2000) *A Genre based Approach to Talk on Daytime Television* (Valencia: Universitat De Valencia).

Signorielli, N. (2003) 'Prime-Time Violence 1993–2001: Has the Picture Really Changed?' *Journal of Broadcasting & Electronic Media*, 47.

Silverstone R. (1994) *Television and Everyday Life* (London: Routledge).

Simmel, G. (1950 [1903]) 'The Metropolis and Mental Life', in K. H. Wolff (ed.), *The Sociology of Georg Simmel* (New York: Free Press).

Simmons, J. and Dodds, T. (2003) *Crime in England and Wales 2002/03* (London: Home Office).

Simon, R. (2002) *Ibn Khaldūn: History as Science and the Patrimonial Empire. Translated by Klára Pogátsa*. (Budapest: Akadémiai Kiadó).

Simpson, G. E. and Yinger, J. M. (1986) *Racial and Cultural Minorities: An Analysis of Prejudice and Discrimination* (New York: Plenum Press).

Simpson, J. H. (1985) 'Socio-Moral Issues and Recent Presidential Elections', *Review of Religious Research*, 27.

Sinclair, P. (1987) *Unemployment: Economic Theory and Evidence* (Oxford: Blackwell).

Sjoberg, G. (1960) *The Pre-Industrial City: Past and Present* (New York: Free Press).

Sjoberg, G. (1963) 'The Rise and Fall of Cities: A Theoretical Perspective', *International Journal of Comparative Sociology*, 4.

Skeggs, B. (1997) *Formations of Class and Gender: Becoming Respectable* (London: Sage).

Skidmore, P. and Harkin, J. (2003) *Grown-up Trust* (London: Demos). Available at: www.demos.co.uk/TRUSprovocationfinal_pdf_media_public.aspx.

Skinner, Q. (ed.) (1990) *The Return of Grand Theory in the Human Sciences* (Cambridge: Cambridge University Press).

Skocpol, T. (1979) *States and Social Revolutions: A Comparative Analysis of France, Russia and China* (Cambridge: Cambridge University Press).

Slapper, G. and Tombs, S. (1999) *Corporate Crime* (Essex: Longman).

Smart, C. (2007) *Personal Life: New Directions in Sociological Thinking* (Cambridge: Polity)

Smart, C. and Neale, B. (1999) *Family Fragments?* (Cambridge: Polity).

Smith, A. (1991 [1776]) *The Wealth of Nations* (London: Everyman's Library).

Smith, A. and Twomey, B. (2002) 'Labour Market Experiences of People with Disability', *Labour Market Trends*, 110(8).

Smith, A. D. (1986) *The Ethnic Origins of Nations* (Oxford: Blackwell).

Smith, D. (1990) *Stepmothering* (London: Harvester).

Smith, D. (1997) 'Job Insecurity and Other Myths', *Management Today*.

Smith, M. J. (1998) *Ecologism: Towards Ecological Citizenship* (Buckingham: Open University Press).

Smith, M. J. and Pangsapa, P. (2008) *Environment and Citizenship: Integrating Justice, Responsibility and Civic Engagement* (London: Zed Books).

So, A. (1990) *Social Change and Development: Modernization, Dependency, and World-Systems Theories* (Newbury Park, CA: Sage).

Social Exclusion Unit (1998a) *Bringing Britain Together* (London: HMSO).

Social Exclusion Unit (1998b) *Rough Sleeping* (London: HMSO).

Sokolovsky, J. (1990) *The Cultural Context of Aging: Worldwide Perspectives* (New York: Bergin and Garvey).

Solomos, J. and Back, L. (1996) *Racism and Society* (Basingstoke: Macmillan).

Soule, A., Babb, P., Evandrou, M., Balchin, S. and Zealey, L. (2005) *Focus on Older People* (Basingstoke: Palgrave Macmillan).

Spender, D. (1982) *Invisible Women: The Schooling Scandal* (London: Writers and Readers Publishing Cooperative Society).

Spenner, K. (1983) 'Deciphering Prometheus: Temporal Change in the Skill Level of Work', *American Sociological Review*, 48.

Sreberny-Mohammadi, A., Winseck, D., McKenna, J. and Boyd-Barrett, O. (eds) (1997) *Media in Global Context: A Reader* (London: Hodder Arnold).

Stanton, E. C. (1985 [1895]) *The Woman's Bible: The Original Feminist Attack on the Bible* (Edinburgh: Polygon Books).

Stanworth, M. (1983) *Gender and Schooling* (London: Hutchinson).

Stanworth, M. (1984) 'Women and Class Analysis: A Reply to John Goldthorpe', *Sociology*, 18.

Stark, R. and Bainbridge, W. S. (1980) 'Towards a Theory of Religious Commitment', *Journal for the Scientific Study of Religion*, 19.

Stark, R. and Bainbridge, W. S. (1985) *The Future of Religion: Secularism, Revival, and Cult Formation* (Berkeley: University of California Press).

Stark, R. and Bainbridge, W. S. (1987) *A Theory of Religion* (New Brunswick, NJ: Rutgers University Press).

Statham, J. (1986) *Daughters and Sons: Experiences of Non-Sexist Childraising* (Oxford: Blackwell).

Stead, W. E. and Stead, J. G. (1996) *Management for a Small Planet: Strategic Decision Making and the Environment* (Thousand Oaks, CA, and London: Sage).

Steele, C. M. (1997) 'A Threat in the Air: How Stereotypes Shape Intellectual Identity and Performance', *American Psychologist*, 52.

Steele, C. M. and Aronson, J. (1995) 'Stereotype Threat and the Intellectual Test Performance of African Americans', *Journal of Personality and Social Psychology*, 69.

Steinberg, R. (1990) 'Social Construction of Skill: Gender, Power and Comparable Worth', *Work and Occupations*, 17.

Stern, V. (1989) *Bricks of Shame: Britain's Prisons* (London: Penguin Books).

Stiglitz, J. E. (2002) *Globalization and Its Discontents* (London: Allen Lane).

Stillwagon, E. (2001) 'HIV Transmission in Latin America: Comparison with Africa and Policy Implications', *South African Journal of Economics*, 68(5).

Stone, L. (1980) *The Family, Sex, and Marriage in England, 1500–1800* (New York: Harper and Row).

Stonewall (2003) *Profiles of Prejudice: The Nature of Prejudice in England* (London: Stonewall).

Storr, M. (2002) 'Sociology and Social Movements: Theories, Analyses and Ethical Dilemmas' in P. Hamilton and K. Thompson (eds), *Sociology and Society*. Vol. 4: *The Uses of Sociology* (Buckingham: Open University Press).

Strategy Unit (2003) *Ethnic Minorities and the Labour Market* (London: HMSO).

Straus, M. A and Gelles, R. J. (1986) 'Societal Change and Change in Family Violence from 1975 to 1985 as Revealed by Two National Surveys', *Journal of Marriage and the Family*, 48.

Sullivan, A. (1995) *Virtually Normal: An Argument About Homosexuality* (London: Picador).

Sullivan, O. (1997) 'Time Waits for No Woman: An Investigation of the Gendered Experience of Domestic Time', *Sociology*, 31.

Sullivan, O. (2000) 'The Domestic Division of Labour: Twenty Years of Change', *Sociology*, 34(3).

Sunday Times (2007) *Rich List 2007*.

Sunday Times (2008) *Rich List 2008*.

Sutherland, E. H. (1949) *Principles of Criminology* (Chicago: Lippincott).

Sutton, P. W. (2000) *Explaining Environmentalism: In Search of a New Social Movement* (Aldershot: Ashgate Publishing).

Sutton, P. W. (2004) *Nature, Environment and Society* (Basingstoke: Palgrave Macmillan).

Sutton, P. W. (2007) *The Environment: A Sociological Introduction* (Cambridge: Polity).

Sutton, P. W. and Vertigans, S. (2005) *Resurgent Islam: A Sociological Approach* (Cambridge: Polity).

Sutton, P. W. and Vertigans, S. (2006) 'Islamic "New Social Movements"? Radical Islam, Al-Qa'ida and Social Movement Theory', *Mobilization: An International Journal*, 11(1).

Svensson, N. L. (2004) *Extraterritorial Accountability: An Assessment of the Effectiveness of Child Sex Tourism Laws*, United Nations Special Report. Available at: Szasz, A. (1994) *EcoPopulism: Toxic Waste and the Movement for Environmental Justice* (Minneapolis: University of Minneapolis Press).

Tan, A. and Ramakrishna, K. (eds) (2002) *The New Terrorism* (Singapore: Eastern Universities Press).

Tarrow, S. (1998) *Power in Movement: Social Movements, Collective Action and Politics* (Cambridge: Cambridge University Press).

Tawney R. H. (1964 [1931]) *Equality* (London: Unwin Books).

Taylor, C. (1992) *Sources of the Self: The Making of the Modern Identity* (Cambridge: Cambridge University Press).

Taylor, I., Evans, K. and Fraser, P. (1996) *A Tale of Two Cities. Global Change, Local Feeling and Everyday Life in the North of England: A Study in Manchester and Sheffield* (London: Routledge).

Taylor, I., Walton, P. and Young, J. (1973) *The New Criminology for a Social Theory of Deviance* (London: Routledge & Kegan Paul).

Taylor, M. W. (1992) *Men Versus the State: Herbert Spencer and Late-Victorian Individualism* (Oxford: Clarendon Press).

Tempest, R. (1996) 'Barbie and the World Economy', *Los Angeles Times*, 22 September.

Therborn, G. (2004) *Between Sex and Power: Family in the World, 1900–2000* (London and New York: Routledge).

Thomas, C. (1999) *Female Forms: Experiencing and Understanding Disability* (Buckingham: Open University Press).

Thomas, C. (2002) 'Disability Theory: Key Ideas, Issues and Thinkers', in C. Barnes, L. Barton and M. Oliver (eds), *Disability Studies Today* (Cambridge: Polity).

Thomas, G. M. (1987) *Institutional Structure: Constituting State, Society and the Individual* (Newbury Park, CA: Sage).

Thomas, K. (1984) *Man and the Natural World: Changing Attitudes in England 1500–1800* (London: Penguin Books).

Thomas, W. I. (with Thomas, D.S.) (1928) *The Child in America: Behavior Problems and Programs* (New York: Knopf).

Thomas, W. I. and Znaniecki, F. (1966 [1918–20] *The Polish Peasant in Europe and America: Monograph of Our Immigrant Group*, 5 vols (New York: Dover).

Thompson, J. B. (1990) *Ideology and Modern Culture* (Cambridge: Polity).

Thompson, J. B. (1995) *The Media and Modernity: A Social Theory of the Media* (Cambridge: Polity).

Thompson, P. and Findlay, P. (1999) 'Changing the People: Social Engineering in the Contemporary Workplace', in A. Sayer and L. Ray (eds), *Culture and Economy after the Cultural Turn* (London: Sage).

Thompson, W. S. (1929) 'Population', *American Journal of Sociology*, 34.

Thorne, B. (1993) *Gender Play: Girls and Boys in School* (New Brunswick, NJ: Rutgers University Press).

Tilly, C. (1978) *From Mobilization to Revolution* (London: Longman Higher Education).

Tilly, C. (1995) 'Globalization Threatens Labor's Rights', *International Labor and Working Class History*, 47.

Tizard, B. and Hughes, M. (1984) *Young Children Learning, Talking and Thinking at Home and at School* (London: Fontana).

Toke, D. (2004) *The Politics of GM Food: A Comparative Study of the UK, USA, and EU* (New York: Routledge).

Tolson, A. (2005) *Media Talk: Spoken Discourse on TV and Radio* (Edinburgh: Edinburgh University Press).

Tolson, A. (ed.) (2001) *Media Talk: Spoken Discourse on TV and Radio* (Edinburgh: Edinburgh University Press)

Tomlinson, J. (1991) *Cultural Imperialism: A Critical Introduction* (London: Pinter).

Tonkiss, F. (2006) *Contemporary Economic Sociology: Globalisation, Production, Inequality* (London: Routledge).

Tönnies, F. (2001 [1887]) *Gemeinschaft Und Gesellschaft [Community and Civil Society]* (New York: Cambridge University Press).

Tough, J. (1976) *Listening to Children Talking* (London: Ward Lock Educational).

Touraine, A. (1971) *The Post-Industrial Society: Tomorrow's Social History: Classes, Conflict and Culture in the Programmed Society* (New York: Random House Inc).

Touraine, A. (1981) *The Voice and the Eye: An Analysis of Social Movements* (Cambridge: Cambridge University Press).

Townsend, I. (2002) 'The Burden of Taxation', 9 July, London, House of Commons Library: Research Paper 02/43.

Townsend, P. (1979) *Poverty in the United Kingdom* (Harmondsworth: Penguin).

Toynbee, P. (2003) *Hard Work: Life in Low Pay Britain* (London: Bloomsbury).

Treas, J. (1995) 'Older Americans in the 1990s and Beyond', *Population Bulletin*, 5.

Troeltsch, E. (1981 [1931]) *The Social Teaching of the Christian Churches*, 2 vols (Chicago, IL: University of Chicago Press).

Tuchman, G. (1978) 'Introduction: The Symbolic Annihilation of Women by the Mass Media', in G. Tuchman, A. K. Daniels and J. Benét, *Hearth and Home: Images of Women in the Mass Media* (New York: Oxford University Press).

Tunstall, J. (1977) *The Media Are American: Anglo-American Media in the World* (London: Constable).

Tunstall, J. (2007) *The Media Were American: US Mass Media in Decline* (New York: Oxford University Press, Inc.).

Turner, B. S. (1974) *Weber and Islam: A Critical Study* (London: Routledge).

Turner, B. S. (1990) 'Outline of a Theory of Citizenship', *Sociology*, 24(2).

Turner, B. S. (1995) *Medical Power and Social Knowledge* (London: Sage).

Turner, G. (2004) *Understanding Celebrity* (London: Sage).

UK Christian Handbook (2004) *Religious Trends, No. 4, Christian Research.*

UK Film Council (2003) *Statistical Yearbook 2003.*

UN (2003) *World Population Prospects: The 2002 Revision Highlights* (New York: UN Department of Economic and Social Affairs Population Division).

UN (2006) *World Urbanisation Prospects: The 2005 Revision* (New York: UN Department of Economic and Social Affairs Population Division).

UN Convention on the Rights of Persons with Disabilities (2006). Available at: www.un.org/disabilities/default.asp?id=259.

UN Department of Economic and Social Affairs (2006) *World Population Prospects: The 2006 Revision.* Available at: http://esa.un.org/unpp/.

UN Economic and Social Affairs Division (ESA) (2006) *World Population Prospects: The 2006 Revision* (New York: UN ESA Population Division).

UNDP (1998) *Human Development Report* (New York: UN Development Programme).

UNDP (2001) *Annual Report 2001* (New York: UN Development Programme).

UNDP (2002) *Are the Millennium Development Goals Feasible?* (New York: UN Development Programme). Available at: www.undp.org/dpa/choices/2002/september/Choices0902p7.pdf.

UNDP (2003) *Human Development Report* (New York: UN Development Programme).

UNDP (2004) *Human Development Report: Cultural Liberty in Today's Diverse World* (New York: UN Development Programme).

UNDP (2007a) *Human Development Report* (New York: UN Development Programme).

UNDP (2007b) *United Nations Development Programme, Annual Report 2007* (New York: UNDP).

UNESCO (2007) *Global Education Digest 2007* (Montreal, Quebec: UNESCO Institute for Statistics).

UNESCO (2008) *EFA Global Monitoring Report: Strong Foundations, Early Childhood Care and Education* (Paris: UNESCO Publishing). Available at: www.efareport. unesco.org.

UNESCO Institute for Statistics (2008). Available at: www.uis.unesco.org.

UNFAO (2001) *The Impact of HIV/AIDS on Food Security* (UN Food and Agricultural Organization, Conference on World Food Security)

UNFPA (1998) *State of the World Population 1998.* Available at: www.unfpa.org/swp/1998/index.htm.

UNFPA (2004) *State of the World Population 2004.* Available at: www.unfpa.org/swp/2004/pdf/en_swp04.pdf.

UNICEF (2000a) *The State of the World's Children, 2000* (New York: UN Children's Fund).

UNICEF (2000b) *Domestic Violence against Women and Girls* (Florence: UN Children's Fund)

Union of International Associations (2007) 'Vol. 1: Organization Descriptions and Cross-References', *Yearbook of International Organizations, 2006–7.*

Union, T. E. (2005) *The European Union at a Glance.* Available at: http://europa. eu.int/abc/index_en.htm.

UNMIK (2008) 'Ban Ki-moon urges restraint by all sides after Kosovo declares independence', 18 February. Available at: www.unmikonline.org/news.htm#1802.

UN Millennium Ecosystem Assessment Board (2005) *Living Beyond Our Means: Natural Assets and Human Well-being* (Washington, DC: Island Press).

UNWFP (2001) 'News Release: WFP Head Releases World Hunger Map and Warns of Hunger "Hot Spots" in 2001', January 8 (New York: United Nations World Food Programme).

UPIAS (1976) *Fundamental Principles of Disability* (London: Union of Physically Impaired Against Segregation).

Urban Task Force (1999) *Towards an Urban Renaissance. Final Report of the Urban Task Force, Chaired by Lord Rogers of Riverside* (London: Department of the Environment, Transport and the Regions).

Urry, J. (1990) *The Tourist Gaze: Leisure and Travel in Contemporary Societies* (London: Sage; 2nd edn 2001).

US Bureau of Justice (1998) *Capital Punishment 1997, Statistics Bulletin* (Washington, DC: US Government Printing Office).

US Bureau of Justice (2004) *Capital Punishment 2003* (Washington, DC: Office of Justice Programs, Bureau of Justice Statistics). Available at: www.ojp.usdoj.gov/bjs/pub/pdf/cp03.pdf.

US Department of Health and Human Services (2000) *Child Maltreatment 1998: Reports from the States to the National Child Abuse and Neglect Data System* (Washington, DC: US Government Printing Office)

Usher, R. and Edwards, R. (1994) *Postmodernism and Education* (New York: Routledge).

Vallas, S. and Beck, J. (1996) 'The Transformation of Work Revisited: The Limits of Flexibility in American Manufacturing', *Social Problems*, 43(3).

Van der Veer, P. (1994) *Religious Nationalism: Hindus and Muslims in India* (Berkeley: University of California Press).

Van Dijk, T. A. (1997) *Discourse Studies. A Multidisciplinary Introduction*, 2 vols (London: Sage).

Van Gennep, A. (1977 [1908]) *The Rites of Passage* (London: Routledge & Kegan Paul).

Vatican (2004) Letter to the Bishops of the Catholic Church on the Collaboration of Men and Women in the Church and in the World. Available at: www.vatican.va/roman_curia/congregations/cfaith/documents/rc_con_cfaith_doc_20040731_collaboration_en.html.

Vaughan, D. (1990) *Uncoupling: Turning Points in Intimate Relationships* (New York: Vintage).

Veit-Wilson, J. (1998) *Setting Adequate Standards* (Bristol: The Policy Press).

Vertovec, S. and Cohen, R. (eds) (2002) *Conceiving Cosmopolitanism: Theory, Context and Practice* (Oxford: Oxford University Press).

Vidal, J. (2003) '10 Million Join World Protest Rallies', *Guardian*, 13 February.

Vincent, J. (1999) *Politics, Power, and Old Age* (Buckingham: Open University Press).

Vincent, J. (2003) *Old Age* (London: Routledge).

Viorst, J. (1986) 'And the Prince Knelt Down and Tried to Put the Glass Slipper on Cinderella's Foot', in J. Zipes (ed.), *Don't Bet on the Prince: Contemporary Feminist Fairy Tales in North America and England* (New York: Methuen).

Visgilio, G. R. and Whitelaw, D. M. (eds) (2003) *Our Backyard: A Quest for Environmental Justice* (Lanham, MD and Oxford: Rowman and Littlefield).

Vogler, C. and Pahl, J. (1994) 'Money, Power and Inequality in Marriage', *Sociological Review*, 42.

Voicu, B., Voicu, M. and Strapcova, K. (2007) 'Engendered Housework: A Cross-European Analysis', IRISS Working Paper, May 2007.

Vold, G. B., Bernard, T. J. and Snipes, J. B. (2002) *Theoretical Criminology* (New York: Oxford University Press).

Von Clausewitz, C. (1993[1832]) *On War* (London: Everyman's Library).

Vygotsky, L. (1986 [1934]) *Thought and Language* (Cambridge, MA: The MIT Press).

Waddington, D., Critcher, C., Dicks, B. and Parry, D. (2001) *Out of the Ashes? The Social Impact of Industrial Contraction and Regeneration on Britain's Mining Communities* (London: Routledge).

Wagar, W. (1992) *A Short History of the Future* (Chicago, IL: University of Chicago Press).

Walby, S. A. (1986) 'Gender, Class and Stratification toward a New Approach', in R. Crompton and M. Mann (eds), *Gender and Stratification* (Oxford: Blackwell).

Walby, S. (1990) *Theorizing Patriarchy* (Oxford: Blackwell).

Walby, S. and Allen, J. (2004) *Domestic Violence, Sexual Assault and Stalking: Findings from the British Crime Survey*, Home Office Research Study 276 (London: Home Office).

Walker, C. (1994) 'Managing Poverty', *Sociology Review* (April).

Wall, D. 2007. *Cybercrimes: The Transformation of Crime in the Information Age* (Cambridge: Polity).

Wallerstein, I. (1974) *The Modern World-System*, vol. I (New York: Academic Press).

Wallerstein, I. (1980) *The Modern World-System*, vol. II (New York: Academic Press).

Wallerstein, I. (1989) *The Modern World-System*, vol. III (New York: Academic Press).

Wallis, R. (1984) *The Elementary Forms of New Religious Life* (London: Routledge and Kegan Paul).

Walmsley, R. 2007. *World Prison Population List* (Seventh Edition), International Centre for Prison Studies (London: King's College).

Walter, A. (1994) *The Revival of Death* (London and New York: Routledge).

Walter, A. (1999) *On Bereavement: The Culture of Grief* (Buckingham: Open University Press).

Walton, P. and Young, J. (eds) (1998) *The New Criminology Revisited* (Basingstoke: Palgrave Macmillan).

Warde, A. and Heatherington, K. (1993) 'A Changing Domestic Division of Labour? Issues of Measurement and Interpretation', *Work, Employment and Society*, 7.

Warner, S. (1993) 'Work in Progress toward a New Paradigm for the Sociological Study of Religion in the United States', *American Journal of Sociology*, 98.

Warren, B. (1980) *Imperialism: Pioneer of Capitalism* (London, Verso).

Watkins, S. (2004) 'A Weightless Hegemony: New Labour's Role in the Neoliberal Order', *New Left Review*, 25.

Watson, J. (2003) *Media Communication: An Introduction to Theory and Process* (Basingstoke: Palgrave Macmillan).

Watts, M. (1997) 'Black Gold, White Heat: State Violence, Local Resistance and the National Question in Nigeria', in S. Pile and M. Keith (eds), *Geographies of Resistance* (New York: Routledge).

Weaver, M. (2001) 'Urban Regeneration – the Issue Explained', *Guardian*, 19 March.

Weber, M. (1951) *The Religion of China* (New York: The Free Press).

Weber, M. (1952) *Ancient Judaism* (New York: The Free Press).

Weber, M. (1958 [1921]) *The City* (Glencoe, IL: The Free Press).

Weber, M. (1958) *The Religion of India* (New York: The Free Press).

Weber, M. (1963) *The Sociology of Religion* (Boston, MA: Beacon).

Weber, M. (1979 [1925]) *Economy and Society: An Outline of Interpretive Sociology* (Berkeley: University of California Press).

Weber, M. (1992 [1904–5]) *The Protestant Ethic and the Spirit of Capitalism* (London: Allen and Unwin).

Weeks, J. (1977) *Coming Out: Homosexual Politics in Britain, from the Nineteenth Century to the Present* (New York: Quartet).

Weeks, J. (1986) *Sexuality* (London: Methuen).

Weeks, J., Heaphy, B. and Donovan, C. (2004) 'The Lesbian and Gay Family', in J. Scott, J. Treas and M. Richards (eds), *The Blackwell Companion to the Sociology of Families* (Oxford, Blackwell Publishing).

Weitzer, R. (2000) *Sex For Sale: Prostitution, Pornography, and the Sex Industry* (New York: Routledge).

Weitzman, L. (1972) 'Sexual Socialization in Picture Books for Preschool Children', *American Journal of Sociology*, 77.

Wellman, B. S., Carrington, P. J. and Hall, A. (1988) 'Networks as Personal Communities', in B. Wellman and S. D. Berkowitz (eds), *Social Structures: A Network Approach* (New York: Cambridge University Press).

Westergaard, J. (1995) *Who Gets What? The Hardening of Class Inequality in the Late Twentieth Century* (Cambridge: Polity).

Western, B. (1997) *Between Class and Market: Postwar Unionization in the Capitalist Democracies* (Princeton: Princeton University Press).

Wetherell, M. and Edley, N. (1999) *Negotiating Hegemonic Masculinity: Imaginary Positions and Psycho-Discursive Practices*, Feminism & Psychology, 9(3).

Wheatley, P. (1971) *The Pivot of the Four Quarters* (Edinburgh: Edinburgh University Press).

Wheeler, D. L. (1998) 'Global Culture or Culture Clash: New Information Technologies in the Islamic World – A View from Kuwait', *Communication Research*, 25(4).

White, C., van Galen, F. and Yuan Huang Chow (2003) 'Trends in Social Class Differences in Mortality by Cause, 1986–2000' *Health Statistics Quarterly*, 20.

White, M. and Trevor, M. (1983) *Under Japanese Management: The Experience of British Workers* (London: Heinemann).

Whiteford, P. and Adema, W. (2007) *What Works Best in Reducing Child Poverty? A Benefit or Work Strategy?* (Paris: OECD).

Whittle, A. and Spicer, A. (2008) 'Is Actor-Network Theory Critical?', *Organization Studies*, 29(1).

Wicks, R. (2004) 'Labour's Unfinished Business', in *Overcoming Disadvantage: An Agenda for the Next 20 Years* (York: Joseph Rowntree Foundation).

Widmer, E. D., Treas, R. and Newcomb, R. (1998) 'Attitudes Towards Nonmarital Sex in 24 Countries' *The Journal of Sex Research*, 35.

Wilde, O. (1960) *The Picture of Dorian Gray* (Brown, Watson: London).

Wilkins, L. T. (1964) *Social Deviance: Social Policy Action and Research* (London: Tavistock).

Wilkinson, H. (1994) *No Turning Back* (London: Demos).

Wilkinson, H. and Mulgan, G. (1995) *Freedom's Children: Work, Relationships and Politics for 18–34 Year Olds in Britain Today* (London: Demos).

Wilkinson, R. (1996) *Unhealthy Societies: The Afflictions of Inequality* (London: Routledge).

Will, J., Self, P. and Datan, N. (1976) 'Maternal Behavior and Perceived Sex of Infant', *American Journal of Orthopsychiatry*, 46.

Williams, R. (1987) *Keywords: A Vocabulary of Culture and Society* (London: Fontana Paperbacks).

Williams, S. J. (1993) *Chronic Respiratory Illness* (London: Routledge).

Willis, P. (1977) *Learning to Labour: How Working-Class Kids Get Working-Class Jobs* (London: Saxon House).

Wilson, B. (1982) *Religion in Sociological Perspective* (Oxford: Clarendon Press).

Wilson, E. (2002) 'The Sphinx in the City: Urban Life, the Control of Disorder', in G. Bridge and S. Watson (eds), *The Blackwell City Reader* (Oxford: Blackwell).

Wilson, E. O. (1975) *Sociobiology: The New Synthesis* (Cambridge, MA: Harvard University Press).

Wilson, J. Q. and Kelling, G. L. (1982) 'Broken Windows: The Police and Neighbourhood Safety', *The Atlantic Monthly*, March.

Wilson, W. J. (1978) *The Declining Significance of Race: Blacks and Changing American Institutions* (Chicago, IL: University of Chicago Press).

Wilson, W. J. (1996) *When Work Disappears: The World of the New Urban Poor* (New York: Knopf).

Wilson, W. J. (1999) *The Bridge Over the Racial Divide: Rising Inequality and Coalition Politics* (Berkeley: University of California Press).

Winqvist, K. (2002) *Women and Men Beyond Retirement, Statistics in Focus: Population and Social Conditions, No. 21* (Luxemburg: Eurostat).

Wireless Intelligence (2007) *Annual Cellular Connections Growth 2006, by African Region*. Available at: www.wirelessintelligence.com/Data.aspx.

Wirth, L. (1938) 'Urbanism as a Way of Life', *American Journal of Sociology*, 44.

Women and Equality Unit (2004) *Women and Men in the Workplace* (London: Department of Trade and Industry).

Wood, J. (1984) 'Groping Towards Sexism: Boys' Sex Talk', in A. McRobbie and M. Nava (eds), *Gender and Generation* (London: Macmillan).

Wood, S. (1989) *The Transformation of Work? Skills, Flexibility and the Labour Process* (London: Unwin Hyman).

Woodrum, E. (1988) 'Moral Conservatism and the 1984 Presidential Election', *Journal for the Scientific Study of Religion*, 27.

Woolgar, S. and Pawluch, D. (1985) 'Ontological Gerrymandering: The Anatomy of Social Problems Explanations', *Social Problems*, 32.

World Bank (1995) *Workers in an Integrating World* (New York: Oxford University Press).

World Bank (1996) *Poverty Reduction: The Most Urgent Task* (Washington, DC: World Bank).

World Bank (1997) *World Development Report 1997: The State in a Changing World* (New York: Oxford University Press).

World Bank (2000–1) 'World Development Indicators', in *World Development Report 2000–2001: Attacking Poverty* (New York: Oxford University Press).

World Bank (2001) *Povertynet: Topics Relevant to Social Capital* (New York: Oxford University Press).

World Bank (2003) *World Development Indicators* (New York: Oxford University Press).

World Bank (2004) *World Development Report: Making Services Work for Poor People* (New York: Oxford University Press).

World Bank (2007a) *The Little Green Data Book* (New York: World Bank Publications).

World Bank (2007b) *World Development Indicators* (New York: Oxford University Press).

World Bank Atlas (2003) *World Bank Atlas 2003* (Washington, DC: World Bank).

World Bank Group (2002) *Disability in Developing Countries* (New York: World Bank).

World Health Organization (2001a) *Conquering Depression* (New Delhi: WHO Regional Office for South East Asia).

World Health Organization (2001a) *Rethinking Care from the Perspective of Disabled People*. WHO Conference Report and Recommendations, August.

World Health Organization (2002) *Global Suicide Rates* (Available at: www.who.int/mental_health/prevention/suicide/suicideprevent/en/>.

Worldwatch Institute (2004) *State of the World 2004: Consumption by the Numbers*. Available at: www.worldwatch.org/press/news/2004/01/07/.

Worrall, A. (1990) *Offending Women: Female Law-Breakers and the Criminal Justice System* (London: Routledge).

Wouters, C. (2002) 'The Quest for New Rituals in Dying and Mourning: Changes in the We-I balance', *Body and Society*, 8(1).

Wouters, C. (2004) *Sex and Manners: Female Emancipation in the West 1890–2000* (London and New York: Sage Publications).

Wright, C. (1992) *Race Relations in the Primary School* (London: David Fulton).

Wright, C. R. (1940) 'Functional Analysis and Mass Communication', *Public Opinion Quarterly*, 24.

Wright, C. R. (1960) 'Functional Analysis and Mass Communication', *Public Opinion Quarterly*, 24.

Wright, E. O. (1978) *Class, Crisis and the State* (London: New Left Books).

Wright, E. O. (1985) *Classes* (London: Verso).

Wright, E. O. (1997) *Class Counts: Comparative Studies in Class Analysis* (Cambridge: Cambridge University Press).

Wright, E. O. (2000) *Class Counts: Student Edition* (New York: Cambridge University Press).

Wrigley, E. A. (1968) *Population and History* (New York: McGraw-Hill).

Wuthnow, R. (1988) 'Sociology of Religion', in N. J. Smelser (ed.), *Handbook of Sociology* (Newbury Park, CA: Sage).

Yeung, W. J., Linver, M. and Brooks-Gunn, J. (2002) 'How Money Matters for Young Children's Development: Parental Investment and Family Processes', *Child Development* 73(6).

Young, I. M. (1980) 'Throwing Like a Girl: A Phenomenology of Feminine Body Comportment, Motility and Spatiality', *Human Studies*, Vol. 3.

Young, I. M. (1990) *Throwing Like a Girl and Other Essays in Feminist Philosophy and Social Theory* (Bloomington: Indiana University Press).

Young, I. M. (2005) *On Female Body Experience: Throwing Like a Girl and Other Essays* (New York: Oxford University Press).

Young, J. (1998) 'Breaking Windows: Situating the New Criminology', in P. Walton and J. Young (eds), *The New Criminology Revisited* (London: Macmillan).

Young, J. (1999) *The Exclusive Society: Social Exclusion, Crime and Difference in Late Modernity* (London: Sage).

Young, M. D. and Willmott, P. (1957) *Family and Kinship in East London* (London: Routledge & Kegan Paul).

Young, M. and Willmott, P. (1973) *The Symmetrical Family: A Study of Work and Leisure in the London Region* (London: Routledge and Kegan Paul).

Zald, M. and McCarthy, J. (1987) *Social Movements in an Organizational Society: Collected Essays* (New Brunswick: Transaction Publishing).

Zammuner, V. L. (1986) 'Children's Sex-Role Stereotypes: A Cross-Cultural Analysis', in P. Shaver and C. Hendrick (eds), *Sex and Gender* (Beverly Hills, CA: Sage).

Zammuner, V. L. (1987) 'Children's Sex-Role Stereotypes: A Cross-Cultural Analysis', in P. Shaver and C. Hendrick (eds), *Sex and Gender* (London: Sage).

Zayani, M. (ed.) (2005) *The Al Jazeera Phenomenon: Critical Perspectives on New Arab Media* (New York: Paradigm Publishers).

Zeitlin, I. (1984) *Ancient Judaism: Biblical Criticism from Max Weber to the Present* (Cambridge: Polity).

Zeitlin, I. (1988) *The Historical Jesus* (Cambridge: Polity).

Zerubavel, E. (1979) *Patterns of Time in Hospital Life* (Chicago, IL: University of Chicago Press).

Zerubavel, E. (1982) 'The Standardization of Time a Sociohistorical Perspective', *American Journal of Sociology*, 88.

Zhang, N. and Xu, W. (1995) 'Discovering the Positive within the Negative: The Women's Movement in a Changing China', in A. Basu (ed.), *The Challenge of Local Feminisms* (Boulder, CO: Westview).

Zimbardo, P. G. (1969) 'The Human Choice: Individuation, Reason, and Order Versus Deindividuation, Impulse, and Chaos', in W. J. Arnold and D. Levine (eds), *Nebraska Symposium on Motivation* (Lincoln: University of Nebraska Press).

Zimbardo, P. G. (1972) 'Pathology of Imprisonment', *Society*, 9.

Zubaida, S. (1996). 'How Successful is the Islamic Republic in Islamizing Iran?' in J. Beinen and J. Stork (eds), *Political Islam Essays from the Middle East Report* (Berkeley: University of California Press).

Zuboff, S. (1988) *In the Age of the Smart Machine: The Future of Work and Power* (New York: Basic Books).

Glossary

Absent father A father who, as a result of divorce or for other reasons, has little or no contact with his children.

Absolute poverty Poverty as defined in terms of the minimum requirements necessary to sustain a healthy existence.

Achieved status Social status based on an individual's effort, rather than traits assigned by biological factors. Examples of achieved status include 'veteran', 'graduate' or 'doctor'.

Actor-network theory (ANT) A theoretical approach to human and non-human relations that insists on the active involvement of non-human things as well as human beings. ANT has been influential in the sociology of organizations.

Affective individualism The belief in romantic attachment as a basis for contracting marriage ties.

Age-grade The system found in small traditional cultures according to which people belonging to a similar age group are categorized together and hold similar rights and obligations.

Ageing The combination of biological, psychological and social processes that affect people as they grow older.

Ageism Discrimination or prejudice against a person on the grounds of age.

Agencies of socialization Groups or social contexts within which processes of socialization take place. The family, peer groups, schools, the media and the workplace are all arenas in which cultural learning occurs.

Agrarian societies Societies whose means of subsistence is based on agricultural production (crop-growing).

Alienation The sense that our own abilities, as human beings, are taken over by other entities. The term was originally used by Feuerbach to refer to the projection of human powers onto gods. Subsequently, Karl Marx employed the term to refer to the loss of control on the part of workers over labour tasks, the products of their labour, other workers and the separation of workers from their essential 'species being'. In later sociology, alienation has been seen as involving feelings of powerlessness and, as such, has been used in a social-psychological way.

Al-Qaeda 'The base' – a network of terrorist activists across the world, whose stated ideology is 'radical Islamist', seeking to install a new Islamic Caliphate and remove foreign influence from Muslim countries. Founded in Afghanistan in 1988/9, the network's most well-known figure is Osama bin Laden.

Alternative medicine Sometimes referred to as complementary medicine, this approach to the treatment and prevention of disease encompasses a wide range of healing techniques which lie outside, or overlap with, orthodox medical practices. Alternative or complementary medicine embodies a holistic approach to health, addressing both physical and psychological elements of an individual's well-being.

Animism The belief that events in the world are mobilized by the activities of spirits.

Anomie A lack of social norms. The concept was used by Durkheim to describe feelings of aimlessness and despair provoked by the rapid social change in the modern world which results in social norms losing their hold.

Apartheid The official system of racial segregation established in South Africa in 1948 and practised until 1994.

Applied social research Research which aims not just to understand a social problem, but also to make a contribution to solving it. Much criminological research, for example, is applied research, aiming to reduce levels of crime. Applied social research is a feature of all social science disciplines and often demands the involvement of multi-disciplinary teams.

Ascribed status Social status based on biological factors, such as race, sex or age.

Assimilation The acceptance of a minority

group by a majority population, in which the group takes on the values and norms of the dominant culture.

Asylum-seeker A person who has applied for refuge in a foreign country because of fear of religious or political persecution in his or her country of origin.

Atavism In criminology, the nineteenth-century argument that criminals displayed traits held over from the history of human evolution, which accounted for their criminality.

Authoritarian states Political systems in which the needs and interests of the state take priority over those of average citizens, and popular participation in political affairs is severely limited or denied.

Authority Following Max Weber, many sociologists have argued that authority is the legitimate power which one person or a group holds over another. The element of legitimacy is vital to this understanding of authority and is the main means by which authority is distinguished from the more general concept of power. Power can be exerted by the use of force or violence. Authority, by contrast, depends on the acceptance by subordinates of the right of those above them to give them orders or directives.

Automation Production processes monitored and controlled by machines with only minimal supervision from people.

Back region An area away from 'front region' performances, characterized by Erving Goffman, where individuals are able to relax and behave in an informal way.

Bias Generally a preference or an inclination, especially one that inhibits impartial judgement. In statistical sampling or testing, an error caused by systematically favouring some outcomes over others.

Bilateral 'On both sides' – used to describe political negotiations between two parties.

Binuclear families A family structure in which a child has parents living in two different homes after separating, both of whom are involved in the child's upbringing.

Biodiversity The diversity of species of life forms on planet Earth.

Biographical research Research that takes individual lives or life histories as its main focus of interest. Biographical methods involve oral histories, life stories, autobiographies, biographies and more. Biographical research tries to find out how people make sense of their lives and relationships with others.

Biomedical model The set of principles underpinning Western medical systems and practices. The biomedical model of health defines diseases objectively, in accordance with the presence of recognized symptoms, and believes that the healthy body can be restored through scientifically based medical treatment. The human body is likened to a machine that can be returned to working order with the proper repairs.

Bisexual An orientation of sexual activities or feelings towards other people of either sex.

Black feminism A strand of feminist thought which highlights the multiple disadvantages of gender, class and race that shape the experiences of non-white women. Black feminists reject the idea of a single unified gender oppression that is experienced evenly by all women, and argue that early feminist analysis reflected the specific concerns of white, middle-class women.

Bureaucracy An organization of a hierarchical sort, which takes the form of a pyramid of authority. The term 'bureaucracy' was popularized by Max Weber. According to Weber, bureaucracy is the most efficient type of large-scale human organization. As organizations grow in size, Weber argued, they inevitably tend to become more and more bureaucratized.

Capital punishment The state-sanctioned execution of a person who has been convicted of a crime that is punishable by death. Capital punishment is commonly known as the 'death penalty'.

Capitalism A system of economic enterprise based on market exchange. 'Capital' refers to any asset, including money, property and machines, which can be used to produce commodities for sale or invested in a market with the hope of achieving a profit. Nearly all industrial societies today are capitalist in orientation – their economic systems are based on free enterprise and on economic competition.

Capitalists Those who own companies, land or stocks and shares, using these to generate economic returns.

Caste A form of stratification in which an individual's social position is fixed at birth and cannot be changed. There is virtually no intermarriage between the members of different caste groups.

Causal relationship A relationship in which one state of affairs (the effect) is brought about by another (the cause).

Causation The causal influence of one factor on another. Causal factors in sociology include the reasons individuals give for what they do, as well as external influences on their behaviour.

Childhood The early period of a person's life, usually divided into stages (such as infant, child, youth) leading towards adulthood. Definitions of childhood differ across time and place, which means that childhood is, in some measure, always socially constructed.

Church A large body of people belonging to an established religious organization. Churches normally have a formal structure, with a hierarchy of religious officials, and the term is also used for the building where their religious ceremonials are held.

Citizen A member of a political community, having both rights and duties associated with that membership.

Civil inattention The process whereby individuals who are in the same physical setting of interaction demonstrate to one another that they are aware of each other's presence, without being either threatening or over-friendly.

Civil partnership A legally sanctioned relationship between two people of the same sex. It gives same-sex couples legal recognition for their relationship and some or all of the rights of married couples.

Civil society The realm of activity which lies between the state and the market, including the family, schools, community associations and non-economic institutions. 'Civil society', or civic culture, is essential to vibrant democratic societies.

Class Although it is one of the most frequently used concepts in sociology, there is no clear agreement about how the notion should best be defined. For Marx, a class was a group of people standing in a common relationship to the means of production. Weber also saw class as an economic category, but stressed its interaction with social status and the affinities of 'party'. In recent times, some social scientists have used *occupation* extensively as an indicator of social class, others have stressed *ownership of property* and other wealth; still others are looking to *lifestyle* choices.

Clock time Time as measured by the clock – that is, assessed in terms of hours, minutes and seconds. Before the invention of clocks, time reckoning was based on events in the natural world, such as the rising and setting of the sun.

Cognition Human thought processes involving perception, reasoning, and remembering.

Cohabitation Two people living together in a sexual relationship of some permanence, without being married to each other.

Cohort A group of people sharing some common experiences within a certain period of time, usually used in relation to 'birth cohorts' – people born in the same years or few years.

Cold War The situation of conflict between the United States and the Soviet Union, together with their allies, which existed from the late 1940s until 1990. It was a 'cold' war because the two sides never actually engaged in military confrontation with each other.

Collective behaviour Activities of people and social groups that normally emerge spontaneously (such as crowds, riots and so on) rather than arising from processes of socialization leading to conformity to social rules and norms.

Collective consumption A concept used by Manuel Castells to refer to processes of consumption of common goods promoted by the city, such as transport services and leisure amenities.

Collective effervescence The sense of heightened energy created in collective gatherings and rituals, used by Durkheim to explain the religious experience as essentially social.

Colonialism The process whereby Western nations established their rule in parts of the world away from their home territories.

Communication The transmission of information from one individual or group to another. Communication is the necessary basis of all social interaction. In face to face contexts, communication is carried on by the use of language, but also by many bodily cues which individuals interpret in understanding what others say and do. With the development of writing and of electronic media such as radio, television or computer transmission systems, communication becomes, to varying degrees, detached from immediate contexts of face-to-face social relationships.

Communism A set of political ideas associated with Karl Marx, as developed particularly by Lenin, and institutionalized in China and, until 1990, in the Soviet Union and Eastern Europe.

Comparative questions Questions concerned with the drawing of comparisons between one context in a society and another, or contrasting examples from different societies, for the purposes of sociological theory or research.

Comparative research   Research that compares one set of findings on one society with the same type of findings on other societies.

Complicit masculinity   A term associated with R. W. Connell's writings on the gender hierarchy in society. Complicit masculinity is embodied by the many men in society who do not themselves live up to the ideal of hegemonic masculinity, yet benefit from its dominant position in the patriarchal order.

Compulsion of proximity   The need felt by individuals to interact with others in face-to-face settings.

Concrete operational stage   A stage of cognitive development, as formulated by Piaget, in which the child's thinking is based primarily on physical perception of the world. In this phase, the child is not yet capable of dealing with abstract concepts or hypothetical situations.

Conflict theories   A sociological perspective that focuses on the tensions, divisions and competing interests present in human societies. Conflict theorists believe that the scarcity and value of resources in society produces conflict as groups struggle to gain access to and control those resources. Many conflict theorists have been strongly influenced by the writings of Marx.

Confluent love   Active and contingent love, as opposed to the 'forever' qualities of romantic love.

Consumer society   A type of society which promotes the consumption of mass-produced products. Consumer societies also generate an ideology of consumerism, which assumes that ever increasing mass consumption is beneficial.

Control theory   A theory which sees crime as the outcome of an imbalance between impulses towards criminal activity and controls which deter it. Control theorists hold that criminals are rational beings who will act to maximize their own reward unless they are rendered unable to do so through either social or physical controls.

Controls   A statistical or experimental means of holding some variables constant in order to examine the causal influence of others.

Conurbation   A clustering of towns or cities into an unbroken urban environment.

Convenience sample   The arbitrary selection of respondents for a study, based on simple opportunity rather than a rigorous quest for representativeness. Used in much applied social research with practical applications.

Conversation analysis   The empirical study of conversations, employing techniques drawn from ethnomethodology. Conversation analysis examines details of naturally occurring conversations to reveal the organizational principles of talk and its role in the production and reproduction of social order.

Core countries   According to world-systems theory, the most advanced industrial countries, which take the lion's share of profits in the world economic system.

Corporate crime   Offences committed by large corporations in society. Examples of corporate crime include pollution, false advertising and violations of health and safety regulations.

Corporate culture   A branch of management theory that seeks to increase productivity and competitiveness through the creation of a unique organizational culture involving all members of a firm. A dynamic corporate culture – involving company events, rituals and traditions – is thought to enhance employee loyalty and promote group solidarity.

Corporation   A type of organization that is a legal entity in its own right and has both rights and responsibilities. Business corporations are created by groups of shareholders who own the corporation and organize its effective management to generate dividends for shareholders

Correlation   A regular relationship between two dimensions or variables, often expressed in statistical terms. Correlations may be positive or negative. A positive correlation between two variables exists where a high rank on one variable is regularly associated with a high rank on the other. A negative correlation exists where a high rank on one variable is regularly associated with a low rank on the other.

Correlation coefficient   A measure of the degree of correlation between two variables.

Cosmopolitanism   In sociology, a term describing a theoretical approach that moves beyond nation-state based thinking towards analysing the human world as a single community.

Created environment   Those aspects of the physical world deriving from the application of technology. Cities are created environments, featuring constructions established by human beings to serve their needs – including roads, railways, factories, offices, private homes and other buildings.

Crime Any action that contravenes the laws established by a political authority. Although we may tend to think of 'criminals' as a distinct subsection of the population, there are few people who have not broken the law in one way or another during the course of their lives. While laws are formulated by state authorities, it is by no means unknown for those authorities to engage in criminal behaviour in certain contexts.

Criminology The study of forms of behaviour that are sanctioned by criminal law.

Crisis of masculinity The argument that traditional forms of masculinity are being undermined by a combination of contemporary influences, provoking a critical phase in which men are unsure of themselves and their role in society.

Critical management studies Critical, usually neo-Marxist, studies of existing management studies approaches. Critical management studies draws from the Frankfurt School of Critical Theory, but is also influenced by the poststructuralist approach of Michel Foucault and others.

Critical realism An approach to science which insists on the existence of an objective external reality which is amenable to investigation (contrast with social constructionism). Critical realists see the task of science as bringing to light the underlying causes of observable events, which are not usually directly observable.

Crude birth rate A statistical measure representing the number of births within a given population per year, normally calculated in terms of the number of births per 1,000 members. Although the crude birth rate is a useful index, it is only a general measure, because it does not specify numbers of births in relation to age distribution.

Crude death rate A statistical measure representing the number of deaths that occur annually in a given population per year, normally calculated as the ratio of deaths per 1,000 members. Crude death rates give a general indication of the mortality levels of a community or society, but are limited in their usefulness because they do not take into account the age distribution.

Cult A fragmentary religious grouping, to which individuals are loosely affiliated, but which lacks any permanent structure. Cults quite often form round an inspirational leader.

Cultural capital Types of knowledge, skills and education which confer advantages on those who acquire them. Cultural capital can be embodied (in forms of speech or bodily comportment), objectified (in cultural products such as works of art) or institutionalized (in educational qualifications).

Cultural pluralism The coexistence of several subcultures within a given society on equal terms.

Cultural reproduction The transmission of cultural values and norms from generation to generation. Cultural reproduction refers to the mechanisms by which continuity of cultural experience is sustained across time. The processes of schooling in modern societies are among the main mechanisms of cultural reproduction, and operate in profound ways through the hidden curriculum – aspects of behaviour learnt by individuals in an informal way while at school.

Culture of poverty The thesis, popularized by Oscar Lewis, that poverty is not a result of individual inadequacies, but the outcome of a larger social and cultural atmosphere into which successive generations of children are socialized. The 'culture of poverty' refers to the values, beliefs, lifestyles, habits and traditions that are common among people living under conditions of material deprivation.

Culture The values, ceremonies and ways of life characteristic of a given group. Like the concept of society, the notion of culture is very widely used in sociology, as well as in the other social sciences (particularly anthropology). Culture is one of the most distinctive properties of human social association.

Cybercrime Criminal activities by means of electronic networks, or involving the use of new information technologies. Electronic money laundering, personal identity theft, electronic vandalism and monitoring of electronic correspondence are all emergent forms of cybercrime.

Cyberspace Electronic networks of interaction between individuals at different computer terminals, linking people at a level – in a dimension – that has no regard for territorial boundaries or physical presence.

Debureaucratization Decline in the predominance of Weberian-style bureaucracies as the typical organizational form within modern society.

Decommodification In the context of welfare provision, the degree to which welfare services are free of the market. In a predominantly decommodified system, welfare services such as education and healthcare are provided to all and are not linked to market processes. In a commodified system, welfare services are treated as commodities to be sold on the market like other goods and services.

Deforestation The destruction of forested land, often by commercial logging.

Degree of dispersal The range or distribution of a set of figures.

Deinstitutionalization The process by which individuals cared for in state facilities are returned to their families or to community-based residences.

Democracy A political system providing for the participation of citizens in political decision-making, often by the election of representatives to governing bodies.

Demographic transition An interpretation of population change, which holds that a stable ratio of births to deaths is achieved once a certain level of economic prosperity has been reached. According to this notion, in pre-industrial societies there is a rough balance between births and deaths, because population increase is kept in check by a lack of available food, and by disease or war. In modern societies, by contrast, population equilibrium is achieved because families are moved by economic incentives to limit the number of children.

Demography The study of the characteristics of human populations, including their size, composition and dynamics.

Denomination A religious sect which has lost its revivalist dynamism, and has become an institutionalized body, commanding the adherence of significant numbers of people.

Dependency culture A term popularized by Charles Murray to describe individuals who rely on state welfare provision rather than entering the labour market. The dependency culture is seen as the outcome of the 'nanny state', which undermines individual ambition and people's capacity for self-help.

Dependency ratio The ratio of people of dependent ages (children and the elderly) to people of economically active ages.

Dependency theory Theory of economic development derived from Marxism arguing that the poverty of low-income countries stems directly from their exploitation by wealthy countries and the transnational corporations that are based in wealthy countries.

Dependent variable A variable, or factor, causally influenced by another (the independent variable).

Desertification Instances of intense land degradation resulting in desert-like conditions over large areas.

Deskilling The process through which the skills of workers are downgraded or, over time, eliminated, and taken over by machines and/or managers.

Developmental questions Questions posed by sociologists when looking at the origins and path of development of social institutions from the past to the present.

Deviance Modes of action which do not conform to the norms or values held by most of the members of a group or society. What is regarded as 'deviant' is as widely variable as the norms and values that distinguish different cultures and subcultures from one another. Many forms of behaviour which are highly esteemed in one context, or by one group, are regarded negatively by others.

Deviancy amplification The unintended consequences that can result when, by labelling a behaviour as deviant, an agency of control actually provokes more of the same behaviour. For example, the reactions of police, the media and the public to perceived acts of deviance can 'amplify' the deviance itself, creating a 'spiral of deviancy'.

Deviant subculture A subculture whose members have values which differ substantially from those of the majority in a society.

Diaspora The dispersal of an ethnic population from an original homeland into foreign areas, often in a forced manner or under traumatic circumstances.

Disability studies A field of enquiry that investigates the position of disabled people in societies, including the experiences, history and campaigns of disabled people and their organizations.

Discourse analysis A general term covering several approaches to the study of language whether this is spoken or written. Most sociological versions of discourse analysis aim to understand language use within specific social and historical contexts.

Discourses The frameworks of thinking in a particular area of social life. For instance, the discourse of criminality means how people in a given society think and talk about crime.

Discrimination Activities that deny to the members of a particular group resources or rewards which can be obtained by others. Discrimination has to be distinguished from prejudice, although the two are usually quite closely associated. It can be the case that individuals who are prejudiced against others do not engage in discriminatory practices against them; conversely, people may act in a discriminatory fashion even though they are not prejudiced against those subject to such discrimination.

Disengagement theory A functionalist theory of ageing that holds that it is functional for society to remove people from their traditional roles when they become elderly, thereby freeing up those roles for others.

Displacement The transferring of ideas or emotions from their true source to another object.

Division of labour The division of a production system into specialized work tasks or occupations, creating economic interdependence. All societies have at least a rudimentary division of labour, especially between the tasks allocated to men and those performed by women. With the development of industrialism, however, the division of labour became vastly more complex than in any prior type of production system. In the modern world, it is now global in scope.

Documentary research The study of written texts including personal diaries, government policies, fictional works and mass media output.

Doubling time The time it takes for a particular level of population to double.

Dramaturgical analysis An approach to the study of social interaction based on the use of metaphors derived from the theatre.

Dysfunction Features of social life that challenge or create tensions in a social system.

Eco-efficiency The development of technologies that generate economic growth, but which do so at minimal cost to the environment.

Ecological citizenship A relatively recent extension of citizenship to include the rights and responsibilities of people towards the natural environment or 'nature'.

Ecological modernization Economic growth and development that incorporate positive policies to protect the environment. Supporters of ecological modernization argue that industrial development and ecological protection are not incompatible.

Economic capital In Pierre Bourdieu's work, resources such as money and property that form part of a system of material exchange. The ownership of economic capital brings significant advantages in itself and can also be exchanged for other forms of capital.

Economic interdependence The outcome of specialization and the division of labour, when self-sufficiency is superseded and individuals depend on others to produce many or most of the goods they need to sustain their lives.

Economy The system of production and exchange which provides for the material needs of individuals living in a given society. Economic institutions are of key importance in all social orders. What goes on in the economy usually influences many other aspects of social life. Modern economies differ very substantially from traditional ones, because the majority of the population is no longer engaged in agricultural production.

Education A social institution which promotes and enables the transmission of knowledge and skills across generations.

Egocentric According to Piaget, the characteristic quality of a child during the early years of her life. Egocentric thinking involves understanding objects and events in the environment solely in terms of the child's own position.

Elaborated code A form of speech involving the deliberate and constructed use of words to designate precise meanings, and adaptable to various cultural settings.

Embodiment In sociology, the notion that self-experience and identity are bounded by individual bodies, which express and partly shape self identities.

Embourgeoisement thesis The process by which bourgeois aspirations, and a bourgeois standard and style of life, becomes institutionalized in the working class. Marxists have argued that this phenomenon undermines working-class consciousness and frustrates working-class attempts to create social change.

Emigration The movement of people out of one country in order to settle in another.

Emotional intelligence The ability of individuals to use their emotions to develop qualities such as empathy, self-control, enthusiasm and persistence.

Emphasized femininity A term associated with R. W. Connell's writings on the gender hierarchy in society. Emphasized femininity forms an important complement to hegemonic masculinity, because it is oriented to accommodating the interests and needs of men. Many representations of women in the media and advertising embody emphasized femininity.

Empirical investigation Factual inquiry carried out in any given area of sociological study.

Encounter A meeting between two or more individuals in a situation of face-to-face interaction. Our day-to-day lives can be seen as a series of different encounters strung out across the course of the day. In modern societies, many of the encounters we have with others involve strangers rather than people we know well.

Endogamy The forbidding of marriage or sexual relations outside one's social group.

Endogenous In sociology, things which develop or originate within the society being studied rather than being introduced from outside (exogenous).

Entrepreneur Someone who starts or owns a business venture and takes personal responsibility for the risks involved and the potential rewards gained.

Environment The non-human, natural world within which human societies exist. In its broadest sense, the environment is the planet Earth.

Environmental issues All of those issues in society which involve *both* social relations and non-human, natural phenomena. Environmental issues can be seen as hybrids of society and nature.

Environmental justice The notion that all people have the right to a healthy and sustainable environment. Environmental justice campaigns have focused on removing the disproportionate risk of environmental pollution being borne by poor communities.

Epidemiology The study of the distribution and incidence of disease and illness within the population.

Estate A form of stratification involving inequalities between groups of individuals established by law.

Ethical religions Religions which depend on the ethical appeal of a 'great teacher' (like Buddha or Confucius), rather than on a belief in supernatural beings.

Ethnic cleansing The creation of ethnically homogeneous territories through the mass expulsion of other ethnic populations.

Ethnicity Cultural values and norms which distinguish the members of a given group from others. An ethnic group is one whose members share a distinct awareness of a common cultural identity, separating them from other groups around them. In virtually all societies ethnic differences are associated with variations in power and material wealth. Where ethnic differences arc also regarded as racial, such divisions are sometimes especially pronounced.

Ethnie A term used by Anthony Smith to describe a group that shares ideas of common ancestry, a common cultural identity and a link with a specific homeland.

Ethnocentric Understanding the ideas or practices of another culture in terms of those of one's own culture. Ethnocentric judgements fail to recognize the true qualities of other cultures. An ethnocentric individual is someone who is unable, or unwilling, to look at other cultures in their own terms.

Ethnography The study of people at firsthand using participant observation or interviewing.

Ethnomethodology The study of how people make sense of what others say and do in the course of day-to-day social interaction. Ethnomethodology is concerned with the 'ethnomethods' by means of which human beings sustain meaningful interchanges with one another.

Eugenics Attempts to improve the fitness of the human race through selective reproduction methods.

Evangelicalism A form of Protestantism characterized by a belief in spiritual rebirth (being 'born again').

Experiment A research method in which a hypothesis can be tested in a controlled and systematic way, either in an artificial situation constructed by the researcher, or in naturally occurring settings.

Exploitation A social or institutional relationship in which one party benefits at the expense of the other through an imbalance in power.

Extended family A family group consisting of close relatives extending beyond a couple and their children living either within the same household or in a close and continuous relationship with one another.

External risk Dangers that spring from the natural world and are unrelated to the actions of humans. Examples of external risk include droughts, earthquakes, famines and storms.

Factual questions   Questions that raise issues concerning matters of fact (rather than theoretical or moral issues).

Family   A group of individuals related to one another by blood ties, marriage or adoption who form an economic unit, the adult members of which are responsible for the upbringing of children. All known societies involve some form of family system, although the nature of family relationships is widely variable. While in modern societies the main family form is the nuclear family, a variety of extended family relationships are also often found.

Family capitalism   Capitalistic enterprise owned and administered by entrepreneurial families.

Fecundity   A measure of the number of children that it is biologically possible for a woman to produce.

Feminist theories   A sociological perspective which emphasizes the centrality of gender in analysing the social world, and particularly the uniqueness of the experience of women. There are many strands of feminist theory, but they all share in common the desire to explain gender inequalities in society and to work to overcome them.

Fertility   The average number of live-born children produced by women of childbearing age in a particular society.

Field   In Pierre Bourdieu's work – the social contexts within which people struggle for competitive advantage and dominance using various forms of capital. Each field has its own set of rules: for instance, the field of art and art appreciation has a very different set of rules to that of business.

First World   The group of nation-states that possesses mature industrialized economies, based on capitalistic production.

Flexible production   Process in which computers design customized products for a mass market.

Focus group   Originally used in market research, a focus group is a small group of people, selected from a larger sample, to take part in a discussion on topics of interest to the researcher.

Focused interaction   Interaction between individuals engaged in a common activity or a direct conversation with one another.

Fordism   The system pioneered by Henry Ford, involving the introduction of the moving assembly line, and crucially linking methods of mass production to the cultivation of a mass market for the goods produced – in Ford's case particularly his famous Model T Ford car.

Formal operational stage   According to Piaget's theory, a stage of cognitive development at which the growing child becomes capable of handling abstract concepts and hypothetical situations.

Formal relations   Relations which exist in groups and organizations laid down by the norms or rules of the 'official' system of authority.

Front region   A setting of social activity in which individuals seek to put on a definite 'performance' for others.

Functionalism   A theoretical perspective based on the notion that social events can best be explained in terms of the functions they perform – that is, the contributions they make to the continuity of a society – and on a view of society as a complex system whose various parts work in a relationship to each other in a way that needs to be understood.

Fundamentalism   A belief in returning to the literal meanings of scriptural texts. Fundamentalism may arise as a response to modernization and rationalization, insisting on faith-based answers, and defending tradition by using traditional grounds.

Gender inequality   The differences in the status, power and prestige women and men have in groups, collectivities and societies.

Gender order   A term associated with the writings of R. W. Connell, the gender order represents patterns of power relations between masculinities and femininities that are widespread throughout society.

Gender regime   The configuration of gender relations within a particular setting, such as a school, a family or a neighbourhood.

Gender relations   The societally patterned interactions between men and women.

Gender roles   Social roles assigned to each sex and labelled as masculine or feminine.

Gender   Social expectations about behaviour regarded as appropriate for the members of each sex. Gender does not refer to the physical attributes in terms of which men and women differ, but to socially formed traits of masculinity and femininity. The study of gender relations has become one of the most important areas of sociology in recent years, although for a long time they received little attention.

Gender socialization   How individuals develop different gender characteristics in the course of socialization processes.

Generalized other A concept in the theory of George Herbert Mead, according to which the individual takes over the general values of a given group or society during the socialization process.

Generation The whole group of individuals who are born and are living at the same time. Generations are not only born into but their experience is also shaped by a particular society.

Genetically modified organisms GMOs are plants or crops that have been produced through manipulation of the genes that compose them.

Genocide The systematic, planned attempt to destroy a racial, political or cultural group.

Genre A concept applied in media studies to refer to a distinct type of media product or cultural item. In the world of television, for example, different genres include soap opera, comedy, news programmes, sport and drama.

Gentrification A process of urban renewal in which older, decaying housing is refurbished by affluent people moving into the area.

Global city A city, such as London, New York or Tokyo, which has become an organizing centre of the new global economy.

Global commodity chains A worldwide network of labour and production processes yielding a finished product.

Global economic inequality Inequalities of income and material standards of life between the nation states of the world. Many studies of global economic inequality concentrate on the differences between the developed and developing worlds.

Global governance The framework of rules needed to tackle global problems, and the diverse set of institutions (including both international governmental organizations and national governments) needed to guarantee this framework of rules.

Global village A notion associated with the Canadian writer Marshall McLuhan, who saw the spread of electronic communication as binding the world into a small community. Thus, people in many different parts of the world follow the same news events through television programming.

Global warming The gradual increase in temperature of planet Earth. Although the 'greenhouse effect' occurs naturally as carbon dioxide traps the sun's rays and heats up the earth, global warming implies an enhanced greenhouse effect as a result of human activity. The effects of global warming are potentially devastating, including floods, droughts and other changes to the world's climate.

Globalization Growing interdependence between different peoples, regions and countries in the world as social and economic relationships come to stretch worldwide.

Glocalization The mix of globalizing processes and local contexts which often leads to a strengthening rather than diminishing of local and regional cultures.

Government The regular enactment of policies, decisions and matters of state by officials within a political apparatus. We can speak of 'government' as a process, or 'the government' to refer to the political authorities overseeing the implementation of their policies by officials. While in the past virtually all governments were headed by monarchs or emperors, in most modern societies the political authorities are elected and their officials are appointed on the basis of expertise and qualifications.

Grand theories Theories which attempt to arrive at an overall explanation of social life and/or social development. Karl Marx's theory of successive class conflicts as the driving force of history is an example of grand theorizing.

Greenhouse effect The build-up of heat-trapping gases within the earth's atmosphere. While a 'natural' greenhouse effect keeps the earth's temperatures at a comfortable level, the build-up of high concentrations of greenhouse gases through human activities has been linked to more rapid global warming.

Greying A term used to indicate that an increasing proportion of a society's population is becoming elderly.

Gross domestic product (GDP) All the goods and services on record as being produced by a country's economy in a particular year, regardless of who owns these factors.

Gross national income (GNI) GDP plus net property income (interest, rent, dividends and profits) from abroad. (The term GNI is now used in preference to GNP – gross national product – which is an older but similar measure.)

Group closure The means whereby a group establishes a clear boundary for itself and thereby separates itself from other groups.

Group production Production organized by means of small groups rather than individuals.

Habitus In Pierre Bourdieu's work – the set of dispositions (including ways of thinking and acting), which members of particular social groups and social classes acquire, largely unconsciously, by virtue of living in the same objective conditions.

Health transition   The shift from acute, infectious diseases to chronic non-infectious diseases as the main cause of death in a society. In industrialized societies which have undergone the health transition, infectious diseases such as tuberculosis, cholera and malaria have been practically eradicated and chronic diseases such as cancer and heart disease have become the most common cause of death.

Hegemonic masculinity   A term first introduced by R. W. Connell, hegemonic masculinity refers to the dominant form of masculinity within the gender hierarchy. Although hegemonic masculinity subordinates other masculinities and femininities, it can be challenged by them. In most Western societies today, hegemonic masculinity is associated with whiteness, heterosexuality, marriage, authority and physical toughness.

Heterosexuality   An orientation in sexual activity or feelings towards people of the opposite sex.

Hidden curriculum   Traits of behaviour or attitudes that are learned at school, but which are not included within the formal curriculum. The hidden curriculum is the 'unstated agenda' involved in schooling – conveying, for example, aspects of gender differences.

Higher education   Education beyond school level, in colleges or universities.

High-trust systems   Organizations, or work settings, in which individuals are permitted a great deal of autonomy and control over the work task.

Homeless   People who have no place to sleep and either stay in free shelters or sleep in public places not meant for habitation.

Homophobia   An irrational fear or disdain of homosexuals.

Homosexual masculinity   According to R. W. Connell's model of gender relations, homosexual masculinity is stigmatized and located at the bottom of the gender hierarchy for men. In the prevailing gender order, homosexuals are seen as the opposite of the 'real man' embodied by hegemonic masculinity.

Homosexuality   An orientation of sexual activities or feelings towards others of the same sex.

Household   All of the people occupying and residing in a housing unit, sharing common living rooms and making common provision for the essentials such as food.

Housework   Unpaid work carried out, usually by women, in the home: domestic chores such as cooking, cleaning and shopping.

Human resource management (HRM)   A branch of management theory that regards employee enthusiasm and commitment as essential to economic competitiveness. The HRM approach seeks to develop in workers the sense that they have an investment in company products and in the work process itself.

Hunting and gathering societies   Societies whose mode of subsistence is gained from hunting animals, fishing and gathering edible plants.

Hyperreality   An idea associated with the French author Jean Baudrillard, who argued that, as a result of the spread of electronic communication, there is no longer a separate 'reality' to which TV programmes and other cultural products refer. Instead, what we take to be 'reality' is structured by such communication itself. So the items reported on the news are not just about a separate series of events, but actually themselves define and construct what those events are.

Hypothesis   An idea, or an educated guess, about a given state of affairs, put forward in exact terms to provide the basis for empirical testing.

Ideal type   A 'pure type', constructed by emphasizing certain traits of a given social item into an analytical model which does not necessarily exist anywhere in reality. The traits are defining, not necessarily desirable, ones. An example is Max Weber's ideal type of bureaucratic organization.

Identity   The distinctive characteristics of a person's character or the character of a group which relate to who they are and what is meaningful to them. Some of the main sources of identity include gender, sexual orientation, nationality or ethnicity, and social class. An important marker of an individual's identity is his or her name, and naming is also important for group identity.

Ideology   Shared ideas or beliefs which serve to justify the interests of dominant groups. Ideologies are found in all societies in which there are systematic and ingrained inequalities between groups. The concept of ideology has a close connection with that of power, since ideological systems serve to legitimize the differential power held by groups.

Immigration　The movement of people into one country from another for the purpose of settlement.

Impression management　An idea associated with the American sociologist Erving Goffman. People 'manage' or control the impressions others have of them by choosing what to conceal and what to reveal when they meet other people.

Incest　Sexual activity between close family members.

Independent variable　A variable, or factor, that causally influences another (the dependent variable).

Individual model of disability　A theory that holds that individual limitations are the main cause of the problems experienced by disabled people: bodily 'abnormality' is seen as causing some degree of 'disability' or functional limitation. This functional limitation is seen as the basis for a wider classification of an individual as 'an invalid'. The individual model of disability has been criticized by supporters of the social model of disability.

Industrial Revolution　The broad spectrum of social and economic transformations that surrounded the development of modern forms of industry. The Industrial Revolution of the mid-eighteenth century launched the long-term process of industrialization.

Industrial societies　Societies in which the vast majority of the labour force works in industrial production.

Industrialization　The development of modern forms of industry – factories, machines and large-scale production processes. Industrializ-ation has been one of the main sets of processes influencing the social world over the past two centuries. Those societies which are industrialized have characteristics quite different from those of the less developed countries. For instance, with the advance of industrialization only a tiny proportion of the population works in agriculture – a major contrast with pre-industrial countries.

Infant mortality rate　The number of infants who die during the first year of life, per 1,000 live births.

Informal economy　Economic transactions carried on outside the sphere of orthodox paid employment.

Informal relations　Relations which exist in groups and organizations developed on the basis of personal connections; ways of doing things that depart from formally recognized modes of procedure.

Informalization　The social process through which the formal codes of manners and behaviour, characteristic of an earlier period, lose their hold amongst a population, resulting in a wider range of acceptable behaviours.

Information poverty　The 'information poor' consist of those who have little or no access to information technology, such as computers.

Information society　A society no longer based primarily on the production of material goods but on the production of knowledge. The notion of the information society is closely bound up with the rise of information technology.

Information technology　Forms of technology based on information processing and requiring microelectronic circuitry.

Institutional capitalism　Capitalistic enterprise organized on the basis of institutional shareholding.

Institutional racism　Patterns of discrimination based on ethnicity that have become structured into existing social institutions.

Intelligence　Level of intellectual ability, particularly as measured by IQ (intelligence quotient) tests.

Interactional vandalism　The deliberate subversion of the tacit rules of conversation.

Intergenerational mobility　Movement up or down a social stratification hierarchy from one generation to another.

International governmental organization (IGO)　An international organization established by treaties between governments for the purpose of conducting business between the nations making up its membership.

International non-governmental organizations (INGOs)　An international organization established by agreements between the individuals or private organizations making up its membership.

Internet　A global system of connections between computers allowing people to communicate with one another and find information on the World Wide Web by visuals, sounds and text in a way that escapes the time and space, and the cost, limitations of distance – and also the control of territorial governments.

Internet-based learning　Educational activity connected through the medium of the Internet.

Interpretative sociology　Several approaches to the study of society, including symbolic interactionism and phenomenology, which investigate the meaningful character of social life for its participants.

Interviews   One-to-one conversations aimed at eliciting information about some aspect of social life. Interviews usually involve a predetermined schedule of questions and can be structured, semi-structured or open-ended depending on the kind of information required.

Intragenerational mobility   Movement up or down a social stratification hierarchy within the course of a personal career.

IQ   Short for 'intelligence quotient', a score attained on tests consisting of a mixture of conceptual and computational problems.

Iron law of oligarchy   A term coined by Weber's student Roberto Michels, meaning that large organizations tend towards the centralization of power in the hands of the few, making democracy difficult.

Job insecurity   A sense of apprehension experienced by employees about both the stability of their work position and their role within the workplace.

Kinship   A relation which links individuals through blood ties, marriage or adoption. Kinship relations are by definition involved in marriage and the family, but extend much more broadly than these institutions. While in most modern societies few social obligations are involved in kinship relations extending beyond the immediate family, in many other cultures kinship is of vital importance for most aspects of social life.

Knowledge economy   A society no longer based primarily on the production of material goods but on the production of knowledge. Its emergence has been linked to the development of a broad base of consumers who are technologically literate and have made new advances in computing, entertainment and telecommunications part of their lives.

Knowledge society   Another common term for information society – a society based on the production and consumption of knowledge and information.

Kuznets Curve   A formula showing that inequality increases during the early stages of capitalist development, then declines, and eventually stabilizes at a relatively low level; advanced by the economist Simon Kuznets.

Labelling theory   An approach to the study of deviance which suggests that people become 'deviant' because certain labels are attached to their behaviour by political authorities and others.

Latent functions   Functional consequences that are not intended or recognized by the members of a social system in which they occur.

Lateral mobility   Movement of individuals from one region of a country to another, or across countries.

Left Realism   A strain of criminology, popularized in the 1980s by the work of Jock Young, that focused on the victims of crime and called for criminology to engage practically with issues of crime control and social policy.

Legitimacy   A particular political order gains legitimacy if most of those governed by it recognize it as just and valid.

Lesbianism   Homosexual activities or attachment between women.

Liberal democracy   A system of democracy based on parliamentary institutions, coupled to the free market system in the area of economic production.

Liberal feminism   A form of feminist theory that believes that gender inequality is produced by reduced access for women and girls to civil rights and certain social resources, such as education and employment. Liberal feminists tend to seek solutions through changes in legislation that ensure the rights of individuals are protected.

Life expectancy   The length of time people can on average expect to live when born. Specifically, the concept refers to the number of years a newborn infant can be expected to live if prevailing patterns of mortality at the time of its birth stay the same throughout its life, regardless of gender.

Life histories   Studies of the overall lives of individuals, often based both on self-reporting and on documents such as letters.

Life-course   The various transitions people experience during their entire life. Sociologists have found that such transitions vary widely across history and cultures, thus the life-course is socially as well as biologically shaped (contrast with life-cycle).

Life-cycle   The common-sense view that all human beings pass through the same biological stages from birth to death (contrast with life-course).

Lifelong learning   The idea that learning and the acquisition of skills should occur at all stages of an individual's life, not simply in the formal educational system early in life. Adult continuing education programmes, mid-career training, Internet-based learning opportunities and community-based 'learning banks' are all ways in which individuals can engage in lifelong learning.

Life-span   The maximum length of life that is biologically possible for a member of a given species.

Lifestyle choices   Decisions made by individuals about their consumption of goods, services and culture. Lifestyle choices have been seen by many sociologists as important reflections of class positions.

Literacy   The ability to read and write.

Low-trust systems   An organizational or work setting in which individuals are allowed little responsibility for, or control over, the work task.

Macrosociology   The study of large-scale groups, organizations or social systems.

Male breadwinner   Until recently in many industrialized societies, the traditional role of the man in providing for the family through employment outside the home. The 'male breadwinner model' has declined in significance with changes in family patterns and the steady growth in the numbers of women entering the labour market.

Male inexpressiveness   The difficulties men have in expressing, or talking about, their feelings to others.

Malthusianism   The idea, first advanced by Thomas Malthus two centuries ago, that population growth tends to outstrip the resources available to support it. Malthus argued that people must limit their frequency of sexual intercourse in order to avoid excessive population growth and a future of misery and starvation.

Managerial capitalism   Capitalistic enterprises administered by managerial executives rather than by owners.

Manifest functions   The functions of a type of social activity that are known to and intended by the individuals involved in the activity.

Manufactured risk   Dangers that are created by the impact of human knowledge and technology upon the natural world. Examples of manufactured risk include global warming and genetically modified foods.

Market-oriented theories   Theories about economic development that assume that the best possible economic consequences will result if individuals are free to make their own economic decisions, uninhibited by governmental constraint.

Marriage   A socially approved sexual relationship between two individuals. Marriage almost always involves two persons of opposite sexes, but in some cultures, certain types of homosexual marriage are allowed. Marriage normally forms the basis of a family of procreation – that is, it is expected that the married couple will produce and bring up children. Many societies permit polygamy, in which an individual may have several spouses at the same time.

Mass customization   The large-scale production of items designed for particular customers through the use of new technologies.

Mass media   Forms of communication, such as newspapers, magazines, radio and television, designed to reach mass audiences.

Mass production   The production of long runs of goods using machine power. Mass production was one outcome of the Industrial Revolution.

Master status   The status or statuses that generally take priority over other indicators of social standing and determine a person's overall position in society.

Materialist conception of history   The view developed by Marx according to which 'material' or economic factors have a prime role in determining historical change.

Maternal deprivation   The absence of a stable and affectionate relationship between a child and its mother early in life. John Bowlby argued that maternal deprivation can lead to mental illness or deviant behaviour later in life.

Matrilineal   Relating to, based on, or tracing ancestral descent through the maternal line.

Matrilocal   Family systems in which the husband is expected to live near the wife's parents.

Mean   A statistical measure of central tendency, or average, based on dividing a total by the number of individual cases.

Means of production   The means whereby the production of material goods is carried on in a society, including not just technology but the social relations between producers.

Means-tested benefits   Welfare services that are available only to citizens who meet certain criteria based not only on need but also on levels of income and savings.

Measures of central tendency   These are ways of calculating averages, the three most common being the mean, the median and the mode.

Media imperialism   A version of imperialism enabled by communications technology, claimed by some to have produced a cultural empire in which media content originating in the industrialized countries is imposed on less developed nations which lack the resources to maintain their cultural independence.

Media regulation   The use of legal means to control media ownership and the content of media communications.

Median   The number that falls halfway in a range of numbers – a way of calculating central tendency that is sometimes more useful than calculating a mean.

Medical gaze   In modern medicine, the detached and value-free approach taken by medical specialists in viewing and treating a sick patient.

Megacities   A term favoured by Manuel Castells to describe large, intensely concentrated urban spaces that serve as connection points for the global economy. It is projected that by 2015, there will be 36 'megacities' with populations of more than eight million residents.

Megalopolis   The 'city of all cities', a term coined in ancient Greece to refer to a city-state that was planned to be the envy of all civilizations, but used in modern times to refer to very large – or overlarge – conurbations.

Melting pot   The idea that ethnic differences can be combined to create new patterns of behaviour drawing on diverse cultural sources.

Meritocracy   A system in which social positions are filled on the basis of individual merit and achievement, rather than ascribed criteria such as inherited wealth, sex or social background.

Metanarratives   Broad, overarching theories or beliefs about the operation of society and the nature of social change. Marxism and functionalism are examples of metanarratives that have been employed by sociologists to explain how the world works. Postmodernists reject such 'grand theories', arguing that it is impossible to identify any fundamental truths underpinning human society.

Microsociology   The study of human behaviour in contexts of face-to-face interaction.

Middle class   A broad spectrum of people working in many different occupations, from employees in the service industry to school teachers to medical professionals. Because of the expansion of professional, managerial and administrative occupations in advanced societies, the middle class may encompass the majority of the population in countries like Britain.

Minority group   A group of people in a minority in a given society who, because of their distinct physical or cultural characteristics, find themselves in situations of inequality within that society. Such groups include ethnic minorities.

Mixed methods   The use of both quantitative and qualitative research methods as part of a single research study.

Mode of production   Within Marxism, the constitutive characteristic of a society based on the socio-economic system predominant within it – for example, capitalism, feudalism or socialism.

Mode   The number that appears most often in a given set of data. This can sometimes be a helpful way of portraying central tendency.

Modernity   The period following the mid-eighteenth-century European Enlightenment, which is characterized by the combination of secularization, rationalization, democratization, individualism and the rise of scientific thinking.

Modernization theory   A version of market-oriented development theory that argues that low-income societies develop economically only if they give up their traditional ways and adopt modern economic institutions, technologies, and cultural values that emphasize savings and productive investment.

Monarchies   Those political systems headed by a single person whose power is passed down through their family across generations.

Monogamy   A form of marriage in which each married partner is allowed only one spouse at any given time.

Monopoly   A situation in which a single firm dominates in a given industry.

Monotheism   Belief in one single God.

Moral consensus   The shared values emphasized by functionalists which, they argue, are necessary for a well ordered society.

Moral panic   A term popularized by Stanley Cohen to describe a societal overreaction to a certain group or type of behaviour that is taken as symptomatic of general social disorder. Moral panics often arise around events that are in fact relatively trivial in terms of the nature of the act and the number of people involved.

Mortality   The number of deaths in a population.

Multiculturalism Ethnic groups exist separately and share equally in economic and political life.

Multilateral Involving many different sides or parties, normally used to describe relations and meetings involving a number of national governments.

Multimedia The combination of what used to be different media requiring different technologies (for instance, visuals and sound) on a single medium, such as a CD-ROM, which can be played on a computer.

Nanotechnology The science and technology of building electronic circuits and devices with, according to a broad definition, dimensions of less than 100 nanometres (one nanometre is one-billionth of a metre).

Nation A group of people bound together by a strong sense of shared values, cultural characteristics such as language and religion and a perceived common history.

Nationalism A set of beliefs, political ideas and movements expressing identification with a given national community and pursuing the interests of that community.

Nations without states Instances in which the members of a nation lack political sovereignty over the area they claim as their own.

Nation-state A particular type of state, characteristic of the modern world, in which a government has sovereign power within a defined territorial area, and the mass of the population are citizens who know themselves to be part of a single nation. Nation-states are closely associated with the rise of nationalism, although nationalist loyalties do not always conform to the boundaries of specific states that exist today. Nation-states developed as part of an emerging nation-state system, originating in Europe, but in current times spanning the whole globe.

Nature A difficult word to pin down, but today generally taken to be the non-human environment of animals, plants, seas and land. Its meaning has changed several times; previously, it was thought to be the essential character of things or the forces that direct life.

Neoliberalism The economic belief that free market forces, achieved by minimizing government restrictions on business, provide the only route to economic growth.

Neo-local residence Involves the creation of a new household each time a child marries or when she or he reaches adulthood and becomes economically active.

Network A set of informal and formal social ties that links people to each other.

New Age movement A general term to describe the diverse spectrum of beliefs and practices oriented on inner spirituality. Paganism, Eastern mysticism, shamanism, alternative forms of healing, and astrology are all examples of 'New Age' activities.

New criminology A branch of criminological thought, prominent in Britain in the 1970s, that regarded deviance as deliberately chosen and often political in nature. The 'new criminologists' argued that crime and deviance could only be understood in the context of power and inequality within society.

New Labour The reforms introduced by Tony Blair when he assumed leadership of the British Labour Party, and by means of which he sought to move the party in new directions, particularly a successful campaign to abolish Clause 4, which committed the party to public ownership of industry.

New migration A term referring to changes in patterns of migration in Europe in the years following 1989. New migration has been influenced by the end of the Cold War and the fall of the Berlin Wall, the prolonged ethnic conflict in the former Yugoslavia and the process of European integration, altering the dynamics between traditional 'countries of origin' and 'countries of destination'.

New racism Racist outlooks, also referred to as cultural racism, that are predicated on cultural or religious differences, rather than biological ones.

New religious movements (NRMs) The broad range of religious and spiritual groups, cults and sects that have emerged alongside mainstream religions. NRMs range from spiritual and self-help groups within the New Age movement to exclusive sects such as the Hare Krishnas.

New social movements A set of social movements that have arisen in Western societies since the 1960s, such as student movements, second-wave feminism, environmentalism, the anti-nuclear movement and 'anti-globalization' demonstrations. They differ from earlier social movements in their new social issues, loose organizational form, new middle-class base and non-violent action repertoire. They are said to reflect the postmaterial values emerging in the relatively rich countries after 1945.

Newly industrializing countries Third World economies which over the past two or three decades have begun to develop a strong industrial base, such as Brazil and Singapore.

Non-verbal communication Communication between individuals based on facial expression or bodily gesture, rather than on the use of language.

Norms Rules of behaviour that reflect or embody a culture's values, either prescribing a given type of behaviour, or forbidding it. Norms are always backed by sanctions of one kind or another, varying from informal disapproval to physical punishment or execution.

Nuclear family A family group consisting of mother, father (or one of these) and dependent children.

Occupation Any form of paid employment in which an individual works in a regular way.

Occupational gender segregation The way that men and women are concentrated in different types of jobs, based on prevailing understandings of what is appropriate 'male' and 'female' work.

OECD Organization for Economic Co-operation and Development, based in Paris. An international organization formed in 1961 to take over the work of the post-war OEEC (Organization for European Economic Cooperation). The OECD aims to assist its members to achieve 'sustainable economic growth' and employment.

Oligopoly The domination of a small number of firms in a given industry.

Oral history Interviews with people about events they witnessed or experienced earlier in their lives.

Organic solidarity According to Emile Durkheim, the social cohesion that results from the various parts of a society functioning as an integrated whole.

Organization A large group of individuals, involving a definite set of authority relations. Many types of organization exist in industrial societies, influencing most aspects of our lives. While not all organizations are bureaucratic in a formal sense, there are quite close links between the development of organizations and bureaucratic tendencies.

Outsourcing The contracting out of a company's work tasks, which were previously carried out internally. Outsourcing can involve simple tasks such as the production of one part of a product, but can extend to contracting out whole departments, as when companies outsource their entire IT operation.

Participant observation A method of research widely used in sociology and anthropology, in which the researcher takes part in the activities of a group or community being studied.

Participatory democracy A system of democracy in which all members of a group or community participate collectively in the taking of major decisions.

Party A group of individuals who work together because they have common backgrounds, aims or interests. According to Weber, party is one of the factors, alongside class and status, that shape patterns of social stratification.

Pastoral societies Societies whose subsistence derives from the rearing of domesticated animals; there is often a need to migrate between different areas according to seasonal changes or to seek fresh grazing.

Pathologies Literally, the scientific study of the nature of diseases, their causes, processes, development and consequences.

Patriarchy The dominance of men over women. All known societies are patriarchal, although there are variations in the degree and nature of the power men exercise, as compared with women. One of the prime objectives of women's movements in modern societies is to combat existing patriarchal institutions.

Patrilineal Relating to, based on, or tracing ancestral descent through the paternal line.

Patrilocal Family systems in which the wife is expected to live near the husband's parents.

Pauperization Literally, to make a pauper of, or impoverish. Marx used the term to describe the process by which the working class grows increasingly impoverished in relation to the capitalist class.

Peer group A friendship group composed of individuals of similar age and social status.

Peripheral countries Countries that have a marginal role in the world economy and are thus dependent on the core-producing societies for their trading relationships.

Personal space The physical space individuals maintain between themselves and others; it may vary between intimate distance for close relationships, social distance for formal encounters and public distance when confronted by an audience.

Personality stabilization According to functionalists, the family plays a crucial role in assisting its adult members emotionally. Marriage between adult men and women is the arrangement through which adult personalities are supported and kept healthy.

Pilot studies   Trial runs in survey research.

Plastic sexuality   Sexuality freed from the needs of reproduction and moulded by the individual.

Political party   An organization established with the aim of achieving governmental power by electoral means and using that power to pursue a specific programme.

Politics   The means by which power is employed and contested to influence the nature and content of governmental activities. The sphere of the 'political' includes the activities of those in government, but also the actions and competing interests of many other groups and individuals.

Polyandry   A form of marriage in which a woman may simultaneously have two or more husbands.

Polycentric transnationals   Transnational corporations whose administrative structure is global but whose corporate practices are adapted according to local circumstances.

Polygamy   A form of marriage in which a person may have two or more spouses simultaneously.

Polygyny   A form of marriage in which a man may have more than one wife at the same time.

Polytheism   Belief in two or more gods.

Population   In the context of social research, the people who are the focus of a study or survey.

Portfolio worker   A worker who possesses a diversity of skills or qualifications and is therefore able to move easily from job to job.

Positivism   In sociology, the view that the study of the social world should be conducted according to the principles of natural science. A positivist approach to sociology holds that objective knowledge can be produced through careful observation, comparison and experimentation.

Post-Fordism   A general term used to describe the transition from mass industrial production, characterized by Fordist methods, to more flexible forms of production favouring innovation and aimed at meeting market demands for customized products.

Post-industrial society   A notion advocated by those who believe that processes of social change are taking us beyond the industrialized order. A post-industrial society is based on the production of information rather than material goods. According to post-industrialists, we are currently experiencing a series of social changes as profound as those that initi-

ated the industrial era some two hundred years ago.

Postmodern feminism   Postmodern feminism draws on the general features of postmodernism in rejecting the idea of single explanations or philosophies. Feminist postmodernism involves, amongst other things, opposition to essentialism (the belief that differences between men and women are innate rather than socially/experientially constructed), and a belief in more plural kinds of knowledge.

Postmodernism   The belief that society is no longer governed by history or progress. Postmodern society is highly pluralistic and diverse, with no 'grand narrative' guiding its development.

Poststructuralism   An approach to social science derived from the field of linguistics and popularized in sociology in the work of Michel Foucault. Poststructuralists reject the idea that absolute truths about the world can be discovered, arguing instead that plural interpretations of reality are inevitable.

Poverty line   An official measure used by governments to define those living below this income level as living in poverty. Many states have an established poverty line, although Britain does not.

Power   The ability of individuals, or the members of a group, to achieve aims or further the interests they hold. Power is a pervasive aspect of all human relationships. Many conflicts in society are struggles over power, because how much power an individual or group is able to achieve governs how far they are able to realize their own wishes at the expense of the wishes of others.

Precautionary principle   The presumption that, where there is sufficient doubt about the possible risks of new departures, it is better to maintain existing practices than to change them.

Prejudice   The holding of preconceived ideas about an individual or group, ideas that are resistant to change even in the face of new information. Prejudice may be either positive or negative.

Pre-operational stage   A stage of cognitive development, in Piaget's theory, in which the child has advanced sufficiently to master basic modes of logical thought.

Primary deviance   In the sociology of deviance, an initial act of crime or deviance. According to Edwin Lemert, acts at the level of primary deviance remain marginal to an individual's self-identity. A process usually occurs by which the deviant act is normalized.

Primary socialization The process by which children learn the cultural norms of the society into which they are born. Primary socialization occurs largely in the family.

Primary source All those sources that are originally produced in the time period which researchers are interested in studying (contrast with secondary source).

Profane That which belongs to the mundane, everyday world.

Proletariat To Karl Marx, the working class under capitalism.

Prophets Religious leaders who mobilize followers through their interpretation of sacred texts.

Prostitution The sale of sexual favours.

Psychopathic A specific personality type. Such individuals lack the moral sense and concern for others that most normal people have.

Public sphere An idea associated with the German sociologist Jürgen Habermas. The public sphere is the arena of public debate and discussion in modern societies.

Pure relationship A relationship of sexual and emotional equality.

Push and pull factors In the early study of global migration, these were the internal and external forces believed to influence patterns of migration. 'Push factors' refer to dynamics within the country of origin, such as unemployment, war, famine or political persecution. 'Pull factors' describe features of destination countries, such as a buoyant labour market, lower population density and a high standard of living.

Qualitative research methods Those methods which gather detailed, rich data with the aim of gaining a better understanding of the social phenomena being studied.

Quality circle (QC) Types of industrialized group production, where workers use their expertise to actively participate in decision-making.

Quantitative research methods Those sociological methods which allow social phenomena to be measured and analysed using mathematical models and statistical techniques.

Queer theory Queer theory argues that sociology and other disciplines are prejudiced towards heterosexuals, and that non-heterosexual voices must be brought to the fore in order to challenge the heterosexual assumptions that underlie much contemporary thinking.

Race A set of social relationships which allow individuals and groups to be located, and various attributes or competencies assigned, on the basis of biologically grounded features.

Racialization The process by which understandings of race are used to classify individuals or groups of people. Racial distinctions are more than ways of describing human differences: they are important factors in the reproduction of patterns of power and inequality.

Racism The attributing of characteristics of superiority or inferiority to a population sharing certain physically inherited characteristics. Racism is one specific form of prejudice, focusing on physical variations between people. Racist attitudes became entrenched during the period of colonial expansion by the West, but seem also to rest on mechanisms of prejudice and discrimination found in very many contexts of human societies.

Radical feminism Form of feminist theory that believes that gender inequality is the result of male domination in all aspects of social and economic life.

Random sampling A sampling method in which a sample is chosen so that every member of the population has the same probability of being included.

Rationalization A concept used by Max Weber to refer to the process by which modes of precise calculation and organization, involving abstract rules and procedures, increasingly come to dominate the social world.

Recidivism Reoffending by individuals previously found guilty of a crime.

Reconstituted family A family in which at least one of the adults has children from a previous union, either living in the home or nearby. Reconstituted families are also known as 'step-families'.

Reflexivity This describes the connections between knowledge and social life. The knowledge we gain about society can affect the way in which we act in it. For instance, reading a survey about the high level of support for a political party might lead an individual to express support for that party too.

Regionalization Divisions of time and space which may be used to 'zone' activities at a very local, domestic level; or the larger division of social and economic life into regional settings or zones at a scale either above or below that of the nation-state.

Reincarnation Rebirth of the soul in another body or form. This belief is most often associated with Hindus and Buddhists.

Relative deprivation The thesis that people's subjective feelings of deprivation are not absolute, but related to their assessment of themselves in comparison with others.

Relative poverty Poverty defined by reference to the overall standard of living in any given society.

Religion A set of beliefs adhered to by the members of a community, involving symbols regarded with a sense of awe or wonder, together with ritual practices in which members of the community engage. Religions do not universally involve a belief in supernatural entities. Although distinctions between religion and magic are difficult to draw, it is often held that magic is primarily practised by individuals rather than being the focus of community ritual.

Religious economy A theoretical framework within the sociology of religion, which argues that religions can be fruitfully understood as organizations in competition with one another for followers.

Representative democracy A political system in which decisions affecting a community are taken, not by its members as a whole, but by people they have elected for this purpose.

Representative sample A sample from a larger population that is statistically typical of that population.

Reproductive technology Techniques of influencing the human reproductive process.

Research methods The diverse methods of investigation used to gather empirical (factual) material. Numerous different research methods exist in sociology, but perhaps the most commonly used are fieldwork (or participant observation) and survey methods. For many purposes it is useful to combine two or more methods within a single research project.

Resistant femininity A term associated with R. W. Connell's writings on the gender hierarchy in society. Women embodying resistant femininity reject the conventional norms of femininity in society ('emphasized femininity') and adopt liberated lifestyles and identities. Feminism and lesbianism, for example, are forms of resistant femininity that are not subordinated to the dominant role of hegemonic masculinity.

Resource allocation How different social and material resources are shared out between and employed by social groups or other elements of society.

Resource mobilization theory (RMT) An American approach to social movement studies which begins from the theoretical premise that movements require resources to be successful. Studying how movements gather the varied resources they need in a competitive social movement field is the basis of RMT.

Response cries These seemingly involuntary exclamations individuals make when, for example, being taken by surprise, dropping something inadvertently or expressing pleasure may be part of our controlled management of the details of social life, studied by ethnomethodologists and conversation analysts.

Restorative justice A branch of criminal justice which rejects punitive measures in favour of community-based sentences that attempt to raise awareness among offenders of the effects of their actions.

Restricted code A mode of speech that rests on strongly developed cultural understandings, so that many ideas do not need to be – and are not – put into words.

Revolution A process of political change, involving the mobilizing of a mass social movement, which by the use of violence successfully overthrows an existing regime and forms a new government. A revolution is distinguished from a coup d'état because it involves a mass movement and the occurrence of major change in the political system as a whole. A coup d'état refers to the seizure of power through the use of arms by individuals who then replace the existing political leaders, but without otherwise radically transforming the governmental system. Revolutions can also be distinguished from rebellions, which involve challenges to the existing political authorities, but again aim at the replacement of personnel rather than the transformation of the political structure as such.

Right realism In criminology, right realism grew out of control theory and political conservatism. It links the perceived escalation of crime and delinquency to a decline in individual responsibility and moral degeneracy. To right realists, crime and deviance are an individual pathology – a set of destructive lawless behaviours actively chosen and perpetrated by individual selfishness, a lack of self-control and morality. Right realists are dismissive of the 'theoretical' approaches to the study of crime.

Risk society   A notion associated with the German sociologist Ulrich Beck. Beck argues that industrial society has created many new dangers of risks unknown in previous ages. The risks associated with global warming are one example.

Rituals   Formalized modes of behaviour in which the members of a group or community regularly engage. Religion represents one of the main contexts in which rituals are practised, but the scope of ritual behaviour extends well beyond this particular sphere. Most groups have ritual practices of some kind or another.

Romantic love   As distinct from passionate love, the idea of romantic love emerged in the eighteenth century, and involves the idea that marriage is based on mutual attraction, rather than on economic reasons. It is a prelude to, but is also in tension with, the idea of a pure relationship.

Sacred   That which inspires attitudes of awe or reverence among believers in a given set of religious ideas.

Sampling   Studying a proportion of individuals or cases from a larger population as representative of that population as a whole.

Sanction   A mode of reward or punishment that reinforces socially expected forms of behaviour.

Scapegoating   Blaming an individual or group for wrongs that were not of their doing.

Schooling   A formal process of instruction, usually in specialized organizational settings – schools. Schooling transmits the types of skills and knowledge thought necessary in particular societies, normally via a designated curriculum.

Science   In the sense of physical science, the systematic study of the physical world. Science – and sociology as a scientific endeavour – involves the disciplined marshalling of empirical data, combined with the construction of theoretical approaches and theories which illuminate or explain those data. Scientific activity combines the creation of bold new modes of thought with the careful testing of hypotheses and ideas. One major feature which helps distinguish science from other types of idea system (such as that involved in religion) is the assumption that all scientific ideas are open to mutual criticism and revision by members of the scientific community.

Second World   The industrialized, formerly communist societies of Eastern Europe and the Soviet Union.

Secondary deviance   An idea associated with the American criminologist Edwin Lemert. Primary deviance refers to an initial act which contravenes a norm or law – for instance, stealing an item from a shop. Secondary deviance is where a label becomes attached to the individual who carried out the act, as where the person stealing from the shop is labelled a 'shoplifter'.

Secondary source   All those sources which discuss, interpret or re-present material that originated at an earlier time (contrast with primary source).

Sect   A religious movement which breaks away from orthodoxy.

Secularization   A process of decline in the influence of religion. Although modern societies have become increasingly secular, tracing the extent of secularization is a complex matter. Secularization can refer to levels of involvement with religious organizations (such as rates of church attendance), the social and material influence wielded by religious organizations, and the degree to which people hold religious beliefs.

Self-consciousness   Awareness of one's distinct social identity, as a person separate from others. Human beings are not born with self-consciousness but acquire an awareness of self as a result of early socialization. The learning of language is of vital importance to the processes by which the child learns to become a self-conscious being.

Self-identity   The ongoing process of self-development and definition of our personal identity through which we formulate a unique sense of ourselves and our relationship to the world around us.

Semi-peripheral countries   Countries that supply sources of labour and raw materials to the core industrial countries and the world economy but are not themselves fully industrialized.

Sensorimotor stage   According to Piaget, a stage of human cognitive development in which the child's awareness of its environment is dominated by perception and touch.

Service class   A term adopted by John H. Goldthorpe to describe those whose employment is based on a code of service rather than a labour contract, and whose work therefore involves a high degree of trust and autonomy. In Goldthorpe's account, the service class (which he categorizes as Class I) refers to professional, senior administrative, and senior managerial employees. (Members of the service class are not those employed in the service industries.)

Sex The anatomical differences which separate men from women. Sociologists often contrast sex with gender. Sex refers to the physical characteristics of the body; gender concerns socially learned forms of behaviour. Sex and gender divisions are not the same. A transvestite, for example, is someone who is physically a man but sometimes assumes the gender of a woman.

Sex tourism The term used to describe international travel oriented on prostitution. It is most highly developed in the countries of the Far East, where groups of men from abroad travel for the opportunity to engage in inexpensive sexual liaisons with women and young children.

Sex work All forms of work involving the provision of sexual services in a financial exchange between consenting adults.

Sexual harassment Unwanted sexual advances, remarks or behaviour by one person towards another, persisted in even though it is made clear that the other person is resistant.

Sexual orientation The direction of one's sexual or romantic attraction.

Sexuality A broad term which refers to the sexual characteristics, and sexual behaviour, of human beings.

Shaman An individual believed to have special magical powers; a sorcerer or witch doctor.

Shared understandings The common assumptions which people hold and which allow them to interact in a systematic way with one another.

Sick role A term, associated with the American functionalist Talcott Parsons, to describe the patterns of behaviour which a sick person adopts in order to minimize the disruptive impact of his or her illness on others.

Simulacra In the world of hyperreality evoked by the French author Jean Baudrillard, simulacra are copies of items for which there is no original. For example, a 'mock Tudor' house looks nothing like original Tudor buildings.

Situational crime prevention An approach to crime prevention that focuses on the creation of crime-resistant environments and communities to reduce the opportunities for committing crimes. It is based on the principles of surveillance and target hardening.

Slavery A form of social stratification in which some individuals are literally owned by others as their property.

Snowball sampling A method of gathering a sample for research studies based on research participants recruiting acquaintances and friends for the study.

Social age The norms, values and roles that are culturally associated with a particular chronological age.

Social capital The social knowledge and connections that enable people to accomplish their goals and extend their influence.

Social change Alteration in the basic structures of a social group or society. Social change is an ever-present phenomenon in social life, but has become especially intense in the modern era. The origins of modern sociology can be traced to attempts to understand the dramatic changes shattering the traditional world and promoting new forms of social order.

Social constraint A term referring to the fact that the groups and societies of which we are a part exert a conditioning influence on our behaviour. Social constraint was regarded by Durkheim as one of the distinctive properties of 'social facts'.

Social constructionism An approach to sociological research which sees social reality as the creation of the interaction of individuals and groups.

Social evolution A theory originally used by nineteenth-century scholars who sought to use evolutionary theory from biology to study the long-term development of societies.

Social exclusion The outcome of multiple deprivations which prevent individuals or groups from participating fully in the economic, social and political life of the society in which they are located.

Social facts According to Emile Durkheim, the aspects of social life that shape our actions as individuals. Durkheim believed that social facts could be studied scientifically.

Social gerontology The study of ageing and the elderly.

Social group Collection of individuals who interact in systematic ways with one another.

Groups may range from very small associations to large-scale organizations or societies. Whatever their size, it is a defining feature of a group that its members have an awareness of a common identity. Most of our lives are spent in group contact; in modern societies, most people belong to groups of many different types.

Social interaction Any form of social encounter between individuals. Most of our lives are made up of social interaction of one type or another. Social interaction refers to both formal and informal situations in which people meet one another. An illustration of a formal situation of social interaction is a school classroom; an example of informal interaction is two people meeting in the street or at a party.

Social mobility Movement of individuals or groups between different socio-economic positions. Vertical mobility refers to movement up or down a hierarchy in a stratification system. Lateral mobility is physical movement of individuals or groups from one region to another. When analysing vertical mobility, sociologists distinguish between how far people are mobile in the course of their career, and how far the position they reach differs from that of their parents.

Social model of disability A theory that locates the cause of disability within society, rather than the individual. It is not individual limitations that cause disability but the barriers that society places in the way of full participation for disabled people.

Social movement Collective attempts to further a common interest or secure a common goal through action outside the sphere of established political institutions. Social movements seek to bring about or block social change and normally exist in relations of conflict with organizations whose objectives and outlook they frequently oppose. However, movements that successfully challenge for power, once they become institutionalized, can develop into formal organizations.

Social position The social identity an individual has in a given group or society. Social positions may be general in nature (those associated with gender roles) or may be more specific (occupational positions).

Social role The expected behaviour of an individual occupying a particular social position. The idea of social role originally comes from the theatre, referring to the parts which actors play in a stage production. In every society, individuals play a number of different social roles, according to the varying contexts of their activities.

Social self The basis of self-consciousness in human individuals, according to the theory of G. H. Mead. The social self is the identity conferred upon an individual by the reactions of others. A person achieves self-consciousness by becoming aware of this social identity.

Social stratification The existence of structured inequalities between groups in society, in terms of their access to material or symbolic rewards. While all societies involve some forms of stratification, only with the development of state-based systems do wide differences in wealth and power arise. The most distinctive form of stratification in modern societies involves class divisions.

Social structure Patterns of interaction between individuals or groups. Most of our activities are structured: they are organized in a regular and repetitive way. Although the comparison can be misleading, it is handy to think of the social structure of a society as rather like the girders which underpin a building and hold it together.

Social unrest The stage of dissatisfaction with existing society, which can give rise to more focused collective behaviour and social movements.

Socialist feminism The beliefs that women are treated as second-class citizens in patriarchal capitalist societies and that both the ownership of the means of production and women's social experience need to be transformed because the roots of women's oppression lie in the total economic system of capitalism. Socialist feminists have criticized some socialists' gender-blind understanding of class.

Socialization The social processes through which children develop an awareness of social norms and values and achieve a distinct sense of self. Although socialization processes are particularly significant in infancy and childhood, they continue to some degree throughout life. No human individuals are immune from the reactions of others around them, which influence and modify their behaviour at all phases of the life cycle.

Socialization of nature The process by which we control phenomena regarded as 'natural', such as reproduction.

Society The concept of society is one of the most important of all sociological notions. A society is a system of structured social relationships connecting people together according to a shared culture. Some societies, like those of hunters and gatherers, are very small, numbering no more than a few dozen people. Others are very large, involving many millions – modern Chinese society, for instance, has a population of more than a billion individuals.

Sociological imagination The application of imaginative thought to the asking and answering of sociological questions. The sociological imagination involves one in 'thinking oneself away' from the familiar routines of day-to-day life.

Sociology The study of human groups and societies, giving particular emphasis to the analysis of the industrialized world. Sociology is one of a group of social sciences, which also includes anthropology, economics, political science and human geography. The divisions between the various social sciences are not clear-cut, and all share a certain range of common interests, concepts and methods.

Sociology of the body The branch of sociology that focuses on how our bodies are affected by social influences. Health and illness, for instance, are determined by social and cultural influences.

Sociology of deviance The branch of sociology concerned with the study of deviant behaviour and with understanding why some behaviour is identified as deviant.

Soil degradation The process by which the quality of the earth is worsened and its valuable natural elements are stripped away through over-use, drought or inadequate fertilization.

Solidarity For Durkheim, the internal forces of social cohesion. More generally, a term often used by the left to describe the political consciousness of an emerging class struggling against oppression – e.g. working-class solidarity.

Source A publication, passage from a publication, or other information that is referred to.

Sovereignty The title to supreme power of a monarch, leader or government over an area with a clear-cut border.

Standard deviation A way of calculating the spread of a group of figures.

State A political apparatus (government institutions, plus civil service officials) ruling over a given territory, with an authority backed by law and the ability to use force. Not all societies are characterized by the existence of a state. Hunting and gathering cultures, and smaller agrarian societies, lack state institutions. The emergence of the state marks a distinctive transition in human history, because the centralization of political power involved in state formation introduces new dynamics into processes of social change.

State-centred theory Development theories that argue that appropriate government policies do not interfere with economic development, but rather can play a key role in bringing it about.

Status set An individual's group of social statuses.

Status The social honour or prestige accorded to a person or a particular group by other members of a society. Status groups normally involve distinct styles of life – patterns of behaviour which the members of a group follow. Status privilege may be positive or negative. 'Pariah' status groups are regarded with disdain, or treated as outcasts, by the majority of the population.

Stereotype A fixed and inflexible characterization of a group of people.

Stigma Any physical or social characteristic believed to be demeaning.

Strike A stoppage of work/withdrawal of labour by a group of workers for specific ends.

Structural functionalism A theoretical perspective in sociology rooted in the work of Talcott Parsons. Structural functionalism analyses societies as social systems in which various social institutions perform specific functions ensuring the smooth operation of the system as a whole.

Structuration The two-way process by which we shape our social world through our individual actions but are ourselves reshaped by society.

Subculture Any segment of the population which is distinguishable from the wider society by its cultural pattern.

Suburbanization The development of suburbia, areas of low-rise housing outside inner cities.

Surplus value In Marxist theory, the value of an individual's labour power which is 'left over' when an employer has repaid the cost involved in hiring a worker.

Surveillance The supervising of the activities of some individuals or groups by others in order to ensure compliant behaviour.

Surveillance society A society in which individuals are regularly watched and their activities documented. The increase in the number of video cameras on motorways, in streets and shopping centres is one aspect of the expansion of surveillance.

Survey A method of sociological research usually involving the administration of questionnaires to a population being studied, and the statistical analysis of their replies to find patterns or regularities.

Sustainable development The notion that economic growth should proceed only insofar as natural resources are recycled rather than depleted, biodiversity is maintained, and clean air, water and land are protected.

Sweatshop A derogatory term for a factory or shop in which employees work long hours for low pay under poor conditions.

Symbol One item used to stand for or represent another – as in the case of a flag which symbolizes a nation.

Symbolic capital In the work of Pierre Bourdieu – those resources that confer high status, distinction, honour and social prestige on people. For example, voluntary charity work may lead to a person being held in high esteem that would not otherwise have accrued from their formal employment or business ownership.

Symbolic interactionism A theoretical approach in sociology developed by G. H. Mead, which places strong emphasis on the role of symbols and language as core elements of all human interaction.

Taliban A fundamentalist Islamic militia; by 1996 the Taliban had taken control of Afghanistan and set up an Islamic government that enforced a strict Muslim code of behaviour. They were overthrown by an American-led international coalition in 2001 after being linked to groups responsible for the September 2001 attacks on New York and Washington.

Talk The carrying on of conversations or verbal exchanges in the course of day-to-day social life. Increasingly, this has been seen as a subject for scrutiny by sociologists, particularly ethnomethodologists.

Target hardening Crime deterrence techniques that aim to make it more difficult for crime to take place through direct interventions into potential crime situations. Steering locks in cars, for example, are required in some areas in order to reduce the attractiveness of car theft.

Taylorism A set of ideas, also referred to as 'scientific management', developed by Frederick Winslow Taylor, according to which productivity could be immensely increased by breaking down industrial tasks into a series of simple operations that could be precisely timed and optimally coordinated.

Technology The application of knowledge to production from the material world. Technology involves the creation of material instruments (such as machines) used in human interaction with nature.

Telecommunications The communication of information, sounds or images at a distance through a technological medium.

Terrorism Usually, violent acts designed to instil fear into a population for political ends. The use of terrorism as a social scientific concept is hotly debated. Some see it as politically loaded against those groups opposed to established states and thus not suitable for scientific work.

Thatcherism The doctrines associated with the former British Prime Minister Margaret Thatcher. These doctrines emphasize the importance of economic enterprise coupled to a cutback in the reach of the state, while maintaining a core role for strong national government.

Theism A belief in a god or gods.

Theoretical questions Questions posed by the sociologist when seeking to explain a particular range of observed events. The asking of theoretical questions is crucial to allowing us to generalize about the nature of social life.

Theory An attempt to identify general properties that explain regularly observed events. Theories are an essential part of all sociological work. While theories tend to be linked to broader theoretical approaches, they are also strongly influenced by the research results they help generate.

Theory of broken windows The idea that there is a connection between the *appearance* of disorder, such as a broken window or vandalism, and actual crime.

Third age The years in later life when people are free from both parenting responsibilities and the labour market. In contemporary societies, the third age is longer than ever before, allowing older people to live active and independent lives.

Third way A political philosophy, pioneered by New Labour and favoured by other centrist democratic leaders, that is committed to preserving the values of socialism while endorsing market policies for generating wealth and dispelling economic inequality.

Third World The less developed societies, in which industrial production is either virtually non-existent or only developed to a limited degree. The majority of the world's population live in Third World countries.

Total institutions A term popularized by Erving Goffman to refer to facilities such as asylums, prisons and monasteries that impose on their residents a forcibly regulated system of existence in complete isolation from the outside world.

Totemism A system of religious belief which attributes divine properties to a particular type of animal or plant.

Transnational corporations (TNCs) Business corporations located in two or more countries. Even when TNCs have a clear national base, they are oriented to global markets and global profits.

Triangulation The use of multiple research methods as a way of producing more reliable empirical data than is available from any single method.

Typification A concept used by Alfred Schutz to describe the way that people make judgements of individuals, based on prior assumptions about the typical character and behaviour of categories of people.

Underclass A class of individuals situated right at the bottom of the class system, often composed of people from ethnic minority backgrounds.

Underdevelopment A concept used in social science to describe the economic state of societies that were exploited and/or previously colonized by Western countries. Underdevelopment suggests a process through which powerful, wealthy states actively exploit the poor and less powerful.

Unemployment Rates of unemployment measure the proportion of people who are 'economically active' and available for work but cannot get a paid job. A person who is 'out of work' is not necessarily unemployed in the sense of having nothing to do. Housewives, for instance, don't receive any pay, but they usually work very hard.

Unfocused interaction Interaction occurring among people present in the same setting but where they are not engaged in direct face-to-face communication.

Universal benefits Welfare benefits that are available equally to all citizens, regardless of level of income or economic status. Access to the National Health Service in Britain is an example of a universal benefit, as all Britons have the right to use it on an ongoing basis for regular healthcare.

Upper class A social class broadly composed of the more affluent members of society, especially those who have inherited wealth, own large businesses or hold large numbers of stocks and shares.

Urban ecology An approach to the study of urban life based on an analogy with the adjustment of plants and organisms to the physical environment. According to ecological theorists, the various neighbourhoods and zones within cities are formed as a result of natural processes of adjustment on the part of urban populations as they compete for resources.

Urban recycling The refurbishing of deteriorating neighbourhoods by encouraging the renewal of old buildings and the construction of new ones on previously developed land, rather than extending out to fresh sites.

Urban renewal Reviving deteriorating neighbourhoods by such processes as recycling land and existing buildings, improving the urban environment, managing local areas better and with the participation of local citizens, and using public funds both to regenerate the area and to attract further private investment.

Urbanism A term used by Louis Wirth to denote distinctive characteristics of urban social life, such as its impersonality.

Urbanization The development of towns and cities.

Value-added model of social movements Neil Smelser's stage-model of social movement development in which each succeeding stage 'adds value' to the movement's overall development.

Values Ideas held by human individuals or groups about what is desirable, proper, good or bad. Differing values represent key aspects of variations in human culture. What individuals value is strongly influenced by the specific culture in which they happen to live.

Variable A dimension along which an object, individual or group may be categorized, such as income or height, allowing specific comparisons with others or over time.

Vertical mobility Movement up or down a hierarchy of positions in a social stratification system.

Victimization studies Surveys aimed at revealing the proportion of the population that has been victimized by crime during a certain period. Victim surveys attempt to compensate for the 'dark figure of unreported crime' by focusing directly on people's actual experience of crime.

Virtual community   Internet-based groups, rooted in public discussions which are long lasting and contain sufficient human feeling to constitute personal relationships in cyberspace.

War   The clash of two organized armed forces that seek to destroy each other's power and especially their will to resist, principally by killing members of the opposing force.

Welfare capitalism   Practice in which large corporations protect their employees from the vicissitudes of the market.

Welfare dependency   A situation where people on welfare, such as those receiving unemployment benefit, treat this as a 'way of life' rather than attempting to secure a paid job.

Welfare state   A political system that provides a wide range of welfare benefits for citizens.

White-collar crime   Criminal activities carried out by those in white-collar or professional jobs.

Work   The activity by which human beings produce from the natural world and so ensure their survival. Work should not be thought of exclusively as paid employment. In traditional cultures, there was only a rudimentary monetary system, and very few people worked for money payments. In modern societies, there remain many types of work, including housework, which do not involve direct payment of wages or salary.

Working class   A social class broadly composed of people involved in blue-collar or manual occupations.

World-accommodating movement   A religious movement that emphasizes the impor-

tance of inner religious life and spiritual purity over worldly concerns.

World-affirming movement   A religious movement that seeks to enhance followers' ability to succeed in the outside world by helping them to unlock their human potential.

World-rejecting movement   A religious movement that is exclusive in nature, highly critical of the outside world, and demanding of its members.

World-systems theory   Pioneered by Immanuel Wallerstein, this theory emphasizes the interconnections among countries based on the expansion of a capitalist world economy. This economy is made up of core countries, semi-peripheral countries and peripheral countries.

Young adulthood   A life-course stage between adolescence and mature adulthood. Given the variability of social and economic contexts over time and across cultures, young adulthood is not seen as a universal life-course stage, but has some currency in the developed societies.

Youth culture   The specific cultural attributes exhibited by many young people in any given period. Youth culture involves behavioural norms, dress codes, language use and other aspects, many of which tend to differ from the adult culture of the time.

Zero tolerance policing   An approach to crime prevention and control that emphasizes the ongoing process of maintaining order as the key to reducing serious crime. In targeting petty crime and minor disturbances, zero tolerance policing reflects the principles underlying the theory of broken windows.

Illustration credits

Index